1998
NOVEL &
SHORT STORY
WRITER'S
MARKET

2,200 PLACES TO SELL YOUR FICTION

EDITED BY

BARBARA KUROFF

ASSISTED BY

DONYA DICKERSON

MEGAN LANE

WRITER'S DIGEST BOOKS
CINCINNATI, OHIO

If you are a publisher of fiction and would like to be considered for a listing in the next edition of *Novel & Short Story Writer's Market*, send a SASE (or SAE and IRC) with your request for a questionnaire to *Novel & Short Story Writer's Market*—QR, 1507 Dana Ave., Cincinnati OH 45207. Questionnaires received after July 15, 1998, will be held for the 2000 edition.

Managing Editor, Annuals Department: Cindy Laufenberg

International Standard Serial Number ISSN 0897-9812
International Standard Book Number 0-89879-818-3

Cover illustration: Brenda Grannan

Attention Booksellers: This is an annual directory of F&W Publications.
Return deadline for this edition is April 30, 1999.

Contents

Writing Fiction

Craft and Technique

Personal Views

Writing and Publishing

The Markets

Resources

Articles in the Craft and Technique section focus this year on creating memorable, multi-dimensional characters that bring life to your fiction. Award-winning private eye novelist **Sue Grafton** provides clues on how to transform your free writing into tightly structured plots and richly formed characters (page 9). Successful author **Robin Hemley** reveals valuable techniques for turning your Uncle Lou (or anyone else) into a unique and believable character—without offending your source of inspiration in the process (page 14). **Tom Chiarella**, fiction writer and professor, guides you step-by-step through different strategies for creating authentic, tension-filled dialogue (page 22). And **Ann Hood**, author of six novels, outlines techniques that compel readers to experience your characters' emotions (page 33).

In our Writing and Publishing section, editors of four top literary journals—**Richard Burgin** (*Boulevard*); **Linda Burmeister Davies** (*Glimmer Train*); **Joseph Kruppa** (*American Short Fiction*); and **Greg Michalson** (*The Missouri Review*)—offer advice on the etiquette of submitting stories, including their criteria for the perfect cover letter (page 68). Writer and teacher **Geoff Schmidt** takes a humorous and helpful look at how writers can convert pesky rejection slips into useful tools for getting their work published (page 73). In The Business of Fiction, you will learn crucial elements of the fiction business, from manuscript preparation and rights to copyright, cover letters and mailing tips (page 77). The annual Fiction Report, takes a look at the current marketplace for all types of novel-length fiction.

Our Personal Views section features informative and inspirational interviews with published writers who tell how they do it and how you can too. **Greg Sarris**'s novel *Grand Avenue* was chosen by Robert Redford as his film company's first made-for-TV project (page 41). Interestingly, Sarris cites Faulkner as the writer whose work most inspired him to translate his own experiences into fiction. **William Heffernan** turned a family experience with corporate downsizing into *The Dinosaur Club* and a $1 million movie deal (page 46). **Isabel Allende**, author of *The House of the Spirits* and *The Stories of Eva Luna*, endured political chaos and the loss of a beloved daughter, but remained committed to her craft of writing (page 52). Successful romance novelist **Jennifer Crusie** says "the only reason to write a novel is because you can't *not* write it" (page 57).

Throughout the book, Insider Reports with editors, publishers and writers provide a wealth of inside information on writing and publishing your fiction. And, in our popular First Bylines feature, four writers share their experiences of being published for the first time.

Our expanded Contest section offers hundreds of opportunities to show off your commitment to writing and at the same time earn recognition, achieve honor and make money. This year, we feature interviews with **Lorian Hemingway**, Ernest Hemingway's granddaughter and director of the Lorian Hemingway Writing Competition (page 542) and with **Lee Deigaard**, the 1997 winner of that competition (page 546).

Maintaining a commitment to writing can be a lonely business. That's why we've included a section of resources for writers (beginning on page 578) to keep you connected with the rest of the writing world. Those resources include conferences and workshops (where I hope to meet some of you this year); and organizations, publications and websites especially for writers.

Have a great 1998 writing—and marketing—your fiction. And please feel free to place a copy of Luke Salisbury's inspiring piece about Faulkner above your desk. Also, if you have any comments or suggestions as to how I can make this book more helpful, I'd love to hear them.

Barbara Kuroff

Editor
nsswm@fwpubs.com

From the Editor

Nothing stopped Faulkner.
He wrote when he wasn't famous;
He wrote after winning the Nobel Prize.
He wrote when his books couldn't make money
*   and when the sale prices of his stories set records.*
He wrote when his books were out of print.
He wrote drunk and sober,
*   and sojourns in Hollywood didn't stop him.*
Phenomenal quantities of alcohol, extramarital affairs,
*   an unhappy marriage, or celebrity never got in his way.*
He was a writer.

Luke Salisbury
The Boston Globe

The above passage is taken from the article "Faulkner and the power of words," written by Luke Salisbury to commemorate the anniversary of William Faulkner's 100th birthday. The entire piece is a beautifully written tribute to Faulkner's genius, but it is the above excerpt I copied and hung above my desk to remind me of what real commitment to the craft of fiction writing entails. It reminds me that Faulkner survived problems and accolades, good times and bad, to write the finest fiction of this century. It reminds me, too, that as writers, we must be committed on a day-to-day basis to our craft.

Commitment to the craft of fiction writing is what this book is about. If you are a fiction writer or are thinking about writing a short story or novel, we've prepared this edition of *Novel & Short Story Writer's Market* with your needs in mind. Whether you are a beginner looking for your first byline, or already published and looking for more places to publish your fiction, you will find the answers to your questions about writing and publishing in today's complex fiction marketplace.

2,200 markets for your fiction appear in this edition of *Novel & Short Story Writer's Market*. Each of those markets represents an opportunity to get your short story or novel into print. 750 markets appear here for the first time, and all listings have been updated to reflect what editors are looking for in 1998. No matter what type of fiction you write—from literary and mainstream to mystery, romance or science fiction—there are editors listed here who want to see your manuscript.

If you're looking for a publisher for your short stories, check our four magazine sections—Literary, Small Circulation, Zines and Commercial Magazines. Literary magazines pride themselves on publishing fine writing by new writers beside works by well-known authors. In the Small Circulation magazine section are publications devoted to almost every topic, every level of writing skill and every type of writer. Our Zines section lists small publications—many of them electronic—that offer the big benefits of self-expression, artistic freedom and niche audiences. In our Commercial Magazines section you'll find today's top-paying, big-circulation magazine markets.

If you're looking for a publisher for your novel, check out our Small Press and Book Publisher sections. The "micropresses" listed in the Small Press section are an increasingly important area of publishing because of their interest in finding new voices. This year, our Book Publisher section has grown by 70 pages to accommodate the 200+ publishers appearing for the first time in *Novel & Short Story Writer's Market*. This section includes all the major publishing houses, from small and independent—but important—presses to the top publishers of mass market fiction.

How to Use This Book to Publish Your Fiction

Like most of the people who use *Novel & Short Story Writer's Market*, chances are you've already put a great deal of time and effort into your writing. Many of you write regularly and are well-read, especially in the area in which you write. Some of you are formally studying writing while some are receiving feedback on your work by sharing it with a writers' group. You've been spending lots of time on writing and rewriting your work, making it the best it can be, and now you feel it's time to share your work with others.

If we could open this book with just one piece of advice it would be this: Take as much care searching for potential markets for your work as you have in crafting it. With this in mind, this book is designed as a tool to help you in your search, and we hope you will use it as a starting place for your overall marketing plan. The temptation when using any book like this is to go straight to the listings and start sending out your work. Perhaps this is the fastest, but it's not the most efficient route to publication.

While we do offer listings of over 2,200 markets and other opportunities for fiction writers, the listings contain only a portion of the information available to you in *Novel & Short Story Writer's Market*. In addition to the listings, we offer interviews with published authors and editors and a wide range of articles on the craft of writing, and information on all aspects of marketing and publishing your work. Reading the material covered here, as well as other books on writing and publishing, will help you make informed decisions that will further your writing career.

WHAT YOU'LL FIND HERE

Novel & Short Story Writer's Market is divided into three parts, each presenting a different type of information. The first part is Writing Fiction. Here we provide articles on the craft of writing, in-depth interviews with established authors, and informational pieces on the business of publishing. This is where you will find the Business of Fiction Writing and the annual fiction report, in addition to other articles on writing and publishing fiction.

Following Writing Fiction is The Markets, the heart of the book. This part is divided into seven sections. The Literary Magazines section includes literary journals of all sizes. Next comes the Small Circulation Magazines section, featuring publications (most paying) with circulations of under 10,000. Our Zines section follows and includes a number of exciting formats that welcome the voices of new writers. The Commercial Magazines section features popular magazines with circulations of more than 10,000. After this is the Small Press section, which includes small presses publishing three or less titles each year. Book Publishers, the next section, features listings of small and mid-size independent presses publishing more than three titles each year, university presses and other nonprofit presses, and publishers of commercial hardcover, trade paperback and mass market books. Finally, the Contests and Awards section offers listings for contests, awards and grants available to fiction writers.

Most of the listings in these market sections are from North America. There are also Canadian listings noted with a maple leaf symbol (❦) and some international markets denoted by an asterisk (*). Many of these international markets are open to writers of English from all over the world.

Throughout The Markets, you'll find features called Insider Reports. These are short interviews with editors, publishers and writers designed to give you an inside look at specific writing areas and a behind-the-scenes look at particular publications or publishers. These pieces offer valuable tips on breaking into markets in their areas of expertise. Our new Writer-to-Writer features in the Book Publishers section offer firsthand advice from published writers on the craft of writing and marketing novel-length fiction.

Resources, the last section of the book, is included for the support and information those listed there provide to writers, including places to make contact with other writers. Here you will find Conferences and Workshops, Retreats and Colonies, Organizations and Resources, Publications of Interest to Fiction Writers and Websites of Interest.

DEVELOPING YOUR MARKETING PLAN

After reading the articles and interviews that interest you, the next step in developing your marketing plan is to use the book to come up with a preliminary list of potential markets. If you are not sure what categories your work falls into or if you just want to explore the possibilities, start by reading the section introductions and browsing through the sections to find markets that interest you. This approach will familiarize you with the many different types of markets for your writing and may lead you to a market you haven't thought of before.

To help you with your market search, we include a Category Index, beginning on page 641. The Category Index is divided into sections corresponding to the major fiction categories. You'll find fiction types such as romance, mystery, religious, regional, etc. Subject headings are then followed by the names of magazines and book publishers expressing an interest in that specific type of fiction.

You may notice that not all the listings in the magazine and book publisher sections appear in the Category Index. Some said they were only interested in very specific topics such as fiction about hiking or hot air ballooning or about the Civil War. Whether your writing subjects are general or specific, we recommend a combination of the browsing method and the Category Index method.

RANKING CODES

To further help you narrow your list of potential markets, we include ranking codes that identify the level of openness of each listing. These codes, Roman numerals **I** through **V**, appear just after each listing's name. In the magazine and book sections, codes indicate whether editors are open to work from writers on all levels, are only open to work by established writers, only accept work by writers from a certain region or who write on a specific subject, or are closed to unsolicited submissions. In the Contest section, ranking codes let you know if entries should be published or unpublished or should be work from certain groups of writers or about certain regions. The ranking codes and explanations for each are given after each section introduction.

You will also notice symbols at the start of some listings. Listings new to our book this year are indicated by a double dagger symbol (‡). Many are newly established markets, and often these are most open to the work of new writers. Some are not new, but have decided to list with us because they have increased their fiction needs.

READING THE LISTINGS

Once you've come up with a list of potential markets, read each listing carefully. You will find you can further streamline your list based on the market's editorial statement, advice, specific needs, terms, payment and reputation.

While different sections contain slightly different listings, there are some things all listings have in common:

After the name and contact information for each listing, you'll find a brief description of the market's publishing philosophy and intended audience. Following this is often a physical description of the magazine or books published. Physical descriptions can tell you a lot about the market's budget and give you hints about its quality and prestige. There is a brief explanation of printing terms to help you get a better picture of the publications as they are described in the listings. This information is included in Printing and Production Terms Defined on page 636. Also check the establishment date, circulation or number of books published.

In some listings, following the profile, we've added our own editorial comment, set off by a bullet. This feature allows us to pass on additional information we've learned about the listing. Included here is information about the market's honors or awards or its treatment of writers. For example, here is the editorial comment for *Ploughshares*:

● Work published in *Ploughshares* has been selected continuously for inclusion in the *Best American Short Stories* and *O. Henry Prize* anthologies. In fact, the magazine has the honor of having the most stories selected from a single issue (three) to be included in *B.A.S.S.* Recent guest editors have included Richard Ford, Tim O'Brien and Ann Beattie.

Next comes the **Needs** section of the listing. In addition to a list or description of the type of work the market is seeking, you'll also find how much work the market receives from writers in a given time, how much it publishes and what percentage of its writing is acquired through agents. This will help you determine your competition. Also included are specifics on length and other requirements.

The **Needs** section of *Ellery Queen's Mystery Magazine* offers the following information:

Needs: "We accept only mystery, crime, suspense and detective fiction." Receives approximately 400 unsolicited fiction mss each month. Accepts 10-15 mss/issue. Publishes ms 6-12 months after acceptance. Agented fiction 50%. Published work by Peter Lovesey, Anne Perry, Marcia Muller and Ruth Rendell. Published new writers within the last year. Length: up to 7,000 words, occasionally longer. Publishes 1-2 short novels of up to 17,000 words/year by established authors; minute mysteries of 250 words; short, humorous mystery verse. Critiques rejected mss "only when a story might be a possibility for us if revised." Sometimes recommends other markets.

After **Needs** comes **How to Contact**, where you'll find out how to approach a market and what material to include with your submission. We suggest you follow the requirements for submission carefully. You will notice some markets have told us they accept disk or e-mail submissions. Although some listings have included e-mail and fax numbers, it is always best to *get permission before submitting a manuscript to a publisher by fax or e-mail*. For more information on submission, presentation and cover letters, see The Business of Fiction Writing on page 77.

Here is how the contact information for a magazine might look:

How to Contact: Send complete ms with a cover letter or send ms in electronic form (disk or e-mail). Include estimated word count, short bio and list of publications. Reports in 3 weeks on queries; 2 months on mss. Send SASE for reply, return of ms or send disposable copy of ms. Simultaneous, reprint and electronic submissions OK. Sample copy for SAE and 5 first-class stamps. Fiction guidelines for 8½ × 11 SAE.

A book publisher might require the following:

How to Contact: Accepts unsolicited mss. Query with outline/synopsis and 3 sample chapters. Include short bio and list of publishing credits. SASE. Reports in 2 weeks on queries; 3-4 months on mss. Simultaneous submissions OK.

Next is the **Payment/Terms** section. When possible, we've provided a range of payment, but note that many publications in the Literary and Zine sections pay only in copies or subscriptions. We also indicate when you will be paid and for what rights. For more on rights and what to look for concerning terms, see the Business of Fiction Writing.

The **Payment/Terms** information for *Asimov's Science Fiction* magazine is:

Payment/Terms: Pays 6-8¢/word for stories up to 7,500 words; 5¢/word for stories over 12,500; $450 for stories between those limits. Pays on acceptance for first North American serial rights plus specified foreign rights, as explained in contract. Very rarely buys reprints. Sends galleys to author.

When an editor provided additional information that might be of benefit, we include that in the **Advice** section at the end of listings. Editor C. Michael Curtis tells writers the following in the **Advice** section of *The Atlantic Monthly*:

Advice: When making first contact, "cover letters are sometimes helpful, particularly if they cite prior publications or involvement in writing programs. Common mistakes: melodrama, inconclusiveness, lack of development, unpersuasive characters and/or dialogue."

LEARNING MORE ABOUT A MARKET

Your marketing research should begin with a careful study of the listings, but it should not end there. Whenever possible obtain a sample copy or catalog. Editors and successful writers agree there is no substitution for reading copies of magazines that interest you. Likewise, you should familiarize yourself with the books of publishers to whom you'd like to submit.

To find out more about a potential market, send a self-addressed, stamped envelope (SASE) for submission guidelines. Most magazines have sample copies available for a modest price. For book publishers, check *Books in Print* at the library to find the publishers of books you admire or feel are similar to the one you are writing. The library also has publishing industry magazines such as *Publishers Weekly* as well as magazines for writers. Some of these magazines are listed in Publications of Interest to Fiction Writers beginning on page 623. These can help keep you informed of new publishers and changes in the field.

THE FOLLOW THROUGH

After carefully studying and narrowing your list of potential markets to those who represent the most suitable places for your work, the next step, of course, is to mail out your work. If you have any questions on how to present your work, see the Business of Fiction Writing. When in doubt, remember to make it as easy as possible for editors to read and respond to your work. They're a busy lot and will not waste time with submissions that are messy and difficult to read. It may be good writing, but the editor may never read a poorly presented manuscript to find that out. If you show you care about your work, the editor will too. For an inside view of editors' perspectives on submissions, see Submission Etiquette: Editors Speak Out, beginning on page 68.

Also keep accurate records. We've asked our listings to indicate how long it will take them to report on a submission, but at times throughout the year the market may get behind. Note that with small magazines and literary journals (especially those published by universities) response time tends to be slower in the summer months. Keeping track of when you send your manuscript will help you decide when it is time to check on the status of your submission.

ABOUT OUR POLICIES

We occasionally receive letters asking why a certain magazine, publisher or contest is not in the book. Sometimes when we contact a listing, the editor does not want to be listed because they: do not use very much fiction; are overwhelmed with submissions; are having financial difficulty or have been recently sold; use only solicited material; accept work from a select group of writers only; do not have the staff or time for the many unsolicited submissions a listing may bring.

Some of the listings do not appear because we have chosen not to list them. We investigate complaints of unprofessional conduct in editors' dealings with writers and misrepresentation of information provided to us by editors and publishers. If we find these reports to be true, after a thorough investigation, we will delete the listing from future editions. See Important Listing Information on page 92 for more about our listing policies.

If a listing appeared in our book last year but is no longer listed, we list it in the Markets Index, beginning on page 667, with a code explaining why it is not listed. The key to those codes is given in the introduction to the Markets Index. Sometimes the listing does not appear because the editor did not respond in time for our press deadline, or it may not appear for any of the reasons previously mentioned above.

Listings appearing in *Novel & Short Story Writer's Market* are compiled from detailed questionnaires, phone interviews and information provided by editors, publishers and awards directors. The publishing industry is volatile and changes of address, editor, policies and needs happen frequently. To keep up with the changes between editions of the book, we suggest you check the monthly Markets column in *Writer's Digest* magazine.

Club newsletters and small magazines devoted to helping writers also list market information. For those writers with access to online services, several offer writers' bulletin boards, message centers and chat lines with up-to-the-minute changes and happenings in the writing community. Some of these resources are listed in our Websites of Interest (page 629). Many magazine and book publishers offer updated information for writers on their websites. Check individual listings for those website addresses.

We rely on our readers as well, for new markets and information about market conditions. Write us if you have any new information or if you have suggestions on how to improve our listings to better suit your writing needs.

Writing Fiction

The Use of the Journal in Writing a Private Eye Novel

BY SUE GRAFTON

The most valuable tool I employ while writing a private eye novel is the working journal. The process is one I began in rudimentary form when I first started work on *"A" Is for Alibi*, though all I retain of that journal now are a few fragmentary notes. With *"B" Is for Burglar*, I began to refine the method and from *"C" Is for Corpse* on, I've kept a daily log of work in progress. This notebook (usually four times longer than the novel itself) is like a letter to myself, detailing every idea that occurs to me as I proceed. Some ideas I incorporate, some I modify, many I discard. The journal is a record of my imagination at work, from the first spark of inspiration to the final manuscript. Here I record my worries and concerns, my dead ends, my occasional triumphs, all the difficulties I face as the narrative unfolds. The journal contains solutions to all the problems that arise in the course of the writing. Sometimes the breakthroughs are sudden; more often the answers are painstakingly arrived at through trial and error.

One of my theories about writing is that the process involves an ongoing interchange between Left Brain and Right. The journal provides a testing ground where the two can engage. Left Brain is analytical, linear, the time keeper, the bean counter, the critic and editor, a valuable ally in the shaping of the mystery novel or any piece of writing for that matter. Right Brain is creative, spatial, playful, disorganized, dazzling, nonlinear, the source of the *Aha*! or imaginative leap. Without Right Brain, there would be no material for Left Brain to refine. Without Left Brain, the jumbled brilliance of Right Brain would never coalesce into a satisfactory whole.

In addition to the yin/yang of the bicameral brain, the process of writing is a constant struggle between the Ego and the Shadow, to borrow Jungian terms. Ego, as implied, is the public aspect of our personality, the carefully constructed personna, or mask, we present to the world as the "truth" about us. The Shadow is our Unconscious, the Dark Side—the dangerous, largely unacknowledged cauldron of "unacceptable" feelings and reactions that we'd prefer not to look at in ourselves and certainly hope to keep hidden from others. We spend the bulk of our lives perfecting our public image, trying to deny or eradicate the perceived evil in our nature.

For the writer, however—especially the mystery writer—the Shadow is crucial. The Shadow gives us access to our repressed rage, the murderous impulses that propel antisocial behavior whether we're inclined to act out or not. Without ingress to our own Shadow, we would have no way to delineate the nature of a fictional killer, no way to penetrate and depict the inner life of the villain in the novels we write. As mystery writers, we probe this emotional black swamp again and again, dredging in the muck for plot and character. As repelled as we may be by the Dark Side of our nature, we're drawn to its power, recognizing that the Shadow contains enormous energy if we can tap into it. The journal is the writer's invitation to the Shadow, a means of beckoning to the Unconscious, enticing it to yield its potent magic to the creative process.

SUE GRAFTON *is the author of the bestselling Kinsey Millhone series, the most recent of which is "M"* Is for Malice. *She has won the Best PI Novel Shamus award an unprecedented three times, with "B," "G" and "K." She is a past president of the Private Eye Writers of America. This article is excerpted from* Writing the Private Eye Novel *copyright © 1997 by The Private Eye Writers of America. Used with permission of Writer's Digest Books, a division of F&W Publications, Inc.*

WHAT GOES INTO THE JOURNAL AND HOW DOES IT WORK?

At the outset of each new novel, the first thing I do is open a document on my word processor that I call "Notes" or "Notes-1." By the end of a book, I have 4 or 5 such documents, averaging 50 single-spaced pages apiece.

In my first act of the writing day, I log into my journal with the date. Usually I begin with a line about what's happening in my life. I make a note if I'm coming down with a cold, if my cat's run away, if I've got company coming in from out of town. Anything that specifically characterizes the day becomes part of the journal on the theory that exterior events have the potential to affect the day's work. If I have a bad day at work, I can sometimes track the problem to its source and try correcting it there. For instance, if I'm consistently distracted every time I'm scheduled for a speaking engagement, I can limit outside events until the book is done.

The second entry in the journal is a note about any idea that's occurred to me in the dead of night, when Shadow and Right Brain are most active. Often, I'm wakened by a nudge from Right Brain with some suggestion about where to go next in the narrative or offering a reminder of a beat I've missed. Sometimes, I'm awakened by emotion-filled dreams or the horror of a nightmare, either one of which can hold clues about the story I'm working on. It's my contention that our writing is a window to all of our internal attitudes and emotional states. If I sit down to write and I'm secretly worried about the progress I'm making, then that worry will infuse the very work itself. If I'm anxious about an upcoming scene, if I'm troubled by the pacing, if I suspect a plot is too convoluted, or the identity of the killer is too transparent, then the same anxiety will inhibit the flow of words. Until I own my worries, I run the risk of self-sabotage or writer's block. The journal serves as a place to off-load anxiety, a verbal repair shop when my internal writing machine breaks down.

Generally, the next step in the journal is to lay out for myself where I am in the book. I talk to myself about the scene I'm working on, or the trouble spots as I see them. It's important to realize that the journal in progress is absolutely private—*for my eyes only*. This is not a literary *oeuvre* in which I preen and posture for some future biographer. This is a nuts-and-bolts format in which I think aloud, fret, whine and wring my hands. There's nothing grand about it and it's certainly not meant to be great writing. Once a novel is finished and out on the shelves, the journal can be opened to public inspection if I so choose.

In the safety of the journal, I can play "Suppose . . ." and "What if . . .", creating an atmosphere of open debate where Ego and Shadow, Left Brain and Right, can all be heard. I write down all the story possibilities . . . all the pros and cons . . . and then check back a day or so later to see which prospects strike a chord. The journal is experimental. The journal functions as a playground for the mind, a haven where the imagination can cavort at will. While I'm working in the journal, I don't have to look good. I can be as dumb or goofy as I want. The journal provides a place where I can let my proverbial hair down and "dare to be stupid," as we used to say in Hollywood.

USING YOUR JOURNAL AS A JUMP-START

The beauty of the journal entry is that before I know it, I'm sliding right into my writing for the day. Instead of feeling resistant or hesitant, the journal provides a jump-start, a way to get the words moving.

To demonstrate the technique, I'll include a few sample pages from the journal I kept during the writing of *"G" Is for Gumshoe*. I do this without embarrassment (she said), though I warn you in advance that what you see is a fumbling process, my tortured mind at work.

"G" Is for Gumshoe is essentially a "road picture." In this seventh novel in the series, Kinsey Millhone discovers she's on Tyrone Patty's hit list, targeted for assassination in retaliation for her part in his arrest and conviction. The following passages of the journal begin some three chapters into the novel. Earlier notes, unfortunately, were lost to me in the transfer of the work from an old computer system to newly acquired equipment. My intention here is not to try to

dazzle you with my song-and-dance work, but to demonstrate the mundane level at which the journal actually functions.

1-2-89

Just checking in to have a little chat. I'm in Chapter 3 and feeling pretty good, but I'm wondering if I don't need some tension or suspense. We know there may be a hit man after her. She's currently on her way to the desert and everything seems really normal . . . nay, even dull. Do I need to pep it up a bit? She's almost at the Slabs. I've been doing a lot of description but maybe I need to weave it into the narrative better. Flipping back and forth from the external to the internal.

What other possibilities are there? I've noticed that with Dick Francis, sometimes when nothing's happening, you sit there expecting something anyway. I could use the external as a metaphor for the internal. I know I'll be doing that when Dietz enters the scene. What could Kinsey be thinking about while she drives down to the Slabs? She's talked briefly . . .

1-4-89

Can't remember what I meant to say in the paragraph above. I did some work last night that I'm really happy with. I'm using a little boy with a toy car at the rest stop. Added a father asleep on the bench. Later, he turns out to be one of the guys hired to kill her.

Want to remember to use a couple of things.

1. When the mother dies, Kinsey goes back down to the desert with Dietz. They search, finding nothing . . . maybe a few personal papers. What they come across, in an old cardboard box under the trailer, is some objects . . . maybe just old cups & saucers (which may trigger memories in Irene Gersh . . .). But the newspapers in which these objects are packed dated back to 1937 . . . Santa Teresa. Obviously, the mother was there at some point.

When Kinsey checks into the mother's background, she realizes Irene's birth certificate is a total fake. The mother has whited out the real information, typed over it, and has done a photocopy. All the information has been falsified. She's not who she says she was during her lifetime . . . father's name is wrong . . . I was thinking it might be Santa Teresa, but then Irene would know at the outset she had some connection with the town. Better she should think she was born in Brawley or someplace like that.

Kinsey tries to track down the original in San Diego . . . or wherever I decide to place the original . . . no record of such a birth. Once Kinsey finds the old newspapers, she decides to try Santa Teresa records, using the certificate # which is the only thing that hasn't been tampered with. Up comes the true certificate.

Must remember that a social security card . . . first three digits indicate where the card was issued. That might be a clue.

Irene Gersh is floored. If mom isn't who she claims she was, then who am I?

Must also remember that mom is frightened to death. That would be a nice murder method.

USING YOUR JOURNAL TO RECORD RESEARCH

In addition to storyboarding ideas, I use my journal to record notes for all the research I've done. I also make a note of any question that occurs to me while I'm writing a scene. Instead of stopping the flow of words, I simply jot down a memo to myself for later action.

Journals often contain the ideas for scenes, characters, plot twists or clever lines of dialogue that don't actually make it into the book I'm working on. Such literary detritus might well provide the spark for the next book in the series.

Often, too, in the pages of a journal, I'll find Right Brain leaping ahead to a later scene in the book. Since I don't actually outline a novel in any format or detailed way, the journal is a road map to the story I'm working on. If dialogue or a descriptive passage suddenly occurs to me, I'll tuck it in the journal and come back to it when I reach the chapter where the excerpt belongs. This way, I find I can do some of my writing in advance of myself. Right Brain, my creative part, really isn't interested in working line-by-line. Right Brain sees the whole picture, like the illustration on the box that contains a jigsaw puzzle. Left Brain might insist that we start at the beginning and proceed in an orderly fashion right through to the end, but Right Brain has its own way of going about its business. The journal is a place to honor Right Brain's ingenuity and nonconformity.

Sometimes I use the journal to write a note directly to Shadow or Right Brain, usually when I'm feeling blocked or stuck. These notes are like writer's prayers and I'm always astonished at how quickly they're answered.

In the *"G" Is for Gumshoe* journal, you can see that by March, some three months later, the book has advanced almost magically. I'll do a hop-skip-and-jump, picking up entries here and there.

3-12-89

Finally got Dietz & Kinsey on the road. They've stopped for lunch. She's asking him about his background & he's being good about that stuff. Want to keep them moving . . . let information surface while they're heading for Santa Teresa. Don't want the story to come to a screeching halt while they chit chat. Must keep defining his character through action . . . not just dialogue. Once I get the book on body-guarding techniques, I can fill in some technical information that will make him seem very knowledgeable. For now, I can do the small touches. At some point, he should give her some rules & regulations.

What else do I want to accomplish on the way up to Santa Teresa? Don't need any action at this point . . . don't need jeopardy per se. Must keep in mind that Dick Francis plays relationships very nicely without jamming incessant screams and chases into the narrative.

3-13-89

I wonder if chapter nine will last all the way to Santa Teresa. What does Kinsey do when she gets home? She'll call Irene to make sure Agnes has arrived, which she will very soon. She'll introduce Dietz to Henry Pitts who'll be briefed about the situation re: the hit man. Security measures (if I knew what they were . . .).

Want to dovetail "A" & "B" plots so both won't come to a ragged stop simultaneously.

Within a day, Agnes Grey will have disappeared from the nursing home.

Soon after, her body will be found.

Haven't quite solved the problem of how Kinsey gets hired to track down the killer.

Can't quite decide what the next beat is in the attempt on Kinsey's life. Dietz will get her a bulletproof vest. Does he jog with her? She won't really feel like it, and he'll advise against. He'll have her take a different route to the office & home every day . . . always in his company.

Maybe Dietz has to make a quick trip to Carson City . . . or someplace. Papa sick? Mama sick? An unavoidable personal emergency. If I played my cards right, his absence might coincide with Kinsey's second trip to the desert. I guess I'll map all this out as I get to it but it does feel like a tricky business to make the story move smoothly through here.

Why do I worry so much about boring the reader? I don't want it to look like I've sacrificed the mystery and the pace for mere romance.

And skipping ahead to August . . .

8-12-89

Trying not to panic here. In the dead of night, Right Brain suggested that maybe Kinsey gets locked in the very storage bin Agnes was locked in. Nice claustrophobic atmosphere.

As a reader, I don't object to being privy to the reasoning process a detective goes through as long as it makes sense to me and seems logical. When the leap comes too fast, then I object. I like for the detective to consider every possible alternative.

My problem here is one of transitions . . . forging the links between the scenes I know are coming up.

8-15-89

Book was due today but so be it. Just closed out Chapter 23 and opened 24. I'm going to write notes to myself for a while and then print pages 30-35 so I can have them handy.

Need to set up "It used to be Sumner. . . ."

Maybe Kinsey & Dietz go back to Irene's & confront her with the true information on the birth certificate. If these aren't my parents, then who am I?

8-16-89

God, I'm tired today. I'd really love to sleep. Let's see what I can accomplish in a stupor. Can't wait for this book to be over and done.

Dear Right Brain,

Please be with me here and help me solve and resolve the remaining questions in the narrative. Help me to be resourceful, imaginative, energetic, inventive. And patient.

Look forward to hearing from you.

Sincerely,

Sue

I could pull up countless other samples, but you get the point I'm sure.

LOOKING BACK

One comfort I take from my journals is that regardless of where I am in the current private eye novel, I can always peek back into the journals I've kept for previous books and discover I was just as confused and befuddled back *then* as I am today. Prior journals are reminders that regardless of past struggles, I did somehow manage to prevail. Having survived through 2 novels, or 5, or even 12, in my case, there's some reason to suppose I'll survive to write the next.

If you haven't already incorporated a journal or its equivalent into your current bag of writing tricks, you might try your hand at one and see how it works for you. Remember, it's your journal and you can do it any way you choose. If you don't use a PC, you can write yours in crayon on 10×14 sheets of newsprint. You can type it, write in longhand, use a code if you need to feel protected. You can log in every day or only once a week. You can use it as a launching pad and then abandon the practice, or use it as I do, as an emotional tether connecting me to each day's work.

To help you get started, I'll give you the first entry just to speed you on your way:

Enter today's date.

Just sitting down here to try my hand at this weird stuff Sue Grafton has been talking about. A lot of it sounds like California psychobabble, but if it helps with the writing, who really cares?

In the book I'm working on what worried me is . . .

Turning Real People Into Fiction

BY ROBIN HEMLEY

We rarely write about other people simply as they're presented to us, mostly because we don't know all the facts of their lives and so we have to make some of them up. There's nothing wrong with that. In many cases, knowing too little about someone is preferable to knowing too much. If you write a story based on a family member, for instance, or a friend, your feelings of affection and friendship for that person can easily get in the way of your story or novel. In other words, you'll leave things out—maybe the best parts of the story, maybe the details that intrigued you about this person in the first place—to protect your friend's privacy. That might be the ethical thing to do—but it might also kill your story.

TRANSFORMATIONS

Usually, there's a middle ground between imagining a character whole cloth and writing something completely biographical about someone you know. You must remember that you're writing fiction, not biography. Fiction, by its nature, involves transformation. If you want to write about Uncle Lou, go ahead, but don't make him Uncle Lou. First of all, think about what makes him so intriguing to you. That central ingredient, of course, is what you'll most likely want to keep. Let's say Uncle Lou believes in ghosts. This is something that's always fascinated you about him. This belief in ghosts sprang from an early childhood experience, when Uncle Lou was allegedly visited in the middle of the night by the ghost of his father. Other than this belief in ghosts, Uncle Lou seems rather plain and unexceptional to you. He's a balding, overweight bachelor. His politics are on the conservative side. He's a quiet man who eats dinner every night with his widowed sister, your Aunt Elena—she does all the cooking and cleaning. While she's in the kitchen fixing dinner, he's out in the living room reading *The Wall Street Journal*. During dinner, he hardly talks to Aunt Elena, and afterward, he departs with hardly a word.

Now you have two characters from your life, and this somewhat strange relationship between them—the kernel of a story. And what about Aunt Elena? Does she believe in ghosts, too? Or does she think Uncle Lou is just a little daffy?

Obviously, there are problems here if you want to write about these people. You may be a little reluctant to change too much about the characters and the situation. At the same time, you don't want to offend Aunt Elena or Uncle Lou. You don't want them to be able to recognize themselves. So you have two choices. Either you can wait until your uncle and aunt pass away to write about them, or you can change them. You can change their ages. But no, what interests you about them is that they're both older, a little lonely, a little dependent on each other, and also obsessed with something that might or might not have occurred when Lou was a little boy: the sighting of his dead father. Okay, so change their sexes. Make Aunt Elena the one who saw

ROBIN HEMLEY *teaches creative writing at Western Washington University in Bellingham. He is a* STORY *magazine contributor whose work has been anthologized in* The Pushcart Prize XV *and* XIX. *He has published two collections of short stories,* All You Can Eat *(Atlantic Monthly Press) and* The Big Ear *(John Blair), and a novel,* The Last Studebaker *(Graywolf Press). This article is excerpted from* Turning Life Into Fiction *copyright © 1994 by Robin Hemley. Used with permission of Story Press, a division of F&W Publications, Inc.*

the ghost. Do they have to be brother and sister? How about husband and wife? Must it be their dead father? What about their mother or a stranger? Can you change the outward appearance of Uncle Lou? Depicting him as balding might offend him more than the way you portray his belief in ghosts. That's what happened to a friend of mine who wrote of a mutual friend in a story. He was cast as a short-order cook, a complete fabrication, but in every other way my friend captured his personality perfectly, from his wise-cracking sense of humor to his receding hairline. The mention of the receding hairline was, of course, what upset him.

The fact is, you can rarely tell what will or won't offend someone in a story you've written about them. The best you can do is to change whatever you can bear to change about them. Make your Uncle Lou a short-order cook. Make Aunt Elena the owner of the diner. Or change the locale. Above all, don't mess with male pattern baldness.

All of this is done not simply to protect Uncle Lou and Aunt Elena's privacy, but for your sake as well. In a way, you must stop thinking of them as your real-life relatives for the story to be successful. You must cut loose from your ties to these people or else your story will seem stilted and you'll be afraid to take risks. The more you transform these people into combinations of your imagination and who they really are, the more liberated you'll feel in writing your story. Remember, just because you *base* a character on Aunt Elena doesn't mean you're restricted to the facts.

Mixing and matching

Another way to transform your characters is by making them into *composites*—that is, a mix of your Uncle Lou and perhaps other real people you know, people who have a certain Lou-ness about them. This way, Uncle Lou will not simply be Uncle Lou, but also perhaps your friend's father, and maybe a pinch of some stranger you once saw in passing and wrote about in your journal. By making a composite character, you actually enrich the character. Real observed detail only enhances a story.

David Michael Kaplan used a composite character in "Anne Rey," a story about an art restorer who goes to live on a sailboat and whose mother is suffering from a mysterious brain ailment. The whole seed idea for "Anne Rey" came from seeing a license plate.

"I was driving along on an L.A. freeway," Kaplan says. "A car passed me and the license plate says Anne Ray. That intrigued me and I wrote it down in my journal, which I had in my car. Just Anne Ray. I changed it to Rey in the story because that had more connotations for me. Over time, I started thinking, 'Who is this Anne Rey?' And that's how the story developed. It was a process of a couple of years.

"As I mulled over the idea, things began to hook up, other seed ideas that I would read in my journal or copy down. I had an idea from a year later about a guy giving up most everything and going off to live on a sailboat. I also copied down some interesting notes from a lecture I heard on art restoration. So, one day, in reviewing my journals and thinking about story ideas, all of a sudden I was reading the-guy-on-the-sailboat story, and I realized it's not a story about a guy living on a sailboat. It's Anne Rey who lives on a sailboat. That's who she is. And then I was reading more and I realized she's an art restorer. That's it! So those three things started coming together, and then the fourth key thing was a year later—I had an experience. I was making films at the time and I was doing a film on radiology. I was interviewing patients for this film, and there was a woman who told me about the experience that she'd had of feeling that there was—and I'm quoting her—'a strange little hat' on her head, the pressure of a little hat on her head. And she'd had a lot of radiological studies done because sometimes the sense of phantom pressure can be the sign of a tumor. So she had a series of CAT scans but they never found anything. She still felt the pressure. That story kind of made an impression on me, and eventually she became the mother, complete with little phantom hats, a woman who was slowly going insane, Anne Rey's mother. So there are about four different things there, things that happened to me, things that I heard people say, things that I saw, that happened over the course of two years, that then came together, mixing and matching, to feed into and become the story 'Anne Rey'."

Here then is the opening of Kaplan's story:

> When Anne Rey was a little girl and her mother read her fairy tales from a large purple book, her favorites had been those in which the hero embarked on a journey by boat; in later years, after consulting the I Ching, Anne always felt a special thrill when she received a hexagram advising "crossing a great sea." So perhaps it was not surprising that shortly after her mother began complaining about the "funny little hat" on the side of her head, Anne Rey—28 years old, single, art restorer, specializing in prints and drawings—decided to give up her small apartment and move onto a sailboat.

That process of mixing and matching is exactly what fiction writers do, whether the story is based on real life or not. This kind of transformation is central to the fiction process. And when you write about someone real, this mixing and matching isn't merely good for self-protection; it deepens your understanding of the character by involving your imaginative process. It makes the character your own "Anne Rey," not the Anne Ray you spotted on a license plate.

One might argue that simply mashing together aspects of different people's personalities is not an act of the imagination at all, but that's a foolish notion. The test of one's imagination is not simply in one's ability to invent details and characters out of thin air, but also in how one orders and overlays real events and people, how one transforms real life into something completely new.

For example, the episode of the ghost I mentioned earlier is something a student and her sister told me once about their father. When he was a boy, he had an uncle who would sometimes stay with the family. The uncle kept a bottle of whiskey hidden in the boy's dresser, and late at night he'd sneak in and take a swig, and the boy would watch him. Then one night, the uncle came into the room and just looked down at the boy in his bed, but didn't take any whiskey or say anything. The next day the boy learned that his uncle had died that night in a car accident. But the story goes on. Every night for a month, the uncle visited the boy, just staring down at him. The family still owns that house, and the father of my student refuses to spend the night there.

The other details I mentioned, about the elderly man whose sister cooks for him every night—that's the relationship between my Uncle Morty and my Grandmother Ida, both of whom are no longer alive. Every night he'd come over and she'd cook dinner for him, and then he'd leave with hardly a word. Of course, there's nothing terribly revealing or troubling or even all that interesting in the situation, and if I'd wanted to write about Morty and Ida and their nightly ritual when they were alive, I would have done so without any compunction whatsoever. It's only when I overlaid something else on top of these people—the ghost sighting—that the story started becoming somewhat intriguing.

Remember that all of these people are or were real, but probably none of them would have recognized themselves in the context in which I placed them. I took my real relatives and added details from the life of a complete stranger, a man I've never even met.

Of course, maybe I'm fooling you again. Maybe I have no Uncle Morty or Grandmother Ida. Maybe I never had a student whose father saw a ghost. The truth of it shouldn't matter to you. Is it interesting? Is it believable? Those are the only issues that count.

WRITING WITHOUT COMPOSITES

Sometimes a writer will bravely, or foolishly, decide to write about a family member or friend without transforming that person much, if at all. It's difficult enough to write in the first place. It's murder when you also have to worry about how Aunt Elena will take it when she inevitably sees the story you've written, based on her life. I'm assuming a negative reaction here, but I've found that people are rarely as upset about being included in your stories as you think they'll be. Often, your Aunt Elena won't recognize herself, or, if she does, she'll ignore those aspects of herself that might have been portrayed negatively.

When Thomas Wolfe first wrote *Look Homeward, Angel*, his hometown of Asheville ostracized him because he wrote about them and told their secrets. He couldn't even show his face in Asheville. A few years after the book was published and he was a world-famous author, the only people who were mad at him were those he didn't include in the book.

Another Asheville native, Gail Godwin, wrote an early novel, *The Old Woman*, in which her younger sister and her mother were cast as characters, though somewhat transformed. In her essay "Becoming a Writer," Godwin recalls that her sister complained, "She'd better never put me in a novel again. I don't like being frozen in print for the rest of my life, forever wearing those silly panties and short skirts; and I'm *not* big like that, she's made me into some sort of Amazon freak." Godwin's mother was more understanding, saying obviously the character based on her was too stupid and passive to be an accurate reflection. The young Godwin responded that the character *was* supposed to be her mother. "Well, there was something left out, then," her mother said.

Novelist Bret Lott hardly transformed his family at all in his novel *Jewel* (Pocket Books), a story based on his grandmother's life. The story is about a woman who finally has to break the spirit and the will of her husband, and to sacrifice much of the childhood of her five other children for the sixth one, a down's syndrome child. When the book was published, he went to his grandmother's house. She was happy to see him, of course, then took him out on the patio behind the house and sat him down at the picnic table and said, "Well, it's a beautiful book, but I just want to tell you I wasn't as hard on your grandfather as you made me out to be." Lott was taken aback. "I said, 'Grandma, it's a novel,' which is always the novelist's excuse, so I was able to weasel my way out of this. Because it was so known in our family that I was writing this book about her and the family, I don't think that she saw a difference between the book and the true family story, which is a dangerous thing—especially since in the novel I used everyone's name. Those are the true names of everyone. I got permission from everyone to do that, but I just couldn't do any better than the real names: Jewel, Leston, Wilman, Burton, Billie Jean, Ann, Brenda Kay. So in her mind, the delineation between fiction and the truth was very blurry. But the other side of the story is that every sibling, every one of her children, all those people involved have said to me at one time or another, 'You got that exactly right.' She, in fact, did break the spirit of her husband, my grandfather. This was a truth she did not necessarily want to face."

With Lott's first novel, *The Man Who Owned Vermont* (Viking), he had to face the disapproval of his father: "*The Man Who Owned Vermont* is about an R.C. Cola salesman. My dad's life was R.C. Cola. He was an R.C. Cola man from 1951 to 1982. When you read that novel, it's a pretty disparaging account of what it's like to be a soda pop salesman. The character doesn't believe in doing what he does, so the whole thing's a sham. There's a line in there about how his whole life has been about selling something that no one in their right mind would want. Chemicals and carbonated water and caramel coloring. Who really needs this? My dad has said on many occasions, 'I know you think that selling soda pop was a waste.' I told him it's not true. All I could say was, 'Dad, it's a novel.' "

Getting permission

Sometimes, you've got to give yourself permission to write about your Aunt Elenas, your Jewels, your moms and dads. If you want to write a story about a relative or close friend, but feel some hesitation, ask yourself why. Are you sure your friend or relative will recognize herself? If so, can you change anything about her to make her less recognizable? If not, maybe you should just go to the person you want to write about and ask for her permission. If she says no, you'll have to respect her wishes or perhaps lose her favor. But part of her response will depend on how you phrase the question. If you act sheepish about it and make it seem like a horrible thing, you can expect a defensive, negative reaction. If you explain a little bit about the story, that it's fiction, and that her life is fascinating to you and worthy of exploration, her reaction will probably be positive. But there's no guarantee.

Remember that there's a certain amount of courage involved in writing, and if you always stay with material that's safe and won't get you into any trouble (even if the trouble is only with your own conflicting emotions about uncovering material that's close to home), your writing might ultimately seem limited and dull. Good writing takes risks and sometimes unsettles the writer as well as the reader. Fiction does not necessarily reflect the world as it should be, but as it is, and that means chronicling conflict. In real life, most of us avoid conflict. But conflict is a crucial element of all fiction, as it is an element of life. Imperfect beings that we are, we thrive on conflict, whether it's the base, reptilian conflict of a car blowing up at the end of a chase scene in a movie, or the more subtle, psychological conflict of a contemporary short story.

Fiction often deals with people making moral choices, and sometimes making the wrong ones. If you write about the world as it is, and not as you'd like it to be, you will definitely offend someone, and not necessarily your Aunt Elena. As Flannery O'Connor put it, storytelling is "an attempt to make someone who doesn't want to listen, listen, and who doesn't want to see, see. We can't change what we see to suit the reader, but we must convey it as whole as possible into his unspacious quarters for his divided and suspicious consideration."

It's important, however, to avoid being too solipsistic in one's writing, thinking that people exist simply as fodder for your brilliant novels and stories. Donald Barthelme explores this notion in his story "The Author," which deals with a mother blithely uncovering the family skeletons of her grown children in her novels. She portrays one of her sons, a doctor, hanging out with a bunch of survivalists in Miami. She also reveals her daughter Virginia's car accident in which Virginia's blood-alcohol ratio was .18 percent. Another son threatens to sue her for writing of his habit of purchasing "U.S. Army morphine syrettes from disaffected Medical Corps master sergeants." The narrator, a former museum-curator-at-large, has been let go because of his mother's uncovering of his theft of several "inconsequential" Native American medicine bundles from the museum. When he confronts his mother, asks her why and how she can do what she does, she answers him coolly, "Because you're mine."

ACTING THE PART

No matter whom you base your characters on, you must think of yourself as much as an actor as a writer. You need to get into the role and learn your part. That's why details are so important, the small details that make up someone's life. One of the best ways to understand characters and motivation is to take an acting class. Of course, most good writers come to their understanding of things such as motivation intuitively; just as many have never read Freud but intuitively understand the concepts of displacement and projection.

A writer, just like an actor, needs to believe the character she is writing about. If you aren't convinced your character is real (whether based on your Uncle Lou or your friend's Uncle Shorty or made up whole cloth), your reader certainly won't believe either.

I'm not saying that the Uncle Shorty in your story should be a photocopy of the real Uncle Shorty. But you should be able to answer any question, no matter how seemingly insignificant, about your character. If asked, "What do the curtains in Shorty's bedroom look like?" you should be able to answer, "There aren't any curtains in his bedroom," or whatever you think best fits his character. It's not necessary that all of these details make it into your story. It's important that you know your character well enough to supply these details. Above all, you want your characters, no matter whom they're based on, to seem as though they lived and breathed before the opening paragraph of your story. You want them to have a sense of history.

Finding the right details

Whether a character in your story or novel is wholly imagined, partly imagined, or a true-to-life representation of someone doesn't matter at all. What matters is the character's believability to the reader. Being believable is not the same as being realistic. Plenty of writers pull off having outlandish characters and plots and settings in their stories, because they make their characters and the worlds they live in believable through *salient details*—that is, physical, sensory details that make the character stand out in the reader's mind. We experience life through our senses, so it stands to reason that if we try to recreate life through the writing of fiction, using sensory details will help create an illusion of real-life experience.

When you write about a character, you must choose the details that will fix him in the reader's mind. Simply writing a sentence like "Uncle Lou was a big man," does not make him a memorable character. How big was he? "The only pants Uncle Lou ever felt comfortable in were second-hand maternity slacks." Now there's a sentence that shows a couple of things about Uncle Lou. It shows perhaps a kind of absurb frugality on his part, as well as giving one a pretty fair idea of how big he is.

When you write about a real person, especially someone you know quite well, a flood of details usually will hit you, many more than you can possibly use in your story. Write as many of those details down in your journal as possible, but select the few that will firmly anchor the character in our minds. If the remarkable thing about Uncle Lou was his shoe size (maybe he wore a size 15), make that the detail that types him. Maybe several things made your uncle remarkable—not only his foot size, but he had an enormous beard, never washed his hair and wore a greasy Cleveland Indians baseball cap. Perhaps you can get away with using all those details, but you might have to toss one or two of them to make him less of a caricature. Which ones would you choose to drop? You'd choose different ones from the ones I'd choose. But the more specific a detail, the more memorable it will be to the reader, and that's a good rule of thumb to use when deciding which details to include in your fiction and which to get rid of.

Likewise, you don't have to give us all these details at once. In fact, if you do, they'll blur, and we'll have as indistinct an impression of your character as if you'd given us no details at all. As a writer of fiction, you must learn to slowly dispense information about your characters, not all in a rush, never to be mentioned again. If, for instance, you decide to keep the greasy baseball cap, it should have some role in the story. Same with the foot size. Not only should it give us some sense of who your character is, but, if possible, make it part of your story's plot. Otherwise, the baseball cap becomes a red herring, a false clue, a detail that serves no purpose other than the author's whim.

TYPE VERSUS STEREOTYPE

Type is different from stereotype. Certain things are typical of people without necessarily being stereotypical. A plumber, for instance, will usually have typical tools of the trade: a plumber's snake, a truck or van, a jumpsuit of some kind for crawling around basements, a flashlight. So what's a stereotype of a plumber? Probably the first two or three images that come to mind are negative, since stereotypes are usually unfair and demeaning—overcharging or falling-down pants. That's not to say that such stereotypes are completely false and nonexistent in real life, just that they're stale, over-used and unfair. That's what a stereotype is, an unoriginal image of a person or group of people, most often used in a derogatory fashion.

Just because you've met someone who fits a stereotype doesn't mean that he'll be less of a stereotype when you place him in a story. In a piece of fiction, *avoid stereotypes*. The reason should seem obvious. Besides the fact that denigrating other people is not the nicest thing in the world, why bother to reinforce old stereotypes, to write about things that have been said a thousand times before? Fictional characters must seem complex for us to believe they're flesh and blood. Real live flesh-and-blood characters don't have to seem complex at all. If you have a friend with a pickup with fat tires, a gun rack, a bumper sticker that reads, "American by birth, Southern by the grace of God," and a blue-tick hound dog named Otis who rides in back, you might say, "Wow, what a stereotype, but he's still my bud." But if you put your bud in a story, I might say, "Sorry, too much of a stereotype. Make him more realistic." And you say, "How? If I make him more realistic, I'll be fictionalizing him." And I'll say, "Exactly!"

HISTORICAL FIGURES AND CELEBRITIES

Sometimes writers of fiction use historical figures or celebrities in their stories. Barry Hannah, while by no means a writer of historical fiction, has made forays into the area. In his acclaimed short story collection, *Airships* (Random House), three stories deal with Jeb Stuart, the Confederate general. "Jeb Stuart attracted me because he was so unlike me," Hannah says. "He was a 29-year-old general. He was a Presbyterian who didn't smoke or drink. He was very dashing, the last of the cavalry heroes. He just about embodies everything good about the South that I know of, and about the cavalier era.

"When I wrote about Jeb after I'd read a good deal about him, I was interested in those around him, the effect that a hero has on those close to him. So I used what I knew about him but I also made up my own cast of folks to put around him. There's one gay guy. I don't think a gay Confederate had ever been written about."

Like any kind of fiction, you must have the confidence to use your imagination, to transform the historical figure or current celebrity—to make the character your own. You're mucking around in history and that can be a daunting challenge to a timid writer. But if you attempt such a story, remember it's fiction you're writing, not history. And, depending on what your goals are in the story, you don't necessarily have to stick to the facts of your subject's life. If your aims are absurdist, you can write a story about how Judy Garland, at the decline of her career, took up sumo wrestling. Obviously, that's nowhere near the truth of her life. But a number of writers have written stories like that to great effect. These stories tend to be more cultural metaphors than actual explorations of someone's life. That's not to say that the two are mutually exclusive. Barry Hannah's stories about Jeb Stuart have as much to do metaphorically with the cultures of the old and new South as they do with the actual life of Jeb Stuart.

"The reason you can use your imagination," says Hannah, "is that most history is not in the books. Their day-to-day life is not in the books. You only get a gloss. It's not that my guess is as good as any, because I try to be educated about the era. But it is up for grabs about what a guy is like in a given hour. People are not always postured and heroic. And they say dreadful things, even the best people. But they sure don't make speeches. And they have to get up and put their pants on. That part of history is never in the books. And I like to give a sense of it."

The main thing to remember when writing this kind of fiction is to do your research. Know something about the era. Know something about the person. Go to the library and look at microfilm of newspaper articles about the person you're writing about. Read biographies about the person, not just one, but two or three. Biographers don't necessarily agree with one another, so you can usually get a couple of different perspectives by reading more than one, and then you can decide which is the most accurate—or you can invent your own perspective. To some degree, you must create your own perspective, or else the story will simply be warmed-over biography.

The way you introduce your famous character in such a story or novel is perhaps of more importance than in any other kind of fiction. If you're not careful, you can easily alienate the reader. If you simply rely on stereotypes of your famous character, or introduce him in a sensational manner, you can be sure that your reader will not be convinced. Consider this opening:

Napoleon sat at his dresser, hand in his jacket, admiring himself in the mirror.

This is a silly opening, starting out in the most obvious fashion. On the other hand, better not to keep your reader unaware of your famous subject's identity too long. Your reader's reaction might be a groan when she discovers after 30 pages who your subject is.

Einstein's Dreams, a novel by Alan Lightman (Pantheon), recreates in an almost impressionistic form Einstein's discovery of the nature of time. Here is the way it opens:

> In some distant arcade, a clock tower calls out six times and then stops. The young man slumps at his desk. He has come to the office at dawn, after another upheaval. His hair is uncombed and his trousers are too big. In his hand, he holds 20 crumpled pages, his new theory of time, which he will mail today to the German journal of physics.

Several things make this opening convincing. Obviously, we know the subject by the title of the book, and in that first paragraph he's not mentioned by name. He doesn't need to be mentioned by name, because Einstein is a universally famous figure, and the reader brings a certain amount of knowledge to the story already. The theory of time is a dead giveaway, as is the slight physical description of the young man's appearance, especially the uncombed hair. The reader instantly recalls the famous photo of an older Einstein with his hair going in all directions at once. The more famous your subject, the less you have to dwell on the obvious facts about that person.

Also notice that the author casts his story in present tense. This strategy gives us a sense of immediacy. It's as though we're watching a movie unfold in slow motion with both sound and sight involved: the distant tolling of the clock, the visual image of the man slumped over his desk. Casting the paragraph in third person, objective, also adds to the sense of a cool authority giving us this information, the facts, as they were, without any interpretation—or so it would seem. It would be hard to come up with a better strategy for introducing such a famous man to us. And it's all done through salient details and a subtle handling of the information we must know about this character.

Writing Effective Dialogue: Examples and Possibilities

BY TOM CHIARELLA

Writing dialogue is so much about the energy and direction of the story at hand that many of the things a writer does are intuitive. A turn here. An exclamation. A silence. I'll often hear experienced writers say they've developed an "ear" for dialogue. The implication is that dialogue exists in the world and writers merely record, with good writers—those with the "ear" for it—recording a little more clearly. The truth is, it's not solely about recording, or listening, but about shaping.

When I speak of the energy and direction of a story, I am referring to its tone and emotion (energy) and tension (direction). Writers craft, or shape, patterns of energy and direction in dialogue. In many ways these become the signatures of their dialogue, the things that make the voices of their characters recognizable and sustainable. Writers may have an ear for dialogue, but what they work with is a voice, shaped and charged by the needs of story. What your character says is directed by the needs of the story.

Classifying dialogue by techniques can be troublesome. Writers don't work that way. Most writers I know despise the very act of naming the things they do. It makes them too self-conscious to think of the patterns they create as they create them. I'm going to do some of that here, but only for the purposes of comparison. You should be looking for the occasional pause, the turn, the reversal, the silence that defines each of these moments. Naming the patterns is unimportant; reading to uncover them is a worthy task.

Thus you must be willing to take dialogue apart to look at what makes it tick. As you read, be willing to isolate moments within a dialogue. Highlight them in your book. Dog-ear the pages. Tear out a page and tape it to the wall above your computer. The idea is to take the dialogue on its own terms, to isolate the specific techniques the writer uses, before returning to the story as a whole to examine the dialogue's function in the larger context.

Begin by looking for the general tension of the dialogue. Some beginning writers confuse tension with conflict, assuming it comes and goes depending on whether characters agree or disagree. Tension is more like the energy between charged particles. It's always there, even when two people agree. Think of 2 cars traveling a reasonable distance apart from one another along an interstate at 65 miles an hour. Safe distance. Same direction. Same speed. No tension, right? Wrong. We all know it only takes one little bump in the road, one touch of the brakes, a doe in the headlights for everything to be completely and suddenly redefined. So you might start by looking for those three qualities when gauging the tension of your dialogue: direction, speed and distance (or separation).

TOM CHIARELLA *is a member of the English department at DePauw University in Greencastle, Indiana. He is the author of a collection of stories,* Foley's Luck *(Knopf). His fiction and nonfiction have appeared in* The New Yorker, Esquire, STORY, The Florida Review *and elsewhere. He has won grants from the NEA and the Indiana Arts Commission. This article is excerpted from* Writing Dialogue *copyright © 1998 by Tom Chiarella. Published by Story Press, a division of F&W Publications, Inc. Reprinted by permission of Brandt & Brandt Literary Agents, Inc.*

TENSION IN DIALOGUE

How do I apply all this talk of direction, speed and distance to a dialogue?

Set two characters up in a blank room—that is, a bare stage, a void, a place not yet defined. Now make a decision. One of them wants something. The other does not have it, or can not get it. How will the first get it, if not by speaking? He must move in the direction of his desire.

    1: Give it to me.

The direction here is clear and declarative. It's a palpable tension. Surely, you can see that this addresses a need in a particular way. Nothing has been named yet, we have no fix on place, or even space, and yet the character speaks out of a sense of what she wants. But it would be no less so if it started this way.

    1: Excuse me.

He's still moving in the direction of his desire, toward what he wants, by breaking the silence, by starting things up. I don't have to move much past that utterance to see a sort of tension filling up the space. Where would you expect this to move from here? Direction is a natural part of dialogue. We expect to be led somewhere by the response. How will the other character deal with this? As the answer to this question becomes clearer, we often start to see the issue of distance, or separation, being defined. The tone of that response will set up speed. You might expect me to say the tension I've set up demands that he reveal everything he wants in the first line. For now, let's have the second character work from a position of total neutrality.

    1: Excuse me.
    2: Yes?
    1: Do you know the time?
    2: No, I don't.
    1: Do you have any sense of how long we've been here?
    2: No.

That's probably as neutral as you're going to get. Still, speaker 2 is resisting. It's possible to read a certain distance into that exchange, an attitude that suggests speaker 2 isn't going to help speaker 1 in any way, shape or form. The brief responses lend an element of increased speed. Play it any way you want. Some element of tension is generally shaped by the act of speaking.

All good dialogue has direction. It's a mishmash of need and desire on the part of an individual character weighed against the tension inherent in the gathering of more than one person. Not convinced? Think there isn't always tension when people speak? "What about families?" you say. "What about people who love each other? There's not always tension there." Some of you are laughing at that already, because for many of us a family (love it as we may) is our greatest tissue of tensions. But I would remind you of my terms. This is not grand conflict here, not man versus nature; nor is it painful tension, nothing one could take care of with a little cup of tea and a foot rub. This is the stuff that fills the spaces between us, even when we don't recognize it. As a writer you have to learn to trust that it's there.

Go back to the conversation in the blank room. Try to make it as free of tension as possible. Would it look something like this?

    1: Hi.
    2: Hi.
    1: How are you?
    2: Fine. How are you?
    1: Great. Nice day.
    2: Really. Nice day.

Sounds hauntingly like those conversations we all have in elevators, or at a chance encounter, or in the hallways at school. Most people say they hate this kind of jabber, and that there's no place for it in fiction. Sure people talk like this in the world, but that's why we must shape dialogue when we write. Good dialogue relies on a stronger tension than we see here. Good dialogue requires sharper word choice, more defined attitudes, more originality. As I said in chapter one, good dialogue should be something of an event unto itself.

But despite the apparent neutrality of the dialogue above, it is not without direction. Look at it again. Chart the direction using arrows if you want. Who starts the conversation? Speaker 1. ("Hi.") It's his energy that plays off the response, too. Here, again, we might use the word "speed," or "pace." ("How are you?") He's the one asking the questions. Speaker 2 is feeding off him. The arrows I'd draw would consistently be moving from 1 toward 2. That's one sort of tension, a sort of tensionless tension. Something that would take a long time to build up to the point where you might call it conflict, the point where 1 would want something from 2. It might end like this.

> 1: Fine then.
> 2: What do you mean?
> 1: Nothing.
> 2: Okay.
> 1: Fine.
> 2: I don't understand.
> 1: You wouldn't.
> 2: Are you angry?
> 1: No.
> 2: You seem angry. Have I done something wrong?
> 1: You just don't care. I'm sorry I ever talked to you.

That's an exaggeration, of course. And I have shaped things to my needs. That's what I believe you must do. But there's no question I have moved from the tension buried in the direction of an apparently neutral conversation and found one result. Could you nag out a neutral conversation for pages and pages, keeping it neutral the whole time? Your answer may be yes. Mine is no. That's the sort of thing we do in life. Jabber about sports, ask about the grandkids, exchange greetings. These are masks we wear. They don't last long before we start to reveal who we are. Put two people in one place, force them to listen to one another and soon they are telling stories or, more aptly for us I guess, telling stories in the act of telling. That is what the writer must believe.

Your challenge is to see stories within the words of your character. Looking for speed, distance and direction and manipulating these is a good place to start. If we accept that all good dialogue has these elements of tension, what is it that sets good dialogue apart from lifeless dialogue? Good dialogue rises out of the way a writer makes use of individual techniques, such as

- interruption
- silences
- echoing
- reversals
- shifts in tone and pace
- idiom
- detail

DIRECTED DIALOGUE

Let's look at an example that begins in a fairly "placeless" place, on the radio airwaves, on a radio talk show. This conversation opens Peter Abrahams' novel *The Fan*. This is one of those conversations we hear all the time. Read it once, then read it again, the second time looking for the tension that's buried in the direction of the speakers. I'll follow with a summary of the novel, and an overview of Gil, the main character, who is also the caller in this dialogue.

"Who's next? Gil on the car phone. What's shakin', Gil?"
Dead air.
"Speak, Gil."
"Is this . . ."
"Go on."
"Hello?"
"You're on the JOC."
"Am I on?"
"Not for long, Gil, the way we're going. This is supposed to be entertainment."
Dead air.
"Got a question or a comment for us, Gil?"
"First-time caller."
"Fantabulous. What's on your mind?"
"I'm a little nervous."
"What's to be nervous? Just three million pairs of ears out there, hanging on your every word. What's the topic?"
"The Sox."
"I like the way you say that."
"How do I say it?"
"Like—what *else* could it be?"
Dead air.
"What about the Sox, Gil?"
"Just that I'm psyched, Bernie."
"Bernie's off today. This is Norm. Everybody gets psyched in the spring. That's a given in this game. Like ballpark mustard."
"This is different."
"How?"
Dead air.
"Gil?"
"I've been waiting a long time."
"For what?"
"This year."
"What's special about it?"
"It's their year."
"Why so tentative?"
"Tentative?"
"Just pulling your leg. The way you sound so sure. Like it's a lead-pipe cinch. The mark of the true-blue fan."
Dead air.
"Gil?"
"Yeah?"
"The Vegas odds are—what are they, Fred? Fred in the control room there, doing something repulsive with a pastrami on rye—10 to 1 on the Sox for the pennant, 20, what is it, 25 to 1 on the whole shebang. Just to give us some perspective on this, Gil, what would you wager at those odds, if you were a wagering man?"
"Everything I owe."
"Owe? Hey. I like this guy. He's got a sense of humor after all. But, Gil—you're setting yourself up for a season of disillusion, my friend."

"Disillusion?"

"Yeah, like—"

"I know what *disillusion* means."

"Do you? Then you must—"

"They went down to the wire last year, didn't they?"

"Ancient history, Gil."

What is the charge that runs through this conversation? How and when do we begin to see the tensions of character revealed? The voice of the talk-show host is the active presence in the conversation, pressing against Gil's nervousness, against his stake in the team, against the public perception of the team, to shake him up, to force him into talking. His direction is clear, and, not surprisingly, Gil is not revealing enough for us to know many real facts about him. This is an openly antagonistic dialogue, one in which the movement of one character is an attempt to drive the tensions to the surface. The teasing, the cajoling, the chiding of the host are all a part of this. But so too is Gil's reluctance to speak, to reveal much about himself. The anonymity of the airwaves is a part of that, sure. But Gil's unwillingness or inability to reveal the tensions within him adds to the antagonism. Not surprising that what would follow is the dark story of Gil's obsessive relationship with a player and Gil's course of self-destruction. In the middle of the dialogue above, when Gil says, "I've been waiting a long time . . . [for] this year," it resonates, like all good dialogue, toward the story ahead, toward the year to come.

This is an example of directed dialogue, in which the writer is attempting to use dialogue as a means of setting up the tensions of the longer work. The particular tensions of this dialogue are reflective of issues that will come into play later. One character (in this case the talk-show host) is used as foil for the other. At first it would appear that the host might be the center of this story, but as we read on, it becomes clear that Gil is the one with the story to tell. It's a fine example of a writer bringing tension directly to the surface through the dialogue itself.

The risk of directed dialogue is that it too often serves the needs of the writer first. It becomes a means of explanation, of exposition, and little more. What Abrahams does well is use the fast, staccato rhythm of the talk-show host to hedge the direction of the piece by employing some specific techniques.

- **Interruption**. When Gil cuts off the host with, "I know what disillusion means," this is another moment where his story is foreshadowed.
- **Silences**. Represented here as "Dead air."
- **Echoing**. "Everything I owe" followed by "Owe? . . ." One speaker often picks up or repeats the last word of the previous speaker.
- **Reversals**. The host moves from sarcasm ("Fantabulous") to challenging ("What's special about it?") to chiding ("Ancient history, Gil.").
- **Shifts in pace**. This is an excellent example of a dialogue that works well without dialogue tags.
- **Shifts in tone**. The dialogue lurches forward when it moves from the host's glib line about "ballpark mustard" to Gil's grim response: "This is different."
- **Convincing use of idiom**. "You're on the JOC."
- **Strong details**. The references to the Sox, ballpark mustard, etc.

These elements hold this dialogue, and the others like it in the book, together, allowing it to work for the writer to advance plot and to serve as a convincing reflection of Gil's world. That's the best effect of directed dialogue.

INTERPOLATED DIALOGUE

The artificial part of directed dialogue is that it requires two characters to be "stuck" in one place long enough for them to open up their lives to the reader through conversation. How many conversations have you had in which all your hopes and fears are revealed, at least in part, within a few exchanges? Odds are not many. Those moments do come, but most often the writer must choose ways to isolate specific moments of dialogues or specific directions within these dialogues to reveal the heart of the character. Often this requires interpolating the dialogue with narrative. Interpolating a dialogue allows the narrative to interrupt and interpret the dialogue. Often a single line of dialogue is interpolated into a far larger moment in the scope of the story than it is in the lives of the characters themselves. Take a simple, one-word response like "Sure." Lines like this pass our way again and again in dialogue, but think for a moment about ways to make this word tie in to the life of a character in some meaningful way. Our character may be saying it unwillingly and with a sense of resignation. To interpolate a moment like this, the narrative might step in, interrupting the dialogue on the page, to unwind the character's life in some way, perhaps touching on all the other times she'd simply given in like that. While this may sound intimidating, it ought to be the stuff writers rub their hands over, as it allows for direct connection from the external world of event to the internal world of the character.

In Anton Chekhov's great story "The Lady With the Pet Dog," a moment of casual conversation becomes a looking glass into a character's soul. The story centers on Dmitry Dmitrovich, a Muscovite in late 19th-century Russia. His public life, and married life, leaves him unsatisfied and melancholy and, on vacation in Yalta, he meets a woman with whom he begins an affair. He is rejuvenated by the relationship, but as it would be destructive to both his life and the woman's, he must keep it a secret. His life is split in two, and while he discovers his humanity in his new love, he is trapped by the world in which he lives. At one point, he leaves a restaurant and feels the urge to share his secret. Read the passage below and notice how little is actually spoken but how much is revealed in the words and reactions of the characters. This interpolated dialogue, brief as it is, has a direction too. Its effect, however, is made clear through the narrative that precedes and follows it.

> Already he was tormented by a strong desire to share his memories with someone. But, in his home it was impossible to talk of his love, and he had no one to talk to outside; certainly he could not confide in his tenants or in anyone at the bank. And what was there to talk about? He hadn't loved then, had he? Had there been anything beautiful, poetical, edifying or simply interesting in his relations with Anna Sergeyevna? And he was forced to talk vaguely of love, of women, and no one guessed what he meant; only his wife would twitch her black eyebrows and say, "The part of the philanderer does not suit you at all, Dmitry."
>
> One evening, coming out of the physician's club with an official with whom he had been playing cards, he could not resist saying:
> "If you only knew what a fascinating woman I became acquainted with at Yalta!"
> The official got into his sledge and was driving away, but turned suddenly and shouted:
> "Dmitry Dmitrovich!"
> "What is it?"
> "You were right this evening: the sturgeon was a bit high."
> These words, so commonplace, for some reason moved Gurov to indignation, and struck him as degrading and unclean. What savage manner, what mugs! What stupid nights, what dull humdrum days! Frenzied gambling, gluttony, drunkenness, continual talk always about the same things! Futile pursuits and conversations always about the same topics take up the better part of one's time, the better part of one's strength, and in the end there is left a life clipped and wingless, an absurd mess, and there is no escaping or getting away from it—just as though one were in a prison.

Although Peter Abrahams would surely cringe at the comparison to a master like Chekhov, it's important to note ways in which this dialogue is completely different from the one cited from *The Fan*. This passage acts as one of the story's moments of clarity, an epiphany in which the character sees his life stripped to its most brutal essence. Yet, the dialogue itself is short and the explicit meaning of what is said would not appear to apply to the protagonist's life in any larger sense. It is a moment that, without the accompanying narrative, might appear to be just another moment of daily jabber. But this brief exchange, in which Dmitry's associate tells him the fish was "high," meaning a bit spoiled, just as Dmitry is about to reveal his heart, represents something far larger, and Chekhov attaches a lyric piece of narrative exposition to the dialogue directly. Like the passage before it, this dialogue reveals, but the interruption and interpretation of the narrative drives home the point of what is *not* said, rather than what is said. This is where the interpolation comes in. The dialogue is realistic; the narrative is expository and interpretive. The two are clearly attached, without apology, by the writer. It's not about filling silences so much as filling the gaps left by our words, the gaps between us.

Interpolation is part of the way we tell stories to one another. It is part of the internal texture of a character. Picture yourself telling someone about an argument you had.

> "Then I said, *'No, I won't have it ready. Not when you want it.'* That's what I told him. My life is a mess. I'm behind in everything, the reports pile up faster than I can get them out and I just hate the new payroll system. I hold everything in, too. I mean I really bury it. I hate it all. I look at everything on my desk and I just want to start fresh."

The sentence in italics represents what was literally said; what follows is interpretation for the intended audience. Maybe you recognize interpolation now. Within the frame of a story, it is tempting to allow the flow of dialogue to take over your pace and treatment of scene. Once again, it is important to think about the way we tell jokes, stories, related memories. Stating what literally happened is often less important than the interpretation of those events. Hitting the dialogue right is a matter of seeing where the tension is in the character's life.

Still, don't overexplain. Go back to real life. Some writers do this sort of interpreting incessantly. Don't they wear you out? Let that serve as your warning. Don't fall into a pattern of interrupting and interpreting every snatch of dialogue. Interpolated dialogue is difficult, and when poorly done can sink your work. Use this tool wisely. A good rule is if you find yourself explaining only for the reader's benefit, then stop. If you are discovering things for yourself, press on.

MISDIRECTED DIALOGUE

What about dialogue where the movement seems random? People don't answer one another. Subjects change without warning. Characters respond to stray thoughts and show no interest in a progression of tensions. Call this type of dialogue misdirected. Misdirected dialogue brings in so many strands of existence that its direction resists diagnosis. It appears to operate without direction, in open defiance of the whole notion. It sounds, quite often, more like real conversations.

Lorrie Moore uses this approach in the following scene from her novel *Who Will Run the Frog Hospital?* Here the narrator and her husband are lying in bed talking. The novel takes place in Paris, where the narrator has come to sort out her life and where her husband has an academic engagement. Read the dialogue below and look for all the different directions presented; the first line appears rather direct, but within moments, the two are speaking in metaphors.

> "I'm not really looking forward to going home," I say now.
> "Really?"
> "I feel disconnected these days, in the house, in town. The neighbors say, 'Hello, how are you?' and sometimes I say, 'Oh, I'm feeling a little empty today. How about you?' "
> "You should get a puppy," he says sleepily.
> "A puppy?"
> "Yeah. It's not like the cat. A puppy you can take for walks around the neighborhood, and people will stop and smile and say, 'Ooooh, look—what's wrong with your puppy?' "

"What is wrong with my puppy?"

"Worms, I think. I don't know. You should have taken him to the vet's weeks ago."

"You're so mean."

"I'm sorry I'm not what you bargained for," Daniel murmurs.

I stop and think about this. "Well, I'm not what you bargained for, either, so we're even."

"No," he says faintly, "you are. You're what I bargained for."

But then he has fallen over the cliff of sleep and is snoring, his adenoids a kind of engine in his face, a motorized unit, a security system like a white flag going up.

The movement here works in waves. The tension between the two characters is high. Just when one character is being direct, the other evades and dances away. The lack of direct response is a sign of intimacy, ironically. There is a code to their language which makes the exchange, with its blend of quiet revelation and gentle chiding, something recognizable and at the same time foreign. Such is the case with misdirected dialogue.

Misdirected dialogue is the type of dialogue that most naturally takes advantage of the rhythms and cadences of language I have been encouraging you to look for. It relies on the fact that life does not always shape itself to the needs of plot, and it turns the mirror on the clamor of voices that surround us, on the natural tendency to leave tensions hanging, rather than march toward resolution. This sort of dialogue sounds more natural and allows tension to build more slowly than in dialogue that's shaped with a heavy sense of direction. It's more surprising, more challenging, and sounds more like the sort of stuff we hear in the world around us. Misdirection is a tool for surprise to be sure, but it brings complexity and ambiguity to our conception of the world within our fiction. Listen for it in the world around you. Use it in the fiction you craft. Its elements include:

- changing the subject
- directing the dialogue "offstage"
- answering questions with answers that aren't quite answers but sound like them
- allowing characters to speak to themselves, for themselves
- carrying on more than one conversation at the same time

Crafting misdirection

Start with three people in a restaurant. Rather than starting with a tension, begin by hearing them speak. You've had lots of practice with this by now. Push them to reveal their tensions. This is the key to creating misdirected dialogue. Allow them to speak in random order, but do not force it.

1: I need a beer. Could I have a beer?

2: I saw Marnie today.

1: Beer, please.

3: Where did you see her?

1: You know. By the fire station.

3: No kidding.

1: Her hair has grown.

3: I would imagine. How do you know?

1: I'm not blind.

2: Are you eating?

3: Did you see her, too?

1: You see her everywhere. She's like That Girl! Those hats!

2: I'm eating. I'm starving.

3: I'm just asking.

1: I saw her last week. As a matter of fact I remarked on her hair.

2: The TV show?

3: You talked to her?

2: Who?

1: Marnie.

3: Marnie.

2: You're kidding. I just saw her today myself.

Not brilliant. But it does follow the rules I suggested. What occurs is that the dialogue moves in different directions as each character starts to respond to the others. Notice the techniques: changing the subject (when speaker 1 brings up the hair); part of it is directing the dialogue "offstage" (when speaker 1 calls for beer); part of it is answering questions with answers that aren't quite answers but sound like them ("How do you know?" followed by "I'm not blind."); another part is allowing characters to speak to themselves, for themselves ("I'm eating. I'm starving."); part of it involves carrying on more than one conversation at the same time.

If you found the conversation difficult to follow, that probably had much to do with the fact that I gave the characters no names, that I attached scenic details and I paced the exchanges to be quick and somewhat sharp. There is, however, a literal direction to this, one that can be better imagined by rewriting the dialogue in columns.

1	2	3
I need a beer. Could I have a beer?		
	I saw Marnie today.	
Beer, please.		
		Where did you see her?
You know. By the fire station.		
		No kidding.
Her hair has grown.		
		I would imagine. How do you know?
I'm not blind.		
	Are you eating?	
		Did you see her too?
You see her everywhere. She's like That Girl! Those hats!		
	I'm eating. I'm starving.	
		I'm just asking.
I saw her last week. As a matter of fact I remarked on her hair.		
	The TV show?	
		You talked to her?
	Who?	
Marnie.		
		Marnie.
	You're kidding. I just saw her today myself.	

Draw arrows from one line to the line that evoked that response and you'll start to see how the patterning works here. Still, it's no parlor trick. Misdirected dialogue often balances tensions against one another in the most explicit fashion. Not for one minute do more voices mean a less diffuse tension. Indeed more voices mean more characters, more characters mean more needs. The key with misdirection is to recognize that it's easy to confuse the reader with evasion and patterning, but you do more to capture a reader when she starts to recognize these unnamable patterns even as the characters continue to speak.

MODULATED DIALOGUE

A fourth type of dialogue, modulated dialogue, uses narrative commentary and scenic detail to extend the complexity of expression. Here the movement is not from one character to another (as in directed dialogue) nor into the life of one character in particular (as in interpolated dialogue). The movement is not particularly between characters either (as in misdirected dialogue). In modulated dialogue, each piece of dialogue becomes a point of entry for the writer to drift toward other details. Memory can be modulated into a dialogue easily and clearly. A character's words call up a forgotten moment, a flashback ensues and at its close, the dialogue begins again. The narrator can comment openly on the "meaning" of the words passing before us on the page.

If all of that sounds pretty bloodless and technical, keep in mind that when memory and place work their way into your dialogues to their fullest measure, your fiction is doing its finest, truest work. You can use modulated dialogue as a means of exploring the tensions more explicitly, of complicating the present, or for advancing the current plot line with a key flashback.

Rich in Love, by Josephine Humphreys, is a novel that explores many of these same connections through the voice and consciousness of a 16-year-old narrator named Lucille Odom, who witnesses the breakup of her parents' marriage and the dissolution of their family with a mixture of fear, wisdom and desire. Many of the dialogues in this book stretch over pages and are interrupted by memory, place and revelation. A good modulated dialogue takes place when she goes to lunch with her erstwhile boyfriend, Wayne Frobiness and his father, who puts Wayne on the spot about money.

". . . and I want you to guess how much I have to pay for liability insurance. Guess."

"I couldn't begin to."

"No, just take a wild guess. What do you think I have to cough up?"

"I don't know." Wayne was stubborn. I knew he wouldn't guess.

"Take a guess, son," Dr. Frobiness insisted.

"A million dollars," I said.

"Heh, no, little lady, not quite that much. No, I'm ponying up *twenty-one thousand* dollars a year for insurance." He pronounced the first syllable of "thousand" with a wide open mouth, and made his eyes big.

"Holy smoke," I said, to be polite. In truth, I thought that was a pretty good bargain. Suppose he botched a liposuction or misaligned an implant? If I were the insurance company, I would not have insured Dr. Frobiness for any amount.

He went on to say that some fathers, himself and Ronald Reagan included, had a lot at stake in the careers of their sons. It wasn't as if the sons of such fathers were free agents. "My heart aches for the President," he said.

"Excuse me," I said. I wanted seconds before they wheeled the roast beef away. It was already three o'clock, and the steamboat round was carved down the middle like a saddle. The waiter in charge of slicing meat was standing over by the aquarium with two other waiters. I waited politely by the meat, plate in hand, but they were engaged in an argument, and a partially melted seahorse made of ice stood between me and them. They didn't notice me. One said, "Maître d' said, get that mother *out*." Another said, "Get him out how?" "I don't know, but get him out." "Shit, man, I ain't reaching my hand in there. It's crabs in there." "He ain't dead yet anyhow." "Sure he is." "Naw, he ain't. His gills is opening and closing, that's his breathing." "Any fish that is upside down is dead in my book." "Said get him out fast before a member sees him." "Get him out, James." "Go for it, James." "All *right, James.*"

There are two types of modulation going on here. The first occurs when the narrator allows the dialogue to fall away and replaces it with the speculation about Dr. Frobiness. In the "present" of our narration, time is passing, yet the dialogue, merely related here, does not reflect that. A similar sort of modulation occurs when Lucille stands and moves to the carving table. In this instance, place, including the fine example of an untagged dialogue (lines that appear without "he said" or specific indication of speaker), takes over, and expands. When the girl returns to the table moments later, more than a page and a half of description has risen to fill up the moments. The dialogue between father and son, to which our narrator is primarily a witness, marches on after the digression, and nothing is lost for the reader in terms of time of understanding.

Writing Dialogue and the exercises within it press you toward modulation. I believe it is the bread and butter of good fiction. A well-modulated dialogue captures scene, tension and an element of the background consciousness in the story and allows the story to rise above the constraints of our artless lives. It allows for the insinuation of beauty and irony. Those things that make a dialogue the backbone of a scene. It is a chance for the narrative consciousness to work in tension with the character's consciousness. Here, unlike interpolated dialogue, the emphasis is not on interpretation but on the collision of details and the art that rises out of it.

THE DANGER OF CLASSIFYING

The danger here is that by defining and classifying these types of dialogue, I have tempted you to think about them as distinctly separate forms of writing, as if one day you will be working with interpolation whereas the next should be saved for directed dialogue only. These forms are not mutually exclusive. When a dialogue is "directed" by a particular need or emotion, that does not mean that scene has to disappear, that memory cannot be modulated into it or that evasion and misdirection cannot be used. Classifications are for biologists, God bless them. Just be aware that dialogue operates around energy and direction. As you write, tune in to the elements. Be aware of the pitfalls of explaining too much and of not explaining at all. Tread a line between too much scene and too little, between too few voices and too many. But *know* the line first.

The key is to read self-consciously, to watch what the writer is doing. Accept nothing as a pure reflection of "real life," as you know by now that dialogue is always shaped. As you read, draw arrows, make charts, watch for patterning. Don't feel the need to ape these patterns straight out, but don't be afraid to either. Soon they will become your signature, as you layer and modulate the voices you create and the world they inhabit in your own distinctive fashion.

Giving Characters Emotion

BY ANN HOOD

It always strikes me as funny that in our daily lives we pass through a whole spectrum of emotions and show them in many ways, some obvious and some subtle, yet in our fiction we often have trouble moving our characters through emotions effectively. I think of this as the curse of writing like a writer. Sometimes we get a tone or a voice in our head and we decide that is how good writers sound.

In a class I took at New York University with E.L. Doctorow, he once mentioned that the curse of his generation was trying to write like Hemingway and that the curse of our generation was trying to write like Raymond Carver. When I got home that night and looked at my own stories that I had been struggling to get right, I saw that Doctorow had hit on an important lesson. I *was* trying to sound like Carver. And at other points in my life, I tried to sound like F. Scott Fitzgerald or Flannery O'Connor or the latest *New Yorker* story. In other words, I was trying to write like a writer.

When we copy a writerly voice, we put up a barrier between us and the emotions of our characters. As a result, the readers get filtered versions of emotion instead of real interpretations and an honest rendering of them. Please don't misunderstand me: There is much to be gained from reading and admiring another writer's work. In fact, it is a necessary part of being a writer. I agree with Saul Bellow who said, "A writer is a reader moved to emulation." However, we must also be able to let go of that writer's voice, or of the voice of that nebulous writer type—the gray-haired man in a tweed coat, the woman in a flowing white dress—whose writerly voice haunts our own work.

So my first piece of advice is to write like yourself. Until you do that, you will not be able to evoke emotion—and therefore character—effectively. Arguably the most important thing a writer can do is get readers to feel emotions. You might believe instead that conveying ideas in fiction is more important. However, I agree with Janet Burroway who, in her classic book *Writing Fiction*, argues that the ideas must be experienced through or with the characters; they must be *felt* or the fiction will fail.

Your goal, then, is to have your characters and your readers feel the necessary emotions, to believe in them, so your ideas will be conveyed convincingly and your fiction will succeed. Put aside the writerly voice. You are now ready to write like the most important writer you will need to create convincing emotions: yourself.

FICTION VS. REAL LIFE

It is important to remember fiction is not real life. We can't rely on easy emotional associations or true stories to render fictional emotional truth; it will inevitably sound false. I remember a

ANN HOOD *is the author of six novels, all published by Bantam/Doubleday, including* Somewhere Off the Coast of Maine, Places to Stay the Night *and* The Properties of Water. *Her short stories and essays have appeared in* STORY, Glimmer Train, The New York Times, The Washington Post, Redbook *and other publications. She has served on the faculty of many universities and writers conferences and presently teaches at New York University. This article is excerpted from* Creating Character Emotions *copyright ©️ 1998 by Ann Hood. Published by Story Press, a division of F&W Publications, Inc. Reprinted by permission of Brandt & Brandt Literary Agents, Inc.*

student of mine who reported events exactly as they happened and called it fiction. One story in particular was about a young couple breaking up. The boy was heartbroken. Each of them said things that were at times meant to be sad, at times filled with despair or jealousy, love or resignation. In between the dialogue was plenty of silence. The story, rather than leaving the reader heartbroken like its main character, was flat and inauthentic. "But this is what happened to me!" the writer said. "And I am heartbroken!" "I believe you," I said. "Now I have to believe that your character is heartbroken."

A brief journey through my own emotional day feels like this: I overslept and so was worried I wouldn't get my son to school on time. I did, but on the way home the road was closed and I felt confused about how to proceed. By the time I found my way home, I couldn't do any of the things I needed to get done before I took my father to a doctor's appointment so I ended up guiltily wasting time at a local cafe. However, the time to myself made me feel quite happy. My father's appointment went well and we both were more hopeful about his recovery than we had been, so we went out for a celebratory lunch at which we both felt a lot of love. When I got home and finally settled down to my computer, my daughter started crying, which irritated me. She settled down for a nap and here I am. It's just three o'clock in the afternoon and I've only told you the major emotions I experienced so far.

But if I were a character in a story, these emotions would have to hold more weight. For example, it would be more important to understand how I reached a hopeful emotional place with my father's illness. I could juxtapose this doctor's visit with one several months ago that left me in despair.

Also, emotions shouldn't be as flat in fiction as they can be in real life. In a story a writer must ask more of emotions. Was the confusion I felt at getting lost this morning important? Why did it matter? What does it say about me, the character? What does it reveal? Perhaps in life it mattered—I had things to do, after all—but in fiction we need to gauge the impact of action against our characters' emotional lives. If confusion in getting lost is only in a story because it sounds real, then don't use it. It has to be important in the fictional life of your character.

Amy Hempel addresses this question of fiction vs. truth in her story "The Harvest." The first half of the story is about a young woman who gets badly hurt in a car accident on her way to dinner with a married man; the last half of the story is the writer telling the reader which events were true and which were made up, and why: "The man of a week, whose motorcycle it was, was not a married man. But when you thought he had a wife, wasn't I liable to do anything? And didn't I have it coming?"

What a good example of demonstrating how a writer manipulates her characters' emotional lives to render certain emotions in the reader. Hempel wanted the reader to think the young woman deserved what she got. Hempel states, "I leave a lot out when I tell the truth. The same when I write a story."

The second important thing you need to do, then, is to separate life from fiction. You need to step into the life of your story, to leave out a lot and still tell the truth.

HOW TO DO IT WRONG

Even after you've managed to close out the voices of those "real" writers who haunt you and to enter your characters' fictional world, there are still a lot of common problems in portraying emotions in fiction. Identifying these problems helps us to avoid them. In fact, after you've read these and thought about them, you'll be surprised how often you'll find them, not just in your own work but in the work of other writers too.

The cliché trap

How easy it is to say that someone is "green with envy," or is so nervous she has "butterflies in her stomach." It's much more difficult to find a fresh way to evoke jealousy or anxiety or any emotion.

One of the problems with this is that clichés simply fall out of our heads and onto the paper. We don't even know it's happening. I remember being at a baseball game with a friend who pointed to a red-faced man walking toward us and said, "His face looks like a boiled ham." What a perfect simile! Not only did it describe the man's face, but ten years later I still remember it. To write one that perfect would take a lot of time. But to write "red as a beet" takes no time and no thought. The same is true with emotions. We have to be alert, like my friend, and reach beyond the obvious cliché.

In her book *The Passionate, Accurate Story*, Carol Bly suggests writing the second thing that comes to your mind rather than the first. Her point is that clichés are always at the forefront of our minds, and therefore are usually what we think of first. But are they effective in our writing? When Bly pushed her students to describe the drab classroom they were sitting in, after they'd used all the obvious descriptions, one of them wrote: "No one ever fell in love in this room."

I think we have to be even more meticulous in our fresh descriptions of emotions. It is easier to forgive "hair as yellow as wheat" than "as happy as a clam." After all, the emotional lives of our characters are the key to our whole story. We must always search for that "boiled ham" description, the one that jumps out at the readers, fits perfectly and stays with them long after the story has ended.

Lack of specificity

Sometimes it is laziness that keeps a writer from doing what Flannery O'Connor called "painting a picture with words." But often this comes from the writer's own insecurity about where the character should be emotionally at this point of the story. The writer knows the character should feel *something*. But what? Instead of considering the plot of the story and the character's own emotional place, the writer relies on a nonspecific emotion and hopes the reader fills in the blanks.

In my novel *Places to Stay the Night*, I had the most trouble with the main character Libby. She just wasn't convincing enough. I knew from the start that Libby is restless and unhappy enough to leave her husband and their two children and go to California. But I lost her authenticity when she got there. I wasn't sure myself how she felt about leaving her family behind. I had her acting out a lot of emotions in the secret hope that a reader might be able to figure out the very thing I couldn't: What did Libby feel once she acted on her other emotions?

It wasn't until I forced out significant details—Where did she work when she got there? Did she make any friends? What did she want from the move?—that I could start to understand her emotional life and to depict it convincingly. Here is an example of what Libby did there and how she felt.

> For her second acting class, Libby wore the electric blue spandex dress. An actress has to be versatile, she'd read. She wanted her teacher, Carl, to see every side of her, how much of a chameleon she could be. When she walked in, the two young blondes in the class glanced at each other. She hated them. They weren't even 21, and they always wore tight black things. They had too much hair, gobs of it. And smooth flawless skin. Their names were Heather and Ashley. Libby decided, as she took her place, that they looked like everybody else, nothing special, just two more California girls. In a way, she thought, she felt bad for them.

The emotional truth here is that Libby is as unhappy in California as she was back in Massachusetts. She just isn't ready to admit it. She has discovered that there are a lot of younger, prettier girls in California and she feels jealous. Notice how the concrete details help the reader understand those emotions. Libby has on a "blue spandex dress"; the other women are wearing "tight black things."

Remember, this is Libby's point of view, so when she notices their "gobs" of hair and "smooth flawless skin," it's important to her emotional state of mind. She tries to convince herself her jealousy is really sympathy—they're not special, they look like everyone else and she actually feels bad for them. But through the specific details, the reader sees that Libby isn't feeling sympathy at all.

How much more effective these concrete details make this scene than if Libby had simply walked into her acting class and noticed the two blonde women there. Even vague descriptions might have led the reader to believe she admired them or that she was happy with herself and her life. Or the reader could simply have been left confused. Think of concrete details as emotional traffic signs, leading the reader to the right place.

Ambiguity

Ambiguity occurs when the writer does not trust her own experience with emotions enough and therefore ignores what it *really* feels like to be sad or in love or angry. A hefty part of writing is being able to explore our own inner lives, to tap into our own emotions and histories, to revisit things that perhaps are unpleasant, like my days as the ninth-grade weirdo. It is this self-exploration that led a student of mine to announce at the end of class, "I signed up for Creative Writing and got Therapy 101 instead!"

If you cannot or will not do some emotional homework, chances are you will create characters who are emotionally ambiguous. Such characters force the reader to look elsewhere in the story for clues to emotional clarification. Those clues should rest within the character. When they don't, your reader will either misunderstand the story or feel confused by it.

One way we fall into ambiguity is by labelling an emotion rather than honestly exploring it. You can avoid this by studying a model from literature. Who is one of your favorite characters? What is his emotional journey? How does the writer take you along without falling into ambiguity? You will see that the character was created without emotional shortcuts or cryptic language to label his emotional self. Clarity and honesty brought this character to life, and that is how you will create believable emotional lives for your characters.

Not trusting your characters

There are times when the writer doesn't trust the characters enough, and this leads to a different set of problems. For one, there can be a lack of consistency. On page 3 the character is mourning his dead wife and on page 4 he's happily shopping for a new pair of jeans, and there is no emotional journey between the two experiences. This leads the reader, of course, to not believing in the story's emotional authenticity. Characters have to work to move from grief to happiness.

Conversely, a writer who doesn't trust the characters enough can write a character who is *too* consistent, who strikes the same note too often, such as a character who is only portrayed as angry or happy. Aristotle says a character should be "consistently inconsistent"; that is important to remember. Consistently inconsistent does not mean characters jump from emotion to emotion recklessly but rather that they believably move from one emotion to the next.

Remember my character Libby? In a way, it takes the entire novel to move her from the unhappy housewife who leaves her family on page 1 to the resigned woman who returns to them on page 275. She moves from hope and excitement to loneliness and even despair before she matures emotionally.

Characters should have a range of emotion to give them depth and complexity. Otherwise, we end up with fiction filled with stereotypes, flat characters moving through an unbelievable world. Had Libby felt the jealousy I showed in the passage above and immediately turned to despair, she would not have been successfully rendered. That jealousy was just one step on an emotional ladder your characters should climb, emotional rung by emotional rung.

HOW TO DO IT RIGHT

The best fiction takes characters through not just an external journey, but an emotional journey, too. As a writer, you do need a bit of "Therapy 101" to help your characters along their own emotional travels. But don't confuse emotional truth with autobiography. You must first give your characters full lives of their own. Edna O'Brien said of Chekhov: "He does not write— he breathes life off the page." Giving your characters authentic, believable emotions is the best way I know to breathe life into them and off the page.

Imagine the characters from literature whom you most believed emotionally. I think of Willa Cather's archbishop, Fitzgerald's Gatsby, Updike's Rabbit, Tolstoy's Anna Karenina. From my childhood I still remember the emotional impact of Jo March from *Little Women*; from adolescence it is Herman Wouk's Marjorie Morningstar. My father likes Tony Hillerman's detective Joe Leaphorn. My husband likes Einstein as he appears in Alan Lightman's *Einstein's Dreams*.

All of these characters have both emotional breath and emotional breadth. They live on long after you've finished the book. Can you create characters who are as emotionally developed? Can you move a character through hope to despair in the way Fitzgerald moves Jay Gatsby?

You don't need to be a literary genius, or even wildly successful, to render emotions effectively. But you do have to work at it. By now you have shut out those other writers' voices, you have successfully separated "real life" from fictional life, and you have considered the common pitfalls writers encounter when writing emotions. It's time to look at what you can do to get it right so your characters breathe off the page too.

Your emotional time line

Conjuring your own emotional memories will certainly help you create emotional lives for your characters, as I did with Rebekah, my teenager from *Somewhere Off the Coast of Maine* who believes her big nose is the cause of her loneliness. Making your own emotional time line will help you do the same for your characters.

Let's look at Rebekah and her nose job again and how my emotional life informed hers. I could say that mine began with a longing to be accepted. My sadness at being excluded from others led to my desire for a change (contact lenses). When I was still excluded, I felt disappointed and confused. But eventually these emotions led to a positive emotion—satisfaction— when I finally grew past the need to be accepted and made friends with the other "Untouchables."

After revisiting my own emotional time line, I could create a believable one for Rebekah, whose longing and sadness mirrored mine. For example, I showed her disappointment: "She sacrificed everything for this day and it was all for nothing. Tomorrow she would don her patched jeans and bicycle to school like before. It didn't matter. Her nose was different, but everything else was still the same."

At the end of *Somewhere Off the Coast of Maine*, Rebekah has a boyfriend and a group of her own friends; she is even happy: "Rebekah had gone so long without friends that she didn't mind that these two weren't part of Sally Perkins' clique. In fact, she liked having her own group, where she was the important one."

It's important to remind yourself that I am not Rebekah. In a way we share an emotional life but all the props are different: She is the daughter of two hippie potters, I'm the daughter of Depression-era, white-collar parents; her mother is critically ill; she has a younger brother; the list goes on and on, all the way to the fact that she's a vegetarian. These external facts do matter. They help create the character of Rebekah and shape her emotions and her reactions to "the havoc they wreak." Our emotional lives only overlap enough to help me convince you, the reader, of authenticity.

Fresh language

This kind of emotional work is only one way you can bring emotional truth to your fiction. There are other technical strategies you can use too. I've already mentioned Carol Bly's advice about writing the *second* thing you think of. But it's worth repeating here and to yourself, over and over. In my classes I refer to this as the Cliché Police and induct all of my students into the force. You can't be too vigilant in your attempts to overcome emotional clichés.

Fresh language and images rather than tired clichés force you—and your reader—to see emotions in a different light. How much better to say, as Susan Taylor Chehak does in her novel *Smithereens*, "I could feel the awkward, scared tumble of my heartbeat" than to say "My heart pounded."

Clichés like this one are a kind of emotional shorthand; they do the work for the writer. Or so the writer thinks. When we read a writer who relies on such emotional shorthand, we don't trust what that writer is trying to say. How can someone who tries to get away with a pounding heart know anything new or enlightening about fear?

One of my favorite clichés is one tear rolling down a cheek. Not only am I not sure if it's physically possible to produce just one tear, but the image is so overused it is now almost comical. A shorthand for sadness? Perhaps. But more likely it shows a writer's unwillingness or inability to work at rendering real emotion.

However, the reason we have read about so many hearts pounding is because there is some morsel of truth in that image. The other night, alone in our big old Victorian house, I thought I heard someone walking around downstairs. My heart did pound, but to say it that way is to cheat the reader and the emotion. That is why pushing past the cliché—using it, in a way—can be effective. If we've read "my heart pounded" enough for it to be the cliché for fear, how can we use that image more effectively? Chehak's "awkward, scared tumble" does just that: It builds on the cliché and creates something fresh.

The power of suggestion

Much emotional work can be done by suggestion. Remember how one pitfall was the problem of stating a character was sad without showing how he wore that sadness? Using props rather than stating the obvious is a good way to avoid that pitfall. Shredded tissues in someone's hand, an open scrapbook on a bedside table, mascara smears under eyes, too many empty wine bottles in a recycling bin—all of these are props that show sadness without the writer having to hit the reader over the head.

How much better to see that character's sadness than to be told he's sad without anything to convince us. These props or suggestions can work in conjunction with something obvious. For example, a character might tell a friend she is sad and then you, the writer, can use many details to suggest that sadness, backing up her statement.

Or the suggestion can give us insights into a character's emotion. Suppose a character wants to hide her sadness from her mother. You can have her state quite blatantly that she's fine, even happy. But everything around her suggests the exact opposite. Description and setting show the reader that in fact the character has done nothing but cry all day. Here is where concrete detail becomes even more important.

Remember my character Libby in her acting class? She wants to hide her jealousy from someone—herself. Those concrete details helped to build the case for the opposite emotion; instead of the sympathy she said she felt, the reader understood her true emotions. I like how this demonstrates that in conveying emotions, as in many facets of good writing, all of the "rules" are interdependent.

Certainly you will sometimes rely on that perfect image or a strong concrete detail or suggestion as a way to show an emotion effectively. Some scenes need one broad stroke to paint that emotional picture. But there are many times when you need to combine a lot of the elements, as in the scene with Libby and her acting class, to drive home your emotional point most effectively.

Point of view

Point of view is a terrific way to render emotion. A character who sees only the tragic stories in the daily paper, for example, or who lies in bed all day watching home shopping channels and crying is clearly conveying sadness. Looking at the world through a character's eyes shapes the reader's perceptions, illustrating the character's emotional self.

One of the most effective uses of point of view to show emotion is through dialogue. The narrative voice can give us emotional readings with great authority, especially when it is backed by strong language, concrete details, and good props that suggest the emotion.

But using dialogue to show emotion helps us to build characters. I'm sure I don't have to remind you that nothing can undermine your story more than weak dialogue. If it's flat or melodramatic or simply sounds false, you will not be able to be emotionally convincing. However, when well written, dialogue can be one of the most authentic ways to show a character's feelings. You give the character a chance to say what she feels in her own voice.

Conversely, dialogue can be a good way to show what a character feels by what he doesn't say. A strong student paper I read showed a couple on the brink of divorce talking about a chipped plate from their wedding china. Feelings are not discussed, yet the scene is emotionally wrought with them—and tension. Had one of them screamed, "I hate you and I want a divorce!" we certainly would have understood the emotions. But *not* saying what they felt made those emotions seem even stronger.

Point of view can also be shaped by interior monologue, which is another excellent way to show a character's emotions. Let's go back to that scene from my novel *Places to Stay the Night* when Libby is in her acting class.

> Acting class made her feel very self-conscious. They had to do things that seemed irrelevant. Like breathe in a particular way that reminded her of her childbirth classes. Then Carl made them say "Ha." Then, "Ha ha." He kept making them add *Has* until they were laughing like crazy people. To Libby, it didn't make any sense. Heather and Ashley really got into it, laughing like mad. Libby watched them. Were they really laughing? Or were they acting? Was that the point?

Libby's interior questioning demonstrates her own feelings of inadequacy, her jealousy of Heather and Ashley, her emotional state. In dialogue she would not have revealed this; she's trying too hard to seem happy and confident to everyone. In this interior monologue, we get a pure emotional reading.

The unpredictable

Indirect action—furiously chopping wood or calling psychics on a 900 number—can also evoke emotion. Don't fall into the trap of stating the emotion you want the reader to see, then forcing your character to act in a predictable emotional way. I've already discussed the dangers of stating an emotion outright without backing it up, but you must carefully choose how you back it up. Like indirect dialogue, indirect action allows the reader to piece together the character's emotional puzzle and keeps the writer from stating the obvious.

This is another overlap of the fictional elements at work in rendering emotion. You can fall into a big cliché trap by stating an emotion and then using an easy or predictable action to illustrate it. For example, stating someone is sad and then showing the person crying can come across as emotionally facile or false rather than reinforcing. Although there is no denying that sadness often results in the action of crying, not all sadness leads there. Can you push the emotional envelope further? Can you take the emotion, the character, and ultimately the reader someplace new?

Not only should you work hard to avoid the predictable, the obvious, and the cliché, but you should even try to subvert the obvious as a way of showing emotion. The obvious response to grief is crying. But what if you had a character respond by laughing? Or making love? I'm not the only person I know who never misses a showing of the *Mary Tyler Moore* episode in which Chuckles the Clown dies and no one can stop laughing.

Let's return again to Libby in her acting class. Her jealousy and unhappiness have been demonstrated in many ways so far: point of view, interior monologue, concrete detail, suggestion. Now look at how the unpredictable brings her to a new emotional place, where she can no longer fool herself about what she feels. Carl, the acting teacher, asks each class member to make a sound that describes his or her center. Libby is worried about being embarrassed. She tries to think of quiet sounds—a sigh or hiccup. But this is what happens.

> And then it was Libby's turn. She hadn't found her center. She was sweaty, panicked. Maybe she had no center. Maybe she was completely hollow, not even a housewife, certainly not a star. The very air in the room seemed to be waiting for her sound. She felt as if someone had ripped out her voice box. Nothing would come out.
> From beside her George farted.
> "Good!" Carl said.
> Heather and Ashley giggled.
> "Wait!" Libby shouted.
> But they were already on to the next exercise. Carl was talking in that slow hypnotic voice. Everyone thought she had farted publicly, that her center was that low and ridiculous. Libby wanted more than anything, in that moment, to be back home.

The scene takes an unpredictable, even comic, turn that leads the reader—and Libby—to an honest emotional place. Libby has a longing for home, a place where she was loved and appreciated, where her center was something substantial.

Indirect action, irony, humor—they all take the reader somewhere fresh and unexpected. They leave cliché behind. Using them forces the writer to look at emotions and the character in a different light.

Emotional complexity

Perhaps the most important thing to remember when searching for emotional honesty is that emotion is not one-dimensional. Emotions are complex and often mixed together. I once had a student who described a woman who was unhappy in her marriage this way: "Chloe was angry. She was also sad and confused. She was disappointed. She felt anxious and afraid." Although the writer did not successfully convey what was at the emotional heart of Chloe, she did stumble upon an important truth in writing emotions: They are complicated and often a mix of many different emotions.

Think of a bride on her wedding day. It would be too easy and too flat to describe her as simply happy. Instead, she is excited, apprehensive, worried, fearful, anxious, joyful, smug—so many emotions! But if you, the writer, can capture her feelings exactly right—with the perfect turn of a phrase, or simile, or fresh image—you will tell the reader more about this character and this story than you can imagine.

One of the things we need to do when rendering emotions is to see our characters as complex beings who experience a range of feelings. If we start a story with a character in despair, we have to move that character through many emotions before our story ends with him hopeful. Also, the faces of despair and hope and every emotion are multifaceted. Just as sadness is not just crying, each emotion is not represented by one dimension. The layers of an emotion often hold other emotions too.

Think again of Libby. She isn't simply jealous of Heather and Ashley; she is disappointed, confused, frightened, worried. She moves through that to longing for home, which also holds layers of other feelings. But for Libby to jump off the page, her emotions have to be rich and complex, to inform the reader of new ideas and authentic feelings. There are times when an emotion is simply rendered. There are even times when the emotion itself is simple. But in evoking character, remember that emotions shape and color your character and demand complexity.

Greg Sarris: Healing the World Through Story

BY JOHN KACHUBA

If writers write what they know, then Greg Sarris has enough knowledge to take him through several lifetimes of writing. That knowledge, his life experiences that are so richly portrayed in his work, springs from his childhood as a poor kid on the mean streets of Santa Rosa, California.

His parents dated secretly, forbidden by racial and socioeconomic differences from seeing each other, and never married. His mother was wealthy, young and white, of Jewish, Irish, and German descent. His father was poor and dark-skinned, descended from Filipino, Coastal Miwok Indian and Pomo Indian ancestors.

Sarris was put up for adoption after his teenaged mother delivered him; she died a few days later from a bad blood transfusion. He spent much of his childhood being shunted from one foster family to another. When he was eight he was taken in by Native Americans, but it wasn't until he was in his twenties that he discovered his true parentage and realized the rich cultural diversity that was his birthright.

Growing up on Grand Avenue in the poor section of Santa Rosa was not easy. By his own admission, Sarris was a wild kid without direction, without hope. For a time, he ran with local gangs in an attempt to fit in, to belong somewhere.

When Sarris met Mabel McKay, a noted Pomo Indian "dreamer" and basket weaver, who was also a healer, storyteller and keeper of Pomo traditions, his life turned around dramatically. Through her influence, he finished high school and went on to get his B.A. from UCLA. After a brief stint in modeling and acting (he made a few appearances in *CHiPs*), he returned to school and eventually earned a Ph.D. from Stanford University.

His fiction debut, *Grand Avenue*, is a collection of ten interconnected stories about the people he grew up with, people of many cultures. The characters reflect the author's own life as they struggle for identity and meaning in a world in which they see themselves powerless. The book was later produced by Robert Redford as a movie for HBO and was nominated for several Emmys.

Sarris is also the author of *Mabel McKay: Weaving the Dream*, *Keeping Slug Woman Alive: A Holistic Approach to American Indian Texts*, and is the editor of *The Sound of Rattles and Clappers*. His latest novel, *Watermelon Nights*, was published by Hyperion.

Greg Sarris is a very busy man; he was scheduled to meet with some TV producers after this interview to pitch some ideas for new shows. He is a professor of English at UCLA and also the elected chief of the Coastal Miwok, a labor of love that takes him back and forth from Los Angeles to Santa Rosa weekly and to Washington, DC, where he is fighting for federal recognition of his tribe.

How does your ethnic diversity shape you as a writer?

It positions me on many borders and when you're on the border, you can look over the different fields. I remember as a kid being between two worlds, a white world and an Indian world, and

JOHN KACHUBA *is a writer and writing teacher based in Loveland, Ohio. His recent credits include:* Connecticut Review, Stoneflower Literary Journal, America's Civil War *and* Poets & Writers.

being surrounded by different people and I would hear what each would say about the other. I was privy to diverse perspectives. What complicated this was that I often didn't know where I belonged, or to whom I belonged. I was always trying to make sense of myself and, while doing so, trying desperately to make sense of the world around me. It was great training as a writer, because I had to listen to everyone around me to find out where I fit in. But, I wouldn't recommend that life for any child.

How do you identify yourself now?

I guess I identify myself with a place, with a language, and as much as anything I'm the history of where I've been and where I am. So much of identity is certainly your family and the culture you've been brought up in but it's that in relationship to place. I'm a boy from a poor part of Santa Rosa, but my identity, and how I understand that place, and the history of that place, and the spirit of that place, and the voices of that place, are Indian. I am also a kid of the streets, so there's some of that in me, too.

How did you feel when you discovered your Native American heritage?

When I found out who my father was, I went running to Mabel McKay and she was particularly unimpressed. I said, "I'm Indian, I'm Indian!" It was finally all coming together and she said, "Just because you've found your father doesn't change who you are, the life you've lived. The life you live is who you are."

You are your experience and what in your experience affects you and moves you profoundly. I'd like to think of myself in the best way as a history of Santa Rosa. My identity is its history and the history starts, and must always come back to, the Indians who lived there for 10 or 20 centuries.

When you read *Grand Avenue* though, you don't necessarily get an Indian point of view. Isn't the hook really just about ordinary people?

Right. They are people who happen to be Indians. We are people first with the same human emotions: the need to be loved, feeling hurt, alone. All those things are human, but they exist in a certain context, in this case, an Indian context.

The stories in *Grand Avenue* begin in despair and hatred, but there is a turnaround by the time we reach the end of the book. There is hope and a return to traditional values. It seems this is a metaphor for your life, perhaps for being Indian.

Yes, exactly. We can't go back and live in the bush, but what we have, and what we carry with us wherever we are, is a set of ethics that can be represented aesthetically through our baskets, through our art, through our spirituality. That is part of my life; I can't live well if I can't practice what is in me, what's good in me, and what Mabel McKay taught me.

That is what Alice [in "The Water Place"] represents, but what she really wants is to pull her family together. She has that desire to hold the family together, not to be spiritual or to be empowered, but to love.

How did your life change after meeting Mabel McKay?

I met Mabel when I was quite young and I think at that point, what she reminded me was that there was a world much bigger than me, much bigger than my problems, a world that I belonged to that had endless, endless possibilities. She taught me that the world wasn't fixed or as small, or as ugly as I was believing it to be. I was an angry, young kid. I was displaced and being around Mabel was a reminder of magic, of beauty and kindness. She reminded me of what every child knows. She reminded me of awe and wonder, and that stopped me from really going over the edge.

How did she affect you as a writer?

She said I had two choices in life. I could let the hatred and poison become whole in my heart and I could infect others with it, or I could use it to doctor, to heal the others around me. I'd like to think that my writing, my art, is an attempt to light the dark, to heal.

Is that what you mean when you say writing is like good medicine?

Yes, and I was thinking primarily of conditions on Indian reservations and hoping my writing might work as a sort of prayer, as a way of healing. However, I have over 2,000 cousins and most of them are not readers. Here I've published four books and probably a couple of my cousins have read one of them. That's one of the reasons I made the movie for HBO, because I thought that would reach them. It fulfilled my dream, which was to get them to go back and read the book.

How about all the non-Indian readers of *Grand Avenue*? Is there a healing process for them as well?

That's a very good question. I act and I write locally from what I know, but if what I know is human, it's relevant universally, isn't it? If it's human, regardless of the context in which it's set, it will speak to all.

My writing is like good water from a well. But just because you drink from the spring that supplies the well, rather than the well itself, doesn't mean the water won't be good wherever it passes, wherever you drink from it.

After your acting and modeling careers, you finally turned to writing. How did that happen?

When I got serious about school it was the Horatio Alger thing. I was going to get into business and I was going to get rich and everybody in the world was going to be sorry they ever abused me . . . but along the way, I fell in love with literature. One of the things studying at school did was to put me in a room alone. That's very lonely for a person used to lots of voices, lots of noises, lots of people around him all the time. The literature reminded me of that, of what I knew best, people telling you stories.

Boy, did I understand Faulkner! As an undergraduate, reading his tales of all those different people talking about each other, it made perfect sense—all those multiple voices. I said this was just like home. It was then I thought I should do this and I dabbled around and tried to write different things. They weren't very good but I would just write, and write, and write.

But my primary influence was oral culture and not the written culture. Many writers will tell you they started reading early and would hide under the covers late at night reading, but I didn't. In fact, I don't think I read a book all the way through until I was a junior in high school. I remember one of the first books I read was Hemingway's *The Old Man and the Sea*, and I remember having felt sorry for the fish.

Which writers have influenced your own work?

Faulkner was certainly important. He made a lot of sense to me because, once again, he wrote about people in a multicultural, multi-historical setting. I love how he did that. We differ fundamentally in lots of different ways, one of which is that Faulkner was recording the demise of the world and I want to somehow record the healing, the building up, the re-creation of the world.

What's the hardest thing about writing fiction?

Getting started with a new voice. There have been times when I have spent every day for a month, working on a paragraph or the first couple of pages just trying to get the voice right. My writing is all about voice and if I don't hear the voice, or the voice doesn't come, or if I can't get the rhythm right, I can't move forward very well. It sometimes takes me quite a while to do that.

One of my colleagues at UCLA told her writing class "if it doesn't come easy, then it's not supposed to be." I was quite alarmed by that. Oh my God, if that were true, we wouldn't have Joyce, James, or Faulkner—we wouldn't have so many great writers. I know when I write, some things come easier than others, but if they're not coming easy, I don't say they're not supposed to be.

What is your writing routine like?

Seven days a week, when I'm home. I try to write at least four hours a day. I'll write from about 11 in the morning until 6 or 7 at night.

How do you gauge your success at the end of the day?

I try to get about three to five pages done each day and if I've gotten five pages and I feel pretty good about them, my work is done. If I have under three pages, I feel I haven't done enough or, if the writing is bad, I don't like what I've done and I have to go back over it, I think I haven't done anything. What I do then is go to the gym and pump iron. I push, push, push so that, no matter how the writing has gone, I can walk out of there and say I've done something constructive today.

Do you work from an outline?

I have a general outline when I start but invariably, I stray. I have an idea where I want to go, but the getting there and where I end up exactly is unplanned.

What is the novel you're working on now about?

It's called *Watermelon Nights* and it's sort of a follow-up to *Grand Avenue*. It takes place in the same locale but it's different in scope. It has three characters who weren't in *Grand Avenue*, although some of the original characters reappear. It's really three novels in one. It starts with a son in a contemporary setting, who is having visions. Then we go back to his mother's story in the '50s, then his grandmother's story about when they first left the reservation. It's basically about how goodness and kindness and angel songs are able to survive and to manifest themselves wherever we go.

Is it difficult for minority writers to get published?

My general sense of things is that, if the work is really good, it can be published, although things are changing rapidly in the publishing world as publishing houses are becoming more accountable to the conglomerates which own them. There's going to be more pressure upon them to make money, but the color of money doesn't have to be green. It can be red or black or yellow as well. I'm not so concerned about what color's going to get published; I'm more concerned about what's going to get published.

What is the best advice you can give to an aspiring writer?

Write from the heart, write what God and Creation have given you and go forward. When I was at Stanford in the early '80s, I was writing some of the stories that went into *Grand Avenue* and a professor there told me I would never be able to sell the stories of people like *that*. I was daunted and put them down for seven or eight years, then came back to them. You have to write what you know, and you have to know what your spirit is and follow that, whether people buy it or not.

William Heffernan: On Downsizing, Dinosaurs and the Million Dollar Deal

BY CINDY LAUFENBERG

Getting offered a one million dollar buyout of a manuscript before your book is even published may seem like a pipe dream to some, but it's reality for William Heffernan, author of *The Dinosaur Club*. This timely, serious-yet-funny novel about corporate downsizing tells the story of Jack Fallon, a corporate worker who finds out within the span of a few days that he's going to be downsized from his job, his wife is leaving him, his kids are more worried about a promised trip to Europe than the impending divorce of their parents, and his domineering mother is willing to take drastic measures to stay in her nursing home if Jack loses his job. Instead of letting these things overwhelm him, Jack decides to fight back—and with the help of spunky lawyer (and love interest) Samantha Moore, Jack rallies the about-to-be-axed employees together to form the Dinosaur Club, battling corporate greed and climaxing in a deliciously over-the-top revenge scene that will have readers cheering by book's end. Called a "wryly twisting, engaging tale . . . a highly entertaining read" by *Publisher's Weekly*, *The Dinosaur Club* was bought by Warner Bros. for a hefty one million dollar sum, and Morrow published the book shortly thereafter.

Heffernan is hardly a newcomer to the writing game, however. Graduating from the University of Dayton in 1962, Heffernan fell into journalism as a way to make a living while writing fiction on the side. "I wrote many short stories, but the only places that would publish them were literary magazines that paid only in copies, so that's what led to journalism. A friend said, 'I know a newspaper that's looking for some feature writers.' I went into it as a means of survival, and kind of fell in love with it. I never really gave up the idea of writing a book; it was just earning a living that kept getting in the way. It's very hard to work and write seriously at the same time." He spent 15 years working at newspapers such as the *New York Daily News* and the *New York Post*, and took a leave of absence in 1978 when his first novel, *Broderick*, was published by Crown. "*Broderick* did well enough for a second book contract to come along, so my leave of absence just sort of extended from there, and now 11 novels later, I'm still at it." Those 11 novels include six mysteries, three international thrillers and two mainstream novels. Many of them, including *The Corsican*, *Blood Rose*, *Ritual* and *Corsican Honor* were international bestsellers, and in 1996 Heffernan won the Edgar Allan Poe Award for his novel *Tarnished Blue*.

I caught up with William Heffernan on a recent book tour to promote *The Dinosaur Club*, and we spoke about his career as a writer.

When did you realize you wanted to write fiction?

Probably in college, my freshman year. Fiction is something that always captivated me, was always my favorite thing to read, so I guess it's something I wished I could do myself. I had an English professor who stunned me by telling me I had talent, and that I should pursue it. Until

CINDY LAUFENBERG *is managing editor of the Annuals Department at Writer's Digest Books, and is a frequent contributor to other Writer's Digest titles. She also plays bass for the Cincinnati-based band 7 Speed Vortex.*

Photo by Stacie Blake

then, I hadn't really given much thought to being able to do it, it was just sort of, well, it would be lovely if I could.

Tell me a little about your first novel.

Broderick was kind of a serious-yet-funny novel, set in 1929, about a real New York City detective who was quite famous during the roaring '20s, and about some criminals he subsequently executes. That was a big scandal at the time, and I fictionalized in a novel. I don't think you could really classify it into a genre other than the fact that it was about a 1929 New York City cop who happened to be the main character. *Broderick* was published by Crown, then my editor left Crown and went to Simon and Schuster and got his own imprint, so my next two books were published by Simon and Schuster, one of which was *The Corsican*. That book did extremely well, made some bestseller lists, and the paperback people at NAL, who bought the paperback rights to *The Corsican*, offered me a very lucrative contract to write two books for them. Those two books generated into 12½ years with that publisher.

Do you outline your novels? Or do you just jump in?

Out of necessity, publishers almost always insist on three chapters and a list or synopsis because publishing today is primarily run by marketing people, rather than editors, and they want to be able to sit there and look at something and say, "How many units of this can we expect to sell?" And it's really a wasted effort because as soon as I have to do it, I throw it away. I've never written a book that's followed course of the synopsis or outline I laid out. It just doesn't happen. Things change; once the characters take over and become real people, to me, they go in directions I hadn't anticipated. You think, "No, no, he wouldn't do that, he'd go this way. . . ."

What would you say has been the toughest thing about being a fiction writer?

It's an enormous roller coaster ride, with peaks and valleys, successes and waiting for something to happen. I think the ups and downs of any career in the arts makes it pretty hard to do; it's hard to keep your mind focused on what you want to do. Publishers aren't exactly enamored with writers—if they could figure out a machine to take their place, they'd be delighted. So, because publishing is a business and writing is an art, they often conflict, and you experience these very extreme ups and downs when dealing with publishers.

When would you say you first felt successful as a writer? And how would you define success for yourself?

I felt successful when I got my first novel published. That's an extraordinary thing to do, because you realize how many people are trying to publish something and how few books are published each year. To achieve that is a success in itself. Of course like anyone else, as soon as one achieves that success, one moves ahead and your ambition takes over. I guess when *The Corsican* received such a tremendous reception from the public, I realized I had arrived. Today, with technology, you're getting so much more feedback from the public so quickly through e-mail and everything else. *The Dinosaur Club* has a website, and I just get overwhelmed with messages from people who bought and read the book.

How was *The Dinosaur Club* published?

When *The Dinosaur Club* became an idea—a novel about corporate downsizing— I sat down with my editor at NAL and discussed it with her. Her advice was to stick to the mysteries, that's where the money is. I'd just finished a series of mysteries, five books, for them. I think a writer has to, at some point, follow the passion in his heart rather than the fear of rejection in his head, and I wanted to do this book. It's the only book I ever wrote without a contract. I wrote before and after and a book in between, and when I finished it and turned it in to my agent, she said, I want to go to Hollywood with this, because I think it will appeal to them. As it turned out, we ended up selling the film rights to Warner Bros. for an astronomical figure, before we even showed it to a publisher.

So you had a movie contract first?

Yeah, and it was not an option, it was a buyout, which is much more impressive because everything gets optioned by someone. But then Morrow picked up on it and did a great job. It's going into its fourth printing now. Oddly enough, Simon and Schuster, who I was with so many years ago, has the floor for the paperback auction. Because of the movie deal, we were able to sell only the North American hardcover rights to Morrow and keep everything else for ourselves. The Japanese just paid a stunning amount of money to put it out in paperback. So it's doing pretty well.

Is there one specific incident that gave you the germ of the idea for this book about downsizing?

In 1993 my wife's uncle was downsized from his job of 28 years. He was midwest regional sales manager for a rather large corporation. He didn't want to retire because he was 52 years old, with not much of a pension—you can't touch it until you're 55, and if you stay a pension accumulates. So they played hardball with him, transferred him to a place on straight commission only, and he didn't earn anywhere near the $160,000 he was earning. So he got beaten down, accepted their offer to leave, and went into a tremendous depression for over two years. He and his wife separated for nine months—fortunately they worked it out, but he lost his home, he didn't have a job, no bank was going to give him a mortgage, and he went through his savings. The next job he got was in the auto department at Sears. I was just fascinated by the brutality these corporations seemed to be using to get rid of people purely on the basis of age, to save money on their pension plans. I started researching it, and person after person, horror story after horror story, emerged. I think one of the things that distressed me the most was that all of these people, to a large degree, were blaming themselves. They understood intellectually it was a greed-based decision but they still felt like failures. And I really wanted to write a novel that might give them a sense of redemption. Early on I realized that the novel had to be humorous because the subject would be too depressing to deal with. So that was the basis of how it got started.

How did you go about researching the novel?

That was the easiest part of all. I used the libraries, of course, and newspapers, to find companies that had downsized, and looked at how they did it, what they offered, and how it effected individuals. But finding people to talk to about the human element of it was the easiest, because they were all over. Between 1993 and 1996 there were almost ten million people who were downsized. You translate that into spouses and children, and you're talking almost 30 million people. You get some very poignant stories about mothers trying to explain to their kids why they no longer have their own home, why the kids can't have their own bedrooms or a treehouse in their backyard, and not knowing when they might be able to have those things again. Most have just given up on the opportunity of paying for college educations for their children, because their savings have been gobbled up. And in most cases the people who are downsized, especially those in middle age, end up taking jobs at less than half of what they were earning before, so savings become a moot point.

Did you find it difficult to add humor to the situation without making fun of it?

No. I would never make fun of the situation, but there's enough humor in people's lives . . . the situation is never funny, it's not funny in the book, it's not anything except horrific. But the individual situations of the lives of the people it's going to affect . . . for example, Jack Fallon is not only about to lose his job but his wife had just run off with a philandering dentist. His kids are very avaricious; they think Jack won't be able to send them to Europe as he promised when they graduate. His mother is in a nursing home, and she's a domineering old woman, and at one point when she thinks Jack isn't going to be able to pay her nursing home bills, she starts claiming she's the Virgin Mary and holding apparitions, so they'll think she's crazy and Medicare will have to pay for it. So really, there are all kinds of elements of humor around the circumference of this story.

What was the most difficult part of writing the book?

To try and keep the anger out of it. I wanted to keep the anger at a satisfactory level, because the more I researched it, the more I heard CEOs talk about what they were doing and justifying it, the angrier I got.

How do you feel about the novel being made into a movie? I'm sure you're happy about it.

It was a lot of money! I hope it's a good film. I think all these people who have endured this [being downsized] will love it if it's a good film, if it's true to the story, to their story, which I think the book is. I really have to reserve judgment and see what happens.

When you were writing the book, did you think in the back of your mind it might make a good movie?

Not really. I don't think that way. Writing a novel is too all-consuming for me, because I really live it for all the time I'm writing it. Even though I'm not sitting at the computer, the characters are still running around in my head. If I started projecting, "Would Hollywood be interested? Will *The New York Times* like it?", it would just get in the way.

So at this point you don't have any input about the screenplay?

John Wells, writer/producer for the TV show *ER*, has been hired to do the screenplay. And I understand he's just about finished, which means they should start casting, I would think, by the end of the summer. I have been advised by a good friend, who is a screenwriter, that novelists should never get involved in writing their own screenplays, because it will only result in a broken heart. A screenplay is a collaboration between director, writer, actors, and everyone who have to take a 420-page manuscript, as this was, and bring it down to a 120-page screenplay. Something you love very deeply and gave birth to has to be cut up into something else. I don't think I would handle that well.

Why do you think this is the one book out of all your books that broke through with the movie deal?

I've had movie deals with other books. *Ritual* was all the way into production as a CBS Movie of the Week when the new president came into CBS and threw out everything that was in production, and then he was fired a year later. I think all but two of my books have been optioned, but you know, as I said, everything's optioned. I think you see such strong attention from Warner Bros. for *The Dinosaur Club* because it's so timely. I think the timeliness of the subject matter has made a great difference. And that's just the luck of the draw.

How did you find your agent?

It was a lot easier for me, because I came out of New York newspapers, and I had an established, recognizable name, so searching around for an agent was a little easier. But I was also smart enough back then to listen to what she had to say, and listen to her instructions exactly. And I think that played a large part in having success so early. A good agent knows all the editors and type of people they work with best. An agent can put you with the right editor and sell the idea to that publishing house, and your work is going to profit by it. I've been very fortunate having some very fine editors. In fact, Liza Dawson, the editor who bought *The Dinosaur Club*, was hired away by Putnam shortly after she bought it, and I insisted they hire an independent editor to edit the book, a guy named Jim Wade, who is just brilliant. Jim had earlier wanted to buy the book at Crown, when he was working there, but he was downsized.

What mistakes have you made in your writing career that you would advise beginning writers not to make?

I think starting to write a series was something of a mistake. I made a lot of money doing it, but I don't think I could do it again, because once you start a series, you're kind of a captive of that publisher. You lose a lot of freedom of movement because of the backlist, and other publishers don't want to pick up on a series. So I think that was a tactical mistake. I had money thrown at me and I succumbed to the temptation. I don't think I would do that again. I'd write each one of those books, but they'd have different lead characters.

What things have you learned about the writing and marketing of fiction that you wish you had known when you first started?

When I first started I had no idea that fiction was so hard to market, so hard to get publicity for, so difficult to gather public attention. I grew up thinking of the Hemingways and the Faulkners and the John O'Haras, the people who were little gods. Now it's just very hard to get any attention for any kind of fiction, whether it's serious fiction or genre fiction or whatever. About writing? I'd read a little too much Henry Miller and thought it was far more glamorous than it is. I've yet to be sitting in a Paris cafe sipping aperitifs while musing about the problems in the world. Life becomes pretty normal and mundane, it's just what you do to make a living. It still beats the hell out of going to work everyday. As my first grade son told his class, my dad works in a bathrobe, so. . . .

Any tips for beginning writers?

I would urge them to be disciplined. If they seriously want to write they must set aside a certain period of time every day, seven days a week. Because if they're not disciplined they're just going to be dabblers, and dabblers always end up as wannabes. If they have that discipline and they have that talent—and you must be able to recognize pretty quickly if you have the talent, otherwise, you should get the hell out and not waste your time. It is really imperative to find a good agent, and that's perhaps harder than finding a publisher. If my children came to me today, and said, Dad, I want to be a writer like you, I'd be complimented and thrilled, and I'd urge them to go to dental school. Because it's a very hard way to make a living. But it's also very rewarding when you occasionally win.

An International Success Story: The Magical World of Isabel Allende

BY JOANNE MILLER

"My life," Isabel Allende says, "is an ongoing soap opera. You wouldn't believe the amazing things that happen." Her characters often view the commonplace through spangled lenses. "I like abundance, baroque things, extremes. My grandmother was a clairvoyant and she experimented with telepathy all her life—it worked better than the telephone. All the richness I've seen appears in my books."

In person, Isabel Allende exhibits strength forged from adversity, feminine sensuality and a quick wit. Her words tumble over each other in gently-accented English. Since 1981, she has published four novels, a collection of short stories and a memoir, several of which have become international bestsellers.

Niece and goddaughter of Salvador Allende, Chile's former president, Allende grew up in isolated comfort in her grandparents' upper-middle-class home. After her mother's second marriage, to a diplomat, the family lived for brief periods in Bolivia, Europe and the Middle East. Allende was 15 when she returned to Chile. Because of continual travel and school changes, she learned to speak French fluently but was barely literate in Spanish. "I had a terrible education," she says, "no consistent formal schooling at all."

In Chile, she found a job as a secretary working for the United Nations Food and Agricultural Program. She often filled in for her aged boss, writing articles on the world hunger campaign, and within a few months became a fulltime writer there. During the next few years, she worked for a women's magazine and other publishers, writing "everything but politics and sports." She began to write humor and interviews for television, and won a grant to study television writing in Belgium.

Allende returned from Europe in 1966. Seven years later, her uncle was assassinated in what was widely held to be a CIA-affiliated coup. With her husband and young family, she continued to live under a brutal military regime in Chile until 1975, then fled to Venezuela, leaving her beloved grandfather and homeland behind. "I couldn't find work in Venezuela as a journalist. I managed to get one humor article published once a week. It didn't pay enough to cover the taxi fare to deliver it. I had to feed my family, so I worked a string of odd jobs, ending up as a school administrator. I hated that job, but it saved our lives."

Allende continued to write, but in her own fashion. When word came from Chile that her grandfather was dying, she began a letter to him; that letter became the basis of her first novel, *The House of the Spirits*. "I wanted to be with him, and this was the only thing I could do. Some people keep journals, a diary. To me, letters are the equivalent of a diary. I still use letters to get into the mood of writing, which is sometimes difficult. Also, I have a bad memory and it helps me remember. Now, I write a letter to my mother every day. I keep my mother's letters and she keeps mine—they're the record of our lives." The transition from journalist to novelist was effortless. "There was no difficulty because I hadn't written journalism in a long time— and I was a lousy journalist. I wasn't objective. I made things up."

JOANNE MILLER *is a fulltime writer of fiction and nonfiction. She recently completed a novel,* Power Lessons, *and is working on another,* Eve.

The House of the Spirits tells the story of three generations of the fictional Trueba family against the backdrop of Chilean history. "I didn't know I was writing a book, and I didn't know what kind it was when I was finished. My mother said, 'It looks like a novel; someone should read it.' So we sent it to five or six publishers in Latin America, and no one even answered. One day, a receptionist—another Chilean exile—from one of the publishers' offices called me and told me I needed an agent, and suggested one. A month later, I had an agent in Spain. I knew so little about the literary world—that people studied it in schools, that it was a huge industry. *The House of the Spirits* was published in Spain and all over Europe, but not in Venezuela. I was still working as a school administrator a year later when I got my first royalty check. I had already begun writing *Of Love and Shadows*; it was the story of my political awakening, but also the story of a crime, one I had become obsessed with. Several people had disappeared from a rural village during the military coup in 1973, and the bodies were found after I had left Chile in 1978. I wanted to tell the story of these villagers and built a fiction around it."

Allende found working with an agent to be indispensable. "I still have the same one, in Barcelona. We have a wonderful but distant relationship. She deals mostly in the European market and also handles my U.S. transactions, which are translations of work already published in Europe. Because of that, I don't have the same editor-writer relationship many American writers have, going over the text together, making changes. European publishers are different. I submit a manuscript, and they either publish or reject it. For me, the center of publishing is in Europe. My work appears in 27 languages; it's the main source of my income."

WRITING BY INSTINCT

"I don't consider myself spiritual, whatever that is. I'm a practical, down-to-earth housewife, very bourgeois. When I write, I like certain discreet rituals, and I meditate, but not for religious reasons. I light a candle, and I always have fresh flowers, because I like them. I don't like clocks, so when the candle burns down, it's time to stop. I have pictures of people I love all around me. This creates an atmosphere in the little room I use for writing; it's no different than when other people bring special things into a place where they make love. I summon the stories and spirits that will tell me their lives. I want them to stay and not be disturbed.

"There is magic in storytelling. You tap into another world. I don't invent anything; the stories are already there, and my job is to find them and bring them to the page. The story is always about some very deep emotion that is important for me. I think that a storyteller is a story hunter. She doesn't make up stories. Out in the world, the role of the storyteller is to ask people about their lives, and then repeat them in some way so those who hear can find particles of truth that will illuminate their own lives.

"I never know what I'm going to write. I'm not the kind of writer who can have an outline. It's as if I am pregnant with something that has been there for a very long time, growing, and when I relax and open myself to the experience, the book comes out."

Allende finds considerable synchronicity in writing. "Sometimes I write something, and I'm convinced it's just my imagination. Months or years later, I discover it was true. It actually happened, somewhere, sometime, to someone."

Concerning decisions in her personal life and her work, Allende trusts her instincts. "When I write and when I live my own life, I try to feel a sense of destiny in my gut. I often make decisions guided by instinct, more than reason or logic or common sense. I think my instinct or my dreams or my unconscious tunes into that part of me that is universal. I don't spend a lot of time in preparation for writing. I generally pour the story out first, then rewrite over and over—many drafts. I never know what the story will be about until I write it. But now, I'm writing a historical novel, which I call "No. 9," because it's the ninth project I've done—it's in sections. I research, then write, then research some more—research can become a labyrinth. I continue to write in Spanish only. Fiction is something that happens in spite of me. I can write a speech in English, and I can cook in English, but I can't make love in English. Spanish is for dreaming and making love."

CATHARSIS

The House of the Spirits, Allende's first novel, helped her to quiet her nostalgic longing for Chile; in her second novel, *Of Love and Shadows*, she overcame a lingering anger at the dictatorship that caused the loss of her home and family. In *The Infinite Plan*, her first work set in America, Allende wrote out her curiosity and wonder after moving to California to be with her American lover (now husband), Willie. "I was in awe of everything I saw. This is such a big country and there is so much diversity. All the races of the planet live here. It's an amazing place." Her novels found an audience in America during the wave of magic realism that included writers such as Gabriel García Márquez, and her work continues to include many magical elements. "It's strange that my work has been classified as magic realism because I see my novels as just being realistic literature. Sometimes I use tricks that are literary devices to exaggerate something, to make it more funny or spectacular, but the essence is always true. There is more magic in California than anywhere. I've never been in a crazier place—crystals, and bondage, and eating tofu! I like crystals if they look like diamonds [she laughs]. America is a very complex, texturized society. Sooner or later, everything ends up here, in the west of the west. There are so many weird stories—just read the personal ads."

Family continues to play an important part in Allende's life and work. She and her husband talked through *The Infinite Plan* before she wrote it; her mother reads and edits each book before it's sent to her agent. *Paula*, a work that also began as a letter, is Allende's most recent book and her first memoir; it is a passionate and moving exploration of her own life entwined with the story of her daughter's death. Allende cared for Paula, victim of a rare genetic illness, during the final year of her life. Like all of Allende's work, it is an affirmation of life, a tale of the honest triumph of spirit over life's inevitable tragedies.

NOVELS, SHORT STORIES AND MOVIES

Primarily a novelist, Allende ventured into short stories only once, with *The Stories of Eva Luna*. "When I moved to the U.S., I had no room of my own in which to write. Novels are, for me, adding up details, just work, work, work, then you're done. Short stories are more difficult— they have to be perfect, complete in themselves, but I could write them in fragments. I would go to Willie's office in San Francisco and write on a yellow pad. *The Stories of Eva Luna* are all love stories, because I was in love myself. I still am."

Two of Allende's novels have been made into big-budget films. *The House of the Spirits* and *Of Love and Shadows* featured well-known actors Meryl Streep, Glenn Close, Jeremy Irons, Vanessa Redgrave, Winona Ryder and Antonio Banderas. Allende's experience with Hollywood was a positive one: "I'm honored they chose my work, and I liked both films very much. I didn't participate in the projects, though; movies are a hectic world, and I don't want any part of it. I feel like the stories in my books are available for anyone to use—I didn't invent them, I just pulled them out of the air. The movie people have every right to tell it their own way."

ON WRITING

Allende's new work, *Aphrodite*, is a nonfiction book about aphrodisiacs, sex and food. "But," says Allende, "a well-told fable tends to be the most powerful aphrodisiac—a tale that has suspense, creates a mood, makes you cry or laugh. Perhaps it introduces a new perspective that changes you, or your opinion of something. Tension is very important—a storyteller carries it all the way through from 'Once upon a time' to the end. Anyone can learn to write, but it's impossible to teach storytelling, just as it's possible to teach someone to play piano, but not how to be Mozart."

Allende has managed to integrate the deeply personal art of writing her stories with the business of the publishing industry. "I'm proud I can make money from writing. It allows me to take care of my family. If I have to make a choice, I never choose the money. I write what I want and don't compromise. Because I was so isolated when I began writing novels, and because I've built up a reputation in America slowly, no one directs me. If I had published *The House of the Spirits* in America first, I probably would have been told to write more family sagas."

A well-known public figure in the San Francisco bay area, Allende generously donates her time to numerous charity events. "I'm very privileged. I think that if I have a voice people will listen to, I should use it wisely. I've been a feminist all my life, and I promote women's issues. In my daughter's name, because she was a teacher, I work for education. So many things touch my life through people I know. To promote research for those who are HIV positive is important, as is the plight of immigrants, because I am one. As an immigrant, my sense of roots is in my memories, and all of those are tied to people."

Allende has credited imagination as her most valuable asset as a writer. "I'm also very disciplined. I walk each morning, then I go to work, whether I'm inspired or not. And when I'm stuck, I have tricks. An example: My mother paints, and sometimes it seems like she's painting the same picture, the same way, over and over. I say, 'Change the format, make the flowers fill the whole picture.' or, 'Instead of the whole palette, use only six colors, and pick them blindly.'

"When I'm writing, I change my boundaries in the same way and make challenges for myself. Sometimes, I'll write something completely unrelated—a love story, even though what I need to work on has nothing to do with a love story. But it's a challenge, and I always learn from it. In *Eva Luna*, there is a girl who is retarded. Because her father does not want to see her, she hides. Where would she hide? Under the bed? Too obvious. Under the table, under a tablecloth! I put a white sheet on my table and spent a day under there. It opened up her world for me."

To writers who are just starting out, or who may be frustrated somewhere along the way, Allende advises, "Don't share your work; it weakens it. That's why I won't talk about the subject matter of 'No. 9.' You need all your energy to write, and if you tell the story to everyone, why write it? Be very patient with yourself. Think of all writing as training, like an athlete trains. You'll destroy a thousand drafts before you have something worthwhile. The joy of the process is what really counts. It's like lovemaking: it's not just the orgasm, it's the getting there."

Jennifer Crusie: Romance Novels are Literature, Too

BY DEBORAH WAY

After thirty-some years, details of the plot escape her, but Jennifer Crusie hasn't forgotten the first romance she read: "It was a young-adult novel called *Green As Spring*. I loved that book. The heroine was so funny and hopeless and real. Life kept slapping her down, and she kept picking herself up. When she finally got the guy, she was so strong, she could love him without needing him to define her. Sometimes I think every novel I've written has been my attempt to do *Green As Spring* again. With sex."

In 1991, Crusie was a Ph.D. candidate studying romances for her dissertation. One day she decided she'd studied enough; the next day, she started writing. The result was *Sizzle*, a novella. "The worst thing I ever wrote," Crusie says. "Really wretched. I couldn't plot at all. But it was funny, and sexy, so I entered it in a contest at Silhouette." It won.

By the time *Sizzle* was released, Crusie had written and published two more romances. By 1997, she'd published nine: one with Silhouette, six with Harlequin, two with Bantam. She's won a Rita ("the Oscar of romance"), for *Getting Rid of Bradley*. Her novels have sold a million copies worldwide. Readers say her books changed their lives.

This year, with the publication of her tenth novel, Crusie's own life will change. *Tell Me Lies* is her first hardcover fiction, for which she'll do her first national tour. Unlike her previous books, *Tell Me Lies* is being sold as a stand-alone title, published by St. Martin's Press. "You won't be picking up a Harlequin Temptation," Crusie says. "There's no line to hang this book on."

Professionally, *Tell Me Lies* means a great deal, but for its author its greater meaning is personal. "Every writer has a book she has to write before she dies, and *Tell Me Lies* is mine. It's about a woman who lives in a small town and always does the right thing, until one day while cleaning out her husband's car she finds another woman's underwear. Really, though, it's about finally walking away from everybody else's script and writing your own, which is very difficult for women to do."

Crusie should know. She's made a habit of not following any single script too closely. Besides novels, she's written short stories, poetry and literary criticism. In 1996, she published *Anne Rice: A Critical Companion* (Greenwood Press). She's earned a master's in business and technical writing and an MFA in creative writing. She's taught pre-school, elementary school, junior high, high school and college. She's run a switchboard. She's waitressed at the Happy Humpty Drive-In.

These days, though, Crusie is content to call herself a romance novelist. She seems amused by writers who, "after a certain amount of success, go around saying, 'I've transcended the genre.' You don't transcend. You may push the boundaries, but it's still romance. For *Tell Me Lies*, I'm insisting on the label. Which does not mean I want reviews that say 'pretty good for a romance.' I want reviews that say 'damn good novel, and, by the way, it's a romance, too.'"

DEBORAH WAY *is a freelance writer living in Cincinnati. Her stories have appeared in* The Missouri Review *(1995 Editors' Prize for Fiction) and* American Short Fiction.

You've published eleven books in six years, which seems pretty prolific. Is writing like breathing for you, or do you sometimes have to force yourself to do it?

I know there are people who sit down at the same time every day and write for X number of hours, week in and week out, and I have to tell you, I'd kill myself first.

I get a contract for a book and stare at the wall, more and more terrified as the weeks tick by. Finally, when the deadline is really bearing down, I jump and write like crazy and rewrite obsessively and weep and rewrite some more. When it's finished, I realize I never want to write again. It's too painful. I'm too stupid. I'll never get another idea. Then I get an idea and noodle around with it, and I send it to my agent and say, "This is really bad." And she sells it and I get another contract.

You sound like your own worst critic. It makes me wonder about the way you describe Sizzle—you said you wrote it when you 'couldn't plot at all.' Was that just an author's self-deprecation, or did your plotting really need work?

Well, this is a cop-out, of course, but I'd say a lot of it goes back to the way women think. We put discrete things together and see patterns, but there's no linear progression there. And fiction, because it's always been in the control of men, is linear: this happens, which logically leads to this happening, which logically leads to this happening, and so on. That's not how I naturally write. I don't write in chronological order. I start with the scenes that are most real to me and then go on to others. Eventually I assemble them like a patchwork quilt and lay the linearity over. At first, though, I didn't know how to lay it over. And fiction-writing books weren't a whole lot of help. They talk about Aristotle's plot curve, Freitag's pyramid, rising action, climax, falling action, denouement—well, fine, but how exactly do those things apply when you're writing 100,000 words and it's all a big mess? What really helped me was studying screenplay structure, which is very rigid and gives you a clear-cut description of what happens at each point in the story. The first act is 25%, the middle is 50%, the last is 25%, and along the way you have turning points. With that in mind, I said, okay, in a 100,000-word novel, I'm going to have four 25,000-word sections, and as long as I'm within roughly 5,000 words when I can spot a major turning point, I'll figure I'm okay. I can look at the sections and see if they're working: do they put more pressure on the character? Do they isolate her more? Essentially, I'm making a four-point tent peg, and once I have it, I can go back and work with the things I really like—individual scenes.

So you figured out a lot of stuff on your own. But you also went through an MFA program. Was that a good move for you?

There's no doubt in my mind that I wouldn't be where I am without the MFA program at Ohio State. Unfortunately, I published five novels before I had the brains and courage to sit in on a workshop. So there are five books out there that I'm not ashamed of, because they were the best I could write with what I knew, but they could have been better.

Nothing can improve your fiction like a good creative writing class, and nothing can destroy your faith in yourself and your work like a bad one. A good instructor doesn't care what you're writing—he or she cares how you're writing: if you're telling the truth on the page, opening a vein and digging deep, or if you're just showing off. A good instructor is brutally honest. I got nailed any number of times for going for the cheap laugh. And then there was the excruciating moment when my teacher, in front of the entire class, pointed to a sentence I'd written and said, "This is the kind of writing that causes cancer in laboratory animals."

Obviously, to get anything out of a workshop, you have to learn not to take criticism as a personal affront. That's made me a much more professional writer. Now when my agent or editors give me feedback, I write down everything as they're saying it, which leaves me no time to argue. Later, I can go over it and calmly decide what to use and what not to. Workshopping teaches you to listen instead of automatically defending—very good training for real life.

But you should never go into a serious writing program unless you're a serious writer, no matter what you write. There are people who say no romance writer is a serious writer, but those people don't understand writing and they're often toxic as teachers. A good instructor is as delighted when you write well as he is when he writes well. A good instructor is excited about fiction, kicks you hard if you shortchange the reader, and hammers craft into you until you're avoiding exposition even in your dreams.

I want to ask you about shortchanging the reader, but first, can you elaborate on what could have been better about your early books?

In *Manhunting*—I hate that title, by the way; it's not mine—I didn't understand point-of-view. I head-hopped like crazy, and it would have been a much tighter book if I hadn't.

Getting Rid of Bradley I wrote before I understood plot and structure; I was simply following my nose. Now I know I could have cut this or done this and it also would have been a lot tighter.

Strange Bedpersons I loved, but I had to rewrite it to tone down the heroine, who was a real smart-mouthed bitch. I see now that that was a mistake on my part, but back then I didn't know enough about writing. When you don't have training, you don't know why you're doing what you're doing, so you end up really leaning on your editor—it's as if she sees everything and you're just blind. Now I can look at a novel and realize a character *has* to do this or say that or make such-and-such decision.

Because otherwise her character would be violated?

Yes.

So it's possible to shortchange characters.

Definitely.

And you said that a good instructor kicks you hard if you shortchange readers, so I guess that's possible, too.

Crusie's rule of fiction: the only reason to write a novel is because you can't *not* write it. You *have* to tell the story. But once you're in a situation where you're getting contracts regularly, it's very easy to shift from this-is-the-book-of-my-heart to this-is-my-book-for-'98. That's when you shortchange your readers. It can happen to anybody. Look at some of Fitzgerald's stories in the *Saturday Evening Post*. But particularly in romance there's this stupid idea that you have to publish three or four books a year. People say things like, "I can't wait until this book is finished, I hate it, the next one's going to be so much better." Well, at that point, jeez, don't write the book.

I've always thought that's why *The Bridges of Madison County* did so well. I think Robert James Waller really believed in that book, and a real reader, a reader who says, "Okay, I'm giving you three hours and I want to be transformed"—that reader will overlook a hell of a lot of bad writing if the writer's heart is on every page.

What do you read? Or whom do you read? And do you think there's a difference between those two questions?

I think there's a huge difference, and it points up a major mistake a lot of writers make today. They ghettoize their reading. They say, "I read romance fiction" or "I read literary fiction." Or "Oh, I never read that stuff." Anytime I hear that, I figure that person's lost, because they're turning down books by type, not by quality or author or any reasonable criteria. They're close-minded, and close-minded is the one thing no decent writer can afford to be.

Then there are people who read soup-can labels if there's nothing else around—people who read current literary fiction, genre fiction, screenplays, poetry, *Beowulf*, *Wuthering Heights*. And they're better writers. Because you can't read all that and come away with a narrow idea of what a story is. The old genre advice of "Write the story you want to read but can't find" takes on deeper meaning when you've read widely.

To get back to your question, Tony Earley is a huge favorite, and so is Toni Cade Bambera. And Geoffrey Chaucer, Patricia Gaffney, Margery Allingham, Terry McMillan, Michael Gilbert,

Susan Elizabeth Phillips, Lee K. Abbott, Georgette Heyer, Jamaica Kincaid, Adrienne Rich, Ron Carlson, Judith Ivory, Melanie Rae Thon, Nora Ephron, Toni Morrison, Elmore Leonard, Valerie Taylor, Dorothy Parker, Justine Dare. This could go on for days.

What things besides reading have served you well in your writing?

I assumed that I got the rejections I got because the editors didn't understand what I was doing. And I decided it made more sense to find an editor who liked my stuff than to try writing stuff an editor would like. Also, I ignored market trends. I started my own trend for romantic comedy. And I chose an agent carefully—one who had a great reputation but who was also a good match personally. Then I listened to her.

I know a lot of people listen to you. You speak at conferences and write opinion pieces on the status of the romance genre. Can you do a bit of that here—comment on the state of the art?

Have you got a couple of hours? The genre is enormous—half the mass-market paperbacks sold worldwide are romances—which means that while a lot of great stuff gets published, a lot of dreck does, too, which is why critics can always find a book with which to indict the entire genre. The fact that the dreck gets read, though, points out the most important thing about romance: women like to read it. It's so empowering. The woman is usually the center of the story, and she always wins.

In my opinion, two things are happening right now that are going to change the shape of romance. The first is the shakedown going on in publishing, which is going to cut the number of titles in print. The second is the slowly increasing respect with which academics are studying romance. It used to be that criticism on romance was blindly sexist, especially from most feminist critics who didn't want to hear that relationships are important to women. But enlightened critics are now starting to look at romance novels as literature, and deciding case-by-case whether they succeed or fail. That kind of criticism has huge potential for improving the genre and luring more good writers to both read and write it.

Our market share increases every year. Our place in the industry is being acknowledged. And our standing in the critical world is beginning to rise. The average romance reader spends over a thousand dollars a year on books. Now all we have to do is write the books she deserves.

First Bylines

BY CHANTELLE M. BENTLEY

What's required to be a writer? A degree in creative writing? Years upon years of exploring the short story or novel form? Hundreds of dusty manuscripts littering bookshelves and hiding under beds? Through the numerous author interviews I've conducted for this article over the past few years, I've come to learn all that's required to be a writer is to write—regardless of whether you've written one story or ten novels.

As a writer, however, you must not only ponder the nature of your being but consider the quality of your work. Is this story/novel worthy of publication? Will it stand out in an editor's slush pile? As you will read in the following four interviews, the keys to seeing your work in print are perseverance and an unwavering belief in your dream. As Eleanor Roosevelt said, "The future belongs to those who believe in the beauty of their dreams."

DAN MONTAGUE
White Wings, *Dutton/Penguin Putnam, Inc.*

An economic analyst for the CIA, an Ensign in the Navy, an Episcopal priest, a counselor, a real estate broker, director of economic development for Alexandria, Virginia, and, finally, director of tourism and marketing for Massachusetts Port Authority—there doesn't seem to be anything that Dan Montague can't do, including writing an unforgettable first novel.

Montague, who is now retired, began writing while still serving as marketing director at Massport. However, it was not fiction that began his writing life but articles for travel magazines. "Because of my position at Massport, I had been doing a lot of traveling around the world. Also, my wife and I had taken a couple of bicycle trips, including one in China. I did articles related to some of my trips and even had one published in the *Boston Globe*." However, Montague found that he wasn't interested in writing articles about where to stay or where to eat; he was more into the "drama" of a locale. "I was getting more into the imaginative side of things. And I was getting rejections from travel magazines saying, 'Look, just give us the facts.' The facts were boring. So that's when I began to think about the idea of doing some creative fictional writing."

Abandoning travel writing, Montague jumped directly into writing novels. Over the next five years, he spent all of his free time writing and managed to complete two and one-half novels while still working fulltime. "They weren't very good, however. My wife wouldn't let me take them out of the house." Then, in 1994, Montague retired from his position at Massport and devoted more time to his latest passion. " 'Now,' my wife said, let's do a good novel.' "

Fourteen months of writing and researching ended with the completion of the manuscript for *White Wings*. The manuscript, which explores the ties that bind three generations of remarkable women, was read not only by Montague's wife but also by his daughters and one of his grand-

---

CHANTELLE BENTLEY *is the editor of* Poet's Market *and production editor of* Guide to Literary Agents.

daughters—three generations of women who could directly relate to the three generations in the book. Says Montague, "I had good readers who could evaluate the manuscript well."

After receiving the women's stamp of approval, Montague created a query package including a letter, sample chapters and background statement and sent it to every agent in Massachusetts. "The reason I limited myself to Massachusetts was, if I did get an agent, I wanted the person to be close enough that I could easily go visit. My plan was if I didn't do anything in Massachusetts, then I would branch out to Connecticut, then Rhode Island, and then, finally, New York."

After "tons" of rejection letters from agents stating either the manuscript wasn't in their focus or that they weren't taking on new clients, Montague heard from an agent who was interested in representing *White Wings*—if Montague would first send the manuscript to an editorial service. "I called the company recommended by the agent and discovered it would cost me $5,600. So I gave up on that [idea]."

At about the same time, Carolyn Jenks, an agent based in Cambridge, Massachusetts, responded to Montague's query and asked to see the entire manuscript. Because Jenks charged a reading fee of $250, Montague went to the library and found out all he could about agents and reading charges before replying.

Deciding the fee was worth a chance at agent representation, he sent the manuscript. Jenks loved the manuscript and asked Montague to send her seven copies right away. "I took the seven copies to her and she said, 'I am going to tell some people I know that I am going to let them read a really hot manuscript we are going to send out all over the market, but I am giving them a break and will hold off for a couple of weeks.' " Of the seven people Jenks contacted, two responded immediately and favorably. One of the two was Penguin Putnam, Inc. "At Jenks's advice, we went with Penguin. And I think that has been a good decision," says Montague.

White Wings landed in the capable hands of editor Al Silverman at Penguin Putnam who, over approximately the next 6 months, did a line-by-line edit of the book and assisted Montague in trimming 30 pages from the manuscript. The manuscript then passed through the keen eyes of a copyeditor and received two proofreads, one from an inhouse proofreader and one from Montague.

As a first book from a new author, *White Wings* received little in the way of publicity when it came off the press in July of 1997. However, Montague put his marketing experience to work and developed a publicity plan for the book. The first thing he did was form a volunteer marketing committee of friends who were in PR in the greater Boston area and who had press contacts. The committee met in April to talk marketing strategy. "Basically what I tried to do was draw these people in to get them excited about the book," says Montague. "I created press kits with photos and background information they could pass on to their newspaper contacts."

Montague then arranged for a reception to be held at the Hampshire House in Boston. (The Hampshire contains the bar where "Cheers" was filmed.) All the local media was invited and Montague's granddaughter was in charge of distributing press kits to them. He says, "We had the *Boston Herald* society editor there, and he did a nice big spread on the reception and the book. It was a great time, a great event."

Now with *White Wings* out in the bookstores and, through his granddaughters' efforts, even in the hands of Oprah Winfrey, Montague is working on revising his second novel and has the beginnings of a third. The second novel was in fact purchased by Penguin Putnam—on the basis of an outline and the first 15 chapters—the February before *White Wings* was released.

And what advice does this author/priest/counselor/marketing director have for those still seeking publication? "I think you have to make your breaks. Do everything you can, everything you can afford and everything you've got time to do to give your manuscript, or even the book itself, the best opportunity. Don't let chances slip by. If you see an opportunity, take advantage of it."

CRAIG ETCHISON
Vietnam Snapshots: Stories of a Conflict, *Mountain State Press*

Twenty years after returning from Vietnam, Craig Etchison, a professor at Allegheny College in Cumberland, Maryland, was visited by memories from the war that insisted on being captured in tangible form. As a flight operations sergeant in a helicopter unit with the First Cavalry Division, Etchison witnessed the real conflict of the Vietnam War. "Our unit went out and reconnaissanced things like B-52 strikes. A B-52 would go in at night and the next morning our unit, with the help of helicopters, would fly over and check what damage had been done. When the guys would come back, I'd take the intelligence report and send it on to division and brigade. So I was in a position to see what was really happening and then to see how the statistics were changed and enlarged by the time they got to the American public."

These memories became a collection of short stories and vignettes not so much about war but about people. "The stories are all based on kernels of something that happened to me during that year [in Vietnam]," says Etchison. "I fleshed each story out of one little incident using, of course, the knowledge I had of the war, the land, the people and how things worked. However, I tried to get a variety of viewpoints—some stories are from the viewpoint of enlisted men, some are from the viewpoint of officers, some are from the viewpoint of the Vietnamese [a child in one case and woman in a couple of other stories]. I don't consider them war stories as much as stories about people caught in war."

The stories, with all their nuances, are quite an ambitious collection, especially when you consider they are Etchison's first works of fiction and that Etchison has had no formal training in creative writing, despite having a Master's degree in English and a Ph.D. in Rhetoric and Linguistics. "I had been doing some academic writing and research kind of stuff since I received my Ph.D. in 1985, but this was my first foray into creative story writing. I was really a novice." So, Etchison started buying books from Writer's Digest and learning more about the craft. "And I really enjoyed it. It was much more fulfilling than the academic writing I had been doing. So I basically bagged the academic writing and, with one or two small exceptions, have been writing fiction."

After completing his stories and vignettes and gathering them into a collection, Etchison first tried contacting a few agents, but none were interested in reading the manuscript. He then submitted the manuscript to a number of university presses who liked the book but didn't have the resources to be able to publish it. Then, when he was just at the point of believing the book would never see the light of day, Etchison received his member's copy of the West Virginia Writer's Association's newsletter. In it he saw a notice saying that Mountain State Press was looking for manuscripts from West Virginia writers. "So I thought what the heck. It really was my last shot. I probably wouldn't have sent it out again."

Mountain State responded very enthusiastically. In fact, the manuscript for *Vietnam Snapshots* went through practically no revision after being accepted. The editor responsible for overseeing the book's production told Etchison it was the best manuscript he had ever seen. Even so, Etchison did run into some tough spots while working on the manuscript. "The toughest decision was the language—how realistic to make it," he says. Etchison finally decided to make the stories very naturalistic and to write the language as it was used in Vietnam, with all the four-letter words. "And I don't regret that [decision]. I think that was the way it had to be."

To validate the stories and test their appeal, Etchison had a number of Vietnam veterans read the manuscript prior to submission. "One of the veterans who read the book said, 'I am collecting books about this [war] so my children will know what it was really like over there—yours is going to be one of them.' I took that as a very high compliment." An unexpected compliment Etchison received is the number of teenagers who have contacted him saying they were enthralled with the stories. "I don't know why they're connecting with the book," he says. "I thought people more my age who were familiar with the war would be interested in reading it, yet quite a bit of interest has been generated with teens."

The teenagers may be connecting with Etchison's style as well as his stories. Because not only does Etchison write adult-oriented stories, he also writes for the younger crowd. Currently, he has a young adult fantasy, the first in a trilogy, that he's preparing for submission. "I have a couple of former students who are now teachers using the story in their classrooms with great success." Also, he has just finished a middle-grade novel that is being evaluated by a nine-year-old who is "a sharp little cookie."

And, for Etchison, being in touch with his readers is what's most important, not necessarily selling to a major publishing house. "It's one thing that helps keep me going," he says. "The reality is most of us never make the big sale. It's fun when people say 'I really liked your book' or 'That touched me' or 'That made me cry or laugh.' I think I am very lucky."

NANCY DICKINSON
"Maternity Leave," *Hurricane Alice, A Feminist Quarterly*

With the addition of a second child and a job she was growing weary of, Nancy Dickinson decided it was finally time to pursue her interest in fiction writing. And, living in the historic district of El Paso, Texas, she applied to the University of El Paso's M.F.A. program by submitting the first story she had ever actually completed. Says Dickinson, "I was always interested in literature and had wanted to write but never found any direction or guidance or support for that [interest]."

So, Dickinson began the three-year program with some catch-up work to do—not having a collection of stories to present for the first of many workshops. "Other people in the workshop seemed to have a body of work, so I had to scrounge to come up with stories for that first workshop. It took about a year before I caught up and had a body of work like the others."

Supported by an understanding professor through that first "nerve-wracking" workshop when her fellow M.F.A. students were "killing her with criticism," Nancy surprised herself by receiving the UTEP Literary Award during her first semester in the program for the story "Maternity Leave." In fact, the award-winning story accomplished many firsts for Dickinson. It was her first story to receive positive feedback during workshop, her first story to receive an award and her first story to achieve publication. "There was a lot of me in 'Maternity Leave,' " she says. "The woman in the story returns to work after having her second child. She works in a PBS station and just doesn't fit in. She's going to the bathroom to pump her breasts and is struggling to bring the milk home to the baby. While she was on maternity leave someone took over her accounts and stole her commission."

And as most of Dickinson's stories are about women, she was naturally attracted to a feminist journal her professor passed around in class with a few other interesting literary magazines. The journal, *Hurricane Alice*, is a quarterly based in Providence, Rhode Island, and published by a 12-member editorial collective.

When the collective voted on Dickinson's story, it received an unanimous "yes" from all the editors. Says *Hurricane Alice*'s executive editor, Maureen Reddy, "We all thought the story was well-written and liked that it covered ground unfamiliar to us. At the same time, it told a story about work and women that is important to many women." [See the Insider Report with Maureen Reddy on page 280.]

This strong response and other similar responses have made Dickinson very keen on small press editors. "I really like small presses because the editors are so kind. They are always positive when they write back. I have received letters from editors who have written three paragraphs about my story; they're rejections, but they've taken the time to write." In fact, one editor wrote Dickinson saying, "No, but send anything else you have." And when she did send other work, he rejected it but still replied with a positive note.

After exhausting the market leads Dickinson obtained through her professor at UTEP, she purchased a copy of *Novel & Short Story Writer's Market*. She uses *NSSWM* not only for locating potential markets, but also for finding journals to read. "I try to do research using *NSSWM* and then, when I see something interesting, I go to the bookstore or send away for a sample copy. I try to stick with the regional publications and have had a lot of success with regional as well as feminist publications." Since the publication of "Maternity Leave," Dickinson has had work included in *Borderlands: Texas Poetry Review, The Shattered Wig Review, Descant: Fort Worth's Journal of Poetry and Fiction* and *Phoebe*.

Dickinson says her acceptance rate improved when she learned the elementary lesson that you need to investigate a publication before submitting to it. "Instead of just taking a guess at what a magazine is about, I read and see which one of my stories would be best," she says. "And if publications don't read during summer, I don't send them my story in summer. If they only publish theme issues, and the story is not in that theme, they are not going to be interested. Before, I was kind of blindly sending things out; now I try to read before I submit something."

Researching and reading publications also aids Dickinson in her writing. "I had a dry spell this past summer, so I wrote away for themes. It was a lot of fun. I got two story ideas when the themes came back. It was like a homework assignment—'Okay, now I have to write about sex and the 21st century.' "

With an M.F.A. and some publication credits under her belt, Dickinson's future writing plans must be focused on trying her hand at a novel, right? Not necessarily. "I really just want to write a good short story. I feel like I still have a lot of work to do there. And, maybe, if I write three great short stories I am proud of, maybe then I'll try a novel. But I really like the short story form, writing and reading it."

BOB BRONGIEL
"Part Time Cop," *Dogwood Tales Magazine*

"Walt Oleksy, a freelance writer from Evanston, Illinois, who hosts the North Shore Writer's Group I attend gave me this advice: Read, write and persevere. Always send a reject out the same day, so you turn a 'no' into a 'maybe.' Well, I think I epitomize what he's been telling me for so long. After 17 years, I finally had my first short story published," says Bob Brongiel, a systems analyst from the Chicago area.

An avid reader of both the *Alfred Hitchcock Mystery Magazine* and *Ellery Queen's Mystery Magazine*, Brongiel was enticed into writing mysteries after winning an award for his nonfiction writing. The year was 1980, and Brongiel had just received an MBA degree from the Lake Forest School of Management. Finally finding time to write, he completed a piece for the trade journal *Production and Inventory Management*. The article, "A Manual/Mechanical Approach to Master Scheduling and Operations Planning," won Best Article of the Year and a cash prize of $500. Says Brongiel, "I think the thrill of winning a prize for my writing was a pretty big incentive, but rather than write nonfiction, my first love was to read and write stories."

His first work of fiction was a short story titled "Just for Once," which he submitted to *Twilight Zone Magazine*. The story was approximately 4 pages long and about a guy who was granted a wish after saying a prayer for 13 consecutive days. "I received a rejection letter several months later with a note saying it was an 'interesting idea, but the characters were wooden.' " That note was enough to encourage Brongiel to give it another try. It also made him realize that maybe he didn't quite know all the mechanics of what constitutes a "good story."

As a result of that insight, Brongiel enrolled in a correspondence course with the Colorado-based National Writers School. "I regularly received lessons requiring a great deal of writing which I immediately completed and sent back," he says. "Lucy Beckstead, my instructor, promptly returned them with critiques. I learned a great deal about writing from those lessons." During this same period, Brongiel also started subscribing to *Writer's Digest* magazine and began attending the North Shore Writer's Group.

With new confidence and skills, he revised "Just for Once" and even increased its length by ten pages. By this time, however, Brongiel became aware that his writing style seemed to "lag behind the times. I was submitting stories to *Twilight Zone Magazine* that had unusual endings, à la Rod Serling, when they were publishing stories more akin to Wes Craven. I submitted stories to *Alfred Hitchcock Mystery Magazine* and *Ellery Queen's Mystery Magazine* in the vein of Jack Richie and Roald Dahl (fairly short with a little 'twist to the tale') when the magazines began printing novelettes, reprints of old classic suspense stories and cozy British mysteries."

Brongiel also wrote a children's book called *Jeffrey and the Fishing Derby*, in the tradition of Beverly Cleary, only to discover that action stories and stories dealing with serious social problems were "hot." "My story was about my kids when they were much younger and it was a joy to write. My problem was that I knew 'the marketplace' but I also knew what I wanted to write, and they weren't the same." Of course, this conflict of interests resulted in Brongiel not publishing any of his stories. "But, I got enormous satisfaction from completing those stories," he says.

In an odd twist of fate, Brongiel's break finally arrived after his short story "Part Time Cop" was rejected by *Pulp: A Fiction Magazine*. "I saw an article in *Writer's Digest* that said the journal *Pulp* was looking for manuscripts. So I submitted my story." And although editor Clancy O'Hara rejected the story because it didn't quite fit the magazine's format, he did attach a note with the following comment: "Bob, it's good work. Another editor might like it. But it's not right for *Pulp*. Thanks, Clancy."

"That might be inconsequential to some, but it gave me the push I needed to resubmit the story somewhere else," says Brongiel. It was then he read about a contest in *Dogwood Tales Magazine* to which he already subscribed. And, several months later, when he was about ready to quit submitting and quit his writer's group, Brongiel received a letter saying "Part Time Cop" had won second place in *Dogwood*'s June 1996 contest. The story was "finally" published, without any changes, in the magazine's July-August 1997 issue. "I took my wife and kids to celebrate at our favorite pizza joint—spent my entire $25 award. I have the award certificate framed and hung in my cubicle at work."

And since Brongiel does much of his writing at work during lunch, his cubicle wall is the perfect place to hang his award. "During the last year, that prize has given me the necessary jolt to continue with my writer's group and write five additional stories about mysteries that take place in my fictitious town of Windy Knolls [the same setting used in the story 'Part Time Cop']. Eventually, I might write enough of those stories to put them in an anthology called *Windy Knolls Mysteries*."

All of Brongiel's five stories have been submitted to a magazine or a contest, but none have, as of yet, received an acceptance. "But they haven't received any rejections either," he says. "My biggest challenge [after the first story was published] was realizing just because you had one story published, the others weren't automatically going to be accepted, too. Each story has to stand on its own merit."

Submission Etiquette: Editors Speak Out

BY DEBORAH WAY

Maybe you can't judge books by their covers, but what about judging manuscripts by their cover letters? Do editors form an impression of your work before they've even read it? If so, what steps can you take to make the impression a good one?

To learn more about the etiquette of submitting to literary magazines, I spoke with Richard Burgin, editor of *Boulevard*; Linda Burmeister Davies, co-editor of *Glimmer Train*; Joseph Kruppa, editor of *American Short Fiction*; and Greg Michalson, managing editor of *The Missouri Review*. All offered opinions on cover letters and more. It's worth noting that, at times, the opinions conflict; like good fictional characters, good editors are idiosyncratic. So, when sending out stories, mind your p's and q's. (And if you find you have committed a submission faux pas, don't lose too much sleep: as Richard Burgin says, "Remember how many magazines are out there. You'd have to try really hard to alienate them all.")

When you open a submission package, what are your expectations for the physical condition of the manuscript?

Greg Michalson: Writers are under the gun here. I don't know if there are more writers these days, but in the last few years the volume of manuscripts has gone up geometrically. You don't know whether to be encouraged or frustrated that there's so much—I hate to use the word "product"—out there that it's sometimes hard to sort through it well. And the fact is, if a manuscript is hard to read, it may not get read as carefully. I would use good, clean, ordinary paper—unused paper: don't put your story on the back of somebody else's. Use a clean typeface. Double space. Make corrections so the thing's not all scribbled over. Make sure your printer has a good ink cartridge. I would prefer not to have a manuscript stapled; I'd rather have it paper-clipped.

Greg Michalson

Linda Burmeister Davies: Personally, we like stories stapled because we carry them with us everywhere: they're in the car, on the bus, under the beds. We'd hate to lose a page.

We've accepted stories with typos and other messy things, but you have to be awfully damn good to get an editor to look beyond the really ugly. Don't send something that's been photocopied to the point where the pages are blackened. Don't send pages with white-out all over them. Do make sure the pages are in order. These are petty things, maybe, but most of the time they turn out to match up with the stories. For instance, if you have a title in gigantic type, or if you use heavy type or sans serif type, somehow we get the feeling that the person is trying to impose a weight on the story, rather than letting it carry its own weight. And like anything unusual in terms of format, it shows that the writer hasn't had much exposure to the process,

DEBORAH WAY *is a freelance writer living in Cincinnati. Her stories have appeared in* The Missouri Review *(1995 Editors' Prize for Fiction) and* American Short Fiction.

very generally. If you follow a somewhat standard physical presentation, we'll know you're a little more committed to writing, a little more experienced, that you've invested enough to find out how it's done.

Joseph Kruppa: Not everything has to be in apple-pie order, but I think there's something to be said for doing things a standard way. I can't remember, for example, ever accepting a story that came folded in thirds in a #10 envelope. And it's better when the manuscript isn't wrinkled or ratty. We get some that look like they've been slept on. The type should be dark enough. It shouldn't be broken. It should be large enough to read; 14 point is easier than 10 or 12. The paragraphs and indents should line up. The title should be done with standard capitalization. And I do mind when pages are missing.

  We don't open the envelope and say, "My God, a paper clip!" Paper clips are fine. So are staples, as long as the staple doesn't interfere with the text.

Richard Burgin: If you're trying to get someone to at least read the opening page of your story, of course you should be neat and well-organized. Undoubtedly, there's a perceived link between appearance and reality. The bottom line, however, is that appearance can only take you so far. In the end, the quality of the stuff has to be there.

How about mechanical infelicities?

Michalson: They're the kiss of death. If you can't write a grammatically clean sentence, if you have three or four misspellings on every page, you haven't bothered to learn your craft. It sends a message that you're either not capable or you just don't care.

Burmeister Davies: Punctuation, I think, is fairly individual. We don't go crazy about it. And, honestly, misspellings don't bother me much. But grammar is important. A consistent tense is important. You want to give the impression of having really thought about your work and taken the time to understand your language.

Kruppa: You've got to have control of the language. I think most editors want to feel they're in the presence of a serious mind, and sloppy mechanics suggest that you aren't very serious.

Susan Burmeister-Brown and
Linda Burmeister Davies

Burgin: It's better to be grammatically correct than not. But, again, the brilliant piece with a few errors is going to be taken, as opposed to the impeccably presented, empty piece.

How personal is too personal in the cover letter?

Kruppa: We get some outlandishly personalized stuff, including letters on colored stationery with cloud scenes and misty mountains. They get tacked up in the office for a couple of weeks, and we get a little laugh, but I can't say we've accepted the accompanying stories.

Michalson: Sometimes we get photographs of the writer or the pet poodle. Or a long, involved history of their family life. I think that's hokey. What we strive for is a professional relationship based on mutual respect. Send your stuff in a straightforward way, and we'll respond in kind.

Burgin: It's completely normal, I think, to want to find out about people, especially if they're offering the information. I suppose some information is too trivial—you know, mentioning that you wrote for your high school newspaper. At one time, I might have been put off by things like that, but now I guess I might be somewhat touched. I did once get a submission from a writer who, in the course of the cover letter, conceded that he was doing time for murder. Maybe that wasn't an apt thing to include, though it did make me think twice about rejecting his work.

Burmeister Davies: We're nosy, Susan and I. We're curious. We enjoy hearing a speck, *just a little speck*, about people. We don't want them to talk our ears off, but they can throw in personal things and we'll get a kick out of it. Personal things about themselves, not us. Not long ago we got a letter that said, 'You know, you guys are really cute.' We hate that. You can be friendly, but be respectful, please.

Is it a good idea to compliment the magazine in your cover letter?

Burgin: I suppose it's implicit that you value the magazine in the fact that you're submitting. But from what I know of human nature, it never hurts to be kind. If you like the magazine, why not say so?

Michalson: It's nice to think people out there read *The Missouri Review* and take it seriously. But, honestly, I'd rather not get an explanation of how much they like it or why they're submitting. We don't need to know that stuff.

Burmeister Davies: I'd say we're slightly more inclined to pay more attention to a story if we know the writer knows *Glimmer Train*. It means right off the bat we're a bit on the same track. So if you read a magazine and like it, mention that. But don't say anything that isn't true; chances are, you'll get caught. A writer who claims to read us but starts the cover letter "Dear Sirs"— that kind of thing is just not good.

Joseph Kruppa

Kruppa: We can usually tell from the story if the writer knows us. And some people are just terribly unconscious about what we're about. They'll send genre pieces—westerns, sci-fi, romance—but we don't do genre stuff.

In some cases I think people just skim through old issues, because we get manuscripts addressed to former editors.

What, if anything, should writers say about their story in the cover letter?

Burgin: I've gotten letters that describe the so-called theme of the story, but not too often. Most letters are pretty mainstream, pretty sophisticated.

Burmeister Davies: If writers want to give a one- or two-liner about the story, fine, but they don't have to. What matters is how the story is carried off. We recognize that a story is important to its writer—at least it should be; it will be if it's any good at all. But you don't have to tell us how much it affects you. We'll know. And don't tell us how great it is. We like to decide that for ourselves. Reading is as personal as writing.

Michalson: Letters that try to explain what a story's about or what an author's trying to accomplish are counterproductive, I think. They can give an editor a chance to make a negative judgment about a story before reading it.

Kruppa: Giving a précis is one of the worst things you can do. It sounds like you're trying to sell something.

How loudly should writers toot their own horn in a cover letter?

Burmeister Davies: It doesn't hurt to say that so-and-so told you to send a story, especially if so-and-so teaches in a respected writing program or is a writer we might know.

Michalson: If Robert Olen Butler read your story and said, "You've just got to send this to *The Missouri Review*," sure, that might be interesting. But I wouldn't make a big deal of it. You don't want it to become something that gets in the way.

Kruppa: It's okay to mention that you got your MFA somewhere, but I'd rather writers didn't name-drop. What does it mean to say you studied with Donald Barthelme? I'm a great admirer of Barthelme, but no matter how closely you worked with him, it doesn't mean your story's any good.

Burgin: I guess I'm skeptical about people's ability to think for themselves. I believe it's natural to be influenced by accomplishments in your field. So if a writer has done an MFA or won a prestigious prize or published in a known magazine, I think they should mention it. Of course, you don't want to send your entire résumé. That's a bit much. So is sending copies of reviews; it seems like you're trying too hard. And it goes without saying that you should never invent publications.

Richard Burgin

As for writers who really are just starting out, I don't think they should despair. Editors want to make discoveries—that's how they achieve reputations.

After waiting months for a response, should writers contact the magazine?

Michalson: If we've kept a manuscript for more than three months, I don't mind a bit getting a query note or phone call. In fact, I'd rather get one at four months than nine, because at four months there's a good chance I can figure out what's going on. At nine, there's a good chance I can't.

But do give us the ten weeks we ask for. We have people who'll send a manuscript once a month, every month, like clockwork, whether they've gotten the last one back or not. Somebody has given them this advice, and it's terrible advice because if we get a little slow, suddenly we can have three or four submissions piling up from the same person. Usually, after about the third one, I'll send a note saying, Listen, I'm happy to read everything you want to send, but let us decide about one story at a time.

Burgin: When I hear how long some people wait just because they're afraid of annoying you, it's sweet, but I always feel bad. Editors aren't precious islands of sacred feeling. If they go on record saying expect to hear from them in this amount of time, and you don't, it's their responsibility to be polite when you inquire. Certainly they shouldn't hold it against you. You're entitled to call because you've already written; you've submitted something. And who knows? In the course of calling, you may get into a nice conversation with the editor.

Kruppa: If we've held the manuscript for too long, it's fine to inquire, but we don't like getting a lot of phone calls.

Burmeister Davies: We get a huge number of manuscripts—many thousands each year—and to read each one attentively, as we like to, we really do need three months. If it's been much longer than that and you haven't heard from us, go ahead and send a note saying so. And do include another copy of the story.

Back to cover letters: once and for all, are they worth agonizing over?

Michalson: I used to say you don't need a cover letter at all, and the truth is, you don't. But it's good to have some sense of human beings on both sides of the transaction. So probably a letter is nice, so long as it's to the point. Really, I wouldn't go more than a paragraph. I'd just say, Hey, here I am, I've published such and such, or, I haven't published—just a small acknowledgement that there's a person there.

I think writers worry so much about cover letters and other things because they feel like it's us versus them. I understand that feeling, but I don't think it's true. Every editor I've known who's worth two dead flies is excited to come across a good manuscript. Most of us are here because we're writers ourselves or because we're dedicated to the idea of literature and want to contribute to the endeavor. We're not out here thinking, "Oh, I get to ruin somebody's life by treating them real bad."

Burgin: I just published my third book of stories [*Fear of Blue Skies*, Johns Hopkins University Press] and I still agonize. Well, I wouldn't say "agonize," because I've become more fatalistic. But I still don't know how to write *the* cover letter, and that insecurity tends to make you over-think. On the other hand, as I get older I'm coming to see that letters don't make a hell of a lot of difference. Since I don't feel I have a gift for writing charming, pithy, original letters of any kind, much less letters accompanying a submission—letters that could in any way make a difference by striking a chord or making someone laugh—since I don't have the knack for any of that, I try to write a totally normal thing, what I imagine to be appropriate, something that won't work against me. I try to impersonate an average person writing an average letter.

Ironically, when I'm reading letters, I feel as though the vast majority of them actually are written by the same person. Hopefully, the stories don't sound that way.

Kruppa: We just like a modest, factual letter that gives a hint of the writer's background. I do think that sort of presentation probably gets the story a slightly better read.

Burmeister Davies: The cover letter is so insignificant. You really shouldn't sweat it. Brief is good.

Accepting—and Using—Rejection

BY GEOFF SCHMIDT

I'm not sure it's exactly flattering to be asked to write an article about rejection (have the legends of my many and spectacular "failures" reached even Cincinnati?), but here I am, and here you are, so we must both have had some experience with the awful business of it. And really, who among us hasn't? Well, okay, Belva Plain, profiled in the *1996 Novel & Short Story Writer's Market*, has only been blessed with acceptance letters throughout her long career. She's the exception, though. If you write, or if you are a writer seeking readers, you have been rejected. We all know the awful fact of our own handwriting on the manila envelope waiting in the mailbox, the terrible heft of it. We have all left that envelope on the kitchen counter or on the table by the front door, unable just yet to open it and confirm the inevitable. We have all read those notes, some of them brisk and professional, some of them almost tender, almost apologetic. Some of us throw them out at once. Some of us keep them in shoeboxes, or paste them to the wall. Some of us burn them.

Some of us use them.

The truth about rejection is this: it is neither benign nor malignant, neither to be feared nor embraced. Rejection is just a force, a fact in a writer's life. How you live with that fact, how you use that force, is what will make rejection a positive or a negative.

The Monday before I was asked to write this article I got this rejection from the editor of a fine literary magazine, one that had published me before: "Geoff—your time is more valuable than this."

At first, I was angry at that note. Not the fact of the rejection but the wording of it, its bluntness and presumption—why, how dare he tell me what was and was not worth my time? It was one of the few times in my life I think I've actually sputtered. My first reaction, in fact, was to commit myself all the more to the piece. Turn it into a series. Perhaps the germ of a novel. I'd show him!

That anger soon faded, of course. Shame took its place: how could I have wasted his time like that? What was I thinking? How could I ever send him anything again? I looked at the story. It was too slight, too easy, immature, written and submitted in haste. I'd never send it out again.

Eventually, I went back to the story, read it with fresh eyes, with the blush of shame and anger both working together, keeping me from either repudiating or blindly committing to the story. I saw the flaws that editor saw. I saw strengths he apparently did not. I realized, though, that it was the wrong piece for the magazine I'd sent it to. It was too slight, too easy for this editor, and this magazine, but I wasn't sure that meant it was without merit. I knew the next piece I sent to this editor would have to be very good, as I'd lost some of his trust, which is so hard for a writer to earn, and so easily lost. And I started to think about other magazines and other editors that might be more open to the piece, once I'd given it the revision it sorely needed.

Had I continued to take that rejection personally, had I never seen past either my anger or

---

GEOFF SCHMIDT *has had stories published in the* Chariton Review, Gettysburg Review, Alaska Quarterly Review, Black Warrior Review, Other Voices, *and the* Crab Orchard Review. *All of those stories were rejected many times before they were accepted. He's about to finish a novel that he says will almost surely be rejected at least once.*

my shame, I might never have begun to think like a writer. I might still be wasting my time.

COPING WITH REJECTION

Before you can use rejection, you have to cope with it. This isn't always easy. There's a great moment in *The Godfather* when, as Sonny Corleone dismisses Michael's plan for revenge as overly emotional, Michael silences his objections with these words: "It's not personal, Sonny. It's just business."

One way to cope with rejection is to not take it personally. Separate your writing self from your business self. This is hard, I know. We all pour so much of ourselves into our stories and books, and draw so much from our lives. When your most secret fears and dreams are at the heart of the piece, when you've sacrificed so many hours in the excruciating crafting of that piece, it's difficult not to take that rejection personally. But that story, no matter how autobiographical, no matter how much you have invested in it emotionally, is not you. The story has gotten rejected, not you.

Another way to cope with rejection is to realize that it happens to almost everyone. From Melville to Elmore Leonard, T.S. Eliot to Stephen King, almost every writer has faced the disappointment of rejection in some form or another. You are not alone.

Still another way to accept rejection is to believe in the process and the notion that eventually good work will get published. Sometimes stories have to find their best readers, and this can be a time-consuming process. Eventually, though, believe that the good writer who perseveres will see print.

A last way to deal with the pain of rejection is to stop submitting. When Emily Dickinson's first publication experiences turned disappointing—when editors rewrote her poems to conform with their notions of what a poem must be—she stopped looking for publication as a way to satisfy herself as an artist. She did not stop writing. If you can not bear the pain of rejection, if it turns you bitter or sends you into depression, and if that depression or anger inhibits your ability to write, then the attempt to publish will have destroyed you as a writer.

WHEN GOOD STORIES GET REJECTED

Stories and novels get rejected for lots of reasons, and not all of them have to do with the worth of the piece. In an age when there are more people writing stories than reading literary magazines, it's no surprise that so many good stories get rejected.

A friend of mine who is both a writer and an editor at a highly respected literary magazine says they accept, on average, "one of every hundred fiction submissions." Often, he says, "we reject good stories because we haven't the room to publish them. We could easily accept twice as many stories as we do, but we would simply accumulate a backlog that would sit for years and decades before getting into print. So we accept only those stories we respond to most. A degree of subjectivity is involved here. Some good stories do not affect a particular reader, an editor, say. They will, however, affect some other editor." Always keep this in mind when your story is turned down at one, or three, or ten magazines.

In my experience, good stories, sent to good literary magazines, will get turned down 11 out of 12 times. I've had stories get rejected as many as 25 times before being accepted by magazines I was proud to have publish my work. One of my stories was returned to me 15 times before it got accepted. It later received a Special Mention in *Pushcart Prize XVI*. My friend the editor says that the writer should keep sending out work as long as he "believes in the manuscript's quality."

Sometimes those good stories will be rejected in a way that gives you hope—there's a sincere handwritten note, or specific comments, or encouragement to submit again. This is one way rejection can be helpful; it allows you to develop a relationship with an editor. You should also take this as a sign that your story will eventually find the right reader at the right magazine. But if you don't get many of those notes, you shouldn't get discouraged. On the day I spoke to my friend the editor, he got 91 manuscripts in the mail. The sheer number of them will prevent him from commenting on all but a few.

In any case, this kind of rejection can have benefits. It will make you feel like part of a larger community, like a professional writer. No longer is your work private, or being read only by uncritical eyes. A professional editor has read and considered that piece. A note with a word of sincere encouragement or criticism can make you feel even more like a part of the literary world. If nothing else, once one story is out and coming back, it can push you to write the next piece just so you don't dwell on that other story getting rejected so often!

Still, merely coping with rejection doesn't seem like it should be enough. There should be ways to use rejection to make yourself a better writer. I think there are.

"IF I'M AS GOOD AS I THINK I AM, WHY HAVEN'T I BEEN PUBLISHED YET?

A few weeks ago, before my first creative writing class, I had a prospective student come into my office. He wanted to get a sense of what to expect from the class. As we talked about what *he* expected from the class, the conversation turned to one reason he was there. "If I'm as good as I think I am," he said, "why haven't I been published yet?"

This is the awful thing about repeated rejection: you start to wonder, "What's wrong with me?" You begin to lose faith in yourself, to doubt your instincts.

It is at this point, this dark night of the writer's soul, that one of three things can happen.

The worst one is this: you will give up. You will begin to believe that everybody else must be right about you. Something is wrong with your writing. Your novel, your stories, must be terrible, because, well, because 20 people haven't wanted to publish them, or 40, or 100. And if nobody wants to publish them, it must mean nobody wants to read them. So you stop writing. You put your novel in a drawer and start using the spreadsheet programs and Web browser on your computer instead of the word-processing program.

I don't think this is always a bad thing. I've known some people who tried to make a living writing fiction and were miserable because of it. After the nth rejection, they gave up, turned to editing or teaching or freelance writing or a hundred other careers they found infinitely more rewarding. They were much happier not writing fiction, and rejection taught them that.

On the other hand, I sorrow for those people who give up what remains, in their heart of hearts, their dream, simply because of rejection. Those people stifle a compulsion, a vital part of themselves, sometimes the best part of themselves. If you burn to write, if it is an ache inside of you, don't let rejection be the thing that makes you abandon what you love. Instead, use rejection to become better at what you love.

REJECTION AS CHALLENGE

This is the second thing that can happen: instead of abandoning your faith in a story, rejection can make you question it. If, as Emerson said, the unexamined life is not worth living, then the unexamined story is probably not worth reading. Blind faith is just as dangerous as the absence of faith. If 20 or 30 or 100 people turn that novel down, though, or if several people tell you that exactly the same thing is wrong with that book, then maybe you should look at it again carefully. Try to revise according to their suggestions. Experiment. If you take rejection not as an insult or a crippling attack but as a challenge, as somebody raising the bar, rejection can push you to do more, to try harder, to take chances. If your safe stories keep getting politely turned down, maybe you'll write a story that feels dangerous, one where you feel like you're taking chances. If your brilliant experimental piece keeps getting the same kinds of rejection, maybe you've let form or style overwhelm story. The point is, rejection will at least let you entertain other possibilities for a piece, and that alone can make you a better writer.

Once, the editor of a magazine rejected a story of mine even though he loved the language of it, and the characters. But, he said, "There's no ending. This is not where this story ends." I reread the story. It was so obvious, suddenly. Inspired, I left the rest of the story intact, added a page-long coda, and sent the story out again. It was accepted by the very next magazine I sent it to—in fact, by the same editor who just rejected me this week with the note I talked about at the start of this article.

REJECTION CAN AFFIRM YOUR FAITH

Finally, rejection may simply strengthen your resolve. So much in writing depends on faith. You reach a point where you must trust your vision, believe in your words. The writers who succeed, often, are not the best writers, but the ones who trust most unshakably their vision.

I once got a smart, detailed rejection from an editor at *The New Yorker* that ended with this post-script: "If you revise this, we'd be pleased to read it again." *The New Yorker*! I attacked that revision. I rewrote that story every way that I knew how. I reconsidered and re-envisioned. But each time I produced a new draft, something had been destroyed, either in the story itself or in my sense of it. I worked for months trying to reshape that story, and in the end I realized I couldn't do it. For better or worse, it was finished, told the only way I could tell it. Rejection, and the subsequent attempt at revision, had reaffirmed my faith in it as it was. Rejection is always a test of faith. And if your faith in a story is not strong, then inevitably, rejection will cause you to lose that faith. You may never return to that story, but you may have learned for the next story, or submission. I know my next submission to the editor who rejected me by saying "Your time is more valuable than this" will have to be good, and will have to be a very different story than the one I gave him. From rejection I have learned a little bit about myself as a writer and a lot about that editor's tastes.

You may, though, use rejection as an opportunity for revision. As your faith in that story is tested, you may actually find a way to improve the story.

A terrible thought nagged at me as I was writing this: what if my article on rejection is rejected? The possibility was too awful; it woke me up in the middle of the night.

If you're reading this now, it means I didn't let the fear of rejection overwhelm me. Instead, I used that fear.

You can, too. Be passionate in your writing. Be reckless. Never lose faith in yourself. Persevere.

The Business of Fiction Writing

It's true there are no substitutes for talent and hard work. A writer's first concern must always be attention to craft. No matter how well presented, a poorly written story or novel has little chance of being published. On the other hand, a well-written piece may be equally hard to sell in today's competitive publishing market. Talent alone is just not enough.

To be successful, writers need to study the field and pay careful attention to finding the right market. While the hours spent perfecting your writing are usually hours spent alone, you're not alone when it comes to developing your marketing plan. *Novel & Short Story Writer's Market* provides you with detailed listings containing the essential information you'll need to locate and contact the markets most suitable for your work.

Once you've determined where to send your work, you must turn your attention to presentation. We can help here, too. We've included the basics of manuscript preparation, along with a compilation of information on submission procedures and approaching markets. In addition we provide information on setting up and giving readings. We also include tips on promoting your work. No matter where you're from or what level of experience you have, you'll find useful information here on everything from presentation to mailing to selling rights to promoting your work—the "business" of fiction.

Approaching magazine markets

While it is essential for nonfiction markets, a query letter by itself is usually not needed by most magazine fiction editors. If you are approaching a magazine to find out if fiction is accepted, a query is fine, but editors looking for short fiction want to see *how* you write. A cover letter can be useful as a letter of introduction, but it must be accompanied by the actual piece. Include basic information in your cover letter—name, address, a brief list of previous publications—if you have any—and two or three sentences about the piece (why you are sending it to *this* magazine or how your experience influenced your story). Keep it to one page and remember to include a self-addressed, stamped envelope (SASE) for reply. See the Sample Short Story Cover Letter on page 79.

Agents: Agents are not usually needed for short fiction and most do not handle it unless they already have a working relationship with you. For novels, you may want to consider working with an agent, especially if marketing to publishers who do not look at unsolicited submissions. For more on approaching agents see *The Guide to Literary Agents* (Writer's Digest Books).

Approaching book publishers

Some book publishers do ask for queries first, but most want a query plus sample chapters or an outline or, occasionally, the complete manuscript. Again, make your letter brief. Include the essentials about yourself—name, address, phone number and publishing experience. Include only the personal information related to your story. Show that you have researched the market with a few sentences about why you chose this publisher. See the Sample Book Query Cover Letter on page 80.

The sample cover letter

A successful cover letter is no more than one page (20 lb. bond paper), single spaced with a double space between paragraphs, proofread carefully, and neatly typed in a standard typeface (not script or italic). The writer's name, address and phone number appear at the top, and it is addressed, ideally, to a specific editor. (If the editor's name is unavailable, address to "Fiction Editor.")

The body of a successful cover letter contains the name and word count of the story, the reason you are submitting to this particular publication, a short overview of the story, and some brief biographical information, especially when relevant to your story. Mention that you have enclosed a self-addressed, stamped envelope or postcard for reply. Also let the editor know if you are sending a disposable manuscript that doesn't need to be returned. (More and more editors prefer disposable manuscripts that save them time and save you postage.) When sending a computer disk, identify the program you are using. Remember, however, that even editors who appreciate receiving your story on a disk usually also want a printed copy. Finally, don't forget to thank the editor for considering your story. See the sample cover letters on pages 79 and 80.

Book proposals

A book proposal is a package sent to a publisher that includes a cover letter and one or more of the following: sample chapters, outline, synopsis, author bio, publications list. When asked to send sample chapters, send up to three *consecutive* chapters. An **outline** covers the highlights of your book chapter by chapter. Be sure to include details on main characters, the plot and subplots. Outlines can run up to 30 pages, depending on the length of your novel. The object is to tell what happens in a concise, but clear, manner. A **synopsis** is a very brief description of what happens in the story. Keep it to two or three pages. The terms synopsis and outline are sometimes used interchangeably, so be sure to find out exactly what each publisher wants.

Manuscript mechanics

A professionally presented manuscript will not guarantee publication. But a sloppy, hard-to-read manuscript will not be read—publishers simply do not have the time. Here's a list of suggested submission techniques for polished manuscript presentation:

• Use white, $8\frac{1}{2} \times 11$ bond paper, preferably 16 or 20 lb. weight. The paper should be heavy enough so it will not show pages underneath it and strong enough to take handling by several people.

• Type your manuscript on a computer using a laser or ink jet printer, or on a typewriter using a new ribbon.

• Proofread carefully. An occasional white-out is okay, but don't send a marked-up manuscript with many typos. Keep a dictionary, thesaurus and stylebook handy and use the spellcheck function of your computer.

• Always double space and leave a $1\frac{1}{4}$ inch margin on all sides of the page. For a short story manuscript, your first page should include your name, address and phone number (single-spaced) in the upper left corner. In the upper right, indicate an approximate word count. Center the name of your story about one-third of the way down, skip two or three lines and center your byline (byline is optional). Skip three lines and begin your story.

• On subsequent pages, put last name and page number in the upper right hand corner.

• For book manuscripts, use a separate cover sheet. Put your name, address and phone number in the upper left corner and word count in the upper right. Some writers list their agent's name and address in the upper right (word count is then placed at the bottom of the page). Center your title and byline about halfway down the page. Start your first chapter on the next page. Center the chapter number and title (if there is one) one-third of the way down the page. Include your last name and page number in the upper right of this page and each page to follow. Start each chapter with a new page.

SAMPLE SHORT STORY COVER LETTER

Jennifer Williamson
8822 Rose Petal Ct.
Norwood OH 45212

January 15, 1998

Rebecca Rossdale
Young Woman Magazine
4234 Market St.
Chicago IL 60606

Dear Ms. Rossdale,

As a teacher and former assistant camp director I have witnessed many a summer romance between teens working at camp. One romance in particular touched me because the young people involved helped each other through a very difficult summer. It inspired me to write the enclosed 8,000-word short story, "Summer Love," a love story about two teens, both from troubled families, who find love and support while working at a camp in upstate New York.

I think the story will fit nicely into your Summer Reading issue. My publishing credits include stories in *Youth Today* and *Sparkle* magazines as well as publications for adults. I am also working on a historical romance.

I look forward to hearing from you.

Sincerely,

Jennifer Williamson
(513)555-5555

Encl.: Manuscript
       SASE

SAMPLE BOOK QUERY COVER LETTER

Bonnie Booth
1453 Nuance Blvd.
Norwood OH 45212

April 12, 1998

Ms. Thelma Collins
Bradford House Publishing
187 72nd St., Fifth Floor
New York NY 10101

Dear Ms. Collins:

I am a published mystery writer whose short stories have appeared in *Modern Mystery* and *Doyle's Mystery Magazine*. I am also a law student and professional hair designer and have brought these interests together in *Only Skin Deep*, my 60,000-word novel set in the glamorous world of beauty care, featuring hair designer to the stars and amateur Norma Haines.

In *Only Skin Deep*, Haines is helping to put together the state's largest hair design show when she gets a call from a friend at the local police station. The body of famed designer Lynette LaSalle has been found in an Indianapolis motel room. She's been strangled and her legendary blonde mane has been shaved off. Later, when the bodies of two other designers are discovered also with shaven heads, it's clear their shared occupation is more than a coincidence.

Your successful series by Ann Smythe and the bestseller *The Gas Pump Murders*, by Marc Crawford, point to the continued popularity of amateur detectives. *Only Skin Deep* would make a strong addition to your line.

I look forward to hearing from you.

Sincerely,

Bonnie Booth
(513)555-5555

Encl.: three sample chapters
synopsis
SASE

• If you work on a computer, chances are your word processing program can give you a word count. If you are using a typewriter, there are a number of ways to count the number of words in your piece. One way is to count the words in five lines and divide that number by five to find an average. Then count the number of lines and multiply to find the total words. For long pieces, you may want to count the words in the first three pages, divide by three and multiply by the number of pages you have.

• Always keep a copy. Manuscripts do get lost. To avoid expensive mailing costs, send only what is required. If you are including artwork or photos, but you are not positive they will be used, send photocopies. Artwork is hard to replace.

• Most publishers do not expect you to provide artwork and some insist on selecting their own illustrators, but if you have suggestions, please let them know. Magazine publishers work in a very visual field and are usually open to ideas.

• If you want a reply or if you want your manuscript returned, enclose a self-addressed, stamped envelope (SASE). For most letters, a business-size (#10) envelope will do. Avoid using any envelope too small for an 8½ × 11 sheet of paper. For manuscripts, be sure to include enough postage and an envelope large enough to contain it. You might also consider sending a disposable manuscript that saves editors time and saves you money. If you are requesting a sample copy of a magazine or a book publisher's catalog, send an envelope big enough to fit.

• When sending electronic (disk or modem) submissions, *contact the publisher first for specific information and follow the directions carefully.* Always include a printed copy with any disk submission. *Fax or e-mail your submissions only with prior approval of the publisher.*

• Keep accurate records. This can be done in a number of ways, but be sure to keep track of where your stories are and how long they have been "out." Write down submission dates. If you do not hear about your submission for a long time—about three weeks to one month longer than the reporting time stated in the listing—you may want to contact the publisher. When you do, you will need an accurate record for reference.

Mailing tips

Manuscripts under five pages long can be folded into thirds and sent in a business-size (#10) envelope. For submissions of five pages or more, however, mail it flat in a 9 × 12 or 10 × 13 envelope. Your manuscript will look best if it is mailed in an envelope only slightly larger. For the return envelope, fold it in half, address it to yourself and add a stamp (or clip IRCs to it with a paper clip). Computer disks may be sent in official mailers or mid-size envelopes with stiffening for 78¢.

Mark both of your envelopes in all caps, FIRST CLASS MAIL or SPECIAL FOURTH CLASS MANUSCRIPT RATE. The second method is cheaper, but it is handled the same as Parcel Post (Third Class). First Class mailing assures fastest delivery and better handling.

Book manuscripts should be mailed in a sturdy box (a ream-size typing paper box works well). Tape the box shut and tape corners to reinforce them. To ensure your manuscript's safe return, enclose a self-addressed and stamped insulated bag mailer. You may want to check with the United Parcel Service (UPS) or other mailing services for rates.

If you use an office or personal postage meter, do not date the return envelope—it could cause problems if the manuscript is held too long before being returned. First Class mail is forwarded or returned automatically. Mark Third or Fourth Class return envelopes with "Return Postage Guaranteed" to have them returned.

It is not necessary to insure or certify your submission. In fact, many publishers do not appreciate receiving unsolicited manuscripts in this manner. Your best insurance is to always keep a copy of all submissions and letters.

When sending return postage to another country, do not send stamps. You must purchase International Reply Coupons (IRCs). The publisher can use the IRCs to buy stamps from his/her own country. In the U.S., IRCs cost $1.05 each and can be purchased at the main branch of your local post office. If you live in Canada, see Canadian Writers Take Note on page 635.

Main branches of local banks will cash foreign checks, but keep in mind payment quoted in our listings by publishers in other countries is usually payment in their currency. Also note reporting time is longer in most overseas markets. To save time and money, you may want to include a return postcard (and IRC) with your submission and forgo asking for a manuscript to be returned.

Rights

Know what rights you are selling. The Copyright Law states that writers are selling one-time rights (in almost all cases) unless they and the publisher have agreed otherwise. A list of various rights follows. Be sure you know exactly what rights you are selling before you agree to the sale.

• **Copyright** is the legal right to exclusive publication, sale or distribution of a literary work. As the writer or creator of a written work, you need simply to include your name, date and the copyright symbol © on your piece in order to copyright it. You can also register your copyright with the Copyright Office for additional protection. Request information and forms from the Copyright Office, Library of Congress, Washington DC 20559. To get specific answers to questions about copyright (but not legal advice), you can call the Copyright Public Information Office at (202)707-3000 weekdays between 8:30 a.m. and 5 p.m. EST. Publications listed in *Novel & Short Story Writer's Market* are copyrighted *unless* otherwise stated. In the case of magazines that are not copyrighted, be sure to keep a copy of your manuscript with your notice printed on it. For more information on copyrighting your work see *The Copyright Handbook: How to Protect and Use Written Works* by Stephen Fishman (Nolo Press, 1992).

• **First Serial Rights**—This means the writer offers a newspaper or magazine the right to publish the article, story or poem for the first time in any periodical. All other rights to the material remain with the writer. The qualifier "North American" is often added to this phrase to specify a geographical limit to the license.

When material is excerpted from a book scheduled to be published and it appears in a magazine or newspaper prior to book publication, this is also called first serial rights.

• **One-time Rights**—A periodical that licenses one-time rights to a work (also known as simultaneous rights) buys the *nonexclusive* right to publish the work once. That is, there is nothing to stop the author from selling the work to other publications at the same time. Simultaneous sales would typically be to periodicals without overlapping audiences.

• **Second Serial (Reprint) Rights**—This gives a newspaper or magazine the opportunity to print an article, poem or story after it has already appeared in another newspaper or magazine. Second serial rights are nonexclusive—that is, they can be licensed to more than one market.

• **All Rights**—This is just what it sounds like. All Rights means a publisher may use the manuscript anywhere and in any form, including movie and book club sales, without further payment to the writer (although such a transfer, or *assignment*, of rights will terminate after 35 years). If you think you'll want to use the material later, you must avoid submitting to such markets or refuse payment and withdraw your material. Ask the editor whether he is willing to buy first rights instead of all rights before you agree to an assignment or sale. Some editors will reassign rights to a writer after a given period, such as one year. It's worth an inquiry in writing.

• **Subsidiary Rights**—These are the rights, other than book publication rights, that should be covered in a book contract. These may include various serial rights; movie, television, audiotape and other electronic rights; translation rights, etc. The book contract should specify who controls these rights (author or publisher) and what percentage of sales from the licensing of these sub rights goes to the author. For more information, see Selling Subsidiary Rights.

• **Dramatic, Television and Motion Picture Rights**—This means the writer is selling his material for use on the stage, in television or in the movies. Often a one-year option to buy such rights is offered (generally for 10% of the total price). The interested party then tries to sell the idea to other people—actors, directors, studios or television networks, etc. Some properties are optioned over and over again, but most fail to become dramatic productions. In such cases, the writer can sell his rights again and again—as long as there is interest in the material. Though dramatic, TV and motion picture rights are more important to the fiction writer than the nonfiction writer, producers today are increasingly interested in nonfiction material; many biographies, topical books and true stories are being dramatized.

• **Electronic Rights**—The marketing of electronic rights to a work, in this era of rapidly expanding capabilities and markets for electronic material, can be tricky. With the proliferation of electronic and multimedia formats, publishers, agents and authors are going to great pains these days to make sure contracts specify exactly *which* electronic rights are being conveyed (or retained).

Compensation for these rights is a major source of conflict between writers and publishers, as many book publishers seek control of them and many magazines routinely include electronic rights in the purchase of all rights, often with no additional payment. Alternative ways of handling this issue include an additional 15% added to the amount to purchase first rights to a royalty system based on the number of times an article is accessed from an electronic database.

Readings

Attending public readings of fiction has become very popular in many cities. The general public seems to be just now catching on to something writers and avid readers have known for years: Readings offer a unique opportunity for those who love literature to experience it together.

If you are comfortable in front of a crowd and you'd like to share your work with others, try giving a reading. Not only does a reading allow you the opportunity to gauge reaction to your unpublished work, it's also an invaluable tool for promoting published short story collections and novels.

While there are some very prestigious reading series such as the "Main Reading Series" sponsored by The Unterberg Poetry Center of the 92nd Street Y in New York City, many readings are local events sponsored by area writers' clubs. You can start small, if you like, with one of the open-mike readings held in most cities in neighborhood coffee houses and taverns or, if you are published, look for bookstores that offer readings by authors whose books they sell.

Other reading outlets include libraries, churches, hospitals, radio stations and public-access cable television stations. Some series are well-established, while in other cases, you may have to approach a location and suggest a reading. It all depends on the amount of time and effort you'd like to invest.

If you decide to create your own reading opportunity, you may have to supply publicity and refreshments as well as a location. Established authors sometimes charge fees to sponsoring organizations, but newer writers usually feel the exposure is enough. If you have published work, however, you may want to bring copies to sell or arrange with your local bookstore to set up a table to sell your books. If you want to join an established series, keep in mind it can be competitive. You may be asked to submit work for consideration and a formal application.

For more information on readings, see *The Writer's Book of Checklists* by Scott Edelstein (Writer's Digest Books).

Promotion tips

Everyone agrees writing is hard work whether you are published or not. Yet, once you arrive at the published side of the equation the work changes. Most published authors will tell you the work is still hard but it is different. Now, not only do you continue working on your next project, you must also concern yourself with getting your book into the hands of readers. It becomes time to switch hats from artist to salesperson.

While even bestselling authors whose publishers have committed big bucks to promotion are asked to help in promoting their books, new authors may have to take it upon themselves to plan and initiate some of their own promotion, sometimes dipping into their own pockets. While this does not mean that every author is expected to go on tour, sometimes at their own expense, it does mean authors should be prepared to offer suggestions for promoting their books.

Depending on the time, money and the personal preferences of the author and publisher, a promotional campaign could mean anything from mailing out press releases to setting up book signings to hitting the talk-show circuit. Most writers can contribute to their own promotion by providing contact names—reviewers, home-town newspapers, civic groups, organizations—that might have a special interest in the book or the writer.

Above all, when it comes to promotion, be creative. What is your book about? Try to capitalize on it. For example, if you've written a mystery whose protagonist is a wine connoisseur, you might give a reading at a local wine-tasting or try to set something up at one of the national wine events. For more suggestions on promoting your work see *The Writer's Guide to Promotion & Publicity*, by Elane Feldman (Writer's Digest Books).

Sample Cover Letter Contest

Unfortunately, there is not a winner in this year's Short Story Cover Letter Contest. Although all the entries had accompanied manuscripts accepted for publication, no one entry exhibited all the basic elements we suggest a cover letter have.

For more on cover letters and formats, see *The Writer's Digest Guide to Manuscript Formats*, by Dian Dincin Buchman and Seli Groves. If you feel you have a successful cover letter, we hope you will consider entering our 1999 Short Story Cover Letter Contest. The winning letter will be published in the next edition. Our criteria is simple: We're looking for a letter that helped lead to the *acceptance* of a short story between May 1997 and May 1998. Keep in mind the letter must include the elements of a good cover letter as outlined. The deadline is May 15, 1998. Send the letter with your address and phone number and proof of acceptance (a copy of the letter of acceptance will do) to Cover Letter, *Novel & Short Story Writer's Market*, 1507 Dana Ave., Cincinnati OH 45207.

In addition to publication in the 1999 edition of *Novel & Short Story Writer's Market*, the writer will receive a small cash payment for publication of the letter, a copy of the book and the opportunity to select two titles from our Writer's Digest Books catalog.

Fiction Report

BY BARBARA KUROFF

With 1996 and 1997 behind us, it seems there is good news ahead for the book publishing industry. At mid-year in 1997, Veronis, Suhler & Associates, a firm that tracks consumer book spending, reported that the long range projection for book sales looks good: readers will increase by 17 percent during the next 5 years and consumer spending on books should increase 5.5 percent and reach $21.2 billion by the year 2001. For the quarter ending July 31, 1997, the 4 major bookselling chains—Barnes & Noble, Borders, Books-A-Million and Crown—reported gains in sales of $2.4 billion, up 15 percent from the previous period. Taking advantage of the upsurge in the bookselling marketplace, Best Buy, a major retailer of music, video and computer hardware, added books to its shelves in late 1997.

The Internet is also giving a boost to book sales. Just halfway through 1997, Amazon.com, pioneer among the emerging Internet booksellers, reported sales of $27.9 million, up from $2.2 million in the same period in 1996. Amazon applied much of that profit toward expanding their infrastructure and consumer awareness. That investment continues to pay off: cumulative customer accounts grew to more than 610,000 (50 percent repeat customers), compared to 340,000 customers during the first quarter of 1997. Vying for the online market is Barnes and Noble at BarnesandNoble@aol.com. Also entering the online bookselling competition is Wal-Mart, the world's largest discounter. Wal-Mart, which previously sold only the bestselling 350 titles in its retail outlets, has added 311,000 titles to its online bookstore (www.walmart.com).

As publishers and booksellers tallied up their end-of-year profits, the general outlook going into 1998 was "cautious optimism." Publishers would continue to publish books by their best-selling authors. Tom Clancy received in excess of $100 million for 2 novels, a 4-year book/multimedia deal and 24 paperbacks to tie in with the ABC miniseries *Tom Clancy's NetForce*. Another sign indicating the industry is serious about carrying on with business is that more than 20 houses who did not attend the 1997 BookExpo America (the largest U.S. book trade show) plan to attend the 1998 show. This includes conglomerates Simon & Schuster and HarperCollins, both noticeably absent in 1997. And, most importantly, all publishers I spoke with said they would continue looking for fresh voices—but they would need to be the best fresh voices—to add to their lines in 1998.

Now, here's a closer look at some specific fiction categories:

CHILDREN'S AND YOUNG ADULT FICTION

The *Publishers Weekly* 1997 fall report on upcoming children's books noted that children's fall releases offered "a number of enduring tendencies in children's book publishing: established, award-winning authors and artists continue to do compelling work; there is always room for talented newcomers; and publishers keep developing innovative formats to appeal to a changing audience and market." In an article entitled "They're Everywhere You Look," written for the same issue of *PW*, Judith Rosen points out that "children's books are available in many places these days—clothing stores, bedding stores, even car washes," with greatest volume of sales (29 percent) coming not from bookstores but from discount stores such as Target, Wal-Mart and Kmart. Large chain bookstores account for 10 percent of the sales of children's books while only 5 percent of children's book sales come from independent and small chain bookstores.

Emily Easton, editor of young adult titles at Walker and Company, admits that "the tightening up of the industry probably will effect writers trying to break into the marketplace. I absolutely think it's gotten a lot tougher to make a go of hardcover fiction overall, and there are fewer houses generally because publishers have been merging and contracting their lists."

Still, Easton is positive. "I think publishers are always looking for somebody with a unique voice and are willing to take a chance on new writers. We're definitely open to new people; that hasn't changed. Our list has gotten slightly smaller, but we were small to begin with. Now we are doing 20-25 new hardcovers a year as opposed to 30 or 35 before. That makes our slots a little tighter to get into."

Easton traces the current tightening up in children's fiction back to the late '80s when "there was over-publishing going on. Everybody thought it was a great idea to get into children's publishing, so there were too many books being published." Now, Easton is concerned that too many children's publishers are relying on "merchandise" rather than books to keep them afloat. "A lot of houses have tightened up their lists and are publishing more merchandising kinds of books—novelty and pop-up books, and media tie-ins. That makes me sad."

At Walker, however, Easton says, "We're still very interested in finding new voices in fiction, primarily middle grade but occasionally young adult. We've done a lot of historical novels, but at this point I am more interested in contemporary material—not necessarily a problem novel, but something fresh, something that speaks to what kids are interested in themselves, rather than something a librarian would have to 'book talk' strongly to get into children's hands."

Scholastic continues to be a dominant force in children's publishing after a 1997 "restructuring" which eliminated 425 positions and netted only $361,000 from sales of $966 million. Its Goosebumps series remains popular, although some parents, teachers and school librarians continue to question the "literary" value of the stories. Scholastic's very full 1997 fall catalogue of paperbacks contained more than a dozen titles written by Ann M. Martin, author of the Baby-Sitters Club series (150 million copies in print since its launch in 1995) along with Martin's new California Diaries books for the 11 to 14 age range.

HORROR

"Horror is alive and doing extraordinarily well on the bestseller lists and at the box office," says author **Janet Berliner**, who became the president of the Horror Writers Association in November 1997. But, says Berliner, "Just don't look for the word 'horror' in caps on the spine or the cover of those books—look for dark fantasy, psychological thriller, or any number of other roses by another name. Why the word horror has become a dirty word I cannot imagine, except that some probably look at it as *Friday the 13th* and other slasher movies, which is not so. Horror goes back to Mary Shelley and even before."

As the focus of her presidency, Berliner has vowed to "reinstate, if you will, the image of horror and horror writers by making it publicly clear that all of those books starting back more recently with *Silence of the Lambs* are in fact horror. The fact is that out of the most famous books of all time, my educated guess is half of them are what normally would be defined as horror except that the word has become a curse word."

Berliner's advice to today's horror writers is "write whatever you need to write and to the best of your ability. But do your homework exceedingly well in terms of direction and for the moment at least, until the cycle swings as it inevitably does, direct it to being called something else."

Currently finishing two novels which she is calling psychological thrillers ("they could as easily be called horror"), Berliner says, "You have two choices: you can sit at a bar whining with your buddies that 'horror is dead' or you can sit at your typewriter working at what you do best, then call it what you wish." And it's true that the big names in horror—Stephen King, Anne Rice, Dean Koontz and John Saul—continue to do well writing novels that are essentially horror but considered mainstream, mass market bestsellers.

MYSTERY

"You can't have trends over a year in mystery—those happen over a decade," says **Otto Penzler**, a former publisher of mystery and owner of The Mysterious Bookshop in New York City, where he sells only mystery, crime and suspense. Penzler has noticed over the last five to six years that "the popular, cozy, soft-boiled books written by women for women with women protagonists—usually with kittens—seem to have leveled off. There is not quite the same growth or demand in that area that there was six or seven years ago. Now books written by women, particularly with women characters, are a little harder-edged, and that is probably because of the success of Patricia Cornwell."

Penzler is seeing more mysteries by foreign authors being translated into English. "It used to be that mysteries were only written by Americans and in English. Now, we're seeing books from South America, France and Japan with settings in those countries. Some of the most wonderful mysteries I've seen are *The Club Dumas* and *The Flanders Panel*, written by Arturo Perez-Reverte from South America.

For those writers wanting to compete in today's mystery marketplace, Penzler advises, "Write brilliantly. I think every third person in America is writing a mystery. And never try to do it with one hand tied behind your back or think that you're writing down or that the mystery is not the highest form of literature being produced in America today. Everything a writer would do to write the great American novel is what he should be doing when writing a mystery novel."

An added note for mystery writers: in fall 1997, Houghton Mifflin published its first *Best American Mystery Stories*, edited by Penzler. This should be a great place to read what is considered today's best mystery fiction and, as a bonus, you will find publishers of mystery and their addresses listed at the back of the anthology.

At Walker and Company, mystery editor **Michael Seidman** does not pay attention to what some might call trends in the mystery marketplace. "Mystery itself is not an easily definable market because there are so many subsets, and people really only read within their subset. You've got a mystery and what you're facing is addressing it to any number of different markets."

Seidman does notice that some paperback publishers are doing minimal print runs these days. "I think what may have happened is that a lot of writers who have been overpaid, based on reviews and not on real sales potential, have reached a point of diminishing returns and publishers are turning them loose. A lot of people are connecting these with the death of the mid-list except these aren't mid-list writers. They weren't selling 15 or 20 thousand copies—that's how I define mid-list. They were selling between 75,000 and 111,000 copies of their novels."

In 1997, Walker cut its number of new mystery titles from 20 to 14, a move Seidman welcomed. "I don't have any help, and it's easier for me to do a good job on less books."

There is no cutting back on titles at Avalon Books, which releases 60 novels each year. "I need a long time to talk about the mysteries we're publishing," says Avalon president **Marcia Markland**. "One of the most exciting things that's come along in a long time is written by physicist Camille Minichino. The series follows the elements table [*Hydrogen*, *Helium* and *Lithium* are Minichino's first titles out]. It's a lovely series."

Another new Avalon mystery title, *Bones*, was written by John Paxson, deputy bureau chief of CBS News in London. "It is so much fun," says Markland, who hopes his book will become a series. "It's about a graduate student who makes a fabulous discovery about dinosaurs, then disappears. We're also having great success with a Milwaukee series, by Kathleen Anne Barrett: *Milwaukee Winters Can be Murder*; *Milwaukee Summers Can Be Deadly*; *Milwaukee Autumns* . . . you get the idea."

Markland advises writers wishing to submit manuscripts to Avalon to send a SASE for guidelines first. "We're always looking for good characters—really likable characters—in the series and writers we take on."

ROMANCE

Olivia M. Hall, president of the Romance Writers of America, who writes as Laurie Paige and has 36 romances to her credit, notes the increasing popularity of inspirational and ethnic romances: "The growth of the inspirational subgenre of romance has been significant, with Harlequin joining the other primarily Christian houses in releasing inspirational romances. The sales of ethnic romances also continues to rise, creating an encouraging outlook for the multicultural subgenre of romance."

Hall is encouraged by the mixing of romance with other genres. "While the romance market seemed to level out at 48 to 52 percent of all mass market paperback fiction published, we are seeing the spread of romantic elements—clearly defined in the behavior of characters and the relationships they are placed into by plot—move into other genres, such as mystery and fantasy. This shows that a majority of readers who are fans of different genres are interested in reading about love, about characters behaving with honor and about good prevailing. The popularity of romance in other genres, such as mystery and fantasy, in addition to romance in other mediums, like film and television, creates more opportunities for romance writers. It creates a broader market, it increases the income of romance writers, and it provides them with other arenas in which to exercise their talents. More respect for romance? We're getting there!"

Marcia Markland, vice president and publisher at Avalon Books, says, "The romance genre is very strong right now. We're expanding all over the place with romance—we're always trying to do more." Current projects include a series set in Hawaii and the Rainbow Rock series, a Native American series by Susan Aylworth. Says Markland, "Aylworth teaches about Native American customs so all the information is culturally and historically accurate." Markland is also publishing a man for the first time in a long time: "We are doing two books by Mike Gaherty, a former creative writing teacher who took early retirement. The first, *More Than a Game*, is about the coach of a girls' soccer team and a football coach who are competing for attention and for their team's sport. They gradually find out they have more in common than they thought."

Markland is also currently looking for Gothics: "I have a hunch we're not finished with that genre." And at a time when many book publishers won't touch a manuscript unless it comes through an agent, Markland stresses that writers don't need a high-powered agent to get published by Avalon. "Here, it's not who you know; it's what you write that matters."

SCIENCE FICTION & FANTASY

Science fiction was a popular media draw in 1996 and 1997, with the release of blockbuster movies *Men in Black* and *Independence Day* and the re-release of the *Star Wars* trilogy yielding millions at the box office and in media tie-ins. At least one popular science fiction writer, however, sees the emphasis on box office glitz and the concern by entertainment conglomerates with huge short term returns as bad news for established science fiction writers. That writer, Spider Robinson, recently used his alt.callahans website to encourage readers to buy his and other new science fiction releases. This was after his publisher, claiming "industry retrenchment," severely cut back the print run of his latest Callahan paperback, *Callahan's Legacy*. Adding to Robinson's concern, his publisher, citing the lower print run, offered him only 60 percent of his usual payment for his next book.

Susan Allison, editor of science fiction and fantasy titles at Walker & Company, also expresses concern about the upswing of recent media tie-ins: "I certainly think the effect media tie-ins have had on the market and on the percentage of science fiction being read is significant, be it an offshoot of *Star Wars* or whatever. It has fragmented the market. The media material seems to draw a particular reader who may or may not read other science fiction, but may want to re-experience that world and those characters. But that leaves a smaller pool of readers who read a book for the first time and want a brand new experience."

Still, Allison is optimistic about the market for new science fiction and says Walker is publishing a few more titles now than during the past several years. "The world of literary science fiction is quite healthy in that there are a lot of wonderful books being published. We would all just like to see the readership for those books broaden."

For those wanting to compete in today's science fiction marketplace, Allison says, "There is no point in writing science fiction unless you read it with love, and a lot of it. And if you read it with love and a lot of it, then you learn the different requirements of the publishers who do the books you read and love. That familiarity with the field is really essential."

In response to domination of media-related books in genre publishing, Avon launched its new science fiction imprint, Avon Eos, in January 1998. Avon publisher **Lou Aronica** sees the new imprint as a way to "redefine and heighten Avon Books' profile within the science fiction and fantasy community" while bringing fresh work into the currently media-heavy science fiction marketplace. "It's time to bring new voices and established writers to the forefront again, time for the literature itself to stir up most of the excitement and controversy." Aronica plans an intensive campaign to promote the new Avon Eos line and to work interactively with booksellers on "an ongoing exchange of advice and information." Eos writers will include both big name science fiction authors as well as talented newcomers.

According to *PW* (June 16, 1997), the fantasy end of the science fiction and fantasy fusion is also strong. The article, written by Robert K. J. Killheffer, quotes **Kuo-Yu Liang**, associate publisher at Del Rey: "There's a timeless appeal to fantasy with its mythic quests and the battle between good and evil." **Shelly Shapiro**, executive editor at Del Rey, says that the broad popularity of fantasy is because it draws on material readers were exposed to as children: dragons and elves, fairies and witches. **Sheila Gilbert**, vice president of DAW, goes so far as to say fantasy is currently easier to sell than science fiction because "in an escapist genre, it's often more of an escape than science fiction." Bantam editor **Anne Lesley Groell** says, "The core audience [for fantasy] does seem to be bigger than for science fiction."

However, just because fantasy is doing well, "doesn't mean that science fiction is down—and certainly not out," reports that same issue of *PW*. It cites new science fiction releases from Tor, HarperPrism, Ace, Bantam and Avon by both established and new writers.

WESTERN

Candy Moulton, editor of *Roundup Magazine*, the publication of the Western Writers of America, says that publishing of western novels has suffered from what has happened in the wholesale book industry during the last several years. "So many wholesalers have consolidated or have gone out of business this year. This has had a ripple-down effect, and we've seen things like all the cutbacks at HarperCollins. Another tremendous blow to the traditional western this year was that Walker & Company, one of the most solid, stable markets for westerns, announced they were discontinuing the traditional western line they published for years."

Moulton is still optimistic about the market for westerns, however. "I think romances with western themes are still very popular and maybe even growing in popularity. The Women of the West books [published by Forge, an imprint of St. Martin's Press] seem to be picking up a bit. Many of the Women of the West books are based on real women, for instance *Ladies of the Goldfield Stock Exchange*, a California Gold Rush story by Sybil Downing." Moulton points out that Downing's book includes a bibliography for people who want to read more about the subject matter. When writing today's western, says Moulton, "absolutely do your research because the stories that seem to be selling are very well-researched and documented."

Moulton also says it's important for writers not to give up. "We have a lot of really good writers right now who are having a hard time selling because the traditional things they were writing are not selling. Write solid stories, but push the envelope a little. Write nontraditional things—a story about Chinese women or other minorities. There are a lot of stories that haven't been told, and I think that's what you need to catch the eye of publishers these days—things that are a little bit different."

Today's publishers of westerns are also looking for humor, says Moulton. "Every time I've been to a western conference there's at least one editor who asks for good humor. If they find someone who can write really good humor with a western theme they will buy it."

Preston Lewis, president of the Western Writers of America, knows firsthand how it feels to be caught in the tightening up of the publishing industry. At the 1997 Cheyenne convention of the WWA, he won the coveted Spur award for his novel *Blood of Texas*, published under his Will Camp pseudonym by Harper Paperbacks. That night, he received the news from his agent that Harper Paperbacks was dropping its western line and would not be publishing the successor to his Spur-winning novel.

"There has been so much turmoil, so many things have changed over the last few years," says Lewis. "The consolidation of the independent distributors and all sorts of other factors have put westerns pretty much in the same boat as other [types of fiction]. I do know that people who criticize westerns haven't read a western in years. If they did, they would see a lot more breadth and complexity than in what was once considered to be western. Traditionally, it's been the stereotype of the western—the guy in the white hat versus the guy in the black hat. And whether they were wearing white or black hats, they were all white guys. This day and age I think western fiction has diversified in a lot of different ways."

Lewis points out that his Spur-winning novel *Blood of Texas* has an Hispanic protagonist. "That illustrates the point that I and other western writers look for ways we can keep the genre fresh. That novel looks at the Texas revolution through the eyes of a Spanish protagonist who is torn between his heritage and what he feels is right."

In agreement with Moulton, Lewis says today's western fiction should be as historically grounded and well-documented as nonfiction. "You are providing history in the form of entertainment. The traditional 'mother lode' for the white hat versus the black hat western has run out; we as writers must look for other areas of the rich western history to tap into."

At Avalon Books, the western continues to do well. "We're having a wonderful time with the westerns—no complaints here," says Avalon vice president **Marcia Markland**. "One exciting thing for us in westerns this year is a new series, Hannah and the Horsemen, written by Johnny D. Boggs." Boggs's western is about a Greek cowboy who carries a copy of Homer and rides a horse named after a Greek god. Markland is equally excited about Terrell Bowers's Broken Spoke series and Avalon's Frontier Justice series.

In an interview written by Sierra Adare for the October 1997 *Roundup*, **Tom Doherty**, publisher of Tor/Forge Books, recommends that writers of any type of fiction write well about what they care about and know. He also advises writers to promote themselves locally: "Local history and heritage is not sufficient to get into the national market, but it proves a strong base to build from."

GOOD ADVICE FOR 1998

Olivia M. Hall maintains her 36 romance novels were published by following three important pieces of advice which she shares with writers of any type of fiction, no matter what "trends" may be occurring in the marketplace:

- Submit, submit, submit. You can't sell anything if you don't have anything out there. If you have a new idea for a story or line, get it down on paper. Today. Now.
- Rewrite, rewrite, rewrite. Hone your craft to the point where it is publishable.
- Try, try, try. A very few writers actually sell on their first try. For every one writer who does, there are 100 who don't.

The Markets

IMPORTANT LISTING INFORMATION

● Listings are not advertisements. Although the information here is as accurate as possible, the listings are not endorsed or guaranteed by the editor of *Novel & Short Story Writer's Market.*
● *Novel & Short Story Writer's Market* reserves the right to exclude any listing that does not meet its requirements.

KEY TO SYMBOLS AND ABBREVIATIONS

‡ New listing in all sections
● Comment by editor of *Novel & Short Story Writer's Market*
✚ Canadian listing
ms—manuscript; **mss**-manuscripts
b&w—black and white
SASE—self-addressed, stamped envelope
SAE—self-addressed envelope
IRC—International Reply Coupon, for use on reply mail from other countries

(See Glossary for definitions of words and expressions used in writing and publishing.)

COMPLAINT PROCEDURE

If you feel you have not been treated fairly by a listing in *Novel & Short Story Writer's Market,* we advise you to take the following steps:
• First try to contact the listing. Sometimes one phone call or a letter can quickly clear up the matter.
• Document all your correspondence with the listing. When you write to us with a complaint, provide the details of your submission, the date of your first contact with the listing and the nature of your subsequent correspondence.
• We will enter your letter into our files and attempt to contact the listing.
• The number and severity of complaints will be considered in our decision whether or not to delete the listing from the next edition.

The Markets

Literary Magazines

This section contains over 500 markets for your literary short fiction. Nearly 100 of these markets are new to this edition, and all listings which appeared in last year's edition have been updated to reflect editors' current needs. While many are university-affiliated and some independently owned, the editors at each have told us they are actively seeking fiction for their respective publications.

Although definitions of what constitutes "literary" writing vary, editors of literary journals agree they want to publish the "best" fiction available today. Qualities they look for in stories include creativity, style, flawless mechanics, and careful attention to detail in content and manuscript preparation. Most of the authors writing such fiction are well-read and well-educated, and many are students and graduates of university creative writing programs.

In this marketplace, however, fine writing will always take precedence over formal training. Adrienne Brodeur, editor of Francis Ford Coppola's literary magazine *Zoetrope*, defines fine fiction on page 260 as stories crafted around "characters you can get involved with, whether you love or hate them . . . a story that takes you somewhere—you're not the same squeeze of toothpaste coming out that you were going in." On page 154, Jack Smith, editor of *The Green Hills Literary Lantern* wants fine fiction "that speaks to the heart, the mind, the soul—fiction that is as complex, as dense, as layered as the most simple of human existences, and as subtle and as provocative as the best literary art." Don Lee, editor of the prestigious journal *Ploughshares* says on page 206, "Something might fall through the cracks, but nonetheless good writing stands out and someone eventually will see it for its merit and its quality."

STEPPING STONES TO RECOGNITION

Some well-established literary journals pay several hundred dollars for a short story. Those paying more include STORY which pays $1,000 per story and $750 per short short story. *Zoetrope* also pays $1,000 per story and $5,000 for stories commissioned by Coppola. Most, though, can only pay with contributor's copies or a subscription to their publication. However, being published in literary journals offers the important benefits of experience, exposure and prestige. As Ronald Spatz, editor of *Alaska Quarterly Review*, says on page 100, literary journals are "the place where new writers try out their works and establish their voices. This is the place where they can establish a reputation that leads them to other publishers." Agents and major book publishers regularly read literary magazines in search of new writers. Work from among these journals is also selected for inclusion in annual prize anthologies such as *The Best American Short Stories, Prize Stories: The O. Henry Awards, Pushcart Prize: Best of the Small Presses,* and *New Stories from the South: The Year's Best.*

You'll find most of the well-known prestigious literary journals listed here. Many, including *Carolina Quarterly* and *Ploughshares*, are associated with universities, while others such as *The Paris Review* are independently published. STORY, published by the publisher of *Novel & Short Story Writer's Market*, won the coveted National Magazine Award for fiction in 1992 and 1995 and was a finalist for that award in 1994, 1996 and 1997.

Among the new listings in this section are a number of electronic literary magazines, an increasingly common trend at a time when paper and publishing costs rise while funding to university presses continues to be cut back or eliminated altogether. These electronic outlets for literary fiction also benefit writers by eliminating copying and postage costs and providing the opportunity for much quicker responses to submissions. *Also notice that some magazines with websites give specific information about what they offer on their websites, including updated writers guidelines and sample fiction from their publications.*

SELECTING THE RIGHT LITERARY JOURNAL

Once you have browsed through this section and have a list of journals you might like to submit to, read those listings again, carefully. Remember that this is information editors present to help you in submitting work that fits their needs. How to Use This Book to Publish Your Fiction, starting on page 3, describes in detail the listing information common to all markets in our book, including information that pertains especially to literary publications.

This is the only section in which you will find magazines that do not read submissions all year long. Whether limited reading periods are tied to a university schedule or meant to accommodate the capabilities of a very small staff, those periods are noted within listings. The staffs of university journals are usually made up of student editors and a managing editor who is also a faculty member. These staffs often change every year. Whenever possible, we indicate this in listings and give the name of the current editor and the length of that editor's term. Also be aware that the schedule of a university journal usually coincides with that university's academic year, meaning that the editors of most university publications are difficult or impossible to reach during the summer.

FURTHERING YOUR SEARCH

It cannot be stressed enough that reading the listing is only the first part of developing your marketing plan. The second part, equally important, is to obtain fiction guidelines and read the actual magazine. Reading copies of a magazine helps you determine the fine points of the magazine's publishing style and philosophy. There is no substitute for this type of hands-on research.

Unlike commercial periodicals available at most newsstands and bookstores, it requires a little more effort to obtain some of the magazines listed here. The new super chain bookstores are doing a better job these days of stocking literaries and you can find some in independent and college bookstores, especially those published in your area. You may, however, need to send for a sample copy. We include sample copy prices in the listings whenever possible.

Another way to find out more about literary magazines is to check out the various prize anthologies and take note of journals whose fiction is being selected for publication there. Studying prize anthologies not only lets you know which magazines are publishing award-winning work, but it also provides a valuable overview of what is considered to be the best fiction published today.

Award-winning publications, as well as other information we feel will help you determine if a listing is the right market for you, are noted in editorial comments identified with a bullet (●). The comments section also allows us to explain more about the special interests or requirements of a publication and any information we've learned from our readers that we feel will help you choose potential markets wisely.

Among the awards and honors we note are inclusion of work in:
- *Best American Short Stories*, published by Houghton Mifflin, 222 Berkeley St., Boston MA 02116.
- *New Stories from the South: The Year's Best*, published by Algonquin Books of Chapel Hill, P.O. Box 2225, Chapel Hill NC 27515.
- *Prize Stories: The O. Henry Awards*, published by Doubleday/Anchor, 1540 Broadway, New York NY 10036.

• *Pushcart Prize: Best of the Small Presses*, published by Pushcart Press, Box 380, Wainscott NY 11975.

The well-respected *Poet* magazine (published by Cooper House Publishing Inc., P.O. Box 54947, Oklahoma City OK 73154) annually honors the best literary magazines (those publishing both fiction and poetry). The program is titled The American Literary Magazine Awards and most recipients of editorial content awards have listings in this section. To find out more about the awards, see the *Poet*'s fall issue.

FOR MORE INFORMATION

See The Business of Fiction Writing for the specific mechanics of manuscript submission. Above all, editors appreciate a professional presentation. Include a brief cover letter and send a self-addressed envelope for a reply or a self-addressed envelope in a size large enough to accommodate your manuscript, if you would like it returned. Be sure to include enough stamps or International Reply Coupons (for replies from countries other than your own) to cover your manuscript's return.

In addition to the double dagger (‡) indicating new listings, we include other symbols to help you in narrowing your search. English-speaking foreign markets are denoted by an asterisk (*). The maple leaf symbol (❋) identifies Canadian presses. If you are not a Canadian writer, but are interested in a Canadian press, check the listing carefully. Many small presses in Canada receive grants and other funds from their provincial or national government and are, therefore, restricted to publishing Canadian authors.

If you're interested in learning more about literary and small magazines, you may want to look at *The International Directory of Little Magazines and Small Presses* (Dustbooks, Box 100, Paradise CA 95967); the *Directory of Literary Magazines*, published by the Council of Literary Magazines and Presses (3-C, 154 Christopher St., New York NY 10014-2839); or *The Association of American University Presses Directory* (584 Broadway, New York NY 10012).

The following is the ranking system we have used to categorize the listings in this section.

I Publication encourages beginning or unpublished writers to submit work for consideration and publishes new writers regularly.

II Publication accepts outstanding work by beginning and established writers.

III Publication does not encourage beginning writers; prints mostly writers with previous publication credits; very few new writers.

IV Special-interest or regional publication, open only to writers in certain genres or on certain subjects or from certain geographical areas.

V Closed to unsolicited submissions.

*THE ABIKO LITERARY PRESS (ALP), 8-1-8 Namiki, Abiko-Shi, Chiba-Ken 270-11 Japan. Phone/fax: (0471)84-7904. Editor: Anna Livia Plulaurelbelle. Fiction Editor: Laurel Sycks. Published irregularly. Circ. 500. Publishes 10 stories/issue. "We are a semi-bilingual (Japanese/English) magazine for Japanese and foreigners living in Japan."
Needs: Artwork, photos, James Joyce's *Finnegan's Wake* criticism and stories influenced by "The Lost Generation" and Joyce. "A story submitted in both English and Japanese receives special consideration. I look for something that I can't forget after reading." Length: 3,000 words average; 5,000 words maximum.
How to Contact: Send manuscript with SAE and IRCs.
Payment/Terms: Pays 1 contributor's copy; writer pays postage. Follow known proper format of small presses and submission procedures. Sponsors contest ($100,000). Write for details. Include IRC for response. 600-page sample copy for $15 plus $15 postage.

‡ABOUT SUCH THINGS, Literary Magazine, (I), 420 W. Walnut Ln., Philadelphia PA 19144. (215)842-3563. E-mail: aboutsuch@juno.com. Editor: Laurel Webster. Fiction Editor: E. Louise Lindinger. Magazine: 8⅜ × 10¾; 28-32 pages; 24 lb. paper; 80 lb. cover stock; illustrations. "We seek to provide a forum for Christian authors to publish work. We receive editorial guidance from a Presbyterian church in Philadelphia. Our audience is primarily very educated, professional, church-going intellectuals who live or have a connection with Philadelphia." Semiannually. Estab. 1996. Circ. 300.

Needs: Ethnic/multicultural, fantasy, historical, humor/satire, literary, regional, religious/inspirational, romance, science fiction (soft/sociological), allegory. No erotica, horror, occult, feminist, gay. Receives 4 unsolicited mss/ month. Accepts 1-3 mss/issue; 2-6 mss/year. Does not read April-June and October-December. Publishes ms 3 months after acceptance. Recently published work by K.D. Mullins and Bryan J. L. Glass. Length: 2,000 words average; 300 words minimum; 3,000 words maximum. Publishes short shorts. Also publishes literary essays, literary criticism and poetry. Always critiques or comments on rejected mss.

How to Contact: Send complete ms with a cover letter. Include estimated word count, SASE, address, phone number, e-mail and submission on diskette in ASCII text. Reports on mss in 12 months. Send SASE for return of ms or send a disposable copy. Simultaneous submissions and reprints OK. Sample copy for $3 and 9×12 SAE with $1.01 postage. Fiction guidelines for #10 SASE.

Payment/Terms: Pays 2 contributor's copies for one-time rights; additional copies for $3. Sends galleys to author. Not copyrighted.

Advice: "Let any moral or spiritual lesson be an outgrowth of a solid plot and real characters. Be willing to let the story have resonance and tension by not tying up every loose end too tightly. Avoid making 'good' characters stereotypically 'churchy.' "

ACM, (ANOTHER CHICAGO MAGAZINE), (II), Left Field Press, 3709 N. Kenmore, Chicago IL 60613. Editor: Barry Silesky. Fiction Editor: Sharon Solwitz. Nonfiction Editor: L. Wisenberg. Magazine: 5½×8½; 200-220 pages; "art folio each issue." Estab. 1977.

● *ACM* is best known for experimental work or work with political slants, clear narrative voices. The editor looks for "engaged and unusual writing." The magazine received an Illinois Arts Council Literary Award in 1997.

Needs: Contemporary, ethnic, experimental, feminist, gay, lesbian, literary, prose poem, political/socio-historical and translations. Receives 300 unsolicited fiction mss each month. Recently published work by Robin Hemley, Maxine Chernoff, Brian Swann, Carol Ascher and Maureen Seaton. Published 1-2 new writers in the last year. Also publishes creative nonfiction.

How to Contact: Unsolicited mss acceptable with SASE. "Send only one story (unless you work short, less than ten pgs.) then we'll read two. We encourage cover letters." Publishes ms 6-12 months after acceptance. Sample copies are available for $8 ppd. Reports in 2-5 months. Receives small press collections.

Payment/Terms: Pays small honorarium plus contributor's copy and 1 year subscription. Acquires first North American serial rights.

Advice: "Get used to rejection slips, and don't get discouraged. Keep introductory letters short. Make sure manuscript has name and address on every page, and that it is clean, neat and proofread. We are looking for stories with freshness and originality in subject angle and style, and work that encounters the world and is not stuck in its own navel."

THE ACORN, a journal of the Western Sierra, (IV), Hot Pepper Press, P.O. Box 1266, El Dorado CA 95623-0039. (916)621-1833. Fax: (916)621-3939. E-mail: jalapep@spider.lloyd.com. Editor: Judy Graham and committee. Fiction Editor: Verma Goodwin. Magazine: 8½×5½; 44 pages. *The Acorn* publishes work about the "western slope of Sierra Nevada and rural lifestyle." Quarterly. Estab. 1993. Circ. 200.

Needs: Adventure, historical, humor/satire, literary, mainstream/contemporary, regional, senior citizen/retirement. "No porn or erotica." "We usually try to choose subjects or topics that fit the season." Receives 2-3 unsolicited mss/month. Accepts 5-6 mss/issue; 24 mss/year. Publishes ms 1 month after acceptance. Recently published work by Tom Gartner, Robert Reid, Drew Cherry, J.K. Colvin and Patty Munter. Length: 1,500 words maximum. Publishes short shorts. Also publishes literary essays and poetry. Often critiques or comments on rejected mss. Sponsors contest; send SASE for information.

How to Contact: Send complete ms with a cover letter. Include 1-paragraph bio and list of publications. Reports in 4 months on mss. Send SASE for reply, return of ms or send a disposable copy of ms. No simultaneous submissions, reprints and electronic submissions OK. Sample copy for $4. Fiction guidelines for #10 SAE.

Payment/Terms: Pays 2 contributor's copy on publication; additional copies for $3.75. Acquires one-time rights. Sometimes sends galleys to author.

Advice: Looks for "memorable work that captures the flavor of our region—its history, landforms and wildlife and rural lifestyle. Good writing helps too."

ACORN WHISTLE, (II), 907 Brewster Ave., Beloit WI 53511. Editor: Fred Burwell. Magazine: 8½×11; 75-100 pages; uncoated paper; light card cover; illustrations; photos. "*Acorn Whistle* seeks accessible and personal writing, art and photography that appeals to readers on both emotional and intellectual levels. Our intended audience is the educated non-academic. Connecting writers with readers is our foremost goal. We also encourage a friendly working relationship between editors and writers." Semiannually. Estab. 1995. Circ. 500.

Needs: Ethnic/multicultural, feminist, historical (general), humor/satire, literary, mainstream/contemporary, regional. No erotica, experimental, fantasy, horror, religious or science fiction. Would like to see more "stories with vivid characterization, compassion for its characters, vivid sense of place. Writing with a commitment to readership." Accepts 5-7 mss/issue; 10-15 mss/year. Publishes ms within a year after acceptance. Recently published work by Paulette Boudreaux, Daniel M. Jaffe and John D. Nesbitt. Publishes 2-6 new writers/year. Length: open. Publishes short shorts. Also publishes memoir and poetry. Often critiques or comments on rejected ms.

How to Contact: Send complete ms. Reports in 2 weeks on queries; 1-12 weeks on mss. Send SASE for reply, return of ms or send a disposable copy of ms. Simultaneous submissions OK. Sample copy for $5. Fiction guidelines for #10 SASE.

Payment/Terms: Pays 2 contributor's copies. Acquires first North American serial rights. Features expanded contributor's notes with personal comments from each author.

Advice: "We prefer realistic story telling, strong characterization, a vivid presentation. Writing that moves both heart and mind has an excellent chance here. Write what matters to you, rather than trying to impress an imaginary audience. Writing fueled by an author's passion *will* reach readers. Don't let rejections discourage you. And, if an editor says, "try again," try again . . . and again!"

ADRIFT, Writing: Irish, Irish American and . . . , (II), 46 E. First St. #4D, New York NY 10003. Editor: Thomas McGonigle. Magazine: 8×11; 32 pages; 60 lb. paper stock; 65 lb. cover stock; illustrations; photos. "Irish-Irish American as a basis—though we are interested in advanced writing from anywhere." Semiannually. Estab. 1983. Circ. 1,000.

Needs: Contemporary, erotica, ethnic, experimental, feminist, gay, lesbian, literary, translations. Receives 40 unsolicited mss/month. Accepts 3 mss/issue. Published work by Francis Stuart; published new writers within the last year. Length: open. Also publishes literary criticism. Sometimes critiques rejected mss.

How to Contact: Send complete ms. Reports as soon as possible. SASE for return of ms. Sample copy for $5. Reviews novels or short story collections.

Payment/Terms: Pays $7.50-300 on publication for first rights.

Advice: "The writing should argue with, among others, James Joyce, Flann O'Brien, Juan Goytisolo, Ingeborg Bachmann, E.M. Cioran, Max Stirner and Patrick Kavanagh."

ADVENTURES OF SWORD & SORCERY, (I, II), Double Star Press, P.O. Box 285, Xenia OH 45385. (937)376-2222. Fax: (937)376-5582. E-mail: double-star@worldnet.att.net. Website: http://www.home.att.net/~double-star/. Editor: Randy Dannenfelser. Magazine: 8½×11; 80 pages; slick cover stock; illustrations. "We publish sword and sorcery, heroic and high fantasy fiction." Quarterly. Estab. 1995. Circ. 7,000.

Needs: Sword and sorcery, heroic and high fantasy fiction. "We want fiction with an emphasis on action and adventure, but still cognizant of the struggles within as they play against the struggles without. Include sexual content only as required by the story, but not excessive/porn." Receives approximately 250 unsolicited mss/month. Accepts 9 mss/issue; 36 mss/year. Publishes ms 1 year after acceptance. Agented fiction 5%. Recently published work by Mike Resnick, Stephen Baxter and Darrell Schweitzer. Publishes 5 new writers/year. Length: 5,000 words average; 1,000 words minimum; 20,000 words maximum. Also publishes literary criticism and book reviews (only solicited). Always critiques or comments on rejected mss.

How to Contact: Send complete ms with a cover letter. Include estimated word count, Social Security number, list of publications, phone number and e-mail address. Reports in 1 month on queries; 2 months on mss. Send SASE for reply, return of ms. No simultaneous submissions. Electronic submissions (e-mail, disk or modem) OK. Sample copy $5.50. Fiction guidelines for #10 SASE. Reviews novels and short story collections.

Payment/Terms: Pays 3-6¢/word on acceptance and 3 contributor's copies; additional copies 40% discount plus shipping. Acquires first North American serial rights. Sends galleys to author.

Advice: "Recently we are looking for more adventuresome work with settings other than generic medieval Europe. We look for real emotion in the prose. Think about the audience we are targeted at, and send us appropriate stories."

ADVOCATE, PKA'S PUBLICATION, (I, II), PKA Publications, 301A Rolling Hills Park, Prattsville NY 12468. (518)299-3103. Editor: Remington Wright. Tabloid: 9⅜×12¼; 32 pages; newsprint paper; line drawings; b&w photographs. "Eclectic for a general audience." Bimonthly. Estab. 1987. Publishes 12,000 copies.

• *PKA's Advocate* editors tend to like positive, upbeat, entertaining material.

Needs: Adventure, contemporary, ethnic, experimental, fantasy, feminist, historical, humor/satire, juvenile (5-9 years), literary, mainstream, mystery/suspense, prose poem, regional, romance, science fiction, senior citizen/

---

‡   **THE DOUBLE DAGGER** before a listing indicates that the listing is new in this edition. New markets are often the most receptive to submissions by new writers.

retirement, sports, western, young adult/teen (10-18 years). Nothing religious, pornographic, violent, erotic, pro-drug or anti-environment. Receives 60 unsolicited mss/month. Accepts 6-8 mss/issue; 36-48 mss/year. Publishes ms 4 months to 1 year after acceptance. Length: 1,000 words preferred; 1,500 words maximum. Sometimes critiques rejected mss.

How to Contact: Send complete ms with cover letter. Reports in 2 weeks on queries; 2 months on mss. SASE. No simultaneous submissions. Sample copy for $4 (US currency for inside US; $5.25 US currency for Canada). Writers guidelines for SASE.

Payment/Terms: Pays contributor's copies. Acquires first rights.

Advice: "The highest criterion in selecting a work is its entertainment value. It must first be enjoyable reading. It must, of course, be original. To stand out, it must be thought provoking or strongly emotive, or very cleverly plotted. Will consider only previously unpublished works by writers who do not earn their living principally through writing."

AETHLON, (I,II,IV), East Tennessee State University, Box 70, 683, Johnson City TN 37614-0683. (423)929-5671. Fiction Editor: John Morefield. Magazine: 6×9; 180-240 pages; illustrations and photographs. "Theme: Literary treatment of sport. We publish articles on that theme, critical studies of author's treatment of sport and original fiction and poetry with sport themes. Most of our readers are academics." Semiannually. Estab. 1983. Circ. 800.

Needs: Sport. "Stories must have a sport-related theme and subject; otherwise, we're wide open." No personal memoirs. Receives 15-20 fiction mss/month. Accepts 6-10 fiction mss/issue; 12-20 fiction mss/year. Publishes ms "about 1 year" after acceptance. Publishes 2-3 new writers/year. Length: 2,500-5,000 words average; 500 words minimum; 7,500 words maximum. Also publishes literary essays, literary criticism, poetry. Sometimes critiques rejected mss.

How to Contact: Send complete ms and brief cover letter with 1-2 lines for a contributor's note. Reports in 6-12 months. SASE in size to fit ms. No simultaneous submissions. Electronic disk submissions OK. Final copy must be submitted on disk (WordPerfect). Sample copy for $12.50. Reviews novels and short story collections. Send books to Prof. Joe Dewey, Dept. of English, University of Pittsburgh-Johnstown, Johnstown PA 15601.

Payment/Terms: Pays 1 contributor's copy and 5 offprints.

Advice: "We are looking for well-written, insightful stories. Don't be afraid to be experimental. Take more care with your manuscript. Please send a legible manuscript free of grammatical errors. Be willing to revise."

AFRICAN AMERICAN REVIEW, (II), Indiana State University, Department of English, Root Hall A218, Terre Haute IN 47809. (812)237-2968. Fax: (812)237-3156. E-mail address: aschoal@ascleco@amber.indstate.edu. Editor: Joe Weixlmann. Fiction Editor: Reginald McKnight. Magazine: 7×10; 176 pages; 60#, acid-free paper; 100# skid stock cover; illustrations and photos. "*African American Review* publishes stories and poetry by African American writers, and essays about African American literature and culture." Quarterly. Estab. 1967. Circ. 4,200.

● *African American Review* is the official publication of the Division of Black American Literature and Culture of the Modern Language Association. The magazine received American Literary Magazine Awards in 1994 and 1995.

Needs: Ethnic/Multicultural: experimental, feminist, gay, lesbian, literary, mainstream/contemporary. "No children's/juvenile/young adult/teen." Receives 10 unsolicited mss/month. Accepts 6-8 mss/year. Publishes ms 1 year after acceptance. Agented fiction 10%. Published work by Clarence Major, Ann Allen Shockley, Alden Reimoneng. Length: 3,000 words average. Also publishes literary essays, literary criticism, poetry. Sometimes critiques or comments on rejected mss.

How to Contact: Send complete ms with a cover letter. Reports in 2 weeks on queries; 3 months on mss. Send SASE for reply, return of ms or send a disposable copy of ms. Sample copy for $6. Fiction guidelines for #10 SASE. Reviews novels and short story collections. Send books to Keneth Kinnamon, Dept. of English, Univ. of Arkansas, Fayetteville, AR 72701.

Payment/Terms: Pays $25-100 and 10 contributor's copies on publication for first North American serial rights. Sends galleys to author.

AGNI, (III), Creative Writing Program, Boston University, 236 Bay State Rd., Boston MA 02215. (617)353-5389. Fax: (617)353-7136. Website: AGNI@acs.bu.edu (includes names of editors, short fiction, poetry and interviews with authors). Editor-in-Chief: Askold Melnyczuk. Magazine: 5½×8½; 320 pages; 55 lb. booktext paper; recycled cover stock; occasional art portfolios. "Eclectic literary magazine publishing first-rate poems and stories." Biannually. Estab. 1972.

● Work from *Agni* has been selected regularly for inclusion in both *Pushcart Prize* and *Best American Short Stories* anthologies. "We tend to be backlogged with fiction."

Needs: Stories, excerpted novels, prose poems and translations. No science fiction. Receives 250 unsolicited fiction mss/month. Accepts 4-7 mss/issue, 8-12 mss/year. Reading period October 1 through April 30 only. Recently published work by Alice Hoffman, Ha Jin, Jill McCorkle and Percival Everett. Publishes 1-10 new writers/year. Rarely critiques rejected mss.

How to Contact: Send complete ms with SASE and cover letter listing previous publications. Simultaneous and electronic (disk) submissions OK. Reports in 1-4 months. Sample copy for $9.

Payment/Terms: Pays $10/page up to $150; 2 contributor's copies; one-year subscription. Pays on publication for first North American serial rights. Sends galleys to author. Copyright reverts to author upon publication.

Advice: "Read *Agni* carefully to understand the kinds of stories we publish. Read—everything, classics, literary journals, bestsellers. People need to read and subscribe to the magazines before sending their work. It's important for artists to support the arts."

THE AGUILAR EXPRESSION, (II), 1329 Gilmore Ave., Donora PA 15033. Editor: Xavier F. Aguilar. Magazine: 8½×11; 10-16 pages; 20 lb. bond paper; illustrations. "We are open to all writers of a general theme—something that may appeal to everyone." Semiannually. Estab. 1989. Circ. 150.

● The editor is particularly interested in stories about the homeless in the U.S. but publishes fiction on other topics as well.

Needs: Adventure, ethnic/multicultural, experimental, horror, mainstream/contemporary, mystery/suspense (romantic suspense), romance (contemporary). No religious or first-person stories. Will publish annual special fiction issue or anthology in the future. Receives 10 unsolicited mss/month. Accepts 1-2 mss/issue; 2-4 mss/year. Recently publishes ms 1 month to 1 year after acceptance. Recently published work by Michael D. Cohen, R.G. Cantalupo and Kent Braithwaite. Length: 1,000 words average; 750 words minimum; 1,500 words maximum. Also publishes poetry.

How to Contact: Send complete ms with cover letter. Reports on queries in 1 week; mss in 1 month. Send SASE for reply to a query or send a disposable copy of ms. No simultaneous submissions. Sample copy for $6. Fiction guidelines for #10 SASE.

Payment/Terms: Pays 1 contributor's copy; additional copies at a reduced rate of $3. Acquires one-time rights. Not copyrighted. Write to publication for details on contests, awards or grants.

Advice: "Clean, clear copy makes a manuscript stand out."

ALABAMA LITERARY REVIEW, (II), Smith 253, Troy State University, Troy AL 36082. (334)670-3286, ext. 3307. Fax: (334)670-3519. Editor: Theron Montgomery. Magazine: 7×10; approximately 100 pages; top paper quality; light card cover; some illustrations. "National magazine for a broad range of the best contemporary fiction, poetry, essays and drama that we can find." Annually. Estab. 1987.

Needs: Contemporary, experimental, humor/satire, literary, prose poem, science fiction, serialized/excerpted novel, translations. "Serious writing." Receives 50 unsolicited fiction mss/month. Accepts 5 fiction mss/issue. Publishes ms 5-6 months after acceptance. Recently published work by John Hodges, Crissa-Jean Chappell, Howard Park and Tom Cody. Published new writers within the last year. Length: 2,000-3,500 words average. Publishes short shorts of 1,000 words. Also publishes literary essays, literary criticism, poetry and drama. Sometimes comments on rejected mss.

How to Contact: Send complete ms with cover letter or submit through agent. Reports on queries in 2 weeks; on mss in 2 months (except in summer). SASE. Simultaneous submissions OK. Sample copy for $4 plus postage. Reviews novels or short story collections. Send to Steve Cooper.

Payment/Terms: Pays in contributor's copies and honorarium when available. First rights returned to author upon publication. Work published in *ALR* may be read on state-wide (nonprofit) public radio program.

Advice: "Read our publication first. Avoid negative qualities pertaining to gimmickry and a self-centered point of view. We are interested in any kind of writing if it is *serious* and *honest* in the sense of 'the human heart in conflict with itself.' "

ALASKA QUARTERLY REVIEW, (II), University of Alaska—Anchorage, 3211 Providence Dr., Anchorage AK 99508. (907)786-4775. Fiction Editor: Ronald Spatz. Magazine: 6×9; 200 pages; 60 lb. Glatfelter paper; 10 pt. C15 black ink varnish cover stock; photos on cover only. *AQR* "publishes fiction, poetry, literary nonfiction and short plays in traditional and experimental styles." Semiannually. Estab. 1982. Circ. 2,200.

● Work appearing in the *Alaska Quarterly Review* has been selected for the *Prize Stories: The O. Henry Awards*, *Best American Essays*, *Best American Poetry* and *Pushcart Prize* anthologies. *The Washington Post* calls the *Alaska Quarterly Review*, "one of the nation's best literary magazines."

Needs: Contemporary, experimental, literary, prose poem, translations. Receives 200 unsolicited fiction mss/ month. Accepts 7-13 mss/issue, 15-24 mss/year. Does not read mss May 15 through August 15. Length: not exceeding 50 pages. Recently published work by William H. Gass, Patricia Hampl, Stuart Dybek, Alan Lightman and Hayden Carruth. Published new writers within the last year. Publishes short shorts.

How to Contact: Send complete mss with SASE. Simultaneous submissions "undesirable, but will accept if

---

MARKET CATEGORIES: (I) Open to new writers; **(II)** Open to both new and established writers; **(III)** Interested mostly in established writers; **(IV)** Open to writers whose work is specialized; **(V)** Closed to unsolicited submissions.

INSIDER REPORT

Alaska Quarterly: preserving the stream of literary fiction

In an environment where competition in top-flight literary magazines is fierce, *Alaska Quarterly Review* prides itself on being a journal where writers who may never have published a word have their work examined closely and are treated as professionals. "It is quite a thrill to find new writers and give them a chance to be heard. We think new voices need to be brought to the fore whenever possible," says Ronald Spatz, editor and co-founder of *Alaska Quarterly Review.* "If there's a compelling piece that's palpable, we are not worried about whether that author has published before or will be published after."

Ronald Spatz

Photo by Benjamin Spatz

Spatz, a transplanted New Yorker, began *AQR* as part of the Department of Creative Writing and Literary Arts at the University of Alaska-Anchorage with the philosophy that literary magazines are "the front lines of the literary arts" and that the contributions of new writers are vital. "This is the place where new writers try out their works and establish their voices. This is the place where they can establish a reputation that leads them to the other publishers. This is producing the core of new literary artists for the nation," he says.

"We've made a serious investment in fiction to produce a journal that is itself art and that is of consequence. Literary journals have a particular place so they need not duplicate what the major magazines like *The New Yorker* and *Harper's* are doing. Their role is bringing to fore a sense of place and vision as well as introducing new work and new voices." It is a role that *AQR* has played superbly. The journal has been described by the *Washington Post Book World* as "one of the nation's best literary magazines."

Spatz's mission, and the goal of *AQR*, is to remain in the forefront of the literary world, to be a leading venue for new and emerging writers. To him the literary magazine is like a stream leading to larger publications, then to the river—major magazines for fiction—and finally emptying into the ocean of national and international publishing houses. Preservation of the stream of literary magazines is essential to ensure a vibrant literary future, and for Spatz, this means providing adequate funding and preserving the National Endowment for the Arts.

"If you cut off the beginning of the continuum, where is the flow going to come from? Down the road you suffer very significant damage. If you don't fund the individual artist or the real artistic works and try to rely on the marketplace alone to try to determine what's appropriate and important, you are going to cut off this initial source. If you look back at what we value in all the arts over time, what you see are works of artists who have been ahead of their time. Their works haven't always gone over well initially, but now we revere them."

INSIDER REPORT, *Spatz*

Preserving the stream by publishing the work of new writers has always been one of the hallmarks of *AQR*. Of the 27 pieces in the "Intimate Voices, Ordinary Lives" issue, four are the writers' very first publishing credits, and another is the first published fiction by a primarily nonfiction writer. "Almost none" of the pieces were solicited from authors; the remainder were chosen from the 3,000 submissions *AQR* receives annually.

While *AQR* has devoted most of its pages to fiction, it has also featured nonfiction, poetry and drama. "Intimate Voices, Ordinary Lives" contains an eclectic mix of fiction and nonfiction, but it doesn't openly advertise which pieces are fiction and which are not, forcing the reader to concentrate on the human experiences portrayed within the pieces themselves. "We look for the demonstration of craft, making the situation palpable and putting it in a form where it becomes emotionally and intellectually complex," says Spatz. "One could look through our pages over time and see that we've taken stories about everyday life. We're not asking our writers to go outside themselves and their experiences to the absolute exotic to catch our interest. Many writers don't realize that they have this wealth of powerful material within them that is not always exotic. They can be freed to do their best work if they're not looking to invent a world completely outside of themselves and their experiences."

Working with so many new writers as *AQR*'s editor and being a creative writing teacher of more than two decades has given Spatz a clear vision about the importance of nurturing new writers in terms of craft, and also about the beginner's role in the literary world as a whole. While many writers are convinced that the perfect plot will get them published, Spatz has different ideas. "The real emphasis, at least for us, would be stories that have an emotional connection. You don't get it simply by having a character face a superficial problem no matter how serious it is. We're not looking for blood on the walls or any kind of sensational, clever approach to get our attention. When the emphasis is on the external, you look at something and go 'Huh, so?'.

"Art is so compelling to us because it takes us on a journey, and the writers are exploring when they write. What happens sometimes with new writers is that they are not confident enough to deal with the unknown and fully explore it, so the stories never really achieve the depth they need. The maturity to care about your subjects and characters, to undertake a writer's exploration by being immersed in characters and language are all elements of the professional writer. And as an editor, you can tell pretty much right away whether a writer has those tools at work."

Spatz also regards professionalism—the serious commitment to one's work—as rule number one of writing. "Writers need to feel that the process itself has some validity, and some writers don't feel validated at all unless they are published. But if they're not validated because they're not published, perhaps the stories they are telling are not significant or compelling to them. Sometimes it seems that writers don't even care about their work." This professional endeavor is just as vital when the writer sends work to be published. "When we say 'read the magazine,' we are talking about a professional approach. The doctor doesn't go into the operating room without a knowledge of absolutely everything necessary to performing surgery."

Spatz's desire for professionalism at *AQR* extends beyond writers into his editorial staff and his own work. "It's an honor to read and be involved in an editorial position as I am. There are so many people involved in a professional enterprise and there are so few arenas for them to get their work published and it's very hard. At *AQR*, we try to treat each author with that level of respect. We try to have our staff be open-minded to a range of

---

INSIDER REPORT, *continued*

presentations. If they happen to come across something they have no tolerance for, say a very unconventional story, then they are not to judge it as damned right then; they are to pass it on to somebody else."

The complexity and connections made by a successful story and the traits of a truly professional writer are of paramount importance to Spatz, and he is eager to showcase those stories and writers in *Alaska Quarterly Review*—whether the writer has a string of publishing credits or the story is the only one the writer will ever produce. "It's conceivable," says Spatz, "that a writer has one story to tell, but if that story touches the heart and mind in important ways, we want to publish it."

Rejection, however, is a fact of life. "Editors make decisions for better or for worse, and they make mistakes," says Spatz. "Luckily, there are a lot of other gate keepers. Pieces we've turned down have later appeared in other magazines. I haven't regretted that we didn't take them. I'm happy to have them published.

"Writers have to be persistent and patient, and that's very hard when you are first starting out. The competition is so intense, and the funding for the front line journals is generally pretty poor, so the staffing is low. It takes time, but new writers need to think in the long term. That way a rejection here and there, or lots of them, should never deter somebody. They can be disappointed but the reality is that they have to stick to it. Will counts as much as talent, and new writers need to have confidence in themselves and be persistent."

—*Andrew Lucyszyn*

---

indicated." Reports in 2-3 months "but during peak periods a reply may take up to 5 months." Publishes ms 6 months to 1 year after acceptance. Sample copy for $5.
Payment/Terms: Pays 1 contributor's copy and a year's subscription. Pays $50-200 honorarium when grant funding permits. Acquires first rights.
Advice: "We have made a significant investment in fiction. The reason is quality; serious fiction *needs* a market. Try to have everything build to a singleness of effect."

ALLEGHENY REVIEW, (IV), Box 32, Allegheny College, Meadville PA 16335. (814)332-6553. E-mail: review@alleg.edu. Website: http://www.alleg.edu/StudentLife/Organizations/AllegReview (includes writer's guidelines, ordering information, information about the editors and the prize winning poem and short story of the previous issue). Editors: Amy Augustyn, Jason Ramsey. Poetry Editor: Beth Hunter. Magazine: 8×5; 82 pages; white paper; illustrations and photos. "The *Allegheny Review* provides a national forum for undergraduate fiction writing. We accept all genres of fiction. Our intended audience is college students, professors and interested readers." Annually. Estab. 1983. Circ. 500.
Needs: Adventure, ethnic/multicultural, experimental, fantasy, feminist, gay, historical (general), horror, humor/satire, lesbian, literary, mainstream/contemporary, mystery/suspense, psychic/supernatural/occult, regional, religious/inspirational, science fiction (soft/sociological), westerns. Receives 40 unsolicited mss/month. Buys 7 mss/issue; 7 mss/year. Does not read mss May-August. Publishes ms 2 months after deadline. Recently published work by David Bernardy and Ander S. Monson. Publishes 2-3 new writers/year. Length: 2,000 words average; 3,000 words maximum. Publishes short shorts. Also publishes poetry.
How to Contact: *Open to work by undergraduate writers only.* Sometimes critiques or comments on rejected ms. Send complete ms with a cover letter. Should include 1 page bio. SASE for reply. Sample copy for $5.
Payment/Terms: Pays free subscription and 1 contributor's copy; additional copies for $4.
Advice: "The story told matters less than the telling. We have no preconceptions of what is publishable or not. Don't moralize. Tell your story and rely on the reader to interpret your work in their own way. The best writing has many interpretations."

ALPHA BEAT PRESS, (I, IV), 31 Waterloo St., New Hope PA 18938. Editor: Dave Christy. Magazine: 7½×9; 95-125 pages; illustrations. "Beat and modern literature—prose, reviews and poetry." Semiannually. Estab. 1987. Circ. 600.

• Work from *Alpha Beat Press* has appeared in *Pushcart Prize* anthologies. Alpha Beat Press also publishes poetry chapbooks and supplements. The magazine is known for writings associated with modern and beat culture.

Needs: Erotica, experimental, literary and prose poem. No religious. Recently published work by Elliott, Joseph Verrilli, Chris Diamant, t.k. splake and Charles Plymell. Published new writers within the last year. Length: 600 words minimum; 1,000 words maximum. Also publishes literary essays, literary criticism, poetry.

How to Contact: Query first. Reports on queries within 2 weeks. SASE. Simultaneous and reprint submissions OK. Sample copy for $10. Reviews novels and short story collections.

Payment/Terms: Pays in contributor's copies. Rights remain with author.

Advice: "*ABP* is the finest journal of its kind available today, having, with 19 issues, published the widest range of published and unpublished writers you'll find in the small press scene."

‡**AMBIGUOUS, (II)**, Ambiguous Inc., 1314 S. Grand #2-146, Spokane WA 99205. (509)325-4809. Editor: Ryan Weldon. Fiction Editor: Kara Beach. Magazine: 8½×11; 137 pages; coated paper; glossy cover; illustrations and photographs. "Ambiguous is a forum for most everyone; a mecca for the people by the people. Our mission is to publish insightful, thought-provoking literary and artistic work. Our intended audience spans from the student, businessperson to practically anyone who cares about 'art.' " Quarterly. Estab. 1997.

Needs: Adventure, condensed/excerpted novel, erotica, ethnic/multicultural, experimental, fantasy, feminist, gay, historical, horror, lesbian, literary, translations. "We also publish essays, poetry and articles of literary quality. We are open to many styles of writing and opinion." Publishes special fiction issues or anthologies. Receives about 30 unsolicited mss/month. Accepts 10-25 mss/issue; 200 or more mss/year. Publishes ms 4-8 months after acceptance. Length: 500-700 words average; 100 words minimum; 5,000-6,000 words maximum. Publishes short shorts. Also publishes literary criticism, essays and poetry. Always critiques or comments on rejected mss.

How to Contact: "The author may send query or complete manuscript with a cover letter." Include estimated word count, 1-page bio, "address and phone number, as well as a SASE if she/he wishes their work to be returned." Reports in 1 month on queries; 2 months on mss. Send SASE for reply, return of ms or send a disposable copy of ms. Simultaneous submissions, reprints and electronic submissions OK. Sample copy for $3. Fiction guidelines for SAE. Reviews novels and short story collections. "Please send them to *Ambiguous* in care of Ryan Weldon."

Payment/Terms: Pays free subscription to the magazine and 3 contributor's copy on publication; additional copies for $6.25. Acquires one-time rights. "Each year, in January we will sponsor a writing contest. To apply, the author must send a manuscript, self stamped envelope and best number or address to contact them at, along with $15. The awards will be as follows: fiction, $500; poetry, $200; essay/article, $200; artwork, $200."

Advice: "We consider the content and how it is presented. If someone represents themselves or their work in a responsible manner and is cohesive we will probably publish the work. We don't have a specific genre. A manuscript stands out if it moves my soul whether I like the story itself or not. I recommend that beginning writers send for guidelines before submitting their work. Always have their work edited and read by several people first. Also, do not be discouraged because one story was not accepted because another may be. I've noticed that there seems to be a trend towards categorizing work. There are few magazines that bring together art, essays, poetry, fiction and articles. This is why we started *Ambiguous*."

AMELIA, (II), 329 E St., Bakersfield CA 93304. (805)323-4064. Editor-in-Chief: Frederick A. Raborg, Jr. Magazine: 5½×8½; 124-136 pages; perfect-bound; 60 lb. high-quality moistrite matte paper; kromekote cover; four-color covers; original illustrations; b&w photos. "A general review using fine fiction, poetry, criticism, belles lettres, one-act plays, fine pen-and-ink sketches and line drawings, sophisticated cartoons, book reviews and translations of both fiction and poetry for general readers with eclectic tastes for quality writing." Quarterly. Plans special fiction issue each July. Estab. 1984. Circ. 1,750.

• *Amelia* sponsors a long list of fiction awards.

Needs: Adventure, contemporary, erotica, ethnic, experimental, fantasy, feminist, gay, historical, humor/satire, lesbian, literary, mainstream, mystery/suspense, prose poem, regional, science fiction, senior citizen/retirement, sports, translations, western. Nothing "obviously pornographic or patently religious." Receives 160-180 unsolicited mss/month. Accepts up to 9 mss/issue; 25-36 mss/year. Recently published work by Michael Bugeja, Jack Curtis, Thomas F. Wilson, Maxine Kumin, Eugene Dubnov, Matt Mulhern and Merrill Joan Gerber. Published new writers within the last year. Length: 3,000 words average; 1,000 words minimum; 5,000 words maximum. Usually critiques rejected mss.

How to Contact: Send complete ms with cover letter with previous credits if applicable to *Amelia* and perhaps a brief personal comment to show personality and experience. Reports in 1 week on queries; 2 weeks to 3 months on mss. SASE. Sample copy for $9.95. Fiction guidelines for #10 SASE. Sends galleys to author "when deadline permits."

Payment/Terms: Pays $35-50 on acceptance for first North American serial rights plus 2 contributor's copies; extras with 20% discount.

Advice: "Write carefully and well, but have a strong story to relate. I look for depth of plot and uniqueness, and strong characterization. Study manuscript mechanics and submission procedures. Neatness does count. There is a sameness—a cloning process—among most magazines today that tends to dull the senses. Magazines like *Amelia* will awaken those senses while offering stories and poems of lasting value."

AMERICAN LITERARY REVIEW, A National Journal of Poems and Stories, (II), University of North Texas, P.O. Box 13827, Denton TX 76203-6827. (940)565-2127. Editor: Barb Rodman. Magazine: 7×10; 128 pages; 70 lb. Mohawk paper; 67 lb. Wausau Vellum cover. "Publishes quality, contemporary poems and stories." Semiannually. Estab. 1990. Circ. 900.
Needs: Mainstream and literary only. No genre works. Receives 50-75 unsolicited fiction mss/month. Accepts 7-10 mss/issue; 14-20 mss/year. Publishes ms within 2 years after acceptance. Published work by Gordon Weaver, Gerald Haslam and William Miller. Length: less than 10,000 words. Critiques or comments on rejected mss when possible. Also accepts poetry and essays.
How to Contact: Send complete ms with cover letter. Reports in 2-3 months. SASE. Simultaneous submissions OK. Sample copy for $8. Fiction guidelines free.
Payment/Terms: Pays in contributor's copies. Acquires one-time rights.
Advice: "Give us distinctive styles, original approaches, stories that are willing to take a chance. We respond to character first, those that have a past and future beyond the page." Looks for "literary quality and careful preparation. There is a sameness to most of the stories that we receive—somebody dies or a relationship ends. We would love to see stories beyond those topics that grab us immediately and keep us interested throughout."

AMERICAN SHORT FICTION, (II), English Dept., Parlin 108, University of Texas at Austin, Austin TX 78712-1164. (512)471-1772. Editor: Joseph Kruppa. Magazine: 5¾×9¼; 128 pages; 60 lb. natural paper; 8015 karma white cover. "*American Short Fiction* publishes fiction *only*, of all lengths, from short short to novella." Quarterly. Estab. 1990. Circ. 1,200.
Needs: Literary. "No romance, science fiction, erotica, mystery/suspense and religious." Receives 500 unsolicited mss/month. Acquires 6 mss/issue; 25-30 mss/year. Accepts mss September 1 through May 31. Publishes ms up to 1 year after acceptance. Agented fiction 20%. Recently published work by Michael Guista, Alyce Miller, Steve Lattimore and Natasha Waxman. Length: open. Sponsors contest. Send SASE for details.
How to Contact: Send complete ms with cover letter. Reports in 3-4 months on mss. Send SASE for reply, return of ms or send disposable copy of the ms. Simultaneous submissions OK if informed. Sample copy for $9.95. Fiction guidelines for #10 SASE.
Payment/Terms: Pays $400/story for first rights. Sends galleys to author.
Advice: "We pick work for *American Short Fiction* along simple lines: Do we love it? Is this a story we will be happy reading four or five times? We comment only *rarely* on submissions because of the volume of work we receive."

‡AMERICAN VOICE, (II), 332 W. Broadway, #1215, Louisville KY 40202. (502)562-0045. Editor: Frederick Smock. Magazine: 6×9; 150 pages; photos. Triannually. Estab. 1985. Circ. 2,000.
Needs: Literary. No children's or romance. Receives 150 unsolicited mss/month. Accepts 5-6 mss/issue. Recently published Isabel Allende, Kyle Potok, Kate Braverman and Leon Rooke. Length: "the shorter the better."
How to Contact: Send complete ms with a cover letter. Include bio. Reports in 6 weeks on mss. Sample copy for $7.
Payment/Terms: Payment varies.

AMERICAN WRITING; A Magazine, (I, II), Nierika Editions, 4343 Manayunk Ave., Philadelphia PA 19128. Editor: Alexandra Grilikhes. Magazine: 8½×5½; 80-88 pages; matte paper and cover stock; photos. "We publish new writing that takes risks. We are interested in the voice of the loner, the artist as shaman, the powers of intuition, exceptional work of all kinds." Semiannually. Estab. 1990. Circ. 2,500.
Needs: Contemporary, excerpted novel, ethnic/multicultural, experimental, feminist, gay, lesbian; literary, translations. No mainstream. Receives 100-200 unsolicited mss/month. Accepts 4-5 mss/issue; 10-11 mss/year. Does not read mss June, December, January. Publishes ms 6-12 months after acceptance. Agented fiction less than 1%. Recently published work by Lara Stapleton, Varda One, Richard Krause, Ayaz Mahmud, John Taylor, Nikki Dillon, Jim Gladstone and Carroll Susco. Publishes 3-6 new writers/year. Length: 3,500 words average; 5,000 words maximum. Publishes short shorts. Also publishes literary essays, literary criticism, poetry. Critiques or comments on rejected mss "when there is time."
How to Contact: Send complete ms with a brief cover letter. Include brief bio and list of publications if applicable. Reports in 1 month on queries; 6-24 weeks on mss. Send SASE for reply, return of ms or send a disposable copy of ms. Simultaneous submissions OK. Sample copy for $6; fiction guidelines for #10 SASE.
Payment/Terms: Pays 2 contributor's copies; additional copies at half price. Acquires first rights or one-time rights.
Advice: "We look for intensity, vision, imaginative use of language, freshness, craft, sophistication; stories that delve. Read not just current stuff, but the odd masters—Dostoyevsky, Chekhov and Hesse. Learn about subtlty and depth. Reading helps you to know who you are as a writer, writing makes you more that person, if you've lucky. Read one or two issues of the magazine *carefully.*"

THE AMERICAS REVIEW, A Review of Hispanic Literature and Art of the USA, (II, IV), University of Washington, Romance Languages, Box 354360, Seattle WA 98195-4360. (206)543-4343. Fax: (206)543-2020. E-mail: lflores@u.washington.edu. Editors: Lauro Flores and Evangelina Vigil-Pinon. Magazine: 5½×8½; 128 pages; illustrations and photographs. "*The Americas Review* publishes contemporary fiction written by U.S.

Hispanics—Mexican Americans, Puerto Ricans, Cuban Americans, etc." Triannually. Estab. 1972.
Needs: Contemporary, ethnic, literary, women's, hispanic literature. No novels. Receives 12-15 fiction mss/month. Accepts 2-3 mss/issue; 8-12 mss/year. Publishes mss 6 months to 1 year after acceptance. Published work by Nash Candelaria, Roberto Fernández, Sheila Ortiz Taylor, Omar Castañeda, Kathleen Alcala and Daniel Orozco. Length: 3,000-4,500 average number of words; 1,500 words minimum; 6,000 words maximum (30 pages maximum, double-spaced). Publishes short shorts. Sometimes critiques rejected mss.
How to Contact: *"You must subscribe upon submitting materials."* Send complete ms. Reports in 3-4 months. SASE. No simultaneous submissions. Accepts electronic submissions via IBM compatible disk. Sample copy for $5; $10 double issue.
Payment/Terms: Pays $50-200; 2 contributor's copies on acceptance for first rights, and rights to 40% of fees if story is reprinted. Sponsors award for fiction writers.
Advice: "There has been a noticeable increase in quality in U.S. Hispanic literature."

♣THE AMETHYST REVIEW, (I, II), Marcasite Press, 23 Riverside Ave., Truro, Nova Scotia B2N 4G2 Canada. (902)895-1345. E-mail: amethyst@auracom.com. Website: http://www.atcon.com/~amethyst (includes writer's guidelines, names of editors, fiction excerpts, subscription info, contest guidelines, Editor's Picks and suggested reading). Editors: Penny Ferguson and Lenora Steele. Magazine: 8¼×6¾; 84 pages; book weight paper; card stock cover; illustrations. "We publish quality contemporary fiction and poetry of interest to the literary reader." Semiannually. Estab. 1993. Circ. 150.
Needs: Literary. Upcoming themes: Harbors (contest theme)—geographical, safe, returning to, leaving (deadline January 31, 1998). Issued in May 1998. List of upcoming themes available for SASE. Receives 10 unsolicited mss/month. Accepts 2-3 mss/issue; 4-6 mss/year. Publishes mss maximum 6 months after acceptance, "usually much sooner." Recently published work by Karen Hood-Caddy, Joanna M. Delong, Gary J. Langguth, Kathleen Schmitt, Byrna Barclay and Pamela Sweeney Jackson. Length: 5,000 words maximum. Publishes short shorts. Also publishes poetry. Sponsors contest; send SASE for information. Always critiques or comments on rejected mss.
How to Contact: Send complete ms with cover letter. Include estimated word count, a 50-word bio and list of publications. Reports in 2-28 weeks on mss. Send SASE or SAE and IRCs for reply, return of mss or send a disposable copy of ms. Sample copy for $6 (current) or $4 (back issues). Fiction guidelines for SASE or SAE and IRCs. Reviews novels and short story collections "only by people we have published."
Payment/Terms: Pays 1 contributor's copy; additional copies $4. Pays on publication. Acquires first North American serial rights.
Advice: "Quality is our criterion. Try to delight us with originality and craft. Send for guidelines and sample. We don't look for a specific type of story. We publish the *best* of what we receive. We are seeking literary quality and accessibility. A story that stands out gives the reader a 'tingle' and stays in your mind for days to come. Pay attention to detail, don't be sloppy. Care about your subjects because if you don't neither will the reader. Dazzle us with quality instead of trying to shock us!"

ANTIETAM REVIEW, (I, II, IV), Washington County Arts Council, 41 S. Potomac St., Hagerstown MD 21740. (301)791-3132. Editor: Susanne Kass. Fiction Editors: Susanne Kass and Ann Knox. Magazine: 8½×11; 54-68 pages; glossy paper; light card cover; photos. A literary journal of short fiction, poetry and black-and-white photographs. "Our audience is primarily in the six state region. Urban, suburban and rural writers and readers, but copies are purchased nationwide, both by libraries as well as individuals. Sales and submissions increase yearly, and we have just celebrated our fifteenth year of continual publication." Annually. Estab. 1982. Circ. 1,800.
- *Antietam Review* has received several awards including First-runner Up (1993-94) for Editorial Content from the American Literary Magazine Awards. Work published in the magazine has been included in the *Pushcart Prize* anthology and *Best American Short Stories*. The magazine also received a grant from the Maryland State Arts Council.
Needs: Condensed/excerpted novel, contemporary, ethnic, experimental, feminist, literary and prose poem. "We read manuscripts from our region—Delaware, Maryland, Pennsylvania, Virginia, West Virginia and Washington D.C. only. We read from September 1 through February 1." No horror, romance, inspirational, pornography. Receives about 100 unsolicited mss/month. Buys 8-10 stories/year. Publishes ms 2-3 months after acceptance. Recently published work by Dick Green, Becky Hagerston, Mario Rossilli, Stephen Murabita, Catherine Mellett, David Conway and Louise Farmer Smith. Publishes 2-3 new writers/year. Length: 3,000 words average. Also publishes poetry.
How to Contact: "Send ms and SASE with a cover letter. Let us know if you have published before and where." Include estimated word count, 1-paragraph bio and list of publications. Reports in 2-4 months. "If we hold a story, we let the writer know. Occasionally we critique returned ms or ask for rewrites." Sample copy for $5.25. Back issue $3.15. Guidelines for legal SAE.
Payment/Terms: "We believe it is a matter of dignity that writers and poets be paid. We have been able to give $50-100 a story and $25 a poem, but this depends on funding. Also 2 copies." Buys first North American serial rights. Sends galleys to author if requested.
Advice: "We seek high quality, well-crafted work with significant character development and shift. We seek no specific theme, but look for work that is interesting, involves the reader and teaches us a new way to view the

world. A manuscript stands out because of its energy and flow. Most of our submissions reflect the times (i.e. the news, current events) more than industry trends. We now require *accepted* stories to be put on disk by the author to cut down on printing costs. We are seeing an increase of first person narrative stories."

♣**THE ANTIGONISH REVIEW, (I, II)**, St. Francis Xavier University, P.O. Box 5000, Antigonish, Nova Scotia B2G 2W5 Canada. (902)867-3962. Fax: (902)867-2389. E-mail: tar@stfx.ca. Editor: George Sanderson. Literary magazine for educated and creative readers. Quarterly. Estab. 1970. Circ. 800.
Needs: Literary, contemporary, prose poem, translations. No erotic or political material. Accepts 6 mss/issue. Receives 50 unsolicited fiction mss each month. Published work by Arnold Bloch, Richard Butts and Helen Barolini. Published new writers within the last year. Length: 3,000-5,000 words. Sometimes comments briefly on rejected mss.
How to Contact: Send complete ms with cover letter. SASE ("U.S. postage not acceptable"). No simultaneous submissions. Electronic (disk compatible with WordPerfect/IBM and Windows or e-mail) submissions OK. Prefers hard copy with disk submission. Reports in 6 months. Publishes ms 3 months to 1 year after acceptance.
Payment/Terms: Pays 2 contributor's copies. Authors retain copyright.
Advice: "Learn the fundamentals and do not deluge an editor."

ANTIOCH REVIEW, (II), Box 148, Yellow Springs OH 45387-0148. (937)767-6389. Editor: Robert S. Fogarty. Associate Editor: Nolan Miller. Magazine: 6×9; 128 pages; 50 lb. book offset paper; coated cover stock; illustrations "seldom." "Literary and cultural review of contemporary issues in politics, American and international studies, and literature for general readership." Quarterly. Published special fiction issue last year; plans another. Estab. 1941. Circ. 5,100.
Needs: Literary, contemporary, experimental, translations. No children's, science fiction or popular market. Accepts 5-6 mss/issue, 20-24 mss/year. Receives approximately 275 unsolicited fiction mss each month. Approximately 1-2% of fiction agented. Recently published work by Ed Falco, Ha Jin, Edith Pearlman and Rick De Mariuis. Published 1-2 new writers/year. Length: generally under 8,000 words.
How to Contact: Send complete ms with SASE, preferably mailed flat. Reports in 2 months. Publishes ms 6-9 months after acceptance. Sample copy for $6. Guidelines for SASE.
Payment/Terms: Pays $10/page; 2 contributor's copies. $3.90 for extras. Pays on publication for first and one-time rights (rights returned to author on request).
Advice: "Our best advice, always, is to *read* the *Antioch Review* to see what type of material we publish. Quality fiction requires an engagement of the reader's intellectual interest supported by mature emotional relevance, written in a style that is rich and rewarding without being freaky. The great number of stories submitted to us indicates that fiction still has great appeal. We assume that if so many are writing fiction, many must be reading it."

APHRODITE GONE BERSERK, (IV), A journal of erotic art, Red Wine Press, 233 Guyon Ave., Staten Island NY 10306. Editors: C. Esposito, E. Eccleston. Magazine: 5½×8½; 48 pages; illustrations and photos. "*AGB* publishes fiction, poetry, essays, photography, etc. that deal with the erotic or sexuality in all styles and from any perspective or orientation." Semiannually. Estab. 1996.
Needs: Erotica: condensed/excerpted novel, experimental, feminist, gay, lesbian, literary, translations. List of upcoming themes available for SASE. Receives 10 unsolicited mss/month. Accepts 3 mss/issue; 6 mss/year. Publishes ms 6-12 months after acceptance. Recently published work by Gerard Malanga, Lyn Lifshin and Arlene Mandell. Publishes short shorts. Also publishes literary essays, literary criticism, poetry.
How to Contact: Send complete ms with a cover letter. Reports in 2 weeks on queries; 1 month on mss. Send SASE for reply, return of ms or send a disposable copy of ms. Simultaneous and reprint submissions OK. Reviews novels or short story collections.
Payment/Terms: Pays 1 contributor's copy. Acquires one-time rights.
Advice: "Stay away from the cliché and tired, and write honestly from the heart. We do not allow industry trends to affect the type of fiction we accept for publication."

APPALACHIAN HERITAGE, (I, II), Hutchins Library, Berea College, Berea KY 40404. (606)986-9341. Fax: (606)986-9494. E-mail: sidney-farr@berea.edu. Editor: Sidney Saylor Farr. Magazine: 6×9; 80 pages; 60 lb. stock; 10 pt. Warrenflo cover; drawings and b&w photos. "*Appalachian Heritage* is a southern Appalachian literary magazine. We try to keep a balance of fiction, poetry, essays, scholarly works, etc., for a general audience and/or those interested in the Appalachian mountains." Quarterly. Estab. 1973. Circ. approximately 600.
Needs: Regional, literary, historical. "We do not want to see fiction that has no ties to Southern Appalachia." Receives 6-8 unsolicited mss/month. Accepts 2-3 mss/issue; 12-15 mss/year. Publishes ms 1-2 years after acceptance. Published work by Garry Barker, James Still and Rhonda Strickland. Published new writers within the last year. Length: 3,000 words maximum. Publishes short shorts. Length: 500 words. Occasionally critiques rejected mss.
How to Contact: Send complete ms with cover letter. Include estimated word count, 2-3-sentence bio and list of publications. Reports in 3-4 weeks on queries; 4-6 weeks on mss. Send SASE for reply, return of ms or send a disposable copy of ms. Simultaneous and electronic submissions OK. Sample copy for $6. Guidelines free.
Payment/Terms: Pays 3 contributor's copies; $6 charge for extras. Acquires first North American serial rights.

Advice: "Get acquainted with *Appalachian Heritage*, as you should with any publication before submitting your work."

‡**ARACHNE, INC., In Praise of America's Grassroots Writers, (I, II, IV)**, 2363 Page Rd., Kennedy NY 14747-9717. Editor: Susan L. Leach. Magazine: 8½ × 5½; 30 pages; 20 lb. cover stock; illustrations and photos. "Rural theme. Sedate, conservative tone." Semiannually. Estab. 1981. Circ. 500.
Needs: Literary, regional, religious/inspirational. No erotica. Publishes special fiction issues or anthologies. Receives 20 unsolicited mss/month. Accepts 1-2 mss/issue; 4-5 mss/year. "Does not read after January and July publications." Publishes ms 3 weeks after acceptance. Recently published work by Anne Thore Beecham. Length: 1,500 words. Publishes short shorts. Also publishes literary essays, literary criticism and poetry. Often critiques or comments on rejected mss.
How to Contact: Query or send complete ms with a cover letter. Include estimated word count and 250 word bio. Reports in 2 weeks on queries. Send SASE for reply, return of ms or send disposable copy of ms. No simultaneous submissions. Sample copy for $5 and 8½ × 5½ SAE with 3 first-class stamps. Fiction guidelines for #10 SASE.
Payment/Terms: Pays 2 contributor's copies for first rights; additional copies $2.50. Sends galleys to author. Not copyrighted.
Advice: "Be willing to work with us to perfect your material. Don't try to do it all in one poem or short story."

ARARAT QUARTERLY, (IV), Ararat Press, AGBU., 585 Saddle River Rd., Saddle Brook NJ 07662. (212)765-8260. Editor: Dr. Leo Hamalian. Magazine: 8½ × 11; 72 pages; illustrations and b&w photographs. "*Ararat* is a forum for the literary and historical works of Armenian intellectuals or non-Armenian writers writing about Armenian subjects."
Needs: Condensed/excerpted novel, contemporary, historical, humor/satire, literary, religious/inspirational, translations. Publishes special fiction issue. Receives 25 unsolicited mss/month. Accepts 5 mss/issue; 20 mss/year. Length: 1,000 words average. Publishes short shorts. Length: 500 words. Also publishes literary essays, literary criticism, poetry. Sometimes critiques rejected mss and recommends other markets.
How to Contact: Send complete ms with cover letter. Reports in 1 month on queries; 3 weeks on mss. SASE. Simultaneous and reprint submissions OK. Sample copy for $7 and $1 postage. Free fiction guidelines. Reviews novels and short story collections.
Payment/Terms: Pays $40-75 plus 2 contributor's copies on publication for one-time rights. Sends galleys to author.

‡**ARBA SICULA, (II, IV)**, St John's University, Jamaica NY 11439. Editor: Gaetano Cipolla. Magazine: 5½ × 8½; 85 pages; top-grade paper; good quality cover stock; illustrations; photos. Bilingual ethnic literary review (Sicilian-English) dedicated to the dissemination of Sicilian culture. Published twice a year. Plans special fiction issue. Estab. 1979. Circ. 1,800.
Needs: Accepts ethnic literary material consisting of various forms of folklore, stories both contemporary and classical, regional, romance (contemporary, historical, young adult) and senior citizen. Material submitted must be in the Sicilian language, with English translation desirable. Published new writers within the last year. Critiques rejected mss when there is time. Sometimes recommends other markets.
How to Contact: Send complete ms with SASE and bio. Reports in 2 months. Publishes ms 1-3 years after acceptance. Simultaneous submissions and reprints OK. Sample copy for $8 with 8½ × 11 SASE and 90¢ postage.
Payment/Terms: 5 free author's copies. $4 for extra copies. Acquires all rights.
Advice: "This review is a must for those who nurture a love of the Sicilian language."

ARKANSAS REVIEW, (II), (formerly Kansas Quarterly), Department of English and Philosophy, P.O. Box 1890, Arkansas State University, State University AR 72467. (501)972-3043. Fax: (501)972-2795. Editor: Norman Lavers. Magazine: 8¼ × 10¾; 84-92 pages; coated, matte paper; matte, 4-color cover stock; illustrations and photos. "We aspire to be a first-rate international journal publishing mainly fiction (stories and novel excerpts) and creative nonfiction. We have no restrictions on length or subject or style, high quality being the only criterion. If you can delight us, and an intelligent sophisticated audience, we'll take it." Triannually. Estab. 1996. Circ. 900.
Needs: Excerpted novel, mainstream/contemporary, translations. "No genre fiction." Receives 65 unsolicited mss/month. Accepts 9-14 mss/issue; 35 mss/year. Publishes ms 6-12 months after acceptance. Agented fiction 1%. Recently published work by George Chambers, Raymond Federman, Carole Glickfeld, Michael Mooney, D.E. Steward, Leslie Edgerton, Marianne Luban, Edra Ziesk, Steve Yates and Lloyd Zimpel. Publishes 3-6 new

---

READ THE BUSINESS OF FICTION WRITING section to learn the correct way to prepare and submit a manuscript.

writers/year. Also publishes literary essays and poetry. Sometimes critiques or comments on rejected mss.

How to Contact: Send complete ms with cover letter. Include a brief list of major publications. Reports in 2 weeks on queries; 2 months on mss. Send SASE for reply, return of ms or send a disposable copy of ms. Simultaneous submissions OK. Sample copy for $6. Fiction guidelines free for #10 SASE.

Payment/Terms: Pays $10-25/page on publication and 2 contributor's copies; additional copies for $6. Acquires first North American serial rights.

Advice: "We publish new writers in every issue. We look for distinguished, mature writing, surprises, a perfect ending and a story that means more than merely what went on in it. We don't like recognizable imitations of currently fashionable writers. Writers with a Kansas connection who are accepted for publication are automatically in the running for the $1,000 Seaton award for best work by a Kansas-connected author (born there, lived there, went to school there). No application. Upon having your work accepted, state your Kansas connection."

‡**THE ARMCHAIR AESTHETE, (I, II)**, Pickle Gas Press, 59 Vinal Ave., Rochester NY 14609. (716)342-6331. E-mail: bypaul@netacc.com. Editor: Paul Agosto. Magazine: 5½×8½; 30-40 pages; 20 lb. paper; 60 lb. color cover; illustrations. The Armchair Aesthete is a new publication providing an outlet for the creative writer while offering our audience (ages 9-90) a "good read." Quarterly. Estab. 1996. Circ. 100.

Needs: Adventure, fantasy (science fantasy, sword and sorcery), historical (general), horror, humor/satire, mainstream/contemporary, mystery/suspense (amateur sleuth, cozy, police procedural, private eye/hardboiled, romantic suspense), science fiction (soft/sociological), westerns (frontier, traditional). Plans to publish special fiction issue. Accepts 8-15 mss/issue; 32-60 mss/year. Publishes ms 3-9 months after acceptance. Agented fiction less than 5%. Length: 1,200 words average; 2,000 words maximum. Publishes short shorts. Also publishes poetry. Sometimes critiques or comments on rejected mss.

How to Contact: Send complete ms with a cover letter. Include estimated word count, 50-100 word bio and list of publications. Reports in 2-3 weeks on queries; 1-3 months on mss. Send SASE for reply, return of ms or send a disposable copy of ms. Simultaneous submissions, reprints and electronic submissions OK. Sample copy for $4 and 2 first-class stamps. Fiction guidelines free for #10 SASE. Reviews novels and short story collections.

Payment/Terms: Pays 1 contributor's copy on publication; additional copies for $3. Acquires one-time rights. Not copyrighted. Accepted works are automatically eligible for an annual contest.

Advice: "A work stands out when the tried and true plots and situations are retold with a fresh, unique twist. Make a professional presentation of your submissions. Spelling, grammar and format all deserve your closest scrutiny."

ARNAZELLA, (II, IV), English Department, Bellevue Community College, 3000 Landerholm Circle SE, Bellevue WA 98007. (206)603-4032. Fax: (425)643-2690. E-mail: arnazella@prostar.com. Advisor: Woody West. Editors change each year; contact advisor. Magazine: 10×9; 104 pages, 70 lb. paper; heavy coated cover; illustrations and photos. "For those interested in quality fiction." Annually. Estab. 1976. Circ. 500.

Needs: Adventure, contemporary, ethnic, experimental, fantasy, feminist, gay, historical, humor/satire, lesbian, literary, mainstream, mystery/suspense, regional. Submit Sept. 1-Dec. 31 for issue published in spring. Recently published work by Judith Skillman, Linda Elegant, Blaine Hammond, Duncan Z. Saffir and Christy Soto. Publishes 25 new writers/year. Publishes short shorts. Also publishes literary essays, poetry. *Northwest contributors only, including British Columbia.*

How to Contact: Send complete ms with cover letter. Electronic submissions (fax and e-mail) OK. "We accept submissions September through December only." Reports on mss in spring. SASE. No simultaneous submissions. Sample copy for $5. Guidelines for SASE.

Payment/Terms: Pays in contributor's copies. Acquires first rights.

Advice: "Read this and similar magazines, reading critically and analytically. Since *Arnazella* does not edit for anything other than very minor problems, we need pieces that are technically sound."

‡**ARSHILE, A Magazine of the Arts, (II)**, 96 Tears Press, P.O. Box 3749, Los Angeles CA 90078. Editor: Mark Salerno. Magazine: 5½×8½; 144 pages; 55 lb. paper; 10 pt c1s cover; illustrations and photos. Publishes "experimental and formally engaged writing for a non-commercial audience. Semiannually. Estab. 1993. Circ. 1,000.

Needs: Receives 100 mss/month. Accepts 1 mss/issue; 1-2 mss/year. Publishes ms 3-6 months after acceptance. Recently published work by Sorrentino, Laskey and McInnis. Publishes short shorts. Also publishes literary essays, literary criticism and poetry.

How to Contact: Send complete ms with a cover letter. Reports in 15 weeks on queries and mss. Send SASE for reply, return of ms or send disposable copy of ms. Reviews novels and short story collections. Send books to editor.

Payment/Terms: Pays free subscription to magazine and 2 contributor's copies for first rights. Sends galleys to author.

ARTFUL DODGE, (II), Dept. of English, College of Wooster, Wooster OH 44691. (216)263-2000. Editor-in-Chief: Daniel Bourne. Magazine: 150-200 pages; illustrations; photos. "There is no theme in this magazine, except literary power. We also have an ongoing interest in translations from Eastern Europe and elsewhere." Annually. Estab. 1979. Circ. 1,000.

Needs: Experimental, literary, prose poem, translations. "We judge by literary quality, not by genre. We are especially interested in fine English translations of significant contemporary prose writers. Translations should be submitted with original texts." Receives 40 unsolicited fiction mss/month. Accepts 5 mss/year. Recently published fiction by Edward Kleinschmidt, Terese Svoboda, David Surface, Greg Boyd and Zbigniew Herbert; and interviews with Tim O'Brien, Lee Smith, Michael Dorris and Stuart Dybek. Published 1 new writer within the last year. Length: 10,000 words maximum; 2,500 words average. Also publishes literary essays, literary criticism, poetry. Occasionally critiques rejected mss.

How to Contact: Send complete ms with SASE. Do not send more than 30 pages at a time. Reports in 1 week to 6 months. No simultaneous or reprint submissions. Sample copies are $5 for older issues; $7 for current issues. Fiction guidelines for #10 SASE.

Payment/Terms: Pays 2 contributor's copies and honorarium. Acquires first North American serial rights.

Advice: "If we take time to offer criticism, do not subsequently flood us with other stories no better than the first. If starting out, get as many *good* readers as possible. Above all, read contemporary fiction and the magazine you are trying to publish in."

ARTISAN, a journal of craft, (I, II), P.O. Box 157, Wilmette IL 60091. (847)673-7246. E-mail: artisanjnl@aol.com. Editor: Joan Daugherty. Tabloid: 8½×11; 36 pages; colored bond paper; illustrations. "The philosophy behind *artisan* is that anyone who strives to express themselves through their craft is an artist and artists of all genres can learn from each other." For artists and the general public. Quarterly. Estab. 1995. Circ. 200.

Needs: Adventure, condensed/excerpted novel, erotica (mild), ethnic/multicultural, experimental, fantasy (science fantasy, sword and sorcery), feminist, horror, humor/satire, literary, mainstream/contemporary, mystery/suspense, psychic/supernatural/occult, science fiction, sports, westerns. "No pornography, or anything too sweet or saccharine." Receives 25 unsolicited mss/month. Accepts 6-8 mss/issue; 40 mss/year. Publishes ms 4-8 months after acceptance. Published work by Crissa-Jean Chappell, Eric Spitznagel, Ruth McLaughlin and Ben Ohmart. Length: 2,000 words average; 4,000 words maximum. Publishes short shorts. Also publishes literary essays, literary criticism, poetry. Sometimes critiques or comments on rejected mss.

How to Contact: Send complete ms with cover letter. Include estimated word count. Reports in 1 month on queries; 3 months on mss. SASE for reply and send a disposable copy of ms. Simultaneous and electronic submissions (e-mail or ASCII) OK. Sample copy for $3.50. Fiction guidelines for #10 SASE. Guidelines also posted on the Internet at http://members.aol.com/artisanjnl. Will sponsor annual short fiction competition: $200 1st prize; $100 2nd prize. Send SASE for guidelines.

Payment/Terms: Pays 3 contributor's copies; additional copies $2. Acquires first rights.

Advice: "Innovative phrasing and subject matter stand out. Strive to use fresh language and situations, but don't disregard the basics of good writing and storytelling."

ASCENT, (II), Dept. 9 English, Concordia College, Moorhead MN 56562. Editor: W. Scott Olsen. E-mail: ascent@cord.edu. Magazine: 6×9; 50-70 pages. Triannually. Estab. 1976. Circ. 1,000.

● *Ascent* has received grants from the Illinois Arts Council. Work published in the magazine has been selected for *Pushcart* Awards and inclusion in the *Best American Short Story Anthology*.

Needs: Literary. Receives 40-50 unsolicited mss/week. Accepts 2-3 mss/issue; 6-9 mss/year. Publishes ms 3-6 months after acceptance. Recently published work by Alvin Greenberg, K.C. Frederick and Edith Pearlman. Length: 3,000 words average. Also publishes poetry and essays. Sometimes critiques or comments on rejected mss.

How to Contact: Send complete ms. Reports in 2 weeks on queries; 2-8 weeks on mss. Send SASE for reply, return of ms or send a disposable copy of ms. Simultaneous submissions OK. Sample copy for $4. Fiction guidelines for SASE.

Payment/Terms: Pays 2 contributor's copies.

Terms: Acquires first rights. Sends galleys to author.

ASIAN PACIFIC AMERICAN JOURNAL, (I, II, IV), The Asian American Writers' Workshop, 37 St. Marks Place, New York NY 10003-7801. (212)228-6718. Fax: (212)228-7718. E-mail: aaww@panix.com. Website: http://www.panix.com/~AAWW. Editor: Eileen Tabios. Magazine: 5½×8½; 150 pages; illustrations. "We are interested in publishing works by writers from all segments of the Asian Pacific American community. The journal appeals to all interested in Asian-American literature and culture." Semiannually. Estab. 1992. Circ. 1,500.

● *Asian Pacific American Journal* received a NEA grant in 1995.

Needs: Adventure, condensed/excerpted novel, erotica, ethnic/multicultural, experimental, feminist, gay, historical (general), humor/satire, lesbian, literary, mainstream/contemporary, regional, serialized novel, translations, Asian-American themes. "We are interested in anything related to the Asian American community." Receives 75 unsolicited mss/month. Accepts 15 mss/issue; 30 mss/year. Does not read September-October, March-April. Publishes ms 3-4 months after acceptance. Agented fiction 5%. Recently published work by Karen Hua, Shawn Wong, Diana Chang and Hun Ohm. Length: 3,000 words average. Publishes short shorts. Also publishes literary essays, poetry. Sometimes critiques or comments on rejected ms.

How to Contact: Send SASE for guidelines. Should include estimated word count, 3-5 sentence bio, list of publications. Reports in 1 month on queries; 4 months on mss. SASE for reply or send a disposable copy of ms.

Simultaneous, reprint, electronic (disk, Macintosh or IBM, preferably Microsoft Word 5 for Mac) submissions OK. Sample copy for $12. Fiction guidelines for SASE. Reviews novels and short story collections.

Payment/Terms: Pays 2 contributor's copies; additional copies at 40% discount. Acquires one-time rights. Sends galleys to author. Sponsors contests, awards or grants for fiction writers. "Send query with SASE."

ASSPANTS, (I, II), Asspants Publications, 1009½ Castro St., San Francisco CA 94114. E-mail: asspants@sirius .com. Editors: Michael Barnett and Chad Lange. Magazine: 8½×8½; 67 pages; illustrations and photos. "We value quality above and beyond any other factor. In addition to fiction, we also publish poetry and black-and-white artwork. Our intention is to show talented writers/artists that publishing *is* possible." Quarterly. Estab. 1996. Circ. 300 (in Bay Area).

Needs: "We consider any material as long as it is intelligent and well-written. We do not like to limit topics." Receives approximately 10 unsolicited mss/month. Accepts 2-3 mss/issue. Publishes ms 4-5 months after acceptance. Published work by Brian Weaver, Constance Bowell Mastores, Chad Lange and Michael Barnett. Length: 10-15 pages maximum.

How to Contact: Send complete ms with a cover letter. Include bio. Send SASE for return of ms or send a disposable copy of ms. Simultaneous and electronic (disk or modem) submissions OK. Sample copy for $7 and 8½×11 SAE. Fiction guidelines for legal-size SASE.

Payment/Terms: Pays 1 contributor's copy; additional copies for $7. Acquires one-time rights; rights revert to author. Not copyrighted.

Advice: "*Asspants* seeks well-written fiction on slightly off-beat, often morbid topics. While we do not adhere to a set style, the editors can tell immediately if manuscript will fit in with the overall feeling of the publication."

ATOM MIND, (II), Mother Road Publications, P.O. Box 22068, Albuquerque NM 87154. Editor: Gregory Smith. Magazine: 8½×11; 128 pages; 60 lb. paper; 80 lb. cover; illustrations and photos. "*Atom Mind* reflects the spirit of the 1960s; it is dedicated to the memory of Steinbeck, Hemingway, Kerouac, Bukowski et al." Quarterly. Estab. 1992. Circ. 1,000.

Needs: Condensed/excerpted novel, erotica, ethnic/multicultural, experimental, humor/satire, literary, mainstream/contemporary, serialized novel, translations. No juvenile, romance, science fiction or young adult/teen. Receives 200-300 unsolicited mss/month. Accepts 5-6 mss/issue; 20 mss/year. Publishes ms 1-2 years after acceptance. Published work by Michael Phillips, Al Masarik, Rick Kempa and Jerry Kamstra. Length: 1,000 words minimum; 6,000 words maximum. Also publishes literary essays, literary criticism, poetry. Sometimes critiques or comments on rejected mss.

How to Contact: Send complete ms with a cover letter. Include estimated word count. Reports in 2 weeks on queries; 1-2 months on mss. Send SASE for reply, return of ms or send a disposable copy of ms. Reprint submissions OK. Sample copy $6. Fiction guidelines free.

Payment/Terms: Pays in contributor's copies. Cash awards to "best of issue," (to subscribers only) as determined by the results of a random readers' poll. Acquires first North American serial rights.

Advice: "*Atom Mind* is very much a one-man operation and therefore subject to the whims and personal biases of the editor. I would like to see more satirical short fiction. Read at least one issue of any magazine you intend to submit to. Writers can save an immense amount of time and money by sending their work ONLY to those journals for which it is suitable—study the markets!"

AURA LITERARY/ARTS REVIEW, (II), University of Alabama at Birmingham, Box 76, Hill University Center, Birmingham AL 35294. (205)934-3354. Fax: (205)934-8050. Editors change each year. Magazine: 6×9; 140 pages; 70 lb. Moistrite matte paper; 80 lb. matte cover; b&w illustrations and photos. "*Aura* is a quality literary and arts review magazine focused on poetry, short fiction and photography." Semiannually. Estab. 1974. Circ. 3,000.

Needs: Adventure, contemporary, ethnic, experimental, fantasy, feminist, gay, historical, horror, humor, lesbian, literary, mystery/suspense, regional, religious/inspirational, romance, senior citizen, science fiction, sports, westerns. Acquires 5-6 mss/issue. Receives 30-40 unsolicited fiction mss each month. Published works by William John Watkins, Vivian Shipley and Holly Day. Published new writers within the last year. Length: up to 5,000 words. Publishes short shorts. Length: 300 words. Also publishes poetry. Critiques rejected mss when there is time.

How to Contact: Send complete ms with SASE. Include estimated word count and 20- to 40-word bio. Simultaneous and electronic (disk) submissions OK. Reports in 3 months. Sample copy for $2.50. "Occasionally" reviews novels and short story collections.

Payment/Terms: Pays 2 contributor's copies. Acquires first rights.

Advice: Looks for "strong verbs, connection and movement."

THE AZOREAN EXPRESS, (I, IV), Seven Buffaloes Press, Box 249, Big Timber MT 59011. Editor: Art Cuelho. Magazine: 6¾×8¼; 32 pages; 60 lb. book paper; 3-6 illustrations/issue; photos rarely. "My overall theme is rural; I also focus on working people (the sweating professions); the American Indian and Hobo; the Dustbowl era; and I am also trying to expand with non-rural material. For rural and library and professor/student, blue collar workers, etc." Semiannually. Estab. 1985. Circ. 600.

Needs: Contemporary, ethnic, experimental, humor/satire, literary, regional, western, rural, working people.

Receives 10-20 unsolicited mss/month. Accepts 2-3 mss/issue; 4-6 mss/year. Publishes ms 1-6 months after acceptance. Length: 1,000-3,000 words. Also publishes short shorts, 500-1,000 words. "I take what I like; length sometimes does not matter, even when longer than usual. I'm flexible."

How to Contact: "Send cover letter with ms; general information, but it can be personal, more in line with the submitted story. Not long rambling letters." Reports in 1-4 weeks. SASE. Sample copy for $6.75. Fiction guidelines for SASE.

Payment/Terms: Pays in contributor's copies. "Depends on the amount of support author gives my press." Acquires first North American serial rights. "If I decide to use material in anthology form later, I have that right." Sends galleys to the author upon request.

Advice: "There would not be magazines like mine if I was not optimistic. But literary optimism is a two-way street. Without young fiction writers supporting fiction magazines the future is bleak because the commercial magazines allow only formula or name writers within their pages. My own publications receive no grants. Sole support is from writers, libraries and individuals."

‡❦**BACKWATER REVIEW, (I, II)**, P.O. Box 222, Stn. B, Ottawa, Ontario K1P 6C4 Canada. E-mail: backwate rs@sympatico.ca/backwaters. Website: http://www3.sympatico.ca/backwaters. Editor: L. Brent Robillard. Assistant Editor: Leslie Holt. Electronic magazine. "We are looking for poetry and prose that interpret the world in new and interesting ways. Our audience is of a literary bend."

● *The Backwater Review* sponsors the Hinterland Award for Prose. Send 1 unpublished short story or play. Entry fee is $9 (includes subscription). Stories cannot exceed 5,000 words. Winning piece will receive $100 plus publication. Deadline is July 31. See website for more details.

Needs: "We publish poetry, short fiction, drama, essays, photography and small press book reviews." No science-fiction, fantasy or formula fiction of any kind. Recently published work by Dan Doyle, Matt Holland and Claire Mulligan. Publishes 24-30 new writers/year.

How to Contact: "We accept electronic submissions; however, we prefer snail mail."

Advice: "Write the truth, the whole truth, and nothing but the truth."

‡**THE BALTIMORE REVIEW, (II)**, Baltimore Writers' Alliance, P.O. Box 410, Riderwood MD 21139. (410)377-5265. Fax: (410)377-4325. Editor: Barbara Diehl. Magazine: 6×9; 128 pages; 60 lb. paper; 10 pt. CS1 gloss film cover. Showcase for the best short stories and poetry by writers in the Baltimore area and beyond. Semiannually. Estab. 1996.

Needs: Ethnic/multicultural, experimental, literary, mainstream/contemporary. No science fiction, westerns, children's, romance, etc. Accepts 8-12 mss/issue; 16-24 mss/year. Publishes ms 1-9 months after acceptance. Recently published work by Elizabeth Mary Larson, Kevin Isom, Lalita Norouha and Oktavi. Length: 3,000 words average; 1,000 words minimum; 6,000 words maximum. Also publishes poetry. Sometimes critiques or comments on rejected mss.

How to Contact: Send complete ms with a cover letter. Include estimated word count, brief bio and list of publications. Reports in 1-3 months. Send SASE for reply, return of ms or send a disposable copy of ms. Simultaneous submissions OK. Sample copy for $8. Fiction guidelines free for #10 SASE.

Payment/Terms: Pays 2 contributor's copies on publication. Acquires first North American serial rights.

Advice: "We look for compelling stories and a masterful use of the English language. We want to feel that we have never heard this story, or this voice, before. Read the kinds of publications you want your work to appear in. Make your reader believe, and care."

❦**B&A: NEW FICTION, (I, II)**, (formerly *Blood & Aphorisms*), P.O. Box 702, Station P, Toronto, Ontario M5S 2Y4 Canada. Phone/fax: (416)535-1233. E-mail: fiction@interlog.com. Website: www.interlog.com/~ficti on. Publisher: Tim Paleczny. Fiction Editor: Michelle Alfano. Managing Editor: Des Harty. Magazine: 8½×11; 48 pages; bond paper; illustrations. "We publish new and emerging writers whose work is fresh and revealing, and impacts on a literary readership." Quarterly. Estab. 1990. Circ. 2,500.

Needs: Experimental, literary. No gratuitous violence, pornography or exploitive fiction. Publishes anthology every 2 years. Receives 100 unsolicited mss/month. Accepts 6-10 mss/issue; 24-40 mss/year. Publishes ms 3-6 months after acceptance. Recently published work by Timothy Findley and Paul Quarrington. Length: 2,500-4,000 words average; 150 words minimum; 5,500 words maximum. Often critiques rejected mss. Sponsors fiction contest: $5,000 in prizes; up to 2,500 words; $18 entry fee includes subscription. SASE for information. Deadline March 11.

How to Contact: Send complete ms with a cover letter. Should include estimated word count, short bio, list of publications with submission. Reports in 1 month on queries; 3 months on mss. SASE for reply to a query or return of ms. Simultaneous (please advise) and electronic (e-mail and disk with hard copy) submissions OK. Sample copy for $6. Fiction guidelines for SASE. Reviews novels and short story collections.

Payment/Terms: Pays subscription to the magazine plus $35/printed page. Additional copies $6. Acquires first North American serial rights, electronic distribution for current issue sampling on Home Page, and the right to use work in anthology.

Advice: "Read *B&A* first. Know what kind of literary magazine you are submitting to. If it is consistent with your work, send us your best."

BARBARIC YAWP, (I, II), Bone World Publishing, 3706 County Rt. 24, Russell NY 13684. (315)347-2609. Editor: John Berbrich. Fiction Editor: Nancy Berbrich. Magazine: digest-size; 40-50 pages; 24 lb. paper; matte cover stock. "We are not preachers of any particular poetic or literary school. We publish any type of quality material appropriate for our intelligent and wide-awake audience." Quarterly. Estab. 1997. Circ. 100.

Needs: Adventure, experimental, fantasy (science, sword and sorcery), historical, horror, humor/satire, literary, mainstream/contemporary, psychic/supernatural/occult, regional, religious/inspirational, science fiction (hard, soft/sociological). "We don't want any pornography, gratuitous violence or whining." Receives 10-15 unsolicited mss/month. Accepts 10-12 mss/issue; 40-48 mss/year. Publishes ms within 6 months after acceptance. Recently published work by Janice Knapp, James Blihar and Michael Barnes. Length: 600 words average; 1,000 words maximum. Publishes short shorts. Also publishes literary essays, literary criticism, poetry. Often critiques or comments on rejected mss.

How to Contact: Send complete ms with a cover letter. Include estimated word count, brief bio and list of publications. Reports in 2 weeks on queries; 1-2 months on mss. Send SASE for reply, return of ms or send a disposable copy of ms. Simultaneous submissions and reprints OK. Sample copy for $3. Fiction guidelines for #10 SASE.

Payment and Terms: Pays 1 contributor's copy; additional copies $3. Acquires one-time rights.

Advice: "We are primarily concerned with work that means something to the author, but which is able to transcend the personal into the larger world. Send whatever is important to you. We will use Yin and Yang. Work must hold my interest and be well-crafted. Read, read, read; write, write, write—then send us your best. Don't get discouraged. Believe in yourself. Take risks."

‡BARNABE MOUNTAIN REVIEW, (I,II), Vital Ink, P.O. Box 529, Lagunitas CA 94938-0529. (415)488-4157. Editor: Gerald Fleming. Magazine: 5×8; 250 pages; 10 pt cover; illustrations and photos. "*Barnabe Mountain Review* publishes only the most carefully crafted fiction. We welcome the 'difficult' and elliptical as well as straightforward work." Annually. Estab. 1995. Circ. 1,000.

Needs: Erotica, ethnic/multicultural, experimental, feminist, gay, humor/satire, lesbian, literary, translations. No "romance, memoir disguised as fiction, fiction using the phrase 'single most,' stories about writers or university professors." Receives 50 unsolicited mss/month. Accepts 6 mss/issue. Does not read August-December. Will not be reading February-June in 1998. Recently published work by Molly Giles, Josephine Carson, Ron Nyren, Thalsa Frank, Ben Brooks and Keith Abbott. Length: open. Publishes short shorts. Also publishes poetry. Sometimes critiques or comments on rejected mss.

How to Contact: Send complete ms with a cover letter. Include estimated word count, 2-sentence bio and list of publications. Reports in 2 weeks on queries; 1-2 months on mss. Send SASE for reply, return of ms. No simultaneous submissions. Electronic (Mac Word disk) submissions OK. Sample copy for $10 and 6×9 SAE with $1.72 postage.

Payment/Terms: Pays 2-3 contributor's copies for one-time rights.

Advice: Looks for "precision, craft, a sense of something at stake, reader under arrest, not a wasted word. Read a copy first. Editorial biases can best be found that way."

*BBR MAGAZINE, P.O. Box 625, Sheffield, S1 3GY, United Kingdom. E-mail: bbr@fdgroup.co.uk. Website: http://www.syspace.co.uk/bbr (includes full contact information, guidelines, review of current issue). Editor: Chris Reed. Annually. Circ. 3,000. Publishes 20,000-30,000 words/issue.

Needs: "*Back Brain Recluse*, the award-winning British fiction magazine, actively seeks new fiction that ignores genre pigeonholes. We tread the thin line between experimental speculative fiction and avant-garde literary fiction."

How to Contact: Enclose a SASE for the return of your manuscript if it is not accepted. "We are unable to reply to writers who do not send return postage. We recommend two IRCs plus disposable ms for non-UK submissions. One US$ is an acceptable (and cheaper!) alternative to IRCs. Please send all submissions to Chris Reed, BBR, P.O. Box 625, Sheffield S1 3GY, UK. We aim to reply to all submissions within 2 months, but sometimes circumstances beyond our control may cause us to take longer. Please enclose SAE if enquiring about a manuscript's status. No responsibility can be accepted for loss or damage to unsolicited material, howsoever caused."

Payment/Terms: "We are currently reading for issue #24, for which we will pay £10 ($15) per 1,000 words on publication. Familiarity with the magazine is strongly advised." Sample copy available in US for $10 from BBR, % Anne Marsden, 31192 Paseo Amapola, San Juan Capistrano CA 92675-2227. (Checks payable to Anne Marsden).

MARKET CONDITIONS are constantly changing! If you're still using this book and it is 1999 or later, buy the newest edition of *Novel & Short Story Writer's Market* at your favorite bookstore or order from Writer's Digest Books.

THE BELLETRIST REVIEW, (I, II), Marmarc Publications, P.O. Box 596, Plainville CT 06062-0596. E-mail: mrlene@aol.com. Editor: Marlene Dube. Fiction Editor: Marc Saegaert. Magazine: 8½×11; 80 pages. "We are interested in compelling, well-crafted short fiction in a variety of genres. Our title *Belletrist*, means 'lover of literature.' This magazine will appeal to an educated, adult audience that appreciates quality fiction." Semiannually.

● The editors would like to see more "light" and humorous fiction.

Needs: Adventure, contemporary, erotica, horror (psychological), humor/satire, literary, mainstream, mystery/suspense, regional. No poetry, fantasy, juvenile, westerns, or overblown horror or confessional pieces. Accepts 10-12 mss/issue; approximately 25 mss/year. Publishes ms within 1 year after acceptance. Recently published work by William John Watkins, Daniel Quinn, Edward Wahl and Mary Overton. Publishes 2-6 new writers/year. Length: 2,500-5,000 words preferred; 1,000 words minimum; 5,000 words maximum. Comments on or critiques rejected mss when time permits. Special fiction contest in September (deadline: July 15). The award is $200. Send SASE for contest rules.

How to Contact: Send complete ms with cover letter including brief biographical note and any previous publications. "Do not send more than one manuscript at a time. The first page of your story should include your name, address and phone number in the upper left hand corner. Center the title and byline one-third of the page down. Three lines after that, begin the body of your work." Reports in 1 month on queries; 2 months on mss. SASE. "We prefer an envelope large enough to accommodate your 8½×11 format without having to fold it. It is not necessary to send your story by certified mail." Simultaneous submissions OK.

Payment/Terms: Pays contributor's copies. Acquires one-time rights.

Advice: "We select fiction that moves us in some fashion, with characters that 'come alive' and involve us in their struggles. Too many stories we receive lack tension or are poorly written. We like to see stories with complex, believable characters whom we care about, and strong writing. We understand it's a tough market for beginning writers, and we provide a forum for writers to have their work published and enhance their portfolios."

THE BELLINGHAM REVIEW, (II), Western Washington University, MS9053, Bellingham WA 98225. Website: http://www.wwu.edu/~bhreview (includes guidelines, poetry, fiction, nonfiction). Editor: Robin Hemley. Magazine: 5½×8; 120 pages; 60 lb. white paper; varied cover stock. "A literary magazine featuring original short stories, novel excerpts, essays, short plays and poetry of palpable quality." Semiannually. Estab. 1977. Circ. 1,500.

● The editors would like to see more humor and literary fiction.

Needs: All genres/subjects considered. Accepts 1-2 mss/issue. Does not read between May 2 and September 30. Publishes short shorts. Recently published work by Robin Parks, Sharon Solwitz, Holiday Reinhorn, Lee Upton and Dori Sanders. Published 2 new writers within the last year. Length: 10,000 words or less. Also publishes poetry.

How to Contact: Send complete ms. Reports in 2 weeks to 3 months. Publishes ms an average of 6 months after acceptance. Sample copy for $5. Reviews novels and short story collections.

Payment/Terms: Pays 1 contributor's copy plus 2-issue subscription and small honorarium when available. Charges $2.50 for extra copy. Acquires first North American serial and one-time rights.

Advice: "We look for work that is ambitious, vital, and challenging both to the spirit and the intellect. We hope to publish important works from around the world, works by older, neglected writers, and works by unheralded but talented new writers."

BELLOWING ARK, A Literary Tabloid, (II), P.O. Box 45637, Seattle WA 98145. (206)545-8302. Editor: R.R. Ward. Tabloid: 11½×16; 32 pages; electro-brite paper and cover stock; illustrations; photos. "We publish material which we feel addresses the human situation in an affirmative way. We do not publish academic fiction." Bimonthly. Estab. 1984. Circ. 500.

● Work from *Bellowing Ark* appeared in the *Pushcart Prize* anthology. The editor says he's using much more short fiction and prefers positive, life-affirming work. Remember, he likes a traditional, narrative approach and "abhors" minimalist and post-modern work.

Needs: Contemporary, literary, mainstream, serialized/excerpted novel. "Anything we publish will be true." No science fiction or fantasy. Receives 600-800 unsolicited fiction mss/year. Accepts 2-3 mss/issue; 12-18 mss/year. Time varies, but publishes ms not longer than 6 months after acceptance. Recently published work by Diane Trzcinski, Jim Bernhard, David Ross, Dave Roberts and Shelley Uva. Published new writers within the last year. Length: 3,000-5,000 words average ("but no length restriction"). Publishes short shorts. Also publishes literary essays, literary criticism, poetry. Sometimes critiques rejected mss.

How to Contact: No queries. Send complete ms with cover letter and short bio. "Prefer cover letters that tell something about the writer. Listing credits doesn't help." No simultaneous submissions. Reports in 6 weeks on mss. SASE. Sample copy for $3, 9×12 SAE and $1.24 postage.

Payment/Terms: Pays in contributor's copies. Acquires all rights, reverts on request.

Advice: "*Bellowing Ark* began as (and remains) an alternative to the despair and negativity of the Workshop/Academic literary scene; we believe that life has meaning and is worth living—the work we publish reflects that belief. Learn how to tell a story before submitting. Avoid 'trick' endings—they have all been done before and better. *Bellowing Ark* is interested in publishing writers who will develop with the magazine, as in an extended community. We find *good* writers and stick with them. This is why the magazine has grown from 12 to 32 pages."

BELOIT FICTION JOURNAL, (II), Box 11, Beloit College WI 53511. (608)363-2028. Editor: Clint McCown. Magazine: 6×9; 150 pages; 60 lb. paper; 10 pt. C1S cover stock; illustrations and photos on cover. "We are interested in publishing the best contemporary fiction and are open to all themes except those involving pornographic, religiously dogmatic or politically propagandistic representations. Our magazine is for general readership, though most of our readers will probably have a specific interest in literary magazines." Semiannually. Estab. 1985.

● Work first appearing in *Beloit Fiction Journal* has been reprinted in award-winning collections, including the *Flannery O'Connor* and the *Milkweed Fiction Prize* collections. The editor says he will not be reading submissions again until Fall 1998.

Needs: Contemporary, literary, mainstream, prose poem, spiritual and sports. No pornography, religious dogma, political propaganda. Receives 400 unsolicited fiction mss/month. Accepts 8-10 mss/issue; 16-20 mss/year. Replies take longer in summer. Publishes ms within 9 months after acceptance. Published work by Nance Van Winckel, Dinty W. Moore, David Milofsky and Debbie Lee Wesselmann. Length: 5,000 words average; 250 words minimum; 10,000 words maximum. Sometimes critiques rejected mss and recommends other markets.

How to Contact: Send complete ms with cover letter. Reports in 1 week on queries; 2-8 weeks on mss. SASE for ms. Simultaneous submissions OK if identified as such. Sample copy for $6. Fiction guidelines for #10 SASE.

Advice: "Many of our contributors are writers whose work we have previously rejected. Don't let one rejection slip turn you away from our—or any—magazine."

✸BENEATH THE SURFACE, (II), McMaster University Society of English, Dept. of English, Chester New Hall, McMaster University, Hamilton, Ontario L8S 4S8 Canada. Contact: Editor. Editors change every April. Magazine: 21cm × 13.5cm; 25-55 pages; illustrations and photos. "Primarily, university audience intended. Also targets general reading public." Semiannually. Estab. 1984. Circ. varies.

Needs: Ethnic/multicultural, experimental, fantasy (non-formula), feminist, gay, historical (general), horror, humor/satire, lesbian, literary, mystery/suspense (non-formula), psychic/supernatural/occult, science fiction (non-formula). Accepts 15 mss/issue; 30 mss/year. Does not read mss during summer months. Publishes ms 1-4 months after acceptance. Published work by William Lantry, Sean Brendan-Brown and Gene Shannon. Length: 3,000 words maximum. Publishes short stories. Also publishes literary essays, poetry.

How to Contact: Send complete ms with a cover letter. Should include short bio and list of publications. Reports in 6 months on mss. Send a disposable copy of ms. Electronic submissions (disk or modem) OK. Sample copy for $4.

Payment/Terms: Pays contributor's copies. Not copyrighted; copyrights belong to authors.

Advice: "Avoid formula fiction. For experimental writers: we are looking for *your* experimentation, not someone else's."

BERKELEY FICTION REVIEW, (II), 201 Heller-ASUC Publications Library, University of California, Berkeley CA 94720. (510)642-2892. E-mail: boogerr@uclink4.berkeley.edu. Website: http://www.OCF.Berkeley.EDU/~bfr/. Editors change yearly. Magazine: 5½ × 8½; 180 pages; perfect-bound; glossy cover; some b&w art; photographs. "We publish a wide variety of contemporary short fiction for a literary audience." Annually. Estab. 1981. Circ. 1,000.

Needs: Contemporary/mainstream, literary, experimental. "Quality, inventive short fiction. No poetry or formula fiction." Receives 60 unsolicited mss/month. Accepts 10-20 mss/issue. Recently published work by Greg Chaimov, Michael Stockham and Caleb Smith. Published work by 10 new writers in the last year. Also publishes short shorts. Occasionally comments on rejected mss.

How to Contact: Send complete ms to "Editor" with very brief cover letter and SASE. Simultaneous submission OK. Usually reports in 2-3 months, longer in summer. Sample copy for $8. Guidelines for SASE.

Payment/Terms: Pays 1 contributor's copy. Acquires first rights. Sponsors short story contest with $100 first prize. Entry fee: $5. Send SASE for guidelines.

Advice: "Our criteria is fiction that resonates. Voices that are strong and move a reader. Clear, powerful prose (either voice or rendering of subject) with a point. Unique ways of telling stories—these capture the editors. Work hard, don't give up. Don't let your friends or family critique your work. Get someone honest to point out your writing weaknesses, and then work on them. Don't submit thinly veiled autobiographical stories—it's been done before—and better. With the proliferation of computers, everyone thinks they're a writer. Not true, unfortunately. The plus side though is ease of transmission and layout and the diversity and range of new work."

‡BIBLIOTECH MAGAZINE, (I, II), Crisp Website Network, E-mail: editorial@crispzine.com. Website: http://www.crispzine.com. Editorial Director: Anthony Tedesco. Electronic magazine. "Our award-winning Bibliotech magazine features established fiction and poetry editors volunteering their creative and connective assistance to new 'under 35' writers, as well as multi-genre excerpts, interviews, information and inspiration for—and from—writers of all ages."

Needs: "Although we publish fiction from established writers of all ages, we only publish new writers who are

18-34. No juvenile, young adult or fiction over 1,000 words." Recently published work by Ben Mezrich, Evan Zall and A. Jake Cooney. Publishes 12 new writers/year.

How to Contact: Electronic submissions only. "Save a text-only copy and paste it into an e-mail message—not as an email attachment."

Advice: "Fiction is more difficult to read online so it needs to be short and fast-paced. Make readers laugh, wail or shriek right from the beginning, and keep them careening to the end. First-person caters to the Net's grassroots and community feel. Include suggestions on where to subtly divvy your fiction into 3-or-4 paragraph sections for easier online reading."

BILINGUAL REVIEW, (II, IV), Hispanic Research Center, Arizona State University, Box 872702, Tempe AZ 85287-2702. (602)965-3867. Editor-in-Chief: Gary D. Keller. Scholarly/literary journal of US Hispanic life: poetry, short stories, other prose and short theater. Magazine: 7×10; 96 pages; 55 lb. acid-free paper; coated cover stock. Published 3 times/year. Estab. 1974. Circ. 2,000.

Needs: US Hispanic creative literature. "We accept material in English or Spanish. We publish original work only—no translations." US Hispanic themes only. Receives 50 unsolicited fiction mss/month. Accepts 3 mss/issue; 9 mss/year. Publishes ms an average of 1 year after acceptance. Published work by Ernestina N. Eger, Leo Romero, Connie Porter and Nash Candelaria. Published work of new writers within the last year. Also publishes literary criticism on US Hispanic themes, poetry. Often critiques rejected mss.

How to Contact: Send 2 copies of complete ms with SAE and loose stamps. Reports in 1-2 months. Simultaneous and high-quality photocopied submissions OK. Sample copy for $6. Reviews novels and short story collections.

Payment/Terms: Pays 2 contributor's copies. 30% discount for extras. Acquires all rights (50% of reprint permission fee given to author as matter of policy).

Advice: "We do not publish literature about tourists in Latin America and their perceptions of the 'native culture.' We do not publish fiction about Latin America unless there is a clear tie to the United States (characters, theme, etc.)."

THE BLACK HAMMOCK REVIEW, A Literary Quarterly, (I, II, IV), 2523 NW Sixth St., Apt. 3, Gainesville FL 32609. (352)335-9612. Editor: Edward A. Nagel. Magazine: $8\frac{1}{2} \times 11$; 40 pages; 20 lb. paper; illustrations and photos. "*The Black Hammock Review* is published by Quantum Press, a Florida non-profit cooperative. It was established to publish works which reflect rural motifs, for example, such settings as Oviedo, Geneva, Chuluota and the Black Hammock area in east-central Florida; however, other 'motifs' will be considered." Quarterly. Estab. 1992.

• Note that *The Black Hammock Review* is published co-operatively with memberships required and members share publishing costs. Editor Edward A. Nagel has published a book, *No Entry*, with Four Walls Eight Windows.

Needs: Ethnic/multicultural, experimental, fantasy (artistic), humor/satire, literary, contemporary, psychic/supernatural, regional, "bucolic themes." Receives 10 unsolicited mss/month. Accepts 4 mss/issue; 16 mss/year. Publishes ms 3 months after acceptance. Recently published work by Tito Perdue, Laura Albritton, Linda L. Dunlap, Kenton S. White and James Ploss. Publishes 6 new writers/year. Length: 2,500 words preferred; 1,500 words minimum; 3,500 words maximum. Also publishes literary essays, literary criticism, poetry. Always critiques or comments on returned mss.

How to Contact: Send complete ms with a cover letter. Should include bio (short), list of publications and brief statement of writer's artistic "goals." Reports in 2 weeks. Send SASE for reply, return of ms or a disposable copy of the ms. No simultaneous submissions. Sample copy for $4 and $8\frac{1}{2} \times 11$ SAE.

Payment/Terms: *Charges membership fee: $25 for individual; $50 for 3 writers.* Fee waivers available for first-rate, first-time writers. Each member of the cooperative is assured publication of at least one carefully edited piece each year, subject to editorial approval. Pays $50-75 *for selected works of established authors* on publication for one-time rights. Pays 6 contributor's copies (or membership contribution); additional copies for $2.

Advice: Looks for "work that evokes in the reader's mind a vivid and continuous dream, vivid in that it has density, enough detail and the right detail, fresh with the author, and shows concern for the characters and the eternal verities. And continuous in that there are no distractions such as poor grammar, purple prose, diction shifts, or change in point of view. Short fiction that has a beginning, middle and end, organically speaking. Immerse yourself in the requested genre, format; work the piece over and over until it is 'right' for you, does what you want it to do; read the masters in your genre on a stylistic and technical level. Transmute your emotions into the work—write about what fascinates you, how people think and act; suspend moral and ethical judgment; 'see' as artist and 'write short.' Use John Gardner's *Art of Fiction*."

BLACK ICE, (I, II, IV), Campus Box 494, Boulder CO 80309-0494. (303)492-8947. Publisher: Ronald Sukenick. Magazine: $5\frac{1}{2} \times 8\frac{1}{2}$; 100 pages; glossy cover; photography on cover. "Publishes the most experimental innovative writing being written today for writers, critics, sophisticated readers." Published 3 times/year. Estab. 1984. Circ. 700.

Needs: Experimental, literary, translations. Does not want to see "anything that's not ground-breaking." Receives 50-75 unsolicited mss/month. Accepts approximately 12-15 mss/issue; approximately 40 mss/year. Pub-

lishes ms 2-4 months after acceptance. Published work by Ursula Molinaro, Eurudice, Ricardo Cruz, Diane Glancy. Sometimes critiques rejected mss and recommends other markets.
How to Contact: Send complete manuscript with cover letter. Reports in 3-6 months on queries; 3-6 months on mss. SASE. Simultaneous submissions OK. Sample copy for $7. Fiction guidelines for #10 SAE and 1 first-class stamp.
Payment/Terms: Pays in contributor's copies. Acquires first rights.
Advice: "Expand your 'institutionalized' sense of what a story should be so that you include (open yourself up to) language play, innovative spatial composition, plots that die trying, de-characterizations whipped up in the food processor, themes barely capable of maintaining equilibrium in the midst of end-of-the-century energy crisis/chaos, etc."

BLACK JACK, (IV), Seven Buffaloes Press, Box 249, Big Timber MT 59011. Editor: Art Cuelho. "Main theme: Rural. Publishes material on the American Indian, farm and ranch, American hobo, the common working man, folklore, the Southwest, Okies, Montana, humor, Central California, etc. for people who make their living off the land. The writers write about their roots, experiences and values they receive from the American soil." Annually. Estab. 1973. Circ. 750.
Needs: Literary, contemporary, western, adventure, humor, American Indian, American hobo, and parts of novels and long short stories. "Anything that strikes me as being amateurish, without depth, without craft, I refuse. Actually, I'm not opposed to any kind of writing if the author is genuine and has spent his lifetime dedicated to the written word." Receives approximately 10-15 unsolicited fiction mss/month. Accepts 5-10 mss/year. Length: 3,500-5,000 words (there can be exceptions).
How to Contact: Query for current theme with SASE. Reports in 1 month on queries and mss. Sample copy for $6.75.
Payment/Terms: Pays 1-2 contributor's copies. Acquires first North American serial rights and reserves the right to reprint material in an anthology or future *Black Jack* publications. Rights revert to author after publication.
Advice: "Enthusiasm should be matched with skill as a craftsman. That's not saying that we don't continue to learn, but every writer must have enough command of the language to compete with other proven writers. Save postage by writing first to find out the editor's needs. A small press magazine always has specific needs at any given time. I sometimes accept material from writers that aren't that good at punctuation and grammar but make up for it with life's experience. This is not a highbrow publication; it belongs to the salt-of-the-earth people."

BLACK LACE, (I, IV), BLK Publishing Co., P.O. Box 83912, Los Angeles CA 90083-0912. (310)410-0808. Fax: (310)410-9250. E-mail: newsroom@blk.com. Website: http://www.blk.com. Editor: Alycee Lane. Magazine: 8⅛×10⅞; 48 pages; book stock; color glossy cover; illustrations and photographs. "*Black Lace* is a lifestyle magazine for African-American lesbians. Published quarterly, its content ranges from erotic imagery to political commentary." Estab. 1991.
● Member of COSMEP. The editor would like to see more full-length erotic fiction, politically-focused articles on lesbians and the African-American community as a whole, and nostalgia and humor pieces.
Needs: Ethnic/multicultural, lesbian. "Avoid interracial stories or idealized pornography." Accepts 4 mss/year. Recently published work by Nicole King, Wanda Thompson, Lynn K. Pannell, Sheree Ann Slaughter, Lyn Lifshin, JoJo and Drew Alise Timmens. Publishes short shorts. Also publishes literary essays, literary criticism, poetry.
How to Contact: Query first with clips of published work or send complete ms with a cover letter. Should include bio (3 sentences). Send a disposable copy of ms. No simultaneous submissions. Electronic submissions OK. Sample copy for $7. Fiction guidelines free.
Payment/Terms: Pays 2 contributor's copies. Acquires first North American serial rights and right to anthologize.
Advice: *Black Lace* seeks erotic material of the highest quality. The most important thing is that the work be erotic and that it feature black lesbians or themes. Study the magazine to see what we do and how we do it. Some fiction is very romantic, other is highly sexual. Most articles in *Black Lace* cater to black lesbians between these two extremes."

BLACK RIVER REVIEW, (II), 855 Mildred Ave., Lorain OH 44052. (216)244-9654. E-mail: brr@freenet.lorain.oberlin.edu. Editors: Deborah Glaefke Gilbert and Kaye Coller. Fiction Editor: Jack Smith. Magazine: 8½×11; 60 pages; glossy cover stock; b&w drawings. "Contemporary writing and contemporary American culture; poetry, book reviews, essays on contemporary literature, short stories." Annually. Estab. 1985. Circ. 400.
Needs: Contemporary, experimental, humor/satire and literary. No "erotica for its own sake, stories directed toward a juvenile audience." Accepts up to 5 mss/year. Does not read mss May 1 through December 31. Publishes ms no later than July of current year. Published work by David Shields, Jeanne M. Leiby and Louis Gallo. Length: up to 3,500 words but will consider up to 4,000 maximum. Publishes short shorts. Also publishes literary essays, literary criticism, poetry. Sometimes critiques rejected mss.
How to Contact: Reports on mss no later than August. SASE. "Will consider simultaneous submissions, but submissions may not be withdrawn after May 1." Sample copy for $3.50 plus $1.50 shipping and handling for back issue; $4 plus $1.50 for current issue. Fiction guidelines for #10 SASE. Reviews novels and short story collections.
Payment/Terms: Pays in contributor's copies. Acquires one-time rights.

Advice: "Since it is so difficult to break in, much of the new writer's creative effort is spent trying to match trends in popular fiction, in the case of the slicks, or adapting to narrow themes ('Gay and Lesbian,' 'Vietnam War,' 'Women's Issues,' etc.) of little and literary journals. An unfortunate result, from the reader's standpoint, is that each story within a given category comes out sounding like all the rest. Among positive developments of the proliferation of small presses is the opportunity for writers to decide what to write and how to write it. My advice is to support a little magazine that is both open to new writers and prints fiction you like. 'Support' doesn't necessarily mean 'buy all the back issues,' but, rather, direct involvement between contributor, magazine and reader needed to rebuild the sort of audience that was there for writers like Fitzgerald and Hemingway."

BLACK WARRIOR REVIEW, (I, II), Box 862936, Tuscaloosa AL 35486-0027. (205)348-4518. Website: http://www.sa.ua.edu/osm/bwr (includes writer's guidelines, names of editors, short fiction). Editor-in-Chief: Christopher Chambers. Fiction Editor: Ariana-Sophia Kartsonis. Magazine: 6×9; 170 pages; illustrations and photos occasionally. "We publish contemporary fiction, poetry, reviews, essays, photography and interviews for a literary audience." Semiannually. Estab. 1974. Circ. 2,000.
● Work that appeared in the *Black Warrior Review* has been included in the *Pushcart Prize* anthology, *Best American Short Stories*, *Best American Poetry* and in *New Short Stories from the South*.
Needs: Contemporary, literary, short and short-short fiction. No genre fiction please. Receives 200 unsolicited fiction mss/month. Accepts 5 mss/issue, 10 mss/year. Approximately 15% of fiction is agented. Recently published work by James Tate, Pamela Ryder and Janet Burroway. Publishes 5 new writers/year. Length: 7,500 words maximum; 2,000-5,000 words average. Also publishes essays, poetry. Occasionally critiques rejected mss. Unsolicited novel excerpts are not considered unless the novel is already contracted for publication.
How to Contact: Send complete ms with SASE (1 story per submission). Simultaneous submissions OK. Reports in 1-4 months. Publishes ms 2-5 months after acceptance. Sample copy for $8. Fiction guidelines for SASE. Reviews novels and short story collections.
Payment/Terms: Pays up to $100 per story and 2 contributor's copies. Pays on publication.
Advice: "Become familiar with the magazine prior to submission. We're increasingly interested in considering good experimental writing and in reading short-short fiction. We read year round."

THE BLACKSTONE CIRCULAR, (II), 26 James St., Suite B-8, Toms River NJ 08753. Editor: Linda Rogers. Magazine: 8½×11; 12-20 pages; copy paper; corner stapled. "Fiction and nonfiction for all interested readers; including gay and lesbian." Monthly. Estab. 1995.
Needs: No juvenile, young adult, psychic/supernatural/occult, erotica. Publishes yearly anthology. Accepts up to 10 mss/issue. Recently published work by Timothy Hodor, Roy Pickering, Jr., Eric Maxim Henning and Catarina Lindstrom. Length: 10 words minimum; 3,000 words maximum. Publishes literary essays and poetry. Often comments on rejected ms.
How to Contact: Send complete ms with a cover letter. Reports on mss in 2 months. Simultaneous, reprint submissions OK. Sample copy for $2. Make check payable to Linda Rogers.
Payment/Terms: Pays 1 contributor's copy. Acquires one-time rights.
Advice: "Strive for universality and write for yourself."

BLUE MESA REVIEW, (I, IV), Creative Writing Program, University of New Mexico, Dept. of English, Albuquerque NM 87131. (505)277-6347. Fax: (505)277-5573. E-mail: bluemesa@unm.edu. Website: http://www. unm.edu/~english/bluemesa/BLUEMESA.HTM (includes writer's guidelines, names of editors, short fiction). Editor: David Johnson. Magazine: 6×9; 300 pages; 55 lb. paper; 10 pt CS1; photos. "*Blue Mesa Review* publishes the best/most current creative writing on the market." Annually. Estab. 1989. Circ. 1,200.
Needs: Adventure, ethnic/multicultural, experimental, feminist, gay, historical, humor/satire, lesbian, literary, mainstream/contemporary, regional, westerns. Contact for list of upcoming themes. Receives 300 unsolicited mss/year. Accepts 100 mss/year. Accepts mss May-September; reads mss November-December; responds in January. Publishes ms 5-6 months after acceptance. Published work by Kathleen Spivack, Roberta Swann and Tony Mares. Publishes short shorts. Also publishes literary essays, poetry.
How to Contact: Send 2 copies of complete ms with a cover letter. Send SASE for reply. Sample copy for $12. Reviews novels, short story collections, poetry and nonfiction.
Payment/Terms: Pays 2 contributor's copies for one-time rights.
Advice: "Get to the point—fast. A short story does not allow for lengthy intros and descriptions. Take a class and get the teacher to edit you! Now that we are using themes, we would like to see theme-related stories. Avoid thought pieces on 'vacations to our enchanting state.' "

THE BLUE MOON REVIEW, (II), P.O. Box 48, Ivy VA 22945-0045. E-mail: editor@thebluemoon.com; fiction@thebluemoon.com. Website: http://www.TheBlueMoon.com. Editor: Doug Lawson. Electronic magazine: Illustrations and photos. Quarterly. Estab. 1994. Circ. 16,000.
Needs: Experimental, feminist, gay, lesbian, literary, mainstream/contemporary, regional, translations. No genre fiction. Receives 40-70 unsolicited mss/month. Accepts 7-10 mss/issue; 28-40 mss/year. Publishes ms up to 9 months after acceptance. Published work by Edward Falco, Deborah Eisenberg, Robert Sward and Eva Shaderow-fsky. Length: open. Publishes short shorts. Also publishes literary essays, literary criticism, poetry. Sometimes critiques or comments on rejected mss.

How to Contact: Send complete ms with a cover letter. Include a brief bio, list of publications and e-mail address if available. Reports in 1-3 months on mss. Send SASE for reply, return of ms or send a disposable copy of ms. Simultaneous and electronic submissions OK. Sample copy and fiction guidelines available at above website. Reviews novels and short story collections.

Payment/Terms: Offers prizes for fiction and poetry. Acquires first electronic rights. Rights revert to author upon request.

Advice: "We look for strong use of language or strong characterization. Manuscripts stand out by their ability to engage a reader on an intellectual or emotional level. Present characters with depth regardless of age and introduce intelligent concepts that have resonance and relevance. We recommend our writers be electronically connected to the Internet."

‡**THE BLUE SKUNK COMPANION, (I, IV)**, The Blue Skunk Society Inc., P.O. Box 8400, MSU 59, Mankato MN 56002-8400. (507)625-7176. Editor: Scott Welvaert. Fiction Editor: Jim Redmond. Magazine: 8×11; 35-45 pages; illustrations and photographs. "We publish fiction, poetry, nonfiction and essays that are inspired by life, not by classic literature, periods or styles. We intend to reach readers that wish to be entertained and moved no matter their age, race or culture." Semiannually. Estab. 1997. Circ. 100-500.
  • *The Blue Skunk Companion* pnly accepts mss from authors who live in Minnesota or who have lived in the state at one time.

Needs: Adventure, condensed/excerpted novel, ethnic/multicultural, experimental, fantasy (contemporary), historical (general), horror, humor/satire, literary, mainstream/contemporary, mystery/suspense (contemporary), psychic/supernatural/occult, regional, romance (contemporary), science fiction (contemporary), translations. "We do not want fiction/prose that falls into clichés." Receives 1-2 unsolicited mss/month. Accepts 5-7 mss/issue; 10-14 mss/year. Publishes ms 4-6 months after acceptance. Recently published work by Roger Sheffer, Brian Batt, Samuel Dollar and Kevin Langton. Length: 1,000-4,000 words average; 1,000 words minimum; 7,000 words maximum. Also publishes literary essays, literary criticism, poetry. Often critiques or comments on rejected mss.

How to Contact: Send complete ms with a cover letter. Include estimated word count, ½-1-page bio and list of publications. Reports in 1 month on queries; 2-3 months on mss. SASE. Simultaneous submissions OK. Sample copy for $3 and 9×12 SAE with 6 first-class stamps. Fiction guidelines for 4×12 SASE. Reviews novels and short story collections.

Payment/Terms: Pays free subscription to the magazine; additional copies for $3. Pays on publication. Acquires first rights. Not copyrighted.

Advice: "We look for a voice that sounds like a 'person' and not like a 'writer.' Good use of language as function, taste and art; not a boastful vocabulary. Try to avoid genre until you have a good grasp of mainstream and contemporary prose. Once that has been achieved, then your genre fiction will be much better. Always be fresh with ideas and themes. We feel that good fiction/prose can be found on the back shelves of bookstores and not on the bestsellers list."

BLUELINE, (II, IV), English Dept., SUNY, Potsdam NY 13676. (315)267-2000. E-mail: tylerao@potsdam.edu. Editor: Tony Tyler. Magazine: 6×9; 112 pages; 70 lb. white stock paper; 65 lb. smooth cover stock; illustrations; photos. "*Blueline* is interested in quality writing about the Adirondacks or other places similar in geography and spirit. We publish fiction, poetry, personal essays, book reviews and oral history for those interested in the Adirondacks, nature in general, and well-crafted writing." Annually. Estab. 1979. Circ. 400.

Needs: Adventure, contemporary, humor/satire, literary, prose poem, regional, reminiscences, oral history, nature/outdoors. Receives 8-10 unsolicited fiction mss/month. Accepts 6-8 mss/issue. Does not read January through August. Publishes ms 3-6 months after acceptance. Published fiction by Jeffrey Clapp. Published new writers within the last year. Length: 500 words minimum; 3,000 words maximum; 2,500 words average. Also publishes literary essays, poetry. Occasionally critiques rejected mss.

How to Contact: Send complete ms with SASE, word count and brief bio. Submit mss August through November 30. Reports in 2-10 weeks. Sample copy for $3.50. Fiction guidelines for 5×10 SASE.

Payment/Terms: Pays 1 contributor's copy for first rights. Charges $3 each for 3 or more extra copies.

Advice: "We look for concise, clear, concrete prose that tells a story and touches upon a universal theme or situation. We prefer realism to romanticism but will consider nostalgia if well done. Pay attention to grammar and syntax. Avoid murky language, sentimentality, cuteness or folksiness. We would like to see more good fiction related to the Adirondacks. If manuscript has potential, we work with author to improve and reconsider for publication. Our readers prefer fiction to poetry (in general) or reviews. Write from your own experience, be specific and factual (within the bounds of your story) and if you write about universal features such as love,

---

CHECK THE CATEGORY INDEXES, located at the back of the book, for publishers interested in specific fiction subjects.

death, change, etc., write about them in a fresh way. Triteness and mediocrity are the hallmarks of the majority of stories seen today."

BOGG, A Magazine of British & North American Writing, (II), Bogg Publications, 422 N. Cleveland St., Arlington VA 22201. (703)243-6019. U.S. Editor: John Elsberg. Magazine: 6×9; 64-68 pages; 70 lb. white paper; 70 lb. cover stock; line illustrations. "American and British poetry, prose poems, experimental short 'fictions,' reviews, and essays on small press." Published triannually. Estab. 1968. Circ. 850.
● The editors at *Bogg* are most interested in short, wry or semi-surreal fiction.
Needs: Very short experimental fiction and prose poems. "We are always looking for work with British/Commonwealth themes and/or references." Receives 25 unsolicited fiction mss/month. Accepts 1-2 mss/issue; 3-6 mss/year. Publishes ms 3-18 months after acceptance. Recently published work by Nigel Hinshelwood. Published 50% new writers within the last year. Length: 300 words maximum. Also publishes literary essays, literary criticism, poetry. Occasionally critiques rejected mss.
How to Contact: Query first or send ms (2-6 pieces) with SASE. Reports in 1 week on queries; 2 weeks on mss. Sample copy for $3.50 or $4.50 (current issue). Reviews novels and short story collections.
Payment/Terms: Pays 2 contributor's copies; reduced charge for extras. Acquires one-time rights.
Advice: "Read magazine first. We are most interested in prose work of experimental or wry nature to supplement poetry, and are always looking for innovative/imaginative uses of British themes and references."

BONE & FLESH, (II), Bone & Flesh Publications, P.O. Box 349, Concord NH 03302-0349. Phone/fax: (603)225-0521. Fiction Editor: Lester Hirsh. Magazine: 8×11; 50 pages; quality paper and cover stock; illustrations. "*Bone & Flesh* publishes diverse prose, poetry and art for an independent, progressive literate audience. We are the longest-lived literary magazine in northern New England." Semiannually. Estab. 1988. Circ. 500. Member CLMP.
● Bone & Flesh is not currently accepting submissions for 1998.
Needs: Experimental, literary. Receives 20 unsolicited mss/month. Accepts 4-6 mss/issue; 6-10 mss/year. Does not read mss June through January. Publishes mss up to one year after acceptance. Published work by Rebecca Rule, Albert Russo and Susan Bartlett. Length: 2,100 words average; 50 words minimum; 2,600 words maximum. Publishes short shorts. Also publishes literary essays, literary criticism, poetry. Often critiques or comments on rejected mss.
How to Contact: Send complete ms with a cover letter. Include estimated word count and bio with submission. Reports in 3 months on mss. SASE for reply. Reprint submissions OK. Sample copy for $7. Fiction guidelines free.
Payment/Terms: Pays free subscription to the magazine and 2 contributor's copies; additional copies 50% off cover price. Acquires first North American serial rights.
Advice: "Excellent use of language is our only criteria. Read a sample copy and follow guidelines closely."

BOOKLOVERS, (I, II), Jammer Publications, P.O. Box 93485, Milwaukee WI 53203-0485. (414)541-7510. E-mail: rjammer@omnifest.uwm.edu. Editor: Jill Lindberg. Magazine: 8½×11; 32 pages; high-grade newsprint paper; photos. "*BookLovers* is a literary magazine aimed at avid readers and writers. Includes book reviews, author interviews, book lists, features on unique book stores and profiles of book discussion groups." Quarterly. Estab. 1992. Circ. 800.
Needs: Adventure, ethnic/multicultural, fantasy (children's), historical, humor/satire, literary, mainstream/contemporary, mystery/suspense (amateursleuth, cozy, police procedural), regional, romance (gothic, historical), serialized novel, sports, young adult/teen (adventure, mystery, science fiction). List of upcoming themes available for SASE. Receives 10 unsolicited mss/month. Buys 3-4 mss/issue; 10-12 mss/year. Publishes ms 6 months after acceptance. Published work by Shirley Mudrick, Lois Schmidt and Jane Farrell. Length: 800-1,000 words average; 500 words minimum; 1,500 words maximum. Also publishes literary essays, literary criticism, poetry.
How to Contact: Send complete ms with a cover letter. Should include estimated word count and bio (200 words maximum). Reports in 2-3 months. Send SASE for reply, return of ms or send a disposable copy of ms. Simultaneous, reprint, electronic (Macintosh only) submissions OK. Sample copy for 9×12 SAE and 5 first-class stamps. Fiction guidelines for #10 SASE.
Payment/Terms: Pays 2-5 contributor's copies. Acquires one-time rights.
Advice: Looking for "unique story line, good grammar, syntax (very important), interesting literature-related articles and book reviews, articles written in succinct manner."

‡BOOKPRESS, The Newspaper of the Literary Arts, (II), The Bookery, 215 N. Cayuga St., Ithaca NY 14850. (607)277-2254. E-mail: clsb@hotmail.com. Editor: Cara Ben-Yaacov. Newspaper: 16 pages; newsprint; Illustrations and photos. Contains book reviews, analysis, fiction and excerpts from published work. Monthly. Estab. 1991. Circ. 20,000.
Needs: Condensed/excerpted novel, feminist, gay, historical, lesbian, literary, regional. No new age. Publishes special fiction issues or anthologies. Receives 3 unsolicited mss/month. Accepts 0-2 mss/issue. Does not read during the summer. Publishes ms 1-3 months after acceptance. Recently published work by Paul Cody, Paul West, Dianne Ackerman, Philip Berrigan and Fred Wilcox. Length: 2,000 words average; 4,000 words maximum. Also publishes literary essays, literary criticism and poetry.

How to Contact: Send complete ms with a cover letter. Include 3-sentence bio. Reports in 1 month on mss. Send SASE for return of ms. Simultaneous submissions OK. Sample copy and guidelines free. Reviews novels or short story collections. Send books to editor.
Payment/Terms: Pays free subscription to newspaper.
Advice: "Send a brief, concise cover letter. No overwriting or overly cerebral academic work. The author's genuine interest and passion for the topic makes for good work."

BOSTON LITERARY REVIEW (BLUR), (I, II), P.O. Box 357, West Somerville MA 02144. (617)666-3080. E-mail: bostonreview@mit.edu. Website: http://www-polisci.mit.edu (includes names of editors, short fiction, back issues going back five years, an interactive form for debate and complete contents of each issue). Editor: Gloria Mindock. Magazine: 24-30 pages. "*Boston Review* is a bimonthly magazine of cultural and political analysis, reviews, fiction and poetry. The editors are committed to a society and culture that foster human diversity and a democracy in which we seek common grounds of principle amidst our many differences. In the hope of advancing these ideals, the *Review* acts as a forum that seeks to enrich the language of public debate." Estab. 1985. Circ. 500.
Needs: Condensed/excerpted novel, experimental, literary, mainstream/contemporary, translations. "We are open to all styles of fiction but especially interested in work that is experimental or takes risks." Receives 100 unsolicited mss/month. Accepts 2 mss/issue; 4 mss/year. Publishes ms 1 year after acceptance. Recently published work by Kiki Delancey, Anndee Huchman, Harry Mathews, Michael Hawley and W.D. Wetherell. Length: 1,500 words average; 2,000 words maximum. Publishes short shorts. Also publishes poetry. Often critiques or comments on rejected mss.
How to Contact: Send complete ms with a cover letter. Include estimated word count, paragraph bio and list of publications. Reports in 1 month on queries; 6 weeks on mss. Send SASE for reply, return of ms or send a disposable copy of ms. Sample copy for $4.
Payment/Terms: Pays 2 contributor's copies. Acquires all rights. Sends galleys to author.
Advice: Looking for "neatness and fiction that takes risks. Send your work out and don't let any rejections stop you. I'm looking for stories that are emotionally and intellectually substantive and also interesting on the level of language. Things that are shocking, dark, lewd, comic, or even insane are fine so long as the fiction is controlled and purposeful in a masterful way."

BOTTOMFISH MAGAZINE, (II), De Anza College, 21250 Stevens Creek Blvd., Cupertino CA 95014. (408)864-8623. Website: http://laws.atc.fhda.edu/documents/bottomfish/bottomfish.html. Editor-in-Chief: David Denny. Magazine: 7×8½; 80-100 pages; White Bristol vellum cover; b&w high contrast illustrations and photos. "Contemporary poetry, fiction, creative nonfiction, b&w graphics and photos." Annually. Estab. 1976. Circ. 500.
Needs: "Literary excellence is our only criteria. We will consider all subjects." Receives 50-100 unsolicited fiction mss/month. Accepts 5-6 mss/issue. Published work by Keith Dawson, Steven Carter and Sarah Hendon. Length: 500 words minimum; 5,000 words maximum; 2,500 words average.
How to Contact: Reads mss September through February. Submission deadline: February 1; publication date: end of March. Submit 1 short story or up to 3 short shorts with cover letter, brief bio and SASE. No reprints. Reports in 3-4 months. Publishes mss an average of 6 months to 1 year after acceptance. Sample copy for $5.
Payment/Terms: Pays 2 contributor's copies. Acquires one-time rights.
Advice: "Strive for originality and high level of craft; avoid clichéd or stereotyped characters and plots."

BOUILLABAISSE, (I, IV), Alpha Beat Press, 31 Waterloo St., New Hope PA 18938. (215)862-0299. Editor: Dave Christy. Magazine: 11×17; 120 pages; bond paper; illustrations and photos. Publishes Beat Generation, post-Beat independent and other modern writings. Semiannually. Estab. 1986. Circ. 600.
● Work included in *Bouillabaisse* has been selected for inclusion in the *Pushcart Prize* anthology.
Needs: Beat generation and modern sub-cultures: adventure, condensed/excerpted novel, erotica, literary. Receives 15 unsolicited mss/month. Accepts 2 mss/issue; 4 mss/year. Publishes ms 6 months after acceptance. Recently published work by A.D. Winans, Ted Joans, Charles Plymell and Daniel Crocker. Length: no limit. Publishes short shorts. Also publishes literary essays, literary criticism, poetry. Sometimes critiques or comments on rejected mss.
How to Contact: Query first. Include bio with submission. Reports in 1 week. Send SASE for reply or return of ms. Simultaneous submissions OK. Sample copy for $10. Reviews novels and short story collections.
Payment/Terms: Pays 1 contributor's copy.
Advice: "Read a sample before submitting."

BOULEVARD, (II), Opojaz Inc., 4579 Laclede Ave. #332, St. Louis MO 63108-2103. (314)361-2986. Editor: Richard Burgin. Magazine: 5½×8½; 150-225 pages; excellent paper; high-quality cover stock; illustrations; photos. "*Boulevard* aspires to publish the best contemporary fiction, poetry and essays we can print. While we frequently publish writers with previous credits, we are very interested in publishing less experienced or unpublished writers with exceptional promise." Published 3 times/year. Estab. 1986. Circ. about 3,000.
Needs: Contemporary, experimental, literary. Does not want to see "anything whose first purpose is not literary." Receives over 400 mss/month. Accepts about 8 mss/issue. Does not accept manuscripts between April 1 and October 1. Publishes ms less than 1 year after acceptance. Agented fiction ⅓-¼. Length: 5,000 words average;

8,000 words maximum. Publishes short shorts. Recently published work by Stephen Dixon, Elizabeth Searle, John Griesemer and Alice Hoffman. Publishes 10 new writers/year. Also publishes literary essays, literary criticism, poetry. Sometimes critiques rejected mss and recommends other markets.

How to Contact: Send complete ms with cover letter. Reports in 2 weeks on queries; 3 months on mss. SASE for reply. Simultaneous submissions OK. Sample copy for $8 and SAE with 5 first-class stamps.

Payment/Terms: Pays $50-150; contributor's copies; charges for extras. Acquires first North American serial rights. Does not send galleys to author unless requested.

Advice: "We are open to different styles of imaginative and critical work and are mindful of Nabokov's dictum 'There is only one school, the school of talent.' Above all, when we consider the very diverse manuscripts submitted to us for publication, we value original sensibility, writing that causes the reader to experience a part of life in a new way. Originality, to us, has little to do with a writer intently trying to make each line or sentence odd, bizarre, or eccentric, merely for the sake of being 'different.' Rather, originality is the result of the character or vision of the writer; the writer's singular outlook and voice as it shines through in the totality of his or her work."

THE BRIAR CLIFF REVIEW, (II), Briar Cliff College, 3303 Rebecca St., Sioux City IA 51104-2100. (712)279-1651 or 279-5321. Fax: (712) 279-5410. E-mail: currans@briar-cliff.edu. Editors: Tricia Currans-Sheehan and Jeanne Emmons. Magazine: 8½×11; 64 pages; 70 lb. matte paper; 10 Pt CIS cover stock; illustrations and photos. "*The Briar Cliff Review* is an eclectic literary and cultural magazine focusing on (but not limited to) Siouxland writers and subjects. We are happy to proclaim ourselves a regional publication. It doesn't diminish us; it enhances us." Annually. Estab. 1989. Circ. 500.
  • *The Briar Cliff Review* has received The Gold Crown and Silver Crown awards from the Columbia Scholastic Press Association and the National Pacemaker Award from the Associated Collegiate Press.

Needs: Ethnic/multicultural, feminist, historical, horror, humor/satire, literary, mainstream/contemporary, regional. No romance, mystery or alien stories. Accepts 5 mss/year. Reads mss only between August 1 and November 1. Publishes ms 3-4 months after acceptance. Recently published work by Dale Evans, Alan Elyshevitz and Thomas McLean. Publishes 10-12 new writers/year. Length: 3,000 words average; 2,500 words minimum; 3,500 words maximum. Also publishes literary essays, literary criticism and poetry. Sometimes critiques or comments on rejected mss.

How to Contact: Send complete ms with a cover letter. Include estimated word count, bio and list of publications. Reports in 3-4 months on mss. Send a SASE for return of ms. Electronic submissions (disk) OK. No simultaneous submissions. Sample copy for $6 and 9×12 SAE. Fiction guidelines free for #10 SASE. Reviews novels and short story collections.

Payment/Terms: Pays 2 contributor's copies for first rights; additional copies available for $3.

Advice: "Send us your best."

‡THE BRIDGE, A Journal of Fiction & Poetry, (II), 14050 Vernon St., Oak Park MI 48237. Editor: Jack Zucker. Fiction Editor: Helen Zucker. Magazine: 160 pages; matte cover. Semiannually. Estab. 1990.
  • *The Bridge* has received grants from CLMP and Michigan Council of the Arts.

Needs: No serious, realistic. Publishes ms 12-18 months after acceptance. Length: 5,000-10,000 words average. Publishes short shorts. Also publishes literary essays, literary criticism, poetry.

How to Contact: Send complete ms with a cover letter. Reports in 4-5 months. SASE for reply, return of ms or send a disposable copy of ms. Simultaneous submissions OK. Sample copy for $7. Fiction guidelines for #10 SASE. Reviews novels and short story collections.

Payment/Terms: Pays 2 contributor's copies; additional copies for $7. Acquires first rights.

‡BRILLIANT CORNERS, A Journal of Jazz & Literature, (II), Lycoming College, Williamsport PA 17701. (717)321-4279. Fax: (717)321-4090. E-mail: feinstei@lycoming.edu. Editor: Sascha Feinstein. Journal: 6×9; 100 pages; 70 lb. Cougar opaque, vellum, natural paper; photographs. "We publish jazz-related literature—fiction, poetry and nonfiction." Semiannually. Estab. 1996. Circ. 500.

Needs: Condensed/excerpted novel, ethnic/multicultural, experimental, literary, mainstream/contemporary, romance (contemporary). Receives 10-15 unsolicited mss/month. Accepts 1-2 mss/issue; 2-3 mss/year. Does not read mss May 15-September 1. Publishes ms 4-12 months after acceptance. Very little agented fiction. Publishes short shorts. Also publishes literary essays, literary criticism and poetry. Often critiques or comments on rejected mss.

How to Contact: Send complete ms with a cover letter. Include 1-paragraph bio and list of publications. Reports in 2 weeks on queries; 1-2 months on mss. SASE for return of ms or send a disposable copy of ms. "Rarely accepts previously published work, and only by very established writers." Sample copy for $7. Reviews novels and short story collections. Send books to editor.

Payment/Terms: Pays $10-25 on publication and 2 contributor's copies. Acquires first North American serial rights. Sends galleys to author when possible.

Advice: "We look for clear, moving prose that demonstrates a love of both writing and jazz. We primarily publish established writers, but we read all submissions carefully and welcome work by outstanding young writers."

THE BROWNSTONE REVIEW, (II), 335 Court St., Suite 114, Brooklyn NY 11231. Website: http://www.quic klink.com/~dawson (includes guidelines, excerpts, masthead, special features). Fiction Editor: Laura Dawson. Magazine: 5½×8½; 60 pages. "We publish any and all types of fiction, so long as the work is of highest quality. Our audience is primarily literary and expects a regular supply of excellent fiction." Semiannually. Estab. 1995. Circ. 250.

Needs: Adventure, erotica, ethnic/multicultural, experimental, feminist, gay, historical, horror, humor/satire, lesbian, literary, mainstream/contemporary, mystery/suspense, regional, science fiction, senior citizen/retirement, sports, westerns. No romance, religious, children's stories or occult/gothic horror. Planning future special fiction issue or anthology. Receives 50 unsolicited mss/month. Accepts 3-6 mss/issue; 6-12 mss/year. Publishes ms 6-9 months after acceptance. Recently published work by Susan Thomas, Dan Hedges, Laura Maffei, Tom Whalen and Hilary Plattner. Length: 1,000-2,000 words average; 250 words minimum; 10,000 words maximum. Publishes short shorts. Also publishes poetry. Sometimes critiques or comments on rejected ms.

How to Contact: Send complete ms with a cover letter. Should include list of publications. Reports in 3 months. Send SASE for reply, return of ms or send a disposable copy of ms. Simultaneous submissions OK.

Payment/Terms: Pays 2 contributor's copies. Acquires first North American serial rights.

Advice: "Strong characters, natural (not expository) dialogue, a non-didactic tone, and a plot that reveals human nature in a way that doesn't clobber the reader over the head—these are qualities we look for in submissions. Avoid workshops and writing by committee. Read voraciously. Revise, revise, revise. We appreciate the drive towards multiple submissions, so long as writers are courteous about letting us know when a piece has been accepted elsewhere."

BURNT ALUMINUM, (II), P.O. Box 3561, Mankato MN 56001. Editors: Ben Hiltner and Sam Dollar. Magazine: 8½×7; 60 pages. "*Burnt Aluminum* is a mainstream fiction magazine. We prefer realistic themes." Semiannually. Estab. 1995. Circ. 150.

Needs: Condensed/excerpted novel, literary, mainstream/contemporary. No horror, mystery or science fiction. Receives 10 unsolicited mss/month. Accepts 6-8 mss/issue; 12-16 mss/year. Publishes ms 6 months after acceptance. Published work by Mike Magnuson and R.J. Bledsoe. No preferred length.

How to Contact: Send complete ms with a cover letter. Include one-paragraph bio and list of publications with submission. Send SASE for reply, return of ms or send a disposable copy of ms. Simultaneous submissions OK. Sample copy for $4 and $1.50 postage.

Payment/Terms: Pays 2 contributor's copies. Acquires first North American serial rights.

Advice: "We prefer stories with strong characters and strong character development. Plot is secondary. We also prefer realistic fiction—like Ray Carver's or Richard Ford's—stories representative of life in today's world. We do not like anything related to fantasy or horror or trivial writing."

BUTTON, New England's Tiniest Magazine of Poetry, Fiction & Gracious Living, (II), P.O. Box 26, Lunenburg MA 01462. E-mail: symboline@juno.com. Editor: S. Cragin. Fiction Editor: Adena Dawes. Magazine: 4×5; 34 pages; bond paper; color cardstock cover; illustrations; photos. Semiannually. Estab. 1993. Circ. 1,500.

Needs: Literary. No genre fiction. Receives 20-40 unsolicited mss/month. Accepts 1-2 mss/issue; 3-5 mss/year. Publishes ms 3-9 months after acceptance. Published work by Sven Birkerts, Stephen McCauley, Wayne Wilson, Romayne Dawney and Lawrence Millman. Length: 500-2,500 words. Also publishes literary essays, poetry. Sometimes critiques or comments on rejected mss "if it shows promise."

How to Contact: Request guidelines. Send ms with bio, list of publications and advise how you found magazine. Reports in 1 month on queries; 2-4 months on mss. SASE. Sample copy for $2. Fiction guidelines for SASE. Reviews novels and short story collections. Send book to editor.

Payment/Terms: Pays honorarium and multiple free subscriptions to the magazine on publication. Acquires first North American serial rights. Sends galleys to author if there are editorial changes.

Advice: "What makes a manuscript stand out? Flannery O'Connor once said, 'Don't get subtle till the fourth page,' and I agree. We publish fiction in the 1,000-3,000 word category, and look for interesting, sympathetic, believable characters and careful setting. I'm really tired of stories that start strong and then devolve into dialogue uninterrupted by further exposition. Also, no stories from a mad person's POV unless it's really tricky and skillful. Advice to prospective writers: continue to read at least ten times as much as you write. Read the best, and read intelligent criticism if you can find it. Find the good authors—Austen, Chekhov, Pym, Ralph Lombreglia and Ruth Rendell—and reread the work. Current trends include the 'My Sordid Upbringing' school of memoir, dreary 'survivor' stories, and 'experimental fiction' which I—personally—find relentlessly turgid and dull, not to mention exasperating to read as one flips pages madly looking for a period, or at least a semicolon. (Gertrude Stein, though a saint, has a lot to answer for!) Too many writing programs are rubber-stamping fee-paying applicants who would never think to use a thesaurus for a more interesting word, or aren't willing to work to create an entire world versus a narrow point-of-view."

BYLINE, (I, II), Box 130596, Edmond OK 73013-0001. (405)348-5591. Website: http://www.bylinemag.com. Editor-in-Chief: Marcia Preston. Managing Editor: Kathryn Fanning. Monthly magazine "aimed at encouraging and motivating all writers toward success, with special information to help new writers." Estab. 1981.

Needs: Literary, genre, general fiction. Receives 100-200 unsolicited fiction mss/month. Accepts 1 ms/issue; 11 mss/year. Published work by Susan McKeague Karnes and Michael Bugeja. Published many new writers

within the last year. Length: 4,000 words maximum; 2,000 words minimum. Also publishes poetry.
How to Contact: Send complete ms with SASE. Simultaneous submissions OK, "if notified. For us, no cover letter is needed." Reports in 6-12 weeks. Publishes ms an average of 3 months after acceptance. Sample copy, guidelines and contest list for $4.
Payment/Terms: Pays $100 on acceptance and 2 contributor's copies for first North American rights.
Advice: "We're very open to new writers. Submit a well-written, professionally prepared ms with SASE. No erotica or senseless violence; otherwise, we'll consider most any theme. We also sponsor short story and poetry contests."

CALLALOO, A Journal of African-American and African Arts and Letters, (I, II, IV), Dept. of English, 322 Bryan Hall, University of Virginia, Charlottesville VA 22903. (804)924-6637. Fax: (804)924-6472. E-mail: callaloo@virginia.edu. Editor: Charles H. Rowell. Magazine: 7×10; 250 pages. Scholarly magazine. Quarterly. Plans special fiction issue in future. Estab. 1976. Circ. 1,500.
● One of the leading voices in African-American literature, *Callaloo* has received NEA literature grants. Work published in *Callaloo* received a 1994 *Pushcart Prize* anthology nomination and inclusion in *Best American Short Stories*.
Needs: Contemporary, ethnic (black culture), feminist, historical, humor/satire, literary, prose poem, regional, science fiction, serialized/excerpted novel, translations. Also publishes poetry and drama. Themes for 1996: Australian Aboriginal Literature; Dominican Arts and Letters. Accepts 3-5 mss/issue; 10-20 mss/year. Length: no restrictions. Published work by Chinua Achebe, Rita Dove, Reginald McKnight, Caryl Philips and John Edgar Wideman.
How to Contact: Submit complete ms in triplicate and cover letter with name, mailing address, e-mail address, if possible, and SASE. Reports on queries in 2 weeks; 3-4 months on mss. Previously published work accepted "occasionally." Sample copy for $8.
Payment/Terms: Pays in contributor's copies. Acquires all rights. Sends galleys to author.
Advice: "We strongly recommend looking at the journal before submitting."

CALYX, A Journal of Art & Literature by Women, (II), Calyx, Inc., P.O. Box B, Corvallis OR 97339. (541)753-9384. Fax: (541)753-0515. E-mail: calyx@proaxis.com. Managing Editor: Margarita Donnelly. Editorial Coordinator: Beverly McFarland. Editors: Teri Mae Rutledge, Linda Varsell Smith, Micki Reaman, Lois Cranston, Dorothy Mack and Yolanda Calvillo. Magazine: 7×8; 128 pages per single issue; 60 lb. coated matte stock paper; 10 pt. chrome coat cover; original art. Publishes prose, poetry, art, essays, interviews and critical and review articles. "*Calyx* exists to publish women's literary and artistic work and is committed to publishing the work of all women, including women of color, older women, working class women, and other voices that need to be heard. We are committed to nurturing beginning writers." Biannually. Estab. 1976. Circ. 6,000.
● *Calyx* received the Oregon Governor's Arts Award and the Bumhershoot Best Journal Award in 1996.
Needs: Receives approximately 1,000 unsolicited prose and poetry mss when open. Accepts 4-8 prose mss/issue, 9-15 mss/year. Reads mss March 1-April 15 and October 1-November 15; submit only during these periods. Recently published work by Rita Marie Nibasa, Marcia T. Jones, Che Rodriguez, Susan Vreeland and Beth Brant. Publishes 10-20 new writers/year. Length: 5,000 words maximum. Also publishes literary essays, literary criticism, poetry.
How to Contact: Send ms with SASE and bio. Simultaneous submissions OK. Reports in up to 8 months on mss. Publishes ms an average of 8 months after acceptance. Sample copy for $9.50 plus $2 postage. Guidelines available for SASE. Reviews novels, short story collections, poetry and essays.
Payment/Terms: "Combination of payment, free issues and 1 volume subscription."
Advice: Most mss are rejected because "the writers are not familiar with *Calyx*—writers should read *Calyx* and be familiar with the publication."

*CAMBRENSIS, 41 Heol Fach, Cornelly, Bridgend, Mid-Glamorgan, CF33 4LN Wales. Editor: Arthur Smith. Quarterly. Circ. 500.
Needs: "Devoted solely to the short story form, featuring short stories by writers born or resident in Wales or with some Welsh connection; receives grants from the Welsh Arts' Council and the Welsh Writers' Trust; uses artwork—cartoons, line-drawings, sketches etc." Length: 2,500 words maximum.
How to Contact: Writer has to have some connection with Wales. SAE and IRCs or similar should be enclosed with "Air mail" postage to avoid long delay.
Payment/Terms: Writers receive 3 copies of magazine. Send IRCs for a sample copy. Subscriptions via Black-

---

 A BULLET INTRODUCES COMMENTS by the editor of *Novel & Short Story Writer's Market* indicating special information about the listing.

well's Periodicals, P.O. Box 40, Hythe Bridge Street, Oxford, OX1 2EU, UK or Swets & Zeitlinger B V, P.O. Box 800, 2160 S Z Lisse, Holland.

❧**CANADIAN AUTHOR, (IV)**, Canadian Author Association, 27 Doxsee Ave. N, Campbellford, Ontario K0L 1L0 Canada. (705)653-0323. Fax: (705)653-0593. E-mail: canauth@redden.on.ca. Editor: Doug Bale. Fiction Editor: Bill Valgardson. Magazine: 8¼ × 10¾; 32 pages; glossy paper; illustrations and photos. "Features in-depth profiles and interviews with the people who influence Canadian literature, as well as articles on the craft and business of writing." Quarterly. Estab. 1919. Circ. 4,000.
Needs: Ethnic/multicultural, experimental, feminist, historical, humor/satire, literary, mainstream/contemporary, regional, senior citizen/retirement. *Must be by a Canadian author only.* Receives 50 unsolicited mss/month. Accepts 1 mss/issue; 4 mss/year. Publishes ms 6-9 months after acceptance. Length: 3,000 words average; 2,000 words minimum; 3,000 words maximum. Also publishes literary essays, poetry.
How to Contact: Send complete ms with a cover letter. Include estimated word count, short bio and list of publication. Reports in 3-5 months. Send SASE for reply, return of ms or send a disposable copy of ms. Simultaneous and reprint submissions OK. Sample copy for $6.50 (Canadian) and 9 × 12 SAE with 88¢ postage.
Payment/Terms: Pays $125 on publication for first rights. Usually sends galleys to author.
Advice: "We look for quality fiction. Read our magazine. Better yet, subscribe."

‡❧**CANADIAN FICTION MAGAZINE, (IV)**, Quarry Press, P.O. Box 1061, Kingston, Ontario K7L 4Y5 Canada. (613)548-8429. Editor: Geoffrey Hancock. Magazine: 6 × 9; 144 pages. Quarterly. Estab. 1971. Circ. 1,200.
Needs: Canadian fiction only.
How to Contact: Reports in 6 weeks on mss.
Payment/Terms: Pays $10/page on publication.

❧**CAPERS AWEIGH MAGAZINE, (I, II, IV), Cape Breton Poetry & Fiction**, Capers Aweigh Small Press, P.O. Box 96, Sydney, Nova Scotia B1P 6G9 Canada. (902)539-9746. Editor: John MacNeil. Magazine: 5 × 8; 80 pages; bond paper; Cornwall-coated cover. "*Capers Aweigh* publishes poetry and fiction of, by and for Cape Bretoners." Publication frequency varies. Estab. 1992. Circ. 500.
Needs: Adventure, ethnic/multicultural, fantasy, feminist, historical, humor/satire, literary, mainstream, contemporary, mystery/suspense, psychic/supernatural/occult, regional, science fiction. List of upcoming themes available for SASE. Receives 2 unsolicited mss/month. Accepts 30 mss/issue. Publishes ms 9 months after acceptance. Published work by C. Fairn Kennedy and Shirley Kiju Kawi. Length: 2,500 words. Publishes short shorts. Also publishes literary criticism, poetry. Sponsors contests only to Cape Bretoners fiction writers.
How to Contact: Query first. Send SASE for reply or send a disposable copy of ms. Electronic submissions OK (IBM). Sample copy for $3 and 6 × 10 SAE.
Payment/Terms: Pays free subscription to the magazine and 1 contributor's copy; additional copies for $3. Acquires first North American serial rights. Sends galleys to author.

❧**THE CAPILANO REVIEW, (II)**, 2055 Purcell Way, North Vancouver, British Columbia V7J 3H5 Canada. (604)984-1712. Fax: (604)983-7520. E-mail: erains@capcollege.bc.ca. Website: http://www.capcollege.bc.ca/dept/TCR/tcr.html (includes complete bibliography of 25 years worth of contributors). Editor: Robert Sherrin. Magazine: 6 × 9; 90-120 pages; book paper; glossy cover; perfect-bound; b&w illustrations and photos. Magazine of "fresh, innovative art and literature for literary/artistic audience." Triannually. Estab. 1972. Circ. 900.
Needs: Experimental, literary and drama. Receives 80 unsolicited mss/month. Accepts 3-4 mss/issue; 10 mss/year. Published works by Philip Russell, Natalee Caple and K.D. Miller. Published new writers within the last year. Length: 4,000 words average. Publishes short shorts. Also publishes literary essays, poetry. Occasionally recommends other markets.
How to Contact: Send complete ms with cover letter and SASE. Include 2- to 3-sentence bio and brief list of publications. Reports on mss in 2-4 months. Send SAE with IRCs for return of ms. Simultaneous submissions OK. Sample copy for $9 (Canadian).
Payment/Terms: Pays $50-200, 2 contributor's copies and one year subscription. Pays on publication. Acquires first North American serial rights.
Advice: "We are looking for exceptional, original style; strong thematic content. Read several issues before submitting and make sure your work is technically perfect."

*THE CARIBBEAN WRITER, (IV)**, The University of the Virgin Islands, RR 02, Box 10,000—Kingshill, St. Croix, Virgin Islands 00850. (809)692-4152. Fax: (809)692-4026. E-mail: ewaters@uvi.edu or qmars@uvi.edu. Website: http://www.uvi.edu/extension/writer/carwrihm.htm. Editor: Erika J. Waters. Magazine: 6 × 9; 272 pages; 60 lb. paper; glossy cover stock; illustrations and photos. "*The Caribbean Writer* is an international magazine with a Caribbean focus. The Caribbean should be central to the work, or the work should reflect a Caribbean heritage, experience or perspective." Annually. Estab. 1987. Circ. 1,500.
Needs Contemporary, historical (general), humor/satire, literary, mainstream and prose poem. Receives 200 unsolicited mss/year. Accepts 15 mss/issue. Length: 1,000 words minimum. Also accepts poetry.
How to Contact: Send complete ms with cover letter. "Blind submissions only. Send name, address and title of

manuscript on separate sheet. Title only on manuscript. Manuscripts will not be considered unless this procedure is followed." Reports "once a year." SASE (or IRC). Simultaneous submissions OK. Sample copy for $5 and $2 postage.
Payment/Terms: Pays 2 contributor's copies. Annual prizes for best story ($400); for best poem ($300); $100 for first publication; best personal essay ($300).
Terms: Acquires one-time rights.
Advice: Looks for "fiction which reflects a Caribbean heritage, experience or perspective."

CAROLINA QUARTERLY, (II), Greenlaw Hall CB #3520, University of North Carolina, Chapel Hill NC 27599-3520. Editor-in-Chief: John R. Black. Fiction Editor: Shannon Wooden. Literary journal: 70-90 pages; illustrations. Triannually. Estab. 1948. Circ. 1,400.
  • Work published in *Carolina Quarterly* has been selected for inclusion in *Best American Short Stories* and in *Short Stories from the South: The Year's Best.*
Needs: Literary. Receives 150-200 unsolicited fiction mss/month. Accepts 5-7 mss/issue; 15-20 mss/year. Publishes ms an average of 4 months after acceptance. Published work by Barry Hannah, Nanci Kincaid and Doris Betts. Published new writers within the last year. Length: 7,000 words maximum; no minimum. Also publishes short shorts, literary essays, poetry. Occasionally critiques rejected mss.
How to Contact: Send complete ms with cover letter and SASE to fiction editor. No simultaneous submissions. Reports in 2-4 months. Sample copy for $5; writer's guidelines for SASE.
Payment/Terms: Pays in contributor's copies for first rights.

‡♥**CAROUSEL LITERARY ARTS MAGAZINE, (I, II)**, % CSA, University Centre, University of Guelph, Guelph, Ontario N1G 2W1 Canada. E-mail: amber@voguelph.ca. Editor: Daniel Evans. Magazine: 5½×8½; 191 pages; illustrations and photographs. Annually. Estab. 1985. Circ. 1,500.
Needs: Contemporary, literary. No solipsisms. Receives 50 unsolicited mss each month. Accepts 5-6 mss per issue. Publishes ms 1-2 months after acceptance. Recently published work by Leon Rooke, Russel Smith, Esta Spalding, Keith Fraser and bill bissett. Publishes new writers. Length: 3,000 words maximum. Also publishes literary essays, interviews, poetry.
How to Contact: Send complete ms. Include bio with manuscript. No simultaneous submissions. Reports in 2 months on queries; 4 months on mss. SASE. Sample copy for $10 (Canadian).
Payment/Terms: Pays in contributor's copies. Acquires one-time rights.
Advice: "We want work which takes chances in style, point of view, characterization. We are open to new writers."

CAYO, A Chronicle of Life in the Keys, (II, IV), P.O. Box 4516, Key West FL 33041. (305)296-4286. Editor: Alyson Simmons. Magazine: 8½×11; 40-48 pages; glossy paper; 70 lb. cover stock; illustrations and photos. Magazine on Keys-related topics or by Keys authors. Quarterly. Estab. 1993. Circ. 1,000.
Needs: Condensed/excerpted novel, experimental, literary, regional. Receives 4-5 unsolicited mss/month. Accepts 2-3 mss/issue; 8-12 mss/year. Published work by Alma Bond, Robin Shanley and Lawrence Ferlinghetti. Length: 3,000 words average; 800 words minimum; 3,000 words maximum. Publishes short shorts. Also publishes literary essays, poetry. Often critiques or comments on rejected mss.
How to Contact: Send complete ms with a cover letter. Include bio and list of publications with submission. Reports in 6 weeks on queries; 3 months on mss. Send SASE for reply, return of ms or send a disposable copy of ms. Simultaneous, reprint and electronic (ASCII text on disk) submissions OK. Sample copy for $4. Fiction guidelines for #10 SASE.
Payment/Terms: Pays in contributor's copies. Acquires one-time rights.
Advice: "The story has to stand on its own and move the reader."

‡***CENCRASTUS**, Unit One, Abbeymount Techbase, Edinburgh, EM8 8EJ Scotland. (031)661-5687. E-mail: 106536.755@compuserve.com. Fiction Editors: Ray Ross and Thom Nairn. Circ. 2,000. Quarterly."
Needs: "Scottish literature arts and affairs magazine with international bias." Publishes 1 or more short stories per issue.
How to Contact: "We look at all copy submitted. SAE."
Payment/Terms: Writers are paid for published fiction and receive contributor's copies.

***CHAPMAN**, 4 Broughton Place, Edinburgh EH1 3RX Scotland. Fiction Editor: Joy Hendry. Quarterly. Circ. 2,000. Publishes 4-6 stories/issue. Estab. 1970.
Needs: "*Chapman*, Scotland's quality literary magazine, is a dynamic force in Scotland, publishing poetry, fiction, criticism, reviews; articles on theatre, politics, language and the arts." Length: 1,000 words minimum; 6,000 words maximum.
How to Contact: Include SAE and return postage (or IRC) with submissions.
Payment/Terms: Pays £9-50/page. Sample copy available for £3.70 (includes postage).

THE CHARITON REVIEW, (II), Truman State University, Kirksville MO 63552. (816)785-4499. Fax: (816)785-7486. Editor: Jim Barnes. Magazine: 6×9; approximately 100 pages; 60 lb. paper; 65 lb. cover stock;

photographs on cover. "We demand only excellence in fiction and fiction translation for a general and college readership." Semiannually. Estab. 1975. Circ. 700.

Needs: Literary, contemporary, experimental, translations. Accepts 3-5 mss/issue; 6-10 mss/year. Published work by Ann Townsend, Glenn DelGrosso, Dennis Trudell and X.J. Kennedy. Published new writers within the last year. Length: 3,000-6,000 words. Also publishes literary essays, poetry. Critiques rejected mss when there is time.

How to Contact: Send complete ms with SASE. No book-length mss. No simultaneous submissions. Reports in less than 1 month on mss. Publishes ms an average of 6 months after acceptance. Sample copy for $5 with SASE. Reviews novels and short story collections.

Payment/Terms: Pays $5/page up to $50 maximum and contributor's copy on publication; additional copies for $5.50. Buys first North American serial rights; rights returned on request.

Advice: "Do not ask us for guidelines: the only guidelines are excellence in all matters. Write well and study the publication you are submitting to. We are interested only in the very best fiction and fiction translation. We are not interested in slick material. We do not read photocopies, dot-matrix, or carbon copies. Know the simple mechanics of submission—SASE, no paper clips, no odd-sized SASE, etc. Know the genre (short story, novella, etc.). Know the unwritten laws. There is too much manufactured fiction; assembly-lined, ego-centered personal essays offered as fiction."

‡CHASM, A Journal of the Macabre, (II, IV), P.O. Box 2549, Jamaica Plain MA 02130. Website: http://www.shore.net/~texas. Editor: Nat Panek. Magazine: 5 × 8½; 50-60 pages; 70 lb. vellum; illustrations and photos. "*Chasm* is a forum for high-quality, dark-themed fiction, poetry, literary journalism and artwork. Aimed at literate horror enthusiasts who want more form the genre than the mass media provides." Estab. 1995. Circ. 300.

Needs: Experimental, horror, psychic/supernatural/occult. No "sword and sorcery fantasy." Receives 40 unsolicited mss/month. Accepts 5-6 mss/issue; 10-12 mss/year. Recently published work by K.S. Hardy, Ben Miller and William Sheldon. Length: 5,000 words average; 100 words minimum; 6,000 words maximum. Publishes short shorts. Also publishes literary essays and poetry. Sometimes comments on or critiques rejected manuscripts.

How to Contact: Send complete manuscript with cover letter. Include 50-75 word bio and estimated word count. Reports in 2-4 weeks on queries; 2-3 months on manuscripts. Send SASE for reply, return of ms or send disposable copy of ms. Simultaneous and electronic (disk only) submissions OK. Sample copy for $5. Fiction guidelines for #10 SASE.

Payment/Terms: Pays 1 contributor's copy; additional copies $3. Sends galleys to author.

Advice: "Restrain your prose but not your imagination. Arresting language, imagery, characterization on the first page are key. Grabbing attention is the hard part—sustaining it only slightly less so. Mass market horror a la King, Barker, Koontz, etc. is a niche that is obviously full to overflowing, and needs no help from a small journal like *Chasm*. Writers who are further out on the fringes in terms of style and content—Harlan Ellison, Angela Carter, Lucius Shepard, Lisa Tuttle—are harder to find. That's where *Chasm* steps in."

THE CHATTAHOOCHEE REVIEW, (I, II), DeKalb College, 2101 Womack Rd., Dunwoody GA 30338. (770)551-3019. Editor: Lawrence Hetrick. Magazine: 6 × 9; 150 pages; 70 lb. paper; 80 lb. cover stock; illustrations; photographs. Quarterly. Estab. 1980. Circ. 1,250.

● Fiction from *The Chattahoochee Review* has been included in *Best New Stories of the South*.

Needs: Literary, mainstream. No juvenile, romance, science fiction. Receives 500 unsolicited mss/month. Accepts 5 mss/issue. Recently published work by Larry Brown, Terry Kay, Merrill Joan Gerber and Mary Ann Taylor-Hall. Published new writers within the last year. Length: 2,500 words average. Also publishes literary essays, literary criticism, poetry. Sometimes critiques rejected mss.

How to Contact: Send complete ms with cover letter, which should include sufficient bio for notes on contributors' page. Reports in 2 months. SASE. May consider simultaneous submission "reluctantly." Sample copy for $5. Fiction and poetry guidelines available on request. Reviews novels and short story collections.

Payment/Terms: Contact Managing Editor for rates. Acquires first rights.

Advice: "Arrange to read magazine before you submit to it." Known for publishing Southern regional fiction.

CHELSEA, (II), Chelsea Associates, Inc., Box 773, Cooper Station, New York NY 10276. Editor: Richard Foerster. Magazine: 6 × 9; 185-235 pages; 60 lb. white paper; glossy, full-color cover; artwork; occasional photos. "We have no consistent theme except for single special issues. Otherwise, we use general material of an eclectic nature: poetry, prose, artwork, etc., for a sophisticated, literate audience interested in avant-garde literature and current writing, both national and international." Annually. Estab. 1958. Circ. 1,800.

● *Chelsea* sponsors the Chelsea Awards. Entries to that contest will also be considered for the magazine, but writers may submit directly to the magazine as well. Fiction originally appearing in *Chelsea* received a *Pushcart* Prize in 1996 and the magazine was the recipient of a New York State Council for the Arts grant in 1996-97.

Needs: Literary, contemporary short fiction, poetry and translations. "No romance, divorce, racist, sexist material or I-hate-my-mother stories. We look for serious, sophisticated literature from writers willing to take risks with language and narrative structure." Receives approximately 200 unsolicited fiction mss each month. Approximately 1% of fiction is agented. Recently published work by Gladys Swan, Rush Rankin, Cary Holladay, K. Margaret Grossman, Joan Connor and Steven Huff. Publishes 1-2 new writers/year. Length: not over 25 printed

pages. Publishes short shorts of 6 pages or less. Sponsors annual Chelsea Award, $750 (send SASE for guidelines).
How to Contact: Send complete ms with SASE and succinct cover letter with previous credits. No simultaneous submissions. Reports in 3 months on mss. Publishes ms within a year after acceptance. Sample copy for $7.
Payment/Terms: Pays contributor's copies and $15 per printed page for first North American serial rights plus one-time non-exclusive reprint rights.
Advice: "Familiarize yourself with issues of the magazine for character of contributions. Manuscripts should be legible, clearly typed, with minimal number of typographical errors and cross-outs, sufficient return postage. Most mss are rejected because they are conventional in theme and/or style, uninspired, contrived, etc. We see far too much of the amateurish love story or romance. We would like to see more fiction that is sophisticated, with attention paid to theme, setting, language as well as plot. Writers should say something that has never been said before or at least say something in a unique way. There is too much focus on instant fame and not enough attention to craft. Our audience is sophisticated, international, and expects freshness and originality."

CHICAGO REVIEW, (II), 5801 S. Kenwood Ave., Chicago IL 60637. Fax: (773)702-0887. E-mail: chicago_review@uchicago.edu. Website: http://humanities.uchicago.edu (includes guidelines, editors' names, subscription information). Fiction Editors: Neda Ulaby and Dawn Marlan. Magazine for a highly literate general audience: 6×9; 128 pages; offset white 60 lb. paper; illustrations; photos. Quarterly. Estab. 1946. Circ. 2,600.
• The *Chicago Review* has won two *Pushcart* prizes.
Needs: Literary, contemporary and experimental. Accepts up to 5 mss/issue; 20 mss/year. Receives 80-100 unsolicited fiction mss each week. Recently published work by Greg Johnson, Tomás Filer, Aleksandar Hermon and Mario Benedetti. Publishes 5 new writers/year. No preferred length, except will not accept book-length mss. Also publishes literary essays, literary criticism, poetry. Sometimes recommends other markets.
How to Contact: Send complete ms with cover letter. SASE. No simultaneous submissions. Reports in 4-5 months on mss. Sample copy for $6. Guidelines with SASE. Reviews novels and short story collections. Send books to Book Review Editor.
Payment/Terms: Pays 3 contributor's copies and subscription.
Advice: "We look with interest at fiction that addresses subjects inventively, work that steers clear of clichéd treatments of themes. We're always eager to read writing that experiments with language, whether it be with characters' viewpoints, tone or style. However, we have been receiving more submissions and are becoming more selective."

CHIRICÚ, (II, IV), Ballantine Hall 849, Indiana University, Bloomington IN 47405. (812)855-5257. Managing Editor: B. Santos. "We publish essays, translations, poetry, fiction, reviews, interviews and artwork (illustrations and photos) that are either by or about Latinos. We have no barriers on style, content or ideology, but would like to see well-written material. We accept manuscripts written in English, Spanish or Portuguese." Annually. Estab. 1976. Circ. 500.
Needs: Contemporary, ethnic, experimental, fantasy, feminist, humor/satire, literary, mainstream, prose poem, science fiction, serialized/excerpted novel, translations. Published new writers within the last year. Length: 7,000 words maximum; 3,000 words average. Occasionally critiques rejected mss.
How to Contact: Send complete ms with cover letter. "Include some personal information along with information about your story." SASE. No simultaneous submissions. Reports in 5 weeks. Publishes ms 6-12 months after acceptance. Sample copy for $5. Guidelines for #10 SASE.
Advice: "Realize that we are a Latino literary journal so, if you are not Latino, your work must reflect an interest in Latino issues or have a Latino focus." Mss rejected "because beginning writers force their language instead of writing from genuine sentiment, because of multiple grammatical errors."

CHIRON REVIEW, (I, II), 522 E. South Ave., St. John KS 67576-2212. (316)549-3933. Editor: Michael Hathaway. Tabloid: 10×13; minimum 24 pages; newsprint; illustrations; photos. Publishes "all types of material, no particular theme; traditional and off-beat, no taboos." Quarterly. Estab. 1982. Circ. 1,200.
• *Chiron Review* is known for publishing experimental and "sudden" fiction.
Needs: Contemporary, experimental, humor/satire, literary. No didactic, religious or overly political writing. Receives 20 mss/month. Accepts 1-3 ms/issue; 4-12 mss/year. Publishes ms within 6-18 months of acceptance. Published work by Albert Huffstickler, James Mechem, Ray Zepeda, Christian Gholson and D.S. Lliteras. Length: 3,500 words preferred. Publishes short shorts. Sometimes recommends other markets to writers of rejected mss.
How to Contact: Query. Reports in 6-8 weeks. SASE. No simultaneous or reprint submissions. Deadlines:

‡ **THE DOUBLE DAGGER** before a listing indicates that the listing is new in this edition.

November 1 (Winter), February 1 (Spring), May 1 (Summer), August 1 (Autumn). Sample copy for $4 ($8 overseas). Fiction guidelines for #10 SASE.
Payment/Terms: Pays 1 contributor's copy; extra copies at 50% discount. Acquires first rights.
Advice: "Research markets thoroughly."

CHRYSALIS READER, Journal of the Swedenborg Foundation, (II), The Swedenborg Foundation, P.O. Box 549, West Chester PA 19381-0549. (610)430-3222. Send mss to: Rt. 1, Box 184, Dillwyn VA 23936. (804)983-3021. Editor: Carol S. Lawson. Book series: 7½×10; 160 pages; archival paper; coated cover stock; illustrations; photos. "A literary magazine centered around one theme per issue. Publishes fiction, essays and poetry for intellectually curious readers interested in spiritual topics." Biannually. Estab. 1985. Circ. 3,000.
Needs: Fiction (leading to insight), contemporary, experimental, historical, literary, mainstream, mystery/suspense, science fiction, spiritual, sports. No religious, juvenile, preschool. Upcoming themes: "Choices" (January 1998); "Education" (September 1999). Receives 100 mss/month. Accepts 15-20 mss/issue; 20-40 mss/year. Publishes ms within 2 years of acceptance. Published work by Robert Bly, Larry Dossey, John Hitchcock, Barbara Marx Hubbard and Linda Pastan. Length: 2,000 words minimum; 3,500 words maximum. Also publishes literary essays, literary criticism, chapters of novels, poetry. Sometimes critiques rejected mss and recommends other markets.
How to Contact: Query first and send SASE for guidelines. Reports in 2 months. SASE. No simultaneous, reprinted or in-press material. Sample copy for $10. Fiction guidelines for #10 SASE.
Payment/Terms: Pays $75-250 and 5 contributor's copies on publication for one-time rights. Sends galleys to author.
Advice: Looking for "1. *Quality*; 2. appeal for our audience; 3. relevance to/illumination of an issue's theme."

‡CHUBBY BUNNY, Putting Feelings into Words, (I), Aman-Ra Productions, 374 Victoria St., San Francisco CA 94132. (415)584-2626. E-mail: daman@sirius.com. Editor: Dennis Aman. Fiction Editor: Daman Sand. Magazine: 9×6; 192 pages; 20 lb. paper; illustrations and photos. "*Chubby Bunny* is interested in the expression of raw emotion—be it love, fear, etc.—in the form of words. Semiannually. Estab. 1995. Circ. 2,000.
Needs: Condensed/excerpted novel, erotica, ethnic/multicultural, experimental, fantasy (sword and sorcery), humor/satire, lesbian, literary, mainstream/contemporary, regional, religious/inspirational, romance, serialized novel, translations. "We need raw power." Receives 30-50 unsolicited mss/month. Accepts 6-10 mss/issue; 20-35 mss./year. Publishes ms 1-3 months after acceptance. Recently published work by Gover Davis, Robert Peters, Maralyn Chen and Arthur Philip Noir. Length: varies. Publishes short shorts. Also publishes literary essays, literary criticism and poetry. Often critiques or comments on rejected mss.
How to Contact: Send complete ms with a cover letter. Include brief bio, estimated word count and names of pets. Reports in 1 week on queries and mss. Send SASE for reply, return of ms or send disposable copy of ms. Simultaneous, reprint and electronic submissions OK. Sample copy free for large SAE with priority mail stamp. Reviews novels or short story collections. Send books to Daman Sand.
Payment/Terms: Pays 3 contributor's copies for one-time rights; additional copies $5.
Advice: "We are less interested in technique than in power. Send us your guts in a box. Submit frequently and don't give up. We respect tenacity."

CICADA, (II, IV), 329 "E" St., Bakersfield CA 93304. (805)323-4064. Editor: Frederick A. Raborg, Jr. Magazine: 5½×8¼; 24 pages; matte cover stock; illustrations and photos. "Oriental poetry and fiction related to the Orient for general readership and haiku enthusiasts." Quarterly. Estab. 1985. Circ. 600.
Needs: *All with Oriental slant*: Adventure, contemporary, erotica, ethnic, experimental, fantasy, feminist, historical (general), horror, humor/satire, lesbian, literary, mainstream, mystery/suspense, psychic/supernatural/occult, regional, contemporary romance, historical romance, young adult romance, science fiction, senior citizen/retirement and translations. "We look for strong fiction with Oriental (especially Japanese) content or flavor. Stories need not have 'happy' endings, and we are open to the experimental and/or avant-garde. Erotica is fine; pornography, no." Receives 30 unsolicited mss/month. Accepts 1 ms/issue; 4 mss/year. Publishes ms 6 months to 1 year after acceptance. Agented fiction 5%. Published work by Gilbert Garand, Frank Holland and Jim Mastro. Length: 2,000 words average; 500 words minimum; 3,000 words maximum. Critiques rejected ms when appropriate. Also publishes poetry.
How to Contact: Send complete ms with cover letter. Include Social Security number and appropriate information about the writer in relationship to the Orient. Reports in 2 weeks on queries; 3 months on mss (if seriously considered). SASE. Sample copy for $4.95. Fiction guidelines for #10 SASE.
Payment/Terms: Pays $10-25 and contributor's copies on publication for first North American serial rights; charges for additional copies. $5 kill fee.
Advice: Looks for "excellence and appropriate storyline. Strong characterization and knowledge of the Orient are musts. Neatness counts high on my list for first impressions. A writer should demonstrate a high degree of professionalism."

CIMARRON REVIEW, (II), Oklahoma State University, 205 Morrill, Stillwater OK 74078-0135. (405)744-9476. Editor: Edward P. Walkiewicz. Magazine: 6×9; 100 pages. "Poetry and fiction on contemporary themes;

personal essay on contemporary issues that cope with life in the 20th century, for educated literary readers. We work hard to reflect quality." Quarterly. Estab. 1967. Circ. 500.
Needs: Literary and contemporary. No collegiate reminiscences or juvenilia. Accepts 6-7 mss/issue, 24-28 mss/year. Published works by Peter Makuck, Mary Lee Settle, W. D. Wetherell, John Timmerman. Published new writers within the last year. Also publishes literary essays, literary criticism, poetry.
How to Contact: Send complete ms with SASE. "Short cover letters are appropriate but not essential, except for providing *CR* with the most recent mailing address available." No simultaneous submissions. Reports in 3 months on mss. Publishes ms within 1 year after acceptance. Sample copy with SASE and $3. Reviews novels, short story collections, and poetry collections.
Payment/Terms: Pays one-year subscription to author, plus $50 for each prose piece. Acquires all rights on publication. "Permission to reprint granted freely."
Advice: "Short fiction is a genre uniquely suited to the modern world. *CR* seeks an individual, innovative style that focuses on contemporary themes."

THE CLIMBING ART, (I, II, IV), 6390 E. Floyd Dr., Denver CO 80222-7638. (303)757-0541. E-mail: rmorrow @dnur.west.net. Editor: Ron Morrow. Fiction Editor: Christiana Langenberg. Magazine: 5½ × 8½; 150 pages; illustrations and photos. "*The Climbing Art* publishes literature, poetry and art for and about the spirit of climbing." Semiannually. Estab. 1986. Circ. 1,200.
Needs: Adventure, condensed/excerpted novel, ethnic/multicultural, experimental, fantasy, historical, literary, mainstream/contemporary, mystery/suspense, regional, science fiction, sports, translations. "No religious, rhyming, or non-climbing related." Receives 50 unsolicited mss/month. Accepts 4-6 mss/issue; 10-15 mss/year. Publishes ms up to 1 year after acceptance. Agented fiction 10%. Publishes 10-15 new writers/year. Length: 500 words minimum; 10,000 words maximum. Publishes short shorts. Also publishes literary essays, literary criticism, poetry. Sometimes critiques or comments on rejected mss. Sometimes sponsors contests.
How to Contact: Send complete ms with a cover letter. Include estimated word count, 1-paragraph bio and list of publications. Reports in 2 weeks on queries; 2-8 weeks on mss. SASE. Simultaneous and electronic submissions OK. Sample copy $7. Reviews novels and short story collections.
Payment/Terms: Pays free subscription and 2 contributor's copies; additional copies for $4. Acquires one-time rights.
Advice: "Read several issues first and make certain the material is related to climbing and the spirit of climbing. We have not seen enough literary excellence."

CLOCKWATCH REVIEW, A Journal of the Arts, (II), Dept. of English, Illinois Wesleyan University, Bloomington IL 61702. (309)556-3352. Editors: James Plath and Zarina Mullan Plath. Magazine: 5½ × 8½; 64-80 pages; glossy cover stock; illustrations; photos. "We publish stories which are *literary* as well as alive, colorful, enjoyable—stories which linger like shadows," for a general audience. Semiannually. Estab. 1983. Circ. 1,500.
   ● *Clockwatch Review* is planning a western issue and would like to see more high-quality genre fiction that breaks the mold.
Needs: Contemporary, experimental, humor/satire, literary, mainstream, prose poem, regional. Receives 50-60 unsolicited mss/month. Accepts 2 mss/issue; 4 mss/year. Published work by Ellen Hunnicutt, Beth Brandt, Charlotte Mandel; published new writers within the last year. Length: 2,500 words average; 1,200 words minimum; 4,000 words maximum. Occasionally critiques rejected mss if requested.
How to Contact: Send complete ms. Reports in 6-12 months. SASE. Publishes ms 3-12 months after acceptance. Sample copy for $4.
Payment/Terms: Pays 3 contributor's copies and small cash stipend (currently $50, but may vary) for first serial rights.
Advice: "*Clockwatch* has always tried to expand the audience for quality contemporary poetry and fiction by publishing a highly visual magazine that is thin enough to invite reading. We've included interviews with popular musicians and artists in order to further interest a general, as well as academic, public and show the interrelationship of the arts. We're looking for high-quality literary fiction that brings something fresh to the page—whether in imagery, language, voice or character. Give us characters with meat on their bones, colorful but not clichéd; give us natural plots, not contrived or melodramatic. Above all, give us your *best* work."

COLLAGES AND BRICOLAGES, The Journal of International Writing, (II), P.O. Box 86, Clarion PA 16214. (814)226-5799. E-mail: fortis@mail.clarion.edu. Editor: Marie-José Fortis. Magazine: 8½ × 11; 100-150 pages; illustrations. "The magazine includes essays, short stories, occasional interviews, short plays, poems that show innovative promise. It is often focus or issue oriented—themes can be either literary or socio-political." Annually. Estab. 1987.
Needs: Contemporary, ethnic, experimental, feminist, humor/satire, literary, philosophical works. "Also symbolist, surrealist b&w designs/illustrations are welcome." Receives about 60 unsolicited fiction mss/month. Publishes ms 6-9 months after acceptance. Recently published work by Rosette Lamont, Eric Basso, Anne Blonstein, Jo Santiago and Kenneth Bernard. Published new writers within the last year. Publishes short shorts. Also publishes literary essays, literary criticism, poetry. Critiques rejected ms "when great potential is manifest."
How to Contact: Send complete ms with cover letter that includes a short bio. Reports in 1-3 months. SASE.

Sample copy for $8.50. Reviews novels and short story collections. "How often and how many per issue depends on reviewers available."

Payment/Terms: Pays 2 contributor's copies. Acquires first rights. Rights revert to author after publication.

Advice: "Avoid following 'industry trends.' Do what you must do. Write what you must write. Write as if words were your bread, your water, a great vintage wine, salt, oxygen. Also, very few of us have a cornucopia budget, but it is a good idea to look at a publication before submitting."

COLORADO REVIEW, (II), English Department, Colorado State University, Fort Collins CO 80523. (970)491-5449. E-mail: creview@vines.colostate.edu. Editor: David Milofsky. Literary journal: 200 pages; 70 lb. book weight paper. Semiannually. Estab. as *Colorado State Review* 1966. Circ. 2,000.

● *Colorado Review*'s circulation has increased from 500 to 2,000.

Needs: Contemporary, ethnic, experimental, literary, mainstream, translations. Receives 300 unsolicited fiction mss/month. Accepts 3-4 mss/issue. Recently published work by Robert Olen Butler, T. Alan Broughton, Susan Welch; published new writers within the last year. Length: under 6,000 words. Does not read mss May through August. Also publishes literary essays, book reviews, poetry. Occasionally critiques rejected mss.

How to Contact: Send complete ms with SASE (or IRC) and brief bio with previous publications. Reports in 3 months. Publishes ms 6-12 months after acceptance. Sample copy for $8. Reviews novels or short story collections.

Payment/Terms: Pays $5/printed page for fiction; 2 contributor's copies; extras for $5. Pays on publication for first North American serial rights. "We assign copyright to author on request." Sends galleys to author.

Advice: "We are interested in manuscripts which show craft, imagination and a convincing voice. If a story has reached a level of technical competence, we are receptive to the fiction working on its own terms. The oldest advice is still the best: persistence. Approach every aspect of the writing process with pride, conscientiousness—from word choice to manuscript appearance."

COLUMBIA: A JOURNAL OF LITERATURE & ART, (II), 415 Dodge Hall, Columbia University, New York NY 10027. (212)854-4391. Editor: Gregory Cowles. Fiction Editor: Diana Katz. Editors change each year. Magazine: 5¼×8¼; approximately 200 pages; coated cover stock; illustrations, photos. "We accept short stories, novel excerpts, translations, interviews, nonfiction and poetry." Biannually.

Needs: Literary and translations. Accepts 3-10 mss/issue. Receives approximately 125 unsolicited fiction mss each month. Does not read mss May 1 to August 31. Recently published work by Stewart O'Nan, Sherman Alexie, Mary Gordon, Elizabeth Graver and Lorrie Moore. Published 5-8 unpublished writers within the year. Length: 20 pages maximum. Publishes short shorts.

How to Contact: Send complete ms with SASE. Accepts computer printout submissions. Reports in 1-2 months. Sample copy for $5.

Payment/Terms: Offers yearly contest with guest editors and cash awards. Send SASE for guidelines.

Advice: "We always look for story—too often, talented writers send nice prose filled with good observations but forget to tell a story. We like writing which is lively, honest, thoughtful, and entertaining. Because our staff changes each year, our specific tastes also change, so our best advice is to write what you want to write."

‡COMPOST NEWSLETTER, (I, II), 11306 Pearl St., #202, Los Angeles CA 90064. E-mail: pbm2@aol.com. Editor: Peter Mooney. Fiction Editor: Daniel Dalessio. Magazine: 7×8½; 24 pages; 20 lb. paper; illustrations. "*Compost Newsletter* is a literary publication of quality writing and art. We primarily publish fiction, poetry and black and white illustrations but we do consider nonfiction: commentary, humor and articles on the craft of writing. *CNL* is intended for a literary/general audience." Quarterly. Estab. 1981. Circ. 100.

Needs: Adventure, condensed/excerpted novel, ethnic/multicultural, experimental, feminist, gay, historical, humor/satire, lesbian, literary, mainstream/contemporary, psychic/supernatural/occult, science fiction, senior citizen/retirement, serialized novel. "No pornography, religious or children's." Receives 8-10 unsolicited mss/month. Accepts 3-4 mss/issue; 12-16 mss/year. Publishes ms 3-6 months after acceptance. Recently published work by Rine Davis, R.M. Host and John Ireland. Length: 2,000 words average; 3,000-4,000 words maximum. Publishes short shorts. Also publishes literary essays, literary criticism, poetry. Sometimes critiques or comments on rejected mss.

How to Contact: Send complete ms with a cover letter. Include estimated word count and 1-paragraph bio. Reports in 3-5 months. Send SASE for reply, return of ms or send a disposable copy of ms. Simultaneous submissions, reprints and electronic submissions OK. Sample copy for $2.50. Fiction guidelines free.

Payment/Terms: Pays 2 contributor's copies on publication; additional copies for $2.50. Acquires one-time rights.

Advice: "Quality is our number one priority. We are primarily interested in mainstream/literary fiction but anything interesting and well-written will catch our attention. Much of the fiction we publish has a clear and distinct voice. Furthermore, it grasps our attention at least by the second paragraph, then sustains its effect. In your cover letter (not necessary), do not brag. That happens all too often and it turns off an editor even before a manuscript is read—not a good start. Always include a SASE if you expect anything in return. Send your most polished work; revise, revise, revise. All successful writers do. Always give a word count. Know our publication, not necessarily to know what we publish, but to know the level at which the work we publish stands. Don't try to catch us off guard with surprising endings. The whole story should surprise us."

CONCHO RIVER REVIEW, (I, II, IV), Fort Concho Museum Press, 630 S. Oakes, San Angelo TX 76903. Fax: (915)942-2155. E-mail: me.hartje@mailserv.angelo.edu. Magazine: 6½×9; 100-125 pages; 60 lb. Ardor offset paper; Classic Laid Color cover stock; b&w drawings. "We publish any fiction of high quality—no thematic specialties—*contributors must be residents of Texas or the Southwest generally.*" Semiannually. Estab. 1987. Circ. 300.

● The magazine is considering featuring "guest editors" with each issue, but manuscripts should still be sent to the editor, Mary Ellen Hartje.

Needs: Contemporary, ethnic, historical, humor/satire, literary, regional and western. No erotica; no science fiction. Receives 10-15 unsolicited mss/month. Accepts 3-6 mss/issue; 8-10 mss/year. Publishes ms 4 months after acceptance. Recently published work by Gordon Alexander, Riley Froh, Gretchen Geralds and Kimberly Willis Holt. Publishes 4 new writers/year. Length: 3,500 words average; 1,500 words minimum; 5,000 words maximum. Also publishes literary essays, poetry. Sometimes critiques rejected mss and recommends other markets.

How to Contact: *Send submissions to Mary Ellen Hartje, English Dept., Angelo State University, San Angelo, TX 76909.* Send complete ms with SASE; cover letter optional. Reports in 3 weeks on queries; 3-6 months on mss. SASE for ms. Simultaneous submissions OK (if noted). Sample copy for $4. Fiction guidelines for #10 SASE. Reviews novels and short story collections. Books to be reviewed should be sent to Dr. James Moore.

Payment/Terms: Pays in contributor's copies; $4 charge for extras. Acquires first rights.

Advice: "We prefer a clear sense of conflict, strong characterization and effective dialogue."

CONFRONTATION, (I), English Dept., C.W. Post of Long Island University, Brookville NY 11548. (516)299-2391, (516)299-2720. Fax: (516)299-2735. Editor: Martin Tucker. Magazine: 6×9; 190-250 pages; 70 lb. paper; 80 lb. cover; illustrations; photos. "We like to have a 'range' of subjects, form and style in each issue and are open to all forms. Quality is our major concern. Our audience is made up of literate, thinking people; formally or self-educated." Semiannually. Estab. 1968. Circ. 2,000.

● *Confrontation* has garnered a long list of awards and honors, including the Editor's Award for Distinguished Achievement from CCLM (now the Council of Literary Magazines and Presses) and NEA grants. Work from the magazine has appeared in numerous anthologies including the *Pushcart Prize, Best Short Stories* and *O. Henry Prize Stories.*

Needs: Literary, contemporary, prose poem, regional and translations. No "proseletyzing" literature. Accepts 30 mss/issue; 60 mss/year. Receives 400 unsolicited fiction mss each month. Does not read June through September. Approximately 10-15% of fiction is agented. Published work by Irving Feldman, David Ray, Lynn Freed and William Styron. Published many new writers within the last year. Length: 500-4,000 words. Publishes short shorts. Also publishes literary essays, poetry. Critiques rejected mss when there is time. Sometimes recommends other markets.

How to Contact: Send complete ms with SASE. "Cover letters acceptable, not necessary. We accept simultaneous submissions but do not prefer it." Accepts diskettes if accompanied by computer printout submissions. Reports in 6-8 weeks on mss. Publishes ms 6-12 months after acceptance. Sample copy for $3. Reviews novels, short story collections, poetry and literary criticism.

Payment/Terms: Pays $20-250 on publication for all rights "with transfer on request to author"; 1 contributor's copy; half price for extras.

Advice: "Keep trying."

CONTEXT SOUTH, (II), Box 4504, Kerrville TX 94927-1315. E-mail: drpoetry@ktc.com. Website: http://www.davidbreeden.com (includes guidelines). Editor: David Breeden. Fiction Editor: Craig Taylor. Magazine: digest sized; 65 pages; illustrations and photos. Annually. Estab. 1988. Circ. 500.

Needs: Experimental, feminist, literary. List of upcoming themes available for SASE. Receives 10-15 unsolicited mss/month. Does not read in summer. Publishes ms up to 1 year after acceptance. Agented fiction 10%. Published work by Thea Caplan and David Vigoda. Length: 500 words minimum; 3,000 words maximum. Publishes short shorts. Also publishes literary essays, literary criticism, poetry. Sometimes critiques or comments on rejected mss.

How to Contact: Send complete ms with a cover letter. Include short bio. Reports in 2 weeks on queries; 3 months on mss. SASE for return of ms. Simultaneous and electronic (disk) submissions OK. Sample copy for $5. Reviews novels and short story collections.

Payment/Terms: Pays 2 contributor's copies. Acquires one-time rights. Sends galleys to author.

Advice: "Read a good deal of fiction, current and past. Avoid sending the trite and that which depends merely on shock."

CORONA, Marking the Edges of Many Circles, (II), Dept. of History and Philosophy, Montana State University, Bozeman MT 59717. (406)994-5200. Co-Editors: Lynda Sexson, Michael Sexson. Managing Editor: Sarah Merrill. Magazine: 7×10; 130 pages; 60 lb. "mountre matte" paper; 65 lb. Hammermill cover stock; illustrations; photos. "Interdisciplinary magazine—essays, poetry, fiction, imagery, science, history, recipes, humor, etc., for those educated, curious, with a profound interest in the arts and contemporary thought." Published occasionally. Estab. 1980. Circ. 2,000.

Needs: Comics, contemporary, experimental, fantasy, feminist, humor/satire, literary, prose poem. "Our fiction ranges from the traditional Talmudic tale to fiction engendered by speculative science, from the extended joke to regional reflection—if it isn't accessible and original, please don't send it." Receives varying number of unsolicited fiction mss/month. Accepts 6 mss/issue. Published work by Rhoda Lerman and Stephen Dixon. Published new writers within the last year. Publishes short shorts. Also publishes literary essays, poetry. Occasionally critiques rejected mss.

How to Contact: Query. Reports in 6 months on mss. Sample copy for $7.

Payment/Terms: Pays 2 free contributor's copies; discounted charge for extras. Acquires first rights. Sends galleys to author upon request.

Advice: "Be knowledgeable of contents other than fiction in *Corona*; one must know the journal."

CRAB CREEK REVIEW, (V), 7265 S. 128th, Seattle WA 98178. (206)772-8489. Editors: Kimberly Allison, Harris Levinson, Laura Sinai and Terri Stone. Magazine: 6×9 paperbound; 50-80 pgs., line drawings. "Magazine publishing poetry, short stories, art and essays for adult, college-educated audience interested in literary, visual and dramatic arts and in politics." Published twice yearly. Estab. 1983. Circ. 450.

Needs: Contemporary, humor/satire, literary and translations. No confession, erotica, horror, juvenile, preschool, religious/inspirational, romance or young adult. Receives 20-30 unsolicited mss/month. Recently published work by David Lee, Joan Fiset, Perle Besserman and Yehuda Amichai. Published new writers within the last year. Length: 3,000 words average; 1,200 words minimum; 5,000 words maximum. Publishes short shorts.

How to Contact: *Not reading unsolicited mss until further notice. Query first.* Send complete ms with short list of credits. Reports in 2-4 months. SASE. No simultaneous submissions. Sample copy for $5. *Anniversary Anthology* $5, *Bread for This Hunger* (1996 anthology) $5.

Payment/Terms: Pays 2 contributor's copies; $4 charge for extras. Acquires first rights. Rarely buys reprints.

Advice: "We appreciate 'sudden fictions.' Type name and address on each piece. Enclose SASE. Send no more than one story in a packet (except for short shorts—no more than three, ten pages total). Know what you want to say and say it in an honest, clear, confident voice."

‡CRAB ORCHARD REVIEW, A Journal of Creative Works, (II), Southern Illinois University at Carbondale, English Department, Faner Hall, Carbondale IL 62901. (618)453-6833. Fax: (618)453-3253. Editor: Richard Peterson. Fiction Editor: Carolyn Alessio. Managing Editor: Jon Tribble. Magazine: 5½×8½; 225 pages; 55 lb. recycled paper, card cover; photo on cover. "This twice-yearly journal will feature the best in contemporary fiction, poetry, creative nonfiction, reviews and interviews. Estab. 1995. Circ. 500.
   • Winner of the 1997 Illinois Arts Council Literary Award and the 1996 CLMP Kolvakos Seed Grant. Member of CLMP.

Needs: Condensed/excerpted novel, ethnic/multicultural, literary, translations. No science fiction, romance, western or children's. List of upcoming themes available for SASE. Receives 50 unsolicited mss/month. Accepts 5-8 mss/issue, 10-16 mss/year. Does not read during the summer. Publishes ms 9-12 months after acceptance. Agented fiction 5%. Recently published work by Cris Mazza, Michael Martone, Jean Thompson, Judy Juanita, Ira Sadoff and Maura Stanton. Length: 2,500 words average; 1,000 word minimum; 6,500 words maximum. Also publishes literary essays and poetry. Rarely critiques or comments on rejected mss.

How to Contact: Send complete ms with a cover letter. Include brief bio and list of publications. Reports in 3 weeks on queries; 4 months on mss. Send SASE for reply, return of ms. Simultaneous submissions OK. Sample copy for $6. Fiction guidelines for #10 SASE. Reviews novels or short story collections. Send books to "Book Review Editor."

Payment/Terms: Pays $75 minimum; $5/page maximum plus 2 contributor's copies for first North American serial rights.

Advice: Looks for "provocative, well-written fiction that engages the reader. Include a self addressed stamped envelope with all submissions, or they will not be returned. Read the journal to determine the range of fiction published."

‡CRANIA, A Literary/Arts Magazine, (II), E-mail: crania@digitaldaze.com. Website: http://www.digitaldaze.com/crania. Editor: Dennis Hathaway. "To bring literary and visual works of art of the highest quality to an audience potentially much larger than the audience reached by print media."

Needs: Fiction, poetry, essays, reviews. No genre fiction. Recently published work by Alyson Hagy, Alex Keegan and Alvin Greenburg.

How to Contact: Electronic submissions only. Send ms by e-mail.

Advice: "*Crania* welcomes submissions from new writers, but the magazine is not a bulletin board kind of site where anyone can get their work into print. We urge potential contributors to read the magazine carefully, and to submit work that shows a facility with craft and a commitment to the idea of writing as an art."

‡CRAZYHORSE, (II), Dept. of English, Univ. of Arkansas, Little Rock, AR 72204. (501)569-3161. Managing Editor: Zabelle Stodola. Fiction Editor: Judy Troy. Magazine: 6×9; 140 pages; cover illustration only. "Publishes original, quality literary fiction." Biannually. Estab. 1960. Circ. 1,000.
   • Stories appearing in *Crazyhorse* regularly appear in the *Pushcart Prize* and *Best American Short Stories* anthologies.

Needs: Literary. No formula (science fiction, gothic, detective, etc.) fiction. Receives 100-150 unsolicited mss/

month. Buys 3-5 mss/issue; 8-10 mss/year. Does not read mss in summer. Published work by Lee K. Abbott, Frederick Busch, Andre Dubus, Pam Durban, H.E. Francis, James Hannah, Gordon Lish, Bobbie Ann Mason and Maura Stanton; published new writers within the last year. Length: Open. Publishes short shorts. Also publishes literary essays, literary criticism, poetry. "Rarely" critiques rejected mss.

How to Contact: Send complete ms with cover letter. Reports in 1-4 months. SASE. No simultaneous submissions. Sample copy for $5. Reviews novels and short story collections. Send books to fiction editor.

Payment/Terms: Pays $10/page and contributor's copies for first North American serial rights. *Crazyhorse* awards $500 to the author of the best work of fiction published in the magazine in a given year.

Advice: "Read a sample issue and submit work that you believe is as good as or better than the fiction we've published."

THE CREAM CITY REVIEW, (I, II), University of Wisconsin-Milwaukee, Box 413, Milwaukee WI 53201. (414)229-4708. Website: http://www.uwm.edu/Dept/English. Editor-In-Chief: Staci Leigh O'Brien. Contact: Fiction Editor. Editors rotate. Magazine: 5½×8½; 200-300 pages; 70 lb. offset/perfect-bound paper; 80 lb. cover stock; illustrations; photos. "General literary publication—an eclectic and electric selection of the best we receive." Semiannually. Estab. 1975. Circ. 2,000.

Needs: Ethnic, experimental, humor/satire, literary, prose poem, regional, translations. Receives approximately 300 unsolicited fiction mss each month. Accepts 6-10 mss/issue. Does not read fiction or poetry May 1 through August 31. Published work by Stephen Dixon, Heather McKey, Carmen Elizaga and Gordon Lish. Published new writers within the last year. Length: 1,000-10,000 words. Publishes short shorts. Also publishes literary essays, literary criticism, poetry.

How to Contact: Send complete ms with SASE. Simultaneous submissions OK if notified. Reports in 6 months. Sample copy for $5 (back issue), $7 (current issue). Reviews novels and short story collections.

Payment/Terms: Pays 1 year subscription or in copies. Acquires first rights. Sends galleys to author. Rights revert to author after publication.

Advice: "Read as much as you write so that you can examine your own work in relation to where fiction has been and where fiction is going. We are looking for strong, consistent voices and fresh voices."

*CREATIVE FORUM, Bahri Publications, 997A Gobindpuri Kalkaj, P.O. Box 4453, New Delhi 110019 India. Telephones: 011-6445710, 011-6448606. Fax: 91.11-6416116. E-mail: bahrius@rocketmail.com and pobox@knowindia.com. Website: http://com/Indianbooks/bahri.htm (includes information on current state/status of the journal, prices, etc.). Fiction Editor: U.S. Bahri. Circ. 1,800. Publishes 8-12 stories annually.

Needs: "We accept short stories for our journal *Creative Forum* in addition to poetry and criticism on fiction and poetry (contemporary only). Novels/novellas accepted if suitable subsidy is forthcoming from the author." Length: 2,000-3,000 words.

How to Contact: Manuscripts should be "neatly typed and not beyond 200 sheets."

Payment/Terms: Pays in copies. Subscriptions $60 US.

Advice: "Short stories accompanied with $50 US towards annual subscription of the journal are given preferential treatment and priority. Be alive to what is happening in the minds of today's men/women and the young generation both at the mental level and social level. Then bring out those problems through your mighty pen so that the world around comes alive to the issues raised in your fiction."

THE CRESCENT REVIEW, (II), The Crescent Review, Inc., P.O. Box 15069, Chevy Chase MD 20825. (301)986-8788. Editor: J.T. Holland. Magazine: 6×9; 160 pages. Triannually. Estab. 1982.

• Work appearing in *The Crescent Review* has been included in *O. Henry Prize Stories*, *Best American Short Stories*, *Pushcart Prize* and *Black Southern Writers* anthologies and in the *New Stories from the South*.

Needs: "Well-crafted stories." Does not read submissions May-June and November-December.

How to Contact: Reports in 1-4 months. SASE. Sample issue for $9.40.

Payment/Terms: Pays 2 contributor's copies; discount for contributors. Acquires first North American serial rights.

CRIPES!, (II), P.O. Box 42302, Lafayette LA 70504-2302. Editor: James Tolan. Magazine: 5½×8½; 52 pages; card cover stock; illustrations; photos. "We look for poetry, prose, art, cartoons and many things in between— as long as it maintains a strong balance between passion (impulse) and craft. Estab. 1994. Circ. 300.

Needs: Condensed/excerpted novel, humor, literary, mainstream/contemporary. Especially looking for short short fiction. No religious or westerns. Receives 20-30 unsolicited mss/month. Accepts 1-2 mss/issue; 4-6 mss/

THE MAPLE LEAF symbol before a listing indicates a Canadian publisher, magazine, conference or contest.

year. Publishes ms within 6 months after acceptance. Recently published work by Tom Whalen, Matthew Firth, Kendall Delacambre, John Fleming and Perry Parks. Length: 1,500-2,000 words maximum. Publishes short shorts. Also publishes poetry. Often critiques or comments on rejected mss.

How to Contact: Send complete ms with a cover letter. Include a 1-paragraph bio and "tell us how you learned about us." Send SASE for reply, return of ms or send 2 disposable copies of ms. Simultaneous submissions OK. Sample copy for $4 and 6×9 SAE with 3 first-class stamps.

Payment/Terms: Pays 2 contributor's copies on publication; addtional copies for $3. Acquires one-time rights.

Advice: Looks for "originality, unpredictability, fresh language, a carefully prepared manuscript, focus and playfullness. Look at *Cripes!* to see what we publish."

‡**CROSSCONNECT, (I, II)**, P.O. Box 2317, Philadelphia PA 19103. (215)898-5324. Fax: (215)898-9348. E-mail: xconnect@ccat.sas.upenn.edu. Website: http://ccat.sas.upenn.edu/xconnect. Editor: David Deifer. "*Cross-Connect* publishes tri-annually on the World Wide Web and annually in print, with the best of our Web issues, plus nominated work from editors in the digital literary community. *xconnect: writers of the information age* is a nationally distributed, full color, journal sized book." 5½×8½; trade paper; 190 pages.

Needs: Literary and experimental fiction. "Our mission—like our name—is one of connection. *CrossConnect* seeks to promote and document the emergent creative artists as well as established artists who have made the transition to the new technologies of the Information Age." Recently published work by H.E. Francis, Doug Lawson, Diane Williams and Tom Harper. Publishes 25 new writers/year.

How to Contact: Electronic and traditional submissions accepted. "We prefer your submissions be cut and pasted into your mail readers and sent to us. No attached files unless requested." Send complete ms (up to three stories) with cover letter and short bio. Previously published and simultaneous submission OK. Rarely comments on rejections.

Payment/Terms: Pays 1 contributor's copy for use in print version. Author retains all rights. Regularly sends prepublication galleys.

Advice: "Persistence."

CRUCIBLE, (I, II), English Dept., Barton College, College Station, Wilson NC 27893. (919)399-6456. Editor: Terrence L. Grimes. Magazine of fiction and poetry for a general, literary audience. Annually. Estab. 1964. Circ. 500.

Needs: Contemporary, ethnic, experimental, feminist, gay, lesbian, literary, regional. Receives 20 unsolicited mss/month. Accepts 5-6 mss/year. Publishes ms 4-5 months after acceptance. Does not normally read mss from April 30 to December 1. Published work by William Hutchins and Guy Nancekeville. Length: 8,000 words maximum. Publishes short shorts.

How to Contact: Send 3 complete copies of ms unsigned with cover letter which should include a brief biography, "in case we publish." Reports in 1 month on queries; 3-4 months on mss (by June 15). SASE. Sample copy for $6. Fiction guidelines free.

Payment/Terms: Pays contributor's copies. Acquires first rights.

Advice: "Write about what you know. Experimentation is fine as long as the experiences portrayed come across as authentic, that is to say, plausible."

‡**CURIO, (I)**, 81 Pondfield Rd., Suite 264, Bronxville NY 10708. (914)961-8649. Fax: (914)779-4033. Editor: M. Teresa Lawrence. Fiction Editor: Mickey Z. Magazine: 8⅜×10½; 45 lb. glossy paper; 60 lb. cover; illustrations and photos. "Written for the young, fashionable and literate American trendsetters. Promotes new ideas, opinions, thoughts and interests through a variety of mixed media art and written words. Quarterly. Estab. 1996.

Needs: Ethnic/multicultural, experimental, gay, humor/satire, literary, psychic/supernatural/occult. List of up-coming themes available for SASE. Receives 300 unsolicited mss/month. Accepts 5-10 mss/issue; 20-40 mss/year. Does not read July 15 to August 31. Publishes ms 4 months after acceptance. Length: 100 words minimum; 3,000 words maximum. Publishes short shorts. Also publishes literary essays, literary criticism and poetry.

How to Contact: Send complete ms with a cover letter. Include estimated word count and Social Security number. Reports in 3 months. Send a disposable copy of ms. Simultaneous, reprint and electronic (disk) submissions OK. Reviews novels and short story collections. Send books to Mickey Z., P.O. Box 522, Bronxville NY 11103.

Payment/Terms: Pays $140/page on publication for first rights.

Advice: "It has to be something that I haven't read anywhere else and that moves me to laugh, cry or simply get outraged. I want people to think about social issues."

‡**CUTBANK, (II)**, English Dept., University of Montana, Missoula MT 59812. (406)243-0211. Editors-in-Chief: Gerri Jardine and Arden Hendric. Fiction Editors: Cat Haglund and Pam Kennedy. Editors change each year. Terms run from June-June. After June, address to "Fiction Editor." Magazine: 5½×8½; 115-130 pages. "Publishes highest quality fiction, poetry, artwork, for a general, literary audience." Semiannually. Estab. 1973. Circ. 600.

Needs: Receives 200 unsolicited mss/month. Accepts 6-12 mss/year. Does not read mss from February 28-August 15. Publishes ms up to 6 months after acceptance. Published new writers within the last year. Length: 40 pages maximum. Also publishes literary essays, literary criticism, poetry. Occasionally critiques rejected mss.

How to Contact: Send complete ms with cover letter, which should include "name, address, publications." Reports in 1-4 months on mss. SASE. Simultaneous submissions OK. Sample copy for $4 (current issue $6.95). Fiction guidelines for SASE. Reviews novels and short story collections. Send books to fiction editor.
Payment/Terms: Pays 2 contributor's copies. Rights revert to author upon publication, with provision that *Cutbank* receives publication credit.
Advice: "Strongly suggest contributors read an issue. We have published stories by David Long, William Kittredge, Rick DeMarinis, Patricia Henley, Melanie Rae Thon and Michael Dorris in recent issues, and like to feature new writers alongside more well-known names. Send only your best work."

‡THE CUTTING EDGE, (I), P.O. Box 1292, Newton IA 50208-1292. Editor: L. McKinney. Magazine: 5×7; pages vary; illustrations. "I believe the smallest presses are the greatest opportunities for writers. I want to see everyone with something to say have a chance at publication." Bimonthly. Estab. 1996.
Needs: Erotica, experimental, gay, horror, lesbian, literary, mainstream/contemporary, psychic/supernatural/occult. Receives several unsolicited mss/month. Accepts 2 mss/issue; 20 mss/year. Publishes ms 2-4 months after acceptance. Length: 500 words minimum; 3,000 words maximum. Publishes short shorts. Also publishes poetry. Often critiques or comments on rejected mss.
How to Contact: Send complete ms with a cover letter. Include estimated word count, brief bio, list of publications and casual cover letter. Reports in 1 month. Send SASE for reply, return of ms or send a disposable copy of ms. Simultaneous and reprint submissions OK. Sample copy for $2. Fiction guidelines for SASE.
Payment/Terms: Pays 2 contributor's copies on publication. Acquires one-time rights.
Advice: "I want to see strong, hard, honest writing. Tell me what it's really like to be on the street, fighting, begging. I don't need to see slick, perfect writing. I want to hear what you really want to say. Don't think of me as an editor. I'm really just a fellow writer who got sick of the system and so created my own. If I could create my perfect world, every writer with something to say would have the space."

✦THE DALHOUSIE REVIEW, (II), Room 114, 1456 Henry St., Halifax, Nova Scotia B3H 3J5 Canada. Editor: Dr. Ronald Huebert. Magazine: 15cm×23cm; approximately 140 pages; photographs sometimes. Publishes articles, book reviews, short stories and poetry. Published 3 times a year. Circ. 650.
Needs: Literary. Length: 5,000 words maximum. Also publishes essays on history, philosophy, etc., and poetry.
How to Contact: Send complete ms with cover letter. SASE (Canadian stamps). Prefers submissions on computer disk (WordPerfect). Sample copy for $8.50 (Canadian) plus postage. Occasionally reviews novels and short story collections.

DAN RIVER ANTHOLOGY, (I), P.O. Box 298, S. Thomaston ME 04861. (207)354-0998. Fax: (207)354-8953. E-mail: olrob@midcoast.com. Editor: R. S. Danbury III. Book: 5½×8½; 156 pages; 60 lb. paper; gloss 65 lb. full-color cover; b&w illustrations. For general/adult audience. Annually. Estab. 1984. Circ. 800.
Needs: Adventure, contemporary, ethnic, experimental, fantasy, historical, horror, humor/satire, literary, mainstream, prose poem, psychic/supernatural, regional, romance (contemporary and historical), science fiction, senior citizen/retirement, suspense/mystery and western. No "evangelical Christian, pornography or sentimentality." Receives 150 unsolicited fiction mss each submission period (January 1 through March 31). "We generally publish 12-15 pieces of fiction." Reads "mostly in April." Length: 2,000-2,400 words average; 800 words minimum; 2,500 words maximum. Also publishes poetry.
How to Contact: *Charges reading fee: $1 for poetry; $3 for prose* (cash only, no checks). Send complete ms with SASE. Reports by May 15 each year. No simultaneous submissions. Sample copy for $12.95 paperback, $19.95 cloth, plus $2.75 shipping. Fiction guidelines for #10 SASE.
Payment/Terms: Pays $5/page, minimum *cash advance on acceptance* against royalties of 10% of all sales attributable to writer's influence: readings, mailings, autograph parties, etc., plus up to 50% discount on copies, plus other discounts to make total as high as 73%. Acquires first rights.
Advice: "Know your market. Don't submit without reading guidelines."

DAVIDS' PLACE JOURNAL, An AIDS Experience Journal, (I, II, IV), P.O. Box 632759, San Diego CA 92103. (619)294-5775. Fax: (619)683-9230. Website: http://www.davidsplace.com. Editor: R. Osborne. Magazine: 8½×7; 125 pages; illustrations and photos. The philosophy of *Davids' Place Journal* is "to communicate the HIV/AIDS experience, to reach the whole community. Submissions may be popular or scholarly." Quarterly. Estab. 1994. Circ. 500.
   ● *Davids' Place Journal* was named for a not-for-profit cafe in San Diego supportive of people with HIV/ AIDS and their friends. A version will be printed on the Internet.
Needs: HIV/AIDS experience. "No erotica." Receives 15 unsolicited mss/month. Accepts 10-15 mss/issue; 40-60 mss/year. Publishes ms 3-6 months after acceptance. Published work by Jameison Currior, Crystal Bacon, Gary Eldon Peter. Length: 5,000 words maximum. Publishes short shorts. Also publishes literary essays, poetry. Sometimes critiques or comments on rejected mss.
How to Contact: Send complete ms with a cover letter. Include 1-paragraph bio with submission. Send SASE for reply. Simultaneous and electronic (modem) submissions, reprints OK. Sample copy $4.
Payment/Terms: Pays 2 contributor's copies. Acquires one-time rights.
Advice: Looking for "authentic experience or artistic relevance to the AIDS experience."

DENVER QUARTERLY, (II, III), University of Denver, Denver CO 80208. (303)871-2892. Editor: Bin Ramke. Fiction Editor: Beth Nugent. Magazine: 6×9; 144-160 pages; occasional illustrations. "We publish fiction, articles and poetry for a generally well-educated audience, primarily interested in literature and the literary experience. They read *DQ* to find something a little different from a strictly academic quarterly or a creative writing outlet." Quarterly. Estab. 1966. Circ. 1,500.

- *Denver Quarterly* received an Honorable Mention for Content from the American Literary Magazine Awards.

Needs: "We are now interested in experimental fiction (minimalism, magic realism, etc.) as well as in realistic fiction and in writing about fiction. No sentimental, science fiction, romance or spy thrillers. No stories longer than 15 pages!" Recently published work by Lucie Broch-Broido, Judith E. Johnson, Stephen Alter and Jorie Graham. Published 5 new writers within the last year. Also publishes poetry.

How to Contact: Send complete ms and brief cover letter with SASE. Does not read mss May-September 15. Do not query. Reports in 3 months on mss. Publishes ms within a year after acceptance. Electronic submissions (disk, Windows 6.0) OK. No simultaneous submissions. Sample copy for $7 (anniversary issue), $6 (all other issues) with SASE.

Payment/Terms: Pays $5/page for fiction and poetry and 2 contributor's copies for first North American serial rights.

Advice: "We look for serious, realistic and experimental fiction; stories which appeal to intelligent, demanding readers who are not themselves fiction writers. Nothing so quickly disqualifies a manuscript as sloppy proofreading and mechanics. Read the magazine before submitting to it. We try to remain eclectic, but the odds for beginners are bound to be small considering the fact that we receive nearly 10,000 mss per year and publish only about ten short stories."

‡❀DESCANT, Descant Arts & Letters Foundation, P.O. Box 314, Station P, Toronto, Ontario M5S 2S8. (416)593-2557. Editor: Karen Mulhallen. Managing Editor: Tracy Jenkins. Quarterly literary journal. Estab. 1970. Circ. 1,200.

Needs: Litarary. Also publishes poetry and literary essays. Submit seasonal material 4 months in advance.

How to Contact: Send complete ms. Sample copy for $8. Writer's guidelines for SASE.

Payment/Terms: Pays $100. Pays on publication.

Advice: "Familiarize yourself with our magazine before submitting."

‡DIRIGIBLE, Journal of Language Art, (II), Dirigible Press, 216 Willow St., New Haven CT 06511. Editors: David Todd and Cynthia Conrad. Magazine: 4¼×7; 40-48 pages; 20 lb. white paper; card stock cover; illustrations. "We seek language-centered poetry, controlled experiments, fiction that is postmodern, paraliterary, nonlinear or subjective, and work that breaks with genre, convention, or form. Hybrid forms of writing and essays on aesthetics, poetics, reader experience and writing processes are also of interest to us." Quarterly. Estab. 1994. Circ. 500-800.

Needs: Experimental, literary, translations, avant garde. No realism or other mainstream genres. Accepts 2-3 mss/issue; 8-12 mss/year. Publishes ms 1 month after acceptance. Recently published work by Fernand Roqueplan, Peoria Melville, Angelica Kaner, Joyce Morral, Tom O'Connell, Mindi Englart, Alexander Shaumyan and Mark Johnston. Length: 1,750 words average; 1 word minimum; 3,600 words maximum. Publishes short shorts. Also publishes literary essays, literary criticism, poetry.

How to Contact: Send complete ms with a cover letter. Reports in 1 month on queries; 1-3 months on mss. Send SASE for reply, return of ms or send a disposable copy of ms. No simultaneous submissions. Sample copy for $2 postage paid. Reviews novels and short story collections.

Payment/Terms: Pays 2 contributor's copies on publication; additional copies for $2 ppd. Acquires first rights.

Advice: "We are grinding an aesthetic ax and acceptance is dependent on our personal vision."

‡THE DISTILLERY: ARTISTIC SPIRITS OF THE SOUTH, (I, II), Motlow St. Community College, P.O. Box 88100, Tullahoma TN 37388-8100. (615)393-1500. Fax: (615)393-1681. Editor: Stuart Bloodworth. Magazine: 88 pages; color cover; photographs. "The editors seek well-crafted, character-driven fiction. Several of us are writers, as well, so we want to see high-quality work that inspires us. In this postmodern-postmodern era, we think epiphanies are back in vogue." Semiannually. Estab. 1994. Circ. 500.

Needs: Literary. Receives 8-10 unsolicited mss/month. Accepts 3-4 mss/issue; 6-8 mss/year. Does not read mss June 1-August 1. Publishes ms 6-12 months after acceptance. Recently published work by Janice Daugharty, William Petrick and Sally Bennett. Length: 3,000-4,000 words average; 4,000 words maximum. Also publishes literary essays, literary criticism, poetry. Sometimes critiques or comments on rejected ms.

How to Contact: Send complete ms with a cover letter. Include estimated word count, brief bio, list of publications. "No third-person bio, please. What a strange thing . . ." Reports 2 weeks on queries; 2-3 months on mss. SASE for reply or send a disposable copy of ms. Sample copy for $6. Fiction guidelines for SASE. Occasionally reviews novels and short story collections. Send books to editor.

Payment/Terms: Pays 3 contributor's copies on publication; additional copies for $6. Acquires first North American serial rights.

Advice: "We want fiction that inspires us, that moves us to laugh or weep. Even though we are jaded old teachers and editors, we still want to feel a chill run down our spines when we read a perfect description or evocative line of dialogue. Revise, revise, revise. Also, do not write for a 'market,' whatever that means. Find your voice. If that voice has something to say, others will find it too, eventually.''

DODOBOBO, A New Fiction Magazine of Washington D.C., (I), Dodobobo Publications, P.O. Box 57214, Washington DC 20037. Editor: Brian Greene. Magazine: 5½×8½; 20-35 pages; illustrations and photos. "We're a literary fiction magazine which intends to give voice to writers the more well-known literary magazines would not be open to." Quarterly. Estab. 1994. Circ. 500.

Needs: Experimental and literary. Receives 20 unsolicited mss/month. Accepts 2-4 mss/issue; 8-16 mss/year. Publishes ms 1-12 months after acceptance. Length: 3,000 words maximum. Sometimes critiques or comments on rejected ms.

How to Contact: "Send complete ms, with or without cover letter." Reports in 2 months on mss. Send SASE for reply, return of ms or send a disposable copy of ms. Simultaneous and reprint submissions OK. Sample copy for $2 (including postage). Fiction guidelines for SASE.

Payment/Terms: Pays 2 contributor's copies. Acquires one-time rights. Sends galleys to author if requested.

Advice: "We like stories which illustrate the reality of the human experience—people's existential crises, their experiences with other people, with their own psyches. Get a copy or two of the magazine and read the stories we've printed.''

DOGWOOD TALES MAGAZINE, For the Fiction Lover in All of Us, (I, II), Two Sisters Publications, P.O. Box 172068, Memphis TN 38187. E-mail: write2me@aol.com. Website: http://www.sftwarestuff.com/dogw ood (includes writer's guidelines, contest information, subscription information, discussion pages for writers and readers). Editor: Linda Ditty. Fiction Editor: Peggy Carman. Magazine: 5½×8½; 52 pages; 20 lb. paper; 60 lb. cover stock; illustrations. "Interesting fiction that would appeal to all groups of people. Each issue will have a Special Feature Story about a Southern person, place or theme." Bimonthly. Estab. 1993.

Needs: Adventure, mainstream/contemporary, mystery/suspense, romance. No erotica, children and westerns. Strong offensive language or subject matter will be automatic rejection. Accepts 7-9 mss/issue; 42-54 mss/year. Publishes ms within 1 year after acceptance. Recently published work by Anne Weatherford, John M. Floyd, Percy Spurlark Parker and L.S. Renye. Length: 1,350 words preferred; 200 words minimum; 4,500 words maximum. Publishes short shorts. Length: 200-500 words. Sometimes critiques or comments on rejected mss.

How to Contact: Send complete ms with a cover letter. Should include estimated word count and list of publications. Reports within 10 weeks on mss. Send SASE for reply, return of ms or send a disposable copy of ms. Simultaneous and electronic submissions (disk, ASCII only, or modem) OK. Sample copy for $3.50. Fiction guidelines for #10 SASE or from website.

Payment/Terms: Pays ¼¢ to ½¢ per word on acceptance plus 1 contributor copy; additional copies at reduced rate. Acquires first serial rights and reprint rights.

Advice: "We like fresh and action moving stories with a strong ending. Must be tightly written and reach out and grab the reader. Revise and send your best. Don't be afraid to submit. Don't be discouraged by rejections.''

‡DOUBLE TAKE, 1317 W. Pettigrew St., Durham NC 27705. Contact: Fiction Editor.

Needs: "Realistic fiction in all of its variety; it's very unlikely we'd ever publish science fiction or gothic horror, for example." Buys 12 mss/year. Length: 3,000-8,000 words.

How to Contact: Send complete ms with cover letter. Accepts simultaneous submissions. Reports in 3 months on mss. Sample copy for $12. Writer's guidelines for #10 SASE.

Payment/Terms: Pays "competitively." Pays on acceptance. Buys first North American serial rights.

Advice: "Use a strong, developed narrative voice. Don't attempt too much or be overly melodramatic, lacking in subtlety, nuance and insight.''

‡DOWN UNDER MANHATTAN BRIDGE, (II), Longhall Productions, 228 East 10th St., #287, New York NY 10003. Editor: Elizabeth Morse. Magazine: 5½×9; 34 pages; 60 lb. cover, illustrations. "We are a serious fine arts publication. Our interests are like life—to create a journalistic and synaesthetic experience." Semiannually. Estab. 1980. Circ. 1,000.

Needs: Feminist, gay, lesbian, literary, mainstream/contemporary. No genre fiction. List of upcoming themes available for SASE. Most material is solicited. Accepts 3 mss/issue; 6-7 mss/year. Publishes ms 6 months to 1 year after acceptance. Recently published work by Ellen Aug Lytle, Janet Sassi and Thaddeus Rutkowski. Length: 3,000 words average. Publishes short shorts. Also publishes literary essays, literary criticism and poetry.

How to Contact: Send complete ms with a cover letter. Include estimated word count. Reports in 3-6 months on mss. Send SASE for reply, return of ms or send disposable copy of ms. Simultaneous submissions OK. Sample copy for $4.89. Fiction guidelines for #10 SASE.

Payment/Terms: Pays 5 contributor's copies for one-time rights.

Advice: "We like irony. Read the magazine and know our taste.''

DOWNSTATE STORY, (II, IV), 1825 Maple Ridge, Peoria IL 61614. (309)688-1409. E-mail: ehopkins@prair ienet.org. Website: http://www.wiu. bqu.edu/users/mfgeh/dss. Editor: Elaine Hopkins. Magazine: illustrations. "Short fiction—some connection with Illinois or the Midwest." Annually. Estab. 1992. Circ. 500.

Needs: Adventure, ethnic/multicultural, experimental, historical, horror, humor/satire, literary, mainstream/contemporary, mystery/suspense, psychic/supernatural/occult, regional, romance, science fiction, westerns. Accepts 10 mss/issue. Publishes ms up to 1 year after acceptance. Length: 300 words minimum; 2,000 words maximum. Publishes short shorts. Also publishes literary essays.

How to Contact: Send complete ms with a cover letter. Reports "ASAP." SASE for return of ms. Simultaneous submissions OK. Sample copy for $8. Fiction guidelines for SASE.

Payment/Terms: Pays $50 maximum on acceptance for first rights.

DROP FORGE, Literature for the Lost, (I, II), Jonestown Press, P.O. Box 4600, Bozeman MT 59772. Editor: Sean Winchester. Magazine: 7×8½; 32 pages; illustrations. "*Drop Forge* focuses on experimental and surreal material. There is a strong emphasis on language and syntax experimentalism. *Drop Forge* wants to know how you communicate with infinity." Published irregularly. Estab. 1993. Circ. 500.

Needs: Experimental and surreal: literary, non-stereotypical, philosophical, translations. "No material conforming to established-genre standards. We are not 'standard.' " Receives 10-15 unsolicited mss/month. Accepts 5-10 mss/issue. Publishes ms 2-8 months after acceptance. Length: 5 words minimum; 3,000 maximum. Publishes short shorts. Length: shorter than 500 words. Also publishes literary essays, poetry. Often critiques or comments on rejected mss.

How to Contact: Send complete ms with a cover letter. Include bio. "Send me a letter that lets me know there's a human on the other side." Reports in 4-5 weeks on queries; 3 months on mss. Send SASE for reply, return of ms or send a disposable copy of ms. No simultaneous submissions. Electronic submissions OK. Sample copy for $2.50. Fiction guidelines for #10 SASE. Reviews novels or short story collections. "Please note: I review only very small press releases, and only those coinciding with the interests of *Drop Forge*."

Payment/Terms: Pays 1 contributor's copy; additional copies available for postage. Acquires one-time rights.

Advice: "I'm interested in works that transcend themselves and the limitations of ordinary type. Take it further than it is willing to go. Don't send imitations. Don't send amusing moral anecdotes."

‡ECHO INK REVIEW, E.I. Publishing Services, (II), 17285 N.E. 70th St., Suite B, Redmond WA 98052. (206)643-6307. Fax: (206)643-6308. E-mail: Balchdrj@juno.com. Editor: Don Balch. Magazine: 6×9; 100-120 pages; 70 lb. paper, 10 pt. ics cover; illustrations and photos. "*Echo Ink Review* publishes short fiction to a general but literate audience of writers and readers. Because we are attempting to help all writers develop their craft, we consider manuscripts from beginning as well as established authors. Beginning writers might find that their manuscripts face stiff competition, but these writers will receive feedback—not the silent rejection." Quarterly. Estab. 1997. Circ. 200.

Needs: Condensed/excerpted novel, erotica, experimental, fantasy, feminist, gay, historical, horror, humor/satire, lesbian, literary, mainstream/contemporary, regional, science fiction, serialized novel. No juvenile, romance westerns or young adult. Publishes special fiction issues or anthologies. Receives 30 unsolicited mss/month. Accepts 6-8 mss/issue; 30 mss/year. Publishes mss 6-9 mss after acceptance. Recently published work by Richard Grayson, Marie Monilia and William J. Cobb. Length: 3,500 words average; 250 words minimum; 10,000 words maximum. Publishes short shorts. Always comments on or critiques rejected manuscripts.

How to Contact: Send complete manuscript with cover letter. Include brief bio, list of publications and estimated word count. Reports in 2 weeks on queries; 4 months on manuscripts. Send SASE for reply, return of ms or send disposable copy of ms. Simultaneous and electronic (disk only) submissions OK. Sample copy for $7.95. Fiction guidelines free.

Payment/Terms: Pays 2 contributor's copies for first rights; additional copies $7.95. Sends galleys to author.

Advice: "We like concrete images, characters amid conflict, structures and stories that cohere. We like an overall sense of change. We like humor, wry or otherwise. We like powerful writing that evokes powerful emotion. Regarding final editorial decisions, however, there remains a measure of subjectivity—we tend to publish only what we like. As we scan manuscripts, clean, typed or laser-printed material is a helpful gesture. Staples, handwritten manuscripts or manuscripts with ink corrections are . . . well . . . less than helpful."

ECHOES, (I, II), Echoes Magazine, P.O. Box 3622, Allentown PA 18106. Fax: (610)776-1634. E-mail: echoesmag@aol.com. Website: http://users.aol.com/echoesmag/. Editor: Peter Crownfield. Magazine: 6×9; 64 pages.; 60 lb. offset paper; 65-80 lb. cover; illustrations and photos. "*Echoes* publishes stories, poetry, and drawings from people in all walks of life—beginners and professionals, students and teachers. We look for writing that affirms the value of the person—either directly or by showing what happens when people are not valued. We like person-centered stories with well-developed characters and a clear story line." Bimonthly. Estab. 1994.

Needs: "*Echoes* will consider any genre as long as the story is well-written and interesting to readers." The following categories are of special interest: ethnic/multicultural, humor/satire, mainstream/contemporary, re-

---

SENDING TO A COUNTRY other than your own? Be sure to send International Reply Coupons instead of stamps for replies or return of your manuscript.

gional, senior citizen/retirement, young adult/teen. "We will not print any work containing gratuitous profanity, sex, or violence." Annual Memorial Day issue "features work that shows how war affects people, with work from veterans and military personnel welcomed." Deadline February 15. Publishes annual special fiction issue or anthology. Receives 100 unsolicited mss/month. Accepts 5 mss/issue; 30 mss/year. Publishes ms 6-40 weeks after acceptance. Recently published work by Carole Bellacera, Ann Mack, Jennifer L. Martin, Gene Moser, Lisa Parker and Donna Walker-Nixon. Length: 3,000 words average; 200 words minimum; 7,500 words maximum. Publishes short shorts. Also publishes poetry and drawings. Usually critiques or comments on rejected mss from subscribers. Sponsors contests. Send SASE for guidelines.

How to Contact: Send complete ms with a cover letter. Include estimated word count and 50-word bio. Reports in 2-3 weeks (subscribers); 8-12 weeks (nonsubscribers). Send SASE for return of ms and/or comments. Reprints and electronic submissions (disk or e-mail) OK. Sample copy $5. Fiction guidelines for SASE or at *Echoes'* website.

Payment/Terms: Pays 5 contributor's copies; additional copies for $4 postage paid.

Advice: "We appreciate stories with a personal viewpoint, well-developed characters and a clear story line—writing that makes us care what happens to the characters. Make your story clear and complete, and make sure it has a point that others will understand. Avoid rambling personal reminiscences."

THE ECKERD REVIEW, Literary Magazine of Eckerd College, (II), (formerly The Siren), Eckerd College, 4200 54th Ave. S., St. Petersburg FL 33711. (813)864-8238. Editor changes each year. Magazine: 9×6; 108 pages; photos. Annually. Estab. 1994. Circ. 1,400.

Needs: Literary, mainstream/contemporary, regional, translations. No science fiction, fantasy, horror, romance. Accepts 2-3 mss/issue. Does not read mss February-August. Publishes ms 2-3 months after acceptance. Published work by Fred Chappell, Elie Wiesel and Chip Greer. Length: 5-10 pages. Also publishes literary essays and poetry.

How to Contact: Send complete ms with a cover letter. Include bio and list of publications. Reports in 1-6 months on mss. Send SASE for return of ms. Simultaneous submissions OK. Sample copy for $6. Reviews novels and short story collections.

Payment/Terms: Pays 2 contributor's copies. Acquires one-time rights.

Advice: "We look for the highest quality, intelligent writing with plot."

‡ECLECTICA MAGAZINE, (II), P.O. Box 82826, Fairbanks AK 99708. (907)474-3494. Fax: (907)474-6841. E-mail: eclecticolarnet.com. Website: http://www2.polarnet.com/~eclectic. Editor: Chris Lott. Fiction Editor: Tom Dooley. Electronic magazine. "We publish the best writing on the World Wide Web. Although we are literary by nature, we publish exceptional work in almost every genre and strive to show the quality and viability of the electronic medium with our high editorial standards." Estab. 1996.

● Sponsors annual, multi-genre contest. See website for details.

Needs: Ethnic/multicultural, experimental, fantasy, humor/satire, literary, mystery/suspense, science fiction, serialized novel, translations. No pornography. Publishes special fiction issues or anthologies. Receives 100 unsolicited mss/month. Accepts 4-6 mss/issue, 72-84 mss/year. Publishes ms 2-3 months after acceptance. Recently published work by Wendy Battin, H. Palmer Hall, Stanley Jenkins and Ingrid Wendt. Length: 10,000 words average; 100 words minimum; 90,000 words maximum. Publishes short shorts. Also publishes literary essays, literary criticism and poetry. Sometimes critiques or comments on rejected mss.

How to Contact: Send complete ms with a cover letter. Include up to 250 word bio and list of publications. Reports in 1 week on queries; 4-6 weeks on mss. Send SASE for reply, return of ms or send disposable copy of ms. Simultaneous, reprint and electronic submissions OK. Reviews novels and short story collections. Send books to "Reviews Editor."

Advice: "A great opening page, consistent mechanics and memorable characters are usually a must. Experimental is good if it goes somewhere. Don't be fooled by the low standards of some web publications. We expect and get work equal to the best literary publications. Many of our authors submit 3-5 times before finding the right piece for us. Our exacting standards (and those of a few others) are proving the web to be a legitimate and fruitful publishing outlet and, like our print counterparts, a credit on our pages is valuable in future endeavors."

8, Dancing With Mr. D, (II), Screaming Toad Press/Dancing With Mr. D Publications, P.O. Box 7030, Falls Church VA 22046. Editor: Llori Steinberg. Magazine: 5×7; illustrations and photos. Monthly. Estab. 1994. Circ. 700.

● The editor says she wants to see more hardcore, irrational, mentally dysfunctional fiction of any subject. She added that the magazine will be going electronic in the future.

Needs: Adventure, erotica, experimental, fantasy (children's, science), horror, humor/satire, literary, mystery/suspense (amateur sleuth, police procedural, private eye/hardboiled. romantic), psychic/supernatural/occult. No gothic or Christian. List of upcoming themes available for SASE. Receives 100 unsolicited mss/month. Accepts 2-5 mss/issue; 6-9 mss/year. Recently published work by Max Thornegould and Jessica Manchester. Publishes 6-10 new writers/year. Length: 5,000 words minimum; 8,000 words maximum. Publishes short shorts. Also publishes literary essays, literary criticism, poetry. Sometimes critiques or comments on rejected mss.

How to Contact: Query with clips of published work and SASE with proper postage. Include bio with list of publications. Reports in 5 weeks on queries; 6-8 weeks on mss. Send SASE for reply. Simultaneous submissions and electronic (Windows only) submissions OK. Sample copy for $6 and 6×9 SAE with 5 first-class stamps. Fiction guidelines free for #10 SAE with 2 first-class stamps.

Payment/Terms: None. Sponsors contests; guidelines for SASE.

Advice: "Be original—don't try to prove a thing other than your honest self. Just send 'talk' to me—tell me your goals and 'loves.' " Does not want to see "Gothic vampire horror. There's already too much of it."

1812, A Literary Arts Magazine, (I, II), P.O. Box 1812, Amherst NY 14226-7812. E-mail: newwriting@aol. com or thebookdoc@aol.com. Website: http://www.1812.simplenet.com. Fiction Editor: Richard Lynch. Magazine: Illustrations and photographs. "We want to publish work that has some *bang*." Annually. Estab. 1994.
   • Work published in *1812* has been described as "experimental, surreal, bizarre."

Needs: Experimental, humor/satire, literary, mainstream/contemporary, translations. Does not want to see "stories about writers, stories about cancer, stories containing hospitals or stories that sound like they've been told before." Also publishes literary essays, literary criticism, poetry. Often critiques or comments on rejected mss.

How to Contact: Send complete ms with a cover letter. Include brief list of publications. Reports in 2 months. SASE for return of ms. Simultaneous, reprint and electronic submissions OK. Reviews novels and short story collections.

Payment/Terms: Payment is "arranged." Acquires one-time rights.

Advice: "Our philosophy can be summed up in the following quote from Beckett: 'I speak of an art turning from it in disgust, weary of its puny exploits, weary of pretending to be able, of being able, of doing a little better the same old thing, of going a little further along a dreary road.' Too many writers copy. We want to see writing by those who aren't on the 'dreary road.' "

ELF: ECLECTIC LITERARY FORUM, (I, II), P.O. Box 392, Tonawanda NY 14150. Phone/fax: (716)693-7006. E-mail: elf@econet.net. Website: http://www.pce.net/elf. Editor: C.K. Erbes. Magazine: 8½×11; 56 pages; 60 lb. offset paper; coated cover; 2-3 illustrations; 2-3 photographs. "Well-crafted short stories, poetry, interviews, reviews, Native American folklore, literary essays for a sophisticated audience." Quarterly. Estab. 1991. Circ. 5,000.

Needs: Adventure, contemporary, ethnic, fantasy, feminism, historical, humor/satire, literary, mainstream, mystery/suspense (private eye), prose poem, regional, science fiction (hard science, soft/sociological), sports, western. No violence and obscenity (horror/erotica). Accepts 4-6 mss/issue; 16-24 mss/year. Publishes ms up to 1 year after acceptance. Recently published work by Vonda McIntyre, Áine Greaney, John Dickson, Gary Earl Ross and R.G. Riel. Length: 3,500 words average. Publishes short shorts. Length: 500 words. Sometimes critiques rejected mss.

How to Contact: Send complete ms with optional cover letter. Reports in 4-6 weeks on mss. SASE. Simultaneous submissions OK (if so indicated). Sample copy for $5.50 ($8 foreign). Fiction guidelines for #10 SASE.

Payment/Terms: Pays contributor's copies. Acquires first North American serial rights.

Advice: "Short stories stand out when dialogue, plot, character, point of view and language usage work together to create a unified whole on a significant theme, one relevant to most of our readers. We also look for writers whose works demonstrate a knowledge of grammar and how to manipulate it effectively in a story. Each story is read by an Editorial Board comprised of English professors who teach creative writing and are published authors."

‡❤EMPLOI PLUS, (V), DGR Publication, 1256 Principale North St., #13, L'Annunciation, Quebec J0T 1T0 Canada. (819)275-3293. Fiction Editor: Daniel G. Reid. Magazine: 7×8½, 12 pages, illustrations and photos. Bilingual (French/English) magazine publishing Canadian and American authors. Every 2 or 3 years. Estab. 1990. Circ. 500.

Needs: Serialized novel. Recently published work by Robert Biro and D.G. Reid. Also publishes poetry.

How to Contact: *Closed to unsolicited submissions.* Sample copy free

EMRYS JOURNAL, (II), The Emrys Foundation, P.O. Box 8813, Greenville SC 29604. Editor: Jeanine Halva-Neubauer. Catalog: 9×9¾; 80 pages; 80 lb. paper (glossy). "We publish short fiction, poetry, and essays. We are particularly interested in hearing from women and other minorities. We are mindful of the southeast but not limited to it." Annually. Estab. 1984. Circ. 400.

Needs: Contemporary, feminist, literary, mainstream and regional. Reading period: August 1-December 1, 1998." Accepts 18 mss/issue. Publishes mss in April. Length: 3,500 words average; 6,000 words maximum. Publishes short shorts. Recently published work by Gil Allen, Margaret Kingery, Arlene McKanic and Kevin Breen.

How To Contact: Send complete ms with cover letter. Reports in 6 weeks. SASE. Sample copy for $15 and 7×10 SAE with 4 first-class stamps. Fiction guidelines for #10 SASE.

Payment/Terms: Pays in contributor's copies. Acquires first rights. "Send to managing editor for guidelines."

Advice: Looks for "fiction by women and minorities, especially but not exclusively southeastern."

‡ENTRE NOUS, (II), Stoneflower Press, 1824 Nacogdoches, Suite 191, San Antonio TX 78209. E-mail: stonflower@aol.com. Managing Editors: Brenda Davidson-Shaddox and Manda Russell. Magazine: 4×5½; approximately 60 pages; 50 lb. white offset paper; 67 lb. Vellum cover; illustrations and photographs. "We try to

help writers find a market for their works and build credentials to help expand exposure." Quarterly. Estab. 1997.
Needs: Ethnic/multicultural, experimental, feminist, literary, mainstream/contemporary. No pornography or religious. Upcoming themes: Relationships/Communication (March); Ethnic Traditions (June); Flying/Birds/Soaring (September); Aging/Growing (December). Guidelines available for SASE. Receives 25 unsolicited mss/month. Publishes ms 3-12 months after acceptance. Length: 2,000 words maximum. Also publishes poetry (line limit 40).
How to Contact: Send complete ms. "Don't try to convince me how good the story is via letter. Let the story speak." Include estimated word count, short paragraph bio, list of publications and awards won or other writing accomplishments. Reports in 2-3 months on mss. Send disposable copy of ms, but send SASE for response. Simultaneous, reprint and electronic submissions OK. Sample copy for $3, 6×9 SAE and 4 first-class stamps. Fiction guidelines for SASE.
Payment/Terms: First 2 copies of journal half price to contributors for SASE (6×9 with $1.24 postage). Acquires one-time rights.
Advice: "We look for technically good writing with good use of language. Study 'how-to' books. Take courses. Read other writers. Learn your craft. You're up against a wall of competitors."

EPOCH MAGAZINE, (II), 251 Goldwin Smith Hall, Cornell University, Ithaca NY 14853. (607)255-3385. Editor: Michael Koch. Submissions should be sent to Michael Koch. Magazine: 6×9; 128 pages; good quality paper; good cover stock. "Top level fiction and poetry for people who are interested in good literature." Published 3 times a year. Estab. 1947. Circ. 1,000.
  • *Epoch Magazine* won the premiere *O. Henry Magazine* Award for best magazine of 1997. Work originally appearing in this quality literary journal has appeared in numerous anthologies including *Best American Short Stories, Best American Poetry, Pushcart Prize, The O. Henry Prize Stories, Best of the West* and *New Stories from the South.*
Needs: Literary, contemporary and ethnic. Accepts 15-20 mss/issue. Receives 400 unsolicited fiction mss each month. Does not read in summer (April 15-September 15). Published work by Denis Johnson, Harriet Doerr, Lee K. Abbott. Published new writers in the last year. Length: no limit. Also publishes literary essays, poetry. Critiques rejected mss when there is time. Sometimes recommends other markets.
How to Contact: Send complete ms with SASE. No simultaneous submissions. Reports in 3-4 weeks on mss. Publishes ms an average of 6 months after acceptance. Sample copy for $5.
Payment/Terms: Pays $5-10/printed page on publication for first North American serial rights.
Advice: "Read the journals you're sending work to."

‡ETCETERA, A Journal of Art & Literature & Thought & Communication & Eclectic et cetera, (I, II), Etcetera Press, P.O. Box 8543, New Haven CT 06531. E-mail: iedit4you@aol.com. Editor: Mindi Englart. Magazine: 5½×8; 32 pages; sandstone cover stock; illustrations and photographs. Semiannually. Estab. 1996. Circ. 500.
Needs: Adventure, condensed/excerpted novel, experimental, feminist, gay, humor/satire, lesbian, literary, romance (contemporary), senior citizen/retirement, serialized novel, translation. No religious or romance. Receives 6-8 unsolicited mss/month. Accepts 2-3 mss/issue; 4-6 mss/year. Publishes ms 2 months after acceptance. Recently published work by Jared Millar, Robert Perchan and Steven Hirsch. Length: 1,200 words average; 1,800 words maximum. Publishes short shorts. Also publishes literary essays, poetry. Often critiques or comments on rejected ms if asked.
How to Contact: Send complete ms with a cover letter. Include estimated word count and 30-word bio. Reports on acceptances/rejections after March 15 and September 15 deadlines. Send SASE for reply, return of ms or send a disposable copy of ms. Simultaneous, reprint and electronic submissions OK. Sample copy for $3. Fiction guidelines for #11 SASE. Reviews novels and short story collections.
Payment/Terms: Pays 1 contributor's copy on publication. Acquires one-time rights. Sometimes sends galleys to author.
Advice: "Experimental, avant-garde, conceptual, thought-provoking, beautiful, ugly, sensitive, strange and humorous works are encouraged."

EUREKA LITERARY MAGAZINE, (I, II), P.O. Box 280, Eureka College, Eureka IL 61530. (309)467-6336. Editor: Loren Logsdon. Fiction Editor: Nancy Perkins. Magazine: 6×9; 100 pages; 70 lb. white offset paper; 80 lb. gloss cover; photographs (occasionally). "No particular theme or philosophy—general audience." Semiannually. Estab. 1992. Circ. 400.
Needs: Adventure, ethnic/multicultural, experimental, fantasy (science), feminist, historical, humor/satire, literary, mainstream/contemporary, mystery/suspense (private eye/hardboiled, romantic), psychic/supernatural/occult, regional, romance (historical), science fiction (soft/sociological), translations. "We try to achieve a balance between the traditional and the experimental. We do favor the traditional, though." Receives 25 unsolicited mss/month. Accepts 4 mss/issue; 8-9 mss/year. Does not read mss mainly in late summer (August). Published work by Samuel Floyd Cross, Leslie Schenk, Catherine Ryan Hyde, John M. Floyd and Joann Azen Bloom. Published new writers within the last year. Length: 4,500 words average; 7,000-8,000 words maximum. Publishes short shorts. Also publishes poetry.
How to Contact: Send complete ms with a cover letter. Should include estimated word count and bio (short

paragraph). Reports in 1 week on queries; 4 months on mss. Send SASE for reply, return of ms or send a disposable copy of ms. Simultaneous submissions OK. Sample copy for $5.

Payment/Terms: Pays free subscription to the magazine and 2 contributor's copies. Acquires first rights or one-time rights.

Advice: "Does the writer tell a good story—one that would interest a general reader? Is the story provocative? Is its subject important? Does the story contain good insight into life or the human condition? We don't want anything so abstract that it seems unrelated to anything human. We appreciate humor and effective use of language, stories that have powerful, effective endings. Take pains with the beginning and ending of the story; both must work. Be sure the voice is genuine. Be sure the manuscript is free from serious surface errors and is easy to read."

‡**EVANSVILLE REVIEW, (I, II)**, University of Evansville, 1800 Lincoln Ave., Evansville IN 47722. (812)488-1114. Website: http://www.evansville.edu/~elrweb. Editor: Ingrid Jendrzejewski. Editors change every 1-2 years. Magazine: 6×9; 120-150 pages; 70 lb. white paper; heavy laminated 4-color cover. Annually. Estab. 1990. Circ. 2,500.

Needs: "We're open to all creativity. No discrimination. All fiction, screenplays, nonfiction, poetry, interviews, photo essays and anything in between." No children or young adult. List of upcoming themes available for SASE. Receives 300 unsolicited mss/year. Does not read mss February-August. Agented fiction 2%. Recently published work by John Updike, Lewis Turco, Felix Stefanile, Dana Gioia, Willis Barnstone, James Ragan, Rachel Hadas and Josephine Jacobsen. Also publishes literary essays, poetry.

How to Contact: Send complete ms with a cover letter, e-mail or fax. Include 150 word or less bio and list of publications. Reports in 2 weeks on queries; 3 months on mss. Send SASE for reply, return of ms or send a disposable copy of ms. Simultaneous and reprint submissions OK. Sample copy for $5. Fiction guidelines free; check website.

Payment/Terms: Pays 5 contributor's copies on publication. Acquires one-time rights. Sends galleys to author if requested. Not copyrighted.

Advice: "Because editorial staffs roll over every 1-2 years, the journal always has a new flavor."

✦**EVENT, (II)**, Douglas College, Box 2503, New Westminster, British Columbia V3L 5B2 Canada. Fax: (604)527-5095. Editor: Calvin Wharton. Fiction Editor: Christine Dewar. Assistant Editor: Bonnie Bauder. Magazine: 6×9; 144 pages; quality paper and cover stock; illustrations; photos. "Primarily a literary magazine, publishing poetry, fiction, reviews; for creative writers, artists, anyone interested in contemporary literature." Triannually. Estab. 1971. Circ. 1,000.

Needs: Literary, contemporary, feminist, humor, regional. "No technically poor or unoriginal pieces." Receives approximately 100 unsolicited fiction mss/month. Accepts 6-8 mss/issue. Recently published work by Julie Keith, Andrew Pyper and Kate Braid. Published new writers within the last year. Length: 5,000 words maximum. Also publishes poetry.

How to Contact: Send complete ms, bio and SAE with Canadian postage or IRC. Reports in 1-4 months on mss. Publishes ms 6-12 months after acceptance. Sample copy for $5.

Payment/Terms: Pays $22/page and 2 contributor's copies on publication for first North American serial rights.

Advice: "A good narrative arc is hard to find."

THE EVERGREEN CHRONICLES, A Journal of Gay, Lesbian, Bisexual & Transgendered Arts & Cultures, (II), P.O. Box 8939, Minneapolis MN 55408-0939. Fax: (612)722-9005. E-mail: evgrnchron@aol.com. Managing Editor: Louisa Castner. Magazine: 7×8½; 90-100 pages; b&w line drawings and photos. "We look for work that addresses the complexities and diversities of gay, lesbian, bisexual and transgendered experiences." Triannually. Estab. 1985. Circ. 1,000.

● The magazine sponsors an annual novella contest; deadline September 30. Send SASE for guidelines.

Needs: Gay or lesbian: adventure, confession, contemporary, ethnic, experimental, feminist, humor/satire, literary, serialized/excerpted novel, suspense/mystery. "We are interested in works by artists in a wide variety of genres. The subject matter need not be specifically lesbian, gay, bisexual or transgender-themed, but we do look for a deep sensitivity to that experience. No sentimental, romantic stuff, fantasy or science fiction." Accepts 10-12 mss/issue; 30-36 mss/year. Publishes ms approximately 2 months after acceptance. Recently published work by Terri Jewel, Doris Grumbach, Alfred Corn and Ruthann Robson. Publishes 10-12 new writers/year. Length: 3,500-4,500 words average; no minimum; 5,200 words maximum. 25 pages double-spaced maximum on prose. Publishes short shorts. Sometimes comments on rejected mss.

How to Contact: Send 4 copies of complete ms with cover letter. "It helps to have some biographical informa-

---

FOR INFORMATION ON ENTERING the *Novel & Short Story Writer's Market* Cover Letter Contest, see page 84.

tion included." Submission deadlines: January 1 and July 1. Reports on queries in 3 weeks; on mss in 3-4 months. SASE. Electronic submissions (fax, e-mail) OK. Sample copy for $8 and $2 postage. Fiction guidelines for #10 SASE.

Payment/Terms: Pays $50 honorarium for one-time rights.

Advice: "We've seen a great increase in the number of unsolicited manuscripts sent to us for consideration. More and more competition in our specific genre of gay and lesbian writing. This means that the quality of the writing we publish is getting better—more readers and writers out there. We're looking for originality in perspective and/or language. Share your writing with others! Join writing groups."

EXPLORATIONS '97, (I, II), University of Alaska Southeast, 11120 Glacier Highway, Juneau AK 99801. (907)465-6418. Fax: (907)465-6406. E-mail: jnamp@acadl.alaska.edu. Editor: Art Petersen. Magazine: 5½ × 8¼; 60 pages; heavy cover stock; b&w illustrations and photographs. "Poetry, prose and art—we strive for artistic excellence." Annually. Estab. 1981. Circ. 750.

Needs: Experimental, humor/satire, traditional quality fiction, poetry, and art. Receives about 1,200 mss/year. Recently published work by William Everson, David Ray, Ania Savage and Nicchia P. Leamer.

How to Contact: *Reading/entry fee $5/story required.* Send name, address and short bio on *back* of first page of each submission. All submissions entered in contest. Submission postmark deadline is March 21. Reports in 2-3 months. Mss cannot be returned. Simultaneous and reprint submissions OK. Sample copy for $5.

Payment/Terms: Pays 2 contributor's copies. Acquires one-time rights (rights remain with the author). Also awards 4 annual prizes of $500 for prose, $500 for poetry and $125 for art ($100, $50 and $25—UAS students only).

Advice: "It is best to send for full guidelines. Concerning poetry and prose, standard form as well as innovation are encouraged; appropriate and fresh *imagery* (allusions, metaphors, similes, symbols . . .) as well as standard or experimental form draw editorial attention. 'Language really spoken by men' and women and authentically rendered experience are encouraged. Unfortunately, requests for criticism usually cannot be met. The prizes for 1997 will be awarded by the poet and critic John Haines."

EXPLORER MAGAZINE, (I), Flory Publishing Co., Box 210, Notre Dame IN 46556. Editor: Raymond Flory. Magazine: 5½ × 8½; approximately 32 pages; 20 lb. paper; 60 lb. or stock cover; illustrations. Magazine with "basically an inspirational theme including love stories in good taste." Christian writing audience. Semiannually. Estab. 1960. Circ. 300.

● The magazine sponsors The Joseph Flory Memorial Award and the Angel Light Award. Awards are $10 and a plaque.

Needs: Literary, mainstream, prose poem, religious/inspirational, romance (contemporary, historical, young adult) and science fiction. No pornography. Accepts 2-3 mss/issue; 5 mss/year. Recently published work by Roger Lee Kenvin, James M. Lane, L.J. Cardin and Terry Peterson. Length: 600 words average; 300 words minimum; 700 words maximum. Also publishes literary essays. Occasionally critiques rejected mss.

How to Contact: Send complete ms with SASE. Reports in 1 week. Publishes ms up to 3 years after acceptance. Simultaneous submissions OK. Sample copy for $3. Fiction guidelines for SASE.

Payment/Terms: Cash prizes of $25, $20, $15 and $10 based on subscribers' votes. The first prize winner also receives a plaque.

Advice: "I need short material, preferably no longer than 700 words—the shorter the better. I always like 'slice of life' with a message, without being preachy. Look for fiction with a 'message' in all styles that are written with feeling and flair. Just keep it short, 'camera-ready' and always in good taste."

EXPRESSIONS, Literature and Art by People with Disabilities and Ongoing Health Problems, (IV), Serendipity Press, P.O. Box 16294, St. Paul MN 55116-0294. (612)552-1209. Fax: (612)552-1209. E-mail: dmamom@worldnet.att.com. Editor: Sefra Kobrin Pitzele. Magazine: 5½ × 8½; 60-84 pages; 60 lb. biodegradable paper; 80 lb. semigloss cover; illustrations and photographs. "*Expressions* provides a quality journal in which to be published when health, mobility, access or illness make multiple submissions both unreachable and unaffordable." Semiannually. Estab. 1993. Circ. 750.

Needs: *Material from writers with disabilities or ongoing health problems only.* Adventure, ethnic/multicultural, experimental, fantasy, feminist, gay, historical, horror, humor/satire, lesbian, literary, mainstream/contemporary, mystery/suspense, psychic/supernatural/occult, regional, religious/inspirational, romance, science fiction, senior citizen/retirement, sports and westerns. "We have no young readers, so all fiction should be intended for adult readers." Does not read mss from December 15 to February 1. Publishes ms 3-5 months after acceptance. Publishes 10-20 new writers/year. Length: 1,500-2,000 words average. Publishes short shorts. Also publishes literary essays, literary criticism, poetry. Sometimes critiques or comments on rejected mss. Sponsors a fiction contest. Send #10 SASE for more information. "Eight to ten reader/scorers from across the nation help me rank each submission on its own merit." Awards are $50 (first place), $25 (second place) and a year's subscription (third place).

How to Contact: *Requires $5 reading fee.* Write for fiction guidelines; include SASE. Submission deadlines: May 15 and November 15. Reports in 2-6 weeks on queries; 2-4 months on mss. SASE for reply to query or return of ms. Simultaneous, reprint and electronic submissions OK. Sample copy for $6, 6 × 9 SAE and 5 first-class stamps.

Payment/Terms: Pays 2 contributor's copies. Acquires one-time rights.
Advice: "Only send clean, new, dark print copy with 1″ margins all around, name and page number on each page. We ask for two copies. Always send a short bio letter and name your submission in that letter. Always send SASE. And be patient."

‡THE FAIRFIELD REVIEW, (I, II), (203)319-0039. Fax: (203)319-0049. E-mail: FairfieldReview@hpmd.com. Website: http://www.fairfieldreview.com. Editor: Edward G.Happ. Electronic magazine. "Our mission is to provide an outlet for poetry, short stories and essays, from both new and established writers and students, which are accessible to the general public."
Needs: Short stories, poetry, essays. Would like to see more stories "rich in lyrical imagery and those that are more humorous." Recently published work by Kelli Willingham and John H. Jennings. Publishes over 20 new writers/year. "We encourage students and first-time writers to submit their work."
How to Contact: Electronic submissions preferred. Fax submissions accepted.
Advice: "In addition to the submission guidelines found in each issue on our website, we recommend reading the essay *Writing Qualities to Keep in Mind* from our Spring 1997 issue."

‡FAN MAGAZINE, A Baseball Literary Magazine, (I, II, IV), 145 15th St. NE, #805, Atlanta GA 30361. (404)607-9489. Fax: (404)607-8639. Editor: Mike Schacht. Magazine: 5½×8½; 64 pages; 60 lb. paper; 65 lb. cover; illustrations and photos. "We believe everyone has a baseball story; we are out to capture the best in poetry, memoir and short fiction." Triannually. Estab. 1989. Circ. 500.
Needs: Historical, literary, sports, nostalgia, memoir. Receives 10 unsolicited mss/month. Accepts 3-5 mss/issue, "depending on quality of submissions." Publishes ms 3 months to 1 year after acceptance. Recently published work by Gene Fehler and Mike Schacht. Length: 1,500 words average. Publishes short shorts. Also publishes literary essays and poetry. Often critiques or comments on rejected mss.
How to Contact: Send complete ms with a cover letter. "A query for guidelines is appreciated." Include estimated word count and 1-2 paragraph bio. Reports in 2 weeks on queries; 2 months on mss. Send SASE for return of ms. Simultaneous submissions and reprints OK. Sample copy for $6. Fiction guidelines free.
Payment/Terms: "Pays 2 contributor's copies; additional copies $3."
Advice: "Please review sample copy and guidelines before submitting. Story must have baseball connection."

FAT TUESDAY, (I, II), 560 Manada Gap Rd., Grantville PA 17028. Editor-in-Chief: F.M. Cotolo. Editors: B. Lyle Tabor and Thom Savion. Associate Editors: Lionel Stevroid and Kristen vonOehrke. Journal: 8½×11 or 5×8; 27-36 pages; bond paper; heavy cover stock; saddle-stitched; b&w illustrations; photos. "Generally, we are an eclectic journal of fiction, poetry and visual treats. Our issues to date have featured artists like Patrick Kelly, Charles Bukowski, Joi Cook, Chuck Taylor and many more who have focused on an individualistic nature with fiery elements. We are a literary mardi gras—as the title indicates—and irreverancy is as acceptable to us as profundity as long as there is fire! Our audience is anyone who can praise literature and condemn it at the same time. Anyone too serious about it on either level will not like *Fat Tuesday*." Annually. Estab. 1981. Circ. 700.

• *Fat Tuesday* is best known for first-person "auto fiction." Their 1997-1998 edition was published in audio format. They may publish future issues in this format.

Needs: Comics, erotica, experimental, humor/satire, literary, prose poem, psychic/supernatural/occult, serialized/excerpted novel and dada. "Although we list categories, we are open to feeling out various fields if they are delivered with the mark of an individual and not just in the format of the particular field." Receives 20 unsolicited fiction mss/month. Accepts 4-5 mss/issue. Published new writers within the last year. Length: 1,000 words maximum. Publishes short shorts. Occasionally critiques rejected mss and usually responds with a personal note or letter.
How to Contact: Send complete ms with SASE. "No previously published material considered." No simultaneous submissions. Reports in 1 month. Publishes ms 3-10 months after acceptance. Sample copy for $5.
Payment/Terms: Pays 1 contributor's copy. Acquires one-time rights.
Advice: "As *Fat Tuesday* crawls through its second decade, we find publishing small press editions more difficult than ever. Money remains a problem, mostly because small press seems to play to the very people who wish to be published in it. In other words, the cast is the audience, and more people want to be in *Fat Tuesday* than want to buy it. It is through sales that our magazine supports itself. This is why we emphasize buying a sample issue ($5) before submitting. As far as what we want to publish—send us shorter works that are 'crystals of thought and emotion which reflect your individual experiences—dig into your guts and pull out pieces of yourself. Your work is your signature; like time itself, it should emerge from the penetralia of your being and recede into the infinite region of the cosmos,' to coin a phrase, and remember *Fat Tuesday* is mardi gras—so fill up before you fast. Bon soir."

FAULT LINES, (I, II), Club Mad Publishing, 107 Demoss Rd., #2, Nashville TN 37209. (615)356-6591. E-mail: jayjones@negia.net. Website: http://www.negia.net/~jayjones/faultlines. Editors: Rex McCulloch, Mark Roberts and Jay Jones. Fiction Editor: Rex McCulloch. Magazine: 5½×8½; 32 pages; 20 lb. white bond paper; 60 lb. cover; photographs and illustrations. Semiannually. Estab. 1994. Circ. 300.

• *Fault Lines* has recently gone to an entirely electronic format.

Needs: Experimental, humor/satire, literary, translations. "Believing that the image resides at the heart of the idea, *Fault Lines* encourages experiments that blend literary and graphical elements." Receives 10-20 unsolicited mss/month. Accepts 4-5 mss/issue; 12 mss/year. Publishes ms 1 month after acceptance. Length: 2,500 words maximum. Publishes short shorts. Also publishes literary essays, poetry, photographs, art. Sometimes critiques or comments on rejected ms.

How to Contact: Send complete ms with a cover letter. Should include estimated word count and brief bio with partial list of previous publications. Reports in 2-3 months on mss. Simultaneous, reprint, electronic (Macintosh compatible) submissions OK. Fiction guidelines for #10 SASE or on website. Reviews novels and short story collections. Send books to Rex McCulloch.

Payment/Terms: Acquires one-time rights.

Advice: "It's better to write interesting fiction about an unassuming subject than to try to fake an exciting story. Neatness and careful editing always make a good impression. In any genre, the elements of good fiction are always the same: idea, character development, and above all, the ability to make the reader care."

FEMINIST STUDIES, (II, IV), Department of Women's Studies, University of Maryland, College Park MD 20742. (301)405-7415. Fax: (301)314-9190. E-mail: femstud@umail.umd.edu. Website: http://www.inform.umd.edu/femstud. Editor: Claire G. Moses. Fiction Editor: Alicia Ostriker. Magazine: journal-sized; about 200 pages; photographs. "Scholarly manuscripts, fiction, book review essays for professors, graduate/doctoral students; scholarly interdisciplinary feminist journal." Triannually. Estab. 1974. Circ. 7,500.

Needs: Contemporary, ethnic, feminist, gay, lesbian. Receives about 15 poetry and short story mss/month. Accepts 2-3 mss/issue. "We review fiction twice a year. Deadline dates are May 1 and December 1. Authors will receive notice of the board's decision by June 30 and January 30, respectively." Published work by Barbara Wilson, Su Fidler Cowling, Frances Webb and Lisa Chewning. Sometimes comments on rejected mss.

How to Contact: Send complete ms with cover letter. No simultaneous submissions. Sample copy for $12. Fiction guidelines free.

Payment/Terms: Pays 2 contributor's copies and 10 tearsheets. Sends galleys to authors.

FICTION, (II), % Dept. of English, City College, 138th St. & Convent Ave., New York NY 10031. (212)650-6319/650-6317. Editor: Mark J. Mirsky. Managing Editor: Michael W. Pollock. Magazine: 6×9; 150-250 pages; illustrations and occasionally photos. "As the name implies, we publish *only* fiction; we are looking for the best new writing available, leaning toward the unconventional. *Fiction* has traditionally attempted to make accessible the unaccessible, to bring the experimental to a broader audience." Biannually. Estab. 1972. Circ. 4,500.

● Stories first published in *Fiction* have been selected for inclusion in the *Pushcart Prize* and *Best of the Small Presses* anthologies.

Needs: Contemporary, experimental, humor/satire, literary and translations. No romance, science-fiction, etc. Receives 200 unsolicited mss/month. Accepts 12-20 mss/issue; 24-40 mss/year. Does not read mss May-October. Publishes ms 1-12 months after acceptance. Agented fiction 10-20%. Published work by Harold Brodkey, Joyce Carol Oates, Peter Handke, Max Frisch, Susan Minot and Adolfo Bioy-Casares. Length: 6,000 words maximum. Publishes short shorts. Sometimes critiques rejected mss and recommends other markets.

How to Contact: Send complete ms with cover letter. Reports in approximately 3 months on mss. SASE. Simultaneous submissions OK, but please advise. Sample copy for $5. Fiction guidelines for SASE.

Payment/Terms: Pays in contributor's copies. Acquires first rights.

Advice: "The guiding principle of *Fiction* has always been to go to terra incognita in the writing of the imagination and to ask that modern fiction set itself serious questions, if often in absurd and comic voices, interrogating the nature of the real and the fantastic. It represents no particular school of fiction, except the innovative. Its pages have often been a harbor for writers at odds with each other. As a result of its willingness to publish the difficult, experimental, unusual, while not excluding the well known, *Fiction* has a unique reputation in the U.S. and abroad as a journal of future directions."

‡❦THE FIDDLEHEAD, (I, II), University of New Brunswick, Campus House, Box 4400, Fredericton, New Brunswick E3B 5A3 Canada. (506)453-3501. Editor: Don McKay. Fiction Editors: Diana Austin, Banny Belyea and Ted Colson. Magazine: 6×9; 104-128 pages; ink illustrations; photos. "No criteria for publication except quality. For a general audience, including many poets and writers." Quarterly. Estab. 1945. Circ. 1,000.

Needs: Literary. No non-literary fiction. Receives 100-150 unsolicited mss/month. Buys 4-5 mss/issue; 20-40 mss/year. Publishes ms up to 1 year after acceptance. Small percent agented fiction. Recently published work by C.R. Crackel; published new writers within the last year. Length: 50-3,000 words average. Publishes short shorts. Occasionally critiques rejected mss.

How to Contact: Send complete ms with cover letter. Send SASE and *Canadian* stamps or IRCs for return of mss. Reprint submissions OK. No simultaneous submissions. Reports in 2-6 months. Sample copy for $7 (US). Reviews novels and short story collections—*Canadian only*.

Payment/Terms: Pays $10-12 (Canadian)/published page and 1 contributor's copy on publication for first or one-time rights.

Advice: "Less than 5% of the material received is published."

‡THE 5TH WALL, a literary gallery for the exhibition of written art, (II), P.O. Box 22161, San Diego CA 92192-2161. (415)831-1514. E-mail: tchad@sfsu.edu. Editor: Chad Mealey. Fiction Editor: Chris Kalidor. Magazine: 4¼×11; 20 pages (varies); paper and cover stock vary. "Artwork created with words has as much value as artwork created with paint or ink or clay. We publish 'artwork' that often evades poetry or prose in a gallery format for the curious." Semiannually. Estab. 1991. Circ. 200.

Needs: Children's/juvenile, condensed/excerpted novel, experimental, humor/satire, literary, mainstream/contemporary, regional, science fiction, translations, unusual. List of upcoming themes available for SASE. Publishes special fiction issues or anthologies. Receives 10-15 unsolicited mss/month. Accepts 10 mss/issue; 20 mss/year. Publishes ms 1-4 months after acceptance. Recently published work by David Horwitz, Richard Kostelanetz and Igor Korneitchouk. Length: 2,000 words average; 1 word minimum; 4,000 words maximum. Publishes short shorts. Also publishes literary essays and poetry. Often critiques or comments on rejected mss.

How to Contact: Query first for long pieces, otherwise send complete ms. Include 1 paragraph bio and list date, medium and price of artwork. Reports in 1 month on queries; 2-4 months on mss. Send SASE for reply, return of ms or send disposable copy of ms. Simultaneous, reprint and electronic submissions OK. Sample copy for $2 and #14 envelope with 2 first-class stamps. Fiction guidelines for #10 SASE.

Payment/Terms: Pays 80% minimum; 90% maximum and 1-10 contributor's copies on publication for one-time rights; additional copies $1 or $2.

Advice: "We view every manuscript as a piece of art. Is it a beautiful landscape? A dynamic abstract? Expressive? Is the piece executed in a way appropriate to the concept or subject? Forget the rules."

‡❀FILLING STATION, (I, II), Filling Station Publications Society, Box 22135, Bankers Hall, Calgary, Alberta T2P 4J5 Canada. E-mail: cybele_cveery@shell. Contact: Editorial Collective. Magazine: 8½×11; 48 pages; 70 lb. offset paper; 80 lb. glossy cover; illustrations and photos. "We're looking for writing that challenges the preconceptions of readers and writers alike, that crosses conventional boundaries and seeks out its own territory. We're particularly interested in new voices." Triannually. Estab. 1993. Circ. 500.

Needs: Ethnic/multicultural, experimental, feminist, gay, lesbian, literary, mainstream/contemporary, regional and translations. Receives 10-15 unsolicited submissions/month. Accepts 3-4 mss/issue; 10 mss/year. Publishes ms within 1 year after acceptance. Recently published work by Thomas Wharton, Golda Fried, Richard Brown, G.R. Gustafson and Robert Majamaa. Publishes 5-6 new writers/year. Length: 2,000 words average; 5,000 words maximum. Publishes short shorts. Also publishes literary essays, literary criticism and poetry.

How to Contact: Send complete ms with cover letter. Should include bio (20-30 words). Reports in 1 month on queries; 3 months on mss. Send SASE for reply, return of ms or send a disposable copy of ms. Simultaneous and electronic submissions OK. Sample copy for $6, 9×12 SAE, 4 first-class stamps or 2 IRCs. Fiction guidelines for #10 SASE. Reviews novels and short story collections.

Payment/Terms: Pays 2 contributor's copies. Acquires first North American serial rights.

Advice: "Fiction must first of all be compositionally solid and show an awareness of, and flexibility within, the language. Beyond this, the writer needs to take risks, to push things a little further. Let your writing stand on its own merit. Don't try to impress editors with flashy cover letters, name-dropping or stacks of credentials. Publishing, especially for small-run magazines, is increasingly expensive and difficult in an era of rising production costs and shrinking funding. The demands on any publisher in any market to seek out higher-quality work are correspondingly greater."

FISH DRUM MAGAZINE, (II), Murray Hill Station, P.O. Box 966, New York NY 10156. Editor: Suzi Winson. Magazine: 5½×8½; 80-odd pages; glossy cover; illustrations and photographs. "Lively, emotional vernacular modern fiction, art and poetry." Annually. Estab. 1988 by Robert Winson (1959-1995). Suzi says, "It is my intention to complete Robert's work and to honor his memory by continuing to publish *Fish Drum*." Circ. 1,000.

Needs: Contemporary, erotica, ethnic, experimental, fantasy, gay, lesbian, literary, prose poem, regional, science fiction. "Most of the fiction we've published is in the form of short, heightened prose-pieces." Receives 6-10 unsolicited mss/month. Accepts 1-2 mss/issue. Also publishes literary essays, literary criticism, poetry.

How to Contact: Send complete manuscript. No simultaneous submissions. Reports on mss in 2-3 months. SASE. Reviews novels and short story collections.

Payment/Terms: Pays in contributor's copies. Charges for extras. Acquires first North American serial rights. Sends galleys to author.

FISH STORIES, Collective II, (II), WorkShirts Writing Center, 3540 N. Southport Ave. #493, Chicago IL 60657-1436. (773)334-8510. Fax: (773)334-6673. Editor: Amy G. Davis. Magazine: 5⅜×8½; 224 pages; 60 lb. white paper; 4-color C1S cover. "We are seeking vivid stories that stand up to a second reading, but don't require it. While our fiction is literary, we have readers outside that audience. *Fish Stories* strives for a diverse collection of work." Annually. Estab. 1995. Circ. 1,200.

• Tobias Wolff's "Powder" published in *Fish Stories: Collective II*, was chosen for *Best American Short Stories* 1997.

Needs: Ethnic/multicultural, experimental, feminist, gay, lesbian, literary, regional. No mainstream, science fiction or any other genre fiction. "We seek experimental or traditional literary work." Receives 65 unsolicited mss/month. Accepts 15-20 mss/issue. Does not read January through July. Publishes ms 2-8 months after acceptance. Recently published work by Tobias Wolff, Yusef Komunyakaa, Rich Bass, Barbara Kingsolver, Stephen

Dixon and Frederick Busch and 5 previously unpublished writers and poets. Length: 3,000-5,000 words average; 10,000 words maximum. Publishes short shorts. Also publishes poetry. Sometimes critiques or comments on rejected mss.

How to Contact: Send for guidelines. "Read a sample copy first, then send mss." Include estimated word count, brief bio, Social Security number, list of publications. Reports in 6 months on mss. Send SASE for reply, return of ms or send a disposable copy of ms. Simultaneous and reprint submissions OK. Sample copy for $10.95. Fiction guidelines free for #10 SASE.

Payment/Terms: Pays 2 contributor's copies; additional copies half-price. Acquires one-time rights.

Advice: Looks for "a strong introduction that is followed through by the rest of the story. The manuscripts that stand out are polished with careful attention to the holistic use of language, point of view, etc."

FLIPSIDE, (I, II), Professional Writing Program, Dixon 109, California University, California PA 15419. (412)938-4586. Editor: Joseph Szejk. Tabloid: 11½×17; 45-60 pages; illustrations; photos. "We publish highly descriptive fiction with characters who 'do something' and are set in scenes which the reader can see." Semiannually. Estab. 1987. Circ. 5,000.

Needs: Contemporary, experimental, literary. No genre fiction. Receives 5-6 unsolicited mss/week. Accepts 2-3 mss/issue; 6-8 mss/year. Publishes ms 1-6 months after acceptance. Publishes 6 new writers/year. Length: 1,000-5,000 words average; 8,000 words maximum. Also publishes literary essays, literary criticism, some poetry.

How to Contact: Send complete ms with cover letter. Reports in 1 month on queries; 2-3 months on mss. SASE. Simultaneous submissions OK. Sample copy and fiction guidelines for 9×12 SAE and $2 postage.

Payment/Terms: Pays 2 contributor's copies. Acquires first North American serial rights.

Advice: "We *do* want heavy description, strong metaphors, highly visible and memorable characters as well as scenes. We do not waste our time with bogus ramblings in a narrator's head in situations or places the reader cannot visualize. Keep writing, rewriting and refining your work. Don't be satisfied by filling pages—make the words create a definite mood or tone."

THE FLORIDA REVIEW, (II), Dept. of English, University of Central Florida, Orlando FL 32816. (407)823-2038. Fax: (407)823-6582. Contact: Russell Kesler. Magazine: 5½×8½; 120 pages; semigloss full-color cover; perfect-bound. "We publish fiction of high 'literary' quality—stories that delight, instruct and aren't afraid to take risks." Semiannually. Estab. 1972. Circ. 1,000.

Needs: Contemporary, experimental and literary. "We welcome experimental fiction, so long as it doesn't make us feel lost or stupid. We aren't especially interested in genre fiction (science fiction, romance, adventure, etc.), though a good story can transcend any genre." Receives 200 mss/month. Accepts 8-10 mss/issue; 16-20 mss/year. Publishes ms within 3-6 months of acceptance. Recently published work by Joey Brown, Emily Meier, Leslie Daniels, Will Allison, Merin Wexler, Lisa Stolley, Anthony Burke Lee and Debbie Lee Wesselmann. Publishes 2-4 new writers/year. Also publishes literary criticism, poetry and essays.

How to Contact: Send complete ms with cover letter. Reports in 2-4 months. SASE required. Simultaneous submissions OK. Sample copy for $6; fiction guidelines for SASE. Reviews novels and short story collections.

Payment/Terms: Pays in contributor's copies. Small honorarium occasionally available. "Copyright held by U.C.F.; reverts to author after publication. (In cases of reprints, we ask that a credit line indicate that the work first appeared in the *F.R.*)"

FLYING HORSE, P.O. Box 445, Marblehead MA 01945. Editor: Dennis Must. Associate Editor: David Wagner. Magazine: 6×9; 100 pages; 50 lb. Finch Opaque paper; 70 lb. cover stock; illustrations; photographs. "*Flying Horse* is an alternative literary journal. Although we welcome contributions from all talented artists, we particularly hope to give voice to those often excluded from the dominant media. For example, we actively encourage submissions from inner city learning centers, community and public colleges, prisons, homeless shelters, social service agencies, unions, the military, hospitals, clinics or group homes, Indian reservations and minority studies programs." Semiannually. Estab. 1996. Circ. 1,000.

Needs: Condensed/excerpted novel, ethnic/multicultural, experimental, literary, mainstream/contemporary, translations. Receives 75-100 unsolicited mss/month. Accepts 20 mss/issue; 40 mss/year. Publishes ms generally in the next issue. Recently published work by Simon Perchik, Lyn Lifshin, David Castleman, Dennis Brutus, Joi Brozek and Zeeva Bukai. Publishes 20 new writers/year. Length: 2,500-5,000 words average; 7,500 words maximum. Publishes short shorts. Also publishes literary essays, literary criticism and poetry. Often critiques or comments on rejected mss.

How to Contact: Send complete ms with a cover letter. Include estimated word count and short bio with

---

* **INTERNATIONAL MARKETS**, those located outside of the United States and Canada, are marked with an asterisk.

submission. Reports in 3 months on mss. Send SASE for reply, return of ms or send a disposable copy of ms. Simultaneous submissions OK. Sample copy for $4. Fiction guidelines for #10 SASE.

Payment/Terms: Pays $10-25 and 2 contributor's copies on publication for one-time rights. Sends galleys to author.

Advice: *"Flying Horse* seeks heterogeneity of voice. Circumstance, class and formal education are not weighed. Nor do we count writing credits. What moves us to say *yes* is the authority of a submitted work, its conviction and originality of expression. The reader will encounter authors from starkly diverse corners of our society in our journal. What unites us, our common fuel, is the *written word*, and our firmly held conviction in its powers of transformation."

THE FLYING ISLAND, (II, IV), Writers' Center of Indianapolis, P.O. Box 88386, Indianapolis IN 46208. (317)955-6336. Editor: Jerome Donahue. Tabloid: 24 pages; illustrations and photos. "A magazine of fiction, essays, reviews and poetry by Indiana-connected writers." Semiannually. Estab. 1979. Circ. 700.

Needs: Ethnic/multicultural, experimental, fantasy, feminist, gay, lesbian, literary, mainstream/contemporary, mystery/suspense, psychic/supernatural/occult, science fiction. Receives 1,000 unsolicited mss/year. Accepts 4-5 mss/issue; 8-10 mss/year. Does not read mss March-May and September-November. Publishes ms 2 months after acceptance. Length: 4,000 words average. Publishes short shorts. Also publishes literary essays, literary criticism and poetry.

How to Contact: Send two copies of complete ms with a cover letter. Should include short bio explaining Indiana connection. Write for guidelines. Reports in 3-5 months on mss. SASE for return of ms. Simultaneous submissions OK. Fiction guidelines for #10 SASE. Reviews novels and short story collections "if story or author has some connection to Indiana."

Payment/Terms: Pays 2 contributor's copies plus honorarium. Pays on publication.

Advice: "We have published work by high school and college students as well as work by 1994 Pulitzer Prize winner Yusef Komunyakaa and Edgar nominee Terence Faherty. Our readers enjoy a wide variety of settings and situations. We're looking for quality and we tend to overlook gimmicky and sentimental writing."

FOLIO: A LITERARY JOURNAL, (II), Department of Literature, American University, Washington DC 20016. (202)885-2990. Editor changes yearly. Send mss to attention: Editor. Magazine: 6×9; 64 pages. "Fiction is published if it is well written. We look for language control, skilled plot and character development." Semiannually. Estab. 1984.

Needs: Contemporary, literary, mainstream, prose poem, translations, essay, b&w art or photography. No pornography. Occasional theme-based issues. See guidelines for info. Receives 150 unsolicited mss/month. Accepts 3-5 mss/issue; 6-40 mss/year. Does not read mss during May-August. Published work by Henry Taylor, Kermit Moyer, Linda Pastan; publishes new writers. Length: 2,500 words average; 4,500 words maximum. Publishes short shorts. Occasionally critiques rejected mss.

How to Contact: Send complete ms with cover letter. Include a brief bio. Reports in 1-2 months. SASE. Simultaneous and reprint submissions OK (if noted). Sample copy for $5. Guidelines for #10 SASE.

Payment/Terms: Pays in contributor's copies. Acquires first North American rights. "$75 award for best fiction and poetry. Query for guidelines."

FOOTWORK, The Paterson Literary Review, (II), Passaic County Community College, One College Blvd., Paterson NJ 07505. (201)684-6555. Editor: Maria Mazziotti Gillan. Magazine: 8½×11; 300 pages; 60 lb. paper; 70 lb. cover; illustrations; photos. Annually.

● *Footwork* was chosen by *Library Journal* as one of the ten best literary magazines in the U.S.

Needs: Contemporary, ethnic, literary. "We are interested in quality short stories, with no taboos on subject matter." Receives about 60 unsolicited mss/month. Publishes ms about 6 months to 1 year after acceptance. Published new writers within the last year. Length: 2,000-3,000 words. Also publishes literary essays, literary criticism, poetry.

How to Contact: Submit no more than 1 story at a time. Submission deadline: March 1. Send SASE for reply or return of ms. "Indicate whether you want story returned." Simultaneous submissions OK. Sample copy for $12. Reviews novels and short story collections.

Payment/Terms: Pays in contributor's copies. Acquires first North American rights.

Advice: Looks for "clear, moving and specific work."

‡FORBIDDEN DONUT, (I), 5101 Valley View Rd., Edina MN 55436. (612)929-0352. E-mail: wwood@earthl ink.net. Editors: Brian Wood and Jon Cazares. Magazine: 8×10; 50 pages; illustrations and photos. "Our continuing mission is to seek out new writers and new artists, to explore strange new ideas and to boldly go where no editors have gone before." Quarterly. Estab. 1995. Circ. 500.

Needs: Adventure, experimental, fantasy (science fantasy, sword and sorcery), horror, humor/satire, literary, mainstream/contemporary, mystery/suspense (amateur sleuth, cozy, police procedural, private eye/hardboiled), psychic/supernatural/occult, science fiction (hard science/soft sociological). No romance or westerns. Receives 2-5 unsolicited mss/month. Accepts 5-10 mss/issue; 20-30 mss year. Publishes ms 1-3 months after acceptance. Length: 3,000 words average; 20,000 words maximum. Publishes short shorts. Also publishes literary essays and literary criticism. Critiques or comments on rejected mss at author's request.

How to Contact: Send complete ms with a cover letter. Include bio. Reports in 1-3 weeks on queries; 2-8 weeks on mss. Send a disposable copy of ms. Simultaneous, reprint and electronic submissions OK. Sample copy for $2. Fiction guidelines free. Reviews novel and short story collections. Send books "Attention: Z.H."
Payment/Terms: Pays $1 and 1 contributor's copy for one-time rights; additional copies $1.
Advice: "The best advice we can give as to what kind of story we might accept is conflict and dialogue. Conflict and dialogue tend to keep the story moving and keep the reader interested, while drawn-out descriptions of everything in sight cause the reader to bog down and become bored. Many great stories don't follow this rule, but those are much more difficult to write. We prefer not to get lengthy submissions through e-mail. Please send recommendations for illustrations or photography to accompany your stories."

FOURTEEN HILLS: The SFSU Review, (II), Dept. of Creative Writing, San Francisco State University, 1600 Holloway Ave., San Francisco CA 94132. (415)338-3083. E-mail: hills@sfsu.edu. Website: http://mercury.s fsu.edu/~hills/14hills.html. Editors change each year. Magazine: 6×9; 160 pages; 60 lb. paper; 10 point C1S cover. "*Fourteen Hills* publishes the highest quality innovative fiction and poetry for a literary audience." Semiannually. Estab. 1994. Circ. 700.
● Two stories from *Fourteen Hills* were included in *Best American Gay Fiction 1997*.
Needs: Ethnic/multicultural, gay, humor/satire, lesbian, literary, mainstream/contemporary, translations. "No sexist or racist work, and no stories in which the plot has been chosen for its shock value. No genre fiction, please." Receives 100 unsolicited mss/month. Accepts 8-10 mss/issue; 16-20 mss/year. Does not usually read mss during the summer. Publishes ms 2-4 months after acceptance. Recently published work by Terese Svoboda, Peter Rock and Stephen Dixon. Publishes 6 new writers/year. Length: 7,000 words maximum. Publishes short shorts. Also publishes literary essays, poetry. Sometimes critiques or comments on rejected mss.
How to Contact: Send complete ms with a cover letter. Include brief bio and list of publications. Reports in 3-5 months on mss. SASE for return of ms. Simultaneous submissions OK. Sample copy for $5. Fiction guidelines for #10 SASE.
Payment/Terms: Pays 2 contributor's copies on publication. Acquires one-time rights. Sends galleys to author.
Advice: "Please read an issue of *Fourteen Hills* before submitting."

‡FREEZER BURN MAGAZINE, (I, II), 8 Piedmont St., Salem MA 01970. (508)745-7379. E-mail: freezburn2 @aol.com. Editor: David Rogers. Magazine: digest sized; 60 pages; 20 lb. paper; glossy card cover; illustrations. "I am most interested in surreal fiction that says something fascinating about human nature." Semiannually. Estab. 1995. Circ. 300.
Needs: Experimental, fantasy (urban), gay, horror, humor/satire, lesbian, literary, mainstream/contemporary, psychic/supernatural/occult, science fiction (soft/sociological). No pornography, straight fantasy. Receives 200 unsolicited mss/month. Accepts 7 mss/issue; 14 mss/year. Publishes ms 6 months after acceptance. Agented fiction 5%. Recently published work by Paul DiFilippo, Lance Olsen, Michael Hemmingson, Jeff Vander Meer, Sue Storm, Mark McLaughlin, Don Webb and Jeffrey Thomas. Length: 2,500 words average; 1,000 words minimum; 4,000 words maximum. Always critiques or comments on rejected mss.
How to Contact: Send complete ms with a cover letter. Include estimated word count, 50-100 word bio and list of publications. Reports in 1-2 weeks on queries; 3-4 weeks on mss. Send SASE for reply, return of ms or send a disposable copy of ms. Simultaneous submissions OK. Sample copy for $5. Fiction guidelines for #10 SASE.
Payment/Terms: Pays $50-100 on acceptance and 1 contributor's copy; additional copies for $5. Acquires first North American serial rights.
Advice: "I look first and foremost for characters that exhibit some sort of change or awareness within the framework of a complete story. Plot is important, but secondary. If I can identify with a character it helps a great deal. Someone once told me that one should read ten times the amount that one writes. Take a pen and a pad of paper everywhere you go and write down anything that you might be able to incorporate in your fiction."

FRONTIERS: A Journal of Women Studies, (II), Washington State University, Frontiers, Women's Studies, Wilson 10, Pullman WA 99164-4007. E-mail: frontier@wsu.edu. Editor: Sue Armitage. Magazine: 6×9; 200 pages; photos. "Women studies; academic articles in all disciplines; criticism; exceptional creative work (art, short fiction, photography, poetry)."
Needs: Feminist, lesbian. Receives 15 unsolicited mss/month. Accepts 7-12 mss/issue. Publishes ms 6-12 months after acceptance. Publishes 10 new writers/year.
How to Contact: Send 3 copies of complete ms with cover letter. Reports in 1 month on queries; 3-6 months on mss. SASE. Writer's guidelines for #10 SASE. Sample copy for $8.
Payment/Terms: Pays 2 contributor's copies. Acquires first North American serial rights.
Advice: "We are a *feminist* journal. *Frontiers* aims to make scholarship in women studies, and *exceptional* creative work, accessible to a cross-disciplinary audience inside and outside academia. Read short fiction in *Frontiers* before submitting."

FUGUE, Literary Digest of the University of Idaho, (I), English Dept., Rm. 200, Brink Hall, University of Idaho, Moscow ID 83844-1102. (208)885-6156. Website: http://www.uidaho.edu/LS/Eng/Fugue (includes writer's guidelines, names of editors, short fiction). Executive Editor: Eric Isaacson. Editors change each year.

Send to Executive Editor. Magazine: 6×9; 60-100 pages; 20 lb. stock paper. "We are interested in all classifications of fiction—we are not interested in pretentious 'literary' stylizations. We expect stories to be written in a manner engaging for anyone, not just academics and the pro-literatae crowd." Semiannually. Estab. 1990. Circ. 500.

Needs: Adventure, ethnic/multicultural, experimental, fantasy, historical, horror, humor/satire, literary, mainstream/contemporary, mystery/suspense, regional, romance, science fiction, sports, westerns. Receives 50 unsolicited mss/month. Accepts 4-8 mss/issue; 8-16 mss/year. Does not read May-September. Publishes ms 1 year after acceptance. Recently published work by Roberta Hill (Whiteman) and Raymond Federman. Publishes 5-10 new writers/year. Length: 3,000 words average; 50 words minimum; 7,000 words maximum. Publishes short shorts. Also publishes literary essays and poetry. Sometimes critiques or comments on rejected mss.

How to Contact: Send complete ms with cover letter. "Obtain guidelines first." Include estimated word count and list of publications. Report in 2 weeks on queries; 2-3 months on mss. SASE for a reply to a query or return of ms. No simultaneous submissions. Sample copy for $5. Fiction guidelines for #10 SASE.

Payment/Terms: Pays $5-20 on publication for first North American serial rights. All contributors receive a copy; extra copies available at a discount.

Advice: Looks for "innovative and somewhat experimental fiction, competent writing, clarity and consideration for the reader above stylism. Do not send us the traditional themes considered to be 'literary.' Be original and inventive. Don't rely on the traditional approaches to fiction or poetry. Take chances, but present your work as a professional. Professionalism is a must. Proper manuscript format is essential."

‡**GARNET, (II)**, Hampden-Sydney College, P.O. Box 655, Hampden-Sydney VA 23943. (904)223-6786. Editor: Brian Gearing. Editors change every year. Magazine: 6×9; 80-100 pages; heavy stock paper; glossy card cover; professionally printed; perfect bound; illustrations and photographs. "We publish quality work from talented beginning and established writers. Our audience includes college students, scholars and the general public." Semiannually. Estab. 1937. Circ. 600; 20 libraries.

Needs: Humor/satire, literary, mainstream/contemporary. No erotica, religious, romance, science fiction. Receives 30-40 unsolicited mss/month. Accepts 3-4 mss/issue; 6-8 mss/year. Publishes ms 1-5 months after acceptance. Agented fiction 5%. Recently published work by George Garrett, William Hoffman, Michael Knight, Susan Pepper Robbins and Richard Stern. Length: 3,000 words average; 5,000 words maximum. Publishes short shorts. Length: 300-500 words. Also publishes literary essays, literary criticism, poetry. Often critiques or comments on rejected mss.

How to Contact: Send complete ms with a cover letter. Include 3-4 sentence bio and list of publications. Reports in 2 weeks on queries; 6-8 weeks on mss. Send SASE for reply, return of ms or send a disposable copy of ms. Simultaneous and electronic submissions OK. Sample copy for $5. Fiction guidelines for SASE. Reviews novels and short story collections. Send books to editor.

Payment/Terms: Pays 2 contributor's copies; additional copies for $5. Acquires one-time rights. "Submissions are automatically considered for contests."

Advice: "We look for well-written, conscientious work with an emphasis on language. Be proud of your work. Show editors that you care about what you've written. It's your child. You've created it; treat it well."

A GATHERING OF THE TRIBES, (II), A Gathering of the Tribes, Inc., P.O. Box 20693, Tompkins Square Station, New York NY 10009. (212)674-3778. Fax: (212)674-5576. E-mail: tribes@pop.interport.net. Website: http://www.tribes.org. Editor: Steve Cannon. Magazine: 8×10; 100-200 pages; glossy paper and cover; illustrations and photos. A "multicultural and multigenerational publication." Estab. 1992. Circ. 2,000-3,000.

● *A Gathering of the Tribes* received a 1995 American Literary Award for editorial content.

Needs: Erotica, ethnic/multicultural, experimental, fantasy (science), feminist, gay, historical, horror, humor/satire, lesbian, literary, mainstream/contemporary, romance (futuristic/time travel, gothic), science fiction (soft/sociological), senior citizen/retirement, translations. "We are open to all; just no poor writing/grammar/syntax." List of upcoming themes available for SASE. Receives 100 unsolicited mss/month. Publishes ms 3-6 months after acceptance. Published work of Carl Watson, Alice Notely and Victor Cruz. Length: 500 words average; 200 words minimum; no maximum. Publishes short shorts. Also publishes literary essays, literary criticism and poetry.

How to Contact: Send complete ms with a cover letter. Include estimated word count, half-page bio, list of publications, phone and fax numbers and address with submission. Send SASE for reply, return of ms or send a disposable copy of ms. Simultaneous, reprint and electronic submissions OK. Sample copy for $10. Reviews novels and short story collections.

Payment/Terms: Pays 1 contributor's copy; additional copies $5. Sponsors contests, awards or grants for fiction writers. "Watch for ads in *Poets & Writers* and *American Poetry Review*."

Advice: Looks for "unique tone and style, offbeat plots and characters, and ethnic and regional work. Type manuscript well: readable font (serif) and no typos. Make characters and their dialogue interesting. Experiment with style, and don't be conventional. Do not send dragged-out, self-indulgent philosophizing of life and the universe. Get specific. Make your characters soar!"

‡❦**GEIST, The Canadian Magazine of Ideas and Culture, (II)**, The Geist Foundation, 103-1014 Homer St., Vancouver, British Columbia V6B 2W9 Canada. (604)681-9161. Fax: (604)669-8250. E-mail: geist@geist.com. Editor: Kevin Barefoot. Magazine: 8×10½; illustrations and photographs. "*Geist Magazine* is particularly inter-

ested in writing that blurs the boundary between fiction and nonfiction. Each issue and most of the writing in *Geist* explores the physical and mental landscape of Canada." Quarterly. Estab. 1990. Circ. 5,000.

Needs: Condensed/excerpted novel, literary. Receives 25 unsolicited mss/month. Accepts 10 mss/issue; 40 mss/ year. Publishes ms 2-12 weeks after acceptance. Length: 200 words minimum; 5,000 words maximum. Publishes short shorts.

How to Contact: Send complete ms with a cover letter. Include estimated word count and 1-2 line bio. Reports in 1 week on queries; 1-2 months on mss. Send SASE for reply, return of ms or send a disposable copy of ms. Reprint submissions OK. Fiction guidelines for SASE. Reviews novels and short story collections. Send books to Dan Geist.

Payment/Terms: Pays $50-250 on publication and 8 contributor's copies; additional copies for $2. Acquires first rights. Send a SASE requesting contest guidelines.

Advice: "Each issue of Geist is a meditation on the imaginary country that we inhabit. Often that imaginary country has something to do with some part of Canada."

‡GEORGE & MERTIE'S PLACE: ROOMS WITH A VIEW, (II), Dick Diver Enterprises, P.O. Box 10335, Spokane WA 99209. (509)325-3738. Editor: Thomas & Duncan. Magazine: 8½×11; 4-8 pages; heavy stock, colored paper; illustrations. "We want well-written fiction and poetry, political and philosophical debate, humor, satire and jeremiad. Our audience will be literate Americans who like to read and to be challenged to think. They will enjoy the use of language." Monthly. Estab. 1995. Circ. 50.

Needs: Anything well written. Receives 5-10 unsolicited mss/month. Accepts 1-2 mss/issue; 10-15 mss/year. "We work 3 months ahead." Recently published work by Geoffrey Peterson and Sharon Clark-Burland. Length: 1,000 words average; 1 word minimum; 2,500 words maximum. Publishes short shorts. Also publishes literary essays, literary criticism, poetry. Rarely critiques or comments on rejected mss.

How to Contact: Send complete ms with a cover letter. Include estimated word count, very brief bio and a comment on the work itself, its gestation. Reports in 1-2 months. Send SASE for reply, return of ms or send a disposable copy of ms. No simultaneous submissions. Sample copy for $2 and SASE. Fiction guidelines for SASE.

Payment/Terms: Pays 1¢/word, $2 minimum on acceptance and 1 contributor's copy; additional copies for $1.50. Acquires first North American serial rights or republication in GMP anthology. Not copyrighted. Each issue has a $10 "best of issue" prize. Published work automatically entered.

Advice: "Read, write, fail and keep going."

GEORGETOWN REVIEW, (II), Milkbone Publishing, P.O. Box 6309, Southern Station, Hattiesburg MS 39406-6309. Phone/fax: (601)818-0148. E-mail: jsfulmer@whale.st.usm.edu. Website: http://www.mindspring. com/~batcat/grwww/ (includes masthead, short fiction, poetry, guidelines). Editor: John Fulmer. Fiction Editor: Victoria Lancelotta. Magazine: 5½×8½; 150-200 pages; smooth offset paper; 10 pt. CS1 cover. "We want to publish quality fiction and poetry." Published twice a year. Estab. 1993. Circ. 600.

Needs: Condensed/excerpted novel, ethnic/multicultural, experimental, feminist, gay, humor/satire, lesbian, literary, science fiction. No romance, juvenile, fantasy. Receives 150 mss/month. Does not read mss May through August. Agented fiction 10%. Recently published work by Terese Svoboda, George Clark, Carolyn Stoloff, Lyn Lifshin, Wendy Brenner and Vivian Shipley. Length: 3,000 words average; 300 words minimum; 6,500 words maximum. Publishes short shorts. Length: 300 words. Also publishes poetry.

How to Contact: Send complete ms with a cover letter. Reports in 2-4 months on mss. SASE. Simultaneous and electronic submissions OK. Sample copy for $5. Guidelines free for SAE and 1 first-class stamp.

Payment/Terms: Pays 2 contributor's copies. Acquires first rights. Sends galleys to author.

Advice: "We simply look for quality work, no matter what the subject or style. Don't follow trends. Write with honesty and heart."

THE GEORGIA REVIEW, (I, II), The University of Georgia, Athens GA 30602-9009. (706)542-3481. Editor-in-Chief: Stanley W. Lindberg. Associate Editor: Stephen Corey. Assistant Editor: Janet Wondra. Journal: 7×10; 208 pages (average); 50 lb. woven old-style paper; 80 lb. cover stock; illustrations; photos. "*The Georgia Review* is a journal of arts and letters, featuring a blend of the best in contemporary thought and literature—essays, fiction, poetry, visual art and book reviews for the intelligent nonspecialist as well as the specialist reader. We seek material that appeals across disciplinary lines by drawing from a wide range of interests." Quarterly. Estab. 1947. Circ. 6,000.

● This magazine has an excellent reputation for publishing high-quality fiction.

Needs: Experimental and literary. "We're looking for the highest quality fiction—work that is capable of sustaining subsequent readings, not throw-away pulp magazine entertainment. Nothing that fits too easily into a 'category.' " Receives about 400 unsolicited fiction mss/month. Accepts 3-4 mss/issue; 12-15 mss/year. Does not read unsolicited mss in June, July or August. Would prefer *not* to see novel excerpts. Published work by Louise Erdrich, Frederick Busch and Barry Lopez. Published new writers within the last year. Length: Open. Also publishes literary essays, literary criticism, poetry. Occasionally critiques rejected mss.

How to Contact: Send complete ms (one story) with SASE. No multiple submissions. Usually reports in 2-3 months. Sample copy for $6; guidelines for #10 SASE. Reviews short story collections.

Payment/Terms: Pays minimum $35/printed page on publication for first North American serial rights, 1 year complimentary subscription and 1 contributor's copy; reduced charge for additional copies. Sends galleys to author.

THE GETTYSBURG REVIEW, (II), Gettysburg College, Gettysburg PA 17325. (717)337-6770. Editor: Peter Stitt. Assistant Editor: Jeff Mock. Magazine: 6¾ × 10; 170 pages; acid free paper; full color illustrations. "Quality of writing is our only criterion; we publish fiction, poetry, and essays." Quarterly. Estab. 1988. Circ. 4,500.
   ● Work appearing in *The Gettysburg Review* has also been included in *Prize Stories: The O. Henry Awards*, the *Pushcart Prize* anthology, *Best American Poetry*, *New Stories from the South*, *Harper's*, and elsewhere. It is also the recipient of a Lila Wallace-Reader's Digest grant and NEA grants.
Needs: Contemporary, experimental, historical, humor/satire, literary, mainstream, regional and serialized novel. "We require that fiction be intelligent, and aesthetically written." Receives 200 mss/month. Accepts 4-6 mss/issue; 16-24 mss/year. Publishes ms within 1 year of acceptance. Published work by Robert Olen Butler, Joyce Carol Oates, Naeem Murr, Tom Perrotta, Jacoba Hood and Tom House. Length: 3,000 words average; 1,000 words minimum; 20,000 words maximum. Occasionally publishes short shorts. Also publishes literary essays, some literary criticism, poetry. Sometimes critiques rejected mss.
How to Contact: Send complete ms with cover letter September through May. Reports in 3-6 months. SASE. No simultaneous submissions. Sample copy for $7 (postage paid). Does not review books per se. "We do essay-reviews, treating several books around a central theme." Send review copies to editor.
Payment/Terms: Pays $25/printed page, subscription to magazine and contributor's copy on publication for first North American serial rights. Charge for extra copies.
Advice: "Reporting time can take more than three months. It is helpful to look at a sample copy of *The Gettysburg Review* to see what kinds of fiction we publish before submitting."

*GHOSTS & SCHOLARS, Flat One, 36 Hamilton St., Hoole, Chester CH2 3JQ England. Fiction Editor: Rosemary Pardoe. Semiannually. Circ. 400. Publishes 6-7 stories/year. "Publishes fiction in the M.R. James tradition, and articles/discussion of same."
Needs: "Submissions should be of ghost stories in the M.R. James tradition only. I will not consider other types of ghost stories." Length: 2,000 words minimum; 8,000 words maximum.
How to Contact: Guidelines for SASE (overseas: 2 IRCs).
Payment/Terms: Pays in copies. Sample copy for $7 cash (US) or £4 cheque (payable to R. Pardoe).

THE GLASS CHERRY, A poetry magazine, (II), The Glass Cherry Press, 901 Europe Bay Rd., Ellison Bay WI 54210-9643. Editor: Judith Hirschmiller. Magazine: 5 × 7; 60 pages; high-tech laser paper; cover stock varies; illustrations and photos. "Our goal is to combine diversity with quality to promote good literature by a variety of writers. New writers are encouraged to submit." Quarterly. Estab. 1994. Circ. 500.
Needs: Condensed/excerpted novel, gay, historical, horror, lesbian, literary, mainstream/contemporary, science fiction, serialized novel, translations. "No pornography." Publishes special fiction issues or anthologies. Receives 6-12 unsolicited mss/month. Accepts 1-2 mss/issue; 4-8 mss/year. Does not read books May-December; reads fiction for magazine all year. Publishes ms 1 year after acceptance. Recently published work by Charles Chaim Wax and Richard Peabody. Length: 1,000 words maximum. Publishes short shorts. Also publishes literary essays, literary criticism and poetry. Critiques or comments on rejected ms "only if requested to do so by author."
How to Contact: Query first. Include short bio and list of publications with submission. Reports in 3 weeks on queries; 3 months on mss. SASE for reply. No simultaneous submissions. Sample copy for $5; back issue, $6. Fiction guidelines for #10 SASE. Reviews novels and short story collections.
Payment/Terms: Pays 1 contributor's copy. Acquires one-time rights.
Advice: "The ordinary, familiar experiences of life are your richest source for writing. Comments without opinions are appreciated and much more interesting. We would like more translations, book reviews, plays and short fiction of personal glimpses (individual, unusual events of a personal nature)."

GLIMMER TRAIN STORIES, (II), Glimmer Train Press, 710 SW Madison St., Suite 504, Portland OR 97205. Fax: (503)221-0836. Website: http://www.glimmertrain.com (includes writer's guidelines and a Q&A section for writers). Editors: Susan Burmeister-Brown and Linda Burmeister Davies. Magazine: 6¾ × 9¼; 160 pages; recycled, acid-free paper; 20 illustrations; 12 photographs. Quarterly. Estab. 1991. Circ. 21,000.
   ● The magazine also sponsors an annual short story contest for new writers and a very short fiction contest.
Needs: Literary. Receives 3,000 unsolicited mss/month. Accepts 10 mss/issue; 40 mss/year. Reads in January, April, July, October. Publishes ms 4-9 months after acceptance. Agented fiction 20%. Recently published work

---

LOOKING FOR A PARTICULAR GENRE? Check our Category Index for magazine and book publishers who want **Mystery/Suspense**, **Romance**, **Science Fiction & Fantasy**, **Thrillers**, **Westerns** and more!

by Kevin Canty, Ellen Gilchrist, Abigail Thomas, Mary Gordon, David Huddle and George Clark. Publishes 2-6 new writers/year. Length: 1,200 words minimum; 8,000 words maximum.

How to Contact: Send complete ms with a cover letter. Include estimated word count and list of publications. Reports in 3 months. Send SASE for return or send a disposable copy of ms (with stamped postcard or envelope for notification). Simultaneous submissions OK. Sample copy for $10. Fiction guidelines for #10 SASE.

Payment/Terms: Pays $500 and 10 contributor's copies on acceptance for first rights.

Advice: "If you're excited about a story you've written, send it to us! If you're not very excited about it, wait and send one that you are excited about. It's usually a good idea to do a lot of reading. This will often improve the quality of your own writing."

✤GRAIN, (II), Saskatchewan Writers' Guild, Box 1154, Regina, Saskatchewan S4P 3B4 Canada. Fax: (306)244-0255. E-mail: grain.mag@sk.sympatico.ca. Website: http://www.sasknet.com/corporate/skwriter (includes history, news, subscription and contest information). Editor: J. Jill Robinson. Literary magazine: 6×9; 128 pages; Chinook offset printing; chrome-coated stock; illustrations; some photos. "Fiction and poetry for people who enjoy high quality writing." Quarterly. Estab. 1973. Circ. 1,500.

● *Grain* received the National Magazine Award-Gold Award for Fiction-1996.

Needs: Contemporary, experimental, literary, mainstream and prose poem. "No propaganda—only artistic/literary writing." No mss "that stay *within* the limits of conventions such as women's magazine type stories, science fiction; none that push a message." Receives 80 unsolicited fiction mss/month. Accepts 8-12 mss/issue; 32-48 mss/year. Length: "No more than 30 pages." Also publishes poetry and creative nonfiction. Occasionally critiques rejected mss.

How to Contact: Send complete ms with SASE (or IRC) and brief letter. Queries by e-mail OK. No simultaneous submissions. Reports within 4 months on mss. Publishes ms an average of 4 months after acceptance. Sample copy for $6.95 plus postage.

Payment/Terms: Pays $30-100 and 2 contributor's copies on publication for first Canadian serial rights. "We expect acknowledgment if the piece is republished elsewhere."

Advice: "Submit a story to us that will deepen the imaginative experience of our readers. *Grain* has established itself as a first-class magazine of serious fiction. We receive submissions from around the world. If Canada is a foreign country to you, we ask that you *do not* use U.S. postage stamps on your return envelope. If you live outside Canada and neglect the International Reply Coupons, we *will not* read or reply to your submission."

GRAND STREET, (V), 131 Varick St., #906, New York NY 10013. (212)807-6548. Fax (212)807-6544. Editor: Jean Stein. Managing Editor: Deborah Treisman. Magazine: 7¾×9½; 240-270 pages; illustrations; art portfolios. "We publish new fiction and nonfiction of all types." Quarterly. Estab. 1981. Circ. 7,000.

● Work published in *Grand Street* has been included in the *Best American Short Stories*.

Needs: Poetry, essays, translations. Receives 400 unsolicited mss/month. Accepts 12 mss/issue; 48 mss/year. Time between acceptance of the ms and publication varies. Agented fiction 90%. Published work by David Foster Wallace, Stephen Millhauser, Dennis Hopper, Paul Auster, John Ashbery, Duong Thu Huong and William T. Vollmann. Length: 4,000 words average; 9,000 words maximum.

How to Contact: *Not accepting unsolicited fiction mss.* Sample copy for $15; $18 overseas and Canada.

Payment/Terms: Pays $250-1,000 and 2 contributor's copies on publication for first North American serial rights. Sends galleys to author.

GRASSLANDS REVIEW, (I, II), P.O. Box 626, Berea OH 44017. E-mail: lkennelly@aol.com. Editor: Laura B. Kennelly. Magazine: 6×9; 80 pages. *Grasslands Review* prints creative writing of all types; poetry, fiction, essays for a general audience. Semiannually. Estab. 1989. Circ. 300.

Needs: Contemporary, ethnic, experimental, fantasy, horror, humor/satire, literary, mystery/suspense, prose poem, regional, science fiction and western. Nothing pornographic or overtly political or religious. Accepts 5-8 mss/issue. Reads only in October and March. Publishes ms 6 months after acceptance. Published work by Paddy Reid, Mary Ann Taylor, Dawn A. Baldwin and Seth Kaplan. Publishes 5-6 new writers/year. Length: 100-3,500 words; 1,500 words average. Publishes short shorts (100-150 words). Also publishes poetry. Sometimes critiques rejected mss and recommends other markets.

How to Contact: Send complete ms in October or March *only* with cover letter. No simultaneous submissions. Reports on mss in 3 months. SASE. Sample copy for $4. May review novels or short story collections.

Payment/Terms: Pays in contributor's copies. Acquires one-time rights. Publication not copyrighted.

Advice: "We are looking for fiction which leaves the reader with a strong feeling or impression—or a new perspective on life. We would like to see more comic fiction. The *Review* began as an in-class exercise to allow experienced creative writing students to learn how a little magazine is produced. It now serves as an independent publication, attracting authors from as far away as the Ivory Coast, but its primary mission is to give unknown writers a start."

‡THE GREAT LAWN, An Art and Literary Journal for Gay Men, (II, IV), The Palm Court Press, P.O. Box 170251, Saint Louis MO 63117-7951. (314)621-6721. E-mail: greatlawn@aol.com. Editor: David Olin Tullis. Magazine: 7½×10½; 56 pages; 70 lb. gloss paper; 80 lb. gloss cover; illustrations and photos. Publishes

INSIDER REPORT

The Green Hills Literary Lantern: a literary light in north central Missouri

The name, thoughtfully chosen in 1990 when Jack Smith and Ken Reger founded the *Green Hills Literary Lantern*, could not be more appropriate. The *Lantern*'s office is Smith's office in the English department of North Central Missouri College, nestled in the bucolic setting of the rolling north central Missouri landscape. Its mission is to "provide a literary market for quality fiction writers, both established and beginners, and provide quality literature for readers from diverse backgrounds." In 1998, the *Lantern* celebrates its eighth year of fulfilling that mission.

Jack Smith

"We wanted to put Trenton, Missouri, on the literary map," says Smith. "We sent out calls for submissions to various colleges and universities, limited pretty much in the beginning to Missouri. We put out a 52-page publication and tried to do it twice a year, but that became difficult because of limited time and funding. Then we went to an annual." Since 1995, the *Lantern* has been an annual literary magazine publishing writers from all over the U.S.

Funding, often a problem for beginning and established journals, became less of a problem when the *Lantern* began receiving grants from the Missouri Arts Council, initially through the local Grundy County Friends of the Arts. MAC funding continues to date, with the journal now being carried under the Council's program assistance category of literature. In 1997, North Central Missouri College began a co-publishing arrangement with the North Central Missouri Writer's Guild, the community group that began the journal under the editorship of Smith and Reger. Arts Council funding and this new co-publishing arrangement, Smith states, have been vital in keeping the journal afloat.

Although Smith sees the *Lantern* as being a cultural resource for north central Missouri, he does not want "obscure" fiction that might appeal only to academics and others with formal training in literature. "We also want to publish good fiction that grabs ordinary readers." It follows then that work accepted for inclusion in the *Lantern* is not written exclusively by academics. Smith says, "We publish people who are in academic programs and who are teachers, but we have published one writer several times who is a factory worker and another who is a lawyer. Most all our writers, though, have in some way studied the craft or are learning what works and what does not as they go along."

The *Lantern* receives an average of 30-40 manuscripts each month, but that number is steadily increasing. "Last review we had over 300 submissions and chose 6 from those." By "we," Smith means co-editor Reger; fiction editor Sara King, who teaches at George Mason University in Virginia; managing editor Mary Jane Smith, Smith's wife; and a group of associate editors composed of members of the North Central Missouri Writer's Guild.

What does it take to get a manuscript accepted by this group of reviewers at the *Lantern*?

INSIDER REPORT, *Smith*

"That strong beginning really helps," says Smith. "And, for me, the bottom line requirement is that the writer is able to handle the language well—the writer should be good with figurative language and with the use of analogy and metaphor that seems natural, not contrived."

But style alone is not enough to get your story onto the pages of the *Lantern*. "There has to be a good plot. The better the story—the better the plot—the more the reader perceives something substantive in that story; it's not just cute, not just self-consciously hip for the sake of being cute or hip," says Smith.

Even when a story shows facility with language and has an engaging plot, Smith says, "Sometimes we get through a story and are really let down by the ending. . . . Endings are even more important than beginnings—sometimes, you can just lop off a bad beginning and let the story start at its 'real' beginning. But endings are really tough. Good writers are able to tie up a story by bringing it to completion with a certain subtlety. That takes a knowledge of the craft, and you have to read a lot of writers and study their techniques to be able to do that successfully."

Unbelievable dialogue and weak characterization are also areas where Smith says writers often fall short. "Dialogue is important and in many stories the language and the characters do not seem real. Writers who don't represent characters as full-dimensional people who seem to step off the pages produce fiction that is artificial and contrived. Writers who submit to us need to get inside their characters, understand their motives and make them real to readers."

To write a story with believable characters who say and do believable things, Smith advises writers to "Observe life, then decide, but not in an obviously calculated fashion, what's going to be 'real' in your story."

To continually improve their craft, Smith says writers should read as much as possible. "Read widely to begin with. Then read a lot of the fiction that appeals to you most, the kind of fiction you write or would like to write. Find out how those writers are doing it, and read some books on the craft, too." Once writers have studied the craft—in the classroom or by reading and writing fiction—and written the best story possible, they should begin submitting work to the publications that seem the most suitable. And, very importantly, the suitability of markets for your stories should be determined by *reading the publications before submitting*. Even then, Smith says, "writers really have to tough it out. Often, they are up against the sheer volume of submissions to places who get thousands of submissions a year and have room to publish only a few in each edition." Writers must also realize that sometimes the difference between acceptance and rejection by a publication may not be the story. "Sometimes it just comes down to an editor's individual taste; one particular editor may not like a story, but an editor at another publication may love it." And sometimes, says Smith, the key to getting published is simply perseverance. "I really do believe that a good story will find its way to the top. Although they may have to send their stories out 20 times or more, good writers are going to get published someplace."

—*Barbara Kuroff*

fictional short stories, poetry, fine art and fine art photography of interest to gay men. Quarterly. Estab. 1997. Circ. 2,000.
Needs: Erotica, gay. Publishes ms. 1-3 months after acceptance. Publishes short shorts. Also publishes literary

essays and poetry. Often critiques or comments on rejected mss.

How to Contact: Send complete ms with a cover letter. Include bio. Send a disposable copy of ms. Simultaneous and electronic submissions OK. Sample copy for $7. Fiction guidelines for #10 SASE.

Payment/Terms: Pays 5 contributor's copies for one-time rights; additional copies $7.

THE GREEN HILLS LITERARY LANTERN, (I, II), Published by North Central Missouri College and The North Central Missouri Writer's Guild, P.O. Box 375, Trenton MO 64683. (816)359-3948, ext. 324. E-mail: jsmith@nc mc.cc.mo.us. Editors: Jack Smith and Ken Reger. Fiction Editor: Sara King. Magazine: 5½ × 8½; 160-170 pages; good quality paper with glossy cover. "The mission of *GHLL* is to provide a literary market for quality fiction writers, both established and beginners, and to provide quality literature for readers from diverse backgrounds. We also see ourselves as a cultural resource for North Central Missouri." Annually. Estab. 1990. Circ. 500.

● *The Green Hills Literary Lantern* received Missouri Arts Council grants in 1997.

Needs: Ethnic/multicultural, experimental, feminist, humor/satire, literary, mainstream/contemporary and regional. "Fairly traditional short stories but we are open to experimental. Our main requirement is literary merit." Receives 30 unsolicited mss/month. Accepts 6-7 mss/issue. Publishes ms 6-12 months after acceptance. Recently published work by Doug Rennie, Walter Cummins, Ian MacMillan and Margaret Hermes. Length: 3,000 words average; 5,000 words maximum. Publishes short shorts. Also publishes poetry. Sometimes critiques or comments on rejected mss.

How to Contact: Send complete ms with a cover letter. Include bio (50-100 words) with list of publications. Accepts queries (only) by e-mail. Reports in 3-4 months on mss. SASE for return of ms. Simultaneous submissions OK. Sample copy for $5.95 (includes envelope and postage).

Payment/Terms: Pays two contributor's copies. Acquires one-time rights. Sends galleys to author.

Advice: "Send stories with all the subtleties of ordinary life. Make sure the language is striking. Don't tell the story. Let the story tell itself. We look for fiction which speaks to the heart, the mind, the soul—fiction which is as complex, as dense, as layered as the most simple of human existences and as subtle and as provocative as the best of literary art. The cost of funding a literary magazine prevents us from publishing longer pieces (over 5,000 words), and it also means we have to reject some publishable fiction due to space limitation."

GREEN MOUNTAINS REVIEW, (II), Johnson State College, Box A-58, Johnson VT 05656. (802)635-2356, ext. 1350. Editor-in-Chief: Neil Shepard. Fiction Editor: Tony Whedon. Magazine: digest-sized; 140-200 pages. Semiannually. Estab. 1975 (new series, 1987). Circ. 1,500.

Needs: Adventure, contemporary, experimental, humor/satire, literary, mainstream, serialized/excerpted novel, translations. Receives 80 unsolicited mss/month. Accepts 6 mss/issue; 12 mss/year. Publishes ms 6-12 months after acceptance. Reads mss September 1 through May 1. Recently published work by W.D. Wetherell, Julia Alvarez, Alix Kates Shulman, Lynne Sharon Schwartz and Carol Emshwille. Length: 25 pages maximum. Publishes short shorts. Also publishes literary criticism, poetry. Sometimes critiques rejected mss.

How to Contact: Send complete ms with cover letter. "Manuscripts will not be read and will be returned between May 1 and September 1." Reports in 1 month on queries; 3-6 months on mss. SASE. Simultaneous submissions OK (if advised). Sample copy for $5.

Payment/Terms: Pays contributor's copies, 1-year subscription and small honorarium, depending on grants. Acquires first North American serial rights. Rights revert to author upon request. Sends galleys to author upon request.

Advice: "The editors are open to a wide spectrum of styles and subject matter as is apparent from a look at the list of fiction writers who have published in its pages. One issue was devoted to Vermont fiction, and another issue filled with new writing from the People's Republic of China. The Spring/Summer 1994 issue was composed entirely of women's fiction."

✤GREEN'S MAGAZINE, Fiction for the Family, (I, II), Green's Educational Publications, Box 3236, Regina, Saskatchewan S4P 3H1 Canada. Editor: David Green. Magazine: 5¼ × 8; 92 pages; 20 lb. bond paper; matte cover stock; line illustrations. Publishes "solid short fiction suitable for family reading." Quarterly. Estab. 1972.

Needs: Adventure, fantasy, humor/satire, literary, mainstream, mystery/suspense and science fiction. No erotic or sexually explicit fiction. Receives 20-30 mss/month. Accepts 10-12 mss/issue; 40-50 mss/year. Publishes ms within 3-6 months of acceptance. Agented fiction 2%. Recently published work by Mary Wallace, Warren Keith Wright and Gerald Standley. Publishes 6 new writers/year. Length: 2,500 words preferred; 1,500 words minimum; 4,000 words maximum. Also publishes poetry. Sometimes critiques rejected mss.

How to Contact: Send complete ms. "Cover letters welcome but not necessary." Reports in 2 months. SASE (or IRC). No simultaneous submissions. Sample copy for $4. Fiction guidelines for #10 SASE (IRC). Reviews novels and short story collections.

Payment/Terms: Pays in contributor's copies. Acquires first North American serial rights.

Advice: "No topic is taboo, but we avoid sexuality for its own sake, and disline material that is needlessly explicit or obscene. We look for strongly written stories that explore their characters through a subtle blending of conflicts. Plots should be appropriate, rather than overly ingenious or reliant on some *deus ex machina* device. It must be a compression of experience or thoughts, in a form that is both challenging and rewarding to the reader. We have no form rejection slip. If we cannot use a submission, we try to offer constructive criticism in our personal reply. Often, such effort is rewarded with reports from our writers that following our suggestions has led to placement of the story or poem elsewhere."

GREENSBORO REVIEW, (I, II), University of North Carolina at Greensboro, Dept. of English, Greensboro NC 27412. (910)334-5459. Fax: (910)334-3281. E-mail: clarkj@fagan.uncg.edu. Website: http://www.uncg.edu/eng/mtal (includes writer's guidelines, literary awards guidelines, address, deadlines, subscription information). Editor: Jim Clark. Fiction Editor: Kathy Flann. Fiction editor changes each year. Send mss to the editor. Magazine: 6×9; approximately 136 pages; 60 lb. paper; 65 lb. cover. Literary magazine featuring fiction and poetry for readers interested in contemporary literature. Semiannually. Circ. 600.
● *Greensboro Review* won a Pushcart Prize in 1997.
Needs: Contemporary and experimental. Accepts 6-8 mss/issue, 12-16 mss/year. Recently published work by Stacey Richter, George Singleton, Robert Olmstead, Ron McFarland and Ivy Goodman. Published 6 new writers within the last year. Length: 7,500 words maximum.
How to Contact: Send complete ms with SASE. No simultaneous submissions. Unsolicited manuscripts must arrive by September 15 to be considered for the winter issue and by February 15 to be considered for the summer issue. Manuscripts arriving after those dates may be held for the next consideration. Reports in 2 months. Sample copy for $4.
Payment/Terms: Pays in contributor's copies. Acquires first North American serial rights.
Advice: "We want to see the best being written regardless of theme, subject or style. Recent stories from *The Greensboro Review* have been included in *The Best American Short Stories*, *Prize Stories: The O. Henry Awards*, *New Stories from the South* and *Best of the West*, anthologies recognizing the finest short stories being published."

GULF COAST, A Journal of Literature & Fine Arts, (II), Dept. of English, University of Houston, Houston TX 77204-3012. (713)743-3013. Contact: Fiction Editors. Editors change each year. Magazine: 6×9; 144 pages; stock paper, gloss cover; illustrations and photographs. "Innovative fiction for the literary-minded." Estab. 1984. Circ. 1,500.
● Work published in *Gulf Coast* has been selected for inclusion in the *Pushcart Prize* anthology.
Needs: Contemporary, ethnic, experimental, literary, regional, translations. No children's, religious/inspirational. Receives 150 unsolicited mss/month. Accepts 8-10 mss/issue; 16-20 mss/year. Publishes ms 6 months-1 year after acceptance. Agented fiction 5%. Published work by Ann Beattie, Madison Smartt Bell, Lee K. Abbott and Tracy Daugherty. Length: no limit. Publishes short shorts. Sometimes critiques rejected mss.
How to Contact: Send complete ms with brief cover letter. "List previous publications; please notify us if the submission is being considered elsewhere." Reports in 3-6 months. Simultaneous submissions OK. Back issue for $6, 7×10 SAE and 4 first-class stamps. Fiction guidelines for #10 SASE.
Payment/Terms: Pays contributor's copies and *small* honorariam for one-time rights.
Advice: "Rotating editorship, so please be patient with replies. As always, please send one story at a time."

GULF STREAM MAGAZINE, (II), Florida International University, English Dept., North Miami Campus, N. Miami FL 33181. (305)940-5599. Editor: Lynne Barrett. Editors change every 1-2 years. Magazine: 5½×8½; 96 pages; recycled paper; 80 lb. glossy cover; cover illustrations. "We publish *good quality*—fiction, nonfiction and poetry for a predominately literary market." Semiannually. Estab. 1989. Circ. 500.
Needs: Contemporary, literary, mainstream. Nothing "radically experimental." Plans special issues. Receives 100 unsolicited mss/month. Accepts 5 mss/issue; 10 mss/year. Does not read mss during the summer. Publishes ms 3-6 months after acceptance. Published work by Alan Cheuse, Ann Hood and David Kranes. Length: 5,000 words average; 7,500 words maximum. Publishes short shorts. Also publishes poetry. Sometimes critiques rejected mss.
How to Contact: Send complete manuscript with cover letter including list of previous publications and a short bio. Reports in 3 months. SASE. Simultaneous submissions OK "if noted." Sample copy for $4. Free fiction guidelines.
Payment/Terms: Pays in gift subscriptions and contributor's copies. Acquires first North American serial rights.
Advice: "Looks for good concise writing—well plotted with interesting characters."

‡HABERSHAM REVIEW, (I, II), Piedmont College, P.O. Box 10, Demorest GA 30535. (706)778-3000. Editor: Frank Gannon. Magazine. "General literary magazine with a regional (Southeastern U.S.) focus for a literate audience." Semiannually. Estab. 1991.
Needs: Contemporary, experimental, literary, mainstream, regional. Receives 100 unsolicited mss/month. Acquires 6-10 mss/issue. Recently published work by Janice Daugharty, James Kilgo, C.R. Crackel, Linda Hartford, Dixie Salazar, George Strange, Marshall Boswell, Steven Carter, Cynthia Morgan Dale and Pat Spears. Publishes short shorts. Sometimes critiques rejected mss.
How to Contact: Send complete ms with cover letter. Reports in 6 months on mss. SASE. No simultaneous submissions. Sample copy for $6.
Payment/Terms: Pays in contributor's copies. Acquires first rights.

HALF TONES TO JUBILEE, (II), English Dept., Pensacola Junior College, 1000 College Blvd., Pensacola FL 32504. (904)484-1416. Editor: Walter Spara. Magazine: 6×9; approx. 100 pages; 70 lb. laid stock; 80 lb. cover. "No theme, all types published." Annually. Estab. 1985. Circ. 500.
Needs: Open. Accepts approx. 6 mss/issue. "We publish in September." Published work by Mark Spencer. Length: 1,500 words average. Publishes short shorts. Also publishes poetry. Sometimes critiques rejected mss and recommends other markets.
How to Contact: Send complete ms with cover letter. SASE. Sample copy for $4. Free fiction guidelines.
Payment/Terms: Pays 2 contributor's copies. Acquires one-time rights.
Advice: We are moving away from linear development; we are noted for innovation in style."

HAPPY, (I, II), The Happy Organization, 240 E. 35th St., 11A, New York NY 10016. (212)689-3142. E-mail: bayardx@aol.com. Editor: Bayard. Magazine: 5½×8; 100 pages; 60 lb. text paper; 100 lb. cover; perfect-bound; illustrations and photos. Quarterly. Estab. 1995. Circ. 500.
• *Happy* was listed in the 1996 *Writer's Digest* "Fiction 50," a list of the top 50 fiction markets. It also received 8 Pushcart Prize nominations for 1996.
Needs: Erotica, ethnic/multicultural, experimental, fantasy, feminist, gay, horror, humor/satire, lesbian, literary, psychic/supernatural/occult, science fiction. Receives 300-500 unsolicited mss/month. Accepts 25-30 mss/issue; 100-120 mss/year. 30-50% of work published is by new writers. Publishes ms 6-12 months after acceptance. Length: 1,000-3,500 words average; 6,000 words maximum. Publishes short shorts. Often critiques or comments on rejected mss.
How to Contact: Send complete ms with a cover letter. Include estimated word count. Reports in 1 week on mss. Send SASE for reply, return of ms or send a disposable copy of ms. Simultaneous submissions OK. Sample copy for $9.
Payment/Terms: Pays 5¢/word, minimum $5 on publication and 1 contributor's copy for one-time rights.
Advice: "No more grumbling about what you should be—become what you intended!"

‡HAWAII REVIEW, (II), University of Hawaii English Dept., 1733 Donaghho Rd., Honolulu HI 96822. (808)956-3030. Fax: (808)956-9962. Editor: Malia E. Gellert. Magazine: 6½×9½; 150-170 pages; illustrations; photos. "We publish short stories as well as poetry and reviews by new and experienced writers. As an international literary journal, we hope to reflect the idea that cultural diversity is of universal interest." For residents of Hawaii and non-residents from the continental US and abroad. Triannually. Estab. 1972. Circ. 5,000.
Needs: Contemporary, ethnic, humor/satire, literary, prose poem, regional and translations. Receives 50-75 mss/month. No more than 40 mss/issue; 130 mss/year. Recently published work by Clint McCown, Ian MacMillan, Robert Shepard, Barbara Phillips, James Spencer an Mark Jarmon. Published new writers within the last year. Length: 4,000 words average; no minimum; 8,000 words maximum. Occasionally critiques mss. Also publishes poetry.
How to Contact: Send complete ms with SASE. Reports in 3-4 months on mss. Sample copy for $5. Fiction guidelines for SASE.
Payment/Terms: Pays 4 contributor's copies and t-shirt.
Advice: "We select fiction based on excellent story, good sentence level writing, attention to detail, no overused story lines, no self-conscious narratives."

HAYDEN'S FERRY REVIEW, (II), Box 871502, Arizona State University, Tempe AZ 85287-1502. (602)965-1243. Fax: (602)965-6704. E-mail: hfr@asuvm.inre.asu.edu. Website: http://news.vpsa.asu.edu/HFR/HFR.html. Managing Editor: Salima Keegan. Editors change every 1-2 years. Magazine: 6×9; 128 pages; fine paper; illustrations and photographs. "Contemporary material by new and established writers for a varied audience." Semiannually. Estab. 1986. Circ. 1,200.
• Work from *Hayden's Ferry Review* has been selected for inclusion in *Pushcart Prize* anthologies.
Needs: Contemporary, ethnic, experimental, fantasy, feminist, gay, historical, humor/satire, literary, mainstream, prose poem, psychic/supernatural/occult, regional, romance (contemporary), science fiction, senior citizen/retirement. Possible special fiction issue. Receives 150 unsolicited mss/month. Accepts 5 mss/issue; 10 mss/year. Publishes mss 3-4 months after acceptance. Published work by T.C. Boyle, Raymond Carver, Ken Kesey, Rita Dove and Rick Bass. Length: No preference. Publishes short shorts. Also publishes literary essays.
How to Contact: Send complete ms with cover letter. No simultaneous submissions. Reports in 3-5 months from deadline on mss. SASE. Sample copy for $6. Fiction guidelines for SAE.
Payment/Terms: Pays 2 contributor's copies. Acquires first North American serial rights. Sends page proofs to author.

---

‡ THE DOUBLE DAGGER before a listing indicates that the listing is new in this edition. New markets are often the most receptive to submissions by new writers.

THE HEARTLANDS TODAY, (II, IV), The Firelands Writing Center, Firelands College of BGSU, Huron OH 44839. (419)433-5560. Editors: Larry Smith and Nancy Dunham. Magazine: 6×9; 160 pages; b&w illustrations; 15 photographs. *Material must be set in the Midwest.* "We prefer material that reveals life in the Midwest today for a general, literate audience." Annually. Estab. 1991.

Needs: Ethnic, humor, literary, mainstream, regional (Midwest). Receives 15 unsolicited mss/month. Accepts 6 mss/issue. Does not read mss August-December. "We edit between January 1 and June 5. Submit then." 1998 theme—"The Midwest: Sirens and Muses." Publishes ms 6 months after acceptance. Published work of Wendell Mayo, Tony Tomassi, Gloria Bowman. Length: 4,500 words maximum. Also publishes literary essays, poetry. Sometimes critiques rejected mss.

How to Contact: Send complete ms with cover letter. Reports in 2 months on mss. Send SASE for ms, not needed for query. Simultaneous submissions OK, if noted. Sample copy for $5.

Payment/Terms: Pays $10-25 on publication and 2 contributor's copies for first rights.

Advice: "We look for writing that connects on a human level, that moves us with its truth and opens our vision of the world. If writing is a great escape for you, don't bother with us. We're in it for the joy, beauty or truth of the art. We look for a straight, honest voice dealing with human experiences. We do not define the Midwest, we hope to be a document of the Midwest. If you feel you are writing from the Midwest, send your work to us. We look first at the quality of the writing."

HEAVEN BONE, (II, IV), Heaven Bone Press, Box 486, Chester NY 10918. (914)469-9018. Editors: Steven Hirsch and Kirpal Gordon. Magazine: 8½×11; 96-116 pages; 60 lb. recycled offset paper; full color cover; computer clip art, graphics, line art, cartoons, halftones and photos scanned in tiff format. "New consciousness, expansive, fine surrealist and experimental literary, earth and nature, spiritual path. We use current reviews, essays on spiritual and esoteric topics, creative stories and fantasy. Also: reviews of current poetry releases and expansive literature." Readers are "scholars, surrealists, poets, artists, musicians, students." Annually. Estab. 1987. Circ. 2,500.

Needs: Esoteric/scholarly, experimental, fantasy, psychic/supernatural/occult, regional, religious/inspirational, spiritual. "No violent, thoughtless or exploitive fiction." Receives 45-110 unsolicited mss/month. Accepts 5-15 mss/issue; 12-30 mss/year. Publishes ms 2 weeks-10 months after acceptance. Published work by Fielding Dawson, Janine Pommy Vega, Charles Bukowski and Marge Piercy. Published new writers within the last year. Length: 3,500 words average; 1,200 words minimum; 5,000 words maximum. Publishes short shorts. Also publishes literary essays, literary criticism, poetry. Sometimes critiques rejected mss.

How to Contact: Query first; send complete ms with cover letter. Include short bio of recent activities. Reports in 3 weeks on queries; 3-40 weeks on mss. Send SASE for reply or return of ms. Reprint submissions OK. Accepts electronic submissions via "Apple Mac versions of Macwrite, Microsoft Word 5.1 or Writenow 3.0." Sample copy for $7. Fiction guidelines free. Reviews novels and short story collections.

Payment/Terms: Pays in contributor's copies; charges for extras. Acquires first North American serial rights. Sends galleys to author, if requested.

Advice: "Read a sample issue first. Our fiction needs are temperamental, so please query first before submitting. We prefer shorter fiction. Do not send first drafts to test them on us. Please refine and polish your work before sending. Always include SASE. We are looking for the unique, unusual and excellent."

HIGH PLAINS LITERARY REVIEW, (II), 180 Adams St., Suite 250, Denver CO 80206. (303)320-6828. Editor-in-Chief: Robert O. Greer, Jr. Magazine: 6×9; 135 pages; 70 lb. paper; heavy cover stock. "The *High Plains Literary Review* publishes poetry, fiction, essays, book reviews and interviews. The publication is designed to bridge the gap between high-caliber academic quarterlies and successful commercial reviews." Triannually. Estab. 1986. Circ. 1,100.

Needs: Most pressing need: outstanding essays, serious fiction, contemporary, humor/satire, literary, mainstream, regional. No true confessions, romance, pornographic, excessive violence. Receives approximately 400 unsolicited mss/month. Accepts 4-6 mss/issue; 12-18 mss/year. Publishes ms usually 6 months after acceptance. Published work by Richard Currey, Joyce Carol Oates, Nancy Lord and Rita Dove. Published new writers within the last year. Length: 4,200 words average; 1,500 words minimum; 8,000 words maximum; prefers 3,000-6,000 words. Also publishes literary essays, literary criticism, poetry. Occasionally critiques rejected mss.

How to Contact: Send complete ms with cover letter. Include brief publishing history. Reports in 4 months. Send SASE for reply or return of ms. Simultaneous submissions OK. Sample copy for $4.

Payment/Terms: Pays $5/page for prose and 2 contributor's copies on publication for first North American serial rights. "Copyright reverts to author upon publication." Sends copy-edited proofs to the author.

Advice: "*HPLR* publishes *quality* writing. Send us your very best material. We will read it carefully and either accept it promptly, recommend changes or return it promptly. Do not start submitting your work until you learn the basic tenets of the game including some general knowledge about how to develop characters and plot and how to submit a manuscript. I think the most important thing for any new writer interested in the short story form is to have a voracious appetite for short fiction, to see who and what is being published, and to develop a personal style."

HILL AND HOLLER: Southern Appalachian Mountains, (II, IV), Seven Buffaloes Press, P.O. Box 249, Big Timber MT 59011. Editor: Art Cuelho. Magazine: 5½ × 8½; 80 pages; 70 lb. offset paper; 80 lb. cover stock; illustrations; photos rarely. "I use mostly rural Appalachian material: poems and stories, and some folklore and humor. I am interested in heritage, especially in connection with the farm." Annually. Published special fiction issue. Estab. 1983. Circ. 750.

Needs: Contemporary, ethnic, humor/satire, literary, regional, rural America farm. "I don't have any prejudices in style, but I don't like sentimental slant. Deep feelings in literature are fine, but they should be portrayed with tact and skill." Receives 10 unsolicited mss/month. Accepts 4-6 mss/issue. Publishes ms 6 months-1 year after acceptance. Length: 2,000-3,000 words average. Also publishes short shorts of 500-1,000 words.

How to Contact: Query first. Reports in 1 month on queries. SASE. Sample copy for $6.75.

Payment/Terms: Pays in contributor's copies. Acquires first North American serial rights "and permission to reprint if my press publishes a special anthology." Sometimes sends galleys to author.

Advice: "In this Southern Appalachian rural series I can be optimistic about fiction. Appalachians are very responsive to their region's literature. I have taken work by beginners that had not been previously published. Be sure to send a double-spaced clean manuscript and SASE. I have the only rural press in North America; maybe even in the world. So perhaps we have a bond in common if your roots are rural."

HOME PLANET NEWS, (II), Home Planet Publications, P. O. Box 415, New York NY 10009. (718)769-2854. Co-editors: Enid Dame and Donald Lev. Tabloid: 11½ × 16; 24 pages; newsprint; illustrations; photos. "*Home Planet News* publishes mainly poetry along with some fiction, as well as reviews (books, theater and art), and articles of literary interest. We see *HPN* as a quality literary journal in an eminently readable format and with content that is urban, urbane and politically aware." Triannually. Estab. 1979. Circ. 1,000.

● *HPN* has received a small grant from the Puffin Foundation for its focus on AIDS issues.

Needs: Ethnic/multicultural, experimental, feminist, gay, historical, lesbian, literary, mainstream/contemporary, science fiction (soft/sociological). No "children's or genre stories (except rarely some science fiction)." Upcoming themes: "AIDS." Publishes special fiction issue or anthology. Receives 12 mss/month. Accepts 1 ms/issue; 3 mss/year. Reads fiction mss only from February to May. Publishes 1 year after acceptance. Published work by Maureen McNeil, Eugene Stein, B.Z. Niditch and Layle Silbert. Length: 2,000 words average; 500 words minimum; 2,500 words maximum. Publishes short shorts. Also publishes literary criticism, poetry.

How to Contact: Send complete ms with a cover letter. Reports in 3-6 months on mss. Send SASE for reply, return of ms or send a disposable copy of the ms. Sample copy for $3. Fiction guidelines for SASE.

Payment/Terms: Pays 3 contributor's copies; additional copies $1. Acquires one-time rights.

Advice: "We use very little fiction, and a story we accept just has to grab us. We need short pieces of some complexity, stories about complex people facing situations which resist simple resolutions."

*HORIZON, Stationsstraat 232A, 1770 Liedekerke Belgium. Fiction Editor: Johnny Haelterman. Semiannually. Circ. 770. Publishes several stories/issue.

Needs: "*Horizon* is a cultural magazine for a general public, therefore fiction should be suitable for a general public." Length: 300 words minimum; 7,500 words maximum. "A realistic treatment is preferred but a touch of fantasy is sometimes acceptable. No extreme violence or sex."

How to Contact: Enclose money or IRCs if you want your work back. "Submitting outside your country is mainly the same as in your own country, except that the postage costs are higher."

Payment/Terms: Payment in Belgian funds for original fiction in Dutch only. No payment for fiction in other languages but the writers receive two copies in that case. English fiction can be translated into Dutch without payment (two copies). Sample copy available for $8 (US).

Advice: "Puns are usually not translatable, so avoid writing stories with an essential part based on puns if you want your work to be translated."

*HRAFNHOH, 32 Strŷd Ebeneser, Pontypridd, CF37 5PB Wales. Fiction Editor: Joseph Biddulph. Circ. 200. Published irregularly. "Now worldwide and universal in scope."

Needs: Fictionalized history, local history, family history. Explicitly Christian approach. "Well-written stories or general prose opposed to abortion, human embryo experimentation and euthanasia particularly welcome."

How to Contact: Suitable work accepted in esperanto, français, español, and other languages, including Creole. "US stamps are of no use to me, but US banknotes acceptable." IRC will cover a brief response, but mss however small are expensive to return, so please send copy.

Payment/Terms: No payment made, but free copies provided. Sample copy free.

Advice: "Be brief, use a lot of local colour and nature description, in a controlled, resonant prose or in dialect."

*HU (THE HONEST ULSTERMAN), 49 Main St., Greyabbey BT22 2NF, Northern Ireland. Fiction Editor: Tom Clyde. 3 times/year. Circ. 1,000. Publishes 1-4 stories/issue. "Northern Ireland's premier literary magazine. Prime focus is poetry, but continues to publish prose (story, novel extract). 3,000 words maximum. "Must include sufficient means of return (IRCs, etc.). If we decide to publish, an IBM-type floppy disk version would be very helpful." Writers receive small payment and two contributor's copies. For 4 issues send UK £14 airmail or sample issue US $7. "Contributors are strongly advised to read the magazine before submitting anything."

‡HUCKLEBERRY PRESS, (II), Huckleberry Press Publishing, 2625 Alcatraz Ave., Suite 268, Berkeley CA 94705-2702. Editor: Melanie Booth. Magazine: 5½×8½; 60 pages; 20 lb. bond paper; card stock cover; illustrations and photographs. "*Huckleberry Press* strives to promote creative individual talents that have not yet been discovered, silenced, mass-marketed who speak with a distinctly literate and contemporary voice." Semiannually. Estab. 1996. Circ. 500.

Needs: Humor/satire, literary, mainstream/contemporary, regional. No science fiction, horror, erotica, juvenile. Receives over 100 unsolicited mss/month. Accepts 4-6 mss/issue; 8-12 mss/year. Publishes ms 2-8 months after acceptance. Agented fiction 5%. Recently published work by Tom Hazuka, Ricia Anne Chansky and Sarah Prynne Cooley. Length: 3,500 words average; 1,000 words minimum; 6,000 words maximum. Also publishes literary essays, poetry. Sometimes critiques or comments on rejected mss.

How to Contact: Send complete ms with a cover letter. Send SASE for guidelines. Include estimated word count and 50-word bio. Reports 2 weeks on queries; 1 month on mss. SASE. Simultaneous and electronic (disk) submissions OK. Sample copy for $4 and 9×6 SAE with 5 first-class stamps. Fiction guidelines for #10 SASE.

Payment/Terms: Pays 2 contributor's copies on publication; additional copies for $3. Acquires first North American serial rights.

Advice: "We look for strong characterization that compels the reader to keep going. Riveting first lines stand out. No multiple submissions or genre pieces. Don't try to dazzle or deceive us; be direct."

‡THE HUDSON REVIEW, (II), 654 Park Ave., New York NY 10021. (212)650-0020. Fax: (212)774-1911. Editors: Paula Deitz and Frederick Morgan. Magazine: 4½×7½; 176 pages; 50 Basis Miami book vellum paper; 65 Basis Torchglow cover. "*The Hudson Review* is a sourcebook of American culture that explores the current trends in literature and the arts. Each issue features poetry and fiction, essays on literary and cultural topics, book reviews, reports from abroad, and chronicles covering recent developments in film, theater, dance, music and art. We encourage and publish new writing in order to bring the creative imagination of today to a varied, responsive audience." Quarterly. Estab. 1948. Circ. 4,500. "Writers who wish to send unsolicited mss outside the normal reading period (June 1 to November 30) must have a subscription."

Needs: Literary. Receives 375 unsolicited mss/month. Accepts 1-2 mss/issue; 4-8 mss/year. Does not read from December 1 through May 31 (except for subscribers). Recently published work by Thomas M. Disch and Julie Keith. Length: 8,000 words average; 10,000 words maximum. Also publishes literary essays, literary criticism and poetry.

How to Contact: Send complete ms with a cover letter. Include estimated word count. Reports in 6 weeks on queries; 12 weeks on mss. Send SASE for reply, return of ms or send disposable copy of ms. No simultaneous submissions. Sample copy for $7. Fiction guidelines free. Reviews novels and short story collections. Send book to editor.

Payment/Terms: Pays 2 contributor's copies; additional copies $3.50. Sends galleys to author.

Advice: "We do not specialize in publishing any particular 'type' of writing; our sole criterion for accepting unsolicited work is literary quality. The best way for you to get an idea of the range of work we publish is to read a current issue."

THE HUNTED NEWS, (I, II), The Subourban Press, P.O. Box 9101, Warwick RI 02889. (401)739-2279 or (401)826-7307. Editor: Mike Wood. Magazine: 8½×11; 30-35 pages; photocopied paper. "I am looking for good writers in the hope that I can help their voices be heard. Like most in the small press scene, I just wanted to create another option for writers who otherwise might not be heard." Annually. Estab. 1991. Circ. 200.

Needs: Experimental, historical, horror, literary, mainstream/contemporary, regional, religious/inspirational, translations. "No self-impressed work, shock or experimentation for its own sake." Would like to see more religious/spiritual fiction. Receives 50-60 unsolicited mss/month. Acquires 3 mss/issue. Publishes ms within 3-4 months after acceptance. Recently published work by Alfred Schwaid, Steve Richmond, Darryl Smyers and Charles Bukowski. Length: 700 words maximum. Publishes short shorts. Also publishes literary essays, literary criticism and poetry. Often critiques or comments on rejected mss.

How to Contact: Send complete ms with cover letter. Reports in 1 month. Send SASE for return of ms. Simultaneous and reprint submissions OK. Sample copy for 8½×11 SAE and 3 first-class stamps. Fiction guidelines free. Reviews novels or short story collections.

Payment/Terms: Pays 3-5 contributor's copies. Acquires one-time rights.

Advice: "I look for an obvious love of language and a sense that there is something at stake in the story, a story that somehow needs to be told. Write what you need to write, say what you think you need to say, no matter the subject, and take a chance and send it to me. A writer will always find an audience if the work is true."

i.e. magazine: A Journal of Literature and the Arts, (II), P.O. Box 73403, Houston TX 77273-3403. E-mail: yoly@flex.net. Managing Editor: Yolande Gottlieb. Fiction Editor: Augusta Griffith. Nonfiction Editor: John Gorman. Nonprofit magazine: digest-sized; 48-50 pages; 70 lb. glossy paper; 80 lb. glossy cover; illustrations and photos. "*i.e. magazine* is open to different themes. We want quality, innovative, imaginative stories for a literary audience." Quarterly. Estab. 1990. Circ. 200.

Needs: Adventure, experimental, fantasy, historical, humor/satire, literary, mainstream/contemporary, mystery/suspense, romance, science fiction, translations, play reviews (with photos; "large metropolitan area theaters only"), visual arts. Receives 50 unsolicited mss/month. Accepts 4-5 mss/issue; 46-48 mss/year. Publishes ms 3-

6 months after acceptance. Published work by Lee Nelson and Eric Muirhead. Publishes short shorts. Also publishes literary essays, literary criticism, poetry. Sometimes critiques or comments on rejected mss.

How to Contact: Send complete ms with a cover letter. Include estimated word count, bio (maximum ½ page), Social Security number, list of publications and 2×2 photo to include with bio when story is printed. Reports in 3-4 weeks on queries; 2-4 months on mss. Send SASE for reply, return of ms or send a disposable copy of ms. No simultaneous submissions. Sample copy for $6 postpaid. Guidelines for #10 SAE and 2 first-class stamps.

Payment/Terms: Pays 1-2 contributor's copies on publication; additional copies available. Acquires one-time rights. Sponsors contests: fiction, nonfiction, poetry, poetry chapbooks and visual arts. Send SASE for contest guidelines.

Advice: "We suggest contributors familiarize themselves with our editorial preferences."

THE ICONOCLAST, (II), 1675 Amazon Rd., Mohegan Lake NY 10547. Editor: Phil Wagner. Journal. 8½×5½; 32-40 pages; 20 lb. white paper; 20 lb. cover stock; illustrations. "*The Iconoclast* is a self-supporting, independent, unaffiliated general interest magazine with an appreciation of the profound, absurd and joyful in life. Material is limited only by *its* quality and *our* space. We want readers and writers who are open-minded, unafraid to think, and actively engaged with the world." Published 8 times/year. Estab. 1992. Circ. 500.
- *The Iconoclast* has grown from a 16-page newsletter to a 32-40-page journal and is, subsequently, buying more fiction.

Needs: Adventure, ethnic/multicultural, humor/satire, literary, mainstream/contemporary, science fiction. "Nothing militant, solipsistic, or silly." Receives 100 unsolicited mss/month. Accepts 3-6 mss/issue; 25-30 mss/year. Publishes ms 6-9 months after acceptance. Recently published work by Stepan Chapman, Peter Love and Hugh Fox. 10-20% of work published is by new writers. Length: 2,000-2,500 words preferred; 100 words minimum; occasionally longer. Publishes short shorts. Also publishes essays, poetry. Sometimes critiques or comments on rejected mss.

How to Contact: Send complete ms. Reports in 1 month. Send SASE for reply, return of ms or send a disposable copy of the ms. Simultaneous and reprint submissions OK, when noted. Sample copy for $2. Reviews novels and short story collections.

Payment/Terms: Pays 1-2 contributor's copies; additional copies $1.20 (40% discount). Acquires one-time rights.

Advice: "We like fiction that has something to say (and not about its author). We hope for work that is observant, intense and multi-leveled. Follow Pound's advice—'make it new.' Write what you want in whatever style you want without being gross, sensational, or needlessly explicit—then pray there's someone who can appreciate your sensibility. Read good fiction. It's as fundamental as learning how to hit, throw and catch is to baseball. With the increasing American disinclination towards literature, stories must insist on being heard."

THE IDIOT, (II), Anarchaos Press, 1706 S. Bedford St., Los Angeles CA 90035. Editor: Sam Hayes. Magazine: 5½×8½; 48 pages; 20 lb. white paper; glossy cardboard cover; illustrations. "For people who enjoy TV shows such as 'The Simpsons' and 'Mystery Science Theater 3000' as well as those who like Woody Allen and S.J. Perelman. I've had letters from engineers to teenagers saying they loved it, so you have to be both funny and weird and sophisticated all at once." Semiannually. Estab. 1993. Circ. 250.

Needs: Humor/satire. Publishes ms 4-8 months after acceptance. Recently published work by Mark Lafferty, Angus Kubrick and Mick Shire. Publishes 2-8 new writers/year. Length: 1,500 words average; 2,500 words maximum. Publishes short shorts. Also publishes poetry. Sometimes critiques or comments on rejected mss.

How to Contact: Send complete ms with a cover letter. Include estimated word count and bio (30-50 words). Reports in 1 month on queries; 3 months on mss. Send SASE for reply, return of ms or send a disposable copy of ms. Simultaneous, reprint and electronic submissions OK. Sample copy for $5.

Payment/Terms: Pays 1-2 contributor's copies. Acquires one-time rights. Sometimes sends galleys to author.

Advice: "Do not send anything if it isn't hilarious. If I don't laugh out loud by the second page I stop reading. It must be consistently funny—most submissions are merely 'cute.' Also, read the magazine to see what we're doing."

IMAGE, A Journal of the Arts & Religion, (II), The Center for Religious Humanism, 323 S. Broad St., P.O. Box 674, Kennett Square PA 19348. Phone/fax: (610)444-8065. E-mail: 73424.1024@compuserve.com. Editor: Greg Wolfe. Magazine: 7×10; 140 pages; glossy cover stock; illustrations and photos. "*Image* is a showcase for the encounter between religious faith and world-class contemporary art. Each issue features fiction, poetry, essays, memoirs, an in-depth interview and articles about visual artists, film, music, etc. and glossy 4-color plates of contemporary visual art." Quarterly. Estab. 1989. Circ. 3,000. Member CLMP.

Needs: Humor/satire, literary, regional, religious/inspirational, translations. Receives 40 unsolicited mss/month. Accepts 2 mss/issue; 8 mss/year. Publishes ms within 1 year after acceptance. Agented fiction 5%. Recently published work by Madison Smartt Bell, Tim Winton, Wally Lamb, Jon Hassler, Ron Hansen and Doris Betts. Length: 5,000 words average; 2,000 words minimum; 8,000 words maximum. Also publishes literary essays and poetry.

How to Contact: Send complete ms with a cover letter. Include bio. Reports in 1 month on queries; 3 months on mss. Send SASE for reply, return of ms or send a disposable copy of ms. Electronic (disk or modem) submissions OK. Sample copy for $10. Reviews novels and short story collections.

Payment/Terms: Pays $100 maximum and 4 contributor's copies on publication; additional copies for $5. Sends galleys to author.

Advice: "Fiction must have a religious aspect to it."

IN THE SPIRIT OF THE BUFFALO, A Literary Magazine (I), In the Spirit of the Buffalo, 1540 S.W. 14th St., Lincoln NE 68522. (402)476-0656. Fax: (402)464-1604. E-mail: buffalo369@aol.com. Editor: Mark A. Reece. Newsletter: 5½×8½; saddle stapled; photocopied; illustrations and photos. "*ITSOTB* showcases the human condition and our ability to survive. We publish poetry, short fiction, essays, cartoons, puzzles and artwork targeted toward adults who enjoy self-expression." Quarterly. Estab. 1996. Circ. 100-200.
- The editor would like to see more science fiction.

Needs: Adventure, fantasy, historical, horror, humor/satire, literary, regional, science fiction (soft/sociological), westerns. "No erotica or sword and sorcery." Receives 4-5 unsolicited mss/month. Accepts 2-3 mss/issue; 8 mss/year. Publishes ms within 6 months after acceptance. Recently published work by Ralph H. Allen, Jr., John Stewart Michael, James C. Sullivan, Barbara J. Less and Lu Motley. Length: 800 words average; no minimum; 1,000 words maximum. Publishes short shorts. Also publishes literary essays and poetry. Sometimes comments on rejected mss.

How to Contact: Send complete ms with a cover letter or send e-mail. Include ½-page bio. Reports in 3 months on mss. SASE for return of ms. Reprints and electronic submissions (e-mail) OK. Sample copy $3. Guidelines for #10 SASE.

Payment/Terms: Pays 1 contributor's copy on publication; additional copies for $1. Acquires one-time rights.

Advice: "I like good dialogue, characters people can relate to and a subtle lesson or moral that makes the story worth reading. Keep the work under 1,000 words and proofread. The story should have a purpose. I haven't seen enough short shorts with impact and development. We prefer e-mail submissions because of the ease of typesetting. Well-prepared paper documents are often scanned and converted to text files. Use standard fonts so the document can be read by OCR software."

*INDIAN LITERATURE, Sahitya Akademi, National Academy of Letters, Rabindra Bhavan, 35 Ferozeshah Rd., New Delhi 110 001 India. Editor: Professor H.S. Shiva Prakash. Circ. 4,100. Publishes 6 issues/year; 200 pages.

Needs: "Presents creative work from 22 Indian languages including Indian English."

Payment/Terms: Sample copy available for $7.

INDIANA REVIEW, (I, II), 465 Ballantine, Bloomington IN 47405. (812)855-3439. Fiction Editor: Laura McCoid. Editors change every 2 years. Magazine: 6×9; 200 pages; 50 lb. paper; Glatfelter cover stock. *Indiana Review* is a "magazine of contemporary fiction and poetry in which there is a zest for language, a relationship between form and content, and awareness of the world. For fiction writers/readers, followers of lively contemporary prose." Semiannually. Estab. 1976. Circ. 3,000.
- *Indiana Review* won the 1996 American Literary Magazine Award. Work published in *Indiana Review* was selected for inclusion in the *O. Henry Prize Stories* anthology.

Needs: Ethnic, literary, regional, translations. Also considers novel excerpts. Receives 300 unsolicited mss each month. Accepts 7-9 prose mss/issue. Published work by Lisa Glait, Danit Braun and Wendell Mays. Length: 1-35 magazine pages. Also publishes literary essays, poetry.

How to Contact: Send complete ms with cover letter. "Cover letters need to be concise and to the point. Encapsulating a piece's theme or content is unacceptable." SASE. Simultaneous submissions OK (if notified *immediately* of other publication). Reports in 3 months. Publishes ms an average of 2-4 months after acceptance. Sample copy for $7.

Payment/Terms: Pays $5/page and 2 contributor's copies for North American serial rights.

Advice: "We look for prose that is well-crafted, socially relevant. We are interested in innovation, unity and social context. All genres that meet some of these criteria are welcome."

‡❧ink magazine, (I, II), P.O. Box 52558, 264 Bloor St. West, Toronto Ontario M5S 1V0 Canada. E-mail: bn096@forfree.net. Editor: John Degen. Magazine: 8×6; 44 pages; card cover; illustrations and photos. "*ink* surveys the mess of creativity. Anything that can be reproduced in ink—poetry, fiction, art, interviews, recipes, postcards, maps, both real and imagined—are reproduced in *ink*." Quarterly. Estab. 1993. Circ. 500.
- Member of the Canadian Magazine Publisher's Association.

Needs: Literary, translations. Publishes special fiction issues or anthologies. Receives 100 unsolicited mss/

MARKET CATEGORIES: **(I)** Open to new writers; **(II)** Open to both new and established writers; **(III)** Interested mostly in established writers; **(IV)** Open to writers whose work is specialized; **(V)** Closed to unsolicited submissions.

month. Accepts 10 mss/issue; 40 mss/year. Recently published work by Al Purdy, Derek McCormack, Alexandra Leggat, Peter McCallum, Chris Chambers and Heidi Greco. Length: 2,000 words average; 1 word minimum; 3,000 words maximum. Publishes short shorts. Also publishes literary essays, literary criticism and poetry. Often critiques or comments on rejected mss.

How to Contact: Query with clips of published work. Include estimated word count and 2-3 sentence bio. Reports in 1-2 months on queries. Send SASE for reply. No simultaneous submissions. Electronic (disk) submissions OK. Sample copy for $3.50. Fiction guidelines for #10 SASE. Reviews novels and short story collections. Send books to editor.

Payment/Terms: Pays free subscription to magazine for first North American serial rights.

INTERIM, (II), Dept. of English, University of Nevada, Las Vegas NV 89154. (702)895-3458. Editor: James Hazen. Magazine: 6×9; 48-64 pages; heavy paper; semigloss cover with illustration. Publishes "poetry and short fiction for a serious, educated audience." However, they focus more on poetry than fiction. Semiannually. Estab. 1944; revived 1986. Circ. 600-800.

Needs: Contemporary, experimental, literary. Accepts 1-2 mss/issue. Publishes ms 6 months to 1 year of acceptance. Recently published work by G.K. Wuori and Mark Wisniewski. Length: 7,500 words maximum.

How to Contact: Send 1 complete ms with cover letter. Reports on mss in 4-6 weeks. SASE. Sample copy for $5.

Payment/Terms: Pays in contributor's copies and two-year subscription to magazine.

Advice: "Don't send excerpts from novels or longer works. We like completed stories, written as such, with the ordinary virtues of the form: strong, interesting characters, movement, resolution, economy, intensity, or wholeness, harmony, radiance. *No simultaneous submissions in either poetry or fiction.* These are unfair to our volunteer, unpaid staff. We cannot study and debate your work only to find at the end that it's been accepted for publication somewhere else. We try to keep our end of the bargain by holding submissions no longer than 60 days."

INTERNATIONAL QUARTERLY, Essays, Fiction, Drama, Poetry, Art, Reviews, (II), P.O. Box 10521, Tallahassee FL 32302-0521. (850)224-5078. Fax: (850)224-5127. Editor: Van K. Brock. Magazine: 7½×10; 176 pages; 50 lb. text paper; 60 lb. gloss cover; fine art illustrations. *"International Quarterly* seeks to bridge boundaries between national, ethnic and cultural identities, and among creative disciplines, by providing a venue for dialogue between exceptional writers and artists and discriminating readers. We look for work that reveals character and place from within." Quarterly. Estab. 1993.

Needs: Ethnic/multicultural, experimental, humor/satire, literary, mainstream/contemporary, regional, translations. "We would consider work in any of the genres that transcends the genre through quality of language, characterization and development. Our sympathies are strongly feminist. Many of the genre categories imply simplistic and limited literary purposes. Any genre can transcend its limits. No issue is limited to work on its regional or thematic focus." Accepts 5 mss/issue; 20 mss/year. "We read all year, but fewer readers are active in July and August." Publishes ms 3-9 months after acceptance. Published work by Kiana Davenport, Edmund Keeley, Iván Mándy, Gary Corseri and S.P. Elledge. Publishes short shorts. Also publishes literary essays, literary criticism (for general readers), poetry. Sometimes critiques or comments on rejected mss.

How to Contact: Query first or send complete ms with a cover letter. Include estimated word count, bio, list of publications. Include rights available. "We prefer first rights for all original English texts." Reports in 1-2 weeks on queries; 2-4 months on mss. Send SASE for reply, return of ms or send a disposable copy of ms. Simultaneous, reprint (please specify) and electronic submissions OK. Sample copy for $6 (a reduced rate) and 4 first-class stamps. Fiction guidelines for #10 SASE. Reviews novels and short story collections. Send books to Book Review Editor.

Payment/Terms: Pays free subscription to magazine and 1 contributor's copy. Acquires first North American serial rights. Sends galleys to author.

Advice: "We would like to see more fiction break out of conventional thinking and set fictional modes without straining or trying to shock and fiction that presents the world of its characters from inside the skin of the culture, rather than those outside of the culture, tourists or short-termers, as it were, commenting on the world of a story's subjects from outside, lamenting that it has fallen into our consumerist ways, etc., lamentable as that may be. Works we publish do not have to be foreign, they may arise out of a profound understanding of any culture or locale, as long as they provide the reader with an authentic experience of that locale, whatever the origin of the author. We have no taboos, but we want writing that understands and creates understanding, writers who want to go beyond cultural givens."

‡INTROVERT ALIVE, (I), (910)297-9755. E-mail: intromag@hotmail.com. Website: http://www.introalive.com. Editors: Brian Wilson and Jeremy Sarine. Electronic magazine. "We are looking for poetry, short stories, journal entries, random thoughts and writings about whatever happens to be in your head or your heart."

Needs: Literary. "We'd prefer not to have anything overly graphic. We want this magazine to be open to all ages." Would like to see more Christian writings. "While this is not a Christian magazine, we would like to have a wide variety of beliefs and religions represented." Recently published work by Richard Krol, Cris Inscoe, Michael Wilson, Adrian Penn, Nick Grimaldi, Anjana Basu and Amanda Pruitt. "We are dedicated to publishing unknown authors."

How to Contact: Electronic and traditional submissions. Send ms by e-mail or postal mail to The Transcending

Embrace, P.O. Box 4343, Eden NC 27289.

Advice: "Our best advice to writers? Be honest with yourself and with others. Be free in your heart and your mind. Don't be afraid to make a mistake or to offend someone. We often get offended by things that we haven't dealt with in ourselves, so offending someone is often only bringing to their attention something that they need to deal with. So next time something offends you, think about why it offends you. Then write about it and send it to us."

THE IOWA REVIEW, (I, II), University of Iowa, 308 EPB, Iowa City IA 52242. (319)335-0462. E-mail: iowa-review@uiowa.edu. Editors: David Hamilton and Mary Hussmann. Magazine: 6×9; 200 pages; first-grade offset paper; Carolina CS1 10-pt. cover stock. "Stories, essays, poems for a general readership interested in contemporary literature." Triannually. Estab. 1970. Circ. 1,500.
- Work published in *Iowa Review* regularly has been selected for inclusion in the *Pushcart Prize* and *Best American Short Stories* anthologies. The editors are especially interested in work from minority writers or those whose "voices have been marginalized."

Needs: Ethnic, experimental, feminist, gay, literary, translations. Receives 300-400 unsolicited fiction mss/month. Agented fiction less than 2%. Accepts 4-6 mss/issue, 12-18 mss/year. Does not read mss April-August. Recently published work by E.J. Graff, Gordon Lish and Jeffrey J. Merrick. Published new writers within the last year. Also publishes literary essays, literary criticism, poetry.

How to Contact: Send complete ms with cover letter. "Don't bother with queries." SASE for return of ms. Simultaneous submissions OK. Reports in 2-4 months on mss. Publishes ms an average of 6-12 months after acceptance. Sample copy for $6. Fiction guidelines for SASE. Reviews novels and short story collections (3-6 books/year).

Payment/Terms: Pays $10/page ($25 minimum) on publication and 2 contributor's copies; additional copies 30% off cover price. Acquires first North American serial rights.

Advice: "We have no set guidelines as to content or length; we look for what we consider to be the best writing available to us. We believe we select and publish some of the best new works written today. In fact, we especially encourage new writers and are pleased when writers we believe we have discovered, from their unsolicited manuscripts, catch on with a wider range of readers. It is never a bad idea either to look through an issue or two of the magazine prior to a submission."

‡IR MAGAZINE, (I), (305) 233-7690. E-mail: BelladonnaFish@Juno.com. Website: http://www.geocities.com/Athens/7119. Editor: Ben Carrasco. Electronic magazine. "A literary magazine focusing on spreading unpublished writer's work to the general public."

Needs: Short stories, all styles and themes except genre fiction (science fiction, horror, fantasy, etc). Would like to see more stories dealing with "character depth and action storylines." Recently published work by Jacques Chester, Scott Millar and Bonnie Beregszaszi. Publishes 15-30 new writers/year.

How to Contact: Electronic and traditional submissions accepted. E-mail for address.

Advice: "Be creative and clever. Be original and don't be concerned by what others might think."

IRIS: A Journal About Women, (II, IV), Box 323 HSC, University of Virginia, Charlottesville VA 22908. (804)924-4500. Fiction Editor: Tristan Seifer. Editor-in-Chief: Susan K. Brady. Magazine: 8½×11; 80 pages; glossy paper; heavy cover; illustrations, artwork and photographs. "Material of particular interest to women. For a feminist audience, college educated and above." Semiannually. Estab. 1980. Circ. 3,500.

Needs: Experimental, feminist, lesbian, literary, mainstream. "I don't think what we're looking for particularly falls into the 'mainstream' category—we're just looking for well-written stories of interest to women (particularly feminist women)." Receives 300 unsolicited mss/year. Accepts 5 mss/year. Publishes ms within 1 year after acceptance. Length: 4,000 words average. Sometimes critiques rejected mss.

How to Contact: Send complete ms with cover letter. Include "previous publications, vocation, other points that pertain. Make it brief!" Reports in 3 months on mss. SASE. Simultaneous submissions OK. Accepts electronic submissions via disk or modem. Sample copy for $5. Fiction guidelines with SASE.

Payment/Terms: Pays in contributor's copies and 1 year subscription. Acquires one-time rights.

Advice: "I select mss which are lively imagistically as well as in the here-and-now; I select for writing which challenges the reader. My major complaint is with stories that don't elevate the language above the bland sameness we hear on the television and everyday. Read the work of the outstanding women writers, such as Alice Munroe and Louise Erdrich."

‡*ISLAND, P.O. Box 210, Sandy Bay 7005 Australia. Contact: Editor. Quarterly. Circ. 1,000. Publishes 6 stories/issue.

Needs: "*Island* is a quarterly of ideas, criticism, fiction and poetry." Length: 4,000 words maximum.

How to Contact: Send double-spaced laser print copy where possible. Include a brief cover letter and SASE.

Payment/Terms: Pays $100 (Australian) minimum. Sample copy available for $8.95 (Australian), back issues $5 plus postage.

‡JACKHAMMER MAGAZINE, (I, II), Introspect Publications, P.O. Box 782047, Wichita KS 67278. (316)681-3195. Editor: Ethan Benda. Magazine: 5½×8½; 36 pages; 30 lb. bond cover stock; illustrations and photos.

"Freedom of emotion through written word and art." Semiannually. Estab. 1994. Circ. 200.

Needs: Erotica, ethnic/multicultural, historical, humor/satire, literary, psychic/supernatural/occult, science fiction (hard science), translations, young adult/teen. No "drug and alcohol glorification or racism." Publishes special fiction issues or anthologies. Receives 1 unsolicited ms/month. Accepts 4 mss/year. Publishes ms 3 months after acceptance. Recently published work by R. Erik Ott, J. Harvey and T. Hibbard. Length: 100 words average; 1,000 words maximum. Publishes short shorts. Also publishes literary essays, literary criticism and poetry.

How to Contact: Query first. Include half-page bio. Reports in 3 weeks on queries. Sample copy for $1 and 2 first-class stamps. Fiction guidelines for #10 SASE.

Payment/Terms: Payment varies for first-rights. Sends galleys to author.

Advice: "The only thing you have to fear is rejection."

JAPANOPHILE, (I, II, IV), Box 223, Okemos MI 48864. (517)669-2109. E-mail: japanlove@aol.com. Editor-in-Chief: Earl Snodgrass. Magazine: 5¼×8½; 58 pages; illustrations; photos. Magazine of "articles, photos, poetry, humor, short stories about Japanese culture, not necessarily set in Japan, for an adult audience, most with a college background and who like to travel." Quarterly. Estab. 1974. Circ. 800.

 • Most of the work included in *Japanophile* is set in recent times, but the magazine will accept material set back as far as pre-WWII.

Needs: Adventure, historical, humor/satire, literary, mainstream, and mystery/suspense. Published special fiction issue last year; plans another. Receives 40-100 unsolicited fiction mss/month. Accepts 12 ms/issue, 20-30 mss/year. Recently published work by Matt Malcomson, Mary Waters and Forrest Johnson. Published new writers within the last year. Length: 3,200 words average; 2,000 words minimum; 6,000 words maximum. Also publishes essays, book reviews, literary criticism and poetry.

How to Contact: Send complete ms with SASE, cover letter, bio and information about story. Simultaneous and reprint submissions OK. Reports in 3 months on mss. Sample copy for $4; guidelines for #10 SASE.

Payment/Terms: Pays $20 on publication for all rights, first North American serial rights or one-time rights (depends on situation). Stories submitted to the magazine may be entered in the annual contest. *A $5 entry fee must accompany each submission* to enter contest. Prizes include $100 plus publication for the best short story. Deadline: December 31.

Advice: "Short stories usually involve Japanese and 'foreign' (non-Japanese) characters in a way that contributes to understanding of Japanese culture and the Japanese people. However, a *good* story dealing with Japan or Japanese cultural aspects anywhere in the world will be considered, even if it does not involve this encounter or meeting of Japanese and foreign characters. Some stories may also be published in an anthology with approval of the author and additional payment."

‡THE JOLLY ROGER, (I, II), P.O. Box 1087, Chapel Hill NC 27514. (919)406-7068. E-mail: drake@jollyroger .com. Website: http://www.jollyroger.com. Editor: Drake Raft. Electronic magazine. "Literature composed in the context of the Western Canon."

Needs: "Conservative and traditional fiction, epic poetry, prose and short stories. Looking for rhyme, meter, words that mean things, plot and character. Publishes an occasional novel or collection of poetry." Recently published work by Drake Raft, Becket Knottingham, Elliot McGucken and Bootsy McClusky. Publishes 10-20 new writers/year.

How to Contact: Electronic and traditional submissions accepted.

THE JOURNAL, (II), Dept of English, Ohio State University, 164 W. 17th St., Columbus OH 43210. (614)292-4076. Editors: Kathy Fagan (poetry); Michelle Herman (fiction). Magazine: 6×9; 150 pages. "We are open to all forms of quality fiction." For an educated, general adult audience. Semiannually. Estab. 1973. Circ. 1,300.

Needs: "Interested in all literary forms." No romance or religious/devotional. Accepts 2 mss/issue. Receives approximately 100 unsolicited fiction mss/month. "Usually" publishes ms within 1 year of acceptance. Agented fiction 10%. Published work by Nell Beram, Kay Sloan, Mark Jacobs and Duncan Greenlaw. Published new writers within the last year. Length: Open. Also accepts poetry. Critiques rejected mss when there is time.

How to Contact: Send complete ms with cover letter. Reports "as soon as possible," usually 3 months. SASE. Sample copy for $5.50; fiction guidelines for SASE.

Payment/Terms: Pays $25 stipend when funds are available; contributor's copies; $5.50 charge for extras.

Terms: Acquires First North American serial rights. Sends galleys to author.

Advice: Mss are rejected because of "lack of understanding of the short story form, shallow plots, undeveloped characters. Cure: read as much well-written fiction as possible. Our readers prefer 'psychological' fiction rather than stories with intricate plots. Take care to present a clean, well-typed submission."

THE JOURNAL, (I, II), Poetry Forum, 5713 Larchmont Dr., Erie PA 16509. Phone/fax: (814)866-2543. (Faxing hours: 8-10 a.m. and 5-8 p.m.) E-mail: 75562.670@compuserve.com. Editor: Gunvor Skogsholm. Journal: 5½×8½; 18-20 pages; light card cover. Looks for "good writing—for late teens to full adulthood." Quarterly. Estab. 1989. Circ. 200.

 • *The Journal* is edited by Gunvor Skogsholm, the editor of *Poetry Forum Short Stories* and *Short Stories Bimonthly*. This magazine is not strictly a pay-for-publication, "subscribers come first.'

Needs: Mainstream. Plans annual special fiction issue. Receives 25-30 unsolicited mss/month. Accepts 1 ms/

issue; 7-10 mss/year. Publishes mss 2 weeks to 7 months after acceptance. Agented fiction 1%. 40% of work published is by new writers. Length: 500 words preferred; 300 words average; 150 words minimum. Publishes short shorts. Length: 400 words. Sponsors contest. Send SASE for details.

How to Contact: Send complete ms. Reports in 2 weeks to 7 months on mss. SASE. Simultaneous submissions OK. Accepts electronic disk submissions. Sample copy for $3. Fiction guidelines for SASE.

Payment/Terms: No payment. Acquires one-time rights. Not copyrighted.

Advice: "Subscribers come first!" Looks for "a good lead stating a theme, support of the theme throughout and an ending that rounds out the story or article. Make it believable, please don't preach, avoid propaganda, and don't say, 'This is a story about a retarded person'; instead, prove it by your writing. Show, don't tell."

‡THE JOURNAL OF AFRICAN TRAVEL-WRITING, (IV), P.O. Box 346, Chapel Hill NC 27514. (919)929-0419. E-mail: ottotwo@email.unc.edu. Editor: Amber Vogel. Magazine: 7×10; 96 pages; 50 lb. paper; illustrations. "*The Journal of African Travel-Writing* presents materials in a variety of genres that explore Africa as a site of narrative." Semiannually. Estab. 1996. Circ. 600.

● Sponsors annual award for best piece published in the journal.

Needs: Adventure, condensed/excerpted novel, ethnic/multicultural, historical, literary, translations. Accepts 1-4 mss/issue. Publishes ms 4-6 months after acceptance. Recently published work by Eileen Drew, Lisa Fugard and Sandra Jackson-Opoku. Also publishes literary essays, literary criticism and poetry. Sometimes critiques or comments on rejected mss.

How to Contact: Send complete ms with a cover letter. Sample copy for $6. Reviews novels and short story collections. Send books to editor.

Payment/Terms: Pays 5 contributor's copies for first rights. Sends galleys to author.

KALEIDOSCOPE: International Magazine of Literature, Fine Arts, and Disability, (II, IV), 701 S. Main St., Akron OH 44311. Phone/fax: (330)762-9755. Editor-in-Chief: Darshan Perusek, Ph.D. Senior Editor: Gail Willmott. Magazine: 8½×11; 56-64 pages; non-coated paper; coated cover stock; illustrations (all media); photos. "*Kaleidoscope* Magazine has a creative focus that examines the experiences of disability through literature and the fine arts. Unique to the field of disability studies, this award-winning publication is not an advocacy or rehabilitation journal. *Kaleidoscope* expresses the experiences of disability from the perspective of individuals, families, healthcare professionals, and society as a whole." Semiannually. Estab. 1979. Circ. 1,000.

● *Kaleidoscope* has received awards from the American Heart Association, the Great Lakes Awards Competition and Ohio Public Images. The editors are looking for more fiction .

Needs: Personal experience, drama, fiction, essay, artwork. Upcoming theme: "Disability and Alternative Healing" (deadline March 1998); "Economics of Disability" (deadline August 1998). Receives 20-25 unsolicited fiction mss/month. Accepts 10 mss/year. Approximately 1% of fiction is agented. Recently published work by Reynolds Price and Lois McMaster Bujold. Published new writers within the last year. Length: 5,000 words maximum. Also publishes poetry.

How to Contact: Query first or send complete ms and cover letter. Include author's educational and writing background and if author has a disability, how it has influenced the writing. Simultaneous submissions OK. Reports in 1 month on queries; 6 months on mss. Sample copy for $4. Guidelines for #10 SASE.

Payment/Terms: Pays $10-125 and 2 contributor's copies on publication; additional copies $5. Acquires first rights. Reprints permitted with credit given to original publication.

Advice: "Read the magazine and get submission guidelines. We prefer that writers with a disability offer original perspectives about their experiences; writers without disabilities should limit themselves to our focus in order to solidify a connection to our magazine's purpose. Do not use stereotypical, patronizing and sentimental attitudes about disability."

KALLIOPE, A Journal of Women's Art, (II), Florida Community College at Jacksonville, 3939 Roosevelt Blvd., Jacksonville FL 32205. (904)381-3511. Editor: Mary Sue Koeppel. Magazine: 7¼×8¼; 76-88 pages; 70 lb. coated matte paper; Bristol cover; 16-18 halftones per issue. "A literary and visual arts journal for women, *Kalliope* celebrates women in the arts by publishing their work and by providing a forum for their ideas and opinions." Short stories, poems, plays, essays, reviews and visual art. Triannually. Estab. 1978. Circ. 1,550.

● Kalliope has received the Frances Buck Sherman Award from the local branch of the National League of Pen Women. The magazine has also received awards and grants for its poetry, grants from the Florida Department of Cultural Affairs and the Jacksonville Club Gallery of Superb Printing Award.

Needs: "Quality short fiction by women writers." Accepts 2-4 mss/issue. Receives approximately 100 unsolicited fiction mss each month. Recently published work by Glynis Kinnan, Rolaine Hoch Stein, Kathleen Spivack

READ THE BUSINESS OF FICTION WRITING section to learn the correct way to prepare and submit a manuscript.

and Connie Mary Fowler. Publishes 3 new writers/year. Published new writers within the last year. Preferred length: 750-2,000 words, but occasionally publishes longer (and shorter) pieces. Also publishes poetry. Critiques rejected mss "when there is time and if requested."

How to Contact: Send complete ms with SASE and short contributor's note. No simultaneous submissions. Reports in 2-3 months on ms. Publishes ms an average of 1-3 months after acceptance. Sample copy: $7 for current issue; $4 for issues from '78-'88. Reviews short story collections.

Payment/Terms: Pays 3 contributor's copies or 1-years subscription for first rights. Discount for extras. "We accept only unpublished work. Copyright returned to author upon request."

Advice: "Read our magazine. The work we consider for publication will be well written and the characters and dialogue will be convincing. We like a fresh approach and are interested in new or unusual forms. Make us believe your characters; give readers an insight which they might not have had if they had not read you. We would like to publish more work by minority writers." Manuscripts are rejected because "1) nothing *happens*!, 2) it is thinly disguised autobiography (richly disguised autobiography is OK), 3) ending is either too pat or else just trails off, 4) characterization is no developed, and 5) point of view falters."

KELSEY REVIEW, (I, II, IV), Mercer County College, P.O. Box B, Trenton NJ 08690. (609)586-4800. E-mail: kelsey.review@mccc.edu. Website: http://www.mccc.edu (includes deadlines, date of publication). Editor: Robin Schore. Magazine: 7×14; 80 pages; glossy paper; soft cover. "Must live or work in Mercer County, NJ." Annually. Estab. 1988. Circ. 2,000.

Needs: Open. Regional (Mercer County only). Receives 120 unsolicited mss/year. Accepts 24 mss/issue. Reads mss only in May. Publishes ms 1-2 months after acceptance. Recently published work by Bruce Petronio, Mary Mallery, Janet Kirk and D.E. Steward. Publishes 3 new writers/year. Length: 2,000 words maximum. Publishes short shorts. Also publishes literary essays, literary criticism and poetry. Always critiques or comments on rejected mss.

How to Contact: Send complete ms with cover letter. SASE for return of ms. No simultaneous submissions. Reports in 1-2 months. Sample copy free.

Payment/Terms: Pays 5 contributor's copies. Rights revert to author on publication.

Advice: Looks for "quality, intellect, grace and guts. Avoid sentimentality, overwriting and self-indulgence. Work on clarity, depth and originality."

KENNESAW REVIEW, (II), Kennesaw State University, Dept of English, 1000 Chastain Rd., Kennesaw GA 30144-5591. (770)423-6346. Editor: Dr. Robert W. Hill. Magazine. "Just good fiction, all themes, for a general audience." Semiannually. Estab. 1987.

Needs: Excerpted novel, contemporary, ethnic, experimental, feminist, gay, humor/satire, literary, mainstream, regional. No romance. Receives 25-60 mss/month. Accepts 2-4 mss/issue. Publishes ms 12-18 months after acceptance. Published work by Julie Brown, Stephen Dixon, Robert Morgan, Carolyn Thorman. Length: 9-30 pages. Length: 500 words. Rarely comments on or critiques rejected mss.

How to Contact: Send complete ms with cover letter. Include previous publications. Reports 2 months on mss. SASE. Simultaneous submissions OK. Sample copy and fiction guidelines free.

Payment/Terms: Pays in contributor's copies. Acquires first publication rights only. Acknowledgment required for subsequent publication.

Advice: "Use the language well and tell an interesting story. Send it on. Be open to suggestions."

‡KENOSIS, (II, IV), P.O. Box 246, Fairfax CA 94978. Editor: Robert Cesaretti. Magazine: 4×6; 50-60 pages; standard paper; card cover; illustrations and photographs. Published "when material permits."

Needs: Experimental, literary. No occult, pornography or erotic. Receives 20 unsolicited mss/month. Length: 2,500 words maximum. Publishes short shorts. Also publishes literary essays, poetry.

How to Contact: Send complete ms with a cover letter. Include spiritual beliefs. Reports in 3 months on mss. SASE for return of ms. Simultaneous and reprint submissions OK.

Payment/Terms: Pays 1 contributor's copy. Acquires one-time rights.

Advice: "I look for spiritual/sacred realities transformed into literature. Read philosophy, theology, mysticism and 'pour' that content into literary form and style. I have not seen enough of the transcendant, existential angst confronting us today. Avoid overtly religosity and conventional style."

THE KENYON REVIEW, (II), Kenyon College, Gambier OH 43022. (614)427-5208. Fax: (614)427-5417. E-mail: kenyonreview@kenyon.edu. Editor: David H. Lynn. "Fiction, poetry, essays, book reviews." Triannually. Estab. 1939. Circ. 5,000.

● Work published in the *Kenyon Review* has been selected for inclusion in *Pushcart Prize* anthologies.

Needs: Condensed/excerpted novel, contemporary, ethnic, experimental, feminist, gay, historical, humor/satire, lesbian, literary, mainstream, translations. Receives 400 unsolicited fiction mss/month. Unsolicited mss read only from September 1 through November 30 and from February 1 through March 31. Publishes ms 12-18 months after acceptance. Recently published work by Joyce Carol Oates, Lewis Hyde, Reginald McKnight and Nancy Zafris. Length: 3-15 typeset pages preferred.

How to Contact: Send complete ms with cover letter. Reports on mss in 2-3 months. SASE. No simultaneous submissions. Sample copy for $8.

Payment/Terms: Pays $10/page on publication for first-time rights. Sends copyedited version to author for approval.

Advice: "Read several issues of our publication. We remain invested in encouraging/reading/publishing work by writers of color, writers expanding the boundaries of their genre, and writers with unpredictable voices and points of view."

KEREM, Creative Explorations in Judaism, (IV), Jewish Study Center Press, Inc., 3035 Porter St. NW, Washington DC 20008. (202)364-3006. Fax: (202)364-3806. Editors: Sara Horowitz and Gilah Langner. Magazine: 6×9; 128 pages; 60 lb. offset paper; glossy cover; illustrations and photos. "*Kerem* publishes Jewish religious, creative, literary material—short stories, poetry, personal reflections, text study, prayers, rituals, etc." Annually. Estab. 1992. Circ. 2,000

Needs: Jewish: feminist, humor/satire, literary, religious/inspirational. Receives 10-12 unsolicited mss/month. Accepts 10-12 mss/issue. Publishes ms 2-10 months after acceptance. Recently published work by Mark Mirsky and Anita Diamant. Length: 6,000 words maximum. Also publishes literary essays, poetry.

How to Contact: Send complete ms with a cover letter. Should include 1-2 line bio. Reports in 2 months on queries; 4-5 months on mss. Send SASE for reply, return of ms or send a disposable copy of ms. Simultaneous submissions OK. Sample copy for $8.50.

Payment/Terms: Pays free subscription and 2-10 contributor's copies. Acquires one-time rights.

Advice: "Should have a strong Jewish content. We want to be moved by reading the manuscript!"

‡KIMERA: A JOURNAL OF FINE WRITING, (I, II), E-mail: kimera@onramp.ior.com. Website: http://www.ior.com/kimera/. Editor: Jan Strever. Electronic magazine. "Kimera attempts to meet John Locke's challenge: Where is the head with no chimeras? We seek fiction that pushes the edge in terms of language use and craft."

Needs: Eclectic, energetic fiction. "Nothing badly conceived without attention to the muscularity of language." Recently published work by J. Bowers, L. Lynch and G. Thomas. Twenty-five percent of work published is by new writers.

How to Contact: Electronic submissions only.

Advice: "Pay attention to how sound echoes the senses in writing."

KIOSK, (II), English Department, S.U.N.Y. at Buffalo, 306 Clemens Hall, Buffalo NY 14260. Editor-in-Chief: Lia Vella. Fiction Editor: Jonathan Pitts. Magazine: 5½×8½; 150 pages; 80 lb. cover; illustrations. "We seek innovative, non-formula fiction and poetry." Annually (may soon be Biannually). Estab. 1986. Circ. 750.

Needs: Literary. "While we subscribe to no particular orthodoxy, our fiction editors are most hospitable to stories with a strong sense of voice, narrative direction and craftsmanship." Receives 50 mss/month. Accepts 10-20 mss/issue. Publishes ms within 6 months of acceptance. Recently published work by Bonnie Jo Campbell, Sheila E. Murphy and Richard Russo. Published new writers within the last year. Length: 3,000 words preferred; 7,500 words maximum. Publishes short shorts, "the shorter the better." Also publishes poetry. Sometimes critiques rejected mss.

How to Contact: Send complete mss with cover letter. Does not read from June through August. Reports in 3-4 months on mss. SASE. Simultaneous and reprint submissions OK. Sample copy for $5. Guidelines for SASE.

Payment/Terms: Pays in contributor's copies. Acquires one-time rights.

Advice: "First and foremost *Kiosk* is interested in sharp writing. There's no need to be dogmatic in terms of pushing a particular style or form, and we aren't. At the same time, we get tired of reading the same old story, the same old poem. Make it new, but also make it worth the reader's effort. Our last issue, 'RUST BELT,' focused upon a pretty specific theme. Because we are anticipating changes in our editorial staff, it would be a good idea to send a self-addressed stamped envelope for the most recent writer's guidelines."

LACTUCA, (I, II), % Mike Selender, 159 Jewett Ave., Jersey City NJ 07304-2003. (201)451-5411. E-mail: lactuca@aol.com. Editor: Mike Selender. Magazine: Folded 8½×14; 72 pages; 24 lb. bond; soft cover; saddle-stapled; illustrations. Plans to change format in 1988. Publishes "poetry, short fiction and b&w art, for a general literary audience." Published annually. Estab. 1986. Circ. 700.

Needs: Adventure, condensed/excerpted novel, confession, contemporary, erotica, literary, mainstream, prose poem and regional. No "self-indulgent writing or fiction about writing fiction." Receives 30 or more mss/month. Accepts 10-12 mss/year. Publishes ms within 12-18 months of acceptance. Published work by Douglas Mendini, Tom Gidwitz and Ruthann Robson; published new writers within the last year. Length: around 12-14 typewritten double-spaced pages. Publishes short shorts. Often critiques rejected mss and recommends other markets.

How to Contact: "Query first to see if we're reading before sending manuscripts. We are dormant and probably won't resume accepting work until late 1998 or later." Cover letter should include "just a few brief notes about yourself. Please no long 'literary' résumés or bios. The work will speak for itself." Reports in 6 weeks-3 months. SASE. No simultaneous or previously published work. Accepts electronic submissions via "MS DOS formatted disk. We can convert most word-processing formats." Sample copy for $4. Fiction guidelines for #10 SASE.

Payment/Terms: Pays 2-5 contributor's copies, depending on the length of the work published. Acquires first North American serial rights. Sends galleys to author. Copyrights revert to authors.

Advice: "We want fiction coming from a strong sense of place and/or experience. Work with an honest emotional depth. We steer clear of self-indulgent material. We particularly like work that tackles complex issues and the impact of such on people's lives. We are open to work that is dark and/or disturbing."

THE LAMPLIGHT, (II), Beggar's Press, 8110 N. 38 St., Omaha NE 68112. (402)455-2615. Editor: Richard R. Carey. Fiction Editor: Sandy Johnsen. Magazine: 8½×11; 60 pages; 20 lb. bond paper; 65 lb. stock cover; some illustrations; a few photographs. "Our purpose is to establish a new literature drawn from the past. We relish foreign settings in the 19th century when human passions transcended computers and fax machines. We are literary but appeal to the common intellect and the mass soul of humanity." Semiannually.

Needs: Historical (general), humor/satire, literary, mystery/suspense (literary), romance (gothic, historical). "Settings in the past. Psychological stories." Plans special fiction issue or anthology in the future. Receives 120-140 unsolicited mss/month. Accepts 2 mss/issue; 4 mss/year. Publishes ms 4-12 months after acceptance. Published work by Frances Hunter, Lucy Streek and Philip Sparacino. Length: 2,000 words preferred; 500 words minimum; 3,500 words maximum. Publishes short shorts. Length: 300 words. Also publishes literary criticism and poetry. Critiques or comments on rejected mss.

How to Contact: Send complete ms with cover letter. Include estimated word count, bio (a paragraph or two) and list of publications. Reports in 1 month on queries; 2½ months on mss. SASE. Simultaneous and reprint submission OK. Sample copy for $10.95, 9×12 SAE. Fiction guidelines for #10 SASE. Reviews novels and short story collections.

Payment/Terms: Pays 1 contributor's copy. Acquires first North American serial rights.

Advice: "We deal in classical masterpieces. Every piece must be timeless. It must live for five centuries or more. We judge on this basis. These are not easy to come by. But we want to stretch authors to their fullest capacity. They will have to dig deeper for us, and develop a style that is different from what is commonly read in today's market."

THE LAMP-POST, of the Southern California C.S. Lewis Society, (II, IV), 29562 Westmont Ct., San Juan Capistrano CA 92675. E-mail: lamppost@ix.netcom.com. Senior Editor: James Prothero. Magazine: 5½×8½; 34 pages; 7 lb. paper; 8 lb. cover; illustrations. "We are a literary review focused on C.S. Lewis and like writers." Quarterly. Estab. 1977. Circ. 200.

● C.S. Lewis was an English novelist and essayist known for his science fiction and fantasy featuring Christian themes. He is especially well-known for his children's fantasy, *The Chronicles of Narnia*. So far, the magazine has found little fiction suitable to its focus, although they remain open.

Needs: "Literary fantasy and science fiction for children to adults." Publishes ms 9 months after acceptance. Recently published work by Susan Lyttek. Length: 2,500 words average; 1,000 words minimum; 5,000 words maximum. Also publishes literary essays, literary criticism and poetry. Sometimes critiques or comments on rejected mss.

How to Contact: Query first or send complete ms with a cover letter. Include 50-word bio. Reports in 6-8 weeks. Send SASE for reply, return of ms or send a disposable copy of ms. No simultaneous submissions. Reprints and electronic (disk) submissions OK. Sample copy for $3. Fiction guidelines for #10 SASE. Reviews fiction or criticism having to do with Lewis or in his vein. Send books to: M.J. Logsdon, Editor, The Lamp-Post, 2294 N. Main St. #48, Salinas CA 93905. E-mail: mjl@ix.netcom.com.

Payment/Terms: Pays 3 contributor's copies; additional copies $3. Acquires first North American serial rights or one-time rights.

Advice: "We look for fiction with the supernatural, mythic feel of the fiction of C.S. Lewis and Charles Williams. Our slant is Christian but we want work of literary quality. No inspirational. Is it the sort of thing Lewis, Tolkien and Williams would like—subtle, crafted fiction? If so, send it. Don't be too obvious or facile. Our readers aren't stupid."

*LANDFALL/UNIVERSITY OF OTAGO PRESS, University of Otago Press, P.O. Box 56, Dunedin, New Zealand. Fax: (64)3 479-8385. E-mail: university.press@otago.ac.nz. Editor: Chris Price.

Needs: Publishes fiction, poetry, commentary and reviews of New Zealand books. Length: maximum 10,000 words but shorter work is preferred. "We concentrate on publishing work by New Zealand writers, but occasionally accept work from elsewhere."

Payment/Terms: Pays NZ $11 per page for fiction plus copy of the issue.

THE LAUREL REVIEW, (III), Northwest Missouri State University, Dept. of English, Maryville MO 64468. (816)562-1265. Co-editors: William Trowbridge, David Slater and Beth Richards. Associate Editors: Nancy Vieira Couto, Randall R. Freisinger, Steve Heller. Reviewer: Peter Makuck. Magazine: 6×9; 124-128 pages; good quality paper. "We publish poetry and fiction of high quality, from the traditional to the avant-garde. We are eclectic, open and flexible. Good writing is all we seek." Biannually. Estab. 1960. Circ. 900.

● A story published in *The Laurel Review* in 1996 was selected for inclusion in the annual *Pushcart Prize* anthology. Two others received special mention.

Needs: Literary and contemporary. Accepts 3-5 mss/issue, 6-10 mss/year. Receives approximately 120 unsolicited fiction mss each month. Approximately 1% of fiction is agented. Recently published work by Karla J. Kuban, William D. Schaefer, Richard Duggin and Becky Bradway. Length: 2,000-10,000 words. Sometimes publishes literary essays; also publishes poetry. Reads September to May.

How to Contact: Send complete ms with SASE. No simultaneous submissions. Reports in 1-4 months on mss. Publishes ms an average of 1-12 months after acceptance. Sample copy for $3.50.

Payment/Terms: Pays 2 contributor's copies and 1 year subscription. Acquires first rights. Copyright reverts to author upon request.

Advice: Send $3.50 for a back copy of the magazine.

LIBIDO, The Journal of Sex and Sensibility, (I, II, IV), Libido, Inc., P.O. Box 146721, Chicago IL 60614. (773)281-5839. E-mail: rune@mcs.com. Website: http://www.SensualSource.com/Libido (includes short fiction, b&w photography, poetry, news and reviews). Editors: Jack Hafferkamp and Marianna Beck. Magazine: 6½×9¼; 88 pages; 70 lb. coated; b&w illustrations and photographs. *"Libido*, to paraphrase Oscar Wilde, is the literary answer to a horizontal urge." Quarterly. Estab. 1988. Circ. 9,000.

● Specializing in "literary" erotica, this journal has attracted a number of top-name writers and was given a Venus Award from Good Vibrations, San Francisco.

Needs: Condensed/excerpted novel, confession, erotica, gay, lesbian. No "dirty words for their own sake, violence or sexual exploitation." Receives 25-50 unsolicited mss/month. Accepts about 5 mss/issue; about 20 mss/year. Publishes ms up to 1 year after acceptance. Recently published work by Larry Tritten, Richard Collins and Sophie du Chien. Publishes 5-10 new writers/year. Length: 1,000-3,000 words; 300 words minimum; 5,000 words maximum. Also publishes literary essays, literary criticism. Sometimes critiques rejected mss and recommends other markets.

How to Contact: Send complete ms with cover letter including Social Security number and brief bio for contributor's page. Reports in 6 months on mss. SASE. No simultaneous submissions. Reprint submissions OK. Sample copy for $8. Free fiction guidelines. Reviews novels and short story collections.

Payment/Terms: Pays $15-50 and 2 contributor's copies on publication for one-time or anthology rights.

Advice: "Humor is a strong plus. There must be a strong erotic element, and it should celebrate the joy of sex. Also, stories should be well written, insightful and arousing. Bonus points given for accuracy of characterization and style."

THE LICKING RIVER REVIEW, (II), University Center, Northern Kentucky University, Highland Heights KY 41076. (606)572-5416. Faculty Editor: Phil Paradis. Fiction Editor: Renee Riegler. Magazine: 7×11; 104 pages; photos. Annually. Estab. 1991. Circ. 1,500.

Needs: Experimental, literary, mainstream/contemporary. Receives 40 unsolicited mss/month. Accepts 7-9 mss/year. Does not read mss February through July. Publishes ms 6 months after acceptance. Recently published work by Dallas Wiebe, Alfred Schwaid, Laurie Jones Neighbor, Brian Howard, Pax Riddle and Dayna marie. Length: 5,000 words maximum. Publishes short shorts. Also publishes poetry.

How to Contact: Send complete ms with a cover letter. Include list of publications. Reports in 3-6 months on mss. SASE for return of manuscript or send disposable copy of ms. No simultaneous submissions. Sample copy for $5.

Payment/Terms: Pays 2 contributor's copies on publication.

Advice: Looks for "good writing and an interesting and well-told story. Read a sample copy first."

LIGHT MAGAZINE, (II), P.O. Box 7500, Chicago IL 60680. Editor: John Mella. Magazine: 8½×11; 32 pages; Finch opaque (60 lb.) paper; 65 lb. color cover; illustrations. "Light and satiric verse and prose, witty but not sentimental. Audience: intelligent, educated, usually 'professional.' " Biannually. Estab. 1992. Circ. 1,000.

Needs: Humor/satire, literary. Upcoming theme: Ogden Nash parody issue. Receives 10-40 unsolicited mss/month. Accepts 2-4 mss/issue. Publishes ms 6-24 months after acceptance. Published work by X.J. Kennedy, J.F. Nims and John Updike. Length: 1,200 words preferred; 600 words minimum; 2,000 words maximum. Publishes short shorts. Also publishes literary essays, literary criticism and poetry. Sometimes critiques or comments on rejected mss.

How to Contact: Query first. Include estimated word count and list of publications. Reports in 1 month on queries; 2-4 months on mss. Send SASE for reply, return of ms or send a disposable copy of ms. No simultaneous submissions. Electronic submissions (disk only) OK. Sample copy for $6 (plus $2 for 1st class). Fiction guidelines for #10 SASE. Reviews novels and short story collections. Send review copies to review editor.

Payment/Terms: Pays contributor's copies (2 for domestic; 1 for foreign). Acquires first North American serial rights. Sends galleys of longer pieces to author.

Advice: Looks for "high literary quality; wit, allusiveness, a distinct (and distinctive) style. Read guidelines first."

LIMESTONE: A LITERARY JOURNAL, (II), University of Kentucky, Dept. of English, 1215 Patterson Office Tower, Lexington KY 40506-0027. (606)257-7008. Magazine: 6×9; 50-75 pages; standard text paper and cover; illustrations; photos. "*Limestone* is a literary magazine edited by University of Kentucky graduate students. It showcases original imaginative and scholarly writing by University of Kentucky students and faculty, by residents of the Bluegrass region and other parts of Kentucky, and by the larger creative and scholarly community." Annually. Estab. 1981. Circ. 1,000.

● The editor would like to see more experimental fiction.

Needs: "Quality poetry and short fiction, literary, mainstream, thoughtful. No fantasy or science fiction. No previously published work." Receives 200 mss/year. Accepts 15 mss/issue. Publishes ms an average of 6 months after acceptance. Publishes 10-15 new writers every year. Length: 3,000-5,000 words preferred; 5,000 words maximum. Publishes short shorts.

How to Contact: Send complete ms with cover letter. Include publishing record and brief bio. Reports in 1 month on queries; 7 months or longer on mss. SASE. Simultaneous submissions OK. Sample copy for $4.

Payment/Terms: Pays 2 contributor's copies. Rights revert to author.

Advice: "Don't beleaguer the obvious—don't think your readers won't get the point. I'm concerned about the slow death of the small independent publishing houses. It makes new, quality fiction and poetry hard to come by outside the literary magazine circuit."

LINES IN THE SAND, (I, II), LeSand Publications, 890 Southgate Ave., Daly City CA 94015. (415)992-4770. E-mail: nsand415@aol.com. Editor: Nina Z. Sanders. Fiction Editors: Nina Z. Sanders and Barbara J. Less. Magazine: 5½×8½; 32 pages; 20 lb. bond; King James cost-coated cover. "Stories should be well-written, entertaining and suitable for all ages. Our readers range in age from 7 to 90. No particular slant or philosophy." Bimonthly. Estab. 1992. Circ. 100.

  • *Lines In The Sand* is known for quirky fiction with surprise endings. Humorous and slice-of-life fiction has a good chance here.

Needs: Adventure, experimental, fantasy, horror, humor/satire, literary, mainstream/contemporary, mystery/suspense (private eye/hard-boiled, amateur sleuth, cozy, romantic), science fiction (soft/sociological), senior citizen/retirement, westerns (traditional, frontier, young adult), young adult/teen (10-18 years). "No erotica, pornography." Receives 70-80 unsolicited mss/month. Accepts 8-10 mss/issue; 50-60 mss/year. Publishes ms 2-4 months after acceptance. Recently published work by Marcella Walker, Harold Huber, Lawrence Casler and Paul Agosto. Publishes 12 new writers/year. Length: 1,200 words preferred; 250 words minimum; 2,000 words maximum. Publishes short shorts. Length: 250 words. Also publishes poetry. Often critiques or comments on rejected mss. Sponsors contests. To enter contest submit 2 copies of story, 2,000 words maximum, double-spaced, typed and $5 reading fee for each story submitted.

How to Contact: Send complete ms with cover letter containing estimated word count and bio (3-4 sentences). Reports in 2-6 months on mss. Send SASE for reply, return of ms or send disposable copy of themes. Simultaneous submissions OK. Sample copy for $3.50. Fiction guidelines for #10 SASE.

Payment/Terms: Pays one contributor's copy. Acquires first North American serial rights.

Advice: "Use fresh, original approach; 'show, don't tell'; use dialogue to move story along; and be grammatically correct. Stories should have some type of conflict. Read a sample copy (or two). Follow guidelines carefully. Use plain language; avoid flowery, 'big' words unless appropriate in dialogue."

LITERAL LATTÉ, Stimulating Prose, Poetry & Art, (II), 61 E. Eighth St., Suite 240, New York NY 10003. (212)260-5532. E-mail: litlatte@aol.com. Website: http://www.literal-latte.com (includes guidelines, staff, samples from past issues, contest info, subscription info, online only specials). Accepts outstanding work by beginning and established writers. Editor: Jenine Gordon Bockman. Fiction Editor: Jeffrey Michael Gordon Bockman. Tabloid: 11×17; 24 pages; 35 lb. Jet paper; 50 lb. cover; illustrations and photos. "*LL* is a high-quality journal of prose, poetry and art distributed free in cafés and bookstores in New York, by subscription ($11/year) and by Ingram Periodicals." Bimonthly. Estab. 1994. Circ. 25,000.

  • *Literal Latté* recently received a *Pushcart Prize*.

Needs: Experimental, fantasy (science), humor/satire, literary, science fiction. Receives 4,000 mss/year. Accepts 30-60 mss/year. Publishes ms within 1 year after acceptance. Published work by Ray Bradbury, Stephen Dixon and Robert Olen Butler. Publishes 4 new writers/year. Length: 6,000 words maximum. Publishes short shorts. Also publishes literary essays, poetry. Sometimes critiques or comments on rejected mss.

How to Contact: Send complete ms with a cover letter. Include estimated word count, bio, list of publications. Reports in 2-3 months on mss. SASE for reply. Simultaneous submissions OK. Sample copy for $5. Fiction guidelines for #10 SASE.

Payment/Terms: Pays free subscription, 5 contributor's copies and a minimum of $25. Acquires first rights. Sponsors contests and awards for fiction writers; send #10 SASE marked "Fiction Contest" or "Poetry Contest."

Advice: "Reading our paper is the best way to determine our preferences. We judge work on quality alone and accept a broad range of extraordinary stories, personal essays, poems and graphics. Include a SASE large enough to house our comments (if any), and news on contests, readings or revised guidelines. Don't send a postcard. Include a phone number, in case we have questions like 'Is this still available?'"

MARKET CONDITIONS are constantly changing! If you're still using this book and it is 1999 or later, buy the newest edition of *Novel & Short Story Writer's Market* at your favorite bookstore or order from Writer's Digest Books.

LITERARY FRAGMENTS, (I, II, III), Cedar Bay Press, L.L.C., P.O. Box 751, Beaverton OR 97075-0751. E-mail questions and comments to Editor: willow-bay@juno.com. Website: www.teleport.com/~cedarbay/ (includes writer's guidelines, names of editors, short fiction, interviews with authors, chat line, news groups, bookstore). Short story collection, soft-cover quarterly and reprints, "more like a quarterly version of an anthology." *Reading fee: $5 per story*; includes free copy of *Literary Fragments* in which story appears if accepted.

Needs: "We publish short stories (5,000 words or less) completely on the basis of literary merit. Open to good quality writing that other publications may have passed up. Must be able to submit well-edited electronic text. Work should match discerning needs of a sophisticated reading audience. Open to all genres. We are interested in the beauty of language and originality. Consider reading *Literary Fragments* first to see what we publish then fill in the genre we are missing." Averages 4 titles/year; receives 8-15 submissions monthly. 50-75% from first-time authors. Accepts 6-8 mss/edition. "We feature contests from time-to-time. See website for details."

How to Contact: Send complete electronic ms (no paper copy) with cover letter (include bio and credits in electronic submission), reading fee (check or money order to Cedar Bay Press, Llc) social security number (USA authors only) and LSASE (no coupons) for notification. Electronic submission on 3.5″ disk in DOS/Windows text only (ASCII or Windows Write or up to version 6 of either WordPerfect or Microsoft Word). "Query not needed; let us see what you have to offer." No print copy. Nonreturnable electronic copy only. Mac Users: Word for Mac files can be e-mailed, however, mail a #10 SASE with reading fee and cover letter to confirm acceptance. All others, please mail diskette. On disk label in upper left corner: your name, Social Security number (USA authors only), address and file name of submission. Reports on queries in 2-4 weeks; on mss in 4-6 weeks. Comments on mss. Simultaneous submission OK.

Payment/Terms: Pays up to 80% of net profits for the volume in which the writer's work appears for the lifetime of the publication, payable annually. Terms: one-time world rights.

Advice: "You have a better chance if you read what we publish and present new ideas that fit into our format. For the first-time writer: a very brief synopsis that states the basic premise of the story gets read. LSASE for reply gets answered." Sample issue: $3.95 plus $1.05 s/h.

THE LITERARY REVIEW, An International Journal of Contemporary Writing, (II), Fairleigh Dickinson University, 285 Madison Ave., Madison NJ 07940. Phone/fax: (973)443-8564. E-mail: tlr@fdu.edu. Website: http://www.webdelsol.com/tlr/ (includes short fiction). Editor-in-Chief: Walter Cummins. Magazine: 6×9; 450 pages; professionally printed on textpaper; semigloss card cover; perfect-bound. "Literary magazine specializing in fiction, poetry, and essays with an international focus." Quarterly. Estab. 1957. Circ. 2,500.

● This magazine has received grants from a wide variety of international sources including the Spanish Consulate General in New York, the Program for Cultural Cooperation between Spain's Ministry of Culture and U.S. Universities, Pro Helvetia, the Swiss Center Foundation, The Luso-American Foundation, Japan-U.S. Friendship Commission. Work published in *The Literary Review* has been included in *Editor's Choice*, *Best American Short Stories* and *Pushcart Prize* anthologies. The editor would like to see more fiction with an international theme.

Needs: Works of high literary quality only. Upcoming theme: "North African Writing" (Winter 1998). Receives 50-60 unsolicited fiction mss/month. Approximately 1-2% of fiction is agented. Recently published work by Maurine O'Neill, Stephen Dixon and Todd Pierce. Published new writers within the last year. Acquires 10-12 mss/year. Also publishes literary essays, literary criticism, poetry. Occasionally critiques rejected mss.

How to Contact: Send 1 complete ms with SASE. "Cover letter should include publication credits." Reports in 3 months on mss. Publishes ms an average of 1½-2 years after acceptance. Sample copy for $5; guidelines for SASE. Reviews novels and short story collections.

Payment/Terms: Pays 2 contributor's copies; 25% discount for extras. Acquires first rights.

Advice: "We want original dramatic situations with complex moral and intellectual resonance and vivid prose. We don't want versions of familiar plots and relationships. Too much of what we are seeing today is openly derivative in subject, plot and prose style. We pride ourselves on spotting new writers with fresh insight and approach."

‡THE LITTLE MAGAZINE, (III), State University of New York at Albany, English Department, Albany NY 12222. E-mail: litmag@csc.albany.edu. Website: http://www.albany.edu/~litmag. Editor: Nancy Dunlop. Magazine: 5½×8½; 200 pages; 70 lb. Nikusa paper; 10 pt. high gloss cover; illustrations. "Fiction and poetry for a literary audience." Annually. Estab. 1965.

● *The Little Magazine* has published entirely on the web since 1995.

Needs: Multi-media, hypertext, experimental, feminist, humor/satire. No romance. Receives "roughly" 600 mss/issue over a 3-month reading period. Accepts 20 mss/issue. Reads only from September 1 to December 15. Publishes ms 6 months after acceptance. Recently published work by Eugene Garber, Lydia Davis, Ralph Lombreglia. Length: 3,000 words. Publishes short shorts.

How to Contact: Send complete ms with SASE (or IRC) *on disk*, but only send between September 1 and December 15. Reports in 2 months on queries; in 4 months on mss. Simultaneous and reprint submissions OK. Sample copy for $15 or by e-mail.

Payment/Terms: Pays 2 contributor's copies (when published on CD-ROM).

Terms: Acquires first North American serial rights.

Advice: "We like a wide variety of work from traditional to experimental."

THE LONG STORY, (II), 18 Eaton St., Lawrence MA 01843. (508)686-7638. E-mail: rpbtls@aol.com. Editor: R.P. Burnham. Magazine: 5½×8½; 150-200 pages; 60 lb. paper; 65 lb. cover stock; illustrations (b&w graphics). For serious, educated, literary people. No science fiction, adventure, romance, etc. "We publish high literary quality of any kind, but especially look for stories that have difficulty getting published elsewhere—committed fiction, working class settings, left-wing themes, etc." Annually. Estab. 1983. Circ. 1,200.
Needs: Contemporary, ethnic, feminist and literary. Receives 30-40 unsolicited mss/month. Accepts 6-7 mss/issue. 50% of writers published are new. Length: 8,000 words minimum; 20,000 words maximum.
How to Contact: Send complete ms with a brief cover letter. Reports in 2 months. Publishes ms an average of 3 months to 1 year after acceptance. SASE. May accept simultaneous submissions ("but not wild about it"). Sample copy for $6.
Payment/Terms: Pays 2 contributor's copies; $5 charge for extras. Acquires first rights.
Advice: "Read us first and make sure submitted material is the kind we're interested in. Send clear, legible manuscripts. We're not interested in commercial success; rather we want to provide a place for long stories, the most difficult literary form to publish in our country."

LOONFEATHER, (II), P.O. Box 1212, Bemidji MN 56619. (218)751-4869. Editor: Betty Rossi. Magazine: 6×9; 48 pages; 60 lb. Hammermill Cream woven paper; 65 lb. vellum cover stock; illustrations; occasional photos. A literary journal of short prose, poetry and graphics. Mostly a market for Northern Minnesota, Minnesota and Midwest writers. Semiannually. Estab. 1979. Circ. 300.
Needs: Literary, contemporary, prose and regional. Accepts 2-3 mss/issue, 4-6 mss/year. Reads mss from September 1 through May 31. Published new writers within the last year. Length: 600-1,500 words (prefers 1,500). Not accepting novel length fiction submissions in the 1998 book year.
How to Contact: Send complete ms with SASE, and short autobiographical sketch. Reports within 4 months. Sample copy for $2 back issue; $5 current issue.
Payment/Terms: Free author's copies. Acquires one-time rights.
Advice: "Send carefully crafted and literary fiction. The writer should familiarize himself/herself with the type of fiction published in literary magazines as opposed to family magazines, religious magazines, etc."

LOST AND FOUND TIMES, (II, IV), Luna Bisonte Prods, 137 Leland Ave., Columbus OH 43214. (614)846-4126. Editor: John M. Bennett. Magazine: 5½×8½; 56 pages; good quality paper; good cover stock; illustrations; photos. Theme: experimental, avant-garde and folk literature, art. Published irregularly (twice yearly). Estab. 1975. Circ. 375.
● The editor would like to see more short, experimental pieces.
Needs: Contemporary, experimental, literary, prose poem. Prefers short pieces. Also publishes poetry. Accepts approximately 2 mss/issue. Published work by Spryszak, Steve McComas, Willie Smith, Rupert Wondolowski, Al Ackerman. Published new writers within the last year.
How to Contact: Query with clips of published work. SASE. No simultaneous submissions. Reports in 1 week on queries, 2 weeks on mss. Sample copy for $6.
Payment/Terms: Pays 1 contributor's copy. Rights revert to authors.

LOUISIANA LITERATURE, A Review of Literature and Humanities, (I, II, IV), Southeastern Louisiana University, SLU 792, Hammond LA 70402. (504)549-5022. E-mail: dhanson@selu.edu. Editor: David Hanson. Magazine: 6¾×9¾; 150 pages; 70 lb. paper; card cover; illustrations. "Essays should be about Louisiana material; preference is given to fiction and poetry with Louisiana and Southern themes, but creative work can be set anywhere." Semiannually. Estab. 1984. Circ. 400 paid; 500-700 printed.
● The editor would like to see more stories with firm closure.
Needs: Literary, mainstream, regional. "No sloppy, ungrammatical manuscripts." Upcoming themes: Louisiana detective fiction, Tennessee Williams, music (jazz, Cajun, blues, etc.), and dog stories (planned for Fall 1997 through Spring 1999). Receives 100 unsolicited fiction mss/month. Accepts mss related to special topics issues. May not read mss June through July. Publishes ms 6-12 months maximum after acceptance. Recently published work by Robert Olen Butler, Patty Friedmann, Albert Davis and Robin Beeman. Published new writers within the last year. Length: 3,500 words preferred; 1,000 words minimum; 6,000 words maximum. Also publishes literary essays (Louisiana themes), literary criticism, poetry. Sometimes comments on rejected mss.
How to Contact: Send complete ms. Reports in 1-3 months on mss. SASE. Sample copy for $5. Reviews novels and short story collections (mainly those by Louisiana authors).
Payment/Terms: Pays usually in contributor's copies. Acquires one-time rights.
Advice: "Cut out everything that is not a functioning part of the story. Make sure your manuscript is professionally presented. Use relevant specific detail in every scene."

THE LOUISVILLE REVIEW, (II), Department of English, University of Louisville, Louisville KY 40292. (502)852-6801. Editor: Sena Jeter Naslund. Managing Editor: Karen J. Mann. Magazine: 6×8¾; 140 pages; Warren's Old Style paper; cover photographs. Semiannually. Estab. 1976. Circ. 750.
Needs: Contemporary, experimental, literary, prose poem. Receives 30-40 unsolicited mss/month. Acquires 6-10 mss/issue; 12-20 mss/year. Publishes ms 2-3 months after acceptance. Published work by Maura Stanton,

Patricia Goedicke and Michael Cadnum. Length: 50 pages maximum. Publishes short shorts. Sponsors contest. SASE for information.

How to Contact: "Manuscripts should be submitted in the Fall." Send complete ms with cover letter. Reports on queries in 2-3 weeks; 2-3 months on mss. SASE. Sample copy for $6. Fiction guidelines for #10 SASE.

Payment/Terms: Pays in contributor's copies. Acquires first North American serial rights.

Advice: Looks for "integrity and vividness in the language."

‡**THE LOWELL PEARL, (II)**, University of Massachusetts Lowell, English Dept., 1 University Ave., Lowell MA 01854. (508)934-4182. Contact: Fiction Editor. Editors revolve each year. Magazine: 5½×8½; 70 pages; heavy cover; illustrations and photographs. "We offer a forum for new and published writers. In addition to distributing the journal to local businesses and libraries, we mail copies to universities across the country. Our philosophy: good writing is good no matter who the author is." Semiannually. Estab. 1989. Circ. 1,500.

Needs: Adventure, condensed/excerpted novel, erotica, ethnic/multicultural, experimental, feminist, gay, historical (general), horror, humor/satire, lesbian, literary, mainstream/contemporary, regional, science fiction (soft/sociological), senior citizen/retirement, sports and translations. Nothing "racist, sexist, discriminatory or violent for no particular reason." Publishes annual special fiction issues or anthologies. Receives 30 unsolicited mss/month. Accepts 2-4 mss/issue; 4-8 mss/year. Publishes ms 1-2 months after acceptance. Agented fiction 2%. Published work by Joseph Zaitchik, Richard Zidonas, Lewis Hamond Stone and Mary Mackic Wiles. Length: 1,000 words average; 5,000 words maximum. Publishes short shorts. Also publishes literary essays, literary criticism and poetry. Sometimes critiques or comments on rejected ms.

How to Contact: Send complete ms with a cover letter. Submission deadlines are September 30 and February 28 each year. Include 2 copies of ms; one with *no* identifying marks on it. Include a separate cover page with name, address, phone and bio (under 50 words). Reports in 2-3 weeks on queries; 1-3 months on mss. SASE for return of ms. Simultaneous and reprint submissions OK. Sample copy free.

Payment/Terms: Pays 2 contributor's copies; additional copies $3. Acquires one-time rights.

Advice: "Has the writer considered every word he/she has written? Is there a reason why an action, thought or description has been included? Revise. Revise. Revise. When I read fiction, I want the story to seem so real and flow so smoothly that I forget it's fiction. I don't want anything like an extraneous detail distracting me from the story. If you haven't thought about every word, every piece of punctuation, don't send it."

LULLWATER REVIEW, (II), Emory University, P.O. Box 22036, Atlanta GA 30322. Editor-in-Chief: Eric Brignac. Associate Editor: Becky Brooks. Fiction Editors: Becky Brooks and Eric Brignac. Magazine: 6×9; 100 pages; 60 lb. paper; photos. "We look for fiction that reflects the issues and lifestyles of today, in whatever form it might arrive, whether as a story, short story or a novel excerpt. We hope to reach the average person, someone who might not ordinarily read a publication like ours, but might be attracted by our philosophy." Semiannually. Circ. 2,000. Member of the Council of Literary Magazines and Presses.

Needs: Condensed/excerpted novel, ethnic/multicultural, experimental, feminist, gay, humor/satire, lesbian, literary, mainstream/contemporary, regional. "No romance, please." Receives 12-14 unsolicited mss/month. Accepts 3-4 mss/issue; 6-7 mss/year. "Response time is slower in the summer, but we are always reading." Publishes ms within 2 months after acceptance. Published work by Lynne Burris Butler, Meghan Keith-Hynes and Patricia Flinn. Length: 10 pages average; 30 pages maximum. Publishes short shorts. Length: 300-500 words. Also publishes poetry. Sometimes critiques or comments on rejected mss. Sponsors contest; send SASE for information in early Fall.

How to Contact: Send complete ms with cover letter. Include bio and list of publications. Reports in 1-2 weeks on queries; 2-3 months on mss. Send SASE for reply, return of ms or send a disposable copy of ms. Simultaneous submissions OK. Sample copy for $5. Fiction guidelines for SASE.

Payment/Terms: Pays 3 contributor's copies; additional copies for $5. Acquires first North American serial rights.

Advice: "We at the *Lullwater Review* look for clear cogent writing, strong character development and an engaging approach to the story in our fiction submissions. Stories with particularly strong voices and well-developed central themes are especially encouraged. Be sure that your manuscript is ready before mailing it off to us. Revise, revise, revise!"

‡**LUMMOX JOURNAL, (IV)**, Lummox Press/Productions, P.O. Box 5301, San Pedro CA 90733-5301. (310)521-9642. E-mail: lumoxraindog@earthlink.net. Editor: Raindog. Magazine: digest size; 20 pages; photocopy paper; illustrations and photos. "*The Lummox Journal* focuses on the process of creativity using interviews, reviews, articles and essays as exploratory tools. Lummox Press plans a yearly anthology of fiction and poetry since the journal doesn't (as a rule) print unsolicited poetry and short fiction. There are always exceptions. . . ." Estab. 1996. Circ. 200.

Needs: Experimental, historical, literary, regional, serialized novel. Publishes special fiction anthology. Receives 1-2 unsolicited mss/month. Accepts 2-3 mss/year. Recently published work by Jay Alamares and Scott Wannberg. Length: 750 words average; 900 words maximum. Publishes short shorts. Also publishes literary essays, literary criticism and poetry.

How to Contact: Query first. Include brief bio and estimated word count. Reports in 1-2 weeks on queries. Send SASE for reply, return of ms or send disposable copy of ms. Simultaneous and electronic (disk only)

submissions OK. Sample copy for $2 and a 6×9 SAE with 2 first-class stamps. Fiction guidelines for #10 SASE. Reviews novels and short story collections. Send books to editor.
Payment/Terms: Pays 1 contributor's copy for one-time rights; additional copies $2. Not copyrighted.
Advice: Looks for "well-written, reality based emotion (not buzzword rants), strength and genuine believability. Make sure it's something you want to see in print."

LUNA NEGRA, (II), S.P.P.C., Kent State University, Box 26, Student Activities, Kent OH 44242. (330)672-2676. Contact: Fiction Editor. Magazine: 6×9; 50 pages; b&w illustrations and photographs. "The *Luna Negra* is a poetry, short story, photography and art biannual." Biannually. Estab. 1956. Circ. up to 2,000.
Needs: Receives 3-4 unsolicited mss/month. Does not read mss in summer months. Publishes short shorts. Sometimes comments on rejected mss.
How to Contact: Send complete ms with cover letter. SASE. Simultaneous, photocopied and reprint submissions OK. Accepts computer printout submissions. Free sample copy. Fiction guidelines for #10 SAE.
Payment/Terms: Pays in contributor's copies. Acquires one-time rights. Rights revert to author after 60 days.

LYNX EYE, (I, II), ScribbleFest Literary Group, 1880 Hill Dr., Los Angeles CA 90041. Editors: Pam McCully and Kathryn Morrison. Magazine: 5½×8½; 120 pages; 60 lb. book paper; varied cover stock. "*Lynx Eye* is dedicated to showcasing visionary writers and artists, particularly new voices." Quarterly. Estab. 1994. Circ. 500.
Needs: Adventure, condensed/excerpted novel, erotica, ethnic/multicultural, experimental, fantasy (science), feminist, gay, historical, horror, humor/satire, lesbian, literary, mainstream/contemporary, mystery/suspense, romance, science fiction, serialized novel, translations, westerns. Receives 500 unsolicited mss/month. Accepts 30 mss/issue; 120 mss/year. Publishes ms approximately 3 months after acceptance (contract guarantees publication within 12 months or rights revert and payment is kept by author). Recently published work by Anjali Banerjee, William J. Cobb, Kel Munger and Gustav Richar. Publishes 10 new writers/year. Length: 2,500 words average; 500 words minimum; 5,000 words maximum. Also publishes artwork, literary essays, poetry. Often critiques or comments on rejected mss.
How to Contact: Send complete ms with a cover letter. Include name and address on page one; name on *all* other pages. Reports in 2-3 months. Send SASE for reply, return of ms or send a disposable copy of ms. Simultaneous submissions OK. Sample copy for $7.95. Fiction guidelines for #10 SASE.
Payment/Terms: Pays $10 on acceptance and 3 contributor's copies for first North American serial rights; additional copies $3.95.
Advice: "We consider any well-written manuscript. Characters who speak naturally and who act or are acted upon are greatly appreciated. Your high school English teacher was correct. Basics matter. Imaginative, interesting ideas are sabotaged by lack of good grammar, spelling and punctuation skills. Most submissions are contemporary/mainstream. We could use some variety. Please do not confuse confessional autobiographies with fiction."

THE MACGUFFIN, (II), Schoolcraft College, Department of English, 18600 Haggerty Rd., Livonia MI 48152. (313)462-4400, ext. 5292 or 5327. Fax: (313)462-4558. E-mail: alindenb@schoolcraft.cc.mi.us. Website: http://www.schoolcraft.cc.mi.us (includes samples, guidelines, editorial contacts and subscription information). Editor: Arthur J. Lindenberg. Fiction Editor: Gary Erwin. Magazine: 6×9; 144 pages; 60 lb. paper; 110 lb. cover; b&w illustrations and photos. "*The MacGuffin* is a literary magazine which publishes a range of material including poetry, nonfiction and fiction. Material ranges from traditional to experimental. We hope our periodical attracts a variety of people with many different interests." Triannual. Quality fiction a special need. Estab. 1984. Circ. 600.
Needs: Adventure, contemporary, ethnic, experimental, fantasy, historical (general), humor/satire, literary, mainstream, prose poem, psychic/supernatural/occult, science fiction, translations. No religious, inspirational, confession, romance, horror, pornography. Upcoming theme: "Short Shorts" (deadline February 1998). Receives 25-40 unsolicited mss/month. Accepts 5-10 mss/issue; 10-30 mss/year. Does not read mss between July 1 and August 15. Publishes ms 6 months to 2 years after acceptance. Agented fiction: 10-15%. Recently published work by Carol J. Pierman, Jay Atkinson, Gary Eberle and Marilyn Trail. Published 30 new writers within the last year. Length: 2,000-2,500 words average; 100 words minimum; 5,000 words maximum. Publishes short shorts. Also publishes literary essays. Occasionally critiques rejected mss and recommends other markets.
How to Contact: Send complete ms with cover letter, which should include: "1. *brief* biographical information; 2. note that this *is not* a simultaneous submission." Reports in 2-3 months. SASE. Reprint and electronic (disk) submissions OK. Sample copy for $4; current issue for $4.50. Fiction guidelines free.
Payment/Terms: Pays 2 contributor's copies. Acquires one-time rights.
Advice: "Be persistent. If a story is rejected, try to send it somewhere else. When we reject a story, we may accept the next one you send us. When we make suggestions for a rewrite, we may accept the revision. There seems to be a great number of good authors of fiction, but there are far too few places for publication. However, I think this is changing. Make your characters come to life. Even the most ordinary people become fascinating if they live for your readers."

THE MADISON REVIEW, (II), Department of English, Helen C. White Hall, 600 N. Park St., University of Wisconsin, Madison WI 53706. (608)263-0566. Rotating Editors. Fiction Editor: Dan Fitzsimons. Poetry Editors:

Erin Hanusa and Trevor Schaid. Magazine: 6×9; 180 pages. "Magazine of fiction and poetry with special emphasis on literary stories and some emphasis on Midwestern writers." Semiannually. Estab. 1978. Circ. 1,000.
Needs: Experimental and literary stories, prose poems, novel excerpts and stories in translation. Receives 10-50 unsolicited fiction mss/month. Acquires approximately 6 mss/issue. Does not read mss May through September. Recently published work by Leslie Pietrzyk, Stephen Shugart and Ira Gold. Published new writers within the last year. Length: 4,000 words average. Also publishes poetry.
How to Contact: Send complete ms with cover letter and SASE. Include estimated word count, 1-page bio and list of publications. "The letters should give one or two sentences of relevant information about the writer—just enough to provide a context for the work." Reports in 6 months on mss. Publishes ms an average of 4 months after acceptance. Sample copy for $2.50.
Payment/Terms: Pays 3 contributor's copies; $2.50 charge for extras.
Terms: Acquires first North American serial rights.

♣MALAHAT REVIEW, University of Victoria, P.O. Box 1700, Victoria, British Columbia V8W 2Y2 Canada. (250)721-8524. Editor: Derk Wynand. Associate Editor: Marlene Cookshaw. Quarterly. Circ. 1,800.
Needs: "General fiction and poetry, book reviews." Reports in 3 months. Publishes 3-4 stories/issue. Length: 10,000 words maximum.
How to Contact: "Enclose proper postage on the SASE." Sample copy: $8 available through the mail; guidelines available upon request. No simultaneous submissions.
Payment/Terms: Pays $25/printed page and contributor's copies.
Advice: Write for information on *Malahat*'s novella and poetry competitions.

MANGROVE, Fiction, Interviews and Poetry from Around the World, (I, II), University of Miami, English Dept., Box 248145, Miami FL 33124-4632. (305)284-2182. Fiction submissions: Fiction Editor. Poetry submissions: Allison Eir Jenks, editor-in-chief. Editors change each year. Magazine: 120 pages. *Mangrove* is "a literary magazine publishing short fiction, poetry, memoirs and interviews." Semiannually. Estab. 1994. Circ. 500.
Needs: Literary, ethnic/multicultural, mainstream/contemporary, regional, translations. Receives 60-100 unsolicited mss/month. Accepts 6-8 mss/issue; 12-15 mss/year. Publishes ms 4-6 months after acceptance. Recently published work by Jamaica Kincaid, Tim O'Brien, Dale Peck and Donald Justice. Length: 5,000 words maximum. Publishes short shorts. Also publishes poetry. Sometimes critiques or comments on rejected ms.
How to Contact: Send complete ms with a cover letter. Include estimated word count, one-paragraph bio and list of publications with submission. SASE for reply. Simultaneous submissions OK. Sample copy for $5, SAE. Fiction guidelines for SASE.
Payment/Terms: Pays 1 contributor's copy. Acquires one-time rights.
Advice: "We look for stories with a distinct voice that make us look at the world in a different way. Send only one story at a time and send us your best work."

manna, The Literary-Professional Quarterly of manna forty, inc., (I, IV), manna forty, inc., Route 1, Box 548, Sharon OK 73857-9761. (405)254-2660 (evenings). Fax: (405)256-2416. Editor: Richard D. Kahoe. Newsletter: 8½×11; 8 pages; 72 lb. recycled paper and cover; illustrations. "*manna* is interested only in nature/religion/psychology, and especially in interfaces of two or three of these subjects." Quarterly. Estab. 1987. Circ. 300-350.
Needs: Ethnic/multicultural, feminist, religious/inspirational, senior citizen/retirement. "We have room for only short-short fiction: parables, personal experience, etc." List of upcoming themes available for SASE. Receives 1 unsolicited mss/month. Accepts 1 mss/issue; 4-8 mss/year. Publishes ms 1-11 months after acceptance. Recently published work by Richard D. Kahoe and Charles Stephens. Publishes 2-5 new writers/year. Length: 500 words average; 150 words minimum; 750 words maximum. Also publishes literary essays, poetry. Always critiques or comments on rejected ms.
How to Contact: Send complete ms with a cover letter "telling who you are," estimated word count and 100-word bio. Reports in 1 month on mss. SASE for return of ms or send a disposable copy of the ms. Simultaneous and reprint submissions OK. Sample copy for SASE.
Payment/Terms: Pays 2 contributor's copies; additional copies for 25¢ plus postage. Acquires one-time rights.
Advice: Looking for "human interest, touching on two or more of our subject areas (nature, religion, psychology) and presuming good literary quality, grammar, word selection, etc. Don't send anything that is not relevant to at least one of our basic subjects. Submit to the periodicals that reflect your style, level of experience/publication record, and content—read guidelines and samples before submitting."

MANOA, A Pacific Journal of International Writing, (II), English Dept., University of Hawaii, Honolulu HI 96822. (808)956-3070. Fax: (808)956-3083. E-mail: mjournal-1@hawaii.edu. Website: http://www2.hawaii.edu/mjournal (includes writer's guidelines, names of editors, short fiction and poetry). Editor: Frank Stewart. Fiction Editor: Ian MacMillan. Magazine: 7×10; 240 pages. "An American literary magazine, emphasis on top US fiction and poetry, but each issue has a major guest-edited translated feature of recent writings from an Asian/Pacific country." Semiannually. Estab. 1989.

• *Manoa* has received numerous awards, and work published in the magazine has been selected for prize anthologies.

Needs: Contemporary, excerpted novel, literary, mainstream and translation (from US and nations in or bordering on the Pacific). "Part of our purpose is to present top U.S. fiction from throughout the US, not only to US readers, but to readers in Asian and Pacific countries. Thus we are not limited to stories related to or set in the Pacific—in fact, we do not want exotic or adventure stories set in the Pacific, but good US literary fiction of any locale." Accepts 8-10 mss/issue; 16-20/year. Publishes ms 6 months-2 years after acceptance. Agented fiction 10%. Recently published work by Robert Olen Butler, Monica Wood and Barry Lopez. Publishes 1-2 new writers/ year. Publishes short fiction. Also publishes essays, book reviews, poetry.

How to Contact: Send complete ms with cover letter or through agent. Reports in 4-6 months. SASE. Simultaneous and electronic submissions OK; query before sending e-mail. Sample copy for $10. Reviews novels and short story collections. Send books or reviews to Reviews Editor.

Payment/Terms: Pays "highly competitive rates so far," plus contributor's copies for first North American serial rights and one-time reprint rights. Sends galleys to author.

Advice: "*Manoa*'s readership is (and is intended to be) mostly national, not local. It also wants to represent top US writing to a new international market, in Asia and the Pacific. Altogether we hope our view is a fresh one; that is, not facing east toward Europe but west toward 'the other half of the world.' Your own writing style and perspective or experience are as individual as fingerprints. Don't con yourself into imitation."

MANY MOUNTAINS MOVING, (II), a literary journal of diverse contemporary voices, 420 22nd St., Boulder CO 80302-7909. (303)545-9942. Fax: (303)444-6510. E-mail: mmmine@concentric.net. Editors: Naomi Horii and Marilyn Krysl. Fiction Editor: Beth Nugent. Magazine: 6×8¾; 200 pages; recycled paper; color/heavy cover; illustrations and photos. "We publish fiction, poetry, general-interest essays and art. We try to seek contributors from all cultures to promote appreciation of diverse cultures." Triannually. Estab. 1994. Circ. 2,000.

• The editor would like to see more experimental, avant garde fiction.

Needs: Ethnic/multicultural, experimental, feminist, gay, historical, humor/satire, lesbian, literary, mainstream/ contemporary, translations. No genre fiction. Plans special fiction issue or anthology. Receives 300 unsolicited mss/month. Accepts 4-6 mss/issue; 12-18 mss/year. Publishes ms 2-8 months after acceptance. Agented fiction 5%. Recently published work by Michael Dorsey, Daniela Kuper, Julie Shigekuni and Michael Ramos. "We try to publish at least one new writer per issue; more when possible." Length: 3,000-5,000 words average. Publishes short shorts. Also publishes literary essays, poetry. Sometimes critiques or comments on rejected mss.

How to Contact: Send complete ms with a cover letter. Include estimated word count, list of publications. Reports in 2 weeks on queries; 1-3 months on mss. Send SASE for reply, return of ms or send a disposable copy of ms. Simultaneous submissions OK. Sample copy for $6.50 and enough IRCs for 1 pound of airmail/printed matter. Fiction guidelines for #10 SASE.

Payment/Terms: Pays 3 contributor's copies; additional copies for $3. Acquires first North American serial rights. Sends galleys to author "if requested." Sponsors a contest, $200 prize. Send SASE for guidelines. Deadline: December 31.

Advice: "We look for top-quality fiction with fresh voices and verve. Read at least one issue of our journal to get a feel for what kind of fiction we generally publish."

MARYLAND REVIEW, (I, II), Department of English and Modern Languages, University of Maryland Eastern Shore, Princess Anne MD 21853-1299. (410)651-6552. E-mail: mandersn@umes-bird.umd.edu. Editor: Mignon H. Anderson. Literary journal: 6×9; 100-150 pages; quality paper stock; heavy cover; illustrations. "We have a special interest in African American and other literature of African orgin, but we welcome all sorts of submissions. Our audience is literary, educated, well-read." Annually. Estab. 1986. Circ. 500.

Needs: Contemporary, humor/satire, literary, mainstream, Black literature. No genre stories; no religious, political or juvenile material. Accepts approximately 12-15 mss/issue. Publishes ms "within 1 year" after acceptance. Recently published work by Errol Miller, Louis Phillips and Nancy Barron. Publishes 4-10 new writers/year. Publishes short shorts. "Length is open, but we do like to include mostly pieces 1,500 words and under." Also publishes poetry.

How to Contact: Send complete ms with cover letter. Include a brief autobiography of approximately 75 words. Reports "as soon as possible." SASE, *but does not return mss*. No simultaneous submissions. "No fax copies, please. No submissions by e-mail." Sample copy for $10.

Payment/Terms: Pays in 2 contributor's copies. Acquires first serial rights only.

Advice: "Think primarily about your *characters* in fiction, about their beliefs and how they may change. Create

---

CHECK THE CATEGORY INDEXES, located at the back of the book, for publishers interested in specific fiction subjects.

characters and situations that are utterly new. We will give your material a careful and considerate reading. Any fiction that is flawed by grammatical errors, misspellings, etc. will not have a chance. We're seeing a lot of fine fiction these days, and we approach each story with fresh and eager eyes. Ezra Pound's battle-cry about poetry refers to fiction as well: 'Make it New!' "

THE MASSACHUSETTS REVIEW, (II), Memorial Hall, South College, University of Massachusetts, Amherst MA 01003. (413)545-2689. Editors: Mary Heath, Jules Chametzky, Paul Jenkins. Magazine: 6×9; 172 pages; 52 lb. paper; 65 lb. vellum cover; illustrations and photos. Quarterly. Estab. 1959. Circ. 1,200.
Needs: Short stories. Does not read fiction mss June 1-October 1. Published new writers within the last year. Recently published work by Stephen Dobyns, Chris Haven, Kim Bridgeford and Martha Conway. Approximately 5% of fiction is agented. Also accepts poetry. Critiques rejected mss when time permits.
How to Contact: Send complete ms. No ms returned without SASE. Simultaneous submissions OK, if noted. Reports in 2 months. Publishes ms an average of 9-12 months after acceptance. Sample copy for $7. Guidelines available for SASE.
Payment/Terms: Pays $50 maximum on publication for first North American serial rights.
Advice: "Shorter rather than longer stories preferred (up to 28-30 pages)."

MATRIARCH'S WAY; JOURNAL OF FEMALE SUPREMACY, (I, II), Artemis Creations, 3395 Nostrand Ave., 2J, Brooklyn NY 11229-4053. Phone/fax: (718)648-8215. E-mail: nohel@aol.com. Editor: Shirley Oliveira. Magazine: 5½×8½; illustrations and photos. *Matriarch's Way* is a "matriarchal feminist" publication. Quarterly. Estab. 1996.
Needs: Condensed/excerpted novel, erotica (quality), ethnic/multicultural, experimental, fantasy (science, sword and sorcery), feminist (radical), horror, humor/satire, literary, psychic/supernatural/occult, religious/inspirational, romance (futuristic/time travel, gothic, historical), science fiction (soft/sociological), serialized novel. Receives 4 unsolicited mss/month. Often critiques or comments on rejected mss. 50% of work published is by new writers.
How to Contact: Query first, query with clips of published work or query with synopsis plus 1-3 chapters of novel. Include estimated word count, bio and list of publications with submission. Reports in 1 week on queries; 6 weeks on mss. SASE for reply or send a disposable copy of ms. Simultaneous, reprint and electronic submissions (3.5 ASCII, DOS) OK. Sample copy for $4. Reviews novels and short story collections and excerpts "We need book reviewers desperately, original or reprints. We supply books."
Payment/Terms: Contributors, $4.50/issue or free tearsheet with request. Acquires one-time rights. Sends galleys to author.
Advice: Looks for "a knowledge of subject, originality and good writing style. Send work on floppy, ASCII or any Microsoft format."

THE MAVERICK PRESS, (II), Box 4915, Rt. 2, Eagle Pass TX 78852. (210)773-9605. Fax: (210)773-8877. E-mail: maupress@adim.hilconet.com. Website: http://www.hilconet.com/~mavpress. Editor: Carol Cullar. Magazine: 7×9; 120 pages; perfect bound; block print cover; illustrations. Semiannually. Estab. 1992. Circ. 200.
Needs: Experimental, literary, mainstream/contemporary, sudden fiction (1-5 pages). "No children's/juvenile, gothic, horror, religious diatribe, young adult/teen." November issue is always thematic; write with SASE for guidelines. Receives 80 mss/month. Accepts 6-8 mss/issue; 12-16 mss/year. Reads mss every 2 months. Publishes ms 6 months-1 year after acceptance. Recently published work by Robert Perchan, Rebecca Davis, Arthur W. Knight, Don Stockard, C.B. Thatcher and John Grey. Length: 1,500 words maximum. Publishes short shorts. Also publishes poetry. Sometimes critiques or comments on rejected mss.
How to Contact: Send complete ms with a cover letter. Include estimated word count, half-page bio and list of publications with submission. Reports immediately on queries; 2 months on mss. Send SASE for reply, return of ms or send a disposable copy of ms. Simultaneous and electronic submissions (IBM formatted disks) OK. Sample copy for $8.50. Fiction guidelines for #10 SASE.
Payment/Terms: Pays 1 contributor's copy. Acquires one-time rights. Occasionally sends galleys to author.
Advice: "We publish sudden or short fiction with little expository writing; *in media res*, bare-bones with prose poem feel to it. Figurative language always attracts this editor. Avoid cliches, pedestrian adjectives or hackneyed adverbs. In fact, avoid adverbs that qualify, weaken or cripple your verbs; use a stronger verb or an original metaphor instead. I see too many stories written from a child's point of view or about children or teens."

MERLYN'S PEN: The National Magazine of Student Writing, Grades 6-12, (I, II, IV), Box 1058, East Greenwich RI 02818. (401)885-5175. Fax: (401)885-5222. E-mail: merlynspen@aol.com. Editor: R. Jim Stahl. Magazine: 8⅜×10⅞; 32 pages; 70 lb. paper; 12 pt. gloss cover; illustrations; photos. Student writing only (grades 6 through 12) for libraries, homes and English classrooms. Annual (each October). Estab. 1985. Circ. 5,000.
● Winner of the Paul A. Witty Short Story Award and Selection on the New York Public Library's Book List of Recommended Reading.
Needs: Adventure, fantasy, historical, horror, humor/satire, literary, mainstream, mystery/suspense, romance, science fiction, western, young adult/teen. Also publishes editorial reviews, poetry. Must be written by students in grades 6-12. Receives 1,200 unsolicited fiction mss/month. Accepts 50 mss/issue; 50 mss/year. Publishes ms 3 months to 1 year after acceptance. Length: 1,500 words average; 25 words minimum; no maximum. Publishes short shorts. Responds to rejected mss.

How to Contact: Send for cover-sheet template. *Charges submission fee: $1/title. For an additional $4, authors receive an extended editorial critique (100 or more words) of their submission in addition to the standard yes/ no response.* Reports in 10 weeks.
Payment/Terms: One copy of *Merlyn's Pen* plus up to 1,000 words $10; over 1,000 words $25; over 3,000 words $50; over 5,000 words $125. Published works become the property of Merlyn's Pen, Inc.
Advice: "Write what you *know*; write where you are. We look for the authentic voice and experience of young adults."

MICHIGAN QUARTERLY REVIEW, University of Michigan, 3032 Rackham, Ann Arbor MI 48109-1070. (313)764-9265. Editor: Laurence Goldstein. "An interdisciplinary journal which publishes mainly essays and reviews, with some high-quality fiction and poetry, for an intellectual, widely read audience." Quarterly. Estab. 1962. Circ. 1,800.
  • Stories from *Michigan Quarterly Review* have been selected for inclusion in *The Best American Short Stories*.
Needs: Literary. No "genre" fiction written for a "market." Receives 200 unsolicited fiction mss/month. Accepts 2 mss/issue; 8 mss/year. Published work by Alice Adams, Alyce Miller and Jim Shepard. Published new writers within the last year. Length: 1,500 words minimum; 7,000 words maximum; 5,000 words average. Also publishes poetry, literary essays.
How to Contact: Send complete ms with cover letter. "I like to know if a writer is at the beginning, or further along, in his or her career. Don't offer plot summaries of the story, though a background comment is welcome." Reports in 6-8 weeks. SASE. No simultaneous submissions. Sample copy for $2.50 and 2 first-class stamps.
Payment/Terms: Pays $8-10/printed page on publication for first rights. Awards the Lawrence Foundation Prize of $1,000 for best story in *MQR* previous year.
Advice: "Read back issues to get a sense of tone; level of writing. *MQR* is very selective; only send the very finest, best-plotted, most-revised fiction."

MID-AMERICAN REVIEW, (II), Department of English, Bowling Green State University, Bowling Green OH 43403. (419)372-2725. Fiction Editor: Michael Czyzniejewski. Magazine: 5½ × 8½; 100-150 pages; 60 lb. bond paper; coated cover stock. "We publish serious fiction and poetry, as well as critical studies in contemporary literature, translations and book reviews." Biannually. Estab. 1981.
  • A story published in the magazine was reprinted in *Best American Short Stories of 1996* and new stories from the South 1997.
Needs: Experimental, literary, memoir, prose poem, traditional and translations. Receives about 120 unsolicited fiction mss/month. Accepts 5-6 mss/issue. Does not read June-August. Approximately 5% of fiction is agented. Recently published work by Stuart Dybeck, François Camoin, Alberto Ríos, H.E. Francis, Nancy Roberts, Jack Driscoll and Mark Wisniewski. Published 2-5 new writers within the last year. Also publishes literary essays and poetry. Occasionally critiques rejected mss. Sponsors the Sherwood Anderson Short Fiction Prize.
How to Contact: Send 1 10-20 page ms with SASE. No simultaneous submissions. Reports in about 3 months. Publishes ms an average of 6 months after acceptance. Sample copy for $5. Reviews novels and short story collections. Send books to editor-in-chief.
Payment/Terms: Payment offered pending funding; usually pays $10-50 on publication and 2 contributor's copies for one-time rights; charges for additional copies.
Advice: "We look for well-written stories that make the reader want to read on past the first page. Clichéd themes and sloppy writing turn us off immediately. Read literary journals to see what's being published in today's market. Also, find authors you like and read as much of their work as you can. Of course, don't give up on a story you believe in. We continue to see quality fiction no matter what is going on, as well as fiction from writers who seem uninformed. We recently published 2 shorts by Stuart Dybeck and would like to see more short short submissions."

MIDLAND REVIEW, (II), Oklahoma State University, English Dept., Morrill Hall, Room 205, Stillwater OK 74078-4068. E-mail: peterst@okstate. Editors change every year. Send to "Fiction Editor." Magazine: 6½ × 9½; 128 pages; 80 lb. paper; perfect bound. Publishes 40% OSU student material." Annually. Estab. 1983. Circ. 300.
Needs: Ecletic, ethnic, experimental, feminist, literary, prose poem, regional, translations. "No dead animal (mammal)/parent stories. No 'when I was a kid' stories. No abstract (in the distance) epiphanies." Receives 35 unsolicited fiction mss/month. Accepts 4 mss/issue. Publishes ms 6-10 months after acceptance. Does not read in May, June or July. Recently published work by Brian Evenson and John Yau. Publishes 18 new writers/year. Length: 4-10 pages double-spaced, typed. Publishes short shorts of 2-4 pages. Also publishes literary essays, poetry.
How to Contact: Send complete ms with cover letter. Reports in 8-10 weeks on queries. SASE for ms. Simultaneous submissions OK. Sample copy for $5 plus 90¢ postage and 9 × 12 SAE. Fiction guidelines for #10 SASE.
Payment/Terms: Pays 1 contributor's copy. Copyright reverts to author.
Advice: "We like something to happen in the story, but don't be cute or clever. Also stories that break the norm catch our eyes and make us glad to be editors. Have something to impart to the world; don't just write stuff down. Reread Flannery O'Connor."

MINAS TIRITH EVENING-STAR, (IV), W.W. Publications, Box 373, Highland MI 48357-0373. (813)585-0985. Editor: Philip Helms. Magazine: 8½×11; 40 pages; typewriter paper; black ink illustrations; photos. Magazine of J.R.R. Tolkien and fantasy—fiction, poetry, reviews, etc. for general audience. Quarterly. Published special fiction issue; plans another. Estab. 1967. Circ. 500.

Needs: "Fantasy and Tolkien." Receives 5 unsolicited mss/month. Accepts 1 ms/issue; 5 mss/year. Published new writers within the last year. Length: 1,000-1,200 words preferred; 5,000 words maximum. Publishes short shorts. Also publishes literary essays, literary criticism, poetry. Occasionally critiques rejected mss.

How to Contact: Send complete ms and bio. Reports in 1-2 months. SASE. No simultaneous submissions. Reprint submissions OK. Sample copy for $1. Reviews novels and short story collections.

Terms: Acquires first rights.

Advice: Goal is "to expand knowledge and enjoyment of J.R.R. Tolkien's and his son Christopher Tolkien's works and their worlds."

MIND IN MOTION, A Magazine of Poetry and Short Prose, (II), Box 7070, Big Bear Lake CA 92315. Editor: Céleste Goyer. Magazine: 5½×8½; 64 pages; 20 lb. paper; 50 lb. cover. "We prefer to publish works of substantial brilliance that engage and encourage the reader's mind." Quarterly. Estab. 1985. Circ. 350.

 • This magazine is known for surrealism and poetic language.

Needs: Experimental, fantasy, humor/satire, literary, prose poem, science fiction. No "mainstream, romance, nostalgia, un-poetic prose; anything with a slow pace or that won't stand up to re-reading." Receives 50 unsolicited mss/month. Acquires 10 mss/issue; 40 mss/year. Reads mss October through July. Publishes ms 2-12 weeks after acceptance. Recently published work by P.G. Palmer, Marc Masse, Jeff Foster and Peter Koelliker. Length: 2,000 words preferred; 250 words minimum; 3,500 words maximum. Also publishes poetry. Sometimes critiques rejected mss.

How to Contact: Send complete ms. "Cover letter or bio not necessary." SASE. Simultaneous (if notified) submissions OK. Sample copy for $3.50. Fiction guidelines for #10 SASE.

Payment/Terms: Pays 1 contributor's copy; charge for additional copies. Acquires first North American serial rights.

Advice: "We're now taking more stories per issue, and they may be a bit longer, due to a format modification. *Mind in Motion* is noted for introspective, philosophical fiction with a great deal of energy and originality."

THE MINNESOTA REVIEW, A Journal of Committed Writing, (I, II), Dept. of English, East Carolina University, Greenville NC 27858. (919)328-6388. Fax: (919)328-4889. Editor: Jeffrey Williams. Magazine: 5¼×7½; approximately 200 pages; some illustrations; occasional photos. "We emphasize socially and politically engaged work." Semiannually. Estab. 1960. Circ. 1,500.

Needs: Experimental, feminist, gay, historical, lesbian, literary. Receives 50-75 mss/month. Accepts 3-4 mss/issue; 6-8 mss/year. Publishes ms within 6 months-1 year after acceptance. Published work by Laura Nixon Dawson, Jameson Currier, Jiqi Kajane and Stephen Guiterrez. Length: 1,500-6,000 words preferred. Publishes short shorts. Also publishes literary essays, literary criticism, poetry. Occasionally critiques rejected mss and recommends other markets.

How to Contact: Send complete ms with optional cover letter. Reports in 2-3 weeks on queries; 2-3 months on mss. SASE. Simultaneous submissions OK. Reviews novels and short story collections. Send books to book review editor.

Payment/Terms: Pays in contributor's copies. Charge for additional copies. Acquires first rights.

Advice: "We look for socially and politically engaged work, particularly short, striking work that stretches boundaries."

MISSISSIPPI MUD, (I, II), 1505 Drake Ave., Austin TX 78704-2440. (512)444-5459. Editor: Joel Weinstein. Magazine: 7¾×10; 96 pages; coated and uncoated paper; coated cover; illustrations; photographs. "*Mississippi Mud* publishes fiction, poetry and artworks reflecting life in America at the end of the 20th century. Good writing is its focus, but it is not for the timid or humorless." Published irregularly. Estab. 1973. Circ. 1,600.

 • Editor would like to see more non-didactic political fiction.

Needs: Excerpted novel, erotica, ethnic/multicultural, experimental, humor/satire, literary, mainstream/contemporary, translations. "No religious or romance." Receives 20-30 unsolicited mss/month. Accepts 8-10 mss/year. Publishes ms 8-18 months after acceptance. Recently published work by Kevin Phelan, Bill U'ren, Willie Smith, Ursula K. Leguin, Matt Sharpe and Toni Graham. Length: 5,000 words average; 100 words minimum; 25,000 words maximum. Publishes short shorts. Also publishes poetry. Sometimes critiques or comments on rejected mss.

How to Contact: Send complete ms with a cover letter. Include list of publications. Reports in 6-8 weeks on queries; 4-6 months on mss. Send SASE for reply, return of ms or send a disposable copy of ms. Simultaneous and electronic (disk) submissions OK. Sample copy for $6.

Payment/Terms: $50-100 and 2 contributor's copies on publication for first North American serial rights.

Advice: "We want good writing, a good yarn, originality. Look for the right markets: magazines where your writing fits."

MISSISSIPPI REVIEW, (III), University of Southern Mississippi, Box 5144, Hattiesburg MS 39406-5144. (601)266-4321. E-mail: fb@netdoor.com. Website: http://www.sushi.st.usm.edu/mrw/. Managing Editor: Rie Fortenberry. "Literary publication for those interested in contemporary literature—writers, editors who read to be in touch with current modes." Semiannually. Estab. 1972. Circ. 1,500.
Needs: Literary, contemporary, fantasy, humor, translations, experimental, avant-garde and "art" fiction. Quality writing. No juvenile or genre fiction. Buys varied amount of mss/issue. Does not read mss in summer. Recently published work by Jason Brown, Terese Svoboda and Barry Hannah. Length: 100 pages maximum.
How to Contact: Not currently reading unsolicited work. Sample copy for $8.
Payment/Terms: Pays in contributor's copies. Acquires first North American serial rights.
Advice: "May I suggest that you enter our annual *Mississippi Review* Prize competition (see Contests section in this book) or submit the work via e-mail to our World Wide Web publication, which is a monthly (except August) and publishes more new work than we are able to in the print version. Send submissions to fb@netdoor. com as ASCII files in the text of your e-mail message, or as Microsoft Word of WordPerfect attachments to your message."

THE MISSOURI REVIEW, (II), 1507 Hillcrest Hall, University of Missouri—Columbia, Columbia MO 65211. (573)882-4474. Fax: (573)884-4671. Website: http://www.missouri.edu/~moreview (includes guidelines, contest information, short fiction, poetry, essays, interviews, features and book reviews). Editor: Speer Morgan. Magazine: 6×9; 212 pages. Theme: fiction, poetry, essays, reviews, interviews, cartoons, "all with a distinctly contemporary orientation. For writers, and the general reader with broad literary interests. We present nonestablished as well as established writers of excellence. The *Review* frequently runs feature sections or special issues dedicated to particular topics frequently related to fiction." Published 3 times/academic year. Estab. 1977. Circ. 6,800.
● The editor would like to see more good comic fiction.
Needs: Condensed/excerpted novel, ethnic/multicultural, humor/satire, literary, contemporary. "No genre or flash fictions; no children's." Receives approximately 400 unsolicited fiction mss each month. Accepts 5-6 mss/issue; 15-20 mss/year. Recently published work by Daniel Akst, Jesse Lee Kercheval, Michael Byers, Talvikki Ansel and Steve Yarbrough. Publishes 6-10 new writers/year. No preferred length. Also publishes personal essays, poetry. Often critiques rejected mss.
How to Contact: Send complete ms with SASE. Include brief bio and list of publications. Reports in 10 weeks. Send SASE for reply, return of ms or send disposable copy of ms. Sample copy for $7.
Payment/Terms: Pays $20/page minimum on signed contract for all rights.
Advice: Awards William Peden Prize in fiction; $1,000 to best story published in *Missouri Review* in a given year. Also sponsors Editors' Prize Contest with a prize of $1,500 for fiction, $1,000 for essays and the Larry Levis Editors' Prize for poetry, with a prize of $1,500; and the Tom McAfee Discovery Prize in poetry for poets who have not yet published a book.

MOBIUS, The Journal of Social Change, (II), 1250 E. Dayton #3, Madison WI 53703. (608)255-4224. E-mail: smfred@aol.com. Editor: Fred Schepartz. Magazine: 8½×11; 32-64 pages; 60 lb. paper; 60 lb. cover. "Looking for fiction which uses social change as either a primary or secondary theme. This is broader than most people think. Need social relevance in one way or another. For an artistically and politically aware and curious audience." Quarterly. Estab. 1989. Circ. 1,500.
Needs: Contemporary, ethnic, experimental, fantasy, feminist, gay, historical, horror, humor/satire, lesbian, literary, mainstream, prose poem, science fiction. "No porn, no racist, sexist or any other kind of ist. No Christian or spiritually proselytizing fiction." Receives 15 unsolicited mss/month. Accepts 3-5 mss/issue. Publishes ms 3-9 months after acceptance. Published work by JoAnn Yolanda Hernández, Patricia Stevens and Rochelle Schwab. Length: 3,500 words preferred; 500 words minimum; 5,000 words maximum. Publishes short shorts. Length: 500 words. Always critiques rejected mss.
How to Contact: Send complete ms with cover letter. Reports in 2-4 months. SASE. Simultaneous and reprint submissions OK. Sample copy for $2, 9×12 SAE and 3 first-class stamps. Fiction guidelines for 9×12 SAE and 4-5 first-class stamps.
Payment/Terms: Pays contributor's copies. Acquires one-time rights and electronic rights for www version.
Advice: "We like high impact, we like plot and character-driven stories that function like theater of the mind." Looks for "first and foremost, good writing. Prose must be crisp and polished; the story must pique my interest and make me care due to a certain intellectual, emotional aspect. Second, *Mobius* is about social change. We want stories that make some statement about the society we live in, either on a macro or micro level. Not that your story needs to preach from a soapbox (actually, we prefer that it doesn't), but your story needs to have *something* to say."

‡MUSE PORTFOLIO, (II), 419 Southwick Rd., Unit Q72, Westfield MA 01085. Editor: Joe Balgassi. Magazine: 5½×8½; 32 pages; 20 lb. paper; color or heavier stock cover. "*M.P.* welcomes submissions from sincere, eloquent freelancers who crave the opportunity to share and support one another's writing through a casual forum. *M.P.* is a non-profit publication." Published 1-2 times/year. Estab. 1992. Circ. 200.
Needs: Ethnic/multicultural, literary, mainstream/contemporary, mystery/suspense (amateur sleuth, cozy, general, romantic suspense), romance (contemporary, young adult, anything tasteful), senior citizen/retirement, young adult/teen (10-18 years). No pornography, vulgarity, excessive violence, profanity. Receives 75 unsolicited mss/

month. Accepts 3-5 fiction mss/issue. Publishes ms 1-3 years after acceptance. Recently published work by Lynn Fessler, Roy Schultz and Larry Bratt. Length: 1,000 words preferred; 300 words minimum; 1,500 words maximum. Publishes short shorts. Length: 300-500 words. Also publishes poetry. Rarely critiques or comments on rejected mss.

How to Contact: Send complete ms with cover letter only in the odd months. "No queries, please." Should include estimated word count, bio (short paragraph), list of publications (optional). Reports in 5 to 12 weeks on mss. SASE or check to cover postage for return of ms. Reprint submissions OK. Sample copy for $3 and 6×9 or larger SAE with 3 first-class stamps. Fiction guidelines for #10 SAE and 1 first-class stamp.

Payment/Terms: Pays 1 contributor's copy.

Terms: Acquires one-time rights. Not copyrighted, but author copyright notices included in issues.

Advice: "Contributors should realize that, because we publish only one issue per year, a year (or longer) wait to publication is not uncommon. Manuscripts not accompanied by SASE will be discarded unread."

THE MUSING PLACE, The Literary & Arts Magazine of Chicago's Mental Health Community, (IV), The Thresholds, 4101 N. Ravenswood, Chicago IL 60613. (773)281-3800, ext. 2465. Fax: (773)281-8790. Editor: Linda Krinsky. Magazine: 8½×11; 36 pages; 60 lb. paper; glossy cover; illustrations. "All material is composed by mental health consumers. The only requirement for consideration of publication is having a history of mental illness." Semiannually. Estab. 1986. Circ. 1,000.

Needs: Adventure, condensed/excerpted novel, ethnic/multicultural, experimental, fantasy (science fantasy, sword and sorcery), feminist, gay, historical (general), horror, humor/satire, lesbian, literary, mainstream/contemporary, mystery/suspense, regional, romance, science fiction and serialized novel. Publishes ms up to 6 months after acceptance. Published work by Allen McNair, Donna Willey and Mark Gonciarz. Length: 500 words average; 700 words maximum. Publishes short shorts. Length: 500 words. Also publishes poetry. Sometimes critiques and comments on rejected mss.

How to Contact: Send complete ms with a cover letter. Include bio (paragraph) and statement of having a history of mental illness. Reports in 6 months. Send a disposable copy of ms. Simultaneous and reprint submissions OK. Sample copy free.

Payment/Terms: Pays contributor's copies. Acquires one-time rights.

NASSAU REVIEW, (II), Nassau Community College, State University of New York, Stewart Ave., Garden City NY 11530-6793. (516)572-7792. Editor: Paul A. Doyle. Magazine: 5½×8½; 80-120 pages; heavy stock paper; b&w illustrations and photographs. For "college teachers, libraries, educated college-level readers." Annually. Estab. 1964.

Needs: Contemporary, fantasy, historical (general), literary, mainstream, serialized novel. Receives 600-800 unsolicited mss/year. Accepts 15 mss/issue. Does not read mss August through November. Publishes ms 6 months after acceptance. Published work by Dick Wimmer, Louis Phillips and Norbert Petsch. Length: 800-1,500 words preferred; 1,000 words minimum; 1,500 words maximum. Publishes short shorts "occasionally."

How to Contact: Send complete ms with cover letter. Include basic publication data. Reports in 1 month on queries; 8 months on mss. SASE. No simultaneous submissions. Sample copy for 9×12 SAE.

Payment/Terms: No payment. Acquires first rights or one-time rights.

Advice: Looks for "imaginative, concrete writing on interesting characters and scenes. Avoid the bizarre."

NEBO, A Literary Journal, (II), Arkansas Tech University, Dept. of English, Russellville AR 72801. (501)968-0256. Editors change each year. Contact Editor or Advisor: Dr. Michael Karl Ritchie. Literary, fiction and poetry magazine: 5×8; 50-60 pages. For a general, academic audience. Annually. Estab. 1983. Circ. 500.

Needs: Literary, mainstream, reviews. Upcoming theme: pop icon fiction and poetry (fiction and poetry that plays with the roles of pop icons). Receives 20-30 unsolicited fiction mss/month. Accepts 2 mss/issue; 6-10 mss/year. Does not read mss May 1-September 1. Published work by Steven Sherrill, J.B. Bernstein, Jameson Currier, Tricia Lande and Joseph Nicholson. Published new writers within the last year. Length: 3,000 words maximum. Also publishes literary essays, literary criticism, poetry. Occasionally critiques rejected mss.

How to Contact: Send complete ms with SASE and cover letter with bio. No simultaneous submissions. Reports in 3 months on mss. Publishes ms an average of 6 months after acceptance. Sample copy for $5. "Submission deadlines for all work are November 15 and January 15 of each year." Reviews novels and short story collections.

Payment/Terms: Pays 1 contributor's copy. Acquires one-time rights.

Advice: "A writer should carefully edit his short story before submitting it. Write from the heart and put everything on the line. Don't write from a phony or fake perspective. Frankly, many of the manuscripts we

● **A BULLET INTRODUCES COMMENTS** by the editor of *Novel & Short Story Writer's Market* indicating special information about the listing.

receive should be publishable with a little polishing. Manuscripts should *never* be submitted with misspelled words or on 'onion skin' or colored paper."

THE NEBRASKA REVIEW, (II), University of Nebraska at Omaha, Omaha NE 68182-0324. (402)554-2771. E-mail: jreed@fa-cpacs.unomaha.edu. Fiction Editor: James Reed. Magazine: 5½×8½; 104 pages; 60 lb. text paper; chrome coat cover stock. "*TNR* attempts to publish the finest available contemporary fiction and poetry for college and literary audiences." Publishes 2 issues/year. Estab. 1973. Circ. 1,000.
● *The Nebraska Review* has published a number of award-winning writers.
Needs: Contemporary, humor/satire, literary and mainstream. No genre fiction. Receives 40 unsolicited fiction mss/month. Accepts 4-5 mss/issue, 8-10 mss/year. Reads for the *Nebraska Review* Awards in Fiction and Poetry September 1 through November 30. Open to submissions January 1 through April 30; does not read May 1 through August 31. Recently published work by Cris Mazza, Mark Wisniewski, Stewart O'Nan, Gerda Sanders and Tom Franklin. Published new writers within the last year. Length: 5,000-6,000 words average. Also publishes poetry.
How to Contact: Send complete ms with SASE. Reports in 1-4 months. Publishes ms an average of 6-12 months after acceptance. Sample copy for $2.50.
Payment/Terms: Pays 2 contributor's copies plus 1 year subscription; $2 charge for extras. Acquires first North American serial rights.
Advice: "Write stories in which the lives of your characters are the primary reason for writing and techniques of craft serve to illuminate, not overshadow, the textures of those lives. Sponsors a $500 award/year—write for rules."

NEOLOGISMS, A Journal of the Written Word, (I, II), Big Snapper Publishing, 1102 Pleasant St., #869, Worcester MA 01602. Editor: Jim Fay. Magazine: 8½×11; 50-80 pages; 60 lb. paper; 80 lb. cover stock; photos. "*Neologisms* is dedicated to the written word in all forms and shapes." Quarterly. Estab. 1996. Circ. 150.
Needs: Experimental, fantasy, literary, science fiction (sociological). "No overly erotic, gay/lesbian, or children-oriented work." Upcoming theme: #7, music (Summer 1998, deadline January 1998). List of upcoming themes available for SASE. Receives 20 unsolicited mss/month. Accepts 5-8 mss/issue; 20-40 mss/year. Recently published work by Leslie Schenk, Greg St. Thomasino, Cheryl Townsend, Robert Ready, Jenny Curtis and Peter McGinn. Publishes 10 new writers/year. Length: 1,100 words average; 50 words minimum; 5,000 words maximum. Publishes short shorts. Also publishes literary essays, literary criticism and poetry.
How to Contact: Send complete ms with a cover letter. Include estimated word count, bio and list of publications. Reports in 2 weeks on queries; 1 month on mss. Send SASE for reply, return of ms or send a disposble copy of ms. Simultaneous submissions OK. Sample copy for $5. Free fiction guidelines. Reviews novels and short story collections.
Payment/Terms: Pays 1 contributor's copy; additional copies for $4. Acquires first rights "and option to use a second time if I ever do a 'Best of' issue." Sends galleys to author only if requested. Not copyrighted.
Advice: "Fiction must have originality and be able to catch my eye. Send stuff that mainstream America would probably not publish."

‡NERVE COWBOY, (II, III), Liquid Paper Press, P.O. Box 4973, Austin TX 78765. Editors: Joseph Shields and Jerry Hagins. Magazine: 7×8½; 52-60 pages; 20 lb. paper; card stock cover; illustrations. "*Nerve Cowboy* publishes adventurous, comical, disturbing, thought-provoking, accessible poetry and fiction. We like to see work sensitive enough to make the hardest hard-ass cry, funny enough to make the most hopeless brooder laugh and disturbing enough to make us all glad we're not the author of the piece." Semiannually. Estab. 1996. Circ. 250.
● Sponsors an annual chapbook contest for fiction or poetry. Deadline January 31. Send SASE for details.
Needs: Literary. Receives 10 unsolicited mss/month. Accepts 2-3 mss/issue; 4-6 mss/year. Publishes ms 6-12 months after acceptance. Recently published work by Albert Huffstickler, Mark Smith, Catfish McDaris, Laurel Speer, Marcy Shapiro and Susanne R. Bowers. Length: 750-1,000 words average; 1,500 words maximum. Publishes short shorts. Also publishes poetry.
How to Contact: Send complete ms with a cover letter. Include bio and list of publications. Reports in 2 weeks on queries; 4-6 weeks on mss. Send SASE for reply, return of ms or send disposable copy of ms. No simultaneous submissions. Reprints OK. Sample copy for $4. Fiction guidelines for #10 SASE.
Payment/Terms: Pays 1 contributor's copy for one-time rights; additional copies $3.50.
Advice: "We look for writing which is very direct and elicits a visceral reaction in the reader. Read magazines you submit to in order to get a feel for what the editors are looking for. Write simply and from the gut."

‡NEW DELTA REVIEW, (II), Creative Writing Programs, English Dept./Louisiana State University, Baton Rouge LA 70803-5001. (504)388-4079. E-mail: wwwndr@unix1.snce.lsu.edu. Contact: Brian Arundel and Tamara Carter. Fiction Editor: Maxine Beach. Editors change every year. Magazine: 6×9; 75-125 pages; high quality paper; glossy card cover; b&w illustrations and artwork. "No theme or style biases. Poetry, fiction primarily; also literary interviews and reviews." Semi-annual. Estab. 1984. Circ. 500.
● The magazine recently won a *Pushcart* Prize. *New Delta Review* also sponsors the Eyster Prizes for fiction and poetry. See the listing in the Contest and Awards Section of this book. Work from the magazine has been included in the *Pushcart Prize* anthology.

Needs: Contemporary, humor/satire, literary, mainstream, prose poem, translations. No novel excerpts. Receives 200 unsolicited mss/ month. Accepts 3-4 mss/issue, 6-8 mss/year. Recently published work by Steve Sterns, Cliff Yudell, Wendy Bremer and Rita Ciresi. Published new writers within the last year. Length: 20 ms pages average; 250 words minimum. Publishes short shorts. Also publishes poetry. Rarely critiques rejected mss.

How to Contact: Send complete ms with cover letter. Cover letter should include estimated word count, bio, Social Security number and "credits, if any; no synopses, please." No simultaneous submissions. Reports on queries in 3 weeks; 3 months on mss. SASE (or IRC). Mss deadlines September 1 for fall; February 15 for spring. Sample copy for $5. Reviews novels and short story collections.

Payment/Terms: Pays in contributor's copies. Charge for extras.

Terms: Acquires first North American serial rights. Sponsors award for fiction writers in each issue. Eyster Prize-$50 plus notice in magazine. Mss selected for publication are automatically considered.

Advice: "Make sparks fly off your typewriter. Send your best work, even if others have rejected it. Don't let our address mislead you: We like fiction and poetry that explore national and international sensibilities, not just Southern regionalism. And don't forget the SASE if you want a response."

NEW ENGLAND REVIEW, (II), Middlebury College, Middlebury VT 05753. (802)443-5075. E-mail: nerevie w@mail.middlebury.edu. Editor: Stephen Donadio. Magazine: 7 × 10; 180 pages; 50 lb paper; coated cover stock. A literary quarterly publishing fiction, poetry and essays with special emphasis on contemporary cultural issues, both in the US and abroad. For general readers and professional writers. Quarterly. Estab. 1977. Circ. 2,000.

● *New England Review* has long been associated with Breadloaf Writer's Conference, held at Middlebury College.

Needs: Literary. Receives 250 unsolicited fiction mss/month. Accepts 5 mss/issue; 20 mss/year. Does not read ms June-August. Published work by Sigrid Nunez, Carolyn Cooke, Jesús Gardea, Cornelia Nixon and Stephen Dobyns. Published new writers within the last year. Publishes ms 3-9 months after acceptance. Agented fiction: less than 5%. Publishes short shorts. Sometimes critiques rejected mss.

How to Contact: Send complete ms with cover letter. "Cover letters that demonstrate that the writer knows the magazine are the ones we want to read. We don't want hype, or hard-sell, or summaries of the author's intentions. Will consider simultaneous submissions, but must be stated as such." Reports in 10-12 weeks on mss. SASE.

Payment/Terms: Pays $10/page, $20 minimum and 2 contributor's copies on publication; charge for extras. Acquires first rights and reprint rights. Sends galleys to author.

Advice: "It's best to send one story at a time, and wait until you hear back from us to try again."

NEW LAUREL REVIEW, (II), New Orleans Poetry Forum/New Laurel Review, P.O. Box 770257, New Orleans LA 70112. (504)947-6001. Editor: Lee Meitzen Grue. Magazine: 6½ × 8; 125 pages; 60 lb. white paper; illustrations and photos. Journal of poetry, fiction, critical articles and reviews. "We have published such internationally known writers as James Nolan, Tomris Uyar and Yevgeny Yevtushenko." Readership: "Literate, adult audiences as well as anyone interested in writing with significance, human interest, vitality, subtlety, etc." Published irregularly. Estab. 1970. Circ. 500. Member of Council of Editors of Learned Journals.

Needs: Literary, ethnic/multicultural, excerpted novel, translations, "cutting edge." No "dogmatic, excessively inspirational or political" material. Acquires 1-2 fiction mss/issue. Receives approximately 25 unsolicited fiction mss each month. Does not read mss during summer months and December. Agented fiction 10%. Length: about 10 printed pages. Publishes short shorts. Also publishes literary essays and poetry. Critiques rejected mss when there is time.

How to Contact: Send complete ms with a cover letter. Include bio and list of publications. Reports in 3 months. Send SASE for reply or return of ms. No simultaneous submissions. Sample copy for $10. "Authors need to look at sample copy before submitting."

Payment/Terms: Pays 1 contributor's copy; additional copies $10, discounted. Acquires first rights.

Advice: "We are interested in fresh, original work that keeps a reader reading. Send a finished manuscript: clean."

NEW LETTERS MAGAZINE, (I, II), University of Missouri-Kansas City, University House, 5101 Rockhill Rd., Kansas City MO 64110. (816)235-1168. Fax: (816)235-2611. Editor: James McKinley. Magazine: 14 lb. cream paper; illustrations. Quarterly. Estab. 1971 (continuation of *University Review*, founded 1935). Circ. 2,500.

Needs: Contemporary, ethnic, experimental, humor/satire, literary, mainstream, translations. No "bad fiction in any genre." Published work by Tess Gallagher, Jimmy Carter and Amiri Baraka; published work by new writers within the last year. Agented fiction: 10%. Also publishes short shorts. Rarely critiques rejected mss.

How to Contact: Send complete ms with cover letter. Does not read mss May 15-October 15. Reports in 3 weeks on queries; 2-3 months on mss. SASE for ms. No simultaneous or multiple submissions. Sample copy: $8.50 for issues older than 5 years; $5.50 for 5 years or less.

Payment/Terms: Pays honorarium—depends on grant/award money; 2 contributor's copies. Sends galleys to author.

Advice: "Seek publication of representative chapters in high-quality magazines as a way to the book contract. Try literary magazines first."

NEW ORLEANS REVIEW, (I, II), Box 195, Loyola University, New Orleans LA 70118. (504)865-2295. Fax: (504)865-2294. E-mail: noreview@beta.loyno.edu. Editor: Ralph Adamo. Magazine: 8½ × 11; 160 pages; 60 lb. Scott offset paper; 12 + King James C1S cover stock; photos. "Publishes poetry, fiction, translations, photographs, nonfiction on literature and film. Readership: those interested in current culture, literature." Quarterly. Estab. 1968. Circ. 1,300.

Needs: "Storytelling between traditional and experimental." Recently published work by Gordon Lish, Alfred Schwaid, C. Semansky, Trudy Lewis, Ellen Gandt, Rodney Jones, William Matthews and Steve Stern. Publishes many new writers/year.

How to Contact: Send complete ms with SASE. Does not accept simultaneous submissions. Accepts disk submissions; inquire about system compatibility. Prefers hard copy with disk submission. Reports in 2-12 weeks. Sample copy for $9.

Payment/Terms: "Inquire." Most payment in copies. Pays on publication for first North American serial rights.

THE NEW PRESS LITERARY QUARTERLY, (II), 65-39 108th St., #E-6, Forest Hills NY 11375. (718)459-6807. Fax: (718)275-1646. Editor-in-Chief: Maria Victoria Figueredo. Prose Editor: Alice Rudensky. Magazine: 8½ × 11; 40 pages; medium bond paper and thick cover stock; b&w illustrations and photographs. "Poems, short stories, commentary, personal journalism. Original, informative and entertaining." Quarterly. Estab. 1984. Circ. 2,000.

Needs: Experimental, humor/satire, mainstream, mystery/suspense. No gratuitous violence. Upcoming themes: Education, self-discovery, nature, spiritual journey, social or political critique. Receives 25 unsolicited mss/month. Accepts 5 mss/issue; 20 mss/year. Publishes ms 12 months after acceptance. Published work by Sol Rubin, Les Haber and Mark Blickley. Published new writers within the last year. Length: 22 double-spaced pages. Also publishes literary essays, literary criticism and poetry.

How to Contact: *Charges reading fee for nonsubscribers. $5/short story (22-double-spaced pages maximum).* Send complete ms with cover letter. Reports in 6 months. SASE. Simultaneous submissions OK. Sample copy for $5.50; fiction guidelines for SASE. $15 for one-year (4 issues) subscription, add $5 for foreign subscription.

Payment/Terms: Pays 2 contributor's copies plus $15 maximum for each prose piece over 500 words ($10 for prose 500 words or less) for first rights.

Advice: "Our approach is eclectic. We want to bring literary participation to as many people as possible. We accept works by established writers and by literary newcomers. Our works appeal to a broad spectrum because they are sensitive to human relationships without prejudice or hatred."

the new renaissance, (II), 26 Heath Rd., #11, Arlington MA 02174-3645. Fiction Editors: Louise T. Reynolds, Michal Anne Kuchauki and Patricia Michaud. Magazine: 6 × 9; 144-182 pages; 70 lb. paper; laminated cover stock; artwork; photos. "An international magazine of ideas and opinions, emphasizing literature and the arts, *tnr* takes a classicist position in literature and the arts. Publishes a variety of diverse, quality and literary fiction which is always well crafted and occasionally experimental. *tnr* is unique for its marriage of the literary and visual arts with political/sociological articles and essays. We publish the beginning as well as the emerging and established writer." Biannually. Estab. 1968. Circ. 1,500.

● Work published in *the new renaissance* has been chosen for inclusion in *Editor's Choice I, Editor's Choice III, Editor's Choice IV* and *Sudden Fiction*.

Needs: Serious, quality literary, humorous, off-beat fiction. Also interested in translations of fiction (send original as well). Accepts 4-5 mss/issue, 6-10 mss/year. Receives approximately 80-140 unsolicited fiction mss each month. Reads only from January 2 through June 30 and from September 1 through October 31. Agented fiction approx. 5-8%. Recently published work by Jeffrey Boyer, Gordon Ekelund and Jan Piper Kornbluth. Length of fiction: 3-36 pages. Also publishes articles, literary essays, literary criticism, poetry and poetry translations. Comments on rejected mss "if we feel we might be helpful, also when we want to encourage writers to submit again."

How to Contact: *"Entry fee of $15 required for non-subscribers," $10 for subscribers.* All fiction mss received without the entry fee are returned unread. Send complete ms with SASE or IRC of sufficient size for return. "Inform us if multiple submission. If you query, enclose SASE, IRC or stamped post card." Reluctantly accepts simultaneous submissions but "we ask that you notify us immediately if the ms has been accepted elsewhere. If we haven't yet read your story, we will accept a substitution either at the time of notification or within 2 months thereafter." Reports in 5-9 months on mss. Publishes ms an average of 12-18 months after acceptance. Reviews novels and short story collections, also biography, poetry collections, etc.

Payment/Terms: Pays $42-85 after publication; 1 contributor's copy. "We offer contributors' discounts for 3 or more copies. All fiction and poetry submissions are now tied into our awards program for the best fiction and poetry published in a three-issue volume of *tnr*. Subscribers: $10 entry fee; non-subscribers: $15 entry fee; writers will receive 2 back issues or a recent issue." Acquires all rights in case of a later *tnr* collection; otherwise, rights return to the writer.

Advice: "This may be preaching to the converted—but we strongly recommend that writers consult current market directories for guidelines on submitting AND that they read listings carefully. In the first six months of 1997, for example, we've had to return more than 140 (fiction) manuscripts UNREAD because writers merely scanned our listings; this includes submissions from Canada and abroad. 'I didn't notice that an entry fee was required,' they write 'but now I've reread your listing and see that it is noted.' Writers who don't read carefully are unlikely to be accepted here. Also, when writers receive an issue of *tnr* or any other litmag that they want to submit to, they should read the fiction very carefully and closely, noting the statement, the style and the craftsmanship. We receive fiction from subscribers and others who have seen at least one or two issues of *tnr* which is absolutely wrong (most frequently in tone or statement but sometimes also in style) for us. Had they understood our fiction, they would never have submitted those manuscripts to us. We have a wide range but we're not 'anything goes.' We favor writing that is personal, compelling, dense so that it holds up to successive readings. We don't want to see well-done, technically proficient 'So what' stories. Learn to edit your own work so that it is not self-indulgent or sloppy. And read—read contemporary fiction, read modern fiction, and read fiction that is not of our time. Good fiction can take us into other worlds, other cultures. At *tnr*, we're looking for a lens, not a mirror. Finally, in cover letter, do not write, 'Please let me hear from you at your earliest convenience' which suggests editors are sitting around waiting for your work to come in. Check a litmag's reporting time beforehand to see if it is acceptable to you.''

‡NEW VIRGINIA REVIEW, 2A, 1306 E. Cary St., Richmond VA 23219. (804)782-1043. Editor: Mary Flinn. Magazine: 6½×10; 180 pages; high quality paper; coated, color cover stock. ''Authors are serious writers of contemporary fiction.'' Published January, May and October. Estab. 1978. Circ. 2,000.
Needs: Contemporary, experimental, literary, mainstream, serialized/excerpted novel. No blue, science fiction, romance, children's. Receives 50-100 unsolicited fiction mss/month. Accepts an average of 15 mss/issue. Does not read from April 1 to September 1. Publishes ms an average of 6-9 months after acceptance. Length: 5,000-6,500 words average; no minimum; 8,000 words maximum. Also publishes poetry. Sometimes critiques rejected mss.
How to Contact: Send complete ms with cover letter, name, address, telephone number, brief biographical comment. Reports in 6 weeks on queries; up to 6 months on mss. ''Will answer questions on status of ms.'' SASE (or IRC). Sample copy for $7 and 9×12 SAE with 5 first-class stamps.
Payment/Terms: Pays $10/printed page; contributor's copies; charge for extras, ½ cover price.
Terms: Pays on publication for first North American serial rights. Sponsors contests and awards for Virginia writers only.
Advice: ''Try to write good strong fiction, stick to it, and try again with another editor.''

NEW WRITING, A Literary Magazine for New Writers, (I), P.O. Box 1812, Amherst NY 14226-7812. E-mail: newwriting@aol.com. Editor: Sam Meade. Electronic magazine: 150 pages; illustrations and photographs. ''We publish work that is deserving.'' Annually. Estab. 1994.
Needs: Work by new writers: action, experimental, horror, humor/satire, literary, mainstream/contemporary, romance, translations, westerns. No waking stories. Length: open. Publishes short shorts. Often critiques or comments on rejected mss. Sponsors an annual award.
How to Contact: Send complete ms with a cover letter. Include *brief* list of publications and *short* cover letter. Reports in 1-2 months. Send SASE for return of ms. Simultaneous submissions OK. Reviews novels and short story collections.
Payment/Terms: Acquires one-time rights.
Advice: ''Don't send first copies of *any* story. Always read over, and rewrite!'' Avoid ''stories with characters who are writers, and death and dying stories—we get too many of them.''

‡NEW YORK STORIES, (I, II), Laguardia Community College, English Department, E-103, 31-10 Thomson Ave., Long Island City NY 11101. (718)482-5677. Editor: Michael Blaine. Fiction Editor: Mark Wisnieski. Magazine: 9×11; 64-96 pages; photos. Quarterly. Estab. 1998.
Needs: Condensed/excerpted novel, erotica, ethnic/multicultural, experimental, feminist, gay, humor/satire, lesbian, literary, mainstream/contemporary, regional, senior citizen/retirement. Receives 300 unsolicited mss/month. Accepts 5-10 mss/issue; 20-40 mss/year. Does not read June through August. Publishes ms 6 months after acceptance. Agented fiction 5%. Length: 2,500-3,000 words average; 100 words minimum. Publishes short shorts. Also publishes literary essays. Sometimes critiques or comments on rejected mss.
How to Contact: Send complete ms with a cover letter. Include 1-paragraph bio and Social Security number. Reports in 2 months on queries; 2-3 months on mss. Send SASE for return of ms or send disposable copy of ms. Simultaneous submissions and reprints OK. Fiction guidelines for #10 SASE.
Payment/Terms: Pays $100 minimum; $1,000 maximum on publication.
Advice: ''Fresh angles of vision, dark humor and psychological complexity are hallmarks of our short stories. Present characters who are 'alive.' Let them breath. To achieve this, revise, revise, revise. Lately, the industry of publishing fiction seems to be playing it safe. We want your best—no matter what.''

✤NeWEST REVIEW, (II, IV), Box 394, R.P.O. University, Saskatoon, Saskatchewan S7N 4J8 Canada. (306)934-1444. Fax: (306)343-8579. E-mail: verne.clemence@sk.sympatico.ca. Editor: Verne Clemence. Magazine: 40 pages; book stock; illustrations; photos. Magazine devoted to western Canada cultural and regional issues; ''fiction, reviews, poetry for middle- to high-brow audience.'' Bimonthly (6 issues per year). Estab. 1975. Circ. 1,000.
Needs: ''We want fiction of high literary quality, whatever its form and content. But we do have a heavy regional

emphasis." Receives 15-20 unsolicited mss/month. Accepts 1 ms/issue; 10 mss/year. Recently published work by Gertrude Story, Thomas Trojiasiek and Don Grafton. Publishes 12-15 new writers/year. Length: 2,500 words average; 1,500 words minimum; 5,000 words maximum. Sometimes recommends other markets.

How to Contact: "We like *brief* cover letters." Reports very promptly in a short letter. SAE, IRCs or Canadian postage. No multiple submissions. Electronic submissions (disk or e-mail) OK. Sample copy for $5.

Payment/Terms: Pays $100 maximum on publication for one-time rights.

Advice: "We don't want unpolished, careless submissions. We do want to be intrigued, entertained and stimulated. Polish your writing. Develop your story line. Give your characters presence. If we, the readers, are to care about the people you create, you too must take them seriously. Be bold and venturesome."

‡NEXUS, (II), Wright State University, W016a Student Union, Dayton OH 45435. (937)775-5533. Editor: Larry Sawyer. Magazine: 7×10; 90-140 pages; good coated paper; heavy perfect-bound cover; b&w illustrations and photography. "International arts and literature for those interested." 3 times per year. Circ. 2,000.

Needs: Contemporary, experimental, literary, regional, translations. No sci-fi, western, romance. Receives 25-30 unsolicited mss/month. Accepts 2-3 mss/issue; 6-10 mss/year. Does not read mss June-Sept. Publishes ms 2-6 months after acceptance. Length: 4,000 words average; 500 words minimum; 7,500 words maximum. Publishes short shorts of any length. Also publishes literary essays, literary criticism and poetry. Sometimes critiques rejected mss and recommends other markets.

How to Contact: Send complete manuscript with cover letter including "any previous publishers of your work. *Do not* explain anything about the story." Reports in 2-4 weeks on queries; 1-2 months on mss. SASE. Simultaneous, photocopied and reprint submissions OK. Sample copy for $5. Fiction guidelines for #10 SASE.

Payment/Terms: Pays contributor's copies. Acquires first North American serial rights.

Advice: "Simplicity and a perfection of style (description, simile, dialogue) always make a lasting impression. Good, careful translations receive favored readings."

NIGHTSUN, (II), Department of English, Frostburg State University, Frostburg MD 21532. Co-editors: Barbara Hurd, Keith Schlegel and Karen Zealand. Magazine: 6×9; 64 pages; recycled paper. "Although *Nightsun* is primarily a journal of poetry and interviews, we are looking for excellent short-short fiction (5 pgs. maximum)." Annually. Estab. 1981. Circ. 300-500.

How to Contact: Send inquiry with SASE. No simultaneous submissions. Reports within 2-3 months. Sample copy for $6.50.

Payment/Terms: Pays 2 contributor's copies. Acquires one-time rights (rights revert to author after publication).

NIMROD, International Journal of Prose and Poetry, (II), University of Tulsa, 600 S. College Ave., Tulsa OK 74104. (918)631-3080. Editor-in-Chief: Francine Ringold. Magazine: 6×9; 160 pages; 60 lb. white paper; illustrations; photos. "We publish one thematic issue and one awards issue each year. A recent theme was "The City," a compilation of poetry and prose from all over the world." We seek vigorous, imaginative, quality writing." Semiannually. Estab. 1956. Circ. 3,000.

● *Nimrod* received an Honorable Mention from the 1995 American Literary Magazine Awards.

Needs: "We accept contemporary poetry and/or prose. May submit adventure, ethnic, experimental, prose poem, science fiction or translations." Upcoming theme: "A Range of Light: The Americas" (1998). Receives 120 unsolicited fiction mss/month. Published work by Janette Turner Hospital, Josephine Jacobson, Alice Walker, Francois Camoin and Gish Jen; published 15 new writers within the last year. Length: 7,500 words maximum. Also publishes poetry.

How to Contact: SASE for return of ms. Reports in 3-5 months. Sample copy: "to see what *Nimrod* is all about, send $8 for a back issue. To receive a recent awards issue, send $8 (includes postage).

Payment/Terms: Pays 2 contributor's copies, plus $5/page up to $25 total per author per issue for one-time rights.

Advice: "We have not changed our fiction needs: quality, vigor, distinctive voice. We have, however, increased the number of stories we print. See current issues. We look for fiction that is fresh, vigorous, distinctive, serious and humorous, seriously-humorous, unflinchingly serious, ironic—whatever. Just so it is quality. Strongly encourage writers to send #10 SASE for brochure for annual literary contest with prizes of $1,000 and $2,000."

96 Inc., (I, II), P.O. Box 15559, Boston MA 02215. (617)267-0543. Fiction Editors: Julie Anderson and Nancy Mehegan. Magazine: 8½×11; 50 pages; 20 lb. paper; matte cover; illustrations and photos. "*96 Inc.* promotes

---

‡ **THE DOUBLE DAGGER** before a listing indicates that the listing is new in this edition.

the process; integrates beginning/young with established writers; reaches out to audiences of all ages and backgrounds." Semiannually. Estab. 1992. Circ. 3,000.

Needs: Gay, historical (general), humor/satire, literary and translations. Receives 200 unsolicited mss/month. Accepts 12-15 mss/issue; 30 mss/year. Agented fiction 10%. Recently published work by Kat Meads, Anesa Miller and Joe Lunevicz. Publishes 8-10 new writers/year. Length: 1,000 words minimum; 7,000 words maximum. Publishes short shorts. Also publishes literary essays, literary criticism and poetry. Sometimes critiques or comments on rejected mss.

How to Contact: Query first. Include estimated word count, bio (100 words) and list of publications. Reports in 3 weeks on queries; 6-12 months on mss. Send SASE for reply, return of ms or send a disposable copy of ms. Simultaneous and electronic submissions OK. Sample copy for $5.50. Fiction guidelines for #10 SASE. Reviews novels and short story collections.

Payment/Terms: Pays modest sum if funds are available, not depending on length or merit, free subscription and 4 contributor's copies on publication for one-time rights.

Advice: Looks for "good writing in any style. Pays attention to the process. Read at least one issue. Be patient—it takes a very long time for readers to go through the thousands of manuscripts."

NITE-WRITER'S INTERNATIONAL LITERARY ARTS JOURNAL, (I, II), Nite Owl Press, 965 Streets Run Rd., Suite 200, Pittsburgh PA 15236-2224. (412)885-9119. E-mail: jthomp7102@aol.com. Editor: John A. Thompson, Sr. Magazine: 8½×11; 30-50 pages; bond paper; illustrations. *"Nite-Writer's International Literary Arts Journal* is dedicated to the emotional intellectual with a creative perception of life." Quarterly. Estab. 1993. Circ. 100.

Needs: Adventure, erotica, historical, humor/satire, literary, mainstream/contemporary, religious/inspirational, romance, senior citizen/retirement, sports, young adult/teen (adventure). Plans special fiction issue or anthology. Receives 3-5 unsolicited mss/month. Accepts 1-2 mss/issue; 5-8 mss/year. Publishes ms within 1 year after acceptance. Published work by Julia Klatt Singer, Jean Oscarson Schoell, Lawrence Keough and S. Anthony Smith. Length: 150 words average; 150 words minimum; 250 words maximum. Publishes short shorts. Also publishes literary essays, literary criticism, poetry. Often critiques or comments on rejected mss.

How to Contact: Send complete ms with a cover letter. Include estimated word count, 1-page bio, list of publications. Reports in 4-6 weeks. SASE for return of ms. Simultaneous submissions OK. Sample copy for $6, 9×13 SAE and 6 first-class stamps. Fiction guidelines for legal size SASE.

Payment/Terms: Does not pay. Acquires first North American serial rights. Sponsors contests.

Advice: "Read a lot of what you write, study the market; don't fear rejection, but use it as a learning tool to strengthen your work before resubmitting. Express what the heart feels."

THE NORTH AMERICAN REVIEW, University of Northern Iowa, Cedar Falls IA 50614. (319)273-6455. E-mail: nar@uni.edu. Website: http://www.cais.net/aesir/NAR/. Editor: Robley Wilson. "The NAR is the oldest literary magazine in America and one of the most respected; though we have no prejudices about the subject matter of material sent to us, our first concern is quality." Bimonthly. Estab. 1815. Circ. 4,500.

Needs: Open (literary). Reads mss from January 1 to April 1 only.

How to Contact: Send complete ms with SASE. Sample copy for $5.

Payment/Terms: Pays approximately $12/printed page; 2 contributor's copies on publication for first North American serial rights. $3.50 charge for extras.

Advice: "We stress literary excellence and read 3,000 manuscripts a year to find an average of 35 stories that we publish. Please *read* the magazine first. Please don't mail your work to us in a Tyvek envelope; it defies letter-openers. Otherwise, our mechanical requirements are the usual ones. Material sent to us must be accompanied by a stamped, self-addressed envelope; the envelope should be large enough to accommodate the manuscript, and the postage should be sufficient to cover the cost of its return to you. If you don't supply postage, or if the envelope isn't large enough to contain the manuscript, we assume that you don't want your work sent back."

NORTH DAKOTA QUARTERLY, (II), University of North Dakota, Box 7209, University Station, Grand Forks ND 58202. (701)777-3322. Editor: Robert W. Lewis. Fiction Editor: William Borden. Poetry Editor: Jay Meek. Magazine: 6×9; 200 pages; bond paper; illustrations; photos. Magazine publishing "essays in humanities; some short stories; some poetry." University audience. Quarterly. Estab. 1910. Circ. 800.

● Work published in *North Dakota Quarterly* was selected for inclusion in *The O. Henry Awards* anthology.

The editors are especially interested in work by Native American writers.

Needs: Contemporary, ethnic, experimental, feminist, historical, humor/satire, literary. Receives 20-30 unsolicited mss/month. Accepts 4 mss/issue; 16 mss/year. Published work by Naguib Mahfouz, Jerry Bumpus, Carol Shields, Rilla Askew and Chris Mazza. Published new writers within the last year. Length: 3,000-4,000 words average. Also publishes literary essays, literary criticism, poetry.

How to Contact: Send complete ms with cover letter. "But it need not be much more than hello; please read this story; I've published (if so, best examples) . . ." SASE. Reports in 3 months. Publishes ms an average of 1 year after acceptance. Sample copy for $8. Reviews novels and short story collections.

Payment/Terms: Pays 3 contributor's copies; 30% discount for extras; year's subscription. Acquires one-time rights.

NORTHEAST ARTS MAGAZINE, (II), P.O. Box 94, Kittery ME 03904. Editor: Mr. Leigh Donaldson. Magazine: 6½×9½; 32-40 pages; matte finish paper; card stock cover; illustrations and photographs. Bimonthly. Estab. 1990. Circ. 750.
Needs: Ethnic, gay, historical, literary, mystery/suspense (private eye), prose poem (under 2,000 words). No obscenity, racism, sexism, etc. Receives 50 unsolicited mss/month. Accepts 1-2 mss/issue; 5-7 mss/year. Publishes ms 2-4 months after acceptance. Agented fiction 20%. Length: 750 words preferred. Publishes short shorts. Sometimes critiques rejected mss.
How to Contact: Send complete ms with cover letter. Include short bio. Reports in 1 month on queries; 2-4 months on mss. SASE. Simultaneous submissions OK. Sample copy for $4.50, SAE and 75¢ postage. Fiction guidelines free.
Payment/Terms: Pays 2 contributor's copies. Acquires first North American serial rights. Sometimes sends galleys to author.
Advice: Looks for "creative/innovative use of language and style. Unusual themes and topics."

NORTHEAST CORRIDOR, (II), Beaver College, 450 S. Easton Rd., Glenside PA 19038. (215)572-2870. E-mail: balee@beaver.edu. Editor: Susan Balée. Magazine: 6¾×10; 120-180 pages; 60 lb. white paper; glossy, perfect-bound cover; illustrations and photos. "Interested in writers and themes treating the Northeast Corridor region of America. Literary fiction, poetry, drama, essays." Annually. Estab. 1993. Circ. 1,000.
 ● *Northeast Corridor* has received grants from the Daphne Foundation, the Ruth and Robert Satter Foundation, the Cottonwood Foundation and the Nicholas Roerich Museum. An essay it published was included in *Best American Essays*.
Needs: Literary: excerpted novel, ethnic/multicultural, feminist, humor/satire, literary, regional, translations. No religious, western, young adult, science fiction, juvenile, horror. List of upcoming themes available for SASE. Planning future special fiction issue or anthology. Receives 100 unsolicited mss/month. Accepts 2-6 mss/issue; 4-12 mss/year. Reads mss infrequently during June, July and August. Publishes ms 6 months after acceptance. Recently published work by Jessica Brilliant, Jason Wilson, Rita Ciresi and Mark Winegardner. Publishes 5-6 new writers/year. Length: 2,500 words average; 1,000 words minimum; 4,500 words maximum. Publishes literary essays, interviews and poetry. Often critiques or comments on rejected mss.
How to Contact: Send complete ms with a cover letter. Include word count, 1-2 line bio and publications list. Reports in 2-4 months on mss. SASE for reply, return of ms or send a disposable copy of ms. Simultaneous submissions OK if indicated. Sample copy for $6, 9×12 SAE and $1.21 postage. Fiction guidelines for #10 SASE.
Payment/Terms: Pays $10-100 and 2 contributor's copies on publication for first North American serial rights; additional copies for $3.50/copy.
Advice: "In selecting fiction we look for love of language, developed characters, believable conflict, metaphorical prose, satisfying resolution. Read everything from Chekov to Alice Munro and write at least 10-20 stories before you start trying to send them out. We would like to see more humor. Writers should avoid sending work that is 'therapy' rather than 'art.' The best fiction is still to be found in small journals. The small tale well told appears here where it can be appreciated if not remunerated."

NORTHWEST REVIEW, (II), 369 PLC, University of Oregon, Eugene OR 97403. (503)346-3957. Editor: John Witte. Fiction Editor: Janice MacCrae. Magazine: 6×9; 140-160 pages; high quality cover stock; illustrations; photos. "A general literary review featuring poems, stories, essays and reviews, circulated nationally and internationally. For a literate audience in avant-garde as well as traditional literary forms; interested in the important writers who have not yet achieved their readership." Triannually. Estab. 1957. Circ. 1,200.
 ● *Northwest Review* has received the Oregon Governor's Award for the Arts. The work included in *Northwest Review* tends to be literary, heavy on character and theme.
Needs: Contemporary, experimental, feminist, literary and translations. Accepts 4-5 mss/issue, 12-15 mss/year. Receives approximately 100 unsolicited fiction mss each month. Published work by Diana Abu-Jaber, Madison Smartt Bell, Maria Flook and Charles Marvin. Published new writers within the last year. Length: "Mss longer than 40 pages are at a disadvantage." Also publishes literary essays, literary criticism, poetry. Critiques rejected mss when there is time. Sometimes recommends other markets.
How to Contact: Send complete ms with SASE. "No simultaneous submissions are considered." Reports in 3-4 months. Sample copy for $4. Reviews novels and short story collections. Send books to John Witte.
Payment/Terms: Pays 3 contributor's copies and one-year subscription; 40% discount on extras. Acquires first rights.

NORTHWOODS JOURNAL, A Magazine for Writers, (I, II), Conservatory of American Letters, P.O. Box 298, Thomaston ME 04861. (207)354-0998. Fax: (207)354-8953. E-mail: olrob@midcoast.com. Editor: R.W. Olmsted. Fiction Editor: Ken Sieben. Magazine: 5½×8½; 32-64 pages; white paper; 65 lb. card cover; offset printing; perfect binding; some illustrations and photographs. "No theme, no philosophy—for people who read for entertainment." Quarterly. Estab. 1993. Circ. 500.
Needs: Adventure, erotica, experimental, fantasy (science fantasy, sword and sorcery), literary, mainstream/contemporary, mystery/suspense (amateur sleuth, police procedural, private eye/hard-boiled, romantic suspense), psychic/supernatural/occult, regional, romance (gothic, historical), science fiction (hard science, soft/sociologi-

cal), sports, westerns (frontier, traditional). Publishes special fiction issue or anthology. Receives 50 unsolicited mss/month. Accepts 12-15 mss/year. Recently published work by Paul A. Jurvie, Richard Vaughn, Bryn C. Gray and Sandra Thompson. Publishes 15 new writers/years. Length: 2,500 words maximum. Also publishes literary essays, literary criticism and poetry.

How to Contact: Read guidelines *before* submitting. Send complete ms with a cover letter. Include word count and list of publications. There is a $3 fee per story. Reports in 1-2 days on queries; by next deadline plus 5 days on mss. Send SASE for reply, return of ms or send a disposable copy of ms. No simultaneous submissions. Sample copies: $5 next issue, $7.75 current issue, $10 back issue (if available), all postage paid. Fiction guidelines for #10 SASE. Reviews novels, short story collections and poetry.

Payment/Terms: Varies, "minimum $4/published page on acceptance for first North American serial rights."

Advice: "Read guidelines, read the things we've published. Know your market."

‡NOTRE DAME REVIEW, (II), University of Notre Dame, English Department, Creative Writing, Notre Dame IN 46556. (219)631-6952. Fax: (219)631-4268. E-mail: tomasula4@nd.edu. Editor: Valerie Sayers. Liter ary magazine: 6×9; 115 pages; 50 lb. smooth paper; illustrations and photographs. "The *Notre Dame Review* is an independent, non-commercial magazine of contemporary American and international fiction, poetry, criticism and art. We are especially interested in work that takes on big issues by making the invisible seen, that gives voice to the voiceless. In addition to showcasing celebrated authors like Seamus Heaney and Czelaw Milosz, the *Notre Dame Review* introduces readers to authors they may have never encountered before, but who are doing innovative and important work. In conjunction with the *Notre Dame Re-View*, the on-line companion to the printed magazine, the *Notre Dame Review* engages readers as a community centered in literary rather than commercial concerns, a community we reach out to through critique and commentary as well as aesthetic experien ce." Semiannually. Estab. 1995. Circ. 2,000.

Needs: Experimental, feminist, historical (literary), translations. "We're eclectic." Upcoming theme issues planned. List of upcoming themes or editorial calendar available for SASE. Receives 15 unsolicited fiction mss/month. Accepts 4-5 mss/issue; 10 mss/year. Does not read mss May through August. Publishes ms 6 months after acceptance. Recently published work by Seamus Heaney, Denise Levertov and Czeslaw Milosz. Length: 3,000 words maximum. Publishes short shorts. Also publishes literary criticism and poetry. Sometimes comments on rejected ms.

How to Contact: Send complete ms with cover letter. Include 4-sentence bio. Reports in 3-4 months. Send SASE for response, return of ms, or send a disposable copy of ms. Simultaneous submissions OK. Sample copy for $6.

Payment/Terms: Pays $5-25 and contributor's copies. Pays on publication. Acquires first North American serial rights.

Advice: "We're looking for high quality work that takes on big issues in a literary way. Please read our back issues before submitting."

‡NOW & THEN, (IV), Center for Appalachian Studies and Services, East Tennessee State University, Box 70556, Johnson City TN 37614-0556. (615)929-5348. Contact: Editor. Magazine: 8½×11; 36-52 pages; coated paper and cover stock; illustrations; photographs. Publication focuses on Appalachian culture, present and past. Readers are mostly people in the region involved with Appalachian issues, literature, education." Triannually. Estab. 1984. Circ. 1,000.

Needs: Ethnic, literary, regional, serialized/excerpted novel, prose poem, spiritual and sports. "Absolutely has to relate to Appalachian theme. Can be about adjustment to new environment, themes of leaving and returning, for instance. Nothing unrelated to region." Upcoming themes: "Food" (Spring 1998, deadline November 1, 1997), "Poetry" (Summer 1998, deadline March 1, 1998); "Transportation" (Winter 1998, deadline July 1, 1998). Buys 2-3 mss/issue. Publishes ms 3-4 months after acceptance. Published work by Lee Smith, Pinckney Benedict, Gurney Norman, George Ella Lyon; published new writers within the last year. Length: 3,000 words maximum. Publishes short shorts. Also publishes literary essays, poetry.

How to Contact: Send complete ms with cover letter. Reports in 3 months. Include "information we can use for contributor's note." SASE (or IRC). Simultaneous submissions OK, "but let us know when it has been accepted elsewhere right away." Sample copy for $5. Reviews novels and short story collections.

Payment/Terms: Pays up to $75 per story, contributor's copies.

Terms: Holds copyright.

Advice: "We're emphasizing Appalachian culture, which is not often appreciated because analysts are so busy looking at the trouble of the region. We're doing theme issues. Beware of stereotypes. In a regional publication like this one we get lots of them, both good guys and bad guys: salt of the earth to poor white trash. Sometimes

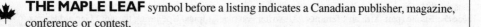

THE MAPLE LEAF symbol before a listing indicates a Canadian publisher, magazine, conference or contest.

we get letters that offer to let us polish up the story. We prefer the author does that him/herself." Send for list of upcoming themes.

*OASIS, Oasis Books, 12 Stevenage Rd., London SW6 6ES United Kingdom. Editor: Ian Robinson. Published 6 times/year. Circ. 400. Publishes usually 1 story/issue.
Needs: "Innovative, experimental fiction." Length: 1,800 words maximum.
Payment/Terms: Pays in copies. Sample copy available for $2.50 check (made payable to Robert Vas Dias) and 4 IRCs.
Advice: "Have a look at a copy of the magazine before submitting."

OASIS, A Literary Magazine, (I, II), P.O. Box 626, Largo FL 33779-0626. (813)449-2186. E-mail: oasislit@a ol.com. Website: http://members.aol.com/wordthis/schvn.htm (or search for "schrapnelvania"). Editor: Neal St-orrs. Magazine: 70 pages. "Literary magazine first, last and always—looking for styles that delight and amaze, that are polished and poised. Next to that, content considerations relatively unimportant—open to all." Quarterly. Estab. 1992. Circ. 500.
Needs: High-quality writing. Receives 150 unsolicited mss/month. Accepts 6 mss/issue; 24 mss/year. Publishes ms 4-6 months after acceptance. Recently published work by Al Masarik and Mark Wisniewski. Publishes 2 new writers/year. Length: no minimum or maximum. Also publishes literary essays and poetry. Occasionally critiques or comments on rejected mss.
How to Contact: Send complete ms with or without a cover letter. Usually reports same day. Send SASE for reply, return of ms or send a disposable copy of ms. Simultaneous, reprint and electronic (e-mail) submissions OK. Sample copy for $6.50. Fiction guidelines for #10 SASE.
Payment/Terms: Pays $15-30 and 1 contributor's copy on publication for first rights.
Advice: "If you want to write good stories, read good stories. Cultivate the critical ability to recognize what makes a story original and true to itself."

OATMEAL & POETRY, Wholesome Nutrition From The Heart, (I, II), Voyager Publishing, P.O. Box 2215, Stillwater MN 55082. (612)578-9589. Editor: Demitra Flanagan. Magazine: 8½×11; 44 pages; bond paper; parchment cover stock; illustrations and photos. "*Oatmeal & Poetry* is a forum for new and growing writers. We publish short stories, articles and poetry that are tasteful, well written and entertaining. Our philosophy is stated in our subtitle 'wholesome nutrition—from the heart.' Our intended audience includes all persons who appreciate well-crafted and well-written stories, shorts, articles, editorials and poetry that deal with both the dark and light side of life while maintaining integrity." Quarterly. Estab. 1994. Circ. 500. "A nominal fee of $2/story or article and $1/poem is charged to offset costs of cash awards granted in each issue."
Needs: Adventure (10-12 years), condensed/excerpted novel, ethnic/multicultural, fantasy (children's, science), historical, humor/satire, literary, mainstream/contemporary, mystery/suspense (amateur sleuth, cozy, police proce-dural, private eye/hardboiled, romantic suspense), psychic/supernatural/occult, regional, religious/inspirational, romance (contemporary, futuristic/time travel, gothic, historical), science fiction, senior citizen/retirement, west-erns (frontier, traditional), young adult/teen (adventure, mystery, romance). "No gay/lesbian plots, explicit sex, erotica, pornography or excessive violence. This is a family magazine. Our magazine generally focuses on the changing seasons, the holidays and how we live through them all." List of upcoming themes available for SASE. Publishes annual special fiction issue or anthology. Receives 15-20 unsolicited mss/month. Accepts 4-6 mss/issue; 24 mss/year. Publishes ms 3-6 months after acceptance. Recently published work by Don Porter, Anne Clayton Fifer and Carolyn Vietenheimer. Publishes 5-10 new writers/year. Length: 1,200-1,500 words average; 500 words minimum; 2,000 words maximum. Publishes short shorts. Also publishes literary essays, literary criticism and poetry. Often critiques or comments on rejected mss.
How to Contact: "First, obtain our complete guidelines, then submit accordingly." Include estimated word count, half-page bio and social security number. "We charge a $2 reading fee which is used to pay an editor's choice award each issue." Reports in 1-2 months on queries. Send SASE for reply, send a disposable copy of ms. No simultaneous submissions. Reprints OK. Query for sample copy price. Fiction guidelines for #10 SASE.
Payment/Terms: Pays contributor's copies on publication; additional copies for $5.50. Acquires first rights or one-time rights. Sends galleys to author. Sponsors contests. Send #10 SASE for guidelines and information on cash prizes for short story and article contests (also poetry and anthology).
Advice: "I must be grabbed in the first paragraph. Stories must be well woven, structured, grammatically correct and have a strong ending. Mostly, make me see, hear, smell and feel the story. Stop trying to be clever—it insults the reader—if you're a clever writer, it will be reflected in the finished product."

OBSIDIAN II: BLACK LITERATURE IN REVIEW, (II, IV), Dept. of English, North Carolina State Univer-sity, Raleigh NC 27695-8105. (919)515-4153. E-mail: krsassan@unity.ncsu.edu. Editor: Afaa M. Weaver. Fiction Editor: Susie R. Powell. Magazine: 6×9; 130 pages. "Creative works in English by black writers, scholarly critical studies by all writers on black literature in English." Published 2 times/year (spring/summer, fall/winter). Estab. 1975. Circ. 500.
Needs: Ethnic (pan-African), feminist. All writers on black topics. Upcoming theme: "Gerrald Barrax." Accepts 7-9 mss/year. Recently published work by Victor Blue, Sean Henry, Lenard D. Moore, Yvonne Jackson, Carolyn Beard Whitlow and Jacki Shelton Green. Published new writers within the last year. Length: 1,500-10,000 words.

How to Contact: Send complete ms in duplicate with SASE. Reports in 3 months. Publishes ms an average of 4-6 months after acceptance. Sample copy for $6.
Payment/Terms: Pays in contributor's copies. Acquires one-time rights. Sponsors contests occasionally; guidelines published in magazine.

‡THE OHIO REVIEW, (II), 209C Ellis Hall, Ohio University, Athens OH 45701-2979. (614)593-1900. Fax: (614)593-2818. Editor: Wayne Dodd. Assistant Editor: Robert Kinsley. Magazine: 6×9; 200 pages; illustrations on cover. "We attempt to publish the best poetry and fiction written today. For a mainly literary audience." Semiannually. Estab. 1971. Circ. 3,000.
Needs: Contemporary, experimental, literary. "We lean toward contemporary on all subjects." Receives 150-200 unsolicited fiction mss/month. Accepts 5 mss/issue. Does not read mss June 1-September 15. Publishes ms 6 months after acceptance. Also publishes poetry. Sometimes critiques rejected mss and/or recommends other markets.
How to Contact: Query first or send complete ms with cover letter. Reports in 6 weeks. SASE. Sample copy for $6. Fiction guidelines for #10 SASE.
Payment/Terms: Pays $5/page, free subscription to magazine and 2 contributor's copies on publication for first North American serial rights. Sends galleys to author.
Advice: "We feel the short story is an important part of the contemporary writing field and value it highly. Read a copy of our publication to see if your fiction is of the same quality. So often people send us work that simply doesn't fit our needs."

OLD CROW REVIEW, (I, II), FKB Press, P.O.Box 403, Easthampton MA 01027-0403. Editor: John Gibney. Magazine: 5½×8½; 100 pages; 20 lb. paper; 90 lb. cover stock; illustrations and photos. Semiannually. Estab. 1991. Circ. 500.
 ● William Monahan's "Experiments in Vacoo" received a *Pushcart* Prize.
Needs: Erotica, experimental, literary, mainstream/contemporary, psychic/supernatural/occult, regional, translations. Receives 400-500 unsolicited mss/month. Accepts 3-5 mss/issue; 6-10 mss/year. Publishes ms 1-3 months after acceptance. Agented fiction 25%. Recently published work by William Monahan, Michael Ventura and Elizabeth Haliwell-Borden. Length: 3,000 words average; 6,000 words maximum. Publishes short shorts. Also publishes literary essays, literary criticism and poetry.
How to Contact: Send complete ms with a cover letter. Should include estimated word count, bio (2-5 sentences) and list of publications. Reports in 1 month on queries; 2 months on mss. Send SASE for reply, return of ms or send a disposable copy of ms. Simultaneous and reprint submissions OK. Sample copy for $5; make check payable to John Gibney. Fiction guidelines for #10 SASE.
Payment/Terms: Pays 1 contributor's copy; additional copies for $5.
Advice: "A piece must seem true to us. If it strikes us as a truth we never even suspected, we build an issue around it. Visions, or fragments of visions, of a new myth emerging at the millennial end are welcome. We haven't seen enough writers taking risks with their stories. Avoid sending pieces which sound just like somebody else's."

THE OLD RED KIMONO, (I, II), Floyd College, Box 1864, Rome GA 30162-1864. (706)295-6363. (706)295-6312. Editor: Jeff Mack. Magazine: 8×11; 65-70 pages; white offset paper; 10 pt. board cover stock. Annually. Estab. 1972. Circ. 1,500.
Needs: Literary. "We will consider good fiction regardless of category." No children's fiction. Receives 200 mss/month. Accepts 3-5 mss/issue. Does not read mss March 1 through September 30. "Issue out in May every year." Recently published work by Ruth Moon Kempher, Ken Anderson, Adam Stanley and Gregg Johnson. Length: 2,500 words maximum. Publishes short shorts. Also publishes poetry.
How to Contact: Send complete ms with cover letter. Reports in 2-4 weeks on queries; 2-3 months on mss. SASE. Simultaneous submissions OK, but "we would like to be told." Sample copy for $3. Fiction guidelines for #10 SASE.
Payment/Terms: Pays 2 contributor's copies. Acquires first rights.

ONIONHEAD, (II), Literary Quarterly, Arts on the Park, Inc., 115 N. Kentucky Ave., Lakeland FL 33801-5044. (941)680-2787. Co-Editors: Susan Crawford and Brenda J. Patterson. Magazine: digest-sized; 40 pages; 20 lb. bond; glossy card cover. "Provocative political, social and cultural observations and hypotheses for a literary audience—an open-minded audience." Estab. 1989. Circ. 250.
Needs: Contemporary, ethnic, experimental, feminist, gay, humor/satire, lesbian, literary, prose poem, regional. "*Onionhead* focuses on provocative political, social and cultural observations and hypotheses. Must have a universal point (international)." Publishes short fiction in each issue. Receives 100-150 unsolicited mss/month. Acquires approximately 28 mss/issue; 100 mss (these numbers include poetry, short prose and essays)/year. Publishes ms within 18 months of acceptance. Recently published work by Mark Ford, Paul F. Wolf and Kay Rhoads. Publishes new writers. Length: 2,500 words average; 3,000 words maximum. Publishes short shorts. Also publishes poetry.
How to Contact: Send complete ms with cover letter that includes brief bio and SASE. Reports in 3 weeks

on queries; 2 months on mss. No simultaneous submissions. Sample copy for $3 postpaid. Fiction guidelines for #10 SASE.

Payment/Terms: Pays in contributor's copy. Charge for extras. Acquires first North American serial rights.

Advice: "Review a sample copy of *Onionhead* and remember *literary quality* is the prime criterion. Avoid heavy-handed approaches to social commentary—be subtle, not didactic. Follow the guidelines and send your best work."

ORACLE STORY, (I, II), Rising Star Publishers, 2105 Amherst Rd., Hyattsville MD 20783-2105. (301)422-2665. Fax: (301)422-2720. Editorial Director: Obi H. Ekwonna. Magazine: 5½×8½; 38 pages; white bond paper; 60 lb. Ibs cover. "Didactic well-made stories; basically adults and general public (mass market)." Quarterly. Estab. 1993. Circ. 500.

• *Oracle Story* is a member of the Association of African Writers. The editors are interested in all genres of fiction but with an African-cultural slant.

Needs: Condensed/excerpted novel, ethnic/multicultural, folklore (African), historical, horror, humor/satire, literary, mainstream/contemporary, mystery/suspense (romantic suspense), serialized novel, young adult/teen (horror and mystery). "No erotic, gay or lesbian writings." List of upcoming themes available for SASE. Publishes annual special fiction issue or anthology. Receives 60 unsolicited mss/month. Accepts 8 mss/issue; 26 mss/year. Publishes ms 6-12 months after acceptance. Recently published work by Branley Allan Branson, Dell R. Lipscomb, Stephanie Stocking, Robert Wexelblatt and Anthony C. Spence. Publishes 20 new writers/year. Length: "not more than 20 typewritten pages." Publishes short shorts. Also publishes literary essays, literary criticism and poetry. Sometimes critiques or comments on rejected mss.

How to Contact: Send complete ms with a cover letter. Include bio with SASE. Reports in 4-6 weeks. SASE for reply or return of ms. No simultaneous submissions. Electronic submissions OK (disks in WordPerfect 5.1, IBM readable format). Sample copy for $5 plus $1.50 postage. Fiction guidelines for SASE. Reviews novels and short story collections.

Payment/Terms: Pays contributor's copy. Acquires first North American seial rights.

Advice: Looks for work that is "well made, well written, and has good language. Take grammar classes." Especially interested in African folklore.

‡ORANGE COAST REVIEW, (II), Dept. of English, 2701 Fairview Rd., Orange Coast College, Costa Mesa CA 92628-5005. (714)432-5043. Advisor: Raymond Obstfeld. Fiction Editor: Angela Powell. Editors change every 6 months. Magazine: 5½×8½; 70 pages; 60 lb. paper; medium/heavy cover; illustrations and photos. "We look for quality, of course. The genre, style, and format take second place to intelligence and depth. Our largest audience consists of students and writers." Annually. Estab. 1990. Circ. 750.

Needs: Condensed novel, ethnic/multicultural, experimental, feminist, gay, humor/satire, lesbian, literary, mainstream/contemporary, serialized novel, translations. No mainstream short fiction and poetry. Receives 100 unsolicited mss/month. Accepts 5-10 mss/issue. Mss accepted December to April only. Publishes ms 6 months after acceptance. Published work by Jo-Ann Mapson, Meredith Moore and Mark Seyi. Length: Open. Publishes short shorts. Also publishes literary essays, poetry. Sometimes critiques or comments on rejected mss.

How to Contact: Send complete ms with a cover letter. Should include estimated word count, short paragraph bio, list of publications with submission. Reports in 2-3 weeks on queries; 2-3 month on mss. SASE for return ms. Simultaneous submissions OK. Sample copy for $4. Fiction guidelines for #10 SASE.

Payment/Terms: Pays $1/published page fiction, 2 contributor's copies on publication for one-time rights.

Advice: "A manuscript stands out when it actually has a beginning, middle and end; a coherent theme that isn't vague or preachy; and characters that come to life. Check your grammar, punctuation, and spelling—three times. If you don't care about the easy stuff, why should we expect you to have cared about the story or poem. Never single space." Looks for "writing that involves their own voice or style, not Raymond Carver's or whoever else impresses them."

OTHER VOICES, (I, II), The University of Illinois at Chicago, Dept. of English (M/C 162), 601 S. Morgan St., Chicago IL 60607. (312)413-2209. Editors: Lois Hauselman, Ruth Canji and Tina Peano. Magazine: 5⅞×9; 168-205 pages; 60 lb. paper; coated cover stock; occasional photos. "Original, fresh, diverse stories and novel excerpts" for literate adults. Semiannually. Estab. 1985. Circ. 1,500.

• *Other Voices* has received 15 Illinois Arts Council Awards since it began.

Needs: Contemporary, excerpted novel, experimental, humor/satire and literary. No taboos, except ineptitude and murkiness. No fantasy, horror, juvenile, psychic/occult. Receives 300 unsolicited fiction mss/month. Accepts 20-23 mss/issue. Recently published work by G.K. Wuvori, Carol Goodman and Keith Dixon. Publishes new writers. Length: 4,000 words average; 5,000 words maximum.

How to Contact: Send ms with SASE October 1 to April 1 only. Mss received during non-reading period are returned unread. Cover letters "should be brief and list previous publications. Also, list title of submission. Most beginners' letters try to 'explain' the story—a big mistake." Simultaneous submissions OK. Reports in 10-12 weeks on mss. Sample copy for $7 (includes postage). Fiction guidelines for #10 SASE.

Payment/Terms: Pays in contributor's copies and modest cash gratuity. Acquires one-time rights.

Advice: "There are so *few* markets for *quality* fiction! We—by publishing 40-45 stories a year—provide new and established writers a forum for their work. Send us your best voice, your best work, your best best."

OUT OF THE CRADLE, An Uncommon Reader, (I, II), P.O. Box 129, South Paris ME 04281-0129. (207)743-6738. Editor: Jeanette Baldridge. Magazine: 8½×11; 48-56 pages; 60 lb. paper; heavy cover stock; illustrations; photos. "*OOTC* has two goals. One is to provide exposure for new writers. Each issue features at least one previously unpublished writer, balancing the stronger work of experienced writers. The second purpose is to provide an uncommon reader for a diverse audience." Quarterly. Estab. 1995. Circ. 700. Member Maine Writers and Publishers Association (MWPA).

Needs: Adventure, ethnic/multicultural, feminist, gay, historical, lesbian, literary, mainstream/contemporary. "No pornography, violence, political propaganda, religious dogma, science fiction or fantasy." Receives 50-100 unsolicited mss/month. Accepts 12-15 mss/issue; 48 mss/year. Publishes ms 1 year after acceptance. Recently published work by David Ackley, Carole Bellacera, Ric B. Edberg and Irving Greenfield. Length: 2,500-3,000 words average; 1,000 words minimum; 5,000 words maximum. Publishes short shorts. Also publishes poetry and creative nonfiction in the form of personal narratives. Often critiques or comments on rejected mss.

How to Contact: Send complete ms with a cover letter. "I like a cover letter that tells me about the writer, not the story which must stand on its own." Include estimated word count, 1-paragraph bio and list of publications. Reports in 6 months on mss. Send SASE for reply, return of ms or send a disposable copy of ms. Simultaneous submissions and reprints OK. Sample copy for $6. Fiction guidelines for #10 SASE.

Payment/Terms: Pays 2 contributor's copies; additional copies for $4. Pays on publication. Acquires one-time rights. Sends galleys to author "if I've made significant changes." Sponsors contests; see notification in magazine.

Advice: "Good writing is a necessity, but not enough in itself. I like stories that keep me interested. The ending doesn't have to be happy, but I do want closure, to feel satisfied and changed (more aware or enlightened) by having read the story. I'm bored with pointlessness and stories that leave the reader hanging. I want well-crafted, high-quality stories that are original in approach and written in a believable voice. Generally I am looking for stories that are an honest portrayal of the human condition. I would like to see more stories that expose prejudice and injustice and show how various people cope with these situations. Aspiring writers should not try to be trendy. Learn to develop your own voice. Pay attention to your craft and strive constantly to develop it by reading and studying other writers, and by getting feedback on your work."

OUTERBRIDGE, (II), English 25-28, The College of Staten Island (CUNY), 2800 Victory Blvd., Staten Island NY 10314. (718)982-3651. Editor: Charlotte Alexander. Magazine: 5½×8½; approximately 110 pages; 60 lb. white offset paper; 65 lb. cover stock. "We are a national literary magazine publishing mostly fiction and poetry. To date, we have had several special focus issues (the 'urban' and the 'rural' experience, 'Southern,' 'childhood,' 'nature and the environment,' 'animals'). For anyone with enough interest in literature to look for writing of quality and writers on the contemporary scene who deserve attention. There probably is a growing circuit of writers, some academics, reading us by recommendations." Annually. Estab. 1975. Circ. 500-700.

Needs: Literary. "No *Reader's Digest* style; that is, very popularly oriented. We like to do interdisciplinary features, e.g., literature and music, literature and science and literature and the natural world." Accepts 8-10 mss/year. Does not read in July or August. Published work by Walter MacDonald, Patricia Ver Ellen and Wally Swist. Published new writers within the last year. Length: 10-25 pages. Also publishes poetry. Sometimes recommends other markets.

How to Contact: Query. Send complete ms with cover letter. "Don't talk too much, 'explain' the work, or act apologetic or arrogant. If published, tell where, with a brief bio." SASE (or IRC). Reports in 8-10 weeks on queries and mss. No multiple submissions. Sample copy for $6 for annual issue.

Payment/Terms: Pays 2 contributor's copies. Charges ½ price of current issue for extras to its authors. Acquires one-time rights. Requests credits for further publication of material used by *OB*.

Advice: "Read our publication first. Don't send out blindly; get some idea of what the magazine might want. A *short* personal note with biography is appreciated. Competition is keen. Read an eclectic mix of classic and contemporary literature. Beware of untransformed autobiography, but *everything* in one's experience contributes."

‡OWEN WISTER REVIEW, (II), ASUW Student Publications Board, P.O. Box 3625, University of Wyoming, Laramie WY 82071. (307)766-3819. Fax: (307)766-4027. Fiction Editors: "Fiction Selection Committee." Editors change each year, contact selection committee. Magazine: 6×9; 92 pages; 60 lb. matte paper; 80 lb. glossy cover; illustrations; photographs. "Though we are a university publication, our audience is wider than just an academic community." Semiannually. Estab. 1978. Circ. 500.

● *Owen Wister Review* has won numerous awards and honors far surpassing many student-run publications. Nine poems from *OWR* were nominated for inclusion in the *Pushcart Prize* anthology (1992-1993). The magazine received Best of Show award from the Associated Collegiate Press/College Media Advisors and six individual Gold Circle Awards from the Columbia Scholastic Press Association.

Needs: Ethnic/multicultural, experimental, humor/satire, literary, translations. No science fiction or fantasy. Plans special fiction issue or anthology. Receives 12-15 unsolicited mss. Acquires 3 mss/issue; 6-8 mss/year. "Summer months are generally down time for *OWR*." Publishes ms 2-3 months after acceptance. Published work by Mark Jenkins, John Bennet, the Kunstwaffen art collaborative, Sue Thornton. Length: 1,300 words average; 7,500 words maximum. Publishes short shorts. Also publishes literary essays, literary criticism and poetry.

How to Contact: Send complete ms with cover letter. Should include bio, list of publications. Reports in 2-3 weeks on queries; 2-3 months on mss. Send SASE for reply, return of ms or send disposable copy of the ms. Sample copy for $5. Free fiction guidelines.

Payment/Terms: Pays 1 contributor's copy. 10% off additional copies. Acquires one-time rights.

Advice: "Our committee likes to hear a fresh voice. Experimental fiction is encouraged. Consistency is very important. We look for and encourage young writers but insist on quality. We want to be hooked and not let go; regardless of subject matter, the approach should be compelling and relentless."

THE OXFORD AMERICAN, The Southern Magazine of Good Writing, (II), P.O. Box 1156, Oxford MS 38655. (601)236-1836. Editor: Marc Smirnoff. Magazine: 8½×11; 100 pages; glossy paper; glossy cover; illustrations and photos. Bimonthly. Estab. 1992. Circ. 25,000.

Needs: Regional (Southern); stories set in the South. Published work by Lewis Nordan, Julia Reed, Florence King and Tony Earley. Also publishes literary essays. Sometimes critiques or comments on rejected mss.

How to Contact: Send complete ms. Send SASE for reply, return of ms or send a disposable copy of ms. No simultaneous submissions. Sample copy for $4.50. "We review Southern novels or short story collections only."

Payment/Terms: Pays $100 minimum on publication for first rights; prices vary.

Advice: "I know you've heard it before—but we appreciate those writers who try to get into the spirit of the magazine which they can best accomplish by being familiar with it."

OXFORD MAGAZINE, (II), Bachelor Hall, Miami University, Oxford OH 45056. (513)529-1954 or 529-5221. Editor: Bret Anthony Johnston. Editors change every year. Send submissions to "Fiction Editor." Magazine: 6×9; 85-100 pages; illustrations. Annually. Estab. 1985. Circ. 500-1,000.

● *Oxford* has been awarded two Pushcart Prizes.

Needs: Literary, ethnic, experimental, humor/satire, feminist, gay/lesbian, translations. Receives 50-60 unsolicited mss/month. May not read mss May 1 through Sepetember 4. Published work by Tony Earley and Ann Harleman. Published new writers within the last year. Length: 2,000-4,000 words average. "We will accept long fiction (over 6,000 words) only in cases of exceptional quality." Publishes short shorts. Also publishes literary essays, literary criticism, poetry.

How to Contact: Send complete ms with cover letter, which should include a short bio or interesting information. Simultaneous submissions OK, if notified. Reports in 3-5 months, depending upon time of submissions; mss received after January 1 will be held over for following year's issue. SASE. Sample copy for $5.

Payment/Terms: Pays in contributor's copies. Acquires one-time rights.

Advice: "*Oxford Magazine* is looking for humbly vivid fiction; that is to say, fiction that illuminates, which creates and inhabits an honest, carefully rendered reality populated by believable, three-dimensional characters. We see far too many glib, sitcom-ish stories, too many saccharine hospital tales, too many brand-name-laden records of GenX angst, too many stories which are really overeager European travelogues. Send us stories that are unique; we want fiction no one else but you could possibly have written."

OXYGEN, A Spirited Literary Magazine, (II), 535 Geary St., #1010, San Francisco CA 94102. (415)776-9681. Editor/Publisher: Richard Hack. Magazine: 5½×8½; 72 pages; 60 lb. vellum paper; glossy cover, perfect-bound. "We are an eclectic, community-spirited magazine looking for vivid, imaginative stories of significance. We welcome fiction and poetry in modes realistic, surreal, expressionist, devotional, erotic, satiric, and invective. We value modern writers like Algren, Böll, H. Miller and Naylor." Publishes 1-2 issues/year. Estab. 1991. Circ. 350.

Needs: Stories, sketches, tales, novel excerpts. "Nothing overly commercial, insincere, or mocking, though we enjoy hard satire." Receives 100 unsolicited mss/month. Accepts 5-6 mss/issue; 10-12 mss/year. Publishes ms up to 6 months after acceptance. Length: 500-7,500 words. Also publishes poetry, occasional essays and reviews.

How to Contact: Send complete ms with optional cover letter, bio and list of publications. Reports in 2-8 weeks. Send SASE for reply or return of ms. Simultaneous submissions OK. Sample copy for $5. Fiction guidelines for #10 SASE.

Payment/Terms: Pays 2 contributor's copies. All rights revert to contributors.

Advice: "Efficiency counts, too: delve, don't vacillate. A thicket of non-profound, tone-deaf, superficial academic qualifications will choke off speech and kill feeling and event before they bloom. No simple journalism, column fluff, first-person experiences, diary entries, or stand-up comedy. We are open to many POVs, but we hope for meaningful writing that is community-spirited, rich and suggestive, a style with a nice feel to it. Does it believe in something, does it love life? Or satirize injustice and abuse? What kind of personal quality does it demonstrate?"

‡OYSTER BOY REVIEW OF FICTION AND POETRY, (I, II), 103B Hanna Street, Carrboro NC 27510. Fax: (919)967-1412. E-mail: oyster-boy@sunsite.unc.edu. Website: http://sunsite.unc.edu/ob. Editors: Damon Sauve and Chad Driscoll. Electronic and print magazine. "An independent literary magazine of poetry and fiction published in North Carolina in print and electronic form. We're interested in the under-rated, the ignored, the misunderstood, and the varietal. We'll make some mistakes. The editors tend to select experimental and traditional narrative fiction. Our audience tends to be young, unpublished writers or writers of considerable talent who have published in the bigger little magazines but like the harder literary edge *Oyster Boy* promotes."

Needs: "Fiction that revolves around characters in conflict with themselves or each other; a plot that has a beginning, a middle, and an end; a narrative with a strong moral center (not necessarily 'moralistic'); a story with a satisfying resolution to the conflict; and an ethereal something that contributes to the mystery of a question, but does not necessarily seek or contrive to answer it." No genre fiction. Recently published work by Kevin McGowin, Lucy Harrison, Thomas Rain Crowe, Michael McNeilley and Pamela Patton. Publishes 15 new writers/year.

How to Contact: Electronic and traditional submissions accepted. "E-mail submissions should be sent as the body-text of the e-mail message, or as an attached ASCII-text file. Attached files of Word 5.1 or later versions are acceptable but not preferred (please indicate version and/or application)."

Advice: "Keep writing, keep submitting, keep revising."

PACIFIC COAST JOURNAL, (I, II), French Bread Publications, P.O. Box 23865, San Jose CA 95153-3868. E-mail: paccoastj@juno.com. Website: http://www.bjt.net/~stgraham (includes guidelines). Editor: Stillson Graham. Fiction Editor: Stephanie Kylkis. Magazine: 5½ × 8½; 56 pages; 20 lb. paper; 67 lb. cover; illustrations; b&w photos. "Slight focus toward Western North America/Pacific Rim." Quarterly (or "whenever we have enough money"). Estab. 1992. Circ. 200.

Needs: Ethnic/multicultural, experimental, feminist, historical, humor/satire, literary, science fiction (soft/sociological, magical realism). Receives 30-40 unsolicited mss/month. Accepts 3-4 mss/issue; 10-12 mss/year. Publishes ms 6-18 months after acceptance. Recently published work by Cris Mazza, Rob Offen and Richard Kostelanetz. Length: 2,500 words preferred; 4,000 words maximum. Publishes short shorts. Also publishes literary essays and poetry. Sometimes critiques or comments on rejected mss. Sponsors contest. Send SASE for details.

How to Contact: Send complete ms with a cover letter. Include 3 other publication titles that are recommended as good for writers. Reports in 2-4 months. Send SASE for reply, return of ms or send a disposable copy of ms. Simultaneous, reprint and electronic submissions OK (Mac or IBM disks or e-mail). Sample copy for $2.50, 6 × 9 SASE. Reviews novels and short story collections.

Payment/Terms: Pays 1 contributor's copy. Acquires one-time rights.

Advice: "We tend to comment more on a story not accepted for publication when an e-mail address is provided as the SASE. Don't worry about trying to 'say' something. Just write. There are very few quality literary magazines that are not backed by big institutions. We don't have those kinds of resources so publishing anything is a struggle. We have to make each issue count."

‡PACIFIC REVIEW, (II), Dept. of English and Comparative Lit., San Diego State University, San Diego CA 92182-0295. (619)594-5443. Contact: Garrick Davis, editor. Magazine: 6 × 9; 75-100 pages; book stock paper; paper back, extra heavy cover stock; illustrations, photos. "There is no designated theme. We publish high-quality fiction, poetry, and familiar essays: we accept one in a hundred stories and never print more than 3 stories in one issue, so fiction is not used as filler." Biannual. Estab. 1973. Circ. 1,000.

Needs: "We do not restrict or limit our fiction in any way other than quality. We are interested in all fiction, from the very traditional to the highly experimental. Acceptance is determined by the quality of submissions." Upcoming themes: "We are accepting essays, pseudo-essays, fiction, ad poetry concerning any aspect of the Unabomber, his manifesto, or the media's role in the malee." Does not read June-August. Published work by Jay Atkinson and Harold Jaffe. Published new writers within the last year. Length: 4,000 words max. Publishes short shorts.

How to Contact: Send original ms with SASE. No unsolicited submissions. Reports in 3-5 months on mss. Sample copy for $3.

Payment/Terms: 1 contributor's copy. "First serial rights are *Pacific Review*'s. All other rights revert to author."

Advice: "We accept work that has clearly been composed in the late twentieth century. That is, the author is aware of the differences between this particular era and every other. In an age radically altered by science, most of the stories we receive look like antiques or unconvincing evasions."

PAINTED BRIDE QUARTERLY, (II), Painted Bride Art Center, 230 Vine St., Philadelphia PA 19106. (215)925-9914. Website: http://www.libertynet.org/pbq~/. Fiction Editor: Kathy Volk-Miller. Literary magazine: 6 × 9; 96-100 pages; illustrations; photos. Quarterly. Estab. 1973. Circ. 1,000.

Needs: Contemporary, ethnic, experimental, feminist, gay, lesbian, literary, prose poem and translations. Recently published work by Lisa Borders, Jeannie Tietja, Kevin Miller, Mark LaMonda and Jennifer Moses. Published new writers within the last year. Length: 3,000 words average; 5,000 words maximum. Publishes short shorts. Also publishes literary essays, literary criticism, poetry. Occasionally critiques rejected mss.

How to Contact: Send complete ms. Reports in 6 months. SASE. Sample copy for $6. Reviews novels and short story collections. Send books to editor.

Payment/Terms: Pays $5/accepted piece and 1 contributor's copy, 1 year free subscription, 50% off additional copies. Acquires first North American serial rights.

Advice: Looks for "freshness of idea incorporated with high-quality writing. We receive an awful lot of nicely written work with worn-out plots. We want quality in whatever—we hold experimental work to as strict standards as anything else. Many of our readers write fiction; most of them enjoy a good reading. We hope to be an outlet for quality. A good story gives, first, enjoyment to the reader. We've seen a good many of them lately, and we've published the best of them."

PALACE CORBIE, (I, II, IV), Merrimack Books, P.O. Box 83514, Lincoln NE 68501-3514. E-mail: we45927@ navix.net. Website: http://www.para-net.com/~palace_corbie (includes writer's guidelines). Editor: Wayne Edwards. Perfect-bound trade paperback: 5½×8½; 180-300 pages; 60 lb. offset paper; illustrations. An annual anthology of fiction and poetry. Estab. 1989. Circ. 1,000.
Needs: Fantasy (dark), horror, psychic/supernatural/occult, science fiction. Publishes ms up to 1 year after acceptance. Agented fiction 5%. Published work by Steve Rasnic Tein, Elizabeth Eugstrom, Douglas Clegg and Yvonne Navarro. Length: 2,000 words minimum; 8,000 words maximum.
How to Contact: Send complete ms. Include estimated word count. Reports in 1 week. Send SASE for reply. No simultaneous submissions. Sample copy for $12.95. Fiction guidelines for #10 SAE and 1 first-class stamp.
Payment/Terms: Variable. Sends galleys to author.
Advice: Looks for "psychologically disturbing stories with high emotional impact."

PALO ALTO REVIEW, A Journal of Ideas, (I, II), Palo Alto College, 1400 W. Villaret, San Antonio TX 78224. (210)921-5255 (or 921-5017). Fax: (210)921-5008. E-mail: eshull@accdum.aced.edu or brichmon@accd um.accd.edu. Editors: Bob Richmond and Ellen Shull. Magazine: 8½×11; 60 pages; 60 lb. natural white paper (50% recycled); illustrations and photographs. "Not too experimental nor excessively avant-garde, just good stories (for fiction). Ideas are what we are after. We are interested in connecting the college and the community. We would hope that those who attempt these connections will choose startling topics and interesting angles with which to investigate the length and breadth of the teaching/learning spectrum." Semiannually (spring and fall). Estab. 1992. Circ. 500-600.
Needs: Adventure, ethnic/multicultural, experimental, fantasy, feminist, historical, humor/satire, literary, mainstream/contemporary, mystery/suspense, regional, romance, science fiction, translations, westerns. Upcoming themes: "Family" (December 1997); "Autobiography" (July 1998). Upcoming themes available for SASE. Receives 100-150 unsolicited mss/month. Accepts 2-4 mss/issue; 4-8 mss/year. Does not read mss March-April and October-November when putting out each issue. Publishes ms 2-15 months after acceptance. Published work by Gayle Silbert, Naomi Chase, Kenneth Emberly, C.J. Hannah, Tom Juvik, Kassie Fleisher and Paul Perry. Length: 5,000 words maximum. Publishes short shorts. Also publishes articles, interviews, literary essays, literary criticism, poetry. Always critiques or comments on rejected mss.
How to Contact: Send complete ms with a cover letter. "Request sample copy and guidelines." Include brief bio and brief list of publications. Reports in 3-4 months. Send SASE for reply, return of ms or send a disposable copy of ms. Simultaneous and electronic (Macintosh disk) submissions OK. Sample copy for $5. Fiction guidelines for #10 SASE.
Payment/Terms: Pays 2 contributor's copies; additional copies for $5. Acquires first North American serial rights.
Advice: "Good short stories have interesting characters confronted by a dilemma working toward a solution. So often what we get is 'a moment in time,' not a story. Generally, the characters are interesting because the readers can identify with them and know much about them. Edit judiciously. Cut out extraneous verbiage. Set up a choice that has to be made. Then create tension—who wants what and why they can't have it."

PANGOLIN PAPERS, (II), Turtle Press, P.O. Box 241, Nordland WA 98358. (360)385-3626. E-mail: trtlbluf@ olympus.net. Editor: Pat Britt. Magazine: 5½×8½; 120 pages; 24 lb. paper; 80 lb. cover. "Best quality literary fiction for an informed audience." Triannually. Estab. 1994. Circ. 500.
Needs: Condensed/excerpted novel, experimental, humor/satire, literary, translations. No "genre such as romance or science fiction." Plans to publish special fiction issues or anthologies in the future. Receives 20 unsolicited mss/month. Accepts 7-10 mss/issue; 20-30 mss/year. Does not read mss in July and August. Publishes ms 4-12 months after acceptance. Agented fiction 10%. Published work by Jack Nisbet and Barry Gifford. Length: 3,500 words average; 100 words minimum; 7,000 words maximum. Publishes short shorts. Length: 400 words. Also publishes literary essays. Sometimes critiques or comments on rejected mss.
How to Contact: Send complete ms with a cover letter. Include estimated word count and short bio. Reports in 2 weeks on queries; 2 months on mss. Send SASE for reply, return of ms or send a disposable copy of ms. No simultaneous submissions. Electronic and reprint submissions OK. Sample copy for $5.95 and $1 postage. Fiction guidelines for #10 SAE.
Payment/Terms: Pays 2 contributor's copies. Offers annual $200 prize for best story. Acquires first North American serial rights. Sometimes sends galleys to author.
Advice: "We are looking for original voices. Follow the rules and be honest in your work."

‡THE PANUS INDEX, (IV), BGB Press, 159 King St., Northampton MA 01060. (413)584-4776. Fax: (413)584-5674. E-mail: stout@javanet.com. Editors: Vincent Bator and Bill Rogers. Magazine: 5½×8½; 120-

---

SENDING TO A COUNTRY other than your own? Be sure to send International Reply Coupons instead of stamps for replies or return of your manuscript.

138 pages; offset/vellum paper; illustrations and photos. "We encourage writers to submit that are working towards the preservation of language and aesthetics. We encourage writers who are anachronistic in their writing, as well as exploring literature's past achievements." Quarterly. Estab. 1996. Circ. 200.

Needs: Condensed/Excerpted Novel, historical, humor/satire, literary, translations. List of upcoming themes available for SASE. Publishes special fiction issues or anthologies. Receives 60-75 mss/month. Accepts 5-10 mss/issue; 25-35 mss/year. Publishes ms 3-4 monthsafter acceptance. Recently published work by Dennis Saleh, Leslie Hedley Wolf, Mark Axelrod, Doug Boiling, Hugh Fox and Richard Gessner. Length: 10,000 words average; no maximum. "We prefer longer pieces." Also publishes literary essays, literary criticism and poetry. Often critiques or comments on rejected mss.

How to Contact: Query with SASE. Include bio. Reports on queries in 2 weeks. Send SASE for reply or send disposable copy of ms. Simultaneous, reprint and disk submissions OK. Sample copy for $5. Fiction guidelines for #10 SASE. Reviews novel and short story collections. Send books to editor.

Payment/Terms: Pays 1 contributor's copy for one-time rights; additional copies $3.

Advice: "To stand out, the writer must have a command of literature history and original non-formulaic ideas."

✤**PAPERPLATES, a magazine for fifty readers," (II)**, Perkolator Kommunikation, 19 Kenwood Ave., Toronto, Ontario M6C 2R8 Canada. (416)651-2551. Fax: (416)651-2910. E-mail: paperplates@perkolator.com. Editor: Bernard Kelly. Magazine: 8½×11; 48 pages; recycled paper; illustrations and photos. Published 2-3 times/year. Estab. 1990. Circ. 500. Member of Toronto Small Press Group and Canadian Magazine Publishers Association.

Needs: Condensed/excerpted novel, ethnic/multicultural, feminist, gay, lesbian, literary, mainstream/contemporary, translations. "No science fiction, fantasy or horror." Receives 2-3 unsolicited mss/month. Accepts 2-3 mss/issue; 6-9 mss/year. Publishes ms 6-8 months after acceptance. Published work by Celia Lottridge, C.J. Lockett, Deirdre Kessler and Marvyne Jenoff. Length: 5,000 words average; 1,500 words minimum; 15,000 words maximum. Publishes short shorts. Also publishes literary essays, literary criticism and poetry.

How to Contact: Send complete ms with a cover letter. Reports in 6 weeks on queries; 3 months on mss. Send SASE for reply, return of ms or send a disposable copy of ms. Simultaneous submissions and electronic submissions OK. Sample copy for $5. Fiction guidelines for #10 SASE.

Payment/Terms: Pays 2 contributor's copies on publication; additional copies for $5. Acquires first North American serial rights.

PARAMOUR MAGAZINE, Literary and Artistic Erotica, (IV), P.O. Box 949, Cambridge MA 02140-0008. (617)499-0069. E-mail: paramour@paramour.com. Website: http://www.paramour.com/. Publisher/Editor: Amelia Copeland. Fiction Editor: Nina Lesser. Magazine: 9×12; 36 pages; matte coated stock; illustrations and photos. "*Paramour* is a quarterly journal of literary and artistic erotica that showcases work by emerging writers and artists. Our goal is to provoke thought, laughter, curiosity and especially, arousal." Quarterly. Estab. 1993. Circ. 12,000.

● Work published in *Paramour* has been selected for inclusion in *Best American Erotica*.

Needs: Erotica. Receives 50 unsolicited mss/month. Accepts 3-5 mss/issue; 12-20 mss/year. Length: 2,000 words average; 1 word minimum; 4,000 words maximum. Publishes short shorts. Also publishes literary essays, literary criticism and poetry.

How to Contact: Request guidelines prior to submissions: call, write or e-mail. Send complete ms with a cover letter. Include estimated word count, name, address and phone number. Reports in 3 weeks on queries; 4 months on mss. SASE for reply only; send disposable copy of ms. No simultaneous submissions. Sample copy for $4.95. Fiction guidelines for #10 SAE and 1 first-class stamp. Reviews novels and short story collections.

Payment/Terms: Pays free subscription to the magazine plus contributor's copies. Acquires first rights.

Advice: "We look for erotic stories which are well-constructed, original, exciting, and dynamic. Clarity, attention to form and image, and heat make a ms stand out. Seek striking and authentic images and make the genre work for you. We see too many derivative rehashes of generic sexual fantasies. We love to see fresh representations that we know will excite readers."

THE PARIS REVIEW, (II), 45-39 171 Place, Flushing NY 11358 (*business office only, send mss to address below*). (212)861-0016. Fax: (212)861-4504. Editor: George A. Plimpton. Managing Editor: Daniel Kunitz. Magazine: 5¼×8½; about 260 pages; illustrations and photographs (unsolicited artwork not accepted). "Fiction and poetry of superlative quality, whatever the genre, style or mode. Our contributors include prominent, as well as less well-known and previously unpublished writers. *The Art of Fiction, Art of Poetry, Art of Criticism* and *Art of Theater* interview series include important contemporary writers discussing their own work and the craft of writing." Quarterly.

Needs: Literary. Receives about 1,000 unsolicited fiction mss each month. Published work by Raymond Carver, Elizabeth Tallent, Rick Bass, John Koethe, Sharon Olds, Derek Walcott, Carolyn Kizer, Tess Gallagher, Peter Handke, Denis Johnson, Bobbie Ann Mason, Harold Brodkey, Joseph Brodsky, John Updike, Andre Dubus, Galway Kinnell, E.L. Doctorow and Philip Levine. Published new writers within the last year. No preferred length. Also publishes literary essays, poetry.

How to Contact: *Send complete ms with SASE to Fiction Editor, 541 E. 72nd St., New York NY 10021.* Reports in 2 months. Simultaneous submissions OK. Sample copy for $11.50.

Payment/Terms: Pays up to $600. Pays on publication for first North American serial rights. Sends galleys to author.

PARTING GIFTS, (II), 3413 Wilshire, Greensboro NC 27408. E-mail: rbixby@aol.com. Website: http://users.a ol.com/marchst (includes guidelines, samples, catalog, news, some artwork and a few java applets just for fun). Editor: Robert Bixby. Magazine: 5×7; 60 pages. "High-quality insightful fiction, very brief and on any theme." Semiannually. Estab. 1988.
Needs: "Brevity is the second most important criterion behind literary quality." Publishes ms within one year of acceptance. Recently published work by David Chorlton, Ben Miller, Deborah Bayer, Tessa Dratt, Mary Rohrer-Dann, Peter Markus and Ray Miller. Length: 250 words minimum; 1,000 words maximum. Also publishes poetry. Sometimes critiques rejected mss.
How to Contact: Send complete ms with cover letter. Simultaneous submissions OK. Reports in 1 day on queries; 1-7 days on mss. SASE.
Payment/Terms: Pays in contributor's copies. Acquires one-time rights.
Advice: "Read the works of Amy Hempel, Jim Harrison, Kelly Cherry, C.K. Williams and Janet Kauffman, all excellent writers who epitomize the writing *Parting Gifts* strives to promote. I need more than ever for my authors to be better read. I sense that many unaccepted writers have not put in the hours reading."

PARTISAN REVIEW, (II), 236 Bay State Rd., Boston MA 02215. (617)353-4260. Editor-in-Chief: William Phillips. Editor: Edith Kurzweil. Magazine: 6×9; 160 pages; 40 lb. paper; 60 lb. cover stock. "Theme is of world literature and contemporary culture: fiction, essays and poetry with emphasis on the arts and political and social commentary, for the general intellectual public and scholars." Quarterly. Estab. 1934. Circ. 8,000.
Needs: Contemporary, experimental, literary, prose poem, regional and translations. Receives 100 unsolicited fiction mss/month. Buys 1-2 mss/issue; 4-8 mss/year. Published work by José Donoso, Isaac Bashevis Singer, Doris Lessing. Published new writers within the last year. Length: open.
How to Contact: Send complete ms with SASE and cover letter listing past credits. No simultaneous submissions. Reports in 4 months on mss. Sample copy for $6 and $1.50 postage.
Payment/Terms: Pays $25-200 and 1 contributor's copy. Pays on publication for first rights.
Advice: "Please, research the type of fiction we publish. Often we receive manuscripts which are entirely inappropriate for our journal. Sample copies are available for sale and this is a good way to determine audience."

PASSAGER, A Journal of Remembrance and Discovery, (I, II, IV), University of Baltimore, 1420 N. Charles St., Baltimore MD 21201-5779. Editors: Kendra Kopelke and Mary Azrael. Magazine: 8¼ square; 32 pages; 70 lb. paper; 80 lb. cover; photographs. "We publish stories and novel excerpts, poems, interviews with featured authors. One of our missions is to provide exposure for new older writers; another is to function as a literary community for writers across the country who are not connected to academic institutions or other organized groups." Quarterly. Estab. 1990. Circ. 750.
Needs: "Special interest in discovering new older writers, but publishes all ages." Receives 200 unsolicited mss/month. Accepts 2-3 prose mss/issue; 8-12/year. Does not read mss June through August. Publishes ms up to 1 year after acceptance. Length: 250 words minimum; 4,000 words maximum. Publishes short shorts. Also publishes poetry.
How to Contact: Send complete ms with cover letter. Reports in 3 months on mss. SASE. Simultaneous submissions OK, if noted. Sample copy for $4. Fiction guidelines for #10 SASE.
Payment/Terms: Pays subscription to magazine and 2 contributor's copies. Acquires first North American serial rights. Sometimes sends galleys to author.
Advice: "*Get a copy* so you can see the quality of the work we use. We seek powerful images of remembrance and discovery from writers of all ages. No stereotyped images of older people—we are interested in promoting complex images of aging that reveal the imagination and character of this stage of life."

PASSAGES NORTH, (I, II), Northern Michigan University, 1401 Presque Isle Ave., Marquette MI 49855. (906)227-2715. Fax: (906)227-1096. Editor: Anne Ohman Youngs. Fiction Editors: Candice Rowe and John Smolens. Magazine: 8×5½; 110-130 pages; 80 lb. paper. "*Passages North* publishes quality fiction, poetry and creative nonfiction by emerging and established writers." Readership: General and literary. Semiannually. Estab. 1979. Circ. 300.
Needs: Ethnic/multicultural, literary, mainstream/contemporary, regional. Receives 100-200 mss/month. Accepts 8-12 fiction mss/year. Does not read May through August. Recently published works by Jim Daniels, Jack Driscoll and Lee Upton. Published new writers within the last year. Length: 5,000 words maximum. Critiques returned mss when there is time. Also publishes interviews with authors.
How to Contact: Send complete ms with SASE and estimated word count. Reports in 6-8 weeks. No simultaneous submissions. Sample copy for $6. Fiction guidelines free.
Payment/Terms: Pays 1 contributor's copy. Rights revert to author on request.

PEARL, A Literary Magazine, (II, IV), Pearl, 3030 E. Second St., Long Beach CA 90803-5163. (562)434-4523. Editors: Joan Jobe Smith, Marilyn Johnson and Barbara Hauk. Magazine: 5½×8½; 96 pages; 60 lb. recycled, acid-free paper; perfect-bound; coated cover; b&w drawings and graphics. "We are primarily a poetry magazine, but we do publish some *very short* fiction and nonfiction. We are interested in lively, readable prose that speaks to *real* people in direct, living language; for a general literary audience." Triannually. Estab. 1974 ("folded" after 3 issues but began publishing again in 1987). Circ. 600.

Needs: Contemporary, humor/satire, literary, mainstream, prose poem. "We will only consider short-short stories up to 1,200 words. Longer stories (up to 4,000 words) may only be submitted to our short story contest. All contest entries are considered for publication. Although we have no taboos stylistically or subject-wise, obscure, predictable, sentimental, or cliché-ridden stories are a turn-off." Publishes an all fiction issue each year. Receives 10-20 unsolicited mss/month. Accepts 1-10 mss/issue; 12-15 mss/year. Submissions accepted September-May *only*. Publishes ms 6 months to 1 year after acceptance. Recently published work by Jerry Wilkerson, Dennis Bartel, Denise Duhamel, Lisa Glatt, Gerald Locklin and Rafael Zepeda. Publishes 3-5 new writers/year. Length: 1,000 words average; 500 words minimum; 1,200 words maximum. Also publishes poetry. Sponsors an annual short story contest. Send SASE for complete guidelines.

How to Contact: Send complete ms with cover letter including publishing credits and brief bio. Simultaneous submissions OK. Reports in 6-8 weeks on mss. SASE. Sample copy for $6 (postpaid). Fiction guidelines for #10 SASE.

Payment/Terms: Pays 2 contributor's copies. Acquires first North American serial rights. Sends galleys to author.

Advice: "We look for vivid, *dramatized* situations and characters, stories written in an original 'voice,' that make sense and follow a clear narrative line. What makes a manuscript stand out is more elusive, though—more to do with feeling and imagination than anything else . . ."

THE PEGASUS REVIEW, (I, IV), P.O. Box 88, Henderson MD 21640-0088. (201)927-0749. Editor: Art Bounds. Magazine: 5½×8½; 6-8 pages; illustrations. "Our magazine is a bimonthly, entirely in calligraphy, illustrated. Each issue is based on specific themes." Estab. 1980. Circ. 180.
 • Because *The Pegasus Review* is done in calligraphy, submissions must be very short. Two pages, says the editor, are the ideal length.

Needs: Humor/satire, literary, prose poem and religious/inspirational. Upcoming themes: "Beginnings" (January/February); "Dreams" (March/April); "Creativity" (May/June); "Country (USA)" (July/August); "Nature" (September/October); "Parents" (November/December). "Themes may be approached by humor, satire, inspirational, autobiographical, prose. Nothing like a new slant on an old theme." Receives 35 unsolicited mss/month. Accepts "about" 50 mss/year. Recently published work by Robert Deluty, Emily C. Long, Hester Dawson and Lawrence W. Thomas. Published work by 10 new writers within the last year. Publishes short shorts of 2-3 pages; 500 words. Themes are subject to change, so query if in doubt. "Occasional critiques."

How to Contact: Send complete ms. SASE "a must." Brief cover letter with author's background, name and prior credits, if any. Simultaneous submissions acceptable, if so advised. Reports in 1-2 months. Sample copy for $2.50. Fiction guidelines for SAE. Subscription: $10/year.

Payment/Terms: Pays 2 contributor's copies. Occasional book awards. Acquires one-time rights.

Advice: "Write daily; read works of the past as well as of the present; think of your audience and never underestimate them. As a writer be aware of taste and quality in your writing. Above all, even though often said—persevere!"

PEMBROKE MAGAZINE, (I, II), Box 60, Pembroke State University, Pembroke NC 28372. (910)521-6000. Editor: Shelby Stephenson. Fiction Editor: Stephen Smith. Magazine: 6×9; approximately 200 pages; illustrations; photos. Magazine of poems and stories plus literary essays. Annually. Estab. 1969. Circ. 500.

Needs: Open. Receives 120 unsolicited mss/month. Publishes short shorts. Published work by Fred Chappell, Robert Morgan. Published new writers within the last year. Length: open. Occasionally critiques rejected mss and recommends other markets.

How to Contact: Send complete ms. No simultaneous submissions. Reports in up to 3 months. SASE. Sample copy for $5 and 9×10 SAE.

Payment/Terms: Pays 1 contributor's copy.

Advice: "Write with an end for *writing*, not publication."

‡PENNSYLVANIA ENGLISH, (I), Penn State DuBois, College Place, DuBois PA 15801. (814)375-4814. Fax: (814)375-4784. Magazine: 5½×8½; 100 pages; 20 lb. bond paper; 65 lb. matte cover. "Open to any interested readers." Semiannually. Estab. 1985. Circ. 300.

Needs: Literary, contemporary mainstream. No genre fiction or romance. Publishes ms an average of 6 months after acceptance. Recently published work by David C. Kress and Dinty W. Moore. Length: 5,000 words maximum. Publishes short shorts. Also publishes literary essays, literary criticism, poetry. Sometimes critiques rejected mss.

How to Contact: Send complete ms with cover letter. Reports in 2 months. SASE. Simultaneous submissions OK.

Payment/Terms: Pays in contributor's copies. Acquires first North American serial rights.

Advice: Looks for "stories that tend to be realistic in nature; stories that are shorter rather than longer (because of space limitations)."

‡PEQUOD, A Journal of Contemporary Literature and Literary Criticism, (II), 19 University Place, Room 200, New York University, New York NY 10003. General Editor: Mark Rudman. Managing Editor: John Curley. Magazine 8½×5½; 150 pages; glossy cover. Semiannually. Estab. 1974. Circ. 4,000.
Needs: Condensed/excerpted novel, ethnic/multicultural, literary, mainstream/contemporary, translations. List of upcoming themes available for SASE. Publishes annual special fiction issue or anthology. Receives 150 unsolicited mss/month. Accepts 2 mss/issue; 4 mss/year. Does not read mss May-August. Publishes ms 3-6 months after acceptance. Recently published work by Stephen Dixon, John Harvey and Joyce Carol Oates. Publishes short shorts. Also publishes literary essays, literary criticism and poetry. Sometimes critiques or comments on rejected ms.
How to Contact: Send complete ms with a cover letter. Include estimated word count and list of publications. Reports in 6-8 weeks on queries; 3-4 months on mss. Send SASE for reply, return of ms or send a disposable copy of ms. Simultaneous and electronic submissions OK. Sample copy for $5. Reviews novels and short story collections.
Payment/Terms: Pays 2 contributor's copies. Rights revert back to author upon publication.
Advice: "Please subscribe to or get a sample copy of *Pequod* first to see what we're about."

PEREGRINE, The Journal of Amherst Writers & Artists Press, (II), AWA Press, P.O. Box 1076, Amherst MA 01004-1076. (413)253-7764. Fax: (413)253-7764. Managing Editor: Nancy Rose. Magazine: 6×9; 120 pages; 60 lb. white offset paper; glossy cover. "*Peregrine* has provided a forum for national and international writers for sixteen years, and is committed to finding excellent work by new writers as well as established authors. We publish what we love, knowing that all editorial decisions are subjective, and that all work has a home somewhere." Annually.
Needs: Poetry and prose—short stories, short short stories, personal essays. No previously published work. No children's stories. Publishes 2 pages in each issue of work in translation. "We welcome work reflecting diversity of voice." Accepts 6-12 fiction mss/issue. Publishes ms an average of 6 months after acceptance. No previously published work. No children's stories. Published work by Martín Espada, Sue Walker, Janet Aalfs, Gene Zeiger, Jim Bell and Lyn Lifshin. Published new writers within the last year. "We like to be surprised. We look for writing that is honest, unpretentious, and memorable." Length: 4,200 words maximum. Short pieces have a better chance of publication. *Peregrine* sponsors an annual contest (The *Peregrine* Prize) and awards $500 each for fiction and poetry.
How to Contact: #10 SASE to "Peregrine Guidelines." Send ms with cover letter; include 40-word biographical note, prior publications and word count. Simultaneous submissions OK. Enclose sufficiently stamped SASE for return of ms; if disposable copy, enclose #10 SASE for response. Deadline for submission: February 28, 1998. Mss received after deadline are held for consideration in the following year. Read October-February. Sample copy $8. Reviews books.
Payment/Terms: Pays contributor's copies. All rights return to writer upon publication.
Advice: "We look for heart and soul as well as technical expertise. Trust your own voice. Familiarize yourself with *Peregrine*." Every ms is read by three or more readers.

PHOEBE, An Interdisciplinary Journal of Feminist Scholarship, (II, IV), Theory and Aesthetics, Women's Studies Program, State University of New York, College at Oneonta, Oneonta NY 13820-4015. (607)436-2014. Fax: (607)436-2656. E-mail: phoebe@oneonta.edu. Editor: Kathleen O'Mara. Journal: 7×9; 140 pages; 80 lb. paper; illustrations and photos. "Feminist material for feminist scholars and readers." Semiannually. Estab. 1989. Circ. 400.
● Editor would like to see more experimental fiction.
Needs: Feminist: ethnic, experimental, gay, humor/satire, lesbian, literary, translations. Upcoming theme: "Youth and Sexuality." Receives 25 unsolicited mss/month. "One-third to one-half of each issue is short fiction and poetry." Does not read mss in summer. Publishes ms 3-4 months after acceptance. Recently published work by Elaine Hatfield, Betty A. Wilder, Jenny Potts, Kristan Ruona and Sylvia Van Nooten. Length: 1,500-2,500 words preferred. Publishes short shorts. Sometimes critiques rejected mss and recommends other markets.
How to Contact: Send complete ms with cover letter. Reports in 1 month on queries; 15 weeks on mss. Electronic (WordPerfect/Microsoft Word disk, e-mail) submissions OK. Sample copy for $7.50. Fiction guidelines free.
Payment/Terms: Pays in contributor's copies. Acquires one-time rights.
Advice: "We look for writing with a feminist perspective. *Phoebe* was founded to provide a forum for cross-cultural feminist analysis, debate and exchange. The editors are committed to providing space for all disciplines and new areas of research, criticism and theory in feminist scholarship and aesthetics. *Phoebe* is not committed to any one conception of feminism. All work that is not sexist, racist, homophobic, or otherwise discriminatory, will be welcome. *Phoebe* is particularly committed to publishing work informed by a theoretical perspective which will enrich critical thinking."

PHOEBE, A Journal of Literary Arts, (II), George Mason University, MSN 2D6, 4400 University Dr., Fairfax VA 22030. (703)993-2915. E-mail: phoebe@gmu.edu. Website: http://www.gmu.edu/pubs/phoebe (includes writer's guidelines, fiction and poetry contest guidelines, subscription information, past issue descriptions, etc.). Contact: Fiction Editor. Editors change each year. Magazine: 6×9; 116 pages; 80 lb. paper; 0-5 illustrations;

0-10 photographs. "We publish mainly fiction and poetry with occasional visual art." Published 2 times/year. Estab. 1972. Circ. 3,000.

Needs: "Looking for a broad range of fiction and poetry. We encourage writers and poets to experiment, to stretch the boundaries of genre." No romance, western, juvenile, erotica. Receives 30 mss/month. Accepts 3-5 mss/issue. Does not read mss in summer. Publishes ms 3-6 months after acceptance. Recently published work by Merin Wexler, Sybil Smith, Jessica Neely, Stephen Graham Jones and Carol Goodman. 50% of work published is by new writers. Length: no more than 35 pages of fiction, no more than 15 pages of poetry.

How to Contact: Send complete ms with cover letter. Include "name, address, phone. Brief bio." SASE. Simultaneous submissions OK. Sample copy for $6.

Payment/Terms: Pays 2 contributor's copies. Acquires one-time rights. All rights revert to author.

Advice: "We are interested in a variety of fiction and poetry. We suggest potential contributors study previous issues. Each year *Phoebe* sponsors fiction and poetry contests, with $500 awarded to the winning short story and poem. The deadline for both the Greg Grummer Award in Poetry and the Phoebe Fiction Prize is December 15. E-mail or send SASE for complete contest guidelines."

‡PIEDMONT LITERARY REVIEW, (II), Piedmont Literary Society, 3750 Woodside Ave., Lynchburg VA 24503. Production Editor: Betty Paige. Fiction Editor: Olga Kronmeyer. Magazine: 5½×8; 42 pages; 20 lb. bond paper; 65 lb. card stock cover. Quarterly. Estab. 1976. Circ. 240.

Needs: Humor/satire, literary, mainstream/contemporary. No erotica, experimental, juvenile, sci-fi. Receives 10-15 unsolicited mss/month. Accepts 1 ms/issue; 4 mss/year. Publishes ms 3 months after acceptance. Recently published work by Mary Larkin, J.S. Demel, Robert E. Brown and Morris Smith. Length: 2,200 words average; 1,000 words minimum; 2,500 words maximum. Also publishes essays, articles, literary criticism, poetry. Sometimes critiques or comments on rejected mss.

How to Contact: Send complete ms with a short cover letter. Include estimated word count. Reports in 1 month on queries; 3 months on mss. SASE for reply, return of ms or send a disposable copy of ms. Simultaneous submissions OK if prompt notice is given of acceptance elsewhere. Sample copy for $4 domestic and Canada. Fiction guidelines free for #10 SASE.

Payment/Terms: Pays 1 contributor's copy on publication; additional copies for $3. Acquires first North American serial rights.

Advice: "Stay within our 2,500 word limit, work on consistent character development and plot, come to satisfactory natural end."

PIG IRON, (II), Box 237, Youngstown OH 44501. (330)747-6932. Fax: (330)747-0599. Editor: Jim Villani. Annual series: 8½×11; 128 pages; 60 lb. offset paper; 85 pt. coated cover stock; b&w illustrations; b&w 120 line photographs. "Contemporary literature by new and experimental writers." Annually. Estab. 1975. Circ. 1,000.

Needs: Literary and thematic. No mainstream. Upcoming themes: "Religion in Modernity" (December 1998); "The 20th Century" (December 1999). Accepts 10-20 mss/issue. Receives approximately 75-100 unsolicited mss/month. Recently published work by Frank Polite, Chris Yambar, William Greenway, E.G. Hallaman and Nancy Bizarri. Length: 8,000 words maximum. Also publishes literary nonfiction, poetry. Sponsors contest. Send SASE for details.

How to Contact: Send complete ms with SASE. No simultaneous submissions. Reports in 4 months. Sample copy for $4.

Payment/Terms: Pays $5/printed page and 2 contributor's copies on publication for first North American serial rights; $5 charge for extras.

Advice: "Looking for work that is polished and compelling. We reject manuscripts that read like old stuff out of some old chest."

PIKEVILLE REVIEW, (I), Pikeville College, Sycamore St., Pikeville KY 41501. (606)432-9200. Editor: James Alan Riley. Magazine: 8½×6; 120 pages; illustrations and photos. "Literate audience interested in well-crafted poetry, fiction, essays and reviews." Annually. Estab. 1987. Circ. 500.

Needs: Ethnic/multicultural, experimental, feminist, humor/satire, literary, mainstream/contemporary, regional, translations. Receives 25 unsolicited mss/month. Accepts 3-4 mss/issue. Does not read mss in the summer. Publishes ms 6-8 months after acceptance. Length: 5,000 words average; 15,000 words maximum. Publishes short shorts. Also publishes literary essays and poetry. Often critiques rejected mss. Sponsors occasional fiction award: $50.

How to Contact: Send complete ms with cover letter. Include estimated word count. Send SASE for reply,

---

FOR INFORMATION ON ENTERING the *Novel & Short Story Writer's Market* Cover Letter Contest, see page 84.

return of ms or send a disposable copy of ms. Simultaneous submissions OK. Sample copy for $3. Reviews novels and short story collections.

Payment/Terms: Pays 5 contributor's copies; additional copies for $3. Acquires first rights.

Advice: "Send a clean manuscript with well-developed characters."

THE PINK CHAMELEON, (I, II, IV), 170 Park Ave., Hicksville NY 11801. Editor: Dorothy (Paula) Freda. Magazine: 5½×8½; 100 pages; 20 lb. bond paper; laminated card stock cover; illustrations and photographs. *The Pink Chameleon* is an "upbeat, family-oriented magazine that publishes any genre as long as the material submitted is in good taste and gives hope for the future, even in sadness." Biennially. Estab. 1985.

Needs: Adventure, condensed/excerpted novel, ethnic/multicultural, experimental, fantasy, historical, humor/satire, literary, mainstream/contemporary, mystery/suspense (amateur sleuth, cozy, romantic), religious/inspirational, romance (contemporary, futuristic/time travel, gothic, historical), science fiction (soft/sociological), senior citizen/retirement, sports, westerns (frontier, traditional), young adult/teen (adventure, mystery, romance, science fiction, western), children's/juvenile (1-12 years). "No pornography or graphic language." Accepts 12 mss/year. Publishes ms 18-24 months after acceptance. Published work by Karen Blicker, Al Manachino and Jené. 50% of work published is by new writers. Length: 3,500 words maximum. Publishes short shorts. Also publishes literary essays and poetry. Often critiques or comments on rejected mss.

How to Contact: *Subscribers only* should send complete ms with a cover letter. Subscription $10; make check payable to Dorothy P. Freda. Send SASE for reply, return of ms or send a disposable copy of ms. Reprint submissions OK. Fiction guidelines free.

Payment/Terms: Acquires one-time rights.

Advice: "Avoid wordiness; use simple, evocative language, and remember that *The Pink Chameleon* is a family-oriented magazine."

*PLANET-THE WELSH INTERNATIONALIST, P.O. Box 44, Aberystwyth, Ceredigion, Cymru/ Wales UK. Fiction Editor: John Barnie. Bimonthly. Circ. 1,400. Publishes 1-2 stories/issue.

Needs: "A literary/cultural/political journal centered on Welsh affairs but with a strong interest in minority cultures in Europe and elsewhere." Length: 1,500-4,000 words maximum.

How to Contact: No submissions returned unless accompanied by an SAE. Writers submitting from abroad should send at least 3 IRCs.

Payment/Terms: Writers receive 1 contributor's copy. Payment is at the rate of £40 per 1,000 words (in the currency of the relevant country if the author lives outside the UK). Sample copy: cost (to USA & Canada) £2.87. Writers' guidelines for SAE.

Advice: "We do not look for fiction which necessarily has a 'Welsh' connection, which some writers assume from our title. We try to publish a broad range of fiction and our main criterion is quality. Try to read copies of any magazine you submit to. Don't write out of the blue to a magazine which might be completely inappropriate to your work. Recognize that you are likely to have a high rejection rate, as magazines tend to favor writers from their own countries."

*THE PLAZA, A Space for Global Human Relations, U-Kan Inc., Yoyogi 2-32-1, Shibuya-ku, Tokyo 151, Japan. Tel: +81-(3)-3379-3881. Fax: +81-(3)-3379-3882. E-mail: plaza@u-kan.co.jp. Website: http://u-kan.co.jp (includes contribution guide, contents of the current and back issues, representative works by *The Plaza* writers). Editor: Leo Shunji Nishida. Fiction Editor: Roger Lakhani. Quarterly. Circ. 4,000. Publishes about 2 stories/issue. "*The Plaza* is an intercultural and bilingual magazine (English and Japanese). Our focus is the 'essence of being human.' All works are published in both Japanese and English (translations by our staff if necessary). The most important criteria is artistic level. We look for works that reflect simply 'being human.' Stories on intercultural (not international) relations are desired. *The Plaza* is devoted to offering a spiritual *Plaza* where people around the world can share their creative work. We introduce contemporary writers and artists as our generation's contribution to the continuing human heritage." Length: Less than 1,000 words, minimalist short stories are welcomed. Send complete ms with cover letter. Sample copy and guidelines free. "The most important consideration is that which makes the writer motivated to write. If it is not moral but human, or if it is neither a wide knowledge nor a large computer-like memory, but rather a deep thinking like the quietness in the forest, it is acceptable. While the traditional culture of reading of some thousands of years may be destined to be extinct under the marvellous progress of civilization, *The Plaza* intends to present contemporary works as our global human heritage to readers of forthcoming generations."

PLEIADES, (II), Department of English & Philosophy, Central Missouri State University, Martin 336, Warrensburg MO 64093. (816)543-4425. Fax: (816)543-8006. E-mail: rmk8708@cmsu2.cmsu.edu. Website: http://www.cmsu.edu/academics/arts&sciences/Engl/Phil/Pleiades (includes guidelines, editors, sample poetry or prose). Executive & Fiction Editor: R.M. Kinder. Managing Editor: Kevin Prufer. Magazine: 5½×8½; 120 pages; 60 lb. paper; perfect-bound; 8 pt. color cover. "*Pleiades* emphasizes cultural diversity, publishes poetry, fiction, literary criticism and reviews for a general educated audience." Semiannually. Estab. 1939. Circ. 500.

Needs: Ethnic/multicultural, experimental, feminist, gay, humor/satire, literary, mainstream/contemporary, regional, translations. "No westerns, romance, mystery, etc. Nothing pretentious, didactic or overly sentimental." Receives 40 unsolicited mss/month. Accepts 8 mss/issue; 16 mss/year. "We're slower at reading manuscripts in the summer." Publishes ms 3-8 months after acceptance. Recently published work by Harriet Zinnes, Howard R. Wolf and Simone Poirer-Bures. Length: 3,000-6,000 words average; 800 words minimum; 8,000 words maximum. Also publishes literary essays, literary criticism and poetry. Sometimes critiques or comments on rejected mss.

How to Contact: Send complete ms with a cover letter. Include 75-100 bio, Social Security number and list of publications. Reports in 3 weeks on queries; 4 months on mss. Send SASE for reply, return of ms or send a disposable copy of ms. Simultaneous submissions OK. Sample copy (including guidelines) for $6.

Payment/Terms: Pays $10 and 1 contributor's copy on publication. Acquires first North American serial rights. Plans a contest for 1998.

Advice: Looks for "a blend of language and subject matter that entices from beginning to end. Send us your best work. Don't send us formula stories. While we appreciate and publish well-crafted traditional pieces, we constantly seek the story that risks, that breaks form and expectations and wins us over anyhow."

PLOUGHSHARES, (II), Emerson College, 100 Beacon St., Boston MA 02116. (617)824-8753. Editor: Don Lee. "Our mission is to present dynamic, contrasting views on what is valid and important in contemporary literature, and to discover and advance significant literary talent. Each issue is guest-edited by a different writer. We no longer structure issues around preconceived themes." Triquarterly. Estab. 1971. Circ. 6,000.

● Work published in *Ploughshares* has been selected continuously for inclusion in the *Best American Short Stories* and *O. Henry Prize* anthologies. In fact the magazine has the honor of having the most stories selected from a single issue (three) to be included in *B.A.S.S.* Guest editors have included Richard Ford, Tim O'Brien and Ann Beattie.

Needs: Literary. "No genre (science fiction, detective, gothic, adventure, etc.), popular formula or commercial fiction whose purpose is to entertain rather than to illuminate." Buys 25 mss/year. Receives 400-600 unsolicited fiction mss each month. Published work by Rick Bass, Joy Williams and Andre Dubus. Published new writers within the last year. Length: 300-6,000 words.

How to Contact: Reading period: postmarked August 1 to March 31. Cover letter should include "previous pubs." SASE. Reports in 3-5 months on mss. Sample copy for $8. (Please specify fiction issue sample.) Current issue for $9.95. Fiction guidelines for #10 SASE.

Payment/Terms: Pays $25/page, $50 minimum per title; $250 maximum, plus copies and a subscription on publication for first North American serial rights. Offers 50% kill fee for assigned ms not published.

Advice: "Be familiar with our fiction issues, fiction by our writers and by our various editors (e.g., Sue Miller, Tobias Wolff, Rosellen Brown, Richard Ford, Jayne Anne Phillips, James Alan McPherson) and more generally acquaint yourself with the best short fiction currently appearing in the literary quarterlies, and the annual prize anthologies (*Pushcart Prize, O. Henry Awards, Best American Short Stories*). Also realistically consider whether the work you are submitting is as good as or better than—in your own opinion—the work appearing in the magazine you're sending to. What is the level of competition? And what is its volume? (In our case, we accept about one ms in 200.) Never send 'blindly' to a magazine, or without carefully weighing your prospect there against those elsewhere. Always keep a log and a copy of the work you submit."

❧THE PLOWMAN, (I, II), Box 414, Whitby, Ontario L1N 5S4 Canada. Editor: Tony Scavetta. Tabloid: 20 pages; illustrations and photos. Quarterly. Estab. 1988. Circ. 10,000.

Needs: "An international journal publishing all holocaust, relition, didactic, ethnic, eclectic, love and other stories." No science fiction. Recently published work by B. Fleming, P. Larty, B. Lilley, B. McCann Jr., Y. Nair and D. Garza. Publishes 125 new writers/year. Length: 7,000 words maximum.

How to Contact: Send complete ms with cover letter. Reports in 1 week. Simultaneous and reprint submissions OK. Sample copy and fiction guidelines for SAE.

Payment/Terms: Pays in contributor's copies; charges for extras. Acquires one-time rights. Sends galleys to author.

Advice: "No satanic or rude language."

*PLURILINGUAL EUROPE/EUROPE PLURILINGUE, % Nadine Dormoy, 44, rue Perronet, 92200 Neuilly, France. Fiction Editors: Nadine Dormoy, Albert Russo. Semiannually. Circ. 1,000. 20% of published content/ issue is fiction.

Needs: "Fiction in English must involve or be set in one of the 15 nations of the European Union. *Plurilingual Europe* is a pluridisciplinary journal that purports to foster understanding between the countries of the EU. All articles, essays and literary work should be written in any of the EU's 12 official languages. High specialization is required for the non-literary material. Excellence in every field always considered." Recently published work by George Steiner, Umberto Eco, Hugo Claus, Albert Russo, Jacques Darras, Renzo Titone, Eduardo Lourenço, Santiago Orontobbio and Norberto Luis Romero. Length: 500 words minimum; 3,000 words maximum.

Payment/Terms: Pays 2 contributor's copies. Subscription rate: US $22 (for 2 issues, postage included). U.S. check made out and sent to Liliane Lazar, 37 Hill Lane, Roslyn Heights, NY 11517, U.S.A. Sample copy for 6 IRCs; send to French address.

Advice: "Have a good knowledge of the country's customs you describe or at least an original viewpoint of that country and its people."

INSIDER REPORT

Ploughshares: a literary adventure

"It's a literary adventure." That's the advertising slogan intrinsic to the philosophy of *Ploughshares*, a triquarterly journal guest-edited every issue. Since 1988, Don Lee has been the editor behind the editor. "You never know quite what an issue will present; there are always real surprises," Lee says.

The founding premise of the journal was to present arguments about what constitutes good writing. Each issue is defined by the guest editor's personal visions, aesthetics and literary circles. When the journal was started in 1971 by Harvard Ph.D. students, Irish expatriates and Black Mountain poets, it became evident that individual editorial tastes made it impossible to have any kind of consensus. And so, says Lee, "it was decided to rotate editors. That policy eventually expanded to invite outsiders to edit the journal. Now we have guest editors from across the country."

Rotating editors works to the journal's advantage. Stories published in *Ploughshares* have been consistently selected for inclusion in *Best American Short Stories* and O. Henry Prize anthologies. "Our main criterion has always been quality of writing," says Lee. "Beyond that, we take some fresh approach to each issue. We have different editors who can have varying tastes, but that's not to say each issue is wildly different, because we do pick the guest editors. Nonetheless, they're certainly going to select or reject certain material. Some decisions might surprise us—and often they do."

Guest editors are allowed to solicit up to half of each issue from their colleagues or friends. But most, says Lee, never take the full percent; they rely on the unsolicited material submitted to the journal. Guest editors, however, only see a very small percentage of the unsolicited submissions—about 100 stories. It's the editorial staff's job to screen the 1,000 manuscripts that arrive in the *Ploughshares* office each month.

"We learn the guest editors' tastes as we go along with the editorial process," says Lee. "Anything we believe is of literary merit, even though it might not meet our individual tastes, is passed to the guest editors if we think it might meet theirs." But, Lee says, a big mistake many people make is to time their submissions with a particular guest editor. "Don't try to think of who's editing and submit a story for that particular reading period. We don't know when an issue will wrap up and how much of a backlog we'll have. If you feel you have something good and in line with our general literary standards, then send it at any time."

If one story is particularly well-liked by the staff, but is rejected by the guest editor, it is often sent on to the next guest editor. Sometimes, says Lee, the next editor accepts it and the story ends up winning awards. "And if a manuscript is rejected by one guest editor and passed on to another and is rejected again, we may encourage that writer to keep sending to us—that way, a writer whose work our staff likes gets a jump on the next reading period."

Besides Lee, the *Ploughshares* editorial staff consists of an assistant editor, poetry editor and two interns. There are also about 20 volunteer readers who pick up batches of

INSIDER REPORT, *Lee*

submissions and read them at home. Those readers are usually MFA graduates or in their second year of an MFA program. Sometimes they are professional editors who work for publishers like Houghton-Mifflin or *The Atlantic* but want an additional connection with the literary world.

Lee himself is a fiction writer, and although he doesn't consider it a full-time pursuit, he has been published in *Glimmer Train*, *Gentlemen's Quarterly* and *American Short Fiction*. While working on his MFA in creative writing at Emerson College, he became involved with *Ploughshares* by volunteering as a fiction reader.

Lee's advice to writers seeking to attract an editor's attention is to refrain from inane summaries of the work in the cover letter. "I think this started with people taking advice from nonfiction writers to heart. They'll describe the story in what they think is punchy language, and most of the time it comes off as ludicrous. Any kind of synopsis of a short story or any description of poetry works against your favor nine times out of ten. What I want to see in a cover letter is a list of writing credentials and previous publications. If there is some familiarity with *Ploughshares*, demonstrate it quickly, because the other big mistake writers make is that they really don't read our magazine."

Beyond the cover letter, Lee doesn't like to make generalizations about "good" writing. "It's really the uniqueness of the writing. What that means is not necessarily to be quirky— not necessarily to have some sort of startling hook or first line. Giving writers a roster or a checklist of things that I think make a story work is the wrong approach. As a writer, you have to write what comes from within yourself."

And the writing, says Lee, should be the writer's main concern.

"There are too many people out there who are more concerned with the business of writing than the writing itself. I see a lot of people who submit their manuscripts as if they were products and not as something they own completely and that they have their hearts in. If you work on your writing, you will eventually make it. You will get published. Something might fall through the cracks, but nonetheless good writing stands out and someone eventually will see it for its merit and its quality."

—*Jane Friedman*

POETIC SPACE, A Magazine of Poetry & Fiction, (I, II), Poetic Space Press, P.O. Box 11157, Eugene OR 97440. E-mail: poeticspac@aol.com. Editor: Don Hildenbrand. Fiction Editor: Thomas Strand. Magazine: 8½×11; 32 pages; bond paper; heavy cover; b&w art. "Social, political, avant-garde, erotic, environmental material for a literary audience." Biannually (summer and winter). Estab. 1983. Circ. 600.
Needs: Erotica, ethnic, experimental, feminist, gay, lesbian, literary. No sentimental, romance, mainstream. Receives about 20 unsolicited mss/month. Accepts 3-4 mss/issue; 8-10 mss/year. Publishes ms 6 months after acceptance. Publishes 5 new writers/year. Recently published work by David Scott Martin, Bruce Holland Rogers, Robert Weaver and Laton Carter. Length: 10 double-spaced pages. Publishes short shorts. Also publishes literary essays, literary criticism, poetry. Often critiques rejected mss and recommends other markets.
How to Contact: Send complete ms with cover letter that includes estimated word count, short bio and list of publications. Queries/mss by e-mail OK. Reports in 1 week on queries; 2 months on mss. SASE. Simultaneous, reprint and electronic submissions OK. Sample copy for $3, 4×9 SAE and 45¢ postage. Fiction guidelines for #10 SAE and 1 first-class stamp (or IRC). Reviews novels and short story collections. Send books to Don Hildenbrand.
Payment/Terms: Pays 1 contributor's copy. Acquires one-time rights or "reserves anthology rights."

POETRY FORUM SHORT STORIES, (I, II), Poetry Forum, 5713 Larchmont Dr., Erie PA 16509. (814)866-2543. Fax: (814)866-2543 (fax hours 8-10 a.m., 5-8 p.m.). E-mail: 75562.670@compuserve.com. Editor: Gunver Skogsholm. Newspaper: 7×8½; 34 pages; card cover; illustrations. "Human interest themes (no sexually explicit or racially biased or blasphemous material) for the general public—from the grassroot to the intellectual." Quarterly. Estab. 1989. Circ. 400.

Needs: Confession, contemporary, ethnic, experimental, fantasy, feminist, historical, literary, mainstream, mystery/suspense, prose poem, religious/inspirational, romance, science fiction, senior citizen/retirement, young adult/teen. "No blasphemous, sexually explicit material." Publishes annual special fiction issue. Receives 50 unsolicited mss/month. Accepts 12 mss/issue; 40 mss/year. Publishes ms 6 months after acceptance. Agented fiction less than 1%. 40% of work published is by new writers. Length: 2,000 words average; 500 words minimum; 5,000 words maximum. Also publishes literary essays, literary criticism, poetry.

How to Contact: *This magazine charges a "professional members" fee of $36 and prefers to work with subscribers.* The fee entitles you to publication of a maximum of 3,000 words. Send complete ms with cover letter. Reports in 3 weeks to 2 months on mss. SASE. Simultaneous and reprint submissions OK. "Accepts electronic submissions via disk gladly." Sample copy for $3. Fiction guidelines for SASE. Reviews novels and short story collections.

Payment/Terms: Preference given to submissions by subscribers. Acquires one-time rights.

Advice: "Tell your story with no padding as if telling it to a person standing with one hand on the door ready to run out to a meeting. Have a good lead. This is the 'alpha & omega' of all good story writing. Don't start with 'This is a story about a boy and a girl.'"

POETRY IN MOTION MAGAZINE, (II), National Poet's Association, P.O. Box 173, Bayport MN 55003-0173. (612)779-6952. E-mail: poem@winternet.com. Website: http://www.winternet.com/~poem/pim.html (includes guidelines and poetry). Editor: Nadia Giordana. Magazine: 8½×11; 64 pages; 35 lb. web paper; color or b&w; glossy cover stock; illustrations; photos. "We include numerous local advertising to fund circulation. We publish a wide variety of subjects in each issue. We have national subscribers across the country and very heavy distribution throughout Minnesota and Wisconsin—those are our readers. Our contributors are from all over the country." Quarterly. Estab. 1994. Circ. 5,000.

Needs: Adventure, experimental, fantasy (science, sword and sorcery), mainstream/contemporary, mystery/suspense (amateur sleuth, private eye/hardboiled), psychic/supernatural/occult, regional, science fiction, westerns (frontier, traditional). Receives 10-20 unsolicited mss/month. Accepts 6-9 mss/issue; 50-100 mss/year. Publishes ms 2-6 months after acceptance. Published work by Robert Mariani, Marian Ford Park, Lain McNeill and Ken Cook. Length: 1,500 words average; 250 words minimum; 2,000 words maximum. Publishes short shorts. Also publishes literary essays and poetry.

How to Contact: Send complete ms with a cover letter. Include estimated word count, short bio and list of publications. Reports in 2-5 months on mss. Send SASE for reply, return of ms or send a disposable copy of ms. Sample copy for $5. Fiction guidelines for #10 SASE.

Payment/Terms: Pays 1 contributor's copy on publication; additional copies for $5. Acquires one-time rights and one-time electronic rights.

Advice: "An interesting twist at the end rather than a predictable ending will put a manuscript at the top of the stack. Avoid clichés. Be patient; my response time can take 2-5 months. Since we use an editable text scanner, manuscripts submitted using a sans serif font such as Helvetica are read first."

‡✽POETRY WLU, (I), Wilfrid Laurier University, Waterloo, Ontario N2L 3C5 Canada. (519)884-1970. Managing Editor: Ed Jewinski. Editors change each year. Magazine: 8½×7; 50-60 pages; standard bond paper; illustrations. "*Poetry WLU* is a place for the new, young, unknown and talented." Annually. Estab. 1981. Circ. 250.

Needs: Literary. Receives 5-10 unsolicited mss/month. Accepts 2-3 mss/issue. "All reading and assessing is done between January and March." Publishes ms 2 months after acceptance. Length: 100 words minimum; 1,500 words maximum. Publishes short shorts. Also publishes poetry.

How to Contact: Send complete ms with a cover letter and SASE. Reports in 2 months. SASE for reply or return of ms. Sample copy for $2.

Payment/Terms: Pays 1 contributor's copy; additional copies for $2. Sponsors contests, awards or grants for fiction writers. "The applicant must be a registered Wilfrid Laurier University student."

POET'S FANTASY, (I), 227 Hatten Ave., Rice Lake WI 54868-2030. (715)234-7472. Editor: Gloria Stoeckel. Magazine: 8½×4½; 40 pages; 20 lb. paper; colored stock cover; illustrations. *Poet's Fantasy* is a magazine of "fantasy, but not conclusive." Bimonthly. Estab. 1992. Circ. about 250.

Needs: Fantasy (science), literary. Receives 2-3 unsolicited mss/month. Accepts 6 mss/year. Recently published work by Richard Hay, Andy Marshall and Betty Lou Hebert. Publishes "several hundred" new writers/year. Length: 1,000 words average; 500 words minimum; 1,500 words maximum. Publishes short shorts. Also publishes literary essays and poetry. Sometimes critiques or comments on rejected mss.

How to Contact: Send complete ms with a cover letter. Include estimated word count and list of publications. Reports in 3 weeks. Send SASE for reply or return of ms. Simultaneous submissions OK. Sample copy for $3. Fiction guidelines free.

Payment/Terms: Pays $3 coupon on publication toward purchase of subscription for first North American serial rights. Subscribers are given preference.

Advice: Wants fiction with "tight writing, action and ending twist. Edit and re-edit before sending."

THE POINTED CIRCLE, (II), Portland Community College-Cascade, 705 N. Killingsworth St., Portland OR 97217. (503)978-5230. E-mail: jranck@pcc.edu. Editors: Student Editorial Staff. Magazine: 80 pages; b&w illustrations and photographs. "Anything of interest to educationally/culturally mixed audience." Annually. Estab. 1980.
Needs: Contemporary, ethnic, literary, prose poem, regional. "We will read whatever is sent, but encourage writers to remember we are a quality literary/arts magazine intended to promote the arts in the community." Acquires 3-7 mss/year. Accepts submissions only December 1-February 15, for October 1 issue. Recently published work by Klarice Westley, Joyful Freeman and DC Palter. Length: 3,000 words maximum.
How to Contact: Send complete ms with cover letter and brief bio. "The editors consider all submissions without knowing the identities of the contributors, so please do not put your name on the works themselves." SASE. Sample copy for $4.50. Fiction guidelines for #10 SASE.
Payment/Terms: Pays in contributor's copies. Acquires one-time rights.
Advice: "Looks for quality—topicality—nothing trite. The author cares about language and acts responsibly toward the reader, honors the reader's investment of time and piques the reader's interest."

PORCUPINE LITERARY ARTS MAGAZINE, (II), P.O. Box 259, Cedarburg WI 53012-0259. (414)375-3128. E-mail: ppine259@aol.com. Website: http://members.aol.com/ppine259 (includes writer's guidelines, cover art, subscription information, table of contents). Editor: W.A. Reed. Fiction Editor: Chris Skoczynski. Magazine: 5×8½; 100 pages; glossy color cover stock; illustrations and photos. Publishes "primarily poetry and short fiction. Novel excerpts are acceptable if self-contained. No restrictions as to theme or style." Semiannually. Estab. 1996. Circ. 1,500.
  ● *Porcupine Literary Arts Magazine* was named Best Literary/Arts Magazine by *Milwaukee Magazine* (1997).
Needs: Condensed/excerpted novel, ethnic/multicultural, literary, mainstream/contemporary. No pornographic or religious. Receives 10 unsolicited mss/month. Accepts 3 mss/issue; 6 mss/year. Publishes ms within 6 months of acceptance. Recently published work by Dennis Must and Mary Ann Cain. Publishes 4-6 new writers/year. Length: 3,500 words average; 2,000 words minimum; 7,500 words maximum. Publishes literary essays and poetry. Sometimes critiques or comments on rejected mss.
How to Contact: Send complete ms with a cover letter. Include estimated word count, 5-line bio and list of publications. Reports in 2 weeks on queries; 2 months on mss. Send SASE for reply, return of ms or send a disposable copy of ms. No simultaneous submissions. Sample copy for $5. Fiction guidelines for #10 SASE.
Payment/Terms: Pays 1 contributor's copy on publication; additional copies for $8.95. Acquires one-time rights.
Advice: Looks for "believable dialogue and a narrator I can see and hear and smell. Form or join a writers' group. Read aloud. Rewrite extensively."

PORTLAND REVIEW, (I, II), Portland State University, Box 347, Portland OR 97207-0347. (503)725-4533. Fax: (503)725-5860. E-mail: review@vanguard.vg.pdx.edu. Editor: Misty Sturgeon. Magazine: 9×6; 200 pages; linen stock paper; heavy linen cover stock; b&w drawings and photos. "We seek to publish fiction in which content takes precedence over style." Quarterly. Estab. 1955. Circ. 1,500.
  ● The editors say they are looking for experimental work "dealing with the human condition."
Needs: Adventure, erotica, ethnic/multicultural, experimental, fantasy (science), feminist, gay, historical, humor/satire, lesbian, literary, mainstream/contemporary, mystery/suspense, regional, science fiction (hard sf), serialized novel, translation. "We could do without all the vampire submissions." Receives about 100 mss each month. Accepts 4-6 mss/issue; 25-30 mss/year. Also publishes critical essays, poetry, drama, interviews and reviews.
How to Contact: Submit complete ms with short bio. Manuscripts returned only if SASE is supplied. Simultaneous and electronic submissions OK (if noted). Reports in 1 month. Sample copy for $5 plus $1 postage.
Payment/Terms: Pays contributor's copies. Acquires one-time rights.
Advice: "Our editors, and thus our tastes/biases change annually, so keep trying us."

POTATO EYES, (II), Nightshade, P.O. Box 76, Troy ME 04987-0076. (207)948-3427. Fax: (207)948-5088. E-mail: potatoeyes@uninet.net. Website: http://www.maineguide.com/giftshop/potatoeyes (includes book listings, mission statement, update on Nightshade Press and Potato Eyes Foundation happenings). Editors: Carolyn Page and Roy Zarucchi. Magazine: 5½×8½; 120 pages; 60 lb. text paper; 80 lb. Curtis flannel cover. "We look for stories/essays with good tension and imagery." Estab. 1988. Circ. 800.
Needs: Contemporary, humor/satire, literary, mainstream, regional, feminist and ecological themes. Receives

---

✳ **INTERNATIONAL MARKETS**, those located outside of the United States and Canada, are marked with an asterisk.

200 unsolicited mss/month. Accepts 5 mss/issue; 10 mss/year. Publishes ms 2 months-2 years after acceptance. Recently published work by Richard Abrons, George Katznelson and Shirley Cochrane. Length: 5,000 words maximum; 2,000 average. Publishes short shorts. Length: 450 words. Also publishes poetry. Sometimes critiques rejected mss.

How to Contact: Send complete ms with cover letter. Reports in 1-2 months on mss. SASE. Sample copy for $5, including postage. Fiction guidelines for #10 SAE.

Payment/Terms: Pays in contributor's copies. Acquires first North American serial rights.

Advice: "We care about the larger issues, including pollution, ecology, bio-regionalism, uncontrolled progress and 'condominia,' and women's issues, as well as the rights of the individual. We care about television, the great sewer pipe of America, and what it is doing to America's youth. We are exploring these issues with writers who have originality, a reordered perspective, and who submit to us generous sprinklings of humor and satire. Although we do occasionally comment on valid fiction, we have walked away unscathed from the world of academia and refuse to correct manuscripts. We respect our contributors and treat them as professionals, however, and write personal responses to every submission if given a SASE. We expect the same treatment—clean copy without multi folds or coffee stains or corrections. We like brief non-Narcissistic cover letters containing the straight scoop. We suggest that beginning fiction writers take the money they have set aside for creative writing courses or conferences and spend it instead on subscriptions to good little literary magazines."

POTOMAC REVIEW, The Quarterly with a Conscience—and a Sense of Humor, (I, II), Potomac Review, Inc., P.O. Box 354, Port Tobacco MD 20677. (301)934-1412. Website: http://www.meral.com/potomac (includes editor's note, contents page, contact information, some sampling of stories, poems). Editor: Eli Flam. Magazine: 5½ × 8½; 96 pages; 50 lb. paper; 65 lb. cover; illustrations. "*Potomac Review* is a mainstream literary quarterly with a challenging diversity." Estab. 1994. Circ. 1,500.

Needs: Excerpted novel—"stories with a vivid, individual quality that get at 'the concealed side' of life. Regionally rooted, with an area or theme focus each issue (e.g., 'Across the Watershed,' spring 1997); we also keep an eye on the wider world." Upcoming themes (subject to change): Northern Virginia, The Play's the Thing, Writing Contest Winners, *The Potomac*: Fifty Years Later. Receives 100 unsolicited mss/month. Accepts 20-30 mss/issue of all sorts; 80-120 mss/year. Publishes ms within a year after acceptance as a rule. Agented fiction 5%. Recently published work by Gerda Antti, Henry Louis Gates Jr., Elisavietta Ritchie and Mark Blickley. Length: 2,000 words average; 100 words minimum; 3,000 words maximum. Publishes short shorts. Length: 250 words. Also publishes poetry, essays and cogent, issue-oriented nonfiction. Humor is welcome.

How to Contact: Send complete ms with a cover letter. Include estimated word count, 2-3 sentence bio, list of publications and SASE. Reports in 2 weeks on queries; 2-3 months on mss. Send SASE for reply, return of ms or send a disposable copy of ms. Simultaneous and reprint submissions OK. Sample copy for $5. Submission guidelines for #10 SASE. Reviews novels, short story collections, other books.

Payment/Terms: Pays 1 contributor's copy; additional copies for $3.

Advice: "Send your best work—though our nonprofit quarterly is regionally rooted in the Potomac River basin, which reaches from Virginia and West Virginia up through Maryland into Pennsylvania, with Washington, DC, and Baltimore two polar sites—we are open to good writing from all points. A manuscript should be well-carpentered, but unobtrusively so, it should flow, in effect letting the story tell itself. In our own exceedingly modest way, we keep plugging along, ever on the search for *the* story (and poem, etc.) as well as decent levels of financial and moral support."

POTPOURRI, (II), P.O. Box 8278, Prairie Village KS 66208. (913)642-1503. Fax: (913)642-3128. E-mail: potpourpub@aol.com. Senior Editor: Polly W. Swafford. Magazine: 8 × 11; 72 pages; glossy cover. "Literary magazine: short stories, verse, essays, travel, prose poetry for a general adult audience." Quarterly. Estab. 1989. Circ. 4,500.

Needs: Adventure, contemporary, ethnic, experimental, fantasy, historical (general), humor/satire, literary, mainstream, suspense, prose poem, romance (contemporary, historical, romantic suspense), science fiction (soft/sociological), western (frontier stories). "*Potpourri* accepts a broad genre; hence its name. Guidelines specify no religious, confessional, racial, political, erotic, abusive or sexual preference materials unless fictional and necessary to plot." Receives 75 unsolicited fiction mss/month. Accepts 10-12 fiction mss/issue; 60-80 prose mss/year. Publishes ms 6-8 months after acceptance. Agented fiction 1%. Recently published work by Thomas E. Kennedy, David Ray, Seymour Shubin, Lyn Lifshin, Carol Hamilton, Walter Cummins, Deborah Shouse, John Sokol and Arthur Winfield Knight. Length: 3,500 words maximum. Also publishes poetry and literary essays. Sometimes critiques rejected mss. *Potpourri* offers annual awards (of $100 each) in fiction and poetry, more depending on grants received, and sponsors the Annual Council on National Literatures Award of $100 each for poetry and fiction on alternating years. "Manuscripts must celebrate our multicultural and/or historic background." 1998 fiction entry deadline: August 31, 1998. Reading fee: $5. Send SASE for guidelines.

How to Contact: Send complete ms with cover letter. Include "complete name, address, phone number, brief summary statement about submission, short author bio." Reports in 2-4 months. SASE. Simultaneous submissions OK when advised at time of submission. Sample copy for $4.95 with 9 × 12 envelope. Fiction guidelines for #10 SASE.

Payment/Terms: Pays contributor's copies. Acquires first rights.

Advice: "We look for well-crafted stories of literary value and stories with reader appeal. First, does the manuscript spark immediate interest and the introduction create the effect that will dominate? Second, does the action in dialogue or narration tell the story? Third, does the conclusion leave something with the reader to be long remembered? We look for the story with an original idea and an unusual twist. We are weary of excessive violence and depressing themes in fiction and are looking for originality in plots and some humorous pieces."

❦**POTTERSFIELD PORTFOLIO, (I, II)**, The Gatsby Press, P.O. Box 27094, Halifax, Nova Scotia B3H 4M8 Canada. Phone/fax: (902)443-9178. E-mail: icolford@is.dal.ca or gaundc@auracom.com. Website: http://www.auracom.com/~saundc/potters.html. Editor: Ian Colford. Fiction Editor: Karen Smythe. Magazine: 6×9; 100 pages; recycled acid-free paper and cover; illustrations. "Literary magazine interested in well-written fiction and poetry. No specific thematic interests or biases." Triannually. Estab. 1979. Circ. 500.
Needs: Receives 30-40 fiction mss/month. Buys 4-8 fiction mss/issue. Recently published work by Steven Heighton, Sheree Fitch and Jean McMeil. Length: 3,500 words average; 500 words minimum; 5,000 words maximum. Publishes short shorts. Sometimes comments on rejected mss.
How to Contact: Send complete ms with cover letter. Include estimated word count and 50-word bio. No simultaneous submissions. Reports in 3 months. SASE. Sample copy for $7 (US), 10½×7½ SAE and 4 first-class stamps.
Payment/Terms: Pays contributor's copy plus $5 Canadian per printed page to a maximum of $25 on publication for first Canadian serial rights.
Advice: "Provide us with a clean, proofread copy of your story. Include a brief cover letter with biographical note, but don't try to sell the story to us. *Always* include a SASE with sufficient *Canadian* postage, or IRCs, for return of the manuscript or a reply from the editors."

*****THE PRAGUE REVIEW**, Bohemia's Journal of International Literature, Prague Publishers Group, V jámě 7, 110 00 Prague 1, Czech Republic. (0042)(2)90000412. Fax: (0042)(2)90000413. E-mail: revue@terminal.cz. Editor: Jason Penazzi-Russell. Fiction Editors: Max Munson and David Leslie Conhaim. Magazine: 130 pages; 80 weight paper; 180 weight cover stock with dust jacket; illustrations and photos. Quarterly. Estab. 1995. Circ. 1,500.
● Recipient of a grant from the Czech Ministry of Culture. Member of the Prague Publishers Group.
Needs: "*The Prague Revue* is Bohemia's English language, international quarterly of contemporary fiction, poetry, performance text and nonfiction. We will publish any genre. Editorial decisions are based solely on the quality of submissions. Our quarterly English language issue brings Central European writers together with international writers for world exposure. We also publish non-English anthologies to bring the works to greater audiences." Recently published work by Ivan Klíma, Arnőst Lustig, Joe Sulton, Robert Menasse, Igor Pomerantsev and Abdullah al-Udhari. Publishes 5 new writers/year. Length: 6,000 words average; 10,000 words maximum.
How to Contact: Submit complete ms with a cover letter. Include estimated word count, 1-paragraph bio, Social Security number and list of publications. SASE for reply or send a disposable copy of the ms. Queries by e-mail OK. Reports in 3 weeks on queries; 2 months on mss. Simultaneous submissions, reprints and electronic submissions OK.
Payment/Terms: Pays $5-150 on acceptance "for those pieces which are also selected for our foreign language issues" and 2 contributor's copies; additional copies for $3. Sample copy available for $7. Fiction guidelines for SAE and IRCs.
Advice: "We keep an eye out for pieces which would contribute also to our foreign language anthologies—particularly our Czech language annual. Prague themes do not contribute to the piece's chances for publication."

PRAIRIE DOG, A Magazine for the Somewhat Eccentric, (II, III), P.O. Box 470757, Aurora CO 80047-0757. Phone/fax: (303)753-0956. E-mail: jrhart@pcisys.net. Editor-in-Chief: John Hart. Magazine: 8½×11; 90 pages; bond paper; parchment cover; illustrations and photos. Biannual. Estab. 1988 as *Infinity Limited*. Circ. 1,000.
Needs: Adventure, contemporary, erotica, ethnic, experimental, fantasy, historical, humor/satire, literary, prose poem, regional, science fiction, translations. "No space opera, gratuitous violence, or pornography." Receives approximately 50 unsolicited mss/month. Acquires 7-12 mss/issue; 20-28 mss/year. Publishes ms 12-16 months after acceptance. Recently published work by Hugh Fox, Simon Perchik, James Gallant, Charles Rampp and W.S. Mayo. Length: 10,000 words maximum. Publishes short shorts, poetry, essays and occasional book reviews. Sometimes critiques rejected mss.
How to Contact: Send complete ms with cover letter. Include brief bio and $2 reading fee per story, essay or ten poems. Reports in 3-5 months on mss. SASE. Simultaneous (if noted in cover letter) and electronic (disk) submissions OK. Sample copy for $6.95 plus $1 p&h and 9×12 SAE. Fiction guidelines for #10 SASE.
Payment/Terms: Pays 1 contributor's copy; additional copies at $2 discount. Acquires one-time rights.
Advice: "We read everything and will respond if you provide an SASE. We accept double-sided and photocopied manuscripts (save the trees) but will not read faint dot matrix and single-spaced manuscripts. Don't summarize your plot in your cover letter. We would like to feature one 'youthful new voice' (under 25, just beginning to be published) per issue, but our standards are high. Mass submissions based on class assignments are sure to be rejected. Because we are entirely unsupported by any institution and accept only minimal advertising, we must, regrettably, return manuscripts unread which are not accompanied by the $2 reading fee."

✤**THE PRAIRIE JOURNAL OF CANADIAN LITERATURE, (I, II)**, Prairie Journal Press, Box 61203, Brentwood Postal Services, Calgary, Alberta T2L 2K6 Canada. Editor: A.E. Burke. Journal: 7 × 8½; 50-60 pages; white bond paper; Cadillac cover stock; cover illustrations. Journal of creative writing and scholarly essays, reviews for literary audience. Semiannually. Published special fiction issue last year. Estab. 1983.
Needs: Contemporary, literary, prose poem, regional, excerpted novel, novella, double-spaced. Canadian authors given preference. Publishes "a variety of types of fiction—fantasy, psychological, character-driven, feminist, etc. We publish authors at all stages of their careers from well-known to first publication." No romance, erotica, pulp. Publishes anthology series open to submissions: *Prairie Journal Poetry II* and *Prairie Journal Fiction III*. Receives 20-40 unsolicited mss each month. Accepts 10-15 mss/issue; 20-30 mss/year. Suggests sample issue before submitting ms. Published work by Nancy Ellen Russell, Carla Mobley, Patrick Quinn. Published many new writers within the last year. Length: 2,500 words average; 100 words minimum; 3,000 words maximum. Deadlines: April 1 for spring/summer issue; October 1 for fall/winter. Also publishes literary essays, literary criticism, poetry. Sometimes critiques rejected mss and recommends other markets.
How to Contact: Send complete ms. Reports in 1 month. SASE. Sample copy for $6 (Canadian) and SAE with $1.10 for postage or IRC. Include cover letter of past credits, if any. Reply to queries for SAE with 52¢ for postage or IRC. No American stamps. Reviews novels and short story collections.
Payment/Terms: Pays contributor's copies and modest honoraria. Acquires first North American serial rights. In Canada author retains copyright.
Advice: Interested in "innovational work of quality. Beginning writers welcome. There is no point in simply republishing known authors or conventional, predictable plots. Of the genres we receive fiction is most often of the highest calibre. It is a very competitive field. Be proud of what you send. You're worth it."

PRAIRIE SCHOONER, (II), University of Nebraska, English Department, 201 Andrews Hall, Lincoln NE 68588-0334. (402)472-0911. E-mail: lrandolp@unlinfo2.unl.edu. Website: http://www.unl.edu/schooner/psmain. htm (includes guidelines, editors, table of contents for current issue). Editor: Hilda Raz. Magazine: 6 × 9; 200 pages; good stock paper; heavy cover stock. "A fine literary quarterly of stories, poems, essays and reviews for a general audience that reads for pleasure." Quarterly. Estab. 1926. Circ. 3,200.
    ● *Prairie Schooner*, one of the oldest publications in this book, has garnered several awards and honors over the years. Work appearing in the magazine has been selected for anthologies including *Pushcart Prizes* and *Best American Short Stories*.
Needs: Good fiction (literary). Accepts 4-5 mss/issue. Receives approximately 200 unsolicited fiction mss each month. Mss are read September through May only. Recently published work by Ursula Hgi, Josip Novakovitch, Rebecca Goldstein, Robin Hemley and Susan Fromberg Schaeffer. Published new writers within the last year. Length: varies. Also publishes poetry. Offers annual prize of $1,500 for best fiction, $500 for best new writer (poetry or fiction), two $500 awards for best poetry.
How to Contact: Send complete ms with SASE and cover letter listing previous publications—where, when. Reports in 3-4 months. Sample copy for $5. Reviews novels and short story collections.
Payment/Terms: Pays in contributor's copies and prize money awarded. Acquires all rights. Will reassign rights upon request after publication.
Advice: "*Prairie Schooner* is eager to see fiction from beginning and established writers. Be tenacious. Accept rejection as a temporary setback and send out rejected stories to other magazines. *Prairie Schooner* is not a magazine with a program. We look for good fiction in traditional narrative modes as well as experimental, meta-fiction or any other form or fashion a writer might try. We are receiving record numbers of submissions. Prospective contributors must sometimes wait longer to receive our reply."

PRESS, (III), Daniel Roberts Inc., 2124 Broadway, Suite 323, New York NY 10023. (212)579-0873. Fax: (212)579-0776. E-mail: pressltd@aol.com. Editor: Daniel Roberts. Magazine: 6¾ × 10; 160 pages; cougap-opaque paper; loe cream cover. Features fiction, poetry and "articles about writing and writers; features that humanize literature, celebrate talent and beauty, and expose fraudulence and pomposity. *Press* will stand not only as the most absolute record of contemporary, American, literary talent, but as a means by which the public can commune with literature." Quarterly. Estab. 1996. Circ. 15,000.
Needs: Receives 800 unsolicited mss/month. Accepts 10 mss/issue; 40 mss/year. Publishes ms 6-10 weeks after acceptance. Agented fiction 10%. Published work by Joyce Carol Oates, Anthony Hecht, Philip Levine, William J. Cobb, James Gallant, Gordon Lish and Harry Mathews. Also publishes poetry. Sometimes comments on or critiques rejected mss.
How to Contact: Send complete ms with a cover letter. Include a short bio and list of publications. Reports in 2 months on queries; 4 months on mss. Send SASE for reply, return of ms or send a disposable copy of ms. Sample copy for $8. Fiction guidelines free.
Payment/Terms: Pays $100 minimum and 1 contributor's copy; additional copies for $6. Pays on acceptance for first rights, first North American serial rights or one-time rights. Sends galleys to the author.
Advice: "While almost all forms are acceptable, prose poems and more experimental writing (stories that don't actually tell a story) are discouraged. We are looking for a strong and specific plot (where 'something' actually happens); one that makes a reader want to turn the page. We want stories where the author's style does not interfere with the plot, but strengthens the expression of that plot."

PRIMAVERA, (II, IV), Box 37-7547, Chicago IL 60637. (312)324-5920. Editorial Board. Magazine: 5½×8½; 128 pages; 60 lb. paper; glossy cover; illustrations; photos. Literature and graphics reflecting the experiences of women: poetry, short stories, photos, drawings. Readership: "an audience interested in women's ideas and experiences." Annually. Estab. 1975. Circ. 1,000.
   ● *Primavera* has won grants from the Illinois Arts Council, the Puffin Foundation and from Chicago Women in Publishing.
Needs: Literary, contemporary, fantasy, feminist, gay/lesbian, humor and science fiction. "We dislike slick stories packaged for more traditional women's magazines. We publish only work reflecting the experiences of women, but also publish manuscripts by men." Accepts 6-10 mss/issue. Receives approximately 40 unsolicited fiction mss each month. Recently published work by Amy Stuber, Carol Kopec, L. Hluchan Sintetos and Sucha Cardoza. Published new writers within the last year. Length: 25 pages maximum. Also publishes poetry. Critiques rejected mss when there is time. Often gives suggestions for revisions and invites re-submission of revised ms. Occasionally recommends other markets.
How to Contact: Send complete ms with SASE. No post cards. Cover letter not necessary. No simultaneous submissions. Reports in 1-6 months on mss. Publishes ms up to 1 year after acceptance. Sample copy for $5; $10 for recent issues. Guidelines for SASE.
Payment/Terms: Pays 2 contributor's copies. Acquires first rights.
Advice: "We're looking for artistry and deftness of untrendy, unhackneyed themes; an original slant on a well-known theme, an original use of language, and the highest literary quality we can find."

✤PRISM INTERNATIONAL, (I, II), E462-1866 Main Mall, University of British Columbia, Vancouver, British Columbia V6T 1Z1 Canada. (604)822-2514. E-mail: prism@unixg.ubc.ca. Website: http://www.arts.ubc.ca/prism/. Executive Editor: S.L. McFerran. Editors: Sioux Browning and Melanie Little. Magazine: 6×9; 72-80 pages; Zephyr book paper; Cornwall, coated one side cover; photos on cover. "An international journal of contemporary writing—fiction, poetry, drama, creative nonfiction and translation." Readership: "public and university libraries, individual subscriptions, bookstores—a world-wide audience concerned with the contemporary in literature." Quarterly. Estab. 1959. Circ. 1,200.
   ● PRISM *international* has won the Journey Prize Award and stories first published in PRISM have been included in the *Journey Prize Anthology* every year since 1991.
Needs: New writing that is contemporary and literary. Short stories and self-contained novel excerpts. Works of translation are eagerly sought and should be accompanied by a copy of the original. No gothic, confession, religious, romance, pornography, or sci-fi. Also looking for creative nonfiction that is literary, not journalistic, in scope and tone. Buys approximately 70 mss/year. Receives over 100 fiction unsolicited mss each month. PRISM publishes both new and established writers; our contributors have included Franz Kafka, Gabriel Garcia Marquez, Michael Ondaatje, Margaret Laurence, Mark Anthony Jarman, Gail Anderson-Dargatz and Eden Robinson. Submissions should not exceed 5,000 words "though flexible for outstanding work" (only one long story per submission, please). Publishes short shorts. Also publishes poetry and drama. Sponsors annual short fiction contest with $2,000 (Canadian) grand prize: send SASE for details.
How to Contact: Send complete ms with SASE or SAE, IRC and cover letter with bio, information and publications list. "Keep it simple. U.S. contributors take note: Do note send U.S. stamps, they are not valid in Canada. Send International Reply Coupons instead." Reports in 2-6 months. Electronic submissions OK (e-mail, web). Sample copy for $5 (U.S./Canadian).
Payment/Terms: Pays $20 (Canadian)/printed page, 1 year's subscription on publication for first North American serial rights. Selected authors are paid an additional $10/page for digital rights.
Advice: "Read several issues of our magazine before submitting. We are committed to publishing outstanding literary work in all genres. We look for strong, believeable characters; real voices; attention to language; interesting ideas and plots. Send us fresh, innovative work which also shows a mastery of the basics of good prose writing. Poorly constructed or sloppy pieces will not receive serious consideration. We welcome e-mail submissions and are proud to be one of few print literary journals who offer additional payment to select writers for digital publication. Too many e-mail submissions, however, come to us unpolished and unprepared to be published. Writers should craft their work for e-mail submission as carefully as they would for submissions through traditional methods. They should send one piece at a time and wait for our reply before they send another."

‡PROCREATION: A JOURNAL OF TRUTHTELLING IN POETRY & PROSE, (I), Silent Planet Publishing, Ltd., 6300-138 Creedmoor Rd., Raleigh NC 27612. Phone/fax: (919)510-9010. E-mail: slntplanet@aol.com. Editor: Stephen A. West. Fiction Editor: Peter Shedor. Journal: digest-sized; 30-36 pages; high-quality paper; matte card cover; photographs. "We are a literary journal dedicated to the pursuit and expression of artfully encapsulated truth. We believe that in creating we echo the Creator's own imaginative and creative activity and, so, become more fully human. We are interested in all kinds of truth, including spiritual truth, but we do not accept propaganda (however truthful), or religious or abstract prose not rooted in real-life experience." Triannually. Estab. 1997. Circ. 500.
Needs: Condensed/excerpted novel, experimental, humor/satire, literary, mainstream/contemporary, religious/inspirational. No erotica or "preachy or sentimental fiction." Receives 50 unsolicited mss/month. Accepts 4 mss/issue; 12 mss/year. Publishes ms 3 months after acceptance. Recently published work by Antonia Lilley and Stephen Robinson. Length: 1,500 words average; 250 words minimum; 2,000 words maximum. Publishes short

shorts. Length: 250 words. Also publishes poetry. Often critiques or comments on rejected mss.
How to Contact: Send complete ms with a cover letter. Include estimated word count, 1 page bio, list of publications "whether, if published, they desire to have contact information listed along with their byline. We seek interaction with the readership, if writers consent, so as to facilitate dialogue and community." Reports in 2 months. SASE for reply, return of ms or send a disposable copy of ms. Electronic submissions OK. Sample copy for $2 (US), $8 (foreign) and 5 first-class stamps or 2 IRCs. Fiction guidelines for #10 SASE or SAE and 1 IRC or by e-mail. Reviews novels and short story collections. Send books to Peter Sheder.
Payment/Terms: Pays 1 contributor's copy on publication; additional copies for $4. Acquires first North American serial rights.
Advice: "We look for strong imagery and well-written prose which reveals truth rather than simply states it in a didactic fashion. We are especially interested in fiction that strongly connects to human experience, whether tragic, comic or beautiful, yet which points to a larger truth outside itself, something transcendent. Look for the extraordinary in the ordinary. Write out of experience, with strong attention to the particulars of time, place, and character but at the same time capturing some universal, some shared truth, to which readers can relate."

PROVINCETOWN ARTS, (II), Provincetown Arts, Inc., 650 Commercial St., P.O. Box 35, Provincetown MA 02657. (508)487-3167. Editor: Christopher Busa. Magazine: 9×12; 184 pages; 60 lb. coated paper; 12 pcs. cover; illustrations and photographs. "*PA* focuses broadly on the artists, writers and theater of America's oldest continuous art colony." Annually. Estab. 1985. Circ. 8,000.
   • *Provincetown Arts* is a recipient of a CLMP seed grant. Provincetown Arts Press has an award-winning poetry series.
Needs: Plans special fiction issue. Receives 300 unsolicited mss/year. Buys 5 mss/issue. Publishes ms 3 months after acceptance. Published work by Carole Maso and Hilary Masters. Length: 3,000 words average; 1,500 words minimum; 8,000 words maximum. Publishes short shorts. Also publishes literary essays, literary criticism, poetry. Sometimes critiques rejected mss and recommends other markets.
How to Contact: Send complete ms with cover letter including previous publications. No simultaneous submissions. Reports in 2 weeks on queries; 3 months on mss. SASE. Sample copy for $7.50. Reviews novels and short story collections.
Payment/Terms: Pays $75-300 on publication for first rights. Sends galleys to author.

PUCKERBRUSH REVIEW, (I, II), Puckerbrush Press, 76 Main St., Orono ME 04473. (207)866-4868/581-3832. Editor: Constance Hunting. Magazine: 9×12; 80-100 pages; illustrations. "We publish mostly new Maine writers; interviews, fiction, reviews, poetry for a literary audience." Semiannually. Estab. 1979. Circ. approx. 500.
Needs: Belles-lettres, experimental, gay (occasionally), literary. "Nothing cliché." Receives 30 unsolicited mss/month. Accepts 6 mss/issue; 12 mss/year. Publishes ms 1 year after acceptance. Recently published work by David Fickett, Farnham Blair and Bethany Round. Sometimes publishes short shorts. Also publishes literary essays, literary criticism, poetry. Sometimes critiques rejected mss.
How to Contact: Send complete ms with cover letter. Reports in 2 months. SASE. Simultaneous submissions OK. Sample copy for $2. Fiction guidelines for SASE. Sometimes reviews novels and short story collections.
Payment/Terms: Pays in contributor's copies.
Advice: "I don't want to see tired plots or treatments. I want to see respect for language—the right words."

PUERTO DEL SOL, (I), New Mexico State University, Box 3E, Las Cruces NM 88003. (505)646-3931. Fax: (505)646-7725. Editors: Kay West, Antonya Nelson and Kevin McIlvoy. Magazine: 6×9; 200 pages; 60 lb. paper; 70 lb. cover stock; photos sometimes. "We publish quality material from anyone. Poetry, fiction, art, photos, interviews, reviews, parts-of-novels, long poems." Semiannually. Estab. 1961. Circ. 1,500.
Needs: Contemporary, ethnic, experimental, literary, mainstream, prose poem, excerpted novel and translations. Receives varied number of unsolicited fiction mss/month. Acquires 8-10 mss/issue; 12-15 mss/year. Does not read mss March through August. Recently published work by Dagobeuto Gilb, Wendell Mayo and William H. Cobb. Published 8-10 new writers/year. Also publishes poetry. Occasionally critiques rejected mss.
How to Contact: Send complete ms with SASE. Simultaneous submissions OK. Reports in 3 months. Sample copy for $7.
Payment/Terms: Pays 2 contributor's copies. Acquires one-time rights (rights revert to author).
Advice: "We are open to all forms of fiction, from the conventional to the wildly experimental, as long as they

---

LOOKING FOR A PARTICULAR GENRE? Check our Category Index for magazine and book publishers who want **Mystery/Suspense**, **Romance**, **Science Fiction & Fantasy**, **Thrillers**, **Westerns** and more!

have integrity and are well written. Too often we receive very impressively 'polished' mss that will dazzle readers with their sheen but offer no character/reader experience of lasting value."

*QUADRANT, P.O. Box 1495, Collingwood, Victoria 3066 Australia. Fiction Editor: Mr. Les Murray. Monthly. Circ. 6,000. Publishes 1-2 stories/issue.
Needs: "Magazine of current affairs, culture, politics, economics, the arts, literature, ideas; stories: general and varied." Length: 800 words minimum; 5,000 words maximum.
Payment/Terms: Pays contributor's copies and a minimum of $100 (Australian). For sample copy "write to us, enclosing cheque for $6 U.S. or equivalent."

‡✷QUARRY, (II), Quarry Press, Box 1061, Kingston, Ontario K7L 4Y5 Canada. (613)548-8429. Contact: Fiction Editor. Magazine: 7¼×9¼; 120 pages; #1 book 120 paper; 160 lb. Curtis Tweed cover stock; illustrations; photos. "Quarterly anthology of new Canadian poetry, prose. Also includes travelogues and book reviews. We seek readers interested in vigorous, disciplined, new Canadian writing." Estab. 1952. Circ. 1,700.
Needs: Experimental, fantasy, literary. "We do not want highly derivative or clichéd style." Receives 80-100 unsolicited fiction mss/month. Buys 4-5 mss/issue; 20 mss/year. Does not read in July. Less than 5% of fiction is agented. Published work by Diane Schoemperlen, David Helwig, Joan Fern Shaw; published new writers within the last year. Length: 3,000 words average. Publishes short shorts. Usually critiques rejected mss and recommends other markets.
How to Contact: Send complete ms with SAE, IRC and brief bio. Publishes ms an average of 3-6 months after acceptance. Sample copy for $6.95 Canadian with 4×7 SAE and 46¢ Canadian postage or IRC.
Payment/Terms: Pays $10/page; 1 year subscription to magazine and 1 contributor's copy on publication for first North American serial rights.
Advice: "Read previous *Quarry* to see standard we seek. Read Canadian fiction to see Canadian trends. We seek aggressive experimentation which is coupled with competence (form, style) and stimulating subject matter. Our annual prose issue (spring) is always a sellout. Many of our selections have been anthologized. *Don't send US stamps or SASE if outside Canada! Use IRCs.* Submit with brief bio."

QUARTERLY WEST, (II), University of Utah, 200 S. Campus Dr., Room 317, Salt Lake City UT 84112-9109. (801)581-3938. Editor: Margot Schilpp. Fiction Editor: Charlotte Freeman. Editors change every 2 years. Magazine: 6×9; 200 pages; 60 lb. paper; 5-color cover stock; illustrations and photographs rarely. "We try to publish a variety of fiction and poetry from all over the country based not so much on the submitting author's reputation but on the merit of each piece. Our publication is aimed primarily at an educated audience interested in contemporary literature and criticism." Semiannually. "We sponsor a biennial novella competition." (Next competition held in 1998). Estab. 1976. Circ. 1,800.
● *Quarterly West* is a past recipient of a grant from the NEA and was awarded First Place for Editorial Content from the American Literary Magazine Awards. Work published in the magazine has been selected for inclusion in the *Pushcart Prize* anthology and *The Best American Short Stories* anthology.
Needs: Literary, contemporary, experimental, translations. Accepts 6-10 mss/issue, 12-20 mss/year. Receives 250 unsolicited fiction mss each month. Recently published work by H.E. Francis, Alan Chense, Ron Carlson, Karen Brennan, William T. Vollmann, David Kranes and Antonya Nelson. Publishes 10-15 new writers/year. No preferred length; interested in longer, "fuller" short stories, as well as short shorts. Critiques rejected mss when there is time.
How to Contact: Send complete ms. Brief cover letters welcome. Send SASE for reply or return of ms. Simultaneous submissions OK with acknowledgement. Reports in 2-3 months; "sooner, if possible." Sample copy for $6.50.
Payment/Terms: Pays $15-500 and 2 contributor's copies on publication for all rights (negotiable).
Advice: "We publish a special section of short shorts every issue, and we also sponsor a biennial novella contest. We are open to experimental work—potential contributors should read the magazine! We solicit quite frequently, but tend more toward the surprises—unsolicited. Don't send more than one story per submission, but submit as often as you like."

‡RAFALE, Supplement Littéraire, (II, IV), Franco-American Research Organization Group, University of Maine, Franco American Center, 164 College Ave., Orono ME 04473-1578. (207)581-3764. Fax: (207)581-1455. E-mail: lisam@maine.maine.edu. Contact: Lisa Michaud, co-editor/secretary. Editor: Rhea Cote Robbins. Tabloid size, magazine format: 4 pages; illustrations and photos. Publication was founded to stimulate and recognize creative expression among Franco-Americans, all types of readers, including literary and working class. This publication is used in university classrooms. Circulated internationally. Quarterly. Estab. 1986. Circ. 5,000.
Needs: "We will consider any type of short fiction, poetry and critical essays having to do with Franco-American experience. They must be of good quality in French as well as English. We are also looking for Canadian writers with French-North American experiences." Receives about 10 unsolicited mss/month. Accepts 2-4 mss/issue. Published work by Robert Cormier; published new writers within the last year. Length: 1,000 words average; 750 words minimum; 2,500 words maximum. Occasionally critiques rejected mss.
How to Contact: Send complete ms with cover letter. Include a short bio and list of previous publications.

Reports in 3 weeks on queries; 1 month on mss. SASE. Simultaneous, reprint and electronic submissions (e-mail, fax) OK.

Payment/Terms: Pays $10 and 3 copies for one-time rights.

Advice: "Write honestly. Start with a strongly felt personal Franco-American experience. If you make us feel what you have felt, we will publish it. We stress that this publication deals specifically with the Franco-American experience."

RAG MAG, (II), Box 12, Goodhue MN 55027-0012. (612)923-4590. Publisher/Editor: Beverly Voldseth. Magazine: 6×9; 60-112 pages; varied paper quality; illustrations; photos. "We are eager to print poetry, prose and art work. We are open to all styles." Semiannually. Estab. 1982. Circ. 300.

Needs: Adventure, comics, contemporary, erotica, ethnic, experimental, fantasy, feminist, literary, mainstream, prose poem, regional. "Anything well written is a possibility. It has to be a good adult story, tight, with plot and zip. I also like strange but well done. No extremely violent or pornographic writing." Receives 100 unsolicited mss/month. Accepts 4 mss/issue. Recently published work by Karen Herseth Wee, Riki Kölbl Nelson, Larry Schug, Kerry Bolander and Greg Komicki. Published new writers within the last year. Length: 1,000 words average; 2,200 words maximum. Occasionally critiques rejected mss.

How to Contact: Send 3-6 pages, brief bio and brief cover letter. SASE. Reports in 3-4 weeks. Simultaneous and previously published submissions OK. Single copy for $6.

Payment/Terms: Pays 1 contributor's copy; $4.50 charge for extras. Acquires one-time rights.

Advice: "Submit clean copy on regular typing paper (no tissue-thin stuff). We want fresh images, sparse language, words that will lift us out of our chairs. I like the short story form. I think it's powerful and has a definite place in the literary magazine."

RAMBUNCTIOUS REVIEW, (I, II), Rambunctious Press, Inc., 1221 W. Pratt Blvd., Chicago IL 60626. Editor: Mary Alberts. Fiction Editor: Nancy Lennon. Magazine: 10×7; 48 pages; illustrations and photos. Annually. Estab. 1983. Circ. 300.

Needs: Experimental, feminist, humor/satire, literary, mainstream/contemporary. List of upcoming themes available for SASE. Receives 30 unsolicited mss/month. Accepts 4-5 mss/issue. Does not read mss May through August. Publishes ms 5-6 months after acceptance. Published work by Sharon Sloan Fiffer, Hugh Fox, Lyn Lifshin and Stephen Schroder. Length: 12 double-spaced pages. Publishes short shorts. Also publishes poetry. Sometimes critiques or comments on rejected mss. Sponsors contest. Send SASE for details.

How to Contact: Send complete ms with a cover letter. Include estimated word count. Reports in 9 months. Send SASE for reply, return of ms or send a disposable copy of ms. Simultaneous submissions OK. Sample copy for $4.

Payment/Terms: Pays 2 contributor's copies. Acquires one-time rights.

‡RASKOLNIKOV'S CELLAR and THE LAMPLIGHT, (I, II), The Beggars's Press, 8110 N. 38th St., Omaha NE 68112-2018. (402)455-2615. Editor: Richard Carey. Fiction Editor: Roberta Gardner. Magazine: 8½×12; 60-150 pages; 20 lb. bond paper; 12pt soft cover. "Our purpose is to encourage writing in the style of the past masters and to hold back illiteracy in our generation." Semiannually. Estab. 1952. Circ. 1,200.

● Member of the International Association of Independent Publishers and the Federation of Literary Publishers.

Needs: Historical, horror, humor/satire, literary, romance (gothic), serialized novels, translations. No "religious, sentimental, folksy, science fiction or ultra modern." Publishes special fiction issue or anthologies. Receives 135 unsolicited mss/month. Accepts 15 mss/issue; 30-45 mss/year. Publishes ms 2-6 months after acceptance. Agented fiction 5%. Recently published work by Frances Downing Hunter, Lucy Streeter, Richard Davignon and Philip Sparacino. Length: 1,500-2,000 words average; 50 words minimum; 3,000 words maximum. Publishes short shorts. Also publishes literary essays, literary criticism and poetry. Always critiques or comments on rejected mss.

How to Contact: Send complete ms with a cover letter. Include estimated word count and 1 page bio. Reports in 2 months on queries; 4 months on mss. Simultaneous submissions OK. Sample copy for $10 plus 9×12 SAE with 2 first-class stamps. Fiction guidelines for #10 SAE with 2 first-class stamps. Reviews novels or short story collections. Send books to Danielle Staton.

Payment/Terms: Pays 1 contributor's copy for first North American serial rights.

Advice: "We judge on writing style as well as content. If your style of writing and your word usage do not attract us at once, there is faint hope of the content and the plot saving the story. Read and learn from the great writers of the past. Set your stories in the un-computer age, so your characters have time to think, to feel, to react. Use your glorious language to the fullest. Our subscribers can read quite well. The strongest way to say anything is to never quite say it."

THE RAVEN CHRONICLES, A Magazine of Multicultural Art, Literature and the Spoken Word, (I, II), The Raven Chronicles, P. O. Box 95918, Seattle WA 98145. (206)543-0249. Fax: (206)543-1104. E-mail: ravenchron@speakeasy.org. Website: http://www.speakeasy.org/ravenchronicles (includes guidelines, editors, short fiction, prose, poetry, separate monthly topics for online publication). Managing Editor: Phoebe Bosché. Fiction Editors: Annie Hansen and Lourdes Orive. Poetry Editors: Tiffany Midge and Jody Aliesan. Webmaster:

Matt Briggs. Magazine: 8½ × 11; 48-64 pages; 50 lb. book paper; glossy cover; b&w illustrations; photos. "*The Raven Chronicles* is designed to promote multicultural art, literature and the spoken word." Triannually. Estab. 1991. Circ. 2,500-5,000.

● This magazine is a frequent winner of Bumbershoot Bookfair awards. The magazine also received grants from the Washington State Arts Commission, the Seattle Arts Commission, the King County Arts Commission and ATR, a foundation for social justice projects.

Needs: Ethnic/multicultural, literary, regional. Upcoming theme: The writer in contemporary society. Receives 300-400 mss/month. Buys 2-3 mss/issue; 8 mss/year. Publishes 3-6 months after acceptance. Published work by David Romtvedt, Sherman Alexie, D.L. Birchfield, Nancy Redwine, Greg Hischak and Sharon Hashimoto. Length: 2,000 words average; 2,500 words maximum. Publishes short shorts. Length: 300-500 words. Also publishes literary essays, literary criticism, poetry. Sometimes critiques rejected mss.

How to Contact: Send complete ms with a cover letter. Include estimated word count. Reports in 4-8 months on manuscripts. Send SASE for return of ms. Simultaneous submissions OK. Sample copy for $3. Fiction guidelines for #10 SASE.

Payment/Terms: Pays $10-40 plus 2 contributor's copies; additional copies at half cover cost. Pays on publication for first North American serial rights. Sends galleys to author.

Advice: Looks for "clean, direct language, written from the heart. Read sample copy, or look at *Before Columbus* anthologies, *Greywolf Annual* anthologies."

READER'S BREAK, (I), Pine Grove Press, P.O. Box 40, Jamesville NY 13078. (315)423-9268. Editor: Gertrude S. Eiler. Annual anthology with an "emphasis on short stories written with style and ability. Our aim has always been to publish work of quality by authors with talent, whether previously published or not."

Needs: "We welcome stories about relationships, tales of action, adventure, science fiction and fantasy, romance, suspense and mystery. Themes and plots may be historical , contemporary or futuristic. No "pornography, sexual perversion, incest or stories for children." Length: 3,500 words maximum. Also publishes "poems to 75 lines in any style or form and on any subject with the above exceptions."

How to Contact: Accepts unsolicited mss. Include SASE. Reports in 3-5 months "since the stories are considered by a number of editorial readers." Reviews novels. SASE for details.

Terms: Pays 1 contributor's copy for one-time rights; additional copies at 20% discount.

Advice: "We prefer fiction with a well-constructed plot and well-defined characters of any age or socio-economic group. Upbeat endings are not required. Please check the sequence of events, their cause-and-effect relationship, the motivation of your characters, and the resolution of plot."

RE:AL, The Journal of Liberal Arts, Stephen F. Austin State University, P.O. Box 13007, Nacogdoches TX 75925. (409)468-2059. Fax: (409)468-2614. E-mail: real@sfasu.edu. Website: http://www.sfasu.edu (includes writer's guidelines). Editor: W. Dale Hearell. Academic journal: 6 × 10; perfect-bound; 120-150 pages; "top" stock. Editorial content: 30% fiction, 30% poetry, 30% scholarly essays and criticism; an occasional play, book reviews (assigned after query) and interviews. "Work is reviewed based on the intrinsic merit of the scholarship and creative work and its appeal to a sophisticated international readership (U.S., Canada, Great Britain, Ireland, Brazil, Puerto Rico, Italy)." Semiannually. Estab. 1968. Circ. 400.

Needs: Adventure, contemporary, genre, feminist, science fiction, historical, experimental, regional. Receives 1,400-1,600 unsolicited mss/2 issues. Accepts 2-5 fiction mss/issue. Publishes 1-12 months after acceptance. Recently published work by John M. Clarke, Linda L. Dunlap, Lucas Carpenter and William Herman. Publishes as many new writers as possible. Length: 1,000-7,000 words. Occasionally critiques rejected mss and conditionally accepts on basis of critiques and changes.

How to Contact: Send complete ms with cover letter. No simultaneous submissions. Reports in 2 weeks on queries; 3-4 weeks on mss. SASE. Sample copy and writer's guidelines for $6.50. Guidelines for SASE.

Payment/Terms: Pays 2 contributor's copies; charges for extras. Rights revert to author.

Advice: "Please study an issue. Have your work checked by a well-published writer—who is not a good friend. Also proofread for grammatical and typographical errors. A manuscript must show that the writer is conscious of what he or she is attempting to accomplish in plot, character and theme. A short story isn't written but constructed; the ability to manipulate certain aspects of a story is the sign of a conscious storyteller."

RED CEDAR REVIEW, (II), Dept. of English, 17C Morrill Hall, Michigan State University, East Lansing MI 48824. (517)355-9656. Editors change. Fiction Editor: David Sheridan. Magazine: 5½ × 8½; 100 pages. Theme: "literary—poetry and short fiction." Biannual. Estab. 1963. Circ. 400.

Needs: Literary. "Good stories with character, plot and style, any genre, but with a real tilt toward literary fiction." Accepts 3-4 mss/issue, 6-10 mss/year. Published work by Diane Wakoski, Tom Paine and Mark Jacobs. Length: Open. Also publishes poetry, 4 poems per submission.

How to Contact: Query with unpublished ms with SASE. No simultaneous submissions. Reports in 2-3 months on mss. Publishes ms up to 4 months after acceptance. Sample copy for $5.

Payment/Terms: Pays 2 contributor's copies. $5 charge for extras. Acquires first rights.

Advice: "It would be nice to see more stories that self-confidently further our literary tradition in some way, stories that 'marry artistic vision with moral insight.' What does your story discover about the human condition? What have you done with words and sentences that's new? Hundreds of journals get hundreds of manuscripts in the mail each month. Why does yours need to get printed? I don't want to learn yet again that innocent people suffer, that life is hollow, that the universe is meaningless. Nor do I want to be told that a warm kitten can save one from the abyss. I want an honest, well crafted exploration of where and what we are. Something after which I can no longer see the world in the same way."

REED MAGAZINE, (I, II), % English Dept., San Jose State University, 1 Washington Square, San Jose CA 95192-0090. (408)924-4493. Fax: (408)924-4580. E-mail: channah817@aol.com. Website: http://www.SJSU.edu. Contact: Fiction Editor. Editors change each year. Magazine: 5×8; 120 pages; matte paper; glossy cover; illustrations; photos. "We publish the highest quality material we can find." Annually. Estab. 1946. Circ. 500.
  ● *Reed Magazine* would like to see more literary science fiction.
Needs: Experimental, humor/satire, literary, regional. "All quality work is considered." No genre romance. Receives 7-10 unsolicited mss/month. Accepts 40-50 mss/issues. Does not read mss May through August. Publishes ms each May. Recently published work by Pearl Mary Wilshaw, Gary J. Langguth, Lyn Lifshin, Dr. Nora Ruth Roberts and Simon Perchik. Length: 4,000 words average. Publishes short shorts. Also publishes literary essays and poetry.
How to Contact: Send complete ms with a cover letter. Include estimated word count and list of publications. Reports in 6 weeks on queries; 3 months on mss. Send SASE for reply, return of ms or send a disposable copy of ms. Electronic submissions OK; include hard copy. E-mail/fax submissions OK. Sample copy for $4.95 and 6×9 SASE with 3 first-class stamps. Fiction guidelines given in the magazine.
Payment/Terms: Pays 2 contributor's copies. Author retains all rights.
Advice: Looks for "quality and originality. Most of all, we're looking for a distinctive voice. Read the best magazines and make yourself an expert in what makes a story work. We'd like to see more lovingly obsessive attention to detail. We don't want to see generic and undetailed five-page stories."

REFLECT, (II, IV), 3306 Argonne Ave., Norfolk VA 23509. (804)857-1097). Editor: W.S. Kennedy. Magazine: 5½×8½; 48 pages; pen & ink illustrations. "Spiral Mode fiction and poetry for writers and poets—professional and amateur." Quarterly. Estab. 1979.
Needs: Spiral fiction. "The four rules to the Spiral Mode fiction form are: (1) The story a situation or condition. (2) The outlining of the situation in the opening paragraphs. The story being told at once, the author is not overly-involved with dialogue and plot development, may concentrate on *sound*, *style*, *color*—the superior elements in art. (3) The use of a concise style with euphonic wording. Good poets may have the advantage here. (4) The involvement of Spiral Fiction themes—as opposed to Spiral Poetry themes—with love, and presented with the mystical overtones of the Mode." No "smut, bad taste, socialist. . . ." Accepts 2-6 mss/issue; 8-24 mss/year. Publishes ms 3 months after acceptance. Published work by Ruth Wildes Schuler, Greg Smith and Gurattan Khalsa. Length: 1,500 words average; 2,500 words maximum. Publishes short shorts. Sometimes critiques rejected mss.
How to Contact: Send complete ms with cover letter. Reports in 2 months on mss. SASE. No simultaneous submissions. Sample copy for $2. (Make checks payable to W.S. Kennedy.) Fiction guidelines in each issue of *Reflect*.
Payment/Terms: Pays contributor's copies. Acquires one-time rights. Publication not copyrighted.
Advice: "Subject matter usually is not relevant to the successful writing of Spiral Fiction, as long as there is some element or type of *love* in the story, and provided that there are mystical references. (Though a dream-like style may qualify as 'mystical.')"

REVIEW: LATIN AMERICAN LITERATURE AND ARTS, 680 Park Ave., New York NY 10021. (212)249-8950, ext. 366. Editor: Alfred MacAdam. Managing Editor: Daniel Shapiro. "Magazine of Latin American fiction, poetry and essays in translation for academic, corporate and general audience." Biannual.
Needs: Literary. No political or sociological mss. Receives 5 unsolicited mss/month. Accepts 20 mss/year. Length: 1,500-2,000 words average. Occasionally critiques rejected mss.
How to Contact: Query first. Reports in 3 months. "Submissions must be previously unpublished in English." Simultaneous submissions OK, if notified of acceptance elsewhere. Sample copy free. Reviews novels and short story collections. Send books to Daniel Shapiro, Managing Editor.
Payment/Terms: Pays $50-200 and 2-3 contributor's copies on publication.
Advice: "We are always looking for good translators."

‡RIO GRANDE REVIEW, UT El Paso's literary magazine, (II), Student publications, 105 E. Union, University of Texas at El Paso, El Paso TX 79968. (915)747-5161. Fax: (915)747-8031. E-mail: rgr@mail.utep.edu. Editors: Skipper Warson and Magdoline Asfahan. Editors change each year. Magazine: 6×9; approximately 100 pages; 70 lb. paper; 85 lb. cover stock; illustrations and photographs. "We publish any work that challenges writing and reading audiences alike. The intended audience isn't any one sect in particular; rather, the work forcing readers to think as opposed to couch reading is encouraged." Semiannually. Estab. 1984. Circ. 1,000.
Needs: Experimental, feminist, gay, humor/satire, lesbian, mainstream/contemporary, flash fiction, short drama. No regional, "anything exclusionarily academic." Receives 40-45 unsolicited mss/month. Accepts 3-4 mss/issue; 6-8 mss/year. Does not read mss March 2-July 31; October 2-December 31. Publishes ms approximately 1 month after acceptance. Recently published work by Lawrence Dunning, James J. O'Keeffe and Carole Bubash. Length:

1,750 words average; 1,100 words minimum; 2,000 words maximum. Publishes short shorts. Also publishes poetry. Sometimes critiques or comments on rejected mss.

How to Contact: Send complete ms with a cover letter. Include estimated word count, 40-word bio and list of publications. Reports in 3 months on queries; 4 months on mss. Send SASE for reply and disposable copy of ms. Electronic submissions OK. Sample copy for $3.

Payment/Terms: Pays 2 contributor's copies on publication; additional copies for $3. Acquires "one-time rights that revert back to the author but the *Rio Grande Review* must be mentioned."

Advice: "Be patient. If the beginning fiction writer doesn't make it into the edition the first time, re-submit. Be persistent. One huge category that the *RGR* is branching into is flash fiction. Because the attention span of the nation is dwindling, thereby turning to such no-brain activities as television and movies, literature must change to accommodate as well."

‡RIVER CITY, (II), Dept. of English, The University of Memphis, Memphis TN 38152. (901)678-4509. Editor: Paul Naylor. Magazine: 6×9; 150 pages. Semiannually. Estab. 1980. Circ. 1,200.

Needs: Novel excerpts, short stories. Upcoming themes: "The Southern/Caribbean Connection." Recently published work by Fred Busch and Lucille Clifton; published new writers within the last year.

How to Contact: Send complete ms with SASE. Reports in 2 months on ms. Sample copy for $7.

Payment/Terms: Awards an annual $100 prize for best poem or best short story and 2 contributor's copies. "We pay if grant monies are available." Acquires first North American serial rights.

Advice: "We're soliciting work from writers with a national reputation, and are occasionally able to pay, depending on grants received. I would prefer no cover letter. *River City* Writing Awards in Fiction: $2,000 1st prize, $500 2nd prize, $300 3rd prize. See magazine for details."

RIVER STYX, (I, II), Big River Association, 3207 Washington Ave., St. Louis MO 63103-1218. Editor: Richard Newman. Magazine: 6×9; 90 pages; color card cover; perfect-bound; b&w visual art. "No theme restrictions; only high quality, intelligent work." Triannual. Estab. 1975.

Needs: Excerpted novel chapter, contemporary, ethnic, experimental, feminist, gay, satire, lesbian, literary, mainstream, prose poem, translations. Receives 15 unsolicited mss/month. Accepts 1-3 mss/issue; 3-8 mss/year. Reads only May through November. Recently published work by Richard Burgin, Leslie Pietrzyk and Peggy Shinner. Length: no more than 20-30 manuscript pages. Publishes short shorts. Also publishes poetry. Sometimes critiques rejected mss and recommends other markets.

How to Contact: Send complete ms with name and address on every page. SASE required. Reports in 3-5 months on mss. Simultaneous submissions OK, "if a note is enclosed with your work and if we are notified immediately upon acceptance elsewhere." Sample copy for $7.

Payment/Terms: Pays 2 contributor's copies, 1-year subscription and $8/page "if funds available." Acquires first North American serial rights.

Advice: "We want high-powered stories with well-developed characters. Strong plots usually with at least three memorable scenes. No thin, flimsy fiction with merely serviceable language."

RIVERSEDGE, A Journal of Art & Literature, (II), CAS 266, UT-PA, 1201 W. University Dr., Edinburg TX 78539-2999. (210)381-3638. Fax: (210)381-2177. E-mail: bookworm@panam.edu. Editor: Dorey Schmidt. Magazine: 100 pages; b&w illustrations and photos. "As a 'Third Coast' publication, *RiverSedge* prints regional and national creative voices whose origin or content speaks specifically to the unique multicultural reality of the Southwest, while retaining a commitment to the universality of quality art and literature." Semiannually. Estab. 1972. Circ. 300.

Needs: Ethnic/multicultural, experimental, feminist, historical, literary, mainstream/contemporary, regional, translations. Upcoming theme: "International" (November '97). List of upcoming themes available for SASE. Plans annual special fiction issue or anthology in the future. Receives 10-12 unsolicited mss/month. Accepts 6-8 mss/issue; 12-16 mss/year. Does not read mss in summer. Publishes ms 4-6 weeks after acceptance. Published work by Jan Epton Seale, Greg Garrett, Amy Hatfield, Stephen Porter and Jeffrey DeLotto. Publishes 5-6 new writers/year. Length: 1,600 words preferred; 100 words minimum; 2,500 words maximum. Also publishes literary essays and poetry. Sometimes critiques or comments on rejected mss.

How to Contact: Send complete ms with a cover letter and bio (not over 200 words). Submission deadlines: April 15 and November 15. Reports in 4 months on mss. Send SASE for reply, return of ms or send a disposable copy of ms. Simultaneous (if noted) and electronic (Mac disk) submissions OK. Sample copy for SASE.

Payment/Terms: Pays 2 contributor's copies; additional copies for $6. Acquires one-time rights.

Advice: Looks for "general literariness—a sense of language as link, not lectern. Characters who look and act and speak in believable ways. Stories which are not simply outpourings of human angst, but which acknowledge life. Find some positive aspects of life to write about. Read several issues of the publication first!" Would like to see more "stories which do not depend on excessive profanity, violence, pain and sexist attitudes. If everyone is screaming at a high pitch, no one hears anything. How about just a few quiet helpful whispers?"

RIVERWIND, (I, II), General Studies/Hocking College, 3301 Hocking Pkwy., Nelsonville OH 45764. (614)753-3591 (ext. 2375). Editors: Deni Naffziger and Jane Ann Devol-Fuller. Fiction Editor: Robert Clark Young.

Magazine: 7×7; 60 lb. paper; cover illustrations; "College press, small literary magazine." Annually. Estab. 1975.

● In addition to receiving funding from the Ohio Arts Council since 1985, *Riverwind* has won the Septa Award and a Sepan Award.

Needs: Contemporary, ethnic, feminist, historical, humor/satire, literary, mainstream, prose poem, spiritual, sports, regional, translations. No juvenile/teen fiction. Receives 30 mss/month. Does not read during the summer. Published work by Roy Bentley and Greg Anderson; published new writers within the last year. Sometimes critiques rejected mss.

How to Contact: Send complete ms with a cover letter. No simultaneous submissions. Reports on mss in 1-4 months. SASE. Sample back issue: $1.

Payment/Terms: Pays in contributor's copies.

Advice: "Your work must be strong, entertaining. It helps if you are an Ohio/West Virginia writer. We hope to print more fiction. We now publish mainly regional writers (Ohio, West Virginia, Kentucky)."

ROCKET PRESS, (I, II), (formerly *Literary Rocket*), P.O. Box 730, Greenport NY 11944. E-mail: rocketusa@d elphi.com. Editor: Darren Johnson. 16-page newspaper. "A Rocket is a transcendental, celestial traveler—innovative and intelligent fiction and poetry aimed at opening minds—even into the next century." Biannually. Estab. 1993. Circ. 500-2,000.

Needs: Erotica, experimental, humor/satire, literary, special interests (prose poetry). "No genre, autobiographical fiction, writing without a story, anything derivative in the least." Publishes annual special fiction issue or anthology. Receives 20 unsolicited mss/month. Accepts 2-4 mss/issue; 8-16 mss/year. Recently published work by Chris Woods, Roger Lee Kenvin and Ben Ohmart. Length: 1,000 words average; 500 words minimum; 2,000 words maximum. Publishes short shorts. Length: 400 words. Also publishes poetry. Sometimes critiques or comments on rejected mss.

How to Contact: Reports in 2 weeks on queries; 1 month on mss. Send SASE for reply, return of ms or send a disposable copy of ms. Simultaneous submissions OK. Current issue $2, past issue $1.

Payment/Terms: Pays 1 copy or free subscription to the magazine; additional copies for $1. Acquires one-time rights.

Advice: "We've changed our dateline to 2050 A.D. and publish straight, newspaper-style stories that fit that time frame. Send anything that could also be publishable fifty years from now. Zany is okay."

THE ROCKFORD REVIEW, (I, II), The Rockford Writers Guild, Box 858, Rockford IL 61105. Editor-in-Chief: David Ross. Magazine: 5⅜×8½; 50 pages; b&w illustrations; b&w photos. "We look for prose and poetry with a fresh approach to old themes or new insights into the human condition." Triquarterly. Estab. 1971. Circ. 750.

Needs: Ethnic, experimental, fantasy, humor/satire, literary, regional, science fiction (hard science, soft/sociological). Published work by Valerie Ann Leff, Tom Deiker, William Gorman and Melanie Coronetz. Length: Up to 1,300 words. Also publishes one-acts and essays.

How to Contact: Send complete ms. "Include a short biographical note—no more than four sentences." Simultaneous submissions OK. Reports in 6-8 weeks on mss. SASE. Sample copy for $5. Fiction guidelines for SASE.

Payment/Terms: Pays contributor's copies. "Two $25 editor's choice cash prizes per issue." Acquires first North American serial rights.

Advice: "Any subject or theme goes as long as it enhances our understanding of our humanity." Wants more "satire and humor, good dialogue."

‡*ROMANIAN REVIEW, Redactia Publicatiilor Pentru Strainatate, Piata Presei Libere NR1, 71341 Bucuresti Romania. Fiction Editor: Mrs. Andreea Ionescu. Monthly. Fiction 40%.

Needs: "Our review is scanning the Romanian history and cultural realities, the cooperation with other countries in the cultural field and it is also a mean of acquaintance with Romanian and overseas writers. We publish the *Romanian Review* in three languages (English, German, French). Fiction related to Romanian civilization may enter the pages of the *Review*." Length: 2,000 words minimum; 5,000 words maximum.

Payment/Terms: "As we do not have the possibility of payment in foreign currency, we can only offer "lei" 2,000-10,000/story, depending on its length and qualities. The exchange may be done on the writer's account." Sample copies available; write for information.

‡SALAMANDER, a magazine for poetry, fiction & memoirs, (II), 48 Ackers Ave., Brookline MA 02146. (617)232-0031. Editor: Jennifer Barber. Fiction Editor: Peter Brown. Magazine: 5½×8½; 80 pages; illustrations

 THE DOUBLE DAGGER before a listing indicates that the listing is new in this edition. New markets are often the most receptive to submissions by new writers.

and photos. "We publish outstanding work by new and established writers for a literary audience." Semiannually. Estab. 1992. Circ. 1,000.

 • Received a grant from the National Endowment for the Arts. Member of CLMP.

Needs: Ethnic/multicultural, experimental, feminist, gay, historical, literary, mainstream/contemporary. "Open to most categories." Receives 20 unsolicited mss/month. Accepts 3 mss/issue; 6 mss/year. Does not read during the summer. Publishes ms 3-6 months after acceptance. Agented fiction 1%. Recently published work by Peter Ho Davies, Susan Monsky, Rebecca McClanahan and Marc Bookman. Length: 10-15 pages. Publishes short shorts. Also publishes literary essays and poetry.

How to Contact: Send complete ms with a cover letter or submit through an agent. Include bio and list of publications. Reports in 1 month on queries, 4 months on mss. Send SASE for return of ms. Sample copy for $3 and 6×9 SAE with $1.47 postage. Fiction guidelines for #10 SASE.

Payment/Terms: Pays $25/two pages printed in magazine plus 2 contributor's copies for one-time rights. Sometimes sends galleys to author.

‡**SALT HILL JOURNAL, (II)**, Salt Hill Literary Association, English Dept., Syracuse University, Syracuse NY 13210. E-mail: jsparker@mailbox.syr.edu. Editor: Peter S. Fendrick. Fiction Editor: Deborah Olin Unferth. Editors change each year. Magazine: 5½×8½; 96 pages; 70 lb. paper; 80 lb. gloss cover; illustrations and photos. Publishes fiction with "fresh imagery, original language and tonal and structural experimentation." Semiannually. Estab. 1994. Circ. 700.

 • Member of CLMP. Sponsors short short fiction contest. Deadline September 15. Send SASE for details.

Needs: Erotica, ethnic/multicultural, experimental, gay, humor/satire, lesbian, literary, translations. No genre fiction. Receives 40-50 unsolicited mss/month. Accepts 3-5 mss/issue; 6-10 mss/year. Does not read April-June. Publishes ms 2-8 months after acceptance. Recently published work by Lydia Davis, Adrienne Clasky and Elizabeth May. Length: 4,500 words maximum. Publishes short shorts. Also publishes literary essays, literary criticism and poetry.

How to Contact: Send complete ms with a cover letter. Include 3-5 sentence bio and estimated word count. Reports in 2-6 months on mss. Send SASE for reply, return of ms or send disposable copy of ms. Simultaneous submissions OK. Sample copy for $7. Fiction guidelines for #10 SASE. Reviews novels or short story collections. Send books to "Book Review Editor."

Payment/Terms: Pays 2 contributor's copies for first North American serial rights and web rights; additional copies $7. Sends galleys to author.

SALT LICK PRESS, (II), Salt Lick Foundation, Salt Lick Press/Lucky Heart Books, 1900 West Hwy. 6, Waco TX 76712. Editor: James Haining. Magazine: 8½×11; 100 pages; 70 lb. offset stock; 65 lb. cover; illustrations and photos. Irregularly. Estab. 1969.

Needs: Contemporary, erotica, ethnic, experimental, feminist, gay, lesbian, literary. Receives 25 unsolicited mss each month. Accepts 4 mss/issue. Length: open. Occasionally critiques rejected mss.

How to Contact: Send complete ms with cover letter. Reports in 2 weeks on queries; 1 month on mss. SASE. Simultaneous and reprint submissions OK. Sample copy for $6, 9×12 SAE and 3 first-class stamps.

Payment/Terms: Pays in contributor's copies. Acquires first North American serial rights. Sends galleys to author.

SAMSARA, The Magazine of Suffering, (IV), P.O. Box 367, College Park MD 20741-0367. Website: http://members.aol.com/rdfgoalie/sammain.htm (includes writer's guidelines and tips to writers). Editor: R. David Fulcher. Magazine: 8½×11; 50-80 pages; Xerox paper; poster stock cover; illustrations. "*Samsara* publishes only stories or poems relating to suffering." Semiannually. Estab. 1994. Circ. 250.

 • *Samsara* is a member of the Small Press Genre Association.

Needs: Condensed/excerpted novel, erotica, experimental, fantasy (science fantasy, sword and sorcery), horror, literary, mainstream/contemporary, science fiction (hard science, soft/sociological). Receives 40 unsolicited mss/month. Accepts 17-20 mss/issue; 40 mss/year. "*Samsara* closes to submission after the publication of each issue. However, this schedule is not fixed." Publishes ms 4 months after acceptance. Recently published work by D.F. Lewis, D. Ceder and Harrison Wein. Length: 2,000 words average; no minimum or maximum. Publishes short shorts. Also publishes poetry. Sometimes critiques or comments on rejected ms.

How to Contact: Send complete ms with a cover letter. Include estimated word count, 1-page bio and list of publications. Reports in 3 months on queries. Send SASE for reply, return of ms or send a disposable copy of ms. Simultaneous, reprint and electronic submissions OK. Sample copy for $2.50. Fiction guidelines for #10 SASE.

Payment/Terms: Pays 1 contributor's copy. Acquires first North American serial rights and reprint rights.

Advice: "Symbolism and myth really make a manuscript stand out. Read a sample copy. Too many writers send work which does not pertain to the guidelines. Writers should avoid sending us splatter-punk or gore stories."

SANSKRIT, Literary Arts Publication of UNC Charlotte, (II), University of North Carolina at Charlotte, Highway 49, Charlotte NC 28223. (704)547-2326. Contact: Literary Editor. Magazine: 9×12, 60-90 pages. "We are a general lit/art mag open to all genres, if well written, for college students, alumni, writers and artists across the country." Annually. Estab. 1968.

• *Sanskrit* has received the Pacemaker Award, Associated College Press, Gold Crown Award and Columbia Scholastic Press Award.

Needs: "Not looking for any specific category—just good writing." Receives 6-10 unsolicited mss/month. Acquires 3-6 mss/issue. Publishes in late March. Deadline: first Friday in November. Published work by Chaim Bertman, Kat Meads and Kerry Madden-Lunsford. Length: 250 words minimum; 5,000 words maximum. Publishes short shorts. Also publishes poetry. Sometimes critiques rejected mss.

How to Contact: Send complete manuscript with cover letter. SASE. Simultaneous submissions OK. Sample copy for $9; additional copies $7. Fiction guidelines for #10 SAE.

Payment/Terms: Pays contributor's copies. Acquires one-time rights. Publication not previously copyrighted.

Advice: "We have actually been noted for our poetry. Fiction tends to be '*New Yorker*'-esque, but we are encouraging more provocative styles. We ask that you be original and creative, but not so avant-garde that we'd need a team of linguists to decipher your work."

SANTA BARBARA REVIEW, Literary Arts Journal, (II), P.O. Box 808, Summerland CA 93067-0808. (805)969-0861. Editor: Patricia Stockton Leddy. Magazine: 6×9; 160 pages, 60 lb. opaque paper; 10 pt. CS1; illustrations and photos. "The goal of *The Santa Barbara Review* is to find stories that entertain, surprise, and shed light on the vast human condition." Triannually. Estab. 1993.

• *Santa Barbara Review* is a member of the Council of Literary Magazines and Presses.

Needs: Literary. "No children's fiction. We try to avoid topics for their news value or political correctness." Receives 50-100 unsolicited fiction mss/month. Accepts 6-8 mss/issue; 24 mss/year. Publishes ms 1 year after acceptance. Length: 3,500-4,000 words average. Occasionally publishes short shorts. Length: 500 words. Also publishes literary essays and poetry. Often critiques or comments on rejected mss. Sponsors annual contest. First place: $350. Send SASE for details.

How to Contact: Send complete ms with a cover letter. Include 2-3 line bio and list of publications. "Always send a disk upon acceptance, Macintosh or IBM." Reports in 2 weeks on queries; 6 months on mss. Send SASE for reply, return of ms or send a disposable copy of ms. Electronic (disk) submissions OK. Sample copy for $7. Reviews novels and short story collections.

Payment/Terms: Pays 2 contributor's copies. Acquires one-time rights.

Advice: "First thing we look for is voice. Make every word count. We want to see immediate involvement, convincing dialogue, memorable characters. Show us connection between things we had previously thought disparate. The self-indulgent, feel sorry for yourself polemic we really don't like. We are very fond of humor that is not mean spirited and wish to see more."

‡SANTA MONICA REVIEW, (II), Santa Monica College, 1900 Pico Blvd., Santa Monica CA 90290. (310)450-5150. Editor: Lee Montgomery. Magazine: 250 pages; photos. "The editors are committed to fostering new talent as well as presenting new work by established writers. There is also a special emphasis on presenting and promoting writers who make their home in Los Angeles." Estab. 1989. Circ. 1,000.

Needs: Literary. Publishes special fiction issues or anthologies. Receives 250 unsolicited mss/month. Accepts 10 mss/issue; 20 mss/year. Does not read during the summer. Agented fiction 10%. Recently published work by Carolyn See, T.C. Boyle, Amy Berstler, Stacey Levine, Steve Katz, Lawrence Thornton, Juith Freeman and Bernard Cooper. Also publishes literary essays and poetry.

How to Contact: Send complete ms with a cover letter. Reports in 3 months. Send a disposable copy of ms. Simultaneous submissions OK. Sample copy for $7. Reviews novels and short story collections. Send books to editor.

Payment/Terms: Pays 3 contributor's copies for first North American serial rights. Sends galleys to author.

SATIRE, (I, II), C&K Publications, P.O. Box 340, Hancock MD 21750-0340. (301)678-6999. E-mail: satire@intr epid.net. Website: http://www.intrepid.net/satire. Editor: Larry Logan. Magazine: 5½×8½; 100 pages; bond paper; illustrations. "We hope that our quarterly provides a home for contemporary literary satire that might make you laugh . . . make you squirm . . . and make you think." Quarterly. Estab. 1994. Circ. 500.

Needs: Humor/satire, literary. "We will consider all categories as long as a satiric treatment is incorporated." Receives 150 unsolicited mss/month. Accepts 20 mss/issue; 80 mss/year. Publishes ms within 6 months after acceptance. Recently published work by Lewis H. Lapham, Lawrence Casler, Madeline Begun Kane, Jesse Bier, Stephen Gross, Terry Stawar, Dean Blehert, Jim Siergey and Tom Roberts. Length: 6,000 words maximum. Publishes short shorts. Also publishes literary essays, condensed/excerpted novel, poetry and 3-6 cartoons/issue. Sometimes critiques or comments on rejected mss.

How to Contact: Send complete ms with cover letter. Include estimated word count, a short bio and list of publications. Reports in 3 months on mss. Send SASE for reply, return of ms or send a disposable copy of ms. Simultaneous, reprint and electronic submissions OK. Sample copy for $5 and #10 SASE. Fiction guidelines free.

Payment/Terms: Pays 2 contributor's copies for works over 1 page; additional 5 copies at cost to authors. Acquires one-time rights. Sends galleys to author.

Advice: "Think and write with quality, and be sure that a 'well-read' audience can identify the satiric target(s). Clever humor and wit is prized within a well-developed story. Study an issue or two before you submit."

*SCARP, New Arts & Writing, % Faculty of Creative Arts, University of Wollongong, Northfields Ave., Wollongong Australia. Editor: Ron Pretty. Circ. 1,000. Publishes 3-6 fiction ms annually. Published twice a year.
Needs: "We look for fiction in a contemporary idiom, even if it uses a traditional form. Preferred length: 2,000 words. We're looking for energy, impact, quality."
How to Contact: "Submit to reach us in April and/or August." Include SASE.
Payment/Terms: Payment: $80 (Australian); contributor's copies supplied.
Advice: "In Australia the beginning writer faces stiff competition—the number of paying outlets is not increasing, but the number of capable writers is."

SCREAMING TOAD PRESS, Dancing with Mr. D. Publications, (II), 809 W. Broad St. #221, Falls-Church VA 22046. Editor: Llori Steinberg. Magazine: 6×9; 20-30 pages; 60 lb. cover; illustrations and photos. "Fiction/nonfiction—usually warped, gore or truelife experience." Quarterly. Estab. 1993. Circ. 500.
Needs: Erotica (horror), experimental, fantasy (children's fantasy, science fantasy), horror, humor/satire, mystery/suspense (amateur sleuth). No religion/Christian. List of upcoming themes available for SASE. Receives 100-350 unsolicited mss/month. Accepts 2 mss/issue; 2-8 mss/year. Recently published work by George Steinberg, Dave Green and Sharon Aldana. Publishes 6 new writers/year. Length: 1,000 words average; 300-500 words minimum; 1,000 words maximum. Publishes short shorts. Also publishes literary essays and literary criticism. Sometimes critiques or comments on rejected mss.
How to Contact: Send complete ms. Include bio (any length). Reports in 2-6 weeks on queries; 6-12 weeks on mss. Send SASE for reply, return of ms or send a disposable copy of ms. Simultaneous and reprint submissions OK. Sample copy for $5 (payable to Llori Steinberg), #10 SAE and 2 first-class stamps. Fiction guidelines for #10 SAE and 2 first-class stamps.
Payment/Terms: No payment. Copies $5. All rights revert to author.
Advice: "I got to enjoy it—it's gotta be you! Don't copy! I want nothing to do with impersonators! I get too many. Knock me out by being unheard of—in anything you write."

♣SCRIVENER CREATIVE REVIEW, (II), 853 Sherbrooke St. W., Montreal, Quebec H3A 2T6 Canada. (514)398-6588. Fax: (514)398-8146. E-mail: bqgc@musicb.mcgillica. Editors: Michelle LeLievre, Lia Barsotti and Michelle Syba. Magazine: 8×9; 100 pages; matte paper; illustrations; b&w photos. "*Scrivener* is a creative journal publishing fiction, poetry, graphics, photography, reviews, interviews and scholarly articles. We publish the best of new and established writers. We examine how current trends in North American writing are rooted in a pervasive creative dynamic; our audience is mostly scholarly and in the writing field." Annually. Estab. 1980. Circ. 500.
Needs: Open, "good writing." Receives 10 unsolicited mss/month. Accepts 20 mss/year. Does not read mss May 1-Sept 1. Publishes ms 2 months after acceptance. Recently published work by J.A. Ross, Lyla Miller and David Bezmozgis. Published new writers within the last year. Length: 25 pages maximum. Occasionally publishes short shorts. Also publishes literary essays, literary criticism, poetry. Often critiques rejected mss. Rarely recommends other markets.
How to Contact: Send complete ms with a cover letter and SASE. Include 50-100 word bio and list of publications. "If piece is in simultaneous circulation, include the titles of the other journals/magazines." Order sample copy ($5); send complete ms with cover letter with "critical statements; where we can reach you; biographical data; education; previous publications." Reports in 4 months on queries and mss. SASE/IRC preferred but not required. Simultaneous and photocopied submissions OK. Accepts computer printouts. Sample copy for $5 (US in USA; Canadian in Canada). Fiction guidelines for SAE/IRC. Reviews novels and short story collections. Send books to Nonfiction Editor.
Payment/Terms: Pays contributor's copies; charges for extras. Rights retained by the author.
Advice: "Send us your best stuff. Don't be deterred by rejections. Sometimes a magazine just isn't looking for your *kind* of writing. Don't neglect the neatness of your presentation."

SE LA VIE WRITER'S JOURNAL, (I), Rio Grande Press, P.O. Box 71745, Las Vegas NV 89170. Editor: Rosalie Avara. Magazine: 8½×5½; 68-74 pages; bond paper; illustrations. *SLVWJ* accepts work through its short short story contests. "Manuscripts should reflect the 'that's life' (Se La Vie) theme, intended for young adult to adult readers. We also publish *The Story Shop*, an annual anthology of short stories. For *The Story Shop*, we accept any type of wholesome stories (no porn or erotica)." Quarterly. Estab. 1987. Circ. 150.
Needs: Adventure, ethnic/multicultural, humor/satire, literary, mystery/suspense (amateur sleuth, private eye/hardboiled, romantic suspense), regional. "No science fiction, porn or erotica; nothing political or feminist; no alternate lifestyles; no extreme religious (although some spiritual)." Receives 8-10 unsolicited mss/month. Accepts 2 mss/issue for *SLVWJ*; 12-15 mss/issue for *The Story Shop*. Publishes ms 3 months after acceptance; 1 year after acceptance for *The Story Shop*. Published work by Marian Ford Park, Edgar H. Thompson and Michael R. Drury. Length: 500 words average; 300 words minimum; 500 words maximum. Length (for *The Story Shop*): 1,500 words average; 1,000 words minimum; 1,500 words maximum. Also publishes literary essays and poetry. Sometimes critiques or comments on rejected mss.
How to Contact: Send SASE first for guidelines, then send complete ms with cover letter. Include estimated word count. Reports in 2 weeks on queries and mss. Send SASE for reply, return of ms or send a disposable copy of ms. Sample copy for $2. Contest and fiction guidelines for #10 SASE. Reviews short story collections.

Payment/Terms: Pays $5-25 to contest winners; copies of *The Story Shop* available for $6.95 each. Pays on publication. Acquires first North American serial rights.

Advice: *Se La Vie* looks for stories with surprise endings. *The Story Shop* looks for "any story that can hold my interest for the first three pages." For both publications, "believable characters, good dialogue, good description, good plot, etc."

THE SEATTLE REVIEW, (II), Padelford Hall Box 354330, University of Washington, Seattle WA 98195. (206)543-9865. Editor: Colleen J. McElroy. Fiction Editor: Charles Johnson. Magazine: 6×9. "Includes general fiction, poetry, craft essays on writing, and one interview per issue with a Northwest writer." Semiannual. Published special fiction issue. Estab. 1978. Circ. 1,000.

Needs: Contemporary, ethnic, experimental, fantasy, feminist, gay, historical, horror, humor/satire, lesbian, literary, mainstream, prose poem, psychic/supernatural/occult, regional, science fiction, excerpted novel, mystery/suspense, translations, western. "We also publish a series called Writers and their Craft, which deals with aspects of writing fiction (also poetry)—point of view, characterization, etc., rather than literary criticism, each issue." Does not want to see "anything in bad taste (porn, racist, etc.)." Receives about 100 unsolicited mss/month. Buys about 3-6 mss/issue; about 4-10 mss/year. Does not read mss June through September. Agented fiction 25%. Published work by David Milofsky, Lawson Fusao Inada and Liz Rosenberg; published new writers within the last year. Length: 3,500 words average; 500 words minimum; 10,000 words maximum. Publishes short shorts. Sometimes critiques rejected mss. Occasionally recommends other markets.

How to Contact: Send complete ms. Reports in 6-8 months. SASE. Sample copy "half-price if older than one year." Current issue for $6; some special issues $7.50.

Payment/Terms: Pays 0-$100, free subscription to magazine, 2 contributor's copies; charge for extras. Pays on publication for first North American serial rights. Copyright reverts to writer on publication; "please request release of rights and cite *SR* in reprint publications." Sends galleys to author.

Advice: "Beginners do well in our magazine if they send clean, well-written manuscripts. We've published a lot of 'first stories' from all over the country and take pleasure in discovery."

SEEMS, (II), Lakeland College, Box 359, Sheboygan WI 53082-0359. (414)565-3871. Editor: Karl Elder. Magazine: 7×8½; 40 pages. "We publish fiction and poetry for an audience which tends to be highly literate. People read the publication, I suspect, for the sake of reading it." Published irregularly. Estab. 1971. Circ. 300.

Needs: Literary. Accepts 4 mss/issue. Receives 12 unsolicited fiction mss each month. Published work by John Birchler; published new writers within the last year. Length: 5,000 words maximum. Publishes short shorts. Also publishes poetry. Critiques rejected mss when there is time.

How to Contact: Send complete ms with SASE. Reports in 2 months on mss. Publishes ms an average of 1-2 years after acceptance. Sample copy for $4.

Payment/Terms: Pays 1 contributor's copy; $4 charge for extras. Rights revert to author.

Advice: "Send clear, clean copies. Read the magazine in order to help determine the taste of the editor." Mss are rejected because of "lack of economical expression, or saying with many words what could be said in only a few. Good fiction contains all of the essential elements of poetry; study poetry and apply those elements to fiction. Our interest is shifting to story poems, the grey area between genres."

SENSATIONS MAGAZINE, (I, II), 2 Radio Ave., A5, Secaucus NJ 07094-3843. Founder: David Messineo. Magazine: 8½×11; 200 pages; 20 lb. paper; full color cover; color photography. "We publish short stories and poetry, no specific theme." Magazine also includes the Rediscovering America in Poetry research series. Semiannually. Estab. 1987.

  • *Sensations Magazine* was a First Place winner in the 1996 American Literary Magazine Awards. This is one of the few markets accepting longer work. They would like to see more mysteries, well-researched historical fiction.

Needs: Fantasy, gay, historical, horror, humor/satire, lesbian, literary, mystery/suspense (private eye), science fiction, western (traditional). No sexually graphic. "We're not into gratuitous profanity, pornography, or violence. Sometimes these are needed to properly tell the tale. We'll read anything unusual, providing it is submitted in accordance with our submission policies. No abstract works only the writer can understand." Theme for October 1998 issue: the 350th Anniversary of American Witchhunts. Accepts 2-4 mss/issue. Publishes ms 2 months after acceptance. Recently published work by Phil Hardin and Phoebe Otis. Length: 35 pages maximum.

How to Contact: Send SASE for guidelines. Simultaneous submissions OK. Accepts electronic submissions (Macintosh only). *Must first make $12 advance payment.* Check payable to David Messineo. *"Do not submit material before reading submission guidelines."* Next deadline: August 15, 1997.

Payment/Terms: Pays $25-75 per story on acceptance for one-time rights.

Advice: "Each story must have a strong beginning that grabs the reader's attention in the first two sentences. Characters have to be realistic and well-described. Readers must like, hate, or have some emotional response to your characters. Setting, plot, construction, attention to detail—all are important. We work with writers to help them improve in these areas, but the better the stories are written before they come to us, the greater the chance for publication. Purchase sample copy first and read the stories."

*SEPIA, Poetry & Prose Magazine, Kawabata Press, Knill Cross House, Knill Cross, Millbrook, Nr Torpoint, Cornwall England. Editor-in-Chief: Colin David Webb. Published 3 times/year.
Needs: "Magazine for those interested in modern un-clichéd work." Contains 32 pages/issue. Length: 200-4,000 words (for short stories).
How to Contact: Always include SAE with IRCs. Send $1 for sample copy and guidelines. Subscription $5; "no cheques!"
Payment/Terms: Pays 1 contributor's copy.

THE SEWANEE REVIEW, (III), University of the South, Sewanee TN 37383. (931)598-1245. Editor: George Core. Magazine: 6×9; 192 pages. "A literary quarterly, publishing original fiction, poetry, essays on literary and related subjects, book reviews and book notices for well-educated readers who appreciate good American and English literature." Quarterly. Estab. 1892. Circ. 3,200.
Needs: Literary, contemporary. Buys 10-15 mss/year. Receives 100 unsolicited fiction mss each month. Does not read mss June 1-August 31. Published new writers within the last year. Length: 6,000-7,500 words. Critiques rejected mss "when there is time." Sometimes recommends other markets.
How to Contact: Send complete ms with SASE and cover letter stating previous publications, if any. Reports in 6 weeks on mss. Sample copy for $6.25.
Payment/Terms: Pays $10-12/printed page; 2 contributor's copies; $4 charge for extras. Pays on publication for first North American serial rights and second serial rights by agreement. Writer's guidelines for SASE.
Advice: "Send only one story at a time, with a serious and sensible cover letter. We think fiction is of greater general interest than any other literary mode."

SHADOW, Between Parallels, (I, II), Shadow Publications, P.O. Box 5464, Santa Rosa CA 95402. Phone/fax: (707)542-7114. E-mail: brianwts@aol.com. Editor-in-Chief: Brian Murphy. Magazine: 8½×5½; white paper; card stock cover. "*Shadow* is aimed at teen readers. Our goal is to provide well-written fiction for young adults. We also support teen writers and make a special point to respond to their work." Annual. Estab. 1995.
Needs: Young adult/teen. Receives 20-45 unsolicited mss/month. Accepts 5-25 mss/year. Publishes ms 1 year after acceptance. Agented fiction 6%. Recently published work by Susan Sanchez, Guilford Barton and John Downing. Length: 3,000 words average; 750 words minimum; 5,000 words maximum. Also publishes literary essays and literary criticism. Often critiques or comments on rejected mss.
How to Contact: Send complete ms. Include estimated word count, bio (1 page or less), Social Security number and list of publications. Reports in 3 weeks on queries; 6-8 weeks on mss. Send SASE for reply. Simultaneous, reprint and electronic submissions OK. Sample copy for $2 and 2 first-class stamps. Fiction guidelines for #10 SASE.
Payment/Terms: Pays 2-3 contributor's copies; additional copies for a reduced price. Acquires one-time rights.
Advice: "We want fiction that has depth to it and that will make our readers stop and think. Work that leaves a lasting impression. New writers should make sure their work is polished before submitting. We still make a point to comment often on work from new writers."

SHATTERED WIG REVIEW, (I, II), Shattered Wig Productions, 425 E. 31st, Baltimore MD 21218. (410)243-6888. Editor: Collective. Attn: Sonny Dodkin. Magazine: 8½×8½; 70 pages; "average" paper; cardstock cover; illustrations and photos. "Open forum for the discussion of the absurdo-miserablist aspects of everyday life. Fiction, poetry, graphics, essays, photos." Semiannually. Estab. 1988. Circ. 500.
Needs: Confession, contemporary, erotica, ethnic, experimental, feminist, gay, humor/satire, lesbian, literary, prose poem, psychic/supernatural/occult, regional. Does not want "anything by Ann Beattie or John Irving." Receives 15-20 unsolicited mss/month. Publishes ms 2-4 months after acceptance. Published work by Al Ackerman, Kim Harrison and Mok Hossfeld. Published new writers within the last year. Publishes short shorts. Also publishes literary criticism, poetry. Sometimes critiques rejected mss and recommends other markets.
How to Contact: Send complete ms with cover letter. Reports in 2 months. Send SASE for return of ms. Simultaneous and reprint submissions OK. Sample copy for $4.
Payment/Terms: Pays in contributor's copies. Acquires one-time rights.
Advice: "The arts have been reduced to imploding pus with the only material rewards reserved for vapid stylists and collegiate pod suckers. The only writing that counts has no barriers between imagination and reality, thought and action. Send us at least three pieces so we have a choice."

SHENANDOAH, The Washington and Lee Review, (II), 2nd Floor, Troubadour Theater, Lexington VA 24450. (540)463-8765. Editor: R.T. Smith. Magazine: 6×9; 124 pages. "We are a literary journal devoted to excellence." Quarterly. Estab. 1950. Circ. 2,000.
Needs: Literary. Receives 400-500 unsolicited fiction mss/month. Accepts 4 mss/issue; 16 mss/year. Does not read mss during summer. Publishes ms 6 months to 1 year after acceptance. Published work by Kent Nelson, Barry Gifford, Nicholas Delbanco and Reynolds Price. Publishes short shorts. Also publishes literary essays, literary criticism and poetry.

How to Contact: Send complete ms with cover letter. Include a 3-sentence bio and list of publications ("just the highlights"). Reports in 10 weeks on mss. Send a disposable copy of ms. Sample copy for $3. Fiction guidelines for #10 SASE. Reviews novels and short story collections.

Payment/Terms: Pays $25/page and free subscription to the magazine on publication. Acquires first North American serial rights. Sends galleys to author. Sponsors contest.

Advice: Looks for "thrift, precision, originality. As Frank O'Connor said, 'Get black on white.' "

SHORT STORIES BIMONTHLY, (I, II), Poetry Forum, 5713 Larchmont Dr., Erie PA 16509. Phone/fax: (814)866-2543. E-mail: 75562.670@compuserve.com. Editor: Gunvor Skogsholm. Newsletter: 11 × 17; 14 pages; 20 lb. paper; illustrations. Estab. 1992. Circ. 400.

Needs: Literary, mainstream. Receives 30 unsolicited mss/month. Accepts 8-10 mss/issue; 48-60 mss/year. Publishes ms 1-9 months after acceptance. Recently published work by Roger Goodfriend, Dave Yoon and Pete Kinnar. 40% of work published is by new writers. Length: 1,800 words average; 600 words minimum; 4,000 words maximum. Publishes short shorts. Length: 600 words. Also publishes literary essays and literary criticism.

How to Contact: Send complete ms with a cover letter. Include estimated word count. Reports in 3 weeks to 6 months on mss. Send SASE for reply, return of ms or send a disposable copy of ms. Simultaneous and electronic submissions OK. Sample copy for $3. Fiction guidelines free. Favors submissions from subscribers. "We exist by subscriptions and advertising." Reviews novels and short story collections.

Payment/Terms: Acquires one-time rights. Sponsors contests, awards or grants for fiction writers. Send SASE.

Advice: "Be original, be honest. Write from your deepest sincerity—don't play games with the readers. Meaning: we don't want the last paragraph to tell us we have been fooled."

SHORT STUFF MAGAZINE FOR GROWN-UPS, (I, II), Bowman Publications, P.O. Box 7057, Loveland CO 80537. (970)669-9139. Editor: Donna Bowman. Magazine: 8½ × 11; 40 pages; bond paper; enamel cover; b&w illustrations and photographs. "Nonfiction is regional—Colorado and adjacent states. Fiction and humor must be tasteful, but can be any genre, any subject. We are designed to be a 'Reader's Digest' of fiction. We are found in professional waiting rooms, etc." Publishes 6 issues/year; "we combine July/August and January/ February."

Needs: Adventure, contemporary, historical, humor/satire, mainstream, mystery/suspense (amateur sleuth, English cozy, police procedural, private eye, romantic suspense), regional, romance (contemporary, gothic, historical), western (frontier). No erotica. "We use holiday themes. Need 3 month lead time. Issues are Valentine (January/February); East and St. Patrick's Day (March/April); Mom's and Dad's (May/June); Americana (July/ August); Halloween (September/October); and Holiday (November/December). Receives 150 unsolicited mss/ month. Accepts 9-12 mss/issue; 76 mss/year. Publishes accepted work immediately. Recently published work by Susanne Shaphren, William Hallstead, Eleanor Sherman, Guy Bellerante, Birdie Etcheson, Guy Belleranti and Jane McBride Choate. Length: 1,000 words average; 1,600 words maximum.

How to Contact: Send complete ms with cover letter. SASE. Reports in 3-6 months. Sample copies for $1.50 and 9 × 12 SAE with $1.50 postage. Fiction guidelines for SASE.

Payment/Terms: Pays $10-50 and subscription to magazine on publication for first North American serial rights. $1-5 for fillers (less than 500 words). "We do not pay for single jokes or poetry, but do give free subscription if published."

Advice: "We seek a potpourri of subjects each issue. A new slant, a different approach, fresh viewpoints—all of these excite us. We don't like gore, salacious humor or perverted tales. Prefer third person. Be sure it is a story with a beginning, middle and end. It must have dialogue. Many beginners do not know an essay from a short story. Essays frequently used if *humorous*. We'd like to see more young (25 and over) humor; 'clean' humor is hard to come by."

SIDE SHOW, 8th Short Story Anthology, (II), Somersault Press, P.O. Box 1428, El Cerrito CA 94530-1428. (510)215-2207. E-mail: jisom@crl.com. Editor: Shelley Anderson, Kathe Stolz and Marjorie K. Jacobs. Book (paperback): 5½ × 8½; 300 pages; 50 lb. paper; semigloss card cover with color illustration; perfect-bound. "Quality short stories for a general, literary audience." Annually. Estab. 1991. Circ. 3,000.

● Work published in *Side Show* has been selected for inclusion in the *Pushcart Prize* anthology.

Needs: Contemporary, ethnic, feminist, gay, humor/satire, literary, mainstream. Nothing genre, religious, pornographic. Receives 50-60 unsolicited mss/month. Accepts 25-30 mss/issue. Publishes ms up to 9 months after acceptance. Recently published work by Dorothy Bryant, Susan Welch, Ericka Lutz, Marianne Rogoff and Miguel Rios. Publishes 5-10 new writers/year. Length: Open. Critiques rejected mss, if requested.

How to Contact: All submissions entered in contest. *$10 entry fee* (includes subscription to next *Side Show*).

✝ THE DOUBLE DAGGER before a listing indicates that the listing is new in this edition. New markets are often the most receptive to submissions by new writers.

No guidelines. Send complete ms with cover letter and entry fee. Reports in 1 month on mss. SASE. Simultaneous submissions OK. Multiple submissions "in same envelope" encouraged. Sample copy for $10 and $2 postage and handling ($.83 sales tax CA residents).

Payment/Terms: Pays $10/printed page on publication for first North American serial rights. Sends galleys to author. All submissions entered in our contest for cash prizes of $500 (1st), $200 (2nd) and $100 (3rd).

Advice: Looks for "readability, vividness of characterization, coherence, inspiration, interesting subject matter, imagination, point of view, originality, plausibility. If your fiction isn't inspired, you probably won't be published by us (i.e., style and craft alone won't do it)."

SIDEWALKS, (II), P.O. Box 321, Champlin MN 55316. (612)421-3512. Editor: Tom Heie. Magazine: 5½ × 8½; 60-75 pages; 60 lb. paper; textured recycled cover. "*Sidewalks* . . . place of discovery, of myth, power, incantation . . . places we continue to meet people, preoccupied, on our way somewhere . . . tense, dark, empty places . . . place we meet friends and strangers, neighborhood sidewalks, place full of memory, paths that bring us home." Semiannually. Estab. 1991. Circ. 500.

Needs: Experimental, humor/satire, literary, mainstream/contemporary, regional. No violent, pornographic kinky material. Accepts 6-8 mss/issue; 12-16 mss/year. Work is accepted for 2 annual deadlines: May 31 and December 31. Publishes ms 10 weeks after deadline. Published work by Jonathan Gillman and Jean Ervin. Length: 2,500 words preferred; 3,000 words maximum. Publishes short shorts. Also publishes poetry.

How to Contact: Send complete ms with cover letter. Include estimated word count, very brief bio, list of publications. Reports in 1 week on queries; 1 month after deadline on mss. Send SASE for reply, return of ms or send a disposable copy of ms. No simultaneous submissions. Accepts electronic submissions. Sample copy for $5.

Payment/Terms: Pays 1 contributor's copy; additional copies $5. Acquires one-time rights.

Advice: "We look for a story with broad appeal, one that is well-crafted and has strong narrative voice, a story that leaves the reader thinking after the reading is over."

SIERRA NEVADA COLLEGE REVIEW, (I, II), Sierra Nevada College, P.O. Box 4269, Incline Village NV 89450. (702)831-1314. Editor: June Sylvester. Magazine: 5½ × 8½; 50-100 pages; coated paper; card cover; saddle-stitched. "We are open to many kinds of work but avoid what we consider trite, sentimental, contrived. . . ." Annually. Estab. 1990. Circ. 200-250 (mostly college libraries).

● The majority of work published in this review is poetry.

Needs: Experimental, literary, mainstream/contemporary, regional. Receives about 50 unsolicited mss/month. Accepts 2-3 mss/year. Does not read mss April 1 through September 1. Work is published by next issue (published in May, annually). Published work by Jamie Andree and James Braziel. Length: 500 words average; 1,000 words maximum. Publishes short shorts. Also publishes literary essays, literary criticism and poetry. Sometimes critiques or comments on rejected mss.

How to Contact: Send complete ms with a cover letter. Include estimated word count and bio. Send SASE for reply, return of ms or send a disposable copy of ms. Simultaneous submissions OK. Sample copy for $2.50.

Payment/Terms: Pays 2 contributor's copies. Acquires one-time rights.

Advice: Looks for "memorable characters, close attention to detail which makes the story vivid. We are interested in flash fiction. Also regional work that catches the flavor of place and time—like strong characters. No moralizing, inspirational work. No science fiction. No children's stories. Tired of trite love stories—cynicism bores us."

THE SILVER WEB, A Magazine of the Surreal, (II), Buzzcity Press, Box 38190, Tallahassee FL 32315. (904)385-8948. Fax: (904)385-4063. E-mail: annkl9@mail.idt.net. Editor: Ann Kennedy. Magazine: 8½ × 11; 80 pages; 20 lb. paper; full color; perfect bound; glossy cover; b&w illustrations and photographs. "Looking for unique character-based stories that are off-beat, off-center and strange, but not inaccessible." Semiannually. Estab. 1989. Circ. 2,000.

● Work published in *The Silver Web* has appeared in *The Year's Best Fantasy and Horror* (DAW Books) and *The Year's Best Fantastic Fiction*.

Needs: Experimental, horror, science fiction (soft/sociological). No "traditional storylines, monsters, vampires, werewolves, etc." *The Silver Web* publishes surrealistic fiction and poetry. Work too bizarre for mainstream, but perhaps too literary for genre. This is not a straight horror/sci-fi magazine. No typical storylines." Receives 500 unsolicited mss/month. Accepts 8-10 mss/issue; 16-20 mss/year. Does not read mss October through December. Publishes ms 6-12 months after acceptance. Recently published work by Brian Evenson, Jack Ketchum and Joel Lane. Length: 6,000 words average; 100 words minimum; 8,000 words maximum. Publishes short shorts. Also publishes poetry. Sometimes critiques rejected ms.

How to Contact: Send complete ms with a cover letter. Include estimated word count. Reports in 1 week on queries; 6-8 weeks on mss. Send SASE for reply, return of ms or send a disposable copy of ms plus SASE for reply. Simultaneous and reprint submissions OK. Sample copy for $7.20. Fiction guidelines for #10 SASE. Reviews novels and short story collections.

Payment/Terms: Pays 2-3¢/word and 2 contributor's copies; additional copies for $4. Acquires first North American serial rights, reprint rights or one-time rights.

Advice: "I have a reputation for publishing excellent fiction from newcomers next to talented, established writers, and for publishing cross-genre fiction. No traditional, standard storylines. I'm looking for beautiful writing with plots that are character-based. Tell a good story; tell it with beautiful words. I see too many writers writing for the marketplace and this fiction just doesn't ring true. I'd rather read fiction that comes straight from the heart of the writer." Read a copy of the magazine, at least get the writer's guidelines.

SILVERFISH REVIEW, (II), Box 3541, Eugene OR 97403. (503)344-5060. Editor: Rodger Moody. High quality literary material for a general audience. Published in June and December. Estab. 1979. Circ. 1,000.
Needs: Literary. Accepts 1-2 mss/issue. Published work by Sherrie Flick, Lidia Yuknavitch and Dennis Duhamel. Also publishes literary essays, poetry, interviews, translations and reviews.
How to Contact: Send complete ms with SASE. No simultaneous submissions. Reports in 2-3 months on mss. Sample copy for $4 and $1.50 postage.
Payment/Terms: Pays 2 contributor's copies and one year subscription; $5/page when funding permits. Rights revert to author.
Advice: "We publish primarily poetry. We will, however, publish good quality fiction. *SR* is mainly interested in the short short story (one-minute and three-minute)."

SING HEAVENLY MUSE!, Women's Poetry and Prose, (I, II, IV), Box 13320, Minneapolis MN 55411. Contact: Editorial Circle. Magazine: 6×9; 100 pages; 55 lb. acid-free paper; 10 pt. glossy cover stock; illustrations; photos. "We foster the work of women poets, prose writers and artists and work that shows an awareness of women's consciousness." Annually. Estab. 1977. Circ. 300.
Needs: Literary, feminist, prose poem and ethnic/minority. List of upcoming themes and reading periods available for SASE. Receives approximately 30 unsolicited fiction mss each month. Accepts 3-6 mss/issue. Published work by Patricia Dubrava, Jana Zvibloman and Alison Townsend. Length: 10,000 words maximum. Publishes short shorts. Also publishes literary essays, poetry. Sometimes critiques or comments on rejected mss.
How to Contact: Query for information on theme issues, reading periods or variations in schedule. No simultaneous submissions. Reports in 1-2 months on queries; 3-9 months on mss. Publishes ms an average of 1 year after acceptance. Sample copy for $4. Fiction guidelines for #10 SASE.
Payment/Terms: Pays 2 contributor's copies and honorarium, depending on funding. Acquires one-time rights. Sends galleys to author.

SKYLARK, (II), Purdue University Calumet, 2200 169th St., Hammond IN 46323. (219)989-2262. Fax: (219)989-2581. E-mail: skylark@nwi.calumet.purdue.edu. Editor-in-Chief: Pamela Hunter. Magazine: 8½×11; 100 pages; illustrations; photos. Fine arts magazine—short stories, poems and graphics for adults. Annually. Estab. 1971. Circ. 600-1,000.
Needs: Contemporary, ethnic, experimental, fantasy, feminist, humor/satire, literary, mainstream, mystery/suspense (English cozy), prose poem, regional, romance (gothic), science fiction, serialized/excerpted novel, spiritual, sports and western (frontier stories). Upcoming theme: "Old Age" (submit by April 1998). Receives 20 mss/month. Accepts 8 mss/issue. Recently published work by Karl Harshbarger, Kristin Jensen, Paddy Reid and Joanne Zimmerman; published new writers within the last year. Length: 4,000 words maximum. Also publishes essays and poetry.
How to Contact: Send complete ms. Send SASE for return of ms. Reports in 4 months. No simultaneous submissions. Sample copy for $8; back issue for $6.
Payment/Terms: Pays 1 contributor's copy. Acquires first rights. Copyright reverts to author.
Advice: "We seek fiction that presents effective imagery, strong plot, and well-developed characterization. Graphic passages concerning sex or violence are unacceptable. We're looking for dramatic, closely-edited short stories. We receive too many stories from writers who do not know how to copyedit. Manuscripts *must* be carefully prepared and proofread."

SLIPSTREAM, (II, IV), Box 2071, New Market Station, Niagara Falls NY 14301. (716)282-2616. Website: http://www.wings.buffalo.edu/libraries/units/pl/slipstream (includes guidelines, editors, current needs, info on current and past releases, sample poems, contest info.). Editor: Dan Sicoli. Fiction Editors: R. Borgatti, D. Sicoli and Livio Farallo. Magazine: 7×8½; 80-100 pages; high quality paper; card cover; illustrations; photos. "We use poetry and short fiction with a contemporary urban feel." Estab. 1981. Circ. 500.
Needs: Contemporary, erotica, ethnic, experimental, humor/satire, literary, mainstream and prose poem. No religious, juvenile, young adult or romance. Occasionally publishes theme issues; query for information. Receives over 75 unsolicited mss/month. Accepts 2-4 mss/issue; 6 mss/year. Recently published work by John Richards, Richard Kostelanetz and B.D. Love. Length: under 15 pages. Publishes short shorts. Rarely critiques rejected mss. Sometimes recommends other markets.
How to Contact: "Query before submitting." Reports within 2 months. Send SASE for reply or return of ms. Sample copy for $5. Fiction guidelines for #10 SASE.
Payment/Terms: Pays 2 contributor's copies. Acquires one-time rights.
Advice: "Writing should be honest, fresh; develop your own style. Check out a sample issue first. Don't write for the sake of writing, write from the gut as if it were a biological need. Write from experience and mean what you say, but say it in the fewest number of words."

THE SMALL POND MAGAZINE, (II), Box 664, Stratford CT 06497. (203)378-4066. Editor: Napoleon St. Cyr. Magazine: 5½×8½; 42 pages; 60 lb. offset paper; 65 lb. cover stock; illustrations (art). "Features contemporary poetry, the salt of the earth, peppered with short prose pieces of various kinds. The college educated and erudite read it for good poetry, prose and pleasure." Triannually. Estab. 1964. Circ. 300.

Needs: "Rarely use science fiction or the formula stories you'd find in *Cosmo, Redbook, Ladies Home Journal,* etc." Accepts 10-12 mss/year. Longer response time in July and August. Receives approximately 40 unsolicited fiction mss each month. Recently published work by Margaret Haller and Alice Ingram. Length: 200-2,500 words. Critiques rejected mss when there is time. Sometimes recommends other markets.

How to Contact: Send complete ms with SASE and short vita. Reports in 2 weeks to 3 months. Publishes ms an average of 2-18 months after acceptance. Sample copy for $3; $2.50 for back issues.

Payment/Terms: Pays 2 contributor's copies for all rights; $3/copy charge for extras, postage paid.

Advice: "Send for a sample copy first. All mss must be typed. Name and address and story title on front page, name of story on succeeding pages and paginated." Mss are rejected because of "tired plots and poor grammar; also over-long—2,500 words maximum. Don't send any writing conference ms unless it got an A or better."

SNAKE NATION REVIEW, (II), Snake Nation Press, Inc., #2 West Force St., 110, Valdosta GA 31601. (912)249-8334. Fax: (912)242-6690. Editor: Roberta George. Fiction Editor: Nancy Phillips. 6×9; 110 pages; acid free 70 lb. paper; 90 lb. cover; illustrations and photographs. "We are interested in all types of stories for an educated, discerning, sophisticated audience." Quarterly. Estab. 1989. Circ. 2,000.

● *Snake Nation Review* receives funding from the Georgia Council of the Arts, the Georgia Humanities Council and the Porter/Fleming Foundation for Literature.

Needs: "Short stories of 5,000 words or less, poems (any length), art work that will be returned after use." Condensed/excerpted novel, contemporary, erotica, ethnic, experimental, fantasy, feminist, gay, horror, humor/satire, lesbian, literary, mainstream, mystery/suspense, prose poem, psychic/supernatural/occult, regional, science fiction, senior citizen/retirement. "We want our writers to have a voice, a story to tell, not a flat rendition of a slice of life." Plans annual anthology. Receives 50 unsolicited mss/month. Buys 8-10 mss/issue; 40 mss/year. Publishes ms 6 months after acceptance. Agented fiction 1%. Recently published work by Robert Earl Price and O. Victor Miller. Length: 3,500 words average; 300 words minimum; 5,500 words maximum. Publishes short shorts. Length: 500 words. Also publishes literary essays, poetry. Reviews novels and short story collections. Sometimes critiques rejected mss and recommends other markets.

How to Contact: Send complete ms with cover letter. Reports on queries in 3 months. SASE. Sample copy for $6, 8×10 SAE and 90¢ postage. Fiction guidelines for SASE.

Payment/Terms: Pays 2 contributor's copies for one-time rights. Sends galleys to author.

Advice: "Looks for clean, legible copy and an interesting, unique voice that pulls the reader into the work." Spring contest: short stories (5,000 words); $300 first prize, $200 second prize, $100 third prize; entry fee: $5 for stories, $1 for poems. Contest Issue with every $5 fee.

SNOWY EGRET, (II), The Fair Press, P.O. Box 9, Bowling Green IN 47833. E-mail: 00pcrepp@bsu.edu. Publisher: Karl Barnebey. Editor: Philip Repp. Magazine: 8½×11; 50 pages; text paper; heavier cover; illustrations. "Literary exploration of the abundance and beauty of nature and the ways human beings interact with it." Semiannually. Estab. 1922. Circ. 500.

Needs: Nature writing, including 'true' stories, eye-witness accounts, descriptive sketches and traditional fiction. "We are particularly interested in fiction that celebrates abundance and beauty of nature, encourages a love and respect for the natural world, and affirms the human connection to the environment. No works written for popular genres: horror, science fiction, romance, detective, western, etc." Receives 25 unsolicited mss/month. Accepts up to 6 mss/issue; up to 12 mss/year. Publishes ms 6 months to 1 year after acceptance. Published works by Jane Candia Coleman, Tama Janowitz, David Abrams and Eva LaSalle Caram. Length: 1,000-3,000 words preferred; 500 words minimum; 10,000 words maximum. Publishes short shorts. Length: 400-500 words. Sometimes critiques rejected mss.

How to Contact: Send complete ms with cover letter. "Cover letter optional: do not query." Reports in 2 months. SASE. Simultaneous (if noted) and electronic (Mac, ASCII) submissions OK. Sample back issues for $8 and 9×12 SAE. Send #10 SASE for writer's guidelines.

Payment/Terms: Pays $2/page and 2 contributor's copies on publication; charge for extras. Acquires first North American serial rights and reprint rights. Sends galleys to author.

Advice: Looks for "honest, freshly detailed pieces with plenty of description and/or dialogue which will allow the reader to identify with the characters and step into the setting. Characters who relate strongly to nature, either positively or negatively, and who, during the course of the story, grow in their understanding of themselves and the world around them."

THE SOFT DOOR, (I, II), 202 S. Church St., Bowling Green OH 43402. Editor: T. Williams. Magazine: 8½×11; 100 pages; bond paper; heavy cover; illustrations and photos. "We publish works that explore human relationships and our relationship to the world." Irregularly.

Needs: Literary, mainstream/contemporary. No science fiction or romance. Upcoming theme: "Custer And The Indians" (deadline October '97). Receives 25 mss/month. Accepts 5 mss/year. Does not read mss November through December. Publishes ms up to 2 years after acceptance. Published work by Mark Sa Franko, Simon Peter Buehrer, E.S. Griggs, Jennifer Casteen and Jim Feltz. Publishes 3 new writers/year. Length: 5,000 words average; 10,000 words maximum. Publishes short shorts. Also publishes poetry. Sometimes critiques or comments on rejected mss.

How to Contact: Send complete ms with a cover letter. Include "short statement about who you are and why you write, along with any successes you have had. Please write to me like I am a human being." Send SASE for reply, return of ms or send a disposable copy of ms. "Please include SASE with all correspondence. Do not send postcards." Simultaneous submissions OK. Sample copy for $12. Make checks payable to T. Williams.

Payment/Terms: Pays 1 contributor's copy. Acquires one-time rights.

Advice: "Read as much contemporary fiction and poetry as you can get your hands on. Write about your deepest concerns. What you write can, and does, change lives. Always interested in works by Native American writers. I also don't get enough work by and about women. Be patient with the small presses. We work under terrific pressure. It's not about money; it's about the literature, caring about ideas that matter."

‡✹**SOLAS, (II)**, Mediasolas Publishing, 0151-32500 South Fraser Way, Suite 130, Abbotsford British Columbia V2T 4W1 Canada. E-mail: wonko@uniserve.com. Website: http://users.univserve.com/~wonko/solas/. Editor: Darren James Harkness. Electronic magazine. "Providing publishing space for new and unpublished poets, writers and artists."

Needs: Short stories, novelettes, poetry and artwork. No erotica. Recently published work by Christopher Anne and Michael Largo. Publishes 2-3 new writers/year.

How to Contact: Electronic and traditional submissions accepted. Send e-mail in standard ASCII format or as attachment in MIME format.

Advice: "Be original, not cliched. We prefer writers in the style of Michael Ondaatje, Franz Kafka, George Orwell, Margaret Atwood. Be descriptive. Grab your audience by the ears, and never let go."

SONORA REVIEW, (I, II), University of Arizona, Department of English, Tucson AZ 85721. (520)626-8383. Co-Editors: Eric Burger and Jeremy Bushnell. Fiction Editors: Mari Muki and Robin Lauzon. Editors change each year. Magazine: 6×9; 150 pages; 16 lb. paper; 20 lb. cover stock; photos seldom. *Sonora Review* publishes short fiction and poetry of high literary quality. Semiannually. Estab. 1980. Circ. 900.
- Work published in *Sonora Review* has been selected for inclusion in the *Pushcart Prize*, *O. Henry Awards*, *Best of the West* and *Best American Poetry* anthologies.

Needs: Literary. "We are open to a wide range of stories with accessibility and vitality being important in any case. We're not interested in genre fiction, formula work." Acquires 4-6 mss/issue. Agented fiction 10%. Recently published work by David Huddle, Ira Sadoff and Jane Mead. Length: open, though prefers work under 25 pages. Also publishes literary essays, literary criticism and poetry.

How to Contact: Send complete ms with SASE and cover letter with previous publications. Simultaneous submissions OK. Reports in 3 months on mss, longer for work received during summer (May-August). Publishes ms an average of 2-6 months after acceptance. Sample copy for $6.

Payment/Terms: Pays a small honorarium and 2 contributor's copies; $5 charge for extras. Acquires first North American serial rights. Annual short story contest: 1st prize, $500. Send #10 SASE for submission guidelines.

Advice: "All mss are read carefully, and we try to make brief comments if time permits. Our hope is that an author will keep us interested in his or her treatment of a subject by using fresh details and writing with an authority that is absorbing." Mss are rejected because "we only have space for 6-8 manuscripts out of several hundred submissions annually." See the listing for their fiction contest in the Contests and Awards section.

SOUTH CAROLINA REVIEW, (I, II), Strode Tower, Clemson University, Clemson SC 29634-1503. (864)656-3151. Editors: Frank Day and Wayne Chapman. Magazine: 6×9; 200 pages; 60 lb. cream white vellum paper; 65 lb. cream white vellum cover stock. Semiannually. Estab. 1967. Circ. 700.

Needs: Literary and contemporary fiction, poetry, essays, reviews. Receives 50-60 unsolicited fiction mss each month. Does not read mss June through August or December. Published work by Joyce Carol Oates, Rosanne Coggeshall and Stephen Dixon. Published new writers within the last year. Rarely critiques rejected mss.

How to Contact: Send complete ms with SASE. Requires text on disk upon acceptance in WordPerfect or Microsoft Word format. Reports in 6-9 months on mss. "No unsolicited reviews." Sample copy for $5.

Payment/Terms: Pays in contributor's copies.

SOUTH DAKOTA REVIEW, (II), University of South Dakota, Box 111, University Exchange, Vermillion SD 57069. (605)677-5966. Website: http://www.usd.edu/englisdr/index.html (includes masthead page with editors' names and submission/subscription guidelines, sample covers, sample story and essay excerpts and poems).

MARKET CATEGORIES: (I) Open to new writers; **(II)** Open to both new and established writers; **(III)** Interested mostly in established writers; **(IV)** Open to writers whose work is specialized; **(V)** Closed to unsolicited submissions.

Editor: Brian Bedard. Editorial Assistant: Geraldine Sanford. Magazine: 6×9; 160-180 pages; book paper; glossy cover stock; illustrations sometimes; photos on cover. "Literary magazine for university and college audiences and their equivalent. Emphasis is often on the American West and its writers, but will accept mss from anywhere. Issues are generally essay, fiction, and poetry with some literary essays." Quarterly. Estab. 1963. Circ. 500.

 • A story by Richard Plant, published in *SDR* was selected for inclusion in the *Sudden Fiction* anthology published in Spring 1996; *SDR* has been selected for inclusion in the *Writer's Digest* "Fiction 50" list of top fiction markets, and two poems, one story, one essay were nominated for a *Pushcart Prize* Anthology.

Needs: Literary, contemporary, ethnic, excerpted novel, regional. "We like very well-written, thematically ambitious, character-centered short fiction. Contemporary western American setting appeals, but not necessary. No formula stories, horror, or adolescent 'I' narrator." Receives 40 unsolicited fiction mss/month. Accepts about 40 mss/year. Assistant editor accepts mss in June through July, sometimes August. Agented fiction 5%. Publishes short shorts of 5 pages double-spaced typescript. Recently published work by Steve Heller, H.E. Francis, James Sallis, Ronna Wineberg, Lewis Horne and Rita Welty Bourke. Publishes 3-5 new writers/year. Length: 1,000-1,300 words minimum; 6,000 words maximum. (Has made exceptions, up to novella length.) Sometimes recommends other markets.

How to Contact: Send complete ms with SASE. "We like cover letters that are not boastful and do not attempt to sell the stories but rather provide some personal information about the writer." Reports in 6-10 weeks. Publishes ms an average of 1-6 months after acceptance. Sample copy for $5.

Payment/Terms: Pays 1-year subscription, plus 2-4 contributor's copies, depending on length of ms; cover price charge for extras while issue is current, $3 when issue becomes a back issue.. Acquires first and reprint rights.

Advice: Rejects mss because of "careless writing; often careless typing; stories too personal ('I' confessional), aimlessness, unclear or unresolved conflicts; subject matter that editor finds clichéd, sensationalized, pretentious or trivial. We are trying to use more fiction and more variety."

SOUTHERN CALIFORNIA ANTHOLOGY, (III), Master of Professional Writing Program—USC, MPW-WPH 404 USC, Los Angeles CA 90089-4034. (213)740-3252. Fax: (213)740-5775. Contact: Editor. Magazine: 5½×8½; 142 pages; semigloss cover stock. "The *Southern California Anthology* is a literary review that is an eclectic collection of previously unpublished quality contemporary fiction, poetry and interviews with established literary people, published for adults of all professions; of particular interest to those interested in serious contemporary literature." Annually. Estab. 1983. Circ. 1,500.

Needs: Contemporary, ethnic, experimental, feminist, historical, humor/satire, literary, mainstream, regional, serialized/excerpted novel. No juvenile, religious, confession, romance, science fiction or pornography. Receives 40 unsolicited fiction mss each month. Accepts 10-12 mss/issue. Does not read February through September. Publishes ms 4 months after acceptance. Recently published work by Stuart Dybek, Larry Heinemann, Aram Saroyan, Susan Fromberg Schaeffer, Robley Wilson and Ross Talarico. Length: 10-15 pages average; 2 pages minimum; 25 pages maximum. Publishes short shorts.

How to Contact: Send complete ms with cover letter or submit through agent. Cover letter should include list of previous publications. Reports on queries in 1 month; on mss in 4 months. Send SASE for reply or return of ms. Sample copy for $4. Fiction guidelines for #10 SASE.

Payment/Terms: Pays in contributor's copies. Acquires first rights.

Advice: "The *Anthology* pays particular attention to craft and style in its selection of narrative writing."

SOUTHERN EXPOSURE, (II, IV), Institute for Southern Studies, P.O. Box 531, Durham NC 27702. (919)419-8311. Editor: Jo Carson. Magazine: 8½×11; 64 pages. "Southern politics and culture—investigative reporting, oral history, fiction for an audience of Southern changemakers—scholars, journalists, activists." Quarterly. Estab. 1972. Circ. 5,000.

 • *Southern Exposure* has won numerous awards for its reporting including the Sidney Hillman Award for reporting on racial justice issues.

Needs: Contemporary, ethnic, feminist, gay, humor/satire, lesbian, literary, regional. Receives 50 unsolicited mss/month. Buys 1 mss/issue; 4 mss/year. Publishes ms 3-6 months after acceptance. Agented fiction 25%. Published work by Clyde Egerton, Jill McCorkle and Larry Brown. Length: 3,500 words preferred.

How to Contact: Send complete ms with cover letter. No simultaneous submissions. Reports in 4-6 weeks on mss. SASE for ms. Sample copy for $4, 8½×11 and $1.85 postage. Fiction guidelines for #10 SASE.

Payment/Terms: Pays $250, subscription to magazine and contributor's copies on publication for first rights.

SOUTHERN HUMANITIES REVIEW, (II, IV), Auburn University, 9088 Haley Center, Auburn University AL 36849. Co-editors: Dan R. Latimer and Virginia M. Kouidis. Magazine: 6×9; 100 pages; 60 lb. neutral pH, natural paper; 65 lb. neutral pH med. coated cover stock; occasional illustrations and photos. "We publish essays, poetry, fiction and reviews. Our fiction has ranged from very traditional in form and content to very experimental. Literate, college-educated audience. We hope they read our journal for both enlightenment and pleasure." Quarterly. Estab. 1967. Circ. 800.

Needs: Serious fiction, fantasy, feminist, humor and regional. Receives approximately 25 unsolicited fiction mss each month. Accepts 1-2 mss/issue, 4-6 mss/year. Slower reading time in summer. Published work by Anne Brashler, Heimito von Doderer and Ivo Andric; published new writers within the last year. Length: 3,500-

15,000 words. Also publishes literary essays, literary criticism, poetry. Critiques rejected mss when there is time. Sometimes recommends other markets.

How to Contact: Send complete ms (one at a time) with SASE and cover letter with an explanation of topic chosen—"special, certain book, etc., a little about author if he/she has never submitted." Reports in 3 months. Sample copy for $5. Reviews novel and short story collections.

Payment/Terms: Pays 2 contributor's copies; $5 charge for extras. Rights revert to author upon publication. Sends galleys to author.

Advice: "Send us the ms with SASE. If we like it, we'll take it or we'll recommend changes. If we don't like it, we'll send it back as promptly as possible. Read the journal. Send typewritten, clean copy carefully proofread. We also award annually the Hoepfner Prize of $100 for the best published essay or short story of the year. Let someone whose opinion you respect read your story and give you an honest appraisal. Rewrite, if necessary, to get the most from your story."

THE SOUTHERN REVIEW, (II), Louisiana State University, 43 Allen Hall, Baton Rouge LA 70803. (504)388-5108. Fax: (504)388-5098. E-mail: bmacon@unix1.sncc.lsu.edu. Editors: James Olney and Dave Smith. Magazine: 6¾ × 10; 240 pages; 50 lb. Glatfelter paper; 65 lb. #1 grade cover stock. "A literary quarterly publishing critical essays, poetry and fiction for a highly intellectual audience." Quarterly. Estab. 1935. Circ. 3,100.

Needs: Literary. "We emphasize style and substantial content. No mystery, fantasy or religious mss." Accepts 4-5 mss/issue. Receives approximately 300 unsolicited fiction mss each month. Does not read mss June through August. Publishes ms 6-9 months after acceptance. Agented fiction 1%. Recently published work by Rick Bass, Robert Olen Butler, Ellen Douglas, Pam Durban, Ehud Havazel, Joyce Carol Oates, Richard Rubin, Gerald Shapiro, June Spence and Scott Ely. Publishes 4-6 new writers/year. Length: 2,000-10,000 words. Also publishes literary essays, literary criticism, poetry. Sponsors annual contest for best first collection of short stories published during the calendar year.

How to Contact: Send complete ms with cover letter and SASE. "Prefer brief letters giving information on author concerning where he/she has been published before, biographical info and what he/she is doing now." Reports in 2 months on mss. Sample copy for $6. Fiction guidelines free for SAE. Reviews novels and short story collections.

Payment/Terms: Pays $12/printed page; 2 contributor's copies on publication for first North American serial rights. Sends galleys to author.

Advice: "Develop a careful, clear style."

‡SOUTHERN VOICES, (I, IV), Cedar Creek School, 2400 Cedar Creek Drive, Ruston LA 71270. (318)255-7707. E-mail: gingram@linknet.net. Website: http://www4.linknet.net. Editor: Gaye Ingram. " *Southern Voices* is an annual literary journal that publishes the finest fiction, poetry & imaginative essays of high school students in Alabama, Arkansas, Florida, Georgia, Louisiana, Mississippi, North and South Carolina, Tennessee, and Texas. Prizes are awarded in the categories of short story, poetry, essay. The purpose of *Southern Voices* is to build pride, high ambition, and superior achievement among students from the Southern states by encouraging their active participation in the rich literary heritage of their region." Journal is distributed free to nearly 1,500 public and private school classrooms and libraries throughout 10 Southern states.

Needs: Short stories, poetry, imaginative essays. Publishes 30-40 new writers/year.

How to Contact: "Work must be submitted with submission form signed by high school English teacher or other school official, verifying originality. Postmark deadline: January 25th. Please see web page for specific guidelines and submission form.

Advice: "For an idea of the kind of creative writing published in *Southern Voices*, please secure a copy from a high school English teacher or by sending $10.00 (check or money order) to address above. May also see selected pieces on web page. We look for good quality, regardless of genre. We would like to have more reflective essays dealing with the way young Southerners respond to the history and traditions of their region."

SOUTHWEST REVIEW, (II), Box 374, 307 Fondren Library West, Southern Methodist University, Dallas TX 75275. (214)768-1037. Editor: Willard Spiegelman. Magazine: 6 × 9; 144 pages. "The majority of our readers are college-educated adults who wish to stay abreast of the latest and best in contemporary fiction, poetry, literary criticism and books in all but the most specialized disciplines." Quarterly. Estab. 1915. Circ. 1,600.

Needs: "High literary quality; no specific requirements as to subject matter, but cannot use sentimental, religious, western, poor science fiction, pornographic, true confession, mystery, juvenile or serialized or condensed novels." Receives approximately 200 unsolicited fiction mss each month. Published work by Brad Barkley, E. Shaskan Bumas, Hilary Steinitz, Richard Stern and Wakako Yamauchi. Length: prefers 3,000-5,000 words. Also publishes literary essays and poetry. Occasionally critiques rejected mss.

How to Contact: Send complete ms with SASE. Reports in 6 months on mss. Publishes ms 6-12 months after acceptance. Sample copy for $5. Guidelines for SASE.

Payment/Terms: Payment varies; writers receive 3 contributor's copies. Pays on publication for first North American serial rights. Sends galleys to author.

Advice: "We have become less regional. A lot of time would be saved for us and for the writer if he or she looked at a copy of the *Southwest Review* before submitting. We like to receive a cover letter because it is some reassurance that the author has taken the time to check a current directory for the editor's name. When there isn't a cover letter, we wonder whether the same story is on 20 other desks around the country."

SOU'WESTER, (II), Southern Illinois University—Edwardsville, Edwardsville IL 62026-1438. (618)692-3190. Managing Editor: Fred W. Robbins. Magazine: 6×9; 120 pages; Warren's Olde Style paper; 60 lb. cover. General magazine of poetry and fiction. Biannually. Estab. 1960. Circ. 300.
  • The *Sou'wester* is known for publishing traditional, well-developed and carefully crafted short stories. Work published here has received an Illinois Arts Council Literary Award for "Best Illinois Fiction" and the Daniel Curley Award.
Needs: "The best work we can find, no matter who the author is." No science fiction or fantasy. Receives 50-100 unsolicited fiction mss/month. Accepts 6 mss/issue; 12 mss/year. Recently published work by Robert Wexelblatt, Julie Simon, John Pesta, Ellen Slezak and David Starkey. Publishes 3-4 new writers/year. Length: 10,000 words maximum. Also publishes poetry. Occasionally critiques rejected mss.
How to Contact: Send complete ms with SASE. Simultaneous submissions OK. Reports in 6-8 months. Publishes ms an average of 6 months after acceptance. Sample copy for $5.
Payment/Terms: Pays 2 contributor's copies; $5 charge for extras. Acquires first serial rights.
Advice: "Work on polishing your sentences."

‡SPARKS, (I, II), E-mail: sparks@las.alfred.edu. Website: http://las.alfred.edu/~sparks. Editor: Jim Esch. Electronic magazine. "*Sparks* is aimed at creative, critically-aware people who thirst for quality and perspective."
Needs: Experimental, literary. "Literature of the imagination. Art is key. Beauty as cause and effect." No genre fiction. Recently published work by Frank Ford, Richard Russell, Larry Lynch and Ro London. Publishes 15-20 new writers/year.
How to Contact: Electronic submissions only.
Advice: "Read back issues. Build your fiction around interesting, intriguing characters. Don't be afraid of imagery and imaginative exploration."

SPELUNKER FLOPHOUSE, (II), P.O. Box 617742, Chicago IL 60661. E-mail: spelunkerf@aol.com. Website: members.aol.com/spelunkerf/ (includes guidelines, excerpts, magazine history, how to subscribe, etc.). Editors: Chris Kubica and Wendy Morgan. Magazine: 8½×7; 96 pages; offset print; perfect-bound; 4-color glossy card cover. "We offer the best poetry, fiction and artwork we can in an inventive, original format. We cooperate regularly with other literary magazines." Quarterly. Estab. 1996. Press run: 1,500.
Needs: Ethnic/multicultural, experimental, feminist, humor/satire, literary, translations. "We are especially interested in fiction and poetry exploring small details of everyday life." Receives 100 unsolicited mss/month. Accepts 3-6 mss/issue; 12-24 mss/year. Publishes ms 4 months after acceptance. Agented fiction: 5%. Recently published work by Edward Falco, Stephen Dixon, Julie Checkoway, Cris Mazza, W.P. Kinsella, Denise Duhamel and Carolyn Alessio. Publishes 5-20 new writers/year. Length: 100 words minimum; 10,000 words maximum. Publishes short shorts. Also publishes poetry. Often critiques or comments on rejected mss. Sponsors contest. Look for guidelines in the magazine.
How to Contact: Send complete ms with a cover letter. Include bio, list of publications if available and any brief interesting information about yourself. Reports in 4-10 weeks on mss. Send SASE for return of the ms or send a disposable copy of the ms. Simultaneous submissions OK, if noted. Sample copy for $6.95 postpaid. Fiction guidelines free with #10 SASE. Occasionally reviews fiction or poetry in book form.
Payment/Terms: Pays "depending on current cash flow" and 2 contributor's copies. Pays on publication. Acquires first North American serial rights. Sends galleys to author.
Advice: "We are interested in stories that have a strong sense of character, technique, language, realistic dialogue, unique style/voice, and (if possible) a plot. No restrictions on length or subject matter except no genre work or 'statements.' Nothing patently cute. Support this necessary forum for the arts by purchasing copies of literary magazines, reading them, and increasing local awareness of magazines/forums such as ours whenever possible. Study the market; then submit. And keep in touch. We love to hear from members/supporters of the literary community."

SPINDRIFT, (II), Shoreline Community College, 16101 Greenwood Ave. North, Seattle WA 98133. (206)546-4785. Editor: Carol Orlock, adviser. Magazine: 140 pages; quality paper; photographs; b&w artwork. "We look for fresh, original work that is not forced or 'straining' to be literary." Annually. Estab. around 1967. Circ. 500.
  • *Spindrift* has received awards for "Best Literary Magazine" from the Community College Humanities Association both locally and nationally and awards from the Pacific Printing Industries.
Needs: Contemporary, ethnic, experimental, historical (general), prose poem, regional, science fiction, serialized/excerpted novel, translations. No romance, religious/inspirational. Receives up to 150 mss/year. Accepts up to 20 mss/issue. Does not read during spring/summer. Publishes ms 3-4 months after acceptance. Published work by David Halpern and Jana Harris; published new writers within the last year. Length: 250 words minimum; 3,500-4,500 words maximum. Publishes short shorts.
How to Contact: Send complete ms, and "bio, name, address, phone and list of titles submitted." Reports in 2 weeks on queries; juries after February 1 and responds by March 15 with SASE. Sample copy for $6, 8×10 SAE and $1 postage.
Payment/Terms: Pays in contributor's copies; charge for extras. Acquires first rights. Publication not copy-

righted.

Advice: "The tighter the story the better. The more lyric values in the narrative the better. Read the magazine, keep working on craft. Submit by February 1."

‡THE SPIRIT (OF WOMAN IN THE MOON), A New Age Literary Magazine, (I, II), 1409 The Alameda, San Jose CA 95126. (408)279-6626. Fax: (408)279-6636. Magazine: 8×11; 36 pages; 60 lb. white paper; glossy cover stock; illustrations and photos. "*The Spirit* is a positive, upbeat and informative publication. We are particularly interested in material on current New Age feminist topics." Semiannually. Estab. 1993. Circ. 3,000. Member Publishing Triangle. "Every submission must include the reading fee which includes a current issue of *The Spirit*: Poetry (3-poem packet), $8; Fiction and nonfiction, $12 up to 5 pages, $3 for each additional page."

Needs: Ethnic/multicultural, feminist, gay, lesbian, literary, psychic/supernatural/occult, religious/inspirational, science fiction (soft/sociological), serialized novel, African-American, new age views. No narrative, futuristic, humanist. Receives 5-30 unsolicited mss/month. Accepts 3-5 mss/issue; 60 mss/year. Publishes mss 2 quarters after acceptance. Recently published work by Wu Hsien. Length: 500-1,500 words average. Publishes short shorts. Also publishes poetry. Always critiques or comments on rejected mss.

How to Contact: Query first. Include word count, 1-paragraph bio, Social Security number, list of publications (10 best) and photo (for publication) with submission. Reports in 2 weeks on queries; 6 weeks on mss. Send SASE for reply, return of ms or send a disposable copy of ms. Simultaneous, reprint and electronic submissions (disk or modem) OK. Sample copy for $4.50 and 6×10 SAE (no IRCs, please). Fiction guidelines free. Reviews novels and short story collections. Send books to Scott Shuker, review editor.

Payment/Terms: Pays $10-100, free subscription to magazine and 2 contributor's copies; additional copies $4.50. Pays on publication. Acquires first North American serial rights or reprint rights.

Advice: "Don't send us things that are meant to be appreciated by the majority culture. We are a niche for new age ideas given the explosive interest in science fiction, psychic phenomenon and angels."

SPITBALL, (I), 5560 Fox Rd., Cincinnati OH 45239. (513)385-2268. Editor: Mike Shannon. Magazine: 5½×8½; 96 pages; 55 lb. Glatfelter Natural, neutral pH paper; 10 pt. CS1 cover stock; illustrations; photos. Magazine publishing "fiction and poetry about *baseball* exclusively for an educated, literary segment of the baseball fan population." Biannually. Estab. 1981. Circ. 1,000.

Needs: Confession, contemporary, experimental, historical, literary, mainstream and suspense. "Our only requirement concerning the type of fiction written is that the story be *primarily* about baseball." Receives 100 unsolicited fiction mss/year. Accepts 16-20 mss/year. Published work by Dallas Wiebe, Michael Gilmartin and W.P. Kinsella; published new writers within the last year. Length: 20 typed double-spaced pages. "The longer it is, the better it has to be."

How to Contact: Send complete ms with cover letter and SASE. Include brief bio about author. Reporting time varies. Publishes ms an average of 3 months after acceptance. Sample copy for $6.

Payment/Terms: "No monetary payment at present. We may offer nominal payment in the near future." 2 free contributor's copies per issue in which work appears. Acquires first North American serial rights.

Advice: "Our audience is mostly college educated and knowledgeable about baseball. The stories we have published so far have been very well written and displayed a firm grasp of the baseball world and its people. In short, audience response has been great because the stories are simply good as stories. Thus, mere use of baseball as subject is no guarantee of acceptance. We are always seeking submissions. Unlike many literary magazines, we have no backlog of accepted material. Fiction is a natural genre for our exclusive subject, baseball. There are great opportunities for writing in certain areas of fiction, baseball being one of them. Baseball has become the 'in' spectator sport among intellectuals, the general media and the 'yuppie' crowd. Consequently, as subject matter for adult fiction it has gained a much wider acceptance than it once enjoyed."

SPOUT, (I, II), Spout Press, 28 W. Robie St., St. Paul MN 55107. (612)298-9846. E-mail: colb0018@gold.tc.umn.edu. Editors: John Colburn and Michelle Filkins. Fiction Editor: Chris Watercott. Magazine: 8½×11; 40 pages; 70 lb. flat white paper; colored cover; illustrations. "We like the surprising, the surreal and the experimental. Our readers are well-read, often writers." Triannually. Estab. 1989. Circ. 300-500.

● *Spout* editors submit work to the *Pushcart* anthology. They would like to see more sudden fiction.

Needs: Condensed/excerpted novel, ethnic/multicultural, experimental, feminist, gay, humor/satire, lesbian, literary, regional, translations. No horror. Publishes special fiction issues or anthologies. Receives 25-30 unsolicited mss/month. Accepts 4-5 mss/issue; 15 mss/year. Publishes ms 1-3 months after acceptance. Agented fiction 5%. Recently published work by Mario Benedetti, Gayle Silbert, Stephen Gutierrez and Michael Little. Length: open. Publishes short shorts and "sudden" fiction. Also publishes poetry. Often comments on rejected mss.

How to Contact: Send complete ms with a cover letter. Include short bio and list of publications with submission. Reports in 1 month on queries; 2-3 months on mss. Send SASE for reply, return of ms or send a disposable copy of ms. Simultaneous submissions OK. Sample copy for $2, 8½×11 SAE and 5 first-class stamps. Fiction guidelines for SASE.

Payment/Terms: Pays 1 contributor's copy; additional copies for $2 plus postage. Acquires one-time rights.

Advice: Looks for "imagination, surprise and attention to language. We often publish writers on their third or fourth submission, so don't get discouraged. We need more weird, surreal fiction that lets the reader make his/her own meaning. Don't send moralistic, formulaic work."

SPRING FANTASY, (I), Women In The Arts, P.O. Box 2907, Decatur IL 62524. Contact: Vice President (newly elected each year). Magazine. "An annual anthology of short stories, juvenile fiction, poetry, essays and black & white artwork; *Spring Fantasy* aims to encourage beginners, especially women." Estab. 1994.
Needs: Adventure, children's/juvenile, fantasy, feminist, historical, horror, humor/satire, literary, mystery/suspense (amateur sleuth, cozy, police procedural, private eye/hardboiled, romantic suspense), romance, science fiction, young adult/teen (adventure, horror, mystery, romance, science fiction, western). Length: 750 words maximum.
How to Contact: Send complete ms without a cover letter. Reports in 4 months. Send SASE for reply, return of ms or send a disposable copy of ms. Simultaneous submissions and reprints OK. Sample copy for $6. Guidelines for #10 SASE.
Payment/Terms: Pays $5-30 honorarium on publication and 1 contributor's copy; 20% discount on additional copies. Acquires first and reprint rights. Sponsors annual contest with cash prizes; send SASE for information.

SPSM&H, (II, IV), *Amelia* Magazine, 329 "E" St., Bakersfield CA 93304. (805)323-4064. Editor: Frederick A. Raborg, Jr. Magazine: 5½ × 8¼; 24 pages; matte cover stock; illustrations and photos. "*SPSM&H* publishes sonnets, sonnet sequences and fiction, articles and reviews related to the form (fiction may be romantic or Gothic) for a general readership and sonnet enthusiasts." Quarterly. Estab. 1985. Circ. 600.
● This magazine is edited by Frederick A. Raborg, Jr., who is also editor of *Amelia* and *Cicada*.
Needs: Adventure, confession, contemporary, erotica, ethnic, experimental, fantasy, feminist, gay, historical, horror, humor/satire, lesbian, literary, mainstream, mystery/suspense, regional, romance (contemporary, historical), science fiction, senior citizen/retirement, translations and western. All should have romantic element. "We look for strong fiction with romantic or Gothic content, or both. Stories need not have 'happy' endings, and we are open to the experimental and/or avant-garde. Erotica is fine; pornography, no." Receives 30 unsolicited mss/month. Accepts 1 ms/issue; 4 mss/year. Publishes ms 6 months to 1 year after acceptance. Agented fiction 5%. Published work by Brad Hooper, Mary Louise R. O'Hara and Clara Castelar Bjorlie. Length: 2,000 words average; 500 words minimum; 3,000 words maximum. Critiques rejected ms when appropriate; recommends other markets.
How to Contact: Send complete ms with cover letter. Include Social Security number. Reports in 2 weeks. SASE. Sample copy for $4.95. Fiction guidelines for #10 SASE.
Payment/Terms: Pays $10-25 and contributor's copies on publication for first North American serial rights; charge for extra copies.
Advice: "A good story line (plot) and strong characterization are vital. I want to know the writer has done his homework and is striving to become professional."

*STAND MAGAZINE, 179 Wingrove Rd., Newcastle Upon Tyne, NE4 9DA England. Fiction Editor: Lorna Tracy. Circ. 4,500. Quarterly. Averages 16-20 stories/year.
Needs: "*Stand* is an international quarterly publishing poetry, short stories, reviews, criticism and translations." Length: 5,000 words maximum.
How to Contact: "Read copies of the magazine before submitting. Enclose sufficient IRCs for return of mss/reply. No more than 6 poems or 2 short stories at any one time. Avoid specific genre writing—e.g. science fiction, travel, etc. Should not be under consideration elsewhere."
Payment/Terms: £25 per 1,000 words of prose on publication (or in US dollars); contributor's copies. Sponsors biennial short competition: First prize, £1,500. Send 2 IRCs for information. Sample copy: $6.50. Guidelines on receipt of 2 IRCs/SASE (U.K. stamps).

*STAPLE, Tor Cottage 81, Cavendish Rd., Matlock DE4 3HD United Kingdom. Fiction Editor: Don Measham. Published 3 times/year. Circ. up to 600. Publishes up to 50% fiction. *Staple* is "about 90 pages, perfect-bound; beautifully designed and produced."
Needs: "Stories used by *Staple* have ranged from social realism (through autobiography, parody, prequel, parable) to visions and hallucinations. We don't use unmodified genre fiction, i.e., adventure, crime or westerns. We are interested in extracts from larger works—provided author does the extraction." Length: 200 words minimum; 5,000 words maximum.
How to Contact: Adequate IRCs and large envelope for return, if return is required. Otherwise IRC for decision only. The monograph series *Staple First Editions* is a biennial. IRC for details. Please note that *Staple* requires stories to be previously unpublished worldwide.
Payment/Terms: Pays complimentary copy plus subscription for US contributors. Get a specimen copy of one of the issues with strong prose representation. Send $10 for airmail dispatch, $5 for surface mail.

STONE SOUP, The Magazine By Young Writers and Artists, (I, IV), Children's Art Foundation, Box 83, Santa Cruz CA 95063. (408)426-5557. E-mail: gmandel@stonesoup.com. Website: http://www.stonesoup.com (includes writer's guidelines, sample copy, links, curriculum matrix, international children's art). Editor: Gerry Mandel. Magazine: 7 × 10; 48 pages; high quality paper; photos. Stories, poems, book reviews and art by children through age 13. Readership: children, librarians, educators. Published 6 times/year. Estab. 1973. Circ. 20,000.

• This is known as "the literary journal for children." *Stone Soup* has previously won the Edpress Golden Lamp Honor Award and the Parent's Choice Award.

Needs: Fiction by children on themes based on their own experiences, observations or special interests. Also, some fantasy, mystery, adventure. No clichés, no formulas, no writing exercises; original work only. Receives approximately 1,000 unsolicited fiction mss each month. Accepts approximately 15 mss/issue. Published new writers within the last year. Length: 150-2,500 words. Also publishes literary essays and poetry. Critiques rejected mss upon request.

How to Contact: Send complete ms with cover letter. "We like to learn a little about our young writers, why they like to write, and how they came to write the story they are submitting." SASE. No simultaneous submissions. Reports in 1 month on mss. Does not respond to mss that are not accompanied by an SASE. Publishes ms an average of 3-6 months after acceptance. Sample copy for $4. Guidelines for SASE. Reviews children's books.

Payment/Terms: Pays $10 plus 2 contributor's copies; $2.50 charge for extras. Buys all rights.

Advice: Mss are rejected because they are "derivatives of movies, TV, comic books; or classroom assignments or other formulas."

‡STONEFLOWER LITERARY JOURNAL, (II), Stoneflower Press, 1824 Nacogdoches, Suite 191, San Antonio TX 78209. E-mail: stonflower@aol.com. Editor: Brenda Davidson-Shaddox. Fiction Coordinator: Coley Scott. Journal: 5½×4; 125 pages; 50 lb. white offset paper; 8 pt. carolina C1S cover stock; illustrations (ink drawings only) and photographs (b&w only). Annually. Estab. 1996.

Needs: Experimental, feminist, humor/satire, literary, mainstream/contemporary, regional. "Any category or style will be considered if the writing is good." Receives 125 unsolicited mss/month. Accepts 6-10 mss/issue; 6-10 mss/year. Publishes ms the next issue, never longer than 1 year. Recently published work by Don Feigert, Jaclyn Rivers, Louis R. Service and Carolyn Veitenheimer. Length: 2,500 words maximum (will not read longer works). Publishes short shorts. Also publishes poetry. "We also publish one interview or profile each issue. Subject should be writer, editor, agent, artist, publisher, photographer or other professional whose primary career is creative." Sometimes (but rarely) critiques or comments on rejected mss.

How to Contact: "Send complete ms with or without a cover letter. But *always* send a bio. Saves time if work is accepted for publication." Include estimated word count, 1-paragraph bio, list of publications, contests won and other writing accomplishments. Reports in 3 months. SASE for reply; send a disposable copy of ms. "No response to any correspondence/inquiry without SASE." Simultaneous submissions, reprints and electronic submissions (e-mail only) OK. Sample copy for $5, 6×9 SASE and $1.24 in postage or 2 IRCs. Fiction guidelines for 9″ SASE or IRC.

Payment/Terms: "Short story writers receive $10/story; interview $10/work; poetry $5/poem." Pays on publication. Acquires one-time rights. Sponsors contest; "send SASE (9″ envelope with one first-class stamp for guidelines. First place fiction winner $75; 2nd place $25. First place poetry $50; 2nd place $10. All honorable mentions receive free copy of journal. Winners names announced in the journal."

Advice: "Technically correct writing combined with colorful, exciting use of the language helps. A story must draw us in quickly. If we lose interest by the end of the first page, we quit reading. In addition to good writing, clean, professionally prepared manuscripts are a must. Will not read handwritten manuscripts. Don't use clichés. Watch spelling. Stay away from passive verbs. Don't choose an exotic topic; write about what people care about. Above all, study creative writing—either on your own or in classes—and read, read, read. Nothing improves one's writing more than exposure to other good writers. The only trend currently affecting us is electronic submissions. We now accept e-mail submissions and generally respond to those quicker than postal submissions. We strive to cut paper use and handling time. Electronic submissions help us accomplish that."

STORY, (II), F&W Publications, 1507 Dana Ave., Cincinnati OH 45207. (513)531-2222. Editor: Lois Rosenthal. Magazine: 6¼×9½; 128 pages; uncoated, recycled paper; uncoated index stock. "We publish the finest quality short stories. Will consider unpublished novel excerpts if they are self-inclusive." Quarterly. Estab. 1931.

• STORY won the National Magazine Award for Fiction in 1992 and 1995, and was a finalist in 1994, 1996 and 1997. STORY holds an annual contest for short short fiction.

Needs: Literary, experimental, humor, mainstream, translations. No genre fiction—science fiction, detective, young adult, confession, romance, etc. Accepts approximately 12 mss/issue. Agented fiction 50-60%. Published work by Joyce Carol Oates, Carol Shields, Tobias Wolff, Madison Smartt Bell, Rick DeMarinis, Antonya Nelson, Rick Bass, Charles Baxter, Tess Gallagher, Rick Moody, Ellen Gilchrist, and Thom Jones; published new writers within the last year. Length: up to 8,000 words.

How to Contact: Send complete ms with or without cover letter, or submit through agent. SASE necessary

---

READ THE BUSINESS OF FICTION WRITING section to learn the correct way to prepare and submit a manuscript.

for return of ms and response. "Will accept simultaneous submissions as long as it is stated in a cover letter." Sample copy for $6.95, 9×12 SAE and $2.40 postage. Fiction guidelines for #10 SASE.

Payment/Terms: Pays $1,000 for stories; $750 for short shorts plus 5 contributor's copies on acceptance for first North American serial rights. Sends galleys to author.

Advice: "We accept fiction of the highest quality, whether by established or new writers. Since we receive more than 300 submissions each week, the competition for space is fierce. We look for original subject matter and fresh voices. Read issues of STORY before trying us."

STORYQUARTERLY, (II), Box 1416, Northbrook IL 60065. (847)564-8891. Co-editors: Anne Brashler and Diane Williams. Magazine: approximately 6×9; 130 pages; good quality paper; illustrations; photos. A magazine devoted to the short story and committed to a full range of styles and forms. Semiannually. Estab. 1975. Circ. 3,000.

Needs: Receives 200 unsolicited fiction mss/month. Accepts 12-15 mss/issue, 20-30 mss/year. Recently published work by Paul Buchanan, Brian Bufkin, Martha Davis, Steve Dixon, Brian Evenson, Steve Harker, Gary Lutz, Ben Marcus, Dawn Raffel, Victoria Redel and Rachel Sherman. Published new writers within the last year.

How to Contact: Send complete ms with SASE. Simultaneous submissions OK. Reports in 3 months on mss. Sample copy for $6.

Payment/Terms: Pays 3 contributor's copies for one-time rights. Copyright reverts to author after publication.

Advice: "Send one manuscript at a time, subscribe to the magazine, send SASE."

STREET BEAT QUARTERLY, (I, II), Wood Street Commons, 301 Third Ave., Pittsburgh PA 15222. (412)765-3302. Fax: (412)765-2646. Editor: Christine Springer. Contact: Sharon Thorp. Magazine: 8½×11; 32 pages; newsprint paper; newsprint cover; illustrations and photos. "*Street Beat Quarterly* publishes (primarily) literary works by those who have experienced homelessness or poverty. We reach those interested in literary magazines and others interested in homelessness issues." Quarterly. Estab. 1990. Circ. 2,000-3,000.

Needs: Adventure, ethnic/multicultural, experimental, fantasy, feminist, historical, humor/satire, literary, mainstream/contemporary, mystery/suspense, stories by children. "No religious." Receives 2 unsolicited mss/month. Accepts 2-5 mss/issue. Publishes ms 1-3 months after acceptance. Published work by Freddy Posco, James Burroughs and Mel Spivak. Length: 750 words average; 100 words minimum; 10,000 words maximum. Publishes short shorts. Also publishes literary essays and poetry. Sometimes critiques or comments on rejected mss.

How to Contact: Send complete ms with a cover letter including bio. Reports in 1 month on mss. Send a disposable copy of ms. Simultaneous, reprint and electronic submissions OK. Sample copy for 3 first-class stamps.

Payment/Terms: Pays $3 plus 1 contributor's copy on publication for one-time rights.

Advice: "We are pretty flexible. Our mission is to publish work by those who have experienced homelessness and poverty; we will consider a limited amount of works by others if it is on the topic (homelessness/poverty). Don't be afraid of us! We are very much a grass-roots publication. Be patient with us; as we sometimes take a short while to respond. We publish some very polished work; we also publish some very 'rough' yet energetic work. We are looking for stories that truly capture the experience of homelessness and poverty on a personal level."

STRUGGLE, A Magazine of Proletarian Revolutionary Literature, (I, II), Box 13261, Detroit MI 48213-0261. Editor: Tim Hall. Magazine: 5½×8½; 36-72 pages; 20 lb. white bond paper; colored cover; illustrations; occasional photographs. Publishes material related to "the struggle of the working class and all progressive people against the rule of the rich—including their war policies, racism, exploitation of the workers, oppression of women, etc." Quarterly. Estab. 1985.

Needs: Contemporary, ethnic, experimental, feminist, historical (general), humor/satire, literary, prose poem, regional, science fiction, senior citizen/retirement, translations, young adult/teen (10-18). "The theme can be approached in many ways, including plenty of categories not listed here." No romance, psychic, western, erotica, religious. Receives 10-12 unsolicited fiction mss/month. Publishes ms 6 months or less after acceptance. Recently published work by P.J. Jason, Namrata Patel, Ken Pell, Alex Shishin and Billie Louise Jones. Published new writers within the last year. Length: 1,000-3,000 words average; 4,000 words maximum. Publishes short shorts. Normally critiques rejected mss.

How to Contact: Send complete ms; cover letter optional. "Tries to" report in 3-4 months. SASE. Simultaneous and reprint submissions OK. Sample copy for $2.50. Make checks payable to Tim Hall-Special Account.

Payment/Terms: Pays 2 contributor's copies. No rights acquired. Publication not copyrighted.

Advice: "Write about the oppression of the working people, the poor, the minorities, women, and if possible, their rebellion against it—we are not interested in anything which accepts the status quo. We are not too worried about plot and advanced technique (fine if we get them!)—we would probably accept things others would call sketches, provided they have life and struggle. For new writers: just describe for us a situation in which some real people confront some problem of oppression, however seemingly minor. Observe and put down the real facts. Experienced writers: try your 'committed'/experimental fiction on us. We get poetry all the time. We have increased our fiction portion of our content in the last few years. The quality of fiction that we have published has continued to improve. If your work raises an interesting issue of literature and politics, it may get discussed in letters and in my editorial. I suggest ordering a sample."

✤**SUB-TERRAIN, (II)**, P.O. Box 1575, Bentall Centre, Vancouver BC V6C 2P7 Canada. (604)876-8710. Fax: (604)879-2667. E-mail: subter@pinc.com. Fiction Editors: D.E. Bolen and Brian Kaufman. Magazine: 8½×11; 40 pages; offset printed paper; illustrations; photos. "*Sub-Terrain* provides a forum for work that pushes the boundaries in form or content." Estab. 1988.

Needs: "Primarily a literary magazine; also interested in erotica, experimental, humor/satire." Receives 100 unsolicited mss/month. Accepts 15-20 mss/issue. Publishes ms 1-4 months after acceptance. Publishes 6-10 new writers/year. Recently published work by Steven Heighton, Clark Timmins, J. Jill Robinson, Derek McCormack, Billie Livingston and Mark Jarman. Length: 200-3,000 words. Publishes short shorts. Length: 200 words. Also publishes literary essays, literary criticism, poetry. Sometimes critiques rejected mss and "at times" recommends other markets.

How to Contact: Send complete ms with cover letter. Simultaneous submissions OK, if notified when ms is accepted elsewhere. Reports in 3-4 weeks on queries; 2-3 months on mss. SASE. Sample copy for $5. Also features book review section. Send books marked "Review Copy, Managing Editor."

Payment/Terms: Pays (for solicited work) $25/page; $20/poem. Acquires one-time rights.

Advice: "We look for contemporary, modern fiction with something special in the voice or style, not simply something that is a well-written story—a new twist, a unique sense or vision of the world, the stuff that every mag is hoping to find. Write about things that are important to you: issues that *must* be talked about; issues that frighten or anger you. The world has all the cute, well-made stories it needs. Read a sample copy before submitting."

SULPHUR RIVER LITERARY REVIEW, (II), P.O. Box 19228, Austin TX 78760-9228. (512)447-6809. Editor: James Michael Robbins. Magazine: 5½×8½; 130 pages; illustrations and photos. "*SRLR* publishes literature of quality—poetry and short fiction with appeal that transcends time. Audience includes a broad spectrum of readers, mostly educated, many of whom are writers, artists and educators." Semiannually. Estab. 1978. Circ. 400.

Needs: Ethnic/multicultural, experimental, feminist, humor/satire, literary, mainstream/contemporary and translations. No "religious, juvenile, teen, sports, romance or mystery." Receives 10-12 unsolicited mss/month. Accepts 2-3 mss/issue; 4-6 mss/year. Publishes ms 1-2 years after acceptance. Recently published work by Aris Fioretos, Ivan A. Bunin, Kevin Meaux and Jamie Brown. Publishes short shorts. Also publishes literary essays, literary criticism and poetry. Often critiques or comments on rejected mss.

How to Contact: Send complete ms with a cover letter. Include short bio and list of publications. Reports in 1 week on queries; 1 month on mss. Send SASE for reply, return of ms or send a disposable copy of ms. No simultaneous submissions. Sample copy for $6.

Payment/Terms: Pays 2 contributor's copies; additional copies for $6. Acquires first North American serial rights.

Advice: Looks for "originality, mastery of the language, imagination. Revise, revise, revise."

A SUMMER'S READING, A Journal of Fiction, Nonfiction, Poetry & Art, (I, II), 804 Oakland Ave., Mt. Vernon IL 62864. (618)242-8364. Fax: (618)244-8047. Editors: Ted Morrissey and Barbara Hess. Magazine: 5½×8½; 40-60 pages; 20 lb. paper; card cover stock; b&w illustrations. "There is so much excellent writing being produced and, by comparison, so few opportunities to publish—we want to provide one more well-edited, attractive outlet." Annually. Estab. 1997. Circ. 300.

Needs: Excerpted novel, literary, translations (provide copy of original). "We have absolutely no taboos in subject matter or imagery." Prefers to read April to September. "One of our reasons for emerging in the summer is to provide a place for writers to send material when the majority of journals are not accepting submissions. We select, edit, produce and distribute during the 'academic' year." Publishes ms 6 months after acceptance. Recently published work by Hoag Holmgren and Kristine Somerville. Length: 100 words minimum; 8,000 words maximum. Publishes short shorts. Also publishes poetry and narrative nonfiction (e.g., autobiography, biography). Would like to see more translations. Sometimes critiques or comments on rejected mss.

How to Contact: Send complete ms with a concise cover letter. Include estimated word count, brief bio (under 100 words) and list of publications. "Do not explain the piece or what inspired it; allow it to speak for itself." Reports in 1-3 months on mss. Send SASE for reply or send a disposable copy of the ms. "No reply without SASE." Simultaneous submissions OK, "but please inform us." Sample copy for $5. Fiction guidelines for #10 SASE.

Payment/Terms: Pays 2 contributor's copies. Acquires one-time rights. Sends galleys to the author.

Advice: Looks for "excellence, which in our collective mind means a combination of practiced writing style and subject which keeps us turning the pages. The chances of your work getting published are better if it's on our desk rather than on yours. Send easy-to-read, error-free material, and we'll give it fair, unbiased consideration. As long as it's 'serious,' we want to see it, from the tightly structured traditional to the wildly experimental. We're seeing too many divorce and war stories—not enough narrative experimentation."

SUN DOG: THE SOUTHEAST REVIEW, (II), English Department, 406 Williams, Florida State University, Tallahassee FL 32306. (904)644-4230. Editors: Ron Wiginton and Michael Trammell. Magazine: 6×9; 60-100 pages; 70 lb. paper; 10 pt. Krome Kote cover; illustrations; photos. Biannually. Estab. 1979. Circ. 2,000.

Needs: "We want stories which are well written, beautifully written, with striking images, incidents and characters. We are interested more in quality than in style or genre." Accepts 20 mss/year. Receives approximately 60 unsolicited fiction mss each month. Reads less frequently during summer. Critiques rejected mss when there is time. Occasionally recommends other markets (up to 5 poems or 1 story.)

How to Contact: Send complete ms with SASE. "Short bio or cover letter would be appreciated." Publishes ms an average of 2-6 months after acceptance. Sample copy for $4.

Payment/Terms: Pays 2 contributor's copies. $2 charge for extras. Acquires first North American serial rights which then revert to author.

Advice: "Avoid trendy experimentation for its own sake (present-tense narration, observation that isn't also revelation). Fresh stories, moving, interesting characters and a sensitivity to language are still fiction mainstays. Also publishes winner and runners-up of the World's Best Short Short Story Contest sponsored by the Florida State University English Department."

‡THE SUNFLOWER DREAM, (I, II), Sunflower Press, 216 Riversview Dr., Carpentersville IL 60110-1743. (847)836-8716. Editor: M.L. Moeller. Magazine: 8½ × 11; 100-200 pages; illustrations and photographs. "I want poetry/short stories most people can say, 'Hey, I understand that.' " Quarterly. Estab. 1996. Circ. 200.

Needs: Adventure, fantasy (science fantasy, sword and sorcery), historical, horror, humor/satire, literary, mainstream/contemporary, mystery/suspense (amateur sleuth, romantic suspense), psychic/supernatural/occult, religious/inspirational, romance (contemporary, futuristic/time travel, gothic, historical), science fiction (soft/sociological), westerns (frontier), young adult/teen (adventure, horror, mystery, romance, science fiction). No pornography. Publishes special fiction issues or anthologies. Receives 35 unsolicited mss/month. Accepts 10-15 mss/issue; 40-60 mss/year. Publishes ms 3-4 months after acceptance. Recently published work by Debbie Klump, Marshall Myers, Kevin Ashby and Dolores Malaschak. Length: 2,000 words average; 3,000 words maximum. Publishes short shorts. Also publishes literary essays, literary criticism, poetry.

How to Contact: Send complete ms with a cover letter. Include estimated word count, bio and list of publications. Reports in 1-2 months on queries; 4-6 weeks on mss. Send SASE for reply, return of ms or send a disposable copy of ms. Simultaneous submissions and reprints OK. Sample copy for $5. Fiction guidelines free. Reviews novels and short story collections.

Payment/Terms: Acquires first rights or one-time rights. Sponsors contest. "The magazine guidelines include the contest, which is ongoing."

Advice: "I look for quality, pace, and whether it catches my interest and holds it. Write your best . . . and keep on trying. It's very unusual for the first thing you ever write to be accepted. Even very good writers get rejection slips. I see a lot of 'stories' that show how much popular reading the writer does. Reading is very important."

SURPRISE ME, (I, IV), Surprise Me Publications, P.O. Box 1762, Claremore OK 74018-1762. Editor: Lynda J. Nicolls. Magazine: 8½ × 11; 20-30 pages; illustrations. "*Surprise Me* is founded on the hope of providing a home for those souls who believe life's purpose is to serve Truth and Beauty. Our main interests are mysticism, the arts and nature. Prisoners, teenagers, the disabled and the elderly are especially welcomed here. Our intended audience is college students, college professors, prisoners, teenagers, the disabled, the elderly and people who do not like most of what is being published now." Biannual. Estab. 1994. Circ. 40.

● Please note that *Surprise Me* now accepts work from subscribers only. The editor would like "to see more children's literature and fantasy stories, like C.S. Lewis' *Chronicles of Narnia*."

Needs: Adventure, children's/juvenile, fantasy, literary, psychic/supernatural/occult, religious/inspirational, romance (futuristic/time travel, gothic), science fiction, senior citizen/retirement, young adult/teen (adventure, romance, science fiction), art, music, mysticism, nature, dance. "I am not interested in profanity, pro-violence, racism, intolerance and pornography. I'm very open to style, form and subject matter." Receives 50 unsolicited mss/month. Accepts 3 mss/issue; 6 mss/year. Publishes ms 6 months after acceptance. Recently published work by Donna Pearson, Ed Mello, Carol Chipps Carlson and Janie Quinn Storck. Length: under 6 typed, double-spaced pages. Also publishes poetry.

How to Contact: *Accepts work from subscribers only.* Send complete ms with a cover letter. Include 5-line bio and list of publications. "Submissions without cover letters are too impersonal for me, so at least please include a note just to say, 'Hi. This is what I'm sending you.' " Send SASE for reply, return of ms or send a disposable copy of ms. Simultaneous, reprint and electronic submissions OK. "Disks are OK, but please send manuscript, too." Sample copy for $6. Fiction guidelines for #10 SASE.

Payment/Terms: Pays 1 contributor's copy. Acquires one-time rights.

Advice: "I would suggest a beginning fiction writer examine a sample copy of our magazine before submitting to us. Writers also should not take a rejection too hard, since it is only one person's opinion. One editor may call it trash and another editor may call it a masterpiece. I would also suggest reading James Joyce, Hermann Hesse, Colin Wilson, Thomas Moore and Rollo May. I'm very open to subject matter, style and form, but I don't like a lot of what is being published now because it often lacks spirituality and has shock value as its motive. I would like to see more writing about the visual arts (i.e. Vincent van Gogh, Georgia O'Keeffe, Ansel Adams and Edward Weston), as well as more writing about philosophy and poetry (i.e. Soren Kierkegaard, William James, William Blake and W.B. Yeats). I would also like to see more children's literature (for or by children)."

SYCAMORE REVIEW, (II), Department of English, Purdue University, West Lafayette IN 47907. (765)494-3783. Fax: (765)494-3780. E-mail: sycamore@expert.cc.purdue.edu. Website: http://www.sla.purdue.edu/acade

mic/engl/sycamore (includes back and current issues, index, submission guidelines, subscription information, journal library). Editor-in-Chief: Sarah Griffiths. Editors change every two years. Send fiction to Fiction Editor, poetry to Poetry Editor, all other correspondence to Editor-in-Chief. Magazine: 5½ × 8½; 150-200 pages; heavy, textured, uncoated paper; heavy laminated cover. "Journal devoted to contemporary literature. We publish both traditional and experimental fiction, personal essay, poetry, interviews, drama and graphic art. Novel excerpts welcome if they stand alone as a story." Semiannually. Estab. 1989. Circ. 1,000.

● Work published in *Sycamore Review* has been selected for inclusion in the *Pushcart Prize* anthology. The magazine was also named "The Best Magazine from Indiana" by the *Clockwatch Review*.

Needs: Contemporary, experimental, humor/satire, literary, mainstream, regional, translations. "We generally avoid genre literature, but maintain no formal restrictions on style or subject matter. No science fiction, romance, children's." Publishes ms 3 months to 1 year after acceptance. Recently published work by Susan Neville, Gordon Lisch and Abraham Rodriguez, Jr. Publishes 6 new writers/year. Length: 3,750 words preferred; 250 words minimum. Also publishes poetry, "this most recently included Charles Wright, Sandra Gilbert and Caroline Knox." Sometimes critiques rejected mss and recommends other markets.

How to Contact: Send complete ms with cover letter. Cover letter should include previous publications and address changes. Does not read mss May through August. Reports in 4 months. SASE. Simultaneous submissions OK. Sample copy for $7. Fiction guidelines for #10 SASE.

Payment/Terms: Pays in contributor's copies; charge for extras. Acquires one-time rights.

Advice: "We publish both new and experienced authors but we're always looking for stories with strong emotional appeal, vivid characterization and a distinctive narrative voice; fiction that breaks new ground while still telling an interesting and significant story. Avoid gimmicks and trite, predictable outcomes. Write stories that have a ring of truth, the impact of felt emotion. Don't be afraid to submit, send your best."

‡SYLVIA, A Journal of Literature & Art, (I, II), P.O. Box 654, Maple Shade NJ 08052. (609)667-0494. E-mail: sylvia@marketavenue.com. Editors: Susan Mauddi and Michelle Wittle. Magazine: 8½ × 5½; 80-100 pages; 60 lb. paper; glossy cover; illustrations and photos. "We publish poetry, short fiction, personal essays and literary criticisms of modern works. We admire the work of Sylvia Plath, but are open to all styles, not just those that emulate hers." Semiannually. Estab. 1996. Circ. 300.

Needs: Condensed/excerpted novel, ethnic/multicultural, experimental, feminist, gay, historical, lesbian, mainstream/contemporary, translations. No romance. Receives 15 unsolicited mss/month. Accepts 2-3 mss/issue; 4-6 mss/year. Publishes ms 6 months to 1 year after acceptance. Length: 5,000 words average; 2,000 words minimum; 6,000 words maximum. Publishes short shorts. Also publishes literary essays, literary criticism and poetry. Sometimes critiques or comments on rejected mss.

How to Contact: Send complete ms with a cover letter. Included estimated word count, 50-word bio, Social Security number, list of publications and how you heard about the magazine. Reports in 6-12 months on mss. Send SASE for return of ms. Sample copy for $5. Reviews novels and short story collections. Send books to Susan Muaddi with a brief bio and information about how readers can purchase copies.

Payment/Terms: Pays 1 contributor's copy for first rights; additional copies $3.50.

Advice: "We like to see stories that are well-crafted and use details well. Make sure the manuscript is error free and that you've re-thought and revised. We like stories that reflect multi-cultural and social themes."

‡TALKING RIVER REVIEW, (I, II), Lewis-Clark State College, Division of Literature and Languages, 500 8th Ave., Lewiston ID 83501. (208)799-2307. Fax: (208)799-2324. E-mail: triver@lcsc.edu. Editor: Dennis Held. Fiction Editor: Claire Davis. Magazine: 6 × 9; 150 pages; 60 lb. paper; coated, color cover; illustrations and photos. "We publish the best work by well-known and unknown authors; our audience is literary but unpretentious." Semiannually. Estab. 1994. Circ. 500.

Needs: Condensed/excerpted novel, ethnic/multicultural, experimental, feminist, gay, historical, humor/satire, lesbian, literary, mainstream/contemporary, regional. Receives 200 unsolicited mss/month. Accepts 5-8 mss/issue; 10-15 mss/year. Does not read March to September. Publishes ms up to 1 year after acceptance. Agented fiction 10%. Recently published work by Gary Gibluer, David Cates, Pete Fromn, Kate Gadbow, David Romtvedt, Rita Cires and Charlene L. Curry. Length: 3,000 words average; 7,500 words maximum. Publishes short shorts. Also publishes literary essays and poetry. Sometimes critiques or comments on rejected mss.

How to Contact: Send complete manuscript with a cover letter. Include estimated word count, 2-sentence bio, Social Security number and list of publications. Reports in 3 months on mss. Send SASE for reply, return of ms or send disposable copy of ms. Simultaneous submissions OK if indicated. Sample copy for $4. Fiction guidelines for #10 SASE.

Payment/Terms: Pays 2 contributor's copies for one-time rights; additional copies $4.

Advice: "Write well; submit one manuscript at a time; send only your best work."

TAMPA REVIEW, (I, II), 401 W. Kennedy Blvd., Box 19F, University of Tampa, Tampa FL 33606-1490. (813)253-3333, ext. 6266. Fax: (813)258-7593. E-mail: mathews@alpha.utampa.edu. Editor: Richard Mathews. Fiction Editor: Lisa Birnbaum. Magazine: 7½ × 10½; approximately 70 pages; acid-free paper; visual art; photos. "Interested in fiction of distinctive literary quality." Semiannually. Estab. 1988.

Needs: Contemporary, ethnic, experimental, fantasy, historical, humor/satire, literary, mainstream, prose poem, translations. "We are far more interested in quality than in genre. Nothing sentimental as opposed to genuinely moving, nor self-conscious style at the expense of human truth." Buys 4-5 mss/issue. Publishes ms within 7 months-1 year of acceptance. Agented fiction 60%. Published work by Elizabeth Spencer, Lee K. Abbott, Lorrie Moore, Tim O'Connor and Naomi Nye. Length: 250 words minimum; 10,000 words maximum. Publishes short shorts "if the story is good enough." Also publishes literary essays (must be labeled nonfiction), poetry.

How to Contact: Send complete ms with cover letter. Include brief bio. No simultaneous submissions. SASE. Reads September through December; reports January through March. Sample copy for $5 (includes postage) and 9×12 SAE. Fiction guidelines for #10 SASE.

Payment/Terms: Pays $10/printed page on publication for first North American serial rights. Sends galleys to author upon request.

Advice: "There are more good writers publishing in magazines today than there have been in many decades. Unfortunately, there are even more bad ones. In T. Gertler's *Elbowing the Seducer*, an editor advises a young writer that he wants to hear her voice completely, to tell (he means 'show') him in a story the truest thing she knows. We concur. Rather than a trendy workshop story or a minimalism that actually stems from not having much to say, we would like to see stories that make us believe they mattered to the writer and, more importantly, will matter to a reader. Trim until only the essential is left, and don't give up belief in yourself. And it might help to attend a good writers' conference, e.g. Wesleyan or Bennington."

TAPROOT LITERARY REVIEW, (I, II), Taproot Writer's Workshop, Inc., Box 204, Ambridge PA 15003. (412)266-8476. E-mail: taproot10@aol.com. Editor: Tikvah Feinstein. Magazine: 5½×8½; 93 pages; #20 paper; card cover; attractively printed; saddle-stitched. "We select on quality, not topic. We have published excellent work other publications have rejected due to subject matter, style or other bias. Variety and quality are our appealing features." Annually. Estab. 1987. Circ. 500.

Needs: Literary. The majority of mss published are received through their annual contest. Receives 20 unsolicited mss/month. Accepts 6 fiction mss/issue. Recently published work by Jacquelyn Spangler, John Vanderslice, Paul E. Perry and Sally Levin. Publishes 10 new writers/year. Length: 2,000 words preferred; 250 words minimum; 3,000 words maximum (no longer than 10 pages, double-spaced maximum). Publishes short shorts. Length: 300 words preferred. Sometimes critiques or comments on rejected mss. Also publishes poetry. Sponsors annual contest. Entry fee: $10/story. Deadline: December 31. Send SASE for details.

How to Contact: Send for guidelines first. Send complete ms with a cover letter. Include estimated word count and bio. Reports in 6 months. Send SASE for return of ms or send a disposable copy of ms. No simultaneous submissions. Sample copy for $5, 6×12 SAE and 5 first-class stamps. Fiction guidelines for #10 SASE.

Payment/Terms: Awards $100 in prize money for first place fiction and poetry winners each issue; $25 for 2nd place; 1 contributor's copy. Acquires first rights.

Advice: "Our contest is a good way to start publishing. Send for a sample copy and read it through. Ask for a critique and follow suggestions. Don't be offended by any suggestions—just take them or leave them and keep writing."

♣**"TEAK" ROUNDUP, The International Quarterly, (I)**, West Coast Paradise Publishing, #5-9060 Tronson Rd., Vernon, British Columbia V1T 6L7 Canada. (250)545-4186. Fax: (250)545-4194. Editors: Yvonne and Robert Anstey. Magazine: 5½×8½; 60 pages; 20 lb. copy paper; card stock cover; illustrations and photos. " '*Teak' Roundup* is a general interest showcase for prose and poetry. No uncouth material." Quarterly. Estab. 1994. Circ. 100.

Needs: Adventure, children's/juvenile, condensed/excerpted novel, ethnic/multicultural, historical, humor/satire, literary, mainstream/contemporary, mystery/suspense (police procedural), regional, religious/inspirational, romance (contemporary, historical), sports, westerns, young adult/teen (adventure). "No uncouth or porn." List of upcoming themes available for SASE. Receives 25 unsolicited mss/month. Accepts 20 mss/issue. Publishes ms 3-6 weeks after acceptance. Recently published work by Percy Harrison and Siegfried Zick. Publishes 6 new writers/year. Length: 1,000 words maximum. Also publishes literary essays, literary criticism and poetry. Often critiques or comments on rejected ms.

How to Contact: *Accepts work from subscribers only.* Subscription for $17 (Canadian); $13 (US). Query first or send complete ms with a cover letter. Include estimated word count and brief bio. Reports in 1 week. Send SASE for reply, return of ms or send a disposable copy of ms. Simultaneous, reprint and electronic submissions OK. Sample copy for $5 (Canadian); $3 (US). Fiction guidelines for #10 SASE. Reviews novels and short story collections.

Payment/Terms: Acquires one-time rights (unreserved reprint if "Best of" edition done later.)

Advice: "Subscribe and see popular work which is enjoyed by our growing audience. Many good writers favor us with participation in subscribers-only showcase for prose and poetry. No criticism of generous contributors."

*TEARS IN THE FENCE, (II), 38 Hod View, Stourpaine, Nr. Blandford Forum, Dorset DT11 8TN England. Editor: David Caddy. Biannual.

Needs: A magazine of poetry, fiction, criticism and reviews, open to a variety of contemporary voices from around the world. Publishes short and long fiction. Publishes 1-2 stories/issue.

Payment/Terms: Pays £7.50 per story plus complimentary copy of the magazine. Sample copy for $5 (US).

TENNESSEE REVIEW, (II), Belmont University, Department of Literature and Language, 1900 Belmont Blvd., Nashville TN 37212-3757. (615)460-6412. Fax: (615)460-5720. E-mail: painej@belmont.edu. Editors: Anthony Lombardy and J.H.E. Paine. Magazine: 6×9; 60-90 pages; quality paper; light matte cover stock. "We publish the best fiction, poetry and criticism we receive for a very sophisticated literary readership." Triannually. Estab. 1994.
Needs: Literary. "No genre fiction." Accepts 3-4 mss/issue; 7-9 mss/year. Does not read mss June 15-August 30. Publishes ms 6 months after acceptance. Published work by David Weisberg, Gary Fincke, Sherri Sizeman and Adrienne Sharp. Length: 5,000-10,000 words. Publishes short shorts. Also publishes literary essays, literary criticism and poetry. Sometimes critiques or comments on rejected mss.
How to Contact: Send complete ms with a cover letter. Include a brief letter of introduction. Reports in 2 months on mss. Send SASE for reply, return of ms or send a disposable copy of ms. Sample copy for $5.
Payment/Terms: Pays 2 contributor's copies on publication. Acquires first North American serial rights.
Advice: Looks for "the quality of the prose, vivid characters and coherent narrative. Read back copies."

THE TEXAS REVIEW, (II), Sam Houston State University Press, Huntsville TX 77341. (409)294-1992. Editor: Paul Ruffin. Magazine: 6×9; 148-190 pages; best quality paper; 70 lb. cover stock; illustrations; photos. "We publish top quality poetry, fiction, articles, interviews and reviews for a general audience." Semiannually. Estab. 1976. Circ. 700.
Needs: Literary and contemporary fiction. "We are eager enough to consider fiction of quality, no matter what its theme or subject matter. No juvenile fiction." Accepts 4 mss/issue. Receives approximately 40-60 unsolicited fiction mss each month. Does not read June-August. Published work by George Garrett, Ellen Gilchrist and Fred Chappell; published new writers within the last year. Length: 500-10,000 words. Critiques rejected mss "when there is time." Recommends other markets.
How to Contact: Send complete ms with cover letter. SASE. Reports in 3 months on mss. Sample copy for $5.
Payment/Terms: Pays contributor's copies plus one year subscription. Acquires all rights. Sends galleys to author.

✤**TEXTSHOP, A Collaborative Journal of Writing, (I, II)**, Dept. of English, University of Regina, Regina, Sasketchewan S4S 0A2 Canada. (306)585-4316. Editors: Andrew Stubbs, Judy Chapman and Richelle Leonard. Magazine: 8½×11; 50 pages; illustrations. *Textshop* is "eclectic in form and open to fiction, poetry and mixed genres, including creative nonfiction." Annually. Estab. 1993.
Needs: Ethnic/multicultural, experimental, literary. Plans special fiction issues or anthologies. Receives 20-25 unsolicited mss/month. Accepts 15-20 mss/issue. Publishes ms in next issue after acceptance. Length: 500 words minimum; 1,000 words maximum. Also publishes literary essays, literary criticism and poetry. Sometimes critiques or comments on rejected ms.
How to Contact: Send complete ms with a cover letter. Include estimated word count and 25-word bio with submission. Reports in 1 month on queries; 3 months on mss. SASE. Sample copy for $2. Reviews material published in each issue.
Payment/Terms: Pays 1 contributor's copy; additional copies for $2. Rights remain with the writer.
Advice: Looks for "risk-taking, mixed genre, experimental fiction. Trust your own voice and idiom. Blur the distinction between life and writing."

THEMA, (II), Box 74109, Metairie LA 70033-4109. Editor: Virginia Howard. Magazine: 5½×8½; 200 pages; Grandee Strathmore cover stock; b&w illustrations. "Different specified theme for each issue—short stories, poems, b&w artwork must relate to that theme." Triannually. Estab. 1988.
  • *Thema* received a Certificate for Excellence in the Arts from the Arts Council of New Orleans.
Needs: Adventure, contemporary, experimental, humor/satire, literary, mainstream, mystery/suspense, prose poem, psychic/supernatural/occult, regional, science fiction, sports, western. "Each issue is based on a specified premise—a different unique theme for each issue. Many types of fiction acceptable, but must fit the premise. No pornographic, scatologic, erotic fiction." Upcoming themes: "Don't call me Thelma!" (March 1, '98); "Magnolias in my briefcase" (July 1, '98); "A postcard not received" (November 1, '98). Publishes ms within 3-4 months of acceptance. Recently published work by Richard Goldstein, James Penha, Jane N. Hyatt, James M. Huggins and Merilyn Wakefield. Publishes 10-15 new writers/year. Length: fewer than 6,000 words preferred. Also publishes poetry. Sometimes critiques rejected mss and recommends other markets.
How to Contact: Send complete ms with cover letter, include "name and address, brief introduction, specifying

---

MARKET CONDITIONS are constantly changing! If you're still using this book and it is 1999 or later, buy the newest edition of *Novel & Short Story Writer's Market* at your favorite bookstore or order from Writer's Digest Books.

the intended target issue for the mss." Simultaneous submissions OK. Reports on queries in 1 week; on mss in 5 months after deadline for specified issue. SASE. Sample copy for $8. Free fiction guidelines.

Payment/Terms: Pays $25; $10 for short shorts on acceptance for one-time rights.

Advice: "Do not submit a manuscript unless you have written it for a specified premise. If you don't know the upcoming themes, send for guidelines first, before sending a story. We need more stories told in the Mark Twain/O. Henry tradition in magazine fiction."

THIN AIR, (II), The Right Kind of Trouble, Graduate Creative Writing Association of Northern Arizona University, P.O. Box 23549, Flagstaff AZ 86002. Contact: Fiction Editor. Editors change each year. Magazine: 8½×11; 50-60 pages; illustrations; photos. Publishes "contemporary voices for a literary-minded audience." Semiannually. Estab. 1995. Circ. 500.

Needs: Condensed/excerpted novel, ethnic/multicultural, experimental, literary, mainstream/contemporary. "No children's/juvenile." Editorial calendar available for SASE. Receives 75 unsolicited mss/month. Accepts 5-8 mss/issue; 10-15 mss/year. Does not read mss May-September. Publishes ms 6-9 months after acceptance. Solicited fiction 35%. Recently published work by Stephen Dixon, Henry H. Roth, Brian Evenson, Charles Bowden, Sean Caughlin, Patricia Lawrence and Craig Rullman. Publishes 3-8 new writers/year. Length: 6,000 words maximum. Publishes short shorts. Also publishes literary essays, literary criticism, creative nonfiction, poetry and interviews. Recent interviews include Thom Jones, Alan Lightman and Rick Bass

How to Contact: Send complete ms with a cover letter. Include estimated word count and list of publications. Reports in 1 month on queries; 3 months on mss. Send SASE for reply, return of ms or send a disposable copy of ms. Simultaneous submissions OK. Sample copy for $4.95. Fiction guidelines free. Reviews novels and short story collections.

Payment/Terms: Pays 2 contributor's copies; additional copies for $4. Pays on publication. Acquires first North American serial rights. Sends galleys to author. Sponsors contest; send SASE for guidelines.

Advice: Looks for "writers who know how to create tension and successfully resolve it. This is 'the right kind of trouble.' "

*THE THIRD ALTERNATIVE, 5 Martins Lane, Witcham, Ely, Cambs CB6 2LB England. Phone: 01353 777931. Fiction Editor: Andy Cox. Quarterly. Publishes 8 stories/issue. A4, 60 pages, lithographed, color glossy.

Needs: "Modern fiction: no mainstream or genre clichés. Innovative, quality science fiction/fantasy/horror and slipstream material (cross-genre)." Length: No minimum; no maximum (no serials).

How to Contact: Only send one story at a time, mailed flat or folded no more than once. USA stamps are not acceptable as return postage (UK stamps or 2 IRCs only). "A covering letter is appreciated." Standard ms format and SAE (overseas: disposable ms and 2 IRCs). No simultaneous submissions. Reprints only in exceptional circumstances.

Payment/Terms: Payment is £20 per 1,000 words. Guidelines, ad rates, etc. all available for 2 IRCs. $6 sample copy, $22 four-issue subscription. US checks acceptable, payable to TTA Press.

THIRD COAST, (II), Dept. of English, Western Michigan University, Kalamazoo MI 49008-5092. (616)387-2675. Managing Editor: Kathleen McGookey. Fiction Editors: Matt Mullins and Carla Vissers. Magazine: 6×9; 150 pages; illustrations and photos. "We will consider many different types of fiction and favor that exhibiting a freshness of vision and approach." Semiannually. Estab. 1995. Circ. 500.

• *Third Coast* has received *Pushcart Prize* nominations. The editors of this publication change with the university year.

Needs: Literary. "While we don't want to see formulaic genre fiction, we will consider material that plays with or challenges generic forms." Receives approximately 100 unsolicited mss/month. Accepts 6-8 mss/issue; 15 mss/year. Does not read mss May to September. Publishes ms 3-6 months after acceptance. Recently published work by Peter Ho Davies, Sarah J. Smith, Wang Ping and Chris Currie. Length: no preference. Publishes short shorts. Also publishes literary essays and poetry. Sometimes critiques or comments on rejected mss.

How to Contact: Send complete ms with a cover letter. Include list of publications. Reports in 1 month on queries; 2 months on mss. Send SASE for reply, return of ms or send a disposable copy of ms. Simultaneous submissions OK. Sample copy for $6. Fiction guidelines for #10 SASE.

Payment/Terms: Pays 2 contributor's copies as well as subscription to the publication and payment, dependent upon available funding; additional copies for $4. Acquires one-time rights. Not copyrighted.

Advice: "Of course, the writing itself must be of the highest quality. We love to see work that explores non-western contexts, as well as fiction from all walks of American (and other) experience."

*THE THIRD HALF MAGAZINE, "Amikeco," 16, Fane Close, Stamford, Lincolnshire PE9 1HG England. Fiction Editor: Kevin Troop. Published irregularly (when possible).

Needs: "*The Third Half* literary magazine publishes mostly poetry, but editorial policy is to publish as much *short* short story writing as possible in each issue. Each issue will now have over 100 pages. Short stories especially for children, for use in the classroom, with 'questions' and 'work to do' are occasionally produced, along with poetry books, as separate editions. I wish to expand on this." Length: 2,500 words maximum.

Payment/Terms: Pays in contributor's copies. Sample copy £4.95; £5.50 by post in England; £7 overseas.

13TH MOON, A Feminist Magazine, (IV), Dept. of English, University at Albany, Albany NY 12222. (518)442-4181. Editor: Judith Johnson. Magazine: 6×9; 250 pages; 50 lb. paper; heavy cover stock; photographs. "Feminist literary magazine for feminist women and men." Annually. Estab. 1973. Circ. 2,000.
Needs: Excerpted novel, experimental, feminist, lesbian, literary, prose poem, science fiction, translations. No fiction by men. Plans two volumes on feminist poetics (one volume on narrative forms and one on poetry). Submissions should be accompanied by a statement of the author's poetics (a paragraph to a page long). Accepts 1-3 mss/issue. Does not read mss May-September. Time varies between acceptance and publication. Published work by F.R. Lewis, Jan Ramjerdi and Wilma Kahn. Length: Open. Publishes short shorts. Also publishes poetry. Sometimes critiques rejected mss.
How to Contact: Send complete ms with cover letter and SASE (or IRC); "no queries." Reports in 8 months on mss. SASE. Accepts electronic submissions via disk (WordPerfect 5.1 only). Sample copy for $10.
Payment/Terms: Pays 2 contributor's copies.
Terms: Acquires first North American serial rights.
Advice: Looks for "*unusual* fiction with feminist appeal."

‡32 PAGES, (I, II), Rain Crow Publishing, 2127 W. Pierce Ave. Apt. 2B, Chicago IL 60622-1824. (773)276-9005. E-mail: 32pp@rain-crow-publishing.com. Website: http://www.rain-crow-publishing.com/32pp/. Editor: Michael S. Manley. Magazine: 7×10; 32 pages; 40 lb. white paper; illustrations. "*32 Pages* publishes new and experienced writers in many styles and genres. I look for well-crafted poetry and fiction that entertains and strives toward art." Bimonthly. Estab. 1997. Circ. 1,000.
Needs: Adventure, erotica, ethnic/multicultural, experimental, fantasy, feminist, gay, historical (general), horror, humor/satire, lesbian, literary, mainstream/contemporary, mystery/suspense, regional, science fiction, translations. No pornography, propaganda, formula fiction. No children's/juvenile. Receives 25-50 unsolicited mss/month. Accepts 3-4 mss/issue; 18-24 mss/year. Publishes ms within 6 months after acceptance. Recently published work by Susan Neville, Stanley Jenkins, William Stuckey, Peter Johnson, Murray Shugars, John McDermott, Carolyn Alessio, Christine Butterworth, Rob Davidson and Maija Kroeger. Length: 4,000 words average; 250 words minimum; 8,000 words maximum. Publishes short shorts. Also publishes personal essays, poetry. Sometimes critiques or comments on rejected mss.
How to Contact: Send complete ms with a cover letter. May also e-mail submissions. Include estimated word count and bio. Reports in 3 months. Send SASE for reply, return of ms or send a disposable copy of ms. Simultaneous submissions, reprints and electronic submissions OK. Sample copy for $2.50. Fiction guidelines for #10 SASE (1 IRC).
Payment/Terms: Pays $5 per page on publication, free subscription to magazine and 2 contributor's copies; additional copies for $2. Acquires one-time rights and one-time electronic rights. Sends galleys to author. Sponsors "fiction chapbook contest annually. Watch for announcements in writer's publications and on our website."
Advice: "I look for attention to craft: voice, language, character and plot working together to maximum effect. Unique yet credible settings and situations that entertain will get the most attention. Write to the best of your abilities and submit your best work. Present yourself and your work professionally. Get used to rejections. Literary magazines must change if they are to survive in today's market. Contemporary fiction must do the same. *32 Pages* is an experiment in *different* literary magazine publishing—we're out to build a new kind of poetry and fiction periodical."

✦THIS MAGAZINE, (II), Red Maple Foundation, 401 Richmond St. W., Suite 396, Toronto, Ontario M5V 3A8 Canada. (416)979-8400. Editor: Andrea Curtis. Magazine: 8½×11; 48 pages; bond paper; non-coated cover; illustrations and photographs. "Alternative general interest magazine." Bimonthly. Estab. 1966. Circ. 7,000.
Needs: Ethnic, contemporary, experimental, feminist, gay, lesbian, literary, mainstream, prose poem, regional. No "commercial/pulp fiction." Published work by Margaret Atwood and Erika de Vasconcelos. Length: 1,500 words average; 2,500 words maximum.
How to Contact: "We no longer accept unsolicited poetry or fiction." Sample copy for $4.50 (plus GST). Fiction guidelines for #9 SASE with Canadian stamps or IRC.
Payment/Terms: Pays $150 (Canadian) fiction; $50/poem published for one-time rights.
Advice: "It's best if you're familiar with the magazine when submitting work; a large number of mss that come into the office are inappropriate. Style guides are available. Manuscripts and queries that are clean and personalized really make a difference. Let your work speak for itself—don't try to convince us."

THE THREEPENNY REVIEW, (II), P.O. Box 9131, Berkeley CA 94709. (510)849-4545. Editor: Wendy Lesser. Tabloid: 10×17; 40 pages; Electrobrite paper; white book cover; illustrations. "Serious fiction." Quarterly. Estab. 1980. Circ. 9,000.
• *The Threepenny Review* has received GE Writers Awards, CLMP Editor's Awards, NEA grants, Lila Wallace grants and inclusion of work in the *Pushcart Prize Anthology.*
Needs: Literary. "Nothing 'experimental' (ungrammatical)." Receives 300-400 mss/month. Accepts 3 mss/issue; 12 mss/year. Does *not* read mss June through August. Publishes 6-12 months after acceptance. Agented fiction 5%. Published Sigrid Nunez, Dagoberto Gilb, Gina Berriault and Leonard Michaels. Length: 5,000 words maximum. Publishes short shorts. Also publishes literary essays, literary criticism, poetry.
How to Contact: Send complete ms with a cover letter. Reports in 2-4 weeks on queries;1-2 months on mss.

Send SASE for reply, return of ms or send a disposable copy of the ms. No simultaneous submissions. Sample copy for $6. Fiction guidelines for #10 SASE. Reviews novels and short story collections.

Payment/Terms: Pays $200 on acceptance plus free subscription to the magazine; additional copies at half price. Acquires first North American serial rights. Sends galleys to author.

TIMBER CREEK REVIEW, (III), 612 Front St. East, Glendora NJ 08029-1133. (609)863-0610. E-mail: jmfreier@aol.com. Editor: J.M. Freiermuth. Newsletter: 5½×8½; 76-84 pages; copy paper; some illustrations and photographs. "Fiction, satire, poetry of all types and travel for a general audience —80% of readers read above the 6th grade level." Quarterly. Circ. 120.

Needs: Adventure, contemporary, ethnic, feminist, historical, humor/satire, mainstream, mystery/suspense (cozy, private eye), regional, western (adult, frontier, traditional). No religion, children's, gay, romance. Plans fifth "All Woman Author" issue (October 1998). Receives 50-60 unsolicited mss/month. Accepts 15-20 mss/issue; 60-70 mss/year. Publishes ms 4-12 months after acceptance. Recently published work by Paul T. Sweeney, Jo-Anne Watts, Roslyn Willett, Judith Marcus, Bill Garten, Mikhammad Abdel-Ishara, Mary Winters, Kathleen Spirack and Laurel Speer. Publishes 0-3 new writers/year. Length: 2,000-3,000 words average; 1,200 words minimum; 9,000 words maximum. Publishes short shorts. Length: "Long enough to develop a good bite." Sometimes critiques rejected mss and recommends other markets.

How to Contact: Send complete ms and/or DOS disk (uses MS Word) with cover letter including "name, address, SASE." Reports in 3-6 weeks on mss. SASE. Simultaneous submissions OK. Accepts electronic submissions. Sample copy for $4 postpaid. Reviews short story collections.

Payment/Terms: Pays subscription to magazine for first publication and contributor's copies for subsequent publications. Acquires one-time rights. Publication not copyrighted.

Advice: "If your story has a spark of life or a degree of humor that brings a smile to my face, you have a chance here. Most stories lack these two ingredients. Don't send something you wrote ten years ago. Spend more time reading and writing and less time marketing."

TOMORROW Speculative Fiction, (www.tomorrowsf.com) (I), Unifont Co., P.O. Box 6038, Evanston IL 60204. (708)864-3668. E-mail: abudrys@tomorrowsf.com. Editor and Publisher: Algis Budrys. Electronic magazine. "Any good science fiction, fantasy and horror, for an audience of fiction readers, plus science articles, poems and cartoons." Bimonthly. Estab. 1992.

● *Tomorrow* has twice been nominated for the Hugo and twice has appeared in the *Writer's Digest* Top 50 Markets. A collection of articles on writing, originally published in *Tomorrow*, is now available.

Needs: Fantasy, horror, science fiction—any kind. Receives 300 mss/month. Accepts 10-12 mss/issue; 60-82 mss/year. Publishes within 18 months of acceptance. Agented fiction 2%. Published works by Robert Reed, Michael Shea, Nina Kiriki Hoffman, Robert Frazier, Yves Meynard and Elisabeth Vonarburg. Length: 4,000 words average. Publishes short shorts.

How to Contact: On fiction, send complete ms. Include estimated word count and Social Security number. On nonfiction, query. No covering letters. "Creased manuscripts and/or single spaced manuscripts will not be read." Reports in 2 weeks. Send SASE for reply, return of ms if desired. No simultaneous submissions. Sample copy of print issue for $5 plus 9×12 SASE.

Payment/Terms: Pays $75 minimum; 7¢/word maximum. Buys First World electronic English language print rights.

Advice: "Read my book, *Writing to the Point*, $10.50 from Unifont Co."

TRAFIKA, (I, II), P.O. Box 250413, Columbia Station, New York NY 10025-1536. Contact: Editors. Magazine: 6×9; 224 pages. "An international periodical of current prose and poetry from new and emerging writers." Quarterly. Estab. 1993. Circ. 7,000.

Needs: Quality short stories, excerpted novels, translations. Receives 50 unsolicited mss/month. Accepts 10-15 mss/issue; 40-60 mss/year. Publishes ms 1-6 months after acceptance. Agented fiction less than 10%. Published work by Lars Jakobson, Do Phuoc Tien, Kristien Hemmerechts, Yves Simon and Mia Couto. Length: 10,000 words maximum. Also publishes literary essays and poetry. Sometimes critiques or comments on rejected mss.

How to Contact: Send ms. Include bio and list of publications. Reports in 2-3 weeks on queries; 2-3 months on mss. SASE for reply only. Simultaneous submissions must be identified. Sample copy for $10. Fiction guidelines for #10 SASE.

Payment/Terms: Pays $15 per printed page plus 2 contributor's copies. Acquires first world serial rights in English.

TRIQUARTERLY, (II), Northwestern University, 2020 Ridge Ave., Evanston IL 60208-4302. (847)491-7614. Editor: Susan Hahn. Magazine: 6×9¼; 240-272 pages; 60 lb. paper; heavy cover stock; illustration; photos. "A general literary quarterly especially devoted to fiction. We publish short stories, novellas or excerpts from novels, by American and foreign writers. Genre or style is not a primary consideration. We aim for the general but serious and sophisticated reader. Many of our readers are also writers." Triannual. Estab. 1964. Circ. 5,000.

● Stories from *Triquarterly* have been reprinted in *The Best American Short Stories*, *Pushcart Prizes* and *O'Henry Prize* Anthologies.

Needs: Literary, contemporary and translations. "No prejudices or preconceptions against anything *except* genre fiction (romance, science fiction, etc.)." Accepts 10 mss/issue, 30 mss/year. Receives approximately 500 unsolicited fiction mss each month. Does not read April 1 through September 30. Agented fiction 10%. Recently published work by Steve Fisher, Michael Collins, Hélène Cixous, Charles Baxter, Margot Livesey and Robert Girardi. Publishes 1-5 new writers/year. Length: no requirement. Publishes short shorts.

How to Contact: Send complete ms with SASE. No simultaneous submissions. Reports in 4 months on mss. Publishes ms an average of 6-12 months after acceptance. Sample copy for $5.

Payment/Terms: Pays 2 contributor's copies on publication for first North American serial rights. Cover price less 40% discount for extras. Sends galleys to author. Honoraria vary, depending on grant support.

TUCUMCARI LITERARY REVIEW, (I, II), 3108 W. Bellevue Ave., Los Angeles CA 90026. Editor: Troxey Kemper. Magazine: 5½ × 8½; about 40 pages; 20 lb. bond paper; 67 lb. cover stock; few illustrations; photocopied photographs. "Old-fashioned fiction that can be read and reread for pleasure; no weird, strange pipe dreams and no it-was-all-a-dream endings." Bimonthly. Estab. 1988. Circ. monthly.

Needs: Adventure, contemporary, ethnic, historical, humor/satire, literary, mainstream, mystery/suspense, regional (southwest USA), senior citizen/retirement, western (frontier stories). No science fiction, drugs/acid rock, pornography, horror, martial arts or children's stories. Accepts 6 or 8 mss/issue; 35-40 mss/year. Publishes ms 2-6 months after acceptance. Published work by Roger Coleman, Dawn I. Zapletal, Curtis Nelson and James M. Phelps. Publishes 10-20 new writers/year. Length: 400-1,200 words preferred. Also publishes rhyming poetry.

How to Contact: Send complete ms with or without cover letter. Reports in 2 weeks. SASE. Simultaneous and reprint submissions OK. Sample copy for $2. Fiction guidelines for #10 SASE.

Payment/Terms: Pays in contributor's copies. Acquires one-time rights. Publication not copyrighted.

Advice: "Computers/printers are 'nice' but sometimes handwritten work on 3-hole lined notebook paper is interesting, too. We do not claim to be authorities on anything. Writers should do/say what they feel is right. Some editor somewhere may like it just that way. Do not be discouraged easily. Lastly, we all can learn, study and improve."

TURNSTILE, (I), 175 Fifth Ave., Suite 2348, New York NY 10010-7848. (212)674-5151. Fax: (212)674-6132. E-mail: nelsontaylor@stmartins.com. Editors: Nelson Taylor and Carrie McGinnis. Magazine: 6 × 9; 128 pages; 55 lb. paper; 10 pt. cover; illustrations; photos. "Publishing work by new writers." Biannual. Estab. 1988. Circ. 1,000.

Needs: Contemporary, experimental, humor/satire, literary, regional. No genre fiction. Receives approximately 100 unsolicited fiction mss/month. Publishes approximately 5 short story mss/issue. Recently published work by Jane W. Ellis and Lauren Sarat. Publishes 5-7 new writers/year. Length: 2,000 words average; 4,000 words maximum. Also publishes poetry, nonfiction essays, and interviews with well-known writers. Sometimes comments on rejected mss.

How to Contact: Query first or send complete ms with cover letter. Reports on queries in 3-4 weeks; on mss in 10-14 weeks. SASE. Simultaneous submissions OK. Sample copy for $6.50 and 7 × 10 SAE; fiction guidelines for #10 SASE.

Payment/Terms: Pays in contributor's copies; charge for extras. Acquires one-time rights.

Advice: "More than ever we're looking for *well-crafted* stories. We look for exceptional characterization and plot. We're known for publishing a range of new voices, and favor stories that rely on traditional narrative techniques. Do continue to submit new stories even if previous ones were not accepted; however, do not submit more than two stories at one time. Recognizing that the commercial publishing industry takes increasingly few risks on new, unconventional writers, *Turnstile* dedicates itself to encouraging and publishing fresh voices."

‡*ULITARRA, (II), Ulitarra Literary Association Inc. P.O. Box 195, Armidale, New South Wales 2350 Australia. (02)67729135. Editors: Michael Sharkey (coordinating editor), Stephen Harris and Winifred Belmont. "We also have a panel which referees academic submissions." Magazine: 210mm × 150mm; 140 pages; 80 GSM paper; 240 GSM cover stock; illustrations and photos. "*Ulitarra* seeks original writing, predominantly by Australian writers (in Australia and abroad), but also publishes works by other writers. We particularly encourage Aboriginal writers and translations by Australian writers of works in other languages." Semiannually. Estab 1992, Circ. 600.

Needs: Adventure, erotica, ethnic/multicultural, excerpted novel, experimental, fantasy (science fantasy), feminist, gay, historical, humor/satire, lesbian, literary, mainstream/contemporary, science fiction (hard science), translations. Publishes special fiction issues or anthologies. Receives 30 unsolicited mss/month. Accepts 4-5 mss/issue; 8-10 mss/year. Publishes ms within 6 months after acceptance. Recently published work by Morris Lurie, Bronwyn Minifie and Antonio Casella. Length: 3,500 words average; 1,200 words minimum; 5,000 words maximum. Publishes short shorts. Length: 3,500 words. Also publishes literary essays, literary criticism, poetry. Always critiques or comments on rejected mss.

How to Contact: Send compete ms with a cover letter and SASE (or IRCs). Include estimated word count and 3-line bio. Reports in 1 week on queries; 3 weeks on mss. Send SASE (or IRCs) for reply, return of ms or send a disposable copy of ms. Electronic submissions (disk or modem) OK. Sample copy for $15. Fiction guidelines free. Reviews novels and short story collections.

Payment/Terms: Pays $90 and 1 contributor's copy; additional copies $10 for overseas contributors. Pays on publication. Acquires first rights. Sends galleys to author. Sponsors contests. Writers can participate by buying a copy of January issue (for poetry prize) or July issue (for short story prize). Details and entry forms are in issue.

Advice: "We publish what *we* like; talent is what we're after. We don't follow fashion: we set it."

‡THE UNDERGROUND, (II), P.O. Box 14311, Milwaukee WI 53214. Magazine: 7⅝ × 9⅞; 12 pages; illustrations and photographs. Triannually. Estab. 1996.

Needs: Ethnic/multicultural, experimental, feminist, humor/satire, literary. Receives 20 unsolicited mss/month. Accepts 3 mss/issue; 9 mss/year. Publishes ms 3-4 months after acceptance. Recently published work by Richard Kostelanetz, P.J. Jason and Joe Malone. Publishes short shorts. Also publishes literary essays, poetry.

How to Contact: Send complete ms with a cover letter. Reports in 2 weeks on queries; 4-6 weeks on mss. Send SASE for reply, return of ms or send a disposable copy of ms. Simultaneous submissions OK. Sample copy for $2. Fiction guidelines free.

Payment/Terms: Pays 2 contributor's copies on publication; additional copies for $2. Acquires first North American serial rights. Sends galleys to author.

Advice: "We want writers who take risks, challenge assumptions and subvert authority, including their own. New or unestablished writers are welcome."

UNMUZZLED OX, (III), Unmuzzled Ox Foundation Ltd., 105 Hudson St., New York NY 10013. (212)226-7170. E-mail: mandreox@aol.com. Editor: Michael Andre. Magazine: 5½ × 8½. "Magazine about life for an intelligent audience." Published irregularly. Estab. 1971. Circ. 7,000.

● Recent issues of this magazine have included poetry, essays and art only. You may want to check before sending submissions or expect a long response time.

Needs: Contemporary, literary, prose poem and translations. No commercial material. Receives 20-25 unsolicited mss/month. Also publishes poetry. Occasionally critiques rejected mss.

How to Contact: Not reading unsolicited mss until April 1998. "Please no phone calls. Correspondence by mail *only*. Cover letter is significant." Reports in 1 month. SASE. Sample copy for $10.

Payment/Terms: Contributor's copies.

THE URBANITE, Surreal & Lively & Bizarre, (II, IV), Urban Legend Press, P.O. Box 4737, Davenport IA 52808. Website: http://www.rictus.com/urbanite/index.htm (includes information on current and upcoming issues). Editor: Mark McLaughlin. Magazine: 8½ × 11; 80 pages; bond paper; coated cover; saddle-stitched; illustrations. "We look for quality fiction in an urban setting with a surrealistic tone." Each issue includes a featured writer, a featured poet and a featured artist. Published three times a year. Estab. 1991. Circ. 500-1,000.

● *The Urbanite* ranked as No. 22 on the *Writer's Digest* Fiction 50 list, 1996.

Needs: Experimental, fantasy (dark fantasy), horror, humor/satire, literary, psychic/supernatural/occult, science fiction (soft/sociological). "We love horror, but please, no tired, gore-ridden horror plots. Horror submissions must be subtle and sly." Upcoming themes: "Strange Love," "Strange Nourishment" and "The Zodiac." List of upcoming themes available for SASE. Receives over 800 unsolicited mss/month. Accepts 15 mss/issue; 45 mss/year. Publishes ms 6 months after acceptance. Recently published work by Basil Copper, Hugh B. Cave, Lisa Jean Bothell, Hertzan Chimera, Pamela Briggs and Thomas Ligotti. Publishes at least 2-3 new writers/year. Length: 2,000 words preferred; 500 words minimum; 3,000 words maximum. Publishes short shorts. Length: 350 words preferred. Also publishes poetry. Sometimes critiques or comments on rejected mss.

How to Contact: Include estimated word count, 4- to 5-sentence bio, Social Security number and list of publications. Reports in 1 month on queries; 3-4 months on mss. Send SASE for reply, return of ms or send a disposable copy of ms. Sample copy for $5. Fiction guidelines for #10 SASE.

Payment/Terms: Pays 2-3¢/word and 2 contributor's copies for first North American serial rights and nonexclusive rights for public readings.

Advice: "The tone of our magazine is unique, and we strongly encourage writers to read an issue to ascertain the sort of material we accept. The number one reason we reject many stories is because they are inappropriate for our publication: in these cases, it is obvious that the writer is not familiar with *The Urbanite*. We are known for publishing quality horror—work from *The Urbanite* has been reprinted in *Year's Best Fantasy & Horror* and England's *Best New Horror*. People keep sending amateurish gore-horror, and they are wasting their time and postage. 'Splatter' fiction is on the way out in publishing. We want to see more slipstream fiction and more bizarre (yet urbane and thought-provoking) humor."

URBANUS MAGAZINE, (III), P.O. Box 192921, San Francisco CA 94119-2921. Editor: Peter Drizhal. 5½ × 8½; 96 pages; 60 lb. offset paper; 10 pt. coated cover; perfect bound. "*Urbanus* is a magazine of language,

---

CHECK THE CATEGORY INDEXES, located at the back of the book, for publishers interested in specific fiction subjects.

literature, contemporary visualism, and its offspring arts: the urban pulse in quick-frame prose, as one offshoot; modern and lyric verse, rap, and jazz refrain, as another." Published approximately triquarterly. Estab. 1987. Circ. 2,000.

Needs: "Urban contemporary, multicultural, meta-fiction, alternative lifestyles, humor/satire, also horror, soft science fiction, and maybe a dash of detection and mystery. No romance tales or 'historically-specific' themes such as War or Westerns—simply not our angle." Receives 5,000 mss/year from which 10 stories are selected. Published work by Susan Moon, James Sallis, Sarah Schulman, Thaisa Frank, Robert F. Gish. Length: 6,000 words maximum. (Excerpts up to 7,000 words will be considered, but *only* when slated with a publisher.)

How to Contact: Deadlines vary (mss are generally not considered November-February) so please query for specific reading windows. Send complete ms with a brief cover. Reports in 1-2 months on queries; 1-3 months on mss. Send SASE for reply, return of ms or send a disposable copy of the ms. No multiple, simultaneous or previously published submissions. Sample copy for $6.95 (or $15.95 for a 3 issue subscription). Extended writer's guidelines available for #10 SASE.

Payment/Terms: Pays 1½-2½¢/word ($15 min.-$125 max.) and 5 contributor's copies for first North American serial rights.

Advice: "We want the atypical eye, dark undercurrents; the socially slanted vision without didactic politicizing; also the normal eye immersed in the pseudo-normal (pseudo-mainstream). One source described us as 'contemporary macabre,' which shouldn't be weighed as a genre tag."

USI WORKSHEETS, (II), % Postings, Box 1, Ringoes NJ 08551. (908)782-6492. Editor: Rotating board. Magazine: 11½×17; 20-25 pages. Publishes poetry and fiction. Annually. Estab. 1973.

Needs: "No restrictions on subject matter or style. Good storytelling or character delineation appreciated. Audience does not include children." Recently published work by Alicia Ostriker, Joan Baranow, Lois Marie Harrod, Frederich Tibbetts and Rod Tulloss. Publishes short shorts.

How to Contact: Query first "or send a SAE postcard for reading dates. We read only once a year." Reports on queries "as soon as possible." SASE. Sample copy for $4.

Payment/Terms: Pays in contributor's copies. Acquires one-time rights. Copyright "reverts to author."

‡VERSE UNTO US, (I), VUS Press, 907 Oak Lane Dr., Joshua TX 76058. (817)558-7837. Editor: Alan Steele. Magazine: 8½×11; 30-35 pages; white bond paper; illustrations. "VUS publishes both short fiction and poetry, dedicated to the tradition of style and subject set by Poe, Plath, Hawthorne—the great American Cannon. The light hearted side of man (happy endings and good fortune) do not apply." Quarterly. Estab. 1996. Circ. 100.

Needs: Experimental, horror, humor/satire, literary, mainstream/contemporary, psychic/supernatural/occult. No science fiction or inspirational. Receives 10-25 unsolicited mss/month. Accepts 1-3 mss/issue; 12-17 mss/year. Publishes ms 2-4 months after acceptance. Length: 2,200-2,500 words average; 500 words minimum; 3,750 words maximum. Also publishes poetry. Sometimes critiques or comments on rejected mss.

How to Contact: Send complete ms with a cover letter. Reports in 6 weeks on queries; 2 months on mss. Send SASE for reply, return of ms or send a disposable copy of ms. Simultaneous submissions OK. Sample copy for $5.25. Fiction guidelines for #10 SASE.

Payment/Terms: Pays $5 on publication and 1 contributor's copy; additional copies for $4. Acquires first North American serial rights.

Advice: "We look for the original idea that captivates us, something we identify with. Spelling errors and poor proofreading skills can be a definite turnoff, even when the thought has merit. In most cases, read an issue first to see the type of work we are interested in. For short fiction, obscurity is an interesting thought, but not to a point where the reader is completely lost. For a first time, we do not like to see a bio. In many cases, we look to what the industry is doing, and then go for the opposite. We like the darker, bleak side of literature, and shock value."

VERVE, (I, II), P.O. Box 3205, Simi Valley CA 93093. Editor: Ron Reichick. Fiction Editor: Marilyn Hochheiser. Magazine: Digest-sized, 40 pages, 70 lb. paper, 80 lb. cover, cover illustrations or photographs. "Each issue has a theme." Quarterly. Estab. 1989. Circ. 700.

Needs: Contemporary, experimental, fantasy, humor/satire, literary, mainstream, prose poem. No pornographic material. Receives 100 unsolicited fiction mss/month. Accepts 4-6 mss/issue; 8-12 mss/year. Publishes ms 2 months after deadline (March 1 and August 1). Length: 1,000 words maximum. Publishes short shorts. Also publishes literary criticism, poetry.

How to Contact: "Request guidelines before submitting manuscript." Reports 4-6 weeks after deadline. SASE. Simultaneous submissions OK. Sample copy for $3.50. Fiction guidelines for #10 SASE. Reviews short story collections.

Payment/Terms: Pays in contributor's copies. Acquires one-time rights.

***VIGIL, (II)**, Vigil Publications, 12 Priory Mead, Bruton, Somerset BA10 ODZ England. Editor: John Howard Greaves. Estab. 1979. Circ. 250. "Simply the enjoyment of varied forms of poetry and literature with an informed view of poetic technique."

Needs: Needs: experimental, literary, regional. Plans special fiction issue. Length: 500-1,500 words.

Payment/Terms: Pays in contributor's copies. Contributor guidelines available for IRC.

Advice: "Most of the stories we receive are work in progress rather than finished pieces. Well structured, vibrantly expressed work is a delight when it arrives. Freshness and originality must always find an audience."

THE VINCENT BROTHERS REVIEW, (II), The Vincent Brothers Company, 4566 Northern Circle, Riverside OH 45424-5733. Editor: Kimberly Willardson. Magazine: 5½×8¼; 88-100 perfect-bound pages; 60 lb. white coated paper; 60 lb. Oxford (matte) cover; b&w illustrations and photographs. "We publish at least two theme issues per year. Writers must send SASE for information about upcoming theme issues. Each issue of *TVBR* contains poetry, b&w art, at least six short stories and usually one nonfiction piece. For a mainstream audience looking for an alternative to the slicks." Triannually. Estab. 1988. Circ. 400.

- *TVBR* was ranked #20 in the "1996 *Writer's Digest* Fiction 50," and, subsequently, was the subject of a front-page feature story in the Sunday, July 7th, 1996, issue of *The Dayton Daily News*. It has received grants from the Ohio Arts Council for the last six years. Also received grant from the Montgomery County Regional Arts and Cultural District of Ohio for 1998. Won Special Merit Award in 1996 American Literary Magazine Awards sponsored by *Poet* Magazine and Cooper House Publishing. The magazine sponsors a fall fiction contest; deadline in October. Contact them for details.

Needs: Adventure, condensed/excerpted novel, contemporary, ethnic, experimental, feminist, historical, humor/satire, literary, mainstream, mystery/suspense (amateur sleuth, cozy, private eye), prose poem, regional, science fiction (soft/sociological), senior citizen/retirement, serialized novel, translations, western (adult, frontier, traditional). Upcoming themes: "Dreams and Nightmares" (January 1998); "The Muse" (April 1998); "Dogs" (October 1998). "We focus on the way the story is presented rather than the genre of the story. No racist, sexist, fascist, etc. work." Receives 200-250 unsolicited mss/month. Buys 6-10 mss/issue; 18-30 mss/year. Publishes ms 2-4 months after acceptance. Recently published work by Gordon C. Wilson, Tom D. Ellison, Nikolaus Maack, Laurel Jenkins-Crowe and Ariel Smart. Publishes 8-12 new writers/year. Length: 2,500 words average; 250 words minimum; 7,000 words maximum. Publishes short shorts. Length: 250-1,000 words. Also publishes literary essays, literary criticism, poetry. Often critiques rejected mss and sometimes recommends other markets.

How to Contact: "Send query letter *before* sending novel excerpts or condensations! *Send only one short story at a time*—unless sending short shorts." Send complete ms. Simultaneous submissions OK, but not preferred. Reports in 3-4 weeks on queries; 2-3 months on mss with SASE. Sample copy for $6.50; back issues for $4.50. Fiction guidelines for #10 SASE. Reviews novels and short story collections.

Payment/Terms: Pays $10 minimum and 2 contributor's copies for one-time rights. $200 first place; $100 second; $50 third for annual short story contest. Charge (discounted) for extras.

Advice: "The best way to discover what *TVBR* editors are seeking in fiction is to read at least a couple issues of the magazine. We are typical readers—we want to be grabbed by the first words of a story and rendered unable to put it down until we've read the last word of it. We want stories that we'll want to read again. This doesn't necessarily mean we seek stories that grab the reader via shock tactics; gross-out factors; surface titillation; or emotional manipulation. Good writers know the difference. Research the markets. Read good writing. Dig deep to find original and compelling narrative voices. It's amazing how many dozens and dozens of stories we receive sound/read so very much alike. We've noticed a marked increase in violent and/or socially ill/deviant-themed stories. Hmm. Is this art imitating life or life imitating art or is it just writers desperate to shock the reader into believing this now passes for originality? Incest stories have been done and done well, but that doesn't mean everyone should write one. Same goes for divorce, death-watch, I-killed-my-boss (spouse, etc.) and got-away-with-it stories."

VOX, Pace University Literary Magazine, (I), Pace University, Willcox Hall, Room 43, 4th Floor, Bedford Rd., Pleasantville NY 10553. (914)773-3962. Editor: Edmond D. Reidy. Magazine: 5½×8½; perfect-bound; 80-120 pages; illustrations and photos. "*Vox* is made for and by college students and publishes works that, we hope, will appeal to this readership. Funny, sad, everything in between, we want it if it can keep the attention of a collegian with a full course-load. This doesn't mean just the usual beer, sex and drug stories—there's a lot more to life, and that's what *Vox* is interested in giving to our readers. Just make it real, honest, avoid cliches and stereotypes and it'll be considered." Annually (spring). Estab. 1977. Circ. 500-1,000.

- *Vox* received the Columbia Scholastic Press Association Silver Crown Award, 1994, 1995 and 1996.

Needs: College-age interests, condensed/excerpted novel, ethnic/multicultural, feminist, humor/satire, literary, mainstream/contemporary, mystery/suspense (police procedural, private eye/hardboiled, romantic suspense), romance (contemporary), No erotica, horror, senior citizen, juvenile. Does not read mss June, July, August. Recently published work by students from Pace. Length: 1,600 words average; 750 words minimum; 4,000 words maximum. Also publishes literary essays and poetry.

How to Contact: Send complete ms with a cover letter. Include estimated word count and brief bio. Reports in 4-6 weeks. Send SASE for reply; send a disposable copy of ms. Sample copy for $6, 5½×8½ SAE and 4 first-class stamps.

Payment/Terms: Pays 2 contributor's copies; additional copies for $3 and 4 first-class stamps for each copy. Acquires one-time rights. Not copyrighted.

Advice: "Send a neat, proofread manuscript; at least spell check it and let a friend or two read it over. Send an original manuscript—things that sound 'familiar' are the quickest to be forgotten."

✿WASCANA REVIEW OF CONTEMPORARY POETRY AND SHORT FICTION, (II), University of Regina, Regina, Saskatchewan S4S 0A2 Canada. (306)585-4299. Editor: Kathleen Wall. Fiction Editor: Dr. Jeanne Shaimi. "Literary criticism, fiction and poetry for readers of serious fiction." Semiannually. Estab. 1966. Circ. 500.

Needs: Literary and humor. Upcoming themes: "Landscape & Literature". Buys 8-10 mss/year. Receives approximately 20 unsolicited fiction mss/month. Agented fiction 5%. Publishes 1-2 new writers/year. Length: no requirement. Occasionally recommends other markets.

How to Contact: Send complete ms with SASE. All contributors must include 3.5 floppy disk compatible with one of the following programs: ASCII; WordStar 3.0, 4.0 or 5.0; MS Word; MordPerfect 4.0, 5.0, 5.1, 6.1; SY Write; 8-bit ASCII; Writer; Multimate; DCL. Reports in 2 months on mss. Publishes ms an average of 6 months after acceptance. Sample copy for $5. Guidelines with SASE.

Payment/Terms: Pays $3/page for prose; $10/page for poetry; 2 contributor's copies on publication for first North American rights.

Advice: "Stories are often technically incompetent or deal with trite subjects. Usually stories are longer than necessary by about one-third. Be more ruthless in cutting back on unnecessary verbiage. All approaches to fiction are welcomed by the *Review* editors—but we continue to seek the best in terms of style and technical expertise. As our calls for submission state, the *Wascana Review* continues to seek . . . short fiction that combines craft with risk, pressure with grace."

‡WASHINGTON SQUARE, Literary Review of New York University's Creative Writing Program, (II), (formerly Ark/Angel Review), NYU Creative Writing Program, 19 University Place, 2nd Floor, New York NY 10003-4556. (212)998-8816. Fax: (212)995-4019. Editor: Jeffrey R.W. Kaplan. Fiction Editor: Kristen Martin. Editors change each year. Magazine: 5½×8½; 144 pages; photographs. "*Washington Square* is the literary review produced by New York University's Graduate Creative Writing Program. We publish outstanding works of fiction and poetry by the students and faculty of NYU as well as the work of writers across the country." Semiannually. Estab. 1996 (we were previously called Ark/Angel Review, estab. 1987). Circ. 1,000.

Needs: Condensed/excerpted novel, ethnic/multicultural, experimental, literary, mainstream/contemporary. No adventure, children's, erotica. Receives 50 unsolicited mss/month. Accepts 10 mss/issue; 20 mss/year. Publishes ms 3-5 months after acceptance. Agented fiction 20%. Recently published work by Dika Lam, Sarah Inman, Jessica Anya Blau, Irene Korenfield. Length: 5,000 words average; 7,000 words maximum. Publishes short shorts. Also publishes poetry. Sometimes critiques or comments on rejected mss.

How to Contact: Send complete ms with a cover letter. Include estimated word count (only put name on first page). Reports in 3 months on queries; 4 months on mss. Send SASE for reply, return of ms or send a disposable copy of ms. Simultaneous submissions OK. Sample copy for $6.

Payment/Terms: Pays 3 contributor's copies; additional copies for $6. Acquires first North American serial rights. "Each fall we sponsor a short story contest. Prize $150. Deadline: December 1."

Advice: "We look for compelling, original, outstanding fiction. Please send polished, proofread manuscripts only."

‡WEB DEL SOL, (III), E-mail: mneff@cais.com. Website: http://webdelsol.com. Editor: Michael Neff. Electronic magazine. "The goal of *Web Del Sol* is to use the medium of the Internet to bring the finest in contemporary literary arts to a larger audience. To that end, WDS not only webpublishes collections of work by accomplished writers and poets, but hosts other literary arts publications on the WWW such as *AGNI, Conjunctions, North American Review, Zyzzyva, Flashpoint, Global City Review, The Literary Review* and *The Prose Poem*.

Needs: "WDS publishes work considered to be literary in nature, i.e., non-genre fiction. WDS also publishes poetry, prose poetry, essays and experimental types of writing." Publishes short shorts. Recently published work by Robert Olen Butler, Carole Maso, Michael Martone, Kathleen Hill, Ben Marcus, Bradford Marrow and Diana Abu-Jaber. "Currently, WDS published Featured Writer/Poet websites, approximately 15 per year at this time; but hopes to increase that number substantially in the coming year. WDS also occasionally publishes individual works and plans to do more of these also."

How to Contact: "Submissions by e-mail from September through November and from January through March only. Submissions must contain some brief bio, list of prior publications (if any), and a short work or prortion of that work, neither to exceed 1,000 words. Editors will contact if the balance of work is required."

Advice: "WDS wants fiction that is absolutely cutting edge, unique and/or at a minimum, accomplished with a crisp style and concerning subjects not usually considered the objects of literary scrutiny. Read works in such publications as *Conjunctions* (http://www.conjunctions.com) and *Flashpoint* (http://webdelsol.com/FLASHPOINT) to get an idea what we are looking for."

WEBSTER REVIEW, (II), SLCC—Meramec, Meramec, % English Dept. 11333 Big Bend Rd., St. Louis MO 63122. (314)984-7542. Editors: Greg Marshall, Robert Boyd and Nancy Schapiro. Magazine: 5×8; 120 pages; 60 lb. white paper; 10pt. C1S; cover illustrations and photographs. "Literary magazine, international, contemporary. We publish many English translations of foreign fiction writers for academics, writers, discriminating readers." Annually. Estab. 1974.

Needs: Contemporary, literary, translations. No erotica, juvenile. Receives 100 unsolicited mss/month. Accepts 6-10 mss/year. Publishes ms 1 year or more after acceptance. Agented fiction less than 1%. Published work by

Marco Lodoli and Barbara Eldridge. Publishes short shorts. Sometimes critiques rejected mss.
How to Contact: Send complete manuscript with cover letter. Reports in 2-4 months on mss. SASE. Simultaneous submissions OK. Sample copy for 6×9 SAE and 2 first-class stamps.
Payment/Terms: Pays contributor's copies. Acquires first rights.

WEST BRANCH, (II), Bucknell Hall, Bucknell University, Lewisburg PA 17837. Editors: Karl Patten and Robert Love Taylor. Magazine: 5½×8½; 96-120 pages; quality paper; coated card cover; perfect-bound; illustrations; photos. Fiction and poetry for readers of contemporary literature. Biannually. Estab. 1977. Circ. 500.
Needs: Literary, contemporary, prose poems and translations. No science fiction. Accepts 3-6 mss/issue. Recently published work by Daniel J. Bingley, Cynthia Elliott, Deborah Hodge, Leslie Pietrzyk, Darby Sanders, Steve Moncada Street, Kathleen Wakefield and Jo-Anne A. Watts. Published new writers within the last year. No preferred length. However, "the fiction we publish usually runs between 12-25 double-spaced pages."
How to Contact: Send complete ms with cover letter, "with information about writer's background, previous publications, etc." SASE. No simultaneous submissions. Reports in 6-8 weeks on mss. Sample copy for $3.
Payment/Terms: Pays 2 contributor's copies and one-year subscription; cover price less 25% discount charge for extras. Acquires first rights.
Advice: "Narrative art fulfills a basic human need—our dreams attest to this—and storytelling is therefore a high calling in any age. Find your own voice and vision. Make a story that speaks to your own mysteries. Cultivate simplicity in form, complexity in theme. Look and listen through your characters."

♣WEST COAST LINE, A Journal of Contemporary Writing & Criticism, (II), 2027 E. Academic Annex, Simon Fraser University, Burnaby, British Columbia V5A 1S6 Canada. (604)291-4287. Fax: (604)291-5737. Managing Editor: Jacqueline Larson. Magazine: 6×9; 128-144 pages. "Poetry, fiction, criticism—modern and contemporary, North American, cross-cultural. Readers include academics, writers, students." Triannual. Estab. 1990. Circ. 600.
Needs: Experimental, ethnic/multicultural, feminist, gay, literary. "We do not publish journalistic writing or strictly representational narrative." Receives 30-40 unsolicited mss/month. Accepts 2-3 mss/issue; 3-6 mss/year. Publishes ms 2-6 months after acceptance. Length: 3,000-4,000 words. Publishes short shorts. Length: 250-400 words. Also publishes literary essays and literary criticism.
How to Contact: Send complete ms with a cover letter. "We supply an information form for contributors." Reports in 3 months. Send SAE with IRCs, not US postage, for return of ms. No simultaneous submissions. Electronic submissions OK. Sample copy for $10. Fiction guidelines free.
Payment/Terms: Pays $3-8/page (Canadian); subscription; 2 contributor copies; additional copies for $6-8/copy, depending on quantity ordered. Pays on publication for one-time rights.
Advice: "Special concern for contemporary writers who are experimenting with, or expanding the boundaries of conventional forms of poetry, fiction and criticism; also interested in criticism and scholarship on Canadian and American modernist writers who are important sources for current writing. We recommend that potential contributors send a letter of enquiry or read back issues before submitting a manuscript."

WEST WIND REVIEW, (I), 1250 Siskiyou Blvd., Ashland OR 97520. (503)552-6518. E-mail: westwind@tao. sou.edu. Editor: Ramana Lewis (1997-1998 school year). Editors change each year. Magazine: 5¾×8½; 150-250 pages; illustrations and photos. "Literary journal publishing prose/poetry/art. Encourages new writers, accepts established writers as well, with an audience of people who like to read anthologies." Annually. Estab. 1980. Circ. 500.
Needs: Adventure, erotica, ethnic/multicultural, experimental, fantasy, feminist, gay, historical (general), horror, humor/satire, lesbian, literary, mainstream/contemporary, mystery/suspense, psychic/supernatural/occult, regional, religious/inspirational, romance, science fiction, senior citizen/retirement, sports, translations, westerns, young adult/teen—"just about anything." Receives 6-60 unsolicited mss/month. Accepts 15-20 mss/issue. Does not read mss during summer months. Publishes ms almost immediately after acceptance. Recently published work by Sharon Doubiago, Tee A. Corinne, Norman Fischer and Sean Brendan-Brown. 50% of work published is by new writers. Length: 3,000 words maximum. Publishes short shorts. Also publishes literary essays and poetry. Sometimes critiques or comments on rejected ms.
How to Contact: Send complete ms with a cover letter. Include estimated word count and short bio. Reports in 2 weeks on queries; by March 1 on mss. Send SASE for reply, return of ms or send a disposable copy of ms. No simultaneous submissions. Fiction guidelines free. Rarely reviews novels or short story collections.
Payment/Terms: To enter prize contest include $1 with entry. First place winner in fiction wins $25. Accepted authors receive 1 free copy. Authors retain all rights.
Advice: "Good writing stands out. Content is important but style is essential. Clearly finished pieces whose content shows subtle action, reaction and transformation for the character(s) are what we like."

*WESTERLY, English Dept., University of Western Australia, Nedlands, 6907 Australia. 08 9380 2101. Fax: 08 9380 1030. E-mail: westerly@uniwa.uwa.edu.au. Website: http://www.arts.uwa.edu.au/Englishwww/westerly. html (includes details of current issue, past issues, forthcoming issues and information about subscribing and contributing). Caroline Horobin, Administrator. Quarterly. Circ. 1,000.
Neds: "A quarterly of poetry, prose, reviews and articles of a literary and cultural kind, giving special attention

to Australia and Southeast Asia." No romance, children's science fiction.

How to Contact: Queries by e-mail OK.

Payment/Terms: Pays $50 (AUS) minimum and 1 contributor's copy. Sample copy for $8 (AUS) plus postage.

WESTERN HUMANITIES REVIEW, (III), % English Department, University of Utah, Salt Lake City UT 84112. (801)581-6070. Fax: (801)581-3392. Editor: Barry Weller. Fiction Editor: Karen Brennan. Magazine: 95-120 pages. Quarterly. Estab. 1947. Circ. 1,200.

Needs: Experimental, literary. Receives 75 unsolicited mss/month. Accepts 4-8 mss/issue; 15-25 mss/year. Does not read mss July-September. Publishes ms within 1-4 issues after acceptance. Published work by Stephen Dixon, Mark Halliday, Gary Krist, Diane Lefer and Joyce Carol Oates. Length: open. Publishes short shorts. Also publishes literary essays, literary criticism and poetry. Sometimes critiques or comments on rejected mss.

How to Contact: Send complete ms with a cover letter. Include list of publications. Reports in 3 weeks on queries; 1-6 months on mss. Send SASE for reply, return of ms or send a disposable copy of ms. Simultaneous submissions OK. Sample copy for $6.

Payment/Terms: Pays 2 contributor's copies; additional copies for $3.50. Acquires first North American serial rights. Sends galleys to author.

WESTVIEW, A Journal of Western Oklahoma, (II), Southwestern Oklahoma State University, 100 Campus Dr., Weatherford OK 73096-3098. (405)774-3168. Editor: Fred Alsberg. Magazine: 8½ × 11; 44 pages; 24 lb. paper; slick color cover; illustrations and photographs. Semiannual. Estab. 1981. Circ. 400.

Needs: Contemporary, ethnic (especially Native American), humor, literary, prose poem. No pornography, violence, or gore. No overly sentimental. "We are particularly interested in writers of the Southwest; however, we accept work of quality from elsewhere." Receives 10 unsolicited mss/month. Accepts 5 mss/issue; 10 mss/year. Publishes ms 1 month-2 years after acceptance. Published work by Diane Glancy, Wendell Mayo, Jack Matthews, Mark Spencer and Pamela Rodgers. Length: 2,000 words average. Also publishes literary essays, literary criticism, poetry. Occasionally critiques rejected mss.

How to Contact: Simultaneous submissions OK. Send complete ms with SASE. Reports in 1-2 months. "We welcome submissions on a 3.5 disk formatted for WordPerfect 5.0, IBM or Macintosh. Please include a hard copy printout of your submission."

Payment/Terms: Pays contributor's copy for first rights.

WHETSTONE, (I, II), Barrington Area Arts Council, P.O. Box 1266, Barrington IL 60011. Co-Editors: Sandra Berris, Marsha Portnoy and Jean Tolle. Magazine: 9 × 6; 110 pages; heavy cover stock. "We try to publish the best quality nonfiction, fiction and poetry for the educated reader." Annually. Estab. 1984. Circ. 700. Member CLMP.

● *Whetstone* has received numerous Illinois Arts Council Awards.

Needs: Humor/satire, literary, mainstream/contemporary. "No genre, formula or plot driven fiction." Receives 30 unsolicited mss/month. Accepts 8-10 mss/year. Publishes ms by December 1 of year accepted. Recently published work by Dennis Vannatta, Leslie Pietzyk, James Klise and Scott Blackwood. Publishes 1-2 new writers/year. Length: 3,000 words average; 6,000 words maximum. Also publishes poetry. Sometimes comments on rejected mss "depending on the work. We often write out the readers' responses if they are helpful. A work gets a minimum of two readers and up to four or five."

How to Contact Send complete ms with a cover letter. Include a 50-word bio. Reports in 3-6 months on mss "or sooner depending on the time of the year." Send SASE for return of ms or reply only. Simultaneous submissions OK. Sample copy (including guidelines) for $5.

Payment/Terms: Pays a variable amount and 2 contributor's copies on publication. Acquires first North American serial rights. Sends galleys to author. "We frequently work with writers on their pieces. All submissions are considered for the $500 Whetstone Prize and the $250 McGrath Award."

Advice: "We like strong characterization and a vivid use of language and, of course, a coherent plot. We like texture and a story which resonates. Read the journal and other small literary journals. Study good writing wherever you find it. Learn from editorial comments. Read. Read. Read, but do it as a writer reads. We're seeing too many childhood trauma stories. There are only so many of these we can accept."

✷WHETSTONE, (I, II), English Dept., University of Lethbridge, 4401 University Dr., Lethbridge, Alberta T1K 3M4 Canada. (403)329-2367. Contact: Editorial Board. Magazine: 6 × 9; 90-140 pages; superbond paper; photos. Magazine publishing "poetry, prose, drama, prints, photographs and occasional music compositions for a general audience." Biannually. Estab. 1971. Circ. 500.

Needs: Experimental, literary, mainstream. "Interested in works by all writers/artists. Interested in multimedia works by individuals or collaborators." Write for upcoming themes. Accepts 1-2 mss/issue, 3-4 mss/year. Published work by Madeline Sonik, Serenity Bee, Stephen Guppy and Ronnie R. Brown. Published new writers within the last year. Length: maximum 10 pages. Publishes short shorts. Also publishes poetry, drama and art.

How to Contact: Send 2 short fictions or 6 poems maximum with SASE. Include cover letter with author's background and experience. No simultaneous submissions. Reports in 5 months on mss. Publishes ms an average of 3-4 months after acceptance. Sample copy for $7 (Canadian) and 7½×10½ or larger SAE and 2 Canadian first-class stamps or IRCs.
Advice: "We seek most styles of quality writing. Follow all submission guidelines, including number of pieces and pages. Avoid moralizing."

WHISKEY ISLAND MAGAZINE, (II), Dept. of English, Cleveland State University, Cleveland OH 44115. (216)687-2056. Fax: (216)687-6943. E-mail: whiskeyisland@popmail.csuohio.edu. Website: http://www.csuohio .edu/whiskey_island (includes writer's guidelines, contest guidelines, staff information, history, short fiction, poetry, subscription information). Editor: Pat Stansberry. Editors change each year. Magazine of fiction and poetry, including experimental works, with no specific theme. Biannually. Estab. 1978. Circ. 2,500.
Needs: Receives 100 unsolicited fiction mss/month. Accepts 4-6 mss/issue. Recently published Mary Robison, J.L. Schneider, Brian Lysle and John Fulmer. Publishes 2-4 new writers/year. Length: 6,500 words maximum. Also publishes poetry (poetry submissions should contain no more than 10 pages).
How to Contact: Send complete ms with SASE. No simultaneous or previously published submissions. Reports in 2-4 months on mss. Sample copy for $5.
Payment/Terms: Pays 2 contributor's copies. Acquires one-time rights.
Advice: Looks for "work that does not adhere to that almost universal distant third-person point-of-view so common in literary fiction. A different voice, tone, point of view, etc. A sense of newness and individuality."

WHISPERING WILLOW'S MYSTERY MAGAZINE, (IV), Whispering Willow's LTD., Co., 2517 South Central, P.O. Box 890294, Oklahoma City OK 73189-0294. (405)239-2531. Fax: (405)232-0392. Editor: Peggy D. Farris. Fiction Editor: Trula Johnson. Magazine: 5½×8½; 112 pages; offset paper; 60 lb. gloss enamel cover stock; illustrations and photos. Publishes "mystery stories for mystery readers all ages." Quarterly. Estab. 1996.
Needs: Mystery/suspense (amateur sleuth, cozy, police procedural, private eye/hardboiled), psychic/supernatural/occult. "No romance." List of upcoming themes available for SASE. Publishes special fiction issue or anthology. Receives 25 unsolicited mss/month. Accepts 5-6 mss/issue; 20-24 mss/year. Publishes ms 3-6 months after acceptance. Deadlines: September 1 for January 10 publication; January 10 for April 1 publication; March 1 for July 1 publication; June 1 for October 1 publication. Published "Hide and Seek," by Tim Myers; "Picture Perfect," by Lisa Lepovetsky; and "Sip A Cup of Murder," by Edie Hanes. Length: 1,800 words average; 500 words minimum; 2,500 words maximum. Also publishes poetry.
How to Contact: Send complete ms with cover letter. Include estimated word count, 1-2 paragraph bio and list of publications. Reports in 1 month on mss. Send SASE for reply, return of ms or send a disposable copy of ms. Simultaneous submissions OK. Sample copy for $6. Fiction guidelines for #10 SASE.
Payment/Terms: Pays 4¢/word on publication and 1 contributor's copy; additional copies for $2.97. Acquires first North American serial rights. Sends galleys to author. Sponsors 3 contests annually; send SASE for information.
Advice: Looks for "mystery, with suspense that is believable, holds the reader's interest, moves along and doesn't drag. An unusual approach or a successful twist makes the manuscript stand out. Check facts for accuracy."

✤**WHITE WALL REVIEW**, 63 Gould St., Toronto, Ontario M5B 1E9 Canada. (416)977-9924. Editors change annually. Send mss to "Editors." Magazine: 5¾×8¾; 144-160 pages; professionally printed with glossy card cover; b&w photos and illustrations. "An annual using interesting, preferably spare art. No style is unacceptable." Annually. Estab. 1976. Circ. 500.
Needs: Nothing "boring, self-satisfied, gratuitously sexual, violent or indulgent." Accepts 10 mss/book. Accepts mss from September to 1st week in December of a given year. Published work by Terry Watada, Brendan Landers and Ruth Olsen Latta. Length: 3,000 words maximum.
How to Contact: Send complete ms with cover letter, SASE and *$5 non-refundable reading fee*. Include a short bio. Reports on mss "as soon as we can (usually in April or May)." Always comments on ms. No simultaneous submissions. Sample copy for $8.
Payment/Terms: Pays 1 contributor's copy. Acquires first or one-time rights.
Advice: "Keep it *short*. We look for creativity, but not to the point of obscurity."

WIDENER REVIEW, (II), Widener University, One University Place, Chester PA 19013. (610)499-4342. Editor: Leslie Cronin. Magazine: 5¼×8½; 100 pages. Fiction, poetry for general audience. Annually. Estab. 1984. Circ. 500.

 A BULLET INTRODUCES COMMENTS by the editor of *Novel & Short Story Writer's Market* indicating special information about the listing.

Needs: "Writers should submit one story, 6,000 words or less. We do not publish juvenile fiction, genre fiction or pornography. Otherwise, our standards are the standards of excellent writing." Recently published work by Madison Smartt Bell, Edith Pearlman, Elizabeth Mozier and Robin Beeman. Publishes approximately 5 new writers/year.

How to Contact: "All work submitted for consideration must be typed and double spaced, on 8½×11 sheets of white paper. We accept both photocopies and computer printouts, provided only one side of the paper has been used. Reporting time is about 3 months. *Writers must enclose an SASE with sufficient postage to return the manuscript.*"

Payment/Terms: Pays 1 contributor's copy; charge for extras. Acquires first serial rights.

THE WILLIAM AND MARY REVIEW, (II), P.O. Box 8795, Campus Center, The College of William and Mary, Williamsburg VA 23187-8795. (757)221-3290. E-mail: bbhatl@mail.wm.edu. Contact: Editor. Magazine: 110 pages; graphics; photography. "We publish high quality fiction, poetry, interviews with writers, and art. Our audience is primarily academic." Annually. Estab. 1962. Circ. 3,500.
  ● This magazine has received numerous honors from the Columbia Scholastic Press Association's Golden Circle Awards.

Needs: Literary, contemporary. No horror, hardcore porn, romance. Receives approximately 90 unsolicited fiction mss/month. Accepts 9 mss/issue. Recently published work by Brenda S. Webster and Nicholas Montemarano. Publishes 2-3 new writers/year. Length: 7,000 words maximum; no minimum. Also publishes poetry. Usually critiques rejected mss.

How to Contact: Send complete ms with SASE and cover letter with name, address and phone number. "Cover letter should be as brief as possible." Simultaneous submissions OK. Queries by e-mail OK; no mss. Reports in 2-4 months. All departments closed in June, July and August. Sample copy for $5.50. May review novels, poetry and short story collections.

Payment/Terms: Pays 5 contributor's copies; discounts thereafter. Acquires first rights.

Advice: "We want original, well-written fiction. While we lean towards stories with an almost mathematically refined flavor, our favorites are essentially mental jigsaw puzzles. We believe that, first and foremost, a work of fiction must be an entertaining and compelling story. Page allotment to fiction will rise in relation to the quality of fiction received."

WILLOW REVIEW, (II), College of Lake County, 19351 W. Washington St., Grayslake IL 60030. (847)223-6601 ext. 2956. Fax: (847)548-3383. E-mail: com426@clc.cc.il.us. Editor: Paulette Roeske. Magazine: 6×9; 80 pages; 70 lb. paper; 80 lb. 4-color cover. "*Willow Review* is nonthematic and publishes short fiction, memoir and poetry for a general and literary adult audience." Annually. Estab. 1969. Circ. 1,000.
  ● *Willow Review* is partially funded by the Illinois Arts Council.

Needs: Contemporary, ethnic, experimental, feminist, literary, prose poems, regional. "There is no bias against a particular subject matter, although there is a clear editorial preference for literary fiction." No "popular genre fiction; children/young adult. Although we publish a range of styles and types of fiction, we look for stories that move us presented in a distinctive voice that is stylistically compelling. We prefer a recognizable world with recognizable characters and events that engage the reader both emotionally and intellectually." Accepts 7-8 mss/issue. Accepted mss published in April of each year. Recently published work by Garrett Hongo, Fran Podulka, Elaine Fowler and Palencia. Length: 1,500 words minimum; 4,000 words maximum. Publishes short shorts. Sometimes comments on rejected mss and recommends other markets.

How to Contact: Send complete ms with cover letter. Include complete mailing address, telephone number, list of previous publications and or other recognition etc., if applicable. Reports in 1-2 months on mss. SASE (if writer would like it returned). Sample copy for $4. Fiction guidelines for #10 SAE and 1 first-class stamp.

Payment/Terms: Pays 2 contributor's copies on publication for first North American serial rights. All manuscripts are automatically considered for the annual *Willow Review* awards.

Advice: "*Willow Review*, because of its length, is forced to make word count a factor although we would publish an exceptional story which exceeds our recommended length. Beyond that, literary excellence is our sole criteria. Perhaps voice, more than any other factor, causes a manuscript to distinguish itself. Study the craft—read the best little magazines, subscribe to them, maintain contact with other writers through writer's groups or informally, attend fiction readings and ask the writers questions in the discussion periods which typically follow. Read Eudora Welty's *One Writer's Beginnings* or John Gardner's *On Becoming a Novelist* or Flannery O'Connor's *Mystery and Manners*. Read Chekhov—read the masters."

WILLOW SPRINGS, (II), Eastern Washington University, 526 Fifth St., MS-1, Cheney WA 99004-2431. (509)458-6429. Editor: Nance Van Winckel. Magazine: 9×6; 128 pages; 80 lb. glossy cover. "*Willow Springs* publishes literary poetry and fiction of high quality, a mix of new and established writers." Semiannually. Estab. 1977. Circ. 1,200.
  ● *Willow Springs* is a member of the Council of Literary Magazines and Presses and AWP. The magazine has received grants from the NEA and a CLMP excellence award.

Needs: Parts of novels, short stories, literary, prose poems, poems and translations. "No genre fiction please." Receives 150 unsolicited mss/month. Accepts 2-4 mss/issue; 4-8 mss/year. Does not read mss May 15-September 15. Publishes ms 6 months to one year after acceptance. Recently published work by Alberto Rios, Alison Baker

and Robin Hemley; published new writers within the last year. Length: 5,000 words minimum; 11,000 words maximum. Also publishes literary essays, literary criticism and poetry. Rarely critiques rejected mss.
How to Contact: Send complete ms with cover letter. Include short bio. No simultaneous submissions. Reports in 2 weeks on queries. Sample copy for $5.
Payment/Terms: Pays $20-50 and 2 contributor's copies for first North American rights.
Advice: "We hope to attract good fiction writers to our magazine, and we've made a commitment to publish three-four stories per issue. We like fiction that exhibits a fresh approach to language. Our most recent issues, we feel, indicate the quality and level of our commitment."

WIND MAGAZINE, (II), P.O. Box 24548, Lexington KY 40524. (606)885-5342. E-mail: wind@lit-arts.com. Editors: Charlie Hughes and Leatha Kendrick. Magazine: 5½×8½; 100 pages. "Eclectic literary journal with stories, poems, book reviews from small presses, essays. Readership is students, professors, housewives, literary folk, adults." Semiannually. Estab. 1971. Circ. 450.
Needs: Literary, mainstream/contemporary, translations. Accepts 6 fiction mss/issue; 12 mss/year. Publishes ms less than 1 year after acceptance. Published work by Carolyn Osborn, Jane Stuart, David Shields, Lester Goldberg and Elisabeth Stevens. Length: 5,000 words maximum. Publishes short shorts, length: 300-400 words. Also publishes literary essays, literary criticism and poetry. Sometimes critiques or comments on rejected mss.
How to Contact: Send complete ms with a cover letter. Include estimated word count and 50-word bio. No e-mail submissions accepted. Reports in 2 weeks on queries; 2 months on mss. Send SASE for reply, return of ms or send a disposable copy of ms. No simultaneous submissions. Sample copy for $4.50. Reviews novels and short story collections from small presses.
Payment/Terms: Pays 1 contributor's copy; additional copies for $3.50. Acquires first North American serial rights and anthology reprint rights.
Advice: "The writing must have an impact on the reader; the reader must come away changed, perhaps haunted, or maybe smiling. There is nothing I like better than to be able to say 'I wish I had written that.' "

WISCONSIN REVIEW, (I, II), University of Wisconsin, Box 158, Radford Hall, Oshkosh WI 54901. (414)424-2267. Editor: Debbie Martin. Editors change every year. Send submissions to "Fiction Editor." Magazine: 6×9; 60-100 pages; illustrations. Literary prose and poetry. Triannual. Estab. 1966. Circ. 2,000.
Needs: Literary and experimental. Receives 30 unsolicited fiction mss each month. Publishes 3 new writers/year. Length: up to 5,000 words. Publishes short shorts.
How to Contact: Send complete ms with SASE and cover letter with bio notes. Simultaneous submissions OK. Reports in 2-6 months. Publishes ms an average of 1-3 months after acceptance. Sample copy for $3.
Payment/Terms: Pays in contributor's copies. Acquires first rights.
Advice: "We look for well-crafted work with carefully developed characters, plots and meaningful situations. The editors prefer work of original and fresh thought when considering a piece of experimental fiction."

‡WOMYN'S PRESS, (I, II), P.O. Box 562, Eugene OR 97405. (541)302-8146. Editors: J.R. David and N. Bruckner. Newspaper: 11½×16; 16 pages; newsprint; illustrations and photos. "We publish fiction, news, poetry, reviews and are by, for and about women, with a feminist focus." Bimonthly. Estab. 1970. Circ. 2,000.
Needs: Adventure, erotica, ethnic/multicultural, experimental, feminist, historical, lesbian, literary, psychic/supernatural/occult, regional. Receives 10-30 mss/month. Accepts 1-2 mss/issue, 6-12 mss/year. Publishes ms "anywhere from 2 months to 1 year" after acceptance. Recently published work by Bonita Rinehart, J.R. David, Carolyn Gage and Natascha Bruckner. Length: 2,000 words average; 500 words minimum; 2,000 words maximum. Publishes short shorts. Also publishes literary essays, literary criticism and poetry. Often critiques or comments on rejected manuscripts.
How to Contact: Send complete manuscript with cover letter. Include 1 paragraph bio. Reports in 1-3 months on queries, 1-12 months on mss. Send SASE for reply, return of ms or send disposable copy of ms. Simultaneous submissions and reprints OK. Sample copy for $3. Reviews novels and short story collections. Send books to editor.
Payment/Terms: Pays free subscription to magazine for one-time rights.
Advice: "Be honest. Be true to your intuition and to the dedicated practice of writing. Even if we don't accept your work, keep writing and sending it out."

THE WORCESTER REVIEW, (II), Worcester Country Poetry Association, Inc., 71 Pleasant, Worcester MA 01609. (508)797-4770. Website: www.geocities.com/paris/leftbank/6433. Editor: Rodger Martin. Magazine: 6×9; 100 pages; 60 lb. white offset paper; 10 pt. CS1 cover stock; illustrations and photos. "We like high quality, creative poetry, artwork and fiction. Critical articles should be connected to New England." Annually. Estab. 1972. Circ. 1,000.
Needs: Literary, prose poem. "We encourage New England writers in the hopes we will publish at least 30% New England but want the other 70% to show the best of writing from across the US." Receives 20-30 unsolicited fiction mss/month. Accepts 2-4 mss/issue. Publishes ms an average of 6 months to 1 year after acceptance. Agented fiction less than 10%. Published work by Toni Graham and Carol Glickfeld. Length: 2,000 words average; 1,000 words minimum; 4,000 words maximum. Publishes short shorts. Also publishes literary essays, literary criticism, poetry. Sometimes critiques rejected mss and recommends other markets.

How to Contact: Send complete ms with cover letter. Reports in 6-9 months on mss. SASE. Simultaneous submissions OK if other markets are clearly identified. Sample copy for $5; fiction guidelines free.
Payment/Terms: Pays 2 contributor's copies and honorarium if possible for one-time rights.
Advice: "Send only one short story—reading editors do not like to read two by the same author at the same time. We will use only one. We generally look for creative work with a blend of craftsmanship, insight and empathy. This does not exclude humor. We won't print work that is shoddy in any of these areas."

WORDS OF WISDOM, (II), 612 Front St., Glendora NJ 08029-1133. (609)863-0610. E-mail: jmfreier@aol.c om. Editor: J.M. Freiermuth. Newsletter: 5½×8½; 72-88 pages; copy paper; some illustrations and photographs. "Fiction, satire, humorous poetry and travel for a general audience—80% of readers can read above high school level." Estab. 1981. Circ. 160.
Needs: Adventure, contemporary, ethnic, feminist, historical, humor/satire, mainstream, mystery/suspense (cozy, private eye), regional, western (adult, frontier, traditional). No religion, children's, gay, romance. Fall 1998 issue to feature travel stories in foreign lands. Receives 50-60 unsolicited mss/month. Accepts 15-20 mss/issue; 60-80 mss/year. Publishes ms 2-12 months after acceptance. Recently published work by DC Palter, Roger Coleman, Cynthia Chadwick, Laura L. Post, Mark Devaney, Zoja Paulouskis-Petit, Michael Ceraolo, Celestine Liu and Marc Davignon. Published first time writers last year. Length: 2,000-3,000 words average; 1,200 words minimum; 7,000 words maximum. Publishes short shorts. Length: "Long enough to develop a good bite." Sometimes critiques rejected mss and recommends other markets.
How to Contact: Send complete manuscript copy and/or DOS floppy (uses MSWord) with cover letter including "name, address, SASE. Include author bio that includes titles of magazines you care enough to send the occasional subscription check. We use those instead of the names of the famous zines that have published you in the past. Submissions without cover letters are not read." Reports in 2-12 weeks on mss. SASE. Simultaneous and electronic (disk) submissions OK. Sample copy for $4 postpaid. Reviews short story collections.
Payment/Terms: Pays subscription to magazine for first publication of story. Acquires one-time rights. Publication not copyrighted.
Advice: "If your story has a spark of life or a degree of humor that brings a smile to my face, you have a chance here. Most stories lack these two ingredients. Don't send something you wrote ten years ago. Don't write your stories as if it were an episode of a TV series. Keep the number of characters down to a manageable number. Try to make everything relate to the plot line."

WRITERS' FORUM, (II), University of Colorado at Colorado Springs, Colorado Springs CO 80933-7150. Fax: (719)262-3582. E-mail: kpellow@brain.uccs.edu. Editor: C. Kenneth Pellow. "Ten to fifteen short stories or self-contained novel excerpts published once a year along with 25-35 poems. Highest literary quality only: mainstream, avant-garde, with preference to western themes. For small press enthusiasts, teachers and students of creative writing, commercial agents/publishers, university libraries and departments interested in contemporary American literature." Estab. 1974.
Needs: Contemporary, ethnic (Chicano, Native American, not excluding others), literary and regional (West). Receives approximately 40 unsolicited fiction mss each month and will publish new as well as experienced authors. Recently published fiction by Lanny Ledeboer and Rick Koster. Publishes 2-4 new writers/year. Length: 1,500-8,500 words. Also publishes literary essays, literary criticism, poetry. Critiques rejected mss "when there is time and perceived merit."
How to Contact: Send complete ms and letter with relevant career information with SASE. Prefers submissions July through October. Simultaneous submissions OK. Reports in 3-5 weeks on mss. Publishes ms an average of 6 months after acceptance. Sample back copy $8 to *NSSWM* readers. Current copy $10. Make checks payable to "Writers' Forum."
Payment/Terms: Pays 2 contributor's copies. Cover price less 50% discount for extras. Acquires one-time rights.
Advice: "Read our publication. Be prepared for constructive criticism. We especially seek submissions with a strong voice that show immersion in place (trans-Mississippi West) and development of credible characters. Probably the TV-influenced fiction with trivial dialogue and set-up plot is the most quickly rejected. Our format—a 5½×8½ professionally edited and printed paperback book—lends credibility to authors published in our imprint."

WRITER'S GUIDELINES, A Roundtable for Writers and Editors, (I, II), Salaki Publishing, Box 608, Pittsburg MO 65724. Phone/fax: (417)993-5544. Editor: Susan Salaki. Magazine: 8½×11; 16 pages; 60 lb. opaque; illustrations and photos. Bimonthly. Estab. 1988. Circ. 1,000.
Needs: Open. Receives 20 unsolicited mss/month. Buys 1 ms/issue; 6 mss/year. Publishes ms-3 months after acceptance. Length: 1,000 words maximum. Also publishes literary essays and literary criticism. Critiques or comments on rejected mss.
How to Contact: Send complete ms. Include estimated word count and bio (100 words). Reports in 1 week. SASE for reply or send a disposable copy of ms. Sample copy for $4. Reviews novels or short story collections.
Payment/Terms: Pays $0-25 and 1 contributor's copy on acceptance for first rights.
Advice: "Don't try to write. Just tell a story."

WRITING FOR OUR LIVES, (I, IV), Running Deer Press, 647 N. Santa Cruz Ave., Annex, Los Gatos CA 95032. (408)354-8604. Editor: Janet M. McEwan. Magazine: 5¼×8¼; 80 pages; 70 lb. recycled white paper; 80 lb. recycled cover. "*Writing For Our Lives* is a periodical which serves as a vessel for poems, short fiction, stories, letters, autobiographies, and journal excerpts from the life stories, experiences and spiritual journeys of women. Audience is women and friends of women." Semiannually. Estab. 1992. Circ. 600.

Needs: Ethnic/multicultural, experimental, feminist, humor/satire, lesbian, literary, translations, "autobiographical, breaking personal or historical silence on any concerns of women's lives. *Women writers only, please.* We have no preannounced themes." Receives 15-20 unsolicited mss/month. Accepts 10 mss/issue; 20 mss/year. Publishes ms 2-24 months after acceptance. Recently published work by Andrea Allard, Grita Baliga-Savel, JoAnn Cooke, Kelley Jacquez, Jayatta Jones, Ronda Nielson and Karen X. Tulchinsky. Publishes 3-5 new writers/year. Length: 2,100 words maximum. Publishes short shorts. Also publishes poetry. Rarely critiques or comments on rejected mss.

How to Contact: Send complete ms with a cover letter. "Publication dates are May and November. Closing dates for mss are 2/15 and 8/15. Initial report immediate; next report, if any, in 1-18 months." Send 2 SASE's for reply, and one of them must be sufficient for return of ms if desired. Simultaneous and reprint submissions OK. Sample copy for $6-8 (in California add 8.25% sales tax), $9-11 overseas. Fiction guidelines for #10 SASE.

Payment/Terms: Pays 2 contributor's copies; additional copies for 50% discount and 1 year subscription at 50% discount. Acquires one-time rights in case of reprints and first worldwide English language serial rights.

Advice: "It is in our own personal stories that the real herstory of our time is told. This periodical is a place for exploring the boundaries of our empowerment to break long historical and personal silences. While honoring the writing which still needs to be held close to our hearts, we can begin to send some of our heartfelt words out into a wider circle."

*WRITING WOMEN, P.O. Box 111, Newcastle Upon Tyne NE3 1WF Great Britain. Editors: Andrea Badenoch, Debbie Taylor, Maggie Hannan, Pippa Little.

Needs: "From 1998 *Writing Women* will be published by Virago Press in an annual anthology in book form. This will include 12 stories by writers who have not previously published a collection, or a novel with a mainstream publisher. We are looking for submissions that take risks and break new ground." Length: 4,000 words maximum.

How to Contact: Include SAE for return of ms.

Payment/Terms: Pays £25 per 1,000 words. Sample copies of old format magazine £2. Guidelines available for SAE.

XAVIER REVIEW, (I, II), Xavier University, 7325 Palmetto St., Box 110C, New Orleans LA 70125-1098. (504)483-7303. Fax: (504)485-7197. E-mail: rskinner@mail.xula.edu. Editor: Thomas Bonner, Jr. Managing Editor: Robert E. Skinner. Assistant Editor: Patrice Melnick. Production Consultant: Mark Whitaker. Magazine: 6×9; 75 pages; 50 lb. paper; 12 pt. CS1 cover; photographs. Magazine of "poetry/fiction/nonfiction/reviews (contemporary literature) for professional writers/libraries/colleges/universities." Semiannually. Estab. 1980. Circ. 500.

Needs: Contemporary, ethnic, experimental, historical (general), literary, Latin American, prose poem, Southern, religious, serialized/excerpted novel, translations. Receives 30 unsolicited fiction mss/month. Accepts 2 mss/issue; 4 mss/year. Does not read mss during the summer months. Published work by Randall Ivey, Rita Porteau, John Goldfine and Christine Wiltz. Length: 10-15 pages. Publishes literary criticism, literary essays, books of creative writing and poetry. Occasionally critiques rejected mss.

How to Contact: Send complete ms. Include 150-word bio and brief list of publications. SASE. Reports in 8-10 weeks. Sample copy for $5.

Payment/Terms: Pays 2 contributor's copies.

XTREME, The Magazine of Extremely Short Fiction, P.O. Box 678383, Orlando FL 32867-8383. E-mail: rhowiley@aol.com. Editor: Rho Wiley. Magazine: 8½×11; 4 pages; heavy bond paper and cover. "Xtreme, the magazine of extremely short fiction, publishes fiction of EXACTLY 250 words. Fiction is considered on the basis of merit only. We feel that the 250 word format affords an opportunity for all writers to push the limits of the language." Semiannually. Estab. 1993. Circ. 500.

Needs: Humor/satire, literary, mainstream/contemporary. Receives 25-30 unsolicited mss/month. Accepts 10 mss/issue; 20 mss/year. Publishes ms 6 months after acceptance. Length: exactly 250 words. Sometimes critiques or comments on rejected mss.

How to Contact: Send complete ms with a cover letter. Reports in 6 weeks on queries; up to 6 months on mss. Send SASE for reply or return of ms. No simultaneous submissions. Sample copy for 9×12 SAE and 2 first-class stamps. Fiction guidelines included with sample copy.

Payment/Terms: Pays 3 contributor's copies for first North American serial rights.

Advice: Looks for "the ability to tell a complete story in the boundaries of the 250 word format. A succinct use of the language always stands out. Work with the form. Try to push the limits of what can happen in only 250 words."

‡**THE YALE REVIEW, (II)**, Yale University/Blackwell Publishers Inc., P.O. Box 208243, New Haven CT 06520. (203)432-0499. Fax: (203)432-0510. E-mail: yalerev@yale.edu. Editor: J.D. McClatchy. Fiction Editor: Susan Bianconi. Magazine: 9¼×6; 180-190 pages; book stock paper; glossy cover; illustrations and photographs. "*The Yale Review* is meant for the well-read general reader interested in a variety of topics in the arts and letters, in history, and in current affairs." Quarterly. Estab. 1911. Circ. 7,000.
Needs: Mainstream/contemporary. Receives 50-80 unsolicited mss/month. Accepts 1-3 mss/issue; 7-12 mss/year. Publishes ms 3 months after acceptance. Agented fiction 25%. Recently published work by Paul Brodeur, Deborah Eisenberg, Jeffrey Eugenides, Sheila Kohler, Joe Ashby Porter, Kit Reed, John Barth and James McCourt. Publishes short shorts (but not frequently). Also publishes literary essays, poetry.
How to Contact: Send complete ms with a cover letter. Include estimated word count and list of publications. Reports in 1 month on queries; 2 months on mss. Send SASE for reply, return of ms or send a disposable copy of ms. Always include SASE. No simultaneous submissions. Reviews novels and short story collections. Send books to the editors.
Payment/Terms: Pays $300-400 on publication and 2 contributor's copies; additional copies for $7. Sends galleys to author. "Awards by the editors; cannot be applied for."
Advice: "We find that the most accomplished young writers seem to be people who keep their ears open to other voices; who read widely."

THE YALOBUSHA REVIEW, The Literary Journal of the University of Mississippi, University of Mississippi, P.O. Box 186, University MS 38677-0186. (601)232-7439. E-mail: yalobush@olemiss.edu. Editors change each year. Magazine: 5½×8½; 130 pages; 60 lb. off-white; card cover stock. "We look for high-quality fiction, poetry, and creative essays; and we seek a balance of regional and national writers." Annually. Estab. 1995. Circ. 500.
Needs: Literary. "No genre or formula fiction." List of upcoming themes available for SASE. Receives 30 unsolicited mss/month. Accepts 6 mss/issue. Does not read mss April through August. Published work by Larry Brown, Cynthia Shearer and Eric Miles Williamson. Length: 15 pages average; 35 pages maximum. Publishes short shorts. Also publishes literary essays and poetry. Sometimes critiques or comments on rejected mss.
How to Contact: Send complete ms with a cover letter. Reports in 1 month on queries; reporting time on mss varies. Send SASE for reply, return of ms or send a disposable copy of ms. Electronic submissions OK. Fiction guidelines for #10 SASE.
Payment/Terms: Pays 2 contributor's copies and $100 to the Editor's Choice winner for each issue. Pays on publication. Acquires first North American serial rights.
Advice: "We look for writers with a strong, distinct voice and good stories to tell." Would like to see more "good endings!"

YELLOW SILK: Journal of Erotic Arts, (II), Verygraphics, Box 6374, Albany CA 94706. (510)644-4188. Editor/Publisher: Lily Pond. "We are interested in nonpornographic erotic literature: joyous, mad, musical, elegant, passionate. 'All persuasions; no brutality' is our editorial policy. Literary excellence is a priority; innovative forms are welcomed, as well as traditional ones." Quarterly. Estab. 1981.
Needs: Erotica, ethnic, experimental, fantasy, feminist/lesbian, gay, humor/satire, literary, prose poem, science fiction and translations. No "blow-by-blow" descriptions; no hackneyed writing except when used for satirical purposes. Nothing containing brutality. Accepts 16-20 mss/year. Recently published work by Tobias Wolff, Richard Zimler and Jane Smiley. Publishes 20 new writers/year. Length: no preference. Occasionally critiques rejected ms.
How to Contact: Send complete ms with SASE and include short, *personal* bio notes. No queries. No prepublished material. No simultaneous submissions. Name, address and phone number on each page. Submissions on disk OK *with* hard copy only. Reports in 3 months on mss. Publishes ms up to 3 years after acceptance..
Payment/Terms: Competitive payment on publication for all periodical and anthology rights for one year following publication, at which time rights revert back to author; and nonexclusive reprint, electronic and anthology rights for the duration of the copyright.
Advice: "Read, read, read! Including our magazine—plus Nabokov, Ntozaké Shangé, Rimbaud, Virginia Woolf, William Kotzwinkle, James Joyce. Then send in your story! Trust that the magazine/editor will not rip you off—they don't. As they say, 'find your own voice,' then trust it. Most manuscripts I reject appear to be written by people without great amounts of writing experience. It takes years (frequently) to develop your work to publishable quality; it can take many rewrites on each individual piece. I also see many approaches to sexuality (for my magazine) that are trite and not fresh. The use of language is not original, and the people do not seem real."

‡   **THE DOUBLE DAGGER** before a listing indicates that the listing is new in this edition.

However, the gems come too, and what a wonderful moment that is. Please don't send me anything with blue eye shadow.''

‡**YEMASSEE, The literary journal of the University of South Carolina, (II)**, Department of English, University of South Carolina, Columbia SC 29208. (803)777-4204. Fax: (803)777-9064. Editor: Melissa Johnson. Magazine: 5½ × 8½; 60-80 pages; 60 lb. natural paper; 65 lb. cover; cover illustration. "We are open to a variety of subjects and writing styles. *Yemassee* publishes primarily fiction and poetry, but we are also interested in one-act plays, brief excerpts of novels, essays, reviews and interviews with literary figures. Our essential consideration for acceptance is the quality of the work.'' Semiannually. Estab. 1993. Circ. 375.

● A story from *Yemassee*, "Marrying Aunt Sadie," was selected for *New Stories from the South 1997*.

Needs: Condensed/excerpted novel, ethnic/multicultural, experimental, feminist, gay, historical, humor/satire, lesbian, literary, mainstream/contemporary, regional. No romance, religious/inspirational, young adult/teen, children's/juvenile, erotica. Receives 10 unsolicited mss/month. Accepts 1-3 mss/issue; 2-6 mss/year. "We hold manuscripts until our reading periods—October 1 to November 15 and March 15 to April 30." Publishes ms 2-4 months after acceptance. Recently published work by Gene Able, Thomas David Lisk, Chris Railey, Robert B. Kennedy, Nichole Potts and Michael Cody. Length: 4,000 words or less. Publishes short shorts. Also publishes literary essays and poetry.

How to Contact: Send complete ms with a cover letter. Include estimated word count, brief bio, Social Security number and list of publications. Reports in 2 weeks on queries, 2-4 months after deadlines on mss. Send SASE for reply, return of ms or send disposable copy of ms. Simultaneous submissions OK. Sample copy for $5. Fiction guidelines for #10 SASE.

Payment/Terms: Pays 2 contributor's copies for first rights; additional copies $2.75. All submissions are considered for the *Yemassee* awards—$200 each for the best poetry and fiction in each issue when funding permits.

Advice: "Our criteria are generally based on what we perceive as quality. Generally that is work that is literary. We are interested in subtlety and originality, interesting or beautiful language use as well as craft and precision. Read more, write more and revise more. Read our journal and any other journal before you submit to see if your work seems appropriate. Send for guidelines and make sure you follow them. Don't suck up in the cover letter. Be honest.''

‡***YORKSHIRE JOURNAL, (IV)**, Smith Settle Ltd., Ilkley Road, Otley, W. Yorkshire LS21 3JP England. 01943-467958. Fax: 01943-850057. Editor: Mark Whitley. Magazine: 245mm × 175mm; 120 pages; matt art paper; art board cover stock; illustrations and photos. "We publish historical/factual articles, poetry and short stories by and about the county of Yorkshire in England." Quarterly. Estab. 1993. Circ. 3,000.

Needs: Regional, "anything about Yorkshire." Receives 2-4 unsolicited mss/month. Accepts 2-3 mss/year. Recently published work by Denis Yeadon, Neville Slack, Mary Walsh and Alex Marwood. Length: 1,500 words average. Often critiques or comments on rejected mss.

How to Contact: Query first. Include estimated word count and 50-word bio with submission. Reports in 6 weeks on queries; 10 weeks on mss. Send SASE (or IRCs) for reply, return of ms or send a disposable copy of ms. Reprints and electronic submissions (disk or modem) OK. Sample copy for $10. Fiction guidelines for SASE (or IRC).

Payment/Terms: Pay varies; includes 1 contributor's copy; additional copies $10. Pays on publication. Acquires first rights.

Advice: "Fiction must be about Yorkshire in some way. Send in an outline first, not the completed manuscript.''

ZERO HOUR, "Where Culture Meets Crime," (I), Box 766, Seattle WA 98111. (206)621-8829. Editor: Jim Jones. Newsprint paper; illustrations and photos. "We are interested in fringe culture. We publish fiction, poetry, essays, confessions, photos, illustrations and interviews, for young, politically left audience interested in current affairs, non-mainstream music, art, culture." Semiannually. Estab. 1988. Circ. 3,000.

Needs: Confessions, erotica, ethnic, experimental, feminist, gay, humor/satire, psychic/supernatural/occult and translations. "Each issue revolves around an issue in contemporary culture: cults and fanaticism, addiction, pornography, etc." No romance, inspirational, juvenile/young, sports. Receives 5 unsolicited mss/month. Accepts 3 mss/issue; 9 mss/year. Publishes ms 2-3 months after acceptance. Published work by Billy Childish, Rebecca Brown, Peter Toliver and Vaginal Davis. Publishes 20 new writers/year. Length: 1,200 words average; 400 words minimum; 5,000 words maximum. Publishes short shorts. Length: 400 words. Sometimes critiques rejected mss.

How to Contact: Query first. Reports in 2 weeks on queries; 1 month on mss. SASE. Simultaneous submissions OK. Sample copy for $3, 9 × 12 SAE and 5 first-class stamps. Fiction guidelines free. Reviews novels and short story collections.

Payment/Terms: Pays $25 per short story, $650 for novels for one-time rights. Sends galleys to author.

Advice: Looking for "straight-forward narrative prose—true-to-life experiences told about unique experiences or from an unusual perspective. Ask yourself does it fit our theme? Is it well written, from an unusual point of view or on an unexplored/underexplored topic? In terms of styles we are specifically seeking narrative prose that tells us a story, gives us a glimpse of a bigger picture, but not one that leaves us going, 'Huh?' It can't be too 'literary' or 'high brow' (some of us are refugees from academia), and it shouldn't be too experimental or too heavy on language over substance ('literary masturbation'). Some authors we like are: Jim Thompson, Graham

INSIDER REPORT

"A matter of the right story"

When Adrienne Brodeur heard from a variety of sources that film director Francis Ford Coppola was interested in short fiction, possibly even in beginning a fiction magazine, she realized it might just be "publishing gossip." But she found the rumors intriguing enough to write a letter basically saying, "Dear Mr. Coppola, I love short fiction, too."

That was the spring of '95 and Brodeur really didn't expect a response from Coppola. "But about six months later, I got a call late one night from a man asking, 'Is this Adrienne Brodeur?' I said, 'Yes,' and he said, 'This is Francis.' My response was, 'Francis who?' "

For several months, Brodeur in New York and Coppola in California engaged in an e-mail relationship sharing "our philosophy of short fiction and what we each like in a short story. It was kind of a meeting of the minds, and from that we gave birth to the concept of a magazine."

Adrienne Brodeur

Named after Coppola's film studio, *Zoetrope: All Story* was launched in early 1997. Unlike most literary journals, its 10½ × 14 size and newsprint-quality paper would be at home with other magazines in grocery checkout lines. The premier issue had a print run of 50,000, many times more than most literary magazines. Those copies were distributed in Starbucks coffee shops, high schools and colleges—free for the taking and reading. *Zoetrope* also offers a writing contest, co-sponsored with the Boston Beer Company, in each issue (see listing in the Contests section of this book) and holds an annual writers' workshop at Blancaneux Lodge in Belize where Amy Bloom was the 1997 Writer-in-Residence. All this is in keeping with Coppola's two-fold goal of providing a no-frills place for fine, new short fiction and making that fiction accessible to as many readers as possible.

Editor-in-chief Brodeur says *Zoetrope* will be published triannually in 1998. She and Coppola also plan to continue including approximately 90 percent new fiction and one story commissioned by Coppola in each edition. Stories are optioned as film ideas for two years. Writers of commissioned stories are paid $5,000. Authors of noncommissioned stories receive $1,000. Each issue may also run an essay about the short story form and a reprint of a classic short story that later became a play or movie.

The philosophy of short fiction Brodeur and Coppola share is that a story should tell a story. "My understanding, having now worked for Francis for a while, is that he really loves the short story genre. He particularly loves a good story in the classic sense of the word 'story.' We both like literary stories, but he's not one to want anything too experimental. The critical elements to him are characters you can get involved with, whether you love them or hate them. He also likes a story that takes you somewhere—you're not the same squeeze of toothpaste coming out that you were going in.

"This all sounds very basic, but there are some wonderful literary magazines that focus on really magnificent writing and lovely descriptions, but that isn't exactly what we look for. We're looking more for the classic narrative arc."

Although they work thousands of miles apart, Brodeur maintains that Coppola stays very involved in the *Zoetrope* operation. "Francis likes e-mail and everything we do is on a Lotus Notes computer system. I always let him know what I'm doing. I post stories I'm interested in and he comments. Most often, I buy the stories in advance of when he reads them. It's a big relief, then, when he likes something I bought weeks before."

Brodeur also finds authors for the stories Coppola commissions. "He gives me a general idea of something he'd be interested in reading a story about. Then, because I read all the literary journals and go to readings and that sort of thing, I'll recommend three or four writers I think have the voice for the story. It's a very different process than someone writing a work and handing it to you as a done piece. But it's worked out very well."

Sara Powers's "The Baker's Wife," Coppola's first commissioned piece, was being developed by Coppola's film company soon after its appearance in the premier edition of *Zoetrope*. But Brodeur insists that finding movie material is only an added benefit of the magazine. "If Francis only wanted to find movie scripts, he wouldn't have hired me; he would have found someone with a film background. He could buy stories for potential movies; he wouldn't need to do a magazine—a magazine is an expensive beast. I think he's an artist who's made it and wants to put something back into new writers and new talent, and that's really a large part of his goal. It's certainly a large part of my goal, too."

Currently, all the manuscripts received in the *Zoetrope* office are read with the help of a group of "great first readers," says Brodeur. "We have a first-tier reading and ranking system, then one of the three other editors and I look at everything. Some manuscripts float to the surface and we look at them more carefully. Then every other week we have a dinner meeting with our editorial board where we look at three to six stories again to see how the board feels about them and make our decisions that way. We also try hard, although it's becoming harder, to write a few comments when we send back a manuscript."

Brodeur says the influx of manuscripts has quadrupled since she first put out her word-of-mouth call for stories, but the number of publishable manuscripts has not. "We're getting many more manuscripts, but there are not necessarily that many more stories we would be interested in publishing. In the beginning, since it was all word of mouth, we were hitting very targeted audiences of writers and we found fine manuscripts."

A publishable story to Brodeur is one she will remember the next day or next week. "When you read hundreds of stories, few actually stand out in your mind. But there are some stories you can remember pieces of, that have touched some rod inside you. It's a visceral response that's hard for me to break down, but I think it's characters you can really get involved with, whether you like or don't like them. And it's a story that really takes you somewhere. It's hard to walk away loving a story, even though it might be beautifully written, if it doesn't affect you on some level. Some people assume their writing is so lovely that anyone is going to want to read about them watching the bird walk down the sidewalk for five pages. With us, that just is not so."

As hard as it seems for an unknown to get published today, Brodeur says, "It really is a matter of the right story. It seems a lot of stories by unpublished writers are making it to our editorial board. Just last week we found an interesting and promising story in our slush pile from a writer who learned about us from who knows where. I know it's easy to get discouraged, but if you have faith in your work and you know it's good, you just have to keep sending it out until it gets published."

—Barbara Kuroff

Greene, Cookie Meuller, Dennis Cooper, Flannery O'Connor, Katherine Porter, Paul Bowles, and Harry Crews. Our audience is young, hip and not necessarily people who normally read books.''

‡**ZOETROPE, All Story, (II)**, AZX Publications, 126 Fifth Ave., #300, New York NY 10011. (212)696-5720. Fax: (212)696-5845. Editor: Adrienne Brodeur. Magazine: 10½ × 14; 60 pages; illustrations and photos. Quarterly. Estab. 1997. Circ. 50,000.
Needs: Literary, mainstream/contemporary, one act plays. Receives 500 unsolicited mss/month. Accepts 8-10 mss/issue; 32-40 mss/year. Publishes ms 2-6 months after acceptance. Agented fiction 15%. Length: 7,000 words maximum.
How to Contact: Send complete manuscript (no more than 2) with a cover letter. Include estimated word count and list of publications. Simultaneous submissions OK. Sample copy for 9 × 12 SAE and $1.70 postage. Fiction guidelines for #10 SASE.
Payment/Terms: Pays $2,000 for 2 year option on movie rights for unsolicited submissions; $5,000 for commissioned works.

ZYZZYVA, the last word: west coast writers & artists, (II, IV), 41 Sutter St., Suite 1400, San Francisco CA 94104. (415)752-4393. Fax: (415)752-4391. E-mail: zyzzyvainc@aol.com. Website: http://www.webdelsol.com/ ZYZZYVA (includes guidelines, names of editors, selections from current issues, editor's note). Editor: Howard Junker. Magazine: 6 × 9; 208 pages; graphics; photos. "Literate" magazine. Triquarterly. Estab. 1985. Circ. 4,500.
  ● *Zyzzyva* was recently profiled in *Poet's & Writer's* Magazine.
Needs: Contemporary, experimental, literary, prose poem. West Coast US writers only. Receives 400 unsolicited mss/month. Accepts 5 fiction mss/issue; 20 mss/year. Agented fiction: 10%. Recently published work by Alison Baker, Judy Grahn and Russell Leong. Publishes 20 new writers/year. Length: varies. Also publishes literary essays.
How to Contact: Send complete ms. "Cover letters are of minimal importance." Reports in 2 weeks on mss. SASE. No simultaneous or reprint submissions. Sample copy for $5. Fiction guidelines on masthead page.
Payment/Terms: Pays $50 on acceptance for first North American serial rights.
Advice: "Keep the faith. I don't feel there are any criteria in the abstract. Each manuscript sets its own terms. I like ambitious writers who are willing to take risks."

Small Circulation Magazines

This section of *Novel & Short Story Writer's Market* contains general interest, special interest, regional and genre magazines with circulations of under 10,000. Although these magazines vary greatly in size, theme, format and management, the editors are all looking for short stories for their respective publications. Their specific fiction needs present writers of all degrees of expertise and interests with an abundance of publishing opportunities.

Although not as high-paying as the large-circulation commercial magazines, all the publications listed here do pay writers 1-5¢/word or more. Also unlike the big commercial magazines, these markets are very open to new writers and relatively easy to break into. Their only criteria is that your story be well written, well presented, and suitable for their particular readership.

DIVERSITY IN OPPORTUNITY

Among the diverse publications in this section are magazines devoted to almost every topic, every level of writing and every type of writer. Paying genre magazines include *Marion Zimmer Bradley's Fantasy Magazine* (3-10¢/word); *Worlds of Fantasy & Horror* (3¢/word minimum); and *Mystery Time* (¼-1¢/word).

Some of the markets listed here publish fiction about a particular geographic area or by authors who live in that locale. A few of those regional publications are *Italian Americana*; *Keltic Fringe*; *Big Sky Stories*; and *Texas Young Writers' Newsletter*.

Publications with even more specialized editorial needs than genre and regional fiction include *The Healing Inn*, "geared to encouraging Christians who have been wounded by a church or religious cult"; *Housewife-Writer's Forum*, offering "support for women and house husbands who juggle writing with family life"; *Inner Voices*, publishing literature by prisoners; *Mentor & Protege* wanting stories that are mentoring related; and *Rosebud, For People Who Enjoy Writing*.

SELECTING THE RIGHT MARKET

Your chance for publication begins as you zero in on those markets most likely to be interested in your work. If you write a particular type of fiction, such as mystery, romance or science fiction, check the Category Index (starting on page 641) for the appropriate subject heading. If your work is more general, or, in fact, very specialized, you may wish to browse through the listings, perhaps looking up those magazines published in your state or region. Also check the Zine section for other specialized and genre publications.

In addition to browsing through the listings and using the Category Index, check the ranking codes at the beginning of listings to find those most likely to be receptive to your work. This is especially true for beginning writers, who should look for magazines that say they are especially open to new writers (**I**) and for those giving equal weight to both new and established writers (**II**). For more explanation about these codes, see the end of this introduction.

Once you have a list of magazines you might like to try, read their listings carefully. Much of the material within each listing carries clues that tell you more about the magazine. How to Use This Book to Publish Your Fiction starting on page 3 describes in detail the listing information common to all the markets in our book.

The physical description appearing near the beginning of the listings can give you clues about the size and financial commitment to the publication. This is not always an indication of quality, but chances are a publication with expensive paper and four-color artwork on the cover has more prestige than a photocopied publication featuring a clip art self-cover. For more information on some of the paper, binding and printing terms used in these descriptions, see Printing and Production Terms Defined on page 636.

FURTHERING YOUR SEARCH

It cannot be stressed enough that reading the listing is only the first part of developing your marketing plan. The second part, equally important, is to obtain fiction guidelines and read the actual magazine. Reading copies of a magazine helps you determine the fine points of the magazine's publishing style and philosophy. There is no substitute for this type of hands-on research.

Unlike commercial magazines available at most newsstands and bookstores, it requires a little more effort to obtain some of the magazines listed here. You may need to send for a sample copy. We include sample copy prices in the listings whenever possible.

FOR MORE INFORMATION

See The Business of Fiction Writing for the specific mechanics of manuscript submission. Above all, editors appreciate a professional presentation. Include a brief cover letter and send a self-addressed envelope for a reply or a self-addressed envelope in a size large enough to accommodate your manuscript, if you would like it returned. Be sure to include enough stamps or International Reply Coupons (for replies from countries other than your own) to cover your manuscript's return. Many publishers today appreciate receiving a disposable manuscript, eliminating the cost to writers of return postage and saving editors the effort of repackaging manuscripts for return.

Most of the magazines listed here are published in the US. You will also find some English-speaking markets from around the world. These foreign publications are denoted with an asterisk (*) at the beginning of listings. To make it easier to find Canadian markets, we include a maple leaf symbol (♦) at the start of those listings.

The following is the ranking system we have used to categorize the listings in this section.

   I **Publication encourages beginning or unpublished writers to submit work for consideration and publishes new writers regularly.**

   II **Publication accepts work by established writers and by writers of exceptional talent.**

   III **Publication does not encourage beginning writers; prints mostly writers with previous publication credits; very few new writers.**

   IV **Special-interest or regional publication, open only to writers in certain genres or on certain subjects or from certain geographical areas.**

   V **Closed to unsolicited submissions.**

‡**ABERRATIONS, Science Fiction, Fantasy and Horror, (II)**, Sirius Fiction, P.O. Box 460430, San Francisco CA 94146-0430. Editor: Richard Blair. Magazine: digest size; 64 pages; 80 lb. pulp paper; 40 lb. enamel cover; illustrations and photos. "A magazine of speculative stories running the gamut from pulp-era science fiction/fantasy/horror of the 30s and 40s to the experimental and literary work of today." Monthly. Estab. 1992. Circ. 1,500.
Needs: Experimental, fantasy (science fantasy, sword and sorcery), horror, science fiction (hard science, soft/ sociological). No true-crime stories. Receives 250-300 unsolicited mss/month. Accepts 10 mss/issue; 120 mss/ year. Publishes ms 1 year after acceptance. Agented fiction 1-2%. Recently published work by Paul Di Filippo, Don Webb, Carrie Martin, T. Jackson King, Lois Tilton, Gerard Daniel Houarner, Kent Brewster, Uncle River and Brian Plante. Length: 1 word minimum; 8,000 words maximum. Publishes short shorts. Also publishes literary essays and literary criticism. Sometimes critiques or comments on rejected mss.
How to Contact: Send complete ms with a cover letter. Include estimated word count. Reports in 2 weeks on queries; 4 months on mss. Send SASE for reply, return of ms or send disposable copy of ms. No simultaneous submissions. Sample copy for $4.50. Fiction guidelines for #10 SASE. Reviews novels and short story collections. Send books to "John F.D. Taff, Reviews Editor."

Payment/Terms: Pays½ cent/word plus two contributor's copies for first English language serial rights.
Advice: "We like stories that take chances (whether this be through characterization, plotting or structuring) as well as those that take a more traditional approach to sf/f/h."

ABOVE THE BRIDGE, (IV), Third Stone Publishing, P.O. Box 416, Marquette MI 49855. (906)494-2458. E-mail: classen@mail.portup.com. Website: http://www.portup.com/ABOVE. Editor: Mikel B. Classen. Magazine: 8½×11; 56 pages; 80 lb. text paper; 80 lb. LOE cover stock; illustrations and photos. "For and about the Upper Peninsula of Michigan." Bimonthly. Estab. 1985. Circ. 5,000.
Needs: Regional. "Any stories pertaining to the Upper Peninsula of Michigan." Family-oriented magazine. "We appreciate disk submissions, using fiction online." Receives 15-20 unsolicited mss/month. Accepts 12-13 mss/year. Publishes ms up to 2 years after acceptance. Length: 800-1,000 words average; 300 words minimum; 2,000 words maximum. Publishes short stories and short venues. Length: 300-400 words. Also publishes literary essays and literary criticism.
How to Contact: Send complete ms with a cover letter. Should include estimated word count, bio, name, address, phone number. Reports in 6-8 months. Send SASE for reply, return of ms or send a disposable copy of ms. Simultaneous and reprint submissions OK. Sample copy for $3.50. Fiction guidelines free.
Payment/Terms: Pays 2¢/word on publication. "If your material is used online, you will be paid double (online plus in print)." Buys one-time rights.
Advice: "Make certain that the manuscript pertains to the Upper Peninsula of Michigan. If you've never been there, don't fake it."

‡*ALTAIR, Alternative Airings in Speculative Fiction, (II), Altair Publishing, P.O. Box 475, Blackwood, South Australia 5051. +61 (8)8278 8995. Fax: +61 (8)8278 5585. E-mail: altair@senet.com.au. Website: http://www.ozemail.com.ow/robsteph/fstguide.htm. Editor/Fiction Editor: Robert N. Stephenson. Fiction Editor: Jason Bleckly. Magazine: A5; 152 pages; 80ssm bond paper; 250ssm glossy cover stock; illustrations. "We publish speculative fiction with a focus on science fiction and fantasy; a good mix of the two encouraged. We like character-driven stories."
Needs: Fantasy (science fantasy), mystery/suspense, science fiction (hard science, soft/sociological, some cyberpunk). Accepts 6-10 mss/issue; 12-70/year. Length: 5,000 words average; 2,000 words minimum; 6,500 words maximum. Publishes short shorts (length: 1,500 words). Sometimes critiques or comments on rejected mss.
How to Contact: Send complete ms with a cover letter. Include estimated word count and 5-line bio. "Return postage is essential or e-mail address; not read otherwise." Reports in 2 months on mss. SASE (or IRCs) for reply or return of ms. Sample copy for $10 (US) (includes international postage: air) and A5 SAE with 2 IRCs. As all copies are limited editions the price is projected by age." Fiction guidelines for SASE (or 1 IRC).
Payment/Terms: Pays 3 cents/word and 1 contributor's copy; additional copies $10. Acquires first world serial rights. Issue #1 is a large international competition open to all writers. Information available from website.
Advice: "We want strong characters, good, clear ideas and a believable plot. We are not interested in single-faceted work; localized slang is not good for an international audience. We are looking for cultural influences and this will show through the writer's talent."

*AMMONITE, 12 Priory Mead, Bruton Somerset BA100DZ United Kingdom. Fiction Editor: John Howard-Greaves. Occasionally. Circ. 200.
Needs: "Myth, legend, science fiction to do with the current passage of evolution towards the possibilities of the Aquarian Age." Publishes 3-7 stories/issue. Length: no minimum; 2,500 words maximum.
Payment/Terms: Pays 1 contributor copy.

ANTERIOR FICTION QUARTERLY, (II), Anterior Bitewing Ltd.®, 993 Allspice Ave., Fenton MO 63026-4901. (314)343-1761. E-mail address: 72247.1405@compuserve.com. Editor: Tom Bergeron. Newsletter: 8½×11; 20 pages; 20 lb. bond paper; 20 lb. bond cover; some illustrations. "Good, easy-reading stories with a point or punch line, general interest; audience tends to be over 50." Quarterly. Estab. 1993. Circ. 50.
Needs: Adventure, historical, humor/satire, literary, mainstream/contemporary, mystery/suspense, psychic/supernatural/occult, regional, romance, sports. No "protests, causes, bigotry, sickness, fanatacism, soap." Receives 25 unsolicited mss/month. Accepts 10 mss/issue; 40 mss/year. Publishes ms 1-3 years after acceptance. Recently published work by Mildred Hechler, Marian Ford Park, Wendell Metzger, Lee Wallerstein and Sylvia Roberts. Length: 1,000 words preferred; 500 words minimum; 2,500 words maximum. Occasionally publishes short shorts. Length: 100-500 words. Always critiques or comments on rejected mss.
How to Contact: *Charges $2 reading fee per story to nonsubscribers.* Reports in 1 week on queries; 2 weeks on mss. Send SASE for reply and return of ms. Simultaneous, reprint and electronic submissions OK. Sample copy for $2. Fiction guidelines for SASE.
Payment/Terms: Pays up to $25 on publication for one-time rights; "$25 prize for best story in each issue. No other payments."
Advice: Looks for "good gimmicks; twists; imagination; likeable characters; departures from the everyday. Read Bernard Malamud, James Thurber, Guy De Maupassant, Henry James."

‡ANTHOLOGY, (I, II), Inkwell Press, P.O. Box 4411, Mesa AZ 85211-4411. (602)461-8200. E-mail: anthology@juno.com. Editor: Sharon Skinner. Magazine: 8½×11; 20-28 pages; 20 lb. paper; 60-100 lb. cover stock;

illustrations and photos. "Our intended audience is anyone who likes to read." Bimonthly. Estab. 1994. Circ. 250-500.

Needs: Adventure, children's/juvenile (5-9 and 10-12 years); fantasy (science fantasy, sword and sorcery), humor/satire, literary, mystery/suspense (amateur sleuth, police procedural, private eye/hardboiled), science fiction (hard science, soft/sociological). *Anthology* maintains an ongoing series of short stories based in the Mythical City of Haven. Information in guidelines. Receives 10-20 unsolicited mss/month. Accepts 2 mss/issue; 12 mss/year. Publishes ms 6-12 months after acceptance. Length: 3,000-6,000 words average; Haven stories 3,000-5,000 words. Publishes short shorts. Also publishes poetry.

How to Contact: Send complete ms with a cover letter. Include estimated word count. Reports in 4 weeks on queries; 6 weeks on mss. Send SASE for reply, return of ms or send disposable copy of ms. Simultaneous, reprint and electronic (disk or modem) submissions OK. Sample copy for 9×12 SAE with 5 first-class stamps. Fiction guidelines for 4½×9½ SASE.

Payment/Terms: Pays 2 contributor's copies; additional copies $2. Haven stories pay $5. Acquires one-time rights. *Anthology* retains rights to reprint any Haven story, however, author may submit the story elsewhere for simultaneous publication.

Advice: "Is there passion in the writing? Is there forethought? Will the story make an emotional connection to the reader? Send for guidelines and a sample issue. If you see that your work would not only fit into, but add something to *Anthology*, then send it."

‡ARACHNE, INC., (II), Arachne, hanging by a thread, Inc., 2363 Page Rd., Kennedy NY 14747-9717. Editor: Susan L. Leach. Chapbook: 8½×5; 25 pages; 20 lb. paper; 20 lb. cover; illustrations; b&w photos. Semiannually. Estab. 1980. Circ. 500.

Needs: Regional. "No obscenity, no pornography." List of upcoming themes available for SASE. Receives 50 unsolicited mss/month. Buys 4 mss/issue; 8-10 mss/year. Does not read mss during Christmas. Publishes ms 3 months after acceptance. Recently published work by Anne Thore Beacham. Length: 1,500 words average; 1,200 words minimum; 1,800 words maximum. Also publishes literary criticism, poetry. Sometimes critiques or comments on rejected ms.

How to Contact: Query with or without clips of published work or send complete ms with a cover letter. Should include estimated word count, bio. Reports in 2 weeks on queries; 2 months on mss. Send SASE for reply, return of ms or send a disposable copy of ms. No simultaneous submissions. Sample copy for $2.50.

Payment/Terms: Pays 2 contributor's copies; additional copies for $2. Acquires first rights. Sends galleys to author. Not copyrighted.

Advice: "Send clean laser-printed copy using a simple font—only a few poems at a time. I am not interested in reading seductive poetry or conquer-the-world poetry—so please, read a copy of *Arachne* first."

*AUGURIES, Morton Publishing, P.O. Box 23, Gosport, Hants P012 2XD England. Editor: Nik Morton. Circ. 300.

Needs: "Science fiction and fantasy, maximum length 4,000 words." Averages 15 stories/year. Publishes 6 new writers/year.

Payment/Terms: Pays £2 per 1,000 words plus complimentary copy. "Buy back issues, then try me!" Sample copy for $10. Subscription (2 issues) $30 to 'Morton Publishing.' Member of the New SF Alliance.

Advice: "Rewrite, put it away, rewrite. Be self-critical. Ask yourself: What am I saying—what do I mean?"

‡*AUREALIS, Australian Fantasy and Science Fiction, P.O. Box 2164, Mt. Waverley, Victoria 3149 Australia. Website: http://aurealis.hl.net. Fiction Editors: Dirk Strasser and Stephen Higgins. Semiannually. Circ. 2,500.

Needs: Publishes 6 stories/issue: science fiction, fantasy and horror short stories. Length: 1,500 words minimum; 6,000 words maximum.

How to Contact: "No reprints; no stories accepted elsewhere. Send one story at a time."

Payment/Terms: Pays 2-6¢ (Australian)/word and contributor's copy. Sample copy for $8 (Australian). Writer's guidelines available for SAE with IRC.

Advice: "Read the magazine. It is available in the UK and North America."

‡BANGTALE INTERNATIONAL, (II), Wild Horse Press, P.O. Box 83984, Phoenix AZ 85071. (602)993-4989. E-mail: bangtalerimenet.com. Editor: William Dudley. Magazine: 8½×5½; 64 pages; 70 lb. paper; 80 lb. cover. "To publish work from and about as many different cultures and countries as we can." Semiannually. Estab. 1994. Circ. 500.

Needs: Adventure, children's/juvenile (1-4, 5-9, 10-12 years), condensed/excerpted novel, ethnic/multicultural, historical, humor/satire, literary, mystery/suspense, regional, romance, translations, westerns, young adult/teen. Receives 50 unsolicited mss/month. Accepts 4 mss/issue; 8 mss/year. Publishes ms 4-6 months after acceptance. Recently published work by Gabrielle Banks and Molly Caldwell. Length: 1,500 words average; 500 words minimum; 2,000 words maximum. Publishes short shorts. Also publishes literary essays, literary criticism and poetry. Sometimes critiques or comments on rejected mss.

How to Contact: Send complete ms with a cover letter. Include estimated word count, and bio. Reports in 4-6 months on mss. Send SASE for reply, return of ms or send disposable copy of ms. Simultaneous and electronic submissions OK. Sample copy for $5 and 8½×11 envelope with $1.50 postage. Fiction guidelines for #10 SASE.

Payment/Terms: Pays $10 minimum; $25 maximum on publication for one-time rights. Sometimes sends galleys to author. Not copyrighted.

Advice: "Write what you know and that which you feel strongly about. We want work that can be understood, work that has feeling, as opposed to work that is obscure and evasive."

☘**BARDIC RUNES, (I, IV)**, 424 Cambridge St, Ottawa, Ontario K1S 4H5 Canada. (613)231-4311. E-mail address: bn872@freenet.carleton.ca. Editor: Michael McKenny. Magazine. Estab. 1990.

Needs: Fantasy. "Traditional or high fantasy. Story should be set in pre-industrial society either historical or of author's invention." Recently published work by Frida Westford, D.K. Latta, Cherith Baldry, Ross G. Kouhi, Ceri Jordan and Jeanny Driscoll. Length: 3,500 words or less.

How to Contact: Electronic submissions OK. For e-mail, send plain unencoded ASCII. "Others may not reach me and, if they do, I may not even reply." For disk, send WordPerfect or ASCII. "No need to unencode."

Payment/Terms: Pays ½¢/word on acceptance. Reports in 2 weeks.

Advice: "Writers, pay keen attention to our stated needs or your story will probably be rejected, however good it may be. We now have more subscribers and more contributors from around the world. Read on every continent except Antarctica."

BIG SKY STORIES, (II), P.O. Box 477, Choteau MT 59422. (406)466-5300. Editor: Happy Feder. 8½×11; 48 pages; heavy bond paper; illustrations and photos. "We publish fiction set in Big Sky Country (Montana, Wyoming, North and South Dakota) prior to 1950. Don't fake the history or geography. Our readers want to be entertained and educated!" Bimonthly. Estab. 1996. Circ. 4,000.

Needs: Historical. Publishes special fiction issues or anthologies. Accepts 2-4 mss/issue. Also publishes literary essays. Recently published work by Johnny D. Boggs, Richard Wheeler, Stan Lynde and Gwen Petersen. Publishes 6-10 new writers/year. Often critiques or comments on rejected ms.

How to Contact: Send complete ms with a cover letter. Should include estimated word count and list of publications with submission. Reports in 1-2 months. Send SASE for reply, return of ms or send a disposable copy of ms. Simultaneous and reprint submissions OK. Sample copy for $4, 8½×11 SAE and 2 first-class stamps. Fiction guidelines for SASE. Reviews novels and short story collections.

Payment/Terms: Pays minimum 1¢/word on publication for first publication rights.

Advice: "Your first paragraph should introduce where, when, who and what, and the story must be set in Big Sky Country. Don't bluff or offer 'soft' history, i.e., a story that, with a few name/place changes, could take place in Ohio or Maryland or Okinawa. Know your Big Sky history."

BLACK BOOKS BULLETIN: WORDSWORK, (IV), Third World Press, P.O. Box 19730, Chicago IL 60619-0730. (773)651-0700. Fax: (773)651-7286. Editor: Haki R. Madhubuti. Magazine: 80 pages. "*Black Books Bulletin: WordsWork* publishes progressive material related to an enlightened African-American audience." Annually.

● In addition to publishing fiction, *Black Books Bulletin: WordsWork* is primarily a review publication covering nonfiction, fiction and poetry books by African-American authors.

Needs: Condensed/excerpted novel, ethnic/multicultural, feminist, historical (general). Receives 40 unsolicited mss/month. Accepts 2 mss/issue. Does not read mss January through June. Publishes ms 1 year after acceptance. Agented fiction 20%. Published work by Amiri Baraka, Keorapetse Kgositsile. Also publishes literary essays, literary criticism, poetry. Sometimes critiques or comments on rejected mss.

How to Contact: Query first. Include estimated word count and bio. Reports in 3 weeks on queries; 3 months on mss. Simultaneous and reprint submissions OK. Reviews novels and short story collections. Send books to Assistant Editor David Kelly.

Payment/Terms: Pays on publication. Acquires all rights.

BLACKFIRE, (I, IV), BLK Publishing Co., P.O. Box 83912, Los Angeles CA 90083-0912. (310)410-0808. Fax: (310)410-9250. E-mail: newsroom@blk.com. Website: http://www.blk.com. Editor: Alan Bell. Magazine: 8⅛×10⅞; 48 pages; color glossy throughout; illustrations and photographs. Bimonthly magazine featuring the erotic images, experiences and fantasies of black gay and bisexual men. Estab. 1992.

● BLK is a member of COSMEP.

Needs: Ethnic/multicultural, gay. No interracial stories or idealized pornography. Accepts 4 mss/issue. Recently published work by Terrance 'Kenji' Evans, Geoff Adams, Thomas Dremel, Stefan Collins and Robert Wesley. Publishes short shorts. Also publishes poetry.

How to Contact: Query first, query with clips of published work or send complete ms with a cover letter.

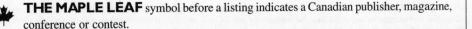

THE MAPLE LEAF symbol before a listing indicates a Canadian publisher, magazine, conference or contest.

Should include bio (3 sentences). Send a disposable copy of ms. No simultaneous submissions; electronic submissions OK. Sample copy for $7. Fiction guidelines free.

Payment/Terms: Pays free subscription, 5 contributor's copies. Acquires first North American serial rights and right to anthologize.

Advice: "*Blackfire* seeks erotic material of the highest quality. The most important thing is that the work be erotic and that it features black gay men or themes. Study the magazine to see what we do and how we do it. Some fiction is very romantic, other is highly sexual. Most articles in *Blackfire* cater to black gay/bisexual men between these two extremes."

‡*BLOODSONGS, P.O. Box 7530, St. Kilda Rd., Melbourne Victoria, 3004, Australia or % Implosion, P.O. Box 533653, Orlando FL 32853. Phone/fax: 03 9380 6840. E-mail: bambada@melbourne.dialix.oz.au. Fiction Editors: Chris A. Masters and Steve Proposch. Quarterly. Circ. 6,000 (Australian), 2,000 (US).

Needs: "Horror magazine." Publishes 4-6 stories/issue. Recently published work by Kaaron Warren, Mary Fortune, Steve Rasnk Tem, Stephen Dedman, Gary Bowen and Carolyn Logan. Length: 1,000 words minimum; 10,000 words maximum.

How to Contact: "Always attach a cover sheet to the front of the ms stating: the name of the piece; the name of the author (if a pen name is used, make it clear which is which); author's address and phone number (phone number not necessary but preferred); if the piece has been published previously or is due to be published elsewhere (include when and where); if it is a multiple submission; who owns the rights, and what rights are being offered. Include a cover letter stating that you are offering the piece for publication. Also include a paragraph or two about yourself (which will be used to make up an author's bio note which will go at the end of each story). Also let us know if the piece is available on computer disk and in what format."

Payment/Terms: Pays $20 (Australian) for first Australian rights and contributor's copies. Writer's guidelines available for SASE (IRC). Sample copy for $8 (US)—surface to anywhere in the world. Make payable to "Barmbada Press."

Advice: "We are only interested in well written, original stories that contain strong elements of horror. It's okay to use a fantasy/science fiction/crime background or setting, but it must be a horror story first to be considered. When dealing with sub-genres (i.e., vampires, Cthulhu Mythos, serial killers, demonic possession, etc.) that have become cliché-ridden, be original. If you can't take an overused genre and offer it something new, turn it inside out, or rework it in such a way to give it your own voice, don't bother."

BOY'S QUEST, (II), The Bluffton News Publishing & Printing Co., P.O. Box 227, Bluffton OH 45817. (419)358-4610. Fax: (419)358-5027. Editor: Marilyn Edwards. Magazine: 7×9; 50 pages; enamel paper; illustrations and photos. Bimonthly. Estab. 1994.

• *Boy's Quest* received an EDPRESS Distinguished Achievement Award for Excellence in Educational Journalism, and a Silver Award-Gallery of Superb Printing.

Needs: Adventure, children's/juvenile (5-9 years, 10-12 years), ethnic/multicultural, historical, sports. Upcoming themes: astronomy, states, US presidents, weather, inventions, Indians. List of upcoming themes available for SASE. Receives 300-400 unsolicited mss/month. Accepts 20-40 mss/year. Agented fiction 2%. Published work by Jean Patrick, Eve Marar and Linda Herman. Length: 300-500 words average; 500 words maximum. Publishes short shorts. Length: 250-400 words. Also publishes poetry. Always critiques or comments on rejected mss.

How to Contact: Send complete ms with a cover letter. Include estimated word count, 1 page bio, Social Security number, list of publications. Reports in 2-4 weeks on queries; 6-10 weeks on mss. Simultaneous and reprint submissions OK. Sample copy for $3. Fiction guidelines for #10 SASE. Reviews novels and short story collections.

Payment/Terms: Pays 5¢/word and 1 contributor's copy on publication for first North American serial rights; additional copies $3, $2 for 10 or more.

Advice: Looks for "wholesome material. Follow our theme list and study copies of the magazine."

MARION ZIMMER BRADLEY'S FANTASY MAGAZINE, (II, IV), Box 249, Berkeley CA 94701-0249. (510)644-9222. Website: http://www.mzlfm.com (includes writer's guidelines, articles on writing, back issue index). Editor and Publisher: Marion Zimmer Bradley. Magazine: 8½×11; 64 pages; 60 lb. text paper; 10 lb. cover stock; b&w interior and 4-color cover illustrations. "Fantasy only; strictly family oriented." Quarterly.

• This magazine is named for and edited by one of the pioneers of fantasy fiction. Bradley is perhaps best known for the multi-volume Darkover series.

Needs: Fantasy. May include adventure, contemporary, humor/satire, mystery/suspense and young adult/teen (10-18) (all with fantasy elements). "No avant-garde or romantic fantasy. No computer games!" Receives 50-200 unsolicited mss/week. Accepts 8-10 mss/issue; 36-40 mss/year. Publishes ms 3-12 months after acceptance. Agented fiction 5%. Recently published work by India Edghill, Steven Piziks, Jo Clayton, Karen Anderson, Marion Zimmer Bradley and Dorothy J. Heydt. Publishes 10 new writers/year. Length: 3,000-4,000 words average; 5,500 words maximum. Publishes short shorts.

How to Contact: Send #10 SASE for guidelines *before* sending ms. Send complete ms. SASE. Reports in 90 days. No simultaneous submissions. Sample copy for $4.

Payment/Terms: Pays 3-10¢/word on acceptance and contributor's copies for first North American serial rights.

Advice: "If I want to finish reading it—I figure other people will too. A manuscript stands out if I care whether the characters do well, if it has a rhythm. Make sure it has characters I will know *you* care about. If you don't care about them, how do you expect me to? Read guidelines *before* sending ms. Beware of 'dime-a-dozen' subjects such as dragons, elves, unicorns, wizards, vampires, writers, sea creatures, brute warriors, ghosts, adventuring sorcerers/sorceresses, thieves/assassins, or final exams for wizards. We get dozens of these kinds of stories every week, and we reject all but the truly unusual and well-written ones."

BRILLIANT STAR, (II), National Spiritual Assembly of the Baha'is of the U.S., Baha'i, National Center, 1233 Central St., Evanston IL 60201. (847)869-9039. Managing Editor: Pepper Peterson Oldziey. Fiction Editor: Cindy Savage. Magazine: 8½×11; 33 pages; matte paper; glossy cover; illustrations; photos. "A magazine for Baha'i children about the history, teachings and beliefs of the Baha'i faith. Manuscripts should reflect spiritual principles of the baha'i" For children approximately 5-12 years old. Bimonthly. Estab. 1969. Circ. 2,300.

Needs: Adventure, children's/juvenile, ethnic, historical, humor/satire, mystery/suspense, spiritual, young adult/teen (10-12 years). "Accepts inspirational fiction if not overtly preachy or moralistic and if not directly Christian and related directly to Christian holidays." Receives 30 unsolicited mss/month. Accepts 1-2 mss/issue; 6-12 mss/year. Publishes ms no sooner than 6 months after acceptance. Published work by Susan Pethick and John Paulits; published new writers within the last year. Length: 100 words minimum; 600 words maximum. "Length should correlate with intended audience—very short mss for young readers, longer mss must be for older readers (ages 10-12), and intended for their interests." Publishes short shorts. Also publishes poetry.

How to Contact: No queries. Send complete ms. Cover letter not essential. Reports in 6-10 weeks on mss. SASE. Simultaneous submissions OK "but please make a notation that it is a simultaneous sub." Sample copy for $2, 9×12 SAE and 5 oz. postage. Fiction guidelines for #10 SASE.

Payment/Terms: Pays in contributor's copies (two); charges for extras.

Terms: "Writer can retain own copyright or grant to the National Spiritual Assembly of the Baha'is of the U.S."

Advice: "We enjoy working with beginning writers and try to develop a constructive collaborative relationship with those who show promise and sensitivity to our aims and focus. We feel that the children's market is open to a wide variety of writers: fiction, nonfiction, science, photo-essays. Our needs for appealing fiction especially for pre-schoolers and young readers make us a good market for new writers. *Please*, have a story to tell! The single main reason for rejection of manuscripts we review is lack of plot to infuse the story with energy and make the reader want to come along, as well as length to age/interest level mismatch. Longer stories must be intended for older children. Only very short stories are useable for young audiences. We love stories about different cultures and ethnic groups. We also welcome submissions that offer solutions to the problems kids face today. We're looking for active, child-oriented writing, not passive, preachy prose."

BURNING LIGHT, (II), A Journal of Christian Literature, Burning Light Press, 4 Robin Lane, West Nilford NJ 07480. (201)208-3087. Editor: Carl Simmons. Magazine: 5½×8½; 32-48 pages; 50 lb. Nekoosa paper; 80 lb. classic laid cover; illustrations. "*Burning Light* publishes fiction, essays and poetry from a Christian perspective. It's worth noting, though, that we want Christians who write and not 'Christian writing.' No one's going to mistake us for *Christianity Today* or *Guideposts*, although hopefully *Kenyon Review*, et al. will come to mind before they catch on to our drift." Quarterly. Estab. 1993.

Needs: Condensed/excerpted novel, experimental, humor/satire, literary, religious/inspirational, science fiction (soft/sociological), serialized novel. No fantasy. Receives 15-20 unsolicited mss/month. Accepts 2-4 mss/issue; 10-15 mss/year. Publishes ms 1-9 months (4-6 months typical) after acceptance. Recently published work by Albert Haley and Sandra Tucker-Maxwell. Publishes 3-6 new writers/year. Length: 1,500-2,000 words average; 10,000 words maximum. Publishes short shorts. Also publishes literary essays, poetry. Sometimes critiques or comments on rejected mss.

How to Contact: Send complete ms with a cover letter. Include estimated word count, 3-4 sentence bio, list of publications. Reports in 3-4 weeks. Send SASE for reply, return of ms or send a disposable copy of ms. Simultaneous and electronic (disk: WordPerfect 5.1, PageMaker 4 or Quark 3.3 preferably) submissions OK. Sample copy for $4. Fiction guidelines free. Reviews novels and short story collections.

Payment/Terms: Pays free subscription to magazine, 5-6 contributor's copies; additional copies for $2.50. Acquires all rights (negotiable).

Advice: "Make sure the writing's coming from you; don't write something because you think it's what a publisher wants."

‡❦CHALLENGING DESTINY, New Fantasy & Science Fiction, (I), Crystalline Sphere Publishing, R.R. #6, St. Mary's Ontario N4X 1C8 Canada. (519)884-7557. E-mail: csp@golden.net. Editors: David M. Switzer and Graham D. Wall. Magazine: 8½×5½; 100 pages; Kallima 10 pt cover; illustrations. "We publish all kinds of science fiction and fantasy short stories." Quarterly. Estab. 1997. Circ. 500.

Needs: Fantasy, science fiction. Receives 15 unsolicited mss/month. Accepts 7 mss/issue, 28 mss/year. Publishes ms 1-3 months after acceptance. Recently published work by Michael Mirolla, James Schellenberg, Timothy Dyck, Gord Zajac and Charles Conrad. Length: 6,000 words average; 1,000 words minimum; 8,000 words maximum. Also publishes literary essays, literary criticism and poetry. Often critiques or comments on rejected mss.

How to Contact: Send complete ms with a cover letter. Include estimated word count. Reports in 1 month on queries, 2 months on mss. Send SASE for reply, return of ms or send disposable copy of ms. Simultaneous, reprint and electronic submissions OK. Sample copy for $5.50. Guidelines for 2 IRCs. Reviews novels and short story collections. Send books to James Schellenberg, R.R. #1, 4421 Spring Creek Rd., Vineland Ontario L0R 2C0 Canada.

Payment/Terms: Pays 2 contributor's copies for first North American serial rights. Sends galleys to author.

Advice: "Manuscripts with a good story and interesting characters stand out. We look for fiction that entertains and makes you think. If you're going to write short fiction, you need to read lots of it. Don't reinvent the wheel. Use your own voice. We've been on the Web since the beginning and are accepting submissions over e-mail. A lot of action is happening online these days."

THE CHINOOK QUARTERLY, (II), Chinook Press, 1432 Yellowstone Ave., Billings MT 59102. (406)245-7704. Editor: Mary Ellen Westwood. Magazine: 7×8½; 60-80 pages; acid-free paper; card cover stock; illustrations; photos. "*The Chinook Quarterly* will be a catalyst for human change and understanding. We want forward-looking and challenging submissions that will be of use to readers in the West." Quarterly. Estab. 1996.

Needs: Adventure, children's/juvenile (10-12 years), condensed/excerpted novel, ethnic/multicultural, experimental, fantasy (science fantasy), feminist, historical, humor/satire, literary, mainstream/contemporary, mystery/suspense (all kinds), regional, romance (contemporary, futuristic/time travel), science fiction (hard science, soft/sociological), sports, translations, westerns, young adult/teen (all kinds). Especially interested in stories about the contemporary West. "No fiction that degrades or discounts human beings." Accepts 4-6 mss/issue; 16-24 mss/year. Publishes ms 1-12 months after acceptance. Length: 1,600 words average; 300 words minimum; 2,000 words maximum. Publishes short shorts. Also publishes literary essays, literary criticism and poetry. Often critiques or comments on rejected mss.

How to Contact: Send complete ms with a cover letter. Include estimated word count, 250-word bio, Social Security number, list of publications and explanation of the piece submitted (why did you write it?)." Send SASE for return of ms. Reprints OK. Sample copy for $7. Fiction guidelines for #10 SASE. Reviews novels and short story collections.

Payment/Terms: Pays $2/printed page and 4 contributor's copies on publication. Acquires one-time rights. Sends galleys to the author.

Advice: "I am looking for a fresh and daring approach and a thinking view of the world. I admire risk takers. I want writing about real people, not just academic musings. I want the true life experiences of humans, not some shallow misinterpretations. Edit, edit, edit . . . after you rewrite, of course."

✤CHRISTIAN COURIER, (II, IV), Calvinist Contact Publishing Limited, Unit 4, 261 Martindale Rd., St. Catharines, Ontario L2W 1A1 Canada. (905)682-8311. Fax: (905)682-8313. E-mail: cceditor@aol.com. Editor: Bert Witvoet. Tabloid: 11½×14; 20 pages; newsprint; illustrations and photos. Weekly. Estab. 1945. Circ. 5,000.

Needs: Adventure, children's/juvenile (10-12 years), historical, religious/inspirational, senior citizen/retirement, sports and translations. No "sentimental 'religious' stuff; superficial moralizing." Receives 5-10 unsolicited mss/month. Accepts 12 mss/year. Does not read mss from the end of July through early August. Publishes ms within a month after acceptance. Length: 1,200 words average; no minimum; 1,400 words maximum. Publishes short shorts. Length 500 words. Also publishes literary essays (if not too technical), literary criticism and poetry. Always critiques or comments on rejected mss.

How to Contact: Send complete ms with a cover letter. Include word count and bio (100 words maximum). Reports in 3 weeks on queries; 4-6 weeks on mss. Send a disposable copy of ms. Simultaneous, reprint and electronic submissions OK. Sample copy free. Fiction guidelines for SASE. Reviews novels and short story collections.

Payment/Terms: Pays $25-60 on publication and 1 contributor's copy (on request). Acquires one-time rights.

Advice: Looks for work "geared to a Christian audience but reflecting the real world, real dilemmas, without pat resolutions—written in an engaging, clear manner."

‡CITIES AND ROADS, a collection of short stories for North Carolina readers and writers, (I, II, IV), P.O. Box 10886, Greensboro NC 27404. E-mail: cities@nr.infi.net. Editor: Tom Kealey. Magazine: 5½×8½; 120 pages; acid-free paper; 70 lb. cover stock. *Cities and Roads* provides a forum for emerging and established North Carolina fiction writers. "We have published a number of the state's finest authors, and there are two slots open, every issue, for previously unpublished writers." Semiannually. Estab. 1995. Circ. 500.

Needs: Open to all genres. "This is a magazine for North Carolina residents and visiting students. Stories with subtle humor and a touch of sadness get our attention quickly. Please don't send us work with the word 'mama' used in the first paragraph. We've only accepted one out of about eighty submissions with that word used at the beginning (and that story was really good)." Publishes a "best of" issue. Receives 200-250 unsolicited mss/year. Accepts 24 mss/year. Publishes ms 2-6 months after acceptance. Recently published work by Sandra Redding, Jon Obermeyer, Kyle Torke, Tom Lanier and HS Mills. Length: 6,000 words maximum. Publishes short shorts. Rarely critiques or comments on rejected mss.

How to Contact: Send complete ms with a cover letter. Include list of publications. "Charm us—we tape some cover letters (lovingly) to the refrigerator." Reports in 3 months on mss. Send SASE for reply, return of ms or send disposable copy of ms. Simultaneous and electronic submissions OK. Sample copy for $7. Fiction guidelines for #10 SASE.

Payment/Terms: Pays 2 contributor's copies for first North American serial rights "and the knowledge that your story has survived a rigorous selection process and will bring happiness to attractive (some might say 'sexy') readers of various age groups and genders."

Advice: "If you want to be published in *Cities and Roads*, write a story about a character most people would like to meet. Put him or her in a situation of peril or opportunity. Add in additional characters to help or hinder the person. Don't wrap it all up nice and neat at the end—life is messy and your story should be too. If you make the editors chuckle or think of a lost love or remember a lovely autumn afternoon, then you get big bonus points. In your short cover letter tell us a little about yourself and why you wrote the story."

CLUBHOUSE MAGAZINE, Focus on the Family, (IV), 8605 Explorer Dr., Colorado Springs CO 80920. (719)531-3400, ext. 1750. Fax: (719)531-3499. Editor: Jesse Florea. Magazine: 24 pages; illustrations and photos. Christian children's magazine. Monthly. Estab. 1987.

Needs: Adventure, children's/juvenile (10-12 years), religious/inspirational, sports. Receives 30 unsolicited mss/month. Accepts 1 ms/issue; 12 mss/year. Length: 400-600 words average. Publishes short shorts. Often critiques or comments on rejected mss.

How to Contact: Send complete ms with a cover letter. Include estimated word count, Social Security number and list of publications. Reports in 4-6 weeks on queries and mss. Send SASE for reply, return of ms or send disposable copy of ms. Simultaneous submissions OK. Sample copy free. Fiction guidelines for $1.50.

Payment/Terms: Pays $25 minimum; $250 maximum on acceptance and 3 contributor's copies for first rights.

Advice: "*Clubhouse* readers are 8- to 12-year-old boys and girls who desire to know more about God and the Bible. Their parents (who typically pay for the membership) want wholesome, educational material with scriptural or moral insight. The kids want excitement, adventure, action, humor or mystery. Your job as a writer is to please both the parent and child with each article."

‡COCHRAN'S CORNER, (I), 1003 Tyler Court, Waldorf MD 20602. (301)870-1664. Editor: Jeanie Saunders. Magazine: 5½×8; 52 pages. "We publish fiction, nonfiction and poetry. Our only requirement is no strong language." For a "family" audience. Quarterly. Estab. 1986. Circ. 500.

Needs: Adventure, children's/juvenile, historical, horror, humor/satire, mystery/suspense, religious/inspirational, romance, science fiction, young adult/teen (10-18 years). "Mss must be free from language you wouldn't want your/our children to read." Plans a special fiction issue. Receives 50 mss/month. Accepts 4 mss/issue; 8 mss/year. Publishes ms by the next issue after acceptance. Recently published work by Pete Kanter, Eric Richardson, Denise O'Brien and Lori Winters. Length: 500 words preferred; 300 words minimum; 1,000 words maximum. Also publishes literary essays, literary criticism, poetry.

How to Contact: "Right now we are forced to limit acceptance to *subscribers only.*" Send complete ms with cover letter. Reports in 3 weeks on queries; 6-8 weeks on mss. SASE for manuscript. Simultaneous and reprint submissions OK. Sample copy for $5, 9×12 SAE and 90¢ postage. Fiction guidelines for #10 SASE.

Payment/Terms: Pays in contributor's copies. Acquires one-time rights.

Advice: "I feel the quality of fiction is getting better. The public is demanding a good read, instead of having sex or violence carry the story. I predict that fiction has a good future. We like to print the story as the writer submits it if possible. This way writers can compare their work with their peers and take the necessary steps to improve and go on to sell to bigger magazines. Stories from the heart desire a place to be published. We try to fill that need. Be willing to edit yourself. Polish your manuscript before submitting to editors."

COLD-DRILL MAGAZINE, (IV), English Dept., Boise State University, 1910 University Dr., Boise ID 83725. (208)385-1999. Editor: Tom Trusky. Faculty Advisor: Dr. Mitchell Wieland. Magazine: box format; various perfect and non-perfect bound inserts; illustrations and photos. Material submitted *must be by Idaho authors or deal with Idaho*. For adult audiences. Annually. Estab. 1970. Circ. 500.

Needs: "The 1997-98 issue will not have a theme; it will be open to all forms of writing and artwork." Length: determined by submissions.

How to Contact: Query first. SASE.

Payment/Terms: Pays in contributor's copies. Acquires first rights.

COMMUNITIES MAGAZINE, (I, IV), P.O. Box 169, Masonville CO 80541-0169. Phone/fax: (970)593-5615. E-mail: communities@ic.org. Website: http://www.ic.org/ (includes samples of articles, ads, from current and back issues). Editor: Diana Christian. Guest editors change with each issue. "Articles on intentional communities—cohousing, ecovillages, urban group houses, student co-ops, rural communes, land-trust communities, and other forms of community (including non-residential)—as well as worker co-ops and workplace democracy. Written for people generally interested in intentional community and cooperative ventures, current and former community members, and people seeking to form or join an intentional community or co-op venture." Quarterly. Estab. 1973. Circ. 4,000.

Needs: "Utopian" stories, science fiction (soft/sociological). "Stories set in intentional communities or cooperatively run organizations." Upcoming themes: "Our Relationship to Money" (March); "Annual Sustainability Issue" (June); "Political Activism in Community" (September). Accepts "1-2 mss/year (more if we got them)." Publishes 25-30 new writers/year. Length: 750 words minimum; 3,000 words maximum.

How to Contact: "To submit an article, please first send for writer's guidelines." Reports in 1 month on queries; 6-8 weeks on mss. Simultaneous and previously published submissions OK. Sample copy for $5. *Communities Magazine*, 138 Twin Oaks Rd., Louisa VA 23093.

Payment/Terms: Pays 1 year subscription (4 issues) or 4 contributor's copies. Acquires first North American rights.

Advice: "We receive too many articles and stories which are completely off topic (in which the writer assumes we are about community in the generic sense, i.e., "community spirit," a neighborhood or town), by people who have no idea what an intentional community is, and/or who have never seen the magazine. We ask that writers read a sample issue first. We like the personal touch; concrete, visual, tightly written, upbeat, or offbeat message; short. No abstract, negative or loosely written, long fiction."

‡THE COMPLEAT NURSE, A Voice of Independent Nursing, (I), Dry Bones Press, P.O. Box 640345, San Francisco CA 94164. Phone/fax: (415)292-7371. Editor: Jim Rankin. Newsletter: 8½×11; 4-6 pages; 60 lb. paper; illustrations and photographs. "We publish themes, ideas, and subjects of interest to nurses and their patients—a definition we view very broadly. Nurses seen as cultural individuals, who practice as well in a profession." Monthly. Estab. 1990.
 • Member of PMA, SPAN.

Needs: Adventure, children's/juvenile, erotica, ethnic/multicultural, fantasy (sexuality and sexual issues), feminist, gay, historical, humor/satire, lesbian, mainstream/contemporary, mystery/suspense, regional, religious/inspirational (historical), science fiction, senior citizen/retirement, translations, young adult/teen, nurse or patient issues. Impact of health care infrastructure changes. Publishes special fiction issues or anthologies. Receives 2-3 unsolicited mss/month. Fiction mss accepted varies; 3-5 mss/year. Publishes ms almost immediately to 1 year after acceptance. Length: 1,500 words average; 3,000 words maximum. Publishes short shorts. Also publishes literary essays, literary criticism, poetry. Always critiques or comments on rejected mss.

How to Contact: Query first or query with clips of published work. Include estimated word count, bio, Social Security number and list of publications. Reports in 1 month on queries; 1-2 months on mss. Send SASE for reply, return of ms or send a disposable copy of ms. Simultaneous submissions, reprints and electronic submissions OK. Reviews novels and short story collections. Send books to editor.

Payment/Terms: Pays in contributor's copies on publication. Rights acquired negotiable. Sends galleys to author.

Advice: "Please consider basic human issues including humor and personal experience and write about those things. We are a shoestring small press—and authors need to work with us to build markets. But we can consider good things others pass up, or unique things."

‡CONTRABAND, (II), (formerly L'Ouverture), P.O. Box 8565, Atlanta GA 31106. (404)572-9141. E-mail: louve@mindspring.com. Editor: Bill Campbell. Fiction Editor: Angela Wiens. Magazine: 8½×11; 44 pages; illustrations and photographs. "Genres are not important to us nor name and reputation. What we are looking for is thought-provoking material that says something about the world in which we live. We abhor yuppie angst, precocious children, and how tough it is to be a writer. Say something important and say it well." Bimonthly. Estab. 1996. Circ. 600.

Needs: Condensed/excerpted novel, ethnic/multicultural, experimental, feminist, gay, historical (general), horror, humor/satire, lesbian, literary, magic realism, mainstream, psychic/supernatural/occult, science fiction (soft/sociological), serialized novel, translations. No romance, adventure. Receives 20 unsolicited mss/month. Accepts 3-5 mss/issue; 18-30 mss/year. Publishes ms 6-12 months after acceptance. Recently published work by Chizoman Okehi, Isaac Webb, Fernand Roqueplan and David Bunch. Publishes short shorts. Also publishes literary essays, literary criticism, poetry. Often critiques or comments on rejected mss.

How to Contact: Send complete ms with a cover letter. Include estimated word count. Reports in 2-3 weeks on queries; 2 months on mss. Send SASE for reply, return of ms or send a disposable copy of ms. Simultaneous submissions, reprints and electronic submissions OK. Sample copy for $4. Fiction guidelines free. Reviews novels and short story collections.

Payment/Terms: Pays 2 contributor's copies on publication; additional copies for $4. Acquires rights to publish in our magazine and on website.

Advice: "We look for a vitality and intensity in any submission. It must say something important to our readers and say it in a unique way. It must intrigue and provoke and stay away from the cliché. I didn't believe this as a beginning writer, but, as an editor, I think it's extremely important to know the market in which one plans to submit. Many editors have unique tastes and are overworked. Purchasing a sample copy first often saves time, postage and fragile egos."

‡THE COZY DETECTIVE, Mystery Magazine, (I), Meager Ink Publishing, 686 Jakes Ct., McMinnville OR 97128. (503)435-1212. Fax: (503) 472-4896. E-mail: detectivemag@onlinemac.com. Editor: David Workman. Fiction Editor: Charlie Bradley. Magazine: 8½×5½; 80 pages; illustrations and photos. Publishes mystery/suspense fiction and true crime stories for mystery buffs. Quarterly. Estab. 1994. Circ. 2,000.

Needs: Condensed/excerpted novel, mystery/suspense (amateur sleuth, cozy, police procedural, private eye/hardboiled), science fiction (mystery), serialized novel, young adult (mystery). No "sex, violence or vulgarity." Publishes special fiction issues or anthologies. Receives 15-25 unsolicited mss/month. Accepts 5 mss/issue; 20 mss/year. Does not read June-August. Recently published work by Kris Neri, Wendy Dager, Ruth Latta, James

Geisert, C. Lester Bradley and Robert W. Kreps. Length: 6,000 words maximum; will consider longer stories for two-part series. Publishes short shorts. Also publishes poetry. Sometimes critiques or comments on rejected ms.
How to Contact: Send complete ms with a cover letter. Include 1-paragraph bio and estimated word count. Reports in 3 weeks on queries; 1-4 months on mss. Send SASE for reply, return of ms or send disposable copy of ms. Simultaneous, reprint and electronic submissions OK. Sample copy for $2.95. Fiction guidelines for #10 SASE. Reviews novels and short story collections. Send books to "Review Editor."
Payment/Terms: Pays 5 contributor's copies for first North American serial rights; additional copies $1.50.
Advice: "Do your best work—don't rush. Try to make your plot secondary to characters in the story. We look for action, crisp dialogue and original use of old ideas. We love a good mystery."

‡**CZ'S MAGAZINE, (I, II)**, CZA, 10035 Douglas Ct., St. Ann MO 63074. (314)890-2060. E-mail: cz@cza.com. Editor: Loretta Nichols. Magazine: 8×10; 20-25 pages; illustrations and photos. "This publication is produced for writers who want to be published in a general subject magazine." Monthly. Estab. 1997. Circ. 200.
Needs: Adventure, children's/juvenile (10-12 years), experimental, fantasy (science fantasy, sword and sorcery), feminist, humor/satire, literary, mainstream/contemporary, mystery/suspense (amateur sleuth, police procedural, romantic suspense), psychic/supernatural/occult, religious/inspirational, romance (contemporary, futuristic/time travel, gothic), science fiction (hard science, soft/sociological), young adult/teen (adventure, mystery, romance, science fiction), interviews. Receives 20 unsolicited mss/month. Accepts 3 mss/issue; 36 mss/year. Publishes ms "up to 3 months" after acceptance. Recently published work by Alice Lance and Gary Leftridge. Length: 1,500 words average; 300 words minimum; 3,000 words maximum. Publishes short shorts. Also publishes literary essays, literary criticism and poetry. Sometimes critiques or comments on rejected mss.
How to Contact: Send complete ms with a cover letter. Include estimated word count, bio and list of publications. Reports in 3 weeks on queries; 2 months on mss. Send SASE for reply, return of ms or send a disposable copy of ms. Simultaneous submissions and reprints OK. Sample copy for $2. Fiction guidelines free. Reviews novels and short story collections. Send books to editor.
Payment/Terms: Pays contributor's copies for one-time rights.
Advice: "Send your work with SASE. I always publish unpublished authors first (unless their work is not fitting)."

DAGGER OF THE MIND, Beyond The Realms Of Imagination, (II), K'yi-Lih Productions (a division of Breach Enterprises), 1317 Hookridge Dr., El Paso TX 79925. (915)591-0541. Executive Editor: Arthur William Lloyd Breach. Magazine. 8½×11; 62-86 pages; hibright paper; high glossy cover; from 5-12 illustrations. Quarterly. Estab. 1990. Circ. 5,000.
● Do not send this publication "slasher" horror. The editor's preferences lean toward "Twilight Zone" and similar material. He says he added mystery to his needs but has received very little quality material in this genre.
Needs: Lovecraftian. Adventure, experimental, fantasy, horror, mystery/suspense (private eye, police procedural), science fiction (hard science, soft/sociological). Nothing sick and blasphemous, vulgar, obscene, racist, sexist, profane, humorous, weak, exploited women stories and those with idiotic puns. Plans special paperback anthologies. Receives 400 unsolicited mss/month. Accepts 8-15 mss/issue; 90-100 mss/year depending upon length. Publishes ms 2 years after acceptance. Agented fiction 30%. Published work by Sidney Williams, Jessica Amanda Salmonson and Donald R. Burleson. All lengths are acceptable; from short shorts to novelette lengths. Also publishes literary essays, literary criticism, poetry. Sometimes comments on rejected mss.
How to Contact: All mail should be addressed to Arthur Breach. Send complete manuscript with cover letter. "Include a bio and list of previously published credits with tearsheets. I also expect a brief synopsis of the story." Reports in 6 months on mss. SASE. Simultaneous submissions OK "as long as I am informed that they are such." Accepts electronic submissions. Sample copy for $3.50, 9×12 SAE and 5 first-class stamps. Fiction guidelines for #10 SASE.
Payment/Terms: Pays ½-1¢/word plus 1 contributor's copy on publication for first rights (possibly anthology rights as well).
Advice: "I'm a big fan of the late H.P. Lovecraft. I love reading through Dunsanian and Cthulhu Mythos tales. I'm constantly on the lookout for this special brand of fiction. If you want to grab my attention immediately, write on the outside of the envelope 'Lovecratian submission enclosed.' There are a number of things which make submissions stand out for me. Is there any sensitivity to the tale? I like sensitive material, so long as it doesn't become mushy. Another thing that grabs my attention are characters which leap out of the pages at you. Move me, bring a tear to my eye; make me stop and think about the world and people around me. Frighten me

---

SENDING TO A COUNTRY other than your own? Be sure to send International Reply Coupons instead of stamps for replies or return of your manuscript.

with little spoken of truths about the human condition. In short, show me that you can move me in such a way as I have never been moved before."

DREAM INTERNATIONAL/QUARTERLY, (I, II, IV), U.S. Address: Charles I. Jones, #H-1, 411 14th St., Ramona CA 92065-2769. E-mail: dreamiq@wizard.com. Editor-in-Chief: Charles I. Jones. Magazine: 5×7; 80-135 pages; Xerox paper; parchment cover stock; some illustrations and photos. "Publishes fiction and nonfiction that is dream-related or clearly inspired by a dream. Also dream-related fantasy." Quarterly. Estab. 1981. Circ. 80-100.
Needs: Adventure, confession, contemporary, erotica, ethnic, experimental, fantasy, historical, horror, humor/satire, literary, mainstream, mystery/suspense, prose poem, psychic/supernatural/occult, romance, science fiction, translations, young adult/teen (10-18). Receives 20-30 unsolicited mss/month. Publishes ms 8 months to 2 years after acceptance. Length: 1,000 words minimum; 2,000 words maximum. Publishes short shorts. Recently published work by Allen Underwood, Tim Scott, Jonathon Bernson, J. Lang Wood and Rowan Wynters. Also publishes literary essays, poetry (poetry submissions to Carmen M. Pursifull, 809 W. Maple St., Champaign IL 61820-2810. Hard copy only for poetry . . . no electronic submissions please! Send SASE for poetry guidelines).
How to Contact: Submit ms. Reports in 6 weeks on queries; 3 months on mss. SASE. Simultaneous and reprint submissions OK. Electronic submissions preferred (except poetry). "If you really want something to have the best chance, send an MS-DOS format IBM-compatible file on a 3.5 disk in MS-Word for Windows format (ASCII and WordPerfect also acceptable). Hardcopy must accompany disk." Sample copy for $10. Guidelines $1 with SAE and 2 first-class stamps. "Accepted mss will not be returned unless requested at time of submission."
Payment/Terms: Pays in contributor's copies (contributors must pay $3 for postage and handling). Offers magazine subscription. Acquires one-time rights.
Advice: "Use your nightly dreams to inspire you to literary flights. Keep a dream journal. Avoid stereotypes and clichés. Submissions should be clear, concise and free (as much as possible) of rambling text. When contacting editor-in-chief, make all checks, money orders and overseas drafts payable to *Charles Jones*. When contacting senior poetry editor, make checks and money orders payable to Carmen M. Pursifull."

✤**DREAMS & VISIONS, New Frontiers in Christian Fiction, (II)**, Skysong Press, 35 Peter St. S., Orillia, Ontario L3V 5AB Canada. Website: http://www.bconnex.net/~skysong. Editor: Steve Stanton. Magazine: 5½×8½; 56 pages; 20 lb. bond paper; glossy cover. "Contemporary Christian fiction in a variety of styles for adult Christians." Triannually. Estab. 1989. Circ. 200.
Needs: Contemporary, experimental, fantasy, humor/satire, literary, religious/inspirational, science fiction (soft/sociological). "All stories should portray a Christian world view or expand upon Biblical themes or ethics in an entertaining or enlightening manner." Receives 20 unsolicited mss/month. Accepts 7 mss/issue; 21 mss/year. Publishes ms 2-6 months after acceptance. Length: 2,500 words; 2,000 words minimum; 6,000 words maximum.
How to Contact: Send complete ms with cover letter. "Bio is optional: degrees held and in what specialties, publishing credits, service in the church, etc." Reports in 1 month on queries; 2-4 months on mss. SASE. Simultaneous submissions OK. Sample copy for $4.95. Fiction guidelines for SASE and online at our website.
Payment/Terms: Pays ½¢/word and contributor's copy. Acquires first North American serial rights and one-time, non-exclusive reprint rights.
Advice: "In general we look for work that has some literary value, that is in some way unique and relevant to Christian readers today. Our first priority is technical adequacy, though we will occasionally work with a beginning writer to polish a manuscript. Ultimately, we look for stories that glorify the Lord Jesus Christ, stories that build up rather than tear down, that exalt the sanctity of life, the holiness of God, and the value of the family."

‡*THE EDGE, (II)**, 1 Nichols Court, Belle Vue, Chelmsford, Essex CM2 OB5 United Kingdom. (01) 245-492561. Editor: Graham Evans. Magazine: A4; 48 pages; 80 GSM bond paper; art gloss cover; illustrations and photos. Publishes genre and non-genre experimental fiction. Bimonthly. Estab. 1995. Circ. 2,000.
Needs: Adventure, erotica, ethnic/multicultural, experimental, fantasy (science fantasy), feminist, gay, historical, horror, humor/satire, lesbian, literary, mainstream/contemporary, mystery/suspense, psychic/supernatural/occult, regional, religious/inspirational, science fiction (hard science, soft/sociological). Receives 80 unsolicited mss/month. Accepts 4-5 mss/issue; 24-30 mss/year. Publishes ms 1 week-6 months after acceptance. Agented fiction 5%. Recently published work by John Shirley, David Kenball, Paul Di Fillipo, Eric Brown, Simon Clark, Keith Brook and Chris Bell. No preferred length. Publishes short shorts. Also publishes literary essays and literary criticism.
How to Contact: Send complete ms with a cover letter. Include estimated word count. Reports in 1 week on queries; 1 month on mss. Send SAE with 2 IRCs for reply or send disposable copy of ms. Disk submissions OK. Sample copy for $6. Fiction guidelines free. Reviews novels or short story collections. Send books to editor.
Payment/Terms: Pays $12 per 1,000 words plus 2 contributor's copies on publication for first rights; additional copies $3. Sends galleys to author.

‡*EIDOLON, The Journal of Australian Science Fiction and Fantasy, (II, IV)**, P.O. Box 225, North Perth, Western Australia 6006. E-mail: eidolon@midnight.com.au. Editors: Jonathan Straman and Jeremy Byrne. Magazine: A5 size; 124 pages; gloss cover; illustrations and photos. "Primarily Australian science fiction, fantasy and horror magazine." Quarterly. Estab. 1990. Circ. 300.

Needs: Fantasy, psychic/supernatural/occult, romance (futuristic/time travel), science fiction, young adult/teen (horror, science fiction). Receives 25 unsolicited mss/month. Accepts 5 mss/issue; 25 mss/year. Publishes ms up to 1 year after acceptance. Agented fiction less than 1%. Recently published work by Terry Dowling, Sean Williams, Simon Brown, Lucy Sussex, Tess Williams and Sara Douglas. Length: 4,000 words average; 10,000 words maximum. Publishes short shorts.

How to Contact: Send complete ms with a cover letter. Include estimated word count, 100-word bio, list of publications and e-mail address. Send SASE for reply and a disposable copy of ms. No simultaneous submissions. Sample copy for $8 AUS. Fiction Guidelines for #10 SASE or SAE with 1 IRC.

Payment/Terms: Pays $20 and 1 contributor's copy for first Australian rights and optional electronic reproduction rights. Sends galleys to author.

Advice: Looks for "sophisticated, original explorations of fantastic themes, surprising plots and intelligent characterization. Proof carefully, work hard on dialogue. Make sure you know the field you're writing in well to avoid rehashing old themes. We expect writers to avoid stereotypical, sexist, racist or otherwise socially unacceptable themes and styles."

ELDRITCH TALES, (II, IV), Yith Press, 1051 Wellington Rd., Lawrence KS 66049. (913)843-4341. Editor-in-Chief: Crispin Burnham. Magazine: 6×9; 120 pages (average); glossy cover; illustrations; "very few" photos. "The magazine concerns horror fiction in the tradition of the old *Weird Tales* magazine. We publish fiction in the tradition of H.P. Lovecraft, Robert Bloch and Stephen King, among others, for fans of this particular genre." Semiannually. Estab. 1975. Circ. 1,000.

Needs: Horror and psychic/supernatural/occult. "No mad slasher stories or similar nonsupernatural horror stories." Receives about 8 unsolicited fiction mss/month. Accepts 12 mss/issue, 24 mss/year. Published work by J.N. Williamson, William F. Wu, Ron Dee and Charles Grant. Published new writers within the last year. Length: 50-100 words minimum; 20,000 words maximum; 10,000 words average. Occasionally critiques rejected mss.

How to Contact: Send complete ms with SASE and cover letter stating past sales. Previously published submissions OK. Prefers letter-quality submissions. Reports in 4 months. Publication could take up to 5 years after acceptance. Sample copy for $7.25.

Payment/Terms: ¼¢/word; 1 contributor's copy. $1 minimum payment. Pays in royalties on publication for first rights.

Advice: "Buy a sample copy and read it thoroughly. Most rejects with my magazine are because people have not checked out what an issue is like or what type of stories I accept. Most rejected stories fall into one of two categories: non-horror fantasy (sword & sorcery, high fantasy) or non-supernatural horror (mad slasher stories, 'Halloween' clones, I call them). When I say that they should read my publication, I'm not whistling Dixie. We hope to up the magazine's frequency to a quarterly. We also plan to be putting out one or two books a year, mostly novels, but short story collections will be considered as well."

THE ELOQUENT UMBRELLA, (I, II, IV), Linn-Benton Community College, 6500 SW Pacific Blvd., Albany OR 97321-3779. (541)753-3335. Contact: Linda Smith. Magazine: illustrations and photos. "*The Eloquent Umbrella*'s purpose is to showcase art, photography, poetry and prose of Linn and Benton Counties in Oregon." Annually. Estab. 1990. Circ. 500.

Needs: Condensed/excerpted novel, ethnic/multicultural, experimental, fantasy, feminist, gay, historical, humor/satire, literary, mainstream/contemporary, mystery/suspense, psychic/supernatural/occult, regional, religious/inspirational, romance, science fiction, senior citizen/retirement, sports, translations, westerns, young adult/teen. "No slander, pornography or other material unsuitable for community reading." Accepts 50-100 mss/issue. Deadline January 15 each year. Reads mss during winter term only; publishes in spring. Length: 1,500 words maximum. Publishes short shorts. Also publishes literary essays, literary criticism and poetry.

How to Contact: Send complete ms with cover letter. Include 1- to 5-line bio. Reports in 6 weeks on mss. SASE for return of ms or send a disposable copy of ms. Simultaneous submissions OK. Sample copy for $2 and 8½×11 SAE.

Payment/Terms: Rights remain with author.

Advice: "The magazine is created by a collective editorial board and production team in a literary publication class."

EPITAPH, Tales of Dark Fantasy & Horror, (II), Pirate Writings Publishing, P.O. Box 329, Brightwaters NY 11718. E-mail: picself@aol.com. Editor: Tom Piccirilli. Managing Editor: Edward J. McFadden. Magazine: digest size; 44 pages; 20 lb. paper; CS1 cover stock; illustrations and photos. Strives "to bring chilling, eerie horror and dark fantasy fiction to the forefront; I want alarming pieces that create an air of unreal authenticity. I will be emphasizing supernatural, occult works with something to say about the mysterious and unknown, but reality-based work is also welcome so long as it contains the flavor of the strange. *Epitaph* will also be actively seeking out new talented writers and those who are gifted, proficient, yet remain under-published in the field." Quarterly. Estab. 1996. Circ. 1,000.

Needs: Fantasy (dark), horror, psychic/supernatural/occult. Receives 150 unsolicited mss/month. Accepts 5-8 mss/issue; 20-36 mss/year. Publishes ms 1 year after acceptance. Length: 2,500 words average; 750 words minimum; 5,000 words maximum. Also publishes poetry. Always critiques or comments on rejected mss.

How to Contact: Send complete ms with a cover letter. Include estimated word count, 1-paragraph bio, Social

Security number and list of publications. Reports in 2 weeks on queries; 2 months on mss. SASE. Simultaneous submissions OK. Sample copy for $3.95. Fiction guidelines for #10 SASE. Pays ½-3¢/word on publication and 2 contributor's copies; additional copies for $3.95. Acquires first North American serial rights.

Advice: "I can always appreciate a well put-together story that attempts to do something unusual and rare, a tight, emotion-packed read that shows an author's confidence and skill. Genuine chills count for much more than easy scenes of carnage. Don't try to impress me with merely gore, grue, or other slimy messes; splatter is fine in the context of an embracing read, but it can't be the sole foundation. Remember that horror is an emotion, a situation, and not simply a setting. It is a means to an end—disturbing and enticing the reader. Don't send tales of vampires, werewolves or other staples of the genre; no killer cats, evil kids who do in everyone they meet, or inspirational narratives of frustrated writers who chop, hack, slice or squash an editor for not accepting a story; no continuations of the H.P. Lovecraft mythos—though I like reading them, I'm not interested in publishing them. Do everything you can to make your story as unpredictable as possible. Learn how to accept constructive criticism."

EYES, (I, II), Apt. 301, 2715 S. Jefferson Ave., Saginaw MI 48601-3830. (517)752-5202. Editor: Frank J. Mueller, III. Magazine: 8½×11; 36 pages; 20 lb. paper; Antiqua parchment, blue 65 lb. cover. "No specific theme. Speculative fiction and surrealism most welcome. For a general, educated, not necessarily literary audience." Estab. 1991. Circ. 30-40.

Needs: Contemporary, horror (psychological), mainstream, prose poem, romance (gothic). "Especially looking for speculative fiction and surrealism. Dark fantasy OK, but not preferred." Nothing pornographic; no preachiness; children's fiction discouraged. Accepts 4-8 mss/issue. Publishes ms up to 1 year or longer after acceptance. Publishes 15 new writers/year. Length: up to 6,000 words. Sometimes critiques rejected mss.

How to Contact: Query first or send complete ms. Reports in 1 month (or less) on queries; 3 months or longer on mss. SASE. No simultaneous submissions. Sample copy for $4; extras $4. Subscriptions $14. (Checks to Frank J. Mueller III.) Fiction guidelines for #10 SASE.

Payment/Terms: Pays one contributor's copy. Acquires one-time rights.

Advice: "Pay attention to character. A strong plot alone, while important, may not be enough to get you in *Eyes*. Atmosphere and mood are also important. Please proofread. If you have a manuscript you like enough to see it in *Eyes*, send it to me. Above all, don't let rejections discourage you. I would encourage the purchase of a sample to get an idea of what I'm looking for."

FIBEROPTIC ETCHINGS, A compilation of teenagers' writing from the information super highway, (IV), Platapus Press, Box 4121 McIntosh, 3001 Broadway, New York NY 10027. (410)730-2319. E-mail: foetchings@aol.com. Website: http://www.geocities.com/Athens/Delphi/7620.foetchings (includes guidelines, editors and contact info, current and past issues, writer and contact info, submission info). Editor: Stacy Cowley. Magazine: 8½×11; 100 pages. "*FiberOptic Etchings* publishes writing by teenagers (13-19), intended for a general audience." Published on the web bimonthly; publishes a print "Best Of" annually in January. Estab. 1995.

Needs: Adventure, condensed/excerpted novel, ethnic/multicultural, experimental, fantasy (science fiction, sword and sorcery), feminist, historical, horror, humor/satire, literary, mainstream/contemporary, mystery/suspense, psychic/supernatural/occult, regional, romance, science fiction, sports, westerns, young adult/teen. "Nothing extraordinarily violent, vulgar, or explicit; no erotica." Receives 5 unsolicited mss/month. Accepts 20-25 mss/issue. Publishes ms 1-2 months after acceptance. Length: 700 words average. Publishes short shorts. Also publishes literary essays, poetry. Always critiques or comments on rejected ms.

How to Contact: Send complete ms with a cover letter (strongly prefer submissions via e-mail). Should include 1-2 paragraph bio, list of publications. Reports in 2 weeks. Simultaneous, reprint, electronic submissions OK. See website for current issue. Fiction guidelines free.

Payment/Terms: Pays 1 contributor's copy; additional copies 50% discount. Acquires one-time rights. Not copyrighted.

Advice: "We look for manuscripts with a unique viewpoint and clear, fluid writing. Don't be afraid to submit unusual or experimental pieces, and don't be afraid to submit again and again. We're always delighted to look at anything that comes our way—we never know where a treasure will be found. We've caught web-fever: rather than publishing just one print issue a year, we're now publishing bimonthly on the web and putting out a past 'Best Of Fiberoptic Etching' issue each December."

‡*THE FIRST WORD BULLETIN, (I, II), Domingo Fernandez 5, Box 500, 28036 Madrid, Spain. United States address: c/o Mary Swain, 2046 Lothbury Dr., Fayetteville NC 28304-5666. E-mail: gw83@correo.interlink. es. Website: http://www.interlink.es/peraso/first. Editor: G.W. Amick. Magazine: 15 cm×21cm; 64 pages; slick paper; 160 grams, slick cover; illustrations. "We want to make the public acutely aware of problems concerning pollution of air, earth and water. Also man's inhumanity to man and animal." Quarterly. Estab. 1995. Circ. 5,000.

Needs: Adventure, historical, humor/satire, literary, mainstream/contemporary, senior citizen/retirement, young adult/teen (adventure, western). No pornography, mystery, science fiction or romance. Receives 15-20 unsolicited mss/month. Accepts 6-8 mss/issue; 24-32 mss/year. Publishes ms 1-2 months after acceptance. Agented fiction 10%. Recently published work by Sheila O'Connor (USA), Jean S. Munro (UK), Rebekah Dahl (Jamaica), Judi Knight (Spain) and Sonya Jason (USA). Length: 800 words minimum; 4,000 words maximum. Publishes short

shorts. Also publishes literary essays, literary criticism and poetry. Often critiques or comments on rejected mss.
How to Contact: Send complete ms with a cover letter or submit through an agent. Include estimated word count, short bio, Social Security number, list of publications. Reports in 6 weeks on queries; 3-4 months on mss. Send disposable copy of ms. Sample copy for $6.50. Fiction guidelines for $2. "We use only overseas airmail postage as surface mail is far too slow."
Payment/Terms: Pays 25 cents/word minimum, $50 maximum plus 1 contributor's copy for one-time world rights.
Advice: "In fiction I like to see the two dogs and a bone theory, well crafted with attention to clarity and precision of language, that is a seamless read. We want to give exposure to emerging writers. First, write from the heart and then revise and revise until it is acceptable. You don't always have to write what you know about but if different pay close attention to detail from research. Study the market you are writing for. Most manuscripts that land on an editor's desk are not suitable because of not being familiar with the magazine or the editor's needs. Some are too long or of the wrong genre. Buy a copy and know the magazine."

*FORESIGHT, (IV), 44 Brockhurst Rd., Hodge Hill, Birmingham B36 8JB England. 0121.783.0587. Editor: John Barklam. Fiction Editor: Judy Barklam. Quarterly.
Needs: Magazine including "new age material, world peace, psychic phenomena, research, occultism, spiritualism, mysticism, UFOs, philosophy, etc. Shorter articles required on a specific theme related to the subject matter of *Foresight* magazine." Length: 300-1,000 words.
How to Contact: Send SAE with IRC for return of ms.
Payment/Terms: Pays in contributor's copies. Sample copy for 75p and 50p postage.

‡THE FRACTAL, Journal of Science Fiction and Fantasy, (I, II, IV), Fractal Ink Press, MS 2D6 4400 University Dr., Fairfax VA 22030. (703)993-2904. E-mail: fractal@gmu.edu. Editors: Jessica Darago and Chris Elliot. Fiction Editor: Lisa Jirousek. Editors change every 2 years. Magazine: 5½ × 8½; 80 pages; 20 lb. paper; 60 lb. glossy cover; illustrations. "*The Fractal* publishes fiction, nonfiction and poetry in the genres of science fiction, fantasy, horror and speculative fiction. Experimental forms and ideas are encouraged; original characters and situations only." Semiannually. Estab. 1992.
Needs: Experimental, fantasy, horror, psychic/supernatural/occult, science fiction. No "media-based, non-original characters/situations." Receives 50 unsolicited mss/month. Accepts 5 mss/issue; 10 mss/year. Does not read during summer. Publishes ms up to 6 months after acceptance. Recently published work by Bentley Little, D.F. Lewis, Lance Olsen, L.H. Crazy Rabbit and Kiel Stuart. Publishes short shorts. Also publishes literary essays, literary criticism and poetry. Always critiques or comments on rejected mss.
How to Contact: Send complete ms with a cover letter. Include estimated word count. Reports in 2 months on queries and mss. Send SASE for reply, return of ms or send disposable copy of ms. Simultaneous and electronic submissions OK. Sample copy for $5. Fiction guidelines for #10 SASE. Reviews novels and short story collections. Send books to editor.
Payment/Terms: Pays $25 for fiction, $5 for poetry and $50 for nonfiction plus 2 contributor's copies for first North American serial rights.
Advice: Looks for "originality, unusual style or subject matter and strong characters."

FREE FOCUS/OSTENTATIOUS MIND, Wagner Press, (I, II), Bowbridge Press, P.O. Box 7415, JAF Station, New York NY 10116-7415. Editor: Patricia Denise Coscia. Editors change each year. Magazine: 8 × 14; 10 pages; recycled paper; illustrations and photos. "*Free Focus* is a small-press magazine which focuses on the educated women of today, and *Ostentatious Mind* is designed to encourage the intense writer, the cutting reality." Bimonthly. Estab. 1985 and 1987. Circ. 100 each.
Needs: Experimental, feminist, humor/satire, literary, mainstream/contemporary, mystery/suspense (romantic), psychic/supernatural/occult, westerns (traditional), young adult/teen (adventure). "X-rated fiction is not accepted." List of upcoming themes available for SAE. Plans future special fiction issue or anthology. Receives 1,000 unsolicited mss/month. Does not read mss February to August. Publishes ms 3-6 months after acceptance. Published work by Edward Janz, A. Anne-Marie Ljung and Christine Warren. Length: 500 words average; 1,000 words maximum. Publishes short shorts. Also publishes literary essays, literary criticism and poetry. Always critiques or comments on rejected mss. Sponsors contest for work submitted to *Free Focus*.
How to Contact: Query with clips of published work or send complete ms with a cover letter. Should Include 100-word bio and list of publications. Reports in 3 months. Send SASE for reply. Simultaneous submissions OK. Sample copy for $3, #10 SAE and $1 postage. Fiction guidelines for #10 SAE and $1 postage. Reviews novels and short story collections.
Payment/Terms: Pays $2.50-5 and 2 contributor's copies on publication for all rights; additional copies for $2. Sends galleys to author.
Advice: "This publication is for beginning writers. Do not get discouraged; submit your writing. We look for imagination and creativity; no x-rated writing."

THE FUDGE CAKE, A Children's Newsletter, (IV), Francora DTP, P.O. Box 197, Citrus Heights CA 95611-0197. Fiction Editor: Jancarl Campi. Newsletter: 5 × 8½; 20 pages; 20 lb. bond paper; illustrations. "Our purpose is to provide a showcase for young writers age 6-17. We value the work of today's children and feel they need an outlet to express themselves." Bimonthly. Estab. 1994. Circ. 250.

Needs: Young adult/teen. No erotica. Receives 2-3 unsolicited mss/month. Accepts 3 mss/issue; 18 mss/year. Publishes ms 2 months after acceptance. Publishes 12 previously unpublished fiction writers/year. Length: 400 words average; 250 words minimum; 500 words maximum. Publishes short shorts. Also publishes poetry. Often critiques or comments on rejected mss.

How to Contact: Send complete ms with a cover letter. Include estimated word count and age. Reports in 1 month. Send SASE for reply, return of ms or send a disposable copy of ms. Simultaneous and reprint submissions OK. Sample copy for $3 and 1 first-class stamp. Fiction guidelines for #10 SASE.

Payment/Terms: Pays 1 contributor's copy; additional copies for $3. Acquires one-time rights.

Advice: "Write then rewrite. Have someone read your work. Check grammar, spelling before submitting."

GAY CHICAGO MAGAZINE, (II), Gernhardt Publications, Inc., 3121 N. Broadway, Chicago IL 60657-4522. (773)327-7271. Publisher: Ralph Paul Gernhardt. Associate Publisher: Jerry Williams. Entertainment Editor: Jeff Rossen. Magazine: 8½ × 11; 80-144 pages; newsprint paper and cover stock; illustrations; photos. Entertainment guide, information for the gay community.

Needs: Erotica (but no explicit hard core), lesbian, gay and romance. Receives "a few" unsolicited mss/month. Acquires 10-15 mss/year. Published new writers within the last year. Length: 1,000-3,000 words.

How to Contact: Send all submissions Attn: Jeff Rossen. Send complete ms with SASE. Accepts 3.5 disk submissions and Macintosh or ASCII Format. Reports in 4-6 weeks on mss. Free sample copy for 9 × 12 SAE and $1.45 postage.

Payment/Terms: Minimal. 5-10 free contributor's copies; no charge for extras "if within reason." Acquires one-time rights.

*GLOBAL TAPESTRY JOURNAL, (II), BB Books, 1 Spring Bank, Longsight Rd., Copster Green, Blackburn, Lancashire BB1 9EU England. Editor: Dave Cunliffe.

Needs: "Post-underground with avant-garde, experimental, alternative, counterculture, psychedelic, mystical, anarchist etc. fiction for a bohemian and counterculture audience." Published fiction by Arthur Moyse, Tina Morris and Jay Lee Findlay. Published work by new writers within the last year.

Payment/Terms: Sample copy for $4 (Sterling Cheque, British Money Order or dollar currency).

HARDBOILED, (I, II), Gryphon Publications, P.O. Box 209, Brooklyn NY 11228-0209. Editor: Gary Lovisi. Magazine: Digest-sized; 100 pages; offset paper; color cover; illustrations. Publishes "cutting edge, hard, noir fiction with impact! Query on nonfiction and reviews." Quarterly. Estab. 1988.

• By "hardboiled" the editor does not mean rehashing of pulp detective fiction from the 1940s and 1950s but, rather, realistic, gritty material. Lovisi could be called a pulp fiction "afficionado," however. He also publishes *Paperback Parade* and holds an annual vintage paperback fiction convention each year.

Needs: Mystery/suspense (private eye, police procedural, noir). Receives 40-60 mss/month. Accepts 20-25 mss/year. Publishes ms within 6 months-2 years of acceptance. Published work by Andrew Vachss, Joe Lansdale, Bill Nolan, Richard Lupoff, Bill Pronzini and Eugene Izzi. Published many new writers within the last year. Length: 2,000 words minimum; 3,000 words maximum. Sometimes critiques rejected mss and recommends other markets.

How to Contact: Query first or send complete ms with cover letter. Query with SASE only on anything over 3,000 words. No full-length novels. Reports in 1 month on queries; 1-2 months on mss. SASE. Simultaneous submissions OK, but query first. Sample copy for $7.

Payment/Terms: Pays $5-50 on publication and 2 contributor's copies for first North American serial rights. Copyright reverts to author.

HAUNTS, Tales of Unexpected Horror and the Supernatural, (II, IV), Nightshade Publications, Box 8068, Cranston RI 02926-0068. (401)781-9438. E-mail: josephkcherkes76520.56@compuserve.com. Editor: Joseph K. Cherkes. Magazine: 6 × 9 digest; 80-100 pages; 50 lb. offset paper; perfect-bound; pen and ink illustrations. "We are committed to publishing only the finest fiction in the genres of horror, fantasy and the supernatural from both semi-pro and established writers. We are targeted towards the 18-35 age bracket interested in tales of horror and the unknown." Triannually. Plans special fiction issue. Estab. 1984. Circ. 3,500.

Needs: Fantasy, horror, psychic/supernatural/occult. No pure adventure, explicit sex or blow-by-blow dismemberment. Receives 700-750 unsolicited fiction mss/month. Accepts 10-12 mss/issue; 40-50 mss/year. Published work by Mike Hurley, Kevin J. Anderson and Frank Ward. Published new writers within the last year. Length:

FOR INFORMATION ON ENTERING the *Novel & Short Story Writer's Market* Cover Letter Contest, see page 84.

3,500 words average; 1,000 words minimum; 8,500 words maximum. Critiques rejected mss and recommends other markets when possible.

How to Contact: Query first. "Cover letters are a nice way to introduce oneself to a new editor." Open to submissions January 1 through June 1, inclusive. Reports in 2-3 weeks on queries; 3-4 months on mss. SASE for query. Accepts magnetic media (IBM PC-MS/DOS 2.0 or higher), and most major word processing formats. Sample copy for $4.95 plus $1 postage and handling. Fiction guidelines for #10 SASE.

Payment/Terms: Pays $5-50 (subject to change) on publication and contributor's copies; charge for additional copies. Acquires first North American serial rights.

Advice: "Follow writers' guidelines closely. They are a good outline of what your publisher looks for in fiction. If you think you've got the 'perfect' manuscript, go over it again—carefully. Check to make sure you've left no loose ends before sending it out. Keep your writing *concise*. If your story is rejected, don't give up. Try to see where the story failed. This way you can learn from your mistakes. Remember, success comes to those who persist."

THE HEALING INN, An Ointment of Love for the Wounded Heart, (I, IV), Christian Airline Personnel Missionary Outreach, 18524 Linden N. #306, Seattle WA 98133. Phone/fax: (206)542-0210. Editor: June Shafhid. Magazine: 8×10; 20 pages. "*The Healing Inn* is geared to encouraging Christians that have been wounded by a church or religious cult. The content or message is to draw people back to God and a balance of healthy Christianity, using fiction stories to encourage their hearts and testimonies to teach them to be individuals before God and man." Estab. 1995. Circ. 2,000.

Needs: Adventure, humor/satire, religious/inspirational. "All stories must have an inspirational message. No judgmental or harsh stories." Publishes ms 3-6 months after acceptance. Length: 2,000 words average; 500 words minimum; 3,000 words maximum. Publishes short shorts. Also publishes poetry.

How to Contact: Send complete ms with a cover letter. Include estimated word count, a short bio and Social Security number. Reports in 2-4 weeks on mss. Send SASE for return of ms. Simultaneous submissions and reprints OK. Sample copy free.

Payment/Terms: Pays free subscription to the magazine and contributor's copies. Acquires first North American serial rights.

Advice: "I look for well-written stories that touch the heart—whether it be humorous or drama. Heartfelt, heartwrenching, life-changing themes catch my eye. Write from your heart; be expressive and honest."

HOPSCOTCH: THE MAGAZINE FOR GIRLS, (II), The Bluffton News Publishing & Printing Co., P.O. Box 164, Bluffton OH 45817. (419)358-4610. Fax: (419)358-5027. Editor: Marilyn Edwards. Magazine: 7×9; 50 pages; enamel paper; pen & ink illustrations; photographs. Publishes stories for and about girls ages 5-12. Bimonthly. Estab. 1989. Circ. 9,000.

● *Hopscotch* is indexed in the *Children's Magazine Guide* and *Ed Press* and has received a Parents' Choice Gold Medal Award and Ed Press Awards.

Needs: Children's/juvenile (5-9, 10-12 years): adventure, ethnic/multicultural, fantasy, historical (general), sports. Upcoming themes: "Good Health"; "Summertime"; "Pets"; "Different Kinds of Schools"; "Cats"; "Poetry"; "Friends"; "Inventions." Receives 300-400 unsolicited mss/month. Accepts 20-40 mss/year. Agented fiction 2%. Published work by Lois Grambling, Betty Killion, Jean Patrick and VaDonna Jean Leaf. Length: 500-750 words preferred; 300 words minimum; 750 words maximum. Publishes short shorts. Length: 250-400 words. Also publishes poetry, puzzles, hidden pictures and crafts. Always comments on rejected mss.

How to Contact: Send complete ms with cover letter. Include estimated word count, 1-page bio, Social Security number and list of publications. Reports in 2-4 weeks on queries; 6-10 weeks on mss. Send SASE for reply, return of ms or send disposable copy of the ms. Simultaneous and reprint submissions OK. Sample copy for $3. Fiction guidelines for #10 SASE. Reviews novels and short story collections.

Payment/Terms: Pays 5¢/word (extra for usable photos or illustrations) before publication and 1 contributor's copy for first North American serial rights; additional copies $3; $2 for 10 or more.

Advice: "Make sure you have studied copies of our magazine to see what we like. Follow our theme list. We are looking for wholesome stories. This is what our publication is all about."

HURRICANE ALICE, A Feminist Quarterly, (II), Hurricane Alice Fn., Inc., Dept. of English, Rhode Island College, Providence RI 02908. E-mail: mreddy@grog.ric.edu. Executive Editor: Maureen Reddy. Fiction is collectively edited. Tabloid: 11×17; 12-16 pages; newsprint stock; illustrations and photos. "We look for feminist fictions with a certain analytic snap, for serious readers, seriously interested in emerging forms of feminist art/artists." Quarterly. Estab. 1983. Circ. 600-700.

Needs: Experimental, feminist, gay, humor/satire, lesbian, science fiction, translations, work by young women. No coming-out stories, defloration stories, abortion stories. Upcoming themes: "Women's health," "the academy" and "the community." Receives 100 unsolicited mss/month. Publishes 8-10 stories annually. Publishes mss up to 1 year after acceptance. Published work by Mary Sharratt, Emily Leider, Joanna Kadi and Toni McNaron. Publishes 3-4 new writers/year. Length: up to 3,000 words maximum. Publishes short shorts. Occasionally critiques rejected mss.

How to Contact: Send complete ms with cover letter. "A brief biographical statement is never amiss. Writers should be sure to tell us if a piece was commissioned by one of the editors." Reports in 3-4 months. SASE for

INSIDER REPORT

Filling the gap in the feminist fiction market

As an original member of the *Hurricane Alice* collective since its establishment in 1983, Maureen Reddy was the perfect candidate to take over as executive editor when the Minneapolis-based collective grew tired of producing the quarterly. "After completing my Ph.D. at the University of Minnesota in 1985, I moved east but stayed involved with *Alice* as the east coast editor and book reviewer. So, about two years ago, when former executive editor Martha Roth needed a new home for *Alice*, I put together a collective here in Providence and moved the publication."

Now, the editorial offices of *Alice* are contained throughout various faculty offices of Rhode Island College, including the College's Writing Center, whose director is a member of the part-time, unpaid editorial collective. The collective

Maureen Reddy

works by dividing the submissions, except reviews, according to genre and having a reading group for each genre. The submission manager, Joan Dagle, receives the submissions, distributes packets to the appropriate groups once a month, and then collects the groups' individual votes. Reddy says, "Any unanimous 'no's' are rejected by me. Any pieces with a majority of yes's are passed on to the whole collective. Then we all read them and vote at our monthly meetings. Often, however, we can be persuaded to take a piece that the majority of people initially vote against, if the piece has a strong enough advocate—just one person who really loves it and can get the rest of us to see why. It's an illuminating process."

Not only an illuminating process but an amazing one, considering the 12-member collective reads approximately 100 manuscripts a month to find the 8 to 10 fiction manuscripts published annually. So, how does a writer attract the attention of editors swamped with submissions? The best way, it almost goes without saying, is to submit a story the editors haven't seen before. "Write a story that is surprising in some way," says Reddy. "I am really tired of coming out stories, discovering feminism stories, and a few other old chestnuts. I'm also getting tired of what one of our editors has taken to calling 'dreary realism.' I like experimental fiction, non-realist fiction, fiction that does something other than plod along from A to B."

Along with "surprise" and "experimentation," writers wanting to submit to *Hurricane Alice* should keep in mind the quarterly's primary focus: feminism. "Our central concerns are to publish feminist work that is serious but not academic and that might not otherwise find a home in print," says Reddy. The collective sees many feminist publications as being fairly restrictive in what they'll print—only academic work or reviews, work by local authors, mostly newsworthy stories or very little fiction. *Alice* is dedicated to filling the gap in the feminist market.

INSIDER REPORT, *Reddy*

And although *Alice*'s main focus is feminist, work submitted does not have to be blatantly so to be accepted. "We look for short, surprising, well-written fiction that has some relation to feminism, although that relation doesn't have to be obvious or directly stated. For instance, in our current issue (12:2) we have a story called 'Courting the Leopard' by Joyce Godlenstern that's a retelling of a fairly obscure fairy tale and is not obviously feminist. However, our editors agreed that it would interest feminist readers, and that its feminism is subtle but definitely there." Reddy also believes that, although they tend to receive many of the same stories every month, "millions" of good story ideas exist in the feminist realm. "A good story stays with me, gets me thinking about it again and again, even days after I've read it."

To really understand the type of work *Alice* is looking for or to see if there is a fit between your work and the journal, Reddy suggests writers request submission guidelines and obtain a sample copy. And although the quarterly does not "pay" its writers, it is very generous with contributors' copies and does offer other benefits: "Samuel Johnson said only a fool would write but for money, but I think he was wrong. Writers write for all kinds of other reasons—to express themselves, to reach readers, to get their voices heard— and *Hurricane Alice* provides all that."

—*Chantelle Bentley*

---

ms. Simultaneous submissions OK, but must be identified as such. Sample copy for $2.50, 11 × 14 SAE and 2 first-class stamps.
Payment/Terms: Pays 6 contributor's copies. Acquires one-time rights.
Advice: "Fiction is a craft. Just because something happened, it isn't a story; it becomes a story when you transform it through your art, your craft."

‡HYBRID MOMENTS MAGAZINE, Literature for Creative Minds, (I, II), Destructive Literature Press, P.O. Box 14, Albertson NY 11507-0014. (718)380-2600. Editor: Peter Edmond. Magazine: 8½×11; 50-100 pages; 24 lb. paper; 24 lb. color cover; illustrations and photos. "Our main theme is diversity. We publish short stories and poetry as well as book/music/movie reviews, comics and articles on anything or anyone unique and interesting." Triannually. Estab. 1995. Circ. 500.
Needs: Adventure, condensed/excerpted novel, experimental, fantasy (science, sword and sorcery), historical, horror, literary, mainstream/contemporary, mystery/suspense (amateur sleuth, police procedural, private eye/hard-boiled, romantic suspense), psychic/supernatural/occult, romance (contemporary, futuristic/time travel, gothic, historical), science fiction (hard science, soft/sociological), serialized novel, westerns (frontier, traditional), young adult/teen (adventure, horror, mystery, romance, science fiction, western). Receives 5 unsolicited mss/month. Accepts 5-8 mss/issue; 15-22 mss/year. Publishes ms 4-8 months after acceptance. Recently published work by Greg Halpern, Jay Travis, Deniese Kennedy, Bonnie Natko, Stephen Corbo, Michael Kurtz, Bryan Jones and Al J. Vermette. Length: 2,500 words average; 250 words minimum; 10,000 words maximum. Publishes short shorts. Also publishes literary essays and poetry. Always critiques or comments on rejected mss.
How to Contact: Send complete ms with a cover letter. Include bio (1 page maximum) and list of publications. Reports in 1 month on queries; 2 months on mss. Send SASE for reply to a query or send a disposable copy of ms. Simultaneous submissions and reprints OK. Sample copy for $3.50. Reviews novels and short story collections. Send books to "Reviews Department."
Payment/Terms: Pays 3 contributor's copies for one-time and reprint rights; additional copies $2.
Advice: "The only criteria we use is originality and thoroughness in the plot and writing. A person's best bet is to write what they know about. If you're writing a story where the main character is a cop, then make sure you research it and know what you need to know about cops. Don't leave gaps in the story either—it kills the flow of the story and we won't publish it."

‡IGNITE, (I, II), Off Center Press, Inc., P.O. Box 2216, New York NY 10009. Phone/fax: (212)677-0508. E-mail: ignite@interport.net. Editor: Dario Stipisic. Magazine: 5½×8½; 64 pages; 50 lb. glossy paper; 10 pt. cover; illustrations and photographs. "Ignite publishes the best in literature and art four times a year to an audience of culturally active urbanites." Quarterly. Estab. 1995. Circ. 2,500.

Needs: Adventure, ethnic/multicultural, experimental, historical (general), humor/satire, literary, mainstream/contemporary, translations. No fantasy and romance. Receives 300 unsolicited mss/month. Accepts 3 mss/issue; 12 mss/year. Does not read mss in the summer. Publishes ms 4 months after acceptance. Recently published work by Janine Pommy Vega and Rudolph Wurlitzer. Length: 1,500 words average; 250 words minimum; 5,000 words maximum. Publishes short shorts. Length: 500 words. Also publishes literary essays, literary criticism, poetry. Often critiques or comments on rejected mss.
How to Contact: Send complete ms with a cover letter. Include estimated word count. Reports in 1 week on queries; 4 months on mss. Send SASE for reply, return of ms or send a disposable copy of ms. Simultaneous submissions OK. Sample copy for $3 and 6 first-class stamps. Fiction guidelines free for #10 SASE. Reviews novels and short story collections.
Payment/Terms: Pays 3 contributor's copies; additional copies for $2. Acquires first rights.

‡IN THE FAMILY, The Magazine for Lesbians, Gays, Bisexuals and their Relations, (I, II, IV), P.O. Box 5387, Takoma Park MD 20913. (301)270-4771. Fax: (301)270-4660. E-mail: lmarkowitz@aol.com. Editor: Laura Markowitz. Fiction Editor: Helena Lipstadt. Magazine: 8½×11, 32 pages; coated paper; coated cover; illustrations and photos. "We use a therapy lens to explore the diverse relationships and families of lesbians, gays, bisexuals and their straight relations." Quarterly. Estab. 1995. Circ. 2,000.
• Received 1997 Excellence in Media Award from the American Association for Marriage and Family Therapy and was nominated twice for Alternative Press awards. Member of IPA.
Needs: Ethnic/multicultural, feminist, gay, humor/satire, lesbian. List of upcoming themes available for SASE. Receives 25 unsolicited mss/month. Accepts 1 ms/issue; 4 mss/year. Publishes ms 3-6 months after acceptance. Recently published work by Ellen Hawley, Daniel Cox, Shoshana Daniel and Martha Davis. Length: 2,000 words average; 2,500 words maximum. Publishes short shorts. Also publishes literary essays and poetry. Sometimes critiques or comments on rejected mss.
How to Contact: Send complete ms with a cover letter. Include estimated word count and 40-word bio. Reports in 6 weeks on queries and mss. Send SASE for reply, return of ms or send disposable copy of ms. Sample copy for $5.50. Fiction guidelines free. Reviews novels and short story collections. Send books to Wayne Scott, Book Review Editor.
Payment/Terms: Pays $25 minimum; $50 maximum plus free subscription to magazine and 5 contributor's copies for first rights.
Advice: "Story must relate to our theme of gay/lesbian/bi relationships and family in some way. Read a few issues and get a sense for what we publish. Shorter is better."

INNER VOICES, A New Journal of Prison Literature, (I, IV), Inner Voices, P.O. Box 4500, #219, Bloomington IN 47402. E-mail: eviltwin@indy.net. Website: http://www.indy.net/~eviltwin (includes mission explanation, guidelines, history, bibliography, publishing announcements, links, subscription information). Editor: C. Nolan Williams. 8½×5½; 50 pages; matte paper; card stock cover; illustrations. Publishes literature written by "prisoners and their loved ones." Semiannually. Estab. 1995. Circ. 200.
Needs: Open to all fiction except children's, young adult and pornography. Receives 20 unsolicited mss/month. Accepts 20-30 mss/issue; 40-60 mss/year. Time between acceptance and publication varies. Recently published work by Salazar, Lyle White and Abu Hasson. Publishes 10 new writers/year. Length: 3,000 words average; 10,000 words maximum. Publishes short shorts. Also publishes poetry. Sometimes critiques or comments on rejected mss.
How to Contact: Send complete ms with a cover letter. Include a personal statement (100-150 words) with submission. Reports in 1 month on queries; 3 months on mss. Send a disposable copy of ms. Simultaneous, reprint and electronic (Mac or modem) submissions OK. Sample copy $4; some free to prisoners. Fiction guidelines free. Reviews novels and short story collections.
Payment/Terms: Pays with free subscription to magazine or 1-2 contributor's copies. Acquires first rights and reprint rights.
Advice: "Find someone who isn't afraid to critique your work and treat that person like gold. Then, give us a try. Please, no position essays or explicit descriptions of crimes or sex. These may be banned from prison libraries. We want to show the range of talent in prisons. I try for a good balance of styles and themes, so do not try to imitate past publications. We get way more religious pieces and midnight meditations than we can use, so the odds are against these. Plenty of love poetry, too. But just give it a try, whatever your best work is." Sometimes enters writers' work in other organizations' contests.

INTUITIVE EXPLORATIONS, A Journal of Intuitive Processes, (I, II, IV), Intuitive Explorations, P.O. Box 561, Quincy IL 62306-0561. (217)222-9082. Editor: Gloria Reiser. Magazine: 8½×11; 28 pages. "*Intuitive Explorations* publishes mind explorations for an audience very interested in exploring the unknown and inner worlds." Bimonthly. Estab. 1987. Circ. 1,000.
Needs: Ethnic/multicultural, psychic/supernatural/occult, religious/inspirational (futuristic/time travel), ancient worlds, future worlds, other realms. Accepts 1 mss/issue; 6 mss/year. Publishes ms 1-2 issues after acceptance. Published work by Father John Groff. Length 700-1,000 words average; 300 words minimum; 2,000 words maximum. Publishes short shorts. Also publishes literary essays, poetry. Sometimes critiques or comments on rejected ms.

How to Contact: Send complete ms with a cover letter. Should include estimated word count and short bio. Reports in 2 months on queries; 2-3 months on mss. Send SASE for reply, return of ms or send a disposable copy of ms. Simultaneous and reprint submissions OK. Sample copy for $1, 9 × 12 SAE and 4 first-class stamps. Reviews novels and short story collections.
Payment/Terms: Pays up to 6 contributor's copies; additional copies 75¢ each. Acquires one-time rights.
Advice: "I'd like to see more fiction in which tarot is woven into the story line as well as stories honoring intuition and/or the earth."

ITALIAN AMERICANA, (I, II, IV), URI/CCE 80 Washington St., Providence RI 02903-1803. (401)277-5306. Editor: Carol Bonomo Albright. Poetry Editor: Dana Gioia. Magazine: 6 × 9; approximately 200 pages; varnished cover; perfect-bound; photographs. "*Italian Americana* contains historical articles, fiction, poetry and memoirs, all concerning the Italian experience in the Americas." Semiannually. Estab. 1974. Circ. 1,200.
Needs: Italian American: literary. No nostalgia. Receives 10 mss/month. Accepts 3 mss/issue; 6-7 mss/year. Publishes up to 1 year after acceptance. Agented fiction 5%. Recently published work by Mary Caponegro and Anthony Ardizzone. Length: 20 double-spaced pages. Publishes short stories. Also publishes literary essays, literary criticism, poetry. Sometimes critiques rejected mss. Sponsors $500-1,000 literature prize annually.
How to Contact: Send complete ms (in triplicate) with a cover letter. Include 3-5 line bio, list of publications. Reports in 1 month on queries; 2-4 months on mss. Send SASE for reply, return of ms or send a disposable copy of ms. No simultaneous submissions. Sample copy for $6. Fiction guidelines for SASE. Reviews novels and short story collections. Send books to Professor John Paul Russo, English Dept., Univ. of Miami, Coral Gables, FL 33124.
Payment/Terms: Awards $250 to best fiction of year and 1 contributor's copy; additional copies $7. Acquires first North American serial rights.
Advice: "Please individualize characters, instead of presenting types (i.e., lovable uncle, aunt, etc.). No nostalgia."

JEWISH CURRENTS MAGAZINE, (IV), 22 E. 17th St., New York NY 10003. (212)924-5740. Editor-in-Chief: Morris U. Schappes. Magazine: 5½ × 8½; 48 pages. "We are a progressive monthly, broad in our interests, printing feature articles on political and cultural aspects of Jewish life in the US and elsewhere, reviews of books and film, poetry and fiction, Yiddish translations; regular columns on Israel, US Jewish community, current events, Jewish women today, secular Jewish life. National audience, literate and politically left, well educated." Monthly. Estab. 1946. Circ. 2,600.
● This magazine may be slow to respond. They continue to be backlogged.
Needs: Contemporary, ethnic, feminist, historical, humor/satire, literary, senior citizen/retirement, translations. "We are interested in *authentic* experience and readable prose; Jewish themes; humanistic orientation. No religious, political sectarian; no porn or hard sex, no escapist stuff. Go easy on experimentation, but we're interested." Upcoming themes (submit at least 3 months in advance): "Black-Jewish Relations" (February); "Holocaust/Resistance" (April); "Israel" (May); "Jews in the USSR & Ex-USSR" (July-August). Receives 6-10 unsolicited fiction mss/month. Accepts 0-1 ms/issue; 8-10 mss/year. Published work by Joyce Charton, Paul Corriel, Rachel Ellner and Jack Levine. Published new writers within the last year. Length: 1,000 words minimum; 3,000 words maximum; 1,800 words average. Also publishes literary essays, literary criticism, poetry.
How to Contact: Send complete ms with cover letter. "Writers should include brief biographical information, especially their publishing histories." SASE. No simultaneous submissions. Reports in 2 months on mss. Publishes ms 2-24 months after acceptance. Sample copy for $3 with SAE and 3 first-class stamps. Reviews novels and short story collections.
Payment/Terms: Pays complimentary one-year subscription and 6 contributor's copies. "We readily give reprint permission at no charge." Sends galleys to author.
Advice: Noted for "stories with Jewish content, especially intergenerational relations, and personal Jewish experience—e.g., immigrant or Holocaust memories, assimilation dilemmas, etc. Matters of character and moral dilemma, maturing into pain and joy, dealing with Jewish conflicts OK. Space is increasingly a problem. Tell the truth, as sparely as possible. Charm us with your insight, wit, intelligence, knowledge and, to an extent, your modesty."

*JEWISH QUARTERLY, P.O. Box 2078, London W1A1JR England. E-mail: jewish.quarterly@ort.org. Website: http://www.ortnet.ort.org/communit/jq/start.htm (includes magazine info, covers, excerpts from articles). Editor: Elena Lappin. Quarterly. Publishes 1-3 contribution of fiction/issue.
Needs: "It deals in the broadest sense with all issues of Jewish interest." Length: 1,500 words minimum; 7,000 words maximum.
Payment/Terms: Payment for accepted items £50.
Advice: "Work should have either a Jewish theme in the widest interpretation of that phrase or a theme which would interest our readership. The question which contributors should ask is 'Why should it appear in the *Jewish Quarterly* and not in another periodical?' "

JOURNAL OF POLYMORPHOUS PERVERSITY, (I), Wry-Bred Press, Inc., 10 Waterside Plaza, Suite 20-B, New York NY 10010. (212)689-5473. Editor: Glenn Ellenbogen. Magazine: 6¾ × 10; 24 pages; 60 lb. paper;

antique india cover stock; illustrations with some articles. "*JPP* is a humorous and satirical journal of psychology, psychiatry, and the closely allied mental health disciplines." For "psychologists, psychiatrists, social workers, psychiatric nurses, *and* the psychologically sophisticated layman." Semiannally. Estab. 1984.

Needs: Humor/satire. "We only consider materials that are funny or that relate to psychology *or* behavior." Receives 50 unsolicited mss/month. Accepts 8 mss/issue; 16 mss/year. Most writers published last year were previously unpublished writers. Length: 1,500 words average; 4,000 words maximum. Comments on rejected mss.

How to Contact: Send complete ms *in triplicate*. Include cover letter and SASE. Reports in 1-3 months on mss. SASE. Sample copy for $7. Fiction guidelines for #10 SASE.

Payment/Terms: Pays 2 contributor's copies; additional copies $7.

Advice: "We will *not* look at poetry. We only want to see intelligent spoofs of scholarly psychology and psychiatry articles written in scholarly scientific language. Take a look at *real* journals of psychology and try to lampoon their *style* as much as their content. There are few places to showcase satire of the social sciences, thus we provide one vehicle for injecting a dose of humor into this often too serious area. Occasionally, we will accept a piece of creative writing written in the first person, e.g. 'A Subjective Assessment of the Oral Doctoral Defense Process: I Don't Want to Talk About It, If You Want to Know the Truth' (the latter being a piece in which Holden Caulfield shares his experiences relating to obtaining his Ph.D. in Psychology). Other creative pieces have involved a psychodiagnostic evaluation of The Little Prince (as a psychiatric patient) and God being refused tenure (after having created the world) because of insufficient publications and teaching experience."

KELTIC FRINGE, (II, IV), Kittatinny Press, Box 3292, RD#3, Uniondale PA 18470. (717)679-2745. Editor: Maureen Williams. Magazine: 8½ × 11; 16 pages; offset printed on quality stock paper; card stock cover; illustrations and photos. Publishes "work by Kelts and/or matters Keltic." Quarterly. Estab. 1986. Circ. 300.
  ● *Keltic Fringe* is interested in the work of writers from the "six Keltic nations": Scotland, Isle of Man, Ireland, Wales, Cornwall, Brittany; Kelts around the world and anyone interested in Keltic culture.

Needs: Keltic: ethnic/multicultural, historical, myth, legend. Looks for "creative retelling of Keltic legends, history, modern Keltic tales." Receives 10-20 unsolicited mss/month. Accepts 1 ms/issue; 4 mss/year. Publishes ms 3-12 months after acceptance. Length: 1,500 words average, 200 words minimum; 3,000 words maximum. Publishes short shorts. Also publishes literary essays, literary criticism, and poetry (only as part of features and themes).

How to Contact: Send complete ms with a cover letter. Include estimated word count, bio (50-words maximum) and statement of Keltic connection. Reports in 2 weeks. Send SASE for reply, return of ms or send a disposable copy of ms. Simultaneous and disk submissions OK. Sample copy for $3.50. Fiction guidelines for #10 SASE. Reviews novels and short story collections.

Payment/Terms: Pays 2-10 contributor's copies; additional copies for $1.75. Acquires first North American serial rights. Sends galleys to author if ms is substantially edited.

Advice: "We want lively, Keltic flavor; not sentimental but poignant. We would like to see fictionalized family memoirs with Keltic setting; magic realism in the form of modern mythology. No trite or mawkish tales. Study sample issue."

*KRAX MAGAZINE, 63 Dixon Lane, Leeds LS12 4RR, Yorkshire, Britain, U.K. Fiction Editor: Andy Robson. Appears 1-2 times/year.

Needs: "We publish mostly poetry of a lighthearted nature but use comic or spoof fiction, witty and humorous essays." Publishes 1 story/issue. Length: 2,000 words maximum.

How to Contact: No specific guidelines.

Payment/Terms: Pays contributor's copies. Sample copy for $1 direct from editor.

Advice: "Don't spend too long on scene-setting or character construction as this inevitably produces an anticlimax in a short piece. Send IRCs or currency notes for return postal costs."

LEFT CURVE, (II), P.O. Box 472, Oakland CA 94604. (510)763-7193. E-mail: leftcurv@wco.com. Website: http://www.wco.com/~leftcurv. Editor: Csaba Polony. Magazine: 8½ × 11; 130 pages; 60 lb. paper; 100 pt. C1S Durosheen cover; illustrations; photos. "*Left Curve* is an artist-produced journal addressing the problem(s) of cultural forms emerging from the crises of modernity that strive to be independent from the control of dominant institutions, based on the recognition of the destructiveness of commodity (capitalist) systems to all life." Published irregularly. Estab. 1974. Circ. 2,000.

Needs: Contemporary, ethnic, experimental, historical, literary, prose poem, regional, science fiction, transla-

---

✳ INTERNATIONAL MARKETS, those located outside of the United States and Canada, are marked with an asterisk.

tions, political. "We publish critical, open, social/political-conscious writing." Upcoming theme: "Cyber-space and Nature." Receives approximately 12 unsolicited fiction mss/month. Accepts approximately 1 ms/issue. Publishes ms a maximum of 12 months after acceptance. Published work by Pēter Lengyel and Michael Filas. Length: 1,200 words average; 500 words minimum; 2,500 words maximum. Publishes short shorts. Sometimes comments on rejected mss.

How to Contact: Send complete ms with cover letter. Include "statement of writer's intent, brief bio and reason for submitting to *Left Curve*." Electronic submissions OK; "prefer 3½ disk and hard copy, though we do accept e-mail submissions." Reports in 3-6 months. SASE. Sample copy for $8, 9 × 12 SAE and $1.24 postage. Fiction guidelines for 1 first-class stamp.

Payment/Terms: Pays in contributor's copies. Rights revert to author.

Advice: "Dig deep; no superficial personalisms, no corny satire. Be honest, realistic and gorge out the truth you wish to say. Understand yourself and the world. Have writing be a means to achieve or realize what is real."

‡LIES MAGAZINE, The Magazine that Contains Children's Stories for Adults, (II), LCN Syndicate, 1112 San Pedro NE #154, Albuquerque NM 87110. (505)268-7316. E-mail: okeefine@aol.com. Editor: Matt Worley. Magazine: 8½ × 11; 44 pages; 50 lb. offset, nonglossy paper; 80 lb. enamel glossy cover; illustrations and photographs. "We strive to make fun of everything, but our fiction is usually less on the humorous side—more gritty—to counter balance sarcasm. We generally attract late teens to early 30s." Estab. 1995. Circ. 2,000.

Needs: Ethnic/multicultural, experimental, humor/satire, literary, mainstream/contemporary, science fiction (soft, sociological). No genre fiction. Receives 10 unsolicited mss/month. Accepts 1-4 mss/issue; 4-16 mss/year. Publishes ms 3 months after acceptance. Recently published work by Stepan Chapman, Michael Wexler, Michael Maiello and Bill Kaul. Length: 2,000 words average; 500 words minimum; 3,000 words maximum. Publishes short shorts. Also publishes literary essays, literary criticism, poetry (very rarely). Sometimes critiques or comments on rejected mss.

How to Contact: Send complete ms with a cover letter. Include 25-50 word bio and list of publications. Reports in 1 month on queries; 2 months on mss. Send SASE for reply, return of ms or send a disposable copy of ms. Electronic submissions OK. Sample copy for $3. Fiction guidelines free for #10 SASE. Reviews novels and short story collections. Send books to Ruth Raymond.

Payment/Terms: Pays 1 contributor's copy on publication; additional copies for $2. Acquires first rights.

Advice: "If you believe in yourself and your writing, someone will eventually understand. Get used to disappointment. Just keep plugging and refining your craft. Nothing happens overnight."

‡LOST WORLDS, The Science Fiction and Fantasy Forum, (I, IV), HBD Publishing, P.O. Box 605, Concord NC 28026-0605. Phone/fax: (704)933-7998. Editor: Holley B. Drye. Newsletter: 8½ × 11; 48 pages; 24 lb. bond paper; full-color cover; b&w illustrations. "General interest science fiction and fantasy, as well as some specialized genre writing. For broad-spectrum age groups, anyone interested in newcomers." Monthly. Estab. 1988. Circ. 150.

Needs: Experimental, fantasy, horror, psychic/supernatural/occult, science fiction (hard science, soft/sociological), serialized novel. Publishes annual special fiction issue. Receives 35-45 unsolicited mss/month. Accepts 10-14 mss/issue; 100 and up mss/year. Publishes ms 1 year after acceptance (unless otherwise notified). Length: 3,000 words preferred; 2,000 words minimum; 5,500 words maximum. Publishes short shorts. Sometimes critiques rejected mss and recommends other markets. "Although we do not publish every type of genre fiction, I will, if asked, critique anyone who wishes to send me their work. There is no fee for reading or critiquing stories."

How to Contact: Query first. "Cover letters should include where and when to contact the author, a pen name, if one is preferred, as well as their real name, and whether or not they wish their real names to be kept confidential. Due to overwhelming response, we are currently unable to predict response time to mss or queries. Phone calls are welcome to check on manuscripts." SASE for return of ms. Simultaneous and reprint submissions OK. Accepts electronic submissions via disk or modem. Sample copy for $5. Fiction guidelines free.

Payment/Terms: Pays contributor's copies. Acquires one-time rights.

Advice: "I look for originality of story, good characterization and dialogue, well-written descriptive passages, and over-all story quality. The presentation of the work also makes a big impression, whether it be good or bad. Neat, typed manuscripts will always have a better chance than hand-written or badly typed ones. All manuscripts are read by either three or four different people, with an eye towards development of plot and comparison to other material within the writer's field of experience. Plagiarism is not tolerated, and we do look for it while reading a manuscript under consideration. If you have any questions, feel free to call—we honestly don't mind. Never be afraid to send us anything, we really are kind people."

MAIL CALL JOURNAL, Where the Spirit of the Civil War Soldier Lives!, Distant Frontier Press, P.O. Box 5031, Dept. N, South Hackensack NJ 07606. Phone: (201)296-0419. E-mail: mcj@historyonline.net. Website: http://www.historyonline.net (includes sample issues, latest editorials, writer's guidelines, poetry and writer's contests). Managing Editor: Anna Pansini. Newsletter: 8½ × 11; 8 pages; 20 lb. paper; illustrations. *Mail Call Journal* publishes pieces on the Civil War. Bimonthly. Estab. 1990. Circ. 500.

Needs: Historical (American Civil War). Receives 20 unsolicited mss/month. Accepts 1 mss/issue; 6 mss/year. Publishes ms up to 1½ years after acceptance. 50% of work published is by new writers. Length: 500 words minimum; 1,500 words maximum. Also publishes literary essays, literary criticism and poetry. Sometimes critiques or comments on rejected ms.

How to Contact: Send complete ms with a cover letter mentioning "any relations from the Civil War period." Reports in 1 year. SASE for return of ms. Simultaneous, reprint and electronic (disk) submissions OK. Sample copy and fiction guidelines are included in a writer's packet for $5.

Payment/Terms: Pays in contributor's copies. Acquires one-time rights for print and Internet publication.

Advice: Wants more "personal accounts" and no "overused themes. We want material written from the heart, not the pocketbook. Flashy is not a part of this publication."

MAJESTIC BOOKS, (I, IV), P.O. Box 19097A, Johnston RI 02919. Fiction Editor: Cindy MacDonald. Bound softcover short story anthologies; 5½ × 8½; 192 pages; 60 lb. paper; C1S cover stock. "Majestic Books is a small press which was formed to give children an outlet for their work. We publish softcover bound anthologies of fictional stories by children, for children and adults who enjoy the work of children." Triannually. Estab. 1993. Circ. 250.

● Although Majestic Books is a small publisher, they are in the market for short fiction for their anthologies. They do a book of stories by children.

Needs: Stories written on any subject by children (under 18) only. Children's/juvenile (10-12 years), young adult (13-18 years). Receives 50 unsolicited mss/month. Accepts 80 mss/year. Publishes ms 1 year maximum after acceptance. Recently published work by Brian Freeman, Gregory Miller and Tiffany Hrach. Publishes 100 new writers/year. Length: 100 words minimum; 2,000 words maximum. Publishes short shorts. Also publishes literary essays. Always critiques or comments on rejected mss.

How to Contact: Send complete ms with a cover letter. Include estimated word count and author's age. Reports in 3 weeks. Send SASE for reply. Simultaneous submissions OK. Sample copy for $3. Fiction guidelines for #10 SASE.

Payment/Terms: Pays 10% royalty for all books sold due to the author's inclusion.

Advice: "We love stories that will keep a reader thinking long after they have read the last word. Be original. We have received some manuscripts of shows we have seen on television or books we have read. Write from inside you and you'll be surprised at how much better your writing will be. Use *your* imagination."

‡MASQUERADE, An Erotic Journal, (II, IV), 801 Second Ave., New York NY 10017. (212)661-7878, ext. 331. Fax: (212)986-7355. E-mail: MasqBks@aol.com. Editor: Marti Hohmann. Magazine: 8½ × 11; gloss paper; gloss cover; illustrations and photos. "*Masquerade* is a pansexual, sex-positive publication expressly interested in work by artists and writers outside the mainstream. We are especially open to contributions from gay, lesbian, bisexual, SM, fetish and transgendered communities."

Needs: Erotica, gay, lesbian. "Stories should contain explicit sexual content. Keep characters and relationships legal: please do not refer to the sexual thoughts, feelings, or actions of characters under eighteen years of age. We do not publish representations of incest or bestiality." Length: 1,000 words average; 5,000 words maximum.

How to Contact: Send complete ms with a cover letter. Reports in 2-3 weeks on mss. Send SASE for reply, return of ms. No simultaneous submissions or reprints. Reviews novels and short story collections. Send books to editor.

Payment/Terms: Pays 3 cents/word; $75 maximum on publication for first North American serial rights.

Advice: "Although our publication will always feature excerpts from recently released Masquerade Books titles, all departments are open to freelance writers."

MEDICINAL PURPOSES, Literary Review, (I, II), Poet to Poet Inc., 86-37 120 St., #2D, ℅ Catterson, Richmond Hill NY 11418. (718)776-8853, (718)847-2150. E-mail: scarptp@worldnet.att.com. Website: http://wsite.com/poettopoet (includes writer's guidelines, samples of published work and announcements for open readings). Editors: Robert Dunn and Thomas M. Catterson. Fiction Editor: Andrew Clark. Magazine: 8½ × 5½; 60 pages; illustrations. "*Medicinal Purposes* publishes quality work that will benefit the world, though not necessarily through obvious means." Ternate-annually (three times per year). Estab. 1995. Circ. 1,000.

Needs: Adventure, erotica, ethnic/multicultural, experimental, fantasy, feminist, gay, historical, horror, humor/satire, lesbian, literary, mainstream/contemporary, mystery/suspense, psychic/supernatural/occult, regional, romance, science fiction, senior citizen/retirement, sports, westerns, young adult/teen. "Please no pornography, or hatemongering." Receives 5 unsolicited mss/month. Accepts 2-3 mss/issue; 8 mss/year. Publishes ms up to four issues after acceptance. Recently published work by Laura Nixon Dawson, Mike Ryan and James Michael Robbins. Length: 2,000 words average; 50 words minimum; 3,000 words maximum. "We prefer maximum of 10 double-spaced pages." Publishes short shorts. Also publishes literary essays, literary criticism, poetry. Sometimes critiques or comments on rejected mss.

How to Contact: Send complete ms with a cover letter. Include estimated word count, brief bio, Social Security number. Reports in 6 weeks on queries; 8 weeks on mss. SASE. Simultaneous and electronic submissions (modem through e-mail) OK. Sample copy for $6, 6 × 9 SAE and 4 first-class stamps. Fiction guidelines free for #10 SASE.

Payment/Terms: Pays 2 contributor's copies. Acquires first rights.

Advice: "One aspect of the better stories we've seen is that the writer enjoys (or, at least, believes in) the tale being told. Also, learn the language—good English can be a beautiful thing. We long for stories that only a specific writer can tell, by virtue of experience or style. Expand our horizons. Clichés equal death around here."

MEDIPHORS, A Literary Journal of the Health Professions, (I, II, IV), P.O. Box 327, Bloomsburg PA 17815. Editor: Eugene D. Radice, MD. Magazine: 8½×11; 73 pages; 20 lb. white paper; 70 lb. cover; illustrations and photos. "We publish broad work related to medicine and health including essay, short story, commentary, fiction, poetry. Our audience: general readers and health care professionals." Semiannually. Estab. 1993. Circ. 900.

Needs: "Short stories related to health." Adventure, experimental, historical, humor/satire, literary, mainstream/contemporary, science fiction (hard science, soft/sociological), medicine. "No religious, erotica, fantasy." Receives 50 unsolicited mss/month. Accepts 14 mss/issue; 28 mss/year. Publishes ms 10 months after acceptance. Agented fiction 2%. Length: 2,500 words average; 4,500 words maximum. Publishes short shorts. Also publishes literary essays and poetry. Sometimes critiques or comments on rejected mss.

How to Contact: Send complete ms with a cover letter. Include estimated word count, bio (paragraph) and any experience/employment in the health professions. Reports in 4 months on mss. Send SASE for reply, return of ms or send a disposable copy of ms. No simultaneous submissions. Sample copy for $6. Fiction guidelines for #10 SASE.

Payment/Terms: Pays 2 contributor's copies; additional copies for $5.50 Acquires first North American serial rights.

Advice: Looks for "high quality writing that shows fresh perspective in the medical and health fields. Accurate knowledge of subject material. Situations that explore human understanding in adversity. Order a sample copy for examples of work. Start with basic quality writing in short story and create believable, engaging stories concerning medicine and health. Knowledge of the field is important since the audience includes professionals within the medical field. Don't be discouraged. We enjoy receiving work from beginning writers."

MENTOR & PROTEGE, Accelerating Personal & Professional Development Through the Art and Practice of Mentoring, (I, IV), P.O. Box 4382, Overland Park KS 66204. (913)362-7889. Editor: Maureen Waters. Newsletter: 8½×11; 12 pages. Quarterly. Estab. 1989. Circ. 250.

Needs: "Submissions must be mentoring related." Receives 1 unsolicited ms/month. "I would run more fiction if I received more." Recently published work by Charles Chaim Wax of Brooklyn. Length: 1,200-3,000 words. Also publishes literary essays. Sometimes critiques or comments on rejected mss.

How to Contact: Query first or send complete ms with a cover letter. Include bio with submission. Reports in 1 month on queries; 2 months on mss. Send SASE for reply, return of ms or send a disposable copy of ms. Simultaneous, reprint and electronic submissions (Mac, IBM disks) OK. Sample copy for $6. Fiction guidelines for #10 SASE.

Payment/Terms: Pays 2 contributor's copies, "but working toward paying 3-5¢ a word."

Advice: "The writer should understand the mentoring concept and the whole story should revolve around mentoring. Readers are professionals involved in mentoring programs, so the fiction we print has to paint a picture that is relevant to them—perhaps helps them understand a new aspect of mentoring or moves them into a new way of thinking. If it's a good or fixable story, I'll work with the writer."

MINDSPARKS, The Magazine of Science and Science Fiction, (I, II, IV), Molecudyne Research, P.O. Box 1302, Laurel MD 20725-1302. (410)715-1703. Editor: Catherine Asaro. Magazine: 8½×11; 44 pages; 20 lb. white paper; 60 lb. cover; illustrations and photos. "We publish science fiction and science articles." Published on a varied schedule. Estab. 1993. Circ. 1,000.

Needs: Science fiction (hard science, soft/sociological), young adult (science fiction). "No pornography." Receives 50 unsolicited submissions/month. Accepts 2-4 mss/issue; 12-14 mss/year. Publishes ms 1-24 months after acceptance. Published work by Hal Clement, G. David Nordley, Lois Gresh and Paul Levinson. Length: 4,000 words average; 8,000 words maximum. Publishes short shorts. Also publishes literary essays, literary criticism and poetry. Often critiques or comments on rejected mss.

How to Contact: Send complete ms with a cover letter. Include estimated word count and list of publications. "Prefers initial contact be made by mail." Reports in 2-3 months. Send SASE for reply, return of ms or send a disposable copy of ms. Simultaneous submissions OK. Sample copy for $4.50, 8½×11 SAE and $1 postage or 2 IRCs. Fiction guidelines for #10 SASE. Reviews novels and short story collections.

Payment/Terms: Pays 2¢/word on publication for first North American serial rights. Sends galleys to author.

Advice: Looks for "well-written, well-researched, interesting science ideas with good characterization and good plot. Read a copy of the magazine. We receive many submissions that don't fit the intent of *Mindsparks*."

‡MINI ROMANCES MAGAZINE, (I, II), P.O. Box 443, San Bernardino CA 92401. (909)421-5151. E-mail: miniromanc@aol.com. Editor: T'La June. Magazine: 65 pages; copy paper; illustrations and photos. "*Mini Romances* is a magazine that allows new and unpublished writers a chance to be published." Bimonthly. Estab. 1997.

Needs: Erotica, romance (contemporary), young adult/teen (romance). No "vulgar language." Receives 10-12 unsolicited mss/month. Accepts 2-3 mss/issue. Publishes ms 2-4 months after acceptance. Length: 2,000 words average; 1,000 words minimum; 2,500 words maximum. Also publishes poetry. Send complete manuscript with a cover letter or e-mail. Include estimated word count. Reports in 3 months on queries and mss. Send SASE for reply, return of ms or send disposable copy of ms. Simultaneous, reprint and electronic submissions OK. Sample copy for $2.50. Fiction Guidelines for #10 SASE.

Payment/Terms: Pays 2 contributor's copies for one-time rights.

Advice: "Make sure that the reader keeps interested in what you're writing. Get to the point in a timely manner, while putting several ups and downs throughout the story."

THE MIRACULOUS MEDAL, (IV), The Central Association of the Miraculous Medal, 475 E. Chelten Ave., Philadelphia PA 19144. (215)848-1010. Editor: Rev. William J. O'Brien, C.M. Magazine. Quarterly.

Needs: Religious/inspirational. Receives 25 unsolicited fiction mss/month. Accepts 2 mss/issue; 8 mss/year. Publishes ms up to two years or more after acceptance.

How to Contact: Query first with SASE. Sample copy and fiction guidelines free.

Payment/Terms: Pays 2¢/word minimum. Pays on acceptance for first rights.

MOUNTAIN LUMINARY, (I), P.O. Box 1187, Mountain View AR 72560-1187. (870)585-2260. Fax: (870)269-4110. E-mail: ecomtn@mutel.net. Editor: Anne Thiel. Magazine; photos. "*Mountain Luminary* is dedicated to bringing information to people about the Aquarian Age; how to grow with its new and evolutionary energies and how to work with the resultant changes in spirituality, relationships, environment and the planet. *Mountain Luminary* provides a vehicle for people to share ideas, philosophies and experiences that deepen understanding of this evolutionary process and humankind's journey on Earth." International quarterly. Estab. 1985.

Needs: Humor/satire, metaphor/inspirational/Aquarian-Age topics. Accepts 8-10 mss/year. Publishes ms 6 months after acceptance. Recently published work by Alan Cohen, Richard Moss, Theresa Dale, Laura V. Hyde, Richard Hill and Dr. Larry Wilson. Publishes 6 new writers/year.

How to Contact: Query with clips of published work. SASE for return of ms. Simultaneous and electronic submissions (Mac IIci, Quark XP) OK. Sample copy and writer's guidelines free.

Payment/Terms: Pays 1 contributor's copy. "We may offer advertising space as payment." Acquires first rights.

Advice: Topical interests include: New Age/Aquarian Age, astrology, crystals, cultural and ethnic concerns, dreams, ecosystems, the environment, extraterrestrials, feminism, folklore, healing and health, holistic and natural health, inspiration, juvenile and teen issues, lifestyle, meditation, men's issues, metaphysics, mysticism, nutrition, parallel dimensions, prayer, psychic phenomenon, self-help, spirituality and women's issues."

MURDEROUS INTENT, Mystery Magazine, (I, IV), Madison Publishing Company, P.O. Box 5947, Vancouver WA 98668-5947. (360)695-9004. Fax: (360)693-3354. E-mail: madison@teleport.com. Website: http://www.teleport.com/~madison (includes writer's guidelines, short fiction, interviews, table of contents, subscription and convention information). Editor: Margo Power. Magazine: 8½×11; 64 pages; newsprint; glossy 2-color cover; illustrations; photos. Quarterly. Estab. 1995. Circ. 7,000.

● *Murderous Intent* was rated 37 in *Writer's Digest* Fiction Top 50.

Needs: Mystery/suspense (amateur sleuth, cozy, police procedural, private eye), psychic/supernatural/occult, science fiction (with mystery) "occasionally." No cannibal stories, no stories with excessive violence, language or sex. Receives 200 unsolicited mss/month. Accepts 10-14 mss/issue; 40-48 mss/year. Publishes ms up to 1 year after acceptance. Recently published work by Barbara Paul, Ed Dorman, Jeremiah Healy, Toni L.P. Kelner, Carol Cail, Michael Mallory, Deborah Adams and Polly Whitney. Publishes 30% new writers/year. Length: 2,000-4,000 words average; 250 words minimum; 5,000 words maximum. Publishes short shorts. Length: 250-400 words. Also publishes mystery-related essays and poetry. Sometimes critiques or comments on rejected mss. Sponsors quarterly contest. SASE for contest guidelines, deadline for submissions September 1, December 1, March 1 and June 1.

How to Contact: Send complete ms with a cover letter. Include estimated word count, brief bio name of story and telephone number and e-mail address. Reports in 3 months on queries, 3-6 months on mss. Send SASE for reply or send a disposable copy of ms. Simultaneous submissions OK. Sample copy for $5, 9×12 SAE and 4 first-class stamps. Guidelines for #10 SASE. "Minisynopsis Corner" for authors to submit minisynopses of their new mystery novels (free).

Payment/Terms: Pays $10 and 2 contributor's copies on acceptance; additional copies for $3.50 (issue their story appears in). Acquires first North American serial rights.

Advice: "The competition is tough so write the mystery you love—build characters people will remember—and surprise us."

MY LEGACY, (I, II), Weems Concepts, HCR-13, Box 21AA, Artemas PA 17211-9405. (814)458-3102. Editor: Kay Weems. Magazine: digest size; 125-150 pages; white paper; 20 lb. colored paper cover; illustrations. "Work must be in good taste. No bad language. Audience is from all walks of life," adults and children. Quarterly. Estab. 1991. Circ. 200.

Needs: Adventure, children's/juvenile (10-12 years), fantasy (children's fantasy, science fantasy), historical, horror, humor/satire, mainstream/contemporary, mystery/suspense (amateur sleuth, cozy, police procedural, private eye/hardboiled, romantic suspense), regional, religious/inspirational, romance (contemporary, futuristic/time travel, gothic, historical), science fiction (hard science, soft/sociological), senior citizen/retirement, westerns (frontier, traditional), young adult/teen (adventure, mystery, science fiction, western). No porno. List of upcoming themes available for SASE. Publishes special fiction issues or anthologies. Receives 15-30 unsolicited mss/ month. Accepts 30-35 mss/issue; 120-140 mss/year. Publishes mss within 6 months after acceptance. Published work by Peter Gauthier, Jel D.Lewis (Jones); Brucie Jacobs, Joseph Farley, Mark Scott and Gerri George. Length: 2,500 words average. Publishes short shorts. Very seldom critiques or comments on rejected mss; "usually don't have time."

How to Contact: Send complete ms with a cover letter. Include estimated word count, bio (short paragraph) and list of publications. Reports within 6 months on mss. Send SASE for reply, return of ms or send a disposable copy of ms (preferable). Simultaneous and reprint submissions OK. Sample copy for $3.50, 9×6½ SAE and $1.70 postage. Fiction guidelines for #10 SASE.

Payment/Terms: Acquires one-time rights.

Advice: Looks for "a good beginning, tight writing, good conversations, believable characters and believable ending."

MYSTERY TIME, An Anthology of Short Stories, (I), Hutton Publications, P.O. Box 2907, Decatur IL 62524. Editor: Linda Hutton. Booklet: 5½×8½; 52 pages; bond paper; illustrations. "Biannual collection of short stories with a suspense or mystery theme for mystery buffs, with an emphasis on women writers and women protagonists." Estab. 1983.

Needs: Mystery/suspense only. Features older women as protagonists. Receives 10-15 unsolicited fiction mss/ month. Accepts 20-24 mss/year. Published work by Leigh Fox, Kristin Neri and Sylvia Roberts. Published new writers within the last year. Length: 1,500 words maximum. Occasionally critiques rejected mss and recommends other markets.

How to Contact: Send complete ms with SASE. "No cover letters." Simultaneous and previously published submissions OK. Reports in 1 month on mss. Publishes ms an average of 6-8 months after acceptance. Reprint submissions OK. Sample copy for $3.50. Fiction guidelines for #10 SASE.

Payment/Terms: Pays ¼-1¢/word and 1 contributor's copy; additional copies $2.50. Acquires one-time rights.

Advice: "Study a sample copy and the guidelines. Too many amateurs mark themselves as amateurs by submitting blindly."

‡NEW ENGLAND WRITERS' NETWORK, (I, II), P.O. Box 483, Hudson MA 01749-0483. (978)562-2946. Fax: (978)568-0497. Editor: Glenda Baker. Fiction Editor: Liz Aleshire. Poetry Editor: Judy Adourian. Magazine: 8½×11; 24 pages; coated cover. "We aim at beginners who want feedback and more experienced writers who need encouragement and support. We are looking for well-written stories that grab us from the opening paragraph." Quarterly. Estab. 1994. Circ. 200.

Needs: Adventure, condensed/excerpted novel, ethnic/multicultural, humor/satire, literary, mainstream/contemporary, mystery/suspense, religious/inspirational, romance. "We will consider anything except pornography." Accepts 5 mss/issue; 20 mss/year. Reads mss only from June 1 through September 1. Publishes ms 4-12 months after acceptance. Recently published work by Mike Lipstock, Steve Burt, Tom Ewart, Michelle Hartman, Janice Lindsay and Amy Weintraub. Length: 2,000 words maximum. Publishes short shorts. Also publishes poetry and 3-4 personal essays per issue. Always critiques or comments on rejected mss.

How to Contact: Send complete ms with a cover letter. Include estimated word count. Bio on acceptance. Reports in 4 months. SASE for return of ms. No simultaneous submissions. Sample copy for $5. Fiction guidelines free. "We do not review story collections or novels. We do publish 2,000 words (maximum) novel excerpts. Writer picks the excerpt—do not send novel."

Payment/Terms: Pays $10 for fiction, $5 for personal essays, $3 per poem on publication and 1 contributor's copy. Acquires first North American serial rights.

Advice: "Give us a try! Please send for guidelines and a sample."

NEW METHODS, The Journal of Animal Health Technology, (IV), P.O. Box 22605, San Francisco CA 94122-0605. (415)379-9065. Editor: Ronald S. Lippert, AHT. Newsletter ("could become magazine again"): 8½×11; 2-4 pages; 20 lb. paper; illustrations; "rarely" photos. Network service in the animal field educating services for mostly professionals in the animal field; e.g., animal health technicians. Monthly. Estab. 1976. Circ. 5,608.

Needs: Animals: contemporary, experimental, historical, mainstream, regional. No stories unrelated to animals. Receives 12 unsolicited fiction mss/month. Accepts one ms/issue; 12 mss/year. Length: Open. "Rarely" publishes short shorts. Occasionally critiques rejected mss. Recommends other markets.

LOOKING FOR A PARTICULAR GENRE? Check our Category Index for magazine and book publishers who want **Mystery/Suspense**, **Romance**, **Science Fiction & Fantasy**, **Thrillers**, **Westerns** and more!

How to Contact: Query first with theme, length, expected time of completion, photos/illustrations, if any, biographical sketch of author, all necessary credits or send complete ms. Report time varies (up to 4 months). SASE for query and ms. Simultaneous submissions OK. Sample copy and fiction guidelines for $2.90.

Payment/Terms: No payment. Acquires one-time rights. Back issue and fiction guidelines only with SASE for $2, must mention Writer's Digest Books.

Advice: Sponsors contests: theme changes but generally concerns the biggest topics of the year in the animal field. "Emotion, personal experience—make the person feel it. We are growing."

‡**NEW THOUGHT JOURNAL, the beat of a thousand drummers, (II, IV)**, Ohl Publishing, Inc. 2520 Evelyn Dr., Dayton OH 45409. (937)293-9717. Fax: (937)866-9603. E-mail: ntjmag@aol.com. Editor: Jeff Ohl. Magazine: 8¼×11; 40 pages; glossy cover; illustrations and photos. "*NTJ* reflects the creative and spiritual intent of authors, artists, musicians, poets and philosophers as they intuitively mirror a silent consensus that is building in our world." Quarterly. Estab. 1994. Circ. 5,000.

Needs: Ethnic/multicultural, fantasy (science fantasy), literary, religious/inspirational, science fiction (soft/sociological), comparative religions, alternative thought, health, living, metaphysics, environment, the arts. List of upcoming themes available for SASE. Receives 12 unsolicited mss/month. Accepts 1-2 mss/issue; 4-8 mss/year. Publishes ms 3-9 months after acceptance. Recently published work by Jesse Wolf Hardin, Jane Stuart, Mel Waldman and Kelly Washburne. Length: 2,500 words average; 1,000 words minimum; 3,500 words maximum. Publishes short shorts. Also publishes literary essays and poetry.

How to Contact: Send complete ms with a cover letter. Include estimated word count and one-sentence bio. Reports in 1 months on queries; 1-3 months on mss. Send SASE for reply, return of ms or send disposable copy of ms. Simultaneous, reprint and electronic submissions OK.

Payment/Terms: Payment negotiable. Pays at least free subscription to magazine and 2 contributor's copies for one-time rights.

Advice: "Submit on-theme; purity of intent; not self-promoting; reflect a spirited/creative lifestyle."

‡**NEWFANGLED FAIRY TALES and GIRLS TO THE RESCUE, (II)**, Meadowbrook Press, 5451 Smetana Dr., Minnetonka MN 55343. (612)930-1100. Editor: Bruce Lansky. Anthology series for children ages 8-12. Semiannually.

Needs: Children's/juvenile (8-12 years). No novels or picture books. Receives 50-60 unsolicited submissions/month for each series. Accepts 10 mss/issue; 20 mss/year. Publishes ms 1 year after acceptance. Length: 1,200-1,500 words average; 1,800 words maximum. Sometimes comments on or critiques rejected mss.

How to Contact: Query first. Include estimated word count and list of publications. Reports in 3 months. Send SASE for reply, return of ms or send disposable copy of ms. Simultaneous submissions and reprints OK. Fiction guidelines for #10 SASE.

Payment/Terms: Pays $500 on publication for nonexclusive worldwide rights. Sends galleys to author.

Advice: "Read our guidelines before submitting."

NEXT PHASE, (I, II), 2520 Evelyn Dr., Dayton OH 45409. (937)293-9717. Fax: (937)866-9603. E-mail: ntjmag@aol.com. Publisher/Editor: Jeff Ohl. 8½×11; 40 pages. "Features the best of fiction, poetry and illustration by up-and-coming writers and artists. We publish quality work as long as it is environmentally and humanely oriented." Triannually. Estab. 1989. Circ. 1,700.

Needs: Experimental, fantasy. Receives 15-25 unsolicited mss/month. Accepts 9 mss/issue; 25 mss/year. Publishes short shorts. Also publishes poetry. Critiques rejected mss.

How to Contact: Send complete manuscript with cover letter. SASE. Simultaneous and reprint submissions OK. Reports in 6 weeks. Sample copy for $4.95 includes postage.

Payment/Terms: Pays contributor's copies. Acquires one-time rights.

Advice: "We accept a broad range of fiction up to 4,000 words. We only accept environmentally or humanely-oriented fiction of all genres."

‡**NIGHT TERRORS, (II)**, 1202 W. Market St., Orrville OH 44667-1710. (330)683-0338. E-mail: DED3548@aol.com. Editor: D.E. Davidson. Magazine: 8½×11; 52 pages; 80 lb. glossy cover; illustrations and photographs. *Night Terrors* publishes quality horror fiction for literate adults. Quarterly. Estab. 1996. Circ. 1,000.

Needs: Horror, psychic/supernatural/occult. "Night Terrors does not accept stories involving abuse, sexual mutulation or stories with children as main characters." Receives 50 unsolicited mss/month. Accepts 12 mss/issue; 46 mss/year. Publishes ms 2-6 months after acceptance. Recently published work by A.R. Morlan, J.N. Williamson, Mort Castle, Nina Kiriki Hoffman, Don D'Ammassa and Dominick Cancilla. Length: 3,000 words average; 2,000 words minimum; 5,000 words maximum. Often critiques or comments on rejected mss.

How to Contact: Send complete ms with a cover letter. Include estimated word count, 50-word bio and list of publications. Reports in 1 week on queries; 2 months on mss. Send SASE for reply, return of ms or send a disposable copy of ms. Simultaneous submissions and reprints OK. Sample copy for $6. Fiction guidelines free for #10 SASE.

Payment/Terms: Pays up to $100 on publication and 1-2 contributor's copy; additional copies for $4.50. Acquires first North American serial rights or second rights for reprints. Sends galleys to author.

Advice: "I publish what I like. I suggest that writers read a copy of the magazine before sending me anything.

Submit a manuscript in appropriate form, proofed for spelling, grammar and punctuation."

NIGHTMARES, (I, II), New Illiad Publishing, P.O. Box 587, Rocky Hill CT 06067. Editor: Ed Kobialka, Jr. Magazine: 8½×11; 64 pages; 20 lb. paper; 80 lb. cover; illustrations. "*Nightmares* publishes horror, from the modern age or gothic. We publish any writer, beginning or established, who submits good material." Published 3 times/year. Estab. 1994. Circ. 375.
Needs: Horror, supernatural/occult. Receives 50-70 unsolicited mss/month. Accepts 8 mss/issue; 35 mss/year. Does not read during December. Publishes ms 1 year after acceptance. Length: 2,500 words average; 500 words minimum; 6,000 words maximum. Usually critiques or comments on rejected mss.
How to Contact: Send complete ms with a cover letter. Include estimated word count, bio (1-2 paragraphs), Social Security number and list of publications. Reports in 1 month on queries; 2 months on mss. Send SASE for reply, return of ms or send a disposable copy of ms. Simultaneous submissions OK. Sample copy for $2.95. Fictions guidelines for #10 SASE.
Payment/Terms: Pays $10 maximum and 2 contributor's copies for first rights.
Advice: "It must be scary! Grab the reader's attention with a good opening; make your characters and places seem real; and don't make your ending predictable. Don't forget about the old, classic monsters—vampires, ghosts and demons still scare people. Graphic brutal violence and descriptive sex are unacceptable. Your goal as a writer should be to terrorize your reader without being disgusting or offensive."

THE NOCTURNAL LYRIC, (I, IV), Box 115, San Pedro CA 90733. (310)519-9220. E-mail: nlyric@webtv.n et. Website: http://www.Angelfire.com/ca/nocturnallyric (includes fiction guidelines, upcoming authors and sample poetry). Editor: Susan Moon. Digest: 5½×8½; 40 pages; illustrations. "We are a non-profit literary journal, dedicated to printing fiction by new writers for the sole purpose of getting read by people who otherwise might have never seen their work." Bimonthly. Estab. 1987. Circ. 400.
Needs: Experimental, fantasy, horror, humor/satire, psychic/supernatural/occult, science fiction, poetry. "We will give priority to unusual, creative pieces." Receives 50 unsolicited mss/month. Publishes ms 10-12 months after acceptance. Recently published work by Mike Bode, Jeff Strand, Denise Longrie and Samantha Reynolds. Length: 2,000 words maximum. Publishes short shorts. Also publishes poetry.
How to Contact: Send complete ms with cover letter. Include "something about the author, areas of fiction he/she is interested in." Reports in 2 weeks on queries; 4-6 months on mss. SASE. Simultaneous and reprint submissions OK. Sample copy for $3 (checks to Susan Moon). Fiction guidelines for #10 SASE.
Payment/Terms: Pays in gift certificates for subscription discounts. Publication not copyrighted.
Advice: "Please stop wasting your postage sending us things that are in no way bizarre. Do send us your wierdest, most unique creations. Don't pretend you've read us when you haven't! I can usually tell! We're getting more into strange, surrealistic horror and fantasy, or silly, satirical horror. If you're avant-garde, we want you! We're mainly accepting things that are bizarre all the way through, as opposed to ones that only have a surprise bizarre ending."

NON-STOP SCIENCE FICTION MAGAZINE, (I, II), Non-Stop Magazine, P.O. Box 981, Peck Slip Station, New York NY 10272-0981. E-mail: nonstop@compuserve.com. Website: http://www.geocities.com/Area51/Corri dor/7174 (includes guidelines, interviews, essays and artwork). Editor: Luis Ortiz. Magazine: 8½×11; 52 pages; glossy 4-color cover, illustrations and photos. Quarterly. Estab. 1993.
Needs: Fantasy (modern), science fiction, translations. Science fiction with strong literary/idea content. Planning special issue on alternative history science fiction. Also planning future special all-fiction issue or anthology. Receives 300-450 unsolicited mss/month. Accepts 3-5 mss/issue; 18 mss/year. Does not read mss July, August or December. Publishes ms 3-18 months after acceptance. Recently published work by Barry N. Malzberg, Charles Platt, L Sprague de Camp and Don Webb. Length: 4,000 words average; 1,000 words minimum; 9,000 words maximum. Publishes literary essays, science articles and literary criticism. Sometimes critiques or comments on mss.
How to Contact: Send complete ms with a cover letter. Include estimated word count, 1- or 2-page bio and list of publications. Reports in 2-3 weeks on queries; 3 months on mss. SASE for reply. Prefers a disposable copy of ms. No simultaneous submissions. Reprint submissions OK from outside North America. Sample copy for $5.95. Reviews novels and short story collections.
Payment/Terms: Pays 3-6¢/word and 2 contributor's copies for first North American serial rights. Sends galleys to author.
Advice: Looks for "strong writing with believable characters and new science extrapolation. Read *Non-Stop* to see what we're publishing. We're seeing too many science fiction ideas coming from watching movies or TV shows. We will reject these instantly. We like to see science and technology used as a springboard for a story. The cost of printing on paper is going to get worse and the advantages of online publishing will seem more attractive."

‡♥NORTHWORDS, Science Fiction, Fantasy & Horror Magazine, (II), The Society for Canadian Content in Speculative Arts and Literature, P.O. Box 5752, Merivale Depot, Nepean Ontario K2C 3M1 Canada. (613)596-4105. Editor: Mark Leslie Lefebure. Magazine: 8½×11; 50 pages; white offset (120m) paper; color cover; illustrations and photos. "*Northwords* publishes great fiction, news, reviews, articles, essays, interviews and poetry by Canadians, with a distinctive Canadian slant, or of general interest to everyone who reads or writes speculative literature." Quarterly. Estab. 1993. Circ. 500.

Needs: Fantasy (science fantasy, sword and sorcery), horror, psychic/supernatural/occult, science fiction. Receives 20 unsolicited mss/month. Buys 3-6 mss/issue; 16-20 mss/year. Publishes ms 2-12 months after acceptance. Recently published work by Robert Sawyer, Charles de Lint, Edo van Belkom and John Buja. Length: 250-8,000 words. Publishes short shorts. Also publishes literary essays, literary criticism and poetry. Often critiques or comments on rejected ms.

How to Contact: Send full ms, SASE or #10 envelope with IRC if from outside Canada with disposable ms. "Response time varies: 2-6 months. We sometimes hold onto submissions we feel are worth re-reading for future issues. If it takes longer for us ro respond, that's probably because the submission itself stands a better chance of being published. Samples copies $5. Queries only may be made through e-mail."

Payment/Terms: Pays 1 copy of magazine. May negotiate other terms if funds are available.

Advice: "Order a sample copy to see what we've already printed. We try to move around and not go anywhere we've already been. If you're not sure, query. Don't just read speculative literature—read everything, and your writing will benefit from it. The world itself is a complex, changing place. Explore characters, explore the sense of wonder in the universe, and always tell an interesting story that demands to be read to the end, never slacking in characterization or progression of plot."

‡**NOW & THEN, The Appalachian Magazine, (I, II, IV)**, Center for Appalachian Studies Services, Box 70556, East Tennessee State University, Johnson City TN 37614-0556. (423)439-5348. Fax: (423)439-6340. E-mail: woodsidj@etsu-tn.edu. Editor: Jane Harris Woodside. Magazine: 8½×11; 40 pages; 70 lb. gloss coated paper; 65 lb. gloss coated cover; illustrations and photos. "Each *Now & Then* is dedicated to a specific theme about life in the Appalachian region. Past themes include Appalachian photography, humor and religion." Triannually. Estab. 1984. Circ. 1,000-1,200.
  ● Member of the Council of Literary Magazines and Presses.

Needs: Ethnic/mulitcultural, experimental, fantasy, feminist, historical, humor/satire, literary, mainstream/contemporary, mystery/suspense, regional, science fiction. Must have some relationship to Appalachia. Upcoming themes: Appalachian food (deadline Nov. 1); Appalachian poetry (deadline March1); Appalachian transportation (deadline July1). List of upcoming themes available for SASE. Receives 7-10 unsolicited mss/month. Accepts 1-2 mss/issue; 3-6 mss/year. Reads only in August, December and April. Publishes ms 4 months after acceptance. Recently published work by Jerry Richardson, Jeff Shearer and Hazel Hale Bostic. Length: 1,500 words average; 1,000 words minimum; 3,000 words maximum. Publishes short shorts. Also publishes literary essays and poetry. Sometimes critiques or comments on rejected mss.

How to Contact: Send complete ms with a cover letter. Include estimated word count and 2-sentence bio. Reports in 4 months on queries; 4-6 months on mss. Send SASE for reply, return of ms or send disposable copy of ms. Simultaneous submissions OK if indicated. Sample copy for $5 plus 8½×11 SAE. Reviews novels and short story collections. Send books to Sandy Ballard, Reviews Editor, Dept. of English, Carson Newman College, Box 2059, Jefferson City TN 37760.

Payment/Terms: Pays $15 minimum; $75 maximum plus 2 contributor's copies for all rights. Sends galleys to author.

Advice: "Fiction needs, first of all, to have some connection to the Appalachian region and the magazine's upcoming theme. I like fiction with precise, vivid use of language and complexity. Read the guidelines."

THE OAK, (I, II), 1530 Seventh St., Rock Island IL 61201. (309)788-3980. Editor: Betty Mowery. 8½×11; 8-14 pages. "To provide a showcase for new authors while showing the work of established authors as well." Bimonthly. Estab. 1991. Circ. 385.

Needs: Adventure, contemporary, experimental, humor/satire, mainstream, prose poem. No erotica. Receives about 25 mss/month. Accepts up to 12 mss/issue. Publishes ms within 3 months of acceptance. Recently published work by Anne Pierre Spangler, Sylvia Roberts and Duane Noecker. Published 25 new writers/year. Length: 500 words maximum. Publishes short shorts. Length: 200 words.

How to Contact: Send complete ms. Reports in 1 week. SASE. Simultaneous and reprint submissions OK. Sample copy for $2. Subscription $10 for 4 issues.

Payment/Terms: None, but not necessary to buy a copy in order to be published. Acquires first rights.

Advice: "I do not want erotica, extreme violence or killing of humans or animals for killing sake. Just be yourself when you write. Please include SASE or manuscripts will be destroyed. Be sure name and address are on the manuscript. Study the markets for length of manuscript and what type of material is wanted."

✽**ON SPEC, The Canadian Magazine of Speculative Writing, (II)**, The Copper Pig Writers' Society, Box 4727, Edmonton, Alberta T6E 5G6 Canada. (403)413-0215. Fax: (403)413-0215. E-mail: onspec@earthling.net. Magazine: 5×8; 96 pages; illustrations. "Provides a venue for Canadian speculative writing—science fiction, fantasy, horror, magic realism." Quarterly. Estab. 1989. Circ. 2,000.

Needs: Fantasy and science fiction. Receives 50 mss/month. Buys 8 mss/issue; 32 mss/year. "We read manuscripts during the month after each deadline: February 28/May 31/August 31/November 30. Please note that we want manuscripts in competition format." Publishes ms 6 months after acceptance. Recently published work by Robert J. Sawyer, Keith Scott, Derryl Murphy, Marianne Nielsen, Kate Riedel, Diane Walton, Michael Stokes and Peter Watts. Length: 4,000 words average; 1,000 words minimum; 6,000 words maximum. Also publishes poetry. Sometimes critiques or comments on rejected mss.

How to Contact: Send complete ms with a cover letter. "No queries!" Include estimated word count, 2-sentence bio and phone number. Reports in 5 months on mss. SASE for return of ms or send a disposable copy of ms plus #10 SASE for response. No simultaneous submissions. Sample copy for $6. Fiction guidelines for #10 SASE.

Payment/Terms: Pays $25-150 and 2 contributor's copies; additional copies for $4. Pays on acceptance for first North American serial rights. Sends galleys to author.

Advice: "Please note we prefer Canadian writers. Tend to prefer character-driven stories. Don't be afraid of rejection, it happens to all of us."

OTHER WORLDS, The Paperback Magazine of Science Fiction-Science Fantasy, (II), Gryphon Publications, Box 209, Brooklyn NY 11228. Editor: Gary Lovisi. Magazine: 5×8; 100+ pages; offset paper; card cover; perfect-bound; illustrations and photographs. "Adventure—or action-oriented SF—stories that are fun to read." Annually. Estab. 1988. Circ. 300.

Needs: Science fiction (hard science, sociological) "with impact." No fantasy, supernatural or sword and sorcery. Receives 24 unsolicited mss/month. Accepts 4-6 mss/issue. Publishes ms 1-2 years (usually) after acceptance. Length: 3,000 words maximum. Publishes short shorts. Length: 500 words. Sometimes critiques rejected mss and recommends other markets.

How to Contact: Send complete ms with cover letter. Simultaneous submissions OK. Reports in 2 weeks on queries; 1 month on mss. SASE. Sample copy for $9.95 (100 pages perfect bound).

Payment/Terms: Pays 2 contributor's copies. Acquires first North American serial rights. Copyright reverts to author.

Advice: Looks for "harder science fiction stories, with *impact*!"

PAPYRUS MAGAZINE, (I, II), Papyrus Literary Enterprises, P.O. Box 270797, West Hartford CT 06127-0797. E-mail: gwhitaker@imagine.com. Website: http://www.readersndex.com/papyrus (includes writer's guidelines, contest rules, samples of *Papyrus* fiction, nonfiction and poetry). Editor-in-Chief: Ginger Whitaker. Magazine: 8½×11; 32 pages. "*Papyrus* is a quarterly periodical for the cultivation of creative works by black writers but we publish work from anyone interested in writing for a black audience. We seek, in particular, work from the unknown, underpublished or unpublished talented writer." Quarterly. Estab. 1994.

Needs: Ethnic/multicultural. Recently published work by Niama Leslie Williams, Melanie Hatter, Evelyn Palfrey, P.J. Jason, Eddie L. Myers, Allison Whittenberg and Priya Satia. Length: 1,500 words minimum; 3,500 words maximum. Also publishes literary essays and poetry. "Looking for insightful book reviews of serious fiction and nonfiction. Pays for book reviews, craft articles."

How to Contact: Send complete ms on 3.5 disk along with a printed copy. Macintosh users should submit files in ClarisWorks, Microsoft Word, WordPerfect or MacWrite II format. IBM users should submit files saved in ASCII or RTF format. SASE. No simultaneous submissions. Electronic submissions OK, query first. Sample copy for $1.75 (back copy) or $2.20 (current issue). Fiction guidelines for #10 SASE.

Payment/Terms: Pays contributor's copies. Acquires first rights.

Advice: "Make sure it is literate, easily accessible (on disk), and of interest to African Americans."

THE PARADOXIST LITERARY MOVEMENT, Anti-literary Journal, (IV), Xiquan Publishing House, 2456 S. Rose Peak Dr., Tucson AZ 85710. Editor: Florentin Smarandache. Magazine: 8½×11; 100 pages; illustrations. "The paradoxist literary movement is an avant-garde movement set up by the editor in the 1980s in Romania. It tries to generalize the art, to make the unliterary become literary." Annually. Estab. 1993. Circ. 500.

Needs: "Crazy, uncommon, experimental, avant-garde"; also ethnic/multicultural. Plans specific themes in the next year. Publishes annual special fiction issue or anthology. Receives 3-4 unsolicited mss/month. Accepts 10 mss/issue. Published work by Arnold Skemer, Marian Barbu and Constantin Urucu. Length: 500 words minimum; 1,000 words maximum. Publishes short shorts. Also publishes literary essays, literary criticism and poetry.

How to Contact: Query with clips of unpublished work. Reports in 2 months on mss. Send a disposable copy of ms. Sample copy for $19.95 and 8½×11 SASE.

Payment/Terms: Pays 1 contributor's copy. Not copyrighted.

Advice: "The Basic Thesis of the paradoxism: everything has a meaning and a non-meaning in a harmony each other. The Essence of the paradoxism: a) the sense has a non-sense, and reciprocally b) the non-sense has a sense. The Motto of the paradoxism: 'All is possible, the impossible too!' The Symbol of the paradoxism: (a spiral—optic illusion, or vicious circle)."

‡✿PARSEC, Canada's Sci-Fi Source, (II), Parsec Publishing Company, Unit G, Suite 108, 1942 Regent St., Sudbury Ontario P3E 3Z9 Canada. (705)523-1831. Fax: (705) 523-5276. E-mail: parsec@vianet.on.ca. Editor: Chris Krejlgaard. Magazine: 8×10¾; 60 pages; newsprint; illustrations and photos. "We accentuate the Canadian content in science fiction, fantasy and horror media projects." Quarterly. Estab. 1995. Circ. 2,000.

● Member of the Canadian Magazine Publishers Association.

Needs: Fantasy (science fantasy, sword and sorcery), horror, science fiction. "No first-person narratives."

Publishes special fiction issues or anthologies. Accepts 16 mss/issue. Publishes ms 6-9 months after acceptance. Length: 2,500 words average; 1,500 words minimum; 5,000 words maximum. Often critiques or comments on rejected mss.

How to Contact: Query first; no unsolicited mss accepted. Include estimated word count. Reports in 3 months on queries. Include SASE for reply. Simultaneous and electronic submissions OK. Sample copy for $3. Fiction guidelines for 4×9 SASE. Reviews novels and short story collections. Send books to editor.

Payment/Terms: Pays $75 minimum; $125 maximum on publication plus 2 contributor's copies for first rights.

Advice: "The writer has four paragraphs to hook me. After that it's an uphill climb. A story must be compelling and relevant. Psuedo-science is frowned upon, but well-researched work that follows current work or trends through to a logical end is applauded. Read and know what type of work appears in *Parsec*. Too many authors submit work that clearly isn't suitable in terms of style and genre."

‡*PEEPING TOM, Menacing and Bizarre Tales of Horror and the Macabre, (I, II), Peeping Tom Magazine, 4 Pottery Close, Belper, Derbyshire DE56 OHU England. 01773 880428. Editor: Stuart Hughes. Magazine: A5; 52 pages; standard paper; illustrations. "We are determined to publish quality horror fiction for an adult audience. We publish one story by a big-name writer in every issue, but we also publish new and upcoming writers." Quarterly. Estab. 1990. Circ. 300.
   • *Peeping Tom* received the British Fantasy Award for Best Small Press 1991 and 1992; nominations for same award 1993-1996.

Needs Horror, psychic/supernatural/occult, science fiction (dark future), psychological horror. If set in suitable genre storyline, also considers erotica, experimental, fantasy (science, sword and sorcery, contemporary), humor/satire, mystery/suspense (police procedural, private eye/hardboiled), romance (futuristic/time travel, gothic), science fiction (hard science, soft/sociological), young adult/teen (horror, science fiction). "We will read anything, but if it doesn't fall loosely into the horror/fantasy/science fiction categories it will almost certainly be returned. Definitely no poetry. We have just published *Ocean Eyes*, a collection of short stories by Stuart Hughes in A5 perfect bound paperback format. If successful we plan one collection per year. No unsolicited material required." Receives 60 unsolicited mss/month. Accepts 8-9 mss/issue; 35 mss/year. Publishes ms up to 18 months after acceptance. "Shorter stories get published sooner on average." Agented fiction 1%. Recently published work by Brian Lumley, Ramsey Campbell and Stephen Gallagher. Length: 3,500 words average; 100 words minimum; 7,000 words maximum. "Stories of more than 3,500 words need to be exceptional to stand any chance."

How to Contact: Query first. Send complete ms with a brief cover letter, no more than a page. Include estimated word count, 2-paragraph bio and list of publications. Reports in 1 month on queries; 3 months on mss. Send SASE (or IRCs) for reply, return of ms or send a disposable copy of ms. No reply or return without return postage. Simultaneous submissions OK (please advise). Reprints OK as long as it has not been U.K. published. Sample copy $6 (send dollar bills if possible). Fiction guidelines for SASE (or 2 IRCs).

Payment/Terms: Pays $2.50/1,000 words and 1 complimentary copy. ("We try to pay American writers in U.S. dollars but not always possible; offer a free subscription as the last resort.") Acquires first British serial rights. Copyright returns to author after one-time publication. "Each year we have a Scaremonger of the Year Award where subscribers vote for their favorite stories and illustrations of that year. No prize—just a certificate and the honor that goes with winning."

Advice: "*Peeping Tom* is a voyeur: we all like to slow down and take a look at car accidents and Tom is no exception. Tom wants to spy on dark deeds of horror and spy into people's darkest and most private thoughts. I really am looking for strong, believable characters. I want to know the character. If the story has strong, realistic characters with a storyline that evolves naturally out of the characters and the situations they find themselves in then it will stand a good chance."

PHANTASM, (I, II), 1530 Seventh St., Rock Island IL 61201. (309)788-3980. Editor: Betty Mowery. 5½×8½; 10 pages; illustrations. "To provide, especially the beginner, a market. Soft horror, fantasy. No gore or violence." Quarterly. Estab. 1993. Circ. 50.

Needs: Fantasy, soft horror. Receives 20 unsolicited mss/month. Accepts 4 mss/issue; 16 mss/year. Publishes ms next issue after acceptance. Publishes 25 new writers/year. Length: 500 words average; 200 words minimum; 500 words maximum. Publishes short shorts. Also publishes poetry.

How to Contact: Send complete ms. Reports in 1 week on queries. SASE for return of ms or send a disposable copy of ms. Simultaneous and reprint submissions OK. Sample copy for $2. Fiction guidelines for #10 SASE. Subscriptions: $10/4 issues.

Payment/Terms: No payment ("but purchase isn't necessary to be published"). Acquires first rights.

Advice: "Either send for a sample and see what has been published—or just go ahead and submit. Always

---

† **THE DOUBLE DAGGER** before a listing indicates that the listing is new in this edition. New markets are often the most receptive to submissions by new writers.

enclose SASE, for there is no response without one."

THE PIPE SMOKER'S EPHEMERIS, (I, II, IV), The Universal Coterie of Pipe Smokers, 20-37 120 St., College Point NY 11356-2128. Editor: Tom Dunn. Magazine: 8½×11; 84-96 pages; offset paper and cover; illustrations; photos. Pipe smoking and tobacco theme for general and professional audience. Irregular quarterly. Estab. 1964.
Needs: Pipe smoking related: historical, humor/satire, literary. Publishes ms up to 1 year after acceptance. Length: 2,500 words average; 5,000 words maximum. Also publishes short shorts. Occasionally critiques rejected mss.
How to Contact: Send complete ms with cover letter. Reports in 2 weeks on mss. Simultaneous and reprints OK. Sample copy for 8½×11 SAE and 6 first-class stamps.
Payment/Terms: Acquires one-time rights.

PIRATE WRITINGS, Tales of Fantasy, Mystery & Science Fiction, (II), Pirate Writings Publishing, P.O. Box 329, Brightwaters NY 11718-0329. E-mail: pwpubl@aol.com. Editor: Edward J. McFadden. Assistant Editor: Tom Piccirilli. Magazine: full size, saddle stapled. "We are looking for poetry and short stories that entertain." Quarterly. Estab. 1992. Circ. 6,000.
Needs: Fantasy (dark fantasy, science fantasy, sword and sorcery), mystery/suspense, science fiction (all types). Receives 300-400 unsolicited mss/month. Accepts 8 mss/issue; 30-40 mss/year. Publishes ms 1-2 years after acceptance. Length: 3,000 words average; 750 words minimum; 8,000 words maximum. Also publishes poetry. Sometimes critiques or comments on rejected mss.
How to Contact: Send complete ms with cover letter. Include estimated word count, 1 paragraph bio, Social Security number, list of publications with submission. Reports in 1 week on queries; 2 months on mss. Send SASE for reply or return of ms or disposable copy of ms. Will consider simultaneous submissions. Sample copy for $5 (make check payable to Pirate Writings Publishing). Fiction guidelines for #10 SAE.
Payment/Terms: Pays 1-5¢/word for first North American serial rights.
Advice: "My goal is to provide a diverse, entertaining and thought-provoking magazine featuring all the above stated genres in every issue. Hints: I love a good ending. Move me, make me laugh, surprise me, and you're in. Read *PW* and you'll see what I mean."

‡PORTABLE PLATEAU, Journal of the Ozark Writer, (I, II, IV), Ridge Runner Press, P.O. Box 755, Joplin MO 64802. (417)624-5061. E-mail: bebop@ipa.net. Editor: Michael Hoerman. Magazine: 11×13; 36 pages; newsprint; illustrations and photos. "*The Portable Plateau* is intended to highlight literary arts on the Ozark Plateau. Ozark themes are not sought necessarily and submissions are welcomed from current or former Ozarkers or anyone with a connection to the region." Triannually. Estab. 1997. Circ. 3,000.
Needs: Adventure, condensed/excerpted novel, erotica, ethnic/multicultural, experimental, historical, humor/satire, literary, mainstream/contemporary, regional, serialized novel, westerns. List of upcoming themes available for SASE. Publishes special fiction issue or anthologies. Publishes ms 2-4 months after acceptance. Length: 3,000 words average; 5,000 words maximum. Publishes short shorts. Also publishes literary essays, literary criticism and poetry. Sometimes critiques or comments on rejected mss.
How to Contact: Query first with clips of published work. Include estimated word count. Reports in 2-4 months. Send SASE for reply. Simultaneous submissions and reprints OK. Sample copy for $5. Fiction guidelines for #10 SASE. Reviews novels and short story collections. Send books to editor.
Payment/Terms: Pays 10 contributor's copies for one-time rights.

POSKISNOLT PRESS, Yesterday's Press, (I, II, IV), Yesterday's Press, JAF Station, Box 7415, New York NY 10116-4630. Editor: Patricia D. Coscia. Magazine: 7×8½; 20 pages; regular typing paper. Estab. 1989. Circ. 100.
Needs: Contemporary, erotica, ethnic, experimental, fantasy, feminist, gay, humor/satire, lesbian, literary, mainstream, prose poem, psychic/supernatural/occult, romance, senior citizen/retirement, western, young adult/teen (10-18 years). "X-rated material is not accepted!" Plans to publish a special fiction issue or anthology in the future. Receives 50 unsolicited mss/month. Accepts 30 mss/issue; 100 mss/year. Publishes ms 6 months after acceptance. Length: 200 words average; 100 words minimum; 500 words maximum. Publishes short shorts. Length: 100-500 words. Sometimes critiques rejected mss and recommends other markets.
How to Contact: Query first with clips of published work or send complete ms with cover letter. Reports in 1 week on queries; 6 months on mss. SASE. Accepts simultaneous submissions. Sample copy for $5 with #10 SAE and $2 postage. Fiction guidelines for #10 SAE and $2 postage.
Payment/Terms: Pays with subscription to magazine or contributor's copies; charges for extras. Acquires all rights, first rights or one-time rights.

THE POST, (II), Publishers Syndication International, P.O. Box 6218, Charlottesville VA 22906-6218. E-mail: asamuels@hombuslib.com. Website: http://www.hombushib.com/. Editor: A.P. Samuels. Magazine: 8½×11; 32 pages. Monthly. Estab. 1988.
Needs: Adventure, mystery/suspense (private eye), romance (romantic suspense), western (traditional). "No explicit sex, gore, extreme violence or bad language." Receives 75 unsolicited mss/month. Accepts 1 ms/issue;

12 mss/year. Time between acceptance and publication varies. Agented fiction 10%. Length: 10,000 words average.

How to Contact: Send complete ms with cover letter. Reports on mss in 5 weeks. No simultaneous submissions. Fiction guidelines for #10 SASE.

Payment/Terms: Pays ½¢ to 4¢/word on acceptance for all rights.

PRAYERWORKS, Encouraging, God's people to do the real work of ministry—intercessory prayer, (I), The Master's Work, P.O. Box 301363, Portland OR 97294-9363. (503)761-2072. Fax: (503)760-1184. E-mail: jayforpryr@aol.com. Editor: V. Ann Mandeville. Newsletter: 5½×8; 4 pages; bond paper. "Our intended audience is 70% retired Christians and 30% families. We publish 300-500 word devotional material—fiction, nonfiction, biographical poetry, clean quips and quotes. Our philosophy is evangelical Christian serving the body of Christ in the area of prayer." Estab. 1988. Circ. 650.

Needs: Religious/inspirational. "Subject matter may include anything which will build relationship with the Lord—prayer, ways to pray, stories of answered prayer, teaching on a Scripture portion, articles that will build faith, or poems will all work. We even use a series occasionally." Publishes 2-6 months after acceptance. Published work by Barb Marshal, Mary Hickey and Vann Mandeville. Length: 350-500 words average; 350 words minimum; 500 words maximum. Publishes short shorts. Also publishes poetry. Often critiques or comments on rejected mss.

How to Contact: Send complete ms with a cover letter. Include estimated word count and a very short bio. Reports in 1 month. Send SASE for reply, return of ms or send a disposable copy of ms. Simultaneous submissions and reprints OK. Sample copy and fiction guidelines for #10 SASE.

Payment/Terms: Pays free subscription to the magazine and contributor's copies on publication. Writer retains all rights. Not copyrighted.

Advice: Stories "must have a great take-away—no preaching; teach through action. Be thrifty with words—make them count."

PRISONERS OF THE NIGHT, An Adult Anthology of Erotica, Fright, Allure and . . . Vampirism, (II, IV), MKASHEF Enterprises, P.O. Box 688, Yucca Valley CA 92286-0688. Editor: Alayne Gelfand. Magazine: 8½×11; 50-80 pages; 20 lb. paper; slick cover; perfect-bound; illustrations. "An adult, erotic vampire anthology of original character stories and poetry. Heterosexual and homosexual situations." Annually. Estab. 1987. Circ. 5,000.

Needs: "All stories must be erotic vampire stories, with unique characters, unusual situations." Adventure, contemporary, erotica, fantasy, feminist, gay, lesbian, literary, mystery/suspense, prose poem, psychic/supernatural/occult, science fiction (soft/sociological). No fiction that deals with anyone else's creations, i.e., no "Dracula" stories. Receives 80-100 unsolicited fiction mss/month. Buys 5-12 mss/issue. Publishes ms 1-11 months after acceptance. Published work by A.R. Morlan, Tom Piccirilli, Della Van Hise and Wendy Rathbone. Publishes 1-5 new writers/year. Length: under 10,000 words. Publishes short shorts. Sometimes critiques rejected mss.

How to Contact: Send complete ms with short cover letter. "A brief introduction of author to the editor; name, address, *some* past credits if available." Reports in 1-3 weeks on queries; 2-4 months on mss. Reads *only* September through March. SASE. No simultaneous submissions. Accepts electronic submissions via IBM Word Perfect (4.2 or 5.1) disk. Sample copy #1-4, $15; #5, $12; #6-#9, $9.95, #10, $7.95. Fiction guidelines for #10 SASE.

Payment/Terms: Pays 1¢/word for fiction on acceptance for first North American serial rights.

Advice: "They say there's nothing new under the sun. Well, maybe . . . but *POTN* is looking for what's new under the *moon*! Although *POTN* is limited in its topic to vampires, there is no limitation within its pages on imagination. *POTN* is looking for new twists on the old theme; new perspectives, unique angles, alien visions and newborn music. *POTN* is *not* looking for re-hashes of old plots and characterizations; no 'counts' or 'count-esses,' please. The pick-up in a singles bar has been beaten into the ground. The hitchhiker-turned-vampire/victim gives new meaning to the word 'boring.' *POTN* wants material that breaks all molds, that severs ties to old concepts of the vampire and creates utterly new images. *POTN* wants to read your story and be delighted, intrigued, startled in fresh, imaginatively new ways. *POTN* does *not* want to be put off by pornography or obscenity. Please do not add sex to an existing story just to fit POTN's definition of itself as 'an erotic vampire anthology'; sex must be an integral part of the tale. Explicitness is not necessary, but it is acceptable. *POTN* stresses the romantic (but not 'gothic') aspects of the vampire as opposed to the bloody, gory, horrific aspects; no 'slasher' stories, please. And, although it is an important, contemporary subject, *POTN* prefers not to address the issue of AIDS as it relates to vampires at this time. Please be sure to SASE for guidelines before submitting; *POTN*'s needs are extremely specific."

PSI, (I, II), P.O. Box 6218, Charlottesville VA 22906-6218. E-mail: asamuels@hombuslib.com. Website: http://www.hombuslib.com/. Editor: A.P. Samuels. Magazine: 8½×11; 32 pages; bond paper; self cover. "Mystery and romance." Bimonthly. Estab. 1987.

Needs: Romance (contemporary, historical, young adult), mystery/suspense (private eye), western (traditional). Receives 35 unsolicited mss/month. Accepts 1-2 mss/issue. Length: 10,000 words average. Critiques rejected mss "only on a rare occasion."

How to Contact: Send complete ms with cover letter. Reports in 2 weeks on queries; 4-6 weeks on mss. SASE.

No simultaneous submissions. Accepts electronic submissions via disk.

Payment/Terms: Pays 1-4¢/word plus royalty on acceptance for first North American serial rights.

Advice: "Manuscripts must be for a general audience. Just good plain story telling (make it compelling). No explicit sex or ghoulish violence."

QUEEN OF ALL HEARTS, (II), Queen Magazine, Montfort Missionaries, 26 S. Saxon Ave., Bay Shore NY 11706. (516)665-0726. Managing Editor: Roger M. Charest, S.M.M. Magazine: 7¾ × 10¾; 48 pages; self cover stock; illustrations and photos. Magazine of "stories, articles and features on the Mother of God by explaining the Scriptural basis and traditional teaching of the Catholic Church concerning the Mother of Jesus, her influence in fields of history, literature, art, music, poetry, etc." Bimonthly. Estab. 1950. Circ. 2,500.

Needs: Religious/inspirational. "No mss not about Our Lady, the Mother of God, the Mother of Jesus." Length: 1,500-2,000 words. Sometimes recommends other markets.

How to Contact: Send complete ms with SASE. No simultaneous submissions. Reports in 1 month on mss. Publishes ms 6-12 months after acceptance. Sample copy for $2.50 with 9 × 12 SAE.

Payment/Terms: Varies. Pays 6 contributor's copies.

Advice: "We are publishing stories with a Marian theme."

♣QUEEN'S QUARTERLY, A Canadian Review, (I, IV), Queen's University, Kingston, Ontario K7L 3N6 Canada. Phone/fax: (613)545-2667. Fax: (613)545-6822. E-mail: qquartly@post.queensu.ca. Website: http://info.queensu.ca./quarterly. Editor: Boris Castel. Magazine: 6 × 9; 800 pages/year; illustrations. "A general interest intellectual review, featuring articles on science, politics, humanities, arts and letters. Book reviews, poetry and fiction." Quarterly. Estab. 1893. Circ. 3,000.

Needs: Adventure, contemporary, experimental, fantasy, historical, humor/satire, literary, mainstream, science fiction and women's. "*Special emphasis on work by Canadian writers.*" Accepts 2 mss/issue; 8 mss/year. Published work by Gail Anderson-Dargatz, Mark Jarman, Rick Bowers and Dennis Bock; published new writers within the last year. Length: 2,000-3,000 words. Also publishes literary essays, literary criticism, poetry.

How to Contact: "Send complete ms with SASE." No simultaneous or multiple submissions. Reports within 3 months. Sample copy for $6.50. Reviews novels and short story collections. Electronic submissions OK.

Payment/Terms: Pays $100-300 for fiction, 2 contributor's copies and 1-year subscription; $5 charge for extras. Pays on publication for first North American serial rights. Sends galleys to author.

RESPONSE, A Contemporary Jewish Review, (II, IV), 114 W. 26th St., Suite 1004, New York NY 10001-6812. (212)620-0350. Fax: (212)929-3459. E-mail: response@panix.com. Editors: David R. Adler and Yigal Schleifer. Magazine: 6 × 9; 120 pages; 70 lb. paper; 10 pt. CS1 cover; illustrations; photos. "Fiction, poetry and essays with a Jewish theme, for Jewish students and young adults." Quarterly. Estab. 1967. Circ. 3,000.

● *Response* received an award from *Jewish Currents Magazine* for outstanding Jewish journalism in 1995.

Needs: Contemporary, ethnic, experimental, feminist, historical (general), humor/satire, literary, prose poem, regional, religious, spirituals, translations. "Stories in which the Holocaust plays a major role must be exceptional in quality. The shrill and the morbid will not be accepted." Receives 10-20 unsolicited mss/month. Accepts 5-10 mss/issue; 10-15 mss/year. Publishes ms 2-4 months after acceptance. Length: 15-20 pages (double spaced). Publishes short shorts. Sometimes recommends other markets.

How to Contact: Send complete ms with cover letter; include brief biography of author. SASE. No simultaneous submissions. Sample copy for $6; free guidelines.

Payment/Terms: Pays in contributor's copies. Acquires all rights.

Advice: "In the best pieces, every word will show the author's conscious attention to the craft. Subtle ambiguities, quiet ironies and other such carefully handled tropes are not lost on *Response*'s readers. Pieces that also show passion that is not marred by either shrillness or pathos are respected and often welcomed. Writers who write from the gut or the muse are few in number. *Response* personally prefers the writer who thinks about what he or she is doing, rather than the writer who intuits his or her stories."

RFD, A Country Journal for Gay Men Everywhere, (I, II, IV), Short Mountain Collective, P.O. Box 68, Liberty TN 37095. (615)536-5176. Contact: The Collective. Magazine: 8½ × 11; 64-80 pages. "Focus on radical faeries, gay men's spirituality—country living." Quarterly. Estab. 1974. Circ. 3,600.

Needs: Gay: Erotica, ethnic/multicultural, experimental, fantasy, feminist, humor/satire, literary, mainstream/contemporary, mystery/suspense, psychic/supernatural/occult, regional, romance. Receives 10 unsolicited mss/month. Accepts 3 mss/issue; 12 mss/year. Length: open. Publishes short shorts. Also publishes literary essays, literary criticism and poetry.

How to Contact: Send complete ms with cover letter and estimated word count. Usually reports in 6-9 months. Send SASE for reply, return of ms or send disposable copy of ms. Sample copy for $6. Free fiction guidelines.

Payment/Terms: Pays 1 or 2 contributor's copies. Not copyrighted.

RIVERSIDE QUARTERLY, (II, IV), P.O. Box 12085, San Antonio TX 78212. (210)734-5424. Editor: Leland Sapiro. Magazine: 5½ × 8½; 64 pages; illustrations. Quarterly. Estab. 1964. Circ. 1,100.

Needs: Fantasy and science fiction. Accepts 1 ms/issue; 4 mss/year. Publishes ms 9 months after acceptance.

Length: 3,000 words average; 3,500 words maximum. Publishes short shorts. Also publishes essays, literary criticism, poetry. Critiques rejected mss.

How to Contact: Send complete ms with a cover letter. Reports in 2 weeks. SASE. Simultaneous submissions OK. Sample copy for $2.50. Reviews novels and short story collections.

Payment/Terms: Pays in contributor's copies. Acquires one-time rights. Sends galleys to author.

Advice: "We print only science fiction and fantasy, with the first requiring no specific 'approach.' However, a fantasy story is deemed relevant only if it expresses some aspect of human behavior that can't be expressed otherwise. See, for example, Kris Neville's 'The Outcasts' in our 2nd issue or Algis Budrys': 'Balloon, Oh, Balloon' in the 3rd."

‡ROMANTIC HEARTS, A Magazine Dedicated to Short Romantic Fiction, (I, II, IV), P.O. Box 450669, Westlake OH 44145-0612. (216)979-9793. E-mail: romharts@aol.com. Editor: Debra L. Krauss. Magazine: 5¼×8; 48 pages; 20 lb. paper; 20 lb. color cover; illustrations and photographs. "Romantic Hearts is dedicated to publishing the finest romantic short fiction written today. Our audience is romance readers and writers. We also publish short romantic essays (500-1,500 words) and love poems of 25 lines of less." Bimonthly. Estab. 1996.

Needs: Romance (contemporary, futuristic/time travel, gothic, historical, all types). No erotica or pornography. Receives 25 unsolicited mss/month. Accepts 5-7 mss/issue; 36-40 mss/year. Publishes ms 8-14 months after acceptance. Recently published work by Holly J. Fuhrmann, Susan Roberts, Michele R. Bardsley and Patricia Morgan. Length: 3,000 words average; 1,500 words minimum; 4,000 words maximum. Also publishes literary essays (must have a romantic theme), poetry. Often critiques or comments on rejected mss.

How to Contact: Send complete ms with a cover letter. Include estimated word count. Reports in 6-8 weeks. Send SASE for reply, return of ms or send a disposable copy of ms. No simultaneous submissions. Sample copy for $4 ppd. Fiction guidelines free for #10 SASE.

Payment/Terms: Pays 3 contributor's copies on publication; additional copies for $2. Acquires first North American serial rights. "Send #10 SASE with request for contest guidelines."

Advice: "The stories I select are uplifting and positive. They must also be a 'romance.' A standout manuscript is one that contains strong characterization and lots of emotion. Always include a cover letter and correctly format your manuscript. Please be sure your story is a romance with a happy ending or the promise of one."

ROSEBUD™, For People Who Enjoy Writing, (I, II), P.O. Box 459, Cambridge WI 53523. Phone/fax: (608)423-9609. Website: http://www.sonatas.com/rosebud (includes writer's guidelines, contests, preview, *Rosebud* bulletin board, teachers guide to current issue, outreach programs and advertising rates). Editor: Roderick Clark. Magazine: 7×10; 136 pages; 60 lb. matte; 100 lb. cover; illustrations. Quarterly. Estab. 1993. Circ. 10,000.

● *Rosebud* was selected for inclusion in the *Writer's Digest* "Fiction 50" list of top fiction markets.

Needs: Adventure, condensed/excerpted novel, ethnic/multicultural, experimental, historical (general), humor/satire, literary, mainstream/contemporary, psychic/supernatural/occult, regional, romance (contemporary), science fiction (soft/sociological), serialized novel, translations. Each submission must fit loosely into one of the following categories to qualify: City and Shadow (urban settings), Songs of Suburbia (suburban themes), These Green Hills (nature and nostalgia), En Route (any type of travel), Mothers, Daughters, Wives (relationships), Ulysses' Bow (manhood), Paper, Scissors, Rock (childhood, middle age, old age), The Jeweled Prize (concerning love), Lost and Found (loss and discovery), Voices in Other Rooms (historic or of other culture), Overtime (involving work), Anything Goes (humor), I Hear Music (music), Season to Taste (food), Word Jazz (wordplay), Apples to Oranges (miscellaneous, excerpts, profiles). Publishes annual special fiction issue or anthology. Receives 1,200 unsolicited mss/month. Accepts 16 mss/issue; 64 mss/year. Publishes ms 1-3 months after acceptance. Recently published work by Seamus Heany, Louis Simpson, Allen Ginsberg and Jimmy Carter. 70% of work published is by new writers. Length: 1,200-1,800 words average. Occasionally uses longer pieces and novel excerpts (prepublished). Publishes short shorts. Also publishes literary essays. Often critiques or comments on rejected mss.

How to Contact: Send complete ms with a cover letter. Include estimated word count and list of publications. Reports in 3 months on mss. SASE for return of ms. Simultaneous and reprints submissions OK. Sample copy for $5.95. Fiction guidelines for legal SASE.

Payment/Terms: Pays $45 and 3 contributor's copies on publication for one-time rights; additional copies for $4.40.

Advice: "Each issue will have six or seven flexible departments (selected from a total of sixteen departments that will rotate). We are seeking stories, articles, profiles, and poems of: love, alienation, travel, humor, nostalgia and unexpected revelation. Something has to 'happen' in the pieces we choose, but what happens inside characters is much more interesting to us than plot manipulation. We like good storytelling, real emotion and authentic voice."

RUBY'S PEARLS, (II), 9832-1 Sandler Rd., Jacksonville FL 32222. E-mail: ruby@gate.net or del.freeman@rub ysbbs.gate.net (for Freeman) and michael.hahn@worldnet.att.net (for Hahn). Editor: Del Freeman. Assistant Editor: Michael Hahn. Electronic magazine; page number varies. "All fiction, no porn, no poetry, general interest." Monthly. Estab. 1991. "Uploaded electronically to BBSs nationwide and internationally, via satellite. Also on the World Wide Web at http://www.gate.net/~ruby/.

● *Ruby's Pearls* has received 3 Digital Quill Awards (sponsored by the Disktop Publishing Association).

By using other bulletin boards and "echoing" across the country the magazine is accessible to the 50 states; available all over the world via Genie, Compuserve and the Internet.

Needs: Contemporary, experimental, humor/satire, mainstream, mystery/suspense. "Stories can be submitted on either size disk, ASCII, IBM format only. Will return if mailer (pre-paid) is enclosed." No porn, erotica. Accepts 1-2 mss/issue; 24-30 mss/year. Publishes ms 1-2 months after acceptance. Publishes short shorts. Length: 250 up (unless it's really killer). Sometimes comments on rejected ms.

How to Contact: Submissions are by 5.25 or 3.5 disk; stories in IBM-ASCII format only or they can be made by modem by calling "Ruby's Joint BBS," 1-904-777-6799 and uploading. Contact by mail or by disk with complete story. Reports in 1-2 months. "Prepaid disk mailer is required." Simultaneous submissions OK. Accepts electronic submissions via disk or modem. For sample copy, access at above website.

Payment/Terms: No payment. Only the privilege to reproduce electronically once. All rights remain with author.

Advice: "Any writer can be seen and judged by the public, sans agent filtering, in the electronic age. Don't worry about who turns you down, but rather who accepts your work."

‡*SHADOWFALL, the magazine of horror & dark fantasy, (II)**, Dark Path Productions, P.O. Box 809, Mt. Ommaney QLD 4074 Australia. 61-414-279184. E-mail: darkpath@powerup.com.au. Website: http://www.powerup.com.au/~darkpath. Editor: M.D. VanElderen. Fiction Editor: Laila Schlack. Magazine: A4; 52 pages; gloss cover; illustrations and photos. "We require stories that are dark, brooding and truly scary. We publish fiction, poetry, book/movie/game reviews, interviews with authors, horror-related non-fiction, artwork and photographs." Quarterly.

Needs: Horror, psychic/supernatural/occult. No children's or new age. Received 30-50 unsolicited mss/month. Accepts 6-8 mss/issue; 24-32 mss/year. Publishes ms 3-12 months after acceptance. Recently published work by Ken Abner, Nancy Kilpatrick, Anthony Plank, Sharen Danbert, John Everson, Jolt Grey, and Darren Latta. Length: 2,500-3,000 words average; 5,000 words maximum. Publishes short shorts. Also publishes poetry. Always critiques or comments on rejected mss.

How to Contact: Send complete ms with a cover letter. Include estimated word count and short bio. Reports in 1 week on queries; 4-6 weeks on mss. Send SASE for reply and a disposable copy of ms. Simultaneous, reprint and electronic submissions OK. Reviews novels and short story collections. Send books to editor.

Payment/Terms: Pays $5 USD minimum; $50 USD maximum and 1 contributor's copy for one-time rights. Sends galleys to author.

Advice: "Go back to the roots of horror-Lovecraft, Poe. Movies to watch: anything with Vincent Price in it, *The Lady in Black, In the Mouth of Madness, The Changeling, Hellraiser*. Don't be frightened to submit-we welcome beginning writers' work. The only problem we experience from time to time is the lack of work from Australian authors due to the low number of markets in our genre in the country. Overseas submissions keep flocking in, forcing us to temporarily close to submissions from those contributors."

SKIPPING STONES: A Multicultural Children's Magazine, (I, II), P.O. Box 3939, Eugene OR 97403. (541)342-4956. Editor: Arun N. Toké. Magazine: 8½×11; 36 pages; recycled 50 lb. halopaque paper; 100 lb. text cover; illustrations and photos. "*Skipping Stones* is a multicultural, international, nature awareness magazine for children 8-16, and their parents and teachers." Published 5 times a year. Estab. 1988. Circ. 3,000.

Needs: Children's/juvenile (8-16 years): ethnic/multicultural, feminist, religious/inspirational, young adult/teen, international, nature. Upcoming themes for 1998: "Living Abroad," "Crosscultural Communications," "Folktales," "Challenging Disability," "Raising Children: Rewards, Punishments." List of upcoming themes available for SASE. Receives 50 mss/month. Accepts 5-8 mss/issue; 25-30 mss/year. Publishes ms 3-6 months after acceptance. Published work by Victoria Collett, Charles Curatalo, Anjali Amit, Lily Hartmann and Peter Chase. Length: 750 words average; 250 words minimum; 1,000 words maximum. Publishes short shorts. Also publishes literary essays and poetry. Often critiques or comments on rejected mss. Sponsors contests, awards or grants for fiction writers under 17 years of age.

How to Contact: Send complete ms with a cover letter. Include 50- to 100-word bio with background, international or intercultural experiences. Reports in 1 month on queries; 3 months on mss. Send SASE for reply, return of ms or send a disposable copy of ms. Simultaneous submissions OK. Sample copy for $5, 9×12 SAE and 4 first-class stamps. Fiction guidelines for #10 SASE.

Payment/Terms: Pays 1-3 contributor's copies; additional copies for $3. Acquires first North American serial rights and nonexclusive reprint rights.

Advice: Looking for stories with "multicultural/multiethnic theme, use of other languages when appropriate.

MARKET CATEGORIES: (I) Open to new writers; **(II)** Open to both new and established writers; **(III)** Interested mostly in established writers; **(IV)** Open to writers whose work is specialized; **(V)** Closed to unsolicited submissions.

Realistic and suitable for 8 to 16 year olds. Promoting social and nature awareness. In addition to encouraging children's creativity, we also invite adults to submit their own writing and artwork for publication in *Skipping Stones*. Writings and artwork by adults should challenge readers to think and learn, cooperate and create."

SLATE AND STYLE, Magazine of the National Federation of the Blind Writers Division, (I, IV), NFB Writer's Division, 2704 Beach Dr., Merrick NY 11566. (516)868-8718. Fax: (516)868-9076. E-mail: stayer @idt.net. Fiction Editor: Loraine Stayer. Newsletter: 8×10; 32 print/40 Braille pages; cassette and large print. "Articles of interest to writers, and resources for blind writers." Quarterly. Estab. 1982. Circ. 200.

● The magazine runs an annual contest for fiction, limit 2,000 words. There is a $5 entry fee and the contest runs from September 1 to May 1. Write for details.

Needs: Adventure, contemporary, fantasy, humor/satire, blindness. No erotica. "Avoid theme of death." Does not read mss in June or July. Recently published work by Carol Archer, Marie Anna Pape and John Gordon Jr. Publishes 2-3 new writers/year. Length: 1,000-3,000 words. Publishes short shorts. Also publishes literary criticism and poetry. Critiques rejected mss only if requested.

How to Contact: Reports in 3-6 weeks. Large print sample copy for $2.50. "Sent Free Matter For The Blind. If not blind, send 2 stamps."

Payment/Terms: Pays in contributor's copies. Acquires one-time rights. Publication not copyrighted. Sponsors contests for fiction writers.

Advice: "Keep a copy. Editors can lose your work. Consider each first draft as just that and review your work before you send it. SASE a must. Although we circulate to blind writers, I do not wish to see articles on blindness by sighted writers unless they are married to, or the son/daughter/parent of a blind person. In general, we do not even print articles on blindness, preferring to publish articles on alternate techniques a blind writer can use to surmount his blindness."

SPACE AND TIME, (I, II), 138 W. 70th St. (4B), New York NY 10023-4468. (212)595-0894. Website: http://www.spacelab.net/~cburns/space&time.html (includes guidelines, staff, current and future contents, back issues/books for sale, schedule of our reading series). Editor: Gordon Linzner. Fiction Editor: Tom Piccirilli. Magazine: 8½×11; 48 pages; 50 lb. paper; index card cover stock; illustrations and photos. "We publish science fiction, fantasy, horror and our favorite, that-which-defies-categorization." Biannually. Estab. 1966. Circ. 2,000. Member of the Small Press Center and the Small Press Genre Organization.

Needs: Fantasy (science, sword and sorcery, undefinable), horror, science fiction (hard science, soft/sociological, undefinable). Receives 100 unsolicited mss/month. Accepts 12 mss/issue; 24 mss/year. Publishes ms 6-18 months after acceptance. Recently published work by Don Webb, Sue Storm, Mary Soon Lee and Stephen Dedhan. Length: 5,000 words average; 10,000 words maximum. Publishes short shorts. Also publishes literary essays, literary criticism and poetry. Send poems to Lawrence Greenberg. Often critiques or comments on rejected mss.

How to Contact: Send complete ms. Include estimated word count. Reports in 1 week on queries; 2-3 months on mss. Send SASE for reply, return of ms or send a disposable copy of ms. Sample copy for $5 and 9×12 SAE with $1.25 postage or 3 IRCs. Fiction guidelines for #10 SASE or SAE and 1 IRC.

Payment/Terms: Pays 1¢/word, $5 minimum and 2 contributor's copies on acceptance; additional copies $3. Acquires first North American serial rights and option to reprint in context of magazine.

Advice: Looks for "good writing, strong characterization and unusual plot or premise."

‡❦SPACEWAYS WEEKLY, The E-mail Magazine of Science Fiction & Fantasy, (I), Chiokis Enterprises, P.O. Box 3023, London Ontario N6A 4H9 Canada. E-mail: spaceways@mirror.org. Editor: Rigel D. Chiokis. Electronic magazine. "We publish science fiction and fantasy short stories and poems in an electronic format." Weekly. Estab. 1997.

Needs: Experimental, Fantasy (science fantasy, sword and sorcery), Feminist (science fiction and fantasy), Gay (science fiction and fantasy), Lesbian (science fiction and fantasy), science fiction (hard science, soft/sociological). Receives 8-12 unsolicited mss/month. Accepts 1 ms/issue; 52 mss/year. Publishes ms 4-6 months after acceptance. Recently published work by Trevon Van Mierlo, Christopher Mehrlein, M.A. Crowley, Max Read, Joanna Van Oorschot and Patricia Read. Length: 2,000-3,000 words average; 5,000 words maximum. Publishes short shorts. Also publishes poetry. Often critiques or comments on rejected mss.

How to Contact: Send complete ms with a cover letter by e-mail in ASCII text. Include estimated word count and copyright notice. Simultaneous submissions OK. Guidelines for #10 SASE.

Payment/Terms: Pays .01/word CDN plus 2 months subscription on acceptance for first Canadian rights.

Advice: "A story must have good characterization first; a good plot, second. Send for my guidelines or read them on our webpage. Follow those guidelines to the letter."

‡STARBLADE, (I, IV), P.O. Box 400672, Hesperia CA 92340. Editor: Stephanie O'Rourke. Magazine: 8½×11; 30 pages; 24 lb. paper; illustrations. "Starblade is for fantasy readers, from science fiction to sword and sorcery." Estab. 1994.

Needs: Fantasy (science fantasy, sword and sorcery) and science fiction. "No porn or gore. No romance." Length: 3,500 words average. Publishes short shorts. Also publishes literary essays, literary criticism and poetry. Always critiques or comments on rejected mss.

How to Contact: Send complete ms and short bio. Include estimated word count. Reports in 4 months on queries; 6 months on mss. Send SASE for reply, return of ms or send a disposable copy of ms. Simultaneous submissions OK. Sample copy for 9×12 SAE and 6 first-class stamps. Reviews novels and short story collections.

Payment/Terms: Pays 2 contributor's copies. Acquires one-time rights.

Advice: "I like good dialogue and a good sense of humor in my stories. I prefer them typed with legible, with a beginning, middle, and ending, hopefully in that order. A writer should remember that the worst thing they can do is not try; after all, I can't accept it if I haven't read it. Even if a story isn't accepted I try to give advice on how to fix it, so send it in!"

‡**STORYHEAD MAGAZINE, (I, II)**, %Mike Brehm, 5701 S. Blackstone Ave. 3N, Chicago IL 60637. (312)702-6674. E-mail: mbrehm@als-popmail.uchicago.edu. Website: http://www.digimark.net/wraith/zines.ht ml. Editors: Mike Brehm and Joe Peterson. Magazine: $7 \times 8\frac{3}{4}$; 40-60 pages; 70 lb. stock paper; 80 lb. stock cover; illustrations and photos. "What we try to do at StoryHead is bring writers and artists together to create illustrated stories and poems. We are therefore looking for *short story* writers, and graphic artists who are interested in illustrating stories. No other magazine exploits the energy and tension between the artist and writer quite like ours does." Quarterly. Estab. 1993. Circ. 300-500.

Needs: Short stories, essays and poetry. Receives 20 unsolicited mss/month. Accepts 3-5 mss/issue; 12-20 mss/year. Publishes ms 3-6 months after acceptance. Published work by David Greenberger, Joe Maynard, Kevin Riordin and Nina Marks. Length: 3,000 words average.

How to Contact: Send complete ms with a cover letter or send electronic mss on ASCII. Reports in 6 months on mss. Send SASE for reply, return of ms or send a disposable copy of ms. Simultaneous and electronic submissions OK. Sample copy for $4.

Payment/Terms: Pays 2 contributor's copies. All rights revert to author.

Advice: "We're interested in the basics: good writing on compelling subjects. Make sure the manuscript is complete. We try not to do too much editing. *StoryHead*'s goal is to publish great work by unknown or little known artists, so that the unknown artist of today can become tomorrow's *known* artist. As an example, in our last issue we published the work of a relatively unknown Polish poet by the name of Wislawa Szymborska. Her poetry came to us because mainstream magazines were not willing to publish an unknown Polish poet. As we were going to press with our eighth issue, Ms. Szymborska was awarded the 1996 Nobel Prize for Literature."

THE STORYTELLER, For Amateur Writers, (I), 2441 Washington Rd., Maynard AR 72444. (501)647-2137. Editor: Regina Cook. Tabloid: $8\frac{1}{2} \times 11$; 50-60 pages; typing paper; illustrations. "This magazine is open to all new writers regardless of age. I will accept short stories in any genre and poetry in any type. Please keep in mind, this is a family publication." Quarterly. Estab. 1996.

Needs: Adventure, historical, humor/satire, literary, mainstream/contemporary, mystery/suspense, regional, religious/inspirational, romance, science fiction (soft/sociological), senior citizen/retirement, sports, westerns, young adult/teen. "I will not accept pornography, erotica, foul language, horror or graphic violence." Publishes ms 3-9 months after acceptance. Recently published work by W.C. Jameson, Bryan Byrd and Randy Offner. Publishes 75-100 new writers/year. Length: 1,500 words average; 200 words minimum. Publishes short shorts. Also publishes literary essays and poetry. Sometimes critiques or comments on rejected mss.

How to Contact: Send complete ms with a cover letter. Include estimated word count and 5-line bio. Reports 2-4 weeks on queries; 1-2 months on mss. Send SASE for reply, return of ms or send a disposable copy of ms. Simultaneous and reprint submissions OK. Sample copy for $6. Fiction guidelines for #10 SASE.

Payment/Terms: "Readers vote quarterly for their favorites in all categories. Winning authors receive certificate of merit and free copy of issue in which their story or poem appeared."

Advice: Looks for "professionalism, good plots and unique characters. Purchase a sample copy so you know the kind of material we look for. Even though this is for amateur writers, don't send us something you would not send to paying markets." Would like more "well-plotted mysteries and suspense and a few traditional westerns. Avoid sending anything that children or young adults would not (or could not) read, such as really bad language."

‡**STRICTLY ROMANCE MAGAZINE, (I, II)**, Indigo Prints, 2599 E. Main St., Suite 181, Bexley OH 43209. E-mail: indigopri@aol.com. Website: http://members.aol.com/IndigoPri/index.html. Editor: Shawna Williams. Magazine: $5\frac{1}{2} \times 8$; 50-80 pages; 60 lb. paper; 67 lb. nonglossy cover stock; illustrations and photos. "We publish and showcase works of new writers as well as established. All stories must have romantic theme and range from sweet to sensual." Quarterly (soon to be bimonthly). Estab. 1996. Circ. under 1,000.

Needs: Romance (contemporary, futuristic/time travel, gothic, historical; all other in romance genre such as mystery, ethnic, paranormal/ghost). No confession type stories. Receives 50-100 unsolicited mss/month. Accepts 7-10 mss/issue; 28-40 mss/year. Publishes ms 3-6 months after acceptance. Recently published work by Karen Jackson, Holly Furhmann and Debra Godfrey. Length: 4,000-5,000 words average; 2,000 words minimum; 6,000 words maximum. Publishes short shorts. Also publishes poetry. Comments on rejected mss when time permits.

How to Contact: Send complete ms with a cover letter. Include estimated word count in top righthand corner of ms and brief bio. Reports in 3 weeks on queries; 2 months on mss. Send SASE (or IRCs) for reply or return of ms. Simultaneous and reprint submissions OK. Electronic submissions OK but query first. Sample copy $4.25 US, $5.25 Canadian, $7.25 overseas. Fiction guidelines for SASE (or IRC). Reviews novels. Send books to "S. Williams, Reviews."

Payment/Terms: Pays $10-20/short story, poem when budget allows; otherwise, pays contributor's copies (2/short story, 1/poetry). Money payments on acceptance, contributor's copies on publication. Acquires one-time rights. After publication, rights revert back to author. Sponsors a yearly contest for fiction writers. Send SASE for information.

Advice: "Stories must be original, imaginative, tight plots. Stories that have a good chance of being published are ones that can move me, make me laugh, cry . . . stir emotions. Make me feel something."

*STUDIO: A JOURNAL OF CHRISTIANS WRITING, (II), 727 Peel St., Albury 2640 Australia. Managing Editor: Paul Grover. Circ. 300. Quarterly. Averages 20-30 stories/year.

Needs: "*Studio* publishes prose and poetry of literary merit, offers a venue for new and aspiring writers, and seeks to create a sense of community among Christians writing." Length: 500-5,000 words.

Payment/Terms: Pays in copies. Sample copy available for $8 (Australian). Subscription $40 (Australian) for 4 issues (1 year). International draft in Australian dollars and IRC required.

TALEBONES, Fiction on the Dark Edge, (II), Fairwood Press, 10531 SE 250th Place, #104, Kent WA 98031. E-mail: talebones@nventure.com. Website: http://www.nventure.com/talebones (includes guidelines, submission requirements, excerpts, news about the magazine, bios). Editors: Patrick and Honna Swenson. Magazine: digest size; 68 pages; standard paper; glossy cover stock; illustrations and photos. "We like stories that have punch, but still entertain. We like dark science fiction and dark fantasy, humor, psychological and experimental works." Quarterly. Estab. 1995. Circ. 300.

 • *Talebones* received the 1995 Genre Writers Association Award for Best New Magazine/Editor.

Needs: Fantasy (dark), humor/satire, science fiction (hard science, soft/sociological, dark). "No straight slash and hack horror." Receives 200 mss/month. Accepts 6-7 mss/issue; 24-28 mss/year. Publishes ms 3-4 months after acceptance. Recently published work by Nina Kinki Hoffman, Bruce Boston, Tom Piccirilli, Leslie What, William John Watkins and Don Webb. Publishes 4-6 new writers/year. Length: 3,000-4,000 words average; 500 words minimum; 5,000 words maximum. Publihses short shorts. Length: 1,000 words. Also publishes poetry. Often critiques or comments on rejected mss.

How to Contact: Send complete ms with a cover letter. Include estimated word count and 1-paragraph bio. Reports in 1 week on queries; 1-3 weeks on mss. Send SASE for reply, return of ms or send a disposable copy of ms. No simultaneous submissions. Electronic submissions (e-mail) OK. Sample copy for $4.50. Fiction guidelines for SASE. Reviews novels and short story collections.

Payment/Terms: Pays $10-80 on acceptance and 1 contributor's copy; additional copies for $3. Acquires first North American serial rights. Sends galleys to author.

Advice: "The story must be entertaining, but should blur the boundary between science fiction and horror. All our stories have a dark edge to them, but often are humorous or psychological. Be polite and know how to properly present a manuscript. Include a cover letter, but keep it short and to the point."

TERRA INCOGNITA, A New Generation of Science Fiction, (II), 52 Windermere Ave. 3rd Floor, Lansdowne PA 19050-1812. E-mail: terraincognita@writeme.com. Editor: Jan Berrien Berends. Magazine: 64 pages; e-brite paper; full-color glossy cover; illustrations; photos. "*Terra Incognita* is devoted to earth-based science fiction stories and relevant nonfiction articles. Readers of quality fiction—even those who are not science fiction fans—enjoy *TI*. Audience ranges from ages 18 and upward. We encourage feminist and socially conscious submissions." Quarterly. Estab. 1996.

Needs: Science fiction (hard science, soft/sociological). "No sexism and gratuitous sex and violence, racism or bias; avoid prose poems and vignettes. We prefer character-driven stories with protagonists and plots." Receives 200-300 unsolicited mss/month. Accepts 6-10 mss/issue; 25-35 mss/year. Publishes ms 3 months to 1 year after acceptance. Published work by L. Timmel Duchamp, Sue Storm, Timons Esais, W. Gregory Stewart, Nicola Griffith, Brian Stableford, Kandis Elliot and Darrell Schweitzer. Length: 5,000 words average; 100 words minimum; 15,000 words maximum. Publishes short shorts. Also publishes literary essays, literary criticism and poetry.

How to Contact: Send complete ms with cover letter. Include estimated word count and anything you think might be interesting in a cover letter. Reports in 1-2 weeks on queries; 1-3 weeks on mss. Send SASE for reply, return of ms or send a disposable copy of ms. "A cover letter is optional; a SASE is not." Sample copy for $5; $6 overseas. Fiction guidelines for #10 SASE. Reviews novels and short story collections.

Payment/Terms: Pays at least 3¢/word and 2 contributor's copies; additional copies $5. Pays on acceptance. Acquires first North American serial rights.

Advice: Looks for "good writing and literary merit; a story that grabs our interest and holds it straight through to the end. Write as well as you can (which means—don't overwrite, but do use the words themselves to advance your story), and tell us a story—preferably one we haven't heard before. Don't get your great idea rejected on account of lousy grammar or poor manuscript format. We take all submissions seriously."

TEXAS YOUNG WRITERS' NEWSLETTER, (I, II, IV), Texas Young Writers' Association, P.O. Box 942, Adkins TX 78101-0942. E-mail: bubbasue@aol.com. Editor: Susan Currie. Newsletter: 8½ × 11; 8 pages; 20 lb. white paper; illustrations. "*TYWN* teaches young writers about the art and business of writing, and also gives them a place to publish their best work. We publish articles by adults with experience in publishing, and poetry and short stories by young writers 12-19." Monthly during summer, bimonthly during school year (August-May). Estab. 1994. Circ. 300.

Needs: Open to authors ages 12-19 only. Adventure, ethnic/multicultural, fantasy (children's fantasy, science fantasy), historical, humor/satire, literary, mainstream/contemporary, mystery/suspense, romance, science fiction, young adult/teen. "Anything by young writers, 12-19. No erotica, horror, gay/lesbian or occult." List of upcoming themes available for SASE. Receives 6 unsolicited mss/month. Accepts 1 ms/issue; 9 mss/year. Publishes ms 6 months after acceptance. Published work by Sarah Elezian, Lillette Hill, Caroline Beever and Anthony Twistt. Length: 900 words average; 500 words minimum; 1,100 words maximum. Publishes short shorts. Also publishes poetry. Always critiques or comments on rejected ms.

How to Contact: Send complete ms with a cover letter. Include estimated word count and 50-100 word bio. Reports in 6 weeks. Send SASE for reply, return of ms or send a disposable copy of ms. Electronic submissions (disk, files in text format) OK. Sample copy for $1. Guidelines for #10 SASE, "please specify adult or young writer's guidelines.

Payment/Terms: Pays 2 contributor's copies for poetry, 5 for articles and short stories. Acquires first North American serial rights. Not copyrighted.

Advice: "Please read back issues and study the sort of fiction we publish, and make sure it fits our newsletter. Since *TYWN* is sent to schools and young people, we prefer upbeat, nonviolent stories. I look for work that is highly original, creative, and appropriate for our audience. Manuscripts that are professional and striking stand out. I haven't seen enough stories with strong characters and involving plots. I don't want to see dull stories with dull characters. We want to show our young writers terrific examples of stories that they can learn from."

‡**THE THRESHOLD, (I, II)**, Crossover Press, P.O. Box 101362, Pittsburgh PA 15237. (412)635-9261. E-mail: lazarro@aol.com. Editors: Don H. Laird and Mike Carricato. Magazine: 8½×11; 48 pages; colored bond paper; card cover; illustrations. "We truly are a magazine 'for writers, by writers.' The editors spent years on the receiving end of rejection. We always give constructive criticism, not a form letter. Our audience is both young and old and they are in search of one thing: imaginative stories and poetry." Quarterly. Estab. 1996. Circ. 150.

Needs: Adventure, condensed/excerpted novel, erotica, experimental, fantasy, gay, horror, humor/satire, lesbian, literary, mainstream/contemporary, mystery/suspense, psychic/supernatural/occult, romance (contemporary, futuristic/time travel/gothic), science fiction, serialized novel, westerns. Publishes special fiction issues or anthologies. Receives 20 unsolicited mss/month. Accepts 6-8 mss/issue, 24-32 mss/year. Publishes ms up to 5 months after acceptance. Recently published work by Mike Watt, Sarah McBride, Tom Hritz, Daine Markham and Nancy Hillen. Length: 3,000-5,000 words average; 8,000 words maximum. Publishes short shorts. Also publishes poetry. Always critiques or comments on rejected mss.

How to Contact: Send complete ms with a cover letter. Include estimated word count and 2-paragraph bio. Reports in 2 weeks on queries; 4 months on mss. Send SASE for reply, return of ms or send disposable copy of ms. Simultaneous, reprint and electronic submissions OK. Sample copy for $5.95. Fiction guidelines for #10 SASE.

Payment/Terms: Pays 1 contributor's copy for one-time rights.

Advice: "If we like it, we print it. Period. If it needs some changes, we send a letter recommending where some revisions would help. It is an open forum between writer and editor. Send in the work. Don't be discouraged by form rejection letters."

THRESHOLDS QUARTERLY, School of Metaphysics Associates Journal, (I, II, IV), SOM Publishing, School of Metaphysics National Headquarters, HCR1, Box 15, Windyville MO 65783. (417)345-8411. Fax: (417)345-6688 (call first, computerized). Website: http://www.som.org. Editor: Dr. Barbara Condron. Senior Editor: Dr. Laurel Fuller Clark. Magazine: 7×10; 32 pages; line drawings and b&w photos. "The School of Metaphysics is a nonprofit educational and service organization invested in education and research in the expansion of human consciousness and spiritual evolution of humanity. For all ages and backgrounds. Themes: dreams, healing, science fiction, personal insight, morality tales, fables, humor, spiritual insight, mystic experiences, religious articles, creative writing with universal themes." Quarterly. Estab. 1975. Circ. 5,000.

● *Thresholds Quarterly* has doubled its circulation.

Needs: Adventure, fantasy, humor/satire, psychic/supernatural/occult, religious/inspirational, science fiction. Upcoming themes: "Dreams, Visions, and Creative Imagination" (February); "Health and Wholeness" (May); "Intuitive Arts" (August); "Man's Spiritual Consciousness" (November). Receives 5 unsolicited mss/month. Length: 4-10 double-spaced typed pages. Publishes short shorts. Also publishes literary essays and poetry. Often critiques or comments on rejected mss.

How to Contact: Query with outline; will accept unsolicited ms with cover letter; no guarantee on time length to respond. Include bio (1-2 paragraphs). Send SASE for reply, return of ms or send a disposable copy of ms. Sample copy for 9×12 SAE and $1.50 postage. Fiction guidelines for #10 SASE.

Payment/Terms: Pays up to 5 contributor's copies. Acquires all rights.

Advice: "We encourage works that have one or more of the following attributes: uplifting, educational, inspirational, entertaining, informative and innovative."

‡**UP DARE?, (I, II, IV)**, la Pierna Tierna Press, P.O. Box 100, Shartlesville PA 19554. (610)488-6894. Editors: Mary M. Towne, Doroteo Estrago and Loring D. Emery. "The only requirement is that all submitted material

must pertain to folks with physical or psychological handicaps-fiction or non-fiction." Magazine: digest-sized. Quarterly. Estab. 1997.

Needs: Fiction and poetry. Looks for "honesty, plain language and message." No smut. Recently published work by Dan Buck, Annette Wilson, Sylvia Mais-Harak and Gordon Graves.

How to Contact: "We will take single-spaced and even double-sided submissions so long as they are legible. We prefer to optically scan all material to avoid typos. We will not insist on an SASE if you truly have financial limitations. We're trying to make it as easy as possible. We will take short (250 words or less) pieces in Braille."

Advice: "We will not use euphemisms—a chair with a leg missing is a 'three-legged chair,' not a 'challenged seat.' We would like to hear from folks who are handicapped, but we aren't closing the door to others who understand and help or just have opinions to share. We will take reprints if the original appearance is identified."

‡**THE VILLAGER**, 135 Midland Ave., Bronxville NY 10708-1800. Phone/fax: (914)337-3252. Editor: Amy Murphy. Fiction Editor: Mrs. Ahmed Hazzah. Magazine: 28-40 pages. "Magazine for a family audience." Monthly. Estab. 1928. Circ. 1,000.

Needs: Adventure, historical, humor/satire, literary, mystery/suspense, prose poem, romance (historical). Recently published work by Bernard Cohen, Rekha Ambardar, Judith Ungan, Mary Hazzan and Sandra Trimble. Length: 1,500-1,800 words. Also publishes poetry.

How to Contact: Send complete ms with cover letter. SASE. Sample copy for $1.25.

Payment/Terms: Pays 2 contributor's copies.

Advice: "*The Villager* is known for it's focus on local history and people."

‡**VINTAGE NORTHWEST, (I, IV)**, Box 193, Bothell WA 98041. (425)823-9189. Editors: Jane Kaake and Sylvia Tacker. Magazine: 7×8½; 68 pages; illustrations. "We are a senior literary magazine, published by Northshore Senior Center, but our focus is to appeal to all ages. All work done by volunteers except printing." Published winter and summer. Estab. 1980. Circ. 500.

Needs: Adventure, comedy, fantasy, historical, humor/satire, inspirational, mystery/suspense, nostalgia, poetry, western (frontier). No religious or political mss. Receives 10-12 unsolicited mss/month. Publishes as many new writers as possible. Length: 1,000 words maximum. Also publishes literary essays. Occasionally critiques rejected mss.

How to Contact: Send complete ms. SASE. Simultaneous and previously published submissions OK. Reports in 3-6 months. Sample copy for $3.25 (postage included). Guidelines with SASE.

Payment/Terms: Pays 1 contributor's copy.

Advice: "Our only requirement is that the author be over 50 when submission is written."

VIRGINIA QUARTERLY REVIEW, (I, II), One West Range, Charlottesville VA 22903. (804)924-3124. Fax: (804)924-1397. E-mail: jco7e@virginia.edu. Editor: Staige Blackford. "A national magazine of literature and discussion. A lay, intellectual audience; people who are not out-and-out scholars but who are interested in ideas and literature." Quarterly. Estab. 1925. Circ. 4,000.

Needs: Adventure, contemporary, ethnic, feminist, humor, literary, romance, serialized novels (excerpts) and translations. "No pornography." Buys 3 mss/issue, 20 mss/year. Length: 3,000-7,000 words.

How to Contact: Query or send complete ms. SASE. No simultaneous submissions. Reports in 2 weeks on queries, 2 months on mss. Sample copy for $5.

Payment/Terms: Pays $10/printed page on publication for all rights. "Will transfer upon request." Offers Emily Clark Balch Award for best published short story of the year.

Advice: Looks for "stories with a somewhat Southern dialect and/or setting. Humor is welcome; stories involving cancer and geriatrics are not."

VOLCANO QUARTERLY, The Village Square of Volcanodom, (I, II, IV), 420 SE Evans Lane, Issaquah WA 98027. (425)392-7858. E-mail: vqjantan@aol.com. Website: http://memberes.aol.com/vqjantan. Editor: Janet Tanaka. Magazine: 8½×11, 16-24 pages; matte paper; illustrations; photos. "After February, 1997, an on-line publication (e-zine), with print copies only for the cyber disadvantaged. Our audience is volcano-people—both professional and amateur volcanologists, geologists, science teachers, students and volcano buffs." Quarterly. Estab. 1992. Circ. 500.

Needs: Adventure, fantasy (science), horror, humor/satire, mystery/suspense, natural disaster, regional, religious/inspirational, romance (contemporary), science fiction (hard science, soft/sociological), serialized novel. "*Stories must deal with volcanoes: past, present or future; earthly or extraterrestrial, and/or volcano scientists, etc. No erotica. Must be in English.*" Publishes ms 3-6 months after acceptance. Length: open. Publishes short shorts.

READ THE BUSINESS OF FICTION WRITING section to learn the correct way to prepare and submit a manuscript.

Also publishes literary criticism and poetry. Always critiques or comments on rejected ms, but "we rarely reject anything that meets our guidelines."

How to Contact: Send complete ms with cover letter. Include brief bio. Reports in 1-2 weeks on queries; 4-6 weeks on mss. Send SASE for reply, return of ms or send a disposable copy of ms. Simultaneous, reprint and electronic submissions OK. Sample copy for $5 and 8½×11 SAE. Fiction guidelines for #10 SASE.

Payment/Terms: Pays 3 contributor's copies. Not copyrighted.

Advice: "All volcanoes and volcanic activity must be scientifically accurate. Non-terrestrial volcanoes can be, of course, purely made up, but with some scientific logic."

‡❧**THE WESTCOAST FISHERMAN, (I, II, IV)**, Westcoast Publishing Ltd., 1496 W. 72nd Ave., Vancouver, British Columbia V6P 3C8 Canada. (640)266-8611. Fax: (604)266-6437. E-mail: fisherman@west-coast.com. Managing Editor: Kevin MacDonell. Magazine: 20cm×27cm; 56-88 pages; newsprint; glossy cover stock; illustrations and photos. "*The Westcoast Fisherman* is a nonpolitical, nonaligned trade magazine serving the commercial fishing industry of Canada's west coast. It is distributed to selected areas of the commercial fishing industry and sold at selected newsstands." Monthly. Estab. 1986. Circ. 8,000.

Needs: Condensed/excerpted novel, historical, humor/satire, regional. "Nothing on sport fishing. Submissions must be closely tied to commercial fishing, preferably in British Columbia. Seasonality is good, e.g., salmon in summer, herring in spring, etc." Receives 1 unsolicited ms/month. Accepts approximately 6 mss/year. Publishes ms 1-3 months after acceptance. Recently published short story by Pete Fletcher. Length: 1,200 words average; 800 words minimum; 2,500 words maximum. Also publishes poetry.

How to Contact: Query with clips of published work or send complete ms with a cover letter. Include 10-20 word bio and where piece has previously appeared, if applicable. Reports in 1 month. Send disposable copy of ms. Simultaneous, reprint and electronic (disk or modem) submissions OK. Sample copy for $3. Fiction guidelines free. Reviews novels or short story collections "if on topic, definitely."

Payment/Terms: Pays 10-15 cents/word and 2-10 contributor's copies; additional copies $3. Pays on publication. Acquires one-time rights. Sponsors annual fiction contest. Timing and conditions change from year to year.

Advice: "We are interested in fiction produced by fishermen or coastal dwellers, or which shows familiarity with their work and world."

❧**WESTERN DIGEST**, Crossbow Publications, 400 Whiteland Dr. NE, Calgary, Alberta T1Y 3M7 Canada. (403)280-3424. Editor: Douglas Sharp. Newsletter: 8½×11; 20 pages; illustrations. Estab. 1995. Circ. 100.

Needs: Westerns (frontier, traditional). "Do not combine westerns with science fiction." Receives 4 unsolicited mss/month. Accepts 5-8 mss/issue; 50 mss/year. Publishes ms 8-12 months after acceptance. Recently published work by Emery Mehok, S.M. Cain, C.K. Eckhardt, Arthur Knight and Dusty Richards. Publishes 10 new writers/year. Length: 3,000 words average; 1,000 words minimum; 5,000 words maximum. Publishes short shorts. Length: 1,000 words. Also publishes literary criticism and poetry. Always critiques or comments on rejected mss.

How to Contact: Send complete ms with a cover letter. Include 10- to 30-word bio. Reports in 1 week on queries; 2 weeks on mss. Send SAE and 2 IRCs for return of ms. Simultaneous submissions, reprints and electronic (Macintosh disk, WordPerfect 5.1) submissions OK. Sample copy for $4. Fiction guidelines free. Reviews novels or short story collections.

Payment/Terms: Pays $10-60 (Canadian funds) and free subscription to the magazine on publication. Acquires one-time rights.

Advice: "I enjoy stories with humorous, ironic or surprise endings. I would like to read more humorous stories. Avoid shoot-'em-ups. One gets tired of reading stories where the fastest gun wins in the end. There are other stories to be told of the pioneers. Rewrite your story until it is perfect. Do not use contractions in narration unless the story is written in first person. Do not send three consecutive pages of dialogue. Be sure to identify the speaker after three or four paragraphs. A reader should not have to reread a passage to understand it. Please, no sex or heavy duty swearing."

WISCONSIN ACADEMY REVIEW, (IV), Wisconsin Academy of Sciences, Arts & Letters, 1922 University Ave., Madison WI 53705. (608)263-1692. Editor-in-Chief: Faith B. Miracle. Magazine: 8½×11; 48-52 pages; 75 lb. coated paper; coated cover stock; illustrations; photos. "The *Review* reflects the focus of the sponsoring institution with its editorial emphasis on Wisconsin's intellectual, cultural, social and physical environment. It features short fiction, poetry, essays, nonfiction articles and Wisconsin-related art and book reviews for people interested in furthering regional arts and literature and disseminating information about sciences." Quarterly. Estab. 1954. Circ. approximately 1,800.

Needs: Experimental, historical, humor/satire, literary, mainstream, prose poem. "Author must have a Wisconsin connection or fiction must be set in Wisconsin." Receives 5-6 unsolicited fiction mss/month. Accepts 1-2 mss/issue; 6-8 mss/year. Published new writers within the last year. Length: 1,000 words minimum; 3,500 words maximum. Also publishes poetry; "will consider" literary essays, literary criticism.

How to Contact: Send complete ms with SAE and state author's connection to Wisconsin, the prerequisite. Sample copy for $2. Fiction guidelines for SASE. Reviews books on Wisconsin themes.

Payment/Terms: Pays 3-5 contributor's copies. Acquires first rights on publication.

Advice: "Manuscript publication is at the discretion of the editor based on space, content and balance. We prefer previously unpublished poetry and fiction. We publish emerging as well as established authors; fiction and poetry, without names attached, are sent to reviewers for evaluation."

WOMAN, (I), Copper Moon Publishing, P.O. Box 1348, Meadville PA 16335. (814)336-4132. E-mail: bwalton @toolcity.net. Editor: Babs Walton. Magazine: 8½×7; 12 or more pages; 20 lb. bond paper; illustrations. "We are a journal, by women and for women, with articles, essays, poetry and fiction on topics of interest to today's modern woman. Monthly. Estab. 1996. Circ. 300.
Needs: Ethnic/multicultural, experimental, feminist, humor/satire, lesbian, literary, mainstream/contemporary, mystery/suspense, psychic/supernatural/occult, religious/inspirational, romance, science fiction. No erotica. Receives 30 unsolicited mss/month. Accepts 1-2 mss/issue; 30 mss/year. Publishes ms 2-6 months after acceptance. Recently published work by Paul Raymond Martin, Mary Chandler and Evan Stubblefield. Length: 1,000 words average; 100 words minimum; 1,500 words maximum. Publishes short shorts. Also publishes poetry. Often critiques or comments on rejected mss.
How to Contact: Query first or send complete ms with cover letter. Include estimated word count and 1-paragraph bio. "If you have a book you want to advertise, add it to your bio. Reports in 2 weeks on queries; 1 month on mss. Send SASE for reply, return of ms or send a disposable copy of ms. Reprints and electronic submissions OK. Sample copy for $1 and #10 SASE with 2 first-class stamps. Fiction guidelines for #10 SASE. Reviews novels and short story collections.
Payment/Terms: Pays 1-year subscription to magazine ($10 value) on acceptance. Acquires first North American serial rights.
Advice: "We look for something different, a special use of language or striking imagery. It can be personal but should also reach out to our whole readership. Be brief!"

WORLDS OF FANTASY & HORROR, (II), Terminus Publishing Co., Inc., 123 Crooked Lane, King of Prussia PA 19406-2570. E-mail: owlswick@netaxs.com. Editor: Darrell Schweitzer. Magazine: 8½×11; 120 pages; white, non-glossy paper; glossy 4-color cover; illustrations. "We publish fantastic fiction, supernatural horror for an adult audience." Quarterly. Estab. 1923 (*Weird Tales);* 1994 (*Worlds of Fantasy & Horror*). Circ. 8,000.
Needs: Fantasy (science, sword and sorcery), horror, psychic/supernatural/occult, translations. "We want to see a wide range of fantasy, from sword and sorcery to supernatural horror. We can use some unclassifiables." Receives 400 unsolicited mss/month. Accepts 8 mss/issue; 32 mss/year. Publishes ms 6-18 months after acceptance. Agented fiction 10%. Published work by Tanith Lee, Thomas Ligotti, Ian Watson and Lord Dunsany. Length: 4,000 words average; 10,000 words maximum (very few over 8,000). "No effective minimum. Shortest we ever published was about 100 words." Publishes short shorts. Also publishes poetry. Always critiques or comments on rejected mss.
How to Contact: Send complete ms with a cover letter. Include estimated word count and list of publications (if relevant). Reports in 2-3 weeks on mss. Send SASE for reply, return of ms or send a disposable copy of ms. No simultaneous submissions. No reprint submissions, "but will buy first North American rights to stories published overseas." Sample copy for $4.95. Fiction guidelines for #10 SASE. Reviews novels and short story collections relevant to the horror/fantasy field.
Payment/Terms: Pays 3¢/word minimum and 2 contributor's copies for first North American serial rights plus anthology option. Sends galleys to author.
Advice: "We look for imagination and vivid writing. Read the magazine. Get a good grounding in the contemporary horror and fantasy field through the various 'best of the year' anthologies. Avoid the obvious cliches of technicalities of the hereafter, the mechanics of vampirism, generic Tolkien-clone fantasy. In general, it is better to be honest and emotionally moving rather than clever. Avoid stories which have nothing of interest save for the allegedly 'surprise' ending."

WRITERS' INTERNATIONAL FORUM, (I, II), Bristol Services International, P.O. Box 516, Tracyton WA 98393. Editor: Sandra E. Haven. "*Writers' International Forum—For Those Who Write to Sell*, will take on a new look in the last quarter of 1997. The new format will expand our most popular features from the past (markets listing, lessons on writing, features about the writing craft) and include a new 'Featured Manuscript' section in which a short story or essay is published with author bio and with a free professional critique of that manuscript. New guidelines will be available for SASE at that time." Monthly. Estab. 1990.
Needs: Adventure, childrens/juvenile (8-12 years), fantasy, historical, humor/satire, mainstream/contemporary, mystery/suspense, psychic/supernatural/occult, regional, romance (contemporary, young adult), science fiction,

senior citizen/retirement, sports, westerns, young adult/teen. "No graphic sex, violence, vignettes or experimental formats." Accepts 20-40 mss/year. Publishes ms an average of 4 months after acceptance. Recently published work by Dede Hammond and Judy S. Dodd. Length: 1,000 words maximum. Publishes short shorts.

How to Contact: Send complete ms with a cover letter. Include brief bio. Reports in 2 months on mss. Send SASE for reply. Fiction guidelines for #10 SASE.

Payment/Terms: Pays $30 plus 2 contributor's copies on acceptance and free professional critique; additional copies for authors at discounted rates. Acquires first rights. Sample copy for $3.

Advice: "The fastest way to know if your story might be suitable for our unique 'Featured Manuscript' column is to read a copy first. If your story is written for children, state the intended age group. If a manuscript is submitted by a young author, please so note. New guidelines and contest information will be available for SASE."

‡*XENOS, Dept. NSS, 29 Prebend St., Bedford MK40 1QN England. E-mail: xenos@xenos.demon.co.uk. Website: http://www.demon.co.uk. Editor: S.V. Copestake. Bimonthly. Circ. 1,000. Founded 1990. Publishes 7-8 stories/issue, many by new writers. "*Xenos* is a glossy-cover story magazine. (No nonfiction, advertisements or illustrations)."

Needs: "We consider science fiction, fantasy, horror, occult, humor, detective, ripping yarns, etc., but submissions *must* be 2,000-10,000 words *and* suitable for the UK. We do not consider purely romantic stories, pornography, blood-and-gore or cyberpunk. We hold two annual short story competitions with cash prizes and publication: open to everyone (subject to an entry fee), no fee and unlimited entries, but subscriber-only."

How to Contact: "Read our guidelines—or take out a subscription—before submitting. Sufficient IRCs (or cash in dollars) for return postage is essential (submissions won't be read without this)."

Advice: "XENOS also publishes *Writer's Tips*, a bimonthly newssheet for writers listing UK markets and competitions. Additionally, XENOS evaluates novels and stories in detail—write for a quote (with 1 IRC)."

YARNS AND SUCH, (I, IV), Creative With Words Publications, Box 223226, Carmel CA 93922. Fax: (408)655-8627. Editors: Brigitta Geltrich (General Editor) and Bert Hower (Nature Editor). Booklet: 5½×8½; 60-90 pages; bond paper; illustrations. Folklore. Annually. Estab. 1975. Circ. varies.

Needs: Ethnic, humor/satire, mystery/suspense (amateur sleuth, private eye), regional, folklore. "Twice a year we publish an anthology of the writings of young writers, titled: *We are Writers Too!*" No violence or erotica, religious fiction. List of upcoming themes available for SASE. Receives 500 unsolicited fiction mss/month. Publishes ms 1-2 months after deadline. Recently published work by Helen Rames Briggs, Jo Ellen Kaminski and Irmgard Mokos; published new writers within the last year. Length: 1,500 words average; limits poetry to 20 lines or less. Critiques rejected mss "when requested, *then we charge $20/prose, up to 1,000 words*."

How to Contact: Query first or send complete ms with cover letter and SASE. "Reference has to be made to which project the manuscript is being submitted. Unsolicited mss without SASE will be destroyed after holding them 1 month." Reports in 2 weeks on queries; 2 months on mss; longer on specific seasonal anthologies. No simultaneous submissions. Accepts electronic (disk) submissions via Macintosh and IBM/PC. Sample copy for $6. Fiction guidelines for #10 SASE.

Payment/Terms: No payment. Acquires one-time rights. 20% reduction on each copy ordered; 30% reduction on each copy on orders of 10 or more.

Advice: "We have increased the number of anthologies we are publishing to 12 per year and offer a greater variety of themes. We look for clean family-type fiction. Also, look at the world from a different perspective, research your topic thoroughly, be creative, apply brevity, tell the story from a character's viewpoint, tighten dialogue, be less descriptive, proofread before submitting and be patient. We will not publish every manuscript we receive. It has to be in standard English, well-written, proofread. We do not appreciate receiving manuscripts where we have to do the proofreading and the correcting of grammar."

YOUNG JUDAEAN, (IV), Hadassah Zionist Youth Commission, 50 W. 58th St., New York NY 10019. (212)303-4575. Editor: Debra Neufeld. National Education Supervisor: Mel Sobell. Magazine: 8½×11; 16 pages; illustrations. "*Young Judaean* is for members of the Young Judaea Zionist youth movement, ages 8-13." Quarterly. Estab. 1910. Circ. 4,000.

Needs: Children's fiction including adventure, ethnic, fantasy, historical, humor/satire, juvenile, prose poem, religious, science fiction, suspense/mystery and translations. "All stories must have Jewish relevance." Receives 10-15 unsolicited fiction mss/month. Publishes ms up to 2 years after acceptance. Accepts 1-2 mss/issue; 10-20 mss/year. Length: 750 words minimum; 1,000 words maximum.

How to Contact: Send complete ms with SASE. Reports in 3 months on mss. Sample copy for 75¢. Free fiction guidelines.

Payment/Terms: Pays five contributor's copies.

Advice: "Stories must be of Jewish interest—lively and accessible to children without being condescending."

*THE ZONE, Pigasus Press, 13 Hazely Combe, Arreton, Isle of Wight, PO30 3AJ England. Fiction Editor: Tony Lee. Published 5 times a year. Publishes 6 stories/issue.

Needs: "*The Zone*: A4-size magazine of quality science fiction plus articles and reviews." Length: 1,000 words minimum; 5,000 words maximum.

How to Contact: "Study recent issues of the magazine. Unsolicited submissions are always welcome but writers must enclose SAE/IRC for reply, plus adequate postage to return ms if unsuitable."

Payment/Terms: Pays in copies. "Token payment for stories and articles of 2,000 words and over." Sample copies available for $9 (cash, US dollars) or 9 IRCs; for UK, £2.75; EC countries, £3 (cheques/eurocheques, should be made payable to: Tony Lee).

Zines

This market section, given its own niche in *Novel & Short Story Writer's Market* for the first time in our 1997 edition, has more than doubled in size this year. And great news for those of you who want to cut paper and postage costs, and eliminate weeks or even months waiting for a response to your query or manuscript submissions: almost all the zines listed here for the first time are electronic zines! Among the e-zines and paper zines listed here are markets for all types of fiction: fantasy, horror, humor, literary, mystery, romance, science fiction and more.

SELF-EXPRESSION AND ARTISTIC FREEDOM

Vastly different from one another in appearance and content, the common source of zines seems to be a need for self-expression. Although this need to voice opinions has always been around, it was not until the '70s, and possibly beginning with the social upheaval of the '60s, that the availability of photocopiers and computers provided an easy, cheap way to produce the self-published and usually self-written "zines." It follows, then, that zines are now springing up in an electronic format.

Although the editorial content of zines runs the gamut from traditional and genre fiction to personal rants to highly experimental work, artistic freedom is a characteristic of all zines. Although zine editors are open to a wide range of fiction that more conventional editors might not consider, don't make the mistake of thinking they expect any less from writers than the editors of other types of publications. Like any good editors, zine editors look for work that is creative and well presented and that shows the writer has taken time to become familiar with the market. And since most zines are highly specialized, familiarity with the niche markets they offer is extremely important. Here are just a few comments from among the "Advice" sections of the zines in this section:

- "I will do minor editorial changes and allow you final approval, but major grammatical errors and/or spelling goofs will be dumped. I have a real-time job that demands a lot of time from me, help me out." (*The Netherreal Horror Cyberzine*)
- "Read your story over a week or two after you've written it. Do you still think anyone wants to read it? If so, then maybe we will too." (*pauper*)
- "Tell a complete tale with strong characters and a plot which draws the reader in from the very first sentence to the very last. The key to good fiction writing is presenting readers with characters they can identify with at some level. . . . Also, be careful with grammar and sentence structure. We get too many submissions which have good plot lines, but are rejected because of poor English skills." (*Pegasus Online*)

Although some of the zines listed here have been published since the early '80s, many are relatively new and some were just starting publication as they filled out the questionnaire to be included in this edition of *Novel & Short Story Writer's Market*. Unfortunately, due to the waning energy and shrinking funds of their publishers (and often a lack of material), few last for more than several issues. Fortunately, though, some have been around since the late '70s and early '80s, and hundreds of new ones are launched every day.

While zines represent the most volatile group of publications in *Novel & Short Story Writer's Market*, they are also the most open to submissions by beginning writers. As mentioned above, the editors of zines are often writers themselves and welcome the opportunity to give others a chance at publication.

SELECTING THE RIGHT MARKET

Your chance for publication begins as you zero in on the zines most likely to be interested in your work. Begin by browsing through the listings. This is especially important since zines are the most diverse and specialized markets listed in this book. Then check the Category Index (starting on page 641) for the appropriate subject heading, such as experimental, fantasy or mystery.

In addition to browsing through the listings and using the Category Index, check the ranking codes at the beginning of listings to find those most likely to be receptive to your work. Most all zines are open to new writers (I) or to both new and established writers (II). For more explanation about these codes, see the end of this introduction.

Once you have a list of zines you might like to try, read their listings carefully. Zines vary greatly in appearance as well as content. Some paper zines are photocopies published whenever the editor has material and money, while others feature offset printing and regular distribution schedules. And a few have evolved into four-color, commercial-looking, very slick publications. The physical description appearing near the beginning of the listings gives you clues about the size and financial commitment to the publication. This is not always an indication of quality, but chances are a publication with expensive paper and four-color artwork on the cover has more prestige than a photocopied publication featuring a clip art self-cover. If you're a new writer or your work is considered avant garde, however, you may be more interested in the photocopied zine or one of the electronic zines. For more information on some of the paper, binding and printing terms used in these descriptions, see Printing and Production Terms Defined on page 636. Also, How to Use This Book to Publish Your Fiction, starting on page 3, describes in detail the listing information common to all markets in our book.

FURTHERING YOUR SEARCH

It cannot be stressed enough that reading the listings is only the first part of developing your marketing plan. The second part, equally important, is to obtain fiction guidelines and a copy of the actual zine. Reading copies of the publication helps you determine the fine points of the zine's publishing style and philosophy. Especially since zines tend to be highly specialized, there is no substitute for this hands-on, eyes-on research.

Unlike commercial periodicals available at most newsstands and bookstores, it requires a little more effort to obtain most of the zines listed here. You will probably need to send for a sample copy. We include sample copy prices in the listings whenever possible.

For a comprehensive listing of zines in a number of categories and reviews of each, check out Seth Friedman's *Factsheet Five* (P.O. Box 170099, San Francisco CA 94117-0099) published twice every year. *Scavenger's Newsletter* (519 Ellinwood, Osage City KS 66523) also lists markets for science fiction, fantasy, horror and mystery. More zines and information on starting your own zine can be found in *The World of Zines: A Guide to the Independent Magazine Revolution*, by Mike Gunderloy and Cari Goldberg Janice (Penguin Books, 375 Hudson St., New York NY 10014). Also check the Websites of Interest section on page 629 for leads to finding great markets on the Internet.

The following is the ranking system we have used to categorize the listings in this section:

   I **Publication encourages beginning or unpublished writers to submit work for consideration and publishes new writers regularly.**

   II **Publication accepts outstanding work by beginning and established writers.**

   III **Hard to break into; publishes mostly previously published writers.**

   IV **Special-interest or regional publication, open only to writers in certain genres or on certain subjects or from certain geographical areas.**

ABSOLUTE MAGNITUDE, Science Fiction Adventures, (I, II, IV), DNA Publications, P.O. Box 910, Greenfield MA 01302. (413)772-0725. Editor: Warren Lapine. Zine: 8½×11; 96 pages; newsprint; color cover; illustrations. "We publish technical science fiction that is adventurous and character driven." Quarterly. Estab. 1993. Circ. 9,000.

Needs: Science fiction: adventure, hard science. No fantasy, horror, funny science fiction. Receives 300-500 unsolicited mss/month. Accepts 7-10 mss/issue; 28-40 mss/year. Publishes ms 3-6 months after acceptance. Agented fiction 5%. Published work by Hal Clement, Chris Bunch, C.J. Cherryh, Barry B. Longyear and Harlan Ellison. Length: 5,000-12,000 words average; 1,000 words minimum; 25,000 words maximum. Publishes very little poetry. Often critiques or comments on rejected ms.

How to Contact: Do NOT query. Send complete ms with a cover letter. Should include estimated word count and list of publications. Send SASE for reply, return of ms or send a disposable copy of ms. Simultaneous and reprint submissions OK. Sample copy for $5. Reviews novels and short story collections.

Payment/Terms: Pays 1-5¢/word on publication for first North American serial rights; 1¢/word for first reprint rights. Sometimes sends galleys to author.

Advice: "We want good writing with solid characterization, also character growth, story development, and plot resolution. We would like to see more character-driven stories."

ABYSS MAGAZINE, "Games and the Imagination," (II, IV), Ragnarok Enterprises, P.O. Box 140333, Austin TX 78714-0333. (512)472-6535. Fax: (512)472-6220. E-mail: ragnarok@aol.com. Website: http://www.ccsi.com/~garball/abyss. Editor: David F. Nalle. Fiction Editor: Patricia Fitch. Zine: 8×10; 48 pages; bond paper; glossy cover; illustrations; photos. "Heroic fantasy fiction: some fantasy, horror, SF and adventure fiction, for college-age game players." Quarterly. Plans special fiction issue. Estab. 1979. Circ. 1,500.

● *Abyss Magazine* can be contacted through Internet online service as well as their own electronic bulletin board.

Needs: Adventure, fantasy, horror, psychic/supernatural/occult, cyberpunk, science fiction, heroic fantasy, sword and sorcery. "Game-based stories are not specifically desired." Upcoming themes: "Horror Issue" (spring); "Review Issue" (summer). Receives 20-30 unsolicited mss/month. Buys 1 ms/issue; 7 mss/year. Publishes ms 1-12 months after acceptance. Published work by Antoine Sadel, Kevin Anderson, Alan Blount; published new writers within the last year. Length: 2,000 words average; 1,000 words minimum; 4,000 words maximum. Publishes short shorts occasionally. Also publishes literary essays and literary criticism. Sometimes critiques rejected mss or recommends other markets.

How to Contact: Send for sample copy first. Reports in 6 weeks on queries; 3 months on mss. "Do send a cover letter, preferably entertaining. Include some biographical info and a precis of lengthy stories." SASE. Simultaneous submissions OK. Prefers electronic submissions by modem or network. Sample copy and fiction guidelines $5. Reviews novels and short story collections (especially fantasy novels).

Payment/Terms: Pays 1-3¢/word or by arrangement, plus contributor's copies. Pays on publication for first North American serial rights.

Advice: "We are particularly interested in new writers with mature and original style. Don't send us fiction which everyone else has sent back to you unless you think it has qualities which make it too strange for everyone else but which don't ruin the significance of the story. Make sure what you submit is appropriate to the magazine you send it to. More than half of what we get is completely inappropriate. We plan to include more and longer stories."

‡APHELION, The Webzine of Science Fiction and Fantasy, (I). (706)543-3408. E-mail: vila@america.net. Website: http://www.america.net/~vila/newzine.html. Editor: Dan L. Hollifield. Electronic zine. "A place for amateur writers to hone their skills and get their work before the public. We wish to provide a forum such that our writers can ready themselves to submit future stories to paying publishers."

Needs: Fantasy (sword and sorcery, high fantasy), horror (Lovecraftian), science fiction (hard science, humorous). "Nothing unsuitable for younger readers. When we do receive submissions that contain this material and are just too good of a story to reject, we feel it necessary to attach an 'Adults Only' warning flag to its link." Recently published work by Roger Bennett, Chad Cottle, Kenneth C. Goldman, Dennis Talent, Thomas Allen Mays, Joe Genswider, Rene Steen, Richie Adams, Brian Gallucci, Cris Lawrence and Neal Williams. Publishes as many new writers as possible.

How to Contact: Electronic submissions only. Send submissions by e-mail as text attachments.

Advice: "Think big. Re-write until it is as good as you can make it. Spellcheck! Read other writers copiously, enjoy what you yourself write. Remember, writing is hard work. Lots of skull-sweat goes into every good story that the pros write."

‡ARTISAN, a journal of craft, (I), P.O. Box 157, Wilmette IL 60091. E-mail: artisanjnl@aol.com. Website: http://members.aol.com/artisanjnl. Editor: Joan Daugherty. Electronic zine. "We were founded with the principle that everyone who strives to improve their craft—from ballet to bricklaying—is an artist, and artists of all disciplines and abilities can learn from each other. We publish a wide variety of genres and styles that should entertain a general reader, although most of our subscribers are themselves writers."

Needs: "We'd love to see more 'literary' stories that appeal to a general audience-stories that are well written and sophisticated without being stuffy. Nothing sexually or violently graphic or with foul language unless it clearly contributes to the story." Recently published work by Joan Harvey, Vivian Choy Edelson, Ed Dougherty and Anne Shultz. Publishes 16 new writers/year.

How to Contact: Electronic and traditional submissions accepted. E-mail submissions should be in ASCII text format; traditional submissions should include a SASE for reply.

Advice: "Send us stories that have well-defined plots, believable characters and a definable 'turning point,' written with just enough words to get the job done-nothing longer than 4,000 words, preferably around 3,000."

ART:MAG, (II), P.O. Box 70896, Las Vegas NV 89170. Editor: Peter Magliocco. Zine: 5½×8½, 8½×14, also 8½×11; 70-90 pages; 20 lb. bond paper; b&w pen and ink illustrations and photographs. Publishes "irreverent, literary-minded work by committed writers," for "small press, 'quasi-art-oriented' " audience. Annually. Estab. 1984. Circ. under 500.

Needs: Condensed/excerpted novel, confession, contemporary, erotica, ethnic, experimental, fantasy, feminist, gay, historical (general), horror, humor/satire, lesbian, literary, mainstream, mystery/suspense, prose poem, psychic/supernatural/occult, regional, science fiction, translations and arts. No "slick-oriented stuff published by major magazines." Receives 1 plus ms/month. Accepts 1-2 mss/year. Does not read mss July-October. Publishes ms within 3-6 months of acceptance. Recently published work by Mike Newirth, Mark Wisniewski, Diana Lee Goldman, Monika Conroy, Joan Elizabeth Blum, Anne Helen Jupiter and Abigail Davis. Length: 2,000 words preferred; 250 words minimum; 3,000 words maximum. Also publishes literary essays "if relevant to aesthetic preferences," literary criticism "occasionally," poetry. Sometimes critiques rejected mss.

How to Contact: Send complete ms with cover letter. Reports in 3 months. SASE for ms. Simultaneous submissions OK. Sample copy for $5, 6×9 SAE and 79¢ postage. Fiction guidelines for #10 SASE.

Payment/Terms: Pays contributor's copies. Acquires one-time rights.

Advice: "Seeking more novel and quality-oriented work, usually from solicited authors. Magazine fiction today needs to be concerned with the issues of fiction writing itself—not just with a desire to publish or please the largest audience. Think about things in the fine art world as well as the literary one and keep the hard core of life in between."

ATROCITY, Publication of the Absurd Sig of Mensa, (II), 2419 Greensburg Pike, Pittsburgh PA 15221. Editor: Hank Roll. Zine: 5½×8½; 30 pages; offset 20 lb. paper and cover; illustrations. Humor and satire for "high IQ-Mensa" members. Monthly. Estab. 1976. Circ. 250.

Needs: Humor/satire: Liar's Club, parody, jokes, funny stories, comments on the absurdity of today's world. Receives 30 unsolicited mss/month. Accepts 2 mss/issue. Publishes ms 6-12 months after acceptance. Published work by John Smethers, Sheryll Watt, Dolph Wave and Ellen Warts. Published new writers within the last year. Length: 50-150 words preferred; 650 words maximum.

How to Contact: Send complete ms. "No cover letter necessary if ms states what rights (e.g. first North American serial/reprint, etc.) are offered." Reports in 1 month. SASE. Simultaneous and reprint submissions OK. Sample copy for $1.

Payment/Terms: Pays contributor's copies. Acquires one-time rights.

Advice: Do not submit mss exceeding 650 words. Manuscript should be single-spaced and copy ready in a horizontal format to fit on one 5½×8½ sheet. "If you don't read the specs, you get it back. Don't waste our time."

‡AURICULAR IMMERSION MEDIA ONLINE MAGAZINE, (I, II). (415)664-6302. E-mail: aherrick@auricular.com. Website: http://www.auricular.com/AIM. Editor: Alan Herrick. Electronic zine. "An online magazine fueled mostly by submissions and developed as a support mechanism for beginning and experienced writers and reporters. Very little editorial discretion is exercised making this sort of an open forum, or testing ground for many contributors. Intended audience is 18-45. Magazine offers fiction, serial fiction, reviews (film and music) political articles, rants, raves and the like. Much of the reported material has a sarcastic edge."

Needs: "Completely open. Nothing offensively hateful. We would like to see more women writers' works." Recently published work by Ted Rosen, Ben Ohmart, Henry Warwick, John Humphries, Alan Herrick, Cliff Neighbors. Publishes as many new writers "as are willing to contribute material."

How to Contact: Electronic submissions only. Send mss via email in ASCII format or as a MS word RTF attachment.

Advice: "Be open minded, have an edge, and be willing to see your material presented in a fashion that is unconventional to other publications in attitude and appearance. Quite a few of our writers have scored weekly columns and paid publishing ventures with their submission to AIM on their CV. Although we can't afford to pay . . . we update the publication online regularly . . . all past submissions are available as archived material and we do our best to get word of our publication out to the masses without cluttering it with advertising and fluff."

‡AUTOMAT, (I). E-mail: mtzadrogaseudo.com. Website: http://pseudo.com/automat/. Editor: Mark T. Zadroga. Electronic zine. "Our focus is people 25-35 with a similar skewed view of the world." Bi-monthly.

Needs: "We accept all sorts of short stories, fiction, prose, poetry."

How to Contact: "We read all submissions. They can be sent to me in care of the above e-mail address."

Payment/Terms: "The author retains all right to the piece. No payment is offered, only the chance to publish your work."

Advice: "You can either e-mail your submissions or you can use the form on the website. If you'd like to run an idea by us before sending it in, check one of the department categories on the form and type a brief description of your idea in the box."

babysue, (II), P.O. Box 8989, Atlanta GA 31106-8989. (404)875-8951. E-mail: lmnop@babysue.com. Website: http://www.babysue.com (includes comics, poetry, fiction and a wealth of music reviews). Editor: Don W. Seven. Zine: 8½ × 11; 32 pages; illustrations and photos. "*babysue* is a collection of music reviews, poetry, short fiction and cartoons for anyone who can think and is not easily offended." Biannually. Estab. 1983. Circ. 5,000.
● Sometimes funny, very often perverse, this 'zine featuring mostly cartoons and "comix" definitely is not for the easily offended.

Needs: Erotica, experimental and humor/satire. Receives 5-10 mss/month. Accepts 3-4 mss/year. Publishes ms within 3 months of acceptance. Recently published work by Daniel Lanette, Massy Baw, Andrew Taylor and Barbara Rimshaw. Publishes short shorts. Length: 1-2 single-spaced pages.

How to Contact: Query with clips of published work. SASE. Simultaneous submissions OK. No submissions via e-mail.

Payment/Terms: Pays 1 contributor's copy.

Advice: "Create out of the love of creating, not to see your work in print!"

BACKSPACE, A Collection of Queer Poetry & Fiction (I, II), Lock the Target Media, 25 Riverside Ave., Gloucester MA 01930-2552. (978)282-5422. E-mail: charkim@tiac.net. Website: http://www.tiac.net/users/charkim. Editor: Kimberley Smith. Fiction Editor: Charlotte Stratton. Zine: 5½ × 8½; 48 pages; copy paper; glossy cover; illustrations and photos. "*Backspace* is a literary zine for the gay, lesbian, bisexual and transgender community." Quarterly. Estab. 1991. Circ. 400-600.

Needs: Experimental, gay, humor/satire, lesbian, literary. "No sexually explicit or violent material." Plans to publish special fiction issues or anthologies. Receives 8-10 unsolicited mss/month. Accepts 4-8 mss/issue; 16-20 mss/year. Publishes ms 6 months after acceptance. Agented fiction 85%. Published work by B.Z. Niditch, Beth Brant, Monika Arnett, Robert Klein Engler and Leah Erickson. Length: 1,500 words minimum; 2,500 words maximum. Also publishes literary essays, poetry.

How to Contact: Send complete ms with a cover letter. Include estimated word count, 30-word bio, list of publications. Reports in 2 weeks on queries; 3-6 weeks on mss. Send SASE for reply, return of ms or send a disposable copy of ms. Simultaneous, reprint, electronic submissions (3.5 diskette, Word, QuarkXPress, Page-maker, ASCII; or e-mail) OK. Sample copy for $2.50. Fiction guidelines for #10 SASE. Reviews novels and short story collections. Send books to Charlotte Stratton.

Payment/Terms: Pays 1 contributor's copy; additional copies $4. Acquires one-time rights. Not copyrighted.

Advice: "Fully formed characters are important; topical allusions are distracting."

BAHLASTI PAPERS, The Newsletter of the Kali Lodge, O.T.O., (I), P.O. Box 3096, New Orleans LA 70177-3096. E-mail: simbi317@concentric.net. Editor: Soror Chén. Zine: 8½ × 11; 12 pages; 20 lb. paper; 20 lb. cover; 2 illustrations; occasional photographs. "Occult, mythological, artistic, alternative and political material for the lunatic fringe." Monthly. Estab. 1986. Circ. 200.

Needs: Condensed/excerpted novel, erotica, ethnic, experimental, fantasy, feminist, gay, horror, humor/satire, lesbian, literary, psychic/supernatural/occult, science fiction, serialized novel, "however our emphasis is on the occult. We do not publish poetry." Plans special compilation issues. Receives 10 unsolicited mss/month. Accepts 2 mss/issue; 24 mss/year. Publishes mss approximately 12-18 months after acceptance. Recently published work by Darius James, Sallie Ann Glassman and Colin Robinson. Publishes 20 new writers/year. Publishes short shorts. Also publishes literary essays, literary criticism.

How to Contact: Send complete ms with cover letter telling "why author is interested in being published in *Bahlasti Papers*." Reports in 1 month on queries and mss. SASE. Simultaneous, reprint and electronic (disk-Microsoft Publisher program) submissions OK. Sample copy for $2.25 with 6 × 9 SAE and 2 first-class stamps. Occasionally reviews novels and short story collections.

Payment/Terms: Pays subscription to magazine. Publication not copyrighted.

Advice: "We do not wish to read hackneyed, Hollywood treatments of voodoo or the occult. Our readers are interested in the odd point-of-view that creates new, empowering, and healing archetypes for the lunatic fringe. Our writers are willing to make an initial descent into shadow regions in order to sing for the gods. And please watch your grammar! Be professional in your presentation and let your writing speak for itself—don't be too cutesy or familiar with the editor."

‡THE BLACK LILY, Fantasy and Medieval Review, (I, II, IV), Southern Goblin Productions, 8444 Cypress Circle, Sarasota FL 34243-2006. (941)351-4386. E-mail: gkuklew@lxnetcom.com. Editor: Vincent Kuklewski. Fiction Editor: Michael Nauton. Zine specializing in Pre-1600 A.D. World: 64 pages; 50 lb. paper; card cover; illustrations and photos. Quarterly. Estab. 1996. Circ. 475.

Needs: Ethnic/Multicultural, fantasy (sword and sorcery), gay, horror, humor/satire, lesbian, literary, mystery/suspense (police procedural, magic/wizard), serialized novel, translations, folktales. No science fiction, erotica or gratuitous gore. Upcoming themes: "Byzantine Empire" (January); "1001 Arabian Nights" (August). List of upcoming themes available for SASE. Publishes special fiction issues or anthologies. Receives 20-30 unsolicited mss/month. Accepts 3-5 mss/issue; 25-30 mss/year. Publishes ms 2-4 months after acceptance. Recently published work by Scott Urban, Jim Lee, D.F. Lewis, Lori J. Paxton, Nancy Bennett, Jones Rada, Jr., Uncle River and Ken Goldman. Length: 3,000-4,000 words average; 1,500 words minimum; 120,000 words maximum. Publishes short shorts. Also publishes literary essays, literary criticism and poetry. Often critiques or comments on rejected manuscripts.

How to Contact: Send complete manuscript with a cover letter or e-mail submission with cover letter. Include estimated word count and 2-line bio. Reports in 1 month on queries; 3 months on mss. Send SASE for reply and send a disposable copy of ms. Reprints and electronic submissions OK. Reviews novels and short story collections. Send books to Vincent Kuklewski.

Payment/Terms: Pays $5 minimum; $50 maximum on acceptance and 1 contributor's copy for one-time or first international serial rights.

Advice: "Avoid tales in which Evil is unbelievably unopposed, in which the characters are so flat they are interchangeable, in which there are elements of magic (overt or implied). A glut of goth and vampire themes is making dark fiction cliché and far too many beginning writers are jumping on the bandwagon. We try to keep open markets for heroic fiction by steering new writers to h.f. themes and other h.f. zines."

‡BLACK PETALS, (I, II, III), 1319 Marshall St., Manitowoc WI 54220. (920)684-7901. Editor: D.M. Yorton. Zine specializing in horror/fantasy: digest size; 30-40 pages; photocopied; illustrations. "A little something special for those special readers of oddity and terror." Bimonthly. Estab. 1997. Circ. 200.

Needs: Experimental, fantasy (sword and sorcery, fairies, elves), horror, psychic/supernatural/occult; science fiction (soft/sociological). No children's or romance. List of upcoming themes available with guidelines. Receives 10-20 unsolicited mss/month. Accepts 6-8 mss/issue. Recently published work by June Harmon, Jeffrey Oetting, Sunny D. and S. Stevens. Length: 1,500 words average; 250 word minimum; 2,500 words maximum. Publishes short shorts. Also publishes poetry. Always critiques or comments on rejected mss.

How to Contact: Send complete ms. Include estimated word count and list of publications. Reports in 2-4 weeks on queries and mss. Send SASE for return of ms. Simultaneous submissions and reprints OK. Sample copy for $2. Fiction guidelines for #10 SASE.

Payment/Terms: Pays contributor's copies; additional copies $1.

Advice: "I like something new and original. Grab my attention by drowning me in words. I love a good scare. Read guidelines first. Ask for sample copy, $1. Remember SASE and enjoy what you're doing, don't force it. There are a lot of good new writers out there who have trouble finding a magazine to start in. I give them an opportunity and ask some to submit each issue."

BLACK SHEETS, (II), % Black Books, P.O. Box 31155-NS2, San Francisco CA 94131-0155. (415)431-0171. Fax: (415)431-0172. E-mail: blackb@queernet.org. Editor: Bill Brent. Zine: 8½×11; 52 pages; illustrations and photos. "We are a humorous zine of sex and popular culture for a polysexual audience. Our motto is 'kinky/queer/intelligent/irreverent.' We are bisexual owned and operated." Quarterly. Estab. 1993.

● Fiction published in *Black Sheets* was included in 1995, 1996 and 1997 volumes of *Best American Erotica* (Simon & Schuster).

Needs: Bi/polysexual, popular culture-based: erotica, ethnic/multicultural, experimental, feminist, gay, humor/satire, lesbian, psychic/supernatural/occult. List of upcoming themes available for SASE. Receives 20 mss/month. Accepts 2-4 mss/issue; 6-12 mss/year. Publishes ms 3 months to 1 year after acceptance. Published work by Paul Reed, Thomas Roche, M. Christian, Carol Queen and Lawrence Livermore. Length: 1,000 words average; 3,000 words maximum (longer can be serialized). Publishes short shorts. Also publishes essays, literary criticism and poetry. Occasionally critiques or comments on rejected mss.

How to Contact: "You should purchase at least 1 copy of *Black Sheets* before sending us your work." Send complete ms with a cover letter. Include estimated word count and a brief bio. Reports in 1 month on queries; 2-3 months on mss. Send a disposable copy of ms. Electronic (IBM or MAC diskette OK) submissions OK. Sample copy for $6 with age statement. Fiction guidelines free. Requests for guidelines may be made via e-mail, but submissions are *not* accepted through e-mail. Reviews novels and short story collections.

Payment/Terms: Pays $10-50 and 1 contributor's copy on publication for one-time rights; additional copies for $3.

Advice: "Read our magazine. *Black Sheets* has a very specific attitude and a growing stable of regular writers. If your piece matches our style and you have read at least one issue (We know who you are!), then we can talk. We love e-mail for that, but *not* for submissions."

BLOODREAMS MAGAZINE, (II, IV), 1312 W. 43rd St., North Little Rock AR 72118. Editor-in-Chief: Kelly Gunter Atlas. Managing Editor: Jeffrey A. Stadt. Zine: Digest sized; 40-60 pages; 20 lb. paper; card stock cover; b&w drawings. "*Bloodreams* is dedicated to the preservation, continuance, and enhancement of the vampire and the werewolf legends, as well as other supernatural legends, for adult fans of the genre." Irregular publishing schedule. Estab. 1991. Circ. 75-100.

Needs: Vampires, werewolves, supernatural horror. "We do not want to see excessive gore or pornography." Receives 20-25 unsolicited mss/month. Accepts 12-20 mss/issue. Does not read mss October through January. Publishes ms in May and October only. Published work by Steve Eller, Dale Patricia Hochstein and Jeffrey A.

Stadt. Length: 1,500 words average; 250 words minimum; 3,500 words maximum. Publishes short shorts. Length: 250-500 words. Also publishes poetry. Sometimes critiques rejected mss and recommends other markets.

How to Contact: Query first. SASE. "We will be publishing on an irregular basis and will be focusing on theme issues in the future." Reports in 1-4 weeks on queries; 6-12 weeks on mss. SASE. Simultaneous submissions OK. Sample copy for $4 (payable to Kelly Atlas). Fiction guidelines for #10 SASE.

Payment/Terms: Pays in contributor's copies. Charges for extras.

Terms: Acquires one-time rights.

Advice: "We look for well-written, concise short stories which are complete within themselves. We like writers who have their own sense of style and imagination who write with their own 'voice' and do not try to copy others' work. We are open to a variety of interpretations of supernatural legends. For example, we like anything ranging from Stephen King to Anne Rice to Robert R. McCammon to Brian Lumley."

THE BLUE LADY, A Magazine Of Dark Fiction, (I, II), Blue Lady Publishing, 307 Stratford Place., Murrells Inlet SC 29576. E-mail: bluelady@prodigy.net. Editor Donna T. Burgess. Zine: digest size; 60-80 pages; illustrations. Publishes "dark fiction of all genres. Explicit material okay, if tasteful. Enjoys the surreal and bizarre—think Clive Barker, Poppy Brite, Stephen King, Anne Rice and Joe Lansdale." Estab. 1995. Circ. 100.

Needs: Experimental, fantasy (science fiction, fantasy), horror, psychic/supernatural/occult, science fiction (cyberpunk). "We do not want to see fiction that is not dark in tone or 'quiet' horror." Publishes special fiction issue or anthology. Receives 35 unsolicited mss/month. Accepts 10-12 mss/issue; 60 mss/year. Publishes ms 3-12 months after acceptance. Published work by James S. Dorr, Charlee Jacob, John Grey, D.F. Lewis, Deidra Cox and Scott Urban. Length: 3,000 words average; 8,000 words maximum. Publishes short shorts. Also publishes poetry.

How to Contact: Send complete ms with a cover letter. Include estimated word count and list of publications. Reports in 2 weeks on queries; 3 months on mss. Send SASE for reply, return of ms or send a disposable copy of ms. Simultaneous submissions and reprints OK. Sample copy for $5. Fiction guidelines for SASE. Reviews other zines.

Payment/Terms: Pays 1 contributor's copy on publication; additional copies for $4. Acquires one-time rights.

Advice: Looks for "good use of language and interesting characters and settings. Try experimenting with different time periods. Try me—especially if your idea is universal. I might like it. Unlike many horror publications around lately, I do want to see strong material. Don't follow trends."

BOTH SIDES NOW, Journal of Spiritual Alternatives, (I, II, IV), Free People Press, 10547 State Highway 110 N., Tyler TX 75704-3731. (903)592-4263. Editor: Elihu Edelson. Zine: 8½×11; 10 pages; bond paper and cover; b&w line illustrations. "*Both Sides Now* explores the Aquarian frontier as the world witnesses the end of an old order and enters a New Age. Its contents include opinion, commentary, philosophy and creative writing for all who are interested in New Age matters." Published irregularly. Estab. 1969. Circ. 200.

Needs: Material with New Age slant, including fables, fantasy, humor/satire, myths, parables, psychic/supernatural, religious/inspirational, romance (futuristic/time travel), science fiction (utopian, soft/sociological). Length: "about 2 magazine pages, more or less." Also publishes literary essays, book reviews and poetry. Often comments on rejected mss with "brief note."

How to Contact: Send complete ms with SASE. Include brief bio and list of publications. Simultaneous submissions and previously published work OK. Reports in 3 months on mss. Send SASE for reply, return of ms or send a disposable copy of ms. Sample copy for $1. Reviews "New Age fiction."

Payment/Terms: Pays 5 contributor's copies. "Authors retain rights."

Advice: Looks for "tight, lucid writing that leaves the reader with a feeling of delight and/or enlightenment. Heed our editorial interests. Short pieces preferred as space is very limited. We plan to publish more fiction; emphasis has been on nonfiction to date."

‡THE BRINK, (I). E-mail: sandy@brink.com. Website: http://www.brink.com. Editor: Sandy Wilder. Electronic zine. Publishes "marginal writing with extreme energy for a kinky neurotic audience."

Needs: "Fiction, poetry, astronomy, porn. We'll look at anything, but we may not read it." Would like to see more "real stories about people, their pets and their cars." Recently published work by George Rosenburg, Danny Vinik and Craig Baldwin. Publishes 6-10 new writers/year.

How to Contact: "Send attachments in Microsoft Word if possible. Manuscripts in HTML are given strong preference for publication."

Advice: "Bombard us with your poop. Send naked pictures of yourselves."

MARKET CONDITIONS are constantly changing! If you're still using this book and it is 1999 or later, buy the newest edition of *Novel & Short Story Writer's Market* at your favorite bookstore or order from Writer's Digest Books.

‡*BRV MAGAZINE, (IV),** Flat 1, 112 St. Georges Terrace, Newcastle upon Tyne NE2 2DP United Kingdom. 0044 (0)191-240-3800. E-mail: brvmag@aol.com. Zine specializing in gothic/darkwave/alternative music: A4 size; 56 pages; illustrations and photos. "The UK's longest running bi-monthly gothic/darkwave/alternative music magazine." Estab. 1991. Circ. 3,000.

Needs: Erotica, horror, psychic/supernatural/occult. Receives 2-3 unsolicited mss/month. Accepts 1 mss/issue; 6 mss/year. Publishes ms up to 2 years after acceptance "due to huge backlog." Recently published work by D.F. Lewis and Brian Stableford. Length: 1,000 words average; 2,000 words maximum. Publishes short shorts. Also publishes literary criticism.

How to Contact: Send complete ms with a cover letter. Reports in 4 weeks. Send SASE for reply, return of ms. Electronic submissions OK. Sample copy for $10 and size A4 envelope. Guidelines free. Reviews novels and short story collections. Send books to editor.

Payment/Terms: Pays 1 contributor's copy for one-time rights; additional copies $5. Not copyrighted.

‡**THE CAT'S EYE, (I)**. (615)228-8639. E-mail: Thecatseye@aol.com. Website: http://members.aol.com/thecats eye/index.htm. Editor: Lysa Fuller. Electronic zine. "A literary e-zine to provide readers and writers a place to submit their creations for possible web publication."

Needs: "Poetry, short fiction and some non-fiction." Would like to see more romance, science fiction and fantasy. No pornography. Recently published work by Ben Stivers and Toni Visage. Publishes 80-100 new writers/year.

How to Contact: Electronic submissions only. "Send submission either in the e-mail itself or attached in a .doc file."

Advice: "Just be yourself, write about what you know and like. We like to help young authors and new authors get a break."

‡**CETERIS PARIBUS, (I, II)**. E-mail: ceteris@intrepid.net. Website: http://www.intrepid.net/ceteris/paribus.h tm. Editor: Jeff Edmonds. Electronic zine. "Good writing with heart. Works by a circle of core writers, supplemented by select unsolicited contributions, have sustained a warm and entertaining intellectual and cultural exchange. The magazine strives to be unique, not bizarre; thought provoking, not iconoclastic; hospitable, not factional; literate, but not pedantic." Bimonthly.

Needs: "Fiction, poetry, personal narratives, topical essays, reviews and criticism for the discerning reader. Our editors are not usually enthusiastic about experimental fiction or writing that is weird for weird's sake. We will consider any well written story with the almost hypnotic ability to transport the reader into its world. We favor traditional literary fiction, but we also welcome genre fiction." Publishes at least 6 new writers/year.

How to Contact: Electronic and traditional submissions accepted. "Manuscripts should be copied and pasted into e-mail. Don't use attachments! For the internet-impaired, paper manuscripts can be sent to Ceteris Paribus/ 1410 N. Quinn St. #3/Arlington, Virginia 22209—but the response time will unavoidably be longer for such submissions."

Advice: "First, send only material that has not appeared previously. We are a unique Web magazine, not a recycling center. Second, we look for more than clever word-spinning. Style should be cultivated to enhance content; it can never compensate the lack. Write about what matters to you, not what might excite others. We look for writers who, through humor or drama, have something of value to say about the human experience."

A COMPANION IN ZEOR, (I, II, IV), 307 Ashland Ave., Egg Harbor Township NJ 08234. E-mail: karenlitma n@juno.com. Website: http://www.geocities.com/~rmgiroux/CZ (includes guidelines, back issue flyers, etc.). Editor: Karen Litman. Fanzine: 8½×11; 60 pages; "letter" paper; heavy blue cover; b&w line illustrations; occasional b&w photographs. Publishes science fiction based on the various Universe creations of Jacqueline Lichtenberg. Occasional features on Star Trek, and other interests, convention reports, reviews of movies and books, recordings, etc. Published irregularly. Estab. 1978. Circ. 300.

- *Companion in Zeor* is one fanzine devoted to the work and characters of Jacqueline Lichtenberg. Lichtenberg's work includes several future world, alien and group culture novels and series including the Sime/ Gen Series and The Dushau trilogy. She's also penned two books on her own vampire character and she co-authored *Star Trek Lives*.

Needs: Fantasy, humor/satire, prose poem, science fiction. "No vicious satire. Nothing X-rated. Homosexuality prohibited unless *essential* in story. We run a clean publication that anyone should be able to read without fear." Occasionally receives one manuscript a month. Accepts "as much as can afford to print." Publication of an accepted ms "can take years, due to limit of finances available for publication." Occasionally critiques rejected mss and recommends other markets.

How to Contact: Query first or send complete ms with cover letter. "Prefer cover letters about any writing experience prior, or related interests toward writing aims." Reports in 1 month. SASE. Simultaneous submissions OK. Sample copy price depends on individual circumstances. Fiction guidelines for #10 SASE. "I write individual letters to all queries. No form letter at present." SASE for guidelines required. Reviews science fiction/fantasy collections or titles.

Payment/Terms: Pays in contributor's copies. Acquires first rights. Acquires website rights as well.

Advice: "Send concise cover letter asking what the author would like me to do for them if their manuscript can not be used by my publication. They should follow guidelines of the type of material I use, which is often not done. I have had many submissions I can not use as it is general fiction which was sent instead. Ask for guidelines before submitting to a publication. Write to the best of your ability and work with your editor to develop your work to a higher point than your present skill level. Take constructive criticism and learn from it. Electronic web publishing seems the way the industry is heading. I would not have thought of a website a few years ago."

COSMIC LANDSCAPES, An Alternative Science Fiction Magazine, (I, IV), % Dan Petitpas, D & S Associates, 19 Carroll Ave., Westwood MA 02090. (617)329-1344. Fax: (617)329-1344. E-mail: enewsr@ix.netc om.com. Website: http://www.neponset.com/cltur. Editor: Dan Petitpas. Zine: on-line publication; illustrations; photos occasionally. "A magazine which publishes science fiction for science-fiction readers; also articles and news of interest to writers and science fiction fans. Occasionally prints works of horror and fantasy." Annually. Estab. 1983.
  • *Cosmic Landscapes* is published totally on the World Wide Web.
Needs: Science fiction (hard science, soft/sociological). "We would like to see more hard science fiction." Receives 15-20 unsolicited mss/month. Accepts 8 mss/issue. Recently published work by Alex Raikhel, Bill Cole, Laura Jimenez and B. Elwin Sherman. Published new writers in the last year. Length: 2,500 words average; 25 words minimum. Will consider all lengths. "Every manuscript receives a personal evaluation by the editor." Sometimes recommends other markets.
How to Contact: Send complete ms with bio. Reports usually in 1 month. SASE. Simultaneous and electronic submissions OK. Sample copy for $3.50. Fiction guidelines for SASE.
Payment/Terms: Acquires one-time rights.
Advice: "We're interested in all kinds of science fiction stories. We particularly like stories with ideas we've not seen before. Don't be influenced by TV or movie plots. Be original. Take an imaginative idea and craft a story from it. Be wild. Ask yourself 'what if?' and then follow through with the idea. Tell the story through the actions of a character or characters to give the readers someone to identify with. Be careful of creating scientific theories if you don't know much science. Let your imagination go!"

‡COSMIC VISIONS, The Online Magazine of Science Fiction and Fantasy, (I). E-mail: winner8@spryn et.com. Website: http://www.cosmicvisions.com. Editor: John R. Fultz. Electronic zine. "*Cosmic Visions* publishes science fiction, fantasy and some horror with sci-fi/fantasy elements. We look for stories which are inspired by the great pulp fiction of the 30s and 40s but with a cutting edge flavor."
Needs: Fantasy, science fiction. Would like to see more 'cosmic' fantasy. No straight horror. Recently published work by Robert Silverberg, Thomas Ligotti, Darrell Schweitzer, Mark Rainey, Karl Shroeder, Robert M. Price, Stan C. Sargent and Lin Carter. "We are constantly looking for bright new writers. The majority of our fiction comes from fresh talent."
How to Contact: Electronic submissions only. "E-mail in MS Word format; ASCII format is also acceptable if MS Word is unavailable."
Advice: "We like stories with strange or exotic settings, action/adventure, mind-bending fiction, multi-dimensional tales, space opera, etc. Any type of sci-fi/fantasy story with originality and good writing technique will be considered. We love stories where the line between science fiction and fantasy is blurred and the boundaries are stretched. Read these writers: Clark Ashton Smith, William Gibson, Robert Silverberg, H.P. Lovecraft, Darrell Schweitzer, Robert E. Howard, Thomas Ligotti, Michael Moorcock, Edgar Rice Burroughs and Lord Dunsany."

‡CREATIO EX NIHILO, The Technology of Terror, (II), Palimpsest Productions, 816 Elm St., #227, Manchester NH 03101-2101. E-mail: editor@palimpsest.com. Website: http://www.palimpsest.com/cxn/index.h tm. Editor: Heather G. Wells. Electronic zine. "*Creatio ex Nihilo* is entirely electronic and accessible for free. We publish horror and dark science fiction, poetry, essays and reviews." Monthly. Estab. 1997.
Needs: Horror, science fiction (dark). Accepts 3-5 mss/issue; 30-50 mss/year. Publishes ms 1 week-2 months after acceptance. Recently published work by David Niall Wilson, Don Webb, Gerard Daniel Hournaur. Length: 800 words average; 1,500 words maximum. Publishes short shorts. Also publishes literary essays, literary criticism and poetry.
How to Contact: Send complete manuscript with a cover letter. Include estimated word count. Reports in 2-4 months on manuscripts. Send SASE for reply, return of ms or send disposable copy of ms. Reprints and electronic submissions OK. Fiction Guidelines free. Reviews novels and short story collections. Send books to editor.
Payment/Terms: Pays $3 minimum; $10 maximum on acceptance for one-time electronic rights.
Advice: "We look for a compelling story with credible characters. The WWW has opened a brand new, cost-effective method of bringing information and entertainment to a wider audience of people. We at *CXN* are thrilled at the success we've had at doing just that."

CROSSROADS . . . Where Evil Dwells, (I, II), 911 Haw Branch Rd., Beaulaville NC 28518-9539. Fax: (910)324-2657. Editor: Pat Nielsen. Zine: digest-sized; approximately 68 pages; 20 lb. paper; 64 lb. index cover. "All stories must be about people at a *Crossroad* in their lives, or set at the crossroads themselves—or both. I strongly encourage writers to do research about the crossroad legends. This is an *adult* horror magazine." Triannually. (Published February, June and October.) Estab. 1992. Circ. 100.
  • Work appearing in *Crossroads* received three Honorable Mentions in *The Year's Best Horror and Fantasy*.

Needs: Horror, psychic/supernatural/occult for adults. "No futuristic or fiction set in the past. No sex or violence involving small children. Every October issue is the Halloween issue—all material must have a Halloween theme," deadline: October 15. Receives 20 unsolicited mss/month. Accepts 10-15 mss/issue; 30 mss/year. Publishes ms 1-6 months after acceptance. Recently published work by John Maclay, Charlee Jacob, Beecher Smith, David Shtogryn, Barbara Malenky and Donna Taylor Burgess. Length: 1,500 words average; 500 words minimum; 3,500 words maximum. Also publishes literary criticism and poetry. "I also need good artists." Often critiques or comments on rejected mss.

How to Contact: Send complete ms with a cover letter. Include estimated word count. Reports in 2 weeks on queries; 2-4 weeks on mss. Send SASE for reply, return of ms or send a disposable copy of ms. "I don't like IRCs—please use US stamps whenever possible." No simultaneous submissions. Reprints OK. Sample copy for $4.50. Fiction guidelines for #10 SASE.

Payment/Terms: Pays 1 contributor's copy; additional copies for $3.50 plus postage for multiple copies. Acquires first North American serial rights. Sends galleys to author (time permitting).

Advice: "I publish many kinds of horror, from the mild to the hard core horror. Don't copy well-known or any other writers. Find your own voice and style and go with it to the best of your ability. I don't go by any trends. I know what I like and I publish as I see fit. Do not send science fiction or fantasy in any form."

CURRICULUM VITAE, (I), Simpson Publications, Grove City Factory Stores, P.O. Box 1309, Grove City PA 16127. (814)671-1361. E-mail: simpub@hotmail.com. Editor: Michael Dittman. Zine: digest-sized; 75-100 pages; standard paper; card cover stock; illustrations. "We are dedicated to new, exciting writers. We like essays, travelogues and short stories filled with wonderful, tense, funny work by writers who just happen to be underpublished or beginners. Our audience is young and overeducated." Quarterly. Estab. 1995. Circ. 2,000.

Needs: Condensed/excerpted novel, erotica, ethnic/multicultural, experimental, humor/satire, literary, mainstream/contemporary, serialized novel, sports, translations. "No sentimental 'weepers' or Bukowski-esque material." List of upcoming themes available for SASE. Publishes special fiction issues or anthologies. Receives 45 unsolicited mss/month. Accepts 7 mss/issue; 28 mss/year. Publishes mss 2-3 months after acceptance. Recently published work by Lyn Lifshin, Jay Ponteri and Todd Karman. Publishes 20 new writers/year. Publishes short shorts. Also publishes literary essays, literary criticism, poetry. Often critiques or comments on rejected mss.

How to Contact: Send complete ms with cover letter. Reports in 1 month on queries and mss. Send SASE for reply, return of ms or send a disposable copy of ms. Simultaneous, reprint and electronic submissions OK. Sample copy for $3. Fiction guidelines for #10 SASE. Reviews novels and short story collections. Send books to Amy Kleinfelder.

Payment/Terms: Pays minimum 2 contributor's copies to $125 maximum on publication. Acquires one-time rights.

Advice: "Looks for quality of writing, a knowledge of past works of literature and a willingness to work with our editors. Submit often and take criticism with a grain of salt."

‡DARK STARR, (I, II, IV), Navarro Publications, P.O. Box 1107, Blythe CA 92226-1107. (888)922-0835. Editor: Richard Navarro. Fiction Editor: Marjorie Navarro. Zine specializing in horror/sci-fi/mystery/occult: digest size; 30-50 pages; laminated cover. Quarterly. Estab. 1998. Circ. 200.

Needs: Condensed/excerpted novel, erotica, fantasy (science fantasy, sword and sorcery), horror, mystery/suspense (private eye/hardboiled, romantic suspense), psychic/supernatural/occult, science fiction (hard science). Publishes special fiction issues or anthologies. Receives 100 unsolicited mss/month. Accepts 8-10 mss/issue, 32 mss/year. Publishes mss 3 months after acceptance. Agented fiction 5 %. "We are bringing back a publication last published in 1990, so all writers/authors will be new to this publication." Length: 2,500 word average; 300 words minimum; 8,500 words maximum. Publishes short shorts. Also publishes poetry. Sometimes critiques or comments on rejected mss.

How to Contact: Send ms with a cover letter. Include estimated word count and bio. Reports in 2 months on mss. Send SASE for reply, return of ms or send disposable copy of ms. Simultaneous and reprint submissions OK. Sample copy for $5 and 6×9 envelope with 2 first-class stamps. Fiction guidelines for #10 SASE.

Payment/Terms: Pays ¼ cent/word on acceptance for first North American serial rights.

Advice: Looks for "excellence in the genre submitted. If it's horror scare me; if it's fantasy let me live it; if it's sci-fi take me there; if it's supernatural give me 'goosebumps.' Please make sure manuscript is clean/legible and check spelling/sentence structure."

‡DIXIE PHOENIX, Exploration in the Southern Tradition, (I, II, IV), 3888 N. 30th St., Arlington VA 22207. E-mail: srimichel@delphi.com. Editors: Mike & Bjorn Munson. Zine specializing in literature/essays: 5½×8½; 52-72 pages; 20 lb. standard paper; 20-70 lb. color cover; illustrations. "Our audience appears to be of all religious and political persuasions from fringe to mainstream. We try to make each issue intriguing, informative, edifying and entertaining. We're a 'Mom & Pop publication' not a corporate operation." Semiannually. Estab. 1992. Circ. 200-300.

Needs: Historical (general), humor/satire, literary, mainstream/contemporary, regional, religious/inspirational, translations, travel essays, Celtic and Southern themes, Southern ghost stories. No children's/juvenile, erotica (no profanity in general), feminist, gay, lesbian, psychic/occult, romance. Upcoming themes: Travel essays from around the world (slated so far: Indonesia, Lesotho), January 1998, July 1998. Receives 5 unsolicited mss/month.

Accepts 1-2 mss/issue; 3-4 mss/year. Publishes ms 6-18 months after acceptance. Length: 1,500 words average; 250 words minimum; 7,000 words maximum. Publishes short shorts. Also publishes literary essays, literary criticism, poetry. "We have regular columns concerning history, culture and spirituality." Sometimes critiques or comments on rejected mss.

How to Contact: Query first or e-mail. Include a "nice friendly letter telling us about themselves and/or their writing." Reports in 1 month on queries; e-mail queries are often quicker; 3-4 months on mss. Send a disposable copy of ms. Simultaneous submissions, reprints and electronic submissions OK. Sample copy for $2. Reviews novels and short story collections.

Payment/Terms: Pays 2 contributor's copies on publication; additional copies for $2. Acquires one-time rights.

Advice: "We value sincerity over shock value. Fiction with a 'Phoenix Flavor' has a subject of personal explora-tion/discovery/epiphany/subjectivity whether spiritual, emotional, intellectual, etc. Definitely get a sample copy of our publication to get an idea of what we're about."

DREAMS & NIGHTMARES, The Magazine of Fantastic Poetry, (IV), 1300 Kicker Rd., Tuscaloosa AL 35404. (205)553-2284. E-mail: davidkm@ogb.gsa.tuscaloosa.al.us. Website: http://ourworld.compuserve.com/homepages/Anamnesis/dn.htm (includes guidelines, poetry, history of magazine). Editor: David C. Kopaska-Merkel. Zine: 5½×8½; 24 pages; ink drawing illustrations. "*DN* is mainly a poetry magazine, but I *am* looking for short-short stories. They should be either fantasy or science fiction." Estab. 1986. Circ. 250.

Needs: Experimental, fantasy, humor/satire, science fiction. "Try me with anything *except*: senseless violence, misogyny or hatred (unreasoning) of any kind of people, sappiness." Receives 4-8 unsolicited fiction mss/month. Accepts 1-2 mss/issue; 1-5 mss/year. Publishes ms 1-9 months after acceptance. Recently published work by Nancy Bennett, Bob Cook and Blythe Ayne. Length: 500 words average; 1,000 words maximum. Publishes short shorts. Length: 500 or fewer words. Sometimes critiques rejected mss. Also publishes poetry.

How to Contact: Send complete ms. Reports in 1-3 weeks on queries; 1-6 weeks on mss. SASE. No simultane-ous submissions. Electronic submissions (ASCII or Mac WordPerfect 5.1) OK. Sample copy for $2. Fiction guidelines for #10 SASE.

Payment/Terms: Pays $3 on acceptance and 2 contributor's copies for one-time rights.

Advice: "I don't want pointless violence or meandering vignettes. I do want extremely short science fiction or fantasy fiction that engages the reader's interest from word one. I want to be *involved*. Start with a good first line, lead the reader where you want him/her to go and end with something that causes a reaction or provokes thought."

‡DREAMS OF A LIME GREEN CATSUIT, (I). E-mail: catsuit@rudolf.canberra.edu.au. Website: http://rudolf.canberra.edu.au/catsuit. Editors: Kelly Jones and Christian Szabo. Electronic zine "looking for young writers and artists who are ignored by other 'mainstream' literary magazines, due to their writing being too experimental or because 'they don't have a name.' "

Needs: "Any and everything. We publish poetry, prose and artworks and things we've labeled 'uninstitutionaliza-ble.' While we aim to be as open-minded as possible, we do draw the line at racial discrimination, homophobia, etc." Publishes 50-70 new writers/year. "We are a stepping stone."

How to Contact: "Australian writers can send us material via mail (12 Greene Place, Emu Ridge 2617, Belconnen ACT) be it hard copy or on IBM formatted disk. Overseas writers have a better chance of reaching us via e-mail."

Advice: "You know you're good, but sending us some cash helps . . . seriously, everyone has a very good chance to get in. We reject very few pieces."

DREAMS OF DECADENCE, Vampire Poetry and Fiction, (I, II, IV), DNA Publications, Inc., P.O. Box 910, Greenfield MA 01302-0013. (413)772-0725. E-mail: dreams@shaysnet.com. Editor: Angela G. Kessler. Zine: digest size; 80 pages; illustrations. Specializes in "vampire fiction and poetry for vampire fans." Quarterly. Estab. 1995. Circ. 1,000.

Needs: Vampires. "I am not interested in seeing the clichés redone." Receives 150 unsolicited mss/month. Accepts 4 mss/issue; 12 mss/year. Publishes ms 1-6 months after acceptance. Length: 4,000 words average; 1,000 words minimum; 5,000 words maximum. Also publishes poetry. Always critiques or comments on rejected mss.

How to Contact: Send complete ms with cover letter. Include estimated word count, 1-paragraph bio and list of publications. Reports in 1 month on queries; 2 months on mss. Send SASE for reply, return of ms or send a disposable copy of ms. Simultaneous submissions OK. Sample copy for $5. Fiction guidelines for #10 SASE. Reviews novels and short story collections.

Payment/Terms: Pays 1-5¢/word on publication and 1 contributor's copy; additional copies for $2.50. Acquires first North American serial rights.

Advice: "I like stories that take the traditional concept of the vampire into new territory, or look at it (from within or without) with a fresh perspective. Don't forget to include a SASE for reply or return of manuscript. Also, to see what an editor wants, *read an issue.*"

THE DRINKIN' BUDDY MAGAZINE: A Magazine for Art and Words, (I), Pimperial Productions, P.O. Box 720608, San Jose CA 95172. (714)452-8720. E-mail: brad2871@sundance.sjsu.edu. Website: http://www.mathcs.sjsu.edu/student/Brad2871 (includes names of editors, short fiction, interviews with authors, interviews with bands, reviews, fashion). Editor: KC! Bradshaw. Webzine. Monthly. Estab. 1994. Circ. 1,000.

Needs: Adventure, condensed/excerpted novel, erotica, ethnic/multicultural, fantasy, gay, historical, horror, humor, lesbian, literary, mainstream, mystery/suspense, psychic/supernatural, regional, romance, science fiction, serialized novel, sports, westerns, young adult/teen. Receives 30-40 unsolicited mss/month. Publishes short shorts.

How to Contact: Send complete ms. Send a disposable copy of the ms. Simultaneous, electronic submissions OK.

Payment/Terms: Acquires one-time rights.

Advice: "A manuscript stands out when its subject and writing style are unique. Shorter stories have a greater chance of being published. If I enjoy the story, it goes in."

‡efil, (I, II). (617)847-6204. E-mail: webmaster@efil.com. Website: http://www.efil.com. Editor: Kelly Bower. Electronic zine that "looks at life a little differently."

Needs: "Anything goes." Would like to see more historical and science fiction. Recently published work by M. Francis Janosco and Bridget Lehane. Publishes 10-12 new writers/year.

How to Contact: Electronic submissions only. Send ms as an e-mail message or as a Claris Works document.

EIDOS: Sexual Freedom and Erotic Entertainment for Consenting Adults, (IV), P.O. Box 96, Boston MA 02137-0096. (617)262-0096. Fax: (617)364-0096. E-mail: eidos@eidos.org. Website: http://www.eidos.org (includes feature articles, interviews, poetry, short fiction, photos). Editor: Brenda Loew Tatelbaum. Zine: 10 × 14; 96 pages; web offset printing; illustrations and photos. Zine specializing in erotica for women, men and couples of all sexual orientations, preferences and lifestyles. "Explicit material regarding language and behavior formed in relationships, intimacy, moment of satisfaction—sensual, sexy, honest. For an energetic, well informed, international erotica readership." Quarterly. Estab. 1984. Circ. 7,000.

• *Eidos* was nominated for Erotic Publication of the Year in the 1996 Erotic Oscars competition in London, England. The editor was awarded Factor Press's Third Annual Golden Phallus Award.

Needs: Erotica. Upbeat erotic fiction is especially wanted. Publishes at least 10-12 pieces of fiction/year. Recently published work by George Painter, Susan Brown-Tischler and Ronald D. Lankford, Jr. 30% of work published is by new writers. Length: 1,000 words average; 500 words minimum; 2,000 words maximum. Also publishes literary criticism, poetry. Occasionally critiques rejected mss.

How to Contact: Send complete ms with SASE. "Cover letter with history of publication or short bio is welcome." Reports in 1 month on queries; 1 month on mss. Simultaneous submissions OK. Sample copy for $5. Fiction guidelines for #10 SASE. Reviews novels and short story collections, "if related to subject of erotica (sex, politics, religion, etc.)."

Payment/Terms: Pays in contributor's copies. Acquires first North American serial rights.

Advice: "We receive more erotic fiction manuscripts now than in the past. Most likely because both men and women are more comfortable with the notion of submitting these manuscripts for publication as well as the desire to see alternative sexually-explicit fiction in print. Therefore we can publish more erotic fiction because we have more material to choose from. There is still a lot of debate as to what erotic fiction consists of. This is a tough market to break into. Manuscripts must fit our editorial needs and it is best to order a sample issue prior to writing or submitting material. Honest, explicitly pro-sex, mutually consensual erotica lacks unwanted power, control and degradation—no unwanted coercion of any kind."

‡ENTERZONE, (I). E-mail: conway@aimnet.com. Website: http//www.ezone.org/ez. Story Editor: Martha Conway. "*Enterzone* is a hyperzine of writing, art and new media publishing fiction and nonfiction stories, essays, criticism, personal commentary, poetry, computer-generated and scanned artwork, photography, audio art, comics, and cartoons for the internet-enabled adult reading public." Recently published work by David Alexander, Levi Asher, Frederick Barthelme and Lisa Solod. Publishes 4-8 new writers/year.

Needs: Would like to see more short stories and hyperfiction. No science fiction or fantasy.

How to Contact: Query through e-mail: query@ezone.org.

Advice "We are actively seeking new metaphors for the dissemination and sharing of creative work. The interactive nature of the World Wide Web allows us to link responses to our articles. This adds the dimension of a symposium or a salon to the magazine."

FAYRDAW, (I), P.O. Box 100, Shartlesville PA 19554. (610)488-6894. Editors: Loring D. Emery, Mary M. Towne and Dorotéo M. Estrago. Zine: 5½ × 8½; about 40 pages; 20 lb. paper; saddle-stitched; illustrations. Bimonthly. Estab. 1994. Circ. 50.

Needs: Adventure, experimental, historical, humor/satire, literary, mainstream/contemporary. "Nothing derivative or overly cute." Receives 10-20 unsolicited mss/month. Accepts 0-3 mss/issue; 20-25 mss/year. Publishes ms 3-4 months after acceptance. Recently published work by Connie Pursell, Ram Krishna Singh and Jim Sullivan. Length: 1,500 words maximum. Publishes short shorts. Also publishes literary essays, literary criticism. Often critiques or comments on rejected mss.

How to Contact: Send complete ms with a cover letter. Include estimated word count, bio (3-5 lines) and list of publications. "Anything chatty." Reports in 1 month. SASE for reply or send a disposable copy of ms. Simultaneous, reprint and electronic (3.5 or 5.25 disk) submissions OK. Sample copy for $2. Fiction guidelines for #10 SASE.

Payment/Terms: Pays $5 (fiction only). Pays on acceptance for one-time rights. Not copyrighted.

Advice: "Look at a sample. Read our guidelines. Fayrdaw is for scratching that itch, bitching that bitch, spreading oil on burning waters, a forum where you can rant in prose about things that really tee you off. With luck it will become the literary 'bird' to all the stupidity, cruelty, injustice and just plain cussedness in our world. We are ultra-Conservative but welcome Progressive contributions, warning the submitter that his work may be set against critical contrary commentary."

THE FIFTH DI/THE SIXTH SENSE/STARFLITE, (II), Promart Writing Lab's Small Press Family, P.O. Box 1094, Carmichael CA 95609-1094. (916)973-1020. Website: http://www.arrowweb.com/promimart (includes writer's guidelines, subscription information, sample fiction). Editor: James B. Baker. Three zines: 5½ × 8½; 48 pages; 20 lb. paper; 24 lb. cover stock. Specializes in science fiction. "My intended audience is made up of those desiring to see man going to the stars. *The Fifth Di* is adult; *The Sixth Sense* is family (no excessive sex or bad language); and *Starflite* is our feature zine." Bimonthly. Estab. 1995. Circ. 192. Member of The Writers' Alliance and The National Writer's Association.

Needs: Science fiction, serialized novel. "No horror and only minimal fantasy." Receives 15-20 unsolicited mss/month. Accepts 10 mss/issue; 180 mss/year. Publishes ms 6-12 months after acceptance. Recently published work by James S. Dorr, Brian A. Hopkins, Joan Tobin, Paul Gates and Gail Hayden. Publishes 10 new writers/year. Length: 3,500 words average. Publishes short shorts. Also publishes literary essays and poetry. Always critiques or comments on rejected mss. Sponsors "Novette" contest (25,000 words or more). Entry fee: $19. Send SASE for information.

How to Contact: Send complete ms with cover letter. Include estimated word count and bio. Reports in days on queries; weeks on mss. SASE or SAE and IRCs if out of U.S. No simultaneous submissions. Sample copy for $1 and 5×9 SASE.

Payment/Terms: Pays $5-40 (.0115/word) on publication and contributor's copy; additional copies for $1.50. Acquires first rights.

Advice: "Do your own thing—ignore the trends. You must do your own editing—too many glitches and your excellent manuscript will be rejected."

‡THE GARRETT COUNTY JOURNAL, (I), P.O. Box 896, Madison WI 53701. E-mail: garrett@gcpress.com. Website: http://www.cyborganic.com/people/garrett/. Editor: Alee Michod. Electronic zine. Publishes "good fiction and essays."

Needs: "Avant-pop, Pynchon-Burrow-Kathy Acker inspired fiction." No anthology fiction. Recently published work by Justin Hall, Ernest Slyman and Cory Kapczinski. Publishes 10 new writers/year.

How to Contact: Electronic and traditional submissions accepted.

Advice: "Don't listen to the advice of editors. They're only frustrated writers."

GENERATOR, Local Literary & Arts Magazine, (I), P.O. Box 980363, Ypsilanti MI 48197. (313)482-2895. E-mail: generator@sprintmail.com. Editors: Kimberly Baker and Michelle McGrath. Zine specializing in local arts and literature: 8 × 14; 52 pages; 20 lb. paper; glossy cover; illustrations and photos. "*Generator* is a literary magazine aimed at exposing new literary talents, as well as local artists from the Ypsilanti area. We have an eclectic format with material ranging from comics, poetry, short stories to memoirs and travel journals." Quarterly. Estab. 1995. Circ. 500.

• *Generator* combines the 'zine revolution with the structural format of a literary arts magazine.

Needs: Condensed/excerpted novel, ethnic/multicultural, experimental, feminist, gay, humor/satire, lesbian, literary, mainstream/contemporary, regional, science fiction (hard science, soft/sociological), translations. No children's/juvenile, fantasy, religious. Receives 15-20 unsolicited mss/month. Accepts 4-5 mss/issue; 16-20 mss/year. Publishes ms 2 months after acceptance. Recently published work by Keith Taylor, Josie Kearns, Bob Hicok, Laura Kosischke, Errol Miller and Mary Winters. Publishes 10 new writers/year. Length: 500-1,000 words average; 1,500 words maximum. Publishes short shorts. Also publishes literary essays, literary criticism and poetry. Sponsors short fiction contest. Send SASE for information.

How To Contact: Send complete ms with a cover letter. Include bio (a few sentences). Reports in 2 months on queries; 3 months on mss. Send SASE for reply, return of ms or send a disposable copy of ms. "Material returned only upon request." Simultaneous, reprint and electronic (disk) submissions OK. Sample copy for $3. Fiction guidelines for #10 SASE. Reviews novels and short story collections.

Payment/Terms: Pays 1 contributor's copy; additional copies for $3. Acquires one-time rights. Not copyrighted.

Advice: "We generally choose work which is well-written, interesting and experimental or that which strays from the conventional norms. We are receptive to many different styles and encourage new writers to submit for

---

CHECK THE CATEGORY INDEXES, located at the back of the book, for publishers interested in specific fiction subjects.

publication. Be original, proofread and take care to edit your own work until it is your best possible copy. The 'Zine Revolution' as it has been called, has been a goldmine in terms of resources and positive energy. Through trades with other small publications we have made valuable connections with other editors and writers.''

‡**GERBIL, A Queer Culture Zine, (II)**, P.O. Box 10692, Rochester NY 14610. (716)262-3966. E-mail: gerbilzine@aol.com. Editors: Tony Leuzzi and Brad Pease. Zine specializing in queer culture: 9½ × 7½; 32 pages; opaque quality paper; opaque cover stock; illustrations and photos. "We provide a forum for queer-identified writers who want to express ideas, views, aesthetics that aren't covered in the mainstream gay press." Quarterly. Estab. 1994. Circ. 2,800.
Needs: Condensed/excerpted novel, erotica, ethnic/multicultural, gay, humor/satire, lesbian, literary, mainstream/contemporary, psychic/supernatural/occult. Receives 5 unsolicited mss/month. Accepts 1 ms/issue; 5 mss/year. Publishes ms 4-6 months after acceptance. Recently published work by Kevin Killian, Bo Huston, Lawrence Braithwaite, Liam Brosnaham and Gysbert Menninga. Length: 250 words minimum; 5,000 words maximum. Publishes short shorts. Also publishes literary essays and poetry. Always critiques or comments on rejected mss.
How to Contact: Send complete ms with a cover letter. Include brief bio. Reports in 2 weeks on queries; 1-3 months on mss. Send SASE for return of ms or send disposable copy of ms. No simultaneous submissions. Electronic submissions OK. Sample copy for $4. Fiction guidelines for #10 SASE. Reviews novels or short story collections. Send books to editor.
Payment/Terms: Pays 3 contributor's copies for one-time rights.
Advice: "Always keep in mind a strong sense of story. Keep an open mind and always read. If you're honest and work hard, someone somewhere will accept your work."

‡**GOPHER, Writings from the rodents of the underground, (I)**. E-mail: gopher@washout.com. Website: http://www.washout.com/gopher. Editor: Rewired. Electronic zine. "Discussion of fringe topics through fiction, sometimes in a humorous way."
Needs: Short fiction. Must be "in almost good taste." Would like to see more occult, supernatural themed pieces as well as abstract fiction. Publishes 10-15 new writers/year.
How to Contact: Electronic submissions only.
Advice: "Send in a submission!"

GOTTA WRITE NETWORK LITMAG, (I, II), Maren Publications, 515 E. Thacker, Hoffman Estates IL 60194-1957. E-mail: netero@aol.com. Editor: Denise Fleischer. Magazine: 8½ × 11; 48-64 pages; saddle-stapled ordinary paper; matte card or lighter weight cover stock; illustrations. Magazine "serves as an open forum to discuss new markets, successes and difficulties. Gives beginning writers their first break into print and promotionally supports established professional novelists." Distributed through the US, Canada and England. Semiannually. Estab. 1988. Circ. 200.
   ● In addition to publishing fiction, *Gotta Write Network Litmag* includes articles on writing techniques, small press market news, writers' seminar reviews, science fiction convention updates, and features a "Behind the Scenes" section in which qualified writers can conduct mail interviews with small press editors and professional writers. Writers interviewed in this manner in the past have included Frederik Pohl, Jody Lynn Nye, Lawrence Watt-Evans and artist Michael Whelan.
Needs: Adventure, contemporary, fantasy, historical, humor/satire, literary, mainstream, prose poem, romance (gothic), science fiction (hard science, soft/sociological). "Currently seeking work with a clear-cut message or a twist at the very end. All genres accepted with the exception of excessive violence, sexual overtones or obscenity." Receives 75-150 unsolicited mss per month. Accepts 1-6 mss per issue; up to 20 mss a year. Publishes mss 6-12 months after acceptance. Recently published Debora Ann Belardino, Guilford Barton, Richard Goodwin and Eugene C. Flinn. Length: 10 pages maximum for short stories. Also publishes poetry.
How to Contact: Send complete ms with cover letter. Include "who you are, type of work submitted, previous publications and focused area of writing." Reports in 2-4 months (later during publication months). SASE ("no SASE, no repsonse"). Reports on fax submissions within days. Responds by fax. No simultaneous submissions or reprints. Electronic (e-mail) submissions OK. Sample copy for $5. Fiction guidelines for SASE.
Payment/Terms: Pays $10 or 2 contributor's copies for first North American serial rights.
Advice: "If I still think about the direction of the story after I've read it, I know it's good. Organize your thoughts on the plot and character development (qualities, emotions) before enduring ten drafts. Make your characters come alive by giving them a personality and a background, and then give them a little freedom. Let them take you through the story."

‡**GROWING PAINS MAGAZINE, (I, II)**, 168 Orient Ave., Pawtucket RI 02861. E-mail: grpain@aol.com. Website: http://members.aol.com/grpain/. Editor: Kevin Ridolfi. Electronic zine. "Works should deal with the 'growing' problems that are inherent and common to everyone, both young and old."
Needs: Short fiction, serial fiction, poetry, essays, humor, young adult. "No lewd, adult fiction." Publishes 15 new writers/year.
How to Contact: Electronic and traditional submissions accepted.
Advice: "Browse through *Growing Pains'* past issues for content tendencies and submission requirements. Don't be afraid to go out on a short limb, but please limit yourself to our already existing categories."

‡♥**THE GUL, A Journey Beyond, (I, IV)**, Abraxis Publications, Box 746, Chesterville, Ontario K0C 1H0 Canada. (613)448-3176. E-mail: p&h@abraxis-publications.com. Editor: Heather O'Neil. Zine: 8½×11; 12 pages; bond paper and cover; illustrations. Specializes in science fiction/fantasy: prose and poetry "with a slant towards the Trekkies. Audience: teen-adult." Quarterly. Estab. 1997. Circ. 200.

Needs: Fantasy (science, sword and sorcery), science fiction (hard science, soft/sociological, *Star Trek*). No erotica, horror, abusive/foul language. "This is a family-oriented zine." Editorial calendar for SASE (IRC). Publishes ms 1-3 months after acceptance. Length: 300 words minimum; 1,000 words maximum. Publishes short shorts. Also publishes literary essays. Always critiques or comments on rejected mss.

How to Contact: Send complete ms with a cover letter. Include short bio. Reports in 3 weeks on queries; 2 months on mss. SASE (IRCs) for reply, return of ms or send a disposable copy of ms. Sample copy for $3 and SAE with 4 first-class stamps (or IRCs). Fiction guidelines for SASE (IRC).

Payment/Terms: Pays free subscription to the magazine. All rights remain with the author.

Advice: "We look for color, imagination, probability of the event being possible in the future, how well the author knows the subject. Have a good main character that can stand alone, a believable scenario and short, to-the-point descriptions that enhance the story without overpowering it."

‡**GZ, Intercultural Home Page, (I, II)**. (31)020-6238935. E-mail: adboit@pi.net. Website: http://home.pi.net/~adboit/home.html. Editors: Adriaan Boiten and Arnout Kors. "Our platform is open for writers from every culture, language or country. We want to show the different cultural experiences as well as the universal feelings, thoughts and aspirations.

Needs: Short stories, travel stories, poems. Would like to see more travel and exotic stories. Recently published work by Marc Swan, Victor Saunders, Donald Unger, David Groulx, John Gardiner, Guadalupe Sequeira Malespin, Carmen Scheicher and Gerla Weidema. Publishes 10 new writers/year.

How to Contact: Electronic submissions only. Send mss by e-mail as enclosed text or attached in a .txt file.

Advice: "Express yourself."

‡**HERETIC HOLLOW, (I, II, IV)**, Box 5511, Pasadena CA 91117. (818)584-0008. Editor: Capella. Zine specializing in occult, magic and metaphysical: 8½×11; 8 pages; white stock paper; grey stock cover; illustrations and photographs. Themes include occult, magical, metaphysical, shamanic, wiccan, psychic. Monthly. Estab. 1996. Circ. 250.

Needs: Erotica, experimental, feminist, gay, horror, lesbian, psychic/supernatural/occult, romance (futuristic/time travel), science fiction. No religious/inspirational. Receives 0-1 unsolicited mss/month. Accepts 0-1 mss/issue. Publishes ms within 3 months after acceptance. Length: 500 words average; 250 words minimum; 5,000 words maximum. Publishes short shorts. Also publishes literary essays, poetry. Always critiques or comments on rejected mss.

How to Contact: Send complete ms with a cover letter. Include half page bio and phone number. Reports in 1 month. Send disposable copy of ms. Simultaneous submissions, reprints and electronic submissions OK. Sample copy for $2. Fiction guidelines free.

Payment/Terms: Pays free subscription to the magazine, 1 contributor's copy on publication; additional copies for $2. Acquires first rights. Sends galleys to author if local.

Advice: "We look for uniqueness and off-the-wall temporal irony. Beginners should send some. Don't hold back. You really are a good writer. We just haven't met—yet!"

HOBSON'S CHOICE, (I, II), Starwind Press, Box 98, Ripley OH 45167. (513)392-4549. Editor: Susannah West. Zine: 8½×11; 16 pages; 60 lb. offset paper and cover; b&w illustrations; line shot photos. "We publish science fiction and fantasy for young adults and adults with interest in science, technology, science fiction and fantasy." Quarterly. Estab. 1974. Circ. 2,000.

Needs: Fantasy, science fiction (hard science, soft/sociological). "We like science fiction that shows hope for the future and protagonists who interact with their environment rather than let themselves be manipulated by it." No horror, pastiches of other authors, stories featuring characters created by others (i.e. Captain Kirk and crew, Dr. Who, etc.). Receives 50 unsolicited mss/month. Accepts 2-4 mss/issue; 16-24 mss/year. Publishes ms 4-24 months after acceptance. Published work by Paul Haspel, Barb Rosen and Barb Myers. Published new writers within the last year. Length: 2,000-10,000 words. Also publishes literary criticism and some literary essays. Occasionally critiques rejected mss.

How to Contact: Send complete ms. Reports in 2-3 months. "If an author hasn't heard from us by 4 months, he/she should feel free to withdraw." Send SASE for return of ms. No simultaneous submissions. Accepts electronic submissions via disk for the IBM PC or PC compatible in ASCII format and Macintosh. Sample copy for $2.50. Fiction guidelines for #10 SASE. Tipsheet packet (all guidelines plus tips on writing science fiction) for $1.50 and SASE. Checks should be payable in U.S. funds only.

Payment/Terms: Pays 1-4¢/word (25% on acceptance, 75% 30 days after publication) and contributor's copies. "We pay 25% kill fee if we decide not to publish story." Rights negotiable. Sends galleys to the author.

Advice: "I certainly think a beginning writer can be successful if he/she studies the publication *before* submitting and matches the submission with the magazine's needs. With regards to writing, get your story going right away; lengthy introductions will lose your reader's interest. Tell your story through action and conversation, not static description."

‡HOLOGRAM TALES, (I). (0181)649-8148. E-mail: stephenhunt@easynet.co.uk. Website: http://www.sf-fantasy.com. Editor: Stephen Hunt. Electronic zine. Publishes science fiction and fantasy including short fiction, film/tv reviews, book reviews, author interviews and convention reports.
Needs: Science fiction and fantasy (sword and sorcery). Would like to see more space opera and high adventure. No horror. Recently published work by Arthur C. Clarke, J.D. Ballard, Greg Bear and Kim Newman. Publishes 30 new writers/year.
How to Contact: Electronic submissions only. Send mss by e-mail.
Advice: "Make sure you have read the publication before you submit to it."

‡I LIKE MONKEYS, (I). (909)624-2525. E-mail: parango@pomona.edu. Website: http://pages.pomona.edu/~parango/monkeys/. Editor: Padgett Arango. Electronic zine. "A wide range of fiction that runs from absurdism to fairly middle-of-the-road postmodernism. A sense of humor is always a plus, but a good grasp of innate futility of modern existence will more than make up for that."
Needs: "Prose of every length is preferred, but poetry is also accepted." No non-experimental genre fiction. Recently published work by Andrew Wood, Anne Paulsen and Alex Cabrera. Publishes as many new writer as possible/year.
How to Contact: Electronic submissions only.
Advice: "It's not hard. Write something vaguely interesting and it will probably be published."

IDIOT WIND, (I, IV), P.O. Box 87, Occoquan VA 22125-0087. (703)494-1897. E-mail: idiotwind@radix.net. Website: http://www.radix.net/~idiotwind. Editor: Douglas Carroll (a.k.a. Ed Lynn). Zine specializing in humor: 5½×8½; 16-20 pages; 20 lb. paper; illustrations and photos (sometimes). "We want to provide cheap laughs at an affordable price. We grew up on the great comic magazines of the seventies, like *National Lampoon*, and strive to recapture some of that spirit. We publish humor fiction, short filler-type material, and Letterman-style Top 10 Lists (in what we call our 'crawl space.' Our intended audience doesn't offend easily." Quarterly. Estab. 1984. Circ. 100-200.
Needs: Humor/satire. Recent themes: "Science and Technology"; "Love & Litigation." List of upcoming themes available for SASE. Receives 5-10 unsolicited mss/month. Accepts 2-3 mss/issue; 8-12 mss/year. Publishes ms 3-4 months after acceptance, "sometimes longer if we're saving it for a particular theme issue." Recently published work by Mead Stone, H. Turnip Smith, Eugene Flinn and Bernie Libster. Length: 1,500 words average; no minimum; 3,000 words maximum. Publishes short shorts. Also publishes poetry. Sometimes critiques or comments on rejected mss.
How to Contact: Send complete ms with a cover letter. Include estimated word count and bio (maximum 75 words). Reports in 3-4 months on queries and mss. Send SASE for reply, return of ms or send a disposable copy of ms. Simultaneous and electronic submissions OK. Sample copy and fiction guidelines for 6×9 SAE and 2 first-class stamps.
Payment/Terms: Pays 3 contributor's copies on publication; additional copies for SASE. Acquires one-time rights.
Advice: "It has to be drop-to-the-floor-grasping-your-sides-laughing-so-hard-you-pee-in-your-pants-kind of funny. Okay. That's a little strict. Funny, though, is the key word. We are a humor magazine. We aren't after long missives on the mating habits of the Tse-Tse fly, unless said Tse-Tse fly's habits include truly kinky stuff like dressing up as a priest for the female and shaving its little Tse-Tse fly legs. Take what you know and exaggerate it, parody it, poke fun at it. Read up on current events and exaggerate it, parody it, poke fun at it."

‡IN CELEBRATION OF TREES, (I, II, IV). E-mail: FTFD57A@prodigy.com. Website: http://www.geocities.com/RainForest/9899 or http://pages.prodigy.com/sbarrera/trees.htm. Editor: Sheila Barrera. Electronic zine. "The trees give us so much: paper, wood, shade, cleaner fresher air, but how often do we really see them? The trees pages are dedicated to reminding the world that a world without trees just might not be that great. In fact, it might be downright unsurvivable." Monthly to bimonthly.
Needs: Poetry, short stories, paintings and computer art, quotes, ponderings and thoughts. "Anything about trees." No "erotica or smut." Would like to see more personal stories relating some kind of relationship with a tree or trees. "Alice Pero is probably our most famous contributor, having been performing on the NYC live poetry beat for years. Gym Nasium-Saldutti, award winning poet and artist, is another, his website having won many awards for being in the top % of the web as well as a wonderful one from the Dali Museum for his tribute to the artist."
How to Contact: Electronic submissions only.
Advice: "If you know HTML coding, please do this, and that will save me time trying to figure out where the stanzas end and begin if your server has scrambled them."

‡THE INDITER, (I). (250)386-1663. Fax: (250)995-1872 E-mail: editor@lnditer.com. Website: http://www.inditer.com. Editor: Rill Loeppky. Electronic zine. "The Inditer is an online magazine dedicated to the encouragement of new writers and essayists. Those wishing to submit material of political or social editorial comment are also welcome to submit their work. Our intended audience would include readers, publishers and editors, secondary school and college creative writing departments."

• The editor would like to see more historical and science fiction. He is also interested in contemporary life essays and political commentary.

Needs: "Fiction, non-fiction, lifestyle articles, sci-fi, political or social articles intended to evoke response and alternative views. I do not want to see smut for the sake of smut. If course language is required to portray a character, so be it. Course language used simply for shock value will not be published. I do not want to see radical political or religious philosophy, nor do I want to see proselytism. I do not want to see material which could be deemed to be defaming or derogatory. I do not want to see writing which is esoteric to the point of being inane." Recently published work by Carline Zarlengo Sposto (Memphis), Larry Lynch (New Brunswick, Canada), Victor Wee (Singapore), Moira Moss (Michigan) and Amy Mueller (Iowa). Publishes 40-50 new writers/ year.

How to Contact: Electronic submissions only. Send ms an e-mail attachment in ASCII text. Short pieces can also be sent as part of the body of an e-mail.

Payment/Terms: "There is no pay for manuscripts used, nor is there a charge to the writer. *The Inditer* is intended to be a vehicle which new writers can use to showcase their work. A number of writers who have published with me have found subsequent markets for their work, and two of them earned university credit for published works. Several universities and colleges have made use of *The Inditer*, both to critique its contents, and for students to avail themselves of it."

Advice: "You can either e-mail your submissions or you can use the form on the website. If you'd like to run an idea by us before sending it in, check one of the department categories on the form and type a brief description of your idea in the box."

‡**INTERTEXT, (I, II)**. (510)355-0661. E-mail: jsnell@intertext.com. Website: http://www.intertext.com/Zines/ InterText/. Editor: Jason Snell. Electronic zine. "Our readers are computer literate (because we're online only) and appreciate entertaining fiction. They're usually accepting of different styles and genres—from mainstream to historical to science fiction to fantasy to horror to mystery—because we don't limit ourselves to one genre. They just want to read a story that makes them think or transports them to an interesting new place."

Needs: "Well-written fiction from any genre or setting." Especially looking for intelligent science fiction. No "exploitative sex or violence. We will print stories with explicit sex or violence, but not if it serves no purpose other than titillation." Recently published work by E. Jay O'Connell, Richard Kadrey, Levi Asher, Marcus Eubanks and William Routhier. Publishes 16 new writers/year.

How to Contact: Electronic submissions only. Stories should be in ASCII, HTML, or Microsoft Word (v. 5 or 6) formats.

Advice: "Have a clear writing style—the most clever story we've seen in months still won't make it if it's written badly. Try to make our readers think in a way they haven't before, or take them to a place they've never thought about before. And don't be afraid to mix genres—our readers have come to appreciate stories that aren't easily labeled as being part of one genre or another."

JACK MACKEREL MAGAZINE, (I, II), Rowhouse Press, P.O. Box 23134, Seattle WA 98102-0434. Editor: Greg Bachar. Zine: 5½×8½; 40-60 pages; Xerox bond paper; glossy card cover stock; b&w illustrations and photos. "We publish unconventional art, poetry and fiction." Quarterly. Estab. 1993. Circ. 1,000.

Needs: Condensed/excerpted novel, erotica, experimental, literary, surreal, translations. Publishes special fiction issues or anthologies. Receives 20-100 unsolicited mss/month. Accepts 10-20 mss/issue; 40-75 mss/year. Recently published work by David Berman, William Waltz, Heather Hayes, Brett Ralph, Ann Miller, Paul Dickinson and Carl Faucher. Length: 250 words minimum; 5,000 words maximum. Publishes short shorts. Also publishes literary essays, literary criticism and poetry.

How to Contact: Send complete ms with a cover letter. Include bio with submission. Send SASE for reply, return of ms or send a disposable copy of ms. Sample copy for $4. Reviews novels and short story collections.

Payment/Terms: Pays in contributor's copies.

KEEN SCIENCE FICTION!, Classic Science Fiction, Written by Writers Who Love It, (I, II, IV), Keen Press, P.O. Box 9067, Spokane WA 99209-0067. (509)744-0987. Fax: (509)744-0986. E-mail: zlsk20a@pro digy.com. Website: http://pages.prodigy.com/KeenSciFi. Editor: Teresa Keene. Zine: 8½×5½; 46-66 pages; heavy laser paper; lasercast cover; illustrations. "I've found that real science fiction lovers never get tired of reading the tried and true formats of time-travel, spacefaring, terraforming, parallel universe, and any other trusty old science fiction device. The purpose of this magazine is to bring those formats back to those of us who love and miss them!" Monthly. Estab. 1996. Circ. 200.

Needs: Science fiction (hard science, soft/sociological) and "some gentle fantasy of the 'Twilight Zone'-ish

---

● **A BULLET INTRODUCES COMMENTS** by the editor of *Novel & Short Story Writer's Market* indicating special information about the listing.

nature. No sword and sorcery." Receives 300 unsolicited mss/month. Accepts 6-9 mss/issue; 100-120 mss/year. Publishes mss 1-6 months after acceptance. Agented fiction 1%. Published work by Don D'Ammassa, Timons Esaias, Janet Ford, Arthur Zirul, Michael Ambrose, John B. Rosenman, Terry McGarry, Jonny Duffy, Art Cosing and Gail Hayden. Length: 2,500 words average; 50 words minimum; 4,000 words maximum. Publishes short shorts. Length: 400 words. Publishes literary essays, book reviews and poetry. Always critiques or comments on rejected mss.

How to Contact: Send complete ms with cover letter or send story on IBM-compatible disk. Include estimated word count, bio, Social Security number and list of publications. "Chatty cover letters welcome!" Reports in 1 week on queries; 1 month on mss. Send SASE for reply, return of ms or send a disposable copy of ms. Simultaneous, reprint and electronic submissions (disk only) OK. "No e-mail submissions!" Sample copy for $4. Fiction guidelines for #10 SASE. Reviews novels and short story collections. Send books to: Steven Sawicki, 186 Woodruff Ave., Watertown CT 06795.

Payment/Terms: Pays 1¢/word, minimum $5, maximum $60 and 2 contributor's copies on publication for one-time rights.

Advice: "I look for stories of clarity, with no 'head-scratching.' Stories should have a beginning, middle, a twist or surprise at the end and be fun to read. Please include information about yourself. Be excited about your work, and let it show! Submit the tidiest manuscript you can."

THE LETTER PARADE, (I), Bonnie Jo Enterprises, P.O. Box 52, Comstock MI 49041. Editor: Bonnie Jo. Zine: legal/letter-sized; 6 pages. Quarterly. Estab. 1985. Circ. 113.

Needs: "Anything short. We print very little fiction, actually. We print more essays. But we're open to the fun little story." Receives 25-30 unsolicited mss/month. Accepts 1-2 mss/issue. Publishes ms up to a year after acceptance. Published work by Allison Linden. Length: 250-750 words preferred; 2,000 words maximum. Publishes short shorts. Also publishes any kind of essays.

How to Contact: Send complete ms with a cover letter. "Please single space so I can publish pieces in the form I receive them." Send disposable copy of ms. Reports in 4 months. Simultaneous and reprint submissions OK. Sample copy for $1. Reviews novels or short story collections. Send review copies to Christopher Magson.

Payment/Terms: Pays subscription to magazine. Not copyrighted.

Advice: "We're predisposed to stories about animals so long as the stories aren't sentimental. No stories ending in suicide. We like humor that's not too light, not too dark. What ridiculous thing happened on the way to the hardware store? What did you do when your cows got loose? What makes you think your husband is in love with Maggie Thatcher?"

‡LIQUID OHIO, Voice of the Unheard, (I), Blue Fish Publications, P.O. Box 60265, Bakersfield CA 93386-0265. (805)871-0586. E-mail: liquidohio@aol.com. Editor: Amber Goddard. Magazine: 8×11; 13-25 pages; copy paper; illustrations and photos. "*Liquid Ohio* is a fairly new publication whose goal is to publish new writers that others might toss in the trash. Our main audience is creatively eccentric people who feel what they do." Quarterly. Estab. 1995. Circ. 500.

Needs: Experimental, humor/satire, literary. "No erotica, vampires or any combination of the two." Receives 15-20 unsolicited mss/month. Accepts 2 mss/issue; 24-30 mss/year. Publishes ms 1-3 months after acceptance. Recently published work by Janet Kuypers, Peter Gorman and Christine Brandel. Publishes 40-60 new writers/year. Length: 1,500-1,800 words average; 2,500-3,000 words maximum. Publishes short shorts. Also publishes literary essays, literary criticism, poetry.

How to Contact: Send complete ms with a cover letter. Should include estimated word count. Reports in 3-4 weeks on queries; 3 months on mss. Send SASE for reply, return of ms or send a disposable copy of ms. Simultaneous submissions, reprint and electronic submissions OK. Sample copy for $3, 11×14 SAE and 3 first-class stamps. Fiction guidelines for #10 SASE.

Payment/Terms: Pays 3 contributor's copies. Acquires one-time rights.

Advice: "We like things that are different, but not too abstract or 'artsy' that one goes away saying, 'huh?' Write what you feel, not necessarily what sounds deep or meaningful—it will probably be that naturally if it's real. Send in anything you've got—live on the edge. Stories that are relatable, that deal with those of us trying to find a creative train in the world. We also love stories that are extremely unique e.g., talking pickles, etc."

THE MONTHLY INDEPENDENT TRIBUNE TIMES JOURNAL POST GAZETTE NEWS CHRONICLE BULLETIN, The Magazine to Which No Superlatives Apply, (I), 80 Fairlawn Dr., Berkeley CA 94708-2106. Editor: T.S. Child. Fiction Editor: Denver Tucson. Zine: 5½×8; 8 pages; 60 lb. paper; 60 lb. cover; illustrations and photographs. "We publish short stories, short short stories, plays, game show transcriptions, pictures made of words, teeny-weeny novelinis." Published irregularly. Estab. 1983. Circ. 500.

● The editor would like to see more "Discombobulating" stories.

Needs: Adventure, experimental, humor/satire, mystery/suspense (amateur sleuth, private eye), psychic/supernatural/occult. "If it's serious, literary, perfect, well-done or elegant, we don't want it. If it's bizarre, unclassifiable, funny, cryptic or original, we might." Nothing "pretentious; important; meaningful; honest." Receives 20 unsolicited mss/month. Accepts 3-4 mss/issue. Accepted manuscripts published in next issue. Length: 400 words preferred; 1,200 words maximum. Publishes short shorts. Length: 400 words. Sometimes critiques rejected mss.

How to Contact: Send complete ms with cover letter. Reports in 1 month. SASE. "May" accept simultaneous submissions. Sample copy for 50¢, and SASE.

Payment/Terms: Pays subscription (2 issues); 3 contributor's copies. Not copyrighted.

Advice: "First of all, stories must be *short*—1,200 words maximum, but the shorter the better. They must make us either laugh or scream or scratch our heads, or all three. Things that are slightly humorous, or written with any kind of audience in mind, are returned. If you can think of another magazine that might publish your story, send it to them, not us. Send us your worst, weirdest stories, the ones you're too embarrassed to send anywhere else."

‡THE MOOCHER'S PERIODICAL, A Guide That's Underground to the Underground, (I, II), M.O.O.C.H. (Motivational Organization of Curious Humanity), P.O. Box 410086, San Francisco CA 94141. Editor: Church. Format varies: folded into various shapes and configurations; 11 × 17; 1+ pages; photocopied; illustrations and photos. "The material we publish has to have an edge to it. Grit. Teeth. Something that bites you on the neck and goes home with you. Sleeps with you, and wakes up the next morning. Won't go away no matter how much you try. Can't be forgotten." Estab. 1992. Circ. 50-500.

Needs: All fiction categories. Special interests: "the truth/reality/what's really going on. We want material that walks the line between fact and fiction, transgresses it, and is believable all at the same time." List of upcoming themes available for SASE. Publishes special fiction issue and anthology. Receives a few unsolicited mss/month. Accepts a couple of mss/issue. Publishes ms 1-12 months after acceptance. Agented fiction 10%. Recently published work by g.r. hand, jr., Elizabeth Hall, Frank Kuenstler, Dorothea Towles and Jack Thomas. Length: 500-1,000 words average. Publishes short shorts. Also publishes literary essays, literary criticism and poetry. Always critiques or comments on rejected ms.

How to Contact Send complete ms with a cover letter or submit through agent. Reports in 4-8 weeks on mss. Send SASE (or IRC) for reply, return of ms or send a disposable copy of ms. Simultaneous submissions OK. Sample copy for $1, #10 SAE and 1 first-class stamp. Fiction guidelines for $1, #10 SAE and 1 first-class stamp. Reviews novels and short story collections.

Payment/Terms: Pays in contributor's copies.

Terms: Rights revert to author upon publication.

‡the moonbomb writers' syndicate, (I, II). E-mail: moonbomb@hooked.net. Website: http://www.hooked.net/users/moonbomb. Editor: Paul C. Choi. Electronic zine. "We are contemporary, urban, irreverent, ethnic, random."

Needs: Short stories, poetry, short plays, any fictional format, autobiographical non-fiction, fictional journalism. No children's fiction. Recently published work by Paul Rossi and Sheryl Ridenour. Publishes 3-4 new writers/year.

How to Contact: Electronic submissions only.

Advice: "Be bold."

‡MYSTERY AND MANNERS QUARTERLY, (I, II). E-mail: brandt8@indy.net. Website: http://www.indy.net/-brandt8/mysman/mysman.htm. Editor: Brandt Judson Ryan. Electronic zine. "To provide realistic, short fiction to the world online—fiction that includes all the five senses, forcing the reader to see something they might not have before."

Needs: "Short fiction only—no genre stories, no mysteries (the title of the zine is misleading)." Would like to see more literary fiction. Recently published work by Alex Keegan, Tom Harper and Sylvia Petter. Publishes 3 new writers/year.

How to Contact: Electronic submissions only. Send ms as an e-mail attachment or in the body of the message.

Advice: "In a realistic way, attempt to bring the other-worldly, right down into the worldly."

‡THE NEBULA, (I, II). (412)381-1146. E-mail: drow.queen@nebula.nauticom.net or lance@nebula.nauticom.net. Website: http://nebula.nauticom.net/nebula. Editors: Cindy Henderson and Lance Williams. "It is The Nebulous Association's mission to publish the highest quality special interest fanzine in the Ohio Valley region. We want to provide our subscribers with the most accurate and up-to-date information on the gaming, science fiction and fantasy genres. It is also our mission to hold highly organized and interesting gaming events for the lowest cost possible to the consumer."

Needs: Gaming, science fiction, fantasy, horror. Recently published work by Cindy Henderson, Hugh Barnes, Lance Williams, Owen McPhee, Pat Beck, James Dodd and Rob Burton. Publishes 6-12 new writers/year.

How to Contact: Electronic submissions only. Send ms at text file in e-mail.

‡NEOLOGUE, New Voices for a New Day, (I). E-mail: jtiess@juno.com. Website: http://www.geocities.com/Athens/Acropolis/7101. Editor: Robert J. Tiess. Electronic zine. "Philosophically, the publication was founded on the premise that writing has grown too distant from its literary heritage. The primary editorial impetus is discovering some of the newest and most creative literary voices of the day. The spirit of *NeoLogue* finds definition in a quote from one of my most treasured poems, *Four Quartets* '. . . last year's words belong to last year's language,/ And next year's words await another voice.' "

Needs: Fiction, poetry, essays, prose pieces, drama, historical, biographical, critical. "Stories should be concise and not exceed 1,000 words. Nothing defamatory or of an expressly sexual nature." Would like to see more literary, speculative, experimental, writing that takes intelligent, inspired chances, develops a particular voice, conveys its statements uniquely and sincerely." Recently published work by Gary Kern and Connie Berridge. Publishes 50 to 60 new writers/year. "New writers are always welcome and encouraged to submit material. Writers will only be judged solely on the quality of their material, not by previous publication credits or erstwhile positions held; in fact, the editor prefers not to be informed of such information as it bears no impact on whether a piece is accepted or rejected."

How to Contact: Electronic submissions only. Specify *NeoLogue Submission* in the subject field.

Advice: "Pay attention to every single syllable and structure in your writing. Proof your work, correct grammatical errors before submitting, check spelling and so forth. Submit only your best material and allow it to speak for itself. Occasionally I may request explanations, corrections, clarifications or additional submissions. Response time is generally within a week. Please visit the website for additional insight into the publication's 'Vision Statement,' writer's guidelines, and deadlines for upcoming issues. Writers may publish their work elsewhere after it appears in *NeoLogue*. Payment is an electronic copy of the issue a writer's work appears in. Issues and back-issues are freely available to the public on demand. Requests for issues should be directed to rjtiess@juno.com with *NeoLogue Issue* in the subject field of the message. Please visit the website for back-issue numbers."

‡THE NETHERREAL HORROR CYBERZINE, (I, II). E-mail: rupickman@geocities.com. Website: http://www.geocities.com/~rupickman. Editor: Jim Hawley. Electronic zine "dedicated to the works, art, fiction and material of H.P. Lovecraft and the Cthulhu Mythos."

Needs: Horror in homage to H.P. Lovecraft—short stories, poetry, novellas, serialized novels, literary essays, articles, art and music. "Material must be in the line of the Cthulhu Mythos. The mention of a deity or character in a story does not qualify it as mythos. My test is simple: take away all references to the mythos and if the story still stands, it probably isn't mythos. If it falls apart, I want to see it." Recently published work by Edward Berglund, Bruce Terlish and Stan Sargent. Publishes 20-50 new writers/year. "I offer a place for new writers to show their material with high visibility, where readers e-mail them back with critical reviews."

How to Contact: Electronic submissions only. Follow instructions on website's submissions page or e-mail a query. Accepts material in any PC-based word processor as an attachment.

Payment/Terms: "*The NetherReal Cyberzine* is non-profit, offering new authors a showcase that is gathering quite an audience, while offering accomplished authors a place to experiment. I attempt to let as many folks know about the site to get the authors additional coverage."

Advice: "Stay away from the formula. I get a lot of end of the world stories. I publish them but on an as time permits basis. If you want your stuff up quick and highlighted, surprise me, twist the twisted, make Lovecraft proud. Stories about individuals against the terror are more believable. Additionally, know your grammar. I will do minor editorial changes and allow you final approval, but major grammatical errors and/or spelling goofs will be dumped. I have a real-time job that demands a lot of time from me, help me out."

‡THE NEW WORLD MAGAZINE, (I). (619)562-6476. E-mail: contributions@swcty.net. Website: http://www.swcty.net. Editor: Andrew Caswell. Electronic zine. "A magazine dedicated to the works of amateur artists and writers, as well as a medium for professional artists and writers to act as mentors. The magazine is generally all audiences. All amateur material and professional articles will be considered for publication."

Needs: "All fiction is good fiction." Recently published work by R. Jason Gabouie, Arthur Gales, Craig Kozeluh, Charles Webber, Mike Rodriguez and Corey Evans. Publishes more new writers "than we can count on two hands."

How to Contact: Electronic submissions only.

Advice: "Write good, original material that will keep the reader's attention."

‡NO IRON PERCALE, (I). (973)731-1801. E-mail: Fitzdisc@Prodigy.net. Website: http://www.geocities.com/-fitzdisc. Editor: Fred Melillo. "An e-zine for the helplessly creative. Our material, though a very young e-zine, is geared toward more or less personalized social philosophy in a fictionalized medium. Though this seems particular, sometimes we feel it means nothing at all, so what we look for in reality is good story writing with original twists."

Needs: Essays and short fiction. "Nothing more than 9 or 10 pages. Other than that, everything is considered."

How to Contact: Electronic submissions only.

Advice: "Don't hold back. Tell us what you mean by whatever means necessary."

NOCTURNAL ECSTASY, Vampire Coven, (I, II, IV), Nocturnal Productions, P.O. Box 147, Palos Heights IL 60463-0147. E-mail: vampyr4@juno.com. Editor: Darlene Daniels. Zine: 8½×11; 75 pages; 20 lb. white paper; glossy cover; illustrations and photos. "We publish material on vampires, music, movies, gothic esoteria, erotica, horror, sado-masochism." Triannually. Estab. 1990. Circ. 10,000.

Needs: Vampire related: adventure, erotica, experimental, gay, horror, humor/satire, lesbian, mystery/suspense (romantic suspense), psychic/supernatural/occult; romance (gothic), science fiction (hard science). Plans to publish special fiction issue or anthology. Receives 100 unsolicited mss/month. Accepts 6 mss/issue; 40 mss/year. Published work by PJ Roberts, Jeffrey Stadt and Dale Hochstein. Length: 2,000 words average; 500 words minimum; 3,000 words maximum. Publishes short shorts. Also publishes literary essays, literary criticism and poetry. Sometimes critiques or comments on rejected mss.

How to Contact: Send complete ms with a cover letter. Include estimated word count and ¼-page bio. Reports in 1 month on queries; 2 months on mss. Send SASE for reply, return of ms or send a disposable copy of ms. Simultaneous, reprint and electronic submissions OK. Sample copy for $6. Fiction guidelines for $1 or 4 first-class stamps. "Checks or money orders payable to Darlene Daniels, not NEVC." Reviews novels and short story collections. Send books to NEVC Reviews.

Payment/Terms: No payment. Acquires one-time rights. Not copyrighted.

Advice: Looks for "originality, ability to hold reader's interest." Would like to see "more erotica, originality; no previously established characters of other authors."

NUTHOUSE, Essays, Stories and Other Amusements, (II), Twin Rivers Press, P.O. Box 119, Ellenton FL 34222. E-mail: nuthous499@aol.com. Website: http://members.aol.com/Nuthous499/index.html (includes writer's guidelines, readers' letters, excerpts). Chief of Staff: Dr. Ludwig "Needles" Von Quirk. Zine: digest-sized; 12-16 pages; bond paper; illustrations and photos. "Humor of all genres for an adult readership that is not easily offended." Published every 6 weeks. Estab. 1993. Circ. 100.

Needs: Humor/satire: erotica, experimental, fantasy, feminist, historical (general), horror, literary, main-stream/contemporary, mystery/suspense, psychic/supernatural/occult, romance, science fiction and westerns. Plans annual "Halloween Party" issue featuring humorous verse and fiction with a horror theme. Receives 12-30 unsolicited mss/month. Accepts 3-5 mss/issue; 30 mss/year. Publishes ms 6-12 months after acceptance. Recently published work by Dale Andrew White, Mitchell Nathanson, Rob Loughran, Vanessa Dodge, Ken Rand, Don Hornbostel and Michael McWey. Length: 500 words average; 100 words minimum; 1,000 words maximum. Publishes short shorts. Length: 100-250 words. Also publishes literary essays, literary criticism and poetry. Often critiques or comments on rejected mss.

How to Contact: Send complete ms with a cover letter. Include estimated word count, bio (paragraph) and list of publications. Reports in 2-4 weeks on mss. SASE for return of ms or send disposable copy of ms. Simultaneous and reprint submissions OK. Sample copy for $1 (payable to Twin Rivers Press). Fiction guidelines for #10 SASE.

Payment/Terms: Pays 1 contributor's copy. Acquires one-time rights. Not copyrighted.

Advice: Looks for "laugh-out-loud prose. Strive for original ideas; read the great humorists—Saki, Woody Allen, Robert Benchley, Garrison Keillor, John Irving—and learn from them. We are turned off by sophomoric attempts at humor built on a single, tired, overworked gag or pun; give us a story with a beginning, middle and end."

OF UNICORNS AND SPACE STATIONS, (I, II, IV), %Gene Davis, P.O. Box 97, Bountiful UT 84011-0097. Website: http://www.inconnect.com/~tDavis. Editor: Gene Davis. Zine: 5½×8½; 60 pages; 20 lb. white paper; card cover stock; illustrations. "Positive SF&F is sought. It should be for adults, though graphic sex, violence and offensive language are not considered." Bimonthly. Estab. 1994. Circ. 100.

Needs: Fantasy (science fantasy, sword and sorcery), science fiction (hard science, soft/sociological, utopian). Wants "clear writing that is easy to follow." Receives 10 unsolicited mss/month. Accepts 9-13 mss/issue; approximtely 25 mss/year. Publishes ms 6-12 months after acceptance. Published work by Laura J. Underwood, Vaseleos Garson and John Grey. Length: 3,000 words average. Publishes short shorts. Also publishes poetry. Sometimes critiques or comments on rejected mss.

How to Contact: Send complete ms with a cover letter. Include estimated word count, bio (75 words or less) and writer's classification of the piece (science fiction, fiction, poetry). Reports in 3 months. Send SASE for reply, return of ms or send a disposable copy of ms. Simultaneous, reprint and electronic (disk only) submissions OK. Sample copy for $4. Fiction guidelines for #10 SASE.

Payment/Terms: Pays 1¢/word and 1 contributor's copy for stories; $5/poem and 1 contributor's copy for poetry; additional copies for $4. Acquires one-time rights.

Advice: "Keep trying. It may take several tries to get published."

OFFICE NUMBER ONE, (I, II), 2111 Quarry Rd., Austin TX 78703. E-mail: onocdingus@aol.com. Editor: Carlos B. Dingus. Zine: 8½×11; 12 pages; 60 lb. standard paper; b&w illustrations and photos. "I look for short stories, imaginary news stories or essays (under 400 words) that can put a reader on edge—avoid profanity or obscenity, make a point to jolt the reader away from a consensus view of the world." Quarterly zine specializing in satire, humor and views from alternate realities. Estab. 1989. Circ. 1,000.

Needs: Fictional news articles, experimental, fantasy, horror, humor/satire, literary, psychic/supernatural/occult, also fictional reviews, Limericks. Receives 16 unsolicited mss/month. Buys 1-3 mss/issue; 16 mss/year. Publishes ms 6-12 months after acceptance. Publishes 10-15 new writers/year. Length: 400 words maximum, 150 best. Also publishes literary essays and poetry. Sometimes critiques or comments on rejected mss if requested.

How to Contact: Send complete ms with optional cover letter. Should include estimated word count with submission. Reports in 4-6 weeks on mss. Send SASE for reply, return of ms or send disposable copy of ms. Will consider simultaneous submissions, reprints. Sample copy for $2 with SAE and 3 first-class stamps. Fiction guidelines for SASE.

Payment/Terms: Pays 1 contributor's copy. Additional copies for $1 plus postage. Acquires one-time rights.

Advice: "Clean writing, no unnecessary words, clear presentation. Express *one* good idea. Write for an audience that you can identify. I'm planning to publish more *shorter* fiction. I plan to be more up-beat and to focus on a journalistic style—and broaden what can be accomplished within this style. It seems like the Internet is taking away from print media. However, I also think the Internet cannot replace print media for fiction writing.''

ONCE UPON A WORLD, (IV), 646 W. Fleming Dr., Nineveh IN 46164-9086. E-mail: 107753.2174@compuserve.com. Editor: Emily Alward. Zine: 8½×11; 80-100 pages; white paper; card stock cover; pen & ink illustrations. "A science fiction and fantasy zine with emphasis on alternate-world cultures and stories of idea, character and interaction. Also publishes book reviews and poems for an adult audience, primarily readers of science fiction and fantasy. We're known for science fiction and fantasy stories with excellent wordbuilding and a humanistic emphasis." Annually. Estab. 1988. Circ. 100.

● The science fiction and fantasy published in *Once Upon a World* tends to be "centered on the human element" and explores the individual in society. The editor would like to see more stories set in worlds with alternate political, economic or family arrangements.

Needs: Fantasy, science fiction. No realistic "stories in contemporary settings"; horror; stories using Star Trek or other media characters; stories with completely negative endings. "We're planning an issue of stories with metaphysical or ethical implications, to be published mid-1998. Deadline for story submissions approximately April 30, 1998. We may also publish another issue of science fiction and fantasy love stories, if response to the current issue is good." List of upcoming themes available for SASE. Receives 20 unsolicited mss/month. Accepts 8-12 mss/issue; per year "varies, depending on backlog." Publishes ms from 2 months to 1½ years after acceptance. Recently published work by Jon C. Picciuolo, Denise Tanaka and Tony Chandler. Publishes 5 new writers/year. Length: 3,000 words average; 400 words minimum; 10,000 words maximum. Publishes short shorts. Also publishes poetry. Sometimes critiques rejected mss and recommends other markets.

How to Contact: Send complete manuscript. Reports in 2-4 weeks on queries; 2-16 weeks on mss. SASE. "Reluctantly" accepts simultaneous submissions. Sample copy for $9. Make checks payable to Emily Alward. Fiction guidelines for #10 SASE. Reviews novels and short story collections.

Payment/Terms: Pays contributor's copies. Acquires first rights. "Stories copyrighted in author's name; copyrights not registered."

Advice: "Create your own unique universe, and then show its texture and how it 'works' in the story. This is a good way to try out a world that you're building for a novel. But, don't forget to also give us interesting characters with believable problems. Submit widely, but pay attention to editors' needs and guidelines—don't scattershot. Take on new challenges—i.e., never say 'I only write science fiction, romance, or even fiction in general—you never know where your 'sideline' work is going to impress an editor. It's a tight market for science fiction and fantasy right now, with magazines folding constantly and much competition from established 'name authors' for slots in the remaining ones. For the small press publisher, unable to get newsstand distribution, the best way to build a readership seems to be 'niche' publishing tied into specialized interests. That's one reason we're looking at the idea of becoming the magazine of science fiction and fantasy love stories, as well as some other specialized directions."

OUTER DARKNESS, Where Nightmares Roam Unleashed, (I, II), Rising Star, 1312 N. Delaware Place, Tulsa OK 74110. (918)832-1246. Editors: Dennis Kirk and Keith Stayer. Zine: 8½×5½; 60-80 pages; 20 lb. paper; 60 lb. card stock cover; illustrations. Specializes in imaginative literature. "Variety is something we strive for in *Outer Darkness*. In each issue we present readers with great tales of science and horror along with poetry, artwork, an ongoing column by Illinois author L.P. Van Ness, humorous editorials and cartoons. We seek to provide readers with a magazine which, overall, is fun to read." Quarterly. Estab. 1994. Circ. 500.

● Fiction published in *Outer Darkness* has received honorable mention in *The Year's Best Fantasy and Horror.*

Needs: Fantasy (science), horror, mystery/suspense (with horror slant), psychic/supernatural/occult, romance (gothic), science fiction (hard science, soft/sociological). "We do not publish works with children in sexual situations and graphic language should be kept to a minimum." Upcoming themes: "Darker Side of Outer Darkness"; "Fallen Angels"; "Mythical Creatures." Receives 50-75 unsolicited mss/month. Accepts 7-9 mss/issue; 20-50 mss/year. Recently published work by D.F. Lewis, Barbara Malenky, L.P. Van Ness, Charlene Jacob and Gerard Daniel Houaner. Publishes 4-6 new writers/year. . Length: 3,000 words average; 1,000 words minimum; 5,000 words maximum. Also publishes literary essays and poetry. Always critiques or comments on rejected mss.

How to Contact: Send complete ms with a cover letter. Include estimated word count, 50- to 75-word bio, list of publications and "any awards, honors you have received." Reports in 1 week on queries; 4-6 weeks on mss.

‡ **THE DOUBLE DAGGER** before a listing indicates that the listing is new in this edition.

Send SASE for reply, return of ms or send a disposable copy of ms. Simultaneous submissions and reprints OK. Sample copy for $4.50. Fiction guidelines for #10 SASE.
Payment/Terms: Pays 2 contributor's copies for fiction, 1 for poetry and art; additional copies $2.75. Pays on publication. Acquires one-time rights.
Advice: "We want stories which keep the reader literally glued to his chair. Strong characterization, well-developed plots and twist/surprise endings are also what we seek in manuscripts. Read the works of Robert Bloch, Richard Matheson, Ray Bradbury and other authors from the 'Golden Era' of horror and science fiction. But *don't* try to mimic their styles. Write the way you write best. We publish a lot of work similar to those found in *Weird Tales* and *The Twilight Zone*. So, while we obviously seek a certain degree of originality, we also enjoy reading solid, traditional works. If possible, study a sample copy. If the price of current issues is beyond your budget, back issues may be available for less."

‡**THE OUTPOST, (I, II)**. (609)587-4821. Fax: (609)586-8795. E-mail: thepost@concentric.net. Website: http://www.cris.com/~Thepost/index.htm. Editor: Tom Julian. Electronic zine. "We want writers and artists to take part in the things going on at *The Outpost*."
Needs: Fantasy, science fiction. Would like to see more comedies, plays and stories about relationships. "No copy-cats. No just like the *Hitchhikers Guide* stuff, please." Recently published work by Victor Martin Ivers, John McGerr and Kenneth Newquist. Publishes as many new writers "as cut the mustard."
How to Contact: Electronic submissions only. Send ms by e-mail.
Advice: "Give me something that puts me there and make it a place I'd want to go."

PABLO LENNIS, The Magazine of Science Fiction, Fantasy and Fact, (I, II, IV), Etaoin Shrdlu Press, Fandom House, 30 N. 19th St., Lafayette IN 47904. Editor: John Thiel. Zine: 8½×11; 26 pages; standard stock; illustrations and "occasional" photos. "Science fiction, fantasy, science, research and mystic for scientists and science fiction and fantasy appreciators." Monthly.
Needs: Fantasy, science fiction. Receives 50 unsolicited mss/year. Accepts 4 mss/issue; 48 mss/year. Publishes ms 4 months after acceptance. Recently published work by Lawrence Dagstine, Varda One, Allen Woods and Arto Baltayan. Publishes 36 new writers/year. Length: 1,500 words average; 3,000 words maximum. Also publishes literary criticism, poetry. Occasionally critiques rejected mss and recommends other markets.
How to Contact: "Method of submission is author's choice but he might prefer to query. No self-statement is necessary." No simultaneous submissions. Reports in 2 weeks. Does not accept computer printouts.
Payment/Terms: Pays 1 contributor's copy. Publication not copyrighted.
Advice: "I have taboos against unpleasant and offensive language and want material which is morally or otherwise elevating to the reader. I prefer an optimistic approach and favor fine writing. With a good structure dealt with intelligently underlying this, you have the kind of story I like. I prefer stories that have something to say to those which have something to report."

‡***PAPER TIGERS, A Compilation of Thoughtscrawl, (I, II, IV)**, Crooked Stare, Flat 2, 47 Shortlands Rd., Bromley BR2 0JJ Kent, England. Zine: A5; 20 pages; recycled gray paper; red ink cover; photos. "Poetic creative realms of thought, prose rather than poetry. Offbeat, quirky, insular and dream-like." Published irregularly. Estab. 1993. Circ. 300.
● Member of the National Small Press Centre.
Needs: Experimental, literary (contemporary). Does not want anything mainstream. List of upcoming themes for SASE (IRC). Accepts 5 mss/year. Recently published work by Simon Brown, Matt Haynes and D. Michael McNamara. Length: 100-1,000 words average. Publishes short shorts. Also publishes literary essays and poetry. Often critiques or comments on rejected mss.
How to Contact: Query with clips of published work. Reports in 2-4 weeks on queries and mss. SASE (IRC) for reply or send a disposable copy of ms. Simultaneous submissions OK. Sample copy for $1 and A5 SAE (2 IRCs).
Payment/Terms: Pays 5-10 contributor's copies; additional copies $1. Acquires one-time rights. Sends galleys to author. Not copyrighted.
Advice: "We want originality, talent, fiction that reflects our style. Sample a copy of our zine first."

‡**pauper, (I)**, 1770 Massachusetts Ave., Box 617, Cambridge MA 02140. E-mail: volpi@pauper.com. Website: http://pauper.com. Editor: Matt Volpi. Electronic zine. "*pauper* is dedicated to publishing new and underpublished authors and giving them an opportunity for immediate comment and criticism through our on-line feedback forms. We reach a relatively literary audience with a large group coming from the academic environment." Monthly.
Needs: Literary. "We'll consider anything within our length requirements (>5,000 words)." No "things that aren't spell-checked, suicides, genre fiction with no transcending qualities." Recently published work by Brad Pennington, Kimberly Metz, May Lenzer and Ro London." We publish at least 35 new writers of prose a year, not to mention the poetry."
How to Contact: Electronic or traditional submissions accepted. E-mail submissions may be sent in the body of the message or as an ASCII attachment. Mail submissions must be accompanied by SASE.
Advice: "Read your story over a week or two after you've written it. Do you still think anyone wants to read

it? If so, then maybe we will too. And try your best to avoid those pesky cliches."

PBW, (I, II), 130 W. Limestone, Yellow Springs OH 45387. (513)767-7416. E-mail: rianca@aol.com. Editor: Richard Freeman. Electronic disk zine: 700 pages; illustrations. "*PBW* is an experimental floppy disk that 'prints' strange and 'unpublishable' in an above-ground-sense writing." Quarterly electronic zine. Featuring avant-garde fiction and poetry. Estab. 1988.
  • *PBW* is an electronic zine which can be read on a Macintosh or available over modem on BBS. Write for details.
Needs: Erotica, experimental, gay, lesbian, literary. No "conventional fiction of any kind." Receives 3 unsolicited mss/month. Accepts 40 mss/issue; 160 mss/year. Publishes ms within 3 months after acceptance. Published work by Vern Frazer, Arthur Knight and Dirk Van Nouhuys. Length: open. Publishes short shorts and novels in chapters. Publishes literary essays, literary criticisms and poetry. Always critiques or comments on rejected mss.
How to Contact: Send complete ms with a cover letter. "Manuscripts are only taken if sent on disk." Reports in 2 weeks. Send SASE for reply, return of ms or send a disposable copy of ms. Simultaneous, reprint and electronic (Mac or modem) submissions OK. Sample copy for $2. Reviews novels and short story collections.
Payment/Terms: Pays 1 contributor's copy. All rights revert back to author. Not copyrighted.

‡PEGASUS ONLINE, the Fantasy and Science Fiction Ezine, (I, II). E-mail: editors@pegasusonline.com or ScottMarlow@pegasusonline.com. Website: http://www.pegasusonline.com. Editor: Scott F. Marlowe. Electronic zine. "*Pegasus Online* focuses upon the genres of science and fantasy fiction. We look for original work which inspires and moves the reader, writing which may cause him or her to think, and maybe even allow to pause for a moment to consider the how's and why's of those things around us."
Needs: Fantasy, science fiction. "More specifically, fantasy is to be of the pure fantastic type: dragons, goblins, magic and everything else you can expect from something not of this world. Science fiction can or cannot be of the 'hard' variety." No "excessive profanity or needless gore." Recently published work by Chris Villars, Larry W. Van Guilder, David Wright, Frederick Rustam and Anthony M. Giorgio. Publishes 18 new writers/year.
How to Contact: Electronic submissions only. Send mss by e-mail.
Advice: "Tell a complete tale with strong characters and a plot which draws the reader in from the very first sentence to the very last. The key to good fiction writing is presenting readers with characters they can identify with at some level. Your characters certainly can be larger than life, but they should not be all-powerful. Also, be careful with grammar and sentence structure. We get too many submissions which have good plot lines, but are rejected because of poor English skills. The end-all is this: we as humans read because we want to escape from reality for a short time. Make us feel like we've entered your world and make us want to see your characters succeed (or not, depending on your plot's angle), and you've done your job and made us happy at the same time."

‡PEN & SWORD, (I). (415)626-5179. E-mail: jag@rahul.net. Website: http://www.rahul.net/jag/. Editor: Jim Gardner. Electronic zine. "The best in modern and post-modern fiction, poetry, essays, criticism and reviews."
Needs: "*Pen & Sword* is an equal opportunity publisher and especially welcomes work from the gay/lesbian/bisexual community." Recently published work by Aldo Alvarez and Jim Tushinski. Publishes 6-10 new writers/year.
How to Contact: "Electronic submissions to the editor in MS Word, FrameMaker, HTML (preferred) or ASCII text are acceptable."

‡PENNY DREADFUL, Tales & Poems of Fantastic Terror, (II, IV), Pendragon Publications, 407 West 50th St., #16, Hell's Kitchen NY 10019. (212)765-2116. Editor: Michael Pendragon. Zine specializing in horror: 8½×5½; 40 pages; illustrations and photos. Publication to "celebrate the darker aspects of man, the world and their creator. We seek to address a highly literate audience who appreciate horror as a literary art form." Triannually. Estab. 1996. Circ. 500.
Needs: Fantasy (dark symbolist), horror, psychic/supernatural/occult. List of upcoming themes available for SASE. Receives 50 unsolicited mss/month. Accepts 3-5 mss/issue; 9-15 mss/year. "*Penny Dreadful* reads all year until we have accepted enough submissions to fill more than one year's worth of issues. We are currently filled and will begin reading for our Autumn 1998 issue in June 1998." Recently published work by James S. Dorr, John B. Ford, Amy Grech, Barbara Malenky, Scott Thomas, Christopher Hivner, Mike Allen, Vera Searles, Sheila B. Roark, Jennifer Tobkin, Jack Lent, Mark Blickley and Ben Pastor. Length: 500 words minimum; 2,500 words maximum. Publishes short shorts. Also publishes poetry. Always critiques or comments on rejected mss.
How to Contact: Send complete ms with a cover letter. Include estimated word count, bio and list of publications. Reports in up to 3 months on queries and mss. Send SASE for reply, return of ms or send disposable copy of ms. Simultaneous submissions and reprints OK. Sample copy for 9×6 SASE with 3 first-class stamps. Fiction guidelines for #10 SASE.
Payment/Terms: Pays free subscription to magazine plus 2 contributor's copies for one-time rights. Sends galleys to author. Not copyrighted.
Advice: Looks for "literary dark horror in the tradition of Poe, M.R. James, Shelley and LeFanu—dark, disquieting tales designed to challenge the readers' perceptions of human nature, morality and man's place within the

Darkness. Stories should be set prior to 1910 or possess a timeless quality. Avoid graphic sex, strong language, references to 20th century people, excessive gore and shock elements.''

PEOPLENET DISABILITY DATENET HOME PAGE, "Where People Meet People," (IV), Box 897, Levittown NY 11756-0897. (516)579-4043. E-mail: mauro@colt.net. Website: http://idt.net/~mauro (includes writer's guidelines, articles, stories, poems). Editor: Robert Mauro. "Romance stories featuring disabled characters." Estab. 1995.
Needs: Romance, contemporary and disabled. Main character must be disabled. Upcoming theme: "Marriage between disabled and non-disabled." Accepts 3 mss/year. Publishes immediately after acceptance. Length: 1,500 words. Publishes short shorts. Length: 750 words. Also publishes poetry. Especially looking for book reviews on books dealing with disabled persons and sexuality.
How to Contact: Send complete ms by e-mail. No simultaneous submissions. Fiction guidelines online.
Payment/Terms: Acquires first rights.
Advice: "We are looking for romance stories of under 1,000 words on romance with a disabled man or woman as the main character. No sob stories or 'super crip' stories. Just realistic romance. No porn. Erotica okay. Love, respect, trust, understanding and acceptance are what I want."

‡PERCEPTIONS, (I, II), Garnet Publications, 555 Third St., Fall River MA 02721. (508)672-6707. Editor: Yvonne Bird. Zine specializing in dark literature: 50 pages; format varies; illustrations and photographs. "Perceptions was created for the sole purpose of serving as a forum for true artistic expression and brilliance. We are a publication of dark, tear-soaked literature. Our audience consists of fellow writers, musicians and artists who wish to indulge in the emotion of others." Biannually. Estab. 1997. Circ. 200.
Needs: Experimental, fantasy (surreal), horror, literary, mystery/suspense, psychic/supernatural/occult, romance (dark/doomed), science fiction. Publishes ms up to 6 months after acceptance. Length is open. Publishes short shorts. Also publishes literary criticism, poetry. Always critiques or comments on rejected mss.
How to Contact: Send complete ms with a cover letter. Include "whatever information you judge relevant." Reports in 1 month on queries; 2 months on mss. SASE for reply, return of ms or send a disposable copy of ms. Simultaneous submissions, reprints OK. Sample copy for $2. Fiction guidelines for #10 SASE. Reviews novels and short story collections. Send books to editor. Also reviews other zines and extreme music.
Payment/Terms: Pays free subscription to the magazine and 4 contributor's copies on publication; additional copies for $2. Acquires one-time rights. Sends galleys to author upon request.
Advice: "I publish surreal (often philosophical) fiction that harbors a unique voice, fiction which induces its own personality upon the reader. A writers words must invoke emotion, whether that be of fright, sadness, longing, amazement or apathy. Send in material that you yourself have difficulty defining and limiting to one genre. I am quite open minded as are my readers, and I encourage individuality and experimentation in both fiction and poetry. I also stress the importance of obtaining an issue and/or copy of writer's guidelines. I abhor quaint, trendy fiction and prefer literature that was written to please the writer as opposed to a market."

‡PHRASE ONLINE, (I). Fax: (352)629-3367. E-mail: tsprang@phrase.org. Website: http://www.phrase.org. Editor: Todd Sprang. Electronic zine, "*Phrase* is an open forum for any and all writers who wish to release their work for the world to read." Bimonthly.
Needs: Short and long fiction, poetry. Other media are considered. Would like to see more satire. Recently published work by Jae H. Lee, Robert Brower and Jason Stelzer. Published 3 new writers in last issue.
How to Contact: Provides form on website for electronic submissions.
Advice: "Proofread. Proofread proofread. Proofread some more."

PICA, (I, II), 165 N. Ashbury Ave., Bolingbrook IL 60440. E-mail: green@dls.net. Website: http://www.dls.net/~green/ (includes guidelines, a modified version of the issue currently in print, works from previous issues). Editor: Lisa Green. Zine: 8½×7; 40-80 pages; 24 lb. paper; 65 lb. cover stock. "*Pica* attempts to publish the best of avant-garde and experimental fiction, essays and poetry. Triannually. Estab. 1995. Circ. 100.
Needs: Condensed/excerpted novel, experimental, feminist, gay, humor/satire, lesbian, literary. "No pornography, nothing 'fluffy,' and nothing you would see published in any magazine you'd find in the checkout aisle at the grocery store." Receives 50 unsolicited mss/month. Accepts 9 mss/issue; 30 mss/year. Publishes ms 6-8 months after acceptance. Recently published work by BB Johns, Sheila E. Murphy and Tim Scannell. 30% of work published is by new writers. Length: 10,000 words maximum. Publishes short shorts. Also publishes literary essays, literary criticism and poetry. Often critiques or comments on rejected mss.
How to Contact: Send complete ms. "Only include a cover letter if you are famous. That we need to know." Reports in 2 months on mss. Send SASE for return of ms. Simultaneous, reprint and electronic (Word 7.0 compatible disk) submissions OK. Sample copy for $3. Fiction guidelines for SASE.
Payment/Terms: Pays 3 contributor's copies or 1 year subscription; additional copies for $1. Acquires one-time rights.
Advice: "We are looking for writers with a broad base of knowledge. We love variety and wit, passion and opinion. We adore works that seek out ambiguity and exploit detail. And please read the magazine." The most common reason for rejections: inappropriate style. Needs "more good fiction by women!"

‡PIF, (I). (808)839-9843. E-mail: pif@dimax.com. Website: http://www.dimax.com/pif/. Editor: Richard Luck. Electronic zine. "Pif's goal is to provide a large, supportive audience for emerging writers. We believe that electronic publishing will revolutionize the industry as profoundly as the printing press did, and we aim to usher in this new era with the best and the brightest the Net has to offer. Our audience is a cross-section of the global community. We're read in over 87 different countries. The majority of our readers tend to be educated, culturally aware and open-minded. Quite a few of our readers are writers as well."

Needs: "We publish a wide range of material, including: poetry, fiction, commentary and original artwork. We also include book, movie and music reviews. We are open to most anything, as long as it is well-written and shows a real love for the craft. We especially seek contemporary literary-quality fiction in the style of Douglas Coupland, Erica Jong, Henry Miller, et al. We're particularly interested in writers who are willing to break boundaries, who are honest and believe in themselves and the characters they create." Recently published work by Camille Renshaw, Robert St. James, Stephen J. Frank and Allison Jenks. "There are many more, but these are the only ones I know of who have subsequently gone on to publish novels or collections of poetry with mainstream publishers since appearing in *Pif*." Publishes 15 new fiction writers and 15-20 new poets/year.

How to Contact: Electronic and traditional submissions accepted. "Submit via e-mail, including the story as a MIME attachment in Word for Windows format (PC-based), or cut and paste into the body of the e-mail. To mail in submissions, visit our web site for the current address, or email pifsubs@dimax.com."

Advice: "Be honest and be yourself. Take a chance and see where it leads you. Above all, believe in your characters and the story you're telling. If you're bored while writing the piece, chances are we'll be bored reading it. So be enthusiastic. Be brave. Be willing to go out on a limb."

‡PLAY THE ODDS, (I), The Big Dog Press, 11614 Ashwood, Little Rock AR 72211. (501)224-9452. Editor: Tom Raley. Fiction Editor: Barbra Stone. Zine specializing in gaming/gambling: 8½ × 11; 16 lb. paper; illustrations and photos. "We cover gambling activities all across the country. We offer tips, reviews, instructions and advice. We also cover cruise lines since most have casinos on board." Monthly. Estab. 1997.

• Sponsors several contests both annual and on-going. Details are printed in each issue.

Needs: Adventure, fantasy (science fantasy), horror, mystery/suspense (cozy, private eye/hardboiled, romantic suspense), science fiction (soft sociological), senior citizen/retirement, sports, westerns (traditional). Receives 20-25 unsolicited mss/month. Accepts 1-2 mss/issue; 12-20 mss/year. Publishes ms 2-4 months after acceptance. Recently published work by Jennifer Sinclair and Gary Lewis. Length: 600 words average; 800 words maximum. Publishes short shorts. Also publishes literary criticism and poetry. Always critiques or comments on rejected mss.

How to Contact: Send complete ms with a cover letter. Include estimated word count and 100 word bio. Reports in 2 weeks on queries; 4-6 weeks on mss. Send SASE for reply, return of ms or send disposable copy of ms. Simultaneous submissions OK. Sample copy for $2. Fiction guidelines for #10 SASE. Reviews novels and short story collections. Send books to D.A. Rogers.

Payment/Terms: Pays $1,500 minimum; $3,000 maximum on acceptance for one-time rights.

Advice: "We look for fast paced stories with real characters. The stories should be fun, enjoyable and the main character doesn't need to be trying to save the world. Few, if any of us, do that. We do however get in bad situations. You must write what you enjoy writing about. If you don't want to write a story about gambling or a gambler, it will show in your work. If it is something you do want, that will also show in your work and we will notice it."

PULP: A FICTION MAGAZINE, Lurid Tales of Adventure, (I), Ramrod Productions, P.O. Box 548, Hermosa Beach CA 90254-0548. (310)376-5959. Editor: Clancy O'Hara. Zine: digest size; 50 pages; standard 20 lb. paper; illustrations. Specializes in "genre fiction (mainly crime/horror) with an unusual spin—work that transcends the genre's humble origins." Bimonthly. Estab. 1995. Circ. 100.

• *Pulp* received an honorable mention in the *Year's Best Fantasy and Horror* and the most Human Editor Award from Green Country Ruffriters.

Needs: Fantasy (sword and sorcery), horror, mystery/suspense (private eye/hardboiled), science fiction (hard science, soft/sociological). Receives 20-50 unsolicited mss/month. Accepts 3 mss/issue; 18 mss/year. Publishes ms within 2 months after acceptance. Recently published work by Tony Lawler, Clancy O'Hara, Amos Johnson, Dana Evans and Christine Wyman. Length: 2,000 words average; 100 words minimum; 3,000 words maximum. Publishes short shorts. Also publishes literary criticism. Sometimes critiques or comments on rejected mss.

How to Contact: Send complete ms with cover letter. Include estimated word count, 1-paragraph bio, Social Security number and list of publications. Reports in 3 months on queries; 6 months on mss. SASE for reply or

---

⬥ THE MAPLE LEAF symbol before a listing indicates a Canadian publisher, magazine, conference or contest.

send a disposable copy of ms. Simultaneous submissions OK. Sample copy for $5. Reviews novels and short story collections.

Payment/Terms: Pays ½¢-1¢/word on publication and 2 contributor's copies; additional copies for $5. Acquires first North American serial rights.

Advice: "Original dialogue and real-sounding, quirky characters. I show as much interest in writers' stories as they show in my magazine; i.e., send for guidelines and read a sample copy. Shorter work has a better chance of publication. I publish more crime and horror than fantasy and it's the very rare science fiction piece I publish. Best chance with me: short horror."

‡QECE, Question Everything Challenge Everything, (II, IV), 406 Main St. #3C, Collegeville PA 19426. E-mail: qece@voicenet.com. Editor: Larry Nocella. Zine: 5½×8½; 40 pages; copy paper; copy paper cover; illustrations and photographs. Zine seeking to inspire free thought and action by encouraging a more questioning mentality. Triannually. Estab. 1996. Circ. 300.

Needs: Experimental. "Anything that inspires others to question and challenge conventions of fiction." No genre fiction, no formulas. Receives 15 unsolicited mss/month. Accepts 1 ms/issue; 3 mss/year. Publishes ms 6 months after acceptance. Recently published work by Kiel Stuart, Paula L. Fleming, Charles Chaim Wax and B. Kim Meyer. Length: 1,000 words average. Publishes short shorts. Always critiques or comments on rejected mss.

How to Contact: Send complete ms with a cover letter. Include estimated word count and 25 words or less bio. Reports in 4 months. Send SASE for reply, return of ms or send a disposable copy of ms. Simultaneous and e-mail submissions OK. Sample copy for $3. Fiction guidelines free for #10 SASE.

Payment/Terms: Pays $5 on publication and 2 contributor's copies; additional copies for $3. Acquires one-time rights.

Advice: "Ignore 'trends'; be yourself as much as possible and you'll create something unique. Be as timeless as possible. Avoid obscure, trendy references. Tie comments about a current trend to timeless observation. If it's in the 'news' chances are it won't be in QECE, The 'news' is a joke. Tell me something I need to know. Favor anecdotes and philosophy over intense political opinions. I'd prefer to hear about personal experiences and emotions everyone can relate to. Criticism is welcome, though. QECE can be negative, but remember it is positive too. Just go for it! Send away and let me decide! Get busy!"

‡R'N'R, (I). E-mail: glbeke@panix.com. Website: http://www.panix.com/-glbeke. Editor: George L. Beke. Electronic zine. "Literate writing with a musical bent. Write with attitude."

Needs: "Poems, memoirs, fiction, musings, confessions, critiques that are smart, evocative and surprising. Nothing boring." Publishes "as many new writers as possible."

How to Contact: Electronic submissions only.

Advice: "Send it."

RALPH'S REVIEW, (I), RC Publications, 129A Wellington Ave., Albany NY 12203-2637. (518)459-0883. E-mail: repub@juno.com. Editor: Ralph Cornell. Zine: 8½×11; 20-35 pages; 20 lb. bond paper and cover. "To let as many writers as possible get a chance to publish their works, fantasy, sci-fi, horror, poetry." Quarterly. Estab. 1988. Circ. 200.

Needs: Adventure, fantasy (science fantasy), horror, humor/satire, literary, psychic/supernatural/occult, science fiction, stamp and coin collecting, dinosaurs, environmental, fishing. No extreme violence, racial, gay/lesbian/x-rated. Publishes annual special fiction issue or anthology. Receives 10-15 unsolicited mss/month. Accepts 1-2 mss/issue; 12-15 mss/year. Publishes ms 2-4 months after acceptance. Recently published work by Ralph Cornell, Celeste Plowden, Christopher Alan Thorn and Peter McLaughlin. Publishes 10-20 previously unpublished writer's/year. Length: 500-1,000 words average; 50 words minimum; 2,000 words maximum. Publishes short shorts. Also publishes poetry. Sometimes critiques or comments on rejected mss.

How to Contact: Send complete ms with a cover letter. Include 1-paragraph bio and list of publications. Reports in 2-3 weeks on queries; 2-3 months on mss. Send SASE for reply, return of ms or send a disposable copy of ms. Simultaneous and reprint submissions OK. Sample copy for $2, 9×12 SAE and 5 first-class stamps. Fiction guidelines for #10 SASE. Reviews novels or short story collections.

Payment/Terms: Pays 1 contributor's copy; additional copies for $2. Acquires first North American serial rights.

Advice: Looks for manuscripts "that start out active and continue to grow until you go 'Ahh!' at the end. Something I've never read before. Make sure spelling is correct. Content is crisp and active. Characters are believable. Must be horrific, your worst nightmare, makes you want to look in the corner while sitting in your own living room."

S.L.U.G. FEST, LTD., A Magazine of Free Expression, (I), SF, Ltd., P.O. Box 1238, Simpsonville SC 29681-1238. (864)297-4009. Fax: (864)297-0578. Editor: M.T. Nowak. Fiction Editor: M. Tatlow. Zine: 8½×11; 70 pages; 20 lb. paper; 30 lb. cover stock; illustrations. "We are dedicated to publishing the best poetry and fiction we can find from writers who have yet to be discovered." Quarterly. Estab. 1991. Circ. 1,000.

Needs: Adventure, ethnic/multicultural, experimental, feminist, historical, humor/satire, literary, mainstream/contemporary, regional, "philosophies, ramblings." "No poor writing." Receives 30 unsolicited mss/month. Accepts 5-10 mss/issue; 20-40 mss/year. Publishes mss 3 months after acceptance. Length: 7,000-10,000 words preferred. Publishes short shorts. Also publishes literary essays, literary criticism and poetry. Often critiques and comments on rejected mss.

How to Contact: Send complete ms with a cover letter. Include estimated word count. Reports in 5 weeks. Send SASE for reply, return of ms or send a disposable copy of ms. Simultaneous, reprint and electronic submissions OK. Sample copy for $5. Fiction guidelines free. Reviews novels and short story collections.

Payment/Terms: Pays 1 contributor's copy. Rights revert to author upon publication.

Advice: "We look for humor, quality of imagery. Get our interest. Style and content must grab our editors. Strive for a humorous or unusual slant on life."

‡**SCRIPTIO, (I, II)**, Scriptio International, 8787 Branch Ave., Suite 127, Clinton MD 20735. E-mail: scriptio_inter@rocketmail.com. Website: http://members.tripod.com/~scriptio. Editor: Dee Howle. Electronic zine. "Scriptio International is a non-profit organization dedicated to the literary and performing arts. In addition to our annual contest, we have a website to promote new writers and writing so it may be accessed by all for free." Quarterly. Estab. 1996

Needs: All kinds of fiction. List of upcoming themes available for SASE. Publishes short shorts. Also publishes literary essays, literary criticism and poetry.

How to Contact: Query first by e-mail. Reports in 2 weeks on queries. Simultaneous, reprint and electronic submissions OK.

Advice: "Study the genre you wish to write and know your subject."

‡❦**SCRIPTIO CANADA, (IV)**, 356 N. Ontario St., Suite 135, Stratford Ontario N5A 3H9 Canada. E-mail: scriptiocanada@rocketmail.com. Website: http://members.tripod.com/~scriptio_canada. Electronic zine. "Scriptio Canada is dedicated to encouraging the literary and performing arts throughout Canada. We have an annual Canadian contest in addition to our website." Estab. 1996.

Needs: All kinds of fiction by Canadian writers. Publishes short shorts. Also publishes literary essays, literary criticism and poetry.

How to Contact: Query first by e-mail. Reports in 2 weeks on queries. Simultaneous, reprint and electronic submissions OK.

Advice: "Study the genre you wish to write and know your subject."

‡***SCRIPTIO UK/EUROPE, (IV)**. E-mail: scriptiouk@geocities.com or scriptiouk@rocketmail.com. Website: http://www.geocities.com/Athens/Forum/9212. Electronic zine. Estab. 1996.

Needs: All kinds of fiction by European writers. Length: 15,000 words maximum. Publishes short shorts. Also publishes literary essays, literary criticism and poetry.

How to Contact: Query first by e-mail. Include list of publications. Reports in 2 weeks on queries. Simultaneous, reprint and electronic submissions OK.

Advice: "Do your best work."

‡**SEPULCHRE, (I, IV)**, Koshkovich Press, 5037 Worchester Dr., Dayton OH 45431. (937)253-6517. E-mail: vannar@bigfoot.com. Editor: Scot H.P. Drew. Zine: digest size; 30-60 pages; 28 lb. paper; 67 lb. coverstock; illustrations and photos. "Quarterly zine devoted to bringing new writers of dark fantasy and imaginative horror out into the sunlight of the small press literary scene." Publishes fiction, poetry and eulogies. Estab. 1997.

Needs: Fantasy (dark), horror, psychic/supernatural/occult. Also needs original eulogies. "These should elicit an emotional response from the reader. You may eulogize any entity, real or fictional, living or deceased." Receives 10 unsolicited mss/month. Accepts 5-10 mss/issue; 20-40 mss/year. Length: 2,000-5,000 words average; 10,000 words maximum. Publishes short shorts. Also publishes poetry. Sample copy for $3.00. Fiction guidelines for #10 SASE.

How to Contact: Send complete ms with a cover letter. Include 2-5 line bio. Send disposable copy of ms. Reports in 6 weeks on mss. Simultaneous submissions OK.

Payment/Terms: Pays 1 contributor's copy.

Advice: "Send your darkest, most disturbing pieces."

SORCEROUS MAGAZINE, Sword & Sorcery, Epic Fantasy, (I, IV), Sorcerous Publications, 7325 Palmer House Dr., Sacramento CA 95828-4026. (916)399-1272. Editor: Rebecca Treadway. Zine: digest size; 60-70 pages; 20 lb. bond paper. Specializes in sword & sorcery and medieval renaissance-based fantasy, heroic fantasy, gritty fantasy, adventure, epic fantasy and dark fantasy. "Please note that I *do not* consider dark fantasy to be synonymous with vampires or Gothic themes; rather, I view it as fantasy with sinister, brutally realistic backgrounds and plots." Annually. Estab. 1994. Circ. 200.

Needs: Fantasy (sword and sorcery, epic). "No parody, short shorts, romance, science fiction or hybrid genres such as fantasy westerns and urban fantasy." Receives 20-30 unsolicited mss/month. Accepts 7-8 mss/issue; 24-30 mss/year. Publishes 3-6 months after acceptance. Length: 7,000 words. Also publishes literary essays and literary criticism. Often critiques or comments on rejected mss.

How to Contact: Send complete ms with a cover letter. Include estimated word count and 1-paragraph bio. Reports in 2 weeks on queries; 1 month on mss. Send SASE for reply, return of ms or send a disposable copy of ms. Simultaneous submissions and reprints OK. Sample copy for $5. Fiction guidelines for #10 SASE. Reviews novels and short story collections.

Payment/Terms: Pays $5 and 1-2 contributor's copies; additional copies $3. Acquires one-time rights.

Advice: "When magic is the primary focus of the tale, I notice a manuscript more than the typical 'Barbarian Adventure.' Realistic, details in background and well-developed characters stand out. Read the guidelines thoroughly. This publication is very specific on this matter. If not purchasing a sample copy, be familiar with styles of authors I prefer—Tolkien, Howard, Eddings, etc. Don't listen to anyone but your own instincts—too many people today try to discourage writers, especially young genre-writers. I don't follow industry trends, neither should the writer. I'm not soft-skinned, I'm not easy to offend, but too many of my submissions have been too light hearted with pouty women! I don't need that! Please!"

‡SPUNK, The Journal of Spontaneous Creativity, (I, II), P.O. Box 55336, Hayward CA 94945. (510)278-6689. Editor: Sean Reinhart. Fiction Editor: Spunk Wilson. Zine: 5½ × 8½; 30 pages; photocopied; illustrations and photos. "*Spunk* is dedicated to the publication of short creative outbursts with no pretensions or apprehensions—somewhere along the fine line between matter and energy lies *Spunk*." Semiannually. Estab. 1997. Circ. 500.

Needs: Erotica, experimental, literary. List of upcoming themes available for SASE. Receive 20 unsolicited mss/month. Accepts to 4-8 mss/issue; 10-20 mss/year. Publishes ms 6-12 months after acceptance. Recently published work by Violet Jones and Stephen Gutierrez. Length: 1,000 words average. "We love really good one-pagers." Also publishes literary essays and poetry. Sometimes critiques or comments on rejected mss.

How to Contact: Send complete ms with a cover letter. Reports in 6 months on mss. Send SASE for reply, return of ms. Simultaneous submissions OK. Sample copy for $2. Fiction guidelines for #10 SASE. Reviews novels and short story collections. Send books to editor.

Payment/Terms: Pays 1 contributor's copy for first North American serial rights.

Advice: "All work should be short, unique and above all Spunky. Obtain a sample copy, not necessarily to emulate our style, but to know if we're on the same planet or not."

‡STAR TREK FANZINE, (I, II, IV), P.O. Box 173848, Arlington TX 76003-3848. (817)432-7081. Website: http://www.flash.net/~stfzine. Editor: Art Lopez. Fiction Editor: Andrew Hearn. Zine specializing in Star Trek: 8½ × 11; 24-30 pages; 60 lb. paper; illustrations. "We are dedicated to providing a forum where fans can share their visions of Star Trek with others and become a part of Star Trek history." Quarterly.

Needs: Only Star Trek. No satirical writings or parodies. Accepts 6-10 mss/issue. Publishes ms 4 months after acceptance. Length: 3,000-4,000 words average; 8,000 words maximum. Publishes short shorts. Also publishes poetry. Often critiques or comments on rejected mss.

How to Contact: Send complete ms with a cover letter. Include estimated word count, 2-3-paragraph bio and 3.5 DOS disk. Reports in 2 months. Send SASE for reply, return of ms or send a disposable copy of ms. Simultaneous electronic submissions OK. Sample copy for $5, 9 × 12 SAE and 5 first-class stamps. Fiction guidelines for #10 SASE.

Payment/Terms: Pays 1 contributor's copy on publication. Acquires one time rights. Not copyrighted.

Advice: "All submissions must be Star Trek. We accept stories, poems and art in classic Trek, Next Generation, DS9, and Voyager. Bring out realistic character development. Successful stories are built by conflicts (both internal and external) and on plausible resolutions of those conflicts. Our readers are very familiar with the Star Trek Universe. Be sure there are no mistakes in your work. We encourage new writers to submit their work, but we strongly advise that they send for guidelines first."

‡STARK RAVING SANITY, (I, II), 1835 Cedar River Dr., Jacksonville FL 32210-1301. E-mail: mdubose@mediaone.net. Website: http://www.unf.edu/~mdubos/srs.htm. Editor: Mike S. Dubose. Electronic zine. "We have published short stories, poems, novel excerpts, prose poems, poetic prose, micro-fiction and everything in between. Our intended audience is anyone looking for an entertaining work of substance."

Needs: "Anything goes, as long as it fits our eclectic, ever changing tastes. We want works that illustrate a variant view of reality—but then again all works do just that. So anything of quality is what we like. No idea—only prose, hate prose or porn." Recently published work by Susan Terris, Joe Flowers, C.K. Tower, Anthony John Ciccariello III, Marc Awodey and Richard Fein.

How to Contact: Electronic and traditional submissions accepted. "Send 2-20 pages in the body of an e-mail message or as a text-only attachment (DOS or MS Word). Traditional mail submissions should include SASE for reply."

Advice: "Send, send, send. Rather than giving me a neat situation, give me characters that I should care about in a neat situation. Make me care."

‡STARSHIP EARTH, (I, II, IV), Black Moon Publishing, P.O. Box 484, Bellaire OH 43906. (614)671-3253. Editor: Kirin Lee. Fiction Editor: Silver Shadowhorse. Zine specializing in the sci-fi universe: 8½ × 11; 60 pages; glossy paper and cover; illustrations and photos. "We are mostly non-fiction with one piece of fiction per month." Monthly. Estab. 1995. Circ. 30,000.

● Sponsors contest. Send SASE for details.

Needs: Fantasy (science fantasy), science fiction (hard science, soft/sociological, historical). Publishes special fiction issues or anthologies. Receives 100-200 unsolicited mss/month. Accepts 1 ms/issue; 12 mss/year. Publishes ms 16-18 months after acceptance. Length: 2,000-3,000 words average; 3,000 words maximum. Publishes short shorts. Sometimes critiques or comments on rejected mss.

How to Contact: Query or send complete ms with a cover letter. Include estimated word count, short bio and list of publications. Reports in 3 weeks on queries; 3-4 months on mss. Send SASE for reply, return of ms or send disposable copy of ms. Fiction guidelines for #10 SASE. Reviews novels and short story collections. Send books to Jenna Dawson.

Payment/Terms: Pays 1 cent/word minimum; 3 cents/word maximum plus 1 contributor's copy for first rights.

Advice: "Get our guidelines. Submit in the correct format. Send typed or computer printed manuscripts only. Avoid bad language, explicit sex and violence. Do not include any religious content. Manuscripts stand out when they are professionally presented."

‡**STRONG COFFEE, (I, II)**, 5412 N. Clark Street, Chicago, IL 60640. (773) 989-0799. Fax: (773)989-5934. E-mail: coffee@strong-coffee.com. Website: http://www.strong-coffee.com. Editor: Martin Northway. Electronic and print zine. "*Strong Coffee* is a coffeehouse publication. Everything one would find in a coffeehouse, one can find in *Strong Coffee*: Art, poetry, fiction, photography, music, humor, politics, coffee, satire, whimsy and conversation, in no particular order or proportion. Like a coffeehouse habitué, each time our readers visit they may find old friends and acquaintances, interesting characters, a celebrity or two, or a whole new crop of faces. There is no agenda, only a forum for community and culture." 20,000 copies distributed free to 220 Chicago-area locations. Monthly.

Needs: Fiction; poetry; art; photography; essay; humor; satire; whimsy; interviews; book, music, art, dance and drama reviews; and "anything else we like." No genre fiction.Recently published work by Achy Obejas, Terry Jacobus, Vincent Tinguely, Witold Gombrowicz (Greg Pekala, trans.), Allen Ginsberg, Henry Hardee and Timothy Quinn. Publishes 10-30 new writers/year.

How to Contact: Send complete ms with SASE or send "as e-mail attachment, MS Word 6.0 or lower, WordPerfect 5.2 or lower, or RTF. If none of the above are available, then e-mail text is OK. In all cases, name, address and telephone must be included. Also, the submission must specify whether it is made for electronic publication only, print publication only or both forms of our publication. Those submitted for use in both media are more likely to be accepted."

Advice: "Short pieces are more likely to be published than long pieces, but we publish those too. Usually, nothing over 10 double-spaced pages gets published, but sometimes it does. We are more interested in quality than subject matter, length or genre. We publish conventional, experimental and non-categorizable fiction. If the piece makes us laugh or cry or think, it has a good chance. If it does all three, it's a shoo-in."

‡**SWAGAZINE, (I, II)**. E-mail: swagazine@jamesclark.com. Website: http://www.silcom.com/swagazine/. Editor: Jim Clark. Electronic zine. "*Swagazine* originated within the online community in Santa Barbara at a now defunct BBS we knew as Swagland. The personalities who graced our electronic medium shared messages of such considerable talent that we decided to pool our efforts, take on the world, and start a magazine of our own. Now, several years later, the BBS world has migrated to the Internet and so has our publication."

Needs: "There is no limitation on style, content or subject matter. *Swagazine* focuses on prose and poetry both as art forms and entertainment media. Social, philosophical and liberal political themes are dealt with, but not in a way that mimics news magazines or purely didactic writing. It is not our goal to educate our readers; we presume they are already educated. *Swagazine* attempts to examine the dynamic relationship between the mindand the voice; between the conscience of people and the standards of mass society; between the message of the endangered individual and the moronic giant of popular opinion." Recently published work by Colin Campbell, Jillian Firth, Ricky Garni, Michael Hoerman, AidanButler and Bryan Zepp Jamieson. Publishes 3-4 new writers/year.

How to Contact: Electronic submission only. "Submissions of poetry and prose should be in standard ASCII format as part of the message body. Attachments in alternate word-processor formats will be sent to the bottom of the consideration pile."

Payment/Terms: "Our electronic magazines are vehicles for aesthetic experiments and entertainment; we are not making money, so we cannot offer any to our submitters. What we do offer is participation in an artistic endeavor that will bring writers and artists together and into opposition; the artist becomes the art and the art is let out of the closet, the disk drive, and the soul."

Advice: "While it is our intent to spotlight our local talent, we are open to submissions from anyone, anywhere. If you would like to submit your prose, poetry, dramatic dialogue, or artwork to us, create freely and honestly. Trendiness is not valued; we probably wouldn't even recognize a fashionable approach if we saw it. Take all the risks you want; no subject matters are forbidden prima facie."

SYCAMORE ROOTS: THE REGIONALIST PAPERS, (II, IV), Ice Cube Press, 205 N. Front St., North Liberty IA 52317-9302. E-mail: icecube@inav.net. Website: http://soli.inav.net/~icecube. Editor: S.H. Semken. Zine: 8½ × 11; 8-12 pages; 60 lb. paper; illustrations and photos. "*Sycamore Roots* publishes attentive, perceptive ideas regarding regional, natural and environmental issues." Quarterly. Estab. 1994. Circ. 500.

• *Sycamore Roots* has received 3 *Pushcart* nominations.

Needs: Regional, outdoor. Receives 4 unsolicited mss/month. Accepts 1 ms/issue; 4 mss/year. Publishes ms 1-

6 months after acceptance. Recently published works by Robert Wolf, G. Max Vogt, Susan Scott and Denise Low. Publishes short shorts. Also publishes essays and poetry. Usually critiques or comments on rejected ms "if it's within the ballpark of what we're looking for."

How to Contact: Query or send complete ms with SASE. Include brief bio. Reports in 3-4 weeks. Send SASE for reply, return of ms or send a disposable copy of ms. Simultaneous submissions OK. Sample copy for $1, 6×9 SAE and 2 first-class stamps. Reviews novel and short story collections.

Payment/Terms: Pays 1 contributor's copy. Acquires one-time rights.

Advice: "It is obvious, but really, you should see a copy of *Sycamore Roots* first so we both know what's going on. We may not be as big a deal as you think, and your writing may not even be close to what we mean when we say natural or environmental. We are slowly switching to an online magazine."

‡**SYNAETHESIA PRESS CHAPBOOK SERIES, (II)**, P.O. Box 641083, San Francisco CA 94164-1083. (415)908-6797. E-mail: books@synaethesia.com. Editor: Jim Camp. Zine specializing in fiction: 16 pages; 50 lb. paper; card cover. Publishes fiction by new and established authors "writing outside the margin." Quarterly. Estab. 1995. Circ. 500.

Needs: Erotica, experimental, literary. No romance, children's, westerns. Receives 10 unsolicited mss/month. Accepts 10 mss/year. Publishes ms 1-6 months after acceptance. Recently published work by Jack Micheline, Alin Catlin, Joe Maynard and Jim Pritchard. Length: 2,500 words maximum. Publishes short shorts. Also publishes literary essays, literary criticism and poetry.

How to Contact: Query first. Include estimated word count. Reports in 1 week on queries. Send SASE for reply. Simultaneous, reprint and electronic submissions OK. Sample copy for $5. Fiction guidelines free. Reviews novels or short story collections. Send books to editor.

Payment/Terms: Pays $50 plus 3 contributor's copies. Sends galleys to author.

Advice: "Make it stand out. Hopefully, you are over 'anxiety of influence.' "

‡**SYNTAX INTERGALACTIC, (I)**. (510)628-3968. Fax: (510) 835-1325 E-mail: dgupta@informix.com. Website: http://www.creative.net/-glyplv/si. Editor: Deepak Gupta. Electronic zine. "Multi-cultural fiction with a new avant-garde twist."

Needs: Would like to see more "sci-fi (Fifth Elementish) and naturalist adventures." No erotica.

How to Contact: "Electronic submissions only."

Advice: "Keep it honest, modern, enticing, sensual and intelligent and you're a shoo-in."

T.R.'S ZINE, P.O. Box 489, Milltown NJ 08850-0489. Editor: T.R. Miller. Zine: 5×8; 18 pages; bond paper; illustrations. Quarterly. Estab. 1996. Circ. 50.

Needs: Ethnic/multicultural, gay, humor/satire, lesbian, literary, mainstream/contemporary, mystery/suspense (romantic), religious/inspirational, senior citizen/retirement, sports, westerns (frontier, traditional). Upcoming themes: "Christmas," "Winter" (seasonal), "St. Patrick's Day," "Easter," "Senior Citizens." Accepts 1 ms/issue. Publishes ms in next issue after acceptance. Length: 250 words average; 50 words minimum; 500 words maximum. Also publishes literary essays, literary criticism and poetry.

How to Contact: Send complete ms with a cover letter. Include 1-page bio. Send SASE for reply or send disposable copy of ms. Simultaneous submissions and reprints OK. Sample copy for $1.

Payment/Terms: Pays 1 contributor's copy on publication. Acquires one-time rights.

Advice: Looks for "anything well written—fine use of words and descriptive writing. Each writer is looked upon by his own writing merit and not compared to others. I'd like to see more imaginative writing."

‡**TELETALE, a Playground for Writers, (I)**. E-mail: campbell@highfiber.com. Website: http://www.us1.net/campbell. Editor: Harlen Campbell. Electronic zine. "*TeleTale* offers writers an opportunity to experiment with electronic media and publishing—everything from traditional through post-modernist, experimental and hypertext fiction, poetry or new forms. My desire is to provide a virtual work-bench upon which artists can prototype the literature of the 21st century—whatever that may turn out to be."

Needs: "Anything of interest to a literate, wired mind. Hypertext, linear or any other form. No hard-core porn. Recently published work by Walter Sorrels and Robert Weber.

How to Contact: Electronic submissions only. See website for details.

Advice: "For a work to be valuable, the reader must be more important to the writer than him or herself."

THISTLE, (I, II, IV), P.O. Box 50094, Minneapolis MN 55405-0094. (612)871-3111. E-mail: thistle@iceworld. org. Editor #1: Chelsea. Editor #2: Thaylor. Zine specializing in gothic literature/art: ¼ size, 4¼×5½; 100 pages;

SENDING TO A COUNTRY other than your own? Be sure to send International Reply Coupons instead of stamps for replies or return of your manuscript.

standard photocopy paper; colored paper cover; illustrations and photos. "Our aim is to produce a zine of high literary and artistic quality, for the gothic community, and anyone who has a fascination with the darker, bleaker or romantic side of life." Semiannual to annual. Estab. 1993. Circ. 500.

Needs: Fantasy (sword and sorcery), horror, mystery/suspense (romantic suspense), psychic/supernatural/occult, romance (gothic, historical). "No poorly written cheese-goth." Receives very few mss/month. Recently published work by Gary Jurechka and Michael McClellan. Length: 20,000 words maximum. Publishes short shorts. Also publishes literary essays, literary criticism and poetry.

How to Contact: Send complete ms with SASE for reply, return of ms or send a disposable copy of ms. Simultaneous, reprint and electronic (IBM disk or modem) submissions OK. Sample copy for $1.50 or 5 first-class stamps. Fiction guidelines for #10 SASE. Reviews novels and short story collections. "Very biased reviews—if we like it, we review it."

Payment/Terms: Pays 1 contributor's copy; inquire about additional copies. Rights belong to author. Not copyrighted.

Advice: "Don't write about vampires, dead roses or bleeding hearts. It's trite! No graphic sex."

TRANSCENDENT VISIONS, (II), Toxic Evolution Press, 251 S. Olds Blvd., 84-E, Fairless Hills PA 19030-3426. (215)547-7159. Editor: David Kime. Zine: letter size; 24 pages; xerox paper; illustrations. "*Transcendent Visions* is a literary zine by and for people who have been labeled mentally ill. Our purpose is to illustrate how creative and articulate mental patients are." Quarterly. Estab. 1992. Circ. 200.

• *Transcendent Visions* has received excellent reviews in many underground publications.

Needs: Experimental, feminist, gay, humor/satire, lesbian. Especially interested in material dealing with mental illness. "I do not like stuff one would find in a mainstream publication. No porn." Receives 5 unsolicited mss/ month. Accepts 7 mss/issue; 20 mss/year. Publishes ms 3-4 months after acceptance. Published work by Beth Greenspan, Jonathan Wayne Koerner, Peter Cogne, Steven Elroy and Paul Wenman. Length: under 10 pages typed, double-spaced. Publishes short shorts. Also publishes poetry.

How to Contact: Send complete ms with cover letter. Include half-page bio. Reports in 2 weeks on queries; 1 month on mss. Send disposable copy of ms. Simultaneous submissions and reprints OK. Sample copy for $1 and 2 first class stamps.

Payment/Terms: Pays 2 contributor's copies on publication. Acquires one-time rights.

Advice: "We like unusual stories that are quirky. Please do not go on and on about what zines you have been published in or awards you have won, etc. We just want to read your material, not know your life story. Please don't swamp me with tons of submissions. Send up to five stories. Please print or type your name and address."

‡THE UNIT CIRCLE, (II), Unit Circle Media, P.O. Box 20352, Seattle WA 98102. (206)322-1702. E-mail: zine@unitcircle.com. Website: http://www.unitcircle.com. Editor: Kevin Goldsmith. Fiction Editor: Nita Daniel. Zine specializing in fiction, poetry, art and music: A4; offset cover; illustrations and photos. "We exist to bring interesting new work to a wider audience." Annually. Estab. 1993. Circ. 500.

Needs: Erotica, ethnic/multicultural, experimental, feminist, gay, historical, humor/satire, lesbian, literary, translations. No fantasy, science fiction, romance or religious. Publishes special fiction issues or anthologies. Receives 2-3 unsolicited mss/month. Accepts 2 mss/issue. Publishes ms 6 months after acceptance. Length: 300 words average; 100 words minimum; 500 words maximum. Publishes short shorts. Also publishes literary essays, literary criticism and poetry. Sometimes critiques or comments on rejected mss.

How to Contact: Send complete ms with a cover letter. Include estimated word count and bio. Reports in 1 month on queries; 4 months on mss. Send SASE for reply, return of ms or send disposable copy of ms. Sample copy and guidelines free for 1 first-class stamp. Reviews novels or short story collections. Send books to fiction editor.

Payment/Terms: Pays 5 contributor's copies for one-time rights; additional copies $1.

Advice: "We are looking for work that has an edgy, experimental quality."

THE UNKNOWN WRITER, (I, II), 5 Pothat St., Sloatsburg NY 10974. (914)753-8363. Fax: (914)753-6562. E-mail: rsidor@worldnet.att.net. Editor: D.S. Davis. Zine specializing in fiction, poetry, environmental issues: digest size; 40 pages; 24 lb. fiber paper; 80 lb. fiber cover stock; illustrations and photos. "*The Unknown Writer* is a forum for new writers and artists. Any subject matter and style goes as long as it's interesting." Triannually. Estab. 1995. Circ. 500.

Needs: Adventure, erotica, ethnic/multicultural, experimental, feminist, gay, historical (general), humor/satire, lesbian, literary, mainstream/contemporary, psychic/supernatural/occult, regional, sports, environmental issues. "Our zine is not really appropriate for children or young adults. We have little interest in science fiction, religious and little room for condensed or serialized novels." Receives 20 unsolicited mss/month. Accepts 10 mss/issue; 30 mss/year. Publishes ms 3-5 months after acceptance. Recently published work by Satig Mesropian and David Castleman. Length: 2,500 words average; 5,000 words maximum. Publishes short shorts. Also publishes literary essays, literary criticism and poetry.

How to Contact: Send complete ms with a cover letter. Include 100-word bio and list of publications. Reports in 3 months. Send a disposable copy of ms. Simultaneous and electronic (disk or modem) submissions OK. Sample copy for $3, Writer's guidelines for #10 SASE. Reviews novels and short story collections.

Payment/Terms: Pays 2 contributor's copies; additional copies for $3. Acquires one-time rights. Not copyrighted.

Advice: "Almost anything goes but we prefer tightly written stories with good dialogue that are not impossible to follow. Write, rewrite and keep writing. When submitting your work, start with small stories and small publications and build your way up. If you're good, publishers will notice."

‡URBAN DIALOGUE, (I), Elmhurst A Station, P.O. Box 800059, Elmhurst NY 11380. (718)899-1712. E-mail: edit@unsociables.com. Website: http://www.unsociables.com. Literary Editor: Marc Landas. Electronic zine. "Urban life is made up of an infinite number of experiences, from life in the streets to brushing one's teeth. We want to hear about everything in between."

Needs: All genres. "No particular category. Just quality."

How to Contact: Mail or e-mail submissions to submissions@unsociables.com.

Advice: "Tell me a good story."

VIRGIN MEAT, (I), 2325 W.K 15, Lancaster CA 93536. (805)722-1758. E-mail: virginmeat@aol.com. Editor: Steve Blum. Gothic interactive computer e-zine. Published irregularly. Estab. 1987. Circ. 5,000.

Needs: Horror. Receives 3-4 mss/day. Length: 2,000 words maximum. Also publishes poetry, art, sound and QTM's.

How to Contact: Request writers' guidelines before your first submission. Submit mss via e-mail address above. Sample copy for $5.

Payment/Terms: Pays in contributor's copies. Acquires one-time rights. Publication not copyrighted.

Advice: "Horror fiction should be horrific all the way through, not just at the end. Avoid common settings, senseless violence and humor."

‡VISIONS MAGAZINE FOR THE ARTS, (I), 4576-E5 Pembroke Mall, Virginia Beach VA 23462. (757)518-0102. Fax: (757)518-0200. E-mail: cybervisions@visionsmagazine.com. Website: http://www.visionsmagazine.com. President: James L. Sides. Electronic and print zine. "Art publication both in print and on-line. We cover all of the arts—this includes poetry, short stories and fiction as well as visual art, performance art and all the other arts."

Needs: Poetry, short fiction, reviews of performances and art openings. No porn. Recently published work by Steven Hewitt, Gayle Myers and James Luker. Publishes 25 new writers/year.

How to Contact: Electronic submissions only.

VOX, Because reaction is a sound, (I, II), Cleave Press, 1603 Hazeldine SE, Albuquerque NM 87106. Fax: (505)764-8443. E-mail: cleavepres@aol.com. Website: http://members.aol.com/cleavepres/webstuff (includes guidelines, themes, graphics, excerpts, cover pictures). Editor: Robbyn Sanger. Zine: 8½ × 11; 40 pages; newsprint paper; glossy 2-color cover; illustrations and photos. "Say it like it is. (Enough said.)" Quarterly. Estab. 1994. Circ. 2,000.

Needs: Erotica, ethnic/multicultural, experimental, feminist, gay, humor/satire, lesbian, literary, opinions, translations. "No formula fiction." Upcoming themes: "Revenge" (deadline January 1998); "Sacrifice" (deadline March 1998); "Herspective" (deadline May 1998). Receives 50 mss/month. Buys 30 mss/issue; 90 mss/year. Publishes ms 1-4 months after acceptance. Published work by Thomas Hamill, Laura Lustig and John Goldfine. Publishes 40 new writers/year. Length: 500 words average; 5 words minimum; 1,000 words maximum. Publishes short shorts. Length: 25 plus words. Sometimes critiques or comments on rejected ms.

How to Contact: Send complete ms with a cover letter. Include estimated word count and brief bio. Reports in 2-4 weeks on queries; 1-2 months on mss. Send SASE for reply, return of ms or send a disposable copy of ms. Simultaneous, reprint and electronic submissions OK. Sample copy for $2. Fiction guidelines free for legal SASE.

Payment/Terms: Pays 3 copies. Acquires one-time rights. Sends galleys to author (if requested). Not copyrighted.

Advice: "Get a sample copy before submitting! I love short shorts. Avoid long dull, overdone stuff. I do not want to see any plot-driven stories. At all. Ever. Have a clearly defined writing voice. Interesting characters, too. I see a lot of writing that seems self-important, stuff that says, 'I'm the author, look at what I know and what I can do.' I think writing should be about the piece itself, to make the writing stand out, not the author. If a reader is impressed by the piece, that in itself will draw attention to the author."

THE W!DOW OF THE ORCH!D, (I, II, IV), Maudit Publications, 2101 Hazel Ave., Virginia MN 55792-3730. (218)749-8645. E-mail: booboo_m@northwennet.com. Editor: M. Zine: 7½ × 8; 60 pages; 20 lb. white paper; b&w illustrations, when available. Quarterly. Estab. 1994. Circ. 100.

FOR INFORMATION ON ENTERING the *Novel & Short Story Writer's Market* Cover Letter Contest, see page 84.

Needs: Dark sykotic and experimental tales or poetry of erotica, fantasy, horror and psychic/supernatural/occult with no happy endings . . . . without a price, that is. "All tales must include one of the following: angels, demons, devils, ghouls, gods, monsters, shapeshifters, sykoz (psychos), vampires, wizardry, and whatever your devious mind in an utter state of severe sykosis can devise! None need to be of the supernatural." List of upcoming themes available for SASE. "Themes have no set deadlines and a theme issue will happen only if there are enough manuscripts." Publishes annual fiction issue. Publishes ms 1-5 issues after acceptance. Recently published work by Marcey Jones, Georgette Fox, Heather Silvio, Kathryn Geier, C.S. Faqua, James Newman and Kurt Roth. Publishes 10 new writers/year. Length: 3,000 words average; 100 minimum; 5,000 words maximum. Publishes short shorts. Also publishes poetry. "We are looking for serialized novels and novellas." Often critiques or comments on rejected mss.
How to Contact: Send complete ms with a cover letter or mail disk. "All tales longer than 5 pages send on disk. Can accept: ASCII and Microsoft Works 3.1 or better. Must include estimated word count, bio (more than a list of publications!!) of about 30 words, and words that will blow me off my duff." Reports in 3 weeks on queries; 1-6 months on mss; 2-4 weeks on poetry; 1-2 months on artwork. Send SASE for reply, return of ms or send a disposable copy of ms. No simultaneous submissions. Reprints OK. Sample copy $5 postpaid (make checks payable to Raquel Bober). Fiction/novel guidelines for #10 SASE. (No SASE needed, if ordering copy).
Payment/Terms: Pays 1 contributor's copy; charges for additional copies. Acquires first North American serial rights or one-time rights.
Advice: "Don't worry about offending me. I want tales that are unique, highly imaginative, and well written. Read your work, if it blows your mind, it'll most likely blow mine. And this is to all you new writers out there— never give up, trust in yourself and your talent; and never ever let some jerky type make you doubt yourself! I've noticed that many writers I'm publishing have their own voices. Almost as if they were unaware of 'trends' or just didn't care. That's what I like to see, a writer or poet who doesn't try to mimic the latest greatest, but has decided he/she is."

‡WIT'S END LITERARY CYBERZINE. Fax: (702)648-7296. E-mail: corwalch@skylink.net. Website: http://www.geocities.com/~witsendlc. Editor: Richard A. Vanaman. Electronic zine. "To promote and encourage creativity amongst the Gay/Lesbian/Bisexual/Transgendered community."
Needs: Poetry, short stories, non-fiction, photography, art, comic strips targeted to the G/L/B/T community. No content containing hate, bigotry or prejudice. Recently published work by Hassan Galadari, Jameson Currier and Eric Hansen. Publishes 100 new writers/year.
How to Contact: Electronic submissions only. Ms should be sent as an e-mail attachment.
Advice: "Be creative, be yourself. And don't forget to include your copyright statement."

‡(000)000-0000, (I, II), 1233 G Beacon Parkway East, Birmingham AL 35209. (205)870-5943. Editor: Andre Villanueva. Zine: 5½ × 8½; 30-60 pages; illustrations. "I mostly like experimental fiction, but I'll consider just about anything. I'm very open-minded." Estab. 1998.
Needs: Experimental, horror, humor/satire, literary, mystery/suspense, psychic/supernatural/occult, science fiction. Accepts 5-10 mss/issue. Publishes ms 1-8 months after acceptance. Length: 10,000 words maximum; no minimum—"If you can write a 50-word story, go for it." Publishes short shorts. Also publishes poetry. Always critiques or comments on rejected mss.
How to Contact: Send complete ms with a cover letter. Include ½ page bio. Reports in 1-3 weeks on queries; 1-8 weeks on mss. Send SASE for reply, return of ms or send disposable copy of ms. Simultaneous, reprint and electronic (IBM disk) submissions OK. Reviews other literary magazines, short novels and short story collections. Send non-returnable books and magazines or include SASE.
Payment/Terms: Pays 2 contributor's copies for one-time rights.
Advice: "Make your opening a barbed hook that won't let go. Have fun with your story. I love experimentation with structure. Even hackneyed themes can be made original through manipulation of the story elements. Read works by Kathe Koja, Richard C. Matheson, Harlan Ellison, Barry N. Malzberg, or the *Sudden Fiction* books to see what kinds of fiction I like and what I mean by originality."

*THE ZONE, The Last Word in SF Magazines, (I, II, IV), Pegasus Press, 13 Hazely Combe, Arreton, I.O.W. P030 3AJ Great Britain. 0983-865668. Editor: Tony Lee. Zine specializing in science fiction: A4; 68 pages; bond paper; card cover; illustrations and photos. "Publishes quality fiction, incisive articles, interviews, poetry, art and critical reviews." Semiannually. Estab. 1994.
 ● Member of the New Science Fiction Alliance.
Needs: Adventure, erotica, ethnic/multicultural, experimental, fantasy (science fantasy), feminist, horror, humor/satire, literary, mainstream/contemporary, psychic/supernatural/occult, romance (futuristic/time travel), science fiction (hard science, soft/sociological/slipstream), translations. No "quest fantasy or routine sword and sorcery adventure." List of upcoming themes available for SASE. Accepts 6 mss/issue; 12 mss/year. Publishes ms up to 6 months after acceptance. Recently published work by Bruce Boston, Andrew Darlington and Rhys Hughes. Length: 3,000 words average; 1,000 words minimum; 5,000 words maximum. Publishes short shorts. Also publishes literary essays, literary criticism and poetry. Sometime critiques or comments on rejected mss.
How to Contact: Query with clips or send complete ms with a cover letter. Include estimated word count, 100 word bio and list of publications. Reports in 3 weeks on queries; 6 weeks on mss. Send SASE for reply, return

of ms or send disposable copy of ms. No simultaneous submissions. Reprints OK. Sample copy for $9 and A4 SAE. Guidelines for 2 IRCs. Reviews novels or short story collections. Send books to editor.

Payment/Terms: Pays $10 maximum and 1 contributor's copy for first British serial rights.

Advice: Looks for "originality, style, use of genre theme. Read our magazine before sending manuscipt."

‡*ZOTHIQUE, The Gargoyle Society Journal, (I, II).** E-mail: lwild@mail.usyd.edu.au. Website: http://www.geocities.com/SoHo/3688. Editor: Leon D. Wild. Electronic zine that publishes dark fantasy, weird horror, artificial mythology and the gothic imaginary.

Needs: Very short prose, poetry, articles and reviews. Recently published work by Don Webb, Marie Buckner and Azra Medea. Publishes 9 new writers/year.

How to Contact: Electronic submissions only. Send ms by e-mail.

Advice: "Write it from the perspective of 'the dark side.' Read some earlier issues to get an idea of what we are striving for."

Commercial Magazines

In this section of *Novel & Short Story Writer's Market* are commercial magazines with circulations of more than 10,000. Many have circulations in the hundreds of thousands or millions. Among the oldest magazines listed here are ones not only familiar to us, but also to our parents, grandparents and even great-grandparents: *The Atlantic Monthly* (1857); *Christian Century* (1900); *Redbook* (1903); *The New Yorker* (1925); *Analog Science Fiction & Fact* (1930); *Esquire* (1933); and *Jack and Jill* (1938).

Commercial periodicals make excellent markets for fiction in terms of exposure, prestige and payment. Because these magazines are well-known, however, competition is great. Even the largest commercial publications buy only one or two stories an issue, yet thousands of writers submit to these popular magazines.

Despite the odds, it is possible for talented new writers to break into print in the magazines listed here. Editors at *Redbook*, a top fiction market which receives up to 600 unsolicited submissions a month, say, "We are interested in new voices and buy up to a quarter of our stories from unsolicited submissions." The fact that *Redbook* and other well-respected publications such as *The Atlantic Monthly* and *The New Yorker* continue to list their fiction needs in *Novel & Short Story Writer's Market* year to year indicates that they are open to both new and established writers. Your keys to breaking into these markets are careful research, professional presentation and, of course, top-quality prose.

Featured on page 376 of this section is an interview with Ron Carlson, whose stories have appeared in *Harper's*, *The New Yorker*, *Playboy*, *Ploughshares* and STORY.

TYPES OF COMMERCIAL MAGAZINES

In this section you will find a number of popular publications, some for a broad-based, general-interest readership and others for large but select groups of readers—children, teenagers, women, men and seniors. Just a few of these publications include *Boys' Life*, *American Girl*, *Seventeen*, *Esquire*, *Harper's*, *Ladies' Home Journal* and *Mature Years*. You'll also find regional publications such as *Aloha: The Magazine of Hawaii and the Pacific*, *Florida Wildlife*, *Georgia Journal*, *Yankee Magazine* and *Portland Magazine*.

Religious and church-affiliated magazines include *The Friend Magazine*, *New Era Magazine* and *Guideposts for Kids*. Other magazines are devoted to the interests of particular cultures and outlooks such as *African Voices*, publishing "enlightening and entertaining literature on the varied lifestyles of people of color," and *India Currents*, specializing in the "arts and culture of India as seen in America for Indians and non-Indians with a common interest in India."

Top markets for genre fiction include *Ellery Queen's Mystery Magazine*, *Alfred Hitchcock Mystery Magazine*, *Analog Science Fiction & Fact* and *Asimov's Science Fiction*. These magazines are known to book publishers as fertile ground for budding genre novelists.

Special interest magazines are another possible market for fiction, but only if your story involves a particular magazine's theme. Some of the highly specialized magazines in this section are *Balloon Life* (hot air ballooning); *Adventure Cyclist* (bicycle touring); and *Juggler's World*.

SELECTING THE RIGHT MARKET

Unlike smaller journals and publications, most of the magazines listed here are available at newsstands and bookstores. Many can also be found in the library, and guidelines and sample copies are almost always available by mail. Start your search, then, by familiarizing yourself with the fiction included in the magazines that interest you.

Don't make the mistake of thinking, just because you are familiar with a magazine, that their fiction isn't any different today than when you first saw it. Nothing could be further from the truth—commercial magazines, no matter how well established, are constantly revising their fiction needs as they strive to reach new readers and expand their audience base.

In a magazine that uses only one or two stories an issue, take a look at the nonfiction articles and features as well. These can give you a better idea of the audience for the publication and clues to the type of fiction that might appeal to them.

If you write a particular type of fiction, such as children's stories or mysteries, you may want to look that subject up in the Category Index at the back of this book. There you will find a list of markets that say they are looking for a particular subject. Check also the subcategories given within each listing. For example, a magazine may be in the Category Index as needing mystery fiction, but check the listing to find out if only a particular subcategory interests them such as hard-boiled detective stories or police procedurals or English-style cozies.

You may want to use our ranking codes as a guide, especially if you are a new writer. At the end of this introduction is a list of the Roman numeral codes we use and what they mean.

FURTHERING YOUR SEARCH

See How to Use This Book to Publish Your Fiction (page 3) for information about the material common to all listings in this book. In this section in particular, pay close attention to the number of submissions a magazine receives in a given period and how many they publish in the same period. This will give you a clear picture of how stiff your competition can be.

While many of the magazines listed here publish one or two pieces of fiction in each issue, some also publish special fiction issues once or twice a year. We have indicated this in the listing information. We also note if the magazine is open to novel excerpts as well as short fiction and we advise novelists to query first before submitting long work.

The Business of Fiction Writing, beginning on page 77, covers the basics of submitting your work. Professional presentation is a must for all markets listed. Editors at commercial magazines are especially busy, and anything you can do to make your manuscript easy to read and accessible will help your chances of being published. Most magazines want to see complete manuscripts, but watch for publications in this section that require a query first.

As in the previous section, we've included our own comments in many of the listings, set off by a bullet (●). Whenever possible, we list the publication's recent awards and honors. We've also included any special information we feel will help you in determining whether a particular publication interests you.

The maple leaf symbol (❁) identifies our Canadian listings. You will also find some English-speaking markets from around the world. These foreign magazine are denoted with an asterisk (*) at the beginning of the listings. Remember to use International Reply Coupons rather than stamps when you want a reply from a country other than your own.

FOR MORE INFORMATION

For more on trends in commercial fiction, see our Fiction Report starting on page 85. For more on commercial magazines in general, see issues of *Writer's Digest* and industry trade publications such as *Folio*, available in larger libraries.

For news about some of the genre publications listed here and information about a particular field, there are a number of magazines devoted to genre topics, including *Mystery Scene*, *Locus* (for science fiction) and *Science Fiction Chronicle*. Addresses for these and other industry magazines can be found in the Publications of Interest to Fiction Writers section of this book.

Membership in the national groups devoted to specific genre fields is not restricted to novelists and can be valuable to writers of short fiction in these fields. Many include awards for "Best Short Story" in their annual contests. For information on groups such as the Mystery Writers of America, the Romance Writers of America and the Science Fiction and Fantasy Writers of

America see the Organizations and Resources section of this book.

The following is the ranking system we have used to categorize the periodicals in this section:

I Periodical encourages beginning or unpublished writers to submit work for consideration and publishes new writers regularly.

II Periodical accepts outstanding work by beginning and established writers.

III Hard to break into; periodical publishes mostly previously published writers.

IV Special-interest or regional magazine, open only to writers in certain genres or on certain subjects or from certain geographic areas.

V Periodical closed to unsolicited submissions.

ADVENTURE CYCLIST, (I, IV), The Adventure Cycling Assn., Box 8308, Missoula MT 59807. (406)721-1776. Editor: Daniel D'Ambrosio. Magazine on bicycle touring: 8⅜ × 10⅞; 32 pages; coated paper; self cover; illustrations and b&w photos. Published 9 times annually. Estab. 1974. Circ. 30,000.
Needs: Adventure, fantasy, historical (general), humor/satire and regional and with a bicycling theme. Buys variable number of mss/year. Published new writers within the last year. Length: 2,000 words average; 1,000 words minimum; 2,500 words maximum. Publishes short shorts. Occasionally comments on rejected mss.
How to Contact: Send complete ms with SASE. Reports in 6 weeks. Simultaneous and previously published submissions OK. Accepts electronic submissions; prefers hard copy with disk submission. Sample copy for $1, 9 × 12 SAE and 60¢ postage. Fiction guidelines for #10 SASE.
Payment/Terms: Pays $25-65/published page on publication for first North American serial rights.

AFRICAN VOICES, The Art and Literary Publication With Class & Soul, (I, II), African Voices Communications, Inc., 270 W. 96th St., New York NY 10025. (212)865-2982. Editor: Carolyn A. Butts. Managing Editor: Layding Kaliba. Fiction Editor: Gail Sharbaan. Magazine: 32 pages; illustrations and photos. "*AV* publishes enlightening and entertaining literature on the varied lifestyles of people of color." Quarterly. Estab. 1993. Circ. 20,000.
Needs: African-American: children's/juvenile (10-12 years), condensed/excerpted novel, erotica, ethnic/multicultural, gay, historical (general), horror, humor/satire, literary, mystery/suspense, psychic/supernatural/occult, religious/inspirational, science fiction, young adult/teen (adventure, romance). List of upcoming themes available for SASE. Publishes special fiction issue. Receives 20-50 unsolicited mss/month. Accepts 20 mss/issue. Publishes ms 3-6 months after acceptance. Agented fiction 5%. Published work by Junot Díaz, Michel Marriott and Carol Dixon. Length: 2,000 words average; 500 words minimum; 3,000 words maximum. Occasionally publishes short shorts. Also publishes literary essays and poetry.
How to Contact: Query with clips of published work. Include short bio. Reports in 6-12 weeks depending on backlog of queries; 2-3 months on mss. Send SASE for return of ms. Simultaneous, reprint and electonic submissions OK. Sample copy for $3 and 9 × 12 SASE. Free fiction guidelines. Reviews novels and short story collections. Send books to Book Editor.
Payment/Terms: Pays $25 maximum on publication for first North American serial rights, free subscription and 5 contributor's copies.
Advice: "A manuscript stands out if it is neatly typed with a well-written and interesting story line or plot. Originality encouraged. We are interested in more horror, erotic and drama pieces. *AV* wants to highlight the diversity in our culture. Stories must touch the humanity in us all."

AIM MAGAZINE, (I, II), 7308 S. Eberhart Ave., Chicago IL 60619. (312)874-6184. Editor: Myron Apilado, EdD. Fiction Editor: Mark Boone. Newspaper: 8½ × 11; 48 pages; slick paper; photos and illustrations. "Material of social significance: down-to-earth gut. Personal experience, inspirational." For "high school, college and general public." Quarterly. Estab. 1973. Circ. 10,000.
    ● *Aim* sponsors an annual short story contest.
Needs: Open. No "religious" mss. Published special fiction issue last year; plans another. Receives 25 unsolicited mss/month. Buys 15 mss/issue; 60 mss/year. Published work by Clayton Davis, Kenneth Nunn, Charles J. Wheelan, Estelle Lurie and Jesus Diaz. Published new writers within the last year. Length: 800-1,000 words average. Publishes short shorts. Sometimes comments on rejected mss.
How to Contact: Send complete ms. Include SASE with cover letter and author's photograph. Simultaneous submissions OK. Reports in 1 month. Sample copy for $4 with SAE (9 × 12) and $1.80 postage. Fiction guidelines for #10 SASE.
Payment/Terms: Pays $15-25 on publication for first rights.
Advice: "Search for those who are making unselfish contributions to their community and write about them.

Our objective is to purge racism from the human bloodstream. Write about your own experiences. Be familiar with the background of your characters." Known for "stories with social significance, proving that people from different ethnic, racial backgrounds are more alike than they are different."

ALOHA, The Magazine of Hawaii and the Pacific, (IV), Davick Publications, P.O. Box 3260, Honolulu HI 96801. (808)593-1191. Fax: (808)593-1327. Editorial Director: Lance Tominaga. Magazine about the 50th state. Upscale demographics. Bimonthly. Estab. 1977. Circ. 75,000.
- The publisher of *ALOHA* has published a coffee table book, *The Best of ALOHA*.
Needs: "Only fiction that illuminates the true Hawaiian experience. No stories about tourists in Waikiki or contrived pidgin dialogue." Receives 6 unsolicited mss/month. Publishes ms up to 1 year after acceptance. Length: 1,000-2,000 words average.
How to Contact: Send complete ms. No simultaneous submissions. Reports in 2 months. SASE. Electronic submissions (disk-Microsoft Word format) OK. Sample copy for $2.95—include SASE (postage is $2.90).
Payment/Terms: Pays between $200-400 on publication for first rights.
Advice: "Submit only fiction that is truly local in character. Do not try to write anything about Hawaii if you have not experienced this culturally different part of America."

AMERICAN GIRL, (III), Pleasant Company Publications, 8400 Fairway Place, Middleton WI 53562. (608)836-4848. E-mail: readermail.ag.pleasantco.com. Editor: Judith Woodburn. Magazine: 8½×11; 52 pages; illustrations and photos. "Four-color bimonthly magazine for girls age 8-12." Estab. 1991. Circ. 700,000.
- Pleasant Company is known for its series of books featuring girls from different periods of American history.
Needs: Children's/juvenile (girls 8-12 years): "contemporary, realistic fiction, adventure, historical, problem stories." No romance, science fiction, fantasy. Receives 100 unsolicited mss/month. Accepts 1 ms/year. Length: 2,300 words maximum. Publishes short shorts. Also publishes literary essays and poetry (if age appropriate).
How to Contact: Query with published samples. Include bio (1 paragraph). Send SASE for reply, return of ms or send a disposable copy of ms. Simultaneous submissions OK. Sample copy for $3.95 plus $1.93 postage.
Payment/Terms: Pays in cash; amount negotiable. Pays on acceptance for first North American serial rights. Sends galleys to author.

‡AMERICAN WAY, (III), P.O. Box 619640, Dallas/Fort Worth Airport TX 75261-9640. (817)967-1804. Fax: (817)967-1571. Editor-in-Chief: John H. Ostdick. Senior Editor: Chuck Thompson. Works exclusively with published/established writers. Biweekly inflight magazine for passengers flying with American Airlines. Estab. 1966.
Needs: Publishes ms an average of 4 months after acceptance. Length: 2,500 words maximum.
How to Contact: *American Way* is only accepting fiction queries now. Reports in 5 months.
Payment/Terms: Pays $1,100. Pays on acceptance. Buys first serial rights.

ANALOG SCIENCE FICTION & FACT, (II), Dell Magazines, 1270 Avenue of the Americas, New York NY 10020. (212)698-1381. E-mail: 71154.662@compuserve.com. Editor: Stanley Schmidt. Magazine: 5³⁄₁₆×7⅞; 160 pages; illustrations (drawings); photos. "Well-written science fiction based on speculative ideas and fact articles on topics of the present and future frontiers of research. Our readership includes intelligent laymen and/or those professionally active in science and technology." Published 11 times yearly. Estab. 1930. Circ. 60,000.
- *Analog* is considered one of the leading science fiction publications. The magazine has won a number of Hugos, Chesleys and Nebula Awards.
Needs: Science fiction (hard science, soft sociological) and serialized novels. "No stories which are not truly science fiction in the sense of having a plausible speculative idea *integral to the story*. We would like to see good humor that is also good, solid science fiction. We do one double-size issue per year (July)." Receives 300-500 unsolicited fiction mss/month. Accepts 4-8 mss/issue. Agented fiction 20%. Recently published work by Paul Anderson, Ben Bova, Maya Kaathryn Bonnhoff, Jerry Oltion, Robert J. Sawyer and Timothy Zahn. Publishes 5-10 new writers/year. Length: 2,000-80,000 words. Publishes short shorts. Critiques rejected mss "when there is time." Sometimes recommends other markets.
How to Contact: Send complete ms with SASE. Include cover letter with "anything that I need to know before reading the story, e.g. that it's a rewrite I suggested or that it incorporates copyrighted material. Otherwise, no cover letter is needed." Query with SASE only on serials. Reports in 1 month on both query and ms. No simultaneous submissions. Fiction guidelines for SASE. Sample copy for $4. Reviews novels and short story collections. Send books to Tom Easton.
Payment/Terms: Pays 5-8¢/word on acceptance for first North American serial rights and nonexclusive foreign rights. Sends galleys to author.
Advice: Mss are rejected because of "inaccurate science; poor plotting, characterization or writing in general. We literally only have room for 1-2% of what we get. Many stories are rejected not because of anything conspicuously *wrong*, but because they lack anything sufficiently *special*. What we buy must stand out from the crowd. Fresh, thought-provoking ideas are important. Familiarize yourself with the magazine—but don't try to imitate what we've already published."

✣**THE ANNALS OF ST. ANNE DE BEAUPRÉ, (II)**, Redemptorist Fathers, P.O. Box 1000, St. Anne de Beaupré, Quebec G0A 3C0 Canada. (418)827-4538. Fax: (418)827-4530. Editor: Father Roch Achard, C.Ss.R. Magazine: 8×11; 32 pages; glossy paper; photos. "Our aim is to promote devotion to St. Anne and Catholic family values." Monthly. Estab. 1878. Circ. 50,000.

Needs: Religious/inspirational. "We only wish to see something inspirational, educational, objective, uplifting. Reporting rather than analysis is simply not remarkable." Receives 50-60 unsolicited mss/month. Published work by Beverly Sheresh, Eugene Miller and Aubrey Haines. Publishes short stories. Length: 1,500 maximum. Always critiques or comments on rejected ms.

How to Contact: Send complete ms with a cover letter. Include estimated word count. Reports in 3 weeks. Send SASE for reply or return of ms. No simultaneous submissions. Free sample copy and guidelines.

Payment/Terms: Pays 3-4¢/word on acceptance and 3 contributor's copies on publication for first North American serial rights.

APPALACHIA JOURNAL, (II, IV), Appalachian Mountain Club, 5 Joy St., Boston MA 02108. (617)523-0636. Editor: Sandy Stott. Magazine: 6×9; 160 pages; 50 lb. recycled paper; 10 pt. CS1 cover; 5-10 illustrations; 20-30 photographs. "*Appalachia* is the oldest mountaineering and conservation journal in the country. It specializes in backcountry recreation and conservation topics (hiking, canoeing, cross-country skiing, etc.) for outdoor (including armchair) enthusiasts." Semiannually (June and December). Estab. 1876. Circ. 13,000.

Needs: Prose, poem, sports. Receives 5-10 unsolicited mss/month. Accepts 1-2 mss/issue; 2-4 mss/year. Publishes ms 6-12 months after acceptance. Length: 500-4,000 words average. Publishes short shorts.

How to Contact: Send complete ms with cover letter. No simultaneous submissions. Reports in 1 month on queries; 3 months on mss. SASE (or IRC) for query. Sample copy for $5. Fiction guidelines for #10 SAE.

Payment/Terms: Pays contributor's copies. Occasionally pays $100-300 for a feature—usually assigned.

Advice: "All submissions should be related to conservation, mountaineering, and/or backcountry recreation both in the Northeast and throughout the world. Most of our journal is nonfiction. The fiction we publish is mountain-related and often off-beat. Send us material that says, I went to the wilderness and *thought* this; not I went there and did this."

ASIMOV'S SCIENCE FICTION, (II), 1270 Avenue of the Americas, New York NY 10020. (212)698-1313. E-mail: 71154.662@compuserve.com. Editor: Gardner Dozois. Executive Editor: Sheila Williams. Magazine: 5³⁄₁₆×7⅜ (trim size); 160 pages; 29 lb. newspaper; 70 lb. to 8 pt. C1S cover stock; illustrations; rarely photos. Magazine consists of science fiction and fantasy stories for adults and young adults. Publishes 11 issues/year (with one double issue). Estab. 1977. Circ. 50,000.

● Named for a science fiction "legend," *Asimov's* regularly receives Hugo and Nebula Awards. Editor Gardner Dozois has received several awards for editing including Hugos and those from *Locus* and *Science Fiction Chronicle* magazines.

Needs: Science fiction (hard science, soft sociological), fantasy. No horror or psychic/supernatural. Receives approximately 800 unsolicited fiction mss each month. Accepts 10 mss/issue. Publishes ms 6-12 months after acceptance. Agented fiction 10%. Recently published work by Robert Silverberg, Connie Willis and Greg Egan. Publishes 5 new writers/year. Length: up to 20,000 words. Publishes short shorts. Critiques rejected mss "when there is time."

How to Contact: Send complete ms with SASE. No simultaneous submissions. Reports in 2-3 months. Fiction guidelines for #10 SASE. Sample copy for $3.50 and 9×12 SASE. Reviews novels and short story collections. Send books to Book Reviewer.

Payment/Terms: Pays 6-8¢/word for stories up to 7,500 words; 5¢/word for stories over 12,500; $450 for stories between those limits. Pays on acceptance for first North American serial rights plus specified foreign rights, as explained in contract. Very rarely buys reprints. Sends galleys to author.

Advice: "We are looking for character stories rather than those emphasizing technology or science. New writers will do best with a story under 10,000 words. Every new science fiction or fantasy film seems to 'inspire' writers—and this is not a desirable trend. Be sure to be familiar with our magazine and the type of story we like; workshops and lots of practice help. Try to stay away from trite, cliched themes. Start in the middle of the action, starting as close to the end of the story as you possibly can. We like stories that extrapolate from up-to-date scientific research, but don't forget that we've been publishing clone stories for decades. Ideas must be fresh."

THE ASSOCIATE REFORMED PRESBYTERIAN, (II, IV), The Associate Reformed Presbyterian, Inc., 1 Cleveland St., Greenville SC 29601. (864)232-8297. Editor: Ben Johnston. Magazine: 8½×11; 32-48 pages; 50 lb. offset paper; illustrations; photos. "We are the official magazine of our denomination. Articles generally relate to activities within the denomination—conferences, department work, etc., with a few special articles that would be of general interest to readers." Monthly. Estab. 1976. Circ. 5,900.

Needs: Contemporary, juvenile, religious/inspirational, spiritual, young adult/teen. "Stories should portray Christian values. No retelling of Bible stories or 'talking animal' stories. Stories for youth should deal with resolving real issues for young people." Receives 30-40 unsolicited fiction mss/month. Accepts 1 ms/some months; 10-12 mss/year. Publishes ms within 1 year after acceptance. Published work by Lawrence Dorr, Jan Johnson and Deborah Christensen. Length: 300-750 words (children); 1,250 words maximum (youth). Sometimes critiques rejected mss.

How to Contact: Include cover letter. Reports in 6 weeks on queries and mss. Simultaneous submissions OK. Sample copy for $1.50; fiction guidelines for #10 SASE.

Payment/Terms: Pays $20-75 for first rights and contributor's copies.

Advice: "Currently we are seeking stories aimed at the 10 to 15 age group. We have an oversupply of stories for younger children."

THE ATLANTIC MONTHLY, (I, II), 77 N. Washington St., Boston MA 02114. (617)854-7700. Editor: William Whitworth. Senior Editors: Michael Curtis, Jack Beatty, Barbara Wallrass and Corby Kummer. Managing Editor: Cullen Murphy. General magazine for the college educated with broad cultural interests. Monthly. Estab. 1857. Circ. 500,000.
* Work published in *The Atlantic Monthly* has been selected for inclusion in Best American Short Stories and O. Henry Prize anthologies for 1995. The magazine was also a winner of the 1996 National Magazine Award for Fiction.

Needs: Literary and contemporary. "Seeks fiction that is clear, tightly written with strong sense of 'story' and well-defined characters." Accepts 15-18 stories/year. Receives 1,000 unsolicited fiction mss each month. Published work by Alice Munro, E.S. Goldman, Charles Baxter and T.C. Boyle; published new writers within the last year. Preferred length: 2,000-6,000 words.

How to Contact: Send cover letter and complete ms with SASE. Reports in 2 months on mss.

Payment/Terms: Pays $2,500/story on acceptance for first North American serial rights.

Advice: When making first contact, "cover letters are sometimes helpful, particularly if they cite prior publications or involvement in writing programs. Common mistakes: melodrama, inconclusiveness, lack of development, unpersuasive characters and/or dialogue."

BALLOON LIFE, The Magazine for Hot Air Ballooning, (II, IV), 2336 47th Ave., SW, Seattle WA 98116. (206)935-3649. Fax: (206)935-3326. E-mail: blnlife@scn.org. Editor: Tom Hamilton. Magazine: 8½×11; 48 pages; color, b&w photos. "Sport of hot air ballooning. Readers participate in hot air ballooning as pilots, crew, official observers at events and spectators."

Needs: Humor/satire, related to hot air ballooning. "Manuscripts should involve the sport of hot air ballooning in any aspect. Prefer humor based on actual events; fiction seldom published." Accepts 4-6 mss/year. Publishes ms within 3-4 months after acceptance. Length: 800 words minimum; 1,500 words maximum; 1,200 words average. Publishes short shorts. Length: 400-500 words. Sometimes critiques rejected mss and recommends other markets.

How to Contact: Send complete ms with cover letter that includes Social Security number. Reports in 3 weeks on queries; 2 weeks on mss. SASE. Simultaneous and reprint submissions OK. Sample copy for 9×12 SAE and $1.90 postage. Guidelines for #10 SASE.

Payment/Terms: Pays $25-75 and contributor's copies on publication for first North American serial, one-time or other rights.

Advice: "Generally the magazine looks for humor pieces that can provide a light-hearted change of pace from the technical and current event articles. An example of a work we used was titled 'Balloon Astrology' and dealt with the character of a hot air balloon based on what sign it was born (made) under."

THE BEAR ESSENTIAL MAGAZINE, (I, II), ORLO, 2516 NW 29th, P.O. Box 10342, Portland OR 97296. (503)242-1047. Fax: (503)243-2645. E-mail: orlo@teleport.com. Editor: Thomas L. Webb. Magazine: 11×14; 72 pages; newsprint paper; Kraft paper cover; illustrations and photos. "*The Bear Essential* has an environmental focus, combining all forms and styles. Fiction should have environmental thread to it and should be engaging to a cross-section of audiences. The more street-level, the better." Semiannually. Estab. 1993. Circ. 15,000.
* *The Bear Essential* was a finalist in the 1995 *Utne Reader*'s Alternative Media Awards and was granted a publishing fellowship by Literary Arts Inc.

Needs: Environmentally focused: humor/satire, literary, science fiction. "We would like to see more nontraditional forms." List of upcoming themes available for SASE. Receives 10-20 unsolicited mss/month. Accepts 2-

 INTERNATIONAL MARKETS, those located outside of the United States and Canada, are marked with an asterisk.

3 mss/issue; 4-6 mss/year. Publishes ms 2 months after acceptance. Recently published work by David James Duncan, Janet Goldberg and Frederic Murray. Length: 2,500 words average; 900 words minimum; 4,500 words maximum. Publishes short shorts. Also publishes literary essays, literary criticism, poetry, reviews, opinion, investigative journalism, interviews and creative nonfiction. Sometimes critiques or comments on rejected mss.
How to Contact: Send complete ms with a cover letter. Include estimated word count, 10 to 15-word bio, list of publications, copy on disk, if possible. Reports in 1 month on queries; 3 months on mss. Send a disposable copy of mss. Simultaneous and electronic (disk is best, then e-mail) submissions OK. Sample copy for $3, 7½ × 11 SAE and 5 first-class stamps. Fiction guidelines for #10 SASE. Reviews novels and short story collections. Send SASE for "Edward Abbey" fiction contest.
Payment/Terms: Pays free subscription to the magazine, contributor's copies and 5¢ per published word; additional copies for postage. Acquires first or one-time rights. Sends galleys to author. Not copyrighted. Sponsors contests, awards or grants for fiction writers.
Advice: "Keep sending work. Write actively and focus on the connections of man, animals, nature, etc., not just flowery descriptions. Urban and suburban environments are grist for the mill as well. Have not seen enough quality humor and irony writing. Juxtaposition of place welcome. Action and hands-on great. Not all that interested in environmental ranting and simple 'walks through the park.' Make it powerful, yet accessible to a wide audience."

BEPUZZLED, (II, IV), Lombard Marketing, Inc., 22 E. Newberry Rd., Bloomfield CT 06002. (203)769-5700. Editor: Sue Tyska. "Mystery jigsaw puzzles . . . includes short mystery story with clues contained in puzzle picture to solve the mystery for preschool, 8-12 year olds, adults." Estab. 1987.
● Most of the large bookstore chains and specialty shops carry *bePuzzled* and other mystery puzzles.
Needs: Mystery: Adventure, juvenile, mainstream, preschool, suspense, young adult—all with mystery theme. Receives 3 unsolicited fiction mss/month. Accepts 20 mss/year. Publishes ms 6-18 months after acceptance. Published work by John Lutz, Matt Christopher, Alan Robbins, Henry Slesar and Katherine Hall Page. Length: 4,000 words preferred; 3,000 words minimum; 4,000 words maximum. Sometimes recommends other markets.
How to Contact: Query for submission guidelines. Reports in 2 months. SASE. Simultaneous submissions OK. Fiction guidelines free.
Payment/Terms: Pays $200 minimum on delivery of final ms. Buys all rights.
Advice: "Thoughtful, challenging mysteries that can be concluded with the visual element of a puzzle. Many times we select certain subject matter and then send out these specifics to our pool of writers . . . List clues and red herrings. Then write the story containing supporting information. Play one of our mystery thrillers so you understand the relationship between the story and the picture."

‡BLACK BELT, (II), Rainbow Publications, Inc., 24715 Ave. Rockefeller, Valencia CA 91355. (805)257-4066. Executive Editor: Jim Coleman. Magazine: 154 pages. Emphasizes "martial arts for both practitioner and layman." Monthly. Circ. 100,000.
Needs: Martial arts-related, historical and modern-day. Buys 1-2 fiction mss/year. Publishes ms 3 months to 1 year after acceptance. Published work by Glenn Yancey. Length: 1,000-2,000 words.
How to Contact: Query first. Reports in 2-3 weeks.
Payment/Terms: Pays $100-300 on publication for first North American serial rights; retains right to republish.

BOMB MAGAZINE, (II), New Art Publications, 594 Broadway, Suite 905, New York NY 10012. (212)431-3943. Editor-in-Chief: Betsy Sussler. Senior Editor: Jennifer Berman. Magazine: 11 × 14; 104 pages; 70 lb. glossy cover; illustrations and photographs. "Artist-and-writer-edited magazine." Quarterly. Estab. 1981.
Needs: Contemporary, experimental, serialized novel. Publishes "Summer Reading" issue. Receives 40 unsolicited mss/week. Accepts 6 mss/issue; 24 mss/year. Publishes ms 3-6 months after acceptance. Agented fiction 80%. Published work by Jim Lewis, AM Homes, Sandra Cisneros and Leslie Dick. Length: 10-12 pages average. Publishes interviews.
How to Contact: Send complete ms with cover letter. Reports in 4 months on mss. SASE. Sample copy for $4.50 with $1.67 postage.
Payment/Terms: Pays $100 and contributor's copies on publication for first or one-time rights. Sends galleys to author.
Advice: "We are committed to publishing new work that commercial publishers often deem too dangerous or difficult. The problem is, a lot of young writers confuse difficult with dreadful. Read the magazine before you even think of submitting something."

‡BOSTON REVIEW, (II), Boston Critic Inc., E53-407, MIT, Cambridge MA 02139. (617)253-3642. Publisher/Editor: Joshua Cohen. "A bimonthly magazine of politics, arts and culture." Tabloid: 11 × 17; 48 pages; jet paper. Estab. 1975. Circ. 20,000.
Needs: Contemporary, ethnic, experimental, literary, prose poem, regional, translations. Receives 150 unsolicited fiction mss/month. Buys 4-6 mss/year. Publishes ms an average of 4 months after acceptance. Recently published work by Harry Mathews and W.D. Wetherell. Length: 4,000 words maximum; 2,000 words average. Occasionally critiques rejected ms.
How to Contact: Send complete ms with cover letter and SASE. "You can almost always tell professional

writers by the very thought-out way they present themselves in cover letters. But even a beginning writer should find some link between the work (its style, subject, etc.) and the publication—some reason why the editor should consider publishing it." Reports in 2-4 months. Simultaneous submissions OK (if noted). E-mail address: bostonreview@mit.edu. Sample copy for $4.50. Reviews novels and short story collections. Send books to Matthew Howard, managing editor.

Payment/Terms: Pays $50-100 and 5 contributor's copies after publication for first rights.

Advice: "I'm looking for stories that are emotionally and intellectually substantive and also interesting on the level of language. Things that are shocking, dark, lewd, comic, or even insane are fine so long as the fiction is *controlled* and purposeful in a masterly way. Subtlety, delicacy and lyricism are attractive too."

BOWHUNTER MAGAZINE, The Number One Bowhunting Magazine, (IV), Cowles Enthusiast Media Inc., 6405 Flank Dr., Harrisburg PA 17112. (717)657-9555. Fax: (717)657-9526. Founder/Editor-in-Chief: M.R. James. Associate Publisher/Editorial Director: Richard Cochran. Editor: Dwight Schuh. Magazine: 8×10½; 150 pages; 75 lb. glossy paper; 150 lb. glossy cover stock; illustrations and photographs. "We are a special interest publication for people who hunt with the bow and arrow. We publish hunting adventure and how-to stories. Our audience is predominantly male, 30-50, middle income." Bimonthly. Circ. 200,000.

● Themes included in most fiction considered for *Bowhunter* are pro-conservation as well as pro-hunting.

Needs: Bowhunting, outdoor adventure. "Writers must expect a very limited market. We buy only one or two fiction pieces a year. Writers must know the market—bowhunting—and let that be the theme of their work. No 'me and my dog' types of stories; no stories by people who have obviously never held a bow in their hands." Receives 25 unsolicited fiction mss/month. Accepts 30 mss/year. Publishes ms 3 months to 2 years after acceptance. Length: 1,500 words average; 500 words minimum; 2,000 words maximum. Publishes short shorts. Length: 500 words. Sometimes critiques rejected mss and recommends other markets.

How to Contact: Query first or send complete ms with cover letter. Reports in 2 weeks on queries; 4 weeks on mss. Sample copy for $2 and 8½×11 SAE with appropriate postage. Fiction guidelines for #10 SASE.

Payment/Terms: Pays $100-350 on acceptance for first worldwide serial rights.

Advice: "We have a resident humorist who supplies us with most of the 'fiction' we need. But if a story comes through the door which captures the essence of bowhunting and we feel it will reach out to our readers, we will buy it. Despite our macho outdoor magazine status, we are a bunch of English majors who love to read. You can't bull your way around real outdoor people—they can spot a phony at 20 paces. If you've never camped out under the stars and listened to an elk bugle and try to relate that experience without really experiencing it, someone's going to know. We are very specialized; we don't want stories about shooting apples off people's heads or of Cupid's arrow finding its mark. James Dickey's *Deliverance* used bowhunting metaphorically, very effectively . . . while we don't expect that type of writing from everyone, that's the kind of feeling that characterizes a good piece of outdoor fiction."

BOYS' LIFE, For All Boys, (II), Boy Scouts of America, Magazine Division, Box 152079, 1325 W. Walnut Hill Lane, Irving TX 75015-2079. (214)580-2366. Fiction Editor: Shannon Lowry. Magazine: 8×11; 68 pages; slick cover stock; illustrations; photos. "*Boys' Life* covers Boy Scout activities and general interest subjects for ages 8 to 18, Boy Scouts, Cub Scouts and others of that age group." Monthly. Estab. 1911. Circ. 1,300,000.

Needs: Adventure, humor/satire, mystery/suspense (young adult), science fiction, sports, western (young adult), young adult. "We publish short stories aimed at a young adult audience and frequently written from the viewpoint of a 10- to 16-year-old boy protagonist." Receives approximately 150 unsolicited mss/month. Buys 12-18 mss/year. Published work by Donald J. Sobol, Geoffrey Norman, G. Clifton Wisler and Marlys Stapelbroek; published new writers within the last year. Length: 500 words minimum; 1,500 words maximum; 1,200 words average. "Very rarely" critiques rejected ms.

How to Contact: Send complete ms with SASE. "We'd much rather see manuscripts than queries." Reports in 6-8 weeks. No simultaneous submissions. For sample copy "check your local library." Writer's guidelines available; send SASE.

Payment/Terms: Pays $750 and up ("depending on length and writer's experience with us") on acceptance for one-time rights.

Advice: "*Boys' Life* writers understand the readers. They treat them as intelligent human beings with a thirst for knowledge and entertainment. We tend to use some of the same authors repeatedly because their characters, themes, etc., develop a following among our readers. Read at least a year's worth of the magazine. You will get a feeling for what our readers are interested in and what kind of fiction we buy."

BUFFALO SPREE MAGAZINE, (II, IV), Spree Publishing Co., Inc., 4511 Harlem Rd., Buffalo NY 14226. (716)839-3405. Editor: Johanna Van De Mark. "City magazine for professional, educated and above-average income people." Quarterly. Estab. 1967. Circ. 21,000.

Needs: Adventure, contemporary, ethnic, humor, literary, philosophy, religion. No pornography. Accepts about 15 mss/issue; 60 mss/year. Length: 2,500 words maximum.

How to Contact: Send complete ms with SASE. Reports within 3-6 months. Sample copy for $2, 9×12 SASE and $2.40 postage.

Payment/Terms: Pays $80-150 and 1 contributor's copy on publication for first rights.

BUGLE, Journal of Elk and the Hunt, (II, IV), Rocky Mountain Elk Foundation, P.O. Box 8249, Missoula MT 59807-8249. (406)523-4570. Fax: (406)523-4550. Editor: Dan Crockett. Magazine: 8½×11; 114-172 pages; 55 lb. Escanaba paper; 80 lb. sterling cover; b&w, 4-color illustrations and photographs. "The Rocky Mountain Elk Foundation is a nonprofit conservation organization established in 1984 to help conserve critical habitat for elk and other wildlife. *BUGLE*, the Foundation's quarterly magazine specializes in research, stories (fiction and nonfiction), art and photography pertaining to the world of elk and elk hunting." Quarterly. Estab. 1984.
Needs: Elk-related adventure, children's/juvenile (5-9 years, 10-12 years), historical, human interest, natural history, scientific. "We would like to see more humor." Upcoming themes; "Bowhunting" and "Women in the Outdoors." Receives 10-15 unsolicited mss/month. Accepts 5 mss/issue; 18-20 mss/year. Publishes ms 6 months after acceptance. Published work by Don Burgess and Mike Logan. Length: 2,500 words preferred; 1,500 words minimum; 5,000 words maximum. Publishes short shorts. Also publishes literary essays and poetry.
How to Contact: Query first or send complete ms with a cover letter. Include estimated word count and bio (100 words). Reports in 2-4 weeks on queries; 4-6 weeks on ms. Send SASE for reply, return of ms or send a disposable copy of ms. Sample copy for $5. Writers guidelines free.
Payment/Terms: Pays 25¢/word maximum on acceptance for one-time rights.
Advice: "We accept fiction and nonfiction stories about elk that show originality, and respect for the animal and its habitat. No 'formula' outdoor writing. No how-to writing."

‡CALLIOPE, World History for Young People, (II, IV), Cobblestone Publishing, Inc., 7 School St., Peterborough NH 03458. Editor: Rosalie Baker. Department. Magazine. "*Calliope* covers world history (east/west) and lively, original approaches to the subject are the primary concerns of the editors in choosing material. For 8-14 year olds." Monthly except June, July, August. Estab. 1990. Circ. 11,000.
● Cobblestone Publishing also publishes the children's magazines *Cobblestone, Faces* and *Odyssey* listed in this book.
Needs: Material must fit upcoming theme; write for themes and deadlines. Childrens/juvenile (8-14 years). "Authentic historical and biographical fiction, adventure, retold legends, etc. relating to the theme." Send SASE for guidelines and theme list. Published after theme deadline. Length: 800 words maximum. Publishes short shorts. Also publishes poetry.
How to Contact: Query first or query with clips of published work (if new to *Calliope*). Include a brief cover letter stating estimated word count and 1-page outline explaining information to be presented, extensive bibliography of materials used. Reports in several months (if interested, response 5 months before publication date). Send SASE (or IRC) for reply (writers may send a stamped reply postcard to find out if query has been received). Sample copy for $4.50, 7½×10½ SAE and $1.05 postage. Guidelines for #10 SAE and 1 first-class stamp.
Payment/Terms: Pays 20-25¢/word.
Terms: Pays on publication for all rights.

CAMPUS LIFE MAGAZINE, (II), Christianity Today, Inc., 465 Gundersen Dr., Carol Stream IL 60188. (630)260-6200. Fax: (630)260-0114. E-mail: cledit@aol.com. Website: http://www.christianity.net/campuslife. Managing Editor: Christopher Lutes. Magazine: 8¼×11¼; 100 pages; 4-color and b&w illustrations; 4-color and b&w photos. "General interest magazine with a Christian point of view." Articles "vary from serious to humorous to current trends and issues, for high school and college age readers." Bimonthly. Estab. 1942. Circ. 100,000.
● *Campus Life* regularly receives awards from the Evangelical Press Association.
Needs: Condensed novel, humor/satire, prose poem, serialized/excerpted novel. "All submissions must be contemporary, reflecting the teen experience in the '90s. We are a Christian magazine but are *not* interested in sappy, formulaic, sentimentally religious stories. We *are* interested in well-crafted stories that portray life realistically, stories high school and college youth relate to. Nothing contradictory of Christian values. If you don't understand our market and style, don't submit." Accepts 5 mss/year. Reading and response time slower in summer. Published work by Barbara Durkin and Tracy Dalton. Published new writers within the last year. Length: 1,000-2,000 words average, "possibly longer." Publishes short shorts.
How to Contact: Query with short synopsis of work, published samples and SASE. Does not accept unsolicited mss. Reports in 4-6 weeks on queries. Sample copy for $2 and 9½×11 envelope.
Payment/Terms: Pays "generally" 15-20¢/word; 2 contributor's copies on acceptance for one-time rights.
Advice: "We print finely-crafted fiction that carries a contemporary teen (older teen) theme. First person fiction often works best. Ask us for sample copy with fiction story. Fiction communicates to our reader. We want experienced fiction writers who have something to say to or about young people without getting propagandistic."

CAPPER'S, (II), Ogden Publications, Inc. 1503 S.W. 42nd St., Topeka KS 66609-1265. (785)274-4300. Fax: (785)274-4305. E-mail: npeavler@kspress.com. Website: http://www.cappers.com (includes sample items from publication and subscription information). Editor: Nancy Peavler. Magazine: 24-48 pages; newsprint paper and cover stock; photos. A "clean, uplifting and nonsensational newspaper for families from children to grandparents." Biweekly. Estab. 1879. Circ. 250,000.
● *Capper's* is interested in longer works, 7,000 words or more. They would like to see more stories with older characters.

Needs: Serialized novels suitable for adults to seniors. "We accept novel-length stories for serialization. No fiction containing violence, sexual references or obscenity; no science fiction or mystery. We would like to see more western romance, pioneer stories." Receives 2-3 unsolicited fiction mss each month. Accepts 4-6 stories/year. Recently published work by John Forrest, Loretta Stewart-Williams and Marion K. Taylor. Published new writers within the last year. Length: 7,000 words minimum; 40,000 words maximum.

How to Contact: Send query or complete ms with SASE. Cover letter and/or synopsis helpful. Electronic submissions (disk, Mac format only) OK. Reports in 6-8 months on ms. Sample copy for $1.50.

Payment/Terms: Pays $75-400 for one-time serialization and contributor's copies (1-2 copies as needed for copyright) on acceptance for second serial (reprint) rights and one-time rights.

Advice: "Since we publish in serialization, be sure your manuscript is suitable for that format. Each segment needs to be compelling enough so the reader remembers it and is anxious to read the next installment. Please proofread and edit carefully. We've seen major characters change names partway through the manuscript."

‡CAREER FOCUS, COLLEGE PREVIEW, DIRECT AIM, JOURNEY, VISIONS, (IV), Communications Publishing Group, Inc., 106 W. 11th St., #250, Kansas City MO 64105-1806. (816)960-1988. Fax: (816)960-1989. Editor: Michelle Paige. Magazines: 70 pages; 50 lb. paper; gloss enamel cover; 8×10 or 5×7 (preferred) illustrations; camera ready photographs. *Career Focus*, "For Today's Professionals" includes career preparation, continuing education and upward mobility skills for advanced Black and Hispanic college students and college graduates. Bimonthly. *College Preview*, "For College-Bound Students" is designed to inform and motivate Black and Hispanic high school students on college preparation and career planning. *Direct Aim*, "A Resource for Career Strategies," is designed for Black and Hispanic college students. Discusses career preparation advancement and management strategies as well as life-enhancement skills. Quarterly. Circ. 600,000. *Journey*, "A Success Guide for College and Career-Bound Students" is for Asian American high school and college students who have indicated a desire to pursue higher education through college, vocational/technical or proprietary schools. Semiannually. *Visions*, "A Success Guide for Career-Bound Students" is designed for Native American students who want to pursue a higher education through college, vocational/technical or proprietary schools. Semiannually. Specialized publication limited to certain subjects or themes.

Needs: Adventure, condensed/excerpted novel, contemporary, ethnic, experimental, historical (general), humor/satire, prose poem, romance (contemporary, historical, young adult), science fiction, sports, suspense/mystery. Receives 2-3 unsolicited mss/month. Buys 2-4 mss/year. After acceptance of ms, time varies before it is published. Length: 1,000 words minimum; 4,000 words maximum. Publishes short shorts. Does not usually comment on rejected ms.

How to Contact: Query with clips of published work (include Social Security number) or send copy of resume and when available to perform. Reports in 4-6 weeks. SASE. Simultaneous and reprint submissions OK. Sample copy and fiction guidelines for 9×10 SASE.

Payment/Terms: Pays 10¢ per word on acceptance for first rights and second serial (reprint) rights.

Advice: "Today's fiction market is geared toward stories that are generated from real-life events because readers are more sophisticated and aware of current affairs. But because everyday life is quite stressful nowadays, even young adults want to escape into science fiction and fairytales. Fiction should be entertaining and easy to read. Be aware of reader audience. Material should be designed for status-conscious young adults searching for quality and excellence. Do not assume readers are totally unsophisticated and avoid casual mention of drug use, alcohol abuse or sex. Avoid overly ponderous, overly cute writing styles. We are an ethnic market so fiction cannot be obviously Anglo. Query describing the topic and length of proposed article. Include samples of published work if possible. Must be typed, double spaced on white bond paper (clean copy only)."

*CHAT, King's Reach Tower, Stamford St., London SE1 9LS England. Fiction Editor: Shelley Silas. Weekly. Circ. 550,000.

Needs: Publishes mysteries, thrillers, science fiction and romance. Publishes 1 story/issue; 1-2/Christmas issues; 4-8/Summer specials. Length: 700 words minimum; 1,000 words maximum.

How to Contact: "I accept and buy fiction from anyone, anywhere. Send material with reply coupons if you want your story returned."

Payment/Terms: Payment "negotiated with the fiction editor and made by cheque." Call or write editor for sample copy. Writer's guidelines available for SAE and IRCs.

✤CHICKADEE, The Magazine for Young Children from OWL, (II), Owl Communications, 179 John St., Suite 500, Toronto, Ontario M5T 3G5 Canada. (416)971-5275. Fax: (416)971-5294. E-mail: owlcom@owlkids.com. Website: http://www.owlkids.com. Managing Editor: Catherine Jane Wren. Editor-in-Chief: Nyla Ahmad. Magazine: 8½×11¾; 32 pages; glossy paper and cover stock; illustrations and photographs. "*Chickadee* is created to give children under nine a lively, fun-filled look at the world around them. Each issue has a mix of activities, puzzles, games and stories." Monthly except July and August. Estab. 1979. Circ. 110,000.

- *Chickadee* has won several awards including the EDPRESS Golden Lamp Honor award and the Parents' Choice Golden Seal awards.

Needs: Juvenile. No religious or anthropomorphic material. Accepts 1 ms/issue; 10 mss/year. Publishes ms an average of 1 year after acceptance. Published new writers within the last year. Length: 300-900 words.

How to Contact: Send complete ms and cover letter with $1 to cover postage and handling. Simultaneous

submissions OK. Reports in 2 months. Sample copy for $4.50. Fiction guidelines for SASE.
Payment/Terms: Pays $25-250 (Canadian); 2 contributor's copies on acceptance for all rights. Occasionally buys reprints.
Advice: "Read back issues to see what types of fiction we publish. Common mistakes include: loose, rambling, and boring prose; stories that lack a clear beginning, middle and end; unbelievable characters; and overwriting."

CHILD LIFE, (IV), Children's Better Health Institute, Box 567, 1100 Waterway Blvd., Indianapolis IN 46206. (317)636-8881. Website: www.satevepost.org/kidsonline. Editor: Lise Hoffman. Juvenile magazine for kids aged 9-11. "The publishers, after falling in love with classic *Child Life* stories reprinted during the 75th anniversary year, have decided to make nostalgia the permanent format of the magazine. The content will consist largely of reprinted stories and artwork. They will be accompanied by childrens' submissions and other features that reflect the Children's Better Health Institute's health and fitness mission. The latter will be handled in-house or assigned."

CHILDREN'S DIGEST, (II, IV), Children's Better Health Institute, P.O. Box 567, 1100 Waterway Blvd., Indianapolis IN 46206. Magazine: 6½×9; 48 pages; reflective and preseparated illustrations; color and b&w photos. Magazine with special emphasis on health, nutrition, exercise and safety for preteens.
● Other magazines published by Children's Better Health Institute and listed in this book are *Child Life*, *Children's Playmate*, *Humpty Dumpty*, *Jack and Jill* and *Turtle*. The magazine has become known for stories featuring contemporary situations and sports/fitness stories.
Needs: "Realistic stories, short plays, adventure and mysteries. Humorous stories are highly desirable. We especially need stories that *subtly* encourage readers to develop better health or safety habits. Stories should not exceed 1,500 words." Receives 40-50 unsolicited fiction mss each month. Published work by Judith Josephson, Pat McCarthy, Sharen Liddell; published new writers within the last year.
How to Contact: Send complete ms with SASE. "A cover letter isn't necessary unless an author wishes to include publishing credits and special knowledge of the subject matter." Reports in 3 months. Sample copy for $1.25. Fiction guidelines for SASE.
Payment/Terms: Pays 12¢/word minimum with up to 10 contributor's copies on publication for all rights.
Advice: "We try to present our health-related material in a positive—not a negative—light, and we try to incorporate humor and a light approach wherever possible without minimizing the seriousness of what we are saying. Fiction stories that deal with a health theme need not have health as the primary subject but should include it in some way in the course of events. Most rejected health-related manuscripts are too preachy or they lack substance. Children's magazines are not training grounds where authors learn to write 'real' material for 'real' readers. Because our readers frequently have limited attention spans, it is very important that we offer them well-written stories."

CHILDREN'S PLAYMATE, (IV), Children's Better Health Institute, P.O. Box 567, 1100 Waterway Blvd., Indianapolis IN 46206. (317)636-8881. Editor: Terry Harshman. Magazine: 6½×9; 48 pages; preseparated and reflective art; b&w and color illustrations. Juvenile magazine for children ages 6-8 years. Published 8 times/year.
● *Child Life*, *Children's Digest*, *Humpty Dumpty* *Jack and Jill* and *Turtle* magazines are also published by Children's Better Health Institute and listed in this book.
Needs: Juvenile with special emphasis on health, nutrition, safety and exercise. "Our present needs are for short, entertaining stories with a subtle health angle. Seasonal material is also always welcome." No adult or adolescent fiction. Receives approximately 150 unsolicited fiction mss each month. Published work by Batta Killion, Ericka Northrop, Elizabeth Murphy-Melas; published new writers within the last year. Length: 300-700 words.
How to Contact: Send complete ms with SASE. Indicate word count on material and date sent. Reports in 8-10 weeks. Sample copy for $1.25. Writer's guidelines for SASE.
Payment/Terms: Pays up to 17¢/word and 10 contributor's copies on publication for *all* rights.
Advice: "Stories should be kept simple and entertaining. Study past issues of the magazine—be aware of vocabulary limitations of the readers."

THE CHRISTIAN CENTURY, An Ecumenical Weekly, (I, IV), 407 S. Dearborn St., Chicago IL 60605. (312)427-5380. Fax: (312)427-1302. Editor: James Wall. Magazine: 8¼×10⅞; 24-40 pages; illustrations and photos. "A liberal Protestant magazine interested in the public meaning of Christian faith as it applies to social issues, and in the individual appropriation of faith in modern circumstances." Weekly (sometimes biweekly). Estab. 1884. Circ. 35,000.
● *Christian Century* has received several awards each year from the Associated Church Press, including: best critical review, best written humor, best feature article, etc.
Needs: Religious/inspirational: feminist, mainstream/contemporary. "We are interested in articles that touch on religious themes in a sophisticated way; we are not interested in simplistic pietistic pieces." Receives 80 unsolicited mss/month. Accepts 10% of unsolicited mss. Publishes ms 1-3 months after acceptance. Published work by Robert Drake and Madeleine Mysko. Length: 2,500 words average; 1,500 words minimum; 3,000 words maximum. Also publishes literary essays and poetry.

How to Contact: Send complete ms with a cover letter. Include bio (100 words). Reports in 1 week on queries; 1 month on mss. Send a disposable copy of ms. No simultaneous submissions. Sample copy for $3. Reviews novels and short story collections.

Payment/Terms: Pays $200 maximum and 1 contributor's copy (additional copies for $1) on publication for all rights. Sends galleys to author.

CHRISTIAN SINGLE, (II), Lifeway Press, 127 Ninth Ave. N., MSN 140, Nashville TN 37234. (615)251-2228. Editor-in-Chief: Stephen Felts. Magazine: 8½×11; 50 pages; illustrations; photographs. "We reflect the doctrine and beliefs of evangelical Christian single adults. We prefer positive, uplifting, encouraging fiction written from the single perspective." Monthly. Estab. 1979. Circ. 65,000.

Needs: Religious/inspirational. Receives 100 unsolicited ms/month. Accepts 1 ms/issue; 4-5 mss/year. Length: 600-1,200 words average. Publishes short shorts and poetry.

How to Contact: Send query with SASE. Include estimated word count and opening paragraph. Reports in 1-2 weeks on queries; 3-6 weeks on mss. Send SASE for reply, return of ms or send a disposable copy of the ms. No simultaneous submissions. Accepts reprint and electronic submissions. Sample copy for 9×12 SAE and 4 first-class stamps.

Payment/Terms: Payment is "negotiable." Pays on acceptance. Buys all rights, first rights, first North American serial rights or one-time rights.

Advice: Looks for "manuscripts that are not preachy and intended for a single audience. Write to evoke an emotion. No Pollyanna stories please. I want stories of 'real' life with 'real' people finding real answers using biblical principles. Take a lot of time to draft a well-written query letter that includes a paragraph or two of the actual piece. I can feel by the query letter what quality of an article I can expect to receive."

‡CITYCYCLE MOTORCYCLE NEWS MAGAZINE, (I, IV), Motormag Corp., P.O. Box 808, Nyalk NY 10960-0808. (914)353-MOTO. Fax: (914)353-5240. E-mail: motomag@aol.com. Editor: Mark Kalan. Magazine: tabloid; 40 pages; newsprint; illustrations and photos. Monthly magazine about motorcyling. Estab. 1990. Circ. 45,000.

Needs: "Anything about motorcycles." No "sexual fantasy." Accepts 2 mss/year. Publishes ms 2-6 months after acceptance. Length: 750-1,500 words average. Publishes short shorts. Also publishes literary essays, literary criticism and poetry. Sometimes critiques or comments on rejected mss.

How to Contact: Query with clips of published work. Reports in 4 weeks on queries. Send SASE for reply. Reprints OK. Sample copy for $3 and 9×12 SAE. Fiction guidelines for #10 SASE. Reviews novels and short story collections. Send books to editor.

Payment/Terms: Pays $10 minimum, $75 maximum on publication for one-time rights.

Advice: "Articles, stories and poetry can be about any subject, fiction or non-fiction, as long as the subject pertains to motorcycles or the world of motorcycling. Examples would include fiction or non-fiction stories about traveling cross-country on a motorcycle, biker lifestyle or perspective, motorcycling/biker humor, etc."

CLUBHOUSE, Focus on the Family, (II, III), 8605 Explorer Dr., Colorado Springs CO 80920. (719)531-3400. Editorial Consultant: Lisa Brock. Assistant Editor: Annette Brashler Bourland. Magazine: 8×11; 24 pages; illustrations and photos. Publishes literature for kids ages 8-12. "Stories must have moral lesson included. *Clubhouse* readers are 8- to 12-year-old boys and girls who desire to know more about God and the Bible. Their parents (who typically pay for the membership) want wholesome, educational material with Scriptual or moral insight. The kids want excitement, adventure, action, humor or mystery. Your job as a writer is to please both the parent and child with each article." Monthly. Estab. 1989. Circ. 100,000.

Needs: Children's/juvenile (8-12 years), religious/inspirational, young adult/teen (adventure, western). No science fiction. Receives 150 unsolicited ms/month. Accepts 3-4 mss/issue. Agented fiction 15%. Recently published work by Sigmund Brower and Nancy Rue. Length: 1,200 words average; 400 words minimum; 2,500 words maximum. "Sometimes we'll run two-part fiction."

How to Contact: Send complete ms with cover letter. Include estimated word count, bio and list of publications. Reports in 6 weeks. Send SASE for reply, return of ms or send a disposable copy of ms. Sample copy for $1.50. Fiction guidelines free.

Payment/Terms: Pays $400 maximum on acceptance and 2 contributor's copies; additional copies for $1.50. Acquires all rights, first rights, first North American serial rights or one-time rights.

Advice: Looks for "humor with a point, historical fiction featuring great Christians or Christians who lived during great times; contemporary, exotic settings; holiday material (Christmas, Thanksgiving, Easter, President's

---

LOOKING FOR A PARTICULAR GENRE? Check our Category Index for magazine and book publishers who want **Mystery/Suspense**, **Romance**, **Science Fiction & Fantasy**, **Thrillers**, **Westerns** and more!

Day); parables; fantasy (avoid graphic descriptions of evil creatures and sorcery); mystery stories; choose-your-own adventure stories and westerns. No contemporary, middle-class family settings (we already have authors who can meet these needs) or stories dealing with boy-girl relationships."

COBBLESTONE, The History Magazine for Young People, (I, II), 7 School St., Peterborough NH 03458. Editor: Margaret Chorlian. Magazine. "Historical accuracy and lively, original approaches to the subject are primary concerns of the editors in choosing material. For 8-14 year olds." Monthly (except July and August). Estab. 1979. Circ. 36,000.
  • *Cobblestone* has received Ed Press and Parent's Choice awards.
Needs: Material must fit upcoming theme; write for theme list and deadlines. Childrens/juvenile (8-14 years). "Authentic historical and biographical fiction, adventure, retold legends, etc., relating to the theme." Upcoming themes available for SASE (or IRC). Published after theme deadline. Accepts 1-2 fiction mss/issue. Length: 800 words maximum. Publishes short shorts. Also publishes poetry.
How to Contact: Query first or query with clips of published work (if new to *Cobblestone*). Include estimated word count. "Include detailed outline explaining the information to be presented in the article and bibliography of material used." Reports in several months. If interested, responds to queries 5 months before publication date. Send SASE (or IRC) for reply or send self-addressed postcard to find out if query was received. Electronic submissions (disk, Microsoft Word or MS-DOS) OK. Sample copy for $4.50, 7½×10½ SAE and $1.05 postage. Fiction guidelines for #10 SAE and 1 first-class stamp.
Payment/Terms: Pays 20-25¢/word on publication for all rights.
Advice: Writers may send $8.95 plus $3 shipping for *Cobblestone*'s index for a listing of subjects covered in back issues.

CONTACT ADVERTISING, (IV), Box 3431, Ft. Pierce FL 34948. (561)464-5447. Editor: Herman Nietzche. Magazines and newspapers. Publications vary in size, 56-80 pages. "Group of 26 erotica, soft core publications for swingers, single males, married males, gay males, transgendered and bisexual persons." Bimonthly, quarterly and monthly. Estab. 1975. Circ. combined is 2,000,000.
  • This a group of regional publications with *very* explicit sexual content, graphic personal ads, etc. Not for the easily offended.
Needs: Erotica, fantasy, swinger, fetish, gay, lesbian. Receives 8-10 unsolicited mss/month. Accepts 1-2 mss/issue; 40-50 mss/year. Publishes ms 1-3 months after acceptance. Length: 2,000 words minimum; 3,500 words maximum. Sometimes critiques rejected mss.
How to Contact: Query first, query with clips of published work or send complete ms with cover letter. Reports in 1-2 weeks on queries; 3-4 weeks on mss. SASE. Simultaneous and reprint submissions OK. Sample copy for $6. Fiction guidelines with SASE.
Payment/Terms: First submission, free subscription to magazine; subsequent submissions $25 on publication for all rights or first rights; all receive 3 contributor's copies.
Advice: "Know your grammar! Content must be of an adult nature but well within guidelines of the law. Fantasy, unusual sexual encounters, swinging stories or editorials of a sexual bend are acceptable. Read Henry Miller!"

CORNERSTONE MAGAZINE, (I, II), Cornerstone Communications, Inc., 939 W. Wilson Ave., Chicago IL 60640. (773)561-2450 ext. 2394. Fax (773)989-2076. Editor: Jon Trott. Fiction Editor: Joyce Paskewich. Magazine: 8½×11; 64 pages; 35 lb. coated matie paper; self cover; illustrations and photos. "For adults, 18-45. We publish nonfiction (essays, personal experience, religious), music interviews, current events, film and book reviews, fiction, poetry. *Cornerstone* challenges readers to look through the window of biblical reality. Known as avant-garde, yet attempts to express orthodox belief in the language of the nineties." Approx. quarterly. Estab. 1972. Circ. 38,000.
  • *Cornerstone Magazine* has won numerous awards from the Evangelical Press Association.
Needs: Ethnic/multicultural, fantasy (science fantasy), humor/satire, literary, mainstream/contemporary, religious/inspirational. Special interest in "issues pertinent to contemporary society, seen with a biblical worldview." No "pornography, cheap shots at non-Christians, unrealistic or syrupy articles." Receives 60 unsolicited mss/month. Accepts 1 mss/issue; 3-4 mss/year. Does not read mss during Christmas/New Year's week and the month of July. Published work by Dave Cheadle, C.S. Lewis and J.B. Simmonds. Length: 1,200 words average; 250 words minimum; 2,500 words maximum. Publishes short shorts. Length: 250-450 words. Also publishes literary essays, literary criticism and poetry.
How to Contact: Send complete ms. Include estimated word count, bio (50-100 words), list of publications, and name, address, phone and fax number on every item submitted. Send disposable copy of the ms. Will consider simultaneous submissions, reprints and electronic (disk or modem) submissions. Reports in up to 6 months, only on acceptance. Sample copy for 8½×11 SAE and 6 first-class stamps. Reviews novels and short story collections.
Payment/Terms: Pays 8-10¢/word maximum; also 6 contributor's copies on publication. Purchases first serial rights.
Advice: "Articles may express Christian world view but shouldn't be unrealistic or syrupy. We're looking for high-quality fiction with skillful characterization and plot development and imaginative symbolism." Looks for "mature Christian short stories, as opposed to those more fit for church bulletins. We want fiction with bite and an edge but with a Christian worldview."

COSMOPOLITAN MAGAZINE, (III), The Hearst Corp., 224 W. 57th St., New York NY 10019. (212)649-2000. Editor: Bonnie Fuller. Fiction Editor: Alison Brower. "Most novel excerpts and stories feature young, contemporary female protagonists and traditional plots, characterizations." Single career women (ages 18-34). Monthly. Circ. just under 3 million.
Needs: Adventure, contemporary, mystery and romance. Buys current novel or book excerpts and occasional short fiction. Agented fiction 98%. Published excerpts by Danielle Steel, Mario Puzo, Louise Erdrich and Lisa Scottoline.
How to Contact: Accepts submissions from agents and publishers only. Guidelines for #10 SASE. Reports in 8-10 weeks.
Payment/Terms: Open to negotiation with author's agent or publisher.

COUNTRY WOMAN, (IV), Reiman Publications, Box 643, Milwaukee WI 53201. (414)423-0100. Editor: Ann Kaiser. Managing Editor: Kathleen Pohl. Magazine: 8½×11; 68 pages; excellent quality paper; excellent cover stock; illustrations and photographs. "Articles should have a rural theme and be of specific interest to women who live on a farm or ranch, or in a small town or country home, and/or are simply interested in country-oriented topics." Bimonthly. Estab. 1971.
Needs: Fiction must be upbeat, heartwarming and focus on a country woman as central character. "Many of our stories and articles are written by our readers!" Published work by Edna Norrell, Millie Thomas Kearney and Rita Peterson. Published new writers within last year. Publishes 1 fiction story/issue. Length: 1,000 words.
How to Contact: Send $2 and SASE for sample copy and writer's guidelines. All manuscripts should be sent to Kathy Pohl, Managing Editor. Reports in 2-3 months. Include cover letter and SASE. Simultaneous and reprint submissions OK.
Payment/Terms: Pays $90-125 on acceptance for one-time rights.
Advice: "Read the magazine to get to know our audience. Send us country-to-the-core fiction, not yuppie-country stories—our readers know the difference! Very traditional fiction—with a definite beginning, middle and end, some kind of conflict/resolution, etc. We do not want to see contemporary avant-garde fiction—nothing dealing with divorce, drugs, etc., or general societal malaise of the '90s."

CREATIVE KIDS, (I, IV), Prufrock Press, P.O. Box 8813, Waco TX 76714-8813. (800)998-2208. Fax: (800)240-0333. E-mail: creative_kids@prufrock.com. Website: http://www.prufrock.com (includes catalog, submission guidelines and information about our staff). Editor: Libby Lindsey. Magazine: 7×10½; 36 pages; illustrations; photos. Material by children for children. Published 4 times/year. Estab. 1980. Circ: 45,000.
 • *Creative Kids* featuring work by children has won Edpress and Parents' Choice Gold and Silver Awards.
Needs: "We publish work by children ages 8-14." Publishes short stories, essays, games, puzzles, poems, opinion pieces and letters. Accepts 3-4 mss/issue; 12-16 mss/year. Publishes ms up to 2 years after acceptance. Published new writers within the last year. No novels.
How to Contact: Send complete ms with cover letter, include name, age, birthday, home address, school name and address, grade, statement of originality signed by teacher or parent. Must include SASE for response. Do not query. Reports in 1 month on mss. SASE. No simultaneous submissions. Sample copy for $3. Guidelines for SASE.
Payment/Terms: Pays 1 contributor's copy. Acquires all rights.
Advice: "*Creative Kids* is designed to entertain, stimulate and challenge the creativity of children ages 8 to 14, encouraging their abilities and helping them to explore their ideas, opinions and world. We would like more opinion pieces."

CRICKET MAGAZINE, (II), Carus Corporation, P.O. Box 300, Peru IL 61354. (815)224-6656. Editor-in-Chief: Marianne Carus. Magazine: 8×10; 64 pages; illustrations; photos. Magazine for children, ages 9-14. Monthly. Estab. 1973. Circ. 83,000.
 • *Cricket* has received a Parents Choice Award, a Paul A. Witty Short Story Award and awards from Edpress.
Needs: Adventure, contemporary, ethnic, fantasy, historic fiction, folk and fairytales, humorous, juvenile, mystery, science fiction and translations. No adult articles. All issues have different "mini-themes." Receives approximately 1,100 unsolicited fiction mss each month. Publishes ms 6-24 months or longer after acceptance. Accepts 180 mss/year. Agented fiction 1-2%. Published work by Peter Dickinson, Mary Stolz and Jane Yolen. Published new writers within the last year. Length: 500-2,000 words.
How to Contact: Do not query first. Send complete ms with SASE. List previous publications. Reports in 3 months on mss. Sample copy for $4; guidelines for SASE.
Payment/Terms: Pays up to 25¢/word; 2 contributor's copies; $2 charge for extras on publication for first rights. Sends edited mss for approval. Buys reprints.
Advice: "Do not write *down* to children. Write about well-researched subjects you are familiar with and interested in, or about something that concerns you deeply. Children *need* fiction and fantasy. Carefully study several issues of *Cricket* before you submit your manuscript." Sponsors contests for readers of all ages.

‡CRUSADER MAGAZINE, (II), Calvinist Cadet Corps, Box 7259, Grand Rapids MI 49510. (616)241-5616. Fax: (616)241-5558. Editor: G. Richard Broene. Magazine: 8½×11; 24 pages; 50 lb. white paper and cover stock; illustrations; photos. Magazine to help boys ages 9-14 discover how God is at work in their lives and in the world around them. 7 issues/year. Estab. 1958. Circ. 12,000.

• *Crusader Magazine* won an Award of Merit in the Youth Category from the Evangelical Press Association in 1995. The magazine is noted for getting the message across with humor.

Needs: Adventure, comics, juvenile, religious/inspirational, spiritual and sports. List of upcoming themes available for SASE. Receives 60 unsolicited fiction mss/month. Buys 3 mss/issue; 18 mss/year. Publishes ms 4-11 months after acceptance. Published work by Sigmund Brouwer, Douglas DeVries and Betty Lou Mell. Length: 800 words minimum; 1,500 words maximum. Publishes short shorts.

How to Contact: Send complete ms and SASE with cover letter including theme of story. Reports in 4-8 weeks. Simultaneous and previously published submissions OK. Sample copy with a 9×12 SAE and 3 first-class stamps. Fiction guidelines for #10 SASE.

Payment/Terms: Pays 2-5¢/word and 1 contributor's copy. Pays on acceptance for one-time rights. Buys reprints.

Advice: "On a cover sheet, list the point your story is trying to make. Our magazine has a theme for each issue, and we try to fit the fiction to the theme. All fiction should be about a young boy's interests—sports, outdoor activities, problems—with an emphasis on a Christian multiracial perspective. No simple moralisms. Avoid simplistic answers to complicated problems."

DIALOGUE, A World of Ideas for Visually Impaired People of All Ages, (I, II), Blindskills Inc., P.O. Box 5181, Salem OR 97304-0181. (800)860-4224. (503)581-4224. Fax: (503)581-0178. E-mail: blindskl@telepo rt.com. Editor/Publisher: Carol McCarl. Magazine: 9×11; 130 pages; matte stock. Publishes information of general interest to visually impaired. Quarterly. Estab. 1961. Circ. 15,000.

Needs: Contemporary, humor/satire, literary, mainstream, senior citizen/retirement. No erotica, religion, confessional or experimental. Receives approximately 10 unsolicited fiction mss/month. Accepts 3 mss/issue, 12 mss/year. Publishes ms an average of 6 months after acceptance. Published work by Kim Rush, Diana Braun and Eric Cameron. Published new writers within the last year. Length: 1,000 words average; 500 words minimum; 1,300 words maximum. Publishes short shorts. Occasionally critiques rejected mss. Sometimes recommends other markets. "We give top priority to blind or visually impaired (legally blind) authors."

How to Contact: Query first or send complete ms with SASE. Also send statement of visual disability. Reports in 2 weeks on queries; 6 weeks on mss. Reprint submissions OK. Accepts electronic submissions on disk; IBM and compatible; Word Perfect 5.1 or 6.0 preferred. Sample copy for $6 and #10 SAE with 1 first-class stamp. Fiction guidelines free.

Payment/Terms: Pays $5-25 and contributor's copy on acceptance for first rights.

Advice: "We prefer contemporary problem stories in which the protagonist solves his or her own problem. We are looking for strongly-plotted stories with definite beginnings, climaxes and endings. Characters may be blind, sighted or visually in-between. Because we want to encourage any writer who shows promise, we may return a story for revision when necessary."

DISCOVERIES, (II), WordAction Publishing Company, 6401 The Paseo, Kansas City MO 64131. (816)333-7000 ext. 2359. Fax: (816)333-4439. Contact: Assistant Editor. Story paper: 8½×11; 4 pages; illustrations. "Committed to reinforce the Bible concept taught in Sunday School curriculum, for ages 8-10 (grades 3-4)." Weekly.

Needs: Religious, puzzles, Bible trivia, 100-200 words. "Avoid fantasy, science fiction, personification of animals and cultural references that are distinctly American." Accepts 1-2 stories and 1-2 puzzles/issue. Publishes ms 1-2 years after acceptance. Publishes 5-10 new writers/year. Length: 500 words.

How to Contact: Send complete ms with cover letter and SASE. Send SASE for sample copy and guidelines.

Payment/Terms: Pays 5¢/word for multiple rights on acceptance or on publication.

Advice: "Stories should vividly portray definite Christian emphasis or character building values, without being preachy."

ELLERY QUEEN'S MYSTERY MAGAZINE, (II), Dell Magazines, 1270 Avenue of the Americas, New York NY 10020. (212)698-1313. Editor: Janet Hutchings. Magazine: digest-sized; 160 pages with special 288-page combined September/October issue. Magazine for lovers of mystery fiction. Published 11 times/year. Estab. 1941. Circ. 500,000 readers.

• *EQMM* has won numerous awards and sponsors its own award for Best Stories of the Year, nominated by its readership.

Needs: "We accept only mystery, crime, suspense and detective fiction." Receives approximately 400 unsolicited fiction mss each month. Accepts 10-15 mss/issue. Publishes ms 6-12 months after acceptance. Agented fiction 50%. Published work by Peter Lovesey, Anne Perry, Marcia Muller and Ruth Rendell. Published new writers within the last year. Length: up to 7,000 words, occasionally longer. Publishes 1-2 short novels of up to 17,000 words/year by established authors; minute mysteries of 250 words; short, humorous mystery verse. Critiques rejected mss "only when a story might be a possibility for us if revised." Sometimes recommends other markets.

How to Contact: Send complete ms with SASE. Cover letter should include publishing credits and brief

biographical sketch. Simultaneous submissions OK. Reports in 3 months or sooner on mss. Fiction guidelines with SASE. Sample copy for $2.95.
Payment/Terms: Pays 3¢/word and up on acceptance for first North American serial rights. Occasionally buys reprints.
Advice: "We have a Department of First Stories and usually publish at least one first story an issue—i.e., the author's first published fiction. We select stories that are fresh and of the kind our readers have expressed a liking for. In writing a detective story, you must play fair with the reader, providing clues and necessary information. Otherwise you have a better chance of publishing if you avoid writing to formula."

EMPHASIS ON FAITH AND LIVING, (IV), Missionary Church, Inc., P.O. Box 9127, Fort Wayne IN 46899-9127. (219)747-2027. Fax: (219)747-5331. Editor: Robert L. Ransom. Magazine: 8½×11; 16 pages; offset paper; illustrations and photos. "Religious/church oriented." Bimonthly. Estab. 1969. Circ. 14,000.
Needs: Religious/inspirational. Receives 10-15 unsolicited mss/month. Accepts 2 mss/year. Publishes ms 3-6 months after acceptance. Published work by Debra Wood and Denise George. Length: 500 words average; 200 words minimum; 1,000 words maximum. Publishes short shorts. Length: 200-250 words.
How to Contact: Send complete ms with a cover letter. Include estimated word count, bio and Social Security number. Reports in 2-3 months on mss. Send SASE for reply, return of ms or send a disposable copy of ms. Simultaneous reprint and electronic submissions OK. Sample copy for 9×12 SAE.
Payment/Terms: Pays $10-50 and 5 contributor's copies on publication.

ESQUIRE, The Magazine for Men, (III), Hearst Corp., 250 W. 55th St., New York NY 10019. (212)649-4020. Editor: Edward Kosner. Fiction Editors: Will Blythe and Rust Hills. Magazine. Monthly. Estab. 1933. Circ. 750,000. General readership is college educated and sophisticated, between ages 30 and 45.
• *Esquire* is well-respected for its fiction and has received several National Magazine Awards. Work published in *Esquire* has been selected for inclusion in the *Best American Short Stories* anthology.
Needs: No "pornography, science fiction or 'true romance' stories." Publishes special fiction issue in July. Receives "thousands" of unsolicited mss/year. Rarely accepts unsolicited fiction. Published work by Cormac McCarthy, Richard Ford, Robert Stone, Martin Amis, Don DeLillo, Mark Helprin and Will Self.
How to Contact: Send complete ms with cover letter or submit through an agent. Simultaneous submissions OK. Fiction guidelines for SASE.
Payment/Terms: Pays in cash on acceptance, amount undisclosed. Publishes ms an average of 2 months after acceptance.
Advice: "Submit one story at a time. Worry a little less about publication, a little more about the work itself."

EVANGEL, (I, II, IV), Light & Life Communications, P.O. Box 535002, Indianapolis IN 46253-5002. (317)244-3660. Editor: Julie Innes. Sunday school take-home paper for distribution to adults who attend church. Fiction involves couples and singles coping with everyday crises, making decisions that show growth. Magazine: 5½×8½; 8 pages; 2- and 4-color illustrations; color and b&w photos. Weekly. Estab. 1897. Circ. 22,000.
Needs: Religious/inspirational. "No fiction without any semblance of Christian message or where the message clobbers the reader." Receives approximately 300 unsolicited fiction mss/month. Accepts 3-4 mss/issue, 156-200 mss/year. Recently published work by Karen Leet and Dennis Hensley. 40% of work published is by new writers. Length: 1,000-1,200 words.
How to Contact: Send complete ms with SASE. Reports in 2 months. Electronic submissions (3½ inch disk-WordPerfect) OK; send hard copy with disk. Sample copy and writer's guidelines with #10 SASE.
Payment/Terms: Pays 4¢/word and 2 contributor's copies on publication; charge for extras.
Advice: "Choose a contemporary situation or conflict and create a good mix for the characters (not all-good or all-bad heroes and villains). Don't spell out everything in detail; let the reader fill in some blanks in the story. Keep him guessing." Rejects mss because of "unbelievable characters and predictable events in the story."

FACES, People, Places, Culture, A Cobblestone Publication, (II, IV), Cobblestone Publishing, Inc., 7 School St., Peterborough NH 03458. (603)924-7209. Fax: (603)924-7380. Managing Editor: Denise Babcock. Magazine. *Faces* is a magazine about people and places in the world for 8-14 year olds. Estab. 1984. Circ. 15,000. Monthly, except June, July and August.
Needs: All material must relate to theme; send for theme list. Children's/juvenile (8-14 years), "retold legends, folk tales, stories from around the world, etc., relating to the theme." Length: 800 words preferred. Publishes short shorts.
How to Contact: Query first or query with clips of published work (send query 6-9 months prior to theme issue publication date). Include estimated word count and bio (2-3 lines). Reports 4 months before publication date. Send SASE for reply. Sample copy for $4.50, 7½×10½ SAE and $1.05 postage. Fiction guidelines for SASE.
Payment/Terms: Pays 20-25¢/word on publication for all rights.

FIRST HAND, Experiences for Loving Men, (II, IV), First Hand Ltd., Box 1314, Teaneck NJ 07666. (201)836-9177. Fax: (201)836-5055. E-mail: firsthand3@aol.com. Editor: Bob Harris. Magazine: digest size; 130 pages; illustrations. "Half of the magazine is made up of our readers' own gay sexual experiences. Rest is fiction and columns devoted to health, travel, books, etc." Publishes 13 times/year. Estab. 1980. Circ. 60,000.

• First Hand Ltd. also publishes *Guys* and *Manscape*, listed in this book.

Needs: Erotica, gay. "Should be written in first person." No science fiction or fantasy. Erotica should detail experiences based in reality. Receives 75-100 unsolicited mss/month. Accepts 6 mss/issue; 72 mss/year. Publishes ms 9-18 months after acceptance. Length: 3,000 words preferred; 2,000 words minimum; 3,750 words maximum. Sometimes critiques rejected mss.

How to Contact: Send complete ms with cover letter. Include name, address, telephone and Social Security number and "advise on use of pseudonym if any. Also whether selling all rights or first North American rights." No simultaneous submissions. Reports in 1-2 months. SASE. Sample copy for $5. Fiction guidelines for #10 SASE.

Payment/Terms: Pays $100-150 on publication for all rights or first North American serial rights.

Advice: "Avoid the hackneyed situations. Be original. We like strong plots."

FLORIDA WILDLIFE, (IV), Florida Game & Fresh Water Fish Commission, 620 S. Meridian St., Tallahassee FL 32399-1600. (850)488-5563. Fax: (850)488-1961. Website: http://www.state.Fl.us/gfc/gfchome. Editor: Dick Sublette. Associate Editor: Frank H. Adams. Magazine: 8½×11; 32 pages. "Conservation-oriented material for an 'outdoor' audience." Bimonthly. Estab. 1947. Circ. 26,000.

• *Florida Wildlife* received the Governor's Environmental Communication Award in 1994 and it received the Florida Magazine Association and Association of Conservation Information awards.

Needs: Adventure, sports. "Florida-related adventure or natural history only. We rarely publish fiction." Accepts 24 mss/year. Length: 1,200 words average; 500 words minimum; 2,000 words maximum.

How to Contact: Send complete ms, double spaced, with cover letter including Social Security number. "We prefer to review article. Response time varies with amount of material on hand." Sample copy for $3.50. Will send writer's guidelines and how to submit memo upon request.

Payment/Terms: Pays minimum of $50 per published page on publication for one-time rights.

Advice: "Send your best work. It must *directly* concern Florida wildlife."

*FORUM, Northern and Shell Tower, Box 381, City Harbour, London E14 9GL England. E-mail: ecoldwell@nor shellco.uk. Fiction Editor: Elizabeth Coldwell. Circ. 30,000. Publishes 26 stories/year.

Needs: "*Forum* is the international magazine of human relations, dealing with all aspects of relationships, sexuality and sexual health. We are looking for erotic stories in which the plot and characterization are as important as the erotic content. Detailed descriptions of sexual encounters are often very erotic, but *Forum* is also concerned with the art of fiction. Try hard to avoid 'The Norm', wherein the narrator, who typically 'never used to believe those stories in magazines' suddenly and implausibly encounters their dream sexual partner at the door saying they have come to borrow a cup of sugar/mend the video/ask directions; and promptly bonks their lights out." Length: 2,000-3,000 words.

How to Contact: "Try not to ask for the manuscript to be returned, just a letter of acceptance/rejection as this saves on your return postage. Anything which is very 'American' in language or content might not be as interesting to readers outside America."

Payment/Terms: Pays £125 plus contributor's copy. "Writers can obtain a sample copy by saying they saw our listing."

THE FRIEND MAGAZINE, (II), The Church of Jesus Christ of Latter-day Saints, 50 E. North Temple, 23rd Floor, Salt Lake City UT 84150. (801)240-2210. Editor: Vivian Paulsen. Magazine: 8½×10½; 50 pages; 40 lb. coated paper; 70 lb. coated cover stock; illustrations; photos. Publishes for 3-11 year-olds. Monthly. Estab. 1971. Circ. 275,000.

Needs: Children's/juvenile: adventure, ethnic, some historical, humor, mainstream, religious/inspirational, nature. Length: 1,000 words maximum. Publishes short shorts. Length: 250 words.

How to Contact: Send complete ms. "No query letters please." Reports in 6-8 weeks. SASE. Sample copy for $1.50 with 9½×11 SAE and four 32¢ stamps.

Payment/Terms: Pays 9-13¢/word on acceptance for all rights.

Advice: "The *Friend* is particularly interested in stories with substance for tiny tots. Stories should focus on character-building qualities and should be wholesome without moralizing or preaching. Boys and girls resolving conflicts is a theme of particular merit. Since the magazine is circulated worldwide, the *Friend* is interested in stories and articles with universal settings, conflicts, and character. Other suggestions include rebus, picture, holiday, sports, and photo stories, or manuscripts that portray various cultures. Very short pieces (up to 250 words) are desired for younger readers and preschool children. Appropriate humor is a constant need."

---

‡   **THE DOUBLE DAGGER** before a listing indicates that the listing is new in this edition. New markets are often the most receptive to submissions by new writers.

THE GEM, (II), Churches of God, General Conference, Box 926, Findlay OH 45839. (419)424-1961. E-mail: cggc@bright.net. Website: http://www.rareyroth.com/cggc. Editor: Evelyn Sloat. Magazine: 6×9; 8 pages; 50 lb. uncoated paper; illustrations (clip art). "True-to-life stories of healed relationships and growing maturity in the Christian faith for senior high students through senior citizens who attend Churches of God, General Conference Sunday Schools." Weekly. Estab. 1865. Circ. 7,000.

Needs: Adventure, humor, mainstream, religious/inspirational, senior citizen/retirement. Nothing that denies or ridicules standard Christian values. Prefers personal testimony or nonfiction short stories. Receives 30 unsolicited fiction mss/month. Accepts 1 ms every 2-3 issues; 20-25 mss/year. Publishes ms 4-12 months after submission. Published work by Betty Steele Everett, Todd Lee and Betty Lou Mell. Length: 1,500 words average; 500 words minimum; 1,700 words maximum.

How to Contact: Send complete ms with cover letter ("letter not essential, unless there is information about author's background which enhances story's credibility or verifies details as being authentic"). Reports in 6 months. SASE. Simultaneous and reprint submissions OK. Sample copy and fiction guidelines for #10 SASE. "If more than one sample copy is desired along with the guidelines, will need 2 oz. postage."

Payment/Terms: Pays $10-15 and contributor's copies on publication for one-time rights. Charge for extras (postage for mailing more than one).

Advice: "Competition at the mediocre level is fierce. There is a dearth of well-written, relevant fiction which wrestles with real problems involving Christian values applied to the crisis times and 'passages' of life. Humor which puts the daily grind into a fresh perspective and which promises hope for survival is also in short supply. Write from your own experience. Avoid religious jargon and stereotypes. Conclusion must be believable in terms of the story—don't force a 'Christian' ending. Avoid simplistic solutions to complex problems. Listen to the storytelling art of Garrison Keillor. Feel how very particular experiences of small town life in Minnesota become universal."

GENT, (II), Dugent Publishing Corp., 14411 Commerce Way, Suite 420, Miami Lakes FL 33016. (305)557-0071. Editor: Bruce Arthur. "Men's magazine designed to have erotic appeal for the reader. Our publications are directed to a male audience, but we do have a certain percentage of female readers. For the most part, our audience is interested in erotically stimulating material, but not exclusively." Monthly. Estab. 1959. Circ. 175,000.

Needs: Erotica: contemporary, science fiction, horror, mystery, adventure, humor. *Gent* specializes in "D-Cup cheesecake," and fiction should be slanted accordingly. "Most of the fiction published includes several sex scenes. No fiction that concerns children, religious subjects or anything that might be libelous." Receives 30-50 unsolicited fiction mss/month. Accepts 2 mss/issue; 26 mss/year. Publishes ms an average of 3 months after acceptance. Agented fiction 10%. Published new writers within the last year. Length: 2,000-3,500 words. Critiques rejected mss "when there is time."

How to Contact: Send complete ms with SASE. Reports in 1 month. Sample copy for $7. Fiction guidelines for #10 SASE.

Payment/Terms: Pays minimum $200 on publication and 1 contributor's copy for first North American serial rights.

Advice: "Since *Gent* magazine is the 'Home of the D-Cups,' stories and articles containing either characters or themes with a major emphasis on large breasts will have the best chance for consideration. Study a sample copy first." Mss are rejected because "there are not enough or ineffective erotic sequences, plot is not plausible, wrong length, or not slanted specifically for us."

GEORGIA JOURNAL, (I, IV), The Indispensable Atlanta Co. Inc., P.O. Box 1604, Decatur GA 30031-1604. (404)377-4275. Fax: (404)377-1820. E-mail: georgiajournal@compuserve.com. Editor: David R. Osier. Magazine: 8½×11; 80 pages; free sheet paper; 60 lb. cover stock; photographs. Stories must have Georgia themes or settings. Bimonthly. Estab. 1980. Circ. 40,000.

Needs: Adventure, condensed/excerpted novel, regional. List of upcoming themes available for SASE. Receives 12 unsolicited mss/month. Accepts 3 mss/year. Publishes ms 6 months after acceptance. Published work by Paul Hemphill, Ferrol Sams and Terry Kay. Length: 5,000 words average; 2,500 words minimum; 6,000 words maximum. Also publishes literary essays, literary criticism, poetry. Often critiques or comments on rejected mss.

How to Contact: Query first or query with clips of published work. Include estimated word count, 1-page bio, Social Security number, list of publications. Reports on queries/mss in 2 months. Send SASE for reply, return of ms or send a disposable copy of ms. Reprint and electronic submissions OK. Sample copy for $5. Reviews novels and short story collections.

Payment/Terms: Pays $150-500 on publication. Acquires first rights, first North American serial rights and one-time rights.

Advice: Looks for "strong point of view and well-defined beginning, middle and end with well-defined characters. Avoid passive voice."

‡GOLD AND TREASURE HUNTER, (II), 27 Davis Rd., P.O. Box 47, Happy Camp CA 96039. (916)493-2029. E-mail: goldgold@snowcrest.net. Editor: Dave McCracken. Fiction Editor: Marcie Stumpf. Magazine: 8×10⅞; 56 pages; 40 lb. coated #5 paper; 70 lb. Westvaco Marva cover; pen-and-ink illustrations; photographs. "Recreational and small-scale gold mining, treasure and relic hunting. All stories must be related to these topics. For recreational hobbyists, adventure loving, outdoor people." Bimonthly. Estab. 1988. Circ. 50,000.

● *Gold and Treasure Hunter* was awarded the *BONE* "Prospecting Magazine of the Year" the last two years in a row. They are currently overstocked with fiction.

Needs: Adventure, experimental, historical, humor, mystery/suspense, senior citizen/retirement. "Subject-related futuristic stories OK, but not sci-fi. No erotica, gay, lesbian--absolutely no 'cussing!' " Buys 1-2 mss/issue; 6-16 mss/year. Publishes ms 6-8 months after acceptance. Published work by Ken Hodgson and Michael Clark. Length: 1,500 words preferred; 500 words minimum; 2,000 words maximum. Publishes short shorts. Length: 400-500 words. Sometimes critiques or comments on rejected mss.

How to Contact: Send complete ms with cover letter. Include Social Security number, "brief outline of the story and something about the author." Reports in 4-6 weeks on queries; 8-10 weeks on mss. SASE for mss. "When submitting fiction material, please include any photos or illustrations available to enhance the story." Macintosh formatted 3.5 and IBM compatible 5.25 or 3.5 disks, along with computer printout, are also acceptable. Sample copy for $3.50 (U.S.), $4.50 (Canada). Free fiction guidelines.

Payment/Terms: Pays 3¢/word and contributor's copy on publication for all rights. "We reserve the right to republish any of our previously-published and paid for material inside our Internet publication, *Wonderful World of Gold and Treasure Hunting*. Any material which we publish on the Internet that has not yet been printed in our magazine will be paid at a rate of 2¢/word and $10/photo used, with the balance of magazine rates to be paid if and when the same material, or a portion of it, is published in the printed magazine."

Advice: Looks for "as always, quality writing. We can edit small changes but the story has to grab us. Our readers love 'real life' fiction. They love exploring the 'that could happen' realm of a good fiction story. Keep your story geared to gold mining or treasure hunting. Know something about your subject so the story doesn't appear ridiculous. Don't try to dazzle readers with outlandish adjectives and keep slang to a minimum." Sponsors fiction contest—look for rules in upcoming issues.

GOLF JOURNAL, (II), United States Golf Assoc., Golf House, P.O. Box 708, Far Hills NJ 07931-0708. (908)234-2300. Fax: (908)781-1112. Editor: Brett Avery. Managing Editor: Rich Skyzinski. Magazine: 48-56 pages; self cover stock; illustrations and photos. "The magazine's subject is golf—its history, lore, Rules, equipment and general information. The focus is on amateur golf and those things applying to the millions of American golfers. Our audience is generally professional, highly literate and knowledgeable; they read *Golf Journal* because of an interest in the game, its traditions, and its noncommercial aspects." Published 9 times/year. Estab. 1948. Circ. 600,000.

Needs: Poignant or humorous essays and short stories. "Golf jokes will not be used." Accepts 12 mss/year. Published new writers within the last year. Length: 1,000-2,000 words. Recommends other markets.

How to Contact: Send complete ms with SASE. Reports in 2 months on mss. Sample copy for SASE.

Payment/Terms: Pays $500-1,000 on acceptance and 5 contributor's copies.

Advice: "Know your subject (golf); familiarize yourself first with the publication." Rejects mss because "fiction usually does not serve the function of *Golf Journal*, which, as the official magazine of the United States Golf Association, deals chiefly with the history, lore and Rules of Golf."

GOOD HOUSEKEEPING, (II), 959 Eighth Ave., New York NY 10019. Contact: Fiction Editor. "It is now our policy that all submissions of unsolicited fiction received in our offices will be read and, if found to be unsuitable for us, destroyed by recycling. If you wish to introduce your work to us, you will be submitting material that will not be critiqued or returned. The odds are long that we will contact you to inquire about publishing your submission or to invite you to correspond with us directly, so please be sure before you take the time and expense to submit it that it is our type of material."

Advice: "We welcome short fiction submissions (1,000-3,000 words). We look for stories with strong emotional interest—stories revolving around, for example, courtship, romance, marriage, family, friendships, personal growth, coming of age. The best way to gauge whether your story might be appropriate for us is to read the fiction in several of our recent issues. (We are sorry but we cannot furnish sample copies of the magazine.) We prefer double-spaced, typewritten (or keyboarded) manuscripts, accompanied by a short cover letter listing any previous writing credits. (We're sorry, but no e-mailed or faxed submissions will be accepted.) Make sure that your name and address appear on the manuscript and that you retain a copy for yourself."

GRAND TIMES, Exclusively for Active Retirees, (I, II), 403 Village Dr., El Cerrito CA 94530-3355. (510)527-4337. Website: http://www.grandtimes.com (includes recent and past articles and writer's guidelines). Editor: Kira Albin. Magazine: 8½×11; 40 pages; illustrations and photographs. "All items must be upbeat in tone and written on subjects of interest to an older audience (60+), but don't necessarily have to be about older people. Clarity should be the hallmark, and humor is always welcome. Please do not submit articles that have a newspaper format where seniors are referred to as 'them' or as a statistical group." Bimonthly. Estab. 1992. Circ. 45,000.

Needs: Senior citizen/retirement: adventure, historical (general), humor/satire, mainstream/contemporary, mystery/suspense (mature adult), romance (mature adult), sports. "All pieces should be of special interest to readers aged 60+." Receives 60-80 unsolicited mss/month. Accepts 1 ms/issue; 6-8 mss/year. Publishes ms 1-12 months after acceptance. Published work by Marie Sadro, Mike Lipstock and Richard Kerckhoff. Length: 800-1,200 average; 250 words minimum; 1,700 words maximum.

How to Contact: "It is recommended that manuscripts be submitted only after obtaining Writers' Guidelines."

Send complete ms with a cover letter. No queries. Include estimated word count and very short bio. Reports in 3 months on mss. SASE for return of ms or send a disposable copy of ms. Must send SASE for editor's reply. Simultaneous and reprint submissions OK. Sample copy for $2. Writers' guidelines for #10 SASE.

Payment/Terms: Pays 1 contributor's copy. "The amount of additional payment is dependent on subject matter, quality and length. Average payment is $10-35/ms." Pays on acceptance for one-time rights.

Advice: "The characters or plot need to have some relevance to active retirees. Writing should be creative and original but not disorganized and unfocused. Please no more pat romance or mystery stories—we want something different. Beware of any condescension, ageism or stereotyping." *Please* obtain Writers' Guidelines before making a submission.

GREEN EGG, A Journal of the Awakening Earth, (IV), Church of All Worlds, Box 1542, Ukiah CA 95482. (707)984-7062. Fax: (707)984-7063. E-mail: gemagazine@aol.com (general business); maerian@aol.com (to the editor). Editor: Maerian "Sun" Morris. Magazine: 8½×11; 76 pages; recycled paper; 4-color glossy cover; b&w illustrations; and photographs. "Magical fantasy, ecological, historical having to do with pagan civilizations." Bimonthly. Estab. 1968. Circ. 12,000.

• *Green Egg* has won both Gold and Bronze awards from the Wiccan Pagan Press Alliance including a Gold Award in 1994 for Best Publication.

Needs: Erotica, ethnic/multicultural, experimental, fantasy (science fantasy), historical, humor/satire, psychic/supernatural/occult, religious/inspirational (pagan). "No porn, sports, western, evil and painful." Upcoming themes: "Druids" (January-February), "Science Fiction" (March-April), "Modern Primitives" (May-June), "Native Americans" (July-August), "Witchcraft" (September-October). Receives 15-18 unsolicited mss/month. Accepts 30 mss/year. Published work by Luisah Teish, Robert Anton Wilson, Deana Metzger and Annie Sprinkle. Length: 600 words minimum; 3,000 words maximum. Publishes short shorts. Length: 500 words. Also publishes poetry. Sometimes critiques or comments on rejected mss.

How to Contact: Send complete ms with cover letter. Should include estimated word count and bio (1 paragraph—50 words). Reports in 2 months. Send SASE for reply, return of ms or send disposable copy of the ms. Include photo of author, if possible, and graphics, if available. Electronic submissions OK. Sample copy of *Green Egg* $6. Fiction guidelines for SASE. Reviews novels and short story collections.

Payment/Terms: Pays subscription to the magazine or contributor's copies. Acquires one-time rights.

Advice: "Looks for economy of prose, artistic use of language, but most important is that the subject matter be germaine to our pagan readership. Magical stories teaching ethics for survival as healthy biosphere heroines, human/animal/otherworld interface; transformative experiences; tidy plots; good grammar, spelling, punctuation; humor; classical deities and ethnic stuff. We're especially fond of science fiction and fantasy."

‡GRIT, American Life & Traditions, (II), Ogden Publications, Inc., 1503 S.W. 42nd St., Topeka KS 66609-1265. (913)274-4300. E-mail: grit@kspress.com. Website: http://www.oweb.com/grit (includes cover story from current issue plus titles of other features and book and products store). Editor-in-Chief: Donna Doyle. Note on envelope: Attn: Fiction Department. Tabloid: 50 pages; 30 lb. newsprint; illustrations and photos. "*Grit* is a 'good news' publication and has been since 1882. Fiction should be approx. 2,500 words and interesting, inspiring, perhaps compelling in nature. Audience is *conservative*; readers tend to be 40 + from smaller towns, rural areas." Biweekly. Estab. 1882. Circ. 400,000.

• *Grit* is considered one of the leading family-oriented publications.

Needs: Adventure, nostalgia, condensed novelette, mainstream/contemporary (conservative), mystery/suspense, light religious/inspirational, romance (contemporary, historical), science fiction, westerns (frontier, traditional). "No sex, violence, obscene words, abuse, alcohol, or negative diatribes." Upcoming themes: "Gardening" (January/February); "Love & Romance (February); "Presenting the Harvest" (June); "Back to School" (August); "Health Issue" (September); "Home for the Holidays" (November); "Christmas Theme" (December). Buys 1 mss/issue; 26 mss/year. Recently published work by Richard Lloyd, George Chaffee and Terri Pelger. Publishes 20 new writers/year. Length: 2,500 words average; 2,300 words minimum; 2,700 words maximum. Also publishes poetry.

How To Contact: Send complete ms with cover letter. Include estimated word count, brief bio, Social Security number, list of publications with submission. Reports in 6 months. Send SASE for return of ms. No simultaneous submissions. Sample copy for $4 postage/appropriate SASE.

Payment/Terms: 15-22¢/word.

Terms: Purchases first North American serial rights or all rights as negotiated.

Advice: Looks for "well-written, fast-paced adventures, lessons of life, wholesome stories with heart."

‡GUIDE MAGAZINE, (I, II, IV), Review & Herald Publishing Association, 55 W. Oak Ridge Dr., Hagerstown MD 21740. (301)791-7000. Fax: (301)790-9734. Editor: Carolyn Rathbun. Magazine: 6×9; 32 pages; glossy (coated) paper; illustrations; photographs. "*Guide* is a weekly Christian journal geared toward 10- to 14-year-olds. Stories and other features presented are relevant to the needs of today's young person and emphasize positive aspects of Christian living." Weekly. Estab. 1953. Circ. 34,000.

Needs: Religious/inspirational: adventure (10-14 years), humor, sports. No romance, science fiction, horror, etc. "We use four general categories in each issue: spiritual/devotional; personal growth; adventure/nature; humor. We need more true stories. No stories that lack clear spiritual application." Receives 80-100 unsolicited mss/

month. Buys 2-3 mss/issue; 150 mss/year. Publishes ms 3-12 months after acceptance. Length: 1,000-1,200 words average. Publishes short shorts. Often critiques or comments on rejected mss.

How to Contact: Send complete ms. Include estimated word count, Social Security number. Reports in 3-4 weeks. SASE for return of ms or send disposable copy. Simultaneous and reprint submissions OK. Sample copy for #10 SAE and 2 first-class stamps. Writer's guidelines for #10 SASE.

Payment/Terms: Pays 3-6¢/word and 3 contributor's copies. Additional copies 50¢ each. Buys first, first North American serial, one-time, reprint or simultaneous rights.

Advice: "The aim of *Guide* magazine is to reflect in creative yet concrete ways the unconditional love of God to young people 10 to 14 years of age. Believing that an accurate picture of God is a prerequisite for wholeness, our efforts editorially and in design will be focused on accurately portraying His attributes and expectations."

GUIDEPOSTS FOR KIDS, (II), P.O. Box 638, Chesterton IN 46304. Editor: Mary Lou Carney. Magazine: 8¼ × 10¼; 32 pages. "Value-centered bimonthly for kids 7-12 years old. Not preachy, concerned with contemporary issues." Bimonthly. Estab. 1990. Circ. 200,000.

● The magazine publishes many new writers but is primarily a market for writers who have already been published. *Guideposts for Kids* received an Award of Excellence from the Ed Press Association in 1995, 1996 and 1997.

Needs: Children's/juvenile: fantasy, historical (general), humor, mystery/suspense, religious/inspirational, westerns, holidays. "No 'adult as hero' or 'I-prayed-I-got' stories." Upcoming themes: Choices, Animals, Humor, Courage. Receives 200 unsolicited mss/month. Accepts 1-2 mss/issue; 6-10 mss/year. Recently published work by Michael McWey and Pam Zollman. Length: 1,300 words preferred; 600 words minimum; 1,400 words maximum. Publishes short shorts. Also publishes small amount of poetry. Sometimes critiques rejected mss; "only what shows promise."

How to Contact: Send complete ms with cover letter. Include estimated word count, Social Security number, phone number and SASE. Reports in 6-8 weeks. Send SASE for reply, return of ms or send disposable copy of ms. Simultaneous submissions OK. Sample copy for $3.25. Fiction guidelines for #10 SASE.

Payment/Terms: $250-600 on acceptance for all rights; 2 contributor's copies. Additional copies available.

Advice: "We're looking for the good stuff. Fast-paced, well-crafted stories aimed at kids 8-12 years of age. Stories should reflect strong traditional values. Don't preach. This is not a Sunday School handout, but a good solid piece of fiction that reflects traditional values and morality. Build your story around a solid principle and let the reader gain insight by inference. Don't let adults solve problems. While adults can appear in stories, they can't give the characters life's answers. Don't make your kid protagonist grateful and awed by sage, adult advice. Be original. We want a good mix of fiction—contemporary, historical, fantasy, sci-fi, mystery—centered around things that interest and concern kids. A kid reader should be able to identify with the characters strongly enough to think. '*I know just how he feels!*' Create a plot with believable characters. Here's how it works: the story must tell what happens when someone the reader likes (character) reaches an important goal (climax) by overcoming obstacles (conflict). Let kids be kids. Your dialogue (and use plenty of it!) should reflect how the kids sound, think and feel. Avoid slang, but listen to how real kids talk before you try and write for them. Give your characters feelings and actions suitable for the 4th to 6th grader."

GUYS, (I, II), FirstHand Ltd., Box 1314, Teaneck NJ 07666. (201)836-9177. Fax: (201)836-5055. E-mail: firsthand3@aol.com. Editor: William Spencer. Magazine: digest size; 130 pages; illustrations; photos. "Fiction and informative departments for today's gay man. Fiction is of an erotic nature, and we especially need short shorts and novella-length stories." Estab. 1988.

Needs: Gay. "Should be written in first person. No science fiction or fantasy. No four-legged animals. All characters must be over 18. Stories including members of ethnic groups are especially welcome. Erotica should be based on reality." Accepts 6 mss/issue; 66 mss/year. Publishes ms 6-12 months after acceptance. Published work by Robert H. Fletcher, Davem Verne and Biff Cole. Published new writers within the last year. Length: 3,000 words average; 2,000 words minimum; 3,750 words maximum. For novellas: 7,500-8,600 words. Publishes short shorts. Length: 750-1,250 words. Sometimes critiques rejected mss and recommends other markets.

How to Contact: Send complete ms with cover letter, include writer's name, address, telephone number and Social Security number and whether selling all rights or first North American serial rights. Reports in 6-8 weeks on ms. SASE. Accepts diskette or e-mail submissions. Sample copy for $5.50. Fiction guidelines for #10 SASE. Reviews novels and short story collections.

Payment/Terms: Pays $100-150; $75 for short shorts (all rights); $250 for novellas (all rights). Acquires all rights or first North American serial rights.

MARKET CATEGORIES: (I) Open to new writers; **(II)** Open to both new and established writers; **(III)** Interested mostly in established writers; **(IV)** Open to writers whose work is specialized; **(V)** Closed to unsolicited submissions.

Advice: "Keep it simple, keep it sexy. If it turns you on, it will turn the reader on."

HADASSAH MAGAZINE, (IV), 50 W. 58th St., New York NY 10019. E-mail: hadamag@aol.com. Executive Editor: Alan M. Tigay. Senior Editor: Zelda Shluker. Jewish general interest magazine: 8½×11; 48-70 pages; coated and uncoated paper; slick, medium weight coated cover; drawings and cartoons; photos. Primarily concerned with Israel, the American Jewish community, Jewish communities around the world, Jewish women's issues and American current affairs. Monthly except combined June/July and August/September issues. Circ. 300,000.
- *Hadassah* has been nominated for a National Magazine Award and has received numerous Rockower Awards for Excellence in Jewish Journalism.
Needs: Ethnic (Jewish). Receives 20-25 unsolicited fiction mss each month. Published fiction by Joanne Greenberg, Anita Desai and Lori Ubell. Published new writers within the last year. Length: 1,500-2,000 words.
How to Contact: Query first with writing samples. Reports in 3-4 months on mss. "Not interested in multiple submissions or previously published articles." Must submit appropriate size SASE.
Payment/Terms: Pays $300 minimum on acceptance for U.S. publication rights.
Advice: "Stories on a Jewish theme should be neither self-hating nor schmaltzy."

HARPER'S MAGAZINE, (II, III), 666 Broadway, 11th Floor, New York NY 10012. (212)614-6500. Website: http://www.harpers.org (includes submission guidelines). Editor: Lewis H. Lapham. Magazine: 8×10¾; 80 pages; illustrations. Magazine for well-educated, widely read and socially concerned readers, college-aged and older, those active in political and community affairs. Monthly. Circ. 218,000.
- This is considered a top but tough market for contemporary fiction.
Needs: Contemporary and humor. Stories on contemporary life and its problems. Receives 600 unsolicited fiction mss/year. Accepts 1 ms/year. Recently published work by David Guterson, David Foster Wallace, Johnathan Franzen, Steven Millhauser, Lisa Roney, Rick Moody and Steven Dixon. Published new writers within the last year. First published David Foster Wallace. Length: 1,000-5,000 words.
How to Contact: Query to managing editor, or through agent. Reports in 6 weeks on queries.
Payment/Terms: Pays $500-1,000 on acceptance for rights, which vary on each author materials and length. Sends galleys to author.
Advice: Buys very little fiction but *Harper's* has published short stories traditionally.

HIGHLIGHTS FOR CHILDREN, 803 Church St., Honesdale PA 18431. (717)253-1080. Editor: Kent L. Brown, Jr. Address fiction to: Beth Troop, Manuscript Coordinator. Magazine: 8½×11; 42 pages; uncoated paper; coated cover stock; illustrations; photos. Monthly. Circ. 2.8 million.
- *Highlights* is very supportive of writers. The magazine sponsors a contest and a workshop each year at Chautauqua (New York). Several authors published in *Highlights* have received SCBWI Magazine Merit Awards.
Needs: Juvenile (ages 2-12). Unusual stories appealing to both girls and boys; stories with good characterization, strong emotional appeal, vivid, full of action. "Begin with action rather than description, have strong plot, believable setting, suspense from start to finish." Length: 400-900 words. "We also need easy stories for very young readers (100-400 words)." No war, crime or violence. Receives 600-800 unsolicited fiction mss/month. Accepts 6-7 mss/issue. Also publishes rebus (picture) stories of 125 words or under for the 3- to 7-year-old child. Published work by Virginia Kroll, Harriett Diller and Vashanti Rahaman; published new writers within the last year. Critiques rejected mss occasionally, "especially when editors see possibilities in story."
How to Contact: Send complete ms with SASE and include a rough word count and cover letter "with any previous acceptances by our magazine; any other published work anywhere." No simultaneous submissions. Reports in 1 month. Free guidelines on request.
Payment/Terms: Pays 14¢ and up/word on acceptance for all rights. Sends galleys to author.
Advice: "We accept a story on its merit whether written by an unpublished or an experienced writer. Mss are rejected because of poor writing, lack of plot, trite or worn-out plot, or poor characterization. Children *like* stories and learn about life from stories. Children learn to become lifelong fiction readers by enjoying stories. Feel passion for your subject. Create vivid images. Write a child-centered story; leave adults in the background."

ALFRED HITCHCOCK MYSTERY MAGAZINE, (I, II), Dell Magazines, 1270 Avenue of the Americas, 10th Floor, New York NY 10020. (212)698-1313. Editor: Cathleen Jordan. Mystery fiction magazine: 5¹⁄₁₆×7⅜; 160 pages; 28 lb. newsprint paper; 60 lb. machine-/coated cover stock; illustrations; photos. Published 11 times/year, including 1 double issue. Estab. 1956. Circ. 615,000 readers.
- Stories published in *Alfred Hitchcock Mystery Magazine* have won Edgar Awards for "Best Mystery Story of the Year," Shamus Awards for "Best Private Eye Story of the Year" and Robert L. Fish Awards for "Best First Mystery Short Story of the Year."
Needs: Mystery and detection (amateur sleuth, private eye, police procedural, suspense, etc.). No sensationalism. Number of mss/issue varies with length of mss. Length: up to 14,000 words. Also publishes short shorts.
How to Contact: Send complete ms and SASE. Reports in 2 months. Guideline sheet for SASE.
Payment/Terms: Pays 8¢/word on acceptance.

HOME TIMES, (I, II, IV), Neighbor News, Inc., 3676 Collin Dr. #12, West Palm Beach FL 33406. (561)439-3509. E-mail: hometimes@aol.com. Editor: Dennis Lombard. Newspaper: tabloid; 24 pages; newsprint; illustrations and photographs. "Conservative news, views, fiction, poetry, sold to general public." Weekly. Estab. 1980. Circ. 5,000.

• The publisher offers "101 Reasons Why I Reject Your Manuscript," a 120-page report for a cost of $19.

Needs: Adventure, historical (general), humor/satire, literary, mainstream, religious/inspirational, romance, sports. "All fiction needs to be related to the publication's focus on current events and conservative perspective—we feel you must examine a sample issue because *Home Times* is *different*." Nothing "preachy or doctrinal, but Biblical worldview needed." Receives 50 unsolicited mss/month. Accepts 5-10 mss/issue. Publishes ms 1-9 months after acceptance. Published work by Cal Thomas, Chuck Colson and Don Feder. Publishes many previously unpublished writers/year. Length: 700 words average; 500 words minimum; 800 words maximum.

How to Contact: Send complete manuscript with cover letter including Social Security number and word count. "Absolutely no queries." Include in cover letter "One to two sentences on what the piece is and who you are." Reports on mss in 1 month. SASE. Simultaneous and reprint submissions OK. Sample current issues for $3. Guidelines for #10 SASE.

Payment/Terms: Pays $5-25 for one-time rights.

Advice: "We are very open to new writers, but read our newspaper—get the drift of our rather unusual conservative, pro-Christian, but non-religious content. Looks for "historical, issues, or family orientation; also like creative nonfiction on historical and issues subjects." Send $10 for a writer's 1-year subscription (12 current issues).

HORIZONS, The Magazine of Presbyterian Women, (II, IV), 100 Witherspoon St., Louisville KY 40202-1396. (502)569-5379. Fax: (502)569-8085. Magazine: 8×11; 40 pages; illustrations and photos. Magazine owned and operated by Presbyterian Women with material on women's issues—religious perspective. Bimonthly. Estab. 1988. Circ. 30,000.

Needs: Ethnic/multicultural, feminist, gay, historical, humor/satire, lesbian, literary, mainstream/contemporary, religious/inspirational, senior citizen/retirement, translations. "No sex/violence." List of upcoming themes available for SASE. Receives 50 unsolicited mss/month. Accepts 1 ms/issue. Publishes ms 4 months after acceptance. Length: 1,500-2,000 words maximum. Publishes short shorts. Length: 500 words. Also publishes literary essays, literary criticism and poetry. Sometimes critiques or comments on rejected mss.

How to Contact: Send complete ms with cover letter. Include estimated word count and Social Security number. Reports in 1 week on queries; 2 weeks on mss. SASE or send a disposable copy of ms. Simultaneous submissions OK. Sample copy for 9×12 SAE. Fiction guidelines for #10 SASE. Reviews novels and short story collections. Send books to Paul Hansen.

Payment/Terms: Pays $50/page and 2 contributor's copies on publication for all rights; additional copies for $2.50.

Advice: "Stories with a religious slant related to women, parenting, mission and family situations fit our mag best."

HUMPTY DUMPTY'S MAGAZINE, (II), Children's Better Health Institute, Box 567, 1100 Waterway Blvd., Indianapolis IN 46206. (317)636-8881. Website: http://www.satevepost.org/kidsonline. Editor: Lisa Hoffman. Magazine: 7⅝×10⅛; 36 pages; 35 lb. paper; coated cover; illustrations; some photos. Children's magazine stressing health, nutrition, hygiene, exercise and safety for children ages 4-6. Publishes 8 issues/year.

Needs: Juvenile health-related material and material of a more general nature. No inanimate talking objects. Rhyming stories should flow easily with no contrived rhymes. Receives 250-300 unsolicited mss/month. Accepts 2-3 mss/issue. Length: 300 words maximum.

How to Contact: Send complete ms with SASE. No queries. Reports in 3 months. Sample copy for $1.25. Editorial guidelines for SASE.

Payment/Terms: Pays up to 22¢/word for stories plus 10 contributor's copies on publication for all rights. (One-time book rights returned when requested for specific publication.)

Advice: "In contemporary stories, characters should be up-to-date, with realistic dialogue. We're looking for health-related stories with unusual twists or surprise endings. We want to avoid stories and poems that 'preach.' We try to present the health material in a positive way, utilizing a light humorous approach wherever possible." Most rejected mss "are too wordy. Need short, short nonfiction."

HUSTLER BUSTY BEAUTIES, (I, IV), HG Publications, Inc., 8484 Wilshire Blvd., Suite 900, Beverly Hills CA 90211. (213)651-5400. Editor: N. Morgen Hagen. Magazine: 8×11; 100 pages; 60 lb. paper; 80 lb. cover; illustrations and photographs. "Adult entertainment and reading centered around large-breasted women for an over-18 audience, mostly male." Published 13 times/year. Estab. 1988. Circ. 150,000.

Needs: Adventure, erotica, fantasy, mystery/suspense. All must have erotic theme. Receives 25 unsolicited fiction mss/month. Accepts 1 ms/issue; 6-12 mss/year. Publishes mss 3-6 months after acceptance. Published work by Mike Dillon and H.H. Morris. Length: 1,600 words preferred; 1,000 words minimum; 2,000 words maximum.

How to Contact: Query first. Then send complete ms with cover letter. Reports in 2 weeks on queries; in 2-4 weeks on mss. SASE. Sample copy for $5. Fiction guidelines free.

Payment/Terms: Pays $350-500 (fiction) and $50 (erotic letters) on publication for all rights.
Advice: Looks for "1. plausible plot, well-defined characters, literary ingenuity; 2. hot sex scenes; 3. readable, coherent, grammatically sound prose."

‡IDEALS MAGAZINE, (IV), Ideals Publications Incorporated, 535 Metroplex Blvd., Suite 250, Nashville TN 37211. (615)781-1421. Fax: (615)781-1447. Editor: Lisa Ragan. Magazine: 96 pages; illustrations and photos. "Magazine for women over 30 years old—poetry, inspirational, beauty of nature, light-hearted views of the past, slice-of-life vignettes." Bimonthly.
Needs: Religious/inspirational, nostalgia, beauty, nature. Upcoming themes include Easter, Mother's Day, Country, Friendship, Thanksgiving and Christmas. Receives 15 unsolicited mss/month. Accepts 1-2 mss/issue; 6 mss/year. Agented fiction less than 1%. Length: 800 words minimum; 1,000 words maximum. Publishes short shorts. Also publishes poetry.
How to Contact: First send request for guidelines, SASE and $4 for sample issue.
Payment/Terms: Pays $10 minimum plus 1 contributor's copy for one-time rights; additional copies $2.95.
Advice: "Think about submitting things your grandmother would like."

IMPLOSION, A Journal of the Bizarre and Eccentric, (II), P.O. Box 533653, Orlando FL 32853. (407)645-3924. E-mail: smudge21@aol.com. Editor: Cynthia Conlin. Magazine: 8½ × 11; 68 pages; 50 lb. glossy paper; 80 lb. glossy cover stock; illustrations and photos. "*Implosion* explores the odd and bizarre side of human existence. It seeks out all things highly unusual." Quarterly. Estab. 1995. Circ. 17,000.
Needs: Adventure, experimental (science fantasy), horror, psychic/supernatural/occult, science fiction (hard science, soft/sociological). Especially interested in "material with weird and bizarre themes and overtones." Receives 100 mss/month. Accepts 5-7 mss/issue; 25-30 mss/year. Publishes ms 4-7 months after acceptance. Published work by J. Spencer Dreischarf, Bert Benmeyer, D.F. Lewis and Rick Reed. Length: 2,000 words average; 12,000 words maximum. Publishes short shorts. Also publishes literary criticism. Sometimes critiques or comments on rejected mss.
How to Contact: Send complete ms with cover letter. Include estimated word count and list of publications. Reports in 2-3 months on mss. Send SASE for reply, return of ms or send a disposable copy of ms. Simultaneous and reprint submissions OK. Sample copy for $5. Guidelines for SASE. Reviews novels and short story collections. Send books to editor.
Payment/Terms: Pays 1-2¢/word on acceptance and 2 contributor's copies; additional copies for $3. Acquires first or one-time rights. Sends galleys to author.
Advice: "We want new ideas and concepts, not clichéd rehashes of 'Twilight Zone' plots. A bit of humor doesn't hurt, either. Remember that 'bizarre' doesn't mean silly or pointless. Check your work for grammatical errors and the like—there's no greater turnoff than poorly constructed manuscripts."

IN TOUCH FOR MEN, (I, IV), 13122 Saticoy St., North Hollywood CA 91605. (818)764-2288. Fax: (818)764-2307. E-mail: glentouch@aol.com. Website: http://www.intouchformen.com (includes information about current issues, subscription rates, hyperfiction and hyperpoetry). Editor: Alan W. Mills. Magazine: 8 × 10¾; 100 pages; glossy paper; coated cover; illustrations and photographs. "*In Touch* is a magazine for gay men. It features five to six nude male centerfolds in each issue, but is erotic rather than pornographic. We include fiction. We now have a second publication, *Indulge*, and our fiction needs have doubled." Monthly. Estab. 1973. Circ. 70,000.
Needs: Confession, gay erotica, romance (contemporary, historical). All characters must be over 18 years old. Stories must have an explicit erotic content. No heterosexual or internalized homophobic fiction. Accepts 6 mss/month; 72 mss/year. Publishes ms 3 months after acceptance. Publishes 20 new writers/year. Length: 2,500 words average; up to 3,500 words maximum. Sometimes critiques rejected mss and recommends other markets.
How to Contact: Send complete ms with cover letter, name, address and Social Security number. Reports in 2 weeks on queries; 2 months on mss. SASE. Simultaneous and reprint submissions, if from local publication, OK. Disk submissions OK (call before sending by modem). Sample copy for $5.95. Fiction guidelines free. Reviews novels and short story collections.
Payment/Terms: Pays $25-75 (except on rare occasions for a longer piece) on publication for one-time rights.
Advice: Publishes "primarily erotic material geared toward gay men. Periodically (but very seldom) we will run fiction of a non-erotic nature (but still gay-related), but that's not the norm. I personally prefer (and accept) manuscripts that are not only erotic/hardcore, but show a developed story, plot and concise ending (as opposed to just sexual vignettes that basically lead nowhere). If it's got a little romance, too, that's even better. Emphasis still on erotic, though. We now only use 'safe sex' depictions in fiction, hoping that it will prompt people to act responsibly. We have a new interest in experimental fiction as long as it does not violate the standards of the homoerotic genre. All fiction must conform to the basic rules of the genre. Beyond that, we look for inventive use of language, unique content, exciting themes and, on occasion, experimental structures or subversion issues. If you're writing for a genre, know that genre, but don't be afraid to twist things around just enough to stand out from the crowd. Our website is becoming increasingly important to us. We have our eyes open for interesting hyperfiction because we want people to keep returning to our site, hoping that they might subscribe to the magazine."

INDIA CURRENTS, (II,IV), The Complete Indian American Magazine, Box 21285, San Jose CA 95151. (408)274-6966. Fax: (408)274-2733. Editor: Vandana Kumar. E-mail: editor@indiacur.com. Magazine: 8½×11; 104 pages; newsprint paper; illustrations and photographs. "The arts and culture of India as seen in America for Indians and non-Indians with a common interest in India." Monthly. Estab. 1987. Circ. 25,000.
  • Editor Arvind Kumar was honored by KQED Channel 9, the local PBS affiliate, as an "Unsung Hero" during Lesbian and Gay Pride Month of June 1995.
Needs: All Indian content: contemporary, ethnic, feminist, historical (general), humor/satire, literary, mainstream, prose poem, regional, religious/inspirational, romance, translations (from Indian languages). "We seek material with insight into Indian culture, American culture and the crossing from one to another." Receives 12 unsolicited mss/month. Accepts 1 ms/issue; 12 mss/year. Publishes ms 2-6 months after acceptance. Published work by Chitra Divakaruni, Jyotsna Sreenivasan and Rajini Srikanth. Published new writers within the last year. Length: 1,800 words.
How to Contact: Send complete ms with cover letter and clips of published work. Reports in 2-3 months on mss. SASE. Simultaneous and reprint submissions OK. Accepts electronic submissions. Sample copy for $3.
Payment/Terms: Pays in subscriptions on publication for one-time rights.
Advice: "Story must be related to India and subcontinent in some meaningful way. The best stories are those which document some deep transformation as a result of an Indian experience, or those which show the humanity of Indians."

‡INSIDE, The Magazine of the Jewish Exponent, (II), Jewish Federation, 226 S. 16th St., Philadelphia PA 19102. (215)893-5700. (215)546-3957. E-mail: expent@netaxs.com. Editor-in-Chief: Jane Biberman. Magazine: 175-225 pages; glossy paper; illustrations; photos. Aimed at middle- and upper-middle-class audience, Jewish-oriented articles and fiction. Quarterly. Estab. 1980. Circ. 75,000.
Needs: Contemporary, ethnic, humor/satire, literary and translations. No erotica. Receives approximately 10 unsolicited fiction mss/month. Buys 1-2 mss/issue; 4-8 mss/year. Published new writers within the last year. Length: 1,500 words minimum; 3,000 words maximum; 2,000 words average. Occasionally critiques rejected mss.
How to Contact: Query first with clips of published work. Reports on queries in 3 weeks. SASE. Simultaneous submissions OK. Sample copy for $5 and 9×12 SAE. Fiction guidelines for SASE.
Payment/Terms: Pays $100-600 on acceptance for first rights. Sometimes buys reprints. Sends galleys to author.
Advice: "We're looking for original, avant-garde, stylish writing but we buy very little."

JACK AND JILL, (II, IV), The Children's Better Health Institute, P.O. Box 567, 1100 Waterway Blvd., Indianapolis IN 46206. (317)636-8881. Editor: Daniel Lee. Children's magazine of articles, stories and activities, many with a health, safety, exercise or nutritional-oriented theme, ages 7-10 years. Monthly except January/February, April/May, July/August, October/November. Estab. 1938.
Needs: Science fiction, mystery, sports, adventure, historical fiction and humor. Health-related stories with a subtle lesson. Published new writers within the last year. Length: 500-800 words.
How to Contact: Send complete ms with SASE. Reports in 3 months on mss. Sample copy for $1.25. Fiction guidelines for SASE.
Payment/Terms: Pays up to 20¢/word on publication for all rights.
Advice: "Try to present health material in a positive—not a negative—light. Use humor and a light approach wherever possible without minimizing the seriousness of the subject. We need more humor and adventure stories."

JIVE, BLACK CONFESSIONS, BLACK ROMANCE, BRONZE THRILLS, BLACK SECRETS, (I, II), Sterling/Mcfadden, 233 Park Ave. S., Fifth Floor, New York NY 10003. (212)780-3500. Editor: Marcia Mahan. Magazine: 8½×11; 72 pages; newsprint paper; glossy cover; 8×10 photographs. "We publish stories that are romantic and have romantic lovemaking scenes in them. Our audience is basically young. However, we have a significant audience base of housewives. The age range is from 18-49." Bimonthly (*Jive* and *Black Romance* in odd-numbered months; *Black Confessions* and *Bronze Thrills* in even-numbered months). 6 issues per year. Estab. 1962. Circ. 100,000.
Needs: Confession, romance (contemporary, young adult). No "stories that are stereotypical to black people, ones that do not follow the basic rules of writing, or ones that are too graphic in content and lack a romantic element." Receives 20 or more unsolicited fiction mss/month. Accepts 6 mss/issue (2 issues/month); 144 mss/year. Publishes ms an average of 2-3 months after acceptance. Published work by Linda Smith; published new writers within the last year. Length: 18-24 pages.
How to Contact: Query with clips of published work or send complete ms with cover letter. "A cover letter should include an author's bio and what he or she proposes to do. Of course, address and phone number." Reports in 3 months. SASE. Simultaneous submissions OK. "Please contact me if simultaneously submitted work has been accepted elsewhere." Sample copy for 9×12 SAE and 5 first-class stamps; fiction guidelines for #10 SAE and 2 first-class stamps.
Payment/Terms: Pays $75-100 on publication for all rights.
Advice: "Our five magazines are a great starting point for new writers. We accept work from beginners as well as established writers. Please study and research black culture and lifestyles if you are not a black writer.

Stereotypical stories are not acceptable. Set the stories all over the world and all over the USA—not just down south. We are not looking for 'the runaway who gets turned out by a sweet-talking pimp' stories. We are looking for stories about all types of female characters. Any writer should not be afraid to communicate with us if he or she is having some difficulty with writing a story. We are available to help at any stage of the submission process. Also, writers should practice patience. If we do not contact the writer, that means that the story is being read or is being held on file for future publication. If we get in touch with the writer, it usually means a request for revision and resubmission. Do the best work possible and don't let rejection slips send you off 'the deep end.' Don't take everything that is said about your work so personally. We are buying all of our work from freelance writers."

JUGGLER'S WORLD, (I, II, IV), International Juggler's Association, Box 443, Davidson NC 28036. (704)892-1296. Fax: (704)892-2499. E-mail: bigiduz@davidson.edu. Editor: Bill Giduz. Fiction Editor: Ken Letko. Magazine: 8½×11; 40 pages; 70 lb. paper and cover stock; illustrations and photos. For and about jugglers and juggling. Quarterly.
Needs: Historical (general), humor/satire, science fiction. No stories "that don't include juggling as a central theme." Receives "very few" unsolicited mss/month. Accepts 8 mss/year. Publishes ms an average of 6-12 months to 1 year after acceptance. Length: 2,000 words average; 1,000 words minimum; 2,500 words maximum. Sometimes critiques rejected mss.
How to Contact: Query first. Reports in 1 week. Simultaneous submissions OK. Prefers electronic submissions via IBM or Macintosh compatible disk. Sample copy for $2.50.
Payment/Terms: Pays up to $100, free subscription to magazine and 3 contributor's copies on acceptance for first rights.
Advice: "Submit a brief story outline to the editor before writing the whole piece."

JUNIOR TRAILS, (I, II), Gospel Publishing House, 1445 Boonville Ave., Springfield MO 65802. (417)862-2781. Elementary Editor: Sinda S. Zinn. Magazine: 5¼×8; 8 pages; 36 lb. coated offset paper; art illustrations; photos. "A Sunday school take-home paper of nature articles and fictional stories that apply Christian principles to everyday living for 10-to 12-year-old children." Weekly. Estab. 1954. Circ. 70,000.
Needs: Contemporary, juvenile, religious/inspirational, spiritual, sports. Adventure stories and serials are welcome. No Biblical fiction or science fiction. Accepts 2 mss/issue. Recently published work by Melissa Knight, O.B. Comer, Russell Lewis and Theresa E. Calvin. Published new writers within the last year. Length: 1,200-1,500 words. Publishes short shorts.
How to Contact: Send complete ms with SASE. Reports in 4-6 weeks. Free sample copy and guidelines with SASE.
Payment/Terms: Pays 5¢/word and 3 contributor's copies on acceptance for first rights.
Advice: "Know the age level and direct stories relevant to that age group. Since junior-age children (grades 5 and 6) enjoy action, fiction provides a vehicle for communicating moral/spiritual principles in a dramatic framework. Fiction, if well done, can be a powerful tool for relating Christian principles. It must, however, be realistic and believable in its development. Make your children be children, not overly mature for their age. We would like more stories with a *city* setting. Write for contemporary children, using setting and background that includes various ethnic groups."

LADIES' HOME JOURNAL, (III), Published by Meredith Corporation, 125 Park Ave., New York NY 10017. (212)557-6600. Editor-in-Chief: Myrna Blyth. Fiction/Articles Editor: Mary Moklev. Managing Editor: Carolyn Noyes. Magazine: 190 pages; 34-38 lb. coated paper; 65 lb. coated cover; illustrations and photos.
  ● *Ladies' Home Journal* has won several awards for journalism.
Needs: Book mss and short stories, *accepted only through an agent*. Return of unsolicited material cannot be guaranteed. Published work by Fay Weldon, Anita Shreve, Jane Shapiro and Anne Rivers Siddons. Length: approximately 2,000-2,500 words.
How to Contact: Send complete ms with cover letter (credits). Simultaneous submissions OK. Publishes ms 4-12 months after acceptance.
Payment/Terms: Acquires First North American rights.
Advice: "Our readers like stories, especially those that have emotional impact. Stories about relationships between people—husband/wife—mother/son—seem to be subjects that can be explored effectively in short stories. Our reader's mail and surveys attest to this fact: Readers enjoy our fiction and are most keenly tuned to stories dealing with children. Fiction today is stronger than ever. Beginners can be optimistic; if they have talent,

---

MARKET CATEGORIES: (I) Open to new writers; **(II)** Open to both new and established writers; **(III)** Interested mostly in established writers; **(IV)** Open to writers whose work is specialized; **(V)** Closed to unsolicited submissions.

I do believe that talent will be discovered. It is best to read the magazine before submitting."

LADYBUG, (II, IV), The Cricket Magazine Group, P.O. Box 300, Peru IL 61354. (815)224-6656. Editor-in-Chief: Marianne Carus. Editor: Paula Morrow. Magazine: 8×10; 36 pages plus 4-page pullout section; illustrations. "*Ladybug* publishes original stories and poems and reprints written by the world's best children's authors. For young children, ages 2-6." Monthly. Estab. 1990. Circ. 130,000.
  • *Ladybug* has received the Parents Choice Award; the Golden Lamp Honor Award and the Golden Lamp Award from the Educational Press Association, and Magazine Merit awards from the Society of Children's Book Writers and Illustrators.
Needs: Fairy tales, fantasy (children's), folk tales, juvenile, picture stories, preschool, read-out-loud stories. Length: 300-750 words preferred. Publishes short shorts.
How to Contact: Send complete ms with cover letter. Include word count on ms (do not count title). Reports in 3 months. SASE. Reprints are OK. Fiction guidelines for SASE. Sample copy for $4. For guidelines *and* sample send 9×12 SAE (no stamps required) and $4.
Payment/Terms: Pays up to 25¢/word (less for reprints) on publication for first publication rights or second serial (reprint) rights. For recurring features, pays flat fee and copyright becomes property of The Cricket Magazine Group.
Advice: Looks for "well-written stories for preschoolers: age-appropriate, not condescending. We look for rich, evocative language and sense of joy or wonder."

LIGUORIAN, (I, IV), "A Leading Catholic Magazine," Liguori Publications, 1 Liguori Dr., Liguori MO 63057. (314)464-2500. Fax: (314)464-8449. Editor-in-Chief: Allan Weinert, CSS.R. Magazine: 5×8½; 64 pages; b&w illustrations and photographs. "*Liguorian* is a Catholic magazine aimed at helping our readers to live a full Christian life. We publish articles for families, young people, children, religious and singles—all with the same aim." Monthly. Estab. 1913. Circ. 330,000.
  • *Liguorian* received Catholic Press Association awards for 1996 including Honorable Mention for General Excellence and for fiction.
Needs: Religious/inspirational, young adult and senior citizen/retirement (with moral Christian thrust), spiritual. "Stories submitted to *Liguorian* must have as their goal the lifting up of the reader to a higher Christian view of values and goals. We are not interested in contemporary works that lack purpose or are of questionable moral value." Receives approximately 25 unsolicited fiction mss/month. Accepts 12 mss/year. Recently published work by Sharon Helgens and Jon Ripslinger. Published new writers within the last year. Length: 1,500-2,000 words preferred. Also publishes short shorts. Occasionally critiques rejected mss "if we feel the author is capable of giving us something we need even though this story did not suit us."
How to Contact: Send complete ms with SASE. Accepts disk submissions compatible with IBM, using a WordPerfect 5.1 program; prefers hard copy with disk submission. Reports in 10-12 weeks on mss. Sample copy and guidelines for #10 SASE.
Payment/Terms: Pays 10-12¢/word and 5 contributor's copies on acceptance for all rights. Offers 50% kill fee for assigned mss not published.
Advice: "First read several issues containing short stories. We look for originality and creative input in each story we read. Since most editors must wade through mounds of manuscripts each month, consideration for the editor requires that the market be studied, the manuscript be carefully presented and polished before submitting. Our publication uses only one story a month. Compare this with the 25 or more we receive over the transom each month. Also, many fiction mss are written without a specific goal or thrust, i.e., an interesting incident that goes nowhere is *not a story*. We believe fiction is a highly effective mode for transmitting the Christian message and also provides a good balance in an unusually heavy issue."

‡LILITH MAGAZINE, The Independent Jewish Women's Magazine, (I, II, IV), 250 W. 57th St., Suite 2432, New York NY 10107. (212)757-0818. E-mail: lilithmag@aol.com. Editor: Susan Weidman Schneider. Fiction Editor: Faye Moskowitz. Magazine: 48 pages; 80 lb. cover; b&w illustrations; b&w and color photos. Publishes work relating to Jewish feminism, for Jewish feminists, feminists and Jewish households. Quarterly. Estab. 1976. Circ. 25,000.
Needs: Ethnic, feminist, lesbian, literary, prose poem, psychic/supernatural/occult, religious/inspirational, senior citizen/retirement, spiritual, translation, young adult. "Nothing that does not in any way relate to Jews, women or Jewish women." Receives 15 unsolicited mss/month. Accepts 1 ms/issue; 3 mss/year. Publishes ms up to 1 year after acceptance. Published work by Lesléa Newman and Gloria Goldreich. Publishes short shorts.
How to Contact: Send complete ms with cover letter, which should include a 2-line bio. Reports in 2 months on queries; 2-6 months on mss. SASE. Simultaneous and reprint submissions OK but must be indicated in cover letter. Sample copy for $6. Writer's guidelines for #10 SASE. Reviews novels and short story collections. Send books to Susan Weidman Schneider.
Payment/Terms: Varies. Acquires first rights.
Advice: "Read the magazine to be familiar with the kinds of material we publish."

LIVE, (II, IV), Assemblies of God, 1445 Boonville, Springfield MO 65802-1894. (417)862-2781. Editor: Paul W. Smith. "A take-home story paper distributed weekly in young adult/adult Sunday school classes. *Live* is a story paper primarily. Stories in both fiction and narrative style are welcome. Poems, first-person anecdotes and humor are used as fillers. The purpose of *Live* is to present in short story form realistic characters who utilize biblical principles. We hope to challenge readers to take risks for God and to resolve their problems scripturally." Weekly. Circ. 130,000.

Needs: Religious/inspirational, prose poem and spiritual. "Inner city, ethnic, racial settings." No controversial stories about such subjects as feminism, war or capital punishment. Accepts 2 mss/issue. Recently published work by M.G. Baldwin, Robert Robeson, Clarence Trowbridge, Alan Cliburn, Kevin Dawson, Betty Lou Mell, Linda Hutton and Rhonda Stapleton. Publishes 5-10 new writers/year. Length: 500-1,700 words.

How to Contact: Send complete ms. Social Security number and word count must be included. Simultaneous submissions OK. Reports in 6-8 weeks. Sample copy and guidelines for SASE.

Payment/Terms: Pays 5¢/word (first rights); 3¢/word (second rights) on acceptance.

Advice: "Study our publication and write good, inspirational true to life or fiction stories that will encourage people to become all they can be as Christians. Stories should go somewhere! Action, not just thought—life; interaction, not just insights. Heroes and heroines, suspense and conflict. Avoid simplistic, pietistic conclusions, preachy, critical or moralizing. We don't accept science or Bible fiction. Stories should be encouraging, challenging, humorous. Even problem-centered stories should be upbeat." Reserves the right to change titles, abbreviate length and clarify flashbacks for publication.

‡MAGAZINE OF FANTASY AND SCIENCE FICTION, (II), P.O. Box 1806, New York NY 10159-1806. Phone/fax: (212)982-2676. Editor: Gordon Van Gelder. Magazine: illustrations on cover only. Publishes "science fiction and fantasy. Our readers are age 13 and up who are interested in science fiction and fantasy." Monthly. Estab. 1949. Circ. 50,000.

• *Magazine of Fantasy and Science Fiction* has won numerous awards including two Nebulas in 1991. The magazine ranks #5 on the latest *Writer's Digest* Fiction 50 list.

Needs: Fantasy and science fiction. Receives "hundreds" of unsolicited fiction submissions/month. Buys 8 fiction mss/issue ("on average"); 100-140 mss/year. Time between acceptance and publication varies; up to 3 years. Recently published work by Ray Bradbury, Esther M. Friesner, Stephen King and Gene Wolf. Length: 25,000 words maximum. Publishes short shorts. Critiques rejected ms, "if quality warrants it." Sometimes recommends other markets.

How to Contact: Send complete ms with cover letter. Reports in 1 month on queries; 6-8 weeks on mss. SASE (or IRC). No simultaneous submissions. Sample copy for $5. Fiction guidelines for SASE.

Payment/Terms: Pays 5-7¢/word.

Terms: Pays on acceptance for first North American serial rights; foreign, option on anthology if requested.

MANSCAPE, (I, IV), First Hand Ltd., Box 1314, Teaneck NJ 07666. (201)836-9177. Fax: (201)836-5055. E-mail: firsthand3@aol.com. Editor: Mick Cody. Magazine: digest sized; 130 pages; illustrations. "Magazine is devoted to gay male sexual fetishes; publishes fiction and readers' letters devoted to this theme." Monthly. Estab. 1985. Circ. 60,000.

Needs: Erotica, gay. Should be written in first person. No science fiction or fantasy. Erotica must be based on real life. Receives 25 unsolicited fiction mss/month. Accepts 5 mss/issue; 60 mss/year. Publishes ms an average of 12-18 months after acceptance. Published new writers within the last year. Length: 3,000 words average; 2,000 words minimum; 3,750 words maximum. Sometimes critiques rejected ms.

How to Contact: Send complete ms with cover letter. SASE. Sample copy for $5; guidelines for #10 SASE.

Payment/Terms: Pays $100-150 on publication for all rights or first North American serial rights.

Advice: "Keep story interesting by exhibiting believability and sexual tension."

MASSAGE MAGAZINE, Keeping Those Who Touch In Touch, (IV), Company of Touch, 1315 W. Mallon Ave., Spokane WA 99201. (509)324-8117. Fax: (509)324-8606. Managing Editor: Karen Menehan. Magazine: 8¼ × 11; 130 pages; 70 lb. gloss paper; 80 lb. gloss cover; illustrations and photographs. "The philosophy is to spread the good word about massage therapy and other healing arts. Material published includes pieces on technique, business advice, experiential pieces and interviews/profiles on pioneers/leaders in the field. Intended audience is those who practice massage and other allied healing arts." Bimonthly. Estab. 1985. Circ. 42,000.

Needs: "We only accept fiction that places massage or bodywork in a positive light." Receives 10 unsolicited ms/month. Accepts 1 ms/issue; 6 mss/year. Publishes ms within 1 year after acceptance. Published work by Erik Lee and Mary Bond. Length: 2,000 words preferred; 1,500 words minimum; 3,000 words maximum. Always critiques or comments on rejected mss.

How to Contact: Query first. Include bio (2-3 sentences). Reports in 2 months. Send SASE for reply or send a disposable copy of ms. Writer's guidelines and sample copy free.

Payment/Terms: Pays $150 maximum and 2 contributor's copies 30 days after publication for first rights; additional copies for $3.

Advice: "Looking for stories that will touch the reader emotionally by showing the importance of human contact—which doesn't mean they have to be melodramatic. Humor is appreciated, as are descriptive detail and vibrant characterizations."

‡**MATURE LIVING, (II)**, Sunday School Board of the Southern Baptist Convention, MSN 140, 127 Ninth Ave. North, Nashville TN 37234-0140. (615)251-2191. Fax: (615)251-5008. E-mail: matureliving@bssb.com. Editor: Al Shackleford. Magazine: 8½×11; 52 pages; non-glare paper; slick cover stock; full color illustrations and photos. "Our magazine is Christian in content and the material required is what would appeal to 55 and over age group: inspirational, informational, nostalgic, humorous. Our magazine is distributed mainly through churches (especially Southern Baptist churches) that buy the magazine in bulk and distribute it to members in this age group." Monthly. Estab. 1977. Circ. 360,000.

● *Mature Living* received the bronze award in the 1996 National Mature Media Awards.

Needs: Humor, religious/inspirational and senior citizen/retirement. Avoid all types of pornography, drugs, liquor, horror, science fiction and stories demeaning to the elderly. Receives 10 mss/month. Buys 1-2 mss/issue. Publishes ms an average of 1 year after acceptance. Published work by Burndean N. Sheffy, Pearl E. Trigg, Joyce M. Sixberry; published new writers within the last year. Length: 600-1,200 words (prefers 1,000).

How to Contact: Send complete ms with SASE. Include estimated word count and Social Security number. Reports in 2 months. Sample copy for $1. Guidelines for SASE.

Payment/Terms: Pays $75 on acceptance; 3 contributor's copies. $1 charge for extras. First rights only.

Advice: Mss are rejected because they are too long or subject matter unsuitable. "Our readers seem to enjoy an occasional short piece of fiction. It must be believable, however, and present senior adults in a favorable light."

MATURE YEARS, (II, IV), United Methodist Publishing House, 201 Eighth Ave. S., Nashville TN 37202. (615)749-6292. Fax: (615)749-6512. Editor: Marvin W. Cropsey. Magazine: 8½×11; 112 pages; illustrations and photos. Magazine "helps persons in and nearing retirement to appropriate the resources of the Christian faith as they seek to face the problems and opportunities related to aging." Quarterly. Estab. 1953.

Needs: Humor, intergenerational relationships, nostalgia, older adult issues, religious/inspirational, spiritual (for older adults). "We don't want anything poking fun at old age, saccharine stories or anything not for older adults. Must show older adults (age 55 plus) in a positive manner." Accepts 1 ms/issue, 4 mss/year. Publishes ms 1 year after acceptance. Published work by Ann S. Gray, Betty Z. Walker and Vickie Elaine Legg. Published new writers within the last year. Length: 1,000-1,800 words.

How to Contact: Send complete ms with SASE and Social Security number. No simultaneous submissions. Reports in 2 months. Sample copy for 10½×11 SAE and $4.50.

Payment/Terms: Pays 5¢/word on acceptance.

Advice: "Practice writing dialogue! Listen to people talk; take notes; master dialogue writing! Not easy, but well worth it! Most inquiry letters are far too long. If you can't sell me an idea in a brief paragraph, you're not going to sell the reader on reading your finished article or story."

MESSAGE MAGAZINE, (I, II), Review and Herald Publishing Association, 55 W. Oak Ridge Dr., Hagerstown MD 21740. (301)791-7000, ext. 2565. Fax: (301)714-1753. Editor: Stephen P. Ruff. Magazine: 8½×11; 31 pages; illustrations and photos. *MESSAGE* is a "Christian outreach magazine dealing with a variety of topics. Our primary audience is African-American." Bimonthly. Estab. 1798. Circ. 70,000.

● *MESSAGE* is the recipient of numerous awards from the Evangelical Press Association.

Needs: Religious/inspirational, young adult/teen. Upcoming theme: "Educational Issue" (importance of education). Receives 5 mss/month. Accepts 1 ms/issue; 7 mss/year. Length: 500-700 words average.

How to Contact: Send complete ms with cover letter. SASE. Include maximum 40-word bio, Social Security number, address and telephone number. Reports in 6-10 months on mss. Send a disposable copy of ms or SASE for return of ms. Electronic submissions OK. "We prefer not to reprint articles." Sample copy and fiction guidelines free.

Payment/Terms: Pays $50-300 and 3 contributor's copies on acceptance. Acquires first North American serial rights.

Advice: "*MESSAGE* does not accept a lot of fiction. The one department we might accept fiction for is our MESSAGE Jr. section. This department is for elementary-aged children and usually teaches some sort of biblical or moral lesson. However, the lessons are sometimes taught via fictitious stories."

♣**MESSENGER OF THE SACRED HEART, (II)**, Apostleship of Prayer, 661 Greenwood Ave., Toronto, Ontario M4J 4B3 Canada. (416)466-1195. Editors: Rev. F.J. Power, S.J. and Alfred DeManche. Magazine: 7×10; 32 pages; coated paper; self-cover; illustrations; photos. Magazine for "Canadian and U.S. Catholics interested in developing a life of prayer and spirituality; stresses the great value of our ordinary actions and lives." Monthly. Estab. 1891. Circ. 16,000.

Needs: Religious/inspirational. Stories about people, adventure, heroism, humor, drama. No poetry. Accepts 1 ms/issue. Length: 750-1,500 words. Recommends other markets.

How to Contact: Send complete ms with SAE. No simultaneous submissions. Reports in 1 month. Sample copy for $1.50 (Canadian).

Payment/Terms: Pays 4¢/word, 3 contributor's copies on acceptance for first North American serial rights. Rarely buys reprints.

Advice: "Develop a story that sustains interest to the end. Do not preach, but use plot and characters to convey the message or theme. Aim to move the heart as well as the mind. If you can, add a light touch or a sense of humor to the story. Your ending should have impact, leaving a moral or faith message for the reader."

‡**MIDSTREAM, A Monthly Jewish Review, (II, IV)**, Theodor Herzl Foundation, 110 E. 59th St., New York NY 10022-1304. (212)339-6046. Editor: Joel Carmichael. Magazine: 8½×11; 48 pages; 50 lb. paper; 65 lb. white smooth cover stock. "We are a Zionist journal; we publish material with Jewish themes or that would appeal to a Jewish readership." Published 9 times/year. Estab. 1955. Circ. 10,000.
   • Work published in *Midstream* was included in the *O. Henry Award* prize anthology.
Needs: Historical (general), humor/satire, literary, mainstream, translations. Receives 15-20 unsolicited mss/month. Accepts 1 mss/issue; 10 mss/year. Publishes ms 6-18 months after acceptance. Agented fiction 10%. Published work by I. B. Singer, Anita Jackson and Enid Shomer. Length: 2,500 words average; 1,500 words minimum; 4,500 words maximum. Sometimes critiques rejected mss.
How to Contact: Send complete ms with cover letter, which should include "address, telephone, or affiliation of author; state that the ms is fiction." Reports in "up to 6 months." SASE.
Payment/Terms: Pays 5¢/word and contributor's copies on publication for first rights.
Advice: "Be patient—we publish only one piece of fiction per issue and we have a backlog."

‡**MIRABELLA**, A Hachette Filipacchi Magazines, Inc. Publication, 1633 Broadway, New York NY 10019. (212)767-5800. Publisher: Audrey Daniels-Arnold. Bimonthly magazine. "*Mirabella* is a fashion and beauty magazine that serves the busy woman's guide to the good life. In addition to journalistic pieces and profiles, *Mirabella* provides extensive coverage on fashion and beauty, investigative reporting on health, and reflections on personal subjects." Estab. 1989. Circ. 31,480. This magazine did not respond to our request for information. Query before submitting.

‡**MONTANA SENIOR CITIZENS NEWS, (II,IV)**, Barrett-Whitman Co., Box 3363, Great Falls MT 59403. (406)761-0305. Editor: Jack Love. Tabloid: 11×17; 60-80 pages; newsprint paper and cover; illustrations; photos. Publishes "everything of interest to seniors, except most day-to-day political items like Social Security and topics covered in the daily news. Personal profiles of seniors, their lives, times and reminiscences." Bimonthly. Estab. 1984. Circ. 25,000.
Needs: Historical, senior citizen/retirement, western (historical or contemporary). No fiction "unrelated to experiences to which seniors can relate." Buys 1 or fewer mss/issue; 4-5 mss/year. Publishes ms within 6 months of acceptance. Published work by Anne Norris, Helen Clark, Juni Dunklin. Length: 500-800 words preferred. Publishes short stories. Length: under 500 words.
How to Contact: Send complete ms with cover letter and phone number. Only responds to selected mss. SASE. Simultaneous and reprint submissions OK. Accepts electronic submission via WordPerfect disk. Sample copy for 9×12 SAE and $2 postage and handling.
Payment/Terms: Pays 4¢/word on publication for first rights or one-time rights.

MS MAGAZINE, MacDonald Communications, Inc., 135 W. 50th St., 16th Floor, New York NY 10020. (212)445-6162. Fax: (212)586-7441. E-mail: ms@echonyc.com. Contact: Marcia Gillespie, editor-in-chief. Executive Editors: Barbara Findlen, Gloria Jacobs. 85% freelance written. Bimonthly magazine on women's issues and news. Estab. 1972. Circ. 200,000.
How to Contact: No unsolicited fiction.
Payment/Terms: Sample copy for $6. Writer's guidelines for #10 SASE.

MY FRIEND, The Catholic Magazine for Kids, (II), Pauline Books & Media, 50 St. Paul's Ave., Boston MA 02130. (617)522-8911. Editor: Sister Anne Joan. Magazine: 8½×11; 32 pages; smooth, glossy paper and cover stock; illustrations; photos. Magazine of "religious truths and positive values for children in a format which is enjoyable and attractive. Each issue contains Bible stories, lives of saints and famous people, short stories, science corner, contests, projects, etc." Monthly during school year (September-June). Estab. 1979. Circ. 12,000.
   • *My Friend* was honored by Catholic Press Association for General Excellence, Best Short Story and Best Illustration in 1994; General Excellence in 1995; General Excellence and Best Short Story (Honorable Mention) in 1996.
Needs: Juvenile, religious/inspirational, spiritual (children), sports (children). Receives 60 unsolicited fiction mss/month. Accepts 3-4 mss/issue; 30-40 mss/year. Published work by Eileen Spinelli, Bob Hartman and M. Donaleen Howitt. Published new writers within the past year. Length: 200 words minimum; 900 words maximum; 600 words average.
How to Contact: Send complete ms with SASE. Reports in 1-2 months on mss. Publishes ms an average of 1 year after acceptance. Sample copy for $2 and 9×12 SAE ($1.24 postage).
Payment/Terms: Pays $20-150 (stories, articles).

READ THE BUSINESS OF FICTION WRITING section to learn the correct way to prepare and submit a manuscript.

Advice: "We are looking for stories that immediately grab the imagination of the reader. Good dialogue, realistic character development, current lingo are necessary. Fiction can entertain, inspire or teach. Fiction stories do not have to do all three. We have a need for each of these types at different times. We prefer child-centered stories in a real-world setting. We are particularly interested in media-related articles and stories that involve healthy choices regarding media use. Try to write visually—be 'graphics-friendly.' "

*MY WEEKLY, For Women Everywhere, (I), 80 Kingsway East, Dundee DD4 8SL Scotland. 01382 223131. Fax: 01382 452471. Editor: H.G. Watson.
Needs: "*My Weekly* is a widely read magazine aimed at 'young' women of all ages. We are read by busy young mothers, active middle-aged wives and elderly retired ladies." Historical, humor/satire, mainstream/contemporary, romance, serialized novel. Accepts 4-5 mss/issue. Agented fiction 10%. Recently published work by Lavyrle Spencer. Fiction "should deal with real, down-to-earth themes that relate to the lives of our readers. Complete stories can be of any length from 1,500 to 4,000 words. Serials from 3 to 10 installments."
How to Contact: Send complete ms with cover letter. Include estimated word count. Simultaneous submissions OK.
Payment/Terms: Our rates compare favourably with other British magazines. Sample copy and guidelines free. Pays in contributor's copies. Acquires first British rights.

NA'AMAT WOMAN, Magazine of NA'AMAT USA, The Women's Labor Zionist Organization of America, (IV), 200 Madison Ave., New York NY 10016-3903. (212)725-8010. Editor: Judith A. Sokoloff. "Magazine covering a wide variety of subjects of interest to the Jewish community—including political and social issues, arts, profiles; many articles about Israel; and women's issues. Fiction must have a Jewish theme. Readers are the American Jewish community." Published 5 times/year. Estab. 1926. Circ. 20,000.
Needs: Contemporary, literary. Receives 10 unsolicited fiction mss/month. Accepts 3-5 fiction mss/year. Length: 1,500 words minimum; 3,000 words maximum. Also buys nonfiction.
How to Contact: Query first or send complete ms with SASE. Reports in 3 months on mss. Free sample copy for 9 × 11½ SAE and $1.20 postage.
Payment/Terms: Pays 10¢/word and 2 contributor's copies on publication for first North American serial rights; assignments on work-for-hire basis.
Advice: "No maudlin nostalgia or romance; no hackneyed Jewish humor and no poetry."

NEW ERA MAGAZINE, (I, II, IV), The Church of Jesus Christ of Latter-day Saints, 50 E. North Temple St., Salt Lake City UT 84150. (801)532-2951. Fax: (801)240-5997. Editor: Richard M. Romney. Magazine: 8 × 10½; 51 pages; 40 lb. coated paper; illustrations and photos. "We will publish fiction on any theme that strengthens and builds the standards and convictions of teenage Latter-day Saints ('Mormons')." Monthly. Estab. 1971. Circ. 200,000.
  ● *New Era* is a recipient of the Focus on Excellence Award from Brigham Young University. The magazine also sponsors a writing contest.
Needs: Stories on family relationships, self-esteem, dealing with loneliness, resisting peer pressure and all aspects of maintaining Christian values in the modern world. "All material must be written from a Latter-day Saint ('Mormon') point of view—or at least from a generally Christian point of view, reflecting LDS life and values." Receives 30-35 unsolicited mss/month. Accepts 1 ms/issue; 12 mss/year. Publishes ms 3 months to 3 years after acceptance. Published work by Jack Weyland and Alma Yates. Length: 1,500 words average; 250 words minimum; 2,000 words maximum.
How to Contact: Query letter preferred; send complete ms. Reports in 6-8 weeks. SASE. Disk submissions (WordPerfect, MacIntosh) OK. Sample copy for $1.50 and 9 × 12 SAE with 2 first-class stamps. Fiction guidelines for #10 SASE.
Payment/Terms: Pays $50-375 and contributor's copies on acceptance for all rights (reassign to author on request).
Advice: "Each magazine has its own personality—you wouldn't write the same style of fiction for *Seventeen* that you would write for *Omni*. Very few writers who are not of our faith have been able to write for us successfully, and the reason usually is that they don't know what it's like to be a member of our church. You must study and research and know those you are writing about. We love to work with beginning authors, and we're a great place to break in if you can understand us." Sponsors contests and awards for LDS fiction writers. "We have an annual contest; entry forms are in each September issue. Deadline is January; winners published in August."

‡NEW MYSTERY, (III), The Best New Mystery Stories, 175 Fifth Ave., #2001, New York NY 10010-7703. (212)353-1582. E-mail: newmyst@aol.com. Website: http://www.NewMystery.com (includes book reviews and short shorts. Editor: Charles Raisch III. Magazine: 8½ × 11; 96 pages; illustrations and photographs. "Mystery, suspense and crime." Quarterly. Estab. 1990. Circ. 90,000.
  ● Response time for this magazine seems to be slower in summer months. The mystery included here is varied and realistic.
Needs: Mystery/suspense (cozy to hardboiled). Plans special annual anthology. Receives 350 unsolicited mss/month. Buys 6-10 ms/issue. Agented fiction 50%. Published work by Stuart Kaminsky, Andrew Greeley and

Rosemary Santini. Publishes 1 new writer/issue. Length: 3,000-5,000 words preferred. Also buys short book reviews 500-3,000 words. Sometimes critiques rejected mss.
How to Contact: Send complete ms with cover letter. "We cannot be responsible for unsolicited manuscripts." Reports on ms in 1 month. SASE. Accepts electronic submissions. Sample copy for $5, 9×12 SAE and 4 first-class stamps.
Payment/Terms: Pays $25-1,000 on publication for all rights.
Advice: Stories should have "believable characters in trouble; sympathetic lead; visual language." Sponsors "Annual First Story Contest."

‡NEW SPY, (II, IV), New Spy, Inc., 175 Fifth Ave., Suite 2001, New York NY 10010-7703. Editor: Charles Raisch III. Magazine: 8½×11; 56 pages; illustrations and photos. Publishes "the world's best spy, thriller, intrigue and adventure short stories and book reviews." Quarterly. Estab. 1997. Circ. 70,000.
Needs: "Modern and historical spy fiction of the highest quality. Most international theaters acceptable, especially Europe, the Middle East and Asia. Offbeat situations and characters encouraged, but the use of solid principles of foreign intelligence intrigue is a central consideration. Military themes okay, as long as at some point, the uniform comes off and secretive plainclothes work carries the day." Published work by James Frey, Leslie Horvitz and Josh Pachter. Length: 3,000-6,000 words preferred. Also buys short book reviews of 250-2,000 words. "See examples in our coverage of Ambler, DeMille, Harris, Ludlum, Truscott and others, I#1."
How to Contact: Send complete ms with a cover letter. If no report in 60 days, consider ms rejected. "*New Spy* magazine is not responsible for unsolicited manuscripts, drawings or other material." Sample copy for $5, 9×12 SAE and 4 first-class stamps.
Payment/Terms: Pays $25-250 on publication for all rights.

THE NEW YORKER, (III), The New Yorker, Inc., 20 W. 43rd St., New York NY 10036. (212)536-5800. Fiction Department. A quality magazine of interesting, well-written stories, articles, essays and poems for a literate audience. Weekly. Estab. 1925. Circ. 750,000.
How to Contact: Send complete ms with SASE. Reports in 10-12 weeks on mss. Publishes 1 ms/issue.
Payment/Terms: Varies. Pays on acceptance.
Advice: "Be lively, original, not overly literary. Write what you want to write, not what you think the editor would like. Send poetry to Poetry Department."

‡NORTHEAST, the Sunday Magazine of the Hartford Courant, (IV), 285 Broad St., Hartford CT 06115. (203)241-3700. Website: http://www.courant.com. Editor: Lary Bloom. Magazine: 10×11½; 20-40 pages; illustrations; photos. "A regional (New England, specifically Connecticut) magazine, we publish stories of varied subjects of interest to our Connecticut audience" for a general audience. Weekly. Published special fiction issue and a special college writing issue for fiction and poetry. Estab. 1982. Circ. 16,000.
● Ranked as one of the best markets for fiction in the last *Writer's Digest* magazine's annual "Fiction Fifty."
Needs: Contemporary and regional. No children's stories or stories with distinct setting outside Connecticut. Receives 150 unsolicited mss/month. Buys 1 ms/issue; 2 mss/month. Publishes short shorts. Length: 750 words minimum; 1,500 words maximum.
How to Contact: Send complete ms with 10×12 SASE. Reports in 8-10 weeks. Simultaneous submissions OK. No reprints or previously published work. Sample copy and fiction guidelines for 10×12 or larger SASE.
Payment/Terms: Pays $250-1,000 on acceptance for one-time rights.

*NOVA SF, (IV), Perseo Libri srl, Box 1240, I-40100 Bologna Italy. Fiction Editor: Ugo Malaguti. Bimonthly. Circ. 5,000.
Needs: "Science fiction and fantasy short stories and short novels."
How to Contact: "No formalities required, we read all submissions and give an answer in about 20 weeks."
Payment/Terms: Pays $50-200, depending on length, and 2 contributor's copies on publication. Buys first Italian serial rights on stories."

NUGGET, (II), Firestone Publishing Inc., 14411 Commerce Way, Suite 420, Miami Lakes FL 33016. (305)557-0071. Editor-in-Chief: Christopher James. A newsstand magazine designed to have erotic appeal for a fetish-oriented audience. Published 12 times a year. Estab. 1956. Circ. 100,000.
Needs: Offbeat, fetish-oriented material encompassing a variety of subjects (B&D, TV, TS, spanking, amputee-ism, golden showers, infantalism, catfighting, etc.). Most of fiction includes several sex scenes. No fiction that concerns children or religious subjects. Accepts 2 mss/issue. Agented fiction 5%. Length: 2,000-3,500 words.
How to Contact: Send complete ms with SASE. Reports in 1 month. Sample copy for $3.50. Guidelines for legal-sized SASE.
Payment/Terms: Pays minimum $200 and 1 contributor's copy on publication for first rights.
Advice: "Keep in mind the nature of the publication, which is fetish erotica. Subject matter can vary, but we prefer fetish themes."

ODYSSEY, Adventures in Science, Cobblestone Publishing, Inc., 7 School St., Peterborough NH 03458. (603)924-7209. Editor: Elizabeth E. Lindstrom. Magazine. "Scientific accuracy, original approaches to the subject

INSIDER REPORT

Ron Carlson: writing from personal experiences

Ron Carlson's short stories have appeared in *Harper's*, *Gentlemen's Quarterly*, *Ploughshares*, *The New Yorker*, *Playboy*, STORY and many other journals and anthologies. Two collections of his work, *The News of the World* (1987) and *Plan B for the Middle Class* (1992) were featured on *The New York Times* "best books of the year" lists. His affection for his characters, ability to capture the complexity of their inner lives, and humor with which he portrays their small dramas make his work distinctive and irresistible. Though he's authored two novels, Carlson considers himself primarily a short story writer, and has just published his third collection, *The Hotel Eden*. "But in the last five years," he says, "some of my stories have been trying to get longer. They've been trying to crawl up and make trouble for me, and I'm going to let them." He's currently working on a novel, *Junior Achievement*, and a couple of short stories, and continues to teach in the Creative Writing Program at Arizona State University.

Ron Carlson

Photo by Connie McGovern

So much of your work portrays a belief in the basic strength and goodness of people. Margot Livesey in her *New York Times* review of *Hotel Eden* wrote, ". . . this writer . . . is a master of that rarity in contemporary fiction, the happy ending. Throughout the stories, disaster hovers, with despair in the wings, but sometimes the characters do win through, and when that happens we are glad." What's the primary influence on your point of view?
I had a great childhood: long, hot days playing ball in empty lots, wild bike rides, hours spent fishing or just throwing stones in the river. I've also been lucky—I've had many long-term relationships in my life. My parents, whom I'm close to, are still alive, and I've been married for 30 years—I've had my truck for 25!

Writing requires honesty, and honesty comes from the evidence. My evidence has been that people can shine. Life has many faces; it's possible to take an honest look at the affirmative side of life and still have drama. Every person, every event has a shadow, and that's what interests me. I ask, "What makes a person stand taller after certain events?" The goal at all times, though, for a story that's affecting, is honesty. I do think the best of people, and I tell the truth.

Your stories are so varied. Where do your story ideas come from?
Odd little collisions: one came from a strange lunch I had; one came when my father mentioned a name that stuck with me. *Place* is very important to me. To develop a story, I create a place in my mind and stay there. If it's authentic to me, something happens. I

INSIDER REPORT, *Carlson*

often use real places because it helps me believe in the story—"Hotel Eden" is based on a room I knew in London long ago. It left a powerful impression on me, so I set a story there.

When did you decide to become a writer?

I was always writing. I got it from my mother; she's a word person, a famous contester of those "25 words or less" things. She won a lot of prizes. But I didn't think of writing as a career choice. In my last two years of college, I looked at everything. I liked physics and math, but I also read Emily Dickinson. I took my first real teaching job in 1969, and by then I'd begun writing for myself. Like many other writers, I balance two jobs, teaching and writing. I write by the project. Short stories fit in my life better.

Did you publish in small journals first? How did you find markets, what did you look for?

I started out writing and selling short nonfiction articles to small publications. Nonfiction was easier to place. When I had some success with that, I started sending stories to small local literary magazines. I'm a big believer in small literary journals, university publications. The *Hayden Ferry Review* is a literary magazine published at Arizona State University. For all writers, study of the marketplace should be ongoing. It leads to new markets, and opens writers' minds to all the things a story can be. I took the "low-rent approach" to research: I went to newsstands, picked up copies—when I traveled, I looked in bookstores for literary journals. A good place to look for titles is the list at the back of *Best American Short Stories*, and of course *Novel & Short Story Writer's Market*. I read the copies I picked up and looked for stories that were kindred to my own.

When you send your work out, there are going to be rejections and false starts. Sometimes, the rejection makes no sense, because the publication seems perfect. Other times you have a clue: I sent a story about an old janitor and his wife talking in bed—a gentle story about a long marriage—to *TriQuarterly*, and they sent back a rejection saying it wasn't right for their "Men in Combat" issue.

Do you spend a lot of time on research or in rewrites?

Once I start a story, I stay in it and keep it warm, but I do have days away. If research is involved, I do it after I've begun. The stories are about the characters, anyway. I rewrite and rewrite, and I'm a good editor. I feel great after I've cut something that doesn't work—it's like getting a haircut; I feel young again. I've published around 100 stories, and as I tell my students, you live and die by the body of work, by the ability to work, not by a single story. Make it as good as you can, then get away. There's no such thing as sitting in the perfect room, writing the perfect story with a silver pen.

As a teacher, what do you find to be common errors or misconceptions about writing among your students?

The most common misconceptions are that every story has to have a strong plot or thematic arc, and that the story exists outside the writer. Stories are about how the writer feels about something or someone. That's what's important: the unique perception. A student will come to me and say, "I want to write like John Grisham." If someone else can write like Grisham, let him. But if you're writing for other people, stop. Passion is what writing is about. Often, if writers get what they expected, they may not have done a credible job.

INSIDER REPORT, *continued*

The part only they can invent may be the truest. It's about passion and discipline.

What's been most valuable to you in your own writing?

I can tolerate not knowing where I'm going. I have the stubbornness to stay in stories that are odd or perplexing. If I stood back and looked at them, evaluated them in terms of the market, I'd have said, "Oh you idiot!" An example is the Halloween story "Chromium Hook" (from *The Hotel Eden*). I wrote it for myself; it's idiosyncratic, yet it met with broad positive response. When writing, I've been able to stay in a mind-set that's very particular and true for me or whatever character I'm occupying. It's important to occupy that space, to send yourself on that journey.

Do you work with an agent?

I have an agent in New York. She found me, which is why I encourage writers to try to publish in small journals where they can be seen. Agents are looking for writers, and can create opportunities that writers alone can't. But a writer should have a viable inventory first—a book or two or several short stories. Writing must be a continuous thread, a way of life, or an agent won't be interested. Market always comes second.

What would you advise those who are just starting out, and who might not be able to benefit from formal training?

I'm not sure there's such a thing as formal training. As a teacher, what I hope to do is enable young writers to read their work more diagnostically. All critiques are about the next story. The twentieth story is better than the fifth, but not in a linear way. Be careful of your impulse to write what matters to you out of your writing. It's all about the work, so if you're planning to be a writer, it better be a trip you want to take.

If you keep at it, the market will find it. Write five or ten stories before you begin to send them. Muscle your way past the rejections. Most importantly, a writer is always working on a new story, so there's always another opportunity down the line. I feel lucky. I still want and love to write. No matter what you've sold or what award you've won, you'll always have to work on something new; you'll always have to go somewhere and type. During the writing day, there'll come a time when you want to get up and leave the room. But the *writer* is the one who stays. The coffee shop on the corner is full of failed writers. That's why there's been such a proliferation of special coffee shops in this country. They're full of writers who quit. So, keep at it.

—*Joanne Miller*

---

are primary concerns of the editors in choosing material. For 8-14 year olds." Monthly (except July and August). Estab. 1991. Circ. 30,000.

Needs: Material must match theme; send for theme list and deadlines. Children's/juvenile (8-14 years), "authentic historical and biographical fiction, science fiction, retold legends, etc., relating to theme." List of upcoming themes available for SASE. Length: 750 words maximum.

How to Contact: Query first or query with clips of published work (if new to *Odyssey*). "Include estimated word count and a detailed 1-page outline explaining the information to be presented; an extensive bibliography of materials authors plan to use." Reports in several months. Send SASE for reply or send stamped postcard to find out if ms has been received. Sample copy for $4.50, 9 × 12 SAE and $1.05 postage. Fiction guidelines for SASE.

Payment/Terms: Pays 20-25¢/word on publication for all rights.

Advice: "We also include in-depth nonfiction, plays and biographies."

OMNI, (II), General Media, 277 Park Ave. 4th Floor, New York NY 10172-0003. Website: http://www.omnimag. com. Fiction Editor: Ellen Datlow. Magazine: online exclusively; illustrations; photos. "Magazine of science and science fiction with an interest in near future; stories of what science holds, what life and lifestyles will be like in areas affected by science for a young, bright and well-educated audience between ages 18-45."
 • Ellen Datlow has won numerous awards (see "Advice" below). She also co-edits *The Year's Best Fantasy and Horror* (a reprint anthology).
Needs: Science fiction and contemporary fantasy. No sword and sorcery, horror or space opera. Receives approximately 400 unsolicited fiction mss/month. Accepts 20 mss/year. Agented fiction 1%. Recently published work by Kathleen Ann Gorman, Paul Park, James P. Blaylock and Michael Bishop. Length: 2,000 words minimum, 15,000 words maximum. Critiques rejected mss that interest me "when there is time." Sometimes recommends other markets.
How to Contact: Send complete ms with SASE. No simultaneous or online submissions. Reports within 2 months. Publishes ms 3 months to 1 year after acceptance.
Payment/Terms: Pays $1,250-2,500. Acquires first electronic rights exclusive for 6 months then can resell to print.
Advice: "Beginning writers should read a lot of the best science fiction short stories today to get a feeling for what is being done. Also, they should read outside the field and nonfiction for inspiration. We are looking for strong, well-written stories dealing with the next 100 years. When submitting your stories, don't be cute, don't be negative in your cover letter. Keep it simple. If you have credentials (writing or workshopping or whatever may be relevant), mention them in the letter. Never tell the plot of your story in a cover letter. Send the full story. I don't know any editor of short fiction who wants a query letter. Rewrite and learn to be your own editor. Don't ever call an editor on the phone and ask why he/she rejected a story. You'll either find out in a personal rejection letter (which means the editor liked it or thought enough of your writing to comment) or you won't find out at all (most likely the editor won't remember a form-rejected story)." Ellen Datlow has been nominated in Best Professional editor category of the Hugos 8 years running and she has won 5 World Fantasy Awards.

ON THE LINE, (II), Mennonite Publishing House, 616 Walnut Ave., Scottdale PA 15683-1999. (412)887-8500. Editor: Mary Meyer. Magazine: 7×10; 28 pages; illustrations; b&w photos. "A religious take-home paper with the goal of helping children grow in their understanding and appreciation of God, the created world, themselves and other people." For children ages 9-14. Weekly. Estab. 1970. Circ. 6,500.
Needs: Adventure and problem-solving stories with Christian values for older children and young teens (9-14 years). Receives 50-100 unsolicited mss/month. Accepts 52 mss/year. Published work by O.B. Comer, Eileen Spinelli and Russell Lewis. Published new writers within the last year. Length: 800-1,500 words.
How to Contact: Send complete ms noting whether author is offering first-time or reprint rights. Reports in 1 month. SASE. Simultaneous and previously published work OK. Free sample copy and fiction guidelines.
Payment/Terms: Pays on acceptance for one-time rights.
Advice: "We believe in the power of story to entertain, inspire and challenge the reader to new growth. Know children and their thoughts, feelings and interests. Be realistic with characters and events in the fiction. Stories do not need to be true, but need to *feel* true."

OPTIONS, The *Bi*-Monthly, (I, IV), AJA Publishing, Box 470, Port Chester NY 10573. E-mail: dianaeditr@a ol.com. Associate Editor: Diana Sheridan. Magazine: digest-sized; 114 pages; newsprint paper; glossy cover stock; illustrations and photos. Sexually explicit magazine for and about bisexuals. "Please read our Advice subhead." 10 issues/year. Estab. 1982. Circ. 100,000.
Needs: Erotica, bisexual, gay, lesbian. "First person as-if-true experiences." Accepts 6 unsolicited fiction mss/ issue. "Very little" of fiction is agented. Published new writers within the last year. Length: 2,000-3,000 words. Sometimes critiques rejected mss.
How to Contact: Send complete ms with or without cover letter. No simultaneous submissions. Reports in approximately 3 weeks. SASE. Electronic submissions (disk or e-mail as textfiles) OK. "Submissions on Macintosh disk welcome and can often use IBM submissions, but please include hard copy too." Sample copy for $2.95 and 6×9 SAE with 5 first-class stamps. Fiction guidelines for SASE.
Payment/Terms: Pays $100 on publication for all rights. Will reassign book rights on request.
Advice: "Read a copy of *Options* carefully and look at our spec sheet before writing anything for us. That's not new advice, but to judge from some of what we get in the mail, it's necessary to repeat. We only buy two bi/ lesbian pieces per issue; need is greater for bi/gay male mss. Though we're a bi rather than gay magazine, the emphasis is on same-sex relationships. If the readers want to read about a male/female couple, they'll buy another magazine. Gay male stories sent to *Options* will also be considered for publication in *Beau*, our gay male magazine. Must get into the hot action by 1,000 words into the story. (Sooner is fine too!) *Most important:* We *only* publish male/male stories that feature 'safe sex' practices unless the story is clearly something that took place pre-AIDS."

ORANGE COAST MAGAZINE, The Magazine of Orange County, (IV), 3701 Birch St., Suite 100, Newport Beach CA 92660. (714)862-1133. Fax: (714)862-0133. E-mail: ocmag@aol.com. Editor: Martin V. Smith. Managing Editor: Sharon Chan. Magazine: 8½×11; 175 pages; 50 lb. Sonoma gloss paper; Warrenflo cover; illustrations and photographs. *Orange Coast* publishes articles offering insight into the community for its affluent, well-educated Orange County readers. Monthly. Estab. 1974. Circ. 38,000.

Needs: Fiction rarely published. Fiction submissions must have Orange County setting or characters or be relevant to local sensibilities. Receives 30 unsolicited mss/month. Accepts 2 mss/year. Publishes ms 4-6 months after acceptance. Length: 2,500 words average; 1,500 words minimum; 3,000 words maximum.

How to Contact: Send complete ms with cover letter that includes Social Security number. Electronic submissions OK. Reports in 3 months. SASE. Simultaneous submissions OK. Sample copy for 9 × 12 SASE.

Payment/Terms: Pays $25-800 on acceptance for first North American serial rights.

Advice: "Read the magazine. Tell us why a specific piece of fiction belongs there. Convince us to make an exception."

*PEOPLE'S FRIEND, 80 Kingsway East, Dundee DD4 8SL Scotland. 01382 223131. Fax: 01382 452491. Fiction Editor: Margaret McCoy. Weekly. Circ. 470,000.

Needs: Specializes in women's fiction. "British backgrounds preferred (but not essential) by our readership." Recently published work by Betty McInnes, Shirley Worral and Christina Jones. Publishes 5 stories/issue. Length: 1,000-3,000 words.

Payment/Terms: Pays $75-85 and contributor's copies. Sample copy and guidelines available on application.

Advice: Looks for manuscript with "emotional content and characterization."

PLAYBOY MAGAZINE, 680 N. Lake Shore Dr., Chicago IL 60611. (312)751-8000. Contact: Fiction Editor. Monthly magazine. "As the world's largest general-interest lifestyle magazine for men, *Playboy* spans the spectrum of contemporary men's passions. From hard-hitting investigative journalism to light-hearted humor, the latest in fashion and personal technology to the cutting edge of the popular culture, *Playboy* is and always has been both guidebook and dream book for generations of American men . . . the definitive source of information and ideas for over 10 million readers each month. In addition, *Playboy*'s 'Interview' and '20 Questions' present profiles of politicians, athletes and today's hottest personalities." Estab. 1953, Circ. 3,283,000. Writer's guidelines for SASE. Query before submitting.

POCKETS, Devotional Magazine for Children, (II), The Upper Room, 1908 Grand Ave., Box 189, Nashville TN 37202. (615)340-7333. E-mail: pockets@upperroom.org. Website: http://www.upperroom.org (includes themes, guidelines and contest guidelines). Editor-in-Chief: Janet R. Knight. Magazine: 7 × 9; 48 pages; 50 lb. white econowrite paper; 80 lb. white coated, heavy cover stock; color and 2-color illustrations; some photos. Magazine for children ages 6-12, with articles specifically geared for ages 8 to 11. "The magazine offers stories, activities, prayers, poems—all geared to giving children a better understanding of themselves as children of God." Published monthly except for January. Estab. 1981. Estimated circ. 99,000.

  • *Pockets* has received honors from the Educational Press Association of America. The magazine's fiction tends to feature children dealing with real-life situations "from a faith perspective."

Needs: Adventure, contemporary, ethnic, historical (general), juvenile, religious/inspirational and suspense/mystery. "All submissions should address the broad theme of the magazine. Each issue will be built around one theme with material which can be used by children in a variety of ways. Scripture stories, fiction, poetry, prayers, art, graphics, puzzles and activities will all be included. Submissions do not need to be overtly religious. They should help children experience a Christian lifestyle that is not always a neatly-wrapped moral package, but is open to the continuing revelation of God's will. Seasonal material, both secular and liturgical, is desired. No violence, horror, sexual and racial stereotyping or fiction containing heavy moralizing." No talking animal stories or fantasy. Receives approximately 200 unsolicited fiction mss/month. Accepts 4-5 mss/issue; 44-60 mss/year. Publishes short shorts. A peace-with-justice theme will run throughout the magazine. Published work by Peggy King Anderson, Angela Gibson and John Steptoe. Published new writers last year. Length: 600 words minimum; 1,600 words maximum; 1,200 words average.

How to Contact: Send complete ms with SASE. Previously published submissions OK, but no simultaneous or faxed submissions. Reports in 1 month on mss. Publishes ms 1 year to 18 months after acceptance. Sample copy free with SAE and 4 first-class stamps. Fiction guidelines and themes with SASE. "Strongly advise sending for themes before submitting."

Payment/Terms: Pays 14¢/word and up and 2-5 contributor's copies on acceptance for first North American serial rights. $1.95 charge for extras; $1 each for 10 or more.

Advice: "Listen to children as they talk with each other. Please send for a sample copy as well as guidelines and themes. Many ms we receive are simply inappropriate. Each issue is theme-related. Please send for list of themes. New themes published in December of each year. Include SASE." Sponsors annual fiction writing contest. Deadline: Aug. 15. Send for guidelines. $1,000 award and publication.

PORTLAND MAGAZINE, Maine's City Magazine, (I, II), 578 Congress St., Portland ME 04101. (207)775-4339. Editor: Colin Sargent. Magazine: 56 pages; 60 lb. paper; 80 lb. cover stock; illustrations and photographs. "City lifestyle magazine—style, business, real estate, controversy, fashion, cuisine, interviews and art relating to the Maine area." Monthly. Estab. 1986. Circ. 100,000.

Needs: Contemporary, historical, literary. Receives 20 unsolicited fiction mss/month. Accepts 1 mss/issue; 10 mss/year. Publishes short shorts. Published work by Janwillem van de Wetering, Sanford Phippen and Mame Medwed. Length: 3 double-spaced typed pages.

How to Contact: Query first. "Fiction below 700 words, please." Send complete ms with cover letter. Reports in 6 months. SASE. Accepts electronic submissions.

Payment/Terms: Pays on publication for first North American serial rights.

Advice: "We publish ambitious short fiction featuring everyone from Frederick Barthelme to newly discovered fiction by Edna St. Vincent Millay."

POWER AND LIGHT, (I, II), Word Action Publishing Company, 6401 The Paseo, Kansas City MO 64131-1284. (816)333-7000. Fax: (816)333-4439. E-mail: mhammer@nazarene.org. Editor: Beula J. Postlewait. Associate Editor: Melissa Hammer. Story paper: 5½×8; 8 pages; storypaper and newsprint; illustrations and photos. "Relates Sunday School learning to preteens' lives. Must reflect theology of the Church of the Nazarene." Weekly. Estab. 1993. Circ. 740,000.

• *Power and Light* would like to see fiction with more natural, contemporary, positive situations.

Needs: Children's/juvenile (1-4 years; 10-12 years): adventure, fantasy (children's fantasy), religious/inspirational. List of upcoming themes available for SASE. Receives 40 mss/month. Accepts 10 mss/year. Publishes ms 2 years after acceptance. Recently published work by Bob Hostetler and Evelyn Horan. Publishes 10 new writers/year. Length: 700 words average; 500 words minimum; 800 words maximum. Often critiques or comments on rejected mss.

How to Contact: Query first ("E-mail response is much quicker and more convenient for queries"). Include estimated word count and Social Security number. Reports in 1 month on queries; 3 months on mss. SASE for reply or return or ms. Simultaneous, reprint and electronic (IBM disk or e-mail) submissions OK. Sample copy for #10 SASE. Fiction guidelines for #10 SASE.

Payment/Terms: Pays 5¢/word and 4 contributor's copies on publication for multi-use rights.

Advice: Looks for "creativity—situations relating to preteens that are not trite such as shoplifting, etc."

POWERPLAY MAGAZINE, (II, IV), Brush Creek Media, Inc., 2215R Market St., #148, San Francisco CA 94114. (415)552-1506. Fax: (415)552-3244. E-mail: jwbean@brushcreek.com. Editor: Bob Fifield. Magazine: 8½×11; 64 pages; white husky paper; gloss cover; b&w photos. "Geared toward gay men. *Powerplay* is kink-oriented. All of our fiction is sexual and frank; quite raw and confrontational." Quarterly. Estab. 1992. Circ. 38,000.

• This publisher also publishes *Bear, GBM, Interleather Man, Hombres Latinos, FQ, Mach, Bunkhouse*.

Needs: Gay: erotica, humor/satire. Looking for "unapologetic, bold sexual experiences, real or imagined." Published Tim Brough and Cord Odebolt. Receives 5-10 unsolicited mss/month. Buys 2-3 mss/issue; 15-20 mss/year. Length: Open. Sometimes critiques or comments on reject mss.

How To Contact: Send complete ms with cover letter. Accepts electronically transmitted submissions (disks for PC; "e-mail accepted in emergencies.") Include bio and Social Security number with submission. Send SASE for return or send disposable copy of the ms. Will consider simultaneous submissions and electronic (disk or modem) submissions. Sample copy for $6.50. Fiction guidelines free.

Payment/Terms: Pays $75 minimum; $125 maximum on publication. Purchases first North American serial rights. Also pays 2-3 contributor's copies.

PURPOSE, (I, II), Herald Press, 616 Walnut Ave., Scottdale PA 15683-1999. (412)887-8500. Fax: (412)887-3111. Editor: James E. Horsch. Magazine: 5⅜×8⅜; 8 pages; illustrations; photos. "Magazine focuses on Christian discipleship—how to be a faithful Christian in the midst of tough everyday life complexities. Uses story form to present models and examples to encourage Christians in living a life of faithful discipleship." Weekly. Estab. 1968. Circ. 14,000.

Needs: Historical, religious/inspirational. No militaristic/narrow patriotism or racism. Receives 100 unsolicited mss/month. Accepts 3 mss/issue; 140 mss/year. Published work by Kayleen Reusser, Crane Delbert Bennett and Margaret Hook. Length: 600 words average; 900 words maximum. Occasionally comments on rejected mss.

How to Contact: Send complete ms only. Reports in 2 months. Simultaneous and previously published work OK. Sample copy for 6×9 SAE and 2 first-class stamps. Writer's guidelines free with sample copy only.

Payment/Terms: Pays up to 5¢/word for stories and 2 contributor's copies on acceptance for one-time rights.

Advice: Many stories are "situational—how to respond to dilemmas. Write crisp, action moving, personal style, focused upon an individual, a group of people, or an organization. The story form is an excellent literary device to use in exploring discipleship issues. There are many issues to explore. Each writer brings a unique solution. Let's hear them. The first two paragraphs are crucial in establishing the mood/issue to be resolved in the story. Work hard on developing these.''

R-A-D-A-R, (I, II), Standard Publishing, 8121 Hamilton Ave., Cincinnati OH 45231-9943. (513)931-4050. Editor: Gary Thacker. Magazine: 12 pages; newsprint; illustrations; a few photos. "*R-A-D-A-R* is a take-home paper, distributed in Sunday school classes for children in grades 3-4. The stories and other features reinforce the Bible lesson taught in class. Boys and girls who attend Sunday school make up the audience. The fiction stories, Bible picture stories and other special features appeal to their interests.'' Weekly. Estab. 1978.
Needs: Fiction—The hero of the story should be an 9-11-year-old in a situation involving one or more of the following: history, mystery, animals, sports, adventure, school, travel, relationships with parents, friends and others. Stories should have believable plots and be wholesome, Christian character-building, but not "preachy." No science fiction. List of upcoming themes available for SASE. Published new writers within the last year. Length: 900-1,000 words average.
How to Contact: Send complete ms. Prefers for authors to send business-size SASE and request theme sheet. "Writing for a specific topic on theme sheet is much better than submitting unsolicited." Reports in 6-8 weeks on mss. SASE for ms. Simultaneous submissions permitted but not desired; reprint submissions OK. Sample copy and guidelines with SASE.
Payment/Terms: Pays 3-7¢/word on acceptance for first rights, reprints, etc.; 4 contributor's copies sent on publication.
Advice: "Send SASE with two first-class stamps for sample copy, guidelines and theme list. Follow the specifics of guidelines. Keep your writing current with the times and happenings of our world. Our needs change as the needs of 3rd-4th graders change. Writers must keep current."

RADIANCE, The Magazine for Large Women, (II), Box 30246, Oakland CA 94604. (510)482-0680. Website: http://www.radiancemagazine.com. Editor: Alice Ansfield. Fiction Editors: Alice Ansfield and Catherine Taylor. Magazine: 8½ × 11; 56 pages; glossy/coated paper; 70 lb. cover stock; illustrations; photos. "Theme is to encourage women to live fully now, whatever their body size. To stop waiting to live or feel good about themselves until they lose weight." Quarterly. Estab. 1984. Circ. 13,000. Readership: 50,000.
Needs: Adventure, contemporary, erotica, ethnic, fantasy, feminist, historical, humor/satire, mainstream, mystery/suspense, prose poem, science fiction, spiritual, sports, young adult/teen. "Want fiction to have a larger-bodied character; living in a positive, upbeat way. Our goal is to empower women." Receives 150 mss/month. Accepts 40 mss/year. Publishes ms within 1 year of acceptance. Published work by Marla Zarrow, Sallie Tisdale and Mary Kay Blakely. Length: 2,000 words average; 800 words minimum; 3,500 words maximum. Publishes short shorts. Sometimes critiques rejected mss.
How to Contact: Query with clips of published work and send complete ms with cover letter. Reports in 3-4 months. SASE. Reprint submissions OK. Sample copy for $3.50. Guidelines for #10 SASE. Reviews novels and short story collections "with at least one large-size heroine."
Payment/Terms: Pays $35-100 and contributor's copies on publication for one-time rights. Sends galleys to the author if requested.
Advice: "Read our magazine before sending anything to us. Know what our philosophy and points of view are before sending a manuscript. Look around within your community for inspiring, successful and unique large women doing things worth writing about. At this time, prefer fiction having to do with a larger woman (man, child). *Radiance* is one of the leading resources in the size-acceptance movement. Each issue profiles dynamic large women from all walks of life, along with articles on health, media, fashion and politics. Our audience is the 30 million American women who wear a size 16 or over. Feminist, emotionally-supportive, quarterly magazine."

RANGER RICK MAGAZINE, (II), National Wildlife Federation, 8925 Leesburg Pike, Vienna VA 22184. (703)790-4000. Editor: Gerald Bishop. Fiction Editor: Deborah Churchman. Magazine: 8 × 10; 48 pages; glossy paper; 60 lb. cover stock; illustrations; photos. "*Ranger Rick* emphasizes conservation and the enjoyment of nature through full-color photos and art, fiction and nonfiction articles, games and puzzles, and special columns. Our audience ranges in ages from 6-12, with the greatest number in the 7 and up. We aim for a fourth grade reading level. They read for fun and information." Monthly. Estab. 1967. Circ. 850,000.
  ● *Ranger Rick* has won several EdPress awards. The editors say the magazine has had a backlog of stories recently, yet they would like to see more *good* mystery and science fiction stories (with nature themes).
Needs: Adventure, fantasy, humor, mystery (amateur sleuth), science fiction and sports. "Interesting stories for kids focusing directly on nature or related subjects. Fiction that carries a conservation message is always needed, as are adventure stories involving kids with nature or the outdoors. Moralistic 'lessons' taught children by parents or teachers are not accepted. Human qualities are attributed to animals only in our regular feature, 'Adventures of Ranger Rick.' '' Receives about 150-200 unsolicited fiction mss each month. Accepts about 6 mss/year. Published fiction by Leslie Dendy. Length: 900 words maximum. Critiques rejected mss "when there is time."
How to Contact: Query with sample lead and any clips of published work with SASE. May consider simultaneous submissions. Reports in 3 months on queries and mss. Publishes ms 8 months to 1 year after acceptance, but sometimes longer. Sample copy for $2. Guidelines for legal-sized SASE.

Payment/Terms: Pays $550 maximum/full-length ms on acceptance for all rights. Very rarely buys reprints. Sends galleys to author.

Advice: "For our magazine, the writer needs to understand kids and that aspect of nature he or she is writing about—a difficult combination! Manuscripts are rejected because they are contrived and/or condescending—often overwritten. Some manuscripts are anthropomorphic, others are above our readers' level. We find that fiction stories help children understand the natural world and the environmental problems it faces. Beginning writers have a chance equal to that of established authors *provided* the quality is there. Would love to see more science fiction and fantasy, as well as mysteries."

REDBOOK, (II), The Hearst Corporation, 224 W. 57th St., New York NY 10019. (212)649-2000. Fiction Editor: Dawn Raffel. Magazine: 8 × 10¾; 150-250 pages; 34 lb. paper; 70 lb. cover; illustrations; photos. "*Redbook*'s readership consists of American women, ages 25-44. Most are well-educated, married, have children and also work outside the home." Monthly. Estab. 1903. Circ. 3,200,000.

Needs: "*Redbook* generally publishes one or two short stories per issue. Stories need not be about women exclusively; but must appeal to a female audience. We are interested in new voices and buy up to a quarter of our stories from unsolicited submissions. Standards are high: Stories must be fresh, felt and intelligent; no formula fiction." Receives up to 600 unsolicited fiction mss each month. Published new writers within the last year. Length: up to 22 ms pages.

How to Contact: Send complete ms with SASE. No queries, please. Simultaneous submissions OK. Reports in 8-12 weeks.

Payment/Terms: Pays on acceptance for first North American serial rights.

Advice: "Superior craftsmanship is of paramount importance: We look for emotional complexity, dramatic tension, precision of language. Note that we don't run stories that look back on the experiences of childhood or adolescence. Please read a few issues to get a sense of what we're looking for."

‡REFORM JUDAISM, (II, IV), Union of American Hebrew Congregations, 838 5th Ave., New York NY 10021. (212)650-4240. Editor: Aron Hirt-Manheimer. Managing Editor: Joy Weinberg. Magazine: 8 × 10¾; 96 pages; illustrations; photos. "We cover subjects of Jewish interest in general and Reform Jewish in particular, for members of Reform Jewish congregations in the United States and Canada." Quarterly. Estab. 1972. Circ. 295,000.

● Recipient of The Simon Rockower Award for Excellence in Jewish Journalism for feature writing, graphic design and photography. The editor says they would publish more stories if they could find excellent, sophisticated, contemporary Jewish fiction.

Needs: Humor/satire, religious/inspirational. Receives 75 unsolicited mss/month. Buys 3 mss/year. Publishes ms 6 months after acceptance. Length: 1,200 words average; 600 words minimum; 3,000 words maximum.

How to Contact: Send complete ms with cover letter. Reports in 6 weeks. SASE for ms. "For quickest response send self addressed stamped postcard with choices: Yes, we're interested in publishing; Maybe, we'd like to hold for future consideration; No, we've decided to pass on publication." Simultaneous submissions OK. Sample copy for $3.50.

Payment/Terms: Pays 30¢/word on publication for first North American serial rights.

ST. ANTHONY MESSENGER, (I, II), 1615 Republic St., Cincinnati OH 45210-1298. E-mail: stanthony@americancatholic.org. Website: http://www.AmericanCatholic.org (includes Saint of the day, selected articles, product information). Editor: Norman Perry, O.F.M. Magazine: 8 × 10¾; 56 pages; illustrations; photos. "*St. Anthony Messenger* is a Catholic family magazine which aims to help its readers lead more fully human and Christian lives. We publish articles which report on a changing church and world, opinion pieces written from the perspective of Christian faith and values, personality profiles, and fiction which entertains and informs." Monthly. Estab. 1893. Circ. 358,000.

● This is a leading Catholic magazine, but has won awards for both religious and secular journalism and writing from the Catholic Press Association, the International Association of Business Communicators and the Cincinnati Editors Association.

Needs: Contemporary, religious/inspirational, romance, senior citizen/retirement and spiritual. "We do not want mawkishly sentimental or preachy fiction. Stories are most often rejected for poor plotting and characterization; bad dialogue—listen to how people talk; inadequate motivation. Many stories say nothing, are 'happenings' rather than stories." No fetal journals, no rewritten Bible stories. Receives 70-80 unsolicited fiction mss/month. Accepts 1 ms/issue; 12 mss/year. Publishes ms up to 1 year after acceptance. Recently published work by Arthur Powers, Darlene Beck-Jacobsen and Kari Sharp hill. Length: 2,000-3,000 words. Critiques rejected mss "when there is time." Sometimes recommends other markets.

How to Contact: Send complete ms with SASE. No simultaneous submissions. Reports in 6-8 weeks. Sample copy and guidelines for #10 SASE. Reviews novels and short story collections. Send books to Barbara Beckwith, book review editor.

Payment/Terms: Pays 15¢/word maximum and 2 contributor's copies on acceptance for first serial rights; $1 charge for extras.

Advice: "We publish one story a month and we get up to 1,000 a year. Too many offer simplistic 'solutions' or answers. Pay attention to endings. Easy, simplistic, deus ex machina endings don't work. People have to feel characters in the stories are real and have a reason to care about them and what happens to them. Fiction entertains but can also convey a point in a very telling way just as the Bible uses stories to teach."

ST. JOSEPH'S MESSENGER AND ADVOCATE OF THE BLIND, (II), Sisters of St. Joseph of Peace, 541 Pavonia Ave., Jersey City NJ 07306. (201)798-4141. Magazine: 8½ × 11; 16 pages; illustrations; photos. For Catholics generally but not exclusively. Theme is "religious—relevant—real." Quarterly. Estab. 1903. Circ. 20,000.
Needs: Contemporary, humor/satire, mainstream, religious/inspirational, romance, senior citizen/retirement. Receives 30-40 unsolicited fiction mss/month. Accepts 3 mss/issue; 20 mss/year. Publishes ms an average of 1 year after acceptance. Published work by Eileen W. Strauch. Published new writers within the last year. Length: 800 words minimum; 1,800 words maximum; 1,500 words average. Occasionally critiques rejected mss.
How to Contact: Send complete ms with SASE. Simultaneous and previously published submissions OK. Sample copy for #10 SASE. Fiction guidelines for SASE.
Payment/Terms: Pays $15-40 and 2 contributor's copies on acceptance for one-time rights.
Advice: Rejects mss because of "vague focus or theme. Write to be read—keep material current and of interest. *Do not preach*—the story will tell the message. Keep the ending from being too obvious. Fiction is the greatest area of interest to our particular reading public."

‡SATURDAY NIGHT, Saturday Night Magazine Ltd., 184 Front St. E, Suite 400, Toronto, Ontario M5A 4N3 Canada. (416)368-7237. Fax: (416)368-5112. E-mail: editorial@saturdaynight.ca. Editor: Kenneth Whyte. Contact: Gillian Burnett, assistant to the editor. Monthly magazine. Readership is urban concentrated. Well-educated, with a high disposable income. Average age is 43. Estab. 1887. Circ. 410,000.
Needs: Publishes novel excerpts.
How to Contact: Submit seasonal material 3-4 months in advance. Accepts simultaneous submissions. Sample copy for $3.50. Writer's guidelines free.
Payment/Terms: Pays on receipt of a publishable ms. Buys first North American serial rights.

SEEK, (II), Standard Publishing, 8121 Hamilton Ave., Cincinnati OH 45231-2396. Editor: Eileen H. Wilmoth. Magazine: 5½ × 8½; 8 pages; newsprint paper; art and photos in each issue. "Inspirational stories of faith-in-action for Christian young adults; a Sunday School take-home paper." Weekly. Estab. 1970. Circ. 40,000.
Needs: Religious/inspirational. Accepts 150 mss/year. Publishes ms an average of 1 year after acceptance. 20% of work published is by new writers. Length: 500-1,200 words.
How to Contact: Send complete ms with SASE. No simultaneous submissions. Reports in 2-3 months. Free sample copy and guidelines.
Payment/Terms: Pays 5-7¢/word on acceptance. Buys reprints.
Advice: "Write a credible story with Christian slant—no preachments; avoid overworked themes such as joy in suffering, generation gaps, etc. Most manuscripts are rejected by us because of irrelevant topic or message, unrealistic story, or poor character and/or plot development. We use fiction stories that are believable."

SEVENTEEN, (I, II), III Magazine Corp., 850 Third Ave., New York NY 10022-6258. (212)407-9700. Fiction Editor: Ben Schrank. Magazine: 8½ × 11; 125-400 pages; 40 lb. coated paper; 80 lb. coated cover stock; illustrations; photos. A general interest magazine with fashion; beauty care; pertinent topics such as current issues, attitudes, experiences and concerns of teenagers. Monthly. Estab. 1944. Circ. 2.5 million.
  ● *Seventeen* sponsors an annual fiction contest for writers age 13-21.
Needs: High-quality literary fiction. No science fiction, action/adventure or pornography. Receives 200 unsolicited fiction mss/month. Accepts 6-12 mss/year. Agented fiction 50%. Published work by Margaret Atwood, Joyce Carol Oates, Ellen Gilchrist and Pagen Kennedy. Publishes 4-5 new writers/year. Length: approximately 750-3,500 words.
How to Contact: Send complete ms with SASE and cover letter with relevant credits. Reports in 3 months on mss. Guidelines for submissions with SASE.
Payment/Terms: Pays $700-2,500 on acceptance for one-time rights.
Advice: "Respect the intelligence and sophistication of teenagers. *Seventeen* remains open to the surprise of new voices. Our commitment to publishing the work of new writers remains strong; we continue to read every submission we receive. We believe that good fiction can move the reader toward thoughtful examination of her own life as well as the lives of others—providing her ultimately with a fuller appreciation of what it means to be human. While stories that focus on female teenage experience continue to be of interest, the less obvious possibilities are equally welcome. We encourage writers to submit literary short stories concerning subjects that may not be immediately identifiable as 'teenage,' with narrative styles that are experimental and challenging. Too often, unsolicited submissions possess voices and themes condescending and unsophisticated. Also, writers hesitate to send stories to *Seventeen* which they think too violent or risqué. Good writing holds the imaginable and then some, and if it doesn't find its home here, we're always grateful for the introduction to a writer's work. We're more inclined to publish cutting edge fiction than simple, young adult fiction."

SHOFAR, For Jewish Kids On The Move, (II, IV), 43 Northcote Dr., Melville NY 11747-3924. (516)643-4598. Fax: (516)643-4598. Editor: Gerald H. Grayson, Ph.D. Magazine: 8½ × 11; 32 pages; 60 lb. paper; 80 lb.

cover; illustration; photos. Audience: Jewish children in fourth through eighth grades. Monthly (October-May). Estab. 1984. Circ. 10,000.

Needs: Children's/juvenile (middle reader): cartoons, contemporary, humorous, poetry, puzzles, religious, sports. "All material must be on a Jewish theme." Receives 12-24 unsolicited mss/month. Accepts 3-5 mss/issue; 24-40 mss/year. Published work by Caryn Huberman, Diane Claerbout and Rabbi Sheldon Lewis. Length: 500-700 words. Occasionally critiques rejected mss. Recommends other markets.

How to Contact: Send complete ms with cover letter. Reports in 6-8 weeks. SASE. Simultaneous and reprint submissions OK. Sample copy for 9×12 SAE and $1.01 first-class postage. Fiction guidelines for 3½×6½ SASE.

Payment/Terms: Pays 10¢/word and 5 contributor's copies on publication for first North American serial rights.

Advice: "Know the magazine and the religious-education needs of Jewish elementary-school-age children. If you are a Jewish educator, what has worked for you in the classroom? Write it out; send it on to me; I'll help you develop the idea into a short piece of fiction. A beginning fiction writer eager to break into *Shofar* will find an eager editor willing to help."

SOJOURNER, The Women's Forum, (I, IV), 42 Seaverns, Jamaica Plain MA 02130. (617)524-0415. Editor: Stephanie Poggi. Magazine: 11×17; 48 pages; newsprint; illustrations; photos. "Feminist journal publishing interviews, nonfiction features, news, viewpoints, poetry, reviews (music, cinema, books) and fiction for women." Published monthly. Estab. 1975. Circ. 40,000.

Needs: "Writing on race, sex, class and queerness." Experimental, fantasy, feminist, lesbian, humor/satire, literary, prose poem and women's. Upcoming themes: "Fiction/Arts Issue" (February); "Annual Health Supplement" (March); Pride (June); Sports (May); Femmes (November); Spirituality (December) and Depression (January). Receives 20 unsolicited fiction mss/month. Accepts 10 mss/year. Agented fiction 10%. Published work by Ruth Ann Lonardelli and Janie Adams. Published new writers within the last year. Length: 1,000 words minimum; 4,000 words maximum; 2,500 words average.

How to Contact: Send complete ms with SASE and cover letter with description of previous publications; current works. Simultaneous submissions OK. Reports in 6-8 months. Publishes ms an average of 6 months after acceptance. Sample copy for $3 with 10×13 SASE. Fiction guidelines for SASE.

Payment/Terms: Pays subscription to magazine and 2 contributor's copies, $15 for first rights. No extra charge up to 5 contributor's copies; $1 charge each thereafter.

Advice: "Pay attention to appearance of manuscript! Very difficult to wade through sloppily presented fiction, however good. Do write a cover letter. If not cute, it can't hurt and may help. Mention previous publication(s)."

SPIDER, The Magazine for Children, (II), Carus Publishing Co./The Cricket Magazine Group, P.O. Box 300, Peru IL 61354. 1-800-588-8585. Editor-in-Chief: Marianne Carus. Associate Editor: Laura Fillotson. Magazine: 8×10; 33 pages; illustrations and photos. "*Spider* publishes high-quality literature for beginning readers, mostly children ages 6 to 9." Monthly. Estab. 1994. Circ. 85,000.

Needs: Children's/juvenile (6-9 years), fantasy (children's fantasy). "No religious, didactic, or violent stories, or anything that talks down to children." Accepts 4 mss/issue. Publishes ms 1-2 years after acceptance. Agented fiction 2%. Published work by Lissa Rovetch, Ursula K. LeGuin and Eric Kimmel. Length: 775 words average; 300 words minimum; 1,000 words maximum. Publishes short shorts. Also publishes poetry. Often critiques or comments on rejected ms.

How to Contact: Send complete ms with a cover letter. Include exact word count. Reports in 3 months. Send SASE for return of ms. Simultaneous and reprint submissions OK. Sample copy for $4. Fiction guidelines for #10 SASE.

Payment/Terms: Pays 25¢/word and 2 contributor's copies on publication for first rights or one-time rights; additional copies for $2.

Advice: "Read back issues of *Spider*." Looks for "quality writing, good characterization, lively style, humor. We would like to see more multicultural fiction."

SPIRIT,(I), Good Ground Press, 1884 Randolph Ave., St. Paul MN 55105. (612)690-7012. Fax: (612)690-7039. Editor: Joan Mitchell. Magazine: 8 ½×11; 4 pages; 50 lb. paper. Religious education magazine for Roman Catholic teens. "Stories must be realistic, not moralistic or pietistic. They are used as catalysts to promote teens' discussion of their conflicts." Biweekly (28 issues). Estab. 1988. Circ. 25,000.

Needs: Feminist, religious/inspirational, young adult/teen. Upcoming themes: Christmas and Easter. List of upcoming themes available for SASE. Receives 20 unsolicited mss/month. Accepts 1 mss/issue; 12 mss/year.

CHECK THE CATEGORY INDEXES, located at the back of the book, for publishers interested in specific fiction subjects.

Publishes ms 6-12 months after acceptance. Published work by Margaret McCarthy, Kathleen Y Choi, Heather Klassen, Kathleen Cleberg, Bob Bartlett and Ron LaGro. Length: 1,000 words minimum; 1,200 words maximum. Sometimes critiques or comments on rejected mss.

How to Contact: Send complete ms with a cover letter. Include estimated word count. Reports in 6 months on mss. SASE for return of ms or send a disposable copy of ms. Simultaneous submissions and reprints OK. Sample copy and fiction guidelines free.

Payment/Terms: Pays $150 minimum on publication and 5 contributor's copies. Acquires first North American serial rights.

Advice: Looks for "believable conflicts for teens. Just because we're religious, don't send pious, moralistic work."

STANDARD, (I, II, IV), Nazarene International Headquarters, 6401 The Paseo, Kansas City MO 64131. (816)333-7000. Editor: Everett Leadingham. Magazine: 8½×11; 8 pages; illustrations; photos. Inspirational reading for adults. Weekly. Estab. 1936. Circ. 165,000.

Needs: "Looking for fiction-type stories that show Christianity in action." Publishes ms 14-18 months after acceptance. Published new writers within the last year. Length: 1,200-1,500 words average; 300 words minimum; 1,700 words maximum.

How to Contact: Send complete ms with name, address and phone number. Reports in 2-3 months on mss. SASE. Simultaneous submissions OK but will pay only reprint rates. Sample copy and guidelines for SAE and 2 first-class stamps.

Payment/Terms: Pays 3½¢/word; 2¢/word (reprint) on acceptance; contributor's copies on publication.

‡STORY FRIENDS, (II), Mennonite Publishing House, 616 Walnut Ave., Scottdale PA 15683-1999. (412)887-8500. E-mail: rstutz%mph@mcimail.com. Editor: Rose Mary Stutzman. A magazine which portrays Jesus as a friend and helper. Nonfiction and fiction for children 4-9 years of age. Monthly.

• The Mennonite Publishing House also published *On the Line*, *Purpose* and *With* magazines.

Needs: Juvenile. Stories of everyday experiences at home, in church, in school or at play, which provide models of Christian values. Recently published work by Virginia Kroll and Joyce Moyer Hosetter. Publishes 10-12 new writers/year. Length: 300-800 words.

How to Contact: Send complete ms with SASE. Seasonal or holiday material should be submitted 6 months in advance. Free sample copy.

Payment/Terms: Pays 3-5¢/word on acceptance for one-time rights. Buys reprints. Not copyrighted.

Advice: "It is important to include relationships, patterns of forgiveness, respect, honesty, trust and caring. Prefer exciting yet plausible short stories which offer different settings, introduce children to wide ranges of friends and demonstrate joys, fears, temptations and successes of the readers. Read good children's literature, the classics, the Newberry winner and the Caldecott winners. Respect children you know and allow their resourcefulness and character to have a voice in your writing."

STRAIGHT, (II), Standard Publishing Co., 8121 Hamilton Ave., Cincinnati OH 45231. (513)931-4050. Editor: Heather Wallace. "Publication helping and encouraging teens to live a victorious, fulfilling Christian life. Distributed through churches and some private subscriptions." Magazine: 6½×7½; 12 pages; newsprint paper and cover; illustrations (color); photos. Quarterly in weekly parts. Estab. 1951. Circ. 40,000.

Needs: Contemporary, religious/inspirational, romance, spiritual, mystery, adventure and humor—all with Christian emphasis. "Stories dealing with teens and teen life, with a positive message or theme. Topics that interest teenagers include school, family life, recreation, friends, church, part-time jobs, dating and music. Main character should be a Christian teenager and regular churchgoer, who faces situations using Bible principles." No science fiction. Themes available on a quarterly basis for SASE. Receives approximately 100 unsolicited fiction mss/month. Accepts 2-3 mss/issue; 100-125 mss/year. Publishes ms an average of 1 year after acceptance. Less than 1% of fiction is agented. Published work by Alan Cliburn, Betty Steele Everett and Teresa Cleary. Published new writers within the last year. Length: 900-1,500 words. Recommends other markets.

How to Contact: Send complete ms with SASE and cover letter (experience with teens especially preferred from new writers). Reports in 1-2 months. Sample copy and guidelines for SASE.

Payment/Terms: Pays 5-7¢/word on acceptance for first and one-time rights. Buys reprints.

Advice: "Get to know us before submitting, through guidelines and sample issues (SASE). And get to know teenagers. A writer must know what today's teens are like, and what kinds of conflicts they experience. In writing a short fiction piece for the teen reader, don't try to accomplish too much. If your character is dealing with the problem of prejudice, don't also deal with his/her fights with sister, desire for a bicycle, or anything else that is not absolutely essential to the reader's understanding of the major conflict."

THE SUN, (II), The Sun Publishing Company, Inc., 107 N. Roberson St., Chapel Hill NC 27516. (919)942-5282. Editor: Sy Safransky. Magazine: 8½×11; 40 pages; offset paper; glossy cover stock; illustrations; photos. "*The Sun* is a magazine of ideas. While we tend to favor personal writing, we're open to just about anything—even experimental writing, if it doesn't make us feel stupid. Surprise us; we often don't know what we'll like until we read it." Monthly. Estab. 1974. Circ. 30,000.

Needs: Open to all fiction. Receives approximately 500 unsolicited fiction mss each month. Accepts 3 ms/issue.

Recently published work by Poe Ballantine, John McNally and Jane Webster. Publishes 2-3 previously unpublished writers/year. Published new writers within the last year. Length: 7,000 words maximum. Also publishes poetry.

How to Contact: Send complete ms with SASE. Reports in 3 months. Publishes ms an average of 6-12 months after acceptance. Sample copy for $3.50

Payment/Terms: Pays up to $500 on publication, plus 2 contributor's copies and a complimentary one-year subscription for one-time rights. Publishes reprints.

SWANK MAGAZINE, (II, IV), Swank Publication, 210 Route 4 East, Suite 401, Paramus NJ 07652. Fax: (201)843-8636. Editor: Paul Gambino. Magazine: 8½×11; 116 pages; 20 lb. paper; 60 lb. coated stock; illustrations; photos. "Men's sophisticated format. Sexually-oriented material. Our readers are after erotic material." Published 13 times a year. Estab. 1952. Circ. 350,000.

Needs: High-caliber erotica. "Fiction always has an erotic or other male-oriented theme; also eligible would be mystery or suspense with a very erotic scene. Also would like to see more humor. Writers should try to avoid the clichés of the genre." Receives approximately 80 unsolicited fiction mss each month. Accepts 1 ms/issue, 18 mss/year. Published new writers within the last year. Length: 1,500-2,750 words.

How to Contact: Send complete ms with SASE and cover letter, list previous publishing credits. Electronic submissions OK. Reports in 3 weeks on mss. Sample copy for $5.95 with SASE.

Payment/Terms: Pays $300-500. Buys first North American serial rights. Offers 25% kill fee for assigned ms not published.

Advice: "Research the men's magazine market." Mss are rejected because of "typical, overly simple storylines and poor execution. We're looking for interesting stories—whether erotic in theme or not—that break the mold of the usual men's magazine fiction. We're not only just considering strict erotica. Mystery, adventure, etc. with erotica passages will be considered."

TEEN LIFE, (II), Gospel Publishing House, 1445 Boonville Ave., Springfield MO 65802-1894. (417)862-2781. Fax: (417)862-6059. E-mail: tbicket@ag.org. Editor: Tammy Bicket. Magazine for teenagers (ages 12-19). It focuses on encouraging teens in their commitment to God and challenging them to grow in their relationship with Christ and others. Quarterly. Estab. 1936. Circ. 60,000.

Needs: Religious/inspirational, mystery/suspense, adventure, humor, spiritual and young adult, "with a strong but not preachy Biblical emphasis. We would like to see more humor." Upcoming themes: "Family," "Discipleship," "Ministry," "Dating." Receives 100 unsolicited fiction mss/month. Recently published work by Teresa Cleary, Betty Steele Everett, Joey O'Connor and Christopher Lyon. Publishes 20 new writers/year. Length: up to 1,500 words.

How to Contact: Send complete ms with SASE. "We want manuscripts that reflect our upcoming themes. Please send for guidelines before sending manuscript." Reports in 1-3 months. Simultaneous, reprint and electronic (disk, Mac) submissions OK. Free sample copy and guidelines.

Payment/Terms: Varies. Pays on acceptance for one-time rights.

Advice: "Most manuscripts are rejected because of shallow characters, shallow or predictable plots, and/or a lack of spiritual emphasis. Write stories about real life. Don't make everything into a fairy tale. Be realistic. Send seasonal material approximately 18 months in advance."

‡'TEEN MAGAZINE, (II), Petersen Publishing Co., 6420 Wilshire Blvd., Los Angeles CA 90048-5515. (213)782-2950. Fax: (213)782-2660. Editor: Roxanne Camron. Magazine: 100-150 pages; 34 lb. paper; 60 lb. cover; illustrations and photos. "The magazine contains fashion, beauty and features for the young teenage girl. The median age of our readers is 16. Our success stems from our dealing with relevant issues teens face." Monthly. Estab. 1957. Circ. 1.1 million.

Needs: Adventure, humor, mystery, romance and young adult. Every story, whether romance, mystery, humor, etc., must be aimed at teenage girls. The protagonist should be a teenage girl. No experimental, science fiction, fantasy or horror. Buys 1 ms/issue; 12 mss/year. Generally publishes ms 3-5 months after acceptance. Length: 2,500-3,500 words. Publishes short shorts.

How to Contact: Send complete ms and short cover letter with SASE. Reports in 10 weeks on mss. Sample copy for $2.50. Guidelines for SASE.

Payment/Terms: Pays $200 and up on acceptance for all rights.

Advice: "Try to find themes that suit the modern teen. We need innovative ways of looking at the age-old problems of young love, parental pressures, making friends, being left out, etc. Subject matter and vocabulary should be appropriate for an average 16-year-old reader. 'TEEN would prefer to have romance balanced with a plot, re: a girl's inner development and search for self. Handwritten mss will not be read."

TROIKA MAGAZINE, Wit, Wisdom, and Wherewithal, (I, II), Lone Tout Publications, Inc., P.O. Box 1006, Weston CT 06883. (203)227-5377. Fax: (203)222-9332. E-mail: troikamag@aol.com. Editor: Celia Meadow. Magazine: 8⅛×10⅝; 100 pages; 45 lb. Expression paper; 100 lb. Warren cover; illustrations and photographs. "Our general interest magazine is geared toward an audience aged 30-50 looking to balance a lifestyle of family, community and personal success." Quarterly. Estab. 1994. Circ. 100,000.

• *Troika* received 1995 *Print Magazine* Awards for Excellence (design) and two Ozzie Silver Awards for Excellence (design).

Needs: Humor/satire, literary, mainstream/contemporary. List of upcoming themes available for SASE. Receives 200 unsolicited mss/month. Accepts 2-5 mss/issue; 8-20 mss/year. Publishes ms 3-6 months after acceptance. Recently published work by Nelson DeMille, Gene Perret, Craig Furnals and Chris Boal. Length: 2,000-3,000 words. Also publishes literary essays and literary criticism. Sometimes critiques or comments on rejected ms.

How to Contact: Send complete ms with a cover letter giving address, phone/fax number and e-mail address. Include estimated word count, brief bio, SASE and list of publications with submission. Reports in 1-3 months. Send SASE for reply to query. Send a disposable copy of ms. Simultaneous and electronic submissions OK. Sample copy for $5. Guidelines for #10 SASE.

Payment/Terms: Pays $250 maximum on publication for first North American serial rights.

TURTLE MAGAZINE FOR PRESCHOOL KIDS, (II), Children's Better Health Institute, Benjamin Franklin Literary & Medical Society, Inc., Box 567, 1100 Waterway Blvd., Indianapolis IN 46206. (317)636-8881. Editor: Terry Harshman. Magazine of picture stories and articles for preschool children 2-5 years old.

Needs: Juvenile (preschool). Special emphasis on health, nutrition, exercise and safety. Also has need for "action rhymes to foster creative movement, very simple science experiments, and simple food activities." Upcoming themes: "New Year Nutrition" (January/February); "What's In, What's Out" (March); "Spring Into Action" (April/May); "Safe Play" (June); "Young Champions" (July/August). Receives approximately 100 unsolicited fiction mss/month. Published new writers within the last year. Length: 300 words for bedtime or naptime stories.

How to Contact: Send complete ms with SASE. No queries. Reports in 8-10 weeks. Send SASE for Editorial Guidelines. Sample copy for $1.25.

Payment/Terms: Pays up to 22¢/word (approximate); varies for poetry and activities; includes 10 complimentary copies of issue in which work appears. Pays on publication for all rights.

Advice: "Become familiar with recent issues of the magazine and have a thorough understanding of the preschool child. You'll find we are catering more to our youngest readers, so think simply. Also, avoid being too heavy-handed with health-related material. First and foremost, health features should be fun! Because we have developed our own turtle character ('PokeyToes'), we are not interested in fiction stories featuring other turtles."

TWN, South Florida's Weekly Gay Alternative, (IV), The Weekly News, Inc., 901 NE 79th St., Miami FL 33138. (305)757-6333 ext. 8910. Fax: (305)756-6488. Contact: Editor. Tabloid: 52 pages; newsprint paper; color cover stock; b&w illustrations and photographs. "TWN is a gay newspaper with 92% male readership. No sex stories. We're interested in issue-oriented writing, particularly with South Florida in mind." Weekly. Estab. 1977. Circ. 34,000.

Needs: Experimental, feminist, gay, historical (general), humor/satire, lesbian, literary. Upcoming themes: "National Coming Out Day" (October), "Valentine's Day, Multiculturalism" (February). Receives 3-5 unsolicited mss/month. Accepts 1 ms/issue; 8-12 mss/year. Publishes ms 2-3 months after acceptance. Agented fiction 50%. Length: 1,200 words preferred; 1,000 words minimum; 2,000 words maximum. Publishes short shorts. Length: 400-600 words. Also publishes literary essays and literary criticisms. Always critiques or comments on rejected mss.

How to Contact: Query with clips of published work. Include estimated word count, bio (1 paragraph), Social Security number. Reports in 1 month on queries; 2 months on ms. Send SASE for reply, return of ms or send a disposable copy of ms. Simultaneous, reprint (must not have appeared in a local competitor's product), and electronic submissions are OK. Sample copy for $1.50. Reviews novels or short story collections.

Payment/Terms: Pays $17.50-150 on publication for one-time rights.

Advice: "We choose work that is timely and fits within a product that is mostly news and cultural analysis. Write tight. Word/page length not as important as conciseness, impact and timeliness."

VIRTUE, helping women build Christ-like character, (II), D.C. Cook Foundation, 4050 Lee Vance View, Colorado Springs CO 80918-7102. (719)531-7776. E-mail: virtuemag@aol.com. Contact: Fiction Editor. Magazine: 8⅛ × 10⅞; 80 pages; illustrations; photos. Christian women's magazine focusing on relationships with God, spouse, children, friends, etc.—"real women with everyday problems, etc." Published 6 times/year. Estab. 1978. Circ. 110,000.

Needs: Contemporary, humor, religious/inspirational. "Must have Christian slant." Accepts 1 ms/issue; 6 mss/year (maximum). Length: 1,000 words minimum; 1,500 words maximum; 1,200 words average.

How to Contact: Send mss to Debbie Colclough, associate editor. Reports in 6-8 weeks on ms. Sample copy for 9 × 13 SAE and $3 postage. Writer's guidelines for SASE.

Payment/Terms: Pays 15-25¢/published word on publication for first rights or reprint rights.

Advice: "Read the magazine! Get to know our style. *Please* don't submit blindly. Send us descriptive, colorful writing with good style. *Please*—no simplistic, unrealistic pat endings or dialogue. We like the story's message to be implicit as opposed to explicit. Show us, inspire us—don't spell it out or preach it to us. No romance considered."

WITH: The Magazine for Radical Christian Youth (II, IV), Faith & Life Press, Box 347, Newton KS 67114-0347. (316)283-5100. Editors: Carol Duerksen and Eddy Hall. Editorial Assistant: Delia Graber. Magazine:

8½ × 11; 32 pages; 60 lb. coated paper and cover; illustrations and photos. "Our purpose is to help teenagers understand the issues that impact them and to help them make choices that reflect Mennonite-Anabaptist understandings of living by the Spirit of Christ. We publish all types of material—fiction, nonfiction, teen personal experience, etc." Published 8 times/year. Estab. 1968. Circ. 6,100.
    ● *With* won several awards from the Associated Church Press and the Evangelical Press Association.
Needs: Contemporary, ethnic, humor/satire, mainstream, religious, young adult/teen (15-18 years). "We accept issue-oriented pieces as well as religious pieces. No religious fiction that gives 'pat' answers to serious situations." Upcoming themes: "Play" (March); "Guilt and Grace (Easter)" (April/May); "Conflict Resolution" (June). Receives about 50 unsolicited mss/month. Accepts 1-2 mss/issue; 10-12 mss/year. Publishes ms up to 1 year after acceptance. Recently published work by Nancy Rue, Greg Hatcher and Beth Ruediger. Published new writers within the last year. Length: 1,500 words preferred; 400 words minimum; 2,000 words maximum. Rarely critiques rejected mss.
How to Contact: Send complete ms with cover letter, include short summary of author's credits and what rights they are selling. Reports in 1-2 months on mss. SASE. Simultaneous and reprint submissions OK. Sample copy for 9 × 12 SAE and $1.21 postage. Fiction guidelines for #10 SASE.
Payment/Terms: Pays 3¢/word for reprints; 5¢/word for simultaneous rights (one-time rights to an unpublished story); 5¢ to 7¢/word for assigned stories (first rights). Supplies contributor's copies; charge for extras.
Advice: "Each story should make a single point that our readers will find helpful through applying it in their own lives. Request our theme list and detailed fiction guidelines (enclose SASE). All our stories are theme-related, so writing to our themes greatly improves your odds."

*WOMAN'S DAY, G.P.O. Box 5245, Sydney NSW 2001 Australia.
Needs: "*Woman's Day* looks for two types of short stories: first for Five Minute Fiction page at the back of the magazine, around 850-1,000 words long; longer short stories, between 1,500 and 4,000 words in length, are used less frequently."
How to Contact: "Manuscripts should be typed with double spacing and sufficient margins on either side of the text for notes and editing. They should be sent to the Fiction Editor with SAE and IRC. We accept unsolicited manuscripts, but must point out that we receive around 100 of these in the fiction department each week, and obviously, are limited in the number we can accept."
Payment/Terms: Payment is usually about $300 (Australian) for the Five Minute Fiction, from $350 for longer stories. *Woman's Day* purchases the first Australian and New Zealand rights. After publication, these revert to the author.

WOMAN'S WORLD MAGAZINE, The Woman's Weekly, (I), 270 Sylvan Ave., Englewood Cliffs NJ 07632. E-mail: wwweekly@aol.com. Fiction Editor: Deborah Purcell. Magazine; 9½ × 11; 54 pages. We publish short romances and mini-mysteries for all women, ages 18-68." Weekly. Estab. 1980. Circ. 1.5 million.
Needs: Romance (contemporary), suspense/mystery. No humor, erotica or period pieces. "Romance stories must be light and upbeat. No death or disease. Let your characters tell the story through detail and dialogue. Avoid prolonged descriptive passages in third person. The trick to selling a mystery is to weave a clever plot full of clues that don't stand out as such until the end. If we can guess what's going to happen, we probably won't buy it." Receives 2,500 unsolicited mss/month. Accepts 2 mss/issue; 104 mss/year. Publishes mss 3-6 months after acceptance. Recently published work by Fay Thompson, Martha Johnson, Tim Myers, Gary Alexander, Mary Lyons, Wendy Murray, Melinda Arthur and P.J. Platz. Length: romances—1,500 words; mysteries—1,000 words. Sometimes critiques rejected mss and recommends other markets.
How to Contact: *No queries.* Send complete ms, "double spaced and typed in number 12 font." Cover letter not necessary. Include name, address and phone number on first page of mss. Reports in 2-4 months. SASE. Faxed submissions OK. Fiction guidelines free.
Payment/Terms: Romances—$1,000, mysteries—$500. Pays on acceptance for first North American serial rights only.
Advice: "Hone your craft in short story writing classes or an ongoing workshop; be tough-skinned about rejection; try, try again."

‡WOMEN'S AMERICAN ORT REPORTER, (III,IV), Women's American ORT, 315 Park Ave. S., New York NY 10010. (212)505-7700. Editor: Aviva Patz. 8⅛ × 10⅞; glossy; photographs. "Jewish women's issues; education, for membership." Quarterly. Estab. 1966. Circ. 100,000.
Needs: Condensed/excerpted novel, ethnic, feminist, humor/satire and literary. Receives 8 unsolicited mss/month. Buys 3 mss/year. Publishes ms 3 months after acceptance. Agented fiction 50%. Length: 1,850 words. Possibly publishes short shorts.
How to Contact: Send complete ms with cover letter. Include Social Security number. Reports in 3 weeks. SASE (or IRC). Sample copy for SASE.
Payment/Terms: Varies. Starts at $500.
Terms: Pays within 60 days of publication for first North American serial rights.

*THE WORLD OF ENGLISH, P.O. Box 1504, Beijing China. Chief Editor: Yu-Lun Chen. Monthly. Circ. 300,000.
Needs: "We welcome contributions of short and pithy articles that would cater to the interest of our reading public, new and knowledgeable writings on technological finds, especially interesting stories and novels, etc.
Payment/Terms: "As our currency is regrettably inconvertible, we send copies of our magazines as the compensation for contributions."
Advice: "Aside from literary works, we put our emphasis on the provision of articles that cover various fields in order to help readers expand their vocabulary rapidly and enhance their reading level effectively, and concurrently to raise their level in writing. Another motive is to render assistance to those who, while learning English, are able also to enrich their knowledge and enlarge their field of vision."

YANKEE MAGAZINE, (II, III), Yankee, Inc., P.O. Box 520, Dublin NH 03444. (603)563-8111. Fax: (603)563-8252. E-mail: queries@yankeepub.com. Editor: Judson D. Hale. Fiction Editor: Edie Clark. Magazine: 6×9; 176 pages; glossy paper; 4-color glossy cover stock; illustrations; color photos. "Entertaining and informative New England regional on current issues, people, history, antiques and crafts for general reading audience." Monthly. Estab. 1935. Circ. 700,000.
   • Ranked as one of the best markets for fiction writers in the last *Writer's Digest* magazine.
Needs: Literary. Fiction is to be set in New England or compatible with the area. No religious/inspirational, formula fiction or stereotypical dialect, novels or novellas. Accepts 6 mss/year. Published work by Andre Dubus, H. L. Mountzoures and Fred Bonnie. Published new writers within the last year. Length: 2,500 words.
How to Contact: Send complete ms with SASE and previous publications. "Cover letters are important if they provide relevant information: previous publications or awards; special courses taken; special references (e.g. 'William Shakespeare suggested I send this to you . . . .')" Simultaneous submissions OK, "within reason." Reports in 6-8 weeks.
Payment/Terms: Pays $1,000 on acceptance; rights negotiable. Makes "no changes without author consent."
Advice: "Read previous ten stories in *Yankee* for style and content. Fiction must be realistic and reflect life as it is—complexities and ambiguities inherent. Our fiction adds to the 'complete menu'—the magazine includes many categories—humor, profiles, straight journalism, essays, etc. Listen to the advice of any editor who takes the time to write a personal letter. Go to workshops; get advice and other readings before sending story out cold."

‡YOU! MAGAZINE, Youth for the Next Millenium, (II, IV), Veritas Communications, Inc. 31194 La Baya Dr., Suite 200, Westlake Village CA 91320. (818)991-1813. Fax: (818)991-2024. E-mail: youmag@earthlink.net. Editor: Patrick Lorenz. Fiction Editor: Mary Lovee Varni. Magazine: 35 pages; illustrations and photos. Publication to help Catholic and other Christian youth "to see pop culture through the eyes of faith." Monthly. Estab. 1987. Circ. 35,000.
Needs: Literary, religious/inspirational, sports, young adult/teen. List of upcoming themes available for SASE. Receives 10-20 unsolicited mss/month. Accepts 1-2 mss/issue; 20-30 mss/year. Length: 350 words average; 100 words minimum; 600-700 words maximum. Publishes short shorts. Also publishes literary essays and poetry.
How to Contact: Query first. Include estimated word count. Reports in 2-3 weeks. Send a disposable copy of ms. Simultaneous, reprint and electronic submissions OK. Sample copy for $2.50 and 12×14 SAE with 2 first-class stamps. Reviews novel and short story collections. Send books to "Submissions Editor."
Payment/Terms: Pays contributor's copies for one-time rights.
Advice: "Inspirational and religious testimonials are best."

● A BULLET INTRODUCES COMMENTS by the editor of *Novel & Short Story Writer's Market* indicating special information about the listing.

Small Press

The term "small press" is often used in the broadest sense within the publishing industry. Depending on the person you're talking with, small press can mean one- and two-person operations, small or mid-size independent presses or university presses and other nonprofit publishers.

In today's book publishing industry "small" presses are becoming increasingly more important as they devote themselves to keeping accessible the work of talented fiction writers who are not currently in the limelight or whose work has had limited exposure. This year, we have merged those presses with our "Commercial Book Publisher" section into a new, expanded "Book Publisher" section beginning on page 413. There you will find many smaller—but important—presses, such as Coffee House, Four Walls Eight Windows and Seven Stories along with the huge publishing conglomerates. *This section now contains only small presses publishing three or fewer books per year.*

MICROPRESSES

The very small presses listed here are sometimes called micropresses and are owned or operated by one to three people, often friends or family members. Some are cooperatives of writers and most of these presses started out publishing their staff members' books or books by their friends. Even the most successful of these presses are unable to afford the six-figure advances, lavish promotional budgets and huge press runs possible in the large, commercial houses. These presses can easily be swamped with submissions, but writers published by them are usually treated as "one of the family."

SELECTING YOUR MARKET

Reading the listing should be just your first step in finding markets that interest you. It's best to familiarize yourself with a press' focus and line. Most produce catalogs or at least fliers advertising their books. Whenever possible, obtain these and writers' guidelines.

If possible, read some of the books published by a press that interests you. It is sometimes difficult to locate books published by a small press (especially by micropress publishers). Some very small presses sell only through the mail.

In How to Use This Book to Publish Your Fiction we discuss how to use the Category Index located near the end of this book. If you've written a particular type of novel, look in the Category Index under the type of fiction you write to find presses interested in your specific subject.

We've also included Roman numeral ranking codes placed at the start of each listing to help you determine how open the press is to new writers. The explanations of these codes appear at the end of this introduction.

In addition to the double dagger (‡) indicating new listings, we include other symbols to help you in narrowing your search. English-speaking foreign markets are denoted by an asterisk (*). The maple leaf symbol (✹) identifies Canadian presses. If you are not a Canadian writer, but are interested in a Canadian press, check the listing carefully. Many small presses in Canada receive grants and other funds from their provincial or national government and are, therefore, restricted to publishing Canadian authors.

There are no subsidy book publishers listed in *Novel & Short Story Writer's Market*. By subsidy, we mean any arrangement in which the writer is expected to pay all or part of the cost of producing, distributing and marketing his book. We feel a writer should not be asked to share in any cost of turning his manuscript into a book. All the book publishers listed here told us that they *do not charge writers* for publishing their work. If any of the publishers listed here ask you to pay any part of publishing or marketing your manuscript, please let us know.

Keep in mind most of the presses listed here have very small staffs. We asked them to give themselves a generous amount of response time in their listing, but note it is not unusual for a small press to get behind. Add three or four weeks to the reporting time listed before checking on the status of your submission.

As with commercial book publishers, we ask small presses to give us a list of recent titles each year. If they did not change their title list from last year, it may be that, because they do so few fiction titles, they have not published any or they may be particularly proud of certain titles published earlier. If the recent titles are unchanged, we've altered the sentence to read "Published" rather than "Recently published."

The Business of Fiction Writing gives the fundamentals of approaching book publishers. The listings include information on what the publisher wishes to see in a submission package: sample chapters, an entire manuscript or other material.

Our editorial comments are set off by a bullet (●) within the listing. We use this feature to include additional information on the type of work published by the press, the awards and honors received by presses and other information we feel will help you make an informed marketing decision.

FOR MORE INFORMATION

For more small presses see the *International Directory of Little Magazines and Small Presses* published by Dustbooks (P.O. Box 100, Paradise CA 95967). To keep up with changes in the industry throughout the year, check issues of two small press trade publications: *Small Press Review* (also published by Dustbooks) and *Small Press* (Jenkins Group, Inc., 121 E. Front St., 4th Floor, Traverse City MI 49684).

The ranking codes used in this section are as follows:

I **Publisher encourages beginning or unpublished writers to submit work for consideration and publishes new writers frequently.**

II **Publisher accepts outstanding work by beginning and established writers.**

III **Hard to break into; publishes mostly writers with extensive previous publication credits or agented writers.**

IV **Special-interest or regional publisher, open only to writers in certain genres or on certain subjects or from certain geographic areas.**

V **Closed to unsolicited submissions.**

ACME PRESS, (I, II), P.O. Box 1702, Westminster MD 21158. (410)848-7577. **Acquisitions**: Ms. E.G. Johnston, managing editor. Estab. 1991. "We operate on a part-time basis and publish 1-2 novels/year." Publishes hardcover and paperback originals. Published new writers within the last year. Averages 1-2 novels/year.
Needs: Humor/satire. "We publish only humor novels, so we don't want to see anything that's not funny." Published *She-Crab Soup*, by Dawn Langley Simmons (fictional memoir/humor); *Biting the Wall*, by J. M. Johnston (humor/mystery); and *Hearts of Gold*, by James Magorian (humor/mystery).
How to Contact: Accepts unsolicited mss. Query first, submit outline/synopsis and first 50 pages or submit complete ms with cover letter. Include estimated word count with submission. SASE for reply, return of ms or send a disposable copy of ms. Agented fiction 25%. Reports in 1-2 weeks on queries; 4-6 weeks on mss. Simultaneous submissions OK. Always comments on rejected mss.
Terms: Provides 25 author's copies; pays 50% of profits. Sends galleys to author. Publishes ms 1 year after acceptance. Writer's guidelines and book catalog for #10 SASE.

AGELESS PRESS, (II, IV), P.O. Box 5915, Sarasota FL 34277-5915. Phone/fax: (941)952-0576. E-mail: irishope@juno.com. **Acquisitions**: Iris Forrest, editor. Estab. 1992. Independent publisher. Publishes paperback originals. Books: acid-free paper; notched perfect binding; no illustrations; average print order: 5,000; first novel print order: 5,000. Published new writers within the last year. Averages 1 title each year.

Needs: Experimental, fantasy, humor/satire, literary, mainstream/contemporary, mystery/suspense, New Age/mystic/spiritual, science fiction, short story collections, thriller/espionage. Looking for material "based on personal computer experiences." Stories selected by editor. Published *Computer Legends, Lies & Lore*, by various (anthology); and *Computer Tales of Fact & Fantasy*, by various (anthology).

How to Contact: Does not accept unsolicited mss. Query first. Send SASE for reply, return of ms or send a disposable copy of ms. Reports in 1 week. Simultaneous and electronic (disk, 5¼ or 3.5 IBM) submissions in ASCII format OK. Sometimes comments on rejected mss.

Terms: Offers negotiable advance. Publishes ms 6-12 months after acceptance.

‡*THE AMERICAN UNIVERSITY IN CAIRO PRESS, 113 Kasr El Aini St., Cairo Egypt. Fax: +20 2 356-1440. E-mail: aucpress@acs.auc.eun.es. **Acquisitions**: Werner Mark Linz, director; Pauline Wickhamp, translated Arabic fiction. Averages 2-4 fiction titles/year.

Needs: "Egyptology, Middle East studies, Islamic art and architecture, social anthropology, Arabic literature in translation. The press is the sole agent of Nobel laureate for literature, Naguib Mahjouz. Recently published *Damascus Nights*, by Rafik Schami; *Houses Behind the Trees*, by Mohamed El-Bisatie; and *The Wiles of Men*, Salwa Bakr. The press publishes the journal *Cario Papers*, a quarterly monograph series in social studies. Special series, joint imprints, and/or copublishing programs: Numerous copublishing programs with U.S. and U.K. university presses and other U.S. and European publishers." Length: 30,000 words minimum; 75,000 words maximum.

How to Contact: Send a cover letter and entire ms.

Advice: "Manuscripts should deal with Egypt and/or Middle East."

♣ANVIL PRESS, (I, II), Bentall Centre, P.O. Box 1575, Vancouver, British Columbia V6C 2P7 Canada; or Lee Building, #204-A, 175 E. Broadway, Vancouver, British Columbia V5T 1W2 Canada. (604)876-8710. Fax: (604)879-2667. E-mail: subter@pinc.com. **Acquisitions**: Brian Kaufman and Dennis E. Bolen, fiction editors. Estab. 1988. "1½ person operation with volunteer editorial board. Anvil Press publishes contemporary fiction, poetry and drama, giving voice to up-and-coming Canadian writers, exploring all literary genres, discovering, nurturing and promoting new Canadian literary talent." Publishes paperback originals. Books: offset or web printing; perfect-bound. Average print order: 1,000-1,500. First novel print order: 1,000. Plans 2 first novels this year. Averages 2-3 fiction titles each year. Often comments on rejected mss. Also offers a critique service for a fee.

● Anvil Press received the Shortlisted City of Van Conver Book Prize for *Monday Night Man*, by Grant Buday.

Needs: Experimental, contemporary modern, literary, short story collections. Recently published *Monday Night Man*, by Grant Buday (short stories); and *Salvage King, Ya*, by Mark Jarman (novel). Published new writers within the last year. Publishes the Anvil Pamphlet series: shorter works (essays, political tracts, polemics, treatises and works of fiction that are shorter than novel or novella form).

How to Contact: Canadian writers only. Accepts unsolicited mss. Query first or submit outline/synopsis and 1-2 sample chapters. Include estimated word count and bio with submission. Send SASE for reply, return of ms or a disposable copy of ms. Reports in 1 month on queries; 2-4 months on mss. Simultaneous submissions OK (please note in query letter that manuscript is a simultaneous submission).

Terms: Pays royalties of 15% (of final sales). Average advance: $200-400. Sends galleys to author. Publishes ms within contract year. Book catalog for 9×12 SASE and 2 first-class stamps.

Advice: "We are only interested in writing that is progressive in some way—form, content. We want contemporary fiction from serious writers who intend to be around for awhile and be a name people will know in years to come."

ARIADNE PRESS, (I), 4817 Tallahassee Ave., Rockville MD 20853. (301)949-2514. **Acquisitions**: Carol Hoover, president. Estab. 1976. "Our purpose is to promote the publication of emerging fiction writers." Shoestring operation—corporation with 4 directors who also act as editors. Publishes hardcover and paperback originals. Books: 50 lb. alkaline paper; offset printing; Smyth-sewn binding. Average print order 1,000. First novel print order 1,000. Plans 1 first novel this year. Averages 1 total title each year; only fiction. Distributes titles through mail-order. Promotes titles through voice literary supplement, New York Review of Books, Boston Consortium, Book Reader and Rapport.

Needs: Adventure, contemporary, feminist, historical, humor/satire, literary, mainstream, psychological, family relations, marital, war. Looking for "literary-mainstream" fiction. No poetry, short stories or fictionalized biographies; no science fiction, horror or mystery. Published *The Greener Grass*, by Paul Bourguignon; *A Rumor of Distant Tribes*, by Eugene Jeffers; *Cross a Dark Bridge*, by Deborah Churchman (psychological suspense) and *Steps of the Sun*, bu Eva Thaddeus (love and conflict in a university town).

How to Contact: *Query first*. SASE. Agented fiction 5%. Reports in 1 month on queries; 2 months on mss. Simultaneous submissions OK. Sometimes critiques rejected mss. "We comment on selected mss of superior writing quality, even when rejected."

Terms: Pays royalties of 10%. No advance. Sends galleys to author. Writer's guidelines and list of books in stock for #10 SASE.

Advice: "We exist primarily for nonestablished writers. Try large, commercial presses first. Novels from 175-350 double-spaced pages have the best chance with us. Characters and story must fit together so well that it is hard to tell which grew out of the other. Send query letter with SASE in advance! Never send an unsolicited manuscript without advance clearance."

‡**ARTEMIS CREATIONS PUBLISHING**, 3395 Nostrand Ave., 2-J, Brooklyn NY 11229. **Acquisitions**: Shirley Oliveira, president. Publishes trade paperback originals and reprints. Publishes 3-4 titles/year.
Imprint(s): Fem Suprem, Matriarch's Way.
Needs: Erotica, experimental, fantasy, feminist, gothic, horror, mystery, occult, religious, science fiction. Recently published *Welts*, by Gloria and Dave Wallace (erotica).
How to Contact: Query or submit synopsis and 3 sample chapters with SASE. Reports in 1 month. Simultaneous submissions OK.
Terms: No advance. Publishes ms 18 months after acceptance. Writer's guidelines and book catalog for #10 SASE.
Advice: "Our readers are looking for strong, powerful feminie archetypes in fiction and nonfiction."

‡**B. DAZZLE, INC.**, 500 Meyer Lane, Redondo Beach CA 90278. (310)374-3000. **Acquisitions**: Kathie Gavin, president & CEO. "We publish unique gift books with intrinsic educational, sociological and ecological value." Publishes hardcover and trade paperback originals. Publishes 2 titles/year.
Needs: Adventure, experimental, fantasy, historical, humor, juvenile, picture books, short story collections.
How to Contact: Query first. Reports in 3 months on queries.
Terms: Pays 3-5% royalty on wholesale price. Book catalog free.
Advice: "Our audience consists of intelligent, cultured, educated persons of all ages sensitive to humanity, nature and beauty. Do not expert immediate evaluation and response."

BETHEL PUBLISHING, (IV), 1819 S. Main, Elkhart IN 46516.(219)293-8585. **Acquisitions**: Pam Merillat. Estab. 1903. Mid-size Christian book publisher. Publishes paperback originals and reprints. Averages 3-5 total titles per year. Occasionally critiques or comments on rejected mss.
Needs: Religious/inspirational, young adult/teen. No "workbooks, cookbooks, coloring books, theological studies, pre-school or elementary-age stories."
How to Contact: Accepts unsolicited complete mss. 30,000-50,000 words maximum. Query first. Enclose 8½×11 SAE and 3 first-class stamps. Reports in 2 weeks on queries; 3 months on mss. Accepts simultaneous submissions. Publishes mss 8-16 months after acceptance.
Terms: Pays royalties of 5-10% and 12 author's copies. Writer's guidelines and book catalog on request.

BOOKS FOR ALL TIMES, INC., (III), Box 2, Alexandria VA 22313. Website: http://www.bfat.com. **Acquisitions**: Joe David, publisher/editor. Estab. 1981. One-man operation. Publishes hardcover and paperback originals. Books: 60 lb. paper; offset printing; perfect binding. Average print order: 1,000. "No plans for new writers at present." Has published 2 fiction titles to date.
Needs: Contemporary, literary, short story collections. "No novels at the moment; hopeful, though, of someday soon publishing a collection of quality short stories. No popular fiction or material easily published by the major or minor houses specializing in mindless entertainment. Only interested in stories of the Victor Hugo or Sinclair Lewis quality."
How to Contact: Query first with SASE. Simultaneous submissions OK. Reports in 1 month on queries. Occasionally critiques rejected mss.
Terms: Pays negotiable advance. "Publishing/payment arrangement will depend on plans for the book." Book catalog free with SASE.
Advice: Interested in "controversial, honest books which satisfy the reader's curiosity to know. Read Victor Hugo, Fyodor Dostoyevsky and Sinclair Lewis, for example. I am actively looking for short articles (up to 3,000 words) on contemporary education. I prefer material critical of the public schools when documented and convincing."

‡**BROADMAN & HOLMAN PUBLISHERS, (II)**, 127 Ninth Ave. N., Nashville TN 37234-0115. (615)251-2000. Editorial Director: Richard P. Rosenbaum, Jr. **Acquisitions**: Vicki Crumpton, Matt Jacobson. "Broadman & Holman will be the best provider of distinctive, relevant, high-quality products and services that lead individuals toward: a personal faith in Jesus Christ, a lifestyle of practical discipleship, a world view that is consistent with the historic, Christian Faith. We will accomplish this in a manner that glorifies God and serves His kingdom while making a positive financial contribution." Religious publisher associated with the Southern Baptist Convention. Publishes paperback originals. Books: Offset paper stock; offset printing; perfect binding. Averages 3 total titles each year.
• They are not currently accepting unsolicited submissions in fiction.

CADMUS EDITIONS, (III), Box 126, Tiburon CA 94920. (707)431-8527. Editor: Jeffrey Miller. Estab. 1979. Emphasis on quality literature. Publishes hardcover and paperback originals. Books: Approximately 25% letterpress; 75% offset printing; perfect and case binding. Average print order: 2,000. First novel print order: 2,000. Averages 1-3 total titles.

Needs: Literary. Published *The Wandering Fool*, by Yunus Emre, translated by Edouard Roditi and Guzin Dino; *The Hungry Girls*, by Patricia Eakins; *Zig-Zag*, by Richard Thornley.

How to Contact: No unsolicited mss. Agent representative material only. SASE.

Payment/Terms: Pays negotiated royalty.

CALYX BOOKS, (I, II), P.O. Box B, Corvallis OR 97339. (503)753-9384. Fax: (541)753-0515. E-mail: calyx@ proaxis.com. **Acquisitions:** M. Donnelly, editor; Micki Reaman, fiction editor. Estab. 1986. "Calyx exists to publish women's literary and artistic work and is committed to publishing the works of all women, including women of color, older women, working-class women, and other voices that need to be heard." Publishes hardcover and paperback originals. Books: offset printing; paper and cloth binding. Average print order: 5,000-10,000 copies. First novel print order: 5,000. Published many new writers within the last year. Averages 3 total titles each year. Distributes titles through Consortium. Promotes titles through advertisements in appropriate places, author readings, reviews and radio interviews.

● *Calyx* won the 1996 Oregon Governor's Arts Award. Past anthologies include *Forbidden Stitch: An Asian American Women's Anthology*; *Women and Aging*, and *Present Tense: Writing and Art by Young Women*.

Needs: Contemporary, ethnic, experimental, feminist, lesbian, literary, short story collections, translations. Published *Four Figures in Time*, by Patricia Grossman; *The Adventures of Mona Pinsky*, by Harriet Ziskin; and *Second Sight*, by Rickey Gard Diamond.

How to Contact: Query first. Send SASE for reply. Reports in 4 months on queries.

Terms: Pays royalties of 10% minimum, author's copies, (depends on grant/award money). Average advance: $200-500. Sends galleys to author. Publishes ms 2 years after acceptance. Writer's guidelines for #10 SASE. Book catalog free on request.

Advice: "Read our book catalog and journal. Be familiar with our publications. Follow our guidelines (which can be requested with a SASE) and be patient. Our process is lengthy."

‡CAROLINA WREN PRESS, INC./LOLLIPOP POWER BOOKS, (V), 120 Morris St., Durham NC 27701. (919)560-2738. Estab. 1976. "Small, nonprofit publisher of women and minority writers, including fiction, nonfiction, poetry, essays and children's literature." Publishes paperback originals and reprints. Averages 1-2 titles/year, 1 fiction title/year.

Needs: "We anticipate a search for manuscripts after 1997 for writers of color's submissions of short stories, but will not accept prior to a date to be announced." Recently published *Puzzles*, by Dara Walker (children's picture book).

How to Contact: Only accepts solicited submissions accompanied by SASE. "Only one of 40" submissions is agented. Reports in 9 months on queries. Sometimes critiques or comments on rejected mss.

Payment/Terms: Pays in author's copies.

Advice: "Please do not submit unless in response to advertised call on specific topic."

CHRISTMAS, An Annual Treasury, (I, II, IV), Augsburg Fortress Publishers, Box 1209, Minneapolis MN 55440. (612)330-3300. Fax: (612)330-3215. Editor: Bob Klausmeier. Estab. 1931. An annual Christmas giftbook containing "poetry, fiction and personal essays related to Christmas and incorporating Christian heritage of the holidays. Also includes Christmas crafts and cooking features." Book: 8⅞ × 11¼; 64 pages; cloth cover; illustrations and photos. Print order: 30,000.

Needs: Children's/juvenile (Christmas, Christian). "No sentimental or maudlin stories, or ones that are not rooted in the Christian heritage of Christmas. No Santa stories."

How to Contact: Send complete ms with a cover letter. Include estimated word count, 100-word bio and list of publications. Send SASE for reply, return of ms or send a disposable copy of ms. Reports in 3 months. Simultaneous submissions OK.

Payment/Terms: Pays $150-400 on acceptance and 1 contributor's copy; additional copies 40% off. Acquires one-time rights. Sends galleys to author.

Advice: Looks for "engaging writing, humorous or serious, incorporating Christian heritage of Christmas."

CONFLUENCE PRESS INC., (II), 500 Eighth Ave., Lewis-Clark State College, Lewiston ID 83501. (208)799-2336. **Acquisitions:** James R. Hepworth, fiction editor. Estab. 1976. Small trade publisher. Publishes hardcover and paperback originals and reprints. Books: 60 lb. paper; photo offset printing; Smyth-sewn binding. Average print order: 1,500-5,000 copies. Published new writers within the last year. Averages 3-5 total titles each year. Distributes titles through Midpoint Trade Books.

Imprint(s): James R. Hepworth Books and Blue Moon Press.

● Books published by Confluence Press have received The Idaho Book Award, Western States Book Awards and awards from the Pacific Northwest Booksellers Association.

Needs: Contemporary, literary, mainstream, short story collections, translations. "Our needs favor serious fiction, 1 fiction collection a year, with preference going to work set in the contemporary western United States." Published *Cheerleaders From Gomorrah*, by John Rember; and *Gifts and Other Stories*, by Charlotte Holmes.

How to Contact: Query first. SASE for query and ms. Agented fiction 50%. Reports in 6-8 weeks on queries and mss. Simultaneous submissions OK. *Critiques rejected mss for $25/hour.*

Terms: Pays royalties of 10%. Advance is negotiable. Provides 10 author's copies; payment depends on grant/award money. Sends galleys to author. Book catalog for 6×9 SASE.

Advice: "We are very interested in seeing first novels from promising writers who wish to break into serious print. We are also particularly keen to publish the best short story writers we can find. We are also interested in finding volume editors for our American authors series. Prospective editors should send proposals."

CREATIVITY UNLIMITED PRESS, (II), 30819 Casilina, Rancho Palos Verdes CA 90274. (310)377-7908. **Acquisitions**: Rochelle Stockwell. Estab. 1980. One-person operation with plans to expand. Publishes paperback originals and self-hypnosis cassette tapes. Books: perfect binding; illustrations; average print order: 1,000; first novel print order 1,000. Averages 1 title (fiction or nonfiction) each year.

Needs: Published *Insides Out*, by Shelley Stockwell (plain talk poetry); *Sex and Other Touchy Subjects*, (poetry and short stories); *Timetravel: Do-It Yourself Past Life Regression Handbook*; *Denial is Not a River in Egypt* and *Everything You Ever Wanted to Know About Everything.*

Advice: Write for more information.

CROSS-CULTURAL COMMUNICATIONS, (I, IV), 239 Wynsum Ave., Merrick NY 11566-4725. (516)868-5635. Fax: (516)379-1901. Editorial Director: Stanley H. Barkan. Estab. 1971. "Small/alternative literary arts publisher focusing on the traditionally neglected languages and cultures in bilingual and multimedia format." Publishes chapbooks, magazines, anthologies, novels, audio cassettes (talking books) and video cassettes (video books, video mags); hardcover and paperback originals. Publishes new women writers series, Holocaust series, Israeli writers series, Dutch writers series, Asian-, African- and Italian-American heritage writers series, Native American writers series, Latin American writers series.

● Authors published by this press have received international awards including Nat Scammacca who won the National Poetry Prize of Italy and Gabriel Preil who won the Bialik Prize of Israel.

Needs: Contemporary, literary, experimental, ethnic, humor/satire, juvenile and young adult folktales, and translations. "Main interests: bilingual short stories and children's folktales, parts of novels of authors of other cultures, translations; some American fiction. No fiction that is not directed toward other cultures. For an annual anthology of authors writing in other languages (primarily), we will be seeking very short stories with original-language copy (other than Latin script should be print quality 10/12) on good paper. Title: *Cross-Cultural Review Anthology: International Fiction 1.* We expect to extend our *CCR* series to include 10 fiction issues: *Five Contemporary* (Dutch, Swedish, Yiddish, Norwegian, Danish, Sicilian, Greek, Israeli, etc.) *Fiction Writers.*" Published *Sicilian Origin of the Odyssey*, by L.G. Pocock (bilingual English-Italian translation by Nat Scammacca); *Sikano L'Americano!—Bye Bye America*, by Nat Scammacca; and *Milkrun*, by Robert J. Gress.

How to Contact: Accepts unsolicited mss. Query with SAE with $1 postage to include book catalog. "Note: Original language ms should accompany translations." Simultaneous and photocopied submissions OK. Reports in 1 month.

Terms: Pays "sometimes" 10-25% in royalties and "occasionally" by outright purchase, in author's copies— "10% of run for chapbook series," and "by arrangement for other publications." No advance.

Advice: "Write because you want to or you must; satisfy yourself. If you've done the best you can, then you've succeeded. You will find a publisher and an audience eventually. Generally, we have a greater interest in nonfiction novels and translations. Short stories and excerpts from novels written in one of the traditional neglected languages are preferred—with the original version (i.e., bilingual). Our kinderbook series will soon be in production with a similar bilingual emphasis, especially for folktales, fairy tales, and fables."

‡DEPTH CHARGE, (II), P.O. Box 7037, Evanston IL 60201. (708)733-9554. Fax: (708)733-0928. Editor: Eckhard Gerdes. Estab. 1986. "We are a small independent publisher." Publishes paperback originals. Books: 24 lb. paper; offset printing; perfect binding; average print order: 500; first novel print order: 500. Plans 2 first novels this year. Averages 2-4 fiction titles each year. Often comments on rejected ms.

Needs: Experimental. Looking for "subterficial fiction." No conventional fiction. Published *The Darkness Starts Up Where You Stand*, by Arthur Winfield Knight; *Openings*, by Richard Kostelanetz; and *Ring in a River*, by Eckhard Gerdes. Publishes *The Journal of Experimental Fiction* series.

How to Contact: Accepts unsolicited mss. Query first. Include bio and list of publishing credits with submission. Send SASE for reply, return of ms or send a disposable copy of ms. Agented fiction 10%. Reports in 3 months. Disk submissions OK.

---

‡ **THE DOUBLE DAGGER** before a listing indicates that the listing is new in this edition.

Terms: Pays royalties of 8% minimum; 8% maximum. Sends galleys to author. Publishes ms 18 months after acceptance. Writer's guidelines for #10 SASE. Book catalog for 9×12 SASE and 4 first-class stamps.
Advice: "Much of the work claiming to be 'experimental' or 'innovative' is actually very conventional. Learn all the conventions, then violate them meaningfully. Familiarize yourself with subterficial fiction as well as the earlier movements of experimental fiction (the Noveau Roman, metafiction, etc.)."

‡**DICKENS PRESS**, P.O. Box 4289, Irvine CA 92616. (714)725-0788. **Acquisitions**: Diane Dennis, editorial director. Publishes hardcover and trade paperback originals. Publishes 2-3 titles/year.
Needs: Mainstream/contemporary, suspense.
How to Contact: Query with one-page synopsis. All unsolicited mss returned unopened. Reports in 1 week on queries; 1 month on mss.
Terms: Pays 12-16% royalty on wholesale price or offers work-for-hire. Offers up to $7,500 advance. Writer's guidelines free.
Advice: "Audience consists of people who want to have more control over their lives by being better informed."

DOWN THERE PRESS, (I, II, IV), Subsidiary of Open Enterprises Cooperative, Inc., 938 Howard St., #101, San Francisco CA 94103. (415)974-8985 ext 105. Fax: (415)974-8989. E-mail: goodvibe@well.com. Imprints are Yes Press and Red Alder Books. Managing Editor: Leigh Davidson. Estab. 1975. Small independent press with part-time staff; part of a large worker-owned cooperative. Publishes paperback originals. Books: Web offset printing; perfect binding; some illustrations. Average print order: 5,000. First novel print order: 3,000-5,000. Published new writers within the last year. Averages 1-2 total titles, 1 fiction title each year. Sometimes critiques or comments on rejected mss. Member of Publishers Marketing Association and Northern California Book Publicity and Marketing Association.
Needs: Erotica, feminist, lesbian. Published *Herotica 4*, edited by Marcy Sheiner (anthology); and *Erotic Reading Circle Stories*, edited by Carol Queen and Jack Davis (anthology).
How to Contact: Accepts unsolicited mss. Submit complete ms with cover letter (short stories for anthologies only). Include estimated word count. Accepts queries and correspondence by fax. Send SASE for reply, return of ms or send disposable copy of ms. Reports in 6-9 months on mss. Simultaneous submissions OK.
Terms: Pays royalties and 2 author's copies. Sends galleys to author. Publishes ms 18 months after acceptance. Writer's guidelines and book catalog for #10 SASE.

‡***GERALD DUCKWORTH & CO. LTD.**, 48 Hoxton Square, London N1 6PB U.K. Publisher and Managing Director: Robin Baird-Smith. Averages 10 titles/year. Estab. 1898.
Needs: Literary fiction only (Alice Thomas Ellis, Beryl Bainbridge, John Bayley). Length: 50,000 words minimum; 100,000 words maximum.
How to Contact: Send a cover letter, synopsis and 2 sample chapters.
Terms: Pays advance—½ on signature of agreement; ½ on first hardback publication.
Advice: "Please only submit if work is of excellent literary standard."

ECOPRESS, (IV), 1029 N.E. Kirsten Place, Corvallis OR 97330. (503)758-7545. Fax: (541)758-5380. E-mail: ecopress@peak.org. **Acquisitions**: Chris Beatty, editor/art director. Estab. 1993. Publishes "books and art that enhance environmental awareness." Publishes hardcover and paperback originals. Books: recycled paper; offset printing; perfect binding; illustrations. Average print order 3,000. First novel print order: 2,000. Averages 2 total titles, 1 fiction title each year.
Needs: Adventure, literary, mainstream/contemporary, mystery/suspense, science fiction, thriller/espionage. Fiction "must have an environmental aspect." Published *Journey of the Tern* and *Sapo*, by Robert Beatty.
How to Contact: Accepts unsolicited mss. Query with outline/synopsis and 1 sample chapter. Include estimated word count, half-page bio and list of publishing credits with submission. Send SASE for reply. Agented fiction 10%. Reports in 1 month on queries; 4 months on mss. Simultaneous, disk (ASCII text) and electronic submissions preferred. Often comments on rejected mss.
Terms: Pays royalties; offers negotiable advance. Sends galleys to author. Publishes ms 1 year after acceptance. Writer's guidelines for SASE.
Advice: "I have to be *very* excited about a book's chances to compete to consider publishing it."

‡**EXILE PRESS, (IV,V)**, 112 Chadwick Way, Cotati CA 94931. (707)795-1415. **Acquisitions**: Drew Hedley, editor/publisher. Estab. 1949. Small independent publisher operated on a part-time basis. Publishes paperback originals. Books: offset printing; perfect bound. Average print order: 500-1,200. Published fiction by new author within the last year.
Needs: Experimental, humor/satire, literary, short story collections, novella. Plans anthology, *Contemporary American Satire 3*, in the next year or two.
How to Contact: Send query letter only first. Include estimated word count, bio and list of publishing credits. Send SASE for reply. Simultaneous submissions OK.
Terms: Pays in author's copies. Publish ms 6-10 months after acceptance. Book catalogs available for SASE.
Advice: Looks for "independence, individualism, talent, courage."

✾GRADE SCHOOL PRESS, (I, IV), 3266 Yonge St., #1829, Toronto, Ontario M4N 3P6 Canada. Phone/fax: (416)784-2883. E-mail: jlastman@compuserve.com. Administrative Assistant: Ziny. Estab. 1990. "Part-time/ small press." Publishes paperback originals. Averages 1-3 total titles, 0-1 fiction title/year. Member CANSCAP.
Needs: Children's/juvenile (historical, series, sports, hi/lo), family saga, feminist, historical (children's only), religious (Jewish only, children's), young adult/teen (easy-to-read, historical, problem novels, series), education (special needs, testing/advocacy).
How to Contact: Accepts unsolicited mss. Query with outline/synopsis and several sample chapters. Include estimated word count, list of publishing credits and general author goals. Send a disposable copy of ms. Sometimes critiques or comments on rejected mss.
Payment/Terms: Provides author's copies; payment depends on grants/awards. Sends galleys to author. Publishes ms 6-12 months after acceptance.
Advice: "Be interesting, original, polished, practical."

GRIFFON HOUSE PUBLICATIONS, Box 81, Whitestone NY 11357. (718)767-8380. President: Frank D. Grande. Estab. 1976. Small press. Publishes paperback originals and reprints.
Needs: Contemporary, drama, ethnic (open), experimental, literary, multinational theory, poetry, reprints, theory, translations.
How to Contact: Query with SASE. No simultaneous submissions. Reports in 1 month.
Terms: Pays in 6 free author's copies. No advance.

HARRIS LITERARY AGENCY, (II), (formerly NRG Associates), P.O. Box 6023, San Diego CA 92166. (619)658-0600. Fax: (619)642-7485. E-mail: n@adnc.com. **Acquisitions:** Barbara Harris, president. Estab. 1996.
Needs: Adventure, mainstream/contemporary, mystery/suspense, science fiction. "No horror or erotica." Published work by J. Norman and Barbara Harris. Length: 60,000 words average; 45,000 words minimum.
How to Contact: Query first by e-mail or fax. Include 400-word bio and list of publications. Reports in 3 weeks on queries; 1 month on mss. Send SASE for reply, return of ms or send a disposable copy of ms. Simultaneous and electronic submissions OK.
Terms: Sends galleys to author. Not copyrighted.
Advice: "Looks for originality, quality writing and good plot. Internet exposure, which we offer, will highlight work to 50,000,000 users. Also, author may get feedback from readers. Avoid submitting unedited work."

‡HEARTSONG PRESENTS, (I, II), Subsidiary of Barbour Publishing, Inc., P.O. Box 719, Uhrichsville OH 44683. (614)922-6045. Fax: (614)922-5948. E-mail: barbourbooks.com. Estab. 1992. Book publisher with book club. Member of Evangelical Christian Publishers Association.
Needs: Romance (contemporary, gothic, historical, romantic suspense, inspirational). Recently published work by Colleen L. Reece, Tracie J. Peterson, Peggy Darty, Sally Larty, Yvonne Lehman, Lonee Lough, DeWanna Pace and Norma Jean Lutz.
How to Contact: Query with synopsis. Include estimated word count, list of publishing credits. Send SASE for reply, return of ms or send disposable copy of ms. Reports in 3 months on queries; 3-5 months on mss. Simultaneous submissions OK.
Terms: Pays average advance: $2,000. No royalty. Provides 10 author's copies. Sends galleys to author on special request. Writer's guidelines free for #10 SASE and 1 IRC.
Advice: "We look for sweet romances that emphasize the need for God as part of lasting romance. We like a strong, entertaining story that has an inspirational theme gently woven throughout. Don't dwell on the physical side of romance. Don't preach your inspirational message, but demonstrate it through the lives of your characters. Study our guidelines and published titles."

***HEMKUNT**, Publishers A-78 Naraina Industrial Area Ph.I, New Delhi India 110028. **Acquisitions:** G.P. Singh, managing director; Deepinder Singh/Arvinder Singh, export directors.
Needs: "We would be interested in novels, preferably by authors with a published work. Would like to have distribution rights for US, Canada and UK beside India."
How to Contact: Send a cover letter, brief summary, 3 sample chapters (first, last and one other chapter). "Writer should have at least 1-2 published novels to his/her credit."
Terms: Catalog on request.

HOLLOW EARTH PUBLISHING, (II), P.O. Box 1355, Boston MA 02205-1355. Phone/fax: (603)433-8735. E-mail: hep2@aol.com. **Acquisitions:** Helian Grimes, editor/publisher. Estab. 1983. "Small independent publisher." Publishes hardcover and paperback originals and reprints. Books: acid-free paper; offset printing; Smythe binding.
Needs: Comics/graphic novels, fantasy (sword and sorcery), feminist, gay, lesbian, literary, New Age/mystic/ spiritual, translations. Looking for "computers, Internet, Norse mythology, magic." Publishes various computer application series.
How to Contact: Does not accept unsolicited mss. Contact by e-mail only. Include estimated word count, 1-2 page bio, list of publishing credits. Agented fiction 90%. Reports in 2 months. Accepts disk submissions.
Terms: Pays in royalties. Sends galleys to author. Publishes ms 6 months after acceptance.

Advice: Looking for "less fiction, more computer information."

ICE CUBE PRESS, (III, IV), 205 N. Front St., North Liberty IA 52317-9302. (319)626-2055. E-mail: icecube@ inav.net. Website: soli.inav.net/~icecube (includes essays, creative environmental nonfiction, poetry and book reviews). **Acquisitions**: S. H. Semken, publisher/editor. Estab. 1994. "One-person operation. Uses nature-oriented fiction and creative nonfiction." Publishes paperback originals. Books: naturally acid-free paper; offset and letterpress printing; perfect binding; illustrations possibly. Average print order: 1,500. First novel print order: 1,500. Plans 3 first novels this year. Promotes titles through radio, TV, newspapers and the Internet.
  • Ice Cube Press also publishes an online magazine, *Sycamore Roots*.
Needs: Regional (regionalism themes), nature and environmental.
How to Contact: Accepts unsolicited mss. Query with outline/synopsis and first chapter. Include short bio. Send SASE for reply, return of ms or send a disposable copy of ms. Reports in 3-4 weeks. Simultaneous submissions OK. Payment negotiable. Always critiques or comments on rejected mss.
Payment/Terms: Individual arrangements with author depending on the book. Sends galleys to author. Publishes ms approximately 1 year after acceptance. Writer's guidelines for #10 SASE.
Advice: "Stories of restoration and sense-of-place are always welcome for consideration."

ILLUMINATION PUBLISHING CO., (II, IV), P.O. Box 1865, Bellevue WA 98009. (425)646-3670. Fax: (425)646-4144. E-mail: illumin.com. **Acquisitions:** Ruth Thompson, editorial director. Estab. 1987. "Illumination Arts is a small company publishing high quality children's picture books with spiritual and/or inspirational values." Publishes hardcover originals. Publishes 2 children's picture book/year. Plans 1 first novel this year. Distributes titles through New Leaf, De Vorss, Book People, Quality and Ingram. Promotes titles through direct mailings, website, book shows, flyers and posters. Member of Book Publishers of the Northwest.
  • Illumination Arts received 1996 Awards of Excellence from Body Mind Spirit for two books.
Needs: Children's/juvenile (adventure, inspirational, preschool/picture books).
How to Contact: Accepts unsolicited mss. Query first or submit complete ms with cover letter. Accepts electronically transmitted queries by fax. Include estimated word count, Social Security number and list of publishing credits. Send SASE for reply or return of ms. Reports in 1 week on queries; 1 month on mss. Simultaneous submissions OK. Often critiques or comments on rejected mss.
Terms: Pays royalties. Sends galleys to author. Publishes ms 18 months-2 years after acceptance. Writer's guidelines for SASE.
Advice: "Submit full manuscripts, neatly typed without grammatical or spelling errors. Expect to be edited many times. Be patient. We are very *painstaking*."

IVY LEAGUE PRESS, INC., (II), P.O. Box 3326, San Ramon CA 94583-8326. (510)736-0601 or 800-IVY-PRESS. Fax: (510)736-0602. E-mail: ivyleaguepress@worldnet.att.net. **Acquisitions**: Maria Thomas, editor. Publishes hardcover and paperback originals. Specializes in medical thrillers. Books: perfect binding. First novel print order: 5,000. Plans 1 novel this year. Averages 2 total titles, 1-2 fiction titles/year. Distributes titles through Baker & Taylor and Ingram. Promotes titles through TV, radio and print.
Needs: Mystery/suspense(medical). Published *Allergy Shots*, by Litman.
How to Contact: Accepts unsolicited mss. Query with outline/synopsis. Include estimated word count, bio and list of publishing credits. Send SASE or a disposable copy of the ms. Reports in 2 months on queries. Electronic submissions OK. Always critiques or comments on rejected mss.
Payment/Terms: Royalties vary. Sends galleys to author.
Advice: "If you tell a terrific story of medical suspense, one which is hard to put down, we may publish it."

‡*KARNAK HOUSE, 300 Westbourne Park Road, London W11 1EH England. Fax: 0171-221-6490. **Acquisitions**: Amon Saba Saakana, managing editor. Publishes 3-4 fiction titles annually.
Needs: "An Afro-Caribbean publishing company concerned with global literary concerns of the African community, whether in North and South America, the Caribbean, Africa or Europe. We look for innovative work in the areas outlined above and work which attempts to express the culture, language, mythology—ethos—of the people. No fantasy, science fiction. We are literary publishers. We look for work which tries to break away from standard English as the dominant narrative voice."
Terms: "We rarely pay advances, and if so, very small, but pay a royalty rate of 8-10% on the published price of the book."

*KAWABATA PRESS, (II), Knill Cross House, Knill Cross, Millbrook, Torpoint, Cornwall PL10 1DX England. Fiction Editor: Colln Webb.
Needs: "Mostly poetry—but prose should be realistic, free of genre writing and clichés and above all original in ideas and content." Length: 200-4,000 words (for stories).
How to Contact: "Don't forget return postage (or IRC)."
Terms: Writers receive half of profits after print costs are covered. Write for guidelines and book list.
Advice: "Avoid clichés; avoid obnoxious plots; avoid the big themes (life, death, etc.); be original; find a new angle or perspective; try to be natural rather than clever; be honest."

‡**LANDMINE BOOKS**, P.O. Box 250702, Glendale CA 91225-0702. (213)860-9897. **Acquisitions**: Jack Russell, editor. Publishes trade paperback originals. Publishes 1-3 titles/year.
Needs: Adventure, gothic, horror, literary, mainstream/contemporary, mystery/suspense, science fiction. Recently published *Stripmall Bohemia*, by Jethro Paris (crime).
How to Contact: Query only with SASE. All unsolicited mss returned unopened. Reports in 1 month on queries, 3 months on mss.
Terms: Pays 5-7% royalty on retail price.

‡**LAUGH LINES PRESS, (IV-Specialized: humor & cartoons)**, P.O. Box 259, Bala Cynwyd PA 19004. E-mail: rozwarren@aol.com. **Acquisitions**: Roz Warren, fiction editor. Estab. 1991. Publishes humor by women, with a special emphasis on cartoon collections. Publishes paperback originals. Books: trade paperbacks; illustrations. Average print order: 5,000. Averages 3-4 total titles, 1 fiction title/year.
• *The Butches of Madison County*, by Ellen Orleans, won the Lambda Book Award for best gay/lesbian humor published in 1995.
Needs: Comics/graphic novels, feminist, humor/satire, lesbian, literary (humorous), mystery/suspense (humorous), romance (humorous), science fiction (humorous), humor—comic novels, lesbian humor, feminist humor. Currently looking for a hilarious comic novel written by a woman. Recently published *The Butches of Madison County*, by Ellen Orleans (lesbian novel/parody).
How to Contact: Query first with 2 sample chapters. Send SASE for reply, return of ms or send disposable copy of ms. Reports in 1 week. Simultaneous submissions OK.
Terms: Pays royalties of 7½% minimum of cover price. Sends galleys to author. Publishes ms 1 year after acceptance. Book catalog for standard size SASE.
Advice: "Before you send it to me, let somebody else read it. If it doesn't make them laugh out loud, keep working on it."

‡**LEAPFROG PRESS, (I, II)**, P.O. Box 1495, 110 Commercial St., Wellfleet MA 02667. (508)349-1925. Fax: (508)349-1180. E-mail: leapfrog@capecod.net. **Acquisitions**: Ira Wood and Marge Piercy, publishers. Estab. 1996. "We publish book-length literary fiction and literate nonfiction that reflects a strong personal story. We're a small shop—two editors and an office manager." Publishes hardcover and paperback originals and paperback reprints. Books: acid-free paper; sewn binding. Average print order: 1,000-3,000. First novel print order: 1,500 (average). Plans up to 3 first novels this year. Averages 2-3 total titles, 1-2 fiction titles/year.
• Member of the Publishers Marketing Association and Bookbuilders of Boston.
Needs: Erotica, ethnic (Jewish), feminist, gay, humor/satire, lesbian, literary, mainstream/contemporary, regional (Cape Cod), religious (Jewish), "Genre's often blurry; we're interested in good writing. We'd love to see memoirs as well as fiction that comments on the world through the lens of personal, political or family experience."
How to Contact: Does not accept unsolicited mss. Query first with outline/synopsis and 2-4 sample chapters (50 pages). Unsolicited queries/correspondence by e-mail and fax OK. Include bio, list of publishing credits and a brief description of the book with submission. Send SASE for reply, return of ms or send a disposable copy of ms. Reports in 6 weeks on queries; 6 months on mss. Simultaneous submissions OK. Sometimes critiques or comments on rejected mss.
Payment/Terms: Pays royalties of 5% minimum; 8% maximum. Offers negotiable advance. Provides negotiable number of author's copies. Sends galleys to author. Publishes ms 1-2 years after acceptance.
Advice: "We love books with a strong personal story to tell and are willing to work with writers who are less experienced but who can accept editing advice. We strongly push sales of secondary rights (translations, foreign sales) and expect the author and publisher to both participate in the process. This may be one of the saving graces of small press publishing. Writers must be willing to accept and incorporate editorial advice and cannot shirk their responsibility to publicize their own work by giving readings, contacting book stores, drumming up local media attention, etc. We believe in strong marketing with an author who can publicize him/herself."

LOLLIPOP POWER BOOKS, (II), 120 Morris St., Durham NC 27701. (919)560-2738. Editor: Ruth A. Smullin. Estab. 1970. "Children's imprint of the Carolina Wren Press, a small, nonprofit press which publishes non-sexist, multi-racial picture books." Publishes paperback originals. Averages 1 title (fiction) each year. Average first book run 3,000 copies.
Needs: Not currently reviewing mss. Recently published *Maria Teresa*, by Mary Atkinson (bilingual); *In Christina's Toolbox*, by Diane Homan; and *Grownups Cry Too*, by Nancy Hazen (bilingual).
Terms: Pays royalties of 10%.
Advice: "Lollipop Power Books must be well-written stories that will appeal to children. We are not interested

---

🍁 **THE MAPLE LEAF** symbol before a listing indicates a Canadian publisher, magazine, conference or contest.

in preachy tales where 'message' overpowers plot and character. We look for good stories told from a child's point of view. Our books present a child's perspective and feelings honestly and without condescension."

LUCKY HEART BOOKS, (II), Subsidiary of Salt Lick Press, Salt Lick Foundation, Inc., 1900 West Hwy. 6, Waco TX 76712. **Acquisitions:** James Haining, editor/publisher. Estab. 1969. Small press with significant work reviews in several national publications. Publishes paperback originals and reprints. Books: offset/bond paper; offset printing; hand-sewn or perfect-bound; illustrations. Average print order: 500. First novel print order: 500.
Needs: Open to all fiction categories. Published *Catch My Breath*, by Michael Lally.
How to Contact: Accepts unsolicited mss. SASE. Agented fiction 1%. Reports in 2 weeks to 4 months on mss. Sometimes critiques or comments on rejected mss.
Terms: Pays 10 author's copies. Sends galleys to author.
Advice: "Follow your heart. Believe in what you do. Use the head, but follow the heart."

MADWOMAN PRESS, (I, II, IV), P.O. Box 690, Northboro MA 01532. (508)393-3447. E-mail: 76620.460@compuserve.com. Editor/Publisher: Diane Benison. Estab. 1991. "Lesbian/feminist press; one-person operation running on a part-time basis." Publishes paperback originals. Books: perfect binding. Average print order: 4,000-6,000. Averages 2-4 total titles, 2 fiction titles each year. Sometimes comments on rejected mss.
● Madwoman Press published *Thin Fire* and *Lesbians in the Military Speak Out*, which were nominated for American Library Association Gay and Lesbian Book awards. This press is becoming known for its lesbian mysteries.
Needs: "All must have lesbian themes: adventure, erotica, ethnic, feminist, mystery/suspense (amateur sleuth, police procedure, private eye), romance, science fiction (hard science, soft sociological), thriller/espionage, western. Especially looking for lesbian detective stories." No horror. No gratuitous violence. Published *Fertile Betrayal*, by Becky Bohan (mystery); and *The Grass Widow*, by Nanci Little (novel).
How to Contact: Query first. Include brief statement of name, address, phone, previous publication and a 1-2 page precis of the plot. SASE. Reports in 2 months on queries; 3 months on solicited mss. Simultaneous submissions OK.
Terms: Pays royalties of 8-15% "after recovery of publications costs." Provides 20 author's copies. Sends galleys to author. Publishes ms 1-2 years after acceptance. Writer's guidelines for #10 SASE.
Advice: "Your query letter will often cause your manuscript to be rejected before it's even read. Write clearly, succinctly, tell the publisher how the book ends and save the hype for the jacket copy. We're looking to form long-term relationships with writers, so talented first novelists are ideal for us. We want to publish an author regularly over the years, build an audience for her and keep her in print. We publish books by, for and about lesbians, books that are affirming for lesbian readers and authors."

‡MERRIMACK BOOKS, (II), P.O. Box 702, Richmond IN 47375. **Acquisitions:** Wayne Edwards, editor. Estab. 1986. Independent publisher of fiction and poetry. Publishes hardcover and paperback originals. Published new writers within the last year.
Needs: Experimental, fantasy (dark), horror (dark fantasy, futuristic, psychological), literary, mystery/suspense (police procedural, private eye/hardboiled), science fiction (hard science/technological, soft/sociological), short story collections. Publishes anthology, *Palace Corbie*. Writers may submit to Anthology Editor.
How to Contact: Accepts unsolicited mss. Submit complete ms. Unsolicited queries/correspondence by e-mail OK. Include estimated word count with submission. Send a disposable copy of ms. Reports in 1 week. No simultaneous submissions.
Payment/Terms: Payment variable; individual arrangement with author. Sends galleys to author. Writer's guidelines for SASE.

MID-LIST PRESS, (I, II), Jackson, Hart & Leslie, Inc., 4324-12th Ave. S., Minneapolis MN 55407-3218. (612)822-3733. **Acquisitions:** Marianne Nora, associate publisher; Lane Stiles, senior editor. Estab. 1989. Non-profit literary small press. Publishes hardcover originals and paperback originals and hardcover reprints. Books: acid-free paper; offset printing; perfect or Smyth-sewn binding. Average print order: 2,000. Plans 1 first novel this year. Averages 3 fiction titles each year. Rarely comments on rejected mss.
● The publisher's philosophy is to nurture "mid-list" titles—books of literary merit that may not fit "promotional pigeonholes"—especially by writers who were previously unpublished.
Needs: General fiction. No children's/juvenile, romance, young adult, religious. Published *Part of His Story*, by Alfred Corn (novel); *The Sincere Cafe: Stories*, by Leslee Becker (short fiction collection); and *The Latest Epistle of Jim*, by Roy Shepard (novel). Publishes First Series Award for the Novel and First Series Award for Short Fiction.
How to Contact: Accepts unsolicited mss. Query first for guidelines. Include #10 SASE. Send SASE for reply, return of ms or send a disposable copy of the ms. Agented fiction less than 10%. Reports in 1-3 weeks on queries; 1-3 months on mss. Simultaneous submissions OK.
Terms: Pays royalty of 40% minimum; 50% maximum of profits. Average advance: $1,000. Sends galleys to author. Publishes ms 6-12 months after acceptance. Writer's guidelines for #10 SASE.
Advice: "Take the time to read some of the books the publisher you're submitting to has put out. And remember

that first impressions are very important. If a query, cover letter, or first page is sloppily or ineptly written, an editor has little hope for the manuscript as a whole."

‡MILKWEEDS FOR YOUNG READERS, Imprint of Milkweed Editions, 430 First Ave. N., Suite 400, Minneapolis MN 55401-1743. (612)332-3192. Fax: (612)332-6248. **Acquisitions:** Elisabeth Fitz, children's reader. Estab. 1984. "Milkweeds for Young Readers are works that embody humane values and contribute to cultural understanding." Publishes hardcover and trade paperback originals. Publishes 25% previously unpublished writers/year. Publishes 1 title/year.
Needs: For ages 8-12: adventure, animal, fantasy, historical, humor, juvenile, mainstream/contemporary, religious, romance, sports. Recently published *Behind the Bedroom Wall*, by Laura E. Williams (historical); *The Boy with Paper Wings*, by Susan Lowell; and *Summer of the Bonepile Monster*, by Aileen Kilgore Henderson (adventure).
How to Contact: Query with 2-3 sample chapters and SASE. Agented fiction 30%. Reports in 2 months on queries, 6 months on mss. Simultaneous submissions OK.
Terms: Pays 7½% royalty on retail price. Advance varies. Publishes ms 1 year after acceptance. Writer's guidelines for #10 SASE. Book catalog for $1.50.

‡MISTY HILL PRESS, (II), 5024 Turner Rd., Sebastopol, CA 95472. (707)823-7437. **Acquisitions**: Sally S. Karste, managing editor. Estab. 1985. Two person operation on a part-time basis. Publishes paperback originals. Books: illustrations; average print order: 2,000; first novel print order: 500-1,000. Plans 1 first novel this year. Publishes 1 title each year.
Needs: Juvenile (historical). Looking for "historical fiction for children, well researched for library market." Published *Trails to Poosey*, by Olive R. Cook (historical fiction); and *Tales Fledgling Homestead*, by Joe Armstrong (nonfiction portraits).
How to Contact: Accepts unsolicited mss. Submit outline/synopsis and sample chapters. Reports within weeks. Simultaneous submissions OK. Sometimes critiques rejected mss; *$15/hour charge for critiques*.
Terms: Pays royalties of 5%. Sends prepublication galleys to author. Writer's guidelines and book catalog for SASE (or IRC).

MOUNTAIN STATE PRESS, (IV), 2300 MacCorkle Ave. SE, Charleston WV 25304. (304)357-4767. Fax: (304)357-4715. **Acquisitions**: Kitty Lamb. Estab. 1978. "A small nonprofit press run by a Board of 13 members who volunteer their time. We specialize in books about West Virginia or by authors from West Virginia." Publishes paperback originals and reprints. Published new writers within the last year. Plans 2-3 first novels this year. Averages 3 total titles, 1-2 fiction titles each year. Promotes titles through newspapers, book signings and mailings.
Needs: Family saga, historical (West Virginia), military/war, New Age/mystic/spiritual, religious. Currently compiling an anthology. Recently published *House Calls in the Hills*, by Dr. Jay Banks; *Vietnam Snapshots*, by Craig Etchison; and *Best of West Virginia Writers*, by various (anthology).
How to Contact: Accepts unsolicited mss. Query with outline/synopsis and 3 sample chapters or submit complete ms with cover letter. Include estimated word count and bio. Send SASE for reply, return of ms or send disposable copy of ms. Reports in 6 months on mss. Electronic submissions OK. Often critiques or comments on rejected mss.
Terms: Pays royalties.
Advice: "Send your manuscript in and it will be read and reviewed by the members of the Board of Mountain State Press."

OUR CHILD PRESS, P.O. Box 74, Wayne PA 19087-0074. (610)964-0606. CEO: Carol Hallenbeck. Estab. 1984. Publishes hardcover and paperback originals and reprints. Plans 2 first novels this year. Plans 2 titles this year.
Needs: Adventure, contemporary, fantasy, juvenile (5-9 yrs.), preschool/picture book and young adult/teen (10-18 years). Especially interested in books on adoption or learning disabilities. Published *Don't Call Me Marda*, by Sheila Welch (juvenile); *Oliver—An Adoption Story*, by Lois Wickstrom; and *Blue Ridge*, by Jon Patrick Harper.
How to Contact: Does not accept unsolicited mss. Query first. Reports in 2 weeks on queries; 2 months on mss. Simultaneous submissions OK. Sometimes comments on rejected mss.
Terms: Pays royalties of 5% minimum. Publishes ms up to 6 months after acceptance. Book catalog free.

OUTRIDER PRESS, (I, II), 1004 E. Steger Rd., Suite C-3, Crete IL 60417. (708)672-6630. Fax: (708)672-5820. E-mail: outriderpr@aol.com. **Acquisitions:** Phyllis Nelson, president; Whitney Scott, fiction editor. Estab. 1988. "Small operation to support feminist voices regardless of race, gender, orientation. Known for publishing new authors." Publishes trade paper originals. Books: offset printing; perfect binding; average print order: under 5,000. Averages 2 total titles, 1 fiction title each year. Distributes titles through Baker & Taylor. Promotes titles through readings, book fairs, publishing parties, book stores and paid ads.
Needs: Feminist, gay, lesbian, literary, New Age/mystic/spiritual, short story collection. No Christian/religious work. Publishes anthologies. "Our anthologies are contests with cash prizes in addition to publication and high-profile readings. Therefore, we charge a $16 reading fee for poetry and fiction." Guidelines for SASE. Scheduled

for 1998 publication: *Freedom's Just Another Word . . .*, poetry and short fiction on freedoms earned and yearned for. Published *Dancing to the End of the Shining Bar*, by Whitney Scott; and *Prairie Hearts—Women View the Midwest*.

How to Contact: Accepts unsolicited mss with SASE. Submit complete ms with cover letter (with short stories). Include estimated word count and list of publishing credits. SASE for return of ms. Reports in 1 month on queries; 2 months on mss. Simultaneous submissions OK. Accepts electronic submissions (3.5 IBM compatible—WordPerfect 5.0, 5.1, 5.2 or 6.0 for DOS; Microsoft Word '97; Rich Text format. No ASCII, no Macs). Sometimes comments on rejected mss; *charges $2 double-spaced pages with 10-page minimum, prepaid and SASE for return*.

Terms: Payment depends on award money.

Advice: "We have a need for short and super-short fiction with pace and flair and poetry with texture and imagery. Give me fresh, honest writing that reflects craft, focus and sense of place; character-driven writing exploring the terrain of human hearts exploring the non-traditional. Follow our guidelines."

PAGES PUBLISHING GROUP, (I, II), (formerly Willowisp Press), Division of PAGES Book Fairs, Inc., 801 94th Ave. N., St. Petersburg FL 33702-2426. (813)578-7600. Address material to Acquisitions Editor. Estab. 1984. "Children's mid-size press." Publishes paperback originals for children. Published new writers within the last year.

Imprint(s): Willowisp Press, Worthington Press, Hamburger Press, Riverbank Press.

• Ruth E. Kelley's *Boomer's Journal* was nominated for the 1996 Arizona State Award Book.

Needs: "Children's fiction and nonfiction, K-8." Adventure, contemporary, romance, for grades 5-8; preschool/picture book. No "violence, sex; romance must be very lightly treated." Riverbank Press is specifically for professional storytellers." Recently published *Mixed-Up Michael*, by Rick Rossiter (picture book); and *Innocent Victim*, by Karle Dickerson (fiction, grades 5-8).

How to Contact: Accepts unsolicited mss. Query (except picture books) with outline/synopsis and 3 sample chapters. Must send SASE. Reporting time on queries varies; 2 months on mss. Simultaneous submissions OK. "Prefer hard copy for original submissions; prefer disk for publication."

Terms: Pay "varies." Publishes ms 6-12 months after acceptance. Writer's guidelines for #10 SASE.

Advice: "We need *fresh* ideas that speak to children. Our consumer is *the child*, so the story must appeal to him or her at a kid's level. 'Fun' and 'engaging' are the watchwords."

PAPYRUS PUBLISHERS & LETTERBOX LITERARY SERVICE, (II), P.O. Box 27383, Las Vegas NV 89126-1383. (702)256-3838. **Acquisitions:** Geoffrey Hutchison-Cleaves, editor-in-chief; Jessie Rosé, fiction editor. Estab. London 1946; USA 1982. Mid-size independent press. Publishes hardcover originals. Audio books; average print order 2,500. Averages 3 total titles each year. Promotes titles through mail, individual author fliers, author tours.

Imprint(s): Letterbox Literary Service, Anthony Wade.

Needs: "No erotica, gay, feminist, children's, spiritual, lesbian, political. Published *Is Forever Too Long?* by Heather Latimer (romantic fiction); *Violet*, by Joan Griffith; and *Louis Wain—King of the Cat Artists 1860-1939*, by Heather Latimer (dramatized biography).

How to Contact: "Not accepting right now. Fully stocked."

Terms: Pays royalties of 10% minimum. Advance varies. Publishes ms 1 year after acceptance.

Advice: "Don't send it, unless you have polished and polished and polished. Absolutely no established author sends off a piece that has just been 'written' once. That is the first draft of many!"

‡PEACHTREE CHILDREN'S BOOKS, Imprint of Peachtree Publishers, Ltd. 494 Armour Circle NE, Atlanta GA 30324. (404)876-8761. Fax: (404)875-2578. **Acquisitions:** Helen Harriss, managing editor. "We publish a broad range of subjects and perspectives, with emphasis on innovative plots and strong writing." Publishes hardcover and trade paperback originals. Publishes 25% previously unpublished writers/year.

Needs: Juvenile, picture books, young adult. Recently published *Under the Backyard Sky*, by Neil Shulman and Sibley Fleming (middle reader).

How to Contact: Submit ms with SASE. Reports in 3 months on queries, 4 months on mss. Simultaneous submissions OK.

Terms: Pays royalty on retail price. Advance varies. Publishes ms 18 months after acceptance. Writer's guidelines for #10 SASE. Book catalog free.

*DAVID PHILIP PUBLISHERS, P.O. Box 23408, Claremont 7735 Cape Province South Africa.

Needs: "Fiction with Southern African concern or focus. Progressive, often suitable for school or university prescription, literary, serious."

How to Contact: Send synopsis and 1 sample chapter.

Terms: Pays royalties. Write for guidelines.

Advice: "Familiarize yourself with list of publisher to which you wish to submit work."

THE POST-APOLLO PRESS, (I, II), 35 Marie St., Sausalito CA 94965. (415)332-1458. Fax: (415)332-8045. E-mail: tpapress@dnai.com. Website: http://www.dnai.com/~tpapress/ (includes excerpts, catalog, reviews and ordering links). **Acquisitions**: Simone Fattal, publisher; Margaret Butterfield, editorial assistant. Estab. 1982. Specializes in "women writers published in Europe or the Middle East who have been translated into English for the first time." Publishes paperback originals. Book: acid-free paper; lithography printing; perfect-bound. Average print order: 2,000. First novel print order: 2,000. Published new writers within the last year. Averages 2 total titles, 1 fiction title each year. Distributes titles through Small Press Distribution, Berkeley, California. Promotes titles through advertising in selected literary quarterlies, SPD catalog, Feminist Bookstore News & Catalog, ALA and ABA and SF Bay Area Book Festival participation.

Needs: Feminist, lesbian, literary, spiritual, translations. No juvenile, horror, sports or romance. "Many of our books are first translations into English." Recently published *Josef Is Dying*, by Ulla Berkéwicz (novel); and *A Beggar At Damascus Gate*, by Yasmine Zahran.

How to Contact: Send query or sample chapter with SASE. Reports in 3 months. Sometimes comments on rejected mss.

Terms: Pays royalties of 6½% minimum or by individual arrangement. Sends galleys to author. Publishes ms 1½ years after acceptance. Book catalog free.

Advice: "We want to see serious, literary quality, informed by an experimental aesthetic."

❧**PRESS GANG PUBLISHERS, (II, IV)**, 225 E. 17 Ave., Suite 101, Vancouver, British Columbia V5V 1A6 Canada. (604)876-7787. Fax: (604)876-7892. Website: http://www.pressgang.bc.ca. Estab. 1974. Feminist press, 3 full-time staff. Publishes paperback originals and reprints. Books: paperback; offset printing; perfect-bound. Average print order: 3,500. First novel print order: 2,000.

• Press Gang Publishers received the 1995 Small Press Award from the Lambda Literary Awards for *Her Tongue on My Theory*, by Kiss & Tell.

Needs: Feminist fiction, nonfiction, mystery, short stories. Subjects and themes include lesbian, women and psychiatry, women and the law, native studies, women of color, erotica, literary. No children/young adult/teen. No poetry. Priority given to Canadian writers. Recently published *Sunnybrook*, by Persimmon Blackridge; *Beyond the Pale*, by Elana Dykewomon; and *When Fox Is A Thousand*, by Larissa Lai.

How to Contact: Accepts unsolicited mss. Query first. SASE. Reports in 2 months on queries; 3-4 months on mss. Simultaneous submissions OK.

Terms: Pays 8-10% royalties. Sends galleys to author. Book catalog free on request.

PUCKERBRUSH PRESS, (I, II), 76 Main St., Orono ME 04473. (207)581-3832 or 866-4808. **Acquisitions**: Constance Hunting, publisher/editor. Estab. 1971. Small, independent press. Publishes paperback originals. Books: laser printing; perfect-bound; sometimes illustrations. Average print order: 1,000. Published new writers within the last year. Publishes 1 previously unpublished writer/year. Averages 3 total titles each year. Distributes titles through MWPA and mail order. Promotes titles through advertising in Maine in Print and Small Press.

Needs: Contemporary, experimental, literary, high-quality work. Published *An Old Pub Near the Angel*, by James Kelman (short stories); *A Stranger Here, Myself*, by Tema Nason (female stories); and *Dorando*, by James Boswell (novel).

How to Contact: Accepts unsolicited mss. Submit complete ms with cover letter. SASE. Reports in 2 weeks on queries; 2 months on mss. Sometimes comments on rejected mss. *If detailed comment, $500.*

Terms: Pays royalties of 10%; 20 author's copies. Sends galleys to author. Publishes ms usually 1 year after acceptance. Writer's guidelines for #10 SASE. "I have a book list and flyers."

Advice: "Write for yourself."

‡**PUDDING HOUSE PUBLICATIONS, (II)**, 60 N. Main St., Johnstown OH 43031. (614)967-6060. **Acquisitions**: Jennifer Bosveld, editor. Estab. 1979. "Small independent publisher seeking outrageously fresh short shorts stories." Publishes paperback originals. Books: paper varies; side stapled; b&w illustrations. Published new writers within the last year.

Needs: Ethnic/multicultural, experimental, humor/satire, literary, the writing experience, liberal/alternative politics or spirituality, new approaches. Recently published *Karmic 4-Star Buckaroo*, by John Bennett (short stories); and *Maggie Lynn & Her Perpetual State of Fulfillment in Johnstown Ohio*, by Jennifer Bosweld (novella).

How to Contact: Accepts unsolicited mss. Submit complete ms with cover letter and ample SASE. Include short bio and list of publishing credits. Send SASE for return of ms. Reports in 1 week. No simultaneous submissions. Sometimes critiques or comments on rejected mss for various fee, if close.

Terms: Pays in author's copies. Sends galleys to author for chapbooks. Publishes ms 2-24 months after acceptance. Writer's guidelines free for SASE. Publication list available.

Advice: "Send dense, rich, pop-culture-placed pieces that sound like the best poetry (gives us an economy of words)."

‡**RASPBERRY PUBLICATIONS, INC., (I, II)**, P.O. Box 925, Westerville OH 43086. (614)841-4353. Fax: (614)899-6147. **Acquisitions**: Susan B. Schmidt or Curt E. Jenkins, fiction editors. Estab. 1993. "Small independent publisher who publishes books written and illustrated by children and students, K-12." Publishes hardcover and paperback originals. Books: 80 lb. offset paper; sheet fed printing; library binding; full color illustrations. Average print order: 2,000; first novel print order: 2,000. Published new writers within the last year. Plans 2 first novels this year. Averages 2-3 total titles, 1-2 fiction titles/year.

● 1994—2nd place in Written & Illustration National Contest for "Whale Dancers." 1995—1st place in Texas Rising Star Writing Contest for "Magic Pencil."

Needs: Children's/juvenile (adventure, animal, easy-to-read, fantasy, historical, mystery, preschool/picture book, series, sports), young adult (adventure, easy-to-read, fantasy/science fiction, historical, mystery/suspense, problem novels, romance, series, sports, western). No horror. Recently published *Monster In My Mouth*, by Kaitlain Rasburry (adventure); *Magic Pencil*, by Ariel Gonzalez (fantasy); and *Whale Dancers*, by Anne Kafoure (animal).

How to Contact: Accepts unsolicited mss. Submit query letter. Include half paragraph bio and list of publishing credits. Send SASE for reply, return of ms or send disposable copy of ms. Reports in 2-4 weeks on queries; 3-6 months on mss. Simultaneous submissions OK. Always critiques or comments on rejected mss. *$5 fee.*

Terms: Pays royalties. Provides 3-5 author's copies; payment depends on grant/award money. Sends galleys to author. Publishes ms 8-24 months after acceptance. Writer's guidelines and book catalog free.

Advice: "Just read our mission statement and stay within our philosophy."

♣RONSDALE PRESS, (II, IV), 3350 W. 21 Ave., Vancouver, British Columbia V6S 1G7 Canada. (604)738-1195. Fax: (604)731-4548. E-mail: ronhatch@pinc.com. Website: ronsdalepress.com (includes guidelines, catalog, events). **Acquisitions**: Ronald B. Hatch, president. Estab. 1988. Ronsdale Press is "dedicated to publishing books that give Canadians new insights into themselves and their country." Publishes paperback originals. Books: 60 lb. paper; photo offset printing; perfect binding. Average print order: 1,000. First novel print order: 1,000. Plans 1 first novel this year. Averages 3 fiction titles each year. Distributes titles through General Distribution, LPC/Inbook and Partner. Promotes titles through ads in BC Bookworld and Globe & Mail, and interviews on radio.

Needs: Experimental and literary. Recently published *The Seventh Circle*, by Benet Davetian (short stories); *Willobe of Wuzz*, by Sandra Glaze; and *Darmma Days*, by Terry Watada.

How to Contact: *Canadian authors only.* Accepts unsolicited mss. Submit outline/synopsis and first 100 pages. SASE. Short story collections must have some magazine publication. Reports in 2 weeks on queries; 2 months on mss. Sometimes comments on rejected mss.

Terms: Pays royalties of 10%. Provides author's copies. Sends galleys to author. Publishes ms 6 months after acceptance.

Advice: "We publish both fiction and poetry. Authors *must* be Canadian. We look for writing that shows the author has read widely in contemporary and earlier literature. Ronsdale, like other literary presses, is not interested in mass-market or pulp materials."

♣ST. AUGUSTINE SOCIETY PRESS, (I, IV), 68 Kingsway Crescent, Etobicoke, Ontario M8X 2R6 Canada. (416)239-1670. **Acquisitions**: Frances Breckenridge, editor. Estab. 1994. "We are a small press, independent of any church. We seek manuscripts which can expand the circle of light detailed by St. Augustine, either fiction or nonfiction." Publishes paperback originals. Average print order: 500 (depends on the type of final product). Averages 1 total title, variable number of fiction titles each year. Member of Toronto Small Press Group.

Needs: Literary, mainstream/contemporary. Recently published *Maledetti (The Forsaken)*, by Michael Gualtieri (novel).

How to Contact: Accepts unsolicited mss. Query with outline/synopsis and 2 sample chapters. Send SASE for reply, return of ms or send a disposable copy of ms. Reports in 3 weeks on queries. Simultaneous submissions OK.

Payment/Terms: Negotiable. Sends galleys to author. Publishes ms 6 months after acceptance. Free writer's guidelines.

Advice: "We welcome works by writers who have, through years of study, gained insights into the human condition. A book that is just a 'good read' is of no interest to us."

SAND RIVER PRESS, (I), 1319 14th St., Los Osos CA 93402. (805)543-3591. Fax: (805)543-7432. Editor: Bruce Miller. Estab. 1987. "Small press." Publishes paperback originals. Books: offset printing; b&w or color illustrations. Average print order: 3,000. First novel print order: 2,000. Averages 2-3 total titles, 1 fiction title each year.

Needs: Native American, lesbian, literary, regional (west).

How to Contact: Accepts unsolicited mss. Submit outline/synopsis and 3 sample chapters. Include list of publishing credits. SASE for return of ms or a disposable copy of the ms. Reports in 3 weeks on queries; 6 weeks on mss. Simultaneous submissions OK. Sometimes comments on rejected mss.

Terms: Pays royalties of 8% minimum; 15% maximum. Average advance: $500-1,000. Provides 10 author's copies. Sends galleys to author. Publishes ms 1 year after acceptance. Book catalog for SASE.

SENDING TO A COUNTRY other than your own? Be sure to send International Reply Coupons instead of stamps for replies or return of your manuscript.

SANDPIPER PRESS, (V), Box 286, Brookings OR 97415-0028. (541)469-5588. **Acquisitions**: Marilyn Reed Riddle, editor. Estab. 1979. One-person operation specializing in low-cost large-print 18 pt. books. Publishes paperback originals. Books: 70 lb. paper; saddle-stitched binding, perfect-bound; 84 pgs. maximum; leatherette cover; b&w sketches or photos. Average print order 2,000; no novels. Averages 1 title every 2 years.
Needs: Unusual quotations, sayings.
How to Contact: *Does not accept unsolicited mss.* Query first or submit outline/synopsis. SASE. Reports in 1 month on queries; 1 month on mss. Simultaneous submissions OK. Occasionally comments on rejected mss.
Terms: Author may buy any number of copies at 40% discount and postage. Book catalog for #10 SASE.
Advice: Send SASE for more information.

‡SANS SOLEIL, (I,II), Subsidiary of Pociao's Books, P.O. Box 130 136, Bonn, Germany 53037. 0228 229583. Fax: 0228 219507. E-mail: pociao@compuserve.com. **Acquisitions:** Pociao, director. Estab. 1995. Small, independent publisher specializing in female writing. Publishes paperback originals. Published new writers within the last year. Plans 1 first novel this year. Averages 2 total titles, 1 fiction title/year.
Needs: Feminist, lesbian, literary. Recently published *Hunger*, by Katharina Franck.
How to Contact: Accepts unsolicited mss. Query first. Unsolicited queries/correspondence by e-mail and fax OK. Include bio with submission. SASE or IRCs for reply or send a disposable copy of ms. Reports in 1 month on queries; 3 months on mss. Simultaneous submissions OK.
Payment/Terms: Pays royalties of 7% minimum; 10% maximum. Advance is negotiable. Sends galleys to author. Publishes ms up to 1 year after acceptance.

THE SAVANT GARDE WORKSHOP, (II, IV), a privately-owned affiliate of The Savant Garde Institute, Ltd., P.O. Box 1650, Sag Harbor NY 11963-0060. (516)725-1414.**Acquisitions**: Vilna Jorgen II, publisher. Estab. 1953. "Literary multiple-media publisher." Publishes hardcover and paperback originals and reprints. First novel print order: 1,000. Averages 2 total titles.
  ● Be sure to look at this publishers' guidelines first. Works could best be described as avant-garde/post modern, experimental.
Needs: Contemporary, futuristic, humanist, literary, philosophical. "We are open to the best, whatever it is." No "mediocrity or pot boilers." Published *01 or a Machine Called SKEETS*, by Artemis Smith (avant-garde). Series include "On-Demand Desktop Collectors' Editions," "Artists' Limited Editions," "Monographs of The Savant Garde Institute."
How to Contact: Do not send unsolicited mss. Query first with SASE and biographical statement. Agented fiction 1%. Reports in 6 weeks on queries ("during academic year"); 2 months on invited mss. Sometimes comments on rejected mss. Critiques rejected mss for $50.
Terms: Average advance: $500, provides author's copies, honorarium (depends on grant/award money). Terms set by individual arrangement with author depending on the book and previous professional experience. Sends galleys to author. Publishes ms 18 months after acceptance. Writer's guidelines free.
Advice: "Most of the time we recommend authors to literary agents who can get better deals for them with other publishers, since we are looking for extremely rare offerings. We are not interested in the usual commercial submissions. Convince us you are a real artist, not a hacker." Would like to see more "thinking for the 21st Century of Nobel Prize calibre. We're expanding into multimedia CD-ROM co-publishing and seek multitalented authors who can produce and perform their own multimedia work for CD-ROM release. We are overbought and underfunded—don't expect a quick reply or fast publication date."

SHIELDS PUBLISHING/NEO PRESS, (V), 301 E. Liberty, Suite 120, Ann Arbor MI 48104. (313)996-9229. Fax: (313)996-4544. Website: neopress.com (includes writer's guidelines, titles and sample contract). **Acquisitions**: Maria C. Allen, editor. "Small, independent press." Publishes hardcover and paperback originals. Plans 1 first novel this year. Averages 1 fiction title each year. Distributes titles through Baker & Taylor. Promotes titles through speaking engagements, radio, TV and authors tours.
Imprint(s): Revolutionary Words, edited by Marva Allen; and Sweet Sweet Back, edited by Lois Douglas.
  ● Shields is known for works focusing on minorities and women.
Needs: Ethnic/multicultural, experimental, feminist, gay, historical, humor/satire, lesbian, literary, religious/inspirational, romance, short story collections. Recently published *Protégé*, by C.C. Arram (novel); and *Reflections & Revolutionary Words*, by Tiffany Edwards.
How to Contact: *Does not accept unsolicited mss.* Query with outline/synopsis and 2 sample chapters. Include list of publishing credits with submission. Send SASE for reply, return of ms or send a disposable copy of ms.
Terms: Pays "variable" royalties. Offers negotiable advance.
Advice: "We are looking for fiction and self-help books that hold out the view that people can better their lives. We are accepting works of fiction that feature characters who take personal responsibility for making things happen with positive rather than negative role models. Neo Press seeks writers whose work indicates what they stand for rather than what they are against. In return, we are able to give our authors more than the usual level of editorial, marketing and distribution support to maximize the success of each book we publish. Proofread and edit your work! There's nothing worse than error-ridden manuscripts. We focus on more select audiences rather than the mainstream. 'Formula' writing has no place with us."

THE SMITH, (I, II), 69 Joralemon St., Brooklyn NY 11201-4003. (718)834-1212. **Acquisitions**: Harry Smith, editor; Michael McGrinder, associate editor. Estab. 1964. Books: 70 lb. vellum paper for offset and 80 lb. vellum for letterpress printing; perfect binding; often uses illustrations. Average print order: 1,000. First novel print order: 1,000. Plans 2 fiction titles this year.

- The Poor Richard Award was presented to publisher Harry Smith for his "three decades of independent literary publishing activities."

Needs: *Extremely limited* book publishing market—currently doing only 3-5 books annually, and these are of a literary nature, usually fiction or poetry. Published *The Cleveland Indian* (novel) and *Blue Eden* (connected long stories), both by Luke Salisbury; and *Bodo*, by John Bennett (novel).

Payment/Terms: Pays royalties. Average advance: $500-1,000. Publishes ms 9 months after acceptance. Writer's guidelines and book catalog for SASE.

Advice: "We find most synopses are stupid. Send one or two chapters, or one to three stories, depending on length. Complete manuscripts may not be read. Our list is our only guide and our motto is: Anything goes as long as it's good. Remember that we publish outside the mainstream, and do not publish any self-help, recovery or inspirational books. And SASE, please! Because of unusual working hours, we are unable to accept registered or certified mail or bulky packages which will not fit through our mail slot. The post office is not conveniently located for us to pick up mail."

♣SNOWAPPLE PRESS, (I, II), P.O. Box 66024, Heritage Postal Outlet, Edmonton, Alberta T6J 6T4 Canada. (403)437-0191. **Acquisitions**: Vanna Tessier, editor. Estab. 1991. "We focus on topics that are interesting, unusual and controversial." Small independent literary press. Publishes hardcover and paperback originals. Books: non-acid paper; offset printing; illustrations. Average print order: 500. First novel print order: 500. Plans 1 first novel this year. Averages 3-4 total titles, 1-2 fiction titles each year. Distributes titles through bookseller and library wholesalers. Promotes titles through press releases and reviews.

Needs: Adventure, children's/juvenile (adventure, fantasy, mystery), experimental, historical, literary, mainstream/contemporary, short story collections, translations, young adult/teen (adventure, mystery/suspense). Recently published *Gypsy Drums*, by Vanna Tessier (short stories); *Salamander Moon*, by Cecelia Frey (short stories); and *Missing Bones*, by Vanna Tessier (young adult).

How to Contact: Does no accept unsolicited mss. Query first with 1-page cover letter. Include estimated word count, 300-word bio and list of publishing credits. SASE with sufficient IRCs. Reports in 3-4 weeks on queries; 3 months on mss. Simultaneous submissions OK.

Terms: Pays honorarium; provides 10-25 author's copies. Sends galleys to author. Publishes ms 12-18 months after acceptance.

Advice: "Query first to obtain guidelines with proper SASE and IRCs."

THE SPIRIT THAT MOVES US PRESS, (II), P.O. Box 720820-N, Jackson Heights NY 11372-0820. (718)426-8788. **Acquisitions**: Morty Sklar, editor/publisher. Estab. 1974. Small independent literary publisher. Publishes hardcover and paperback originals. "We do, for the most part, simultaneous clothbound and trade paperbacks for the same title." Books: 60 lb. natural acid-free paper; mostly photo-offset, some letterpress; cloth and perfect binding; illustrations. Average print order: 3,000. Published new writers within the last year. Publishes 20% previously unpublished writers/year. Averages 2 fiction titles, mostly multi-author. Distributes titles directly and through wholesalers. Promotes titles through *Publishers Weekly*, *Kirlens* and advertisements in trade and consumer publications.

- *Patchwork Of Dreams*, was awarded a grant by Jackson Heights City Council representative to place this book in several schools for classroom use. The Spirit That Moves Us Press is known for our having been the first U.S. publisher of Jaroslav Seifert, who won the Nobel Prize a year after they published his *The Casting Of Bells*.

Needs: Literary. "Our choice of 'literary' does not exclude almost any other category—as long as the writing communicates on an emotional level, and is involved with people more than things. Nothing sensational or academic." Published *Patchwork of Dreams: Voices from the Heart of the New America*, a multiethnic collection of fiction and other genres; *Editor's Choice III: Fiction, Poetry & Art from the U.S. Small Press*, biennally, and *Free Parking*, both edited by Morty Sklar.

How to Contact: Accepts unsolicited mss. "We are undergoing major changes. Please query before sending work." Query letter only first "unless he/she sees an announcement that calls for manuscripts and gives a deadline." Include estimated word count, bio and whether or not ms is a simultaneous submission. SASE for reply or return of ms. Reports on mss "if rejected, soon; if under consideration, from 1-3 months." Comments on rejected mss "when author requests that or when we are compelled to by the writing (good or bad)."

Terms: Pays royalties of 10% net and authors copies, also honorarium, depends on finances. Sends galleys to author. Publishes up to 1 year after acceptance. Plans and time-frames for #10 SASE "but the guidelines are only for certain books; we don't use general guidelines." Catalog for 6×9 SAE and 2 first-class stamps.

Advice: "We are interested in work that is not only well written, but that gets the reader involved on an emotional level. No matter how skilled the writing is, or how interesting or exciting the story, if we don't care about the people in it, we won't consider it. Also, we are open to a great variety of styles, so just be yourself and don't try to second-guess the editor. You may have our newest collection *Patchwork of Dreams* as a sample, for $10 (regularly $14.50 with postage).

‡**STORM PEAK PRESS**, 157 Yesler Way, Suite 413, Seattle WA 98104. (206)223-0162. Publishes trade paperback originals and reprints. Publishes 3 books/year.
Needs: Juvenile adventure. Recently published *The Ballad of Big Ben's Boots & Other Tales for Telling*, by John Dashney.
How to Contact: Query with SASE. Reports in 2 months.
Terms: Pays royalty on retail price or net revenues.
Advice: "Get editorial help before sending a manuscript. Be confident the material is well-written."

STORMLINE PRESS, (I, II), P.O. Box 593, Urbana IL 61801. Publisher: Raymond Bial. Estab. 1985. "Small independent literary press operated by one person on a part-time basis, publishing one or two books annually." Publishes hardcover and paperback originals. Books: acid-free paper; paper and cloth binding; b&w illustrations. Average print order: 1,000-2,000. First novel print order: 1,000-2,000. Published new writers within the last year. Averages 1-2 total titles, all fiction each year.
  • Stormline's title, *First Frost*, was selected for a Best of the Small Presses Award.
Needs: Literary. Looks for "serious literary works, especially those which accurately and sensitively reflect rural and small town life." Published *Silent Friends: A Quaker Quilt*, by Margaret Lacey (short story collection).
How to Contact: Accepts unsolicited mss. Query (with SASE), preferably during November or December. Include estimated word count, bio, list of publishing credits. SASE for reply or return of ms. Reports in 2 weeks on queries; 1 month on mss. Simultaneous submissions OK.
Terms: Pays royalties of 10% maximum. Provides author's copies. Sends galleys to author. Publishes ms 6-12 months after acceptance. Writer's guidelines for SASE. Book catalog free.
Advice: "We look for a distinctive voice and writing style. We are always interested in looking at manuscripts of exceptional literary merit. We are not interested in popular fiction or experimental writing. Please review other titles published by the press, notably *Silent Friends: A Quaker Quilt*, to get an idea of the type of books published by our press."

THIRD SIDE PRESS, INC., (II), 2250 W. Farragut, Chicago IL 60625-1863. (773)271-3029. Fax: (773)271-0459. E-mail: thirdside@aol.com. **Acquisitions**: Midge Stocker, publisher. Estab. 1991. "Small, independent press, feminist." Publishes paperback originals. "Experimental and contemporary lesbian novels." Books: 50 lb. recycled, acid-free paper; offset-web or sheet printing; perfect binding. Average print order: 3,000. First novel print order: 2,000. Published new writers within the last year. Averages 4 total titles, 2 fiction titles each year. Distributes titles through Consortium Book Sales & Distribution.
Needs: Lesbian: erotica (lesbian only), feminist, literary, mainstream/contemporary. No "collections of stories; horror; homophobic" material. Recently published *Not So Much the Fall*, by Kerry Hart (first novel); *Speaking in Whispers*, by Kathleen Morris (erotica); and *The Mayor of Heaven*, by Lynn Kanter. Series include Royce Madison mysteries; Women/Cancer/Fear/Power series.
How to Contact: Query first. Queries by e-mail OK. Include bio (1-2 paragraphs) and synopsis. Send SASE for reply, return of ms or send a disposable copy of ms. Reports in 2-3 weeks on queries; 3-6 months on mss. Simultaneous submissions OK with notice. Sometimes comments on rejected mss.
Terms: Pays royalties (varies). Provides 10 author's copies. Publishes ms 6-18 months after acceptance. Writer's guidelines for 9 × 12 SAE and 2 first-class stamps. Book catalog for 2 first-class stamps.
Advice: "Look at our catalog and read one or two of our other books to get a feel for how your work will fit with what we've been publishing. Plan book readings and other appearances to help sell your book. And don't quit your day job."

THIRD WORLD PRESS, P.O. Box 19730, Chicago IL 60619. (773)651-0700. Publisher/Editor: Haki Madhubuti. Estab. 1967. Black-owned and operated independent publisher of fiction and nonfiction books about the black experience throughout the Diaspora. Publishes paperback originals. Plans 1 first novel this year, as well as short story collections. Averages 10 total titles, 3 fiction titles each year. Average first novel print order 15,000 copies.
Needs: Ethnic, historical, juvenile (animal, easy-to-read, fantasy, historical, contemporary), preschool/picture book, short story collections, and young adult/teen (easy-to-read/teen, folktales, historical). "We primarily publish nonfiction, but will consider fiction by and about blacks."
How to Contact: Accepts unsolicited mss October-May each year. Query or submit outline/synopsis and 1 sample chapter with SASE. Reports in 6 weeks on queries; 5 months on mss. Simultaneous submissions OK. Accepts computer printout submissions.
Terms: Individual arrangement with author depending on the book, etc.

✤**THISTLEDOWN PRESS, (II, IV)**, 633 Main St., Saskatoon, Saskatchewan S7H 0J8 Canada. (306)244-1722. Editor-in-Chief: Patrick O'Rourke. **Acquisitions**: Jesse Strothers. Estab. 1975. Publishes paperback originals. Books: Quality stock paper; offset printing; perfect-bound; occasional illustrations. Average print order 1,500-2,000. First novel print order: 1,000-1,500. Publishes 12 titles, 6 or 7 fiction, each year.
  • A story included in the press *The Blue Jean Collection* received a Vicky Metcalf Award, and books published by Thistledown have been selected as "Our Choice" by the Canadian Children's Book Centre and the Arthur Ellis Crime Writers Award (Best Juvenile Story).

Needs: Literary, experimental, short story collections, novels.

How to Contact: "We *only* want to see Canadian-authored submissions. We will *not* consider multiple submissions." No unsolicited mss. Query first with SASE. Photocopied submissions OK. Reports in 2 months on queries. Publishes anthologies. "Stories are nominated." Published *It's A Hard Cow*, by Terry Jordan (short stories); *Soldier Boys*, by David Richards; *The Woman on the Bridge*, by Mel Dagg (short stories); and *The Blue Camaro*, by R.P. MacIntyre. Also publishes The Mayer Mystery Series (mystery novels for young adults) and The New Leaf Series (first books for poetry and fiction).

Payment/Terms: Pays standard royalty on retail price. Publishes ms 2 years after acceptance. Writer's guidelines and book catalog for #10 SASE.

Advice: "We are primarily looking for quality writing that is original and innovative in its perspective and/or use of language. Thistledown would like to receive queries first before submission—perhaps with novel outline, some indication of previous publications, periodicals your work has appeared in. *We publish Canadian authors only.* We are continuing to publish more fiction and are looking for new fiction writers to add to our list. New Leaf Editions line is first books of poetry or fiction by emerging Western Canadian authors. Familiarize yourself with some of our books before submitting a query or manuscript to the press."

‡**THORNGATE ROAD, (II, IV-Specialized: gays, lesbians and bisexuals only)**, Campus Box 4240, English Department, Illinois State University, Normal IL 61790-4240. (309)438-7705. Fax: (309)438-5414. E-mail: jmelled@ilstu.edu. **Acquisitions**: Jim Elledge, director. Estab. 1996. Thorngate Road is a small, one-person operation publishing prose poems, poetry and cross-genre/experimental texts by gays, lesbians or bisexuals only. Publishes paperback originals. Books: 70 lb. paper; offset printing; saddle stitched; cover only illustrations. Average print order: 300. Averages 2 total titles, 1 prose poetry title/year.

Imprint(s): Berdache Chapbook Series and Frank O'Hara Award Chapbook Series.
● Thorngate Road also sponsors the Frank O'Hara Award Chapbook Competition.

Needs: Comics/graphic novels, experimental, feminist, gay, lesbian, literary, prose poetry, short shorts. Recently published *Two Girls*, by Kristy Nielsen (prose poems); and *An Invisible Veil Between Us*, by Larry Wayne Johns (poetry). Publishes the Frank O'Hara Chapbook Series and Berdache Chapbook Series. "In 1997-98, we'll be publishing new books by Karen Lee Osborne, David Trinidad, Maureen Seaton and Reginald Shepherd."

How to Contact: Accepts unsolicited mss only if submitted to the Frank O'Hara Award Chapbook Competition. Query letter only. Unsolicited queries/correspondence by e-mail OK. Include list of publishing credits and acknowledgements page should accompany submissions to the O'Hara contest. Send SASE for reply, return of ms or send disposable copy of ms. Reports in 1 week on queries; 3 months on mss. Simultaneous submissions OK.

Terms: Pays in 25 author's copies; pays honorarium of $500 for winners of the Frank O'Hara Award Chapbook Competition. Sends galleys to author. Writer's guidelines free for #10 SASE.

Advice: Support lesbigay presses and journals by buying copies of their books and issues or with cash donations, even if the donations are small. Don't support us in hopes of getting your work published but because it's a noble endeavor—and because it's necessary in order to get lesbigay voices heard.

‡❦**TURNSTONE PRESS, (II)**, 607-100 Arthur St., Winnipeg, Manitoba R3B 1H3 Canada. (204)947-1555. Fax: (204)942-1555. E-mail: editor@turnstonepress.mb.ca. **Acquisitions**: Manuela Dias, editor. Estab. 1976. "Turnstone Press is a literary press that publishes Canadian writers with an emphasis on writers from, and writing on, the Canadian west." Canadian literary press focusing on eclectic new writing, prairie writers and travel writing. Books: Offset paper; perfect-bound; average first novel print order: 1,500. Published new writers within the last year. Publishes 3 previously unpublished writers/year. Averages 8-10 total titles/year. Distributes titles through General Distribution Services (Canada) and LPC/Login (US). Promotes titles through Canadian national and local print media and select US print advertising.

● Turnstone Press received the Manitoba Book Design of the Year Award. *Summer of My Amazing Luck*, by Miriam Toews was nominated for the Stephen Leacock Award for Humor and the John Hirsch Award for Most Promising Writer.

Needs: Experimental, literary, regional (Western Canada), mystery, noir. "We will be doing only 2-3 fiction titles a year. Interested in new work exploring new narrative/fiction forms, travel/adventure writing of a literary nature and writing that pushes the boundaries of genre." Recently published *How to Get There From Here*, by Michelle Berry (short stories); *A Blue and Golden Year*, by Alison Preston (mystery); and *Summer of My Amazing Luck*, by Miriam Toews (comic novel).

How to Contact: *Canadian authors only.* Accepts unsolicited mss. Query first with 20-40 sample pages and SASE. Include estimated word count and list of publishing credits. Reports in 6 weeks on queries; 2-4 months on mss.

Terms: Pays royalties of 10%; 10 author's copies. Average advance: $500. Publishes ms 1 year after acceptance. Sends galleys to author. Book catalog free on request. Simultaneous submissions OK if notified.

Advice: "Like most Canadian literary presses, we depend heavily on government grants which are not available for books by non-Canadians. Do some homework before submitting work to make sure your subject matter/ genre/writing style falls within the publishers area of interest. Specializes in experimental literary and prairie writing."

TURTLE POINT PRESS, (II), 103 Hog Hill, Chappaqua NY 10514. (800)453-2992. **Acquisitions**: Jonathan Rabinowitz, president. Estab. 1990. "Small press publishing mostly lost literary fiction in quality paperback editions. Beginning in 1994 doing contemporary fiction as well." Publishes paperback originals and reprints. Books: recycled 60 lb. stock paper; sewn binding; occasional illustrations. Average print order: 1,500. First novel print order 800-1,500. Plans 2 first novels this year. Averages 4-5 fiction titles each year.

Needs: Literary, novels, translations. "Literary fiction, *tranlations* particularly from French, Spanish and Italian." Published *The Toys of Princes*, by Ghislain de Diesbach (Richard Howard, translator) (short stories); *Clovis*, by Michael Ferrier (social-satire fiction); and *The Diary of a Forty-Niner*, edited by Jackson/Carfield (journal).

How to Contact: Submit outline/synopsis and sample chapters. Include estimated word count, short bio, list of publishing credits. Send SASE for reply, return of ms or send a disposable copy of ms. Reports in 1 month. Sometimes comments on rejected mss.

Terms: Pays royalty (varies), negotiable advance or honorarium. Publishes ms 4-12 months after acceptance. Book catalogs are free.

Advice: "We are publishers of lost fiction with a keen interest in doing contemporary writing and contemporary translation."

THE UNIVERSITY OF ARKANSAS PRESS, (II), 201 Ozark Ave., Fayetteville AR 72701. (501)575-3246. Fax: (501)575-6044. E-mail: uaprinfo@cavern.uark.edu. Director: John Coghlan. **Acquisitions**: Kevin Brock, acquisitions editor. Estab. 1980. "Regional awareness, national impact . . . through books." Small university press. Publishes hardcover and paperback originals and paperback reprints. Average print order: 750 cloth and 2,000 paper copies. Averages 28 total titles, 2 short fiction titles (a novel only in translation or reprint) each year.

● This press has won the Spur Award for best Western nonfiction. University of Arkansas Press will not be considering fiction this year.

Needs: Literary, mainstream, regional (South Ozarks, Arkansas), short story collections, translations. Publishes anthologies or special editions. Stories are usually selected by the editor. Published *Augustus*, by John Williams (novel); *Horses into the Night*, by Baltasar Porcel, translated by John Getman (novel); and *Overgrown with Love*, by Scott Ely (short story collection).

How to Contact: Query first with SASE. Include estimated word count, 2 paragraph bio and list of publishing credits. Reports in 1 month. Simultaneous and electronic (disk) submissions OK.

Terms: Pays royalties of 10% on hardback, 6% on paperback; 10 author's copies. Publishes ms an average of 1 year after acceptance. Writer's guidelines and book catalog for 9 × 12 SASE.

Advice: "We are looking for fiction—primarily short fiction—written with energy, clarity and economy. Apart from this, we have no predisposition concerning style or subject matter. The University of Arkansas Press does not respond to queries or proposals not accompanied by SASE. Be prepared to submit on disk plus hard copy."

UNIVERSITY OF MISSOURI PRESS, (II), 2910 LeMone Blvd., Columbia MO 65201. (573)882-7641. Fax: (573)884-4498. E-mail: willcoxc@ext.missouri.edu. Website: www.system.missouri.edu/upress (includes authors, titles). **Acquisitions**: Clair Willcox, editor. Estab. 1958. "Mid-size university press." Publishes paperback originals and reprints (short story collections only). Published new writers within the last year. Publishes 1 previously unpublished writer/year. Averages 52 total titles, 4 short story collections each year.

● The University of Missouri Press is a member of the Association of American University Presses.

Needs: Short story collections. No children's fiction. Recently published *Quake*, by Nance Van Winckel (short stories); *Four Decades*, by Gordon Weaver (short stories); and *Lost Women, Banished Souls*, by Garnett Kilberg Cohen (short stories).

How to Contact: Accepts unsolicited mss. Query first. Queries by e-mail OK. Submit cover letter and sample story or two. Include bio/publishing credits. SASE for reply. Reports in 2 weeks on queries; 3 months on mss. Simultaneous submissions OK. Sometimes comments on rejected ms.

Terms: Pays royalties of 6%. Sends galleys to author. Publishes ms 1-1½ years after acceptance. Book catalogs are free.

UNIVERSITY OF NEVADA PRESS, (II, IV), MS 166, Reno NV 89557-0076. (702)784-6573. Fax: (702)784-6200. E-mail: dalrympl@scs.unr.edu. Director: Ronald E. Latimer. Editor-in-Chief: Margaret Dalrymple. **Acquisitions**: Trudy McMurrin, acquisitions editor. Estab. 1961. "Small university press. Publishes fiction that focuses primarily on the American West." Publishes hardcover and paperback originals and paperback reprints. Books: acid-free paper. Publishes approximately 25 total titles, 4 fiction titles/year. Member AAUP.

Needs: Ethnic/multicultural (general), family saga, historical (American West), humor/satire, mystery/suspense (U.S. West), regional (U.S. West). Published *Wild Indians & Other Creatures*, by Adrian Louis (short stories); *Bad Boys and Black Sheep*, by Robert Franklin Gish (short stories); and *The Measurable World*, by Katharine Coles (novel). "We have series in Basque Studies, Gambling Studies, history and humanities, ethnonationalism, Western literature."

How to Contact: Accepts unsolicited mss. Query with outline/synopsis and 2-4 sample chapters. E-mail and fax OK. Include estimated word count, 1-2 page bio and list of publishing credits. Send SASE for reply, return of ms or send a disposable copy of ms. Agented fiction 20%. Reports in 2-3 weeks on queries; 2-4 months on mss. Sometimes critiques or comments on rejected ms.

Payment/Terms: Pays royalties; negotiated on a book-by-book basis. Sends galleys to author. Publishes ms 9-

24 months after acceptance. Writer's guidelines for #10 SASE.

Advice: "We are not interested in genre fiction."

UNIVERSITY PRESS OF COLORADO, (IV), P.O. Box 849, Niwot CO 80544. (303)530-5337. Fax: (303)530-5306. **Acquisitions**: Laura Furney, acquisitions editor; Luther Wilson, director. Estab. 1965. "Small, independent, scholarly publisher, nonprofit." Publishes hardcover and paperback originals and reprints. Books: acid-free paper; offset printing; case bound. Average print order: 1,000. First novel print order: 1,500. Averages 30 total titles, 2 fiction titles each year. Member of The Association of American University Presses.

Needs: Regional (western), western (modern). "All of our fiction projects will be part of our Women's West series." Published *Fire in the Hole*, by Sybil Downing (historical western); and *The Eagle Catcher*, by Margaret Coel (historical Native American).

How to Contact: Query with outline/synopsis and 3 sample chapters. Include estimated word count, bio and list of publishing credits. Send SASE for reply, return of ms or send disposable copy of ms. Agented fiction 90%. Reports in 3 weeks on queries; 4 months on mss. Sometimes critiques or comments on rejected mss.

Terms: Pays royalties of 12% maximum. Provides 10 author's copies. Sends galleys to author. Publishes ms within 2 years after acceptance. Writer's guidelines and book catalog free.

Advice: "We look for high quality fiction that might not appeal to the larger trade houses. We are interested in publishing fiction that fits into our series *Women's West*. Generally, our authors are responsible for proofreading and indexing their own manuscripts. If they do not wish to do so, we will hire proofreaders and/or indexers at the author's expense."

VAN NESTE BOOKS, (I, II), 12836 Ashtree Rd., Midlothian VA 23113-3095. Phone/fax: (804)897-3568. E-mail: kvno@aol.com. **Acquisitions**: Karen Van Neste Owen, publisher. Estab. 1996. "We are a small independent publisher interested in publishing serious fiction." Publishes hardcover originals. Books: 55 lb. acid-free paper; cloth binding; illustrations (cover only). Average print order: 1,500. Plans 2 first novels for 1998 and 2-4 novels per year thereafter. Averages 2-4 total titles, 2-4 fiction titles each year.

Needs: Feminist, historical, humor/satire, literary, mainstream/contemporary, mystery/suspense, regional (southern), thriller/espionage.

How to Contact: Accepts unsolicited mss. Query with "brief" synopsis and 3 sample chapters. Include estimated word count, 2-paragraph bio, Social Security number and list of publishing credits. Send SASE for reply, return of ms or send disposable copy of ms. Reports in 2 months on queries; 6 months on mss. Sometimes critiques or comments on rejected mss.

Terms: Pays royalties of 10-15% minimum on print runs of more than 2,500 copies; half that on print runs under 2,500 copies. Average advance: $500 for finished disk. Sends galleys to author. Publishes ms 12-18 months after acceptance.

Advice: "Write well! And make the copy as clean as possible."

W.W. PUBLICATIONS, (IV), Subsidiary of A.T.S., Box 373, Highland MI 48357-0373. (813)585-0985. Also publishes *Minas Tirith Evening Star*. **Acquisitions**: Philip Helms, editor. Estab. 1967. One-man operation on part-time basis. Publishes paperback originals and reprints. Books: typing paper; offset printing; staple-bound; black ink illustrations. Average print order: 500. First novel print order: 500. Averages 1 title (fiction) each year.

● The publisher is an arm of the American Tolkien Society.

Needs: Fantasy, science fiction, young adult/teen (fantasy/science fiction). "Specializes in Tolkien-related or middle-earth fiction." Published *The Adventures of Fungo Hafwirse*, by Philip W. Helms and David L. Dettman.

How to Contact: Accepts unsolicited mss. Submit complete ms with SASE. Reports in 1 month. Simultaneous submissions OK. Occasionally critiques rejected mss.

Terms: Individual arrangement with author depending on book, etc.; provides 5 author's copies. Free book catalog.

Advice: "We are publishing more fiction and more paperbacks. The author/editor relationship: a friend and helper."

‡WOMAN IN THE MOON PUBLICATIONS, (I, IV), 1409 The Alameda, San Jose CA 95126. (408)279-6626. Fax: (408)279-6636(*). E-mail: sb02701@mercury.fhda.edu. Publisher: Dr. SDiane A. Bogus. Editor-in-Chief: Phillip Lynch. Estab. 1979. "We are a small press with a primary publishing agenda for poetry, New Age and reference books of no more than 1,000 words biannually. For our news magazine *The Spirit* we accept short story manuscripts." Averages 2-4 total titles each year.

Needs: Contemporary, ethnic, fantasy, gay, lesbian, psychic/supernatural/occult, prisoner's stories, short story

---

FOR INFORMATION ON ENTERING the *Novel & Short Story Writer's Market* Cover Letter Contest, see page 84.

collections.

How to Contact: Accepts unsolicited mss between January 1-April 30 only up to 100 mss. Query first or submit outline/synopsis and sample chapters. Query by letter, phone, fax or e-mail. SASE for query. Acknowledges in 1 week; reports during or at end of season. Simultaneous submissions OK. Comments on rejected mss.

Terms: *$45 reading fee required.* Pays royalties of 5% minimum; 10% maximum. Pays $25 plus 2 copies for short stories in quarterly newsletter. Publishes ms within 2 years after acceptance. Writer's guidelines for #10 SASE. Book sample for 6×9 SAE and $4 postage. Book catalog for $5.

Advice: "To the short story writer, write us a real life lesbian gay set of stories. Tell us how life is for an African American person in an enlightened world. Create a possibility, an ideal that humanity can live toward. Write a set of stories that will free, redeem and instruct humanity. The trends in fiction by women have to do with the heroine as physical and capable and not necessarily defended by or romantically linked to a male." Sponsors fiction and nonfiction prose contest in the name of Audre Lorde. Awards two $250 prizes. Contest runs from September 1 to November 30. Winners announced in February.

WOODLEY MEMORIAL PRESS, (IV), English Dept., Washburn University, Topeka KS 66621. (913)234-1032. E-mail: zzlaws@acc.wuacc.edu.Editor: Robert N. Lawson. Estab. 1980. "Woodley Memorial Press is a small, nonprofit press which publishes book-length poetry and fiction collections by Kansas writers only; by 'Kansas writers' we mean writers who reside in Kansas or have a Kansas connection." Publishes paperback originals. Averages 2 titles each year.

● Check for next short story collection contest. Work must be by a Kansas resident only. Most of the fiction the press publishes comes from its short story competition.

Needs: Contemporary, experimental, literary, mainstream, short story collection. "We do not want to see genre fiction, juvenile, or young adult." Published *Gathering Reunion*, by David Tangeman (short stories).

How to Contact: *Charges $5 reading fee.* Accepts unsolicited mss. Accepts unsolicited queries and correspondence by e-mail. Send complete ms. SASE. Reports in 2 weeks on queries; 2 months on mss. Sometimes comments on rejected ms.

Terms: "Terms are individually arranged with author after acceptance of manuscript." Publishes ms one year after acceptance. Writer's guidelines for #10 SASE.

Advice: "We only publish one work of fiction a year, on average, and definitely want it to be by a Kansas author. We are more likely to do a collection of short stories by a single author."

‡YMAA PUBLICATION CENTER, 38 Hyde Park Ave., Jamaica Plain MA 02130. (800)669-8892. Fax: (617)524-4184. **Acquisitions**: Andrew Murray, editor. Estab. 1982. Publishes hardcover originals and trade paperback originals and reprints. Publishes 6 titles/year.

Needs: Must have Asian, particularly Chinese, focus or theme. This is a *new* focus. No children's books.

How to Contact: Submit outline, 1 sample chapter and SASE. Reports in 2 months on proposals.

Terms: Pays royalty on retail price. No advance.

Advice: "If I were a writer trying to market a book today, I would spend a considerable amount of time examining the needs of a publisher *before* sending my manuscript to him. The writer must adhere to our style manual and follow our guidelines exactly."

ZEPHYR PRESS, (III), Subsidiary of Aspect, Inc., 13 Robinson St., Somerville MA 02145. Fax: (617)776-8246. Website: http://world.std.com/~zephyr. **Acquisitions**: Ed Hogan, editorial director. Estab. 1980. Small nonprofit publisher of Russian/Slavic literary and travel books. Publishes hardcover and paperback originals. Books: acid-free paper; offset printing; Smyth-sewn binding; some illustrations. Average print order: 1,500-2,000. First novel print order: 1,000-1,500. Averages 1-2 total titles each year.

● Zephyr Press does not plan to publish fiction in 1998 or 1999.

Needs: Contemporary, ethnic, feminist/lesbian, literary, mainstream, short story collections, translations (Russian, Eastern European fiction). Published *Sleeper at Harvest Time*, by Leonid Latynin; and *From Three Worlds: New Writing from Ukraine*, edited by Ed Hogan et. al.

How to Contact: "We no longer read unsolicited mss outside of our specialty of Russian/Slavic writing. Our focus in fiction is now on contemporary Russian writers in translation. We accept queries from agents, and from authors whose previous publications and professional credits (you must include a summary of these) evince work of exceptional talent and vision. Queries should include vita, list of publications, and up to 10 sample pages, photocopies only. If we are interested, we will request the full manuscript. Otherwise, we will probably not respond."

Terms: Pays royalties of approximately 12% of publisher's net for first edition. "Occasional flexibility of terms." Sends galleys to author. Book catalog for SASE.

Advice: "Seek well qualified feedback from literary magazine editors or agents and/or professionally established writers before submitting manuscripts to book publishers. We regard the author/editor relationship as one of close cooperation, from editing through promotion."

Book Publishers

In this section, you will find many of the "big-name" book publishers—Avon, The Berkley Publishing Group, Harcourt Brace & Company, Harlequin, Alfred A. Knopf, and Little Brown and Company, to name a few. Many of these publishers remain tough markets for new writers or for those whose work might be considered literary or experimental. Indeed, some only accept work from established authors, and then often only through an author's agent.

Also listed here are "small presses" publishing four or more titles annually. Included among them are small and mid-size independent presses, university presses and other nonprofit publishers. Introducing new writers to the reading public has become an increasingly more important role of these smaller presses at a time when the large conglomerates are taking less chances on unknown writers. Many of the successful small presses listed in this section have built their reputations and their businesses in this way and have become known for publishing prize-winning fiction.

These smaller presses also tend to keep books in print longer than larger houses. And, since small presses publish a smaller number of books, each title is equally important to the publisher, and each is promoted in much the same way and with the same commitment. Editors also stay at small presses longer because they have more of a stake in the business—often they own the business. Many smaller book publishers are writers themselves and know first-hand the importance of a close editor-author or publisher-author relationship.

However, although having your novel published by one of the big commercial publishers listed in this section is difficult, it is not impossible. The trade magazine *Publisher's Weekly* regularly features interviews with writers whose first novels are being released by top publishers. Many editors at large publishing houses find great satisfaction in publishing a writer's first novel. In the Insider Report on page 460 with Malle Vallik, editor at Harlequin, Vallik talks with pride about working with new authors in developing their talent: "That's one of the fun parts of the job, reading a manuscript you think has potential and going through the revision process once, twice or more times." And, says Vallik, "the best moment of all is when you can make that phone call and offer the deal. That's one of the things that keeps us editors going, and we do that a lot at Harlequin."

TYPES OF BOOK PUBLISHERS

Large or small, the publishers in this section publish books "for the trade." That is, unlike textbook, technical or scholarly publishers, trade publishers publish books to be sold to the general consumer through bookstores, chain stores or other retail outlets. Within the trade book field, however, there are a number of different types of books.

The easiest way to categorize books is by their physical appearance and the way they are marketed. Hardcover books are the more expensive editions of a book, sold through bookstores and carrying a price tag of around $20 and up. Trade paperbacks are soft-bound books, also sold mostly in bookstores, but they carry a more modest price tag of usually around $10 to $20. Today a lot of fiction is published in this form because it means a lower financial risk than hardcover.

Mass market paperbacks are another animal altogether. These are the smaller "pocket-size" books available at bookstores, grocery stores, drug stores, chain retail outlets, etc. Much genre or category fiction is published in this format. This area of the publishing industry is very open to the work of talented new writers who write in specific genres such as science fiction, romance and mystery.

At one time publishers could be easily identified and grouped by the type of books they do. Today, however, the lines between hardcover and paperback books are blurred. Many publishers known for publishing hardcover books also publish trade paperbacks and have paperback imprints. This enables them to offer established authors (and a very few lucky newcomers) hard-soft deals in which their book comes out in both versions. Thanks to the mergers of the past decade, too, the same company may own several hardcover and paperback subsidiaries and imprints, even though their editorial focuses may remain separate.

CHOOSING A BOOK PUBLISHER

In addition to checking the bookstores and libraries for books by publishers that interest you, you may want to refer to the Category Index at the back of this book to find publishers divided by specific subject categories. The subjects listed in the Index are general. Read the individual listings to find which subcategories interest a publisher. For example, you will find several romance publishers listed under that heading in the Category Index, but read the listings to find which type of romance is considered—gothic, contemporary, Regency or futuristic. See How to Use This Book to Publish Your Fiction for more on how to refine your list of potential markets.

The Roman numeral ranking codes appearing after the names of the publishers will also help you in selecting a publisher. These codes are especially important in this section, because many of the publishing houses listed here require writers to submit through an agent. A numeral **III** identifies those that mostly publish established and agented authors, while a numeral **I** points to publishers most open to new writers. See the end of this introduction for a complete list of ranking codes.

IN THE LISTINGS

As with other sections in this book, we identify new listings with a double-dagger symbol (‡). In this section, many of these are not new publishers, but instead are established publishers who decided to list this year in the hope of finding promising new writers.

In addition to the double dagger (‡) indicating new listings, we include other symbols to help you in narrowing your search. English-speaking foreign markets are denoted by an (*). The maple leaf symbol (✽) identifies Canadian presses. If you are not a Canadian writer, but are interested in a Canadian press, check the listing carefully. Many small presses in Canada receive grants and other funds from their provincial or national government and are, therefore, restricted to publishing Canadian authors.

We continue to include editorial comments set off by a bullet symbol (●) within listings. This is where we tell you of any honors or awards received by publishers or their books. We also include information about any special requirements or circumstances that will help you know even more about the publisher's needs and policies.

Each listing includes a summary of the editorial mission of the house, an overarching principle that ties together what they publish. Under the heading **Acquisitions**: we list one or more editors, often with their specific area of expertise. An imprint listed in boldface type means there is an independent listing arranged alphabetically within this section.

Book editors asked us again this year to emphasize the importance of paying close attention to the Needs and How to Contact subheads of listings for book publishers. Unlike magazine editors who want to see complete manuscripts of short stories, most of the book publishers listed here ask that writers send a query letter with an outline and/or synopsis and several chapters of their novel. The Business of Fiction Writing, beginning on page 77 of this book, outlines how to prepare work to submit directly to a publisher.

There are no subsidy book publishers listed in *Novel & Short Story Writer's Market*. By subsidy, we mean any arrangement in which the writer is expected to pay all or part of the cost of producing, distributing and marketing his book. We feel a writer should not be asked to share in any cost of turning his manuscript into a book. All the book publishers listed here told us that they *do not charge writers* for publishing their work. *If any of the publishers listed here ask you to pay any part of publishing or marketing your manuscript, please let us know.*

A NOTE ABOUT AGENTS

Many publishers are willing to look at unsolicited submissions, but most feel having an agent is to the writer's best advantage. In this section more than any other, you'll find a number of publishers who prefer submissions from agents.

Because the commercial fiction field has become so competitive, and publishers have so little time, more and more are relying on agents. For some publishers, agents act as "first readers," wading through the deluge of submissions from writers to find the very best. For writers, a good agent can be a foot in the door—someone willing to do the necessary work to put your manuscript in the right editor's hands.

Because it is almost as hard to find a good agent as it is to find a publisher, many writers see agents as just one more roadblock to publication. Yet those who have agents say they are invaluable. Not only can a good agent help you make your work more marketable, an agent acts as your business manager and adviser, keeping your interests up front during contract negotiations.

Still, finding an agent can be very difficult for a new writer. Those already published in magazines or other periodicals have a better chance than someone with no publishing credits. Although many agents will read queries, packages and manuscripts from unpublished authors without introduction, referrals from other clients can be a big help. If you don't know any published authors, you may want to try to meet an agent at a conference before approaching them with your manuscript. Some agents even set aside time at conferences to meet new writers.

For listings of agents and more information on how to approach and deal with them, see the 1998 *Guide to Literary Agents*, published by Writer's Digest Books. The book separates nonfee- and fee-charging agents. While many agents do not charge any fees up front, a few charge writers to cover the costs of using outside readers. Be wary of those who charge large sums of money for reading a manuscript. Reading fees do not guarantee representation. Think of an agent as a potential business partner and feel free to ask tough questions about his or her credentials, experience and business practices.

FOR MORE INFORMATION

Some of the mystery, romance and science fiction publishers included in this section are also included in *Mystery Writer's Sourcebook*, *Romance Writer's Sourcebook* or *Science Fiction and Fantasy Writer's Sourcebook* (all published by Writer's Digest Books). These books include in-depth interviews with editors and publishers. Also check issues of *Publishers Weekly* for publishing industry trade news in the U.S. and around the world or *Quill & Quire* for book publishing news in the Canadian book industry.

For more small presses see the *International Directory of Little Magazines and Small Presses* published by Dustbooks (P.O. Box 100, Paradise CA 95967). To keep up with changes in the industry throughout the year, check issues of two small press trade publications: *Small Press Review* (also published by Dustbooks) and *Small Press* (Jenkins Group, Inc., 121 E. Front St., 4th Floor, Traverse City MI 49684).

The ranking system we've used for listings in this section is as follows:

I **Publisher encourages beginning or unpublished writers to submit work for consideration and publishes new writers frequently.**

II **Publisher accepts outstanding work by beginning and established writers.**

III Hard to break into; publishes mostly writers with extensive previous publication credits or agented writers.

IV Special-interest or regional publisher, open only to writers in certain genres or on certain subjects or from certain geographic areas.

V Closed to unsolicited submissions.

WRITER-TO-WRITER

Featured in this section for the first time are Writer-to-Writer quotes from established authors. Placed near the publisher of each author's work, these pieces offer information—and some inspiration, too—on being a fiction writer and surviving the lonesome and often daunting work of completing a novel-length manuscript.

---

‡ABBEVILLE KIDS, Imprint of Abbeville Publishing Group, 488 Madison Ave., New York NY 10022. (212)888-1969. Fax: (212)644-5085. **Acquisitions:** Susan Costello, editorial director/editor-in-chief. Abbeville Kids publishes children's fiction and nonfiction with an emphasis on illustrations and picture books. Publishes hardcover and trade paperback originals.
Needs: Juvenile, picture books. Recently published *Felix Explores Planet Earth*, by Annette Langen and Constanza Droop; The *Silly Shapes* series, by Sophie Fatus.
How to Contact: Rarely publishes unsolicited material. Query with complete ms and SASE. Reports in 3 months on queries. Simultaneous submissions OK.
Terms: Pays royalty. Advance varies. Publishes book 18 months after acceptance of ms. Book catalog and ms guidelines free; call customer service.

‡ABSEY & CO., 5706 Root Rd., Suite #5, Spring TX 77389. E-mail: abseyandco@aol.com. **Acquisitions:** Karen Foster, editorial director. "We are looking primarily for education books, especially those with teaching strategies based upon research." Publishes hardcover, trade paperback and mass market paperback originals. Publishes 5-10 titles/year.
Needs: Juvenile, mainstream/contemporary, short story collections.
How to Contact: Query with SASE. Reports in 3 months on queries. Simultaneous submissions OK.
Terms: Pays 8-15% royalty on wholesale price. Publishes ms 1 year after acceptance. Writer's guidelines for #10 SASE.
Advice: "Since we are a small, new press, we are looking for good manuscripts with a firm intended audience. As yet, we haven't explored this market. We feel more comfortable starting with nonfiction—educational. A mistake we often see in submissions is writers underwrite or overwrite—a lack of balance."

ACADEMY CHICAGO PUBLISHERS, (II), 363 W. Erie St., Chicago IL 60610. (312)751-7302. **Acquisitions:** Anita Miller, senior editor. Estab. 1975. "We are known for our women's studies." Midsize independent publisher. Publishes hardcover and paperback originals and paperback reprints.
● Academy Chicago Publishers is not accepting mss at this time because of "heavy returns from super stores."
Needs: Biography, history, feminist, academic and anthologies. Only the most unusual mysteries, no private-eyes or thrillers. No explicit sex or violence. Serious fiction, not romance/adventure. "We will consider historical fiction that is well researched. No science fiction/fantasy, no religious/inspirational, no how-to, no cookbooks. In general, we are very conscious of women's roles. We publish very few children's books." Published *Hiwassee*, by Charles F. Price; *Murder at the Movies*, by A.E. Eddenden; and *Threshold of Fire*, by Hella Haasse.
How to Contact: Accepts unsolicited mss. Query and submit first three chapters, triple spaced, with SASE and a cover letter briefly describing the content of your work. No simultaneous submissions. "Manuscripts without envelopes will be discarded. *Mailers* are a *must*."
Terms: Pays 5-10% on net in royalties; no advance. Publishes ms 18 months after acceptance. Sends galleys to author.
Advice: "At the moment we are swamped with manuscripts and anything under consideration can be under consideration for months."

ACE SCIENCE FICTION, Berkley Publishing Group, 200 Madison Ave., New York NY 10016. (212)686-9820. Estab. 1977. Publishes hardcover and paperback originals and reprints. See Berkley/Ace Science Fiction.

‡ACROPOLIS BOOKS, INC., (I, II, III), 747 Sheridan Blvd., #1A, Lakewood CO 80214-2551. (303)231-9923. Fax: (303)231-0492. E-mail: acropolisbooks@worldnet.att.net. Website: acropolisbooks.com. **Acquisi-**

tions: Constance J. Wilson, vice president of operations. Midsize trade publisher; full (national) distribution. "It is the mission of Acropolis Books to publish books at the highest level of consciousness, commonly referred to as mysticism. This was the consciousness demonstrated by revelators of every religion in the world." Publishes hardcover and paperback originals and reprints. Publishes 20 titles/year. Imprint publishes 5-10 titles/year.
Imprint(s): I-Level, Awakening and Flashlight.
Needs: Mysticism/inspirational. "Our books encompass the spiritual principles of Omnipresence, Omnipotence and Omniscience; and further bring home the mystical realization that everyone in this world is an individual instrument of God in expression." Recently published *Bunny Bu*, by Dianne Baker (children's book); and *Secret Splendor*, by Charles Essert.
How to Contact: Submit 4 sample chapters with SASE. Include estimated word count, 1 page bio, social security number and list of publishing credits. Reports in 1 month on queries, 3 months on mss.
Terms: Royalties or outright purchases negotable. Advances negotiable. Publishes ms an average of 1 year after acceptance. Book catalog and writer's guidelines for #10 SASE.
Advice: "Clearly understand our focus by reading or understanding books that we have published."

*ADAEX EDUCATIONAL PUBLICATIONS, P.O. Box AK188, Kumasi, Ghana. **Acquisitions**: Asare Konadu Yamoah, publisher/fiction editor.
Needs: Looks for cultural development, romance, literary translators and copyright brokers. "Publication development organization for Ghanaian, African and world literature: novels, workbooks, language development, etc." Average 5-10 fiction titles/year. Length: 8-250 typed pages.
How to Contact: Send brief summary and first and last chapter.
Terms: Pays advance and royalties.

ADVOCACY PRESS, (IV), Box 236, Santa Barbara CA 93102-0236. (805)962-2728. Fax: (805)963-3580. E-mail: advpress@rain.org. **Acquisitions**: Barbara Fierro Lang, executive director. Estab. 1983. "We promote gender equity and positive self-esteem through our publications." Small publisher with 3-5 titles/year. Hardcover and paperback originals. Books: perfect or Smyth-sewn binding; illustrations; average print order: 5,000-10,000 copies; first novel print order: 5,000-10,000. Averages 2 children's fiction (32-48 pg.) titles per year. Promotes titles through catalogs, distributors, schools and bookstores.
● Advocacy Press books have won the Ben Franklin Award and the Friends of American Writers Award. The press also received the Eleanor Roosevelt Research and Development Award from the American Association of University Women for its significant contribution to equitable education.
Needs: Juvenile. Wants only feminist/nontraditional messages to boys or girls—picture books; self-esteem issues. Published *Minou*, by Mindy Bingham (picture book); *Kylie's Song*, by Patty Sheehan (picture book); *Nature's Wonderful World in Rhyme*, by William Sheehan. Publishes the World of Work Series (real life stories about work).
How to Contact: Submit complete manuscript with SASE for return. Reports in 10 weeks on queries. Simultaneous submissions OK.
Terms: Pays in royalties of 5-10%. Book catalog for SASE.
Advice: Wants "only fictional stories for children 4-12-years-old that give messages of self-sufficiency for little girls; little boys can nurture and little girls can be anything they want to be, etc. Please review some of our publications *before* you submit to us. For layout and writing guidelines, we recommend that you read *The Children's Book: How to Write It, How to Sell It* by Ellen Roberts, Writers Digest Books. *Because of our limited focus, most of our titles have been written inhouse.*"

‡*AFRICA CHRISTIAN PRESS, P.O. Box 30, Achimota, Ghana, West Africa. **Acquisitions**: Mrs. Margaret Saah, assistant editor.
Needs: "We are a Christian publishing house specializing in Christian fiction works by Africans or expariates with a long association with Africa." Averages 6 fiction titles/year. Length: 15,000 words minimum.
How to Contact: Submit cover letter, synopsis, brief summary, sample chapter/s and/or entire manuscript. Mss should be "typewritten, double spaced, with generous margins." Send 2 copies and a SAE with IRCs for response/return.
Terms: Pays royalties. Write for catalog and/or writer's guidelines.

ALASKA NATIVE LANGUAGE CENTER, (IV), University of Alaska, P.O. Box 757680, Fairbanks AK 99775-7680. (907)474-7874. **Acquisitions**: Tom Alton, editor. Estab. 1972. Small education publisher limited to books in and about Alaska native languages. Generally nonfiction. Publishes hardcover and paperback originals. Books: 60 lb. book paper; offset printing; perfect binding; photos, line art illustrations; average print order: 500-1,000 copies. Averages 6-8 total titles each year.
Needs: Ethnic. Publishes original fiction only in native language and English by Alaska native writers. Published *A Practical Grammar of the Central Alaskan Yup'ik Eskimo Language*, by Steven A. Jacobson; *One Must Arrive With a Story to Tell*, by the Elders of Tununak, Alaska.
How to Contact: Does not accept unsolicited mss. Electronic submissions via ASCII for modem transmissions or Macintosh compatible files on 3.5 disk.
Terms: Does not pay. Sends galleys to author.

‡ALEXANDER BOOKS, Subsidiary of Creativity, Inc., 65 Macedonia Rd., Alexander NC 28701. (704)252-9515. **Acquisitions:** Vivian Terrell, executive editor. Publishes hardcover originals, and trade paperback and mass market paperback originals and reprints. Publishes 8-10 titles/year.
Imprint(s): Farthest Star (Ralph Roberts, publisher).
Needs: Historical, mainstream/contemporary, mystery, science fiction, western. "We prefer local or well-known authors or local interest settings." Recently published *Six-Gun Ladies*, by Talmage Powell (western); *Compleat Chance Perdue*, by Ross H. Spencer (mystery); and *The Giant Rat of Sumatra*, by Rick Boyer (mystery).
How to Contact: Query or submit synopsis and 3 sample chapters with SASE. Reports in 1 month on queries, 3 months on mss.
Terms: Pays 12-15% royalty on wholesale price. Advances seldom given (minimum $100). Publishes ms 1 year after acceptance. Book catalog and writer's guidelines for #10 SASE with 2 first-class stamps.
Advice: "Always send well-proofed manuscripts in final form. We will not read first rough drafts. Know your market."

ALGONQUIN BOOKS OF CHAPEL HILL, Subsidiary of Workman Publishing, 307 W. Weaver St., Carrboro NC 27510. (919)767-0108. Fax: (919)933-0272. **Acquisitions**: Elisabeth Scharlatt, publisher. Averages 24 total titles/year. Prefers not to share information at this time.
Imprint(s): Front Porch Paperbacks.

ALYSON PUBLICATIONS, INC., (II), 6922 Hollywood Blvd., Suite 1000, Los Angeles CA 90028. (213)871-1225. Fax: (213)467-6805. **Acquisitions**: Julie K. Trevelyan, fiction editor. Estab. 1977. Medium-sized publisher specializing in lesbian- and gay-related material. Publishes paperback originals and reprints. Books: paper and printing varies; trade paper, perfect-bound; average print order: 8,000; first novel print order: 6,000. Published new writers within the last year. Plans 40 total titles, 18 fiction titles each year.
● In addition to adult titles, Alyson Publications has been known for its line of young adult and children's books.
Needs: "We are interested in all categories; *all* materials must be geared toward lesbian and/or gay readers. No poetry." Recently published *3 Plays by Mart Crowley*; *Swords of the Rainbow*, edited by Eric Garber and Jewelle Gomez; and *Daddy's Wedding*, Michael Willhoite. Publishes anthologies. Authors may submit to them directly.
How to Contact: Query first with SASE. Reports in 3-12 weeks.
Terms: "We prefer to discuss terms with the author. Gay and/or lesbian nonfiction and excellent fiction are our focal points." Sends galleys to author. Book catalog for SAE and 3 first-class stamps.

‡AMERICAN DIABETES ASSOCIATION, 1660 Duke St., Alexandria VA 22314. (703)549-1500. Website: http://www.diabetes.org. **Acquisitions:** Susan Reynolds, acquisitions editor. "The mission of the American Diabetes Association is to prevent and cure diabetes and to improve the lives of all people affected by diabetes." Publishes hardcover originals and trade paperback originals. Publishes 15 titles/year.
Needs: Juvenile. "We publish very little fiction—all for juveniles with diabetes." Recently published *The Dinosaur Tamer*, by Marcia Levine Mazur (juvenile fiction).
How to Contact: Query with synopsis and 2 sample chapters. Reports in 2 months.
Terms: Pays 7-10% royalty on retail price. Offers $3,000 advance. Publishes ms 9 months after acceptance. Book catalog free.
Advice: "Our audience consists primarily of consumers with diabetes who want to better manage their illness. Obtain a few of our books to better understand our target audience and appropriate reading level."

♣ANNICK PRESS LTD., (IV), 15 Patricia Ave., Willowdale, Ontario M2M 1H9 Canada. (416)221-4802. Publisher of children's books. Publishes hardcover and paperback originals. Books: offset paper; full-color offset printing; perfect and library bound; full-color illustrations. Average print order: 9,000. First novel print order: 7,000. Plans 18 first picture books this year. Averages approximately 25 titles each year, both fiction and nonfiction. Average first picture book print order 2,000 cloth, 12,000 paper copies. Distributes titles through Firefly Books Lts.
Needs: Children's books only.
How to Contact: "Annick Press publishes only work by Canadian citizens or residents." Does not accept unsolicited mss. Query with SASE. Free book catalog. Occasionally critiques rejected mss.
Terms: No terms disclosed.

‡ARCADE PUBLISHING, (III), 141 Fifth Ave., New York NY 10010. (212)475-2633. Fax: (212)353-8148. President, Editor-in-Chief: Richard Seaver. **Acquisitions**: Cal Barksdale, Richard Seaver, Jeannette Seaver, Tim Bent, Sean McDonald and David Martyn. Estab. 1988. Independent publisher. Publishes hardcover originals and paperback reprints. Books: 50-55 lb. paper; notch, perfect-bound; illustrations; average print order: 10,000; first novel print order: 3,000-5,000. Published new writers within the year. Averages 40 total titles, 12-15 fiction titles each year. Distributes titles through Little, Brown & Co.
Needs: Literary, mainstream/contemporary, mystery/suspense, translations. No romance, science fiction, young adult. Recently published *Trying to Save Piggy Sneed*, by John Irving; *Famine*, by Todd Komarnicki; *Yocandra in the Paradise of Nada*, by Zoé Valdés; and *Divorcing Jack*, by Colin Bateman.

How to Contact: No unsolicited mss; unsolicited mss will be returned (SASE or IRC). Submit through an agent only. Agented fiction 100%. Reports in 2 weeks on queries; 3-4 months on mss. Does not comment on rejected ms.
Terms: Pays negotiable advances and royalties. 10 author's copies. Writer's guidelines and book catalog for SASE.

ARCHWAY PAPERBACKS/MINSTREL BOOKS, (II), Imprint of Pocket Books for Young Readers, 1230 Avenue of the Americas, New York NY 10020. (212)698-7268. **Acquisitions**: Patricia MacDonald, vice president/editorial director. Published by Pocket Books. Publishes paperback originals and reprints. Published new writers this year.
Imprint(s): Minstrel Books (ages 7-12); and **Archway** (ages 12 and up).
Needs: Young adult: mystery, suspense/adventure, thrillers. Young readers (80 pages and up): adventure, animals, humor, family, fantasy, friends, mystery, school, etc. No picture books. Published *Fear Street: The New Boy*, by R.L. Stine; and *Aliens Ate My Homework*, by Bruce Coville.
How to Contact: Submit query first with outline; SASE "mandatory. If SASE not attached, query letter will not be answered."
Payment/Terms: Pays royalties of 6% minimum; 8% maximum. Publishes ms 2 years after acceptance.

ARJUNA LIBRARY PRESS, (II), Subsidiaries include: The Journal of Regional Criticism, 1025 Garner St., D, Space 18, Colorado Springs CO 80905-1774. **Acquisitions**: Count Prof. Joseph A. Uphoff, Jr., director. Estab. 1979. "The Arjuna Library is an artist's prototype press." Publishes paperback originals. Books: 20 lb. paper; photocopied printing; perfect-bound; b&w illustrations. Average print order: 20. Averages 6 total titles, 3 fiction titles each year.
  ● Arjuna Press has had exhibits at the Colorado Springs Fine Arts Center, KTSC Public Television (academic), University of Southern Colorado and The Poets House, New York as well as in Heidelberg, Germany; Cracow, Poland; and Latouille Lentillac, France; as well as numerous other countries. The press is known for its surrealism and science fiction titles.
Needs: Adventure, childrens/juvenile (fantasy), erotica, experimental, fantasy (surrealist), horror (supernatural), lesbian, romance (futuristic/time travel), science fiction (hard science/technological, soft/sociological poetry), young adult/teen (fantasy/science fiction). Nothing obscene or profane. Published *This Sort of Scribble*, by Gregory Moore (short story); *High*, by Michael K. White; and *The March Hare*, by Marosa Di Giorgio, translated by Kathryn A. Kopple.
How to Contact: Accepts unsolicited mss. Submit complete ms with cover letter, resume. Include list of publishing credits, a disposable copy of the ms to be filed; will return samples in envelopes. Simultaneous submissions OK. Sometimes comments on rejected mss.
Terms: Pays 1 author's copy, plus potential for royalties. Writer's guidelines for SASE.
Advice: "Many new writers are impatient to gain acceptance and an income. These people often send letters that are rude or even threatening. It is important to realize that in our civilization everybody has been taught to read and write. Many people think it is an occupation of last resort when a job cannot be obtained elsewhere! It has never been easy to make a living as a writer. All of us should remember that civility is a key to success where hostility obliges the recipient to redress. We should all be patient in each new encounter, but the initiative to decency arises from the pretext of the correspondence."

✸ARSENAL PULP PRESS, (II), 103-1014 Homer St., Vancouver, British Columbia V6B 2W9 Canada. (604)687-4233. Fax: (604)669-8250. E-mail: arsenal@pinc.com. **Acquisitions**: Linda Field, editor. Literary press. Publishes paperback originals. Average print order: 1,500-3,000. First novel print order: 1,500. Published new writers within the last year. Publishes 1-3 previously unpublished writers/year. Averages 12-15 total titles, 2 fiction titles each year. Distributes titles through LPC Group/In Book. Promotes titles through reviews, excerpts and print advertising.
  ● Arsenal Pulp Press has received 3 Alcuin Society Awards for Excellence in Book Design.
Needs: Ethnic/multicultural (general), feminist, gay, lesbian, literary, short story collections. No genre fiction, i.e. westerns, romance, horror, mystery, etc. Recently published *Queer View Mirror*, by Johnston & Tulchinsky, eds. (gay and lesbian anthology); *Hard Core Logo*, by Michael Turner; and *Silence Descends*, by George Case.
How to Contact: Accepts unsolicited mss. Query with cover letter, outline/synopsis and 2 sample chapters. Include list of publishing credits. Send SASE for reply, return of ms or send a disposable copy of ms. Agented

 INTERNATIONAL MARKETS, those located outside of the United States and Canada, are marked with an asterisk.

fiction 10%. Reports in 1 month on queries; 3-4 months on mss. Simultaneous submissions OK. Sometimes comments on rejected mss.

Terms: Pays royalties of 10% minimum; 10% maximum. Negotiable advance. Sends galleys to author. Publishes ms 1 year after acceptance. Writer's guidelines and book catalog free for 9×11 SASE.

Advice: "We very rarely publish American writers."

ARTE PUBLICO PRESS, (II, IV), University of Houston, 4800 Calhoun, Houston TX 77204-2090. (713)743-2841. **Acquisitions:** Dr. Nicolás Kanellos, publisher. Estab. 1979. "Small press devoted to the publication of contemporary U.S.-Hispanic literature. Mostly trade paper; publishes 4-6 clothbound books/year. Publishes fiction and belles lettres." Publishes 30 paperback originals and occasionally reprints. Average print order 2,000-5,000. First novel print order 2,500-5,000.

Imprint(s): Piñata Books featuring children's and young adult literature by U.S.-Hispanic authors and *The Americas Review*.

    • Arte Publico Press received the 1994 American Book Award for *In Search of Bernabé*, by Graciela Limón; the Thorpe Menn Award for Literary Achievement; the Southwest Book Award and others. Arte Publico Press is the oldest and largest publisher of Hispanic literature for children and adults in the United States.

Needs: Childrens/juvenile, contemporary, ethnic, feminist, literary, short story collections, young adult written by US-Hispanic authors. Recently published *A Perfect Silence*, by Alba Ambert; *Song of the Hummingbird*, by Graciela Limón; and *Little Havana Blues: A Cuban-American Literature Anthology*.

How to Contact: Accepts unsolicited mss. Submit outline/synopsis and sample chapters or complete ms with cover letter and SASE. Agented fiction 1%. Sometimes critiques rejected mss.

Terms: Advances negotiated. Provides 20 author's copies; 40% discount on subsequent copies. Sends galleys to author. Publishes ms minimum 2 years after acceptance. Book catalog free on request.

Advice: "Include cover letter in which you 'sell' your book—why should we publish the book, who will want to read it, why does it matter, etc."

ATHENEUM BOOKS FOR YOUNG READERS, (II), Imprint of the Simon & Schuster Children's Publishing Division, 1230 Avenue of the Americas, New York NY 10022. (212)698-2721. Vice President/Editorial Director: Jonathan J. Lanman. Editorial Coordinator: Howard Kaplan. **Acquisitions:** Marcia Marshall, executive director; Ana Cerro, editor; Anne Schwartz, editorial director, Anne Schwartz Books. Second largest imprint of large publisher/corporation. Publishes hardcover originals. Books: Illustrations for picture books, some illustrated short novels. Average print order: 6,000-7,500. First novel print order: 5,000. Averages 50 total titles, 25 middle grade and YA fiction titles each year.

    • Books published by Atheneum Books for Children have received the Newbery Medal (*The View From Saturday*, by E.L. Konigsburg) and the Christopher Award (*The Gold Coin*, by Alma Flor Ada, illustrated by Neal Waldman). Because of the merger of Macmillan and Simon & Schuster, Atheneum Books has absorbed the Scribners imprint of Macmillan.

Needs: Juvenile (adventure, animal, contemporary, fantasy, historical, sports), preschool/picture book, young adult/teen (fantasy/science fiction, historical, mystery, problem novels, sports, spy/adventure). No "paperback romance type" fiction. Published *Albert's Thanksgiving*, by Lesle Tryon (3-6, picture book); *Alice the Brave*, by Phyllis Reynolds Naylor (8-12, middle grade novel); and *Uncle Vampire*, by Cynthia Grant (12 & up young adult novel).

How to Contact: Accepts queries only. SASE. Agented fiction 40%. Reports in 4-6 weeks on queries. Simultaneous submissions OK "if we are so informed and author is unpublished." Very rarely critiques rejected mss.

Terms: Pays in royalties of 10%. Average advance: $3,000 "along with advance and royalties, authors receive ten free copies of their book and can purchase more at a special discount." Sends galleys to author. Writer's guidelines for #10 SASE.

Advice: "We publish all hardcover originals, occasionally an American edition of a British publication. Our fiction needs have not varied in terms of quantity—of the 50-60 titles we do each year, 25 are fiction in different age levels. We are less interested in specific topics or subject matter than in overall quality of craftsmanship. First, know your market thoroughly. We publish only children's books, so caring for and *respecting* children is of utmost importance. Also, fad topics are dangerous, as are works you haven't polished to the best of your ability. (Why should we choose a 'jewel in the rough' when we can get a manuscript a professional has polished to be ready for publication?) The juvenile market is not one in which a writer can 'practice' to become an adult writer. In general, be professional. We appreciate the writers who take the time to find out what type of books we publish by visiting the libraries and reading the books. Neatness is a pleasure, too."

‡AUNT LUTE BOOKS, (IV), P.O. Box 410687, San Francisco CA 94141. (415)826-1300. Fax: (415)826-8300. **Acquisitions:** Shahara Godfrey, first reader. Small feminist and women of color press. Publishes hardcover and paperback originals. Publishes 4 total titles/year.

Needs: Ethnic/multicultural, feminist, lesbian.

How to Contact: Accepts unsolicited mss. Query with outline/synopsis and sample chapters. Send SASE for return of ms. Reports in 4 months.

Terms: Pays in royalties. Guidelines and catalog for free.

Advice: "We seek manuscripts, both fiction and nonfiction, by women from a variety of cultures, ethnic backgrounds and subcultures; women who are self-aware and who, in the face of all contradictory evidence, are still hopeful that the world can reserve a place of respect for each woman in it. We seek work that explores the specificities of the worlds from which we come, and which examines the intersections between the borders which we all inhabit."

AVALON BOOKS, (I, II, IV), Imprint of Thomas Bouregy Company, Inc., 401 Lafayette St., New York NY 10003. (212)598-0222. **Acquisitions:** Marcia Markland, vice president/publisher. Publishes hardcover originals. Averages 60 titles/year.
Needs: "Avalon Books publishes wholesome romances, mysteries, westerns. Intended for family reading, our books are read by adults as well as teenagers, and their characters are all adults. There is no graphic sex in any of our novels. Currently, we publish five books a month: two romances, one mystery, one career romance and one western. All the romances are contemporary; all the westerns are historical." Published *Ride the Rainbow Home*, by Susan Aylworth (career romance); *Even As We Speak*, by Caragh O'Brien (career romance); *The Mysterious Cape Cod Manuscript*, by Marie Lee (mystery); and *Frontier Justice*, by Dan Hepler (western). Books range in length from a minimum of 40,000 words to a maximum of 50,000 words.
How to Contact: Submit the first three chapters. "We'll contact you if we're interested." Publishes many first novels. Enclose ms-size SASE. Reports in about 3 months. "Send SASE for a copy of our tip sheet."
Terms: The first half of the advance is paid upon signing of the contract; the second within 30 days after publication. Usually publishes within 6 to 8 months.

‡AVISSON PRESS, INC., 3007 Taliaferro Rd., Greensboro NC 27408. **Acquisitions:** M.L. Hester, editor. Publishes hardcover originals and trade paperback originals and reprints. Publishes 12-15 titles/year.
Needs: Ethnic, historical, literary. "Upcoming and future titles are market-driven." Recently published *Constellation*, by Greg Mulenhey (novel); *Faith In What?*, by Richard Krawiec (novel); and *In Bed With The Exotic Enemy*, by Daniela Gioseffi (stories/novella).
How to Contact: Query or submit synopsis and 3 sample chapters (30-50 pages). Reports in 1 week on queries, 1-3 months on mss. Simultaneous submissions OK.
Terms: Pays 8-10% royalty on wholesale price or a percentage of print run (for poetry). Offers $200-500 advance. Publishes ms 9 months after acceptance. Book catalog for #10 SASE.
Advice: Audience is public and school libraries.

AVON BOOKS, (II), The Hearst Corporation, 1350 Avenue of the Americas, New York NY 10019. (212)261-6800. Senior Vice President/Publisher: Lou Aronica. Estab. 1941. Large hardcover and paperback publisher. Publishes hardcover and paperback originals and reprints. Averages 300 titles a year.
Imprint(s): Avon, Bard, **EOS**, Camelot, **Flare** and **Science Fiction**.
Needs: Literary, fantasy, historical romance, mainstream, science fiction, war, young adult/teen. No poetry, short story collections, religiou or westerns. Published *Butterfly*, by Kathryn Harvey; *So Worthy My Love*, by Kathleen Woodiwiss; and *Dead to Rights*, by J.A. Jance.
How to Contact: Query letters only. SASE to insure response.
Terms: Vary. Sponsors Flare Novel competition.

‡AVON EOS, (II, V), Imprint of Avon Books, 1350 Avenue of the Americas, New York NY 10019. (212)261-6821. Fax: (212)261-6895. **Acquisitions:** Jennifer Brehl, senior editor. Imprint estab. 1998. Science fiction and fantasy imprint for serious readers. Imprint of major general trade publisher. Publishes mass market and trade hardcover and paperback originals and paperback reprints. Published new writer within the last year. Publishes 70 total titles/year, all fiction.
Needs: Fantasy, science fiction. Recently published *Days of Cain*, by J.R. Dunn; *Rage of a Demon King*, by Raymond E. Feist; *Fairyland*, by Paul J. McAuley.
How to Contact: Does not accept unsolicited mss. Send query with outline/synopsis and 3 sample chapters through agent only. Include estimated word count, bio and list of publishing credits. Send SASE for reply, return of ms or send disposable copy of ms. Agented fiction 99%. Reports in 1 month on queries. Simultaneous submissions OK.
Terms: Pays negotiable advance. Sends galleys to author.

WRITER-TO-WRITER

The words that motivated me were the ones my computer guy put on my screensaver: "A writer is someone who has written today!"

J.A. Jance
Dead to Rights, Avon Books

Advice: "Get an agent."

‡AVON FLARE BOOKS, Imprint of Avon Books, Division of the Hearst Corp., 1350 Avenue of the Americas, New York NY 10019. (212)261-6817. Fax: (212)261-6895. **Acquisitions:** Elise Howard, executive editorial director. Publishes mass market paperback originals and reprints. Imprint publishes 115 new titles/year.
Needs: Adventure, ethnic, humor, mainstream, mystery, romance, suspense, contemporary. "Very selective with mystery." Manuscripts appropriate to ages 12-18. Recently published *The Dark Shore*, by Adam Lee; and *Angela & Diabola*, by Lynne Reidbanks.
How to Contact: Query with sample chapters and synopsis. Reports in 4 months. Simultaneous submissions OK.
Terms: Pays 6-8% royalty. Offers $2,500 minimum advance. Publishes ms 2 years after acceptance. Writer's guidelines and book catalog for 8×10 SAE with 5 first-class stamps.
Advice: "The YA market is not as strong as it was five years ago. We are very selective with young adult fiction. *Avon does not publish picture books,* nor do we use freelance readers."

‡AVON SCIENCE FICTION, (formerly Avon Nova), Imprint of Avon Books, 1350 Avenue of the Americas, New York NY 10019. (212)261-6800. Website: http://www.williammorrow.com. **Acquisitions:** Amy Goldschlager, editorial assistant to Jennifer Brehl, senior editor. "We are a 'small big company.' We can't be all things to all people. We put out a cutting-edge literary science fiction/fantasy line that appeals to people who want to read good books." Publishes hardcover originals, trade paperback and mass market paperback originals and reprints. Publishes 25% previously unpublished writers/year. Publishes 70 titles/year.
Needs: Fantasy, science fiction. No horror or juvenile topics. "We look for cutting-edge, original work that will break traditional boundaries of this genre." Recently published *Rage of a Demon King*, by Raymond Feist (fantasy); *The Family Tree*, by Sheri Tepper (science fiction); and *An Exchange of Hostages*, by Susan R. Matthews (science fiction).
How to Contact: Query with full synopsis of book, 3 sample chapters and SASE. Agented fiction 95%. Reports in 6 months. Simultaneous submissions OK "but we discourage it."
Terms: Pays royalty on retail price, range varies. Publishes ms 18 months after acceptance. Writer's guidelines for #10 SASE. Book catalog for 9×12 SAE with 7 first-class stamps.
Tips: "Having an agent is a good thing. Don't send clones of other books. If you're going to take the time to write a whole book, please submit following our guidelines to the detail. Make sure information is up to date."

BAEN BOOKS, (II), P.O. Box 1403, Riverdale NY 10471. (718)548-3100. Website: http://www.baen.com (includes writer's guidelines, chat line, annotated catalog, author bios, tour information). Publisher and Editor: Jim Baen. **Acquisitions:** Toni Weisskopf, executive editor. Estab. 1983. "We publish books at the heart of science fiction and fantasy." Independent publisher. Publishes hardcover and paperback originals and paperback reprints. Published new writers within the last year. Plans 2-3 first novels this year. Averages 60 fiction titles each year. Distributes titles through Simon & Schuster.
Imprint(s): Baen Science Fiction and Baen Fantasy.
Needs: Fantasy and science fiction. Interested in science fiction novels (based on real science) and fantasy novels "that at least strive for originality." Recently published *Memory*, by Lois McMaster Bugold; *Four and Twenty Blackbirds*, by Mercedes Lachey; and *In Enemy Hands*, by David Webster. Published new writers within the last year.
How to Contact: Accepts unsolicited mss. Submit ms or outline/synopsis and 3 consecutive sample chapters with SASE (or IRC). Reports in 6-9 months. Will consider simultaneous submissions, "but grudgingly and not as seriously as exclusives." Occasionally critiques rejected mss.
Terms: Pays in royalties; offers advance. Sends galleys to author. Writer's guidelines for SASE.
Advice: "Keep an eye and a firm hand on the overall story you are telling. Style is important but less important than plot. Good style, like good breeding, never calls attention to itself. Read *Writing to the Point*, by Algis Budrys. We like to maintain long-term relationships with authors."

BAKER BOOKS, (II, IV), a division of Baker Book House, P.O. Box 6287, Grand Rapids MI 49516-6213. (616)676-9185. Fax: (616)676-9573. Website: http://www.bakerbooks.com (includes guidelines, "Meet Our Editors," book excerpts and features, company history, advance info. on future releases). **Acquisitions:** Jane Schrier, assistant editor, Trade Books. Estab. 1939. "Midsize Evangelical publisher." Publishes hardcover and paperback

---

LOOKING FOR A PARTICULAR GENRE? Check our Category Index for magazine and book publishers who want **Mystery/Suspense**, **Romance**, **Science Fiction & Fantasy**, **Thrillers**, **Westerns** and more!

originals. Books: web offset print; average print order: 5,000-10,000; first novel print order: 5,000. Averages 130 total titles.

Needs: "We are mainly seeking Christian fiction of two genres: Contemporary women's fiction and mystery." No fiction that is not written from a Christian perspective or of a genre not specified. Recently published *Praise Jerusalem!*, by Augusta Trobaugh (contemporary women's fiction); *The Secrets of Barneveld Calvary*, by James Schaap (contemporary women's fiction); and *Familiar Terror*, by Evelyn Minshull (contemporary women's fiction).

How to Contact: Does not accept unsolicited mss. Submit query letter, outline/synopsis and 3 sample chapters. SASE. Agented fiction 80% (so far). Reports in 3-4 weeks on queries. Simultaneous submissions OK. Sometimes comments on rejected ms.

Terms: Pays royalties of 14% (of net). Sometimes offers advance. Sends galleys to author. Publishes ms 1 year after acceptance. Writer's guidelines for #10 SASE. Book catalog for 9½ × 12½ SAE and 3 first-class stamps.

Advice: "We are not interested in historical fiction, romances, science fiction, Biblical narratives, or spiritual warfare novels. Please write for further information regarding our fiction lines. Send a cover letter describing your novel and your credentials as an author. Do not call to 'pass by' your idea. Do not send complete manuscripts."

BALLANTINE BOOKS, 201 E. 50th St., New York NY 10022. Subsidiary of Random House. **Acquisitions**: Doug Grad, editor (historical, thriller); Leona Nevler, editor (all fiction); Peter Borland, executive editor (commercial fiction); Elisa Wares, senior editor (romance, mystery); Joe Blades, associate publisher (mystery); Andrea Schulz, associate editor (literary fiction). Publishes originals (general fiction, mass-market, trade paperback and hardcover). Published new writers this year. Averages over 120 total titles each year.

Needs: Major historical fiction, women's mainstream and general fiction.

How to Contact: Submit query letter or brief synopsis and first 100 pages of ms. SASE required. Reports in 2 months on queries; 4-5 months on mss.

Terms: Pays in royalties and advance.

‡BANKS CHANNEL BOOKS, (IV), P.O. Box 4446, Wilmington NC 28406. (910)762-4677. Fax (910)762-4677. E-mail: bankschan@aol.com. Managing Editor: E.R. Olefsky. Estab. 1993. "We are a tiny regional press doing books by Carolina authors only. We look at fiction through our novel contest only." Publishes hardcover and paperback originals and paperback reprints. Books: 50-60 lb. paper; perfect or hardcase bound; illustrations sometimes. Average print order: 2,000. First novel print order: 2,000-3,000. Published new writer within the last year. Plans 1 first novel this year. Publishes 1 title every other year.

● The publisher's 1996 fiction title, *All We Know of Heaven*, was a finalist for the 1997 Paterson Fiction Prize. Member of the Publishers Association of the South and SPAN.

Needs: Literary. "Our contest will run in 1998 (through July 31) for one novel (literary fiction) by a Carolina author."

How to Contact: Charges entry fee for contest. Send query letter first. Queries/correspondence by e-mail OK. Include 1-paragraph bio and list of publishing credits with submission. SASE for reply or return of ms. Reports in 1 week on queries; 2 months on mss. No simultaneous submissions.

Payment/Terms: Pays royalties of 6% minimum; 10% maximum. Sends galleys to author. Publishes ms 1 year after acceptance. Writer's guidelines for #10 SASE.

Advice: "We are seeing work that ten years ago would have been snapped up by the big New York presses—and we are delighted to have it. Send a beautifully crafted piece of literary fiction to our contest. It doesn't need to have a Carolina setting, but it helps."

WRITER-TO-WRITER

Writers are the only artists I know of who expect to get somewhere by *waiting*. Everyone knows you have to dance to be a dancer, you have to sing to be a singer, you have to paint to be a painter, but far too many people seem to believe that you *don't* have to write to be a writer. So, instead of writing, they wait. Of course, every professional writer, when asked for advice, says the same thing. This is because—no matter how often it's said—it remains *the* one thing that every aspiring writer needs to hear. Issac Asimov said it beautifully in just six words: "It's the writing that teaches you." Writing is what teaches you. Writing is what leads to "inspiration." Writing is what generates ideas. Nothing else—and nothing less. Don't meditate, don't do yoga, don't do drugs. Just write.

Daniel Quinn
The Story of B, Bantam Books

BANTAM BOOKS, (II), Division of Bantam Dell Doubleday Publishing Group, Inc. 1540 Broadway, New York NY 10036. (212)354-6500. Fax: (212)782-9523. Editor: Shauna Summers. Estab. 1945. Complete publishing: hard-cover, trade, mass market. Publishes 35 titles/year.

Imprint(s): Crime Line, Domain, **Fanfare**, **Loveswept**, **Spectra**.

Needs: Contemporary, literary, mystery, historical, western, romance, science fiction, fantasy. Recently published *The Story of B*, by Daniel Quinn; and *The Burning Man*, by Phillip M. Margolin.

How to Contact: Query letter only first. No unsolicited mss. Include estimated word count and list of publishing credits. Simultaneous submissions OK. Reports on queries in 2-3 months.

Terms: Individually negotiated. Publishes ms 8 months after acceptance. Writer's guidelines (for romance only) free for SASE.

BANTAM/DOUBLEDAY/DELL BOOKS FOR YOUNG READERS DIVISION, (III), Bantam/Doubleday/Dell, 1540 Broadway, New York NY 10036. **Acquisitions**: Michelle Poploff, editorial director. Editor-in-Chief to the Young Readers Division: Beverly Horowitz. Estab. 1945. Complete publishing: hardcover, trade, mass market.

Imprint(s): Delacorte, **Doubleday Adult Trade**, Doubleday Picture Books; Paperback line: Dell Yearling, Laurel-Leaf, Skylark, Star Fire, Little Rooster, Sweet Dreams, Sweet Valley High.

 • The Young Readers Division offers two contests, the Delacorte Press Annual Prize for a First Young Adult Novel and the Marguerite DeAngeli Prize.

Needs: Childrens/juvenile, young adult/teen. Published *Baby*, by Patricia MacLachlan; *Whatever Happened to Janie*, by Caroline Cooney; *Nate the Great and the Pillowcase*, by Marjorie Sharmat.

How to Contact: Does not accept unsolicited mss. Submit through agent. Agented fiction 100%. Reports on queries "as soon as possible." Simultaneous submissions OK.

Terms: Individually negotiated; offers advance.

‡✿**BEACH HOLME PUBLISHERS LTD.**, 226-2040 W. 12th Ave., Vancouver, British Columbia V6J 2G2 Canada. (604)773-4868. Fax: (604)733-4860. E-mail: bhp@beachholme.bc.ca. Website: http://www.beachholme. bc.ca. **Acquisitions:** Joy Gugeler, managing editor; Theresa Bubela, editor. Estab. 1971. Publishes trade paperback originals. Publishes 10 titles/year. "Accepting only Canadian submissions." Publishes 40% previously unpublished writers/year.

Needs: Adult literary fiction from authors published in Canadian literary magazines. Young adult (Canada historical/regional). "Interested in excellent quality, imaginative writing." Recently published *Inappropriate Behavior*, by Irene Mock (short fiction).

How to Contact: Send cover letter, SASE, outline and two chapters. Reports in 2 months. Simultaneous submissions OK, if so noted.

Terms: Pays 10% royalty on retail price. Offers $500 average advance. Publishes ms 1 year after acceptance. Writer's guidelines free.

Advice: "Make sure the manuscript is well written. We see so many that only the unique and excellent can't be put down. Prior publication is a must. This doesn't necessarily mean book length manuscripts, but a writer should try to publish his or her short fiction."

‡**BEACON HILL PRESS OF KANSAS CITY**, Book Division of Nazarene Publishing House, P.O. Box 419527, Kansas City MO 64141. Fax: (816)753-4071. E-mail: bjp@bhillkc.com. **Acquisitions:** Bonnie Perry, managing editor. Estab. 1912. "Beacon Hill Press is a Christ-centered publisher that provides authentically

---

WRITER-TO-WRITER

I frequently talk to groups of aspiring writers, and the major piece of advice I give them is they should always write for fun, and never to get published or to make money. It is a fact of life that only a small percentage of people who would like to be published ever see a book in print, and those who do get published rarely make enough money to support themselves. If you write to get published or if you write to make money, you are probably going to end up sad.

On the other hand, I wrote for years without being successful because I love the process of creating a story and following it through to completion. Think of how many people play golf or bridge and never get paid a cent for it. Why are these people playing golf or bridge? Think of writing as a hobby and you'll always be happy.

Phillip M. Margolin
The Burning Man, Doubleday; Bantam Books (paperback)

Christian resources that are faithful to God's word and relevant to life." Publishes hardcover and paperback originals. Publishes 30 titles/year. Accent on holy living; encouragement in daily Christian life.

Needs: Wholesome, inspirational. Considers historical and Biblical fiction, Christian romance, but no teen or children's. Recently published *Turn Northward, Love*, by Ruth Glover; and *Fly Away*, by Lynn Austin.

How to Contact: Query or proposal preferred. Reports in 3 months. Average ms length: 30,000-60,000 words.

Terms: Standard contract is 12% royalty on net sales for first 10,000 copies and 14% on subsequent copies. (Sometimes makes flat rate purchase.) Publishes ms within 1 year after acceptance.

FREDERIC C. BEIL, PUBLISHER, INC., (II), 609 Whitaker St., Savannah GA 31401. E-mail: beilbook@beil .com. Website: http://www.beil.com. **Acquisitions:** Frederic C. Beil III, president; Mary Ann Bowman, editor. Estab. 1983. "Our objectives are (1) to offer to the reading public carefully selected texts of lasting value; (2) to adhere to high standards in the choice of materials and in bookmarking craftsmanship; (3) to produce books that exemplify good taste in format and design; and (4) to maintain the lowest cost consistent with quality." General trade publisher. Publishes hardcover originals and reprints. Books: acid-free paper; letterpress and offset printing; Smyth-sewn, hardcover binding; illustrations. Average print order: 3,000. First novel print order: 3,000. Plans 2 first novels this year. Averages 14 total titles, 4 fiction titles each year.

Imprint(s): The Sandstone Press.

Needs: Historical, literary, regional, short story collections, translations. Published *A Woman of Means*, by Peter Taylor; *An Exile*, by Madison Jones; and *A Master of the Century Past*, by Robert Metzger.

How to Contact: Does not accept unsolicited mss. Query first. Reports in 1 week on queries.

Terms: Payment "all negotiable." Sends galleys to author. Book catalog free on request.

THE BERKLEY PUBLISHING GROUP, (III), Subsidiary of G.P. Putnam's Sons, 200 Madison Ave., New York NY 10016. (212)951-8800. Imprints are Berkley, Jove, Boulevard, Ace Science Fiction. Editor-in-Chief: Leslie Gelbman. Fiction Editors: Natalee Rosenstein, Judith Stern, Tom Lolgan, Gail Fortune, Susan Allison, Ginjer Buchanan, Lisa Consedine and Hillary Cige. Nonfiction: Elizabeth Beier, Denise Silvestro and Hillary Cige. Large commercial category line. Publishes paperback originals, trade paperbacks and hardcover and paperback reprints. Books: Paperbound printing; perfect binding; average print order: "depends on position in list." Plans approx. 10 first novels this year. Averages 1,180 total titles, 1,000 fiction titles each year.

Needs: Fantasy, mainstream, mystery/suspense, romance (contemporary, historical), science fiction. Recently published *Forever Peace*, by Joe Haldeman.

How to Contact: Accepts no unsolicited mss. Submit through agent only. Agented fiction 98%. Reports in 6-8 weeks on mss. Simultaneous submissions OK.

Terms: Pays royalties of 4-10%. Provides 10 author's copies. Publishes ms 2 years after acceptance. Writer's guidelines and book catalog not available.

Advice: "Aspiring novelists should keep abreast of the current trends in publishing by reading *The New York Times* Bestseller Lists, trade magazines for their desired genre and *Publishers Weekly*."

BERKLEY/ACE SCIENCE FICTION, (II), Berkley Publishing Group, 200 Madison Ave., New York NY 10016. (212)951-8800. **Acquisitions:** Susan Allison, editor-in-chief; Anne Sowards. Estab. 1948. Publishes paperback originals and reprints and 6-10 hardcovers per year. Number of titles: 6/month. Buys 85-95% agented fiction.

Needs: Science fiction and fantasy. No other genre accepted. No short stories. Published *The Cat Who Walks Through Walls*, by Robert Heinlein; and *Neuromancer*, by William Gibson.

How to Contact: Submit outline/synopsis and 3 sample chapters with SASE. No simultaneous submissions.

WRITER-TO-WRITER

I get up around 3:30 a.m. and go through an elaborate tea-making ritual. I do my first draft with a fountain pen, writing into blank books. When the weather is warm, I write on the back porch. There's no electricity, so I use oil lamp and candle light.

My wife types the first draft into the computer, and I rewrite on the machine in the afternoon. I also put a book through three "focused" rewrites after it's finished, checking for specific weaknesses.

It takes me about two years to finish a novel. I write other things during those two years, though.

Joe Haldeman
Forever Peace, Berkley

Reports in 2 months minimum on mss. "Queries answered immediately if SASE enclosed." Publishes ms an average of 18 months after acceptance.

Terms: Standard for the field. Sends galleys to author.

Advice: "Good science fiction and fantasy are almost always written by people who have read and loved a lot of it. We are looking for knowledgeable science or magic, as well as sympathetic characters with recognizable motivation. We are looking for solid, well-plotted science fiction: good action adventure, well-researched hard science with good characterization and books that emphasize characterization without sacrificing plot. In fantasy we are looking for all types of work, from high fantasy to sword and sorcery." Submit fantasy and science fiction to Anne Sowards.

‡BETHANY HOUSE PUBLISHERS, Subsidiary of Bethany Fellowship, Inc., 11300 Hampshire Ave. S., Minneapolis MN 55438. (612)829-2500. **Acquisitions:** Cindy M. Alewine, review department. "The purpose of Bethany House Publishers' publishing program is to relate biblical truth to all areas of life, whether in the framework of a well-told story, a challenging book for spiritual growth, or a Bible reference work." Publishes hardcover and trade paperback originals, mass market paperback reprints. Publishes 120-150 titles/year.

Imprint(s): Portraits (Barbara Lilland, editor).

Needs: Adventure, historical, mainstream/contemporary, religious (romance), young adult. Recently published *Drums of Change*, by Janet Oke; *The Shunning*, by Beverly Lewis; and *Mandie & the Courtroom Battle*, by Lois Gladys Leppard.

How to Contact: Submit proposal package including synopsis, 3 sample chapters, author information, educational background and writing experience with SASE. Reports in 3 months. Simultaneous submissions OK.

Terms: Pays negotiable royalty on wholesale price. Offers negotiable advance. Publishes ms 1 year after acceptance. Writer's guidelines free. Book catalog for 9×12 SAE with 5 first-class stamps.

BIRCH BROOK PRESS, (IV), P.O. Box 81, Delhi NY 13753. (212)353-3326. Fax: (212)979-0128. **Acquisitions:** Tom Tolnay, publisher. Estab. 1982. Small publisher of popular culture and literary titles in handcrafted letterpress editions. Publishes fiction anthologies with specific theme. Books: 80 lb. vellum paper; letter press printing; illustrations. Average print order: 500-1,000. Plans 1 first novel this year. Averages 4 total titles, 2 fiction titles each year. Distributes titles through Ingram and Baker and Taylor. Promotes titles through catalogs and direct mail.

Needs: Literary. "We make specific calls for fiction when we are doing an anthology." Plans to publish literary-quality anthology of mystery short stories. Recently published *A Double Play of Baseball Novellas*, by Merritt Clifton and John Sandman; *Kilimanjaro Burning*, by John Robinson (novella); *In Foreign Parts*, by Elisabeth Stevens (short stories) and *Fiction, Flyfishing & The Search for Innocence*, by Lyons/McGuane/Enger, et al.

How to Contact: Does not seek unsolicited mss. Query first. SASE. Reports on queries in 2-6 weeks; mss 2-4 months. Simultaneous submissions OK. Sometimes critiques or comments on rejected mss.

Terms: Modest flat fee as advance against royalties. Writers guidelines for SASE.

Advice: "We mostly generate our own anthologies and print notices to request submissions."

BkMk PRESS, (II), UMKC, University House, 5100 Rockhill Rd., Kansas City MO 64110-2499. (816)235-2558. Fax: (816)235-2611. E-mail: freemank@smtpgate.ssb.umkc.edu. **Acquisitions:** James McKinley, director. Estab. 1971. Small independent press. "Mostly short story collections." Publishes hardback and paperback originals. Books: standard paper; offset printing; perfect- and case-bound; average print order: 600; Averages 6 total titles, 1 fiction title each year. Distributes titles through direct mail and wholesalers (Books in Print). Promotes titles through Books in Print, some magazine/journal advertising, brochure mailings, readings and appearances.

Needs: Contemporary, ethnic, experimental, literary, translations. "Fiction publishing limited to short stories and novellas. Ordinarily prints anthologies or collections by one writer. BkMk Press does not publish commercial novels." Recently published *Drive Dive Dance & Fight*, by Thomas E. Kennedy (short stories); *Body and Blood*, by Philip Russell (episodic novel); and *Mustaches & Other Stories*, by G.W. Clift (short stories).

How to Contact: Query first or submit 2 sample chapters with SASE. Reports in 2-3 months on queries; 6 months on mss.

Terms: Pays royalties of 10% and 20 author's copies. Sends galleys to author. Free book catalog.

Advice: "We value the exceptional, rare, well-crafted and daring." Especially interested in Midwestern writers.

BLACK HERON PRESS, (I, II), P.O. Box 95676, Seattle WA 98145. **Acquisitions:** Jerry Gold, publisher. Estab. 1984. One-person operation; no immediate plans to expand. "We're known for literary fiction. We've done several Vietnam War titles and several surrealistic fictions." Publishes paperback and hardback originals. Average print order: 2,000; first novel print order: 1,500. Averages 4 fiction titles each year. Distributes titles nationally.

- Three books published by Black Heron Press have won awards from King County Arts Commission. This press received Bumbershoot Most Significant Contribution to Literature in 1996. Black Heron Press will not be looking at new material until summer 1998.

Needs: Adventure, contemporary, experimental, humor/satire, literary, science fiction. Vietnam war novel—literary. "We don't want to see fiction written for the mass market. If it sells to the mass market, fine, but we don't see ourselves as a commercial press." Recently published *Charlie & The Children*, by Joanna C. Scott; *The Fruit 'N Food*, by Leonard Chang; and *In A Cold Open Field*, by Sheila Solomon Klass.

How to Contact: Query and sample chapters only. Reports in 3 months on queries. Simultaneous submissions OK.

Terms: Pays standard royalty rates. No advance.

Advice: "A query letter should tell me: 1) number of words; 2) number of pages; 3) if ms is available on floppy disk; 4) if parts of novel have been published; 5) if so, where?"

JOHN F. BLAIR, PUBLISHER, (II, IV), 1406 Plaza Dr., Winston-Salem NC 27103. (910)768-1374. Fax: (910)768-9194. **Acquisitions:** Carolyn Sakowski, president. Estab. 1954. Small independent publisher. Publishes hardcover and paperback originals. Books: Acid-free paper; offset printing; illustrations. Average print order: 5,000. Number of titles: 17 in 1996, 20 in 1997. "Among our 17-20 books, we do one novel a year."

Needs: Prefers regional material dealing with southeastern U.S. No confessions or erotica. "Our editorial focus concentrates mostly on nonfiction." Published *The Big Ear*, by Robin Hemley (short story collection); *How to Get Home*, by Bret Lott; and *Cape Fear Rising*, by Philip Gerard.

How to Contact: Query or submit with SASE. Simultaneous submissions OK. Reports in 1 month. Publishes ms 1-2 years after acceptance. Free book catalog.

Terms: Negotiable.

Advice: "We are primarily interested in nonfiction titles. Most of our titles have a tie-in with North Carolina or the southeastern United States. Please enclose a cover letter and outline with the manuscript. We prefer to review queries before we are sent complete manuscripts. Queries should include an approximate word count."

‡BLUE MOON BOOKS, INC., North Star Line, 61 Fourth Ave., New York NY 10003. (212)505-6880. Fax: (212)673-1039. E-mail: bluoff@aol.com. **Acquisitions:** Barney Rosset, publisher/editor. "Blue Moon Books is strictly an erotic press; largely fetish-oriented material, B&D, S&M, etc." Publishes trade paperback and mass market paperback originals. Publishes 30-40 titles/year.

Imprint(s): North Star Line.

Needs: Erotica. Recently published *J and Seventeen*, by Kenzaburo Oe; and *The Love Run*, by Jay Parini.

How to Contact: Query or submit synopsis and 1-2 sample chapters with SASE. Reports in 2 months. Simultaneous submissions OK.

Terms: Pays 7½-10% royalty on retail price. Offers $500 and up advance. Publishes ms 1 year after acceptance. Writer's guidelines for #10 SASE. Book catalog free.

‡THE BLUE SKY PRESS, Imprint of Scholastic Inc., 555 Broadway, New York NY 10012. (212)343-6100. Fax: (212)343-4535. Website: http://www.scholastic.com. **Acquisitions:** The Editors. Blue Sky Press publishes primarily juvenile picture books. Publishes hardcover and trade paperback originals. Publishes 15-20 titles/year.

● Because of a long backlog of books, The Blue Sky Press is not accepting unsolicited submissions.

Needs: Juvenile: adventure, fantasy, historical, humor, mainstream/contemporary, picture books, multicultural, folktales. Recently published *True North*, by Kathryn Lasky (novel); *Goose*, by Molly Bang (picture book); and *When Birds Could Talk & Bats Could Sing*, by Virginia Hamilton (folktales).

How to Contact: Agented fiction 25%. Reports in 6 months on queries.

Terms: Pays 10% royalty on wholesale price, between authors and illustrators. Publishes ms 2½ years after acceptance.

‡BLUE STAR PRODUCTIONS, Division of Bookworld, Inc., 9666 E. Riggs Rd., #194, Sun Lakes AZ 85248. (602)895-7995. Fax: (602)895-6991. E-mail: bkworld@aol.com. Website: http://www.bkworld.com. **Acquisitions:** Barbara DeBolt, editor. Blue Star Productions publishes metaphysical fiction and nonfiction titles on specialized subjects. "Our mission is to aid in the spiritual growth of mankind." Publishes trade and mass market paperback originals. Publishes 10-12 titles/year.

Needs: Fantasy, spiritual (metaphysical), UFO's. Recently published *The Best Kept Secrets*, by Charles Wright; and *The Antilles Incident*, by Donald Todd.

How to Contact: Query or submit synopsis and the first 3 chapters. SASE a must. Reports in 1 month on queries, 6 months on mss.

WRITER-TO-WRITER

Find your own special voice. Tell *your* story *your* way. Make it sing with your words, your rhythms, your experiences. No one else on earth should be able to tell a story like yours if your story is plugged into your heart and soul.

　　Lynn Plourde
　　Pigs in the Mud in the Middle of the Rud, Scholastic/Blue Sky Press

Terms: Pays 10% royalty on wholesale or retail price. No advance. Writer's guidelines for #10 SASE. Book catalog free.

Advice: "Know our guidelines. We have temporarily restricted our needs to those manuscripts whose focus is metaphysical, ufology, time travel and Native American. Query to see if this restriction has been lifted before submitting other material."

‡BOOKCRAFT, INC., (I), 1848 W. 2300 South, Salt Lake City UT 84119. (801)972-6180. **Acquisitions**: Cory H. Maxwell, editorial manager. Publishes hardcover and softcover originals. Books: 60 lb. stock paper; sheet-fed and web press; average print order: 5,000-7,000; 3,000 for reprints. Published new writers within the last year. "We are always open for creative, fresh ideas."

Imprint(s): Parliament.

- Books published by Bookcraft have received several awards from the Association of Mormon Letters and the 1994 John and Frankie Orton Award for LDS Lierature went to *The Work and the Glory*, by Gerald N. Lund.

Needs: Contemporary, family saga, historical, mystery/suspense (private eye, romantic suspense, young adult), romance (gothic), religious/inspirational, thriller/espionage and western (traditional frontier, young adult). Recently published *The Work and the Glory: Thy Gold to Refine* (vol. 4), by Gerald N. Lund; *A Face in the Shadows*, by Susan Evans McCloud; and *Two Roads*, by Chris Crowe.

How to Contact: Query, submit outline/synopsis and sample chapters, or submit complete ms with SASE (or IRC). Reports in 2 months.

Terms: Pays royalties; no advance. Sends galleys to author. Free book catalog and writer's guidelines.

Advice: "Our principal market is the membership of The Church of Jesus Christ of Latter-Day Saints (Mormons) and manuscripts should relate to the background, doctrines or practices of that church. The tone should be fresh, positive and motivational, but not preachy. We do not publish anti-Mormon works."

BOOKS IN MOTION, (II), 9212 E. Montgomery, Suite #501, Spokane WA 99206. (509)922-1646. **Acquisitions**: Gary Challender, president. Estab. 1980. "Audiobook company, national marketer. Publishes novels in audiobook form *only*." Published new writers within the last year. Plans 12 first novels this year. Averages 70 total titles, 65 fiction titles each year.

- Books in Motion is known for its audio westerns and mysteries. The publisher has received favorable reviews from *Library Journal*, *Kliatt Magazine* and *Audio-File* magazine.

Needs: Action/adventure, westerns, mystery, science fiction (non-technical), some romance. Recently published *Kiahawk*, by Craig Fraley; *The Isle of Venus Mystery*, by Tom Neet; and *Name Witheld*, by J.A. Jance. Have published over 140 new authors in last 3 years.

How to Contact: Accepts unsolicted mss. Submit synopsis and sample chapters (first and middle). SASE for ms. Reports within 3 weeks to 3 months. Simultaneous submissions OK.

Terms: Pays royalties of 10%. "We pay royalties every 6 months. Royalties that are received are based on the gross sales that any given title generates during the 6-month interval. Authors must be patient since it usually takes a minimum of one year before new titles will have significant sales." Publishes ms 6-12 months after acceptance. Book catalog free on request.

Advice: "Our audience is 20% women, 80% men. Many of our audience are truck drivers, who want something interesting to listen to. We prefer a minimum of profanity and no gratuitous sex. We want novels with a strong plot. The fewer the characters, the better it will work on tape. Six-tape audiobooks sell and rent better than any other size in the unabridged format. One hour of tape is equal to 40 pages of double-spaced, 12 pitch, normal margin, typed pages. Manuscript should be between 200 and 400 pages."

✤BOREALIS PRESS, (I, IV), 9 Ashburn Dr., Nepean, Ontario K2E 6N4 Canada. Fax: (613)829-7783. **Acquisitions**: Frank Tierney, editor; Glenn Clever, fiction editor. Estab. 1970. Publishes hardcover and paperback originals and reprints. Books: standard book-quality paper; offset printing; perfect and cloth binding. Average print order: 1,000. Buys juvenile mss with b&w illustrations. Averages 4 total titles each year.

Imprint(s): *Journal of Canadian Poetry*.

- Borealis Press has a "New Canadian Drama," with six books in print. The series won Ontario Arts Council and Canada Council grants.

Needs: Contemporary, literary, juvenile, young adult. "Must have a Canadian content or author; query first." Recently published *Alphabet Soup*, by Kerry Rauch; *Jamie of Fort William*, by Elizabeth Kouhi; and *Sunshine Sketches of a Little Town*, by Stephen Leacock.

How to Contact: Submit query with SASE (Canadian postage). No simultaneous submissions. Reports in 2 weeks on queries, 3-4 months on mss. Publishes ms 1-2 years after acceptance.

Terms: Pays 10% royalties and 3 free author's copies; no advance. Sends galleys to author. Publishes ms 18 months after acceptance. Free book catalog with SASE.

Advice: "Have your work professionally edited. Our greatest challenge is finding good authors, i.e., those who do not fit the popular mode."

THOMAS BOUREGY & COMPANY, INC., 401 Lafayette St., New York NY 10003. Small category line. See Avalon Books.

BOYDS MILLS PRESS, (II), Subsidiary of Highlights for Children, 815 Church St., Honesdale PA 18431. (800)490-5111. **Acquisitions:** Beth Troop, manuscript coordinator. Estab. 1990. "Independent publisher of quality books for children of all ages." Publishes hardcover. Books: Coated paper; offset printing; case binding; 4-color illustrations; average print order varies. Plans 4 fiction titles (novels).
Needs: Juvenile, young adult (adventure, animal, contemporary, ethnic, historical, sports). Recently published *Willie and the Rattlesnake King*, by Clara Gillow Clark; and *Lichee Tree*, by Ching Yeung Russell.
How to Contact: Accepts unsolicited mss. Send first three chapters and synopsis. Reports in 1 month. Simultaneous submissions OK.
Terms: Pays standard rates. Sends pre-publication galleys to author. Time between acceptance and publication depends on "what season it is scheduled for." Writer's guidelines for #10 SASE.
Advice: "We're interested in young adult novels of real literary quality as well as middle grade fiction that's imaginative with fresh ideas. Getting into the mode of thinking like a child is important. We publish very few novels each year, so make sure your story is as strong and as polished as possible before submitting to us. We do not deal with romance, science fiction or fantasy novels, so please do not submit those genres."

BRANDEN PUBLISHING CO., (I, II), Subsidiary of Branden Press, Box 843, 17 Station St., Brookline Village MA 02147. Fax: (617)734-2046. E-mail: branden@branden.com. Website: http://www.branden.com. **Acquisitions:** Adolph Caso, editor. Estab. 1967. Publishes hardcover and paperback originals and reprints. Books: 55-60 lb. acid-free paper; case- or perfect-bound; illustrations; average print order: 5,000. Plans 5 first novels this year. Averages 15 total titles, 5 fiction titles each year.
Imprint(s): I.P.L.
Needs: Ethnic, historical, literary, military/war, short story collections and translations. Looking for "contemporary, fast pace, modern society." No porno, experimental or horror. Published *I, Morgain*, by Harry Robin; *The Bell Keeper*, by Marilyn Seguin; and *The Straw Obelisk*, by Adolph Caso.
How to Contact: Does not accept unsolicited mss. Query *only* with SASE. Reports in 1 week on queries.
Terms: Pays royalties of 5-10% minimum. Advance negotiable. Provides 10 author's copies. Sends galleys to author. Publishes ms "several months" after acceptance.
Advice: "Publishing more fiction because of demand. *Do not make phone or e-mail inquiries.* Do not oversubmit; single submissions only; do not procrastinate if contract is offered. Our audience is a well-read general public, professionals, college students, and some high school students. We like books by or about women."

‡GEORGE BRAZILLER, INC., 171 Madison Ave., Suite 1103, New York NY 10016. (212)889-0909. **Acquisitions:** Adrienne Baxter, editor. Publishes hardcover and trade paperback originals and reprints. Publishes 10-15 titles/year.
Needs: Ethnic, gay, lesbian, literary. "We rarely do fiction but when we have published novels, they have mostly been literary novels." Recently published *Blindsight*, by Herve Guibert; and *Papa's Suitcase*, by Gerhard Kopf.
How to Contact: Submit 4-6 sample chapters with SASE. Reports in 3 months on proposals.
Terms: Pays 2-10% royalty on retail price, or makes outright purchase of $2,000-6,000. Offers $2,500-6,000 advance. Publishes ms 10 months after acceptance. Writer's guidelines and book catalog free.

BRIDGE WORKS PUBLISHING CO., (I, II), 221 Bridge Lane, Box 1798, Bridgehampton NY 11932. (516)537-3418. Fax: (516)537-5092. **Acquisitions:** Barbara Phillips, editorial director. Estab. 1992. "We are very small (3 full-time employees) doing only 4-6 books a year. We publish quality fiction and nonfiction. Our books are routinely reviewed in such papers as *The New York Times*, *Newsday*, *The Washington Post* and *The Boston Globe*." Publishes hardcover originals. Average print order: 5,000. Published new writers within the last year. Plans 4 novels and 2 nonfiction titles this year. Averages 4-6 total titles (75% fiction) each year.
  ● *The Prince of West End Avenue*, published by Bridge Works, was a finalist for the 1995 National Book Critics Circle Award.
Needs Humor/satire, literary, translations. Recently published *Sunrise Shows Late* and *Free Reign*.
How to Contact: Accepts unsolicited mss, but "must send query letter first." Query with outline/synopsis and 4 sample chapters. Include estimated word count and list of publishing credits. Send SASE for reply, return of ms or send a disposable copy of ms. Agented fiction 50%. Reports in 2 weeks on queries; 2 months on mss. Sometimes critiques or comments on rejected mss.
Payment/Terms: Pays royalties of 10% maximum "based on cover price with a reserve against returns." Average advance: $1,000. Sends galleys to author. Publishes ms 1 year after acceptance.
Advice: "It is preferable that an author have published somewhere else (short story collections, journalism, other genres) before trying us."

---

‡ THE DOUBLE DAGGER before a listing indicates that the listing is new in this edition. New markets are often the most receptive to submissions by new writers.

‡**BROADWAY BOOKS**, Division of Bantam Doubleday Dell Publishing Group, Inc. 1540 Broadway, New York NY 10036. (212)354-6500. Publisher: William Shinker. **Acquisitions:** John Sterling, vice president and editor-in-chief (literary fiction, nonfiction). Broadway publishes general interest nonfiction and fiction for adults. Publishes hardcover and trade paperback originals and reprints.
Needs: Publishes commercial literary fiction. Recently published *A Face at the Window*, by Dennis McFarland.
How to Contact: This publisher accepts agented fiction only.

‡♥**BROWN BEAR PRESS**, 122 Felbrigg Ave., Toronto, Ontario M5M 2M5 Canada. **Acquisitions**: Ruth Bradley-St-Cyr, publisher. Publishes trade paperback original nonfiction from Canadian authors only and reprints of Canadian classics. Publishes 4 titles/year.
Needs: Reprints only. "We do not publish new fiction." Canadian literature for adults and children.
How to Contact: Reports in 2 months on proposals.
Terms: Pays 8-10% royalty on retail price. Offers $100-300 advance. Publishes ms 1 year after acceptance. Writer's guidelines free with Canadian SASE.

‡**BRYANT & DILLON PUBLISHERS, INC.**, P.O. Box 39, Orange NJ 07050. (201)675-5668. Fax: (201)675-8443. **Acquisitions:** Gerri Dillon. "We publish books that speak to an African-American audience." Publishes hardcover and trade paperback originals. Publishes 8-10 titles/year.
Needs: Ethnic, mystery/suspense, romance, Main characters must be African-American/or African-American themes. Recently published *Forever Mine*, by Kathryn Williams-Platt (novel); and *Ebony Blood*, by Claire Luna (novel).
How to Contact: Submit cover letter, author's information sheet, marketing information, synopsis and 3 sample chapters with SASE (envelope large enough for contents sent). Reports in 3 months on proposals. Simultaneous submissions OK.
Terms: Pays 6-10% royalty on retail price. Publishes ms 1 year after acceptance.
Tips: "No faxes or phone calls, please!" Audience is majority African-American. No poetry or children's books.

‡**BUZZ BOOKS, (III, IV)**, Subsidiary of St. Martin's Press/Griffin, New York office: 175 Fifth Ave., New York NY 10010. (212)674-5151. Fax: (212)529-0694. **Acquisitions:** Jim Fitzgerald, executive editor. Estab. 1997. "Buzz Books is a joint venture between L.A.'s award-winning *Buzz* magazine and New York's St. Martin's Press. With plans to publish 15-20 fiction and nonfiction hardcover and trade paperback titles/year, Buzz Books captures the dynamic and wide-ranging culture of Southern California. Please note that we are publishing books with a Southern California sensibility for a national audience." Publishes hardcover and paperback originals and paperback reprints. Publishes new writers within the last year. Plans 1 first novel this year. Averages 15-20 total titles; 3-5 fiction titles/year.
Needs: Ethnic/multicultural, feminist, gay, glitz, historical (Southern California topic), literary, mainstream contemporary, regional (Southern California), pop culture. Recently published *Dog Eat Dog*, by Edward Bunker (crime novel); *Nixon Carver*, by Mark Maxwell (literary); and *Loteria & Other Stories*, by Ruben Mendoza (literary).
How to Contact: Accepts unsolicited mss, but "agented manuscripts preferred." Query first. Include bio (100 words), list of publishing credits and specific reference to Southern California connection. If ms is requested, send disposable copy of ms. Agented fiction 100%. Reports on queries in 2 weeks; 3 months on mss. Simultaneous submissions OK.
Terms: Pays in royalties; pays advances.

‡♥**CAITLIN PRESS, INC.**, P.O. Box 2387 Station B, Prince George, British Columbia V2N 2S6 Canada. (604)964-4953. Fax: (604)964-4970. **Acquisitions:** Cynthia Wilson. Estab. 1978. "We publish books about the British Columbia interior or by people from the interior." Publishes trade paperback and soft cover originals. Publishes 6-7 titles/year.
Needs: Adventure, historical, humor, mainstream/contemporary, short story collections, young adult.
How to Contact: Query first with SASE. Reports in 3 months on queries. Simultaneous submissions OK.
Terms: Pays 15% royalty on wholesale price. Publishes ms 18 months after acceptance.
Advice: "Our area of interest is British Columbia and Northern Canada. Submitted manuscripts should reflect our interest area."

AN IMPRINT LISTED IN BOLDFACE TYPE means there is an independent listing arranged alphabetically within this section.

‡**CAMELOT BOOKS**, Imprint of Avon Books, Division of The Hearst Corp., 1350 Avenue of the Americas, New York NY 10019. (212)261-6817. Fax: (212)261-6895. **Acquisitions:** Elise Howard, editorial director; Stephanie Seigel, assistant editor. Camelot publishes fiction for children ages 8-12. Publishes paperback originals and reprints. Publishes 80-100 titles/year.
Imprint(s): Avon Flare (for ages 12 and up).
Needs: Subjects include adventure, humor, juvenile (Camelot, 8-12) mainstream, mystery, ("very selective with mystery"), suspense. Avon does not publish picture books. Recently published *Honus & Me*, by Dan Gutman; and *Christie & Company*, by Katherine Hall Page (mystery).
How to Contact: Submit query letter *only*. Reports back in 3 months.
Terms: Pays 6-8% royalty on retail price. Offers $2,000 minimum advance. Publishes ms 2 years after acceptance. Writer's guidelines and book catalog for 8×10 SAE with 5 first-class stamps.

‡✹**CANADIAN INSTITUTE OF UKRAINIAN STUDIES PRESS**, CIUS Toronto Publications Office, University of Toronto, Dept. of Slavic Languages and Literatures, 21 Sussex Ave., Toronto, Ontario M5S 1A1 Canada. (416)978-8240. Fax: (416)978-2672. E-mail: cius@chass.utoronto.ca. Website: http://www.utoronto.ca/cius. **Acquisitions:** Maxim Tarnawsky, director. Estab. 1976. "We publish scholarship about Ukraine and Ukrainians in Canada." Publishes hardcover and trade paperback originals and reprints. Publishes 5-10 titles/year.
Needs: Ukrainian literary works. "We do not publish fiction except for use as college textbooks." Recently published *Yellow Boots*, by Vera Lysenko.
How to Contact: Query or submit complete ms. Reports in 1 month on queries, 3 months on mss.
Terms: Nonauthor-subsidy publishes 20-30% of books. Pays 0-2% royalty on retail price. Publishes ms 2 years after acceptance. Writer's guidelines and book catalog free.
Advice: "We are a scholarly press and do not normally pay our authors. Our audience consists of University students and teachers and the general public interested in Ukrainian and Ukrainian-Canadian affairs."

‡**CANDLEWICK PRESS**, Subsidiary of Walker Books Ltd. (London), 2067 Massachusetts Ave., Cambridge MA 02140. (617)661-3330. Fax: (617)661-0565. **Acquisitions:** Liz Bicknell, editor-in-chief (nonfiction/fiction); Mary Lee Donovan, senior editor (nonfiction/fiction); Gale Pryor, editor (nonfiction/fiction); Susan Halperin, editor (fiction for young adult, middle grades); Amy Ehrlich, consulting editor (picture books). Candlewick Press publishes high-quality illustrated children's books for ages infant through young adult. "We are a truly child-centered publisher." Estab. 1991. Publishes hardcover originals, trade paperback originals and reprints. Publishes 200 titles/year.
Needs: Juvenile. Recently published *What Do Fish Have To Do With Anything*, by Avi; and *Lone Wolf*, by Kristine Franklin.
How to Contact: Agented submissions only. Reports in 10 weeks on mss. Simultaneous submissions OK, if so noted.
Terms: Pays 10% royalty on retail price. Advance varies. Publishes ms 3 years after acceptance for illustrated books, 1 year for others.

‡***CANONGATE BOOKS LTD.**, 14 High St., Edinburgh EH1 1TE Scotland, UK. Fax: 44 131 557 5211. E-mail: info@canongate.co.uk. **Acquisitions:** Jamie Byng and Emily Dewhurst, fiction editors. Averages 12-15 fiction titles/year. "Cultural contribution rather than just hedonistic exuberance provides the flavor of novels published by Canongate in the past, but this criterion is not inflexible if the exuberance has, in our view, genuine quality." Publishes 4-6 previous unpublished writers/year. Recently published *Hannibal*, by Ross Leccoe (historical); *Justine*, by Alice Thompson (literary); and *Kill Kill Faster Faster*, by Joel Rose (literary). Length: 40,000 words minimum; 500,000 words maximum. Send cover letter, synopsis and 3 sample chapters. Pays advance and 10% royalty. Submitting writers should be sure ms "possesses literary merit and commercial potential."
Imprint(s): Payback Press (African-American and Jamaican culture work) and Rebel Inc. (stems from the underground literary magazine of the same name).
How to Contact: Write for information and guidelines.
Advice: "Be original, be daring, experiment, be conscious, be compelling, make me laugh—don't ever forget you're an independent voice that can speak for many."

‡**CAROLRHODA BOOKS, INC.**, Imprint of Lerner Publications Co., 241 First Ave. N., Minneapolis MN 55401. (612)332-3344. Fax: (612)332-7615. **Acquisitions:** Rebecca Poole, submissions editor. Estab. 1969. Carolrhoda Books seeks creative children's nonfiction and historical fiction with unique and well-developed ideas and angles. Publishes hardcover originals. Publishes 50-60 titles/year.
Needs: Juvenile, historical, picture books. "We continue to add fiction for middle grades and 1-2 picture books per year. Not looking for folktales or anthropomorphic animal stories." Recently published *Come Morning*, by Leslie Davis Guccione (historical); *Fire in the Sky*, by Candice Ransom (historical); and *Fire at the Triangle Factory*, by Holly Littlefield (easy reader historical).
How to Contact: Query with SASE or send complete ms for picture books. Include SASE for return of ms. Reports in 3 months on queries; 5 months on mss. Simultaneous submissions OK.
Terms: Pays royalty on wholesale price, makes outright purchase or negotiates payments of advance against

royalty. Advance varies. Publishes ms 18 months after acceptance. Writer's guidelines and book catalog for 9×12 SASE with $3 in postage. No phone calls.

Advice: "Our audience consists of children ages four to eleven. We publish very few picture books. We prefer manuscripts that can fit into one of our series. Spend time developing your idea in a unique way or from a unique angle; avoid trite, hackneyed plots and ideas."

CARROLL & GRAF PUBLISHERS, INC., (III), 260 Fifth Ave., New York NY 10001. (212)889-8772. Fax: (212)545-7909. **Acquisitions**: Kent Carroll, publisher/executive editor. Estab. 1983. "Carroll and Graf is one of the few remaining independent trade publishers and is therefore able to publish successfully and work with first-time authors and novelists." Publishes hardcover and paperback reprints. Plans 5 first novels this year. Averages 120 total titles, 75 fiction titles each year. Average first novel print order 7,500 copies.

Needs: Contemporary, erotica, fantasy, science fiction, literary, mainstream and mystery/suspense. No romance.

How to Contact: Does not accept unsolicited mss. Query first or submit outline/synopsis and sample chapters. SASE. Reports in 2 weeks. Occasionally critiques rejected mss.

Terms: Pays in royalties of 6% minimum; 15% maximum; advance negotiable. Sends galleys to author. Publishes ms 9 months after acceptance. Free book catalog on request.

‡CARTWHEEL BOOKS, Imprint of Scholastic, Inc., 555 Broadway, New York NY 10012. (212)343-6100. Fax: (212)343-4444. Website: http://www.scholastic.com. **Acquisitions:** Bernette Ford, vice president/editorial director. Estab. 1991. "Cartwheel Books publishes innovative books for children, ages 3-9. We are looking for 'novelties' that are books first, play objects second. Even without its gimmick, a Cartwheel Book should stand alone as a valid piece of children's literature." Publishes hardcover originals. Publishes 85-100 titles/year.

Needs: Fantasy, humor, juvenile, mystery, picture books, science fiction. "The subject should have mass market appeal for very young children. Humor can be helpful, but not necessary. Mistakes writers make are a reading level that is too difficult, a topic of no interest or too narrow, or manuscripts that are too long." Recently published *Little Bill (series)*, by Bill Cosby (picture book); *Dinofours* (series), by Steve Metzger (picture book); and *The Haunted House*, by Fiona Conboy (3-D puzzle storybook).

How to Contact: Agented submissions or previously published authors only. Reports in 2 months on queries; 6 months on mss. Simultaneous submissions OK.

Terms: Pays royalty on retail price. Offers advance. Publishes ms 2 years after acceptance. Book catalog for 9×12 SAE. Writer's guidelines free.

Advice: Audience is young children, ages 3-9. "Know what types of books the publisher does. Some manuscripts that don't work for one house may be perfect for another. Check out bookstores or catalogs to see where your writing would 'fit' best."

CATBIRD PRESS, (II), 16 Windsor Rd., North Haven CT 06473-3015. E-mail: catbird@pipeline.com. Publisher: Robert Wechsler. **Acquisitions**: Mary Mazzara, editor. Estab. 1987. Small independent trade publisher. "Catbird Press specializes in quality, imaginative prose humor and Central European literature in translation." Publishes cloth and paperback originals. Books: acid-free paper; offset printing; paper binding; illustrations (where relevant). Average print order: 4,000. First novel print order: 3,000. Averages 4 total titles, 1-2 fiction titles each year.

Needs: Humor (specialty); literary, translations (specialty Czech, French and German read in-house). No thriller, historical, science fiction, or other genre writing; only writing with a fresh style and approach. Recently published *The Third Lion*, by Floyd Kemske; *It Came With the House*, by Jeffrey Shaffer; and *The Royalscope Fe-As-Ko*, by Randall Beth Platt.

How to Contact: Accepts unsolicited mss but no queries. Submit outline/synopsis with sample chapter. SASE. Reports in 2-4 weeks on mss. Simultaneous submissions OK, "but let us know if simultaneous."

Terms: Pays royalties of 7½-10%. Average advance: $2,000; offers negotiable advance. Sends galleys to author. Publishes ms approximately 1 year after acceptance. Terms depend on particular book. Writer's guidelines for #10 SASE.

Advice: "Book publishing is a business. If you're not willing to learn the business and research the publishers, as well as learn the craft, you should not expect much from publishers. They simply will have no respect for you. If you send genre or other derivative writing to a quality literary press, they won't even bother to look at it. If you can't write a decent cover letter, keep your fiction in your drawer. We are interested in unpublished novelists who combine a sense of humor with a true knowledge of and love for language, a lack of ideology, care for craft and self-criticism."

‡CENTENNIAL PUBLICATIONS, 256 Nashua Ct., Grand Junction CO 81503. (970)243-8780. **Acquisitions:** Dick Spurr, publisher. Publishes hardcover and trade paperback originals and reprints. Publishes 4-5 titles/year.

Needs: Humor, mystery. "We are very selective in this market." Recently published *In Over My Waders*, by Jack Sayer (humor).

How to Contact: Submit synopsis. Reports in 1 week on queries, 1 month on mss.

Terms: Pays 8-10% royalty on retail price. Offers average of $1,000 advance. Publishes ms 8 months after acceptance. Book catalog free.

CENTER PRESS, (III), P.O. Box 16452, Encino CA 91416-6452. (818)377-4301. Website: http://www.concentr ic.net/~medianet/index.html. **Acquisitions**: Gabriella Stone, managing editor. Estab. 1979. "Small three-person publisher with expansion goals." Publishes hardcover and paperback originals, especially short story and poetry collections. Plans 1-2 novels this year. Averages 6 total titles.
 • Center Press has received the Masters Literary Award.
Needs: Erotica, historical, humor/satire, literary, short story collections. *List for novels filled for next year or two.*
How to Contact: Does not accept unsolicited mss. Query through agent only. SASE. Agented fiction 90%. Reports in 2 months on queries. Simultaneous submissions OK. Occasionally critiques or comments on rejected mss; fee varies.
Terms: Payment rate is "very variable." Sends galleys to author.
Advice: "Be competent, be solvent. Know who you are. Target your market."

‡CHAMPION BOOKS INC., P.O. Box 636, Lemont IL 60439. (800)230-1135. **Acquisitions:** Rebecca Rush, president. "In their prime, Kerouac and Ginsberg were never literary stars. They were the unknown and unheard, speaking their minds and breaking new ground. Champion Books seeks obscure and unrenowned authors interested not in following the footsteps of others, but in creating their own new shoes to walk in." Publishes trade paperback originals. Publishes 5 titles/year.
Imprint(s): New Shoes Series.
Needs: Literary, poetry, short story collections. Recently published *Warning This is Not a Book*, by Pete Babones.
How to Contact: Simultaneous submissions OK. Reports in 4 months on mss. Send a query with SASE first.
Terms: Pays 8-10% royalty on retail price. Publishes ms 5 months after acceptance. Book catalog and writer's guidelines for SASE.
Advice: "We are seeking works that deal with contemporary American Society with an emphasis on counterculture and alternative lifestyles."

‡CHARIOT CHILDREN'S BOOKS, Imprint of Chariot Victor Publishing, 4050 Lee Vance View, Colorado Springs CO 80918. (719)536-3271. Fax: (719)536-3269. **Acquisitions:** Liz Duckworth, managing editor. "Chariot Children's Books publishes works of children's inspirational titles, ages 1-12, with a strong underlying Christian theme or clearly stated Biblical value." Publishes hardcover and trade paperback originals. Publishes 50 titles/year.
 • Chariot Children's Books is not accepting unsolicited submissions at this time.
Needs: Historical, juvenile, picture books, religious. "Our age range is 8-12 years old. We're particularly interested in historical Christian juvenile fiction and series." Does not want teen fiction; currently overwhelmed with contemporary fiction. Recently published *Dance of Darkness*, by Sigmund Brouwer (Winds of Light series).
How to Contact: Queries from previously published authors only. Query with SASE. Reports in 4 months on queries. Simultaneous submissions OK if so noted.
Terms: Pays variable royalty on retail price. Offers advance, $1,000 for picture books, $2,500 for juvenile fiction. Publishes ms 2 years after acceptance. Writer's guidelines for #10 SASE. Book catalog on request.

CHARIOT VICTOR PUBLISHING, 4050 Lee Vance View, Colorado Springs CO 80918. (719)536-3280. Fax: (719)536-3269. **Acquisitions**: Lee Hough, senior acquisitions editor; Karl Schaller, editorial director; Kathy Davis (children), editorial assistant; Dave Horton (adult), acquisitions editor. Estab. 1875. Publishes hardcover and paperback originals. Number of fiction titles: 35-40 juvenile, 4-6 adult. Encourages new writers.
Imprint(s): Chariot Books, Victor Books, Lion Publishing.
Needs: Religious/inspirational, juvenile, young adult and adult; sports, animal, spy/adventure, historical, Biblical, fantasy/science fiction, picture book and easy-to-read. Published *California Pioneer* series, by Elaine Schulte; *The Patriots*, by Jack Cavanaugh. Published new writers within the last year.
How to Contact: All unsolicited mss are returned unopened. Send query with SASE to Kathy Davis. Simultaneous submissions OK.
Terms: Royalties vary ("depending on whether it is trade, mass market or cloth" and whether picture book or novel). Offers advance. Writer's guidelines with SASE.
Advice: "Focus on Christians, not Christianity. Chariot Victor Publishing publishes books for toddlers through adults which help people better understand their relationship with God, and/or the message of God's book, the Bible. Interested in seeing contemporary novels (*not* Harlequin-type) adventure, romance, suspense with Christian perspective."

MARKET CATEGORIES: (I) Open to new writers; **(II)** Open to both new and established writers; **(III)** Interested mostly in established writers; **(IV)** Open to writers whose work is specialized; **(V)** Closed to unsolicited submissions.

‡CHARLESBRIDGE PUBLISHING, 85 Main St., Watertown MA 02172. (617)926-0329. **Acquisitions:** Elena Dworkin Wright, editorial director. Estab. 1980. "We are looking for fiction to use as literature in the math curriculum and activity books for kids to make or do some project (not coloring)." Publishes school programs and hardcover and trade paperback originals. Publishes 20 books/year.
Imprint: *Talewinds* (fiction).
Needs: Math concepts in nonrhyming story. Recently published *Sir Cumference and the First Round Table*, by Cindy Neuschwander (a math adventure/picture book).
How to Contact: Reports in 2 months.
Terms: Publishes ms 1 year after acceptance.
Advice: "We market through schools, book stores and specialty stores at museums, science centers, etc."

‡CHICAGO SPECTRUM PRESS, 1571 Sherman Ave., Annex C, Evanston, IL 61201. (847)492-1911. **Acquisitions:** Wanda Johnson-Hall, office administrator. Publishes hardcover and trade paperback originals. Publishes 20 titles/year.
Needs: Ethnic, feminist, historical, humor, juvenile, literary, mainstream/contemporary, mystery/suspense, science fiction, short story collections, young adult. Recently published *Deadly Prayer*, by Pascal Littman (mystery); *Beaned in Boston*, by Gail Farrelley (mystery); and *Into the Arena*, by Corey Kinczewski (politics).
How to Contact: Query first. Reports in 1 month.
Terms: Pays royalty on retail price. No advance. Publishes ms 2 months after acceptance. Book catalog free.

‡CHINA BOOKS & PERIODICALS, INC., 2929 24th St., San Francisco CA 94110-4126. (415)282-2994. Fax: (415)282-0994. Website: http://www.chinabooks.com. **Acquisitions:** Greg Jones, editor. Estab. 1960. "China Books is the main importer and distributor of books and magazines from China, providing an ever-changing variety of useful tools for travelers, scholars and others interested in China and Chinese culture." Publishes hardcover and trade paperback originals. Averages 5 titles/year.
Needs: Ethnic, experimental, historical, literary. "*Must* have Chinese, Chinese-American or East Asian theme. We are looking for high-quality fiction with a Chinese or East Asian theme or translated from Chinese that makes a genuine literary breakthrough and seriously treats life in contemporary China or Chinese-Americans. No fiction that is too conventional in style or treats hackneyed subjects. No fiction without Chinese or Chinese-American or East Asian themes, please." Recently published *The Banker*, by Cheng Naishan.
How to Contact: Query with outline/synopsis and sample chapters. Query for electronic submissions. Reports in 3 months on queries. Simultaneous submissions OK.
Terms: Pays 6-8% royalty on net receipts. Offers $1,000 average advance. Publishes ms 1 year after acceptance. Book catalog free. Writer's guidelines for #10 SASE.
Advice: "We are looking for original ideas, especially in language study, children's education, adoption of Chinese babies, or health issues relating to Traditional Chinese medicine. See our website for author guidelines."

CHINOOK PRESS, (II), 1432 Yellowstone Ave., Billings MT 59102. (406)245-7704. Editor/Publisher: Mary Ellen Westwood. Estab. 1996. "One-person operation on a part-time basis just starting out. I hope to have a catalog of equal parts fiction, nonfiction and poetry." Publishes paperback originals. Books: acid-free paper; printing and binding suitable to product; illustrations. Average print order: 2,000-5,000. First novel print order: 2,000-5,000. Plans 1 first novel this year. Averages 4 total titles, 2 fiction titles each year. Sometimes critiques or comments on rejected mss.
Needs: Adventure, childrens/juvenile (all types), ethnic/multicultural, experimental, family saga, fantasy (all types), feminist, historical, humor/satire, literary, mainstream/contemporary, mystery/suspense (all types), regional (the West), science fiction (all types), short story collections, translations, young adult/teen (all types). "I want fiction that educates and uplifts, that shows real human beings in real or imagined situations that aid in human advancement. I do not want fiction that titillates for the sole purpose of titillation. I want fiction with a definite message and purpose."
How to Contact: Accepts unsolicited mss. Submit complete ms with cover letter. Include estimated word count, 1-page bio, Social Security number, list of publishing credits and "brief explanation of why you wrote what you wrote." Send SASE for return of ms. Reports in 2 months on queries and mss. Simultaneous submissions OK "if identified as such."
Terms: "We make individual arrangements with each author depending on book, but author must provide promotion time." Sends galleys to author. Publishes ms 2 months to 2 years after acceptance. Writer's guidelines for #10 SASE.
Advice: "I am a well-trained and well-practiced editor with 29 years experience in both journalism and law. Bad spelling, incorrect grammar and muddy thinking will not sell your work to me. But your best effort will receive attentive and enthusiastic handling here. I want more new and creative solutions to the human condition. I want fewer 'Oh, woe is me! I just can't do anything with my life.' stories."

CHRONICLE BOOKS, (II), 85 Second St., San Francisco CA 94105. (415)573-3730. Fax: (415)537-4440. E-mail: frontdesk@chronbooks.com. Website: http://www.chronbooks.com. President: Jack Jensen. Publishing Director: Caroline Herter. Associate Publishers: Nion McEvoy, Victoria Rock, Christine Carswell. **Acquisitions:**

Jay Schaefer, editor (fiction); Victoria Rock, editor (children's). Estab. 1966. Publishes hardcover and paperback originals. Averages 150 total titles, 10 fiction this year.

Needs: Open. Looking for novellas, collections and novels. No romances, science fiction, or any genre fiction: no category fiction. Publishes anthologies. Recently published *Griffin & Sabine*, by Nick Bantock; *Lies of the Saints*, by Erin McGraw; *Spirits of the Ordinary*, by Kathleen Alcalá and *The Lonliest Road in America*, by Roy Parvin.

How to Contact: Accepts unsolicited mss. Submit complete ms with cover letter. "No queries, please." Send SASE for reply and return of ms. Agented fiction 50%. Prefers no simultaneous submissions. Sometimes comments on rejected ms.

Terms: Standard rates. Sends galleys to author. Publishes ms 9-12 months after acceptance. No writer's guidelines available.

‡CHRONICLE BOOKS FOR CHILDREN, Imprint of Chronicle Books, 85 Second St., San Francisco CA 94105. (415)537-3730. Fax: (415)537-4460. E-mail: frontdesk@chronbooks.com. Website: http://www.chronbooks.com. **Acquisitions:** Victoria Rock, director of Children's Books (nonfiction/fiction); Erica Jacobs, editor (nonfiction/fiction plus novelty, packaged, buy-ins); Amy Novesky, assistant editor (nonfiction/fiction plus middle grade and young adult). "Chronicle Books for Children publishes an eclectic mixture of traditional and innovative children's books. We're looking for quirky, bold artwork and subject matter." Publishes hardcover and trade paperback originals. Publishes 40-50 titles/year.

Needs: Fiction picture books, middle grades fiction, young adult projects. Mainstream/contemporary, multicultural, picture books, young adult, chapter books. Recently published *The Eyes of Graywolf*, by Jonathan London; *Dem Bones*, by Bob Banner; and *Hush Little Baby*, by Sylvia Long.

How to Contact: Query with synopsis and SASE. Send complete ms for picture books. Reports in 2-18 weeks on queries; 5 months on mss. Simultaneous submissions OK, if so noted.

Terms: Pays 8% royalty. Advance varies. Publishes ms 18 months after acceptance. Writer's guidelines for #10 SASE. Book catalog for 9×12 SAE and 3 first-class stamps.

Advice: "We are interested in projects that have a unique bent to them—be it in subject matter, writing style, or illustrative technique. As a small list, we are looking for books that will lend our list a distinctive flavor. Primarily we are interested in fiction and nonfiction picture books for children ages up to eight years, and nonfiction books for children ages up to twelve years. We publish board, pop-up, and other novelty formats as well as picture books. We are also interested in early chapter books, middle grade fiction, and young adult projects."

CIRCLET PRESS, (IV), 1770 Massachusetts Ave., #278, Cambridge MA 02140. (617)864-0492 (noon-6p.m. EST). Fax: (617)864-0663, call before faxing. E-mail: circlet-info@circlet.com. Website: http://www.circlet.com/ (includes previews of upcoming books, catalog of complete books in print, links to authors' web pages and other publishers). **Acquistions**: Cecilia Tan, publisher. Estab. 1992. Small, independent specialty book publisher. "We are the only book publisher specializing in science fiction and fantasy of an erotic nature." Publishes paperback originals. Books: perfect binding; illustrations sometimes; average print order: 2,500. Published 50 new writers within the last year. Averages 6-8 anthologies each year. Distributes titles through the LPC Group in the US/Canada, Turnaround UK in the UK and Bulldog Books in Australia. Promotes titles through reviews in book trade and general media, mentions in Publishers Weekly, Bookselling This Week and regional radio/TV.

● Stories from Circlet Press appear in *Best American Erotica*, 1995, 1996 and 1997.

Needs: "We publish only short stories of erotic science fiction/fantasy, of all persuasions (gay, straight, bi, feminist, lesbian, etc.). No horror! No exploitative sex, murder or rape. No degradation." No novels. All books are anthologies of short stories. Recently published *The Drag Queen of Elfland*, by Lawrence Schmiel (short stories); *Sex Magick 2* and *Erotica Vampirica*, by various ed. (anthologies).

How to Contact: Accepts unsolicited mss between April 1 and August 31. "Any manuscript sent other than this time period will be returned unread or discarded." Submit complete short story with cover letter. Include estimated word count, 50-100 word bio, list of publishing credits. Send SASE for reply, return of ms or send a disposable copy of ms. Agented fiction 5%. Reports in 2-12 months. Simultaneous and e-mail submissions OK. Always critiques or comments on rejected mss.

Terms: Pays minimum ½¢/word for 1-time anthology rights only, plus 2 copies; author is free to sell other rights. Sends galleys to author. Publishes ms 1-12 months after acceptance. Writer's guidelines for #10 SASE. Book catalog for #10 SAE and 2 first-class stamps.

Advice: "Read what we publish, learn to use lyrical but concise language to portray sex positively. Make sex and erotic interaction integral to your plot. Stay away from genre stereotypes. Use depth of character, internal monologue and psychological introspection to draw me in." Note: "We do not publish novels."

‡CITADEL PRESS, (II), Carol Publishing Group, 120 Enterprise Ave., Secaucus NJ 07094. (212)486-2200 or (212)736-1141. Fax: (201)866-8159. E-mail: info@citadelpublishing.com. Website: http://www.citadelpublishing.com. **Acquisitions**: Allan J. Wilson, executive editor; Marcy Swingler, associate editor. Estab. 1942. Publishes hardcover and paperback originals and paperback reprints. Averages 65 total titles, 4-7 fiction titles each year. Occasionally critiques rejected mss.

Needs: No religious, romantic or detective. Published *The Rain Maiden*, by Jill M. Phillips and *Human Oddities*,

INSIDER REPORT

Erin McGraw: on relationships and writing fiction

Relationships are never easy. The bonds between husbands and wives, parents and children require constant work. The payoffs can be big but are more than often insignificant. In the short stories of Erin McGraw, characters gracefully reveal just how painful and occasionally gratifying our day-to-day existence is. As a writer, McGraw understands the necessity of relationships, both in her fiction and in her professional life. Luckily, the latter has proved more consistently rewarding in her life than in the lives of her characters. Whether it's receiving positive reviews from her readers or looking to her agent for support, discussing problems with her students or even giving advice to beginning writers, these alliances have become an important and beneficial part of her writing process.

Erin McGraw

Photo by Roger Pfingston

McGraw's strongest piece of advice to writers is brief but invaluable: "Write every day." This task may seem challenging for most, but for someone who is "disciplined by nature," McGraw claims, "it is very easy to sit down at the computer every single morning at eight o'clock and get to work. I get up, do my sit-ups, take the dogs out, put in my contacts and boom." At that point, however, her muse gains control: "I do not know what will happen when I sit down, but I do make sure I have my butt in the chair every day. I think about Flannery O'Connor who could only manage two hours a day because of her poor health, but she made sure that she was there if lightning struck anywhere in the [fiction writing] realm so that she could grab it."

With two collections of literary short stories—*Lies of the Saints*, published in 1996 by Chronicle Books, and *Bodies at Sea*, published in 1989 by University of Illinois Press—and a novel with the working title *The Baby Tree* close to completion, the creative lightning has obviously struck McGraw more than once. She started writing seriously in college at University of California Davis, but not writing fiction. "I wanted to be a poet. My biggest single influence is T.S. Eliot." But her first important mentor relationship with poet, Karl Shapiro, helped her discover her true talents. "He said, 'Try fiction. Try writing all the way out to the margin.' I went home with a broken heart for a week and then I took his advice. He saved me a lot of time."

These days McGraw is the one passing advice on to her own students. As a professor at the University of Cincinnati, she not only encourages beginning writers to establish a daily writing schedule but stresses the importance of revising meticulously. "Those sentences have to work. Every time the reader stops and says 'huh?' you've lost him. All of that credibility and momentum you've worked so hard to build up is just shot." Another common mistake McGraw cautions her students about is too much reliance on melodrama. "Students don't trust the inherent drama of our lives, so they tend to pump it up enor-

INSIDER REPORT, *McGraw*

mously. The problem that immediately follows is exactly the opposite effect: writers shun any kind of drama at all and end up writing these flattened-out Prozac stories."

Practical marketing guidance also often enters into McGraw's relationships with her students. Once their work is ready for publishers' eyes, McGraw encourages them to submit to the best markets first: "It's easier, much easier," she says, to get published today than ever before. "There are simply more outlets, there are more magazines than there used to be." But, she says, "Start at the top of your list. There is no point in not sending to *The Atlantic* out of shyness. What happens when you send out to '*Sludge River Quarterly*' and they take it? You sit there and think what if somebody better would have wanted it. It's also not self-defeating to expect your manuscript to come back. My teacher, Scott Sanders, suggested we put together a ranked list of where we'd like our work to appear. Send it out to number one, then have the envelope already addressed and stamped for the next place. Everything that mind-set implies about how to approach publishing is very helpful."

The relationship between students and teacher is often a two-way street. "You get to where teaching and writing feed each other: what I'm working on at home goes straight into the classroom; what we discuss in the classroom I carry straight back home with me. There are times when I'm eager to get into the classroom because I want to talk about what's going on." When obstacles appear in her own fiction, McGraw brings it up in class as a way to "get it out there, look at it, analyze it, and stop doing it." These conversations often turn into craft lectures for conferences or surface in the reviews she writes for *The Georgia Review*.

One recurring topic in McGraw's classroom is the ability of writers to learn from and reflect on their own work; looking at her stories through a critic's eye has been an on-going task for her. "I went through a couple of years retooling my own aesthetic. Almost the minute I was done with my first book, I thought, I'm glad this book was taken, but I don't want to write like this any more. The stories all have a knotted, closed-in, claustrophobic quality. They're filled with solitary people who have largely imposed their own conditions on their lives." It became necessary to redefine her relationship with her writing. "It was hard, like wrestling with a shadow. Finally, I came around the corner and started putting together a different type of structure. It was a complete change in how I approached what fiction does." This struggle resulted in her *Lies of the Saints* collection. A poignant, published victory.

After publication of her two short story collections, McGraw found work on her novel to be a pleasant change. "I was much more comfortable because there wasn't that awful sense you get with stories of things being so heavy. The force of gravity is seven times heavier in a short story because the ending is staring you right in the face. It's difficult just getting your character in and out of the car. That just isn't true with novel writing because you've got much more air."

McGraw points out that the relationship between the writer and the writing can produce some immensely gratifying moments. That's when, says McGraw, "your story takes a turn and you know you're getting it right. Sometimes it is just a tiny thing, a sentence that is gracefully done and you know it's gracefully done. But it makes it all worth it. It's nourishing."

McGraw also notes that a good agent can be beneficial to the writer's comfort zone. When discussing her relationship with her agent, she says, "the only con is that you lose 15 percent off the top. As far as I'm concerned that's not much of a drawback because

INSIDER REPORT, *continued*

it also means you have a top to lose 15 percent from. If an agent has taken on your book in the first place, it's because she thinks there is money to be made from it. You have somebody who has an absolute vested interest in getting you the best possible financial deal and who knows more about the system than you do. It's also somebody you can call and say, 'I'm afraid I can't finish this book.' Again, your agent has a vested interest in bucking you up."

An important personal and professional relationship for McGraw is the one with her husband, poet Andrew Hudgins. "We constantly look at each other's work and we're each other's best reader." In the end, however, McGraw's relationship with her audience is the most significant one as a writer. "When I get a letter out of the blue from someone who has read one of my stories or read my book, I think, there is some kind of payoff from this. It's so consoling to know your work has reached people." With this much experience with relationships, it's no wonder readers are drawn to the genuine encounters between the characters in McGraw's fiction. After all, isn't that what life—and good fiction—are all about?

—Donya Dickerson

by Martin Monestiere.
How to Contact: Accepts unsolicited mss. Query first with SASE (or IRC). Reports in 6 weeks on queries; 2 months on mss. Simultaneous submissions OK.
Terms: Pays in royalties of 10% minimum; 15% maximum; 12-25 author's copies. Advance is more for agented ms; depends on grant/award money.

‡**CITY LIGHTS BOOKS, (II, III)**, 261 Columbus Ave., San Francisco CA 94133. (415)362-1901. Fax: (415)362-4921. **Acquisitions:**Robert Sharrard, editor. Estab. 1955. Publishes paperback originals. Plans 1-2 first novels this year. Averages 12 total titles, 4-5 fiction titles/year.
How to Contact: Accepts unsolicited mss with SASE. Query letter only first. Unsolicited queries/correspondence by fax OK. Send SASE for reply, return of ms or send a disposable copy of ms.

‡**CLARION BOOKS**, Imprint of Houghton Mifflin Company, 215 Park Ave. S., New York NY 10003. **Acquisitions**: Dorothy Briley, editor/publisher; Dinah Stevenson, executive editor; Nina Ignatowicz, senior editor. Estab. 1965. Clarion is a strong presence when it comes to books for young readers. Publishes hardcover originals. Publishes 50 titles/year.
● Clarion is swamped with submissions and is not accepting manuscripts at this time.
Needs: Adventure, humor, mystery/suspense, strong character studies. "We would like to see more distinguished short fiction for readers seven to ten."
How to Contact: *No unsolicited mss.* Accepts fiction translations. Reports in 2 months. Prefers no simultaneous submissions.
Terms: Pays 5-10% royalty on retail price. Advances from $4,000. Publishes ms 2 years after acceptance. Writer's guidelines for #10 SASE.
Advice: Looks for "freshness, enthusiasm—in short, life."

CLEIS PRESS, (II), P.O. Box 14684, San Francisco CA 94114. E-mail: sfcleis@aol.com. **Acquisitions**: Frederique Delacoste, editor. Estab. 1980. Midsize independent publisher. Publishes paperback originals. Published new writers within the last year. Plans 1 first novel every other year. Averages 15 total titles, 5 (3 are anthologies) fiction titles/year.
● Cleis Press has received the Best Lesbian Fiction Lambda Literary Award for *Memory Mambo*, by Achy Obejas, the Fab Award, Firecracker for Outstanding Press; and several Canada Award nominations.
Needs: Comics/graphic novels, erotica, ethnic/multicultural (gay/lesbian), feminist, gay, historical (gay/lesbian), horror (vampire), humor/satire, lesbian, short story collection, thriller/espionage, translations. Recently published *Memory Mambo*, by Achy Obejas (novel); and *Real Live Nude Girl*, by Carol Queen.
How to Contact: Accepts unsolicited mss with SASE. Accepts unsolicited queries by E-mail. Submit complete ms with a cover letter. Include 1- or 2-page bio, list of publishing credits. Send SASE for reply or send a disposable copy of ms. Agented fiction 25%. Reports in 6 weeks. No simultaneous submissions.

Payment/Terms: Pays royalty of 7%. Advance is negotiable. Sends galleys to author. Publishes ms 12-18 months after acceptance. Catalogue for SASE and 2 first-class stamps.

COFFEE HOUSE PRESS, (II), 27 N. Fourth St., Minneapolis MN 55401. (612)338-0125. **Acquisitions**: Allan Kornblum and Chris Fischbach, editors. Estab. 1984. "Nonprofit publisher with a small staff. We publish literary titles: fiction and poetry." Publishes paperback originals. Books: acid-free paper; Smyth-sewn binding; cover illustrations; average print order: 2,500. First novel print order: 3,000-4,000. Published new writers within the last year. Plans 2 first novels this year. Averages 12 total titles, 5-6 fiction titles each year.
  ● This successful nonprofit small press has received numerous grants from various organizations including NEA, the Mellon Foundation and Lila Wallace/Readers Digest.
Needs: Contemporary, ethnic, experimental, satire, literary. Looking for "non-genre, contemporary, high quality, unique material." No westerns, romance, erotica, mainstream, science fiction or mystery. Publishes anthologies, but they are closed to unsolicited submissions. Also publishes a series of short-short collections called "Coffee-to-Go." Published *Ex Utero*, by Laurie Foos (first novel); *Gunga Din Highway*, by Frank Chin (novel); and *A .38 Special & a Broken Heart*, by Jonis Agee (short short stories).
How to Contact: Accepts unsolicited mss. Submit samples with cover letter. SASE. Agented fiction 10%. Reports in 3 months on queries; 9 months on mss. Sometimes critiques rejected mss.
Terms: Pays royalties of 8%. Average advance: $3,000. Provides 15 author's copies. Writer's guidelines for #10 SASE with 55¢ postage.

‡CONCORDIA PUBLISHING HOUSE, 3558 S. Jefferson Ave., St. Louis MO 63118-3968. (314)268-1000. Fax: (314)268-1329. Family and Children's Editor: Ruth Geisler. **Acquisitions:** Dawn Weinstock. Estab. 1869. "We publish Protestant, inspirational, theological, family and juveniles. All manuscripts must conform to the doctrinal tenets of The Lutheran Church—Missouri Synod." Publishes hardcover and trade paperback originals. Publishes 80 titles/year.
  ● Concordia has increased their number of books published from 60 to 80 in the past year.
Needs: Juvenile. "We will consider preteen and children's fiction and picture books. All books must contain Christian content. No adult Christian fiction." Recently published *The Great Meow Mystery*, by Dandi Mackall.
How to Contact: Send a query with SASE first. Reports in 2 months on queries. Simultaneous submissions discouraged.
Terms: Pays royalty or makes outright purchase. Publishes ms 1 year after acceptance. Writer's guidelines for #10 SASE.
Advice: "Our needs have broadened to include writers of books for lay adult Christians and of Christian novels (low-key, soft-sell) for pre-teens and teenagers."

♣COTEAU BOOKS, (IV), Thunder Creek Publishing Co-operative Ltd., 401-2206 Dewdney Ave., Regina, Saskatchewan S4R 1H3 Canada. (306)777-0170. Fax: (306)522-5152. E-mail: coteau@coteau.unibase.com. Website: http://coteau.unibase.com. **Acquisitions**: Geoffrey Ursell, publisher. Estab. 1975. "Coteau Books publishes the finest Canadian fiction, poetry drama and children's literature, with an emphasis on western writers." Small, independent publisher. Publishes hardcover and paperback originals. Books: #2 offset or 60 lb. hi-bulk paper; offset printing; perfect and Smyth-sewn binding; 4-color illustrations. Average print order: 1,500-3,000; first novel print order: approx. 1,500. Published new writers within the last year. Publishes 14 total titles, 6-8 fiction titles each year.
  ● Books published by Coteau Books have received awards including 1995 Fiction Award for *Crosswinds*, 1995 City of Regina Award for *Club Chernobyl* and 1995 Sasketchewan Book of the Year for *Z:A Meditation on Oppression, Desire and Freedom*. The publisher does anthologies and these are announced when open to submissions.
Needs: Middle years and young adult fiction. No science fiction. No children's picture books. Published *Due West: 30 Great Stories From Alberta, Saskatchewan and Manitoba*, edited by Wayne Tefs, et al (anthology); *Inspection of a Small Village*, by Connie Gault (short stories); and *Crosswinds*, by Byrna Barclay.
How to Contact: *Canadian writers only.* Send submissions with query letter and résumé to Acquisitions Editor: Barbara Sapergia. SASE. No simultaneous or multiple submissions. Fiction 12.5%. Reports on queries in 2-3 months; 2-3 months on mss. Sometimes comments on rejected mss.
Terms: "We're a co-operative and receive subsidies from the Canadian, provincial and local governments. We do not accept payments from authors to publish their works." Sends galleys to author. Publishes ms 1-2 years after acceptance. Book catalog for 8½ × 11 SASE.
Advice: "We publish short-story collections, novels, drama, nonfiction and poetry collections, as well as literary

---

READ THE BUSINESS OF FICTION WRITING section to learn the correct way to prepare and submit a manuscript.

interviews and children's books. This is part of our mandate. The work speaks for itself! Be bold. Be creative. Be persistent!"

‡COUNCIL FOR INDIAN EDUCATION, (I,IV), 517 Rimrock Rd., Billings MT 59102. (406)252-7451. **Acquisitions**: Hap Gilliland, president and editor. Estab. 1963. Small, non-profit organization publishing Native American materials for schools. Publishes hardcover and paperback originals. Books: offset printing; perfect-bound or saddle-stitched binding; b&w illustrations; average print order: 1,000; first novel print order: 1,000. Published new writers within the last year; plans 3 first novels this year. Averages 5 total titles, 4 fiction titles each year.
Needs: All must be about Native Americans: adventure, ethnic, family saga, historical, juvenile (adventure, historical and others), preschool/picture book, regional, young adult/teen (easy-to-read, historical, mystery, western), western (frontier). Especially needs "short novels, and short stories accurately portraying Native American life past or present—fast moving with high interest." No sex emphasis. Published *Old Lop Ear Wolf*, by Royce Holland (3 stories); *Mi'ca—Buffalo Hunter*, by Jane Bendix (novel); *Search for Identity*, by various authors (short stories).
How to Contact: No manuscripts accepted between June 1 and October 1 each year. Accepts unsolicited mss. Submit complete ms with SASE (or IRC). Reports in 4 months. Simultaneous submissions OK. Usually critiques rejected ms.
Terms: Pays 10% of wholesale price or 1½¢/word. Publishes ms 1 year after acceptance. Sends galleys to author. Free writer's guidelines and book catalog.
Advice: Mostly publishes original fiction in paperback. "Be sure material is culturally authentic and good for the self-concept of the group about whom it is written. Send us only material on Native-Americans, make sure it is true to the culture and way of life of a particular tribe at a particular time, and that you don't downgrade any group."

‡COUNTERPOINT, 1627 I St. NW, Suite 850, Washington DC 20006. Fax: (202)887-0562. **Acquisitions**: Jack Shoemaker, editor-in-chief. "Counterpoint publishes serious literary work, with particular emphasis on natural history, science, philosophy and contemporary thought, history, art, poetry and fiction. All of our books are printed on acid-free paper, with cloth bindings sewn. In this multimedia age, we are committed to the significant readership that still demands and appreciates well-published and well-crafted books." Publishes hardcover and trade paperback originals and reprints. Publishes 20-25 titles/year.
Needs: Historical, humor, literary, mainstream/contemporary, religious, short story collections. Recently published *Women in Their Beds*, by Gina Berriault (short stories).
How to Contact: Agented submissions only. Reports in 2 months. Simultaneous submissions OK.
Terms: Pays 7.5-15% royalty on retail price. Publishes ms 18 months after acceptance.

CREATIVE ARTS BOOK CO., (II), 833 Bancroft Way, Berkeley CA 94710-2235. (415)848-4777. Fax: (510)848-4844. Publisher: Donald S. Ellis. **Acquisitions**: George Samsa, editor-in-chief; Jennifer Ellis and Victoria Gill, fiction editors. Estab. 1975. Small independent trade publisher. Publishes hardcover originals and paperback originals and reprints. Average print order: 2,500-10,000. Average first novel print order: 2,500-10,000. Published new writers within the last year. Plans 3-6 first novels this year. Averages 10-20 titles each year. Distributes titles through reps, Ingram, Baker-Taylor and book people. Promotes titles through catalogues, review copies, reps, major reviews, newspapers and magazine print.
Imprint(s): Creative Arts Communications Books, Creative Arts Life and Health Books, Saturday Night Specials and Editions 833.
• Books published by Creative Arts have been finalists for the American Book Award. Creative Arts is planning a new edition of *California Childhood*, an anthology of stories about growing up in California. Deadline for submissions is December 1997.
Needs: Contemporary, erotica (literary), feminist, historical, literary, mystery/suspense (Saturday night specials), regional, short story collections, translations, music, western. Publishes anthologies, *Black Lizard Crime Fiction* (Vols. I & II) and *Stolen Moments*, a collection of love stories. Recently published *Fatal Decision*, by Michael Gould (novel); *An Optimist in Hell*, by Stephen Spotte (short stories) and *Fatal Image*, by Jim Hurst (suspense). Publishes the Childhood (growing up) series.
How to Contact: Accepts unsolicited mss. Queries by fax OK. Submit outline/synopsis and 3 sample chapters (approximately 50 pages). SASE. Agented fiction 50%. Reports in 1 month on queries; 6 weeks on mss. Simultaneous submissions OK.
Terms: Pays royalties of 7½-15%; average advance of $1,000-10,000; 10 author's copies. Sends galleys to author. Writers guidelines and book catalog for SASE.
Advice: "Keep writing. Keep trying."

CREATIVE WITH WORDS PUBLICATIONS, (I), Box 223226, Carmel CA 93922. Fax: (408)655-8627. **Acquisitions**: Brigitta Geltrich (general); Bert Hower (nature), fiction editor. Estab. 1975. One-woman operation on part-time basis "with guest editors, artists and readers from throughout the U.S." Books: bond and stock paper; mimeographed printing; saddle-stitched binding; illustrations. Average print order varies. Publishes paperback anthologies of new and established writers. Averages 12-13 anthologies each year. Distributes titles through author, schools and libraries.

Needs: Humor/satire, juvenile (easy-to-read, fantasy), nature. "Editorial needs center on folkloristic items (according to themes): tall tales and such for annual anthologies." Needs seasonal short stories, stories on values and human relationships appealing to general public; "tales" of folklore nature, appealing to all ages, poetry, prose and language art works by children. Recently published anthologies, *Humor*; *Names*; *Sports*; *Space and Skies*."

How to Contact: Accepts unsolicited mss. Query first; submit complete ms (prose no more than 1,500 words) with SASE and cover letter. Electronic submissions (3.5 diskette) OK. Reports in 1 month on queries; 1-2 months on mss after deadline. Publishes ms 1-2 months after deadline. Writer's guidelines and theme list (1 oz.) for SASE. No simultaneous submissions, "no previously published material." *Critiques rejected mss; $10 for short stories (less than 1,000 words); $20 for longer stories, folklore items; $5 for poetry.*

Terms: Pays in 20% reduced author copies (20%: 1-9 copies; 30%: 10 copies); Best of the Month (1 free copy).

Advice: "Our fiction appeals to general public: children—senior citizens. Follow guidelines and rules of Creative With Words Publications and not those the writer feels CWW should have. We only consider fiction along the lines of folklore, seasonal genres and themes set by CWW. We set our themes twice a year: July 1 and January 1. Be brief, sincere, well-informed, patient and proficient! Look at the world from a different perspective, research your topic thoroughly, apply brevity; and write your story through a viewpoint character."

CROSSWAY BOOKS, (II, IV), Division of Good News Publishers, 1300 Crescent, Wheaton IL 60187-5800. Fax: (630)682-4785. **Acquisitions**: Jill Carter. Estab. 1938. " 'Making a difference in people's lives for Christ' as its maxim, Crossway Books lists titles written from an evangelical Christian perspective." Midsize independent evangelical religious publisher. Publishes paperback originals. Average print order 5,000-10,000 copies. Averages 50 total titles, 10-15 fiction titles each year. Distributes through Christian bookstores and catalogs.

- Crossway Books is known as a leader in Christian fiction. Several of their books have received "Gold Medallion" awards from the Evangelical Christian Publishers Association.

Needs: Contemporary, adventure, historical, literary, religious/inspirational, young adult. "All fiction published by Crossway Books must be written from the perspective of evangelical Christianity. It must understand and view the world through a Christian worldview." No sentimental, didactic, "inspirational" religious fiction, heavy-handed allegorical or derivative fantasy. Recently published *The Kill Fee of Cindy LaCoste*, by Stephen Bly (contempory); *Lethal Mercy*, by Harry Kraus (medical thriller); and *Encounter the Light*, by Donna Fletcher Crow (historical).

How to Contact: Does not accept unsolicited mss. Send query with synopsis and sample chapters only. Reports in 6-8 weeks on queries. Publishes ms 1-2 years after acceptance. Electronic submissions (fax) OK.

Terms: Pays in royalties and negotiates advance. Writer's guidelines for SASE. Book catalog for 9×12 SAE and 6 first-class stamps.

Advice: "We feel called to publish fiction in the following categories: Supernatural fiction, Christian realism, historical fiction, intrigue, western fiction and children's fiction. All fiction should include explicit Christian content, artfully woven into the plot, and must be consistent with our statements of vision, purpose and commitment. Crossway can successfully publish and market *quality* Christian novelists. Also read John Gardner's *On Moral Fiction*. We require a minimum word count of 25,000 words."

THE CROWN PUBLISHING GROUP, (II), 201 E. 50th St., New York NY 10022. (212)572-6190. Executive Vice Pres., Editor-in-Chief: Betty A. Prashker. Executive Editor, Crown: Steven Ross. Editorial Director, Harmony Books: Lauren Shakeley. President and Publisher, Clarkson N. Potter: Chip Gibson. Executive Editor: Lauren Shakely.

Imprint(s): Crown, **Harmony Books**, Clarkson N. Potter, Inc.

Needs: Adventure, contemporary, historical, horror, humor/satire, literary, mainstream, science, war. Recently published *Amethyst Dreams*, by Phyllis A. Whitney.

How to Contact: Does not accept unsolicited mss. "Query letters only addressed to the Editorial Department. Complete mss are returned unread . . ." SASE (or IRC). Reports in 3-4 months.

Terms: Pays advance against royalty; terms vary and are negotiated per book.

WRITER-TO-WRITER

I write because I can't help it. Success is nice but a by-product. Your goal isn't to be rich and famous. It is to write a good book. And, if you are collecting a lot of rejection slips, it means you are learning your craft. Go for it!

  Phyllis A. Whitney
  Amethyst Dreams, Crown

‡**CUMBERLAND HOUSE PUBLISHING**, 2200 Abbott Marten Rd., Suite 102, Nashville TN 37215. (615)385-2444. Fax: (615)385-3772. E-mail: cumbhouse@aol.com. **Acquisitions:** Ron Pitkin, president. "We look for unique titles with clearly defined audiences." Publishes hardcover and trade paperback originals, and hardcover and trade paperback reprints. Publishes 35 titles/year. Imprint publishes 5 titles/year.

Imprint(s): Cumberland House Hearthside; Julia M. Pitkin, editor-in-chief.

Needs: Mystery, western. Recently published *A Rumor of Bones*, by Beverly Connor (mystery); and *The Broncbuster*, by Mike Flanagan.

How to Contact: Query first. Writers should know "the odds are really stacked against them." Reports in 2 months on queries; 4 months on mss. Simultaneous submissions OK.

Terms: Pays 10-20% royalty on wholesale price. Offers $1,000-25,000 advance. Publishes ms an average of 8 months after acceptance. Book catalog for 8×10 SAE and 4 first-class stamps. Writer's guidelines free.

Advice: Audience is "adventuresome people who like a fresh approach to things. Writers should tell what their idea is, why it's unique and why somebody would want to buy it—but don't pester us."

‡**CURTIS/STRONGMEN PUBLISHING**, P.O. Box 4306, Grand Central Station, New York NY 10163. (212)544-8592. **Acquisitions:** Antonio M. Monaco, editor. Publishes hardcover, trade paperback and mass market paperback originals. Publishes 11 titles/year; 5-6 imprint titles/year.

Imprint(s): Curtis (James J. Izzo, publisher), Strongmen (Antonio M. Monaco, editor).

Needs: Gay. "We publish quality (and racy) masculine gay fiction. Don't send lengthy sample material."

How to Contact: Query or submit synopsis amd 10-12 sample pages with SASE. Reports in 1 month on queries; 2 months on mss. Simultaneous submissions OK.

Terms: Pays 5-12% royalty on wholesale price. Offers negotiable advance. Publishes ms 5 months after acceptance. Writer's guidelines for #10 SASE. Book catalog free.

Advice: Audience is "mainstream gay males, their friends and families. Keep within our guidelines and only submit material consistent with Curtis/Strongmen themes. Most importantly—keep writing!"

JOHN DANIEL AND COMPANY, PUBLISHERS, (I, II), Division of Daniel & Daniel, Publishers, Inc., Box 21922, Santa Barbara CA 93121-1922. (805)962-1780. Fax: (805)962-8835. E-mail: dandd@silcom.com. **Acquisitions:** John Daniel, fiction editor. Estab. 1980; reestablished 1985. Small independent publisher. Publishes paperback originals. Books: 55-65 lb. book text paper; offset printing; perfect-bound paperbacks; illustrations sometimes. Average print order: 2,000. First novel print order: 2,000. Published new writers within the last year. Plans 2 short story collections this year. Averages 5 total titles, 2-3 fiction titles each year. Distributes titles through Baker & Taylor, Ingram, Bookpeople, Sunbelt, Bookazine, etc. Promotes titles through bound prepub galleys to major reviewers, direct mail, reviews upon publication and sales reps in NY and the western states.

● This press has become known for belles-lettres and literary fiction, and work that addresses social issues.

Needs: "I'm open to all subjects (including nonfiction)." Literary, mainstream, short story collections. No pornographic, exploitive, illegal or badly written fiction. Recently published *Jealous-Hearted Me*, by Nancy Huddleston Packer (short stories); *The Innocent*, by Robert Taylor (novel); and *Drums*, by Brad Henderson (novel).

How to Contact: Accepts unsolicited mss. Query first. SASE. Submit outline/synopsis and 2 sample chapters. Reports in 3 weeks on queries; 2 months on mss. Simultaneous submissions OK. Sometimes critiques rejected mss.

Terms: Pays in royalties of 10% of net minimum. Sends galleys to author.

Advice: "Write for the pleasure and joy of writing. Let us see the writing that meant the most to you in the writing process. There are practical and learnable reasons why good fiction is better (and more publishable) than bad fiction. Give me an SASE and I'll send you twelve such reasons. In the meantime, remember that the real reward of being a writer is the writing itself. Anything else you get out of it (money, love, fame. . .) is gravy."

‡**DANTE UNIVERSITY OF AMERICA PRESS, INC.**, P.O. Box 843, Brookline Village MA 02147-0843. Fax: (617)734-2046. E-mail: danteu@usa1.com. Website: http://www1.usa1.com/~danteu/. **Acquisitions:** Adolph Caso, president. "The Dante University Press exists to bring quality, educational books pertaining to our Italian heritage as well as the historical and political studies of America. Profits from the sale of these publications benefit the Foundation, bringing Dante University closer to a reality." Estab. 1975. Publishes hardcover and trade paperback originals and reprints. Publishes 5 titles/year. Average print order for a first book is 3,000.

Needs: Translations from Italian and Latin. Recently published *Rogue Angel*, by Carol Damioli.

How to Contact: Query first with SASE. Reports in 2 months.

Terms: Pays royalty. Negotiable advance. Publishes ms 10 months after acceptance.

DARK HORSE COMICS, INC., (I, IV), 10956 SE Main St., Milwaukie OR 97222. (503)652-8815. Fax: (503)654-9440. E-mail: jamier@dhorse.com. Website: http://www.dhorse.com (includes guidelines, overview of titles). **Acquisitions:** Jamie S. Rich. Estab. 1986. "Dark Horse publishes all kinds of comics material, and we try not to limit ourselves to any one genre or any one philosophy. Most of our comics are intended for readers 15-40, though we also publish material that is accessible to younger readers." Comic books: newsprint or glossy paper, each title 24-28 pages. Averages 10-30 total titles each year. Publishes 3-5 new writers/year. Distributes through direct market, bookstores and newsstands.

● Dark Horse Press's comics have won several awards including the Eisner, Harvey and Parent's Choice awards.

Needs: Comics: adventure, childrens/juvenile, fantasy (space fantasy, super hero, sword and sorcery), horror, humor/satire, mystery/suspense (private eye/hardboiled), psychic/supernatural, romance (contemporary), science fiction (hard science, soft/sociological), western (traditional). Proposals or scripts for comic books only. Plans anthology. Recently published comics by Stan Sakai, Jay Stephens and Paul Pope. Published short story comic anthologies: *Dark Horse Presents*.

How to Contact: Does not accept unsolicited mss. Query letter first. Include one-page bio, list of publishing credits. Send SASE or disposable copy of ms. Reports in 1-2 months. Simultaneous submissions OK.

Terms: Pays $25-100/page and 5-25 author's copies. "We usually buy first and second rights, other rights on publication." Writer's guidelines free for #10 SASE.

Advice: "Read comics. Know comics. Understand comics. Have a reason to want to publish your story as a comic, beyond it not working as a novel or screenplay. Obtain copies of our Writer's Guidelines before making a submission."

‡MAY DAVENPORT, PUBLISHERS, 26313 Purissima Rd., Los Altos Hills CA 94022. (415)948-6499. Fax: (415)948-6499. **Acquisitions:** May Davenport, editor/publisher. Estab. 1976. "We prefer books which can be *used* in high schools as supplementary readings in English or creative writing courses. Reading skills have to be taught, and novels by humorous authors can be more pleasant to read than Hawthorne's or Melville's novels, war novels, or novels about past generations. Humor has a place in literature." Publishes hardcover and trade paperback originals. Publishes 4 titles/year.

Imprint(s): md Books (nonfiction and fiction).

Needs: Humor, literary. "We want to focus on novels junior and senior high school teachers can share with their reluctant readers in their classrooms." Recently published *Drivers Ed is Dead*, by Pat Delgado; *The Newman Assignment*, by Kurt Haberl; and *When the Dancing Ends*, by Judy Hairfield.

How to Contact: Reports in 1 month.

Terms: Pays 15% royalty on retail price. No advance. Publishes ms 1 year after acceptance. Book catalog and writer's guidelines for #10 SASE.

Advice: "Since the TV-oriented youth in schools today do not like to read or to write, why not create books for that impressionable and captive audience? Great to work with talented writers especially when writers are happy and inspired within themselves."

‡✹ROBERT DAVIES PUBLISHING, #311, 4999 St. Catherine St. W, Montreal, Quebec H3Z 1T3 Canada. Fax: (514)481-9973. E-mail: rdppub@vir.com. Website: http://www.rdppub.com. Publishes trade paperback originals and reprints. Publishes 20% previously unpublished writers/year. Publishes 32 titles/year.

Needs: Adventure, fantasy, gay/lesbian, historical, juvenile, literary, mainstream/contemporary, mystery.

How to Contact: Query with SASE. Reports in 9 months. Simultaneous submissions OK.

Terms: Pays 10-15% royalty on retail price. Offers $2,000 advance if warranted. Publishes ms 1 year after acceptance. Book catalog for 9×12 SAE with 2 first-class Canadian stamps.

Advice: Audience is general to university. "Don't oversell your idea. Present it rationally and neatly."

DAW BOOKS, INC., (I), Division of Penguin Putnam Inc., 375 Hudson St., New York NY 10014. Fax: (212)366-2090. Publishers: Elizabeth R. Wollheim and Sheila E. Gilbert. **Acquisitions**: Peter Stampfel, submissions editor. Estab. 1971. Publishes paperback originals and hardcover originals. Books: Illustrations sometimes; average print and number of first novels published per year vary widely. Averages 40 new titles plus 40 or more reissues, all fiction, each year. Occasionally critiques rejected mss.

Needs: Science fiction (hard science, soft sociological), fantasy and mainstream thrillers only. Recently published *Owl Flight*, by Mercedes Lackey; *Beneath the Vaulted Hills*, by Sean Russell; *Bright Shadow*, by Elizabeth Forrest; and *The Mageborn Traitor*, by Melanie Rawn. Publishes many original anthologies including *Sword &*

WRITER-TO-WRITER

Grow a tough and thick skin. This is a brutal business that doesn't get emotionally easier as you gain success. One horrible letter can erase the good feelings of a hundred positive ones. One negative review can destroy your love of writing for days or weeks. You have to keep an even keel—your feet have to stay on the ground with each positive milestone, such as a best-seller list or a glowing review. And you cannot fall into a hole every time someone tells you your work stinks. Someone is always willing and happy to tell you your work stinks!

R.A. Salvatore
The Demon Awakens, Del Rey Books

Sorceress (edited by Marion Zimmer Bradley); *Cat Fantastic* (edited by Andre Norton and Martin H. Greenberg). "You may write to the editors (after looking at the anthology) for guidelines % DAW."
How to Contact: Submit complete ms with return postage and SASE. Usually reports in 3-5 months on mss, but in special cases may take longer. "No agent required."
Terms: Pays an advance against royalties. Sends galleys to author.
Advice: "We strongly encourage new writers. Research your publishers and submit only appropriate work."

‡**DAWN PUBLICATIONS**, 14618 Tyler Foote Rd., Nevada City CA 95959. (800)545-7475. Website: http://www.dawnpub.com. **Acquisitions:** Glenn J. Hovemann, editor. "Dawn Publications is dedicated to inspiring in children a sense of appreciation for all life on earth." Publishes hardcover and trade paperback originals. Publishes 6 titles/year.
Needs: Childrens/juvenile. Nature awareness and inspiration. Recently published *Walking with Mama*, by Barbara Stynes (shows the sweetness and intimacy of a walk in nature by toddler and mother).
How to Contact: Query with SASE. Reports in 2 months. Simultaneous submissions OK.
Terms: Pays royalty on wholesale price. Publishes ms 1 year after acceptance. Writer's guidelines and book catalog for #10 SASE.

‡**DEAD LETTER**, Imprint of St. Martin's Press, 175 Fifth Ave., New York NY 10010. (212)674-5151. **Acquisitions:** Joe Veltre, editor. Publishes trade paperback originals and reprints, mass market paperback originals and reprints. Publishes 36 titles/year.
Needs: Mystery. Recently published *A Stiff Risotto*, by Lou Jane Temple; and *Mortal Causes*, by Ian Rankin.
How to Contact: Query with synopsis, 3 sample chapters and SASE. Agented fiction 93%. Simultaneous submissions OK.
Terms: Pays variable royalty on net price. Advance varies.

‡**DEL REY BOOKS**, Subsidiary of Ballantine Books, 201 E. 50 St., New York NY 10022. (212)572-2677. E-mail: delray@randomhouse.com. Website: http://www.randomhouse.com/delrey/. **Acquisitions:** Jill Benjamin. Estab. 1977. "In terms of mass market, we basically created the field of fantasy bestsellers. Not that it didn't exist before, but we put the mass into mass market." Publishes hardcover originals and paperback originals and reprints. Plans 6-7 first novels this year. Publishes 60 titles each year, all fiction. Sometimes critiques rejected mss.
Needs: Fantasy and science fiction. Fantasy must have magic as an intrinsic element to the plot. No flying-saucer, Atlantis or occult novels. Published *The Demon Awakens*, by R.A. Salvatore; *The Chronicles of Pern*, by Anne McCaffrey (science fiction/hardcover original); *The Shining Ones*, by David Eddings (fantasy/hardcover original); and *Jack the Bodiless*, by Julian May (science fiction/paperback reprint).
How to Contact: Accepts unsolicited mss. Submit cover letter with complete manuscript or brief outline/synopsis and *first* 3 chapters. Prefers complete ms. Address science fiction to SF editor; fantasy to fantasy editor. Reports in 2 weeks on queries; 2-10 months on mss.
Terms: Pays in royalties; "advance is competitive." Publishes ms 1 year after acceptance. Sends galleys to author. Writer's guidelines for #10 SASE.
Advice: Has been publishing "more fiction and hardcovers, because the market is there for them. Read a lot of science fiction and fantasy, such as works by Anne McCaffrey, David Eddings, Larry Niven, Arthur C. Clarke, Terry Brooks, Frederik Pohl, Barbara Hambly. When writing, pay particular attention to plotting (and a satisfactory conclusion) and characters (sympathetic and well-rounded) because those are what readers look for."

‡**DELACORTE PRESS**, Imprint of Dell Publishing, Division of Bantam Doubleday Dell, 1540 Broadway, New York NY 10036. (212)354-6500. Editor-in-Chief: Leslie Schnur. **Acquisitions**: (Ms.) Jackie Cantor (women's fiction); Steve Ross (commercial nonfiction and fiction). Publishes hardcover and trade paperback originals. Publishes 36 titles/year.
Needs: Mainstream/contemporary. No mss for children's or young adult books accepted in this division. Recently published *Killing Time in St. Cloud*, by Judith Guest; *The Horse Whisperer*, by Nicholas Evans; *Hardcase*, by Bill Pronzin; and *The Magic Bullet*, by Harry Stein.
How to Contact: Query with outline, first 3 chapters or brief proposal. Accepts simultaneous submissions.

WRITER-TO-WRITER

I thought my novel *Errands* was finished, but it wasn't. When I finally realized this, I settled down to do yet another final draft, cut out 100 pages, moved some incidents around; in other words, I let go of the autobiographical and let the novel become true fiction. But it was hard.
Judith Guest
Killing Time in St. Cloud, Delacorte Press

Reports in 3-4 months.

Terms: Pays 7½-12½ royalty. Advance varies. Publishes ms 2 years after acceptance, but varies. Guidelines for 9×12 SASE.

DELACORTE/DELL BOOKS FOR YOUNG READERS/DOUBLEDAY, (II, III, IV), Division of Bantam Doubleday Dell Publishing Group, Inc., 1540 Broadway, New York NY 10036. See listing for Bantam/Doubleday/Dell Books for Young Readers.

DELL PUBLISHING, Division of Bantam Doubleday Dell, 1540 Broadway, New York NY 10036. (212)354-6500. Estab. 1922. Publishes hardcover and paperback originals and paperback reprints.
Imprint(s): Delacorte Press, Delta, Dell, Dial Press, Laurel.
Needs: See below for individual imprint requirements.
How to Contact: Reports in 4-5 months. Simultaneous submissions OK. "Submit entire ms with a cover letter and narrative synopsis. Limit synopsis to 10 pages. Dell is comprised of several imprints, each with its own editorial department. Please review carefully the following information and direct your submissions to the appropriate department. Your envelope must be marked: Attention: (One of the following names of imprints), Dell Editorial Department—Book Proposal. Enclose SASE."
DELACORTE: Publishes in hardcover; looks for top-notch commercial fiction and nonfiction; 35 titles/year.
DELTA: Publishes trade paperbacks including original fiction and nonfiction; 20 titles/year.
DELL: Publishes mass-market and trade paperbacks; looks for family sagas, historical romances, sexy modern romances, adventure and suspense thrillers, mysteries, psychic/supernatural, horror, war novels, fiction and nonfiction. 200 titles/year.
DIAL PRESS: Publishes literary fiction and high-end nonfiction 2 titles/year.
Terms: Pays 6-15% in royalties; offers advance. Sends galleys to author.
Advice: Not presently publishing any fantasy books. "Don't get your hopes up. Query first only with 4-page synopsis plus SASE. Study the paperback racks in your local drugstore. We encourage first novelists. We also encourage all authors to seek agents."

‡**DELL PUBLISHING ISLAND**, Imprint of Dell Publishing, Division of Bantam Doubleday Dell, 1540 Broadway, New York NY 10036. (212)354-6500. **Acquisitions**: Leslie Schnur, editor-in-chief. Publishes trade paperback originals and reprints. Publishes bestseller fiction and nonfiction. Publishes 12 titles/year.
Needs: Mystery, romance, suspense. Recently published *Runaway Jury*, by John Grisham (suspense).
How to Contact: Reports in 4-6 months on queries. Simultaneous submissions OK.
Terms: Pays 7½-12½% royalty on retail price. Advance varies. Publishes ms 1 year after acceptance. Book catalog for 9×12 SAE and 3 first class stamps.

‡**DELTA TRADE PAPERBACKS**, Imprint of Dell Publishing, Division of Bantam Doubleday Dell, 1540 Broadway, New York NY 10036. (212)354-6500. **Acquisitions**: Leslie Schnur, editor-in-chief. Publishes trade paperback originals, mostly light, humorous material and books on pop culture. Publishes 36 titles/year.
Needs: Erotica, literary, short story collections. Recently published *Fast Greens*, by Turk Pipkin; *Last Days of the Dog Men*, by Brad Watson (stories); and *Sacred Dust*, by David Hill.
How to Contact: Query with synopsis, 2-3 sample chapters or complete ms and SASE. Reports in 4-6 months on queries. Simultaneous submissions OK.
Terms: Pays 7½-12½% royalty on retail price. Advance varies. Publishes ms 1 year after acceptance. Book catalog for 9×12 SAE and 3 first class stamps.

‡**DENLINGERS PUBLISHERS, LTD.**, P.O. Box 2300, Centreville VA 20122-8445. **Acquisitions:** William W. Denlinger. Publishes hardcover and trade paperback originals. Publishes 10 titles/year.
Needs: Adventure, feminist, historical, mainstream/contemporary, suspense. "We may consider other subjects. We are always looking for outstanding material."
How to Contact: Query with SASE. Reports in 1 week on queries; 2 months on mss.
Terms: Pays 5-10% royalty on wholesale price or makes outright purchase of $300-3,000. Publishes ms 1 year after acceptance. Book catalog for #10 SASE.
Advice: "We only accept manuscripts that are written on a computer and have a disk available in a program that we can use or convert."

‡**DERRYNANE PRESS**, 348 Hartford Turnpike, Hampton CT 06247. (860)455-0039. **Acquisitions:** Peter Cherici, executive editor. Publishes hardcover and trade paperback originals and reprints. Publishes 4 titles/year, 1 imprint title/year.
Imprint(s): Golden Grove Books.
Needs: Historical, literary. "Irish and Celtic themes only." Published *Under Pegasus*, by David Beckman.
How to Contact: Submit synopsis and 2 sample chapters with SASE. Reports in 1 month on queries and mss. Simultaneous submissions OK.
Terms: Pays 8-12% royalty on wholesale price on discounts of 55% or more. Offers $500-1,000 advance. Publishes ms 9 months after acceptance. Book catalog free.

Advice: "We have an Irish-American ethnic audience, and material must be attuned to our market."

DIAL BOOKS FOR YOUNG READERS, (V), Division of Penguin Putnam Inc., 375 Hudson St., New York NY 10014. (212)366-2000. Editor-in-Chief/Pres./Publisher: Phyllis Fogelman. Editorial Assistant: Victoria Wells. **Acquisitions:** Submissions Editor. Estab. 1961. Trade children's book publisher, "looking for agented picture book mss and novels." Publishes hardcover originals. Plans 1 first novel this year. Averages 100 titles, mainly fiction.
Imprint(s): Pied Piper Books, Easy-to-Read Books.
Needs: Juvenile (1-9 yrs.) including: animal, fantasy, spy/adventure, contemporary and easy-to-read; young adult/teen (10-16 years) including: fantasy/science fiction, literary and commercial mystery and fiction. Published *Sam and the Tigers*, by Julius Lester and Jerry Pinckney; *Language of Doves*, by Rosemary Wells; and *Great Interactive Dream Machine*, by Richard Peck.
How to Contact: Does not accept unsolicited mss. Query with SASE. Occasionally critiques or comments on rejected ms.
Terms: Pays advance against royalties.
Advice: "To agents: We are publishing more fiction books than in the past, and we publish only hardcover originals, most of which are fiction. At this time we are particularly interested in both fiction and nonfiction for the middle grades, and innovative picture book manuscripts. We also are looking for easy-to-reads for first and second graders. Plays, collections of games and riddles, and counting and alphabet books are generally discouraged. Before submitting a manuscript to a publisher, it is a good idea to request a catalog to see what the publisher is currently publishing. We will send a catalog to anyone who sends 4 first-class stamps with a self-addressed, 9 × 12 envelope."

‡DIAL PRESS, Imprint of Dell Publishing, 1540 Broadway, New York NY 10036. (212)354-6500. Fax: (212)782-9698. Website: http://www.bbd.com. **Acquisitions:** Susan Kamil, vice president, editorial director. Estab. 1924. "Dial Press is dedicated to the publication of quality fiction and nonfiction." Publishes 6 titles/year.
Needs: Ethnic, literary. Recently published *Drinking: A Love Story*, by Caroline Knapp (memoir); *The Giant's House*, by Elizabeth McCracken; and *Animal Husbandry*, by Laura Zigman (humorous novel).
How to Contact: Query with SASE. Agented submissions only. Reports in 2 months. Simultaneous submissions OK.
Terms: Pays royalty on retail price. Offers $25,000-500,000 advance. Publishes ms 1-2 years after acceptance.

‡DOUBLEDAY ADULT TRADE, (III), a division of Bantam Doubleday Dell Publishing Group, Inc., 1540 Broadway., New York NY 10036. (212)782-9911. Fax: (212)782-9700. Website: http://www.bdd.com. **Acquisitions:** Patricia Mulcahy, vice president/editor-in-chief. Estab. 1897. Publishes hardcover and paperback originals and paperback reprints.
Imprint(s): Anchor Press (contact Martha Lewis); Currency (contact Harriet Rubin); Main Street (contact Bruce Tracy); **Nan A. Talese** (contact Nan A. Talese); Religious Division (contact Eric Major); Image (contact Trace Murphy).
Needs: "Doubleday is not able to consider unsolicited queries, proposals or manuscripts unless submitted through a bona fide literary agent, except that we will consider fiction for Perfect Crime line, romance and western imprints." Recently published *Simple Justice*, by John Morgan Wilson.
How to Contact: Send copy of complete ms (60,000-80,000 words) to Perfect Crime Editor, Loveswept Editor or Western Editor as appropriate. Sufficient postage (or IRC) for return via fourth class mail must accompany ms. Reports in 2-6 months.
Terms: Pays in royalties; offers advance. Publishes ms 1 year after acceptance.

♣DOUBLEDAY CANADA LIMITED, 105 Bond St., Toronto, Ontario M5B 1Y3 Canada. No unsolicited submissions. Prefers not to share information.

‡DOWN EAST BOOKS, Division of Down East Enterprise, Inc., P.O. Box 679, Camden ME 04843-0679. Fax: (207)594-7215. E-mail: adevine@downeast.com. Managing Editor: Karin Womer. **Acquisitions:** Acquisitions Editor. Estab. 1954. "We are primarily a regional publisher concentrating on Maine or New England."

WRITER-TO-WRITER

In the last moment before waking, in that fuzzy limbo between conscious and subconscious dreaming, I fix on the day's work ahead—a line, a scene, a chapter. I let it play in my mind, see where it goes, what it shows me. Then I go straight to my desk and start writing.

    John Morgan Wilson
    Simple Justice, Doubleday

Publishes hardcover and trade paperback originals and trade paperback reprints. Publishes 20-24 titles/year. Average print order for a first book is 3,000.

- Down East Books has published Elisabeth Ogilvie, Michael McIntosh, Robin Hansen, Peter F. Stevens, Lee Wulff.

Imprint(s): Silver Quill (outdoor sportsmen market).

Needs: Juvenile, regional. "We publish 1-2 juvenile titles/year (fiction and non-fiction), and 1-2 adult fiction titles/year." Recently published *A Show of Hands*, by David Crossman (regional mystery); *A Penny for a Hundred*, by Ethel Pochocki (juvenile); and *Saturday Night at Moody's Diner*, by Tim Sample (humor).

How to Contact: Query first with SASE. Reports in 2 months. Simultaneous submissions OK.

Terms: Pays 10-15% on receipts. Offers $200 average advance. Publishes ms 1 year after acceptance. Writer's guidelines for 9×12 SAE with 3 first-class stamps.

‡DUFOUR EDITIONS, (II,IV), P.O. Box 7, Chester Springs PA 19425. (610)458-5005. Fax: (610)458-7103. **Acquisitions:** Thomas Laudie, associate publisher. Estab. 1940s. Small independent publisher, tending toward literary fiction. Publishes hardcover and paperback originals and reprints. Publishes 6-7 total titles/year; 1-2 fiction titles.

Needs: Feminist, literary, short story collections, translations. Recently published *The Carriage Stone*, by Holmebakk (translation).

How to Contact: Accepts unsolicited mss. Send query letter only first. Include estimated word count, bio and list of publishing credits. Include SASE for reply. Reports in 2-3 weeks on queries; 2-3 months on mss.

♣DUNDURN PRESS, (II), 2181 Queen St. E., #301, Toronto, Ontario M4E 1E5 Canada. (416)698-0454. Fax: (416)698-1102. E-mail: editorial@dundurn.com. Publisher: Kirk Howard; **Acquisitions:** Barry Jowett and Nigel Wood, senior editors. Estab. 1972. Subsidiaries include Hounslow Press, Simon & Pierre, Boardwalk Books and Umbrella Press. Midsize independent publisher with plans to expand. Publishes hardcover and paperback originals.

Needs: Contemporary, literary. Recently published *Love Minus One*, by Norma Harrs; *Grave Deeds*, by Betsy Struthers; and *Sherlock Holmes: Travels in the Canadian West*, by Ronald Weyman.

How to Contact: Accepts unsolicited mss. Submit outline/synopsis and sample chapters. SASE for ms. Simultaneous submissions OK. Accepts electronic submissions. Unsolicited mss *not* accepted by e-mail.

Terms: Pays royalties of 10%; 10 author's copies. Sends galleys to author. Publishes ms 6-9 months after acceptance. Book catalog free on request for SASE.

‡THOMAS DUNNE BOOKS, Imprint of St. Martin's Press, 175 Fifth Ave., New York NY 10010. (212)674-5151. **Acquisitions:** Tom Dunne. Publishes wide range of fiction and nonfiction. Publishes hardcover originals, trade paperback originals and reprints. Publishes 90 titles/year.

Needs: Mainstream/contemporary, mystery/suspense, "women's" thriller. Recently published *Brandenburg*, by Glenn Meade (thriller); and *Birds of Prey*, by Wilbur Smith.

How to Contact: Query or submit synopsis and 100 sample pages with SASE. Reports in 2 months on queries. Simultaneous submissions OK.

Terms: Pays 10-15% royalty on retail price for hardcover, 7½% for paperback. Advance varies with project. Publishes ms 1 year after acceptance. Book catalog and writer's guidelines free.

‡DUTTON CHILDREN'S BOOKS, Imprint of Penguin Putnam Inc., 375 Hudson St., New York NY 10014. (212)366-2000. **Acquisitions:** Lucia Monfried, editor-in-chief. Estab. 1852. Dutton Children's Books publishes fiction and nonfiction for readers ranging from preschoolers to young adults on a variety of subjects. Publishes hardcover originals. Publishes 70 titles/year.

- At press time, Dutton Children's Books was being restructured. Verify current information.

Needs: Dutton Children's Books has a complete publishing program that includes picture books; easy-to-read books; and fiction for all ages, from "first-chapter" books to young adult readers. Recently published *The Iron Ring*, by Lloyd Alexander.

How to Contact: Query with SASE.

Terms: Pays royalty on retail price.

DUTTON SIGNET, (III), Division of Penguin Putnam Inc., 375 Hudson St., New York NY 10014. (212)366-2000. **Acquisitions:** Michaela Hamilton, vice president/publisher (fiction), Signet and Onyx; Arnold Dolin,

MARKET CONDITIONS are constantly changing! If you're still using this book and it is 1999 or later, buy the newest edition of *Novel & Short Story Writer's Market* at your favorite bookstore or order from Writer's Digest Books.

associate publisher, Dutton, publisher, Plume; Laura Gilman, editorial director, Roc; Rosemary Ahern, senior editor (literary fiction); Joe Pittman, editor (mystery); Diedre Mullane, senior editor (multicultural literary fiction); Audrey LeFehr, executive editor (women's fiction). Estab. 1948. Publishes hardcover and paperback originals and paperback reprints. Published new writers within the last year.

Imprint(s): Onyx, Topaz, Mentor, Signet Classic, Plume, Plume Fiction, Meridian, **Roc**.

Needs: "All kinds of commercial and literary fiction, including mainstream, historical, Regency, New Age, western, thriller, science fiction, fantasy, gay. Full length novels and collections." Published *Trial by Fire*, by Nancy Taylor Rosenberg; *Black Cross*, by Greg Iles; and *The Takeover*, by Stephen Frey.

How to Contact: Agented mss only. Queries accepted with SASE. "State type of book and past publishing projects." Simultaneous submissions OK. Reports in 3 months.

Terms: Pays in royalties and author's copies; offers advance. Sends galleys to author. Publishes ms 18 months after acceptance. Book catalog for SASE.

Advice: "Write the complete manuscript and submit it to an agent or agents. We publish The Trailsman, Battletech and other western and science fiction series—all by ongoing authors. Would be receptive to ideas for new series in commercial fiction."

E.M. PRESS, INC., (I, IV), P.O. Box 4057, Manassas VA 20108. (540)439-0304. **Acquisitions**: Beth Miller, editor; Mel Parature, fiction editor. Estab. 1991. "Expanding small press." Publishes paperback and hardcover originals. Books: 50 lb. text paper; offset printing; perfect binding; illustrations. Average print order: 1,200-5,000. Averages 8 total titles, fiction, poetry and nonfiction, each year. Distributes titles through wholesalers and direct sales. Promotes titles through radio and TV, Interview Report, direct mailings and Ingram's catalogs.

Needs: "We are focusing more on Virginia/Maryland/DC authors and subject matter. We're emphasizing nonfiction and we're launching a new children's line, though we still consider 'marketable' fiction. Recently published *The Relationship*, by John Hyman (young adult); *Santa's New Reindeer*, by Judie Schrecker; *I, Anna Kerry*, by William Giannini (literary); and *How Will They Get That Heart Down Your Throat*, by Karen Walton.

How to Contact: Accepts unsolicited mss. Submit outline/synopsis and sample chapters or complete ms with cover letter. Include estimated word count. Send a SASE for reply, return of ms or send a disposable copy of the ms. Agented fiction 10%. Reports in 3 months on queries; 3 months on mss. Simultaneous submissions OK.

Terms: Amount of royalties and advances varies. Sends galleys to author. Publishes ms 18 months after acceptance. Writer's guidelines for SASE.

Advice: Publishing "less fiction, more regional work, though we look for fiction that will do well in secondary rights sales."

‡EAKIN PRESS, (II, IV), P.O. Box 90159, Austin TX 78709-0159. (512)288-1771. Fax: (512)288-1813. **Acquisitions**: Edwin M. Eakin, editorial director; Melissa Roberts, Virginia Messer. Estab. 1978. Eakin specializes in Texana and Western Americana for adults and juveniles. Publishes hardcover originals. Books: Old style (acid-free); offset printing; case binding; illustrations. Average print order 2,000. First novel print order 5,000. Published new writers within the last year. Plans 2 first novels this year. Averages 80 total titles each year.

Imprint(s): Nortex.

Needs: Juvenile. Specifically needs historical fiction for school market, juveniles set in Southwest for Southwest grade schoolers. Published *Wall Street Wives*, by Ande Ellen Winkler; *Jericho Day*, by Warren Murphy; and *Blood Red Sun*, by Stephen Mertz.

How to Contact: Prefers queries, but accepts unsolicited mss. Send SASE for guidelines. Agented fiction 5%. Simultaneous submissions OK. Reports in 3 months on queries.

Terms: Pays royalties; average advance: $1,000. Sends galleys to author. Publishes ms 1-1½ years after acceptance. Writers guidelines for #10 SASE. Book catalog for 75¢.

Advice: "Juvenile fiction only with strong Southwest theme. We receive around 600 queries or unsolicited mss a year."

THE ECCO PRESS, (II), 100 W. Broad St., Hopewell NJ 08525. (609)466-4748. **Acquisitions**: Ruth Greenskin; Daniel Halpern, editor-in-chief. Estab. 1970. Small publisher. Publishes hardcover and paperback originals and reprints. Books: acid-free paper; offset printing; Smythe-sewn binding; occasional illustrations. Averages 60 total titles, 20 fiction titles each year. Average first novel print order: 3,000 copies.

Needs: "We can publish possibly one or two original novels a year." No science fiction, romantic novels, western (cowboy) or historical novels. Published *Where Is Here*, by Joyce Carol Oates; *Have You Seen Me*, by Elizabeth Graver; and *Coming Up Down Home*, by Cecil Brown.

How to Contact: Accepts unsolicited mss. Query first with SASE and 1-page bio. Reports in 3-6 months, depending on the season.

Terms: Pays in royalties. Advance is negotiable. Publishes ms 1 year after acceptance. Writer's guidelines for SASE. Book catalog free on request.

Advice: "We are always interested in first novels and feel it's important they be brought to the attention of the reading public."

‡EDGE BOOKS, Imprint of Henry Holt & Co., 115 W. 18th St., New York NY 10011. (212)886-9200. **Acquisitions:** Marc Aronson, executive editor. Publishes hardcover originals. Publishes 4-5 titles/year.

Needs: Young adult. Recently published *Shizko's Daughter*, by Kyoko Mori; and *The Long Season of Rain*, by Helen Kim (novels).

How to Contact: Query or submit complete ms. Reports in 4 months on queries. Simultaneous submissions OK.

Terms: Pays 6-7½% royalty on retail price. Advance varies. Publishes ms 18 months after acceptance. Book catalog free from Henry Holt (same address).

Advice: "All our titles are international or multicultural coming-of-age fiction and nonfiction. We are very open to new authors, but because we publish so few titles, the standards are very high. The emphasis is on voice and literary quality, rather than subject."

‡♥**LES ÉDITIONS DU VERMILLON**, 305 St. Patrick St., Ottawa, Ontario K1N 5K4 Canada. (613)241-4032. **Acquisitions**: Monique Bertoli, general manager. Publishes trade paperback originals. Publishes 30% previously unpublished writers/year. Publishes 15 books/year.

Needs: Juvenile, literary, religious, short story collections, young adult. Recently published *Beaurivage Tome I Les eaux chantentes Roman*, by Jean-Eudes Dubé; *Une affaire de famille*, by Jean-François Somain; and *Lettres á deux mains*, by Jean-Louis Grosmaire.

How to Contact: Query first. Reports in 1 year on mss.

Terms: Pays 10% royalty. Offers no advance. Publishes ms 18 months after acceptance. Book catalog free.

‡♥**ÉDITIONS LA LIBERTÉ INC.**, 3020 Chemin Ste-Foy, Ste-Foy, Quebec G1X 3V6 Canada. Phone/fax: (418)658-3763. **Acquisitions**: Nathalie Roy, director of operations. Publishes trade paperback originals. Publishes 75% previously unpublished writers/year. Publishes 4-5 titles/year.

Needs: Historical, juvenile, literary, mainstream/contemporary, short story collections, young adult. Recently published *L'espace Montauban/Le Dernier Roman Scout*, by Jean Désy.

How to Contact: Query with synopsis. Simultaneous submissions OK.

Terms: Pays 10% royalty on retail price. Accepts only mss written in French. Publishes ms 4 months after acceptance. Book catalog free.

‡♥**EDITIONS PHIDAL**, 5740 Ferrier, Mont-Royal, Quebec H4P 1M7 Canada. (514)738-0202. **Acquisitions**: Lionel Soussan, chief editor. Publishes hardcover and mass market paperback originals. Publishes 5% previously unpublished writers/year. Publishes 50-70 titles/year.

Needs: Juvenile. "We specialize in children's books ages three and up. Illustrations are very helpful." Recently published *Les Voyelles*, by Nicole Sallenave (children's).

How to Contact: Submit synopsis and 3-5 sample chapters. Reports in 2 months on mss. Simultaneous submissions OK.

Terms: Pays 10% royalty on retail price. Publishes ms 6 months after acceptance.

Advice: Audience is children, both in English and French languages. Ages 3 and up.

WM. B. EERDMANS PUBLISHING CO., (II), 255 Jefferson Ave. SE, Grand Rapids MI 49503-4570. (800)253-7521. Fax: (616)459-6540. **Acquisitions**: Jon Pott, editor-in-chief, fiction editor (adult fiction); Amy De Vries, fiction editor (children). Estab. 1911. "Although Eerdmans publishes some regional books and other nonreligious titles, it is essentially a religious publisher whose titles range from the academic to the semi-popular. Our children's fiction is meant to help a child explore life in God's world and to foster a child's exploration of her or his faith. We are a midsize independent publisher. We publish a few adult novels a year, and these tend to address spiritual issues from a Christian perspective." Publishes hardcover and paperback originals and reprints. Published new writers within the last year. Plans 2-3 first novels this year. Averages 140 total titles, 10-15 fiction titles (mostly for children) each year. Sometimes critiques or comments on rejected ms.

Imprint(s): Eerdmans Books for Young Readers.

● Wm. B. Eerdmans Publishing Co.'s titles have won awards from the American Library Association and The American Bookseller's Association.

Needs: Religious (children's, general, fantasy, mystery/suspense, thriller). Recently published *Come Sunday*, by Nikki Grimes (children's).

How to Contact: Accepts unsolicited mss. Query with outline/synopsis and 2 sample chapters. Accepts unsolicited queries and correspondence by fax. Include 150- to 200-word bio and list of publishing credits. SASE for reply or send a disposable copy of ms. Agented fiction 25%. Reports in 3-4 weeks on queries; 2-3 months on mss. Simultaneous submissions OK, "if notified." Electronic submission (fax) OK.

Terms: Pays royalties of 7% minimum; 10% maximum. Offers negotiable advance. Sends galleys to author. Publishes ms 12-18 months after acceptance. Writer's guidelines and book catalog free.

Advice: "Our readers are educated and fairly sophisticated, and we are looking for novels with literary merit."

♥**EKSTASIS EDITIONS, (IV)**, Box 8474, Main P.O., Victoria, British Columbia V8W 3S1 Canada. Phone/fax: (604)385-3378. **Acquisitions**: Richard Olafson, publisher. Estab. 1982. Independent publisher. Publishes paperback originals. Books: acid free paper; offset printing; perfect/Smyth binding. Average print order: 1,000-3,000. First novel print order: 1,000-2,000. Published new writers within the last year. Plans 3 first novels this year. Averages 14 total titles, 5 fiction titles each year.

Needs: Erotica, experimental, literary, mainstream/contemporary, New Age/mystic/spiritual, short story collections, translations. Published *Bread of the Birds*, by André Carpentier.
How to Contact: Accepts unsolicited mss. Submit complete ms with cover letter. Include estimated word count, bio, list of publishing credits. SASE for reply. Reports in 5 months on queries; 4 months on mss.
Terms: Pays royalties of 6%. Pays 75 author's copies. Sends galleys to author. Publishes ms 6 months after acceptance. Book catalog available for $2.

‡♥**EMPYREAL PRESS**, P.O. Box 1746, Place Du Parc, Montreal, Quebec HZW 2R7 Canada. Website: www.generation.net/~talisher/empyreal. **Acquisitions**: Geof Isherwood, publisher. "Our mission is the publishing of Canadian and other literature which doesn't fit into any standard 'mold'—writing which is experimental yet grounded in discipline, imagination." Publishes trade paperback originals. Publishes 50% previously unpublished writers/year. Publishes 1-4 titles/year.
Needs: Experimental, feminist, gay/lesbian, literary, short story collections. Recently published *Winter, Spring, Summer, Fall*, by Robert Sandiford (short stories).
How to Contact: No unsolicited mss.
Terms: Pays 10% royalty on wholesale price. Offers $300 (Canadian) advance. Book catalog for #10 SASE.

PAUL S. ERIKSSON, PUBLISHER, (II), P.O. Box 62, Forest Dale VT 05745. (802)247-4210 Fax: (802)247-4256. **Acquisitions**: Paul S. Eriksson, editor; Peggy Eriksson, associate publisher/co-editor. Estab. 1960. "We look for intelligence, excitement and saleability." Publishes hardcover and paperback originals. First novel print order: 3,000-5,000.
Needs: Mainstream. Published *The Headmaster's Papers*, by Richard A. Hawley; and *Hand in Hand*, by Tauno Yliruusi.
How to Contact: Query first. Publishes ms an average of 6 months after acceptance.
Terms: Pays 10-15% in royalties; advance offered if necessary. Free book catalog.
Advice: "Our taste runs to serious fiction."

M. EVANS & CO., INC., (II), 216 E. 49th St., New York NY 10017. (212)688-2810. Fax: (212)486-4544. E-mail: mevans@spiynet.com. Contact: Editor. Estab. 1960. Publishes hardcover and trade paper nonfiction and a small fiction list. Publishes 30-40 titles each year.
Needs: "Small general trade publisher specializing in nonfiction titles on health, nutrition, diet, cookbooks, parenting, popular psychology." Published *A Fine Italian Hand*, by William Murray; and *Presumption*, by Julia Barnett.
How to Contact: Query first with outline/synopsis and 3 sample chapters. SASE. Agented fiction: 100%. Simultaneous submissions OK.
Terms: Pays in royalties and offers advance; amounts vary. Sends galleys to author. Publishes ms 6-12 months after acceptance.

FABER AND FABER, INC., (II), 53 Shore Rd., Winchester MA 01890. Fax: (617)729-2783. **Acquisitions**: Daniel Weaver and Valerie Cimino, fiction editors. Estab. 1976. Small trade house which publishes literary fiction and collections. Averages 4-6 fiction titles each year. Distributes titles through Cornell University Press Distributors. Promotes titles through galley mailings, author tours and national publicity compaigns.
Needs: Feminist, gay, lesbian, literary. "No romances, juvenile, please." Allow 2 months for response. Recently published *A Child Out of Alcatraz*, by Tara Ison; *Twilight at the Equator*, by Jaime Manrique (gay interest); and *Leaning Towards Infinity*, by Sue Woolfe (women's).
How to Contact: Send query and 1 or 2 sample chapters with SASE for reply. Requires synopsis/description—cannot consider ms without this. Address to Publishing Assistant.
Terms: Pays royalty on retail price; advance varies. Publishes ms 1 year after acceptance. Writer's guidelines for #10 SASE.

‡**FANFARE**, Imprint of Bantam Books, Division of Bantam Doubleday Dell, 1540 Broadway, New York NY 10036. (212)354-6500. Fax: (212)782-9523. **Acquisition:** Beth de Guzman, senior editor; Wendy McCurdy, senior editor; Stephanie Kip, associate editor; Cassie Goddard, associate editor. Fanfare's mission is "to publish a range of the best voices in women's fiction from brand new to established authors." Publishes 10-15% previously unpublished writers/year. Publishes 30 titles/year.
Needs: Publishes only romance and women's contemporary fiction. Adventure/romance, historical/romance, suspense/romance, western/romance. Length: 90,000-120,000 words. Recently published *The Unlikely Angel*, by

CHECK THE CATEGORY INDEXES, located at the back of the book, for publishers interested in specific fiction subjects.

Betina Krahn (historical romance); *Long After Midnight*, by Iris Johansen (romantic suspense); and *Stolen Hearts*, by Michelle Martin (contemporary romance).

How to Contact: *No unsolicited mss.* Query with SASE. Agented submissions only. Agented fiction 95%. Reports in 2-3 months on queries; 3-4 months on mss (accepted only upon request). Simultaneous submissions OK.

Terms: Royalty and advance negotiable. Publishes ms 12 months after acceptance.

Advice: "Be aware of what we publish and what our needs are in terms of length and content of manuscripts."

FANTAGRAPHICS BOOKS, (II, IV), 7563 Lake City Way NE, Seattle WA 98115. (206)524-1967. Fax: (206)524-2104. Publisher: Gary Groth. Estab. 1976. Publishes comic books, comics series and graphic novels. Books: offset printing; saddle-stitched periodicals and Smythe-sewn books; heavily illustrated. Publishes originals and reprints. Publishes 25 titles each month.

Needs: Comic books and graphic novels (adventure, fantasy, horror, mystery, romance, science, social parodies). "We look for subject matter that is more or less the same as you would find in mainstream fiction." Published *Blood of Palomar*, by Gilbert Hernandez; *The Dragon Bellows Saga*, by Stan Sakai; *Death of Speedy*; *Housebound with Rick Geary*; and *Little Nemo in Slumberland*.

How to Contact: Send a plot summary, pages of completed art (photocopies only) and character sketches. May send completed script if the author is willing to work with an artist of the publisher's choosing. Include cover letter and SASE. Reports in 1 month.

Terms: Pays in royalties of 8% (but must be split with artist) and advance.

FARRAR, STRAUS & GIROUX, (III), 19 Union Square W., New York NY 10003. (212)741-6900. Fax: (212)633-2427. Editor-in-Chief: Jonathan Galassi. **Acquisitions**: John Glusman, executive editor; Elizabeth Dyssegard, executive editor (Noonday Press); Elisabeth Sifton, publisher (Hill and Wang); Ethan Nosowsky, editor (North Point Press). Midsized, independent publisher of fiction, nonfiction, poetry. Publishes hardcover originals. Published new writers within the last year. Plans 2 first novels this year. Averages 100 total hardcover titles, 30 fiction titles each year.

Imprint(s): Hill & Wang, **The Noonday Press** and North Point Press.

Needs: Open. No genre material. Published *The Autobiography of My Mother*, by Jamaica Kincaid; *Smilla's Sense of Snow*, by Peter Hoeg; and *The Laws of Our Fathers*, by Scott Turow.

How to Contact: Does not accept unsolicited mss. Query first. "Vast majority of fiction is agented." Reports in 2 months. Simultaneous submissions OK.

Terms: Pays royalties (standard, subject to negotiation). Advance. Sends galleys to author. Publishes ms one year after acceptance. Writer's guidelines for #10 SASE.

FARRAR, STRAUS & GIROUX/CHILDREN'S BOOKS, (I), 19 Union Square W., New York NY 10003. (212)741-6900. Fax: (212)633-2427. E-mail: remayes@fsgee.com. **Acquisitions**: Margaret Ferguson, editor-in-chief. Estab. 1946. "We publish original and well-written material for all ages." Number of titles: 50. Published new writers within the last year. Buys juvenile mss with illustrations. Buys 25% agented fiction.

Needs: Children's picture books, juvenile novels, nonfiction. Published *Sheep in Wolves' Clothing*, by Satoshi Kitamura; *Remembering Mog*, by Colby Rodowsky; and *Starry Messenger*, by Peter Sis.

How to Contact: Submit outline/synopsis and 3 sample chapters, summary of ms and any pertinent information about author, author's writing, etc. Reports in 2 months on queries, 3 months on mss. Publishes ms 18-24 months after acceptance.

Terms: Pays in royalties; offers advance. Publishes ms 18 months after acceptance. Book catalog with 9×12 SASE and 96¢ postage.

Advice: "Study our list to avoid sending something inappropriate. Send query letters for long manuscripts; don't ask for editorial advice (just not possible, unfortunately); and send SASEs!"

‡FARTHEST STAR, Imprint of Alexander Books, 65 Macedonia Rd., Alexander NC 28701. (704)252-9515. **Acquisitions:** Ralph Roberts, publisher. Publishes trade paperback originals and reprints. Publishes 4 titles/year.

Needs: Science fiction. Recently published *Birthright: The Book of Man*, by Mike Resnick (science fiction reprint).

How to Contact: Query or submit 3 sample chapters with SASE. Reports in 1 month on queries; 3 months on mss. Simultaneous submissions OK.

Terms: Pays 12-15% royalty on wholesale price. Seldom offers advance. Publishes ms 1 year after acceptance. Writer's guidelines for #10 SASE with 2 first-class stamps. Book catalog for #10 SASE with 2 first-class stamps.

FAWCETT, (I, II, III), Division of Random House/Ballantine, 201 E. 50th St., New York NY 10022. (212)751-2600. **Acquisitions:** Leona Nevler, editor-in-chief. Estab. 1955. Major publisher of mass market and trade paperbacks. Publishes paperback originals and reprints. Prints 160 titles annually. Encourages new writers. "Always looking for *great* first novels."

Imprint(s): Ivy, Crest, Gold Medal, Columbine and Juniper.

Needs: Mysteries. Published *Noelle*, by Diana Palmer; *Writing for the Moon*, by Kristin Hannah.
How to Contact: Query with SASE. Send outline and sample chapters for adult mass market. If ms is requested, simultaneous submissions OK. Prefers letter-quality. Reports in 2-4 months.
Terms: Pays usual advance and royalties. Publishes ms 1 year after acceptance.
Advice: "Gold Medal list consists of four paperbacks per month—usually three are originals."

FC2/BLACK ICE BOOKS, (I), Unit for Contemporary Literature, Illinois State University, Normal IL 61790-4241. (309)438-3582. Fax: (309)438-3523. E-mail: ckwhite@rs6000.cmp.ilstu.edu. Co-director: Curtis White. Estab. 1974. "Publisher of innovative fiction." Publishes hardcover and paperback originals. Books: perfect/Smyth binding; illustrations. Average print order: 2,200. First novel print order: 2,200. Published new writers within the last year. Plans 2 first novels this year. Averages 10 total titles, 10 fiction titles each year. Often critiques or comments on rejected mss.
Needs: Feminist, gay, literary, science fiction (cyberpunk), short story collections. Published *Cares of the Day*, by Ivan Webster (minority); *Angry Nights*, by Larry Fondation (literary); and *Little Sisters of the Apocalypse*, by Kit Reed (science fiction).
How to Contact: Accepts unsolicited mss. Query with outline/synopsis. Include 1-page bio, list of publishing credits. SASE. Agented fiction 5%. Reports on queries in 3 weeks. Simultaneous submissions OK.
Terms: Pays royalties of 8-10%; offers $100 advance. Sends galleys to author. Publishes ms 1 year after acceptance. Writer's guidelines for SASE.
Advice: "Be familiar with our list."

THE FEMINIST PRESS AT THE CITY UNIVERSITY OF NEW YORK, City College, Wingate Building, Convent Ave. at 138th St., New York NY 10031. (212)650-8890. Fax: (212)348-1241. **Acquisitions:** Jean Casella, senior editor; Florence Howe, publisher; Sara Clough, assistant editor. Estab. 1970. "Nonprofit, tax-exempt, education and publishing organization interested in changing the curriculum, the classroom and consciousness." Publishes hardcover and paperback reprints. "We use an acid-free paper, perfect-bind our books, four color covers; and some cloth for library sales if the book has been out of print for some time; we shoot from the original text when possible. We always include a scholarly and literary afterword, since we are introducing a text to a new audience. Average print run: 4,000." Publishes no original fiction; exceptions are anthologies and international works. Averages 10-15 total titles/year; 4-8 fiction titles/year (reprints of feminist classics only). Distributes titles through Consortium Book Sales and Distribution. Promotes titles through author tours, advertising, exhibits and conferences.
Needs: Children's, contemporary, ethnic, feminist, gay, lesbian, literary, regional, science fiction, translations, women's. Recently published *Two Dreams: Short Stories*, by Shirley Geok-lin Lim; and *Unpunished: A Mystery*, by Charlotte Perkins Gilman.
How to Contact: Accepts unsolicited mss. Query first. Submit outline/synopsis and 1 sample chapter. SASE. Reports in 1 month on queries; 3 months on mss. Simultaneous submissions OK.
Terms: Pays royalties of 10% of net sales; $100 advance; 10 author's copies. Sends galleys to author. Book catalog free on request.

‡DONALD I. FINE, INC., (III), Imprint of Penguin Putnam Inc., 375 Hudson St., New York NY 10014. (212)727-3270. Fax: (212)727-3277. **Acquisitions:** Thomas Burke, associate editor. Estab. 1983. "Mini-major book publisher." Publishes hardcover originals. Published new writers within the last year. Plans 6 first novels this year. Averages 20 total titles, 12 fiction titles each year.
Needs: Adventure, historical, horror (dark fantasy, psychological), literary, military/war, mystery/suspense, thriller/espionage. Upcoming anthology themes include mystery, sports/literary. Published *A Certain Justice*, by John T. Lescroart (trial novel/mystery); *Collected Short Fiction of Bruce Jay Friedman* (literary fiction); and *Grand Jury*, by Philip Friedman (novel).
How to Contact: No unsolicited mss. Submit through agent only. Agented fiction 100%. Simultaneous submissions OK.
Terms: Pays royalties; offers negotiable advance. Publishes ms 1 year after acceptance.

FIREBRAND BOOKS, (II), 141 The Commons, Ithaca NY 14850. (607)272-0000. **Acquisitions:** Nancy K. Bereano, publisher. Estab. 1985. "Our audience includes feminists, lesbians, ethnic audiences, and other progressive people." Independent feminist and lesbian press. Publishes quality trade paperback originals. Averages 8-10 total titles each year.
　● Firebrand has won the Lambda Literary Award Organization's Publisher's Service Award.

AN IMPRINT LISTED IN BOLDFACE TYPE means there is an independent listing arranged alphabetically within this section.

Needs: Feminist, lesbian. Published *The Gilda Stories*, by Jewelle Gomez (novel); and *Stone Butch Blues*, by Leslie Feinberg (novel).
How to Contact: Accepts unsolicited mss. Submit outline/synopsis and sample chapters or send complete ms with cover letter. SASE. Reports in 2 weeks on queries; 2 months on mss. Simultaneous submissions OK with notification.
Terms: Pays royalties. Publishes ms 1 year after acceptance.

‡FJORD PRESS, (II), P.O. Box 16349, Seattle WA 98116. (206)935-7376. Fax: (206)938-1991. E-mail: fjord@h alcyon.com. Website: http://www.fjordpress.com/fjord. **Acquisitions:** Steven T. Murray, editor-in-chief. Estab. 1981. "We publish only literary novels of the highest quality." Publishes paperback originals and reprints. Books: acid-free paper; offset printing; perfect bound. Average print order: 2-3,000. First novel print order: 1,500-2,000. Published new writers within the last year. Plans 2 first novels this year. Publishes 4 total titles/year; 4 fiction titles.
Needs: Ethnic/multicultural (general, African-American), feminist, gay, lesbian, literary, mainstream/contemporary, mystery suspense (amateur sleuth only), regional (contemporary west), translations. Recently published *Runemaker*, by Tiina Nunnally (ethnic amateur sleuth); *Plenty Good Room*, by Teresa McClain-Watson (African-American mainstream); *Love Like Gumbo*, by Nancy Rawles (Creole family saga).
How to Contact: Send Query letter or query with synopsis and 1 sample chapter (20 pages maximum). Unsolicited queries/correspondence by e-mail OK. Include estimated word count and list of publishing credits. Include SASE for reply, return of ms. Reports in 1-2 months on queries; 2-3 months on mss. Simultaneous submissions OK.
Terms: Pays royalties of 8% minimum; 10% maximum. Pays advance; negotiable. Sends galleys to author. Publishes ms 6-18 months after acceptance. Guidelines and book catalog for #10 SASE or on website.
Advice: "We are picking up midlist authors who have been dumped by large corporate houses—we love it. Check your market carefully. Don't send us anything until you have looked at our books in your local or university library."

FLARE BOOKS, (II), Imprint of Avon Books, Div. of the Hearst Corp., 1350 Avenue of the Americas, New York NY 10019. (212)261-6800. Executive Editor: Elise Howard. Estab. 1981. Small, young adult line. Publishes paperback originals and reprints. Plans 2-3 first novels this year. Averages 24 titles, all fiction each year.
Needs: Young adult (easy-to-read [hi-lo], problem novels, historical romance, spy/adventure), "very selective." Looking for contemporary fiction. No science fiction/fantasy, heavy problem novels, poetry. Published *Nothing But the Truth*, *A Documentary Novel*, by Avi; *Night Cries*, by Barbara Steiner; and *The Weirdo*, by Theodore Taylor.
How to Contact: Accepts unsolicited mss. Submit complete ms with cover letter (preferred) or outline/synopsis and 3 sample chapters. Agented fiction 75%. Reports in 3-4 weeks on queries; 3-4 months on mss. Simultaneous submissions OK.
Terms: Royalties and advance negotiable. Sends galleys to author. Writer's guidelines for #10 SASE. Book catalog for 9×12 SAE with 98¢ postage. "We run a young adult novel competition each year."

‡FOCUS PUBLISHING, INC., 1375 Washington Ave. S., Bemidji MN 56601. (218)759-9817. Website: http://www.paulbunyan.net/focus. **Acquisitions:** Jan Haley, vice president. "Focus Publishing is a small press primarily devoted to Christian books and secular titles appropriate to children and home-schooling families." Publishes hardcover and trade paperback originals and reprints. Publishes 4-6 titles/year.
Needs: Juvenile, picture books, religious, young adult. "We are looking for Christian books for men and young adults. Be sure to list your target audience." Recently published *Butch & the Rooster*, by Judy Hess (children's picture book).
How to Contact: Query and submit synopsis. Reports in 2 months.
Terms: Pays 7-10% royalty on retail price. Publishes ms 1 year after acceptance. Book catalog free.
Advice: "I prefer SASE inquiries, synopsis and target markets. Please don't send 5 lbs. of paper with no return postage."

FORGE BOOKS, (I), Tom Doherty Associates, 175 5th Ave., New York NY 10010. (212)388-0100. Fax: (212)388-0191. **Acquisitions:** Melissa Ann Singer, senior editor; Natalia Aponte, editor; Stephen de las Heras, assistant editor. Estab. 1993. "Midsize company that specializes in genre fiction, mainly thrillers, historicals and mysteries." Publishes hardcover and paperback originals. Published new writers within the last year. Plans 2-3 first novels this year. Averages 130 total titles, 129 fiction titles each year. Sometimes critiques or comments on rejected mss.
Needs: Erotica, historical, horror, mainstream/contemporary, mystery/suspense (amateur sleuth, cozy, police procedural, private eye/hardboiled), thriller/espionage, western (frontier saga, traditional). Plans anthology. Published *Relic*, by Douglas Preston and Lincoln Child (thriller); *Mirage*, by Soheir Khashoggi (contemporary fiction); *1812*, by David Nevin (historical); and *Billy Gashade*, by Loren D. Estleman.
How to Contact: Accepts unsolicited mss. Query with outline/synopsis and 5 sample chapters. Include estimated word count, bio and list of publishing credits. SASE for reply. Agented fiction 90%. Simultaneous submissions OK.

Terms: Pays royalties. Average advance $30,000 negotiable. Sends galleys to author. Publishes ms 9 months after acceptance.
Advice: "The writing mechanics must be outstanding for a new author to break in to today's market."

‡**FOUL PLAY**, Imprint of W.W. Norton, 500 Fifth Ave., New York NY 10110. (212)354-5500. Fax: (212)869-0856. Website: http://www.wwnorton.com. **Acquisitions:** Candace Watt, editor. Estab. 1996. "We publish a broad range of mysteries, from cozies to hard-boiled to traditional." Publishes hardcover originals and reprints. Publishes 6 titles/year.
Needs: Mystery, suspense. Recently published *Death of a Sunday Writer*, by Eric Wright; and *Gospel*, by Bill James (mysteries).
How to Contact: Query with synopsis, 1 sample chapter and SASE. A small percentage of books from first-time authors; agented fiction 90%. Reporting time varies. Simultaneous submissions OK.
Terms: Pays 10-12½-15% royalty on retail price. Advance varies. Publishes ms 6 months after acceptance. Book catalog free from W.W. Norton (same address).

FOUR WALLS EIGHT WINDOWS, (II), 39 W. 14th St., #503, New York NY 10011. (212)206-8965. E-mail: eightwind@aol.com. Website: http://www.fourwallseightwindows.com (includes complete catalog, featured books and ordering information). **Acquisitions:** John Oakes, publisher; Dan Simon, editor. Estab. 1986. "We are a small independent publisher." Publishes hardcover and paperback originals and paperback reprints. Books: quality paper; paper or cloth binding; illustrations sometimes. Average print order: 3,000-7,000. First novel print order: 3,000-5,000. Plans 1 first novel this year. Averages 18 total titles/year; approximately 9 fiction titles/year.
• Four Walls Eight Windows' books have received mention from the *New York Times* as "Notable Books of the Year" and have been nominated for *L.A. Times* fiction and nonfiction prizes.
Needs: Literary, nonfiction.
How to Contact: Does not accept unsolicited submissions. "Query letter accompanied by sample chapter, outline and SASE is best. Useful to know if writer has published elsewhere, and if so, where." Agented fiction 70%. Reports in 2 months. Simultaneous submissions OK. No electronic submissions.
Terms: Pays standard royalties; advance varies. Sends galleys to author. Publishes ms 1-2 years after acceptance. Book catalog free on request.
Advice: "We get 3,000 or so submissions a year: 1. Learn what our taste is, first; 2. Be patient."

FRIENDS UNITED PRESS, (I), 101 Quaker Hill Dr., Richmond IN 47374-1980. (765)962-7573. Fax: (765)966-1293. **Acquisitions:** Ardith Talbot, editor. Estab. 1973. "Friends United Press commits itself to energize and equip Friends and others through the power of the Holy Spirit to gather people into fellowship where Jesus Christ is known, loved and obeyed as teacher and Lord." Quaker Denominated House. Publishes paperback originals. Books: 60 lb. paper; perfect bound. Average print order: 1,000. Averages 7 total titles, 1-2 fiction titles each year. Member of Protestant Church Publishers Association. Promotes titles through magazines.
Needs: Historical (Friends' history), religious (children's, inspirational). Recently published *For The Gift of A Friend*; *For the Love of a Friend*; and *For the Call of a Friend*, by Susan McCracken.
How to Contact: Accepts unsolicited mss. Submit complete ms with cover letter. Send SASE for reply, return of ms or send disposable copy of ms. Simultaneous submissions OK. Sometimes critiques or comments on rejected mss.
Terms: Pays royalties of 7½% maximum. Sends galleys to author. Publishes ms 1 year after acceptance. Writer's guidelines for #10 SASE.
Advice: "Membership in the Society of Friends (Quakers) is preferred. Manuscript should be about Quakers, Quaker history or theology, or about theology or spirituality that is in the realm of the theology and spirituality of Friends."

GAY SUNSHINE PRESS AND LEYLAND PUBLICATIONS, (IV), P.O. Box 410690, San Francisco CA 94141. Fax: (415)626-1802. **Acquisitions:** Winston Leyland, editor. Estab. 1970. Midsize independent press. Publishes hardcover and paperback originals. Books: natural paper; perfect-bound; illustrations. Average print order: 5,000-10,000.
• Gay Sunshine Press has received a Lambda Book Award for *Gay Roots* (volume 1), named "Best Book by a Gay or Lesbian Press."
Needs: Literary, experimental, translations—all gay male material only. "We desire fiction on gay themes of *high* literary quality and prefer writers who have already had work published in literary magazines. We also publish erotica—short stories and novels." Published *Partings at Dawn: An Anthology of Japanese Gay Literature from the 12th to the 20th Centuries*; and *Out of the Blue: Russia's Hidden Gay Literature—An Anthology*.
How to Contact: "Do not send an unsolicited manuscript." Query with SASE. Reports in 3 weeks on queries; 2 months on mss. Send $1 for catalog.
Terms: Negotiates terms with author. Sends galleys to author. Pays royalties or by outright purchase.
Advice: "We continue to be interested in receiving queries from authors who have book-length manuscripts of high literary quality. We feel it is important that an author know exactly what to expect from our press (promotion, distribution, etc.) before a contract is signed. Before submitting a query or manuscript to a particular press, obtain critical feedback on your manuscript from knowledgeable people. If you alienate a publisher by submitting a

manuscript shoddily prepared/typed, or one needing very extensive rewriting, or one which is not in the area of the publisher's specialty, you will surely not get a second chance with that press."

‡LAURA GERINGER BOOKS, Imprint of HarperCollins Children's Books, 10 E. 53rd St., New York NY 10022. (212)207-7000. Website: http://www.harpercollins.com. **Acquisitions:** Laura Geringer, editorial director. "We look for books that are out of the ordinary, authors who have their own definite take, and artists that add a sense of humor to the text." Publishes hardcover originals. Published 5% previously unpublished writers/year. Publishes 15-20 titles/year.
Needs: Adventure, fantasy, historical, humor, literary, picture books, young adult. Recently published *Zoe Rising*, by Pam Conrad (novel); and *The Leaf Men*, by William Joyce (picture book).
How to Contact: Query with SASE for picture books; submit complete ms with SASE for novels. Agented fiction 75%. Reports in 2 weeks on queries; 4 months on mss.
Terms: Pays 10-12½% on retail price. Advance varies. Publishes ms 6-12 months after acceptance for novels, 1-2 years after acceptance for picture books. Writer's guidelines for #10 SASE. Book catalog for 8×10 SAE with 3 first-class stamps.
Advice: "A mistake writers often make is failing to research the type of books an imprint publishes, therefore sending inappropriate material."

GESSLER PUBLISHING COMPANY, (IV), 10 E. Church Ave., Roanoke VA 24011. (703)345-1429. Fax: (540)342-7172. E-mail: gesslerco@aol.com. Website: http://www.gessler.com/gessler (includes company info., teacher activities, links). **Acquisitions:** Richard Kurshan. Estab. 1932. "Publisher/distributor of foreign language educational materials (primary/secondary schools)." Publishes paperback originals and reprints, videos and software. Averages 75 total titles each year. Distributes titles through education dealers and catalog.
Needs: "Foreign language or English as a Second Language." Needs juvenile, literary, preschool/picture book, short story collections, translations. Published *Don Quixote de la Mancha* (cartoon version of classic, in Spanish); *El Cid* (prose and poetry version of the classic, In Spanish); and *Les Miserables* (simplified version of Victor Hugo classic, in French).
How to Contact: Query first, then send outline/synopsis and 2-3 sample chapters; complete ms with cover letter. Agented fiction 40%. Reports on queries in 1 month; on mss in 6 weeks. Simultaneous and electronic (e-mail, fax) submissions OK. Sometimes comments on rejected ms.
Terms: Pay varies with each author and contract. Sends galleys to author. "Varies on time of submission and acceptance relating to our catalog publication date." Publishes ms 9 months after acceptance. Writer's guidelines not available. Book catalog free on request.
Advice: "We specialize in the foreign language market directed to teachers and schools. A book that would interest us has to be attractive to the market. A teacher would be most likely to create a book for us."

‡GODDESS DEAD PUBLICATIONS, (I,II), Damage, Inc., P.O. Box 46277, Los Angeles CA 90046. (213)850-0067. Fax (213)850-5894. **Acquisitions:** Tracey Lee Williams, owner. Estab. 1996. Publishes paperback originals. Books: perfect binding. Average print order: 500. First novel print order: 500. Averages 3-5 total titles, 3 fiction titles/year.
Needs: Erotica, experimental, feminist, literary, mainstream/contemporary.
How to Contact: Accepts unsolicited mss. Query with outline/synopsis. Unsolicited queries/correspondence by fax OK. Include bio and list of publishing credits. SASE for reply or return of ms. Reports in 2 months on queries; up to 6 months on mss. Simultaneous submissions OK.
Payment/Terms: Royalties and advance negotiable; pays author's copies. Sends galleys to author. Publishes ms 6 months minimum after acceptance. Writer's guidelines free.
Advice: "Don't try to please me—just write your best stuff. Be unique, be unafraid."

DAVID R. GODINE, PUBLISHER, INC., (V), P.O. Box 9103, 9 Lewis St., Lincoln MA 01773. Fax: (617)259-9198. E-mail: godine@godine.com. Website: http://www.godine.com. President: David R. Godine. **Acquisitions:** Mark Polizzotti, editorial director. Estab. 1970. Small independent publisher (5-person staff). Publishes hardcover and paperback originals and reprints. Average print order: 2,500-5,000; first novel print order: 2,500. Publishes 1 new writer every 3-5 years.
Imprint(s): Nonpareil Books (trade paperbacks), Verba Mundi (translations), Imago Mundi (photography).
Needs: Literary, historical, children's. Recently published *Last Trolley from Beethovenstraat*, by Grete Weil (novel in translation); and *The Last Worthless Evening*, by Andre Dulous (short stories).
How to Contact: Does not accept unsolicited mss.
Terms: Standard royalties; offers advance. Publishes ms 3 years after acceptance.
Advice: "Have your agent contact us."

♣GOOSE LANE EDITIONS, (II, IV), 469 King St., Fredericton, New Brunswick E3B 1E5 Canada. (506)450-4251. **Acquisitions:** Laurel Boone, editor. Estab. 1957. Publishes hardcover and paperback originals and occasional reprints. Books: some illustrations. Average print run: 2,000. First novel print order: 1,500. Averages 14 total titles, 4-5 fiction titles each year. Distributes titles through General Distribution Services, Literary Press Group (Canada); Stoddart (US).

• Goose Lane has won the Atlantic Booksellers' Association Booksellers' Choice Award and the Friends of American Writers Book Award for *English Lessons,* by Shauna Singh Baldwin and the Small Press Book Awards for *Season of Apples,* by Ann Copeland.

Needs: Contemporary, historical, literary, short story collections. "Not suitable for mainstream or mass-market submissions. No genres i.e.: modern and historical adventure, crime, modern and historical romance, science fiction, fantasy, westerns, confessional works (fictional and autobiographical), and thrillers and other mystery books." Recently published *Dance the Rocks Ashore,* by Lesley Choyce; *Homer in Flight,* by Rabindranath Maharaj; and *Badass on a Softail,* by T.F. Rigelhof.

How to Contact: Considers unsolicited mss; outline or synopsis and 30-50 page sample. Query first. SASE "with Canadian stamps, International Reply Coupons, cash, check or money order. No U.S. stamps please." Reports in 6 months. Simultaneous submissions OK.

Terms: Pays royalties of 8% minimum; 12% maximum. Average advance: $100-200, negotiable. Sends galleys to author. Writers guidelines for 9 × 12 SAE and IRC.

Advice: "We do not usually consider submissions from outside Canada."

GRAYWOLF PRESS, (III), 2402 University Ave., Suite 203, St. Paul MN 55114. (612)641-0077. Website: http://www.graywolfpress.org. Publisher: Fiona McCrae. **Acquisitions:** Jeffrey Shotts. Estab. 1974. "Graywolf Press is an independent, nonprofit publisher dedicated to the creation and promotion of thoughtful and imaginative contemporary literature essential to a vital and diverse culture." Growing small literary press, nonprofit corporation. Publishes hardcover and paperback originals and paperback reprints. Books: acid-free quality paper; offset printing; hardcover and soft binding; illustrations occasionally. Average print order: 3,000-10,000. First novel print order: 2,000-6,000. Averages 18-20 total titles, 6-8 fiction titles each year.

• Graywolf Press books have won numerous awards. Most recently, Josip Novakovich won the Richard J. Margolis Award (1995), and David Treuer won the 1996 Minnesota Book Award for Novels and Short Stories.

Needs: Literary, and short story collections. Literary fiction; no genre books (romance, western, science fiction, suspense). Recently published *The Apprentice,* by Lewis Libby (novel); *Watershed,* by Percival Everett (novel); and *Rainy Lake,* by Mary François Rockcastle (novel).

How to Contact: Query with SASE. Reports in 3 months. Simultaneous submissions OK. Occasionally critiques rejected mss.

Terms: Pays in royalties of 7½-10%; negotiates advance and number of author's copies. Sends galleys to author. Publishes ms 18 months after acceptance. Free book catalog.

‡**GREENE BARK PRESS,** P.O. Box 1108, Bridgeport CT 06601. (203)372-4861. **Acquisitions:** Thomas J. Greene, publisher. "We only publish children's fiction—all subjects, but in reading picture book format appealing to ages 3-9 or all ages." Publishes hardcover originals. Publishes 60% previously unpublished writers/year. Publishes 5 titles/year.

Needs: Juvenile. Recently published *The Butterfly Bandit,* by Ester Hauser Laurence (hardcover picture book).

How to Contact: Submit complete ms with SASE. Does not accept queries or ms by e-mail. Reports in 3 months on mss. Simultaneous submissions OK.

Terms: Pays 10-15% royalty on wholesale price. Publishes ms 1 year after acceptance. Writer's guidelines and book catalog with SASE.

Advice: Audience is "children who read to themselves and others. Mothers, fathers, grandparents, godparents who read to their respective children, grandchildren. Include SASE, be prepared to wait, do not inquire by telephone."

‡**GREENWILLOW BOOKS,** Imprint of William Morrow & Co., Division of Hearst Books, 1350 Avenue of the Americas, New York NY 10019. (212)261-6500. Website: http://www.williammorrow.com. Estab. 1974. "Greenwillow Books publishes quality hardcover books for children." Publishes hardcover originals and reprints. Publishes 1% previously unpublished writers/year. Publishes 70-80 titles/year.

Needs: Juvenile, picture books: fantasy, historical, humor, literary, mystery. Recently published *Lilly's Purple Plastic Purse,* by Kevin Henkes; *Under the Table,* by Marisabina Russo; and *The Missing Sunflowers,* by Maggie Stern.

How to Contact: Reports in 3 months on mss. Agented fiction 70%. Simultaneous submissions OK.

Terms: Pays 10% royalty on wholesale price for first-time authors. Advance varies. Publishes ms 2 years after acceptance. Writer's guidelines for #10 SASE. Book catalog for $2 and 9 × 12 SAE.

● **A BULLET INTRODUCES COMMENTS** by the editor of *Novel & Short Story Writer's Market* indicating special information about the listing.

‡GREYCLIFF PUBLISHING CO., (II, IV), P.O. Box 1273, Helena MT 59722. (406)443-1888. Fax: (406)443-0788. E-mail: gcpub*nitco.net*. **Acquisitions:** Gary LaFontaine, partner. Estab. 1985. "Small independent publisher with Montana novel series." Publishes hardcover and paperback originals and hardcover and paperback reprints. Books: 60 lb. paper; illustrations in nonfiction. Average print order: 5,000. First novel print order: 3,000. Published new writers within the last year. Plans 2 first novels this year. Averages 6 total titles, 2 fiction titles/year. Member of SPAN and the Rocky Mountain Booksellers Association.
Needs: Montana only. Adventure, ethnic/multicultural (Native American), experimental, family saga, historical, literary, mainstream/contemporary, military/war, mystery/suspense, regional (Montana), romance, short story collections, western. Recently published *Queen of the Legal Tender Saloon*, by Eileen Clarke. Publishes the Greycliff Montana novel series.
How to Contact: Accepts unsolicited mss. Submit complete manuscript with cover letter. Unsolicited queries/correspondence by e-mail and fax OK. Include estimated word count, 100-word bio, Social Security number and list of publishing credits. Send SASE for reply or return of mss. Reports in 1 month on queries; 2 months on mss. Simultaneous submissions OK. Sometimes comments on rejected mss.
Payment/Terms: Pays in royalties of 15% minimum. Average advance: $500. Sends galleys to author. Publishes ms 1 year after acceptance. Book catalog for $1 plus SASE.
Advice: "We love Montana. We publish for a large group of people who also believe that this state is special. We want engrossing novels set in Montana."

‡GROLIER PUBLISHING, Grolier Inc., Sherman Turnpike, Danbury CT 06813. (203)797-3500. Fax: (203)797-3197. Estab. 1895. "Grolier Publishing is a leading publisher of reference, educational and children's books. We provide parents, teachers and librarians with the tools they need to enlighten children to the pleasure of learning and prepare them for the road ahead." Publishes hardcover and trade paperback originals.
Imprint(s): Children's Press, Franklin Watts, **Orchard Books**.
Needs: Juvenile, picture books.
How to Contact: Prefers to work with unagented authors. Reports in 4 months on proposals. Simultaneous submissions OK.
Terms: Pays royalty for established authors; makes outright purchase for first-time authors. Advance varies. Publishes ms 18 months after acceptance. Writer's guidelines free. Book catalog for 9 × 12 SAE and $3 postage.

‡GROVE/ATLANTIC, INC., 841 Broadway, New York NY 10003. (212)614-7850, 7860. Fax: (212)614-7886, 7915. **Acquisitions:** Jim Moser, executive editor. "Grove/Atlantic publishes serious nonfiction and literary fiction." Publishes hardcover originals, trade paperback originals and reprints. Publishes 60-70 titles/year.
Imprint(s): Grove Press (Estab. 1952), Atlantic Monthly Press (Estab. 1917).
Needs: Experimental, literary. Recently published *The Ordinary Seaman*, by Francisco Goldman; and *Cold Mountain*, by Charles Frasier.
How to Contact: No unsolicited mss. Query with SASE. "Because of volume of queries, Grove/Atlantic can only respond when interested—though SASE might generate a response." Simultaneous submissions OK.
Terms: Pays 7½-15% royalty on retail price. Advance varies considerably. Publishes ms 1 year after acceptance. Book catalog free.

GRYPHON PUBLICATIONS, (I, II), P.O. Box 209, Brooklyn NY 11228. (718)646-6126 (after 6 pm EST). **Acquisitions:** Gary Lovisi, owner/editor. Estab. 1983. Publishes hardcover and paperback originals and trade paperback reprints. Books: bond paper; offset printing; perfect binding. Average print order: 500-1,000. Published new writers within the last year. Plans 2 first novels this year. Averages 5-10 total titles, 6 fiction titles each year.
Imprint(s): Gryphon Books, Gryphon Doubles.
Needs: Mystery/suspense (private eye/hardboiled, crime), science fiction (hard science/technological, soft/sociological). No horror, romance or westerns. Published *The Dreaming Detective*, by Ralph Vaughn (mystery-fantasy-horror); *The Woman in the Dugout*, by Gary Lovisi and T. Arnone (baseball novel); and *A Mate for Murder*, by Bruno Fischer (hardboiled pulp). Publishes Gryphon Double novel series.
How to Contact: "I am not looking for novels now but will see a *1-page synopsis* with SASE." Include estimated word count, 50-word bio, short list of publishing credits, "how you heard about us." Send SASE. Do not send ms. Agented fiction 5-10%. Reports in 2-4 weeks on queries; 1-2 months on mss. Simultaneous and electronic submissions OK (with hard copy—disk in ASCII). Often critiques or comments on rejected mss.
Terms: For magazines, $5-45 on publication plus 2 contributor's copies; for novels/collections payment varies and is much more. Sends galleys to author. Publishes ms 1-3 years after acceptance. Writers guidelines and book catalog for SASE.
Advice: "I am looking for better and better writing, more cutting-edge material with *impact*! Keep it lean and focused."

♣GUERNICA EDITIONS, (III, IV), P.O. Box 117, Toronto, Ontario M5S 2S6 Canada. (416)658-9888. Fax: (416)657-8885. E-mail: 102026.1331@compuserve.com. **Acquisitions:** Antonio D'Alfonso, editor. Umberto Claudio, fiction editor. Estab. 1978. Publishes paperback originals. Books: offset printing; perfect binding. Average print order: 1,500. Average first novel print order: 1,000. Plans to publish 1 first novel this year. Publishes 16-20 total titles each year.

● The press has recently won the American Booksellers Association Award for *Astoria*, by Robert Viscusi.

Needs: Contemporary, ethnic, literary, translations of foreign novels. Looking for novels about women and ethnic subjects. No unsolicited works. Recently published *Stained Glass*, by Concetta Principe; *Conversation with Johnny*, by Anthony Valerio; *The Loss of the Miraculous*, by Ben Morreale; *Impala*, by Carole David; and *Maude*, by Susanne Jacob.

How to Contact: Does not accept or return unsolicited mss. Query first. IRCs. 100% of fiction is agented. Reports in 6 months. Electronic submissions via IBM WordPerfect disks.

Terms: Pays royalties of 7-10% and 10 author's copies. Book catalog for SAE and $5 postage. (Canadian stamps only).

Advice: Publishing "short novels (150 pages or less)."

‡❋GUTTER PRESS, 118 Peter St., Suite 1, Toronto, Ontario M5V 2G7 Canada. (416)593-7036. E-mail: gutter@io.org. Website: http://www.io.org/~gutter/. **Acquisitions**: Sam Hiyate, publisher. Publishes trade paperback originals and reprints. Publishes 50% previously unpublished writers/year. Publishes 6 titles/year.

Imprint(s): Ken Sparling Books, Eye Press, Kaleyard.

Needs: Literary. "Ultimately, language is what has to be at issue, the issue you address with all your heart. Give us your heart and we'll give you ours back." Recently published *Dark Rides*, by Derek McCormack.

How to Contact: Submit 3 sample chapters with SAE and IRC. Reports in 6 months. Simultaneous submissions OK.

Terms: Pays 10-15% royalty on retail price. Offers $500-1,500 (Canadian) advance. Publishes ms 2 years after acceptance. Writer's guidelines for SAE and IRC.

Advice: "Our audience is people who care about language and what it can accomplish beyond what has already been accomplished."

*ROBERT HALE LIMITED, (II), Clerkenwell House, 45/47 Clerkenwell Green, London EC1R 0HT England. Publishes hardcover and trade paperback originals and hardcover reprints.

Needs: Historical, mainstream and western. Length: 40,000-150,000 words.

How to Contact: Send cover letter, synopsis or brief summary and 2 sample chapters.

‡HAMPTON ROADS PUBLISHING COMPANY, INC., (II, IV), 134 Burgess Ln., Charlottesville VA 22902. (804)296-2772. Fax: (804)296-5096. E-mail: hrpc@hrpub.com. **Acquisitions**: Frank DeMarco, chairman and chief editor. Estab. 1989. Small company that publishes and distributes hardcover and paperback originals on subjects including metaphysics, health, complementary medicine, visionary fiction and other related topics. Average print order: 3,000-5,000. Published new writers within the last year. Averages 30 total titles/year, 5-6 fiction titles/year.

Needs: Literary, New Age/mystic/spiritual, psychic/supernatural/occult. Looking for "visionary fiction, past-life fiction, based on actual memories." Recently published *Naked into the Night*, by Monty Joynes (visionary); *Clear Cut*, by Bill Hunger (visionary); *Dear Companion*, by Kelly Joyce Neff (past-life recall).

How to Contact: Accepts unsolicited mss. Query first. Unsolicited queries/correspondence by e-mail and fax OK. Include description of book. Send SASE for reply, return of ms or send disposable copy of ms. Agented fiction 5%. Reports in 3-4 weeks on queries. Simultaneous submissions OK.

Terms: Pays in royalties; advance is negotiable. Sends galleys to author.

Advice: "We are a cutting-edge publisher. Send us something new and different. Be patient. Sometimes we are slow."

HARCOURT BRACE & COMPANY, (III), 525 B St., Suite 1900, San Diego CA 92101. (619)699-6810. Fax: (619)699-6777. Publisher: Louise Pelan. **Acquisitions**: Michael Stearns (fantasy and general); Diane D'Andrade, executive editor (general fiction); Jeannette Larson (general fiction); Allyn Johnston, editorial director; Linda Zuckerman, editorial director of Browndeer Press; Elizabeth Van Doren, editorial director of Gulliver Books; Paula Wiseman, editorial director of Silver Whistle. Publishes hardcover originals and paperback reprints. Averages 150 titles/year. Publishes "very few" new writers/year.

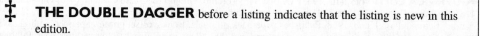

‡ THE DOUBLE DAGGER before a listing indicates that the listing is new in this edition.

Imprint(s): Harcourt Brace Children's Books, Gulliver Books, Browndeer Press, Red Wagon Books and Silver Whistle.
- Books published by Harcourt Brace & Co. have received numerous awards including the Caldecott and Newbery medals and selections as the American Library Association's "Best Books for Young Adults." Note that the publisher only accepts manuscripts through an agent. Unagented writers may query only.

Needs: Nonfiction for all ages, picture books for very young children, historical, mystery. Recently published *Tops and Bottoms*, by Janet Stevens; *Verdi*, by Janell Cannon; *Tangerine*, by Edward Bloor; *Hands*, by Lois Ehlert; and *Merlin* (The Young Merlin Trilogy 3), by Jane Yolen.

How to Contact: No unsolicited mss. Query first. Submit through agent only.

Terms: Terms vary according to individual books; pays on royalty basis. Catalog for 9 × 12 SASE.

Advice: "Read as much current fiction as you can; familiarize yourself with the type of fiction published by a particular house; interact with young people to obtain a realistic picture of their concerns, interests and speech patterns."

‡HARCOURT BRACE & COMPANY, Children's Books Division, 525 B St., Suite 1900, San Diego CA 92101. (619) 699-6810. Fax: (619)699-6777. E-mail: lpelan@harcourtbrace.com. **Acquisitions:** Manuscript Submissions. "Harcourt Brace & Company owns some of the world's most prestigious publishing imprints—which distinguish quality products for the juvenile, educational, scientific, technical, medical, professional and trade markets worldwide." Publishes hardcover originals and trade paperback reprints.

Imprint(s): Gulliver Books, Gulliver Green, Browndeer Press, Red Wagon, Voyager and Odyssey Paperbacks, Magic Carpet and Libros Viajeros.

Needs: Childrens/juvenile, young adult. Recently published *Tangerine*, by Edward Bloor (young adult); *Littlejim's Dreams*, by Gloria Houston (middlegrade); and *The Last Rainmaker*, by Sherry Garland (young adult).

How to Contact: Query first. No phone calls.

‡HARKEY MULTIMEDIA, P.O. Box 20001, Seattle WA 98102. **Acquistions:** Charlotte Bosarge, editor/art director. Publishes hardcover and trade paperback originals. Publishes 3-6 titles/year.

Needs: Adventure, confession, experimental, horror, humor, mystery, picture books, religious, romance, science fiction, young adult.

How to Contact: Query with synopsis and 1-3 sample chapters. Reports in 1 month on queries and mss. Simultaneous submissions OK.

Terms: Pays 6-12% royalty on retail price. Publishes ms 6 months after acceptance. Writer's guidelines for #10 SASE.

Advice: "Fiction writing is your chance to be free and express yourself and try something new! Show us who you really are and we are more likely to be interested in your work."

✦HARLEQUIN ENTERPRISES, LTD., (II, IV), 225 Duncan Mill Rd., Don Mills, Ontario M3B 3K9 Canada. (416)445-5860. President and CEO: Brian E. Hickey. Editorial Director Harlequin: Randall Toye; Silhouette: Isabel Swift; Gold Eagle: Randall Toye. Estab. 1949. Publishes paperback originals and reprints. Books: Newsprint paper; web printing; perfect-bound. Published new writers within the last year. Number of titles: Averages 700/year. Buys agented and unagented fiction.

Imprint(s): Harlequin Romances, Harlequin Presents, Harlequin American Romances, Superromances, Temptation, Intrigue and Regency, **Silhouette**, Worldwide Mysteries, Gold Eagle.
- Harlequin introduced a new imprint, Mira for single-title women's fiction. Query for more information/guidelines.

Needs: Romance, heroic adventure, mystery/suspense (romantic suspense *only*). Will accept nothing that is not related to the desired categories.

How to Contact: Send query letter or send outline and first 50 pages (2 or 3 chapters) or submit through agent with SASE (Canadian). Absolutely no simultaneous submissions. Reports in 1 month on queries; 2 months on mss.

Terms: Offers royalties, advance. Must return advance if book is not completed or is unacceptable. Sends galleys

---

WRITER-TO-WRITER

Exercise the writing muscle every day, even if it is only a letter, notes, a title list, a character sketch, a journal entry. Writers are like dancers, like athletes. Without that exercise, the muscles seize up. Faulkner said: "I write only when I am inspired. Fortunately I am inspired at 9 o'clock every morning."

Jane Yolen
Merlin (The Young Merlin Trilogy, Book 3), Harcourt Brace & Company

INSIDER REPORT

Harlequin: looking for love & laughter

With the publication of the first Love & Laughter books late in 1996, Harlequin Enterprises launched its newest line of short contemporary romance novels. But despite the line being the newest kid on the block, its editor, Malle Vallik, is definitely not. "I've always read romance in one form or another throughout my life," she says. "Even the mysteries I've read had a little bit of romance."

Vallik has worked in publishing since 1982, doing everything from driving a truck and putting the books on the racks to publicity to her current editorial job. She's been with Harlequin for the past seven years, starting as an associate editor for the Temptation line. "I said to myself, I like this business and if I'm going to stay in it, I might as well work for a company that is very successful, that people really respond to and that publishes the books I enjoy so much."

Malle Vallik

Harlequin's success is evident in its growth and its addition of new lines, such as Love & Laughter. For Love & Laughter, Vallik wants 50,000-word, fast-paced, contemporary romantic comedies. "I want to stress that they are contemporary. These are characters who would know what *Seinfeld* is, or *Mad About You*, and have the same concerns that we do going into the next millenium. They're not timeless love stories; they're very specific to our age."

Although 'romantic comedy' should give you a good idea of what Vallik is looking for, she is surprised by the number of unusable manuscripts she receives. "I'm finding people are forgetting the two basic elements of premise and perspective. There has to be a fairly strong comic premise in a Love & Laughter book, as there was in the movie *While You Were Sleeping*. The heroine has daydreamed over this man for quite some time and is in love with him. She saves his life but he goes into a coma, and the family is convinced she is his fiancée. This is a strong romantic-comic premise that you can develop from. The characters go through changes; she learns what he's really like, what his brother is like. There are suspicions that develop. And then the guy actually wakes up and the story goes on from there. This has a very strong comic premise."

In addition to a comic premise, a Love & Laughter book must also have a comic perspective in the voices of the characters and in your voice as author, Vallik says. "It's the way the character looks at the world and finds the humor in the disaster. Meg Ryan's character in *Sleepless In Seattle* is an example of this, even though that film is much more of a drama, with just a bit of a romantic comedy. It's her way of looking at things, the way she looks at love, the slapstick that she does that brings the comedy into the story."

Vallik is surprised at some of the submissions she gets, because they are straight dramas with a few jokes thrown in here and there. "That's not what I'm looking for," she says. "I would love to see more straight screwball comedies, full of misunderstanding and based on an appealing and original idea." Originality is the key. "Don't let the rules hold you

INSIDER REPORT, *Vallik*

back. Write the story as you would like to tell it. The things that really strike an editor's eye are the things that are kind of different and fun."

One author who writes what Vallik is looking for is Jennifer Crusie. "She is great, and she was actually one of the launch authors for the Love & Laughter program. Jennie has a very contemporary voice and a comic perspective." A fine example of her voice is Crusie's Love & Laughter novel *Anyone But You.* (See the interview with Jennifer Crusie on page 57.)

"For every writer that gets published in category romance, it is because she has a strong voice and doesn't sound like anyone else," Vallik says. "The thing we see over and over again are stories that sound exactly like every other one we've published, and of course that's not what we want. We want something new and different and appealing. A lot of people don't seem to go very 'high concept' in Love & Laughter, and to me that seems like a pretty obvious technique: asking 'what if' again and again, putting all the combinations together and seeing what happens. People should not worry about what anyone else is writing and just think of the best idea they can."

Vallik says that when submitting to Love & Laughter, writers should send the first two chapters of their novel plus a synopsis. Established authors should also include a list of recent titles, and both new and established writers should summarize the unique selling point or hook that their book has. "If you can say what the strong hook of your book is in a paragraph, and it's something interesting and appealing, that's fairly impressive."

A strong hook also helps sell a book to the readership, Vallik says. A strong image for the cover, a title and the back cover copy are all things that can be drawn from a strong hook, and if the author considers that in advance, it helps sell the book to the editor. Vallik points to Tiffany White as an author who considers all the angles when submitting a book.

"She is one of our Silhouette Yours Truly launch authors," Vallik says. "The whole concept of Yours Truly is that some kind of written communication starts the story. So she had a bachelor auction, which is kind of a neat hook, and she called it *Male for Sale*, which is good. It was a fun story, because the way the auction worked the heroine wasn't sure which guy she was bidding on. She thought she was picking a very conservative looking fellow, and she got the motorcycle rider. Kind of the fun opposites, which I can talk about on the back cover." The strength of the title and concept of the bachelor auction also made the front cover more effective. "Tiffany considers the whole angle when she first has an idea; what title will work nicely, how can my editor get the story across in a hundred words. She considers what the book will be like on the shelf. And of course, that's backed up by an entertaining story and great characters."

Writers do not need an agent to sell to Love & Laughter. "Our negotiations are pretty much the same across the board. The only benefit to having an agent would be if that agent was one I've dealt with before, and that agent phones me to say, 'I've got something for you that's appropriate for Love & Laughter,' I'm going to read that one first. But we read everything." Vallik adds that it takes a little longer to get to unagented writers, and that 55 to 65 percent of books bought by Harlequin are through agents.

Many writers make the mistake of reading a lot of one type of romance, and then trying to copy that type, Vallik says. "Writers are often told by their critique groups, 'No, no, this will never work. You'll have to change all of this if you want to sell this to Harlequin.' What we actually like is that it is so different or that it's fundamentally your story told your way." Vallik says that although the odds seem to be against unpublished writers, it's important to remember that there are new openings all the time. "We're always beginning

---

new projects and some of our established authors are moving into other programs, so there is opportunity and space. We have never turned away a good book because we didn't have the space; we'll always find the space." Also, since Love & Laughter is newer than the other lines, it's wide open. "Your chance of being bought as a new author is much higher than in Temptation, which is looking but not looking that hard."

"The other thing about Harlequin in general," Vallik says, "is how much we work with unpublished people in developing their talent. That's one of the fun parts of the job, reading a manuscript you think has potential and going through the revision process once, twice or more times. There are many people published with us now that went through several manuscripts before they hit it, but after that they were fine." Vallik says she remembers the names of promising writers and looks forward to hearing from them again. "The best moment of all is when you can make that phone call and offer the deal. That's one of the things that keeps us editors going, and we do that a lot at Harlequin."
—*David Borcherding*

---

to author. Publishes ms 1 year after acceptance. Guidelines available.
Advice: "The quickest route to success is to follow directions for submissions: Query first. We encourage first novelists. Before sending a manuscript, read as many current Harlequin titles as you can. It's very important to know the genre and the series most appropriate for your submission." Submissions for Harlequin Romance and Harlequin Presents should go to: Mills & Boon Limited Eton House, 18-24 Paradise Road, Richmond, Surrey TW9 1SR United Kingdom, Attn: Karin Stoecker; Superromances: Paula Eykelhof, senior editor; Temptation: Birgit Davis-Todd, senior editor. American Romances and Intrigue: Debra Matteucci, senior editor and editorial coordinator, Harlequin Books, 6th Floor, 300 E. 42 Street, New York, NY 10017. Silhouette submissions should also be sent to the New York office, attention Isabel Swift. "The relationship between the novelist and editor is regarded highly and treated with professionalism."

‡*HARLEQUIN MILLS & BOON LTD., (I, II), Subsidiary of Harlequin Enterprises Ltd., Eton House, 18-24 Paradise Rd., Richmond, Surrey TW9 1SR United Kingdom. (44)0181-948-0444. **Acquisitions**: K. Stoecker, editorial director. Estab. 1908-1909. "World's largest publisher of brand name category romance; books are available for translation into more than 20 languages and distributed in more than 100 international markets." Publishes paperback originals. Published new writers within the last year. Plans 3-4 first novels this year.
Imprint(s): Harlequin, Silhouette, MIRA, Mills & Boon.
Needs: Romance (contemporary, historical, regency period, medical). Publishes Christmas anthologies. Closed to outside submissions. Publishes Harlequin Romance, Harlequin Presents (historical romance, medical romance in the UK).
How to Contact: Does not accept unsolicited mss; returns unsolicited mss. Query with outline/synopsis. Unsolicited queries/correspondence by fax OK. Include estimated word count, 1-2 paragraph bio, list of publishing credits and why the story is targeted at the series. Send SASE for reply, return of ms. Agented fiction less than 50%. Reports in 1 month on 12-14 weeks on mss. No simultaneous submissions. Often critiques or comments on rejected mss.
Terms: Advance against royalty. Sends galleys to author. Publishes ms up to 3 years after acceptance. Writer's guidelines free.

HARMONY BOOKS, (V), Subsidiary of Crown Publishers, 201 E. 50th St., New York NY 10022. (212)572-6179. Contact: General Editorial Department. Publishes hardcover and paperback originals.
Needs: Literary fiction. Also publishes serious nonfiction, history, personal growth, media and music fields.
How to Contact: Does not accept unsolicited mss.

‡HARPER LIBROS, Imprint of HarperCollins Publishers, 10 E. 53rd St., New York NY 10022. (212)207-7000. Fax: (212)207-7145. Website: http://www.harpercollins.com. **Acquisitions:** Terry Karten, editorial director. Estab. 1994. "Harper Libros offers Spanish language editions of selected HarperCollins titles, sometimes reprints, sometimes new books that are published simultaneously in English and Spanish. The list mirrors the English-language list of HarperCollins in that we publish both literary and commercial fiction and nonfiction titles including all the different HarperCollins categories, such as self-help, spirituality, etc." Publishes hardcover and trade paperback originals. Publishes 10 titles/year.

Imprint(s): Harper Arco Iris (Jennifer Pasanen) (children's).

Needs: Literary.

How to Contact: Query. *No unsolicited mss.*

Terms: Pays variable royalty on net price. Advance varies. Publishes ms 1 year after acceptance.

‡**HARPER PERENNIAL**, Imprint of HarperCollins Publishers, 10 E. 53rd St., New York NY 10036. (212)207-7000. Website: http://www.harpercollins.com. **Acquisitions:** Hugh Van Dusen, vice president/executive editor. Estab. 1963. "Harper Perennial publishes a broad range of adult fiction and nonfiction paperbacks." Publishes trade paperback originals and reprints. Publishes 100 titles/year.

Needs: Ethnic, feminist, literary. "Don't send us novels—go through hardcover." Recently published *Lying On the Couch*, by Irwin D. Yalom (psycho-thriller novel); *American Pie*, by Michael Lee West (novel); and *Bird Girl and the Man Who Followed the Sun*, by Velma Wallis (fiction/native American studies).

How to Contact: Agented submissions only. Reports in 2 weeks on queries; 1 month on mss.

Terms: Pays 5-7½% royalty. Advance varies. Publishes ms 6 months after acceptance. Book catalog free.

Advice: Audience is general reader—high school, college. "Call and get the name of an editor and they will look at it. Usually an editor is listed in a book's acknowledgments. You should address your submission to an editor or else it will probably be returned."

HARPERCOLLINS CHILDREN'S BOOKS, (II), 10 E. 53rd St., New York NY 10022. (212)207-7044. Senior Vice President/Publisher: Susan Katz. Senior Vice President/Associate Publisher/Editor-in-Chief: Kate Jackson. **Acquisitions**: Joanna Cotler, vice president/editorial director, Joanna Cotler Books; Michael di Capua, vice president/publisher, Michael di Capua Books; Laura Geringer, vice president/editorial director, Laura Geringer Books; Mary Alice Noon, vice president/editorial director, Harper Trophy; Mary Alice Moore, editorial director, HarperFestival; Executive Editors: Sally Doherty, Kate M. Jackson, Ginee Seo, Phoebe Yen and Robert O. Warren. Publishes hardcover trade titles and paperbacks.

Needs: Picture books, easy-to-read, middle-grade, teenage and young adult novels; fiction, fantasy, animal, sports, spy/adventure, historical, science fiction, problem novels and contemporary. Published Harper: *Walk Two Moons*, by Sharon Creech (ages 8-12); *The Best School Year Ever*, by Barbara Robinson (ages 8 up); Harper Trophy (paperbacks): *Catherine, Called Birdy*, by Karen Cushman (ages 12 and up). Also publishes The Danger Guys series by Tony Abbott (ages 7-10).

How to Contact: Query; submit complete ms; submit outline/synopsis and sample chapters; submit through agent. SASE for query, ms. Please identify simultaneous submissions. Reports in 2-3 months.

Terms: Average 10% in royalties. Royalties on picture books shared with illustrators. Offers advance. Publishes novel 1 year; picture books 2 years after acceptance. Writer's guidelines and book catalog for SASE.

Advice: "Write from your own experience and the child you once were. Read widely in the field of adult and children's literature. Realize that writing for children is a difficult challenge. Read other young adult novelists as well as adult novelists. Pay attention to styles, approaches, topics. Be willing to rewrite, perhaps many times. We have no rules for subject matter, length or vocabulary but look instead for ideas that are fresh and imaginative. Good writing that involves the reader in a story or subject that has appeal for young readers is also essential. One submission is considered by all imprints."

‡**HARPERCOLLINS PUBLISHERS**, 10 E. 53rd St., New York NY 10022. (212)207-7000. Website: http://www.harpercollins.com. **Acquisitions**: Joelle Del Bourgo, vice president/editorial director. "HarperCollins, one of the largest English language publishers in the world, is a broad-based publisher with strengths in academic, business and professional, children's, educational, general interest, and religious and spiritual books, as well as multimedia titles." Publishes hardcover and paperback originals and paperback reprints. Trade publishes more than 500 titles/year.

Imprint(s): Harper Adult Trade; Harper Audio, Harper Business, HarperActive, **Harper Libros**, **Harperpaperback**, **Harper Perennial**, **HarperCollins Children's Books**, HarperCollins San Francisco, Regan Books, Westview Press, **Zondervan Publishing House**.

Needs: Adventure, fantasy, gothic, historical, mystery, science fiction, suspense, western, literary. "We look for

---

WRITER-TO-WRITER

Persistence is by far the most important ingredient for writers. Most aspiring writers give up long before their chance arrives. Writing and publishing is like a tug-a-war—you can't let go of the rope and not expect to lose your place.

    Kevin J. Anderson

    X-Files: Ruins, HarperCollins

a strong story line and exceptional literary talent." Recently published *Monkey King*, by Patricia Chao; *The House of Forgetting*, by Benjamin Saenz; *Trading Reality*, by Michael Ridpath (thriller); *X-Files: Ruins*, by Kevin J. Anderson; and *Diamonds Are Forever*, by W.P. Kinsella.

How to Contact: *No unsolicited queries or mss.* Agented submissions only. Reports on solicited queries in 6 weeks.

Terms: Pays standard royalties. Advance negotiable.

Advice: "We do not accept any unsolicited material."

‡✲HARPERCOLLINS PUBLISHERS (CANADA) LIMITED., 55 Avenue Rd., Suite 2900, Toronto, Ontario M5R 3L2 Canada. (416)975-9334. **Acquisitions:** Iris Tupholme, publisher/editor-in-chief. Publishes hardcover originals and reprints, trade paperback originals and reprints, mass market paperback reprints. Publishes 40-60 titles/year.

Needs: Ethnic, experimental, feminist, juvenile, literary, mainstream/contemporary, picture books, religious, short story collections, young adult. Recently published *Let Me Be the One*, by Hanor (short stories).

How to Contact: "We do not accept unsolicited mss. Query first." Reports in 2 months on queries and proposals.

Terms: Offers from $500 to over six figures advance. Publishes ms 18 months after acceptance. Book catalog free on request.

✱HARPERCOLLINS PUBLISHERS (NEW ZEALAND) LIMITED, (IV), P.O. Box 1, Auckland, New Zealand. **Acquisitions:** Ian Watt, publisher. Averages 10-15 fiction titles/year (15-20 nonfiction).

Imprint(s): Flamingo.

Needs: Adult fiction: Flamingo imprint; Teen fiction: 12 years plus; Junior fiction: 8-11 years. Length: Flamingo: 40,000 + words; Teen: 20-35,000 words; Junior: 15-17,000 words.

How to Contact: Full ms preferred.

Terms: Pays royalties. "Write and ask for guidelines."

Advice: "It helps if the author and story have New Zealand connections/content."

HARPERPAPERBACKS, (V), 10 E. 53rd St., New York NY 10022. (212)207-7000. Fax: (212)207-7759. **Acquisitions:** Carolyn Marino, editorial director. Independent publisher. Publishes paperback originals and reprints. Published new writers within the last year.

Imprint(s): HarperPrism.

Needs: Mainstream/contemporary, mystery/suspense, romance (contemporary, historical, romantic suspense), thriller/espionage, young adult/teen.

How to Contact: Query by letter or agent. No unsolicited mss accepted.

Terms: Pays advance and royalties.

HARVEST HOUSE PUBLISHERS, (II, IV), 1075 Arrowsmith, Eugene OR 97402. (541)343-0123. Fax: (541)342-6410. Editorial Manager: LaRae Weikert. Editorial Director: Carolyn McCready. **Acquisitions:** Kristi Hirte, manuscript coordinator. Estab. 1974. "The foundation of our publishing program is to publish books that 'help the hurts of people' and nurture spiritual growth." Midsize independent publisher with plans to expand. Publishes hardcover and paperback originals and reprints. Books: 40 lb. ground wood paper; offset printing; perfect binding; average print order: 10,000; first novel print order: 10,000-15,000. Averages 100 total titles, 6 fiction titles each year.

Needs: Christian living, contemporary issues, family saga, humor, Christian mystery (romantic suspense), religious/inspirational and Christian romance (historical). Especially seeks inspirational, romance/historical and mystery. Recently published *Where the Wild Rose Blooms*, by Lori Wick; *Conquered Heart*, by Lisa Samson; and *Israel, My Beloved*, by Kay Arthur.

How to Contact: No longer accepting unsolicited ms. Recommends using Evangelical Christian Publishers Association or the Writer's Edge.

Terms: Pays in royalties of 14-18%; 10 author's copies. Sends galleys to author. Publishes ms 1 year after acceptance.

✱HEADLINE BOOK PUBLISHING LTD., 338 Euston Road, London NW1 3BH England. **Acquisitions:** Jane Morpeth, publishing director (fiction); Heather Holden-Brown, publishing director (nonfiction). Averages approximately 600 titles/year.

WRITER-TO-WRITER

Use your *imagination*! Trust me, your life is not interesting. Don't write it down.
   W.P. Kinsella
   Diamonds Are Forever, HarperCollins

Needs: Mainstream publisher of popular fiction and nonfiction in hardcover and mass-market paperback. Length: 95,000-150,000 words.
How to Contact: "Send a synopsis/5 consecutive chapters and *curriculum vitae* first, and return postage."
Terms: Pays advance against royalties. Catalog available.
Advice: "Study UK publishers' catalogs to see what is published in both the US and the UK. Read the UK trade press: *The Bookseller* and *Publishing News* to get a feel for our market. *The Writers' & Artists' Yearbook* is useful."

HELICON NINE EDITIONS, (I, II), Subsidiary of Midwest Center for the Literary Arts, Inc., P.O. Box 22412, Kansas City MO 64113. (816)753-1095. **Acquisitions**: Gloria Vando Hickok, publisher/editor. Estab. 1990. Small press publishing poetry, fiction, creative nonfiction and anthologies. Publishes paperback originals. Books: 60 lb. paper; offset printing; perfect-bound; 4-color cover. Average print order: 1,000-5,000. Plans 8 total titles, 2-4 fiction titles this year. Also publishes one-story chapbooks called *feuillets*, which come with envelope, 250 print run.
Needs: Contemporary, ethnic, experimental, literary, short story collections, translations. "We're only interested in fine literature." Nothing "commercial." Published *Knucklebones*, by Annabel Thomas; and *Return to Sender*, by Ann Slegman. Published new writers within the last year.
How to Contact: Does not accept unsolicited mss. Query first. SASE. Reports in 1 week on queries.
Terms: Pays royalties, author's copies or honorarium. "Individual arrangement with author." Sends galleys to author. Publishes ms 1-6 months after acceptance. Writer's guidelines for SASE.
Advice: "Check spelling and grammar before submitting. Be proud of your work. Submit a clean, readable copy in a folder or box—paginated with title and name on each page. Also, do not pre-design book, i.e., no illustrations. We'd like to see books that will be read 50-100 years from now. New classics."

‡♣HERITAGE HOUSE PUBLISHING CO. LTD., Box 115, R.R. #2, Outrigger Rd., Nanoose Bay, British Columbia V0R 2R0 Canada. Fax: (250)468-5318. E-mail: herhouse@island.net. Website: http://www.rapidexmall .com/bc/bc/heritage. **Acquisitions**: Rodger Touchie, publisher/president. Heritage House is primarily a regional publisher of Western Canadiana and the Pacific Northwest. "We aim to publish popular history, contemporary recreational literature and culturally appealing manuscripts." Publishes trade paperback originals. Publishes 50% previously unpublished writers/year. Publishes 10-12 titles/year.
Needs: Juvenile. Recently published *Eagle's Reflection*, by Jim Challenger (children's); and *Orca's Family & More Northwest Coast Stories*, by Jim Challenger (children's).
How to Contact: Query with synopsis and SASE. Reports in 2 months.
Terms: Pays 10-12% royalty. Publishes ms 1 year after acceptance. Book catalog for SASE.
Advice: "Our books appeal to residents and visitors to the northwest quadrant of the continent. Present your material after you have done your best. Double space. Don't worry about getting an agent if yours is a one-shot book. Write for the love it. The rest will take care of itself."

‡HIGHSMITH PRESS, P.O. Box 800, Fort Atkinson WI 53538-0800. (414)563-9571. Fax: (414)563-4801. E-mail: hpress@highsmith.com. Website: http://www.hpress.highsmith.com. **Acquisitions:** Donald J. Sager, publisher. "Highsmith Press emphasizes library reference and professional books that meet the practical needs of librarians, educators and the general public." Publishes hardcover and paperback originals. Publishes 20 titles/year.
Imprint(s): Alleyside Press (creative, time-saving, low-cost resources for teachers and librarians).
Needs: No longer accepting children's picture book ms. "Our current emphasis is on storytelling collections for preschool-grade 6. We prefer stories that can be easily used by teachers and children's librarians, multicultural topics, and manuscripts that feature fold and cut, flannelboard, tangram, or similar simple patterns that can be reproduced." Recently published *Storyteller's Sampler*, by Valerie Marsh.
How to Contact: Reports in 1 month on queries; 3 months on mss. Simultaneous submissions OK.
Terms: Pays 10-12% royalty on net sales price. Offers $250-2,000 advance. Publishes ms 6 months after acceptance. Writer's guidelines and catalog free.

‡HOHM PRESS, P.O. Box 2501, Prescott AZ 86302. **Acquisitions:** Regina Sara Ryan, managing editor. "Our offerings include a range of titles in the areas of psychology and spirituality, herbistry, alternative health methods and nutrition, as well as distinctive children's books. Hohm Press is proud to present authors from the U.S. and Europe who have a clarity of vision and the mastery to communicate that vision." Publishes hardcover and trade paperback originals. Publishes 6-10 titles/year. 50% of books from first-time authors.
How to Contact: Reports in 3 months on queries. Simultaneous submissions OK.
Terms: Pays 10-15% royalty on net sales. No advance. Publishes ms 18 months after acceptance. Book catalog for $1.50.

HOLIDAY HOUSE, INC., (I, II), 425 Madison, New York NY 10017. (212)688-0085. Fax: (212)421-6134. Editor-in-Chief: Regina Griffin. **Acquisitions:** Allison Cunningham, assistant editor. Estab. 1935. "Holiday House has a commitment to publishing first-time authors and illustrators." Independent publisher of children's books, picture books, nonfiction and novels for young readers. Publishes hardcover originals and paperback reprints. Published new writers within the last year. Number of titles: Approximately 50 hardcovers and 15 paperbacks each year.

- *The Wright Brothers: How They Invented the Airplane* by Russell Freedman and published by Holiday House is a Newbery Honor Book.

Needs: Children's books only: literary, contemporary, Judaica and holiday, adventure, humor and animal stories for young readers. Recently published *The Life and Death of Crazy Horse*, by Russell Freedman; *The Golen*, by Barbara Rogasky, illustrated by Trina Schart Hyman; and *The Magic Dreideis*, by Eric A. Kimmel, illustrated by Katya Krenina. "We're not in a position to be too encouraging, as our list is tight, but we're always open to good writing."

How to Contact: "We prefer query letters and three sample chapters for novels; complete manuscripts for shorter books and picture books." Simultaneous submissions OK as long as a cover letter mentions that other publishers are looking at the same material. Reports in 1 month on queries, 3 months on mss. "No phone calls, please."

Terms: Advance and royalties are flexible, depending upon whether the book is illustrated. Publishes ms 1-2 years after acceptance.

Advice: "Please submit only one project at a time."

‡**HOLMES PUBLISHING GROUP**, P.O. Box 623, Edmonds WA 98020. E-mail: jdh@jdh.seanet.com. CEO: J.D. Holmes. **Acquisitions:** L.Y. Fitzgerald. Holmes publishes informative spiritual health titles on philosophy, metaphysical and religious subjects. Publishes hardcover and trade paperback originals and reprints. Publishes 40 titles/year.

Imprint(s): Alchemical Press, Sure Fire Press, Contra/Thought, Alexandria Press.

Needs: Metaphysical, occult.

How to Contact: Query first. Reports in 2 months.

Terms: Pays 10% royalty on wholesale price. Publishes ms 4 months after acceptance.

‡**HENRY HOLT & COMPANY BOOKS FOR YOUNG READERS**, Imprint of Henry Holt & Co., Inc., 115 W. 18th St., New York NY 10011. (212)886-9200. Fax: (212)633-0748. **Acquisitions:** Laura Godwin, associate publisher. Marc Aronson, senior editor (young adult nonfiction and fiction); Christy Ottaviano (picture books, middle grade fiction). Estab. 1866 (Holt). Henry Holt Books for Young Readers publishes excellent books of all kinds (fiction, nonfiction, illustrated) for all ages, from the very young to the young adult. Publishes hardcover and trade paperback originals. Publishes 50-60 titles/year.

Imprint(s): Edge Books (Marc Aronson, senior editor, "a high caliber young adult fiction imprint"); Red Feather Books (Christy Ottaviano, editor, "covers a range between early chapter and younger middle grade readers"); Owlet Paperbacks.

Needs: Juvenile: adventure, animal, contemporary, fantasy, history, humor, multicultural, religion, sports, suspense/mystery. Picture books: animal, concept, history, humor, multicultural, religion, sports. Young adult: contemporary, fantasy, history, multicultural, nature/environment, problem novels, sports. Recently published *Long Season of Rain*, by Helen Kim; and *Winning Ways*, by Sue Macy (both young adult).

How to Contact: Query with SASE. Reports in 5 months on queries and mss. Simultaneous submissions OK.

Terms: Pays royalty on retail price, 6% minimum for paperback, 10% minimum for hardcover. Offers $2,500 and up advance. Publishes ms 18 months after acceptance. Book catalog and writer's guidelines free.

HENRY HOLT & COMPANY, (II), 115 W. 18th St., 6th Floor, New York NY 10011. (212)886-9200. **Acquisitions**: Allen Peacock, senior editor (fiction). Publishes hardcover and paperback originals and reprints. Averages 80-100 total original titles, 35% of total is fiction each year.

Imprint(s): Owl (paper).

- Henry Holt is publishing more titles and more fiction.

How to Contact: Accepts queries; no unsolicited mss. Agented fiction 95%.

Terms: Pays in royalties of 10% minimum; 15% maximum; advance. Sends galleys to author.

‡**HOUGHTON MIFFLIN BOOKS FOR CHILDREN**, Imprint of Houghton Mifflin Company, 222 Berkeley St., Boston MA 02116. (617)351-5959. Fax: (617)351-1111. Website: http://www.hmco.com. **Acquisitions:** Sarah Hines-Stephens, submissions coordinator. "Houghton Mifflin gives shape to ideas that educate, inform, and above all, delight." Publishes hardcover and trade paperback originals and reprints. Firm publishes 100 titles/year.

Needs: Adventure, ethnic, historical, humor, juvenile (early readers), literary, mystery, picture books, suspense,

---

🍁 **THE MAPLE LEAF** symbol before a listing indicates a Canadian publisher, magazine, conference or contest.

young adult, board books. Recently published *Where Are You, Little Zack?*, by Enderle/Tessler (picture book, humorous); *The Woman in the Wall*, by Patrice Kindl (novel); and *Three Stories You Can Read to Your Cat*, by Miller (early reader with illustrations).

How to Contact: Submit complete ms with appropriate-sized SASE. Reports in 2 months. Simultaneous submissions OK.

Terms: Pays 5-10% royalty on retail price. Advance dependent on many factors. Publishes ms 18 months after acceptance. Writer's guidelines for 8×10 SASE. Book catalog for 9×12 SASE with 3 first-class stamps.

Advice: "Faxed manuscripts and proposals are not considered."

HOUGHTON MIFFLIN COMPANY, (III), 222 Berkeley St., Boston MA 02116. (617)351-5940. Fax: (617)351-1202. Website: http://www.hmco.com. **Acquisitions:** Christina Coffin, managing editor; Christine Corcoran, assistant to editorial director. Estab. 1832. Publishes hardcover and paperback originals and paperback reprints. Averages 100 total titles, 50 fiction titles each year.

Needs: None at present.

Terms: Pays royalties of 10% minimum; 15% maximum. Advance varies. Publishes ms 1-2 years after acceptance. Writer's guidelines and book catalog free.

How to Contact: Does not accept unsolicited mss. Buys virtually 100% agented fiction.

‡❧HOUNSLOW PRESS, Subsidiary of Dundurn Press Limited, 2181 Queen St., Suite 301, Toronto, Ontario M4E 1E5 Canada. Fax: (416)698-1102. **Acquisitions:** Tony Hawke, general manager. Estab. 1972. Publishes hardcover and trade paperback originals. Publishes 10% previously unpublished writers/year. Publishes 8 titles/year.

Needs: Literary and suspense. "We really don't need any fiction for the next year or so."

How to Contact: Query first. Reports in 2 months on queries.

Terms: Pays 10-12½% royalty on retail price. Offers $500 average advance. Publishes ms 1 year after acceptance. Book catalog free.

Advice: "If I were a writer trying to market a book today, I would try to get a good literary agent to handle it."

❧HOUSE OF ANANSI PRESS, (II), Affiliate of Stoddart Publishing, 1800 Steeles Ave. W., Concord, Ontario L4K 2P3 Canada. (905)660-0611. Fax: (905)660-0676. E-mail: anansi@irwin-pub.com. Website: www.irwin-pub.com/irwin/anansi. **Acquisitions:** Michael Byron Davis, publisher; Martha Sharpe, editor. Estab. 1967. Small literary press; publishes Canadian literary fiction, poetry and nonfiction. Publishes hardcover and paperback originals and paperback reprints. Average print order: 1,000. Published new writers within the last year. Plans 1 first novel this year. Averages 10-15 total titles, 3-5 fiction titles each year. Member of Literary Press Group and Association of Canadian Publishers. Distributes titles through General Distribution Services.

- House of Anansi Press has received the Governor-General's Award for nonfiction for *The Unconscious Civilization*.

Needs: Erotica, ethnic/multicultural, gay, lesbian, literary, short story collections, translations (from French-Canada only). Publishes anthologies of works by previously published Anansi authors. Recently published *Awake When All the World is Asleep*, by Shree Ghatage (short stories); and *Affairs of Art*, by Lise Bissonnette. Publishes the Spider Line series for new, experimental writing.

How to Contact: Submit outline/synopsis and 2 sample chapters. Include 1-page bio and list of publishing credits. Send SASE for reply, return of ms or send disposable copy of ms. Agented fiction 1%. Reports in 3 months on queries; 6 months on mss. Simultaneous and electronic submissions OK. Sometimes critiques or comments on rejected mss.

Terms: Pays royalties of 8% minimum; 10% maximum. Average advance: $700, negotiable. Sends galleys to author. Publishes ms 9 months after acceptance.

Advice: "We are hoping to expand and improve our fiction list. We will publish mainly in trade paperback with flaps, as this seems to be the market preference. Renewed interest in new Canadian writers (especially fiction) is bolstering our longstanding commitment to publishing excellent new fiction, as well as our previously published authors. It's best for newer writers to build up a publishing record by placing stories and/or poems in good literary journals or magazines before attempting to place a book with a publisher."

‡HOWELLS HOUSE, P.O. Box 9546, Washington DC 20016-9546. (202)333-2182. **Acquisitions:** W.D. Howells, publisher. Estab. 1988. "Our interests are institutions and institutional change." Publishes hardcover and trade paperback originals and reprints. Publishes 4 titles/year; each imprint publishes 2-3 titles/year.

Imprint(s): The Compass Press, Whalesback Books.

Needs: Historical, literary, mainstream/contemporary.

How to Contact: Query first. Reports in 2 months on proposals.

Terms: Pays 15% net royalty or makes outright purchase. May offer advance. Publishes ms 8 months after ms development completed.

‡HUMANICS CHILDREN'S HOUSE, Imprint of Humanics Publishing, 1482 Mecaslin St. NW, Atlanta GA 30309. (404)874-2176. **Acquisitions:** Shattuck Groom, director of trade division. Estab. 1977. "We publish picture books for young children that incorporate a small message about self-development." Publishes hardcover and trade paperback originals and reprints. Publishes 8 titles/year.

Needs: Picture books. "We do not publish many unsolicited manuscripts." Recently published *Giggle E. Goose*, by Al Newman; and *Paz in the Land of Numbers*, by Miriam Bowden.

How to Contact: Query or submit ms with SASE. Agented fiction 10%. Reports in 1 month. Simultaneous submissions OK, if so noted.

Terms: Pays 5-13% royalty on net receipts. Offers $500-1,000 advance. Publishes ms 6-24 months after acceptance. Writer's guidelines for #10 SASE. Book catalog for 9×12 SAE with 7 first-class stamps.

Advice: Audience is young children who need to be read to, or are beginning to read a little. "No phone calls, please."

‡♥**HUMANITAS**, 990 Croissant Picard, Brossard, Quebec J4W 1S5 Canada. Phone/fax: (514)466-9737. **Acquisitions**: Constantin Stoiciu, president. Publishes hardcover originals. Publishes 20% previously unpublished writers/year. Publishes 20 titles/year.

Needs: Fantasy, romance, short story collections. Recently published *La ronde de jour*, by Jean-Louis Le Scouarnec (roman).

How to Contact: Query first. Simultaneous submissions OK.

Terms: Pays 10-12% royalty on wholesale price. Publishes ms 2 months after acceptance. Writer's guidelines and book catalog free on request.

HYPERION, (III), Walt Disney Co., 114 Fifth Ave., New York NY 10011. (212)633-4400. Fax: (212)633-4811. **Acquisitions:** Brian DeFiore; Leslie Wells, executive editor; Rick Kot, executive editor; Laurie Abkemeier, editor; Wendy Lefkon, executive editor. Estab. 1990. "Mainstream commercial publisher." Publishes hardcover and paperback originals. Published new writers within the last year. Averages 110 total titles, 20 fiction titles each year.

Needs: Ethnic/multicultural, gay, literary, mainstream/contemporary, mystery/suspense, religious/inspirational, thriller/espionage. Recently published *Cadillac Jukebox*, by James Lee Burke; *Bone*, by Fae Mynne Ng (literary); and *No Witnesses*, by Ridley Pearson (suspense); and *Cimarron Rose*, by James Lee Burke.

How to Contact: Does not accepted unsolicited mss. Query first. Include bio (1 page) and list of publishing credits. Send SASE for reply, return of ms or send a disposable copy of ms. Agented fiction 100%. Reports in 2 weeks on queries; 1 month on mss. Simultaneous submissions OK.

Terms: Pays royalties; offers negotiable advance. Sends galleys to author. Publishes ms 6 months after acceptance.

‡**HYPERION BOOKS FOR CHILDREN**, Imprint of Hyperion, 114 Fifth Ave., New York NY 10011. (212)633-4400. Fax: (212)633-4833. **Acquisitions:** Lisa Holton, vice president/publisher. "The aim of Hyperion Books for Children is to create a dynamic children's program informed by Disney's creative vision, direct connection to children, and unparalleled marketing and distribution." Publishes hardcover and trade paperback originals. Publishes 210 titles/year.

Needs: Juvenile, picture books, young adult. Recently published *McDuff*, by Rosemary Wells and Susan Jeffers (picture book); and *Split Just Right*, by Adele Griffin (middle grade).

How to Contact: Agented submissions only. Reports in 1 month. Simultaneous submissions OK.

Terms: Pays royalty, "varies too widely to generalize." Advance varies. Publishes ms 1 year after acceptance. Writer's guidelines and book catalog free.

Advice: "Hyperion Books for Children are meant to appeal to an upscale children's audience. Study your audience. Look at and research current children's books. Who publishes what you like? Approach them. We are Disney and are always looking for Disney material."

‡**IDEALS CHILDREN'S BOOKS**, Imprint of Hambleton-Hill Publishing, Inc., 1501 County Hospital Rd., Nashville TN 37218. **Acquisitions:** Suzanne Smith, copy editor. Ideals Children's Books publishes nonfiction, fiction and poetry for toddlers to 10-year-olds. Publishes children's hardcover and trade paperback originals. Publishes 40 titles/year.

WRITER-TO-WRITER

Every day I thank the Higher Power that has given me the opportunity to write every morning that I wake. It's like being on full-tilt with the entire planet. The influence of the artist can be an enormous one. His words can reach thousands, even millions of people and can change their lives for the better. How many people can say that about the work they do?

James Lee Burke
Cimarron Rose, Hyperion

Needs: Childrens/juvenile. Recently published *The Sea Maidens of Japan*, by Lili Bell (Japanese culture, parent-child relationships); and *Sing, Henrietta! Sing!*, by Lynn Downey (friendship/gardening).

How to Contact: This publisher only accepts unsolicited mss from agents and members of the Society of Children's Book Writers & Illustrators, and previously published book authors may submit with a list of writing credits. Query or submit complete ms with SASE. Reports in 6 months on queries and mss.

Terms: Pay determined by individual contract. Publishes ms up to 2 years after acceptance. Book catalog for 9×12 SASE with 11 first-class stamps. Writer's guidelines for #10 SASE.

Advice: Audience is children in the toddler to 10-year-old range. "We are seeking original, child-centered fiction for the picture book format. Innovative nonfiction ideas for easy readers are also being sought."

♣INSOMNIAC PRESS, (II), 378 Delaware Ave., Toronto, Ontario M6H 2T8 Canada. (416)536-4308. Fax: (416)588-4198. E-mail: insomna@pathcom.com. **Acquisitions**: Mike O'Connor, publisher. Estab. 1992. "Small press which publishes new and experimental fiction." Publishes paperback originals. Books: 60 lb. paper; offset printing; perfect binding; illustrations. Average print order: 1,500. First novel print order: 1,500. Published new writers within the last year. Plans 3 first novels this year. Averages 8 total titles, 6 fiction titles each year.

Needs: Experimental, gay, literary, New Age/mystic/spiritual, short story collections. Plans anthology of gay stories. Recently published *What Passes for Love*, by Stan Rogal (short stories); *Beneath the Beauty*, by Philip Arima (poetry); and *Bootlegging Apples*, by Mary Elizabeth Grace (poetry).

How to Contact: Accepts unsolicited mss. Query with outline/synopsis. Accepts electronically transmitted queries by e-mail. Include estimated word count, bio and list of publishing credits. SASE for reply. Reports in 6 months. Simultaneous submissions OK.

Terms: Pays royalties. Sends galleys to author.

‡INTERCONTINENTAL PUBLISHING, (I,II,IV), 6451 Steeple Chase Ln., Manassas VA 20111-2611. (703)369-4992. Fax: (703)670-7825. E-mail: icpub@worldnet.att.net. Publisher: H.G. Smittenaas. Estab. 1992. Small press publisher of hardcover and paperback originals. Average print order: 5,000. Published new writer within the last year. Publishes 6 total titles/year; 6 fiction titles.

Needs: Mystery/suspense (amateur sleuth, cozy, police procedural, private eye/hardboiled). Recently published *Deadly Dreams*, by Schiller (mystery); *Twisted*, by Carmer (mystery).

How to Contact: Query with outline/synopsis and 1-3 sample chapters. Include estimated word count. Send SASE for reply, return of ms or send disposable copy of ms. Reports in 1-2 months on queries and mss. Simultaneous submissions OK.

Terms: Pays royalties of 5% minimum. Sends galleys to author.

Advice: "Be original, write proper English, be entertaining."

INTERLINK PUBLISHING GROUP, INC., (V), 46 Crosby St., Northampton MA 01060. (413)582-7054. Fax: (413)582-7057. E-mail: interpg@aol.com. Contemporary fiction in translation published under Emerging Voices: New International Fiction. **Acquisitions**: Michel Moushabeck, publisher; Phyllis Bennis, fiction editor. Estab. 1987. "Midsize independent publisher specializing in world travel, world literature, world history and politics." Publishes hardcover and paperback originals. Books: 55 lb. Warren Sebago Cream white paper; web offset printing; perfect binding; average print order: 5,000; first novel print order: 5,000. Published new writers within the last year. Plans 5-8 first novels this year. Averages 30 total titles, 5-8 fiction titles each year.

Imprint(s): Interlink Books, Olive Branch Press and Crocodile Books USA.

Needs: "Adult translated fiction from around the world." Recently published *Samarkind*, by Amin Maalof; *The Children Who Sleep by the River*, by Debbie Taylor; *The End Play*, by Indira Mahindra; and *The Silencer*, by Simon Louvish. Publishes the International Folk Tales series.

How to Contact: *Does not accept unsolicited mss.* Submit outline/synopsis only. SASE. Reports in 2 weeks on queries.

Terms: Pays royalties of 6% minimum; 7% maximum. Sends galleys to author. Publishes ms 1-1½ years after acceptance.

Advice: "Our Emerging Voices Series is designed to bring to North American readers the once-unheard voices of writers who have achieved wide acclaim at home, but were not recognized beyond the borders of their native lands. We are also looking for folktale collections (for adults) from around the world that fit in our International Folk Tale Series."

INTRIGUE PRESS, (II, IV), Subsidiary of Columbine Publishing Group, Inc., P.O. Box 456, Angel Fire NM 87710. (505)377-3474. Fax: (505)377-3526. E-mail: publish@intriguepress.com. **Acquisitions**: Lee Ellison, editor. Estab. 1994. "Small independent publisher specializing in mystery, suspense, and adventure fiction. Publishes hardcover and paperback originals and paperback reprints. Books: 50 lb. booktext paper; offset lithography printing; adhesive case or perfect-bound binding. Average print order: 3,000. First novel print order: 3,000. Published new writers within the last year. Plans 2 first novels this year. Averages 4 total titles, 3-4 fiction titles each year. Member of Publishers Marketing Association and Small Publishers of North America.

Imprint(s): Columbine Books (nonfiction).

Needs: Adventure, mystery/suspense (amateur sleuth, police procedural, private eye/hardboiled), thriller/espionage. "Our list is fairly well filled for the next year. Generally, our fiction needs are very specific. We do not publish anything outside those categories." Recently published *Partnerships Can Kill*, by Connie Shelton (mystery series); *Satan's Silence*, by Alex Matthews (mystery series); and *Assault on the Venture*, by Dan Shelton (action/adventure). Publishes The Charlie Parker mysteries, by Connie Shelton and the Cassidy McCabe mysteries by Alex Matthews.

How to Contact: Accepts unsolicited mss. Query with outline/synopsis and 3-4 sample chapters. Include estimated word count, 1-page bio, list of publishing credits and "how you might contribute to marketing the book." Send SASE for reply, return of ms or send disposable copy of ms. Reports in 4-6 weeks. Simultaneous submissions OK. Sometimes critiques or comments on rejected mss.

Terms: Pays royalties of 10% minimum, 15% maximum of net sales price. Offers negotiable advance. Sends galleys to author. Publishes ms 6-18 months after acceptance. Writer's guidelines and book catalog for #10 SASE.

Advice: "We already receive approximately 20 times more submissions than we can buy, so it behooves writers to be sure their work is absolutely top notch before sending it. Having a freelance editor or book doctor look at the manuscript before submitting it is a good idea. Also, we like authors who want to be involved in promotion and publicity. Belonging to writing organizations like Mystery Writers of America or Sisters in Crime is a definite plus because they give members lots of creative promotion tips. Along with your query letter, tell me your marketing plans."

IRONWEED PRESS, (II), P.O. Box 754208, Parkside Station, Forest Hills NY 11375. Phone/fax: (718)268-2394. E-mail: iwpress@aol.com. **Acquisitions:** Jin Soo Kang, publisher. Estab. 1996. Small independent publisher. Publishes hardcover and paperback originals. Plans 1 first novel this year. Averages 4 total titles, 4 fiction titles/year.

Needs: Ethnic/multicultural (Asian-American), experimental, humor/satire, literary.

How to Contact: Accepts unsolicited mss. Submit complete ms with a cover letter. Include list of publishing credits. SASE for return of ms. Reports in 1 month on queries; 2-3 months on mss. Simultaneous submissions OK. Sometimes critiques or comments on rejected mss.

Payment/Terms: Pays royalties of 8% minimum; offers advance; provides author's copies. Sends galleys to author. Publishes ms 6-12 months after acceptance.

ITALICA PRESS, (II, IV), 595 Main St., #605, New York NY 10044. (212)935-4230. Fax: (212)838-7812. E-mail: italica@aol.com. **Acquisitions:** Eileen Gardiner and Ronald G. Musto, publishers. Estab. 1985. Small independent publisher of Italian fiction in translation. Publishes paperback originals. Books: 50-60 lb. natural paper; offset printing; Smythe-sewn binding; illustrations. Average print order: 1,500. "First time translators published. We would like to see translations of Italian writers well-known in Italy who are not yet translated for an American audience." Publishes 6 total titles each year; 2 fiction titles. Distributes titles through direct mail. Promotes titles through catalogs.

Needs: Translations of 20th Century Italian fiction. Published *Bakunin's Son*, by Sergio Atzeni (experimental); *Otronto*, by Maria Corti; and *Sparrow*, by Giovanni Verga.

How to Contact: Accepts unsolicited mss. Query first. Queries by fax OK. Reports in 3 weeks on queries; 2 months on mss. Simultaneous submissions OK. Electronic submissions via Macintosh disk. Sometimes critiques rejected mss.

Terms: Pays in royalties of 5-15% and 10 author's copies. Sends pre-publication galleys to author. Publishes ms 1 year after acceptance. Book catalog free on request.

Advice: "Remember we publish *only* fiction that has been previously published in Italian. A *brief* call saves a lot of postage. 90% of the proposals we receive are completely off base—but we are very interested in things that are right on target. Please send return postage if you want your manuscript back."

‡JAMESON BOOKS, (I, II, IV), Jameson Books, Inc., The Frontier Library, 722 Columbus St., Ottawa IL 61350. (815)434-7905. Fax: (815)434-7907. **Acquisitions:** Jameson G. Campaigne, Jr., publisher/editor Estab. 1986. "Jameson Books publishes conservative, even libertarian politics and economics." Publishes hardcover and paperback originals and reprints. Books: free sheet paper; offset printing; average print order: 10,000; first novel print order: 5,000. Plans 6-8 novels this year. Averages 12-16 total titles, 4-8 fiction titles each year. Occasionally critiques or comments on rejected mss.

Needs: Very well-researched western (frontier pre-1850). No cowboys, no science fiction, mystery, poetry, et al. Published *Yellowstone Kelly*, by Peter Bowen; *Wister Trace*, by Loren Estelman; and *One-Eyed Dream*, by Terry Johnston.

How to Contact: Does not accepted unsolicited mss. Submit outline/synopsis and 3 consecutive sample chap-

---

SENDING TO A COUNTRY other than your own? Be sure to send International Reply Coupons instead of stamps for replies or return of your manuscript.

ters. SASE. Agented fiction 50%. Reports in 2 weeks on queries; 2-5 months on mss. Simultaneous submissions OK.

Terms: Pays royalties of 5% minimum; 15% maximum. Average advance: $1,500. Sends galleys to author. Publishes ms 1-12 months after acceptance. Book catalog for 6×9 SASE.

JOURNEY BOOKS FOR YOUNG READERS, (I, II), (formerly Bob Jones University Press), a division of Bob Jones University Press, Greenville SC 29614. (864)242-5100, ext. 4316. Website: http://www.bju.edu/press/freelnce.html. **Acquisitions:** Mrs. Gloria Repp, editor. Estab. 1974. "Small independent publisher." Publishes paperback originals and reprints. Books: 50 lb. white paper; Webb lithography printing; perfect-bound binding. Average print order: 5,000. First novel print order: 5,000. Published new writers within the last year. Plans 3 first novels this year. Averages 12 total titles, 10 fiction titles each year.

Needs: Children's/juvenile (adventure, animal, easy-to-read, historical, mystery, series, sports), young adults (adventure, historical, mystery/suspense, series, sports, western). Published *The Rivers of Judah*, by Catherine Farnes (contemporary teen fiction); *Arby Jenkins*, by Sharon Hambric (contemporary ages 9-12); and *The Treasure Keeper*, by Anita Williams, (adventure ages 6-10).

How to Contact: Accepts unsolicited mss. Query with outline and 5 sample chapters. Submit complete ms with cover letter. Include estimated word count, short bio, Social Security number and list of publishing credits. Send SASE for reply, return of ms or send a disposable copy of ms. Reports in 3 weeks on queries; 6 weeks on mss. Simultaneous and disk submissions (IBM compatible preferred) OK. "Check our webpage for guidelines." Sometimes comments on rejected mss.

Terms: "Pay flat fee for first-time authors; royalties for established authors." Sends final ms to author. Publishes ms 12-18 months after acceptance. Writer's guidelines and book catalog free.

Advice: Needs "more upper-elementary adventure/mystery or a good series. No picture books. No didactic stories. Read guidelines carefully. Send SASE if you wish to have ms returned. Give us original, well-developed characters in a suspenseful plot with good moral tone."

‡JUST US BOOKS, INC., 356 Glenwood Ave., 3rd Floor, East Orange NJ 07017. Fax: (201)677-7570. E-mail: justusbook@aol.com. Publisher: Cheryl Willis Hudson. **Acquisitions:** Allyson Sherwood, submissions manager. Publishes hardcover and trade paperback and mass market paperback originals. Publishes 3-5 titles/year.

Imprint(s): Afro-Bets®.

Needs: For middle readers and young adults. Looking for "contemporary, realistic, appealing fiction for readers aged 9-12, especially stories involving boys. Stories may take the form of chapter books with a range of 5,000-20,000 words." Recently published *Ziggy and the Black Dinosaurs: Lost in the Tunnel of Time*, by Sharon M. Draper (mystery); and *Annie's Gifts*, by Angela Shelf Medearis, illustrated by Anna Rich.

How to Contact: "Currently accepts queries *only*. Due to proliferation of unsuitable manuscripts, prospective writers must send for guidelines and catalog. Unsolicited manuscripts will be returned *unread*." Query with SASE.

Terms: Pays royalty or makes outright purchase. Offers variable advance. Publishes ms 18 months after acceptance. Book catalog and writer's guidelines for 6×9 SAE with 2 first-class stamps.

Advice: "We want stories for middle readers that appeal to both girls and boys (ages 9-12). This group still has higher priority for us than acquiring picture books."

‡KAYA PRODUCTION, 133 W. 25th St. #3E, New York NY 10001. (212)352-9220. Fax: (212)352-9221. E-mail: kaya@panix.com. Website: http://www.kaya.com. **Asquistions:** Sunyoung Lee, associate editor. "Kaya is a small independent press dedicated to the publication of innovative literature from the Asian diaspora." Publishes hardcover originals and trade paperback originals and reprints.

Needs: Ethnic, regional. "Kaya publishes Asian, Asian-American and Asian diasporic materials. We are looking for innovative writers with a commitment to quality literature." Recently published *East Goes West*, by Younghill Kang (novel reprint).

How to Contact: Submit synopsis and 2-4 sample chapters with SASE. Reports in 6 months on mss. Simultaneous submissions OK.

Terms: Writer's guidelines for #10 SASE. Book catalog free.

Advice: Audience is people interested in a high standard of literature and who are interested in breaking down easy approaches to multicultural literature.

KENSINGTON PUBLISHING CORP., (II), 850 Third Ave., New York NY 10022. (212)407-1500. Fax: (212)935-0699. **Acquisitions:** Monica Harris, senior editor (Arabesque); Tracy Bernstein, executive editor (Kensington Trade Paperbacks); Paul Dinas, executive editor (Pinnacle Books); Ann La Farge, executive editor (Zebra Books and Kensington Mass Market). Estab. 1975. "Kensington focuses on profitable niches and uses aggressive marketing techniques to support its books." Publishes hardcover originals, trade paperbacks and mass market originals and reprints. Averages 400 total titles/year.

Needs: Adventure, contemporary, erotica, mysteries, nonfiction, romance (contemporary, historical, regency, multicultural), thrillers, true crime, women's. No science fiction. Published *Destiny Mine*, by Janelle Taylor; *The Fall Line*, by Mark T. Sullivan; *Cemetary of Angels*, by Noel Hynd; and "Bride Price," in *Irish Magic II*, by Roberta Gellis. Ms length ranges from 100,000 to 125,000 words.
How to Contact: Contact with agent. Reports in 3-5 months.
Terms: Pays royalties and advances. Publishes ms 18 months after acceptance. Free book catalog.
Advice: "We want fiction that will appeal to the mass market and we want writers who want to make a career."

‡♥**KEY PORTER BOOKS LTD.**, 70 The Esplanade, Toronto, Ontario M5E 1R2 Canada. (416)862-7777. President/Editor-in-Chief: Susan Renouf. **Acquisitions**: Michael Mailand, senior editor (nonfiction); Barbara Berson, senior editor (fiction). Publishes hardcover originals and trade paperback originals and reprints. Publishes 50-60 titles/year.
Imprint(s): Firefly Books.
Needs: Humor, mainstream/contemporary, picture books. Recently published *Angel Falls*, by Tim Wynveen; and *Ancestral Suitcase*, by Sylvia Fraser.
How to Contact: Query with SASE. No longer accepts unsolicited mss.

‡♥**KINDRED PRODUCTIONS**, 4-169 Riverton Ave., Winnipeg, Manitoba R2L 2E5 Canada. (204)669-6575. Fax: (204)654-1865. E-mail: kindred@cdnmbconf.ca. Website: http://www.mbconf.org/mbc/kp/kindred.htm, **Acquisitions**: Marilyn Hudson, manager. "Kindred Productions publishes, promotes and markets print and nonprint resources that will shape our Christian faith and discipleship from a Mennonite Brethren perspective." Publishes trade paperback originals and reprints. Publishes 3 titles/year.
Needs: Historical (religious), juvenile, religious. "All our publications are of a religious nature with a high moral content."
How to Contact: Submit synopsis, 2-3 sample chapters and SASE. Reports in 3 months on queries. Simultaneous submissions OK.
Terms: Pays 10-15% royalty on retail price. Publishes ms 18 months after acceptance. Writer's guidelines and book catalog free on request.
Advice: "Most of our books are sold to churches, religious bookstores and schools. We are concentrating on devotional and inspirational books. We are accepting *very* few children's manuscripts."

‡**KITCHEN SINK PRESS**, Subsidiary of Kitchen Sink Entertainment, Inc., 320 Riverside Dr., Northampton MA 01060. (413)586-9525. Fax: (413)586-7040. Website: kitchensp@aol.com. **Acquisitions**: N.C. Christopher Couch, editor; Robert Boyd, editor; Catherine Garnier, associate editor. Estab. 1969. "Kitchen Sink Press publishes graphic novels and comics. It also publishes historical and analytical works on comics, artists, film and animation." Publishes trade paperback originals. Publishes 20 titles/year.
Imprint(s): Kitchen Sink Comix (comic books), Kitchen Sink Kids (children's titles).
Needs: Comics/graphic novels. Holds license for Will Eisner's *The Spirit*, J. O'Barr's *The Crow*. "We are not interested in superheroes. Check current catalog and works by Will Eisner, Alan Moore to get a feel for what we want." Recently published *From Hell*, by Alan Moore; *Cages*, by Dave McKean; and *Xenozoic Tales*, by Mark Schultz.
How to Contact: Query with 1 sample chapter for graphic novels, several pages for comics, and SASE. Reports in 3 months on queries. Simultaneous submissions OK.
Terms: Authors paid royalty on original work; stories based on licensed characters treated as work-for-hire. Publishes ms 18 months after acceptance. Writer's guidelines for #10 SASE. For book catalog call (800)672-7862 or fax request to (413)582-7116.

‡**ALLEN A. KNOLL, PUBLISHERS, (V)**, 200A W. Victoria St., Suite 3, Santa Barbara CA 93101. Estab. 1990. Small independent publisher. Publishes hardcover originals. Books: Offset printing; sewn binding. Member PMA, SPAN, ABA.
Needs: Recently published *Flip Side*, by Theodore Roosevelt Gardner II (suspense); *The Unlucky Seven*, by Alistair Boyle (mystery); and *Nobody Roots for Goliath*, by David Champion (courtroom drama). Publishes A Bomber Hanson Mystery (courtroom drama series) and A Gil Yates Private Investigator Novel (P.I. series).

WRITER-TO-WRITER

Put the seat of the pants (or skirt) on the seat of the chair and write. Hoping won't help; dreaming won't help; wanting won't help. Only writing and writing and writing (and, if necessary, rewriting) will make a writer.

Roberta Gellis
"Bride Price" in *Irish Magic II*, Kensington

How to Contact: Does not accept unsolicited mss. Book catalog free.

ALFRED A. KNOPF, (II), Division of Random House, 201 E. 50th St., New York NY 10022. (212)751-2600. Vice President: Judith Jones. **Acquisitions:** Senior Editor. Estab. 1915. Publishes hardcover originals. Number of titles: approximately 46 each year. Buys 75% agented fiction. Published new writers in the last year. Also publishes nonfiction.
Needs: Contemporary, literary, suspense and spy. No western, gothic, romance, erotica, religious or science fiction. Published *Silent Witness*, by Richard North Patterson; *Mystery Ride*, by Robert Boswell; *The Night Manager*, by John Le Carre; and *Lasher*, by Anne Rice. Published new writers within the last year.
How to Contact: Submit outline or synopsis with SASE. Reports within 1 month on mss. Publishes ms an average of 1 year after acceptance.
Terms: Pays 10-15% in royalties; offers advance. Must return advance if book is not completed or is unacceptable. Publishes ms 1 year after acceptance.
Advice: Publishes book-length fiction of literary merit by known and unknown writers.

KNOPF BOOKS FOR YOUNG READERS, (II), Division of Random House, 201 E. 50th St., New York NY 10022. (212)751-2600. Website: http://www.randomhouse.com/Knopf/index. **Acquisitions:** Sinion Boughton, publishing director. "Knopf is known for high quality literary fiction, and is willing to take risks with writing styles. It publishes for children ages 5 and up." Publishes hardcover and paperback originals and reprints. Averages 30 total titles, approximately 7 fiction titles each year.
Imprint(s): Dragonfly Books (picture books) and Knopf paperbacks (fiction).
Needs: "High-quality contemporary, humor, picture books, middle grade novels." Recently published *Merl and Jasper's Supper Caper*, by Laura Rankin, *The Squiggle*, by Carole Lexa Shaefer and Piers Morgan, *Crash*, by Jerry Spinelli; and *The Golden Compass*, by Philip Pullman.
How to Contact: Query with outline/synopsis and 2 sample chapters with SASE. Simultaneous submissions OK. Reports in 6-8 weeks on queries.
Terms: Pays royalties of 4% minimum; 10% maximum. Average advance: $3,000 and up. Sends galleys to author. Publishes ms 1-2 years after acceptance.

‡LAUREL BOOKS, Imprint of Dell Publishing, Division of Bantam Doubleday Dell, 1540 Broadway, New York NY 10036. (212)354-6500. **Acquisitions:** Leslie Schnur, editor-in-chief. Publishes trade paperback originals, mostly light, humorous material and books on pop culture. Publishes 4 titles/year.
Needs: Literary.
How to Contact: Query with synopsis, 2-3 sample chapters or complete ms and SASE. Reports in 4-6 months on queries. Simultaneous submissions OK.
Terms: Pays 7½-12½% royalty on retail price. Advance varies. Publishes ms 1 year after acceptance. Book catalog for 9×12 SAE and 3 first class stamps.

LEE & LOW BOOKS, (I, II), 95 Madison Ave., New York NY 10016. (212)779-4400. Fax: (212)683-1894. Editor-in-Chief: Elizabeth Szabla. **Acquisitions:** Renee Schultz. Estab. 1991. "Our goals are to meet a growing need for books that address children of color, and to present literature that all children can identify with. We only consider multicultural children's picture books. Of special interest are stories set in contemporary America." Publishes hardcover originals—picture books only. Averages 8-10 total titles each year.
Needs: Children's/juvenile (historical, multicultural, preschool/picture book for children ages 4-10). "We do not consider folktales, fairy tales or animal stories." Published *Dear Ms. Parks: A Dialogue With Today's Youth*, by Rosa Parks (collection of correspondence); *Giving Thanks: A Native American Good Morning Message*, by Chief Jake Swamp (picture book); and *Sam and the Lucky Money*, by Karen Chinn (picture book).
How to Contact: Accepts unsolicited mss. Send complete ms with cover letter or through an agent. Send SASE for reply, return of ms or send a disposable ms. Agented fiction 30%. Reports in 1-3 months. Simultaneous submissions OK. Sometimes critiques or comments on rejected mss.
Terms: Pays royalties. Offers advance. Sends galleys to author. Publishes ms 18 months after acceptance.

WRITER-TO-WRITER

Be a professional. Remember that your first word often isn't your best word, and that writing is re-writing. Don't wait for inspiration—write steadily and regularly, in a disciplined schedule that fits your life. If you can manage to write five polished pages a week, by the end of a year you'll have 250 pages. That's not bad.

Richard North Patterson
Silent Witness, Alfred A. Knopf

Writer's guidelines for #10 SASE. Book catalog for SASE with $1.01 postage.

Advice: "Writers should familiarize themselves with the styles and formats of recently published children's books. Lee & Low Books is a multicultural children's book publisher. We would like to see more contemporary stories set in the U.S. Animal stories and folktales are not considered at this time."

LEISURE BOOKS, (I, II), Division of Dorchester Publishing Co., Inc., 276 Fifth Ave., Suite 1008, New York NY 10001. (212)725-8811. Fax: (212)532-1054. E-mail: timdy@aol.com. **Acquisitions:** Jennifer Bonnell, editorial assistant; Christopher Keeslar, assistant editor. Mass-market paperback publisher—originals and reprints. Books: Newsprint paper; offset printing; perfect-bound; average print order: variable; first novel print order: variable. Plans 25 first novels this year. Averages 150 total titles, 145 fiction titles each year.

Needs: Historical romance, horror, techno-thriller, western. Looking for "historical romance (90,000-115,000 words)." Published *Pure Temptation*, by Connie Mason (historical romance); and *Frankly My Dear*, by Sandra Hill (time-travel romance).

How to Contact: Accepts unsolicited mss. Query first. SASE. Agented fiction 70%. Reports in 1 month on queries; 2 months on mss. "All mss must be typed, double-spaced on one side and left unbound." Comments on rejected ms "only if requested ms requires it."

Terms: Offers negotiable advance. Payment depends "on category and track record of author." Sends galleys to author. Publishes ms within 2 years after acceptance. Romance guidelines for #10 SASE.

Advice: Encourages first novelists "if they are talented and willing to take direction, *and* write the kind of category fiction we publish. Please include a brief synopsis if sample chapters are requested."

‡LERNER PUBLICATIONS COMPANY, (II), 241 First Ave. N., Minneapolis MN 55401. (612)332-3344. **Acquisitions:** Jennifer Martin, editor. (612)332-3344. Estab. 1959. "Midsize independent *children's* publisher." Publishes hardcover originals and paperback reprints. Books: Offset printing; reinforced library binding; perfect binding; average print order: 5,000-7,500; first novel print order: 5,000. Averages 70 total titles, 1-2 fiction titles each year.

Imprint(s): First Avenue Editions.

● Lerner Publication's joke book series is recommended by "Reading Rainbow" (associated with the popular television show of the same name).

Needs: Young adult: general, problem novels, sports, adventure, mystery (young adult). Looking for "well-written middle grade and young adult. No *adult fiction* or single short stories." Recently published *Dancing Pink Flamigos and Other Stories*, by Maria Testa.

How to Contact: Accepts unsolicited mss. Query first or submit outline/synopsis and 2 sample chapters. Reports in 1 month on queries; 2 months on mss. Simultaneous submissions OK.

Terms: Pays royalties. Offers advance. Provides author's copies. Sends galleys to author. Publishes ms 12-18 months after acceptance. Writer's guidelines for #10 SASE. Book catalog for 9×12 SAE with $1.90 postage.

Advice: Would like to see "less gender and racial stereotyping; protagonists from many cultures."

‡ARTHUR LEVINE BOOKS, Imprint of Scholastic Inc., 555 Broadway, New York NY 10012. (212)343-6100. **Acquisitions:** Arthur Levine, publisher. "Arthur Levine Books is looking for distinctive literature, for whatever's extraordinary. This is the first year for our list; we plan to focus on fiction." Publishes 8-10 titles/year.

Needs: Juvenile, picture books. Recently published *When She Was Good*, by Norma Fox Mazer.

How to Contact: Query only, include SASE. "We are willing to work with first-time authors, with or without agent."

Terms: Pays variable royalty on retail price. Advance varies. Book catalog for 9×12 SASE.

LINCOLN SPRINGS PRESS, (II), P.O. Box 269, Franklin Lakes NJ 07417. **Acquisitions:** M. Gabrielle, editor. Estab. 1987. Small, independent press. Publishes poetry, fiction, photography, high quality. Publishes paperback originals. Books: 65 lb paper; offset printing; perfect binding. Average print order: 1,000. "Prefers short stories, but will publish first novels if quality high enough." Averages 4 total titles, 2 fiction titles each year.

Needs: Contemporary, ethnic, experimental, feminist, historical, literary, short story collections. No "romance, Janet Dailey variety." Published *Maybe It's My Heart*, by Abigail Stone (novel); and *Subway Home*, by Justin Vitiello.

How to Contact: Accepts unsolicited mss. Query first with 1 sample chapter. SASE. Reports in 2 weeks to 3 months. Simultaneous submissions OK.

Terms: Authors receive royalties of 5% minimum; 15% maximum "after all costs are met." Provides 10 author's copies. Sends galleys to author.

LINTEL, (II), 24 Blake Lane, Middletown NY 10940. (212)674-4901. Editorial Director: Walter James Miller. Estab. 1977. Two-person organization on part-time basis. Books: 90% opaque paper; photo offset printing; perfect binding; illustrations. Average print order: 1,000. First novel print order: 1,200. Publishes hardcover and paperback originals. Occasionally comments on rejected mss.

Needs: Experimental, feminist, gay, lesbian, regional short fiction. Published second edition (fourth printing)

of *Klytaimnestra Who Stayed at Home*, mythopoeic novel by Nancy Bogen; and *The Mountain,* by Rebecca Rass.
How to Contact: Accepts unsolicited mss. Query with SASE. Simultaneous and photocopied submissions OK. Reports in 2 months on queries; 3 months on mss. Publishes ms 6-8 months after acceptance.
Terms: Negotiated. No advance. Sends galleys to author. Free book catalog.
Advice: "Lintel is devoted to the kinds of literary art that will never make The Literary Guild or even the Book-of-the-Month Club: that is, literature concerned with the advancement of literary art. We still look for the innovative work ignored by the commercial presses. We consider any ms on its merits alone. We encourage first novelists. Be innovative, advance the *art* of fiction, but still keep in mind the need to reach reader's aspirations as well as your own. Originality is the greatest suspense-building factor. Consistent misspelling errors, errors in grammar and syntax can mean only rejection."

‡LIONHEARTED PUBLISHING, INC., (II), P.O. Box 618, Zephyr Cove NV 89448. (702)588-1388. Fax: (702)588-1386. E-mail: admin@lionhearted.com. Website: http://www.LionHearted.com. **Acquisitions**: Historical or Contemporary Acquisitions Editor. Estab. 1994. Independent. Publishes paperback originals. Books: mass market paperback; perfect binding. Published new writers within the last year. Plans 12 first novels this year. Averages 12-72 fiction titles/year.
• LionHearted Publishing received the Wall Street Journal Women Entrepreneurs (book October 1997) award.
Needs: Romance (contemporary, futuristic/time travel, historical, regency period, romantic suspense; over 65,000 words only). Recently published *Undercover Love*, by Lucy Grijalua (romance); *Forever, My Knight*, by Lee Ann Dansby (romance); and *Destiny's Disguise*, by Candice Kohl (romance).
How to Contact: Accepts unsolicited mss. Query with outline/synopsis and 3 sample chapters. Include estimated word count, list of publishing credits, cover letter and 1 paragraph story summary in cover or query letter. Send SASE for reply, return of ms or send disposable copy of ms. Agented fiction less than 10%. Reports in 1 month on queries; 3 months on mss. No simultaneous submissions. Always critiques or comments on rejected mss.
Terms: Pays royalties of 10% maximum. Average advance: $1,000. $5,000 minimum guarantee on royalties. Sends galleys to author. Publishes ms 18-24 months after acceptance. Writer's guidelines free for #10 SASE. Book catalog available for SASE.
Advice: "If you are not an avid reader of romance, don't attempt to write romance, and don't waste your time or an editor's by submitting to a publisher of romance."

*THE LITERATURE BUREAU, P.O. Box CY749 Causeway, Harare Zimbabwe. **Acquisitions**: B.C. Chitsike, fiction editor. Publishes 8 previously unpublished writers/year. Averages 12 fiction titles/year. Distributes titles through booksellers and our tours to schools. Promotes titles through radio programs and book reviews.
Needs: "All types of fiction from the old world novels to the modern ones with current issues. We publish these books in association with commercial publishers but we also publish in our own right. We specialize in Shona and Ndebele, our local languages in Zimbabwe. Manuscripts in English are not our priority." Recently published *Madirativhang*, edited by E. Mari (poetry); *Emdangweni*, edited by E. Bhala (poetry); and *Nelakawibaya*, by D. Phiti (short stories). Length: 7,000-30,000 words.
How to Contact: Send entire manuscript. Reports in 6 months on mss.
Terms: Pays royalties. Obtain guidelines by writing to the Bureau.
Advice: "Send the complete manuscript for assessment. If it is a good one it is either published by the Bureau or sponsored for publication. If it needs any correction, a full report will be sent to the author. We have 'Hints to New Authors,' a pamphlet for aspiring authors. These can be obtained on request."

LITTLE, BROWN AND COMPANY, (II, III), 1271 Avenue of the Americas, New York NY 10020 and 34 Beacon St., Boston MA 02108. (212)522-8700 and (617)227-0730. **Acquisitions**: Editorial Department. Estab. 1837. "The general editorial philosophy for all divisions continues to be broad and flexible, with high quality and the promise of commercial success is always the first considerations." Medium-size house. Publishes adult and juvenile hardcover and paperback originals. Averages 200-225 total adult titles/year. Number of fiction titles varies.
Imprint(s): Little, Brown; Back Bay; Bulfinch Press.
• Send children's submissions to Submissions Editor, Children's Books, at Boston address. Include SASE.
Needs: Open. No science fiction. Published *Along Came a Spider*, by James Patterson; *The Poet*, by Michael Connelly; *The Pugilist at Rest: Stories*, by Thom Jones. Published new writers within the last year.
How to Contact: Does not accept unsolicited adult mss. "We accept submissions from authors who have

FOR INFORMATION ON ENTERING the *Novel & Short Story Writer's Market* Cover Letter Contest, see page 84.

published before, in book form, magazines, newspapers or journals. No submissions from unpublished writers." Reports in 4-6 months on queries. Simultaneous and photocopied submissions OK.

Terms: "We publish on a royalty basis, with advance."

LITTLE, BROWN AND COMPANY CHILDREN'S BOOKS, (III), Trade Division; Children's Books, 34 Beacon St., Boston MA 02108. (617)227-0730. Fax: (617)227-8344. Maria Modugno, editor-in-chief. **Acquisitions**: Erica Stahler, assistant editor; Megan S. Tingley, senior editor; Stephanie Peters, editor. Estab. 1837. Books: 70 lb. paper; sheet-fed printing; illustrations. Sometimes buys juvenile mss with illustrations "if by professional artist." Published "a few" new writers within the last year. Distributes titles through sales representatives. Promotes titles through author tours, book signings, posters, press kits, magazine and newspapers and Beacon Hill Bookbay.

● *Maniac Magee*, by Jerry Spinelli and published by Little, Brown and Company Children's Books, received a Newbery Award. *The Tulip Touch*, by Anne Fine received the Whitbread Award. *The Day Gogo Went to Vote*, by Elinor Sisulu received a 1997 ALA Notable Children's Books award. *Lunch Bunnies*, by Kathryn Lasky was listed in *Publishers Weekly* "Best Books '96."

Needs: Middle grade fiction and young adult. Recently published *Edward and the Pirates*, by David McPhail (picture book); *One of Each*, by Mary Ann Hoberman (picture book); and *The Tulip Touch*, by Anne Fine (young adult). Publishes 3 previously unpublished writers/year.

How to Contact: Submit through agent; authors with previous credits in children's book or magazine publishing may submit directly (include list of writing credits). Inquiries by fax OK.

Terms: Pays on royalty basis. Sends galleys to author. Publishes ms 1-2 years after acceptance.

Advice: "We are looking for trade books with bookstore appeal. We are especially looking for young children's (ages 3-5) picture books. New authors should be aware of what is currently being published. We recommend they spend time at the local library and bookstore familiarizing themselves with new publications." Known for "humorous middle grade fiction with lots of kid appeal. Literary, multi-layered young adult fiction with distinctive characters and complex plots."

LITTLE SIMON, Imprint of Simon & Schuster Children's Publishing Division, 1230 Avenue of the Americas, New York NY 10022. (212)698-7200. Website: http://www.simonandschuster.com. **Acquisitions**: Robin Corey, editor. "Our goal is to provide fresh material in an innovative format for pre-school age. Our books are often, if not exclusively, illustrator driven." Averages 120 total titles/year. This imprint publishes novelty books only (pop-ups, lift-the-flaps board books, etc).

How to Contact: Query for more information. Does not accept unsolicited mss. Reports in 8 months. Accepts simultaneous submissions.

Terms: Pays royalties of 2% minimum; 5% maximum. Publishes ms 6 months after acceptance.

‡**LITTLE TIGER PRESS**, % XYZ Distributors, 12221 W. Feerick St., Wauwatosa WI 53222. (414)466-6900. **Acquisitions**: Amy Mascillino. Publishes hardcover originals. Publishes 8-10 titles/year. Receives 100 queries and 1,200 mss/year.

Needs: Humor, juvenile, picture books. "Humorous stories, stories about animals, children's imagination, or realistic fiction are especially sought." Recently published *Lazy Ozzie*, by Michael Coleman, illustrated by Gwyneth Williamson; *Shhh!*, by Julie Sykes, illustrated by Tim Warnes; and *Dora's Eggs*, by Julie Sykes, illustrated by Jane Chapman.

How to Contact: Send ms with SASE. Agented fiction 15%. Reports in 2 months on queries and proposals, 3 months on mss. Simultaneous submissions OK.

Terms: Pays 7½-10% royalty on retail price or for first-time authors makes outright purchase of $800-2,500. Offers $2,000 minimum advance. Publishes ms 1 year after acceptance. Writer's guidelines for #10 SASE. Book catalog for #10 SASE with 3 first-class stamps.

Advice: "Audience is children 3-8 years old. We are looking for simple, basic picture books, preferably humorous, that children will enjoy again and again. We do not have a multicultural or social agenda."

‡**LIVING THE GOOD NEWS**, a division of the Morehouse Group, 600 Grant St., Suite #400. Denver CO 80203. Fax: (303)832-4971. **Acquisitions:** Liz Riggleman, editorial administrator. "Living the Good News is looking for books on practical, personal, spiritual growth for children, teens, families and faith communities." Publishes hardcover and trade paperback originals. Publishes 15 titles/year.

Needs: Juvenile, picture books, religious, young adult.

How to Contact: Query first. Submit synopsis with SASE. Reports in 2 months on proposals. Simultaneous submissions OK.

Terms: Pays royalty. Publishes ms 1 year after acceptance. Book catalog for 9 × 12 SAE and 4 first-class stamps. Writer's guidelines for #10 SASE.

Advice: Audience is those seeking to enrich their spiritual journey, typically from mainline and liturgical church backgrounds. "We look for original, creative ways to build connectedness with self, others, God and the earth."

‡**LIVINGSTON PRESS, (II)**, Station 22, University of Alabama, Livingston AL 35470. Imprint: Swallows Tale Press. **Acquisitions**: Joe Taylor, editor. Estab. 1982. "Literary press." Publishes hardcover and paperback

originals. Books: acid-free paper; offset printing; perfect binding. Average print order: 1,500. First novel print order: 1,500. Published new writers within the last year. Plans 2 first novels this year. Averages 4-6 total titles, 5 fiction titles each year. Sometimes critiques or comments on rejected mss.

Needs: Literary, short story collections. No genre. Published *Sideshows*, by B.K. Smith; *A Bad Piece of Luck*, by Tom Abrams; and *Alabama Bound*, by Colquitt.

How to Contact: Does not accept unsolicited mss. Query first. Include bio, list of publishing credits. Send SASE for reply, return of ms or send a disposable copy of ms. Agented fiction 10%. Reports in 3 weeks on queries; 6 months on mss. Simultaneous submissions OK.

Terms: Pays royalties of 6% minimum; 7½% maximum. Provides 12 author's copies. Sends galleys to author. Publishes ms 1-2 years after acceptance. Book catalog free.

‡LLEWELLYN PUBLICATIONS, (IV), P.O. Box 64383, St. Paul MN 55164. (612)291-1970. Fax: (612)291-1908. Website: http://www.llewellyn.com. **Acquisitions:** Nancy Mostad, acquisitions and development manager. Midsize publisher of New Age/occult fiction and nonfiction. Publishes paperback originals. Plans 1-2 first novels this year. Publishes 80 total titles/year; 10 fiction titles/year.

Needs: New Age/mystic/spiritual, psychic/supernatural/occult. Recently published *Soothsayer*, by D.J. Conway (occult); and *Ronin*, by D.A. Heeley (fantasy).

How to Contact: Query with outline/synopsis and 3 sample chapters or submit complete ms with a cover letter. Include estimated word count and bio. Send SASE for reply, return of ms or send disposable copy of ms. Replies in 1 week on queries; 2 weeks to 2 months on mss. Simultaneous submissions OK.

Terms: Sends galleys to author. Publishes ms 1 year after acceptance. Fiction guidelines free. Book catalog $3.

♣JAMES LORIMER & CO., PUBLISHERS, 35 Britain St., Toronto, Ontario M5A 1R7 Canada. (416)362-4762. Fax: (416)362-3939. **Acquisitions**: Diane Young, senior editor. "James Lorimer & Co. publishes Canadian authors only, on Canadian issues/topics. For juvenile list, realistic themes only, especially mysteries and sports." Publishes trade paperback originals. Publishes 10% previously unpublished writers/year. Publishes 20 titles/year.

Needs: Juvenile, young adult. "No fantasy, science fiction, talking animals; realistic themes only. Currently seeking chapter books for ages 7-11 and sports novels for ages 9-13 (Canadian writers only)." Recently published *Face Off*, by Chris Forsyth (sports); *Camp All-Star*, by Michael Coldwell (basketball).

How to Contact: Submit synopsis and 2 sample chapters. Reports in 4 months.

Terms: Pays 5-10% royalty on retail price. Offers negotiable advance. Publishes ms 6 months after acceptance. Book catalog for #10 SASE.

LOTHROP, LEE & SHEPARD BOOKS, (III), William Morrow & Co., 1350 Sixth Ave., New York NY 10019. (212)261-6641. Fax: (212)261-6648. **Acquisitions**: Susan Pearson, vice president/editor-in-chief; Melanie Donovan, senior editor. Estab. mid 19th century. "We publish children's books for all ages—about 25 books a year—primarily picture books." Publishes hardcover originals. Published new writers within the last year. Averages 25 total titles, 2-3 fiction titles each year.

Imprint(s): Morrow Junior Books (Contact: Diana Capriotti), **Greenwillow Books** (Contact: Barbara Trueson).
  ● The press received the Coretta Scott King Award for Illustration for *Meet Danitra Brown*, Mildred L. Batchelder Honor Award for Translation for *Sister Shako & Kolo the Goat*, and the Archer/Eckblad Children's Picture Book Award for *Circus of the Wolves*.

Needs: "Our needs are not by category but by quality—we are interested only in fiction of a superlative quality." Published *Sister Shako & Kolo the Goat*, by Vedat Dalokay; *What Kind of Love?*, by Shelia Cole; and *Dreamtime*, by Oodgeroo (anthology of Aboriginal stories).

How to Contact: Does not accept unsolicited mss. Submit through agent only. SASE for return of ms. Agented fiction 100%. Reports in 3-6 months on mss. Sometimes comments on rejected mss.

Terms: Pays royalties of 10% minimum; negotiable advance. Sends galleys to author. Publishes ms within 2 years after acceptance.

Advice: "I'd like to see more quality. More mss that move me to out-loud laughter or real tears—i.e. mss that touch my heart. Find an agent. Work on the craft. We are less able to work with beginners with an eye to the future; mss must be of a higher quality than ever before in order to be accepted."

‡♣LE LOUP DE GOUTTIÈRE, 347 Rue Saint-Paul, Quebec, Quebec G1P 1N5 Canada. (418)694-2224. **Acquisitions**: France Gagné, adjointe a l'édition. Publishes 15% previously unpublished writers/year. Publishes 16 titles/year.

Needs: Literary, short story collections. Recently published *L'Amour Sauce Tomate*, by Sylvie Nicolas; and *Docteur Wincet*, by Jean Désy.

How to Contact: Submit 3 sample chapters in French. Reports in 1 year on mss.

Terms: Pays 10% royalty. Offers no advance. Publishes ms 1 year after acceptance. Book catalog free.

LOVE SPELL, (I, II), Division of Dorchester Publishing Co., Inc., 276 Fifth Ave., Suite 1008, New York NY 10001. (212)725-8811. **Acquisitions**: Christopher Reeslar, assistant editor; Jennifer Bonnell and Mira Son, editorial assistants. "Love Spell publishes quirky sub-genres of romance: time-travel, paranormal, futuristic. Despite the exotic settings, we are still interested in character-driven plots." Mass market paperback publisher—originals and reprints. Books: newsprint paper; offset printing; perfect-bound; average print order: varies; first novel print order: varies. Plans 15 first novels this year.

Needs: Romance (futuristic, time travel, paranormal, historical). Looking for romances of 90,000-115,000 words. Recently published *Hidden Heart*, by Anne Avery (futuristic romance).

How to Contact: Accepts unsolicited mss. Query first. "All mss must be typed, double-spaced on one side and left unbound." SASE for return of ms. Agented fiction 70%. Reports in 1 month on queries; 4 months on mss. Comments "only if requested ms requires it."

Terms: Offers negotiable advance. "Payment depends on category and track record of author." Sends galleys to author. Publishes ms within 2 years after acceptance. Writer's guidelines for #10 SASE.

Advice: "The best way to learn to write a Love Spell Romance is by reading several of our recent releases. The best written stories are usually ones writers feel passionate about—so write from your heart! Also, the market is very tight these days so more than ever we are looking for refreshing, standout original fiction."

LOVESWEPT, (I, II), Bantam Books, 1540 Broadway, New York NY 10036. (212)354-6500. Website: http://www.bdd.com. **Acquisitions**: Susan Bradley and Joy Abella, senior editors. Imprint estab. 1982. Publishes paperback originals. "Our goal is to give you, the reader, stories of consistently high quality that sometimes make you laugh, make you cry, but are always fresh and creative and contain many delightful surprises within their pages." Plans several first novels this year. Averages 72 total titles each year.

Needs: "Contemporary romance, highly sensual, believable primary characters, fresh and vibrant approaches to plot. No gothics, regencies or suspense."

How to Contact: Query with SASE; no unsolicited mss or partial mss. "Query letters should be no more than two to three pages. Content should be a brief description of the plot and the two main characters."

Terms: Pays in royalties of 6%; negotiates advance. Writer's guidelines and book catalog free.

Advice: "Read extensively in the genre. Rewrite, polish and edit your own work until it is the best it can be—before submitting."

‡THE LYONS PRESS, (II), 31 W. 21st St., New York NY 10010. (212)929-1836. **Acquisitions**: Lilly Golden. Estab. 1984. Publishes hardcover and paperback originals and paperback reprints. Published new writers within the last year. Averages 70 total titles.

Needs: Adventure (sports), short story collections, western, outdoors. Recently published *Guiding Elliott*, by Robert Lee (fiction); *Travelers Corners*, by Scott Woldie (short stories); and *Dry Rain*, by Pete Fromm (short stories).

How to Contact: Accepts unsolicited mss. Query with outline/synopsis. Include bio and list of publishing credits. Send SASE for reply. Agented fiction 60%. Reports in 2 months. Simultaneous submissions OK. Critiques or comments on rejected mss.

Terms: Pays royalties; offers advance. Sends galleys to author.

MARGARET K. McELDERRY BOOKS, (V), Imprint of the Simon & Schuster Children's Publishing Division, 1230 Sixth Ave., New York NY 10020. (212)698-2761. **Acquisitions**: Margaret K. McElderry, publisher; Emma D. Dryden, editor. Estab. 1971. Publishes hardcover originals. Books: High quality paper; offset printing; cloth and three-piece bindings; illustrations; average print order: 10,000; first novel print order: 6,000. Published new writers within the last year. Averages 25 total titles each year. Buys juvenile and young adult mss, agented or non-agented.

   ● Books published by Margaret K. McElderry Books have received numerous awards including the Newbery and the Caldecott Awards, and a *Boston Globe/Horn Book* honor award. Because of the merger between Macmillan and Simon & Schuster this imprint (still intact) is under a new division (see above).

Needs: All categories (fiction and nonfiction) for juvenile and young adult: adventure, contemporary, early chapter books, fantasy, literary, mystery and picture books. "We will consider any category. Results depend on the quality of the imagination, the artwork and the writing." Recently published *A Summertime Song*, written and illustrated by Irene Haas; *Dog Friday*, by Hilary McKay; and *The Moorchild*, by Eloise McGraw.

Terms: Pays in royalties; offers advance. Publishes ms 18 months after acceptance.

Advice: "Imaginative writing of high quality is always in demand; also picture books that are original and unusual. Picture book manuscripts written in prose are totally acceptable. Keep in mind that McElderry Books is a very small imprint which only publishes 12 or 13 books per season, so we are very selective about the books we will undertake for publication. The YA market is tough right now, so we're being very picky. We try not to publish any 'trend' books. Be familiar with our list and with what is being published this year by all publishing houses."

AN IMPRINT LISTED IN BOLDFACE TYPE means there is an independent listing arranged alphabetically within this section.

‡McGREGOR PUBLISHING, 118 S. Westshore Blvd., Suite 233, Tampa FL 33609. (813)254-2665 or (888)405-2665. **Acquisitions:** Dave Rosenbaum, acquisitions editor. Publishes hardcover and trade paperback originals. Publishes 4-6 titles/year.
Needs: Mystery/suspense.
How to Contact: Query or submit synopsis with 2 sample chapters. Reports in 1 month on queries, 2 months on mss. Simultaneous submissions OK.
Terms: Pays 10-12% on retail price; 13-16% on wholesale price. Advances vary. Publishes ms 1 year after acceptance. Writer's guidelines and book catalog free.
Advice: "We work closely with an author to produce quality product with strong promotional campaigns."

MACMURRAY & BECK, INC., (II), 1649 Downing St., Denver CO 80218. (303)832-2152. Fax: (303)832-2158. Website: http://www.macmurraybeck.com (includes writer's guidelines, authors, titles). **Acquisitions**: Frederick Ramey, executive editor. Estab. 1991. "We are interested in reflective personal narrative of high literary quality." Publishes hardcover and paperback originals. Books: average print order: 4,000; first novel print order: 4,000. Published new writers within the last year. Plans 3-4 novels this year. Averages 8 total titles, 2-3 fiction titles each year. Distributes titles through major wholesalers and the Internet. Promotes titles through national advertising, direct mail and the Internet.
 • *St. Bull's Obituary*, by Daniel Akst was a PEN Faulkner finalist. MacMurray & Beck received the 1994 Rosenthal Foundation Award.
Needs: Contemporary, literary, short story collections, translations. Looking for "reflective fiction with high literary quality and commercial potential. No genre fiction, plot-driven, traditional, frontier western or mainstream." Recently published *Horace Afoot*, by Frederick Reuss; *Celibates and Other Lovers*, by Walter Keady; and *Perdido*, by Rick Collignon.
How to Contact: Does not accept unsolicited mss. Query first with outline/synopsis and 15 sample pages. Include 1-page bio, list of publishing credits, any writing awards or grants. SASE for reply. Agented fiction 75%. Reports in 3 months on queries. Simultaneous submissions OK. Sometimes critiques or comments on rejected mss.
Terms: Pays royalties; offers negotiable advance. Publishes ms 18 months after acceptance. Book catalog for $2.
Advice: "We are most interested in manuscripts that reflect carefully and emotionally on the ways we live our lives, on the things that happen to us, on what we know and believe. Our editors are also drawn to works that contemplate the roles that geography, culture, family and tradition play in all our efforts to define ourselves. We search for works that are free of the modern habit of accepting the world without thought. We publish a very limited number of novels each year and base our selection on literary quality first. Submit a concise, saleable proposal. Tell us why we should publish the book, not just what it is about."

‡JOHN MACRAE BOOKS, Imprint of Henry Holt & Co., Inc., 115 W. 18th St., New York NY 10011. (212)886-9200. **Acquisitions:** John Macrae, executive editor. Estab. 1991. "We publish literary fiction and nonfiction. Our primary interest is in language; strong, compelling writing." Publishes hardcover and trade paperback originals. Publishes 20-25 titles/year.
Needs: Literary, mainstream/contemporary. Recently published *Burning Your Boats*, by Angela Carter (novel).
How to Contact: Query only with SASE. Reports in 2 months on queries. Simultaneous submissions OK.
Terms: Pays 6-7½% royalty on retail price. Advance varies. Publishes ms 1 year after acceptance.

MAGE PUBLISHERS, (IV), 1032 29th St. NW, Washington DC 20007. (202)342-1642. Fax: (202)342-9269. E-mail: mage1@access.digex.net. Website: http://www.mage.com. **Acquisitions**: Amin Sepehri, assistant to publisher. Estab. 1985. "Small independent publisher." Publishes hardcover originals. Averages 4 total titles, 1 fiction title each year.
Needs: "We publish *only* books on Iran and Persia and translations of Iranian fiction writers." Ethnic (Iran) fiction. Recently published *My Uncle Napolean*, by Iraj Pezeshkzad; *King of the Benighted*, by M. Irani; and *Sutra and Other Stories*, by Simon Daneshvar.
How to Contact: Query first. SASE. Reports in 3 months on queries. Simultaneous and electronic submissions OK.
Terms: Pays royalties. Publishes ms 1 year after acceptance. Writer's guidelines for SASE. Book catalog free.
Advice: "If it isn't related to Persia/Iran, don't waste our time or yours."

‡MAIN STREET BOOKS, Imprint of Doubleday Adult Trade, 1540 Broadway, New York NY 10036. (212)354-6500. **Acquisitions:** Bruce Tracy, editorial director. Estab. 1992. "Main Street Books continues the tradition of Dolphin Books of publishing backlists, but we are focusing more on 'up front' books and big sellers in the areas of self-help, fitness and popular culture." Publishes hardcover originals, trade paperback originals and reprints. Publishes 20-30 titles/year.
Needs: Literary, pop, commercial. Recently published *Outside Providence*, by Peter Farrelly; and *Beeperless Remote*, by Van Whitfield.
How to Contact: Agented submissions only. Reports in 1 month on queries; 6 months on mss. Simultaneous submissions OK, if so noted.

Terms: Offers advance and royalties. Publishes ms 18 months after acceptance. Doubleday book catalog and writer's guidelines free.
Advice: "We have a general interest list."

‡**MARINER BOOKS**, Imprint of Houghton Mifflin, 222 Berkeley St., Boston MA 02116. (617)351-5000. Fax: (617)351-1202. Website: http://www.hmco.com. **Acquisitions:** John Radziewicz. Estab. 1997. "Houghton Mifflin books give shape to ideas that educate, inform and delight. Mariner is an eclectic list that notably embraces fiction." Publishes trade paperback originals and reprints.
Needs: Literary, mainstream/contemporary. Recently published *The Blue Flower*, by Penelope Fitzgerald (historical fiction).
How to Contact: Prefers agented submissions. Submit synopsis with SASE. Reports in 2 months on mss. Simultaneous submissions OK.
Terms: Pays 6% royalty on retail price or makes outright purchase. Advance varies. Book catalog free.

‡**MARIPOSA**, Imprint of Scholastic Inc., 555 Broadway, New York NY 10012. (212)343-6100. Website: http://www.scholastic.com. **Acquisitions:** Susana Pasternac, editor. "There is a great need for children's Spanish-language literature, work that is well done and authentic, that fills a *need*, not just a space." Publishes trade paperback originals and reprints. Publishes 20-25 titles/year (2-3 original titles/year).
Needs: Juvenile, picture books, young adult. "We do Spanish-language translations of the Magic School Bus and Goosebumps series." Recently published *Abuela and the Three Bears*, by Jerry Gello and Anna Lopez Escriva (bilingual picture book).
How to Contact: Query with completed ms and SASE. Reports in 3 months on mss. Simultaneous submissions OK.
Terms: Pays royalty on retail price, varies. Publishes ms 1 year after acceptance. Book catalog for #10 SASE.

‡♥**MARITIMES ARTS PROJECTS PRODUCTIONS**, (formerly M.A.P. Productions), Box 596, Station A, Fredericton, New Brunswick E3B 5A6 Canada. Phone/fax: (506)454-5127. E-mail: jblades@nbnet.nb.ca. **Acquisitions**: Joe Blades, publisher. "We are a small literary and regional (Atlantic Canadian) publishing house." Publishes trade paperback originals and reprints. Publishes 50-75% previously unpublished writers/year. Publishes 8-12 titles/year.
Imprint(s): Broken Jaw Press, Book Rat, SpareTime Editions, Dead Sea Physh Products.
Needs: Literary. Recently published *Diary of a Broken Heart*, by Shane MacDonald.
How to Contact: Query with bio and SASE. Reports in 6 months on mss.
Terms: Pays 10% royalty on retail price or 10% of print run. Offers $0-100 advance. Publishes ms 1 year after acceptance. Writer's guidelines for #10 SASE (Canadian postage or IRC). Book catalog for 6½×9½ SAE with 2 first-class Canadian stamps.

‡**MARLOWE & COMPANY**, Imprint of Marlowe & Thunder's Mouth, 632 Broadway, New York NY 10012. (212)780-0380. **Acquisitions**: John Webber, publisher. "We feature challenging, entertaining and topical titles in our extensive publishing program." Publishes hardcover and trade paperback originals and reprints. Publishes 50 titles/year.
Needs: Literary. "We are looking for literary, rather than genre fiction." Recently published *Fata Morgana*, by William Kotzwinkle; and *Heart's Journey In Winter*, by James Buchaw (winner of the Guardian Fiction Prize).
How to Contact: Query with SASE. "We do not accept unsolicited submissions." Reports in 2 months on queries. Simultaneous submissions OK.
Terms: Pays 10% royalty on retail price for hardcover, 6% for paperback. Offers advance of 50% of anticipated first printing. Publishes ms 1 year after acceptance. Book catalog free.

‡***MAROVERLAG**, Riedingerstrasse 24, D-86153, Augsburg Germany. **Acquisitions**: Benno Käsmayr, editor. Publishes 4-6 novels or story collections/year.
Needs: Publishes "exciting American authors in excellent translations; e.g. Charles Bukowski, Jack Kerouac, William Burroughs, Paul Bowles, Gerald Locklin, Keith Abbott, Raymond Federman and Gilbert Sorrentino."
How to Contact: Send a cover letter, synopsis, brief summary and 2 sample chapters. "Please include SAE and postage."
Terms: Writers paid for published fiction. "Our books and catalogs can be ordered at every German bookstore. Most of them send to the U.S. too."

‡**MASQUERADE BOOKS, (IV)**, Crescent Publishing, 801 Second Ave., New York NY 10017. (212)661-7878. Fax: (212)986-7355. E-mail: masqbks@aol.com. **Acquisitions:** Jennifer Reut, editor. Nation's largest erotic press. Publishes hardcover and paperback originals and paperback reprints. Published new writers within the last year. Plans 25 first novels next year. Publishes 125 total titles; 115 fiction titles.
   ● Press has received multiple Lambda Literary Awards.
Needs: Erotica, fantasy, gay, historical, horror, lesbian, psychic/supernatural/occult, romance, science fiction, short story collections, thriller/espionage. No children's, young adult, religious. "All manuscripts must contain explicit sexual content. No children, incest, bestiality." Prefers SM/fetish erotica. Recently published *The Slave*,

by Laura Antoniou (novel); *Flashpoint: Gay Male Sexual Writing*, by Michael Bronski (anthology); and *The Mad Man*, by Samuel Delany (novel).

How to Contact: Accepts unsolicited submissions. Query or send complete ms with a cover letter. Unsolicited correspondence by e-mail and fax OK. Include estimated word count and list of publishing credits. Send SASE for reply, return of ms or send disposable copy of ms. Agented fiction: 20%. Reports in 2 weeks on queries; 2 months on mss.

Terms: Pays royalties of 5% minimum plus negotiable advance and author's copies. Publishes ms 5-6 months after acceptance. Guideline and catalog free.

Advice: "We are always in the market for well-written, mass-market fiction. Gay market is saturated; no new material until 1998. By contrast, lesbian authors encouraged to submit. Familiarize yourself with our imprints and order a sample copy of our bimonthly magazine before sending us material. Imprints are as follows: Masquerade: straight erotica; Badboy: erotica for gay men; Rosebud: erotica for lesbians; Hard Candy: literary works by gay men with a strong emphasis on sexuality; Rhinoceros: pansexual literary words with a strong emphasis on sexuality."

‡MEADOWBROOK PRESS, 5451 Smetana Dr., Minnetonka MN 55343. (612)930-1100. Fax: (612)930-1940. **Acquisitions:** Jason Sanford, submissions editor. Estab. 1975. "We look for fresh approaches to overcoming traditional problems (e.g. potty training)." Publishes trade paperback originals and reprints. Publishes 12 titles/year.

Needs: Childrens/juvenile. Recently published *Girls to the Rescue*, Book #3, edited by Bruce Lansky (a collection of stories featuring courageous, clever and determined girls).

How to Contact: Query first. Reports in 3 months on queries. Simultaneous submissions OK.

Terms: Publishes ms 1 year after acceptance. Writer's guidelines and book catalog for #10 SASE.

Advice: "We like how-to books in a simple, accessible format and any new advice on parenting."

‡MERCURY HOUSE, (V), 785 Market St., Suite 1500, San Francisco CA 94103. (415)974-0729. Fax: (415)974-0832. **Acquisitions**: K. Janene-Nelson, managing editor; Tom Christensen, executive director. Estab. 1985. Small nonprofit literary house publishing outstanding work overlooked by mainstream presses, especially with a minority viewpoint. Publishes paperback originals. Books: acid-free paper; notch binding; some illustrations. Average print order: 4,000; first novel print order: 3,500. Averages 8 total titles, 1 fiction title/year. Member of Consortium Book Sales & Distribution.

● Recent recognition of Mercury House includes a Carey-Thomas nomination for Severo Sarduy's *Christ on the Rue Jacob*, which was named one of the best books of 1995 by *Publishers Weekly*; a Bay Area Book Reviewers Award for the first-ever English-language edition of George Sand's *Horace*, translated by Zack Rogow; a Firecracker Alternative Book Award for Dale Pendell's *Pharmako/Poeia*; and the Pen West Translation Award for Red Pine's *Guide to Capturing a Plum Blossom* by Sung Po-Jen.

Needs: Ethnic/multicultural, experimental, feminist, gay, lesbian, literary, regional (western), short story collections, translations. Publishes a sacred view of work; black view of jazz anthologies. Recently published *Masters and Servants*, by Pierre Michon, translated by Wyatt A. Mason; *Manhattan Music*, by Meena Alexander (multicultural); and *Conjuring Tibet*, by Charlotte Painter (spiritual quest).

How to Contact: Does not accept unsolicited mss. Query with outline/synopsis and up to 30 pages. Include estimated word count and list of publishing credits. Send SASE for reply, return of ms or send disposable copy of ms. Reports in 1 month on queries; 3 months on mss. No simultaneous submissions.

Terms: Pays royalties of 10% minimum. Average advance is low. Provides 10 author's copies. Sends galleys to author. Publishes ms in the same season after acceptance. Writer's guidelines free for #10 SASE. Book catalog for 6½×8½ SAE and $1.01 postage.

‡MILKWEED EDITIONS, 430 First Ave. N., Suite 400, Minneapolis MN 55401. (612)332-3192. **Acquisitions**: Emilie Buchwald, publisher; Elisabeth Fitz, manuscript coordinator. Estab. 1984. Nonprofit publisher with the intention of transforming society through literature. Publishes hardcover and paperback originals. Books: book text quality—acid-free paper; offset printing; perfect or hardcover binding. Average print order: 4,000. First novel print order depends on book. Averages 14 total titles/year. Number of fiction titles "depends on manuscripts."

● Milkweed Editions books have received numerous awards, including Finalist, *LMP* Individual Achievement Award for Editor Emilie Buchwald, awards from the American Library Association, and several Pushcarts.

✱ INTERNATIONAL MARKETS, those located outside of the United States and Canada, are marked with an asterisk.

Needs: For adult readers: literary fiction, nonfiction, poetry, essays; for children (ages 8-12): fiction and biographies. Translations welcome for both audiences. No legends or folktales for children. No romance, mysteries, science fiction.

How to Contact: Send for guidelines first, then submit complete ms. Reports in 1 month on queries; 6 months on mss. Simultaneous submissions OK. "Send for guidelines. Must enclose SASE."

Terms: Authors are paid in royalties of 7%; offers negotiable advance; 10 author's copies. Sends galleys to author. Publishes ms 1 year after acceptance. Book catalog for $1.50 postage.

Advice: "Read good contemporary literary fiction, find your own voice, and persist. Familiarize yourself with our list before submitting."

*MILLENNIUM, Orion Publishing Group, Orion House, 5 Upper St. Martin's Lane, London WC2H 9EA England. **Acquisitions:** Simon Spanton, editorial director. Averages 12-15 fiction titles/year. "Midsize commercial genre imprint. Hardcover and paperback originals and paperback reprints."

Needs: Science fiction, fantasy, horror. Novel-length material only. Accepts 90% agented submissions.

How to Contact: Send cover letter (including estimated word count and list of publishing credits), synopsis and first 50 sample pages.

Terms: Pays advance plus royalties.

‡MINSTREL BOOKS, Imprint of Pocket Books for Young Readers, Imprint of Simon & Schuster, 1230 Avenue of the Americas, New York NY 10020. (212)698-7000. Fax: (212)698-7007. Website: http://www.simonandschuster.com. Editorial director: Patricia McDonald. **Acquisitions:** Attn: Manuscript proposals. Estab. 1986. "Minstrel publishes fun, kid-oriented books, the kinds kids pick for themselves, for middle grade readers, ages 8-12." Publishes hardcover originals and reprints, trade paperback originals. Publishes 125 titles/year.

Needs: Middle grade fiction for ages 8-12: animal stories, fantasy, humor, juvenile, mystery, suspense. No picture books. "Thrillers are very popular, and 'humor at school' books." Recently published *R.L. Stine's Ghosts of Fear Street,* by R.L. Stine; and *Aliens Ate My Homework,* by Bruce Coville.

How to Contact: Query with synopsis/outline, sample chapters and SASE. Reports in 3 months on queries. Simultaneous submissions OK.

Terms: Pays 6-8% royalty on retail price. Advance varies. Publishes ms 2 years after acceptance. Writer's guidelines and book catalog free.

Advice: "Hang out with kids to make sure your dialogue and subject matter are accurate."

‡MOREHOUSE PUBLISHING CO., 871 Ethan Allen Hwy., Ridgefield CT 06877-2801. Fax: (203)431-3964. E-mail: eakelley@aol.com. **Acquisitions:** E. Allen Kelley, publisher; Deborah Grahame, senior editor. Estab. 1884. Morehouse publishes a wide variety of religious nonfiction and fiction with an emphasis on the Anglican faith. Publishes hardcover and paperback originals. Publishes 15 titles/year.

Needs: Juvenile, picture books, religious, young adult. Small children's list. Artwork essential. Recently published *Bless All Creatures Here Below,* by Judith Gwyn Brown; and *Angel and Me,* by Sara Maitland.

How to Contact: Query with synopsis, 2 chapters, intro and SASE. Note: Manuscripts from outside the US will not be returned. Please send copies only. Reports in 4 months. Simultaneous submissions OK.

Terms: Pays 7-10% royalty. Offers $500-1,000 advance. Publishes ms 8 months after acceptance. Book catalog for 9×12 SAE with $1.01 in postage stamps.

WILLIAM MORROW AND COMPANY, INC., (II), 1350 Avenue of the Americas, New York NY 10019. (212)261-6500. Fax: (212)261-6595. **Acquisitions:** Ann Bramson, editorial director (Hearst Books, Hearst Maine Books); Amy Cohn (Beech Tree Books, Mulberry Books); Susan Pearson, editor-in-chief (Lothrop, Lee & Shepard Books); David Reuther, editor-in-chief (Morrow Junior Books); Toni Sciarra, editor (Quill Trade Paperbacks); Elizabeth Shub (Greenwillow Books). Estab. 1926. Approximately one fourth of books published are fiction.

Imprint(s): Greenwillow Books; Hearst Books; Hearst Marine Books; **Lothrop, Lee & Shepard**; Morrow; **Morrow Junior Books**; Mulberry Books; Quill Trade Paperbacks; Tambourine Books; Tupelo Books and Rob Weisbach Books.

Needs: "Morrow accepts only the highest quality submissions" in contemporary, literary, experimental, adventure, mystery/suspense, spy, historical, war, feminist, gay/lesbian, science fiction, horror, humor/satire and translations. Juvenile and young adult divisions are separate.

How to Contact: Submit through agent. All unsolicited mss are returned unopened. "We will accept queries, proposals or mss only when submitted through a literary agent." Simultaneous submissions OK.

Terms: Pays in royalties; offers advance. Sends galleys to author. Publishes ms 2 years after acceptance. Free book catalog.

Advice: "The Morrow divisions of Greenwillow Books; Lothrop, Lee & Shepard; Mulberry Books and Morrow Junior Books handle juvenile books. We do five to ten first novels every year and about one-fourth of the titles are fiction. Having an agent helps to find a publisher."

MORROW JUNIOR BOOKS, (III), 1350 Avenue of the Americas, New York NY 10019. (212)261-6691. **Acquisitions:** David L. Reuther, editor-in-chief; Meredith Carpenter, executive editor; Andrea Curley, senior editor. Publishes hardcover originals. Plans 1 first novel this year. Averages 55 total titles each year.

Needs: Juvenile (5-9 years) including animal, easy-to-read, fantasy (little), spy/adventure (very little), preschool/picture book, young adult/teen (10-18 years) including historical, sports. Published *Birthday Surprises*, edited by Johanna Horwitz; *My Own Two Feet*, by Beverly Cleary; and *The White Deer*, by John Bierhoust.
How to Contact: Does not accept unsolicited mss.
Terms: Authors paid in royalties; offers variable advance. Books published 12-18 months after acceptance. Book catalog free on request.
Advice: "Our list is very full at this time. No unsolicited manuscripts."

‡**THE MOUNTAINEERS BOOKS**, 1001 SW Klickitat Way, Suite 201, Seattle WA 98134-1162. (206)223-6303. Fax: (206)223-6306. E-mail: mbooks@mountaineers.org. **Acquisitions:** Margaret Foster, editor-in-chief; Thom Votteler, senior acquisitions editor. Estab. 1961. "We specialize in expert, authoritative books dealing with mountaineering, hiking, backpacking, skiing, snowshoeing, canoeing, bicycling, etc. These can be either how-to-do-it or where-to-do-it (guidebooks)." Publishes 95% hardcover and trade paperback originals and 5% reprints. Publishes 40 titles/year. Average print order for a first book is 5,000-7,000.
Needs: Adventure. "We might consider an exceptionally well-done book-length manuscript on mountaineering." No poetry or mystery.
How to Contact: Query first. Reports in 3 months.
Terms: Pays royalty on net sales. Offers advance. Publishes ms 1 year after acceptance. Writer's guidelines and book catalog for 9 × 12 SAE with 3 first-class stamps.
Advice: "The type of book the writer has the best chance of selling our firm is an authoritative guidebook (*in our field*) to a specific area not otherwise covered; or a how-to that is better than existing competition (again, *in our field*)."

MOYER BELL LIMITED, Kymbolde Way, Wakefield RI 02879. (401)789-0074. Fax: (401)789-3793. **Acquisitions**: Jennifer Moyer, president/fiction editor. Estab. 1984. "Small publisher established to publish literature, poetry, reference and art books." Publishes hardcover and paperback originals and reprints. Books: average print order 3,000; first novel print order: 3,000. Averages 25 total titles, 6 fiction titles each year.
Needs: Serious literary fiction. No genre fiction. Recently published *The Orchard on Fire*, by Shena Mackay.
How to Contact: Accepts unsolicited mss. Submit outline/synopsis and 2 sample chapters. SASE. Reports in 2 months on mss. No queries. Simultaneous and electronic submissions OK. Sometimes comments on rejected mss.
Terms: Pays royalties of 10% minimum on hardcover. Average advance $2,500. Sends galleys to author. Publishes ms 12-18 months after acceptance. Book catalog free.

MULTNOMAH PUBLISHERS, INC., (II), P.O. Box 1720, Sisters OR 97759. (541)549-1144. Fax: (541)549-2044. **Acquisitions**: Editorial Dept. Estab. 1987. Midsize independent publisher of evangelical fiction and nonfiction. Publishes paperback originals. Books: perfect binding; average print order: 12,000. Averages 120 total titles, 40-50 fiction titles each year.
  ● Multnomah Books has received several Gold Medallion Book Awards from the Evangelical Christian
   Publishers Association.
Needs: Literary, religious/inspirational issue or thesis fiction. Published *Dominion*, by Randy Alcorn (contemporary); *Virtually Eliminated*, by Jefferson Scott (technothriller); and *Love to Water My Soul*, by Jane Kirkpatrick (historical novel). Publishes "Battles of Destiny" (Civil War series).
How to Contact: Submit outline/synopsis and 3 sample chapters. "Include a cover letter with any additional information that might help us in our review." Send SASE for reply, return of ms or send a disposable copy of ms. Reports in 10 weeks. Simultaneous submissions OK.
Terms: Pays royalties. Provides 100 author's copies. Sends galleys to author. Publishes ms 1-2 years after acceptance. Writer's guidelines for SASE.
Advice: "Looking for clean, moral, uplifting fiction. We're particularly interested in contemporary women's fiction, historical fiction, superior romance, and thesis fiction."

WRITER-TO-WRITER

I can't not write. I couldn't imagine reading a book, good or bad, or walking past an office-supply store without feeling the itch to get back to work. I've found that success of any kind is an aphrodisiac; the more I write and sell, the more ideas I have. I've never been blocked. "Writer's Block" is the last refuge of the failed artist.

   Loren D. Estleman
   Never Street, Mysterious Press; *Billy Gashade*, Forge

THE MYSTERIOUS PRESS, (III), Crime and mystery fiction imprint for Warner Books, 1271 Avenue of the Americas, New York NY 10120. (212)522-7200. Website: http://www.warnerbooks.com. (includes authors, titles, guidelines, bulletin board, tour info., contests). **Acquisitions**: William Malloy, editor-in-chief. Sara Ann Freed, executive editor. Estab. 1976. Publishes hardcover originals and paperback reprints. Books: Hardcover (some Smythe-sewn) and paperback binding; illustrations rarely. Average first novel print order: 5,000 copies. Published new writers within the last year.

• The Mysterious Press's *Up Jumps the Devil*, by Margaret Maron, won the Agatha Award for Best Mystery Novel.

Needs: Mystery/suspense. Published *The Two-Bear Mambo*, by Joe R. Lansdale; *Both Ends of the Night*, by Marcia Muller; *The Ax* by Donald Westlake; and *Never Street*, by Loren D. Estleman.

How to Contact: Agented material only. Critiques "only those rejected writers we wish to encourage."

Terms: Pays in royalties of 10% minimum; offers negotiable advance. Sends galleys to author. Buys hard and softcover rights. Publishes ms 1 year after acceptance.

Advice: "Write a strong and memorable novel, and with the help of a good literary agent, you'll find the right publishing house. Don't despair if your manuscript is rejected by several houses. All publishing houses are looking for new and exciting crime novels, but it may not be at the time your novel is submitted. Hang in there, keep the faith—and good luck."

THE NAIAD PRESS, INC., (I, II, IV), P.O. Box 10543, Tallahassee FL 32302. (904)539-5965. Fax: (904)539-9731. E-mail: naiadpress@aol.com. **Acquisitions**: Barbara Grier, editorial director. Estab. 1973. "Oldest and largest lesbian publishing company." Books: 50 lb. offset paper; sheet-fed offset; perfect-bound. Average print order: 12,000. First novel print order: 12,000. Publishes 30 total titles each year.

• The Naiad Press is one of the most successful and well-known lesbian publishers. They have also produced eight of their books on audio cassette.

Needs: Lesbian fiction, all genres. Recently published *Love's Harvest*, by Peggy Herring; *Northern Blue*, by Tracey Richardson; *First Impressions*, by Kate Calloway; *Chain Letter*, by Claire McNab; and *Out of the Night*, by Kris Bruyer.

How to Contact: Query first only. SASE. Include outline/synopsis, estimated word count, 2-sentence bio. Reports in 3 weeks on queries; 3 months on mss. No simultaneous submissions.

Terms: Pays 15% royalties using a standard recovery contract. Occasionally pays 7½% royalties against cover price. "Seldom gives advances and has never seen a first novel worthy of one. Believes authors are investments in their own and the company's future—that the best author is the author who produces a book every 12-18 months forever and knows that there is a *home* for that book." Publishes ms 1-2 years after acceptance. Book catalog for legal-sized SASE and $1.50 postage and handling.

Advice: "We publish lesbian fiction primarily and prefer honest work (i.e., positive, upbeat lesbian characters). Lesbian content must be accurate . . . a lot of earlier lesbian novels were less than honest. No breast beating or complaining. Our fiction titles are becoming increasingly *genre* fiction, which we encourage. Original fiction in paperback is our main field, and its popularity increases. We publish books BY, FOR AND ABOUT lesbians. We are not interested in books that are unrealistic. You know and we know what the real world of lesbian interest is like. Don't even try to fool us. Short, well-written books do best. Authors who want to succeed and will work to do so have the best shot."

THE NAUTICAL & AVIATION PUBLISHING CO. OF AMERICA INC., (IV), 8 W. Madison St., Baltimore MD 21201. (410)659-0220. E-mail: lkeddie@aol.com or 73244@compuserve.com or ssjb86a@prodigy.com. President: Jan Snouck-Hurgronje. **Acquisitions**: Rebecca Irish, editor. Estab. 1979. Small publisher interested in quality military history and literature. Publishes hardcover originals and reprints. Averages 10 total titles, 1-4 fiction titles each year.

Needs: Military/war (especially military history and Civil War). Looks for "novels with a strong military history orientation." Published *Normandy*, by VADM William P. Mack (military fiction); *Straits of Messina*, by VADM William P. Mack (military fiction); and *The Captain*, by Jan De Hartog (military fiction).

How to Contact: Accepts unsolicited mss. Query first or submit complete mss with cover letter. SASE necessary for return of mss. Agented fiction "miniscule." Reports on queries in 2-3 weeks; on mss in 3 weeks. Simultaneous submissions OK. Sometimes comments on rejected mss.

Terms: Pays royalties of 14%. Advance negotiable. After acceptance publishes ms "as quickly as possible—next season." Book catalog free on request.

Advice: Publishing more fiction. Encourages first novelists. "We're interested in good writing—first novel or last novel. Keep it historical, put characters in a historical context. Professionalism counts. Know your subject. *Convince us.*"

‡NAVAL INSTITUTE PRESS, Imprint of U.S. Naval Institute, 118 Maryland Ave., Annapolis MD 21402-5035. Fax: (410)269-7940. E-mail: esecunda@usni.org. Website: http://www.usni.org. Press Director: Ronald Chambers. **Acquisitions:** Paul Wilderson, executive editor; Mark Gatlin, senior acquisitions editor; Scott Belliveau, acquisitions editor. Estab. 1873. The U.S. Naval Institute Press publishes general and scholarly books of professional, scientific, historical and literary interest to the naval and maritime community. Publishes 80 titles/year. Average print order for a first book is 2,000.

Imprint(s): Bluejacket Books (paperback reprints).
Needs: Limited fiction on military and naval themes. Recently published *Rising Wind*, by Dick Couch (modern military thriller).
How to Contact: Query letter strongly recommended.
Terms: Pays 5-10% royalty on net sales. Publishes ms 1 year after acceptance. Writer's guidelines for #10 SASE. Book catalog free with 9×12 SASE.

THOMAS NELSON PUBLISHERS, (IV), Nelson Place at Elm Hill Pike, P.O. Box 141000, Nashville TN 37214-1000. (615)889-9000. Estab. 1798. "Largest Christian book publishers." Publishes hardcover and paperback originals. Averages 150-200 total titles each year.
Imprint(s): Janet Thoma Books, Oliver-Nelson Books, Thomas Nelson Trade Book Division.
Needs: Adventure, children's/juvenile (adventure), mystery/suspense, religious/inspirational (general), western (frontier saga, traditional). "All work must be Christian in focus." No short stories. Published *A Skeleton in God's Closet*, by Paul Maier (suspense/mystery); *The Twilight of Courage*, by Brock and Bodie Thoene (historical suspense); and *The Secrets of the Roses*, by Lila Peiffer (romance).
How to Contact: Corporate office does not accept unsolicited mss. "No phone queries." Send brief prosaic résumé, 1 page synopsis, an SASE and one sample chapter to acquisitions editors at the following locations: Janet Thoma, Janet Thoma Books, 1157 Molokai, Tega Cay SC 29715, fax: (803)548-2684; Vic Oliver, Oliver-Nelson Books, 1360 Center Dr., Suite 102-B, Atlanta GA 30338, fax: (770)391-9784; for biblical reference books contact: Phil Stoner, Nelson Biblical Reference Publishing, P.O. Box 141000, Nashville TN 37214. Fax: (615)391-5225. Reports in 3 to 12 months.
Terms: Offers negotiable advance. Sends galleys to author. Publishes ms 1-2 years after acceptance. Writer's guidelines for #10 SASE. Simultaneous submissions OK if so stated in cover letter.
Advice: "We are a conservative publishing house and want material which is conservative in morals and in nature."

‡TOMMY NELSON, Thomas Nelson, Inc. Publishers, 404 BNA Dr., Bldg. 200, Suite 508, Nashville TN 37217. **Acquisitions**: Laura Minchew, acquisitions editor. Tommy Nelson publishes children's Christian fiction for boys and girls up to age 14. Publishes hardcover and trade paperback originals. Publishes 5% previously unpublished writers/year. Publishes 50-75 titles/year.
Needs: Adventure, juvenile, mystery, picture books, religious. "No stereotypical characters without depth." Recently published *The Parable of the Lily*, by Liz Curtis Higgs, illustrated by Nancy Munger (picture book, ages 3-7); and *The Younguns of Mansfield*, by Thomas L. Tedrow (fiction, ages 10-14).
How to Contact: Submit synopsis with 3 sample chapters. Agented fiction 50%. Reports in 1 month on queries, 3 months on mss. Simultaneous submissions OK, but prefers not to.
Terms: Pays royalty on wholesale price or makes outright purchase. Pays $1,000 minimum advance. Publishes ms 18 months after acceptance. Manuscript guidelines for #10 SASE.
Advice: "Know the CBA market. Check out the Christian bookstores to see what sells and what is needed." Note: Nelson Children's Books and Word Children's books are now Tommy Nelson.

‡NESHUI PUBLISHING, (I, II), 6447 Alamo Ave. 2W, St. Louis MO 63105. (310)277-5154. Website: http://www.itlives.com. Editor: B. Hodge. Estab. 1995. Midsize, independent publisher of paperback originals. Books: 20 lb. paper; perfect bound. Average print order: 3,000-10,000. First novel print order: 3,000. Published new writers within the last year. Plans 6 first novels this year. Averages 6 total titles/year, 5 fiction titles/year.
Needs: Adventure, children's/juvenile (adventure, animal, easy-to-read, fantasy, historical, mystery, series), comics/graphic novels, experimental, fantasy, feminist, gay, glitz, historical, horror (dark fantasy, futuristic, psychological, supernatural), humor/satire, lesbian, literary, mainstream/contemporary, military/war, mystery/suspense (amateur sleuth, cozy, police procedural, private eye/hardboiled), New Age/mystic/spiritual, short story collections, thriller/espionage, translations, western (frontier saga, traditional), young adult (adventure, easy-to-read, fantasy/science fiction, historical, horror, mystery/suspense, romance, series, western). Especially interested in cyberfiction, graphic novels and experimental work. Publishes experimental anthology, *Faulkner & Third Street*.
How to Contact: Query with outline/synopsis or submit complete ms with cover letter. Include bio. Send SASE for reply or send disposable copy of ms. Agented fiction 6%. Reports in 6 weeks on queries. Simultaneous submissions OK.
Terms: Advance is negotiable. Pays honorarium. Sends galleys to author. Publishes ms 3-6 months after acceptance.

 INTERNATIONAL MARKETS, those located outside of the United States and Canada, are marked with an asterisk.

‡**NEW DIRECTIONS PUBLISHING CORP.**, 80 Eighth Ave., New York NY 10011. (212)255-0230. Fax: (212)255-0231. Website: http://www.wwnorton.com. **Acquisitions:** (Mr.) Declan Spring, managing editor. Estab. 1936. "New Directions publishes experimental, avant-garde works." Publishes hardcover and trade paperback originals and reprints. Averages 30-35 titles/year. Publishes 1% previously unpublished writers/year.
Needs: Experimental, avant-garde. "Become familiar with our catalog before deciding to submit."
How to Contact: Query first. Reports in 4 months.
Terms: Pays royalty on retail price. Offers $200-2,000 advance. Publishes ms 18 months after acceptance.

‡**THE NEW ENGLAND PRESS, INC.**, P.O. Box 575, Shelburne VT 05482. (802)863-2520. Fax: (802)863-1510. E-mail: nep@together.net. **Acquisitions:** Mark Wanner, managing editor. The New England Press publishes regional nonfiction and regional/historical young adult fiction. Publishes hardcover and trade paperback originals. Publishes 50% previously unpublished writers/year. Publishes 6-8 titles/year.
Needs: Regional, young adult. "We look for very specific subject matters based on Vermont history and heritage. We are also interested in historical novels for young adults based in New Hampshire and Maine. We do not publish contemporary adult fiction of any kind." Recently published *The Black Bonnet*, by Louella Bryant (young adult/Vermont history.)
How to Contact: Submit synopsis and 2 sample chapters with SASE. Reports in 3 months on proposals. Simultaneous submissions OK.
Terms: Pays royalty on wholesale price. No advance. Publishes ms 15 months after acceptance. Book catalog free.
Advice: "Our readers are interested in all aspects of Vermont and northern New England, including hobbyists (railroad books) and students (young adult fiction and biography). No agent is needed, but our market is extremely specific and our volume is low, so send a query or outline and writing samples first. Sending the whole manuscript is discouraged. We will not accept projects that are still under development or give advances."

NEW VICTORIA PUBLISHERS, (II, IV), Box 27, Norwich VT 05055. Phone/fax: (802)649-5297. E-mail: newvic@aol.com. Website: http://www.opendoor.com/NewVic/. **Acquisitions:** Claudia Lamperti, editor; ReBecca Béguin, editor. Estab. 1976. Small, three-person operation. Publishes trade paperback originals. Plans 2-5 first novels this year. Averages 8-10 titles/year. Distributes titles through Inbook/LPC Group.
● Books published by New Victoria Publishers have been nominated for Lambda Literary Awards and the Vermont Book Publishers Special Merit Award.
Needs: Lesbian/feminist: adventure, fantasy, historical, humor, mystery (amateur sleuth), romance. Looking for "strong feminist characters, also strong plot and action. We will consider most anything if it is well written and appeals to a lesbian/feminist audience; mostly mysteries." Publishes anthologies or special editions. Query for guidelines. Recently published *Takes One To Know One*, by Kate Allen (mystery); *Outside In*, by Nanisi Barrett D'Arnuk (mystery); and *No Daughter of the South*, by Cynthia Webb (mystery).
How to Contact: Submit outline/synopsis and sample chapters. SASE. Unsolicited queries by fax OK. Reports in 2 weeks on queries; 1 month on mss.
Terms: Pays royalties of 10%. Publishes ms 1 year after acceptance. Book catalog free.
Advice: "We are especially interested in lesbian or feminist mysteries, ideally with a character or characters who can evolve through a series of books. Mysteries should involve a complex plot, accurate legal and police procedural detail, and protagonists with full emotional lives. Pay attention to plot and character development. Read guidelines carefully."

‡**NEW YORK UNIVERSITY PRESS**, 70 Washington Square, New York NY 10012. (212)998-2575. Fax: (212)995-3833. E-mail: nyupmark@elmer2.bobst.nyu.edu. Website: http://www.nyu.edu/pages/nyupress/index.html. **Acquisitions:** Tim Bartlett (psychology, literature); Eric Zinner (cultural studies); Jennifer Hammer (Jewish studies, women's studies); Niko Pfund (business, history, law). Estab. 1916. "New York University Press embraces ideological diversity. We often publish books on the same issue from different poles to generate dialogue, engender and resist pat categorizations." Hardcover and trade paperback originals. Publishes 30% previously unpublished writers/year.
Needs: Literary. "We publish only 1 fiction title per year and don't encourage fiction submissions." Recently published *Bird-Self Accumulated*, by Don Judson (novella).
How to Contact: Submit synopsis and 1 sample chapter with SASE. Reports in 1 month. Simultaneous submissions OK.
Terms: Advance and royalty on net receipts varies. Publishes ms 8 months after acceptance.

✤**NEWEST PUBLISHERS LTD., (IV)**, 201, 8540-109 St., Edmonton, Alberta T6G 1E6 Canada. (403)492-4428. Fax: (403)492-4099. E-mail: newest@planet.eon.net. **Acquisitions:** Liz Grieve, general manager. Estab. 1977. Publishes trade paperback originals. Published new writers within the last year. Averages 8 total titles, fiction and nonfiction.
● NeWest received the Commonwealth Writers Prize for Best First Book in the Caribbean and Canada Region for *Icefields* by Thomas Wharton (1996) and for *Chorus of Mushrooms* by Hiromi Goto (1995).

Needs: Literary. "Our press is interested in western Canadian writing." Published *Diamond Grill*, by Fred Wah (bio fiction); *Icefields*, by Thomas Wharton (novel); and *Moon Honey*, by Suzette Mayr (novel). Publishes the Nunatak New Fiction Series.

How to Contact: Accepts unsolicited mss. Query first or submit outline/synopsis and 3 sample chapters. SASE necessary for return of ms. Reports in 2 months on queries; 4 months on mss. Rarely offers comments on rejected mss.

Terms: Pays royalties of 10% minimum. Sends galleys to author. Publishes ms at least 1 year after acceptance. Book catalog for 9×12 SASE.

Advice: "*We publish western Canadian writers only or books about western Canada.* We are looking for excellent quality and originality."

NIGHTSHADE PRESS, (II), Ward Hill, Troy ME 04987-0076. (207)948-3427. Fax: (207)948-5088. E-mail: potatoeyes@uninet.net. Website: http://www.maineguide.com/giftshop/potatoeyes (includes guidelines, newsletter, book list). Contact: Carolyn Page or Roy Zarucchi. **Acquisitions:** Edward M. Holmes, fiction editor. Estab. 1988. "Fulltime small press publishing literary magazine, poetry chapbooks, plus 1 or 2 nonfiction projects per year. Short stories *only, no novels please.*" Publishes paperback originals. Books: 60 lb. paper; offset printing; saddle-stitched or perfect-bound; illustrations. Average print order: 400. Published new writers within the last year. Plans to publish "dozens" of first novels this year. Averages 6 total titles, plus 19th century history collection. Promotes titles through mailing lists and independent book stores.

● Nightshade Press also publishes the literary magazine *Potato Eyes*.

Needs: Contemporary, feminist, humor/satire, literary, mainstream, regional. No religious, romance, preschool, juvenile, young adult, psychic/occult. Published *Two If By Sea*, by Edward M. Holmes; *Nightshade Nightstand Short Story Reader*, foreward by Fred Chappell; and *Every Day A Visitor*, by Richard Abrons.

How to Contact: Accepts unsolicited mss—short stories only. "Willing to read agented material." Unsolicited queries by e-mail OK. Reports in 1 month on queries; 3-4 months on mss. Sometimes comments on rejected mss.

Terms: Pays 2 author's copies. Publishes ms about 1 year after acceptance. Writer's guidelines and book catalog for SASE. Individual contracts negotiated with authors.

Advice: "Would like to see more real humor; less gratuitous violence—the opposite of TV. We have overdosed on heavily dialected southern stories which treat country people with a mixture of ridicule and exaggeration. We prefer treatment of characterization which offers dignity and respect for folks who make do with little and who respect their environment. We are also interested in social criticism, in writers who take chances and who color outside the lines. We also invite experimental forms. Read us first. An investment of $5 may save the writer twice that in postage."

‡NOONDAY PRESS, Imprint of Farrar Straus Giroux, Inc., 19 Union Square W., New York NY 10003. (212)741-6900. Fax: (212)633-2427. **Acquisitions:** Judy Klein, executive editor. Noonday emphasizes literary nonfiction and fiction, as well as fiction and poetry reprints. Publishes trade paperback originals and reprints.

Needs: Literary. Mostly reprints of classic authors. Recently published *Annie John*, by Jamaica Kincaid; and *Enemies: A Love Story*, by Isaac Bashevis Singer.

How to Contact: Query with outline. Reports in 2 months on queries. Simultaneous submissions OK.

Terms: Pays 6% royalty on retail price. Advance varies. Publishes ms 1 year after acceptance. Writer's guidelines free.

‡NORTH STAR LINE, Imprint of Blue Moon Books, 61 Fourth Ave., New York NY 10003. (212)505-6880. Fax: (212)673-1039. **Acquisitions:** Barney Rosset, editor/publisher. "North Star Line is aesthetically oriented, publishing poetry and poetic prose." Publishes hardcover originals, trade paperback originals and reprints. Publishes 10-15 titles/year.

Needs: Literary, short story collections, anthologies. Recently published *Stirrings Still*, by Samuel Beckett (reprint).

How to Contact: Query with synopsis and 1-2 sample chapters. Reports in 2 months on queries. Simultaneous submissions OK.

Terms: Pays 7½-10% royalty on retail price. Offers $500 advance. Publishes ms 1 year after acceptance.

‡NORTHLAND PUBLISHING CO., INC., P.O. Box 1389, Flagstaff AZ 86002-1389. (520)774-5251. Fax: (520)774-0592. E-mail: emurphy@northlandpub.com. Website: http://www.northlandpub.com. **Acquisitions:** Erin Murphy, editor-in-chief. Estab. 1958. "We seek authoritative manuscripts on our specialty subjects; no mainstream, general fiction or nonfiction." Publishes hardcover and trade paperback originals. Publishes 30% previously unpublished writers/year.

● This publisher has received the following awards in the past year: National Cowboy Hall of Fame Western Heritage Award for Outstanding Juvenile Book (*The Night the Grandfathers Danced*); Colorado Book Awards—Best Children's Book (*Goose and the Mountain Lion*); Reading Rainbow Book (*It Rained on the Desert Today*).

Imprint(s): Rising Moon (books for young readers).

Needs: Unique children's picture book and middle reader chapter book stories, especially those with Southwest/

West regional theme; Native American folktales (retold by Native Americans only, please). Picture book mss should be 350-1,500 words; chapter book mss should be approximately 20,000 words. Does not want to see "mainstream" stories. Northland does not publish general trade fiction. Recently published *The Night the Grandfathers Danced*, by Linda Theresa Raczek, illustrated by Katalin Ohla Ehling; and *My Name is York*, by Elizabeth Van Steenwyk, illustrated by Bill Farnsworth (children's book).

How to Contact: Query or submit outline and sample chapters. Reports in 1 month on queries; 3 months on mss. No fax or e-mail submissions. Simultaneous submissions OK if so noted.

Terms: Pays 8-12% royalty on net receipts, depending upon terms. Offers $1,000-3,000 average advance. Publishes ms 2 years after acceptance. Writer's guidelines and book catalog for 9 × 12 SAE with $1.50 in postage.

Advice: "Our audience is composed of general interest readers and those interested in specialty subjects such as Native American culture and crafts. It is not necessarily a scholarly market, but it is sophisticated."

‡NORTH-SOUTH BOOKS, affiliate of Nord-Sud Verlag AG, 1123 Broadway, Suite 800, New York NY 10010. (212)463-9736. **Acquisitions:** Julie Amper. Website: http://www.northsouth.com. Estab. 1985. "The aim of North-South is to build bridges—bridges between authors and artists from different countries and between readers of all ages. We believe children should be exposed to as wide a range of artistic styles as possible with universal themes." Publishes 5% previously unpublished writers/year. Publishes 100 titles/year.

● North-South Books is the publisher of the international bestseller, *The Rainbow Fish*.

Needs: Picture books, easy-to-read. "We are currently accepting only picture books; all other books are selected by our German office." Recently published *Wake Up, Santa Claus!*, by Marcus Pfister (picture); *The Other Side of the Bridge*, Wolfram Hänel (easy-to-read); and *A Mouse in the House*, by G. Wagener.

How to Contact: Agented fiction only. Query. Does not respond unless interested. All unsolicited mss returned unopened. Returns submissions accompanied by SASE.

Terms: Pays royalty on retail price. Publishes ms 2 years after acceptance.

W.W. NORTON & COMPANY, INC., (II), 500 Fifth Ave., New York NY 10110. (212)354-5500. Estab. 1924. Midsize independent publisher of trade books and college textbooks. Publishes hardcover originals. Occasionally comments on rejected mss.

Needs: High-quality fiction (preferably literary). No occult, science fiction, religious, gothic, romances, experimental, confession, erotica, psychic/supernatural, fantasy, horror, juvenile or young adult. Published *Seduction Theory*, by Thomas Beller; *Come and Go, Molly Snow*, by Mary Ann Taylor-Hall; and *The Book of Knowledge*, by Doris Grumbach.

How to Contact: Submit query letter to "Editorial Department" listing credentials and briefly describing ms. SASE. Simultaneous submissions OK. Reports in 8-10 weeks. Packaging and postage must be enclosed to ensure safe return of materials.

Terms: Graduated royalty scale starting at 7½% or 10% of list price, in addition to 15 author's copies; offers advance. Free book catalog.

Advice: "We will occasionally encourage writers of promise whom we do not immediately publish. We are principally interested in the literary quality of fiction manuscripts. A familiarity with our current list of titles will give you an idea of what we're looking for. If your book is good and you have no agent you may eventually succeed; but the road to success will be easier and shorter if you have an agent backing the book."

‡NWI, (I, II), Subsidiary of Quality Plus Books, P.O. Box 6314, Lawrenceville NJ 08648-0314. **Acquisitions:** Maria Valentin, editor. Estab. 1915. Midsize independent publisher geared towards publishing new and unpublished writers. Publishes hardcover and paperback originals. Books: 50 lb. white offset paper; electronic pre-press printing; perfect/hardcase binding. Average print order 3,000. Averages 25 total titles, 15 fiction titles/year.

● Member of SPAN, PMA.

Needs: Adventure, children's/juvenile, comics/graphic novels, fantasy, horror, mystery/suspense, New Age/mystic/spiritual, psychic/supernatural/occult, religious, romance, science fiction, short story collections, thriller/espionage, western, young adult/teen. Especially looking for children's books.

How to Contact: Accepts unsolicited mss. Query with outline/synopsis. Send SASE for reply or send a disposable copy of ms. Agented fiction 10%. Reports in 2 weeks. Simultaneous submissions OK. Sometimes critiques or comments on rejected mss.

Payment/Terms: Pays royalties of 8% minimum; 15% maximum. "Payment by individual arrangement at times depending on book." Publishes ms 3 months after acceptance. Writer's guidelines for SASE.

Advice: "We are publishing more paperbacks. Demand is growing. There is a growing need for high quality children's books and we are seeking to fulfill this need. Unpublished writers are encouraged to apply."

‡ONE WORLD, Imprint of Ballantine Publishing, 201 E. 50th St., New York NY 10022. (212)572-2620. Fax: (212)940-7539. Website: http://www.randomhouse.com. **Acquisitions:** Cheryl Woodruff, associate publisher; Gary Brozek, associate editor. Estab. 1992. "One World's list includes books written by and focused on African Americans, Native Americans, Asian Americans and Latino Americans. We concentrate on *American* multicultural experiences." Publishes hardcover and trade paperback originals, trade and mass market paperback reprints. Publishes 25% previously unpublished writers/year.

Needs: Historical. "We are looking for good contemporary fiction. In the past, topics have mostly been 'pre-

Civil rights era and before.' " Recently published *Kinfolks*, by Kristin Hunter Lattany (novel).
How to Contact: Query with synopsis, 3 sample chapters (100 pages) and SASE. Reports in 4 months. Simultaneous submissions OK, if so noted.
Terms: Pays 8-12% royalty on retail price, varies from hardcover to mass market. Advance varies. Publishes ms 2 years after acceptance. Writer's guidelines and book catalog for #10 SASE.
Advice: "For first-time authors, have a completed manuscript. You won't be asked to write on speculation."

‡♥**ORCA BOOK PUBLISHERS LTD., (I, IV)**, P.O. Box 5626, Station B, Victoria, British Columbia V8R 6S4 Canada. (604)380-1229. Fax: (250)380-1892. E-mail: orca@pinc.com. Website: http://www.swiftly.com/ orca. **Publisher:** R.J. Tyrrell. **Estab.** 1984. **Acquisitions:** Ann Featherstone, children's book editor. "Regional publisher of West Coast-oriented titles." Publishes hardcover and paperback originals. Books: quality 60 lb. book stock paper; illustrations Average print order: 3,000-5,000. First novel print order: 2,000-3,000. Plans 1-2 first novels this year. Averages 20-25 total titles, 1-2 fiction titles each year. Sometimes comments on rejected mss.
Needs: Contemporary, juvenile (5-9 years), literary, mainstream, young adult/teen (10-18 years). Looking for "contemporary fiction." No "romance, science fiction."
How to Contact: Query first, then submit outline/synopsis and 1 or 2 sample chapters. SASE. Agented fiction 20%. Reports in 2 weeks on queries; 1-2 months on mss. Publishes Canadian authors only.
Terms: Pays royalties of 10%; $500 average advance. Sends galleys to author. Publishes ms 6 months-1 year after acceptance. Writer's guidelines for SASE. Book catalog for 8½×11 SASE.
Advice: "We are looking to promote and publish Canadians."

‡**ORCHARD BOOKS**, Division of Grolier Publishing, 95 Madison Ave., New York NY 10016. (212)951-2650. **Acquisitions:** Sarah Caguiat, editor; Dominic Barth, associate editor. Orchard specializes in children's illustrated and picture books. Publishes hardcover and trade paperback originals. Publishes 25% previously unpublished writers/year.
Needs: Picture books, young adult, middle reader, board book, novelty. Recently published *Silver Packages*, by Rylant and Soentpiet; and *Mysterious Thelonius*, by Raschka.
How to Contact: Query with SASE. Reports in 3 months on queries.
Terms: Pays 7½-15% royalty on retail price. Advance varies. Publishes ms 1 year after acceptance.
Advice: "Go to a bookstore and read several Orchard Books to get an idea of what we publish. Write what you feel and query us if you think it's 'right.' It's worth finding the right publishing match."

‡**ORLOFF PRESS**, P.O. Box 80774, Athens GA 30608. Phone/fax: (706)548-0701. Fax: (706)548-0701. E-mail: orloffpress@aol.com. **Acquisitions:** John Spencer, editor. Publishes hardcover originals and reprints. Orloff specializes in literary and contemporary fiction. Publishes 50% previously unpublished writers/year. Publishes 4-6 titles/year.
 ● In addition to fiction, Orloff Press recently began publishing (and actively seeking submissions of) creative nonfiction.
Needs: Erotica, historical, humor, literary, mainstream/contemporary, mystery, short story collections. Recently published *Superstoe*, by William Borden (novel); and *Larger Than Death*, by Lynne Murray (mystery).
How to Contact: Submit synopsis, 3 sample chapters and SASE. Reports in 1 month on queries; 2 months on mss. Simultaneous submissions OK.
Terms: Pays 10% royalty on wholesale price. No advance. Publishes ms 9 months after acceptance. Book catalog free.

*‡**PETER OWEN PUBLISHERS**, 73 Kenway Rd., London SW5 0RE England. E-mail: admin@peterowen.u-net.com. **Acquisitions:** Antonia Owen, fiction editor. Averages 15 fiction titles/year.
Needs: "Independent publishing house now 45 years old. Publish fiction from around the world, from Russia to Japan. Publishers of Shusaku Endo, Paul and Jane Bowles, Hermann Hesse, Octavio Paz, Colette, etc."
How to Contact: Send cover letter, synopsis and/or sample chapter. Please include SASE (or IRC).
Terms: Pays advance and standard royalty.
Advice: "Be concise. Always include SASE and/or international reply coupon. Best to work through agent. Writers can obtain copy of our catalogue by sending SASE, and/or international reply coupon. It would help greatly if author was familiar with the list. U.K. bookselling, especially since end of net book agreement, is making new fiction very hard to sell. It is also hard to get fiction reviewed. At the moment we are publishing less fiction than nonfiction."

LOOKING FOR A PARTICULAR GENRE? Check our Category Index for magazine and book publishers who want **Mystery/Suspense, Romance, Science Fiction & Fantasy, Thrillers, Westerns** and more!

‡RICHARD C. OWEN PUBLISHERS INC., P.O. Box 585, Katonah NY 10536. Fax: (914)232-3977. **Acquisitions:** Janice Boland, director of children's books. "Our focus is literacy education with a meaning-centered perspective. We believe students become enthusiastic, independent, life-long learners when supported and guided by skillful teachers. The professional development work we do and the books we publish support these beliefs." Publishes hardcover and paperback originals. Publishes 99% previously unpublished writers/year.
- "We are also seeking manuscripts for our new collection of short, snappy stories for 8-10-year-old children (3rd and 4th grades). Subjects include humor, careers, mysteries, science fiction, folktales, women, fashion trends, sports, music, myths, journalism, history, inventions, planets, architecture, plays, adventure, technology, vehicles."

Needs: Picture books. "Brief, strong story line, real characters, natural language, exciting—child-appealing stories with a twist. No lists, alphabet or counting books." Recently published *There Was a Mouse*, by Blanchard/Suhr; and *Jump the Broom*, by Candy Helmso.
How to Contact: Send for ms guidelines, then submit full ms with SASE. Reports in 1 month on queries; 2 months on mss. Simultaneous submissions OK, if so noted.
Terms: Pays 5% royalty on wholesale price. Publishes ms 3 years after acceptance. Writer's guidelines for SASE with 52¢ postage.
Advice: "We don't respond to queries. Because our books are so brief it is better to send entire ms."

‡OWL BOOKS, Imprint of Henry Holt & Co., Inc., 115 W. 18th St., New York NY 10011. (212)886-9200. **Acquisitions:** Theresa Burns, editor. Estab. 1996. "We are looking for original, great ideas that have commercial appeal, but that you can respect." Publishes 30% previously unpublished writers/year.
Needs: Mainstream/contemporary. Recently published *White Boy Shuffle*, by Paul Beatty; and *The Debt to Pleasure*, by John Lanchester.
How to Contact: Query with synopsis, 1 sample chapter and SASE. Reports in 2 months. Simultaneous submissions OK.
Terms: Pays 6-7½% royalty on retail price. Advance varies. Publishes ms 1 year after acceptance.

‡OWL CREEK PRESS, 2693 SW Camaro Dr., Camaro Island WA 98292. **Acquisitions:** Rich Ives, editor. "We publish selections on artistic merit only." Publishes hardcover originals, trade paperback originals and reprints. Publishes 50% previously unpublished writers/year.
Needs: Literary, short story collections. Recently published *The Body of Martin Aguilera*, by Percival Everett; and *Sailing to Corinth*, by Irene Wanner.
How to Contact: Submit 1 sample chapter. Reports in 3 months.
Terms: Pays 10-15% royalty, makes outright purchase or with a percentage of print run. Publishes ms 2 years after acceptance. Book catalog for #10 SASE.

‡♣PACIFIC EDUCATIONAL PRESS, Faculty of Education, University of British Columbia, Vancouver, British Columbia V6T 1Z4 Canada. Fax: (604)822-6603. E-mail: cedwards@interchange.ubc.ca. **Acquisitions:** Catherine Edwards, director. Publishes trade paperback originals. Publishes 15% previously unpublished writers/year. Publishes 6-8 titles/year.
- Pacific Educational Press considers Canadian authors only for children's titles. Non-Canadian writers may submit educational titles.

Needs: For children: ethnic, historical, juvenile, mystery, science fiction, young adult. For children or teachers: plays. "We select fiction based on its potential for use in language arts classes as well as its literary merit." Recently published *The Reluctant Deckhand*, by Jan Padgett (juvenile novel about a young girl's summer aboard her mother's fishing boat).
How to Contact: Submit synopsis. Reports in 6 months on mss. Simultaneous submissions OK, if so noted.
Terms: Book catalog and writer's guidelines for 9×12 SAE with IRCs.

PANTHEON BOOKS, (III), Subsidiary of Random House, 201 E. 50th St., New York NY 10022. (212)572-2854. **Acquisitions:** Editorial Department. Estab. 1942. "Small but well-established imprint of well-known large house." Publishes hardcover and trade paperback originals and trade paperback reprints. Averages 75 total titles, about one-third fiction, each year.
Needs: Quality fiction and nonfiction.
How to Contact: Query letter and sample material. SASE.
Payment/Terms: Pays royalties; offers advance.

‡PAPER CHASE PRESS, 5721 Magazine St., #152, New Orleans LA 70115. **Acquisitions:** Jennifer Osborn, editor. "Our audience is mainstream—people who read a lot and are open to all kinds of fiction, literary or otherwise." Publishes hardcover and trade paperback originals and reprints. Publishes 90% previously unpublished writers/year.
Needs: Mainstream/contemporary.
How to Contact: Query; submit synopsis and first 2 chapters only. Responds only if interested. Simultaneous submissions OK.
Terms: Pays royalty on retail price; varies from hardcover to trade. Publishes ms 18 months after acceptance

of ms.

Advice: "We don't want to see someone's first draft. Stay in tune with current trends in fiction. The beginning of the story should be strong enough to *immediately* generate interest in the whole book—sympathetic characters with depth and variety. Relationship issues are particularly interesting to us, i.e., family relationhips, personal relationships. Make your characters and your story believable!"

PAPIER-MACHE PRESS, (II), 627 Walker St., Watsonville CA 95076-4119. (408)763-1420. Fax: (408)763-1422. Website: www.ReadersNdex.com/papiermache. **Acquisitions**: Sandra Martz, editor/publisher; Shirley Coe, acquisitions editor. Estab. 1984. "Small women's press." Publishes anthologies, novels. Books: 60-70 lb. offset paper; perfect-bound or case-bound. Average print order: 4,000-8,000. Published new writers within the last year. Publishes 6-10 total titles/year.

● Papier-Mache Press publishes a number of well-received themed anthologies. Their anthology, *I Am Becoming the Woman I've Wanted*, received a 1995 American Book Award. *Late Summer Break*, by Ann Knox was a PMA Benjamin Franklin Award Finalist.

Needs: Contemporary, feminist, women's novels. Published *Late Summer Break*, by Ann Knox; *Creek Walk and Other Stories*, by Molly Giles; and *Flying Horses/Secret Souls*, by Randeane Tetu.

How to Contact: Query first. SASE. Reports in 2 months on queries; 6 months on mss. Simultaneous and photocopied submissions OK. Accepts computer printouts.

Terms: Standard royalty agreements and complimentary copy. Publishes ms 18 months after acceptance. Writer's guidelines and book catalog free.

Advice: "Absolutely essential to send sample chapters with query. Please note on the query whether it's a simultaneous submission."

PASSEGGIATA PRESS, INC., (III, IV), (formerly Three Continents Press), P.O. Box 636, Pueblo CO 81002. (719)544-1038. Fax: (719)546-7889. **Acquisitions**: Donald Herdeck, fiction editor. Estab. 1973. "We search for books that will make clear the complexity and value of non-Western literature and culture." Small independent publisher with expanding list. Publishes hardcover and paperback originals and reprints. Books: library binding; illustrations. Average print order: 1,000-1,500. First novel print order: 1,000. Averages 15 total titles, 6-8 fiction titles each year.

Needs: "We publish original fiction only by writers from Africa, the Caribbean, the Middle East, Asia and the Pacific. No fiction by writers from North America or Western Europe." Published *Lina: Portrait of a Damascene Girl*, by Samar Altar; *The Native Informant*, by Ramzi Salti (stories); and *Repudiation*, by Rachid Boudjedra.

How to Contact: Query with outline/synopsis and sample pages with SASE. State "origins (non-Western), education and previous publications." Reports in 1 month on queries; 2 months on mss. Simultaneous submissions OK. Occasionally critiques ("a few sentences") rejected mss.

Terms: "Send inquiry letter first and ms only if so requested by us. We are not a subsidy publisher, but do a few specialized titles a year with grants. In those cases we accept institutional subventions. Foundation or institution receives 20-30 copies of book and at times royalty on first printing. We pay royalties twice yearly (against advance) as a percentage of net paid receipts." Royalties of 5% minimum; 10% maximum. Offers negotiable advance, $300 average. Provides 10 author's copies. Sends galleys to author. Free book catalog available; inquiry letter first and ms only if so requested by us.

Advice: "Submit professional work (within our parameters of interest) with well worked-over language and clean manuscripts prepared to exacting standards."

‡PATEK PRESS, INCORPORATED, (I), 2193 Capehart Circle NE, Atlanta GA 30345. E-mail: dneuge@aol.com. **Acquisitions:** Dunn Neugebauer, owner/editor. Estab. 1997. Small, independent publisher. Publishes paperback originals. Books: 50 or 60 lb. paper; perfect bound; illustrations when appropriate. Average print order 500-1,000. First novel print order 1,000. Plans 5-10 first novels this year. Plans 12-20 total titles, 8-15 fiction titles this year.

Needs: Adventure, horror, humor/satire, mainstream/contemporary, mystery/suspense, sports, short story collections. No historical, science fiction or children's literature. "We strongly encourage new writers, but exercise other options first. We are a small, independent publisher without the financial capabilities of the big publishers."

How to Contact: Accepts unsolicited mss. Submit complete ms with cover letter. Unsolicited queries/correspondence by e-mail OK. Include bio with submission. SASE for reply or return of ms. Reports in 2 weeks on queries; 2 months on mss. Simultaneous submissions OK. Often critiques or comments on rejected mss.

Payment/Terms: "Payment negotiated individually with each book. Depends upon salability, subject matter, length, etc." Sends galleys to author. Publishes ms 3-6 months after acceptance. Writer's guidelines free.

Advice: "Our philosophy is to give new authors a chance. We will consider their work regardless of publishing background. We do have time for the struggling author. Make sure your copy is clean, edited and work has been put in from your end; otherwise don't expect miracles from ours."

PAULINE BOOKS AND MEDIA, (I), (formerly St. Paul Books and Media), Subsidiary of Daughters of St. Paul, 50 St. Paul's Ave., Jamaica Plain MA 02130-3491. (617)522-8911. Fax: (617)541-9805. E-mail: pbm_edit@interramp.com. **Acquisitions**: Sister Patricia Edward Jablonski, fsp., children's editor. Estab. 1934. "As a Catholic publishing house, Pauline Books & Media communicates the Gospel message through all available forms of media. We serve the Church by responding to the hopes and needs of all people with the Word of God, in the spirit of St. Paul." Roman Catholic publishing house. Publishes hardcover and paperback originals. Averages 25-35 total titles, 2-3 fiction titles each year. Promotes titles through seasonal and annual catalogs, advertisements in various publications such as Christian Retailing and through trade shows such as the CBA.

● The Press won 2 second place awards from the Catholic Press Association in 1997.

Needs: Juvenile (easy-to-read, historical, religion, contemporary). All fiction must communicate high moral and family values. "Our fiction needs are entirely in the area of children's literature. We are looking for pre-teen and teen morals. Would like to see characters who manifest faith and trust in God." Does not want "characters whose lifestyles are not in conformity with Catholic teachings." Recently published *The Mystery of Half Moon Cove*, by Dan Montgomery (pre-teen/teen mystery); *The Mystery of the Aspen Bandits*, by Dan Montgomery (pre-teen/teen mystery); and *Marie of Bayou Teche*, by Billie Touchstone Signer (pre-teen historical novel).

How to Contact: Does not accept unsolicited mss. Query first. SASE. Reports in 3 months.

Terms: Pays royalties of 8% minimum; 12% maximum. Provides negotiable number of author's copies. Publishes ms 2 or 3 years after acceptance. Writer's guidelines for #10 SASE. Book catalog for 9 × 12 SASE with 4 first-class stamps.

Advice: "There is a dearth of juvenile fiction appropriate for Catholics and other Christians. We do not accept any fiction written in the first person."

PEACHTREE PUBLISHERS, LTD., (IV), 494 Armour Circle NE, Atlanta GA 30324. (404)876-8761. President: Margaret Quinlin. **Acquisitions**: Sarah Smith, fiction editor. Estab. 1977. Small, independent publisher specializing in general interest publications, particularly of Southern origin. Publishes hardcover and paperback originals and hardcover reprints. Average first novel print run 5,000-8,000. Averages 12-15 total titles, 1-2 fiction titles each year. Plans 3 first novels this year. Promotes titles through review copies to appropriate publications, press kits and book signings at local bookstores.

Imprint(s): Freestone and Peachtree Jr.

● Peachtree has received the GA Author of the Year for Juvenile Literature for *The Tree That Owns Itself*, by Loretta Hammer and Gail Karwoski; and the Family Channel Seal of Quality for *T.J.'s Secret Pitch*, by Fred Bowen. They recently put a stronger emphasis on books for children and young adults.

Needs: Contemporary, literary, mainstream, regional. "We are primarily seeking Southern fiction: Southern themes, characters, and/or locales, and children's books." No science fiction/fantasy, horror, religious, romance, historical or mystery/suspense. Published *Over What Hill?* and *Out to Pasture*, by Effie Wilder.

How to Contact: Accepts unsolicited mss. Query, submit outline/synopsis and 50 pages, or submit complete ms with SASE. Reports in 1 month on queries; 3 months on mss. Simultaneous submissions OK.

Terms: Pays in royalties. Sends galleys to author. Free writer's guidelines. Publishes ms 2 years after acceptance. Book catalog for 2 first-class stamps.

Advice: "We encourage original efforts in first novels."

‡*PEEPAL TREE PRESS, 17 King's Ave., Leeds LS6 1QS England. E-mail: submissions@peepal.demon.co.uk. **Acquisitions**: Jeremy Poynting, fiction editor. Publishes 3 previously unpublished writers/year. Averages 12-14 fiction titles/year.

Needs: "Peepal Tree publishes primarily Caribbean and Black British fiction, though it has begun to expand into African and South Asian writing. We publish both novels and collections of short stories." Recently published *Unde Obadiah & the Alien*, by Geoffrey Philp (Caribbean/humor); *The View from Belmon*, by Kevyn Alan Arthur (Caribbean/historical); and *Excavation*, by Lean Goulbourne (Caribbean/adventure). Length: 25,000 words minimum; 100,000 words maximum.

How to Contact: Send a cover letter, synopsis and 3 sample chapters.

Terms: Pays 10% royalties, in general no advances.

Advice: "We suggest that authors send for a copy of our catalog to get some sense of the range and parameters of what we do." Peepal Tree publishes an annual catalog and a quarterly newsletter available from the address above.

PELICAN PUBLISHING COMPANY, (IV), Box 3110, Gretna LA 70054-3110. (504)368-1175. Website: http://www.pelicanpub.com (includes writer's guidelines, featured book, index of Pelican books). **Acquisitions**: Nina Kooij, editor-in-chief. Estab. 1926. "We seek writers on the cutting edge of ideas. We believe ideas have consequences. One of the consequences is that they lead to a bestselling book." Publishes paperback reprints and hardcover originals. Books: Hardcover and paperback binding; illustrations sometimes. Buys juvenile mss with illustrations. Distributes titles internationally through distributors, bookstores, libraries. Promotes titles at reading and book conventions, in trade magazines, in radio interviews, print reviews and TV interviews.

● A Pelican book, *Why Cowboys Sleep With Their Boots On*, by Laurie Lazzaro Knowlton won a 1996 Premier Print Award Certificate of Merit.

Needs: Juvenile fiction, especially with a regional and/or historical focus. No young adult fiction, contemporary fiction or fiction containing graphic language, violence or sex. Also no "psychological" novels. Recently published *That Printer of Udell's*, by Harold Bell Wright (reprint); *Great River*, by Glen Pitre, Michelle Benoit (adult historical); and *The South Carolina Lizard Man*, Nancy Rhyre (middle reader historical adventure).

How to Contact: Prefers query. May submit outline/synopsis and 2 sample chapters with SASE. No simultaneous submissions. "Not responsible if writer's only copy is sent." Reports in 1 month on queries; 3 months on mss. Publishes ms 12-18 months after acceptance. Comments on rejected mss "infrequently."

Terms: Pays 10% in royalties; 10 contributor's copies; advance considered. Sends galleys to author. Publishes ms 18 months after acceptance. Catalog of titles and writer's guidelines for SASE.

Advice: "Research the market carefully. Order and look through publishing catalogs to see if your work is consistent with our list. For ages 8 and up, story must be planned in chapters that will fill at least 90 double-spaced manuscript pages. Topic should be historical and, preferably, linked to a particular region or culture. We look for stories that illuminate a particular place and time in history and that are clean entertainment. The only original adult work we might consider is historical fiction, preferably Civil War (not romance). For middle readers, regional historical or regional adventure could be considered. Please don't send three or more chapters unless solicited. Follow our guidelines listed under 'How to Contact.' "

♣PEMMICAN PUBLICATIONS, (II, IV), 1635 Burrows Ave., Unit 2, Winnipeg, Manitoba R2X 0T1 Canada. (204)589-6346. Fax: (204)589-2063. E-mail: pemmicac@fox.nstn.ca. Website: http://fax.nstn.ca/~pemmican. **Acquisitions:** Sue Maclean, managing editor. Estab. 1980. Metis and Aboriginal children's books, some adult. Publishes paperback originals. Books: stapled binding and perfect-bound; 4-color illustrations. Average print order: 2,500. First novel print order: 1,000. Published new writers within the last year. Averages 9 total titles each year. Distributes titles through Pemmican Publications. Promotes titles through press releases, fax, catalogues and book displays.

Needs: Children's/juvenile (American Indian, easy-to-read, preschool/picture book); ethnic/multicultural (Native American). Recently published *Red Parka Mary*, by Peter Eyvindson (children's); *Nanabosho & Kitchie Odjig*, by Joe McLellan (native children's legend); and *Jack Pine Fish Camp*, by Tina Umpherville (children's). Also publishes the Builders of Canada series.

How to Contact: Accepts unsolicited mss. Submit complete ms with cover letter. Send SASE (or IRC) for reply, return of ms or send a disposable copy of ms. Reports in 1 year. Simultaneous and disk submissions OK.

Terms: Pays royalties of 5% minimum; 10% maximum. Average advance: $350. Provides 10 author's copies.

PENGUIN PUTNAM INC., 375 Hudson St., New York NY 10014. See the listing for Dutton Signet.

‡PERFECTION LEARNING CORP., (I, II, IV), (formerly Penguin USA), 10520 New York Ave., Des Moines IA 50322. (515)278-0133. Fax: (515)278-2980. E-mail: perflern@etins.net. **Acquisitions:** Sue Thies, senior editor K-8; Terry Ofner, senior editor 6-12. Midsize, supplemental publisher of educational materials. Publishes hardcover and paperback originals. Published new writers within the last year. Plans 5-10 first novels this year. Publishes 20-30 total titles/year; 10-15 fiction/titles.

Needs: Children's/juvenile (adventure, animal, easy-to-read, fantasy, historical, mystery, preschool/picture book, series, sports), young adult/teen (adventure, easy-to-read, fantasy/science fiction, historical, horror, mystery/suspense, problem novels, series, sports, western). Recently published *Holding the Yellow Rabbit*, by Bonnie Taylor (mystery); *Rocky Mountain Summer*, by Linda Baxter (historical fiction); and *Great Eagles and Small One*, by Ralph Moisa, Jr. (mythic native American)."

How to Contact: Query with outline/synopsis and 3-4 sample chapters or submit complete ms with a cover letter. Include 1-page bio, estimated word count and list of publishing credits. Send SASE for reply, return of ms or send a disposable copy of the ms. Reports in 3-4 weeks on queries; 1-2 months on mss. Simultaneous submissions OK.

Terms: Publishes ms 6-8 months after acceptance. Fiction guidelines free.

Advice: "We are an educational publisher. Check with educators to find out their needs, their students' needs and what's popular.

‡PERSPECTIVES PRESS, P.O. Box 90318, Indianapolis IN 46290-0318. (317)872-3055. E-mail: ppress@iquest.net. Website: http://www.perspectivespress.com. **Acquisitions:** Pat Johnston, publisher. Estab. 1982. "Our purpose is to promote understanding of infertility issues and alternatives, adoption and closely-related child welfare issues, and to educate and sensitize those personally experiencing these life situations, professionals who work with such clients, and the public at large." Publishes hardcover and trade paperback originals. Publishes 95% previously unpublished writers/year.

Needs: "No adult fiction!"

How to Contact: Reports in 1 month on queries to schedule a full reading.

Terms: Pays 5-15% royalty on net sales. Publishes ms 1 year after acceptance. Writer's guidelines and book catalog for #10 SAE with 2 first-class stamps.

Tips: "We will consider adoption or foster care-related fiction manuscripts that are appropriate for preschoolers and early elementary school children. We do not consider YA. No autobiography, memoir or adult fiction."

‡PHILOMEL BOOKS, (II), Imprint of Penguin Putnam Inc., 200 Madison Ave., New York NY 10016. (212)951-8700. **Acquisitions:** Patricia Gauch, editorial director; Michael Green, editor. Estab. 1980. "A high-quality oriented imprint focused on stimulating picture books, middle-grade novels, and young adult novels." Publishes hardcover originals and paperback reprints. Averages 25 total titles, 5-7 novels/year.

● Books published by Philomel have won numerous awards. Their book, *The War of Jenkins Ear*, by

Michael Morpurgo, was selected as the "1995 Top of the List" in the Youth Fiction category by *Booklist*.

Needs: Adventure, ethnic, family saga, fantasy, historical, juvenile (5-9 years), literary, preschool/picture book, regional, short story collections, translations, western (young adult), young adult/teen (10-18 years). Looking for "story-driven novels with a strong cultural voice but which speak universally." No "generic, mass-market oriented fiction." Recently published *The Outcast of Redwall*, by Brian Jacques; *The Merlin Effect*, by T.A. Barron; *Moon of Two Dark Horses*, by Sally Keehn.

How to Contact: Accepts unsolicited mss. Query first or submit outline/synopsis and first 3 chapters. SASE. Agented fiction 40%. Reports in 6-8 weeks on queries; 8-10 weeks on mss. Simultaneous submissions OK. Sometimes comments on rejected ms.

Terms: Pays royalties, negotiable advance and author's copies. Sends galleys to author. Publishes ms anywhere from 1-3 years after acceptance. Writer's guidelines for #10 SASE. Book catalog for 9×12 SASE.

Advice: "We are not a mass-market publisher and do not publish short stories independently. In addition, we do just a few novels a year."

‡PICADOR USA, Imprint of St. Martin's Press, 175 Fifth Ave., New York NY 10010. **Acquisitions:** George Witte. Estab. 1994. "We publish high-quality literary fiction and nonfiction. We are open to a broad range of subjects, well written by authoritative authors." Publishes hardcover originals and trade paperback originals and reprints. Publishes 30% previously unpublished writers/year.

Needs: Literary. Recently published *Human Croquet*, by Kate Atkinson; *The Jade Peony*, by Wayson Choy; and *In The Deep Midwinter*, by Robert Clark.

How to Contact: Query only with SASE. Reports in 2 months on queries. Simultaneous submissions OK.

Terms: Pays 7½-12½% royalty on retail price. Advance varies. Publishes ms 18 months after acceptance. Writer's guidelines for #10 SASE. Book catalog for 9×12 SASE and $2.60 postage.

‡PIÑATA BOOKS, Imprint of Arte Publico Press, University of Houston, Houston TX 77204-2090. (713)743-2841. Fax: (713)743-2847. **Acquisitions:** Nicolas Kanellos, president. Estab. 1994. "We are dedicated to the publication of children's and young adult literature focusing on U.S. Hispanic culture." Publishes hardcover and trade paperback originals. Publishes 60% previously unpublished writers/year.

Needs: Adventure, juvenile, picture books, young adult. Recently published *The Secret of Two Brothers*, by Irene Beltran Hernandez (ages 11-adult); *Pepita Talks Twice*, by Ofelia Dumas Lachtman (picture book, ages 3-7); and *Jumping Off to Freedom*, by Anilu Bernardo (young adult).

How to Contact: Query with synopsis, 2 sample chapters and SASE. Reports in 1 month on queries, 6 months on mss. Simultaneous submissions OK.

Terms: Pays 10% royalty on wholesale price. Offers $1,000-3,000 advance. Publishes ms 2 years after acceptance. Writer's guidelines for #10 SASE. Book catalog free.

Advice: "Include cover letter with submission explaining why your manuscript is unique and important, why we should publish it, who will buy it, etc."

PINEAPPLE PRESS, (II, IV), P.O. Box 3899, Sarasota FL 34230-3899. (941)953-2797. E-mail: info@pineappl epress.com. Website: http://www.pineapplepress.com (includes searchable database of titles, news events, featured books, company profile, and option to request a hard copy of catalog). **Acquisitions:** June Cussen, executive editor. Estab. 1982. Small independent trade publisher. Publishes hardcover and paperback originals and paperback reprints. Books: quality paper; offset printing; Smyth-sewn or perfect-bound; illustrations occasionally. Average print order: 5,000. First novel print order: 2,000-5,000. Published new writers within the last year. Plans 1-2 first novels this year. Averages 20 total titles each year. Distributes titles through Pineapple, Ingram and Baker & Taylor. Promotes titles through reviews, advertising in print media, direct mail, author signings and the World Wide Web.

Needs: "In 1998 we prefer to see only Florida-related novels." Recently published *Power in the Blood*, by Michael Lister (ecclesiastical mystery); *My Brother Michael*, by Janis Owens (Southern drama); *The Thang That Ate My Granddaddy's Dog*, by John Calvin Rainey (African-American); and *Conflict of Interest*, by Terry Lewis (legal thriller).

How to Contact: Prefers query, cover letter listing previous publications, outline or one-page synopsis with sample chapters (including the first) and SASE. Then if requested, submit complete ms with SASE. Reports in 2 months. Simultaneous submissions OK.

Terms: Pays royalties of 7½-15%. Advance is not usually offered. "Basically, it is an individual agreement with each author depending on the book." Sends galleys to author. Publishes ms 18 months after acceptance. Book catalog sent if label and $1.24 postage enclosed.

✝   THE DOUBLE DAGGER before a listing indicates that the listing is new in this edition. New markets are often the most receptive to submissions by new writers.

Advice: "Quality first novels will be published, though we usually only do one or two novels per year. We regard the author/editor relationship as a trusting relationship with communication open both ways. Learn all you can about the publishing process and about how to promote your book once it is published."

PINNACLE BOOKS, 850 Third Ave., New York NY 10022. (212)407-1500. See Kensington Publishing Corp.

PIPPIN PRESS, 229 E. 85th Street, Gracie Station Box 1347, New York NY 10028. (212)288-4920. Fax: (908)225-1562. **Acquisitions:** Barbara Francis, publisher; Joyce Segal, senior editor. Estab. 1987. "Small, independent children's book company, formed by the former editor-in-chief of Prentice Hall's juvenile book division." Publishes hardcover originals. Books: 135-150 GSM offset-semi-matte paper (for picture books); offset, sheet-fed printing; Smythe-sewn binding; full color, black and white line illustrations and half tone, b&w and full color photographs. Averages 5-6 titles each year. Sometimes comments on rejected mss.
Needs: Juvenile only (5-12 yrs. including animal, easy-to-read, fantasy, science, humorous, spy/adventure). "I am interested in humorous novels for children of about 7-12 and in picture books with the focus on humor. Also interested in autobiographical novels for 8-12 year olds and selected historical fiction for the same age group."
How to Contact: No unsolicited mss. Query first. SASE. Reports in 2-3 weeks on queries. Simultaneous submissions OK.
Terms: Pays royalties. Sends galleys to author. Publication time after ms is accepted "depends on the amount of revision required, type of illustration, etc." Writer's guidelines for #10 SASE.

‡PLEASANT COMPANY PUBLICATIONS, (II), Subsidiary of Pleasant Company, 8400 Fairway Place, Middleton WI 53528. (608)836-4848. Fax: (608)836-1999. **Acquisitions:** Jennifer Hirsch, submissions editor. Estab. 1986. Midsize independent publisher. "We are best known for our historical fiction for girls ages 8-12." Publishes hardcover and paperback originals. Averages 10-15 total titles, 3 fiction titles/year.
Imprints: The American Girls Collection and American Girl Library.
Needs: Children's/juvenile (historical, mystery, contemporary for girls 8-12). Pleasant Company Publications also seeks mss for its forthcoming contemporary fiction imprint. "Novels should capture the spirit of contemporary American girls and also illuminate the ways in which their lives are personally touched by issues and concerns affecting America today. We are looking for thoughtfully developed characters and plots, and a discernible sense of place." Stories must feature an American girl, aged 10-12; reading level 4th-5th grade. No science fiction, fantasy or first-romance stories. Recently published *Meet Josefina*, *Josefina Learns a Lesson*, and *Josefina's Surprise*, all by Valerie Tripp (historical middle grade). Publishes The American Girls Collection series; "also, possibly other historical fiction and contemporary fiction for girls 8-12."
How to Contact: Accepts unsolicited mss. Query with outline/synopsis and 3 sample chapters. Include list of publishing credits. "Tell us why the story is right for us." Send SASE for reply, return of ms or send a disposable copy of ms. Agented fiction 5%. Reports in 8-10 weeks on queries; 3-4 months on mss. Simultaneous submissions OK.
Payment/Terms: Vary. Publishes ms 3-12 months after acceptance. Writer's guidelines for SASE.
Advice: For historical fiction "your story *must* have a girl protagonist age 8-12. No first romance, no science fiction/fantasy, no talking animals. No early reader. Our readers are girls 8-12, along with parents and educators. We want to see character development and strong plotting."

‡POCKET BOOKS, (II), Division of Simon & Schuster, 1230 Avenue of the Americas, New York NY 10020. (212)698-7000. **Acquisitions:** Emily Bestler, executive vice President/editorial director; Patricia McDonald, editorial director. Publishes paperback and hardcover originals and reprints. Published new writers within the last year. Averages 300 titles each year. Buys 90% agented fiction. Promotes books through print advertising, radio, TV ads, readings and book signings.
Imprint(s): Washington Square Press and Star Trek.
Needs: Adventure, contemporary, erotica, ethnic, fantasy, feminist, gothic, historical, horror, humor/satire, literary, mainstream, military/war, psychic/supernatural, romance, spy, suspense/mystery, western. Published *Waiting to Exhale*, by Terry McMillan; *The Way Things Ought To Be*, by Rush Limbaugh (hardcover and paperback); *Harvest*, by Tess Gerritsen; and *She's Come Undone*, Wally Lamb.
How to Contact: Query with SASE (or IRC). No unsolicited mss. Reports in 6 months on queries only. Publishes ms 12-18 months after acceptance. Sometimes critiques rejected mss.
Terms: Pays in royalties and offers advance. Sends galleys to author. Writer must return advance if book is not completed or is not acceptable. Publishes ms 2 years after acceptance. Writer's guidelines for #10 SASE.

♣PRAIRIE JOURNAL PRESS, (I, IV), Prairie Journal Trust, P.O. Box 61203, Brentwood Postal Services, Calgary, Alberta T2L 2K6 Canada. **Acquisitions:** Anne Burke, literary editor. Estab. 1983. Small-press, noncommercial literary publisher. Publishes paperback originals. Books: bond paper; offset printing; stapled binding; b&w line drawings. Publishes 5 previously unpublished writers/year. Averages 2 total titles or anthologies/year.
Needs: Literary, short stories. No romance, horror, pulp, erotica, magazine type, children's, adventure, formula, western. Published *Prairie Journal Fiction*, *Prairie Journal Fiction II* (anthologies of short stories); *Solstice* (short fiction on the theme of aging); and *Prairie Journal Prose*.
How to Contact: Accepts unsolicited mss. Query first and send Canadian postage or IRCs and $6 for sample

copy, then submit 1-2 stories with SAE and IRCs. Reports in 6 months or sooner. Occasionally critiques or comments on rejected mss if requested.

Terms: Pays 1 author's copy; honorarium depends on grant/award provided by the government or private/corporate donations. Sends galleys to author. Book catalog free on request to institutions; SAE with IRC for individuals. "No U.S. stamps!"

Advice: "We wish we had the means to promote more new writers. We often are seeking theme-related stories. We look for something different each time and try not to repeat types of stories if possible."

PREP PUBLISHING, (I, II), PREP Inc., 1110½ Hay St., Fayetteville NC 28305. (910)483-6611. Fax: (910)483-2439. **Acquisitions**: Anne McKinney, editor. Estab. 1994. Publishing division affiliated with a 14-year-old company. Publishes hardcover and paperback originals. Books: acid free paper; offset printing; perfect binding; illustrations. Average print order: 5,000. First novel print order: 5,000. Averages up to 15 total titles, 10 fiction titles each year. Distributes titles through Seven Hills Book Distributors, Ingram, Baker & Taylor, Quality Books, Unique Books and others.

Needs: Children's/juvenile (adventure, mystery), religious/inspirational, romance (contemporary, romantic suspense), thriller/espionage, young adult (adventure, mystery/suspense, romance, sports). "Spiritual/inspirational novels are most welcome." Published *Second Time Around*; and *Back in Time*, by Patty Sleem (mysteries); and *About Martha*, by C.B. Guforth (romance).

How to Contact: Send SASE for author's guidelines and current catalog. Often comments on rejected mss.

Terms: Pays negotiable royalties. Advance is negotiable. Individual arrangement with author depending on the book. Sends galleys to author. Publishes ms 1-2 years after acceptance.

Advice: "Rewrite and edit carefully before sending manuscript. We look for quality fiction that will appeal to future generations."

PRESIDIO PRESS, (IV), 505B San Marin Dr., Suite 300, Novato CA 94945. (415)898-1081, ext. 125. Fax: (415)898-0383. **Acquisitions**: E.J. McCarthy, editor-in-chief. Estab. 1976. Small independent general trade—specialist in military. Publishes hardcover originals. Publishes an average of 2 works of fiction per list under its Lyford Books imprint. Regularly publishes new writers. Averages 24 new titles each year.

Imprint(s): Lyford Books.

Needs: Historical with military background, war, thriller/espionage. Recently published *Synbat*, by Bob Mayer; *In a Heartbeat*, by Eric Stone; and *A Murder of Crows*, by Steve Shepard.

How to Contact: Accepts unsolicited mss. Query first. SASE. Reports in 2 weeks on queries; 2-3 months on mss. Simultaneous submissions OK. Critiques or comments on rejected ms.

Terms: Pays in royalties of 15% of net minimum; advance: $1,000 average. Sends edited manuscripts and page proofs to author. Publishes ms 12-18 months after acceptance. Book catalog and guidelines free on request. Send 9×12 SASE with $1.30 postage.

Advice: "Think twice before entering any highly competitive genre; don't imitate; do your best. Have faith in your writing and don't let the market disappoint or discourage you."

‡PRIDE PUBLICATIONS AND IMPRINTS, (I, II), P.O. Box 148, Radnor OH 43066. (888)902-5983. E-mail: pridepblsh@aol.com. **Acquisitions:** Cris Newport, senior editor. Large independent publisher specializing in cutting edge novels and children's books. Publishes paperback originals and reprints. Average and first novel print orders: 5,000. Published new writers within the last year. Plans 2 first novels this year. Averages 10 total titles/year, 8 fiction titles/year.

● Chosen as the "Best Example of an Independent Publisher" by BookWatch (Midwest Book Review).

Needs: Adventure, children's/juvenile (adventure, easy-to-read, fantasy, historical, mystery, series), comics/graphic novels, erotica, ethnic/mulitcultural, experimental, fantasy (space fantasy, sword and sorcery), feminist, gay, historical, horror (dark fantasy, futuristic, psychological, supernatural), humor/satire, lesbian, literary, mainstream/contemporary, mystery/suspense (amateur sleuth), New Age/mystic/spiritual, psychic/supernatural/occult, religious (children's, general, inspirational, thriller, mystery/suspense, thriller), science fiction (hard science, soft/sociological, cyberfiction), young adult/teen (adventure, easy-to-read, fantasy/science fiction, historical, horror, mystery/suspense, problem novels, series). Recently published *Still Life with Buddy*, by Leslie Newman (novel told in poetry); *Shadows of Aggar*, by Chris Anne Wolfe (fantasy); and *The White Bones of Truth*, by Cris Newport (future fiction). Publishes mystery and science fiction series.

How to Contact: Accepts unsolicited mss. Query with outline/synopsis and 3 sample chapters. Unsolicited queries/correspondence by e-mail OK. Include estimated word count, 100 word bio, list of publishing credits.

AN IMPRINT LISTED IN BOLDFACE TYPE means there is an independent listing arranged alphabetically within this section.

Send SASE for reply, return of ms. Agented fiction 20%. Reports in 2 weeks on queries; 3 months on mss. Simultaneous submissions OK.

Terms: Pays royalties of 10% minimum; 60% maximum. Publishes ms 12 months after acceptance. Fiction guidelines for #10 SASE. Catalog for #10 SAE with 2 first-class stamps.

Advice: "We feel there is a lot of poor quality work being published, and so are careful to choose work that is revolutionary and cutting edge. Read our books before you even query us."

‡PUFFIN BOOKS, Imprint of Penguin Putnam Inc., 375 Hudson St., New York NY 10014-3657. (212)366-2000. Website: http://www.penguin.com/childrens. **Acquisitions:** Sharyn November, senior editor; Joy Peskin, editorial assistant. "Puffin Books publishes high-end trade paperbacks and paperback reprints for preschool children, beginning and middle readers, and young adults." Publishes trade paperback originals and reprints.

Needs: Picture books, young adult novels, middle grade and easy-to-read grades 1-3. "We publish mostly paperback reprints. We do few original titles." Recently published *A Gift for Mama*, by Esther Hautzig (Puffin chapter book).

How to Contact: Submit picture book ms or 3 sample chapters with SASE. Reports in 1 month on mss. Simultaneous submissions OK, if so noted.

Terms: Royalty and advance vary. Publishes ms 1 year after acceptance. Book catalog for 9×12 SASE with 7 first-class stamps; send request to Marketing Department.

Advice: "Our audience ranges from little children 'first books' to young adult (ages 14-16). An original idea has the best luck."

‡G.P. PUTNAM'S SONS, (III), Imprint of Penguin Putnam Inc., 200 Madison Ave., New York NY 10016. (212)951-8405. Fax: (212)951-8694. Website: http://www.putnam.com. Managing Editor: David Briggs. **Acquisitions**: Maya Rao, editorial assistant. Publishes hardcover originals. Published new writers within the last year.

Imprint(s): Grosset, **Philomel**, Price Stern Sloan, Putnam, **Riverhead**, Jeremy P. Tarcher.

Needs: Adventure, mainstream/contemporary, mystery/suspense, science fiction. Recently published *Executive Orders*, by Tom Clancy (adventure); *Small Vices*, by Robert B. Parker (mystery/thriller); and *Chromosome 6*, by Robin Cook (medical thriller).

How to Contact: Does not accept unsolicited mss. Reports in 6 months on queries. Simultaneous submissions OK.

Payment/Terms: Pays variable royalties on retail price. Advance varies. Writer's guidelines free.

♣QUARRY PRESS, (I,II), Box 1061, Kingston, Ontario, K7L 4Y5 Canada. (613)548-8429. **Acquisitions**: Bob Hilderley, publisher. Estab. 1965. Small independent publisher with plans to expand. Publishes paperback originals. Books: 1 lb. paper offset sheet; perfect-bound; illustrations. Average print order: 1,200. First novel print order: 1,200. Published new writers within the past year. Plans 1 first novel this year. Averages 20 total titles, 4 fiction titles each year.

Needs: Children's folklore and poetry, experimental, feminist, historical, literary, short story collections. Published *Ritual Slaughter*, by Sharon Drache; *Engaged Elsewhere*, edited by Kent Thompson (includes work by Mavis Gallant, Margaret Laurence, Dougles Glover, Ray Smitz, Keath Fraser and others); published fiction by previously unpublished writers within the last year.

How to Contact: *Does not accept unsolicited mss.* Query first. SASE for query and ms. Reports in 4 months. Simultaneous submissions OK. Sometimes comments on rejected mss.

Terms: Pays royalties of 7-10%. Advance: negotiable. Provides 5-10 author's copies. Sends galleys to author. Publishes ms 6-8 months after acceptance. Book catalog free on request.

Advice: "Publishing more fiction than in the past. Encourages first novelists. Canadian authors only."

‡QUIXOTE PRESS, 3544 Blakeslee St., Wever IA 52658. Phone/fax: (319)372-7480. **Acquisitions:** Bruce Carlson, president. Quixote Press specializes in humorous regional folklore and special interest cookbooks. Publishes trade paperback originals and reprints. Publishes 90% previously unpublished writers/year.

Needs: Adventure, ethnic, experimental, humor, short story collections, children's. Recently published *Out Behind the Barn*, by B. Carlson (rural folklore).

How to Contact: Query with synopsis and SASE. Reports in 2 months. Simultaneous submissions OK.

Terms: Pays 10% royalty on wholesale price. No advance. Publishes ms 1 year after acceptance. Writer's guidelines and book catalog for #10 SASE.

Advice: Carefully consider marketing considerations. Audience is women in gift shops, on farm site direct retail outlets.

♣RAGWEED PRESS INC./gynergy books, (I), P.O. Box 2023, Charlottetown, Prince Edward Island C1A 7N7 Canada. (902)566-5750. Fax: (902)566-4473. E-mail: editor@ragweed.com. **Acquisitions**: Managing Editor. Estab. 1980. "Independent Canadian-owned feminist press." Publishes paperback originals. Books: 60 lb. paper; perfect binding. Average print order: 3,000. Averages 12 total titles, 3 fiction titles each year. Published new writers within the last year.

Needs: *Canadian-authors only.* "We do accept submissions to anthologies from U.S. writers." Children's/juvenile (adventure, picture book, girl-positive), feminist, lesbian, young adult. Recently published *Sudden Death*, by Jackie Manthorne (lesbian mystery); and *Ghostwise*, by Dan Yashinsky (young adult).

How to Contact: Accepts unsolicited mss with cover letter, brief bio, list of publishing credits. SASE for reply. Reports in 6 months. Simultaneous submissions OK.

Terms: Pays royalties of 10%; offers negotiable advance. Provides 5 author's copies. Sends galleys to author. Publishes ms 1-2 years after acceptance. Writer's guidelines for #10 SASE. Book catalog for large SAE and 2 first-class stamps.

Advice: "Specialized market—lesbian novels especially. Be brief, give résumé."

‡**RAIN DANCER BOOKS**, 3211 W. Wadley, Bldg. 3A, Suite 143, Midland TX 79705. **Acquisitions:** T.R. Wayne, acquisitions editor. "We are wide open to publishing the best literature that makes its way to our door. We envision an audience with a zest for life, a love of reading and a copy of our catalog." Publishes 68% previously unpublished writers/year.

Needs: Adventure, ethnic, experimental, fantasy, historical, humor, juvenile, literary, mainstream/contemporary, mystery/suspense, occult, picture books, plays, religious, romance, science fiction, short story collections, western, young adult. "We are interested in books that lend themselves to serialization, especially mysteries." Recently published *Mystery of the Oil Rig*; *Mystery of the Tumbleweed*; and *Mystery of the Lasso*; all by Linda Lee (mysteries for adult literacy students).

How to Contact: Query or submit synopsis and sample chapter. Simultaneous submissions OK.

Terms: Pays 2-20% royalty on wholesale price or makes outright purchase. No advance. Publishes ms 18 months after acceptance. Writer's guidelines and catalog for #10 SASE.

Advice: "Write from solid research. Revise when necessary. Send out simultaneous submissions. We do not return submissions. This saves us time and the author postage."

‡**RAINBOW BOOKS, INC., (I, II)**, P.O. Box 430, Highland City, FL 33813-0430. (800)613-BOOK. Fax: (941)648-4420. E-mail: naip@aol.com. **Acquisitions:** Besty Lampe, editorial director. Estab. 1979. Midsize press. Publishes trade paperback originals. Books: 60 lb. paper; perfect binding. Average print order: 15,000. First novel print order: 2,000-5,000. Plans 2 first novels for January 1998.

● Member of Publishers Association of the South, Florida Publishers Association, National Association of Independent Publishers, Association of American Publishers, Publishers Marketing Association.

Needs: Historical, literary, mainstream/contemporary, military/war, mystery/suspense (amateur sleuth, cozy, police procedural), romance (contemporary, romantic suspense), science fiction (soft/sociological). "We would like to see well-written mystery, adventure, mainstream novels." Will soon publish *Path to Ariquepa*, by Mark Jacoby; and *Pharmacology is Murder*, by Dirk Wyle.

How to Contact: Accepts unsolicited mss. Query first for guidelines. Include estimated word count, bio of 3 pages or less, Social Security number and list of publishing credits. Send SASE for reply, return of ms or send disposable copy of ms. "But tell us." Reports in 2-3 weeks on queries; 8-10 weeks on mss. Simultaneous submissions OK.

Terms: Pays in royalties plus advance and 50 author's copies. Negotiates all arrangements. Sends galleys to author. Publishes ms 1-2 years after acceptance.

Advice: "Since we are just beginning to publish fiction, the future is hard to read. However, we expect to stick with trade softcover, since it covers the most territory. We feel that the very large publishers have closed their doors to the unpublished author—that poor soul who writes well but doesn't have a track record. We'd like to find those folks and give them an opportunity to be published and perhaps find an audience that would follow them through the years. In other words, we're going to look very carefully at each manuscript we call for. Be professional. Come in with that manuscript looking like a pro's manuscript. Please don't tell us, 'I have a great idea for a novel and I've got it on paper. You can clean it up however you want.' That's not to say that we won't help the author that's 'almost there;' we will. Meanwhile, be prepared, if we decide to take on the novel, to provide a PC compatible diskette of the book."

‡**RANDOM HOUSE BOOKS FOR YOUNG READERS**, Imprint of Random House, 201 E. 50th St., New York NY 10022. (212)751-2600. Fax: (212)940-7685. Website: http://www.randomhouse.com. Publishing Director: Kate Klimo. **Acquisitions:** Maria de Seville, assistant. Estab. 1935. Publishes hardcover, trade paperback, and mass market paperback originals and reprints. "Random House Books aim to create books that nurture the hearts and minds of children, providing and promoting quality books and a rich variety of media that entertain and educate readers from 6 months to 12 years."

Needs: Humor, juvenile, mystery, picture books, young adult. Recently published *The Wubbulous World of Dr. Seuss*, by Dr. Seuss; and *Critters of the Night: No Flying in the Hall*, by Mercer Mayer.

How to Contact: Agented fiction only. Reports in 3 weeks-6 months. Simultaneous submissions OK.

MARKET CATEGORIES: (I) Open to new writers; **(II)** Open to both new and established writers; **(III)** Interested mostly in established writers; **(IV)** Open to writers whose work is specialized; **(V)** Closed to unsolicited submissions.

Terms: Pays 1-6% royalty or makes outright purchase. Advance varies. Publishes ms 1 year after acceptance. Book catalog free.
Advice: "Familiarize yourself with our list. We look for original, unique stories. Do something that hasn't been done."

RANDOM HOUSE, INC., 201 E. 50th St., New York NY 10022. (212)751-2600. **Acquisitions:** Sandy Fine, submissions coordinator. Estab. 1925. Publishes hardcover and paperback originals. Encourages new writers.
Imprint(s): Pantheon Books, Panache Press at Random House, **Vintage Books**, Times Books, Villard Books and **Knopf**.
Needs: Adventure, contemporary, historical, literary, mainstream, short story collections, mystery/suspense. "We publish fiction of the highest standards." Authors include James Michener, Robert Ludlum, Mary Gordon.
How to Contact: Query with SASE. Simultaneous submissions OK. Reports in 4-6 weeks on queries, 2 months on mss. Rarely comments on rejected mss.
Terms: Payment as per standard minimum book contracts. Free writer's guidelines and book catalog.
Advice: "Please try to get an agent because of the large volume of manuscripts received, agented work is looked at first."

‡RANDOM HOUSE, INC. JUVENILE BOOKS, 201 E. 50th St., New York NY 10022. (212)572-2600.
Acquisitions: (Juvenile Division): Kate Klimo, publishing director, Random House. Simon Boughton, vice president/publishing director, Andrea Cascardi, associate publishing director, Crown/Knopf. Managing Editor (all imprints): Sue Malone Barber. Publishes hardcover, trade paperback and mass market paperback originals, mass market paperback reprints.
Imprint(s): Random House Books for Young Readers, **Alfred A. Knopf**, Crown Children's Books, Dragonfly Paperbacks.
Needs: Adventure, young adult (confession), fantasy, historical, horror, humor, juvenile, mystery/suspense, picture books, science fiction (juvenile/young adult), young adult.
How to Contact: Agented fiction only.

♣RANDOM HOUSE OF CANADA, (III), Division of Random House, Inc., 33 Yonge St., Suite 210, Toronto, Ontario M5E 1G4 Canada. Publishes hardcover and paperback originals. Publishes 56 titles/year. No unsolicited mss. Agented fiction only. All unsolicited mss returned unopened. "We are *not* a mass market publisher."
Imprint(s): Vintage Imprints.

♣RED DEER COLLEGE PRESS, (II, IV), Box 5005, Red Deer, Alberta T4N 5H5 Canada. (403)342-3321. Fax: (403)357-3639. E-mail: cdearden@rdc.ab.ca. **Acquisitions:** Dennis Johnson, managing editor. Estab. 1975. Publishes adult and young adult hardcover and paperback originals "focusing on books by, about, or of interest to Western Canadians." Books: offset paper; offset printing; hardcover/perfect-bound. Average print order: 5,000. First novel print order: 2,500. Averages 14-16 total titles, 2 fiction titles each year. Distributes titles in Canada, the US and the UK.
Imprint(s): Roundup Books, edited by Ted Stone.
  ● Red Deer College Press has received numerous honors and awards from the Book Publishers Association of Alberta, Canadian Children's Book Centre, the Governor General of Canada and the Writers Guild of Alberta. *The Rose Garden*, by Kristjana Gunnars received the Georges Bugnet Award for Best Novel.
Needs: Contemporary, experimental, literary, young adult. No romance, science fiction. Published anthologies under Roundup Books imprint focusing on stories/poetry of the Canadian and American West. Published *100 Years of Cowboy Stories*, edited by Ted Stone; *A Roundup of Cowboy Humor*, edited by Ted Stone; and *Josepha: A Prairie Boy's Story*, by Jim McGugan, illustrated by Murray Kimber.
How to Contact: *Canadian authors only.* Does not accept unsolicited mss in children's and young adult genres. Query first or submit outline/synopsis and 2 sample chapters. SASE. Reports in 3 months on queries; in 6 months on mss. Simultaneous submissions OK. Final mss must be submitted on Mac disk in MS Word.
Terms: Pays royalties of 8-10%. Advance is negotiable. Sends galleys to author. Publishes ms 1 year after acceptance. Book catalog for 9×12 SASE.
Advice: "We're very interested in literary and experimental fiction from Canadian writers with a proven track record (either published books or widely published in established magazines or journals) and for manuscripts with regional themes and/or a distinctive voice. We publish Canadian authors almost exclusively."

‡RED DRAGON PRESS, (II), 433 Old Town Court, Alexandria VA 22314. **Acquisitions:** Laura Qa, publisher. Estab. 1993. "Small independent publisher of innovative, progressive and experimental works." Publishes paperback originals. Books: quality paper; offset printing; perfect binding; some illustrations. Average print order: 500. Published new writers within the last year. Plans 1 first novel this year. Averages 4 total titles, 1-2 fiction titles/year. Member of Women's National Book Association.
  ● Red Dragon Press received an Individual Artist Project Support Grant in literature from Alexandria Commission for the Arts, 1995-96.
Needs: Experimental, fantasy (space fantasy), feminist, gay, horror (dark fantasy, futuristic, psychological,

supernatural), lesbian, literary, psychic/supernatural/occult, science fiction (hard science/technological, soft/sociological), short story collections. Recently published *True Stories: Fiction by Uncommon Women*.

How to Contact: Accepts unsolicited mss. Submit query letter. Include 1 page bio, list of publishing credits and 1-3 sample stories (up to 36 pages). Send SASE for reply, return of ms or send disposable copy of ms. Reports in 6 weeks. Simultaneous submissions OK. Often critiques or comments on rejected mss *for various fee*.

Terms: Publishes ms 6-12 months after acceptance. Writer's guidelines free for #10 SASE. Book catalog for #10 SASE.

Advice: "Be familiar with the work of one or more of our previously published authors."

*REED PUBLISHING (NEW ZEALAND) LTD., (IV), Private Bag 34901, Birkenhead, Auckland 10, New Zealand. **Acquisitions**: Alison Southby, fiction editor. Averages 3 fiction titles/year. "Reed Publishing NZ has two divisions: Reed Consumer Books (trade publishing); and Heinemann Education."

Needs: "We publish literary fiction and children's books, with a strong bias towards writing by New Zealanders or about New Zealand and the Pacific." Length: 40,000 words minimum.

How to Contact: Send a cover letter with synopsis and 3 sample chapters. SASE (SAE and IRC).

Terms: "Authors are paid a royalty. Advances are negotiable. It is unlikely that we would accept fiction not written by a New Zealander or Pacific Islander or without some content that relates to New Zealand." Catalog available on request.

REVELL PUBLISHING, (III), Subsidiary of Baker Book House, P.O. Box 6287, Grand Rapids MI 49516-6287. (616)676-9185. Fax: (616)676-9573. E-mail: lholland@bakerbooks.com or petersen@bakerbooks.com. Website: http://www.bakerbooks.com. **Acquisitions**: Linda Holland, editorial director; Bill Petersen, senior acquisitions editor; Jane Campbell, senior editor (Chosen Books). Estab. 1870. "Midsize evangelical book publishers." Publishes paperback originals. Average print order: 7,500. Published new writers within the last year. Plans 1 first novel this year. Averages 60 total titles, 8 fiction titles each year.

Imprint(s): Spire Books.

Needs: Religious/inspirational (general). Published *Ordeal at Iron Mountain*, by Linda Rae Rao (historical); *A Time to Weep*, by Gilbert Morris (historical); and *The End of the Age*, by David Dolan (suspense).

How to Contact: Query with outline/synopsis. Include estimated word count, bio and list of publishing credits. Send SASE for reply, return of ms or send a disposable copy of ms. Agented fiction 20%. Reports in 3 weeks on queries; 2 weeks on mss. Simultaneous submissions OK. Sometimes comments on rejected mss.

Terms: Pays royalties. Sends galleys to author. Publishes ms 1 year after acceptance. Writer's guidelines for SASE.

‡REVIEW AND HERALD PUBLISHING ASSOCIATION, 55 W. Oak Ridge Dr., Hagerstown MD 21740. (301)791-7000. **Acquisitions**: Jeannette R. Johnson, editor. "Through print and electronic media, the Review and Herald Publishing Association nurtures a growing relationship with God by providing products that teach and enrich people spiritually, mentally, physically and socially as we near Christ's soon second coming." Publishes hardcover, trade paperback and mass market paperback originals and reprints. Publishes 50% previously unpublished writers/year.

Needs: Adventure, historical, humor, juvenile, mainstream/contemporary, religious, all Christian-living related. Recently published *Shadow Creek Ranch*, by Charles Mills (juvenile adventure series); *The Liberation of Allyson Brown*, by Helen Godfrey Pyke (inspirational); and *The Appearing*, by Penny Estes Wheeler (inspirational).

How to Contact: Submit synopsis and complete ms or 3 sample chapters. Reports in 1 month on queries; 2 months on mss. Simultaneous submissions OK.

Terms: Pays 7-15% royalty. Offers $500-1,000 advance. Publishes ms 18 months after acceptance. Writer's guidelines for #10 SASE. Book catalog for 10×13 SASE.

Advice: "We publish for a wide audience, preschool through adult."

‡THE RIEHLE FOUNDATION, P.O. Box 7, Milford OH 45150. **Acquisitions:** Mrs. B. Lewis, general manager. "We are only interested in materials which are written to draw the reader to a deeper love for God." Publishes trade paperback originals and reprints. Publishes 50% previously unpublished writers/year.

Needs: Religious, short story collections; all with Roman Catholic subjects. Recently published *Six Short Stories on the Via Dolorosa*, by Ernesto V. Laguette (devotional short stories).

How to Contact: Submit entire ms with SASE. Reports in 3 months. Simultaneous submissions OK.

Terms: Pays royalty. Publishes ms 6 months after acceptance. Writer's guidelines and book catalog for #10 SASE.

RIO GRANDE PRESS, (I), P.O. Box 71745, Las Vegas NV 89170. **Acquisitions:** Rosalie Avara, publisher. Estab. 1989. "One-person operation on a half-time basis." Publishes paperback originals. Books: offset printing; saddle-stitched binding. Average print order: 100. Published new writers within the last year. Averages 10 total titles, 2 fiction titles each year.

Imprint(s): *Se La Vie Writer's Journal*.

● The publisher also sponsors a short short story contest quarterly.

Needs: Adventure, contemporary, ethnic, family saga, fantasy, humor/satire, literary, mystery/suspense (amateur sleuth, private eye, romantic suspense), regional, short story collections. Looking for "general interest, slice of life stories; good, clean, wholesome stories about everyday people. No sex, porn, science fiction (although I may consider flights of fantasy, daydreams, etc.), or religious. Any subject within the 'wholesome' limits. No experimental styles, just good conventional plot, characters, dialogue." Published *The Story Shop* I-V (short story anthologies; 13 stories by individual authors).

How to Contact: Submit story after August 1. SASE. Reports in 2 weeks on queries or acceptance. Sometimes comments on rejected mss.

Terms: Pays, if contest is involved, up to $15 plus $5 on honorable mentions.

Advice: "I enjoy working with writers new to fiction, especially when I see that they have really worked hard on their craft, i.e., cutting out all unnecessary words, using action dialogue, interesting descriptive scenes, thought-out plots and well-rounded characters that are believable. Please read listing carefully noting what type and subject of fiction is desired."

RISING TIDE PRESS, (II), 5 Kivy St., Huntington Station NY 11746. (516)427-1289. Fax: (516)423-6642. E-mail: rtpress@aol.com. **Acquisitions:** Lee Boojamra, editor; Alice Frier, senior editor. Estab. 1988. "Independent women's press, publishing lesbian nonfiction and fiction—novels only—no short stories." Publishes paperback trade originals. Books: 60 lb. vellum paper; sheet fed and/or web printing; perfect-bound. Average print run: 5,000. First novel print run: 4,000-6,000. Plans 10-12 first novels this year. Averages 12 total titles. Promotes titles through PW, Girlfriends, Lambda Book Report.

• Rising Tide plans two anthologies: *Women Cruising Women* (short stories) and *How I Met My True Love* (lesbian romance). Deadline is June 1, 1997. SASE for guidelines.

Needs: Lesbian adventure, contemporary, erotica, fantasy, feminist, romance, science fiction, suspense/mystery, western. Looking for romance and mystery. "Minimal heterosexual content." Published *Emerald City Blues*, by Joan Stewart (literary); *Rough Justice*, by Claire Youmans (mystery); and *Playing for Keeps*, by Stevie Rios (romance). Developing a dark fantasy and erotica line.

How to Contact: Accepts unsolicited mss with 1-page outline/synopsis and SASE. Reports in 1 week on queries; 2-3 months on mss. Comments on rejected mss.

Terms: Pays 10-15% royalties. "*We will assist writers who wish to self-publish for a nominal fee.*" Sends galleys to author. Publishes ms 6-18 months after acceptance. Writer's guidelines for #10 SASE. Book catalog for $1.

Advice: "Outline your story to give it boundaries structure, find creative ways to introduce your characters and begin the story in the middle of some action and dialogue. Our greatest challenge is finding quality manuscripts that are well plotted and not predictable, with well-developed, memorable characters. Read your novel before you send it to any publisher."

‡RIVERHEAD BOOKS, Imprint of Penguin Putnam, Inc., 200 Madison Ave., New York NY 10016. (212)951-8400. Fax: (212)779-8236. Website: http://www.putnam.com/putnam. Senior Editors: Julie Grau, Amy Hertz. **Acquisitions:** Kathryn Crosby, editorial assistant. Estab. 1994. "Riverhead aims to help readers open up themselves to new ideas, helpful advice, or healing words. Our books are well-written and try to raise readers' consciousness, not only entertain. Many of our titles deal with spiritual material, especially contemporary, progressive ways to think, act and live. Religion is a specialty." Publishes hardcover originals and reprints, trade paperback originals and reprints. Publishes 60% previously unpublished writers/year.

Needs: Adventure, confession, ethnic, experimental, feminist, gay, lesbian, historical, humor, literary, mainstream/contemporary, plays, religious, short story collections, suspense. Recently published *Going Down*, by Jennifer Belle (mainstream/contemporary); *The Beach*, by Alex Garland (suspense/adventure); and *Drown*, by Junot Diaz (short story/ethnic).

How to Contact: Prefers agented submissions. Query with synopsis and sample chapters. "Many writers submit the entire manuscript, which is daunting to read when there are hundreds in the office. It's best to submit an outline of the story along with a few chapters to give a sample of the writing." Reports in 2 months on queries; 4 months on mss.

Terms: Pays 6-15% royalty on retail price or makes outright purchase of $7,500-1 million. Publishes ms 9 months after acceptance. Book catalog free.

Advice: "We envision our audience to be very literate, curious people who enjoy fine writing and enriching stories or information. Our audience ranges from high-schoolers to the elderly, in all parts of the country. If you're submitting, do some research and find out which editor might be most interested in your work—call the office or look in one of our books that might have a similar style or theme and check the acknowledgments—often the editor is listed. We like first-time novelists with fresh voices or an interesting perspective. Quality writing is our #1 priority."

ROC, (II, III), Imprint of Dutton Signet, a division of Penguin Putnam, Inc., 375 Hudson St., New York NY 10014. (212)366-2000. Fax: (212)366-2888. **Acquisitions:** Laura Anne Gilman, executive editor. Publishes hardcover, trade paperback and mass market originals and hardcover, trade paperback (and mass market) reprints. Published new writers within the last year. Averages 48 (all fiction) titles each year.

Needs: Fantasy, horror (dark fantasy) and science fiction. Publishes science fiction, horror and fantasy anthologies. Anthologies by invitation only. Recently published *Deathstalker War*, by Simon Green (science fiction); *Dragon at World's End*; by Christopher Rowley (fantasy); and *Gallery of Horror*, edited by Charles Grant; and

Giant Bones, by Peter Beagh (fantasy). Publishes the Battletech® and Shadowrun® series.

How to Contact: Query with outline/synopsis and 3 sample chapters. Include list of publishing credits. Not responsible for return of submission if no SASE is included. Agented fiction 99%. Reports in 2 weeks on queries; 3-4 months on mss. Simultaneous submissions OK. Sometimes comments on rejected ms.

Terms: "Competitive with the field." Publishes ms 1 year after acceptance.

‡❤ROUSSAN PUBLISHERS INC., Roussan Editeur Inc., 2110 Decarie Blvd., Suite 100, Montreal, Quebec H4A 3J3 Canada. (514)481-2895. Fax: (514)487-2899. Website: http://www.magnet.ca/roussan. **Acquisitions:** Kathryn Rhoades, editor; Jane Frydenlund, editor-in-chief. Roussan Publishers Inc., specializes in reality-based fiction for young adults and pre-teens. Publishes trade paperback originals. Publishes 40% previously unpublished writers/year. Publishes 12 titles/year; each division publishes 6 titles/year.

● Roussan Publishers Inc. has published such authors as George Bowering, Dayle Gaetz and Beth Goobie.

Needs: Young adult and junior readers only—adventure, fantasy, feminist, historical, juvenile, mystery, science fiction. No picture books. Recently published *Home Child*, by Barbara Haworth-Attard (historical); *The Vampire's Visit*, by David Poulsen; and *Gone to Maui*, by Cherylyn Stacey (young adult).

How to Contact: Submit synopsis and 3 sample chapters. Reports in 3 months. Simultaneous submissions OK.

Terms: Pays 8-10% royalty on retail price. Publishes ms 1 year after acceptance.

ROYAL FIREWORKS PRESS, (I), Box 399, First Avenue, Unionville NY 10988. (914)726-4444. Fax: (914)726-3824. E-mail: rfpress@nyfrontiercomm.net. Website: rfpress@ny.frontiercomm.net. Vice President: Thomas Holland. **Acquisitions:** Charles Morgan, editor (fiction); William Neumann, editor (fiction); Astrid Bismarck (fiction); Myrna Kemnitz, editor (science fiction). Estab. 1978. "For nearly 20 years, we have pursued the purpose of enhancing the educational experience of gifted and talented children. Our goal has been to provide the materials that enable teachers, administrators and parents to enrich the experience and life opportunities of gifted children." Independent publisher. Publishes paperback originals and paperback reprints. Plans 60 first novels this year. Averages 150 total titles, 100 fiction titles each year.

Needs: Young adult/teen (10-18 years): fantasy/science fiction, historical, romance (young adult), sports and mystery/adventure, middle school/young adult (10-18) series, teenage angst. Published the following young adult series: Mystery & Adventure (including historical novels); Growing Up Right (values, relationships, adult development); Science Fiction. Recently published *The Kipton Chronicles*, by Charles Fontray; and *Key to Honor*, by Ron Wattanja.

How to Contact: Accepts unsolicited mss. Include estimated word count and list of publishing credits. SASE. Reports in 4 months on mss. No simultaneous submissions.

Terms: Negotiated "as appropriate." Sends galleys to author. Writer's guidelines for #10 SAE and 1 first-class stamp (or IRC). Book catalog for 9×12 SAE and 3 first-class stamps.

RUBENESQUE ROMANCES, (I, IV), P.O. Box 534, Tarrytown NY 10591-0534. (914)345-7485. E-mail: rubenesque@aol.com. Website: www.Rubenesque.com (includes authors, titles, writer's guidelines). **Acquisitions**: Joanne K. Morse, publisher. Estab. 1995. "Small, independent publisher." Publishes paperback originals. Books: copy paper; perfect-bound. Published new writers within the last year. Plans 10 novels this year. Publishes 90% previously unpublished writers/year. Averages 12 total titles, all fiction, each year. Distributes titles through mail order and local book stores.

Needs: Romance (contemporary, futuristic/time travel, gothic, historical, regency/period, romantic suspense, western). "All light romance for and about large-sized heroines. No alternative lifestyles or pornography." Plans anthology. Recently published *Love in the Pyramid*, by Abigail Sommers; *Moon Love*, by Cynthia MacGregor; and *So Much for Illusion*, by Deborah McClatchey (all light romances).

How to Contact: Accepts unsolicited mss. Send SASE for guidelines first, then query. Include estimated word count and 100-word bio with submissions. "No manuscripts over 50,000 words." Send SASE for reply to query or return of ms. Reports in 1 month on queries; 2 months on mss. Disk submissions OK (prefers MAC, DOS-based OK). Always critiques or comments on rejected mss.

Terms: Pays royalties of 15% maximum. Publishes ms 6 months after acceptance. Writer's guidelines and book catalog for #10 SASE.

Advice: "Send SASE for guidelines—we will not read manuscript without this step. Order our guidelines and follow them. We work closely with new authors, offering a unique opportunity to the novice writer. If your idea is good but your writing is poor, we'll help you redo your manuscript."

‡RUSSIAN HILL PRESS, (II,III), 1250 17th St., 2nd Floor, San Francisco CA 94107. (415)487-0480. Fax: (418)487-0290. E-mail: editors@russianhill.com. **Acquisitions:** Kit Cooley, assistant editor. Estab. 1996. "Small (but growing) independent publisher. Focus: West Coast, irreverent, youthful." Publishes hardcover originals. Average print order 5,000. First novel print order 2,000. Published new writers within the last year. Plans 2 first novels this year. Averages 6-10 total titles, 5-9 fiction titles/year. Member of PMA, IPN.

Needs: Erotica, ethnic/multicultural, feminist, gay, humor/satire, lesbian, literary, mainstream/contemporary, mystery/suspense, regional (west of the Rockies), thriller/espionage. Especially looking for literary, Generation X, thriller, humor. Recently published *Tainted Million*, by Susan Trott (mystery); *Swamp Cats*, by Jeff Love (humorous); and *Funerals for Horses*, by Catherine Ryan Hyde (literary).

How to Contact: Does not accept unsolicited mss. Query letter only first. Unsolicited queries/correspondence by e-mail and fax OK. Include estimated word count, 1-page bio and list of publishing credits with submission. SASE for reply. Agented fiction 90%. Reports in 2 months on queries; 4 months on mss. Simultaneous submissions OK. Sometimes critiques or comments on rejected mss.
Payment/Terms: Pays royalties of 10% minimum; 15% maximum. Offers negotiable advance. Sends galleys to author. Publishes ms 8 months after acceptance. Writer's guidelines for #10 SASE. Book catalog for $2.
Advice: "Get an agent. Pay attention to the types of fiction we publish."

ST. MARTIN'S PRESS, 175 Fifth Ave., New York NY 10010. (212)674-5151. Chairman and CEO: John Sargent. President: Roy Gainsburg. Publishes hardcover and paperback reprints and originals.
Imprint(s): Thomas Dunne.
Needs: Contemporary, literary, experimental, adventure, mystery/suspense, spy, historical, war, gothic, romance, confession, feminist, gay, lesbian, ethnic, erotica, psychic/supernatural, religious/inspirational, science fiction, fantasy, horror and humor/satire. No plays, children's literature or short fiction. Published *The Silence of the Lambs*, by Thomas Harris; *The Shell Seekers* and *September* by Rosamunde Pilcher.
How to Contact: Query or submit complete ms with SASE. Simultaneous submissions OK (if declared as such). Reports in 2-3 weeks on queries, 4-6 weeks on mss.
Terms: Pays standard advance and royalties.

‡J.S. SANDERS & COMPANY, INC., P.O. Box 50331, Nashville TN 37205. **Acquisitions:** John Sanders, publisher. "J.S. Sanders & Company publishes new books in Southern letters and history, as well as a reprint list of 19th and 20th century titles in its Southern Classic series." Publishes hardcover originals and trade paperback originals and reprints. Publishes 25% previously unpublished writers/year.
Imprint(s): Caliban Books.
Needs: Historical, literary. Recently published *Nashville 1864: A Novel*, by Madison Jones (literary/historical); and *The Women on the Porch*, by Caroline Gordon (literary reprint).
How to Contact: Submit 1 sample chapter with SASE. Reports in 1 month on queries. Simultaneous submissions OK.
Terms: Pays 7½-15% royalty. Publishes ms 9 months after acceptance. Book catalog free.

SARABANDE BOOKS, INC., (II), 2234 Dundee Rd., Suite 200, Louisville KY 40205-1845. E-mail: saraband en@aol.com. Website: www.SarabandeBooks.com (includes authors, titles, writer's guidelines, names of editors, author interviews and ordering and contest information). **Acquisitions**: Sarah Gorham, editor-in-chief; Kirkby Tiltle, fiction editor. Estab. 1994. "Small literary press." Publishes hardcover and paperback originals. Averages 6 total titles, 2-3 fiction titles each year. Distributes titles through Consortium Book Sales & Distribution. Promotes titles through sales reps, brochures, newsletters, postcards, national ads, catalogues, sales conferences, book fairs, author tours and reviews.
Needs: Short story collections, 300 pages maximum (or collections of novellas, or single novellas of 150 pages). "Short fiction *only*. We do not publish full-length novels." Recently published *The Least You Need to Know*, by Lee Martin; *Blood and Milk*, by Sharon Solwitz; and *Sparkman in the Sky and Other Stories*, by Brian Griffin.
How to Contact: Submit (in September only.) Query with outline/synopsis and 1 sample story or ten-page sample. Electronic queries OK. Include 1 page bio, listing of publishing credits. SASE for reply. Reports in 3 months on queries; 6 months on mss. Simultaneous submissions OK.
Terms: Pays in royalties, author's copies. Sends galleys to author. Writer's guidelines available for contest only. Send #10 SASE. Book catalog available.
Advice: "Make sure you're not writing in a vacumm, that you've read and are conscious of your competition in contemporary literature. Have someone read your manuscript, checking it for ordering, coherence. Better a lean, consistently strong manuscript than one that is long and uneven. Old fashioned as it sounds, we like a story to have good narrative, or at least we like to be engaged, to find ourselves turning the pages with real interest."

‡✿SCHOLASTIC CANADA LTD., 123 Newkirk Rd., Richmond Hill, Ontario L4C 3G5 Canada. **Acquisitions**: Diane Kerner, Sandra Bogart Johnston, editors, children's books. Publishes hardcover and trade paperback originals. Publishes 30 titles/year.
Imprint(s): North Winds Press (contact Joanne Richter); Les Éditions Scholastic (contact Sylvie Andrews, French editor).
Needs: Children's/juvenile, young adult. Recently published *After the War*, by Carol Matas (juvenile novel).
How to Contact: Query with synopsis, 3 sample chapters and SASE. Reports in 1 month on queries.

READ THE BUSINESS OF FICTION WRITING section to learn the correct way to prepare and submit a manuscript.

Terms: Pays 5-10% royalty on retail price. Offers $1,000-5,000 (Canadian) advance. Publishes ms 1 year after acceptance. Book catalog for 8½×11 SAE with 2 first-class stamps (IRC or Canadian stamps only).

‡**SCHOLASTIC INC.**, 555 Broadway, New York NY 10012. (212)343-6100. Scholastic Inc. **Acquisitions**: Craig Walker, editorial director. Estab. 1920. Publishes trade paperback originals for children ages 4-young adult. "We are proud of the many fine, innovative materials we have created—such as classroom magazines, book clubs, book fairs, and our new literacy and technology programs. But we are most proud of our reputation as 'The Most Trusted Name in Learning.' " Publishes juvenile hardcover picture books, novels and nonfiction.
Imprint(s): Blue Sky Press, **Cartwheel Books**, **Arthur Levine Books**, **Mariposa**, **Scholastic Press**, Scholastic Professional Books.
Needs: Hardcover—open to all subjects suitable for children. Paperback—family stories, mysteries, school, friendships for ages 8-12, 35,000 words. Young adult fiction, romance, family and mystery for ages 12-15, 40,000-45,000 words for average to good readers. Recently published *Her Stories: African American Folktales, Fairy Tales and True Tales*, by Virginia Hamilton, illustrated by Leo and Diane Dillon; and *Pigs in the Middle of the Rud*, by Lynn Plourde.
How to Contact: Queries welcome; unsolicited manuscripts discouraged. Reports in 6 months.
Terms: Pays advance and royalty on retail price. Writer's guidelines for #10 SASE.
Advice: New writers for children should study the children's book field before submitting.

‡**SCHOLASTIC PRESS**, Imprint of Scholastic Inc., 555 Broadway, New York NY 10012. (212)343-6100. Website: http://www.scholastic.com. **Acquisitions:** Brenda Bowen, editor. Scholastic Press publishes a range of picture books, middle grade and young adult novels. Publishes hardcover originals. Publishes 5% previously unpublished writers/year.
Needs: Juvenile, picture books. Recently published *Slam*, by Walter Dean Myers.
How to Contact: Agented submissions only. Reports in 6 months on queries.
Terms: Pays royalty on retail price. Royalty and advance vary. Publishes ms 18 months after acceptance.

‡*****SCOTTISH CULTURAL PRESS, (II, IV)**, Unit 14, Leith Walk Business Centre, 130 Leith Walk, Edinburgh EH6 5DT Scotland. (0131)555-5950. Fax: (0131)555-5018. E-mail: scp@sol.co.uk. Director: Jill Dick. Estab. 1992. Small independent publisher of paperback originals. Mainly concentrates on Scottish authors or Scottish content. Average print order: 1,000-2,000. Published new writers within the last year. Plans 1-2 first novels this year. Averages 35 total titles/year, 5 fiction titles/year.
Needs: Children's/juvenile (all), mainstream/contemporary, short story collections, young adult/teen (adventure, fantasy/science fiction, historical, horror, mystery/suspense, problem novels, romance, series, sports. All should be by a Scottish author or have Scottish content. Recently published *Night Visits*, by Ron Butlin (contemporary); *Now You Must Dance*, by Bruce Leeming (political); and *Summer is Ended*, by Ken Steven (teen historical).
How to Contact: Accepts unsolicited submissions. Query with outline/synopsis and 2 sample chapters. Unsolicited queries/correspondence by e-mail and fax OK. Include 1 page bio and list of publishing credits. Send SASE for return of ms or send disposable copy of ms. Agented fiction 4%. Reports in 3 weeks on queries; 4 months on mss. Simultaneous submissions OK.
Terms: Pays royalties of 10% minimum. Sends galleys to author. Publishes ms 12 months after acceptance. Book catalog free.

SCRIBNER'S, Unit of Simon & Schuster, 1230 Avenue of the Americas, New York NY 10020. (212)698-7000. **Acquisitions**: Jillian Blake, associate editor. Publishes hardcover originals. Published new writers within the last year. Averages 70-75 total titles/year.
Imprint(s): Rawson Associates (contact Eleanor Rawson); Lisa Drew Books (contact Lisa Drew).
Needs: Literary, mystery/suspense. Recently published *Accordion Crimes*, by E. Annie Proulx (novel, Pulitzer Prize winning author); *Underworld*, by Don Delillo; and *Go Now*, by Richard Hell (novel).
How to Contact: Submit through agent. Reports in 3 months on queries. Simultaneous submissions OK.
Terms: Pays royalties of 7½% minimum; 12½% maximum. Advance varies. Publishes ms 9 months after acceptance.

‡**SEAL PRESS, (I, IV)**, 3131 Western Ave., Seattle WA 98121. (206)283-7844. E-mail: sealpress@sealpress.sea net.com. Website: http://www.sealpress.com. **Acquisitions**: Faith Conlon, president. Estab. 1976. "Midsize independent publisher of fiction and nonfiction by women." Publishes hardcover and paperback originals. Books: 55 lb. natural paper; Cameron Belt, Web or offset printing; perfect binding; illustrations occasionally; average print order: 6,500; first novel print order: 4,000-5,000. Averages 15 total titles, 6 fiction titles each year. Sometimes critiques rejected ms "very briefly."
  ● Seal has received numerous awards including Lambda Literary Awards for mysteries, humor and translation.
Needs: Ethnic, feminist, humor/satire, lesbian, literary, mystery (amateur sleuth, cozy, private eye/hardboiled), young adult (easy-to-read, historical, sports). "We publish women only. Work must be feminist, non-racist, non-homophobic." Publishes anthologies. Send SASE for list of upcoming projects. Recently published *An Open*

Weave, by Devorah Major (literary novel); *Faint Praise*, by Ellen Hart (mystery novel); and *The Lesbian Parenting Book*, by D. Menlee Clunis and G. Dorsey Green.

How to Contact: Query with outline/synopsis and 2 sample chapters. SASE. Reports in 2 months.

Terms: Pays royalties; offers negotiable advance. Publishes ms 1-2 years after acceptance. Writer's guidelines and book catalog are free.

SECOND CHANCE PRESS AND THE PERMANENT PRESS, (I, II), 4170 Noyac Rd., Sag Harbor NY 11963. (516)725-1101. **Acquisitions**: Judith and Martin Shepard, publishers. Estab. 1977. Mid-size, independent publisher of literary fiction. Publishes hardcover originals. Books: hardcover. Average print order: 1,500-2,000. First novel print order: 1,500-2,000. Published new writers within the last year. Publishes 75% previously unpublished writers/year. Averages 12 total titles, all fiction, each year. Distributes titles through Ingram, Baker & Taylor and Brodart. Promotes titles through reviews.

Needs: Contemporary, erotica, ethnic/multicultural, experimental, family saga, literary, mainstream. "We like novels with a unique point of view and a high quality of writing." No genre novels. Recently published *Licking Our Hands*, by Elise d'Haere; *Up, Down & Sideways*, by Robert Patton; and *The Geometry of Love*, by Joan Fox Cuccio.

How to Contact: Query with outline and no more than 2 chapters. SASE. Agented fiction 35%. Reports in 6 weeks on queries; 6 months on mss. Simultaneous submissions OK.

Terms: Pays royalties of 10-20%. Advance: $1,000. Sends galleys to author. Book catalog for $3.

Advice: "We are looking for good books, be they tenth novels or first ones, it makes little difference. The fiction is more important than the track record. Send us the beginning of the story, it's impossible to judge something that begins on page 302. Also, no outlines and very short synopsis—let the writing present itself."

‡SEEDLING PUBLICATIONS, INC., 4079 Overlook Dr. E, Columbus OH 43214-2931. Phone/fax: (614)451-2412 or (614)792-0796. E-mail: sales@seedlingpub.com. Website: http://www.seedlingpub.com. **Acquisitions:** Josie Stewart, vice president. Seedling publishes books for young children to "keep young readers growing." Publishes 80% previously unpublished writers/year.

Needs: Juvenile. Recently published *Howie Has a Stomachache*, by Johnny Ray Moore (a pig with a stomachache); *Play Ball, Sherman*, by Betty Erickson; and *Dinosaurs Galore*, by Audrey Eaton and Jane Kennedy.

How to Contact: Submit outline with SASE. Reports in 4-6 months. Simultaneous submissions OK. Reviews artwork/photos as part of ms package. Send photocopies.

Terms: Pays 5% royalty or makes outright purchase of $150-300. Publishes ms 1 year after of acceptance. Writer's guidelines for #10 SASE. Book catalog for #10 SAE and 2 first-class stamps.

Advice: "Follow our guidelines. Do not submit full-length picture books or chapter books. Our books are for children, ages 5-7, who are just beginning to read independently. Try a manuscript with young readers. Listen for spots in the text that don't flow. Rewrite until the text sounds natural to beginning readers."

SERENDIPITY SYSTEMS, (I, II, IV), P.O. Box 140, San Simeon CA 93452. (805)927-5259. E-mail: bookware@thegrid.net. Website: http://www.thegrid.net/bookware/bookware.htm (includes guidelines, sample books, writer's manuscript help, catalog). **Acquisitions**: John Galuszka, publisher. Estab. 1985. "Electronic publishing for IBM-PC compatible systems." Publishes "electronic editions originals and reprints." Books on disk. Published new writers within the last year. Averages 36 total titles, 15 fiction titles each year (either publish or distribute). Often comments on rejected mss.

Imprint(s): Books on Disks™ and Bookware™.

Needs: "Works of fiction which use, or have the potential to use, hypertext, multimedia or other computer-enhanced features. We cannot use on-paper manuscripts." No romance, religion, New Age, children's, young adult, occult. Published *Costa Azul*, by C.J. Newton (humor); *Sideshow*, by Marian Allan (science fiction); and *Silicon Karma*, by Tom Easton (science fiction).

How to Contact: Query by e-mail. Submit complete ms with cover letter and SASE. *IBM-PC compatible disk required*. ASCII files saved under system 7 or higher required unless the work is hypertext or multimedia. Send SASE for reply, return of ms or send disposable copy of ms. Reports in 2 weeks on queries; 1 month on mss.

Terms: Pays royalties of 25%. Publishes ms 2 months after acceptance. Writer's guidelines for SASE.

Advice: "A number of new tools have recently become available, Hypertext publishing programs DART and ORPHEUS, for example, and we look forward to seeing works which can take advantage of the features of these and other programs. Would like to see: more works of serious literature—novels, short stories, plays, etc. Would like to not see: right wing adventure fantasies from 'Tom Clancy' wanna-be's."

SEVEN BUFFALOES PRESS, (II), Box 249, Big Timber MT 59011. **Acquisitions**: Art Cuelho, editor/publisher. Estab. 1975. Publishes paperback originals. Averages 4-5 total titles each year.

Needs: Contemporary, short story collections, "rural, American Hobo, Okies, Native-American, Southern Appalachia, Arkansas and the Ozarks. Wants farm- and ranch-based stories." Published *Rig Nine*, by William Rintoul (collection of oilfield short stories).

How to Contact: Query first with SASE. Reports in 1 month. Sample copy $6.75.

Terms: Pays royalties of 10% minimum; 15% on second edition or in author's copies (10% of edition). No advance. Writer's guidelines and book catalog for SASE.

Advice: "There's too much influence from TV and Hollywood, media writing I call it. We need to get back to the people, to those who built and are still building this nation with sweat, blood and brains. More people are into it for the money, instead of for the good writing that is still to be cranked out by isolated writers. Remember, I was a writer for ten years before I became a publisher."

‡**SEVEN STORIES PRESS, (II)**, 632 Broadway, Seventh Floor, New York NY 10012. (212)995-0908. Fax: (212)995-0720. **Acquisitions:** Daniel Simon. Estab. 1995. "Publishers of a distinguished list of authors in fine literature, journalism, contemporary culture and alternative health." Publishes hardcover and paperback originals and paperback reprints. Average print order: 5,000. Published new writer within the last year. Plans 2 first novels this year. Averages 20 total titles, 10 fiction titles/year. Sometimes critiques or comments on rejected mss.
- Seven Stories Press received the Firecracker Alternative Book Award (nonfiction), 1996 and 1997; the Will Eisner Comic Industry Award (Best Graphic Album-New) 1997; nomination for Best Books for Young Adults by ALA 1997; Nebula Award Finalist, 1995, 1996.

Needs: Literary. Plans anthologies. Ongoing series of short story collections from other cultures (e.g., *Contemporary Fiction from Central America*; from Vietnam, etc. Recently published *The House of Moses All-Stars*, by Charley Rosen (novel); *. . . And Dreams Are Dreams*, by Vassilis Vassilikos (novel); and *Exteriors*, by Annie Ernaux (novel).
How to Contact: Query with outline/synopsis and 1 sample chapter. Include list of publishing credits. SASE for reply. Agented fiction 60%. Reports in 1 month on queries; 4 months on mss. Simultaneous submissions OK.
Payment/Terms: Pays standard royalty; offers advance. Sends galleys to author. Publishes ms 1-2 years after acceptance. Free book catalog.
Advice: "Writers should only send us their work after they have read some of the books we publish and find our editorial vision in sync with theirs."

‡***SEVERN HOUSE PUBLISHERS**, 9-15 High St., Sutton, Surrey SM1 1DF United Kingdom. (0181)770-3930. Fax: (0181)770-3850. **Acquisitions:** Yvette Taylor, editorial assistant. Publishes hardcover and trade paperback originals and reprints. Publishes 120 titles/year.
Needs: Adventure, fantasy, historical, horror, mainstream/contemporary, mystery/suspense, romance, science fiction, short story collections. Recently published *Tender Warrior*, by Fern Michaels (historical romance); *The Geneva Rendezvous*, by Julie Ellis (romance); *Devil May Care*, by Elizabeth Peters (crime and mystery); and *Blood and Honor*, by W.E.B. Griffin (war fiction).
How to Contact: Agented submissions only. Submit synopsis and 3 sample chapters. Reports in 3 months on proposals.
Terms: Pays 7½-15% royalty on retail price. Offers $750-2,500. Simultaneous submissions OK. Book catalog free.

HAROLD SHAW PUBLISHERS, (II, IV), Box 567, 388 Gundersen Dr., Wheaton IL 60189. (603)665-6700. **Acquisitions:** Joan Guest, managing editor. Literary Editor: Lil Copan. Estab. 1968. "Small, independent religious publisher with expanding fiction line." Publishes paperback originals and reprints. Average print order: 5,000. Averages 40 total titles, 1-2 fiction titles each year.
Needs: Literary, religious/inspirational. Looking for religious literary novels for adults. No short stories, romances, children's fiction. Recently published *The Other Side of the Sun* and *Love Letters*, by Madeleine L'Engle; and *The Tower, the Mask, and the Grave*, by Betty Smartt Carter (mystery). Published new writers within the last year.
How to Contact: Accepts unsolicited mss. Query first. Submit outline/synopsis and 2-3 sample chapters. SASE. Reports in 4-6 weeks on queries; 3-4 months on mss. No simultaneous submissions. Sometimes critiques rejected mss.
Terms: Pays royalties of 10%. Provides 10 author's copies. Sends pages to author. Publishes ms 12-18 months after acceptance. Free writer's guidelines. Book catalog for 9×12 SAE and $1.32 postage.
Advice: "Character and plot development are important to us. We look for quality writing in word and in thought. 'Sappiness' and 'pop-writing' don't go over well at all with our editorial department."

‡**SIERRA CLUB BOOKS FOR CHILDREN**, Imprint of Sierra Club Books, 85 Second St., San Francisco CA 94105. (415)977-5500. **Acquisitions:** Helen Sweetland, director. "Sierra Club Books for Children publishes books that offer responsible information about the environment to young readers, with attention to the poetry and magic in nature that so fascinated and inspired John Muir, the poet-philosopher who was the Sierra Club's founder." Publishes hardcover originals and trade paperback originals and reprints. Publishes 2% previously unpublished writers/year. Publishes 15 titles/year.
Needs: Juvenile, nature/environment. Recently published *Desert Trip*, by Barbara A. Steiner; *The Empty Lot*, by Dale H. Fife; and *The Snow Whale*, by Caroline Pitcher.
How to Contact: Query first. Agented submissions preferred. All unsolicited mss returned unopened. Reports in up to 1 year on queries.
Terms: Pays 8-10% royalty on retail price. Advance varies. Publishes ms an average of 2 years after acceptance; works waiting for illustrators may take significantly longer. Book catalog for 9×12 SASE.

SILHOUETTE BOOKS, (I, II, IV), 300 E. 42nd St., 6th Floor, New York NY 10017. (212)682-6080. Fax: (212)682-4539. Website: http://www.romance.net. Editorial Director: Isabel Swift. Senior Editors and Editorial Coordinators (SIM/SYT): Leslie J. Wainger, (SSE/LI), Tara Gavin. **Acquisitions:** Melissa Senate, senior editor (Silhouette Romance); Tracy Farrell, senior editor (Harlequin Historicals). Editors: Gail Chasan, Marica Adirim, Mary Theresa Hussey, Karen Taylor Richman, Melissa Jeglinski, Cristine Grace, Margaret Marbury. Estab. 1979. Publishes paperback originals. Published 10-20 new writers within the last year. Buys agented and unagented adult romances. Averages 360 total titles each year.
Imprint(s): Silhouette Romance, Silhouette Special Edition, Silhouette Desire, Silhouette Intimate Moments, Silhouette Yours Truly, Harlequin Historicals.
  • Books published by Silhouette Books have received numerous awards including Romance Writers of America's Rita Award, awards from Romantic Times and best selling awards from Walden and B. Dalton bookstores.
Needs: Contemporary romances, historical romances. Recently published *Unforgettable Bride*, by Annette Broadrick (SR); *A Baby in His In-Box*, by Jennifer Greene (SD); *Wild Mustang Woman*, by Lindsay McKenna (SSE); *The Proposal*, by Linda Turner (SIM); *Big Bad Daddy*, by Christie Ridgway (SYT); *Lion's Lady*, by Suzanne Barclay (HH); and *Decidedly Married*, by Carole Gift Page (LI).
How to Contact: Submit query letter with brief synopsis and SASE. No unsolicited or simultaneous submissions. Publishes ms 9-36 months after acceptance. Occasionally comments on rejected mss.
Terms: Pays in royalties; offers advance (negotiated on an individual basis). Must return advance if book is not completed or is unacceptable. Publishes ms 3 years after acceptance.
Advice: "You are competing with writers that love the genre and know what our readers want—because many of them started as readers. Please note that the fact that our novels are fun to read doesn't make them easy to write. Storytelling ability, clean compelling writing and love of the genre are necessary."

‡**SILVER PRESS**, Imprint of Silver Burdett Press (Division of Simon & Schuster), 299 Jefferson Rd., Parsippany NJ 07054. **Acquisitions:** Dorothy Goeller, editor. Publishes hardcover originals. Publishes 20 titles/year.
Needs: Picture books K-3.
How to Contact: Not accepting any unsolicited submissions. All unsolicited mss returned unopened. Reports in 6 months on queries; 1 year on mss. Simultaneous submissions OK.
Terms: Pays 3-7½% royalty. Average advance $4,000. Publishes ms 2-3 years after acceptance. Book catalog for 9 × 12 SASE with $2.60 postage.

‡❀**SIMON & PIERRE PUBLISHING CO. LTD., (IV)**, A member of the Dundurn Group, 2181 Queen St. E., Suite 301, Toronto, Ontario M4E 1E5 Canada. (416)698-0454. Fax: (416)698-1102. Publisher: Jean Paton. **Acquisitions:** Carl Brand, director of operations. Estab. 1972. "Small literary press." Publishes paperback originals. Books: Hi Bulk paper; book printer printing; perfect binding; b&w illustrations. Average print order: 2,000. First novel print order: 1,000. Averages 10 total titles, 2 fiction titles each year.
Needs: Literary, mainstream/contemporary, mystery/suspense (amateur sleuth, cozy). Plans Canadian mystery anthologies. Published *Grave Deeds*, by B. Struthers (mystery-cozy); and *Crime in a Cold Climate*, by D. Shene-Melvin (mystery-anthology).
How to Contact: Accepts unsolicited mss. Query first or query with outline/synopsis. Include estimated word count; 1 page bio; list of publishing credits. Send SASE for reply, return of ms or send a disposable copy of ms. Reports in 2 months on queries; 3 months on mss. Simultaneous submissions OK.
Terms: Pays royalties of 10%. Average advance $750. Provides 10 author's copies. Sends galleys to author. Publishes ms 8-12 months after acceptance. Writer's guidelines free. Book catalog for 9 × 12 SASE and $1 postage.

SIMON & SCHUSTER, 1230 Avenue of the Americas, New York NY 10020. (212)698-7000.
Imprint(s): Pocket Books, Poseidon Press.
Needs: General adult fiction, mostly commercial fiction. Recently published *Scaredy Cats* Series, by George

---

WRITER-TO-WRITER

My biggest obstacle was that I wasn't listening to my "writing voice." I started out writing (and publishing) short stories for adults, but it was only after I started writing for children and young adults that I had my success. I really do believe that we have a writing voice and that we have to discover what it is. Often, what we think we want to write is not what we were meant to write.

George Edward Stanley
Scaredy Cats Series, Simon & Schuster

Edward Stanley.
How to Contact: Agented material 100%.

SIMON & SCHUSTER BOOKS FOR YOUNG READERS, (V), Subsidiary of Simon & Schuster Children's Publishing Division, 1230 Avenue of the Americas, New York NY 10020. (212)698-2851. Fax: (212)698-2796. Website: http://www.simonandschuster.com. Vice President/Editorial Director: Stephanie Owens Lurie. Executive Editor: Virginia Duncan. Senior Editor: David Gale. **Acquisitions**: Acquisitions Editor. "Flagship children's imprint of large children's publishing division." Publishes hardcover originals. Published new writers within the last year. Plans 4 first novels this year. Averages 100 total titles, 25 fiction titles each year.
● Books from Simon & Schuster have been the recipients in 1996 of 2 Caldecott honor awards, 1 Coretta Scott King Honor Award, 7 ALA Notable books for children, 8 ALA Best Books for Young Adults and 6 ALA Quick Picks for Reluctant Readers.
Needs: Children's/juvenile, young adult/teen (adventure, historical, mystery, picture book, contemporary fiction). No chapter books. No problem novels. No anthropomorphic characters. Publishes anthologies; editor solicits from established writers. Recently published *Slave Day*, by Rob Thomas (young adult novel); *Running Out of Time*, by Margaret Peterson Haddix (middle school novel); and *Adventures of Sparrowboy*, by Brian Pinkney.
How to Contact: *Does not accept unsolicited mss.* Submit query letter and SASE. Agented fiction 90%. Reports in 2 months on queries. Simultaneous submissions OK.
Terms: Pays royalties. Offers negotiable advance. Sends galleys to author. Publishes ms within 2 years of acceptance. Writer's guidelines for #10 SASE. Book catalog available in libraries.

‡SJL PUBLISHING COMPANY, P.O. Box 152, Hanna IN 46340. (219)324-9678. Publisher/Editor: Sandra J. Cassady. SJL publishes scientific fiction and nonfiction. Publishes hardcover and trade paperback originals. Publishes 40% previously unpublished writers/year. Publishes 8-10 titles/year.
Needs: Humor, juvenile, science fiction.
How to Contact: Query with synopsis and SASE. Reports in 1 month on queries; 2 months on mss. Simultaneous submissions OK.
Terms: Pays 10% royalty. Publishes ms 1 year after acceptance. Writer's guidelines for #10 SASE.

‡SKINNER HOUSE BOOKS, Imprint of The Unitarian Universalist Association, 25 Beacon St., Boston MA 02108. (617)742-2100, ext 601. Fax: (617)742-7025. E-mail: skinner_house@uua.org. Website: http://www.uua. org. **Acquisitions:** Kristen Holmstrand, assistant editor. Audience is Unitarian Universalists, ministers, lay leaders, religious educators, feminists, gay and lesbian activists and social activists. Publishes trade paperback originals and reprints. Publishes 50% previously unpublished writers/year. Publishes 8-10 titles/year.
Needs: Juvenile.
How to Contact: Query first. Reports in 2 months on queries.
Terms: Pays 5-10% royalty on net sales. Offers $100 advance. Publishes ms 1 year after acceptance. Writer's guidelines for #10 SASE. Book catalog for 6×9 SAE with 3 first-class stamps.
Tips: "From outside our denomination, we are interested in manuscripts that will be of help or interest to liberal churches, Sunday School classes, ministers and volunteers. Inspirational/spiritual titles must reflect liberal Unitarian Universalist values. The only fiction we publish is for children, usually in the form of parables or very short stories (500 words) on liberal religious principles or personal development. Fiction for adults is not accepted."

GIBBS SMITH, PUBLISHER/PEREGRINE SMITH, (II, IV), P.O. Box 667, Layton UT 84041. (801)544-9800. Fax: (801)544-5582. **Acquisitions**: Gail Yngve, fiction editor; Theresa Desmond, children's editor; Madge Baird, editorial director (westerns). Estab. 1969. Small independent press. "We publish books that make a difference." Publishes hardcover and paperback originals and reprints. Published new writers within the last year. Averages 40-60 total titles, 1-2 fiction titles each year.
● Gibbs Smith is the recipient of a Western Writers Association Fiction Award.
Needs: Children's (preschool/picture books), comics/graphic novels, ethnic/multicultural, feminist, humor/satire, literary, mainstream/contemporary, new age/mystic/spiritual, science fiction (hard science/technological, soft/sociological), short story collections. Publishes *The Peregrine Reader*, a series of anthologies based upon a variety of themes. Published *The White Rooster and Other Stories*, by Robert Bausch (literary); and *Last Buckaroo*, by Mackey Hedges (western).
How to Contact: Accepts unsolicited mss. Query with outline/synopsis and 2 sample chapters. Include esti-

---

MARKET CONDITIONS are constantly changing! If you're still using this book and it is 1999 or later, buy the newest edition of *Novel & Short Story Writer's Market* at your favorite bookstore or order from Writer's Digest Books.

mated word count, 1-paragraph bio and list of publishing credits. SASE for reply. Reports in 3-4 weeks on queries; 2-4 months on mss. Simultaneous submissions OK. Sometimes critiques or comments on rejected mss.
Terms: Pays royalties; amount depends on author and author's publishing history. Provides 10 author's copies. Sends galleys to author. Publishes ms 1-2 years after acceptance. Writer's guidelines and book catalog for #10 SASE.
Advice: "The fiction editor also holds several other positions within the company. Please be patient about response time."

SOHO PRESS, (I, II), 853 Broadway, New York NY 10003. (212)260-1900. **Acquisitions**: Juris Jurjevics, publisher; Laura M.C. Hruska and Melanie Fleishman, fiction editors. "Soho Press publishes discerning authors for discriminating readers." Publishes hardcover originals and trade paperback reprints. Published new writers within the last year. Publishes 10 previously unpublished writers/year. Averages 25 titles/year. Distributes titles through Farrar, Straus & Giroux. Promotes titles through readings, tours, print ads, reviews, interviews, advance reading copies, postcards and brochures.
Imprint(s): Soho Crime, edited by Laura Hruska and Juris Jurjevics (mystery); and Hera, edited by Laura Hruska (women's historical fiction).
   ● *Woman in Amber*, by Agate Nesaule, received an American Book Awards.
Needs: Ethnic, literary, mainstream, mystery/espionage, suspense. "We do novels that are the very best of their kind." Recently published *My Lucky Face*, by May-lee Chai; *The Gun Seller*, by Hugh Laurie; and *Stone Cowboy*, by Mark Jacobs. Also publishes the Hera series (serious historical fiction reprints with strong female leads).
How to Contact: Submit query with SASE. Reports in 1 month on queries; 6 weeks on mss. Simultaneous submissions OK.
Terms: Pays royalties of 10-15% on retail price. For trade paperbacks pays 7½%. Offers advance. Publishes ms 1 year after acceptance. Book catalog plus $1 for SASE.
Advice: Greatest challenge is "introducing brand new, untested writers. We do not care if they are agented or not. Half the books we publish come directly from authors. We look for a distinctive writing style, strong writing skills and compelling plots. We are not interested in trite expression of mass market formulae."

‡SOUNDPRINTS, Division of Trudy Corporation, 165 Water St., Norwalk CT 06856. Fax: (203)844-1176. **Acquisitions**: Assistant Editor. "Soundprints takes you on an Odyssey of discovery, exploring an historical event or a moment in time that affects our every day lives. Each Odyssey is approved by a Smithsonian Institution curator, so readers experience the adventures as if they were really there." Publishes hardcover originals. Publishes 20% previously unpublished writers/year. Publishes 10-14 titles/year.
Needs: Juvenile.
How to Contact: Query first. Reports on queries in 3 months. Simultaneous submissions OK.
Terms: Makes outright purchase. No advance. Publishes ms 2 years after acceptance. Book catalog for 9×12 SAE with $1.05 postage. Writer's guidelines for #10 SASE.
Advice: "Our books are written for children from ages 4-8. Our most successful authors can craft a wonderful story which is derived from authentic wildlife facts. First inquiry to us should ask about our interest in publishing a book about a specific animal or habitat. We launched a new series in fall of 1996. Stories are about historical events that are represented by exhibits in the Smithsonian Institution's museums. When we publish juvenile fiction, it will be about wildlife and all information in the book *must* be accurate."

SOUTHERN METHODIST UNIVERSITY PRESS, (I, II), P.O. Box 415, Dallas TX 75275. (214)768-1433. Fax: (214)768-1428. **Acquisitions**: Kathryn M. Lang, senior editor. Estab. 1936. "Small university press publishing in areas of film/theater, Southwest life and letters, religion/medical ethics and contemporary fiction." Publishes hardcover and paperback originals and reprints. Books: acid-free paper; perfect-bound; some illustrations. Average print order 2,000. Published new writers within the last year. Averages 10-12 total titles; 3-4 fiction titles each year. Sometimes comments on rejected mss.
Needs: Contemporary, ethnic, literary, regional, short story collections. "We are always willing to look at 'serious' or 'literary' fiction." No "mass market, science fiction, formula, thriller, romance." Recently published *Bitter Lakes*, by Ann Harleman (literary novel); and *The Woman in the Oilfield*, by Tracy Daugherty (stories).
How to Contact: Accepts unsolicited mss. Query first. Submit outline/synopsis and 3 sample chapters. SASE. Reports in 3 weeks on queries; 6-12 months on mss. No simultaneous submissions.
Terms: Pays royalties of 10% net, negotiable advance, 10 author's copies. Publishes ms 1 year after acceptance. Book catalog free.
Advice: "We view encouraging first time authors as part of the mission of a university press. Send query describing the project and your own background. Research the press before you submit—don't send us the kinds of things we don't publish." Looks for "quality fiction from new or established writers."

‡SPECTRA BOOKS, (II, IV), Subsidiary of Bantam Doubleday Dell Publishing Group, 1540 Broadway, New York NY 10036. (212)765-6500. Website: http://www.bdd.com. Executive Editor: Jennifer Hershey. Senior Editor: Tom Dupree. Associate Editor: Anne Groell. Estab. 1985. Large science fiction, fantasy and speculative fiction line. Publishes hardcover originals, paperback originals and trade paperbacks. Averages 60 total titles, all fiction.

● Many Bantam Spectra Books have received Hugos and Nebulas including Connie Willis's *Doomsday Book*, which won both in 1993.

Needs: Fantasy, humor (fantasy, science fiction), literary, science fiction. Needs include novels that attempt to broaden the traditional range of science fiction and fantasy. Strong emphasis on characterization. Especially well written traditional science fiction and fantasy will be considered. No fiction that doesn't have at least some element of speculation or the fantastic. Recently published *Game of Thrones*, by George R. Martin (medieval fantasy); *Assassin's Quest*, by Robin Hobb (coming of age fantasy); and *Blue Mars*, by Stanley Robinson (science fiction).

How to Contact: Query first with 3 chapters and a short (no more than 3 pages double-spaced) synopsis. SASE. Agented fiction 90%. Reports in 6 months. Simultaneous submissions OK if noted.

Terms: Pays in royalties; negotiable advance. Sends galleys to author. Writer's guidelines for #10 SASE.

Advice: "Please follow our guidelines carefully and type neatly."

THE SPEECH BIN, INC., (IV), 1965 25th Ave., Vero Beach FL 32960. (561)770-0007. Fax: (561)770-0006. **Acquisitions**: Jan J. Binney, senior editor. Estab. 1984. Small independent publisher and major national and international distributor of books and material for speech-language pathologists, audiologists, special educators and caregivers. Publishes hardcover and paperback originals. Averages 15-20 total titles/year. "No fiction at present time, but we are very interested in publishing fiction relevant to our specialties."

Needs: "We are most interested in seeing fiction, including books for children, dealing with individuals experiencing communication disorders, other handicaps, and their families and caregivers, particularly their parents, or family members dealing with individuals who have strokes, physical disability, hearing loss, Alzheimer's and so forth."

How to Contact: Accepts unsolicited mss. Query first. SASE. Agented fiction 10%. Reports in 4-6 weeks on queries; 1-3 months on mss. Simultaneous submissions OK, but only if notified by author.

Terms: Pays royalties. Sends galleys to author. Publishes ms 6 months after acceptance. Writer's guidelines for #10 SASE. Book catalog for 9 × 12 SAE with 4 first-class stamps.

Advice: "We are most interested in publishing fiction about individuals who have speech, hearing and other handicaps."

SPINSTERS INK, (II, IV), 32 E. First St., #330, Duluth MN 55802. Fax: (218)727-3119. E-mail: spinsters@aol. com. Website: http://www.lesbian.org/spinsters-ink (includes online catalog, writer's guidelines, staff list, chat rooms, excerpts from books, discussion forums). **Acquisitions**: Nancy Walker. Estab. 1978. Moderate-size women's publishing company growing steadily. "We are committed to publishing works by women writing from the periphery: fat women, Jewish women, lesbians, poor women, rural women, women of color, etc." Publishes paperback originals and reprints. Books: 55 lb. acid-free natural paper; photo offset printing; perfect-bound; illustrations when appropriate. Average print order: 5,000. Published new writers within the last year. Plans 2 first novels this year. Averages 6 total titles, 3-5 fiction titles each year. Distributes titles through InBook/LPC and all wholesalers. Promotes titles through Women's Review of Books, Feminist Bookstore News, regional advertising, author interviews and reviews.

● Spinster Ink won a 1997 Minnesota Women's Consortium Award. They published *Mother Journeys*, by M. Reddy, M. Roth and A. Sheldon, which received a 1995 Minnesota Book Award and also the 1995 Susan Koppelman Award; *Martha Moody*, by Susan Stinson, a 1996 PMA Benjamin Franklin Award Winner; and *Silent Words*, by Joan Drury, received a 1997 Minnesota Book Award, a 1997 PMA Benjamin Franklin Award and a 1997 Northeastern Minnesota Book Award. Spinsters plans an anthology called *Women of Color in the Midwest*.

Needs: Feminist, lesbian. Wants "full-length quality fiction—thoroughly revised novels which display deep characterization, theme and style. We *only* consider books by women. No books by men, or books with sexist, racist or ageist content." Recently published *Silent Words*, by Joan Drury (feminist mystery); *The Activist's Daughter*, by Ellyn Bache (feminist); and *Living at Night*, by Mariana Romo-Carmona (lesbian). Publishes anthologies. Writers may submit directly. Series include: "Coming of Age Series" and "Forgotten Women's Series."

How to Contact: Query or submit outline/synopsis and 2-5 sample chapters not to exceed 50 pages with SASE. Electronic queries OK. Reports in 1 month on queries; 3 months on mss. Simultaneous submissions discouraged. Disk submissions OK (DOS or Macintosh format—MS Word 4.0). Prefers hard copy with disk submission. Occasionally critiques rejected mss.

Terms: Pays royalties of 7-10%, plus 10 author's copies; unlimited extra copies at 40% discount. Publishes ms 18 months after acceptance. Free book catalog.

Advice: "In the past, lesbian fiction has been largely 'escape fiction' with sex and romance as the only required ingredients; however, we encourage more complex work that treats the lesbian lifestyle with the honesty it deserves. Look at our catalog and mission statement. Does your book fit our criteria?"

STARBURST PUBLISHERS, (II), P.O. Box 4123, Lancaster PA 17604. (717)293-0939. Fax: (717)293-1945. E-mail: starbrst@redrose.net. **Acquisitions**: Ellen Hake, editorial director. Estab. 1982. Midsize independent press specializing in inspirational and self-help books. Publishes trade paperback and hardcover originals and trade paperback reprints. Receives 1,000 submission/year. 60% of books by first-time authors. Averages 10-15 total titles each year. Promotes titles through print and all major distributors.

Needs: Religious/inspirational: Adventure, contemporary, fantasy, historical, horror, military/war, psychic/supernatural/occult, romance (contemporary, historical), spiritual, suspense/mystery, western. Wants "inspirational material." Recently published *The Miracle of the Sacred Scroll*, by Johan Christian; and *The Remnant*, by Gilbert Morris (Christian).

How to Contact: Submit outline/synopsis, 3 sample chapters, bio, photo and SASE. Agented fiction less than 25%. Reports in 6-8 weeks on manuscripts; 1 month on queries. Accepts electronic submissions via disk and modem, "but also wants clean double-spaced typewritten or computer printout manuscript."

Terms: Pays royalties of 6% minimum; 16% maximum. "Individual arrangement with writer depending on the manuscript as well as writer's experience as a published author." Publishes ms up to one year after acceptance. Writer's guidelines for #10 SASE. Book catalog for 9 × 12 SAE and 4 first-class stamps.

Advice: "50% of our line goes into the inspirational marketplace; 50% into the general marketplace. We are one of the few publishers that has direct sales representation into both the inspirational and general marketplace."

‡**STEEPLE HILL**, 300 E. 42nd Street, 6th Floor, New York NY 10017. (212)682-6080. Steeple Hill publishes Love Inspired, a line of inspirational contemporary romances with stories designed to lift readers spirits and gladden their hearts. These books feature characters facing the challenge of today's world and learning important lessons about life, love and faith. Set to launch September 1997 with 3 books per month. Editorial Director: Isabel Swift. **Acquisitions**: Tara Gavin, senior editor/editorial coordinator; Anne Canadeo, freelance editor. Melissa Jeglinski, editor. Publishes paperback originals and reprints. Buys agented and unagented inspirational love stories.

• Authors who write for Steeple Hill are a combination of celebrated authors in the Christian women's fiction market such as Jane Peart, Carole Gift Page, Roger Elwood, Sara Mitchell and Irene Brand, as well as talented newcomers to the field of inspirational romance.

Needs: "Wholesome contemporary tales of inspirational romance that include strong family values and high moral standards. Drama, humor and a touch of mystery all have a place in the series." To be published: *The Risk of Loving*, by Jane Peart; *In Search of her Own*, by Carole Gift Page; *Promises*, by Roger Elwood; *Night Music*, by Sara Mitchell; and *Child of Her Heart*, by Irene Brand.

How to Contact: Submit query letter with brief synopsis and SASE or write for detailed submission guidelines/tip sheets. No unsolicited or simultaneous submissions. Publishes 9-36 months after acceptance. Occasionally comments on rejected mss.

Terms: Royalties paid twice-yearly; offers advance (negotiated on an individual basis). Must return advance if book is not completed or unacceptable. Writer's guidelines for #10 SASE.

Advice: "Although the element of faith must be clearly present, it should be well-integrated into the characterizations and plot. Children and humor are welcome; family values and traditional morals are imperative. While there is no premarital sex between characters, a vivid, exciting romance that is presented with a mature prespective is essential."

‡**STILL WATERS POETRY PRESS**, 459 Willow Ave., Galloway Township NJ 08201. Website: http://www2. netcom.com/~salake/stillwaterspoetry.html. **Acquisitions**: Shirley Warren, editor. "Dedicated to significant poetry for, by or about women, we want contemporary themes and styles set on American soil. We don't want gay, patriarchal religion, lesbian, simple rhyme or erotic themes." Publishes trade paperback originals and chapbooks. Publishes 4 titles/year. Publishes 80% previously unpublished writers/year.

Needs: Literary, women's interests. "We seldom publish fiction. Don't send the same old stuff." No long books. Recently published *Grain Pie*, by Anne Lawrence (chapbook).

How to Contact: Short stories only with SASE. Reports in 1 month on queries; 3 months on mss. Simultaneous submissions OK.

Terms: Pays in copies for first press run; 10% royalty for additional press runs. No advance. Publishes ms 4 months after acceptance. Writer's guidelines and book catalog for #10 SASE.

Advice: "Audience is adults with literary awareness. Don't send mss via certified mail."

‡**STONE BRIDGE PRESS, (IV)**, P.O. Box 8208, Berkeley CA 94707. (510)524-8732. Fax: (510)524-8711. E-mail: sbpedit@stonebridge.com. Website: http://www.stonebridge.com (includes complete catalog, contact information, related features, submission guidelines and excerpts). **Acquisitions**: Peter Goodman, publisher. Estab. 1989. "Independent press focusing on books about Japan in English (business, language, culture, literature)." Publishes paperback originals and reprints. Books: 60-70 lb. offset paper; web and sheet paper; perfect-bound; some illustrations; average print order: 3,000; first novel print order: 2,000-2,500. Averages 6 total titles, 2 fiction titles, each year. Distributes titles through Weatherhill and New Holland. Promotes titles through Internet announcements, special-interest magazines and niche tie-ins to associations.

Imprint(s): Rock Spring Collection of Japanese Literature, edited by Peter Goodman.

• Stone Bridge Press received a PEN West Literary Award for Translation and a Japan-U.S. Friendship Prize for *Still Life*, by Junzo Shono, translated by Wayne P. Lammers. Another book, *A Long Rainy Season* received the 1995 Benjamin Franklin Award for Fiction/Poetry from PMA. An anthology of expatriate writers in Japan was published in 1997.

Needs: Japan-themed. No poetry. If not translation, interested in the expatriate experience. "Primarily looking at material relating to Japan. Mostly translations, but we'd like to see samples of work dealing with the expatriate experience." Also Asian- and Japanese-American. Published *Wind and Stone*, by Masaaki Tachihara; *Still Life and Other Stories*, by Junzo Shono; *One Hot Summer in Kyoto*, by John Haylock.

How to Contact: Accepts unsolicited mss. Query first. Submit 1-page cover letter, outline/synopsis and 3 sample chapters. SASE. Agented fiction 25%. Reports in 1 month on queries; 6-8 months on mss. Simultaneous submissions OK. Sometimes comments on rejected ms.

Terms: Pays royalties, offers negotiable advance. Publishes ms 18-24 months after acceptance. Catalog for 1 first-class stamp.

Advice: "As we focus on Japan-related material there is no point in approaching us unless you are very familiar with Japan. We'd especially like to see submissions dealing with the expatriate experience. Please, absolutely no commercial fiction."

‡STONEWALL INN, Imprint of St. Martin's Press, 175 Fifth Ave., New York NY 10010. (212)674-5151. Website: http://www.stonewallinn.com. **Acquisitions:** Keith Kahla, general editor. "Stonewall Inn is the only gay and lesbian focused imprint at a major house . . . and is more inclusive of gay men than most small presses." Publishes trade paperback originals and reprints. Publishes 20-23 titles/year. Publishes 40% previously unpublished writers/year.

Needs: Gay, lesbian, literary, mystery. Recently published *Love Alone*, by Paul Monette; and *Buddies*, by Ethan Mordden.

How to Contact: Query with SASE. Reports in 6 months on queries. Simultaneous submissions OK.

Terms: Pays standard royalty on retail price. Pays $5,000 advance (for first-time authors). Publishes ms 1 year after acceptance. Book catalog free.

Advice: "Anybody who has any question about what a gay novel is should go out and read half a dozen. For example, there are hundreds of 'coming out' novels in print."

STORY LINE PRESS, (II), Three Oaks Farm, Brownsville OR 97327-9718. (541)466-5352. Fax: (541)466-3200. E-mail: slp@ptinet.com. Website: http://www.ptinet.com/~slp. **Acquisitions:** Robert McDowell, editor. Estab. 1985. "Nonprofit literary press." Publishes hardcover and paperback originals and hardcover and paperback reprints. Published new writers within the last year. Plans 1 first novel this year. Averages 10 total titles, 3 fiction titles each year.

• Story Line Press books have received awards including the Oregon Book Award.

Needs: Adventure, ethnic/multicultural, literary, mystery/suspense, regional, short story collections, translations. Recently published *The Open Door*, by Floyd Skloot; and *A Place in Mind*, by Sydney Lea. Publishes Stuart Mallory Mystery series.

How to Contact: Accepts unsolicited mss. Returns mss "if postage is included." Query with outline. Include bio, list of publishing credits and description of work. Send SASE for reply, return of ms or send a disposable copy of ms. Agented fiction 2.7%. Reports in 9-12 weeks on queries; 6-9 months on mss. Simultaneous submissions OK. No electronic submissions.

Terms: Provides author's copies; payment depends on grant/award money. Sends galleys to author. Publishes ms 1-3 years after acceptance. Book catalog for 7×10 SASE.

Advice: "Patience . . . understanding of a nonprofit literary presses' limitations. Be very familiar with our list and only submit accordingly."

‡SUDBURY PRESS, Profitable Technology, Inc., 40 Maclean Dr., Sudbury MA 01776. Fax: (508)443-0734. E-mail: press@intertain.com. Website: http://www.intertain.com. **Acquisitions:** Susan Gray, publisher. Sudbury Press publishes only cozy mysteries and autobiographies and biographies of women. Publishes hardcover and mass market paperback originals. Publishes 8 titles/year. Publishes 100% previously unpublished writers/year.

Needs: "We look for exclusively cozy mysteries in the style of Agatha Christie. We are not interested in thrillers, chillers, horror, legal mysteries or true crime."

How to Contact: Submit synopsis, 2 sample chapters and SASE. Prefers complete ms. Reports in 3 months.

Terms: Pays 10% royalty on wholesale price. Offers $0-3,000 advance. Publishes ms 6 months after acceptance. Book catalog on Internet.

‡THE SUMMIT PUBLISHING GROUP, One Arlington Center, 1112 E. Copeland, 5th Floor, Arlington TX 76011. **Acquisitions:** Len Oszustowicz, publisher; Bill Scott, editor. Summit Publishing Group seeks contemporary books with a nationwide appeal. Publishes hardcover originals, trade paperback originals and reprints. Publishes 35 titles/year. Publishes 40% previously unpublished writers/year.

Needs: Literary, religious. Recently published *The Gospel of Elvis*, by Louie Ludwig (humor).

How to Contact: Submit synopsis, 2 sample chapters and SASE. Reports in 1 month on queries, 3 months on mss. Simultaneous submissions OK.

Terms: Pays 5-20% royalty on wholesale price. Offers $2,000 and up advance. Publishes ms 6 months after acceptance.

SUNSTONE PRESS, (IV), P.O. Box 2321, Santa Fe NM 87504-2321. (505)988-4418. Contact: James C. Smith, Jr. Estab. 1971. Midsize publisher. Publishes hardcover and paperback originals. Average first novel print order: 2,000. Published new writers within the last year. Plans 2 first novels this year. Averages 16 total titles, 2-3 fiction titles, each year.

- ● Sunstone Press published *Ninez*, by Virginia Nylander Ebinger which received the Southwest Book Award from the Border Regional Library Association.

Needs: Western. "We have a Southwestern theme emphasis. Sometimes buys juvenile mss with illustrations." No science fiction, romance or occult. Published *Apache: The Long Ride Home*, by Grant Gall (Indian/Western); *Sorrel*, by Rita Cleary; and *To Die in Dinetah*, by John Truitt.

How to Contact: Accepts unsolicited mss. Query first or submit outline/synopsis and 2 sample chapters with SASE. Reports in 2 weeks. Simultaneous submissions OK. Publishes ms 9-12 months after acceptance.

Terms: Pays royalties, 10% maximum, and 10 author's copies.

‡TAB BOOK CLUB, (TEEN AGE BOOK CLUB), (II), Scholastic Inc., 555 Broadway, New York NY 10012. Editor: Greg Holch. Published new writers within the last year.

Needs: "TAB Book Club publishes novels for young teenagers in seventh through ninth grades. We do not publish short stories, problem novels or standard teenage romances. A book has to be unique, different, and of high literary quality."

How to Contact: "Due to the extremely large number of submissions, we will not be looking at new manuscripts this year."

Advice: "The books we are publishing now are literary works that we hope will become the classics of the future. They are novels that reveal the hearts and souls of their authors."

‡NAN A. TALESE, Imprint of Doubleday, 1540 Broadway, New York NY 10036. (212)782-8918. Fax: (212)782-9261. Website: http://www.bdd.com. **Acquisitions:** Nan A. Talese, editorial director. "Nan A. Talese publishes nonfiction with a powerful guiding narrative and relevance to larger cultural trends and interests, and literary fiction of the highest quality." Publishes hardcover originals. Publishes 15 titles/year.

Needs: Literary. Recently published *The Dancer Upstairs*, by Nicholas Shakespeare (novel); *Alias Grace*, by Margaret Atwood (novel); and *Into the Great Wide Open*, by Kevin Carty (first novel).

How to Contact: Agented fiction only. Reports in 1 week on queries, 1 month on mss. Simultaneous submissions OK.

Terms: Pays royalty on retail price, varies. Advance varies. Publishes ms 8 months after acceptance.

Advice: "We're interested in everything literary—we're not interested in genre fiction. No low-market stuff. Audience is highly literate people interested in literary books. We want well-written material."

‡TEXAS CHRISTIAN UNIVERSITY PRESS, P.O. Box 298300, TCU, Fort Worth TX 76129. (817)921-7822. Fax: (817)921-7333. Director: Judy Alter. **Acquisitions:** Tracy Row, editor. Estab. 1966. Texas Christian publishes "scholarly monographs, other serious scholarly work and regional titles of significance focusing on the history and literature of the American." Publishes hardcover originals, some reprints. Publishes 10% previously unpublished writers/year. Publishes 10 titles/year.

Needs: Regional fiction. Recently published *Hunter's Trap*, by C.W. Smith; *Tales from the Sunday House*, by Minetta Altgelt Goyne (history); and *The Coldest Day in Texas*, by Peggy Pursy Freeman (juvenile).

How to Contact: Considers mss by invitation only. Please do not query. Reports in 3 months.

Terms: Nonauthor-subsidy publishes 10% of books. Pays 10% royalty on net price. Publishes ms 16 months after acceptance.

Advice: "Regional and/or Texana nonfiction or fiction have best chance of breaking into our firm."

THORNDIKE PRESS, (IV), Division of Macmillan U.S.A., Box 159, Thorndike ME 04986. (800)223-6121. **Acquisitions:** Jamie Knobloch. Estab. 1979. Midsize publisher of hardcover and paperback large print *reprints*. Books: alkaline paper; offset printing; Smythe-sewn library binding; average print order: 1,000. Publishes 524 total titles each year.

Needs: *No fiction that has not been previously published*.

How to Contact: Does not accept unsolicited mss. Query.

Terms: Pays 10% in royalties.

Advice: "We do not accept unpublished works."

‡TIDEWATER PUBLISHERS, Imprint of Cornell Maritime Press, Inc., P.O. Box 456, Centreville MD 21617-0456. (410)758-1075. Fax: (410)758-6849. **Acquisitions:** Charlotte Kurst, managing editor. Estab. 1938. "Tidewater Publishers issues adult nonfiction works related to the Chesapeake Bay area, Delmarva or Maryland in

---

CHECK THE CATEGORY INDEXES, located at the back of the book, for publishers interested in specific fiction subjects.

general. The only fiction we handle is juvenile and must have a regional focus." Publishes hardcover and paperback originals. Publishes 41% previously unpublished writers/year. Publishes 7-9 titles/year.

Needs: Regional juvenile fiction only. Recently published *Toulouse: The Story of a Canada Goose*, by Priscilla Cummings (picture book); and *Oyster Moon*, by Margaret Meacham (adventure).

How to Contact: Query or submit outline/synopsis and sample chapters. Reports in 2 months.

Terms: Pays 7½-15% royalty on retail price. Publishes ms 1 year after acceptance. Book catalog for 10×13 SAE with 5 first-class stamps.

Advice: "Our audience is made up of readers interested in works that are specific to the Chesapeake Bay and Delmarva Peninsula area."

TOR BOOKS, (II), Tom Doherty Associates, 175 Fifth Ave., New York NY 10010. (212)388-0100. **Acquisitions**: Patrick Nielsen Hayden, manager of science fiction; Melissa Singer (Forge Books). Estab. 1980. Publishes hardcover and paperback originals, plus some paperback reprints. Books: 5 point Dombook paper; offset printing; Bursel and perfect binding; few illustrations. Averages 200 total titles, mostly fiction, each year. Some nonfiction titles.

Imprint(s): Forge Books.

Needs: Fantasy, mainstream, science fiction and horror. Published *Moving Mars*, by Greg Bear; *Alvin Journeyman*, by Orson Scott Card; *A Crown of Swords*, by Robert Jordan; and *The Two Georges*, by Richard Dreyfuss and Harry Turtledove.

How to Contact: Agented mss preferred. Buys 90% agented fiction. No simultaneous submissions. Address manuscripts to "Editorial," *not* to the Managing Editor's office.

Terms: Pays in royalties and advance. Writer must return advance if book is not completed or is unacceptable. Sends galleys to author. Free book catalog on request. Publishes ms 1-2 years after acceptance.

‡TRIANGLE TITLES, Imprint of Obelesk Books, P.O. Box 1118, Elkton MD 21922. E-mail: obelesk@netgsi.com. Website: www.netgsi.com/~obelesk. **Acquisitions:** Gary Bowen, editor. Publishes science fiction, fantasy and horror books featuring minority characters of all types and strong women characters. Publishes trade paperback originals and reprints. Publishes 10% previously unpublished writers/year. Publishes 4 titles/year.

● Publishes such well-known authors as Edward Lee and Shannah Jay.

Needs: Fantasy, gothic, horror, science fiction, short story collections. "We publish gay/lesbian, bisexual and transgendered science fiction, fantasy and horror. We prefer minority characters: racial, ethnic, sexual, disabled and strong women. No stories about straight, white men. Length: 5,000 words maximum. No novel excerpts or poetry." Recently published *Floating Worlds: Oriental Fantasies (short fiction); Icarus & Angels: Flights of Fantasy* (science fiction); and *Cyber Magic: Lesbian Science Fiction*.

How to Contact: Reports in 1 month on queries and mss. Simultaneous submissions OK.

Terms: Pays $10-20 for one-time rights. Writer's guidelines and book catalog for #10 SASE.

Advice: "Audience are mature, open-minded and multicultural. We are especially looking for minority authors; disabled, racial, ethnic and sexual minorities and women."

‡TSR, INC., Box 756, Lake Geneva WI 53147. (414)248-3625. Executive Editor: Brian Thomsen. **Acquisitions**: Submissions Editor. Estab. 1974. "We publish original paperback and hardcover novels and 'shared world' books." TSR publishes games as well, including the Dungeons & Dragons® role-playing game. Books: standard paperbacks; offset printing; perfect binding; b&w (usually) illustrations; average first novel print order: 75,000. Averages 20-30 fiction titles each year.

Imprint(s): the Dragonlance® series, Forgotten Realms™ series, Dungeons & Dragons® Books, Dark Sun Books, **TSR™ Books**, Ravenloft™ Books.

● TSR also publishes the magazine *Amazing Stories* and *Dragon* listed in this book. For more, see the interviews with Kim Mohan of *Amazing Stories* and Brian Thomsen, executive editor for TSR Books in the 1995 *Science Fiction Writer's Marketplace and Sourcebook*.

Needs: "We most often publish character-oriented fantasy and science fiction; all horror must be suitable for line of Ravenluff™ Books. We work with authors who can deal in a serious fashion with the genres we concentrate on and can be creative within the confines of our work-for-hire contracts." Published *The Legacy*, by R.A. Salvatore; *The Valorian*, by Mary H. Herbert; and *Before the Mask*, by Michael and Teri Williams.

How to Contact: "Because most of our books are strongly tied to our game products, we expect our writers to be very familiar with those products."

Terms: Pays royalties of 4% of cover price. Offers advances. "Commissioned works, with the exception of our TSR™ Books line, are written as work-for-hire, with TSR, Inc., holding all copyrights." Publishes ms 1 year after acceptance.

Advice: "With the huge success of our Dragonlance® series and Forgotten Realms™ books, we expect to be working even more closely with TSR-owned fantasy worlds. Be familiar with our line and query us regarding a proposal."

TYNDALE HOUSE PUBLISHERS, (II, IV), P.O. Box 80, 351 Executive Drive, Wheaton IL 60189-0080. (630)668-8300. Fax: (630)668-8311. E-mail: kv@tyndale.com. Website: http://www.tyndale.com. Vice President of Editorial: Ron Beers. **Acquisitions**: Ken Petersen, acquisition director. Manuscript Review Committee. Estab.

1962. Privately owned religious press. Publishes hardcover and trade paperback originals and paperback reprints. Averages 100 total titles, 20-25 fiction titles each year. Average first novel print order: 5,000-15,000 copies. Distributes titles through catalog houses, rackers and distributors. Promotes titles through prints ads in trade publications, radio, point of sale materials and catalogs.

Imprint(s): Lining Books.

● Three books published by Tyndale House have received the Gold Medallion Book Award. They include *An Echo in the Darkness*, by Francine Rivers; *The Sword of Truth*, by Gilbert Morris; and *A Rose Remembered*, by Michael Phillips.

Needs: Religious: historical, romance. "We primarily publish Christian historical romances, with occasional contemporary, suspense or standalones." Recently published *Treasure of Zanzibar*, by Catherine Palmer (adventure romance); *The Atonement Child*, by Francine Rivers (general); and *Left Behind* series, by Jerry Jenkins and Tim Lattaye (prophecy fiction). Publishes 1 previously unpublished writer/year.

How to Contact: Does not accept unsolicited mss. Queries only. Reports in 6-10 weeks. Publishes ms an average of 9-18 months after acceptance.

Terms: Royalty and advance negotiable. Publishes ms 18 months after acceptance. Writer's guidelines and book catalog for 9×12 SAE and $2.40 for postage.

Advice: "We are a religious publishing house with a primarily evangelical Christian market. We are looking for spiritual themes and content within established genres."

‡**UNITY BOOKS**, Unity School of Christianity, 1901 NW Blue Parkway, Unity Village MO 64065-0001. (816)524-3550 ext. 3190. Fax: (816)251-3552. E-mail: sprice@unityworldhq.org. Website: http://www.unityworl dhq.org. **Acquisitions:** Michael Maday, editor; Brenda Markle, associate editor. "We are a bridge between traditional Christianity and New Age spirituality. Unity School of Christianity is on Christian principles, spiritual values and the healing power of prayer as a resource for daily living." Publishes hardcover and trade paperback originals and reprints. Publishes 30% previously unpublished writers/year. Publishes 16 titles/year.

Needs: Spiritual, inspirational, metaphysical.

How to Contact: Query with synopsis and sample chapter. Reports in 1 month on queries; 2 months on mss.

Terms: Pays 10-15% royalty on net receipts. Publishes ms 13 months after acceptance of final ms. Writer's guidelines and book catalog free.

‡**UNIVERSITY OF CALIFORNIA PRESS**, 2120 Berkeley Way, Berkeley CA 94720. Director: James H. Clark. Associate Director: Lynne E. Withey. **Acquisitions:** Linda Norton, editor (literature, poetry). Estab. 1893. Los Angeles office: 405 Hilgard Ave., Los Angeles CA 90024-1373. UK office: University Presses of California, Columbia, and Princeton, 1 Oldlands Way, Bognor Regis, W. Sussex PO22 9SA England. "Most of our publications are hardcover nonfiction written by scholars." Publishes hardcover and paperback originals and reprints. Publishes 180 titles/year.

Needs: Publishes fiction only in translation.

How to Contact: Queries are always advisable, accompanied by outlines or sample material. Send to Berkeley address. Enclose return postage. Reports in 2 months.

‡**UNIVERSITY OF GEORGIA PRESS**, 330 Research Dr., Athens GA 30602-4901. (706)369-6130. Fax: (706)369-6131. E-mail: ugapress@uga.edu. **Acquisitions:** David Dejardines, acquisition editor. Estab. 1938. University of Georgia Press is a midsized press "with attention to design and production. We can't cover all areas, but what we do, we do well. We are neither conservative nor edgy, but open-minded." Publishes hardcover originals, trade paperback originals and reprints. Publishes 33% previously unpublished writers/year. Publishes 85 titles/year.

Imprint(s): Brown Thrasher Books, David Dejardines, acquisition editor (paperback originals and reprints, Southern history, literature and culture).

Needs: Literary. Recently published *The Quarry*, by Harvey Grossinger (novel); and *Lost in Translation*, by Steven Harvey (essays).

How to Contact: Query with 1-2 sample chapters and SASE. Reports in 2 months on queries.

Terms: Pays 7-10% royalty on net price. Rarely offers advance; amount varies. Publishes ms 1 year after acceptance. Writer's guidelines for #10 SASE. Book catalog free.

‡**UNIVERSITY OF ILLINOIS PRESS**, 1325 S. Oak St., Champaign IL 61820-6903. (217)333-0950. Fax: (217)244-8082. E-mail: uipress@uiuc.edu. Website: http://www.uiuc.edu/providers/uipress. **Acquisitions:** Richard Wentworth, director/editor-in-chief. Estab. 1918. Publishes hardcover and trade paperback originals and reprints. Publishes 50% previously unpublished writers/year. Publishes 100-110 titles/year.

Needs: Ethnic, experimental, mainstream. Recently published *Distant Friends and Intimate Strangers*, by Charles East; *Taking It Home: Stories from the Neighborhood*, by Tony Ardizzone; and *Flights in the Heavenlies*, by Ernest J. Finney.

How to Contact: Query first. Reports in 1 month. "We are not presently looking at unsolicited collections of stories. We do not publish novels."

Terms: Nonauthor-subsidy publishes 10% of books. Pays 0-10% royalty on net sales; offers $1,000-1,500

average advance (rarely). Publishes ms 1 year after acceptance. Book catalog for 9 × 12 SAE with 2 first-class stamps.
Advice: "Serious scholarly books that are broad enough and well-written enough to appeal to non-specialists are doing well for us in today's market."

‡UNIVERSITY OF IOWA PRESS, 119 W. Park Rd., Iowa City IA 52242-1000. (319)335-2000. Fax: (319)335-2055. Website: http://www.uiowa.edu/~uipress. **Acquisitions:** Paul Zimmer, director. Estab. 1969. Publishes hardcover and paperback originals. Publishes 30% previously unpublished writers/year. Publishes 35 titles/year. Average print order for a first book is 1,000-1,200.
Needs: Currently publishes the Iowa Short Fiction Award selections.
How to Contact: Query first. Reports within 4 months.
Terms: Pays 7-10% royalty on net price. Publishes ms 1 year after acceptance. Writer's guidelines and book catalog free.

‡UNIVERSITY OF NEBRASKA PRESS, 312 N. 14th St., P.O. Box 880484, Lincoln NE 68588-0484. (402)472-3581. Fax: (402)472-0308. E-mail: press@unlinfo.unl.edu. Website: http://www.unl.edu./UP/home.htm. **Acquisitions:** Douglas Clayton, editor-in-chief (fiction in translation, humanities). Estab. 1941. "The University of Nebraska Press seeks to encourage, develop, publish and disseminate research, literature and the publishing arts. The Press maintains scholarly standards and fosters innovations guided by referred evaluations." Publishes hardcover and paperback originals and reprints. Publishes 25% previously unpublished writers/year. Average print order for a first book is 1,200.
Imprint(s): Bison Books, Jay Fultz, editor (paperback reprints); Landmark Editions (hardcover reprints).
● University of Nebraska Press has published such authors as N. Scott Momaday, Rolena Adorna (Cabeza de Vaca) and Diane Glancy.
Needs: Accepts fiction translations but no original fiction. Recently published *School Days*, by Patrick Chamoiseau (Caribbean childhood memoir); *Rue Ordener, Rue Labat*, Sarah Kofman (France-Judaism, 20th century); and *Celebration in the Northwest*, by Ana Maria Matute (contemporary Spanish women's fiction).
How to Contact: Query first with outline/synopsis, 1 sample chapter and introduction. Reports in 4 months.
Terms: Pays graduated royalty from 7% on original books. Occasional advance. Writer's guidelines and book catalog for 9 × 12 SAE with 5 first-class stamps.

‡THE UNIVERSITY OF TENNESSEE PRESS, 293 Communications Bldg., Knoxville TN 37996-0325. Fax: (423)974-3724. E-mail: jsiler@utk.edu. Website: http://www.lib.utk.edu/UTKgophers/UT-PRESS. **Acquisitions:** Joyce Harrison, acquisitions editor; Jenifer Siler, director. Estab. 1940. Publishes 35% previously unpublished writers/year. Publishes 30 titles/year. Average print order for a first book is 1,000.
Needs: Regional. Recently published *Sharpshooter*, by David Madden (Civil War novel).
How to Contact: Query with SASE first. Reports in 2 months.
Terms: Nonauthor-subsidy publishes 10% of books. Pays negotiable royalty on net receipts. Publishes ms 1 year after acceptance. Writer's guidelines for SASE. Book catalog for 12 × 16 SAE with 2 first-class stamps.
Advice: "Our market is in several groups: scholars; educated readers with special interests in given scholarly subjects; and the general educated public interested in Tennessee, Appalachia and the South. Not all our books appeal to all these groups, of course, but any given book must appeal to at least one of them."

‡UNIVERSITY OF TEXAS PRESS, P.O. Box 7819, Austin TX 78713-7819. Fax: (512)320-0668. E-mail: castiron@mail.utexas.edu. Website: http://www.utexas.edu/utpress/. **Acquisitions:** Theresa May, assistant director/executive editor (social sciences, Latin American studies); Joanna Hitchcock, director (humanities, classics); Shannon Davies, acquisitions editor (science). Estab. 1952. Publishes 50% previously unpublished writers/year. Publishes 80 titles/year. Average print order for a first book is 1,000.
Needs: Latin American and Middle Eastern fiction only in translation. Recently published *Satan's Stones*, by Moniru Ravanipur (short stories).
How to Contact: Query or submit outline and 2 sample chapters. Reports in up to 3 months.
Terms: Pays royalty usually based on net income. Offers advance occasionally. Publishes ms 18 months after acceptance. Writer's guidelines and book catalog free.
Advice: "It's difficult to make a manuscript over 400 double-spaced pages into a feasible book. Authors should take special care to edit out extraneous material. Looks for sharply focused, in-depth treatments of important topics."

‡UNIVERSITY PRESS OF MISSISSIPPI, 3825 Ridgewood Rd., Jackson MS 39211-6492. (601)982-6205. Fax: (601)982-6217. E-mail: press@ihl.state.ms.us. Director: Richard Abel. Associate Director and Editor-in-Chief: Seetha Srinivasan. **Acquisitions:** Acquisitions Editor. Estab. 1970. Publishes hardcover and paperback originals and reprints. Publishes 20% previously unpublished writers/year. Publishes 55 titles/year.
Imprint(s): Banner Books (literary reprints).
Needs: Commissioned trade editions by prominent writers. Recently published *Skin Deep*, by Diana Wagman; and *Me: A Book of Remembrance*, by Winnifred Eaton.
How to Contact: Submit outline and sample chapters. Reports in 3 months.

Terms: "Competitive royalties and terms." Publishes ms 1 year after acceptance. Catalog for 9×12 SAE with 3 first-class stamps.

‡UNIVERSITY PRESS OF NEW ENGLAND, (includes Wesleyan University Press), 23 S. Main St., Hanover NH 03755-2048. (603)643-7100. Fax: (603)643-1540. Director: Peter Gilbert. **Acquisitions:** Phil Pochoda, editorial director; Phyliss Deutch, editor. Estab. 1970. "University Press of New England is a consortium of six university presses. Some books—those published for one of the consortium members—carry the joint imprint of New England and the member: Wesleyan, Dartmouth, Brandeis, Tufts, University of New Hampshire and Middlebury College. Associate member: Salzburg seminar." Publishes hardcover originals. Publishes 80 titles/year; 4 fiction titles/year.
Imprint(s): HardScrabble.
Needs: Literary, regional (New England) novels and reprints. Recently published *J. Eden*, by Kit Reed; *Water Witches*, by Chris Bohjalian (novel); *A Great Place to Die*, by Sean Connolly; and *Professor Romeo*, by Anne Bernays.
How to Contact: Query first. Submit outline, list of publishing credits, 1-2 sample chapters with SASE. Agented fiction 50%. Simultaneous submissions OK. Reports in 2 months. Sometimes comments on rejected mss.
Terms: Nonauthor-subsidy publishes 80% of books. Pays standard royalty. Offers advance occasionally. Writer's guidelines and book catalog for 9×12 SAE with 5 first-class stamps.

VANDAMERE PRESS, (II), P.O. Box 5243, Arlington VA 22205. **Acquisitions**: Jerry Frank, editor. Estab. press 1984; firm 1976. "Small press, independent publisher of quality hard and softcover books." Publishes hardcover and paperback originals. Published new writers within the last year. Averages 6 total titles, 1 fiction title each year.
Needs: Adventure, erotica, humor/satire, military/war. No children's/juvenile/young adult. Published *Hegemon*, by Alexander M. Grace; and *Ancestral Voices*, by Hugh Fitzgerald Ryan.
How to Contact: Accepts unsolicited mss. Submit outline/synopsis and 3-4 sample chapters or complete ms with cover letter. Include bio (1-2 pages), list of publishing credits. Send SASE for reply, return of ms or send a disposable copy of the ms. Reporting time varies with work load. Simultaneous submissions OK. Sometimes comments on rejected mss.
Terms: Pays royalties; negotiable small advance. Sends galleys to author. Publishes ms 3 months-2 years after acceptance.
Advice: "Submissions must be neat, clean and double spaced. Author should include a résumé. Manuscript package should not take ten minutes to unwrap. And do not send registered or certified."

‡❦VANWELL PUBLISHING LIMITED, 1 Northrup Crescent, P.O. Box 2131, St. Catharines, Ontario L2M 6P5 Canada. (905)937-3100. Fax: (905)937-1760. **Acquisitions:** Angela Dobler, general editor; Simon Kooter, editor (military). Estab. 1983. Publishes trade originals and reprints. Publishes 85% previously unpublished writers/year. Publishes 5-7 titles/year.
  • Vanwell Publishing Ltd. has received awards from Education Children's Book Centre and Notable Education Libraries Association.
Needs: Historical, military/war. Recently published *The Stone Orchard*, by Susan Merritt (historical fiction); *The Wagner Whacker*, by Joseph Romain (baseball, historical fiction).
How to Contact: Query first with SASE. Reports in 3 months on queries.
Terms: Pays 8-15% royalty on wholesale price. Offers $200 average advance. Publishes ms 1 year after acceptance. Book catalog free.
Advice: "The writer has the best chance of selling a manuscript to our firm which is in keeping with our publishing program, well written and organized. Our audience: older male, history buff, war veteran; regional tourist; students. *Canadian* only military/aviation, naval, military/history and children's nonfiction have the best chance with us."

‡VICTOR BOOKS, Adult imprint of Chariot Victor Publishing, 4050 Lee Vance View, Colorado Springs CO 80918. Fax: (719)536-3269. **Acquisitions**: Acquisitions Editor. Estab. 1934. "Victor is interested in both historical

---

WRITER-TO-WRITER

Writing isn't easy. The only way to figure out what you have to say is in process, as you're figuring out the best possible way to say it. You'll never get a hand to play unless you stay at the table. And, even if you do well, you should probably keep your day job.

  Kit Reed
  J. Eden, University Press of New England/HardScrabble Books

and contemporary fiction that is compelling and wholesome, but not preachy." Publishes hardcover and trade paperback originals, both fiction and nonfiction. Averages 40-50 titles/year.

Needs: Religious. Recently published *The Victors*, by Jack Cavanaugh; *My Son, My Savior*, by Calvin Miller; and *Shadows on Stoney Creek*, by Wanda Luttrell.

How to Contact: Reports in 1 month on queries. Simultaneous submissions OK, if specified.

Terms: Pays royalty on all books. Sometimes offers advance. Writer's guidelines for #10 SASE.

Advice: "All books must in some way be Bible-related by authors who themselves are evangelical Christians with a platform. Victor, therefore, is not a publisher for everybody. Only a small fraction of the manuscripts received can be seriously considered for publication. Most books result from contacts that acquisitions editors make with qualified authors, though from time to time an unsolicited proposal triggers enough excitement to result in a contract. A writer has the best chance of selling Victor a well-conceived and imaginative manuscript that helps the reader apply Christianity to his/her life in practical ways. Christians active in the local church and their children are our audience."

‡VIKING, Imprint of Penguin Putnam Inc., 375 Hudson St., New York NY 10014. (212)366-2000. **Acquisitions:** Barbara Grossman, publisher. Publishes a mix of academic and popular fiction and nonfiction. Publishes hardcover and trade paperback originals.

Needs: Literary, mainstream/contemporary, mystery, suspense. Recently published *Out to Canaan*, by John Karon (novel).

How to Contact: Agented fiction only. Reports in 4-6 months on queries. Simultaneous submissions OK.

Terms: Pays 10-15% royalty on retail price. Advance negotiable. Publishes ms 1 year after acceptance.

Advice: "Looking for writers who can deliver a book a year (or faster) of consistent quality."

‡VIKING CHILDREN'S BOOKS, Imprint of Penguin Putnam Inc., 375 Hudson St., New York NY 10014. (212)366-2000. **Acquisitions:** Elizabeth Law, editor-in-chief. "Viking Children's Books publishes the highest quality trade books for children including fiction, nonfiction, and novelty books for pre-schoolers through young adults." Publishes hardcover originals. Publishes 25% previously unpublished writers/year. Publishes 80 books/year.

Needs: Juvenile, young adult. Recently published *The Awful Aardvarks Go to School*, by Reeve Lindbergh (picture book); and *Virtual World*, by Chris Westwood (young adult novel).

How to Contact: Query with synopsis, one sample chapter and SASE. Picture books submit entire ms. Reports in 2 months on queries. Simultaneous submissions OK.

Terms: Pays 10% royalty on retail price. Advance negotiable. Publishes ms 1 year after acceptance.

Advice: Mistakes often made is that "authors disguise nonfiction in a fictional format."

‡VINTAGE, Imprint of Knopf Publishing Group, Division of Random House, 201 E. 50th St., New York NY 10020. **Acquisitions:** Linda Rosenberg, managing editor. Publishes trade paperback originals and reprints. Publishes 5% previously unpublished writers/year.

Needs: Literary, mainstream/contemporary, short story collections. Recently published *Snow Falling on Cedars*, by Guterson (contemporary); and *Martin Dressler*, by Millhauser (literary).

How to Contact: Submit synopsis with 2-3 sample chapters. Reports in 6 months. Simultaneous submissions OK.

Terms: Pays 4-8% on retail price. Offers $2,500 and up advance. Publishes ms 1 year after acceptance.

*VISION BOOKS PVT LTD., Madarsa Rd., Kashmere Gate, Delhi 110006 India. **Acquisitions:** Sudhir Malhotra, fiction editor. Publishes 25 titles/year.

Needs: "We are a large multilingual publishing house publishing fiction and other trade books."

How to Contact: "A brief synopsis should be submitted initially. Subsequently, upon hearing from the editor, a typescript may be sent."

Terms: Pays royalties.

VISTA PUBLISHING, INC., (I, IV), 473 Broadway, Long Branch NJ 07740-5901. (908)229-6500. Fax: (908)229-9647. **Acquisitions:** Carolyn Zagury, president. Estab. 1991. "Small, independent press, owned by women and specializing in nurse authors." Publishes paperback originals. Plans 5 first novels this year. Averages 12 total titles, 6 fiction titles each year. Distributes titles through catalogs, wholesalers, distributors, exhibits and the Internet. Promotes titles through author signings, press releases, author speakings, author interviews and book reviews.

● A BULLET INTRODUCES COMMENTS by the editor of *Novel & Short Story Writer's Market* indicating special information about the listing.

Needs: Adventure, humor/satire, mystery/suspense, romance, short story collections. Recently published *The Web*, by Helen Osterman (psychodrama); *Servant of the Dead*, by Ashland Brown (medical mystery); and *Street Pizza*, by Diane Petit (EMS general fiction).

How to Contact: Accepts unsolicited mss. Query with complete ms. Fax query OK. Include bio. Send SASE for reply, return of ms or send disposable copy of ms. Reports in 2 months on mss. Simultaneous submissions OK. Comments on rejected mss.

Terms: Pays royalties. Sends galleys to author. Publishes ms 2 years after acceptance. Writer's guidelines and book catalog for SASE.

Advice: "We prefer to read full mss. Authors should be nurses or allied health professionals."

WALKER AND COMPANY, (I), 435 Hudson St., New York NY 10014. Fax: (212)727-0984. **Acquisitions**: Michael Seidman (mystery), Jacqueline Johnson (western), Emily Easton (young adult). Estab. 1959. Midsize independent publisher with plans to expand. Publishes hardcover and trade paperback originals. Average first novel print order: 2,500-3,500. Number of titles: 120/year. Published many new writers within the last year.

- Books published by Walker and Company have received numerous awards including the Spur Award (for westerns) and the Shamus Awards for Best First Private Eye Novel and Best Novel.

Needs: Nonfiction, sophisticated, quality mystery (amateur sleuth, cozy, private eye, police procedural), traditional western and children's and young adult nonfiction. Published *The Killing of Monday Brown*, by Sandra West Prowell; *Murder in the Place of Anubis*, by Lynda S. Robinson; and *Who In Hell Is Wanda Fuca*, by G.M. Ford.

How to Contact: *Does not accept unsolicited mss*. Submit outline and chapters as preliminary. Query letter should include "a concise description of the story line, including its outcome, word length of story (we prefer 70,000 words), writing experience, publishing credits, particular expertise on this subject and in this genre. Common mistakes: Sounding unprofessional (i.e. too chatty, too braggardly). Forgetting SASE." Agented fiction 50%. Notify if multiple or simultaneous submissions. Reports in 3-5 months. Publishes ms an average of 1 year after acceptance. Occasionally comments on rejected mss.

Terms: Negotiable (usually advance against royalty). Must return advance if book is not completed or is unacceptable.

Advice: "As for mysteries, we are open to all types, including suspense novels and offbeat books that maintain a 'play fair' puzzle. We are always looking for well-written western novels that are offbeat and strong on characterization. Character development is most important in all Walker fiction. We expect the author to be expert in the categories, to know the background and foundations of the genre. To realize that just because some subgenre is hot it doesn't mean that that is the area to mine—after all, if everyone is doing female p.i.s, doesn't it make more sense to do something that isn't crowded, something that might serve to balance a list, rather than make it top heavy? Finally, don't tell us why your book is going to be a success; instead, show me that you can write and write well. It is your writing, and not your hype that interests us."

‡**WARD HILL PRESS**, P.O. Box 04-0424, Staten Island NY 10304-0008. **Acquisitions**: Elizabeth Davis, editorial director. Estab. 1989. Ward Hill Press publishes fiction and nonfiction for middle readers and young adults (ages 10 and up), with a special focus on American history since 1860, as well as multiculturalism. Publishes hardcover and paperback originals. Publishes 75% previously unpublished writers/year. Publishes 4-6 titles/year.

Needs: Young adult fiction, "set in a contemporary, urban environment, that deals with issues of race or culture."

WRITER-TO-WRITER

- Read. Lots. Everything: fiction, periodicals, newspapers.
- Watch TV, especially talk shows, even the trash shows. Such programming has convinced me that *nothing* is impossible, which should be the mantra of every fiction writer. *Nothing is impossible*.
- Observe people in public places that are microcosms of society, i.e., airports, malls. If I see an interesting individual or situation, I begin asking myself questions. My answers are probably much more colorful than the facts, but that question/answer exercise has sparked ideas.
- Don't place too much stock in trends, most of what you've learned in a creative writing class, even advice from old pros. Listen to your own imagination, write from your heart, your gut, and be willing to take chances.

  Sandra Brown
  Fat Tuesday, Warner Books

Recently published *My Best Defense*, by Bob Riggs (novel, ages 9-14).
How to Contact: Query first. Reports in 2 months on queries. Reviews artwork/photos as part of ms package. Send photocopies. "No phone calls please."
Terms: Pays 6-12% royalty on retail price. Offers advance. Publishes ms 1 year after acceptance. Writer's guidelines for #10 SASE.

‡**WARNER ASPECT**, Imprint of Warner Books, 1271 Avenue of the Americas, New York NY 10020. **Acquisitions**: Betsy Mitchell, editor-in-chief. "We're looking for 'epic' stories in both fantasy and science fiction." Publishes hardcover, trade paperback, mass market paperback originals and mass market paperback reprints. Publishes 5-10% previously unpublished writers/year.
Needs: Fantasy, science fiction. Recently published *Encounter with Tiber*, by Buzz Aldrin and John Barnes (science fiction); and *Finity's End*, by C.S. Cherryh (science fiction).
How to Contact: Agented fiction only. Reports in 10 weeks on mss.
Terms: Pays royalty on retail price. Offers $5,000-up advance. Publishes ms 14 months after acceptance of ms.
Advice: "Think big. Sample our existing titles—we're a fairly new list and pretty strongly focused." Mistake writers often make is "hoping against hope that being unagented won't make a difference. We simply don't have the staff to look at unagented projects."

WARNER BOOKS, 1271 Avenue of the Americas, New York NY 10020. (212)522-7200. Publishes hardcover, trade paperback and mass market paperback originals and reprints. Warner publishes general interest fiction. Averages 350 total titles/year.
Imprint(s): Mysterious Press, Warner Aspect.
Needs: Fantasy, horror, mainstream, mystery/suspense, romance, science fiction, thriller. Recently published *The Celestine Prophecy*, by James Redfield; *Nocturne*, by Ed McBain (mystery); *Mail*, by Mameve Medwed; *Fat Tuesday*, by Sandra Brown; and *The Notebook*, by Nicholas Sparks.

DANIEL WEISS ASSOCIATES, INC., (II), 33 W. 17th St., New York NY 10011. (212)645-3865. Fax: (212)633-1236. **Acquisitions**: Kieran Scott, editorial assistant. Estab. 1987. "Packager of 140 titles a year including juvenile, young adult, and adult fiction as well as nonfiction titles. We package for a range of publishers within their specifications." Publishes paperback originals. All titles by first-time writers are commissioned for established series.
Needs: Juvenile (ballet, friendship, horse, mystery), mainstream, preschool/picture book, beginning readers and young adult (continuity series, romance, romantic suspense, thriller). Publishes Sweet Valley Twins, Sweet Valley High and Sweet Valley University series. "We cannot acquire single-title manuscripts that are not part of a series the author is proposing or submitted specifically according to our guidelines for an established series." Published *Sweet Valley High*, by Francine Pascal (young adult series); *Thoroughbred*, by Joanna Campbell (juvenile horse series); and *Boyfriends & Girlfriends*, by Katherine Applegate (young adult continuity series).
How to Contact: Accepts unsolicited mss. Query first with synopsis/outline and 2 sample chapters. SASE. Agented fiction 60%. Reports in 2 months. Simultaneous submissions OK.
Terms: Pays advance royalty. Advance is negotiable. Publishes ms 1 year after acceptance. Writer's guidelines for #10 SASE.
Advice: "We are always happy to work with and encourage first-time novelists. Being packagers, we often create and outline books by committee. This system is quite beneficial to writers who may be less experienced. Usually we are contacted by the agent rather than the writer directly. Occasionally, however, we do work with writers who send in unsolicited material. I think that a professionally presented manuscript is of great importance."

‡**WESLEYAN UNIVERSITY PRESS**, 110 Mount Vernon St., Middletown CT 06459. (860)685-2420. **Acquisitions:** Suzanna Tamminen, editor. "We are a scholarly press with a focus on cultural studies." Publishes hardcover originals. Publishes 10% previously unpublished writers/year. Publishes 20-25 titles/year.
Needs: Science fiction. "We publish very little fiction." Recently published *Dhalgren*, by Samuel R. Delany.

WRITER-TO-WRITER

Too many writers think all you need to do is write well—but that's only part of what a good book is. Above all, a good book tells a "good story." Focus on the story first—ask yourself, "Will other people find this story so interesting they will tell others about it?" Remember, a bestselling book usually follows a simple rule: "It's a wonderful story, wonderfully told;" not "It's a wonderfully told story."

Nicholas Sparks
The Notebook, Warner Books

How to Contact: Submit outline. Reports in 1 month on queries, 3 months on mss. Simultaneous submissions OK.
Terms: Pays 10% royalty. Offers up to $3,000 advance. Publishes ms 1 year after acceptance. Writer's guidelines for #10 SASE. Book catalog free.
Advice: Audience is the informed general reader to specialized academic reader.

‡**WHISPERING COYOTE PRESS, INC.**, 300 Crescent Court, Suite 860, Dallas TX 75201. Fax: (214)871-5577, (214)319-7298. **Acquisitions:** Mrs. Lou Alpert, publisher. Publishes picture books for children ages 3-10. Publishes 20% previously unpublished writers/year. Publishes 6 titles/year.
Needs: Adventure, fantasy, juvenile picture books. "We only do picture books." Recently published *The Red Shoes*, retold and illustrated by Barbara Bazilian, adapted from a story by Hans Christian Anderson; *Cats on Judy*, by JoAnn Early Macken, illustrated by Judith DuFour Love; and *Hush! A Gaelic Lullaby*, by Carole Gerber, illustrated by Mary Husted.
How to Contact: Submit complete ms. If author is illustrator also, submit sample art. Send photocopies, no original art. Agented fiction 10%. Reports in 3 months. Simultaneous submissions OK.
Terms: Pays 8% royalty on retail price of first 10,000 copies, 10% after (combined author and illustrator). Offers $2,000-8,000 advance (combined author, illustrator). Publishes ms 2 years after acceptance. Writer's guidelines and book catalog for #10 SASE.

WHITE PINE PRESS, (II), 10 Village Square, Fredonia NY 14063-1761. (716)672-5743. Fax: (716)672-4724. E-mail: pine@net.bluemoon.net. Website: www.bluemoon.net/~pine/ (includes recent titles). **Acquisitions:** Dennis Maloney, director; Elaine La Mattina, fiction editor. Estab. 1973. "White Pine Press is your passport to a world of voices, emphasizing literature from around the world." Small literary publisher. Publishes paperback originals and reprints. Books: 60 lb. natural paper; offset; perfect binding. Average print order: 2,000-3,000. First novel print order: 2,000. Publishes 2-3 previously unpublished writers/year. Averages 8-10 total titles, 6-7 fiction titles each year. Distributes titles through Consortium Book Sales & Distribution. Promotes titles through reviews, advertising, direct mailing, readings and signings.
Needs: Ethnic/multicultural, literary, short story collections, translations. Looking for "strong novels." No romance, science fiction. Publishes anthologies. Editors select stories. Recently published *Where This Lake Is*, by Jeff Lodge; *Black Flames*, by Daniel Pearlman; and *I Saw A Man Hit His Wife*, by M. Greenside (short stories). Publishes Dispatches series (international fiction), a Human Rights series, and Secret Weavers series (writing by Latin American Women) and New American Voices Series (first novels by American writer).
How to Contact: Accepts unsolicited mss. Query letter with outline/synopsis and 2 sample chapters. Include estimated word count and list of publishing credits. SASE for reply or return of ms. Agented fiction 10%. Reports in 2 weeks on queries; 3 months on mss. Simultaneous submissions OK.
Terms: Pays royalties of 5% minimum; 10% maximum. Offers negotiable advance. Pays in author's copies; payment depends on grant/award money. Sends galleys to author. Publishes 1-2 years after acceptance. Book catalog free.
Advice: "Follow our guidelines."

‡**WILLOW CREEK PRESS**, P.O. Box 147, 9931 Highway 70 W., Minocqua WI 54548. (715)358-7010. **Acquisitions:** Tom Petrie, editor-in-chief. Publishes hardcover and trade paperback originals and reprints. Publishes 15% previously unpublished writers/year. Publishes 25 titles/year.
Needs: Adventure, humor, picture books, short story collections. Recently published *Cold Noses and Warm Hearts*, edited by Laurie Morrow (short story collection); *Flashes in the River*, by Ed Gray (illustrated fiction); and *Poetry for Guys*, by Kathy Schmook.
How to Contact: Submit synopsis and 2 sample chapters. Reports in 2 months. Simultaneous submissions OK.
Terms: Pays 6-15% royalty on wholesale price. Offers $2,000-5,000 advance. Publishes ms 10 months after acceptance. Book catalog for $1.

‡**WILSHIRE BOOK CO.**, 12015 Sherman Rd., North Hollywood CA 91605-3781. (818)765-8579. **Acquisitions:** Melvin Powers, publisher and Marcia Grad, senior editor. Estab. 1947. "You are not only what you are today, but also what you choose to become tomorrow." Publishes trade paperback originals and reprints. Publishes 80% previously unpublished writers/year. Publishes 25 titles/year.
Needs: Allegories that teach principles of psychological/spiritual growth or offer guidance in living. Min. 30,000 words. Recently published *The Princess Who Believed in Fairy Tales*, by Marcia Grad; *The Knight in Rusty Armor*, by Robert Fisher; and *Greatest Salesman in the World*.
How to Contact: Requires synopsis, 3 sample chapters and SASE. Accepts complete mss. Reports in 2 months.
Terms: Pays standard royalty. Publishes ms 6 months after acceptance.
Advice: "We are vitally interested in all new material we receive. Just as you hopefully submit your manuscript for publication, we hopefully read every one submitted, searching for those that we believe will be successful in the marketplace. Writing and publishing must be a team effort. We need you to write what we can sell. We suggest that you read the successful books mentioned above or others that are similar to the manuscript you want to write. Analyze them to discover what elements make them winners. Duplicate those elements in your own

style, using a creative new approach and fresh material, and you will have written a book we can catapult onto the bestseller list."

‡**WISDOM PUBLICATIONS**, 361 Newbury St., 4th Floor, Boston MA 02115. (617)536-3358. Fax: (617)536-1897. **Acquisitions:** Editorial Project Manager. "Wisdom Publications is a nonprofit publisher for works on Buddhism, Tibet and East-West themes." Publishes hardcover originals, trade paperback originals and reprints. Publishes 50% previously unpublished writers/year. Publishes 12-15 titles/year.
Needs: Children's books with Buddhist themes. Recently published *Her Father's Garden*, by James Vollbracht; and *The Gift*, by Isia Osuchowska.
How to Contact: Query first with SASE.
Terms: Pays 4-8% royalty on wholesale price (net). Publishes ms 2 years after acceptance. Writer's guidelines and book catalog free.
Advice: "We are now publishing children's books with Buddhist themes and contemplative/Buddhist poetry."

***THE WOMEN'S PRESS, (IV)**, 34 Great Sutton St., London EC1V 0DX England. **Acquisitions**: Helen Windrath and Charlotte Cole, fiction editors. Publishes approximately 50 titles/year.
Needs: "Women's fiction, written by women. Centered on women. Theme can be anything—all themes may be women's concern—but we look for political/feminist awareness, originality, wit, fiction of ideas. Includes literary fiction, crime, and teenage list *Livewire*."
Terms: Writers receive royalty, including advance.
Advice: Writers should ask themselves, "Is this a manuscript which would interest a feminist/political press?"

‡♥**WORDSTORM PRODUCTIONS INC.**, Box 49132, 7740 18th St. SE, Calgary, Alberta T2C 3W5 Canada. Phone/fax: (403)236-1275. E-mail: wordstrm@cadvision.com. **Acquisitions:** Perry P. Rose, president; Eileen A. Rose, vice president. "We provide the highest possible quality of works by published and nonpublished authors." Publishes trade and mass market paperback originals. Publishes 90% previously unpublished writers/year. Publishes 5-7 titles/year.
Needs: Adventure, humor, mainstream/contemporary, mystery/suspense, children's books. Recently published *228*, by David E. Weischadle (adventure); and *Kosha*™ *Tells: Orville the Orphan Tree*, by Perry P. Rose and Audrey Lazarus (children 5-9 years.)
How to Contact: Query with synopsis, 3 sample chapters and SASE or SAE and IRCs. All unsolicited mss returned unopened. Reports in 2 months on queries, 6 months on mss.
Terms: Pays 10-12% royalty on retail price. (Works released in USA paid 66% of above.) Publishes ms 1 year after acceptance. Writer's guidelines for #10 SASE.
Advice: When sending self-addressed return envelope, please remember to use an international postal coupon if mailing is originating outside Canada. U.S. stamps cannot be used to mail "from" Canada.

♥**WORLDWIDE LIBRARY, (II)**, Division of Harlequin Books, 225 Duncan Mill Rd., Don Mills, Ontario M3B 3K9 Canada. (416)445-5860. **Acquisitions**: Feroze Mohammed, senior editor/editorial coordinator. Estab. 1979. Large commercial category line. Publishes paperback originals and reprints. Averages 72 titles, all fiction, each year. "Mystery program is reprint; no originals please."
Imprint(s): Worldwide Mystery; Gold Eagle Books.
Needs: "We publish action-adventure series; future fiction." A new future fiction series, *Outlanders*, was recently published.
How to Contact: Query first or submit outline/synopsis/series concept or overview and sample chapters. SAE. U.S. stamps do not work in Canada; use International Reply Coupons or money order. Agented fiction 95%. Reports in 10 weeks on queries. Simultaneous submissions OK. Sometimes critiques rejected ms.
Terms: Advance and sometimes royalties; copyright buyout. Publishes ms 1-2 years after acceptance.
Advice: "Publishing fiction in very selective areas. As a genre publisher we are always on the lookout for innovative series ideas, especially in the men's adventure area."

WRITE WAY PUBLISHING, (I, II), Suite 210, 10555 E. Dartmouth, Aurora CO 80014. (303)695-0001. Fax: (303)368-8004. E-mail: writewy@aol.com. Website: www.writewaypub.com (includes first chapter, reviews and sales information on every title). **Acquisitions**: Dorrie O'Brien, owner/editor. Estab. 1993. "Write Way is a fiction-only small press concentrating on genre publications such as mysteries, soft science fiction, fairy tale/fantasy and horror/thrillers. Small press. Publishes hardcover originals. Average print order: 2,500. First novel print order: 1,000. Published new writers within the last year. Publishes 60% previously unpublished writers/

year. Averages 10-12 total titles, all fiction, each year. Distributes titles through Midpoint Trade Books. Promotes titles through newspapers, magazines and trade shows.

Needs: Fantasy/fairy tale, horror (soft), mystery/suspense (amateur sleuth, cozy, police procedural, private eye/hardboiled), psychic/supernatural, science fiction (soft/sociological, space trilogy/series). Recently published *The Dead Past*, by Tom Piccirilli (mystery); *Fury's Children*, by Seymour Shubin (psychological suspense); and *Fruitcake*, by Jane Rubino (mystery).

How to Contact: Query with short outline/synopsis and 1-2 sample chapters. Include estimated word count, bio (reasonably short) and list of publishing credits. Send SASE for reply, return of ms or send a disposable copy of ms. Agented fiction 10%. Reports in 2-4 weeks on queries; 6-8 months on mss. Simultaneous submissions OK. Often comments on rejected mss.

Terms: Pays royalties of 8% minimum; 10% maximum. Does not pay advances. Sends galleys to author. Publishes ms 3 years after acceptance. Writer's guidelines for SASE.

Advice: "Always have the query letter, synopsis and the first chapters edited by an unbiased party prior to submitting them to us. Remember: first impressions are just as important to a publisher as they might be to a prospective employer."

‡**WRITERS PRESS**, 5278 Chinden Blvd., Boise ID 83714. (208)327-0566. Fax: (208)327-3477. E-mail: writers @cyberhighway.net. Website: www.writerspress.com. **Acquisitions:** John Ybarra, editor. "Our philosophy is to show children how to help themselves and others. By publishing high-quality children's literature that is both fun and educational, we are striving to make a difference in today's educational world." Publishes hardcover and trade paperback originals. Publishes 60% previously unpublished writers/year. Publishes 6 titles/year.

Needs: Adventure, historical, juvenile, picture books, young adult, inclusion, special education. Recently published *Eagle Feather*, by Sonia Gardner, illustrated by James Spurlock (picture book).

How to Contact: Query first. Reports in 1 month on queries, 4 months on mss.

Terms: Pays 4-12% royalty or makes outright purchase of up to $1,500. Publishes ms 6 months after acceptance. Writer's and catalog guidelines free.

‡♦**YORK PRESS LTD.**, 77 Carlton St., Suite 305, Toronto, Ontario M5B 2J7 Canada. (416)599-6652. Fax: (416)599-2675. **Acquisitions:** Dr. S. Elkhadem, general manager/editor. Estab. 1975. "We publish scholarly books and creative writing of an experimental nature." Publishes trade paperback originals. Publishes 10% previously unpublished writers/year. Publishes 10 titles/year.

Needs: "Fiction of an experimental nature by well-established writers." Recently published *The Moonhare*, by Kirk Hampton (experimental novel).

How to Contact: Query first. Reports in 2 months.

Terms: Pays 10-20% royalty on wholesale price. Publishes ms 6 months after acceptance.

‡**ZEBRA BOOKS**, Imprint of Kensington, 850 Third Ave., 16th Floor, New York NY 10022. (212)407-1500. Publisher: Lynn Brown. **Acquisitions**: Ann Lafarge, editor. "Zebra Books is dedicated to women's fiction, which includes, but is not limited to romance." Publishes hardcover originals, trade paperback and mass market paperback originals and reprints. Publishes 5% previously unpublished writers/year. Publishes 140-170 titles/year.

Needs: Romance, women's fiction. Recently published *By Candlelight*; *Love With a Stranger*, by Janell Taylor (romance); and *Darling Jasmine*, by Bertrice Small.

How to Contact: Query with synopsis and SASE. Not accepting unsolicited submissions. Reports in 1 month on queries, in 3 months on mss. Simultaneous submissions OK.

WRITER-TO-WRITER

Don't listen to your family or your friends with regard to your writing. It's true that everyone who writes isn't going to get published; and it's true that everyone who gets published isn't going to be a bestseller. But getting published and becoming a bestseller is a combination of: some talent; getting your manuscript to the right editor; having that editor be wildly enthusiastic about your work; getting promotion so the reading public knows the book's out there; an actively involved guardian angel; and dumb luck. It's a dirty job, but someone has to do it; and no one really knows who will be honestly successful—least of all your family or your friends who will go out of their way to tell you what an impossible task you've set out for yourself. Forget them, and go for it!

Bertrice Small
Darling Jasmine, Kensington/Zebra

Terms: Pays variable royalty and advance. Publishes ms 18 months after acceptance. Book catalog for #10 SASE.

ZOLAND BOOKS, INC., (II, III), 384 Huron Ave., Cambridge MA 02138. (617)864-6252. Fax: (617)661-4998. **Acquisitions:** Roland Pease, publisher/editor. Managing Editor: Michael Lindgren. Marketing Director: Stephen Hull. Estab. 1987. "We are a literary press, publishing poetry, fiction, nonfiction, photography, and other titles of literary interest." Publishes hardcover and paperback originals. Books: acid-free paper; sewn binding; some with illustrations. Average print order: 2,000-5,000. Averages 12 total titles each year.
- Recent awards include: Hemmingway/PEN Award, Kafka Prize for Women's Fiction, National Book Award finalist, New York Times Notable Book, Publishers Weekly Best Book of the Year.

Needs: Contemporary, feminist, literary, African-American interest. Recently published *The Clairvoyant*, by Maria Thurm; *The Old World*, by Jonathan Strong; and *Life Designs*, by Elaine Ford.
How to Contact: Accepts unsolicited mss. Query first, then send complete ms with cover letter. SASE. Reports in 4-6 weeks on queries; 3-6 months on mss.
Terms: Pays royalties of 5-8%. Average advance: $1,500; negotiable (also pays author's copies). Sends galleys to author. Publishes ms 1-2 years after acceptance. Book catalog for 6×9 SAE and 2 first-class stamps.

ZONDERVAN, (III, IV), Division of HarperCollins Publishers, 5300 Patterson SE, Grand Rapids MI 49530. (616)698-6900. E-mail: @zph.com. Website: http://www.zondervan.com. **Acquisitions:** Manuscript Review Editor. Estab. 1931. "Our mission is to be the leading Christian communication company meeting the needs of people with resources that glorify Jesus Christ and promote biblical principles." Large evangelical Christian publishing house. Publishes hardcover and paperback originals and reprints, though fiction is generally in paper only. Published new writers in the last year. Averages 150 total titles, 5-10 fiction titles each year. Average first novel: 5,000 copies.
Needs: Adult fiction, (mainstream, biblical, historical, adventure, sci-fi, fantasy, mystery), "Inklings-style" fiction of high literary quality and juvenile fiction (primarily mystery/adventure novels for 8-12-year-olds). Christian relevance necessary in all cases. Will *not* consider collections of short stories or inspirational romances. Published *The Campaign*, by Marilyn Quayle and Nancy Northcutt (mystery); *Byzantium*, by Steven Lawhead (fantasy); and *Blood of Heaven*, by Bill Myers (suspense).
How to Contact: Accepts unsolicited mss. Write for writer's guidelines first. Include #10 SASE. Query or submit outline/synopsis and 2 sample chapters. Reports in 4-6 weeks on queries; 3-4 months on mss.
Terms: "Standard contract provides for a percentage of the net price received by publisher for each copy sold, usually 14-17% of net."
Advice: "Almost no unsolicited fiction is published. Send plot outline and one or two sample chapters. Most editors will *not* read entire mss. Your proposal and opening chapter will make or break you."

Contests and Awards

In addition to honors and, quite often, cash awards, contests and awards programs offer writers the opportunity to be judged on the basis of quality alone without the outside factors that sometimes influence publishing decisions. New writers who win contests may be published for the first time, while more experienced writers may gain public recognition of an entire body of work.

The contest listings in this section include literary magazines and small presses that have developed award programs to garner attention and to promote writers. Grant programs that lost funding in the past are starting to bounce back with renewed commitment. All this represents increased opportunities for writers.

There are contests for almost every type of fiction writing. Some focus on form, such as STORY's Short Short Fiction Contest, for stories up to 1,500 words. Others feature writing on particular themes or topics including The Isaac Asimov Award for science fiction, the ASF Translation Prize and the Arthur Ellis Awards for crime fiction. Still others are prestigious prizes or awards for work that must be nominated such as the Pulitzer Prize in Fiction and the Whiting Writers' Awards. Chances are no matter what type of fiction you write, there is a contest or award program that may interest you.

SELECTING AND SUBMITTING TO A CONTEST

Use the same care in submitting to contests as you would sending your manuscript to a publication or book publisher. Deadlines are very important and where possible we've included this information. At times contest deadlines were only approximate at our press deadline, so be sure to write or call for complete information.

Follow the rules to the letter. If, for instance, contest rules require your name on a cover sheet only, you will be disqualified if you ignore this and put your name on every page. Find out how many copies to send. If you don't send the correct amount, by the time you are contacted to send more it may be past the submission deadline.

One note of caution: Beware of contests that charge entry fees that are disproportionate to the amount of the prize. Contests offering a $10 prize, but charging $7 in entry fees, are a waste of your time and money.

If you are interested in a contest or award that requires your publisher to nominate your work, it's acceptable to make your interest known. Be sure to leave the publisher plenty of time, however, to make the nomination deadline.

The Roman numeral coding we use to rank listings in this section is different than that used in previous sections. The following is our ranking system:

I   **Contest for unpublished fiction, usually open to both new and experienced writers.**

II   **Contest for published (usually including self-published) fiction, which may be entered by the author.**

III   **Contest for fiction, which must be nominated by an editor, publisher or other nominating body.**

IV   **Contest limited to residents of a certain region, of a certain age or to writing on certain themes or subjects.**

*ABIKO QUARTERLY INTERNATIONAL FICTION CONTEST/TSUJINAKA AWARD (I), 8-1-8 Namiki, Abiko-shi, Chiba-ken 270-11 Japan. Contact: Laurel Sicks, editor. Award to "best short story in English of up to 5,000 words." Award: 100,000 yen. Competition receives 100 submissions. Entry fee $12. Guidelines available after September 1 for SASE. Inquiries by e-mail OK. Open September 1-December 31 each year. Previously unpublished submissions. Word length: up to 5,000 words. "Include SAE with 2 IRCs for notification. No American postage. Send two copies of manuscript. We keep master copy which we treat like gold. The other copy is remailed to judge." Winners announced July 1999. Winners notified by mail.

‡ACW WRITERS CONTEST, (I), American Christian Writers, P.O. Box 110390, Nashville TN 37222. (615)834-0450. Website: http://www.ecpa.org/acw. Director: Reg Forder. Award "to encourage excellence." Annual competition for short stories. Award: Free tuition to writers conference. Competition receives approximately 30 submissions. Judges: ACW staff. Entry fee $10. Guidelines for SASE. Deadline November 30. Unpublished submissions. Word length: 1,000 words maximum. Winners announced every January. "Winners notified by mail and in our magazine, *The Christian Communicator*." List of winners available for SASE.

AIM MAGAZINE SHORT STORY CONTEST, (I), P.O. Box 20554, Chicago IL 60620. (312)874-6184. Contact: Myron Apilado, publisher/editor; Ruth Apilado, associate editor; Mark Boone, fiction editor. Estab. 1984. "To encourage and reward good writing in the short story form. The contest is particularly for new writers." Contest offered annually if money available. Award: $100 plus publication in fall issue. "Judged by *Aim*'s editorial staff." Sample copy for $4. Contest rules for SASE. Unpublished submissions. "We're looking for compelling, well-written stories with lasting social significance."

AKRON MANUSCRIPT CLUB ANNUAL FICTION CONTEST (I), Akron Manuscript Club and A.U., Falls Writer's Workshop, and Taylor Memorial Library, P.O. Box 1101, Cuyahoga Falls OH 44223-0101. (216)923-2094. Contest Director: M.M. LoPiccolo. Award to "encourage writers with cash prizes and certificates and to provide in-depth critique that most writers have never had the benefit of seeing." Annual competition for short stories. Award: $50 (first prize in three fiction categories); certificates for second and third prizes. Competition receives approx. 20-50 submissions per category. Judge: M.M. LoPiccolo. Guidelines will be sent *only* with SASE. Deadline January 1-March 15. Unpublished submissions. Word length: 2,500 words (12-13 pages). Send all mail to: 69 Annual Fiction Contest. "Send *no* manuscript without obtaining current guidelines. *Nothing* will be returned without SASE." Winners announced May 1998. Winners notified by mail. List of winners available for SASE.

‡ALABAMA STATE COUNCIL ON THE ARTS INDIVIDUAL ARTIST FELLOWSHIP, (II, IV), 201 Monroe St., Montgomery AL 36130. (205)242-4076 ext. 226. E-mail: becky@arts.state.al.us. Contact: Becky Mullen. "To provide assistance to an individual artist." Semiannual awards: $5,000 and $10,000 grants awarded in even-numbered years ('96-'98). Guidelines available January 1998 by e-mail or phone. Inquiries by fax and e-mail OK. Competition receives approximately 30 submissions annually. Judges: Independent peer panel. Deadline May 1. Two-year Alabama residency required. Winners announced in September. Winners notified by letter. List of winners available by e-mail, phone or fax.

THE NELSON ALGREN AWARD FOR SHORT FICTION, (I), *Chicago Tribune*, 435 N. Michigan Ave., Chicago IL 60611. Annual award to recognize an outstanding, unpublished short story, minimum 2,500 words, maximum 10,000 words. Awards: $5,000 first prize; 3 runners-up receive $1,000 awards. Publication of 4 winning stories in the *Chicago Tribune*. No entry fee. Entries must be typed, double spaced. For guidelines, send business-size SASE. Guidelines mailed in the fall. Deadline: Entries are accepted only from November 1-February 1. Winners announced August.

AMARILLO TRI-STATE FAIR LITERARY AWARDS, (I), % Cleo Smith, 8303 Broadway, Amarillo TX 79108-2206. (806)383-5772. Annual competition for prose and poetry. Offers small cash awards and Best of Show Awards in Adult and Youth (grades 2 through 12) Divisions. Judges: Different each year. Published authors and professionals in youth literary field. Entries will receive a critique. Entry fee: $5 prose, $3 poetry, students free. Guidelines available after April 1998 for SASE. Deadline: August 1 (adults), August 30 (youth). Unpublished submissions. "Categories and length requirements may change a bit from year to year. Guidelines required. Open. Winners are displayed at Literary Booth at Amarillo Tri-State Fair during Fair Week in September." List of winners available for SASE.

AMATEUR SLEUTH, (I, IV), *Whispering Willow's Mystery Magazine*, 2517 S. Central, P.O. Box 890294, Oklahoma City OK 73189-0294. (405)239-2531. Fax: (405)232-3848. Contact: Peggy D. Farris, editor-in-chief. Annual competition for short stories. Award: $200 (1st place), $125 (2nd place), $100 (3rd place), plus publication. Competition receives approximately 30 submissions. Judge: Trula Johnson. Entry fee $10. Guidelines for SASE. Deadline December 31. Unpublished submissions. Mystery or mystery/suspense stories only. Length: 500-2,500 words. "Your main character is an amateur sleuth involved in a mystery. No explicit sex, gore, or extreme violence. You have freedom in creating exciting mysteries weaving your readers down winding roads of clues."

AMELIA MAGAZINE AWARDS, **(I)**, 329 "E" St., Bakersfield CA 93304. (805)323-4064. Contact: Frederick A. Raborg, Jr., editor. The Reed Smith Fiction Prize; The Willie Lee Martin Short Story Award; The Cassie Wade Short Fiction Award; The Patrick T. T. Bradshaw Fiction Award; and four annual genre awards in science fiction, romance, western and fantasy/horror. Estab. 1984. Annual. "To publish the finest fiction possible and reward the writer; to allow good writers to earn some money in small press publication. *Amelia* strives to fill that gap between major circulation magazines and quality university journals." Unpublished submissions. Length: The Reed Smith—3,000 words maximum; The Willie Lee Martin—3,500-5,000 words; The Cassie Wade—4,500 words maximum; The Patrick T. T. Bradshaw—25,000 words; the genre awards—science fiction, 5,000 words; romance, 3,000 words; western, 5,000 words; fantasy/horror, 5,000 words. Award: "Each prize consists of $200 plus publication and two copies of issue containing winner's work." The Reed Smith Fiction Prize offers two additional awards when quality merits of $100 and $50, and publication; Bradshaw Book Award: $250, 2 copies. Deadlines: The Reed Smith Prize—September 1; The Willie Lee Martin—March 1; The Cassie Wade—June 1; The Patrick T. T. Bradshaw—February 15; *Amelia* fantasy/horror—February 1; *Amelia* western—April 1; *Amelia* romance—October 1; *Amelia* science fiction—December 15. Entry fee: $5. Bradshaw Award fee: $10. Contest rules for SASE. Looking for "high quality work equal to finest fiction being published today."

AMERICAN FICTION AWARDS, **(I)**, New Rivers Press, Moorhead State University, P.O. Box 229, Moorhead MN 56563. (218)236-4681. E-mail: davisa@mhd1.moorhead.msus.edu. Contact: Alan Davis, editor. "To find and publish short fiction by emerging writers." Annual award for short stories. Award: $1,000 (1st prize), $500 (2nd prize), $250 (3rd prize). Competition receives approx. 1,000 submissions. Editor chooses finalists; guest judge chooses winners; past judges have included Tim O'Brien and Wallace Stegner. Entry fee $7.50. Guidelines for SASE. Inquiries by e-mail OK. Deadline May 1. Unpublished submissions. Word length: up to 10,000 words. "We are looking for quality literary or mainstream fiction—all subjects and styles." No genre fiction. For a sample copy, contact your bookstore or New Rivers Press, 420 N. Fifth St., Suite 910, Minneapolis MN 55401. Send ms and cover letter with bio "after reading our ads in *AWP* and *Poets and Writers* each spring." (Previous editions published by Birch Lane Press/Carol Publishing Groups.) Winners announced in September/October 1998. Winners notified by phone/mail. List of winners available for SASE.

AMERICAN SHORT FICTION CONTEST, (I), English Dept., Parlin 108, University of Texas at Austin, Austin TX 78712. (512)471-1772. Contact: Joseph Kruppa, editor. Annual competition for short stories. Award: $1,000 and publication (1st prize); $500 (2nd place); $300 (3rd prize). Entry fee: $20 (includes subscription to *ASF*). Guidelines and entry form in *ASF*. Deadline May 15. Unpublished submissions.

‡ANAMNESIS FICTION AWARD, (I), Anamnesis Press, P.O. Box 51115, Palo Alto CA 94303. (415)255-8366. Fax: (415)255-3190. E-mail: anamnesis@compuserve.com. Website: http://ourworld.compuserve.com/ho mepages/anamnesis. Contact: Keith Allen Daniels, president. Award to "recognize quality writers of short fiction in an era where the novel has become far too commercial and serious short fiction is in short supply." Annual competition for short stories. Award: $1,000 and an award certificate plus chapbook publication of the winning story. Judges: 3 anonymous literary experts. Entry fee $20. Guidelines for SASE or on webpage. Inquiries by fax and e-mail OK. Deadline March 15. Unpublished submissions. Word length: 7,500 words or less. "We want to see stories with emotional/intellectual depth, sensitivity, imaginative ideas and strong characters." Winners notified by mail by June 30. List of winners available on webpage.

SHERWOOD ANDERSON SHORT FICTION PRIZE, (I), *Mid-American Review*, Dept. of English, Bowling Green State University, Bowling Green OH 43403. (419)372-2725. Contact: Michael Czyzniejewski, fiction editor. "Contest is judged by an anonymous judge, who is a well-known fiction writer. Only stories accepted for publication by *Mid-American Review* are considered." Award frequency is subject to availability of funds. Competition receives 3,500 submissions. "To encourage the writer of quality short fiction." No entry fee. No deadline. Unpublished material. Winners announced in the fall 1998 issue. Winners notified by phone or mail.

*ANDREAS-GRYPHIUS-PREIS (LITERATURPREIS DER KÜNSTLERGILDE), (II, IV), Die Kunstler-gilde e.V., Hafenmarkt 2, D-73728 Esslingen a.N., Germany. 0711/39 69 01-0. Chief Secretary: Ramona Rauscher-Steinebrunner. "The prize is awarded for the best piece of writing or for complete literary works." Annual competition for short stories, novels, story collections, translations. Award: 1 prize of DM 25,000; 1 prize of DM 7,000. Competition receives 30-50 entries. Inquiries by fax OK. Judges: Jury members (7 persons). Fiction should be published in the last 5 years. Deadline October 1997. "The prize is awarded to writers who are dealing with the particular problems of the German culture in eastern Europe." Winners announced beginning of 1998. Winners notified by mail.

‡ANISFIELD-WOLF BOOK AWARDS, The Cleveland Foundation, 1422 Euclid Ave., Suite 1400, Cleveland OH 44115-2001. (216)861-3810. Fax: (216)861-1729. E-mail: lwoodman@clevefdn.org. Director of Communications: Lynne E. Woodman. Award to recognize recent books which have made important contributions to our understanding of racism or our appreciation of the rich diversity of human cultures. Annual award for novels and story collections. Award: $10,000, divided equally if multiple winners. Judges: panel of jurors. No entry fee. Guidelines available for SASE. Deadline January 31, 1998 for books published in 1997. Previously published submissions between January 1, 1997 and December 31, 1997. "Only books written in English and published in the preceding calendar year are eligible. Plays and screenplays are not eligible, nor are works in progress. No grants are made for the completion or publication of manuscripts."

‡ANNUAL CAT WRITERS' ASSOCIATION COMMUNICATIONS CONTEST, Cat Writers' Association, 25 Kellycrest Rd., Branford CT 06405. (203)488-3495. Contest Chair: Sally E. Bahner. Awards recognize excellence in works about and related to felines. Annual competition for short stories and novels. Awards: cash for specially sponsored awards, Muse medallion for regular categories. Judges: CWA members. Entry fee $7.50 for members; $15 nonmembers. Guidelines for SASE. Deadline July. Published submissions. Works must be about cats.

‡♣THE ANNUAL/ATLANTIC WRITING COMPETITIONS, (I, IV), Writers' Federation of Nova Scotia, 1809 Barrington St., Suite 901, Halifax, Nova Scotia B3J 3K8 Canada. (902)423-8116. E-mail: writers1@fox. nstn.ca. Website: http://www.chebucto.ns.ca/Culture/WFNS/. Executive Director: Jane Buss. "To recognize and encourage unpublished writers in the region of Atlantic Canada. (Competition only open to residents of Nova Scotia, Newfoundland, Prince Edward Island and New Brunswick, the four Atlantic Provinces.)" Annual competition for short stories, novels, poetry, children's writing and drama. Award: Various cash awards. Competition receives approximately 10-12 submissions for novels; 75 for poetry; 75 for children's; 75 for short stories; 10 for nonfiction. Judges: Professional writers, librarians, booksellers. Entry fee $15/entry. Guidelines available after May 1998 for SASE. Inquiries by fax or e-mail OK. Deadline August 1998. Unpublished submissions. Winners announced February 1999. Winners notified by mail. List of winners available by request from office.

‡ANTHOLOGY ANNUAL CONTEST, (I), P.O. Box 4411, Mesa AZ 85201. (602)461-8200. E-mail: tavara @primenet.com. Contest Coordinator: Sharon Skinner. Annual competition for short stories. Awards: First prize $100, *Anthology* T-shirt, 1-year subscription; second prize, *Anthology* T-shirt, 1-year subscription; third prize, 1-year subscription. All prize-winning stories are published in November/December issue. Entry fee $5/short story. Maximum number of entries: 2/writer. "All stories submitted to contest are eligible to be printed in upcoming issues of *Anthology*, regardless of finish, unless author specifies otherwise. We ask for one-time rights. All copyrights are held by their original owner." Guidelines for SASE. Simultaneous and prepublished submissions OK. Any subject, any genre. Word length: 1,000-6,000 words.

ANTIETAM REVIEW LITERARY AWARD, (I, IV), *Antietam Review*, 41 S. Potomac St., Hagerstown MD 21740. (301)791-3132. Contact: Susanne Kass, executive editor. Annual award to encourage and give recognition to excellence in short fiction. Open to writers from Maryland, Pennsylvania, Virginia, West Virginia, Washington DC and Delaware. "We consider only previously unpublished work. We read manuscripts between June 1 and September 1." Award: $100 for the story; the story is printed as lead in the magazine with citation as winner of Literary Contest. Competition receives 100 submissions. "We consider all fiction mss sent to *Antietam Review* Literary Contest as entries for inclusion in each issue. We look for well-crafted, serious literary prose fiction under 5,000 words." Entry fee $10 for each story submitted. Guidelines available after January for #10 SASE. Winners announced October. Winners notified by phone. List of winners available for SASE.

♣ANVIL PRESS 3-DAY NOVEL WRITING CONTEST, (I), Anvil Press, 204-A 175 E. Broadway, Vancouver, British Columbia V5T 1W2 Canada. (604)876-8710. Fax: (604)879-2667. E-mail: subter@pinc.com. Editor: Brian Kaufman. Annual prize for best novel written in 3 days, held every Labor Day weekend. "Prize is publication plus 15% royalties on sales." Receives 500 entries for each award. Guide available after March 1 for SASE. Judges: Anvil Press editorial board. Entry fee $25. Guidelines for SASE. Deadline August 30. "Entrants must register with Anvil Press. Winner is announced November 30." Winners notified by mail and phone. List of winners available for SASE.

ARIZONA AUTHORS' ASSOCIATION NATIONAL LITERARY CONTEST, (I), 3509 E. Shea Blvd., Suite 117, Phoenix AZ 85028. (602)867-9001. Contact: Gerry Benninger, president. Estab. 1981. Annual award "to encourage writers everywhere to write regularly for competition and publication." Award: "Cash prizes totalling $1,000 for winners and honorable mentions in short stories, nonfiction and poetry. Winning entries are published in the *Arizona Literary Magazine*." Entry fee: $5 for poetry, $7 for nonfiction and short stories. Contest rules for #10 SASE after January 1. Deadline July 29. Unpublished submissions. Looking for "strong concept; good, effective writing, with emphasis on the subject/story." Winners announced October 1-15. Winners notified by phone. List of winners available for SASE.

‡ARIZONA COMMISSION ON THE ARTS CREATIVE WRITING FELLOWSHIPS, (I, IV), 417 W. Roosevelt St., Phoenix AZ 85003. (602)255-5882. E-mail: artscomm@primenet.com. Website: http://az.arts.asu. edu/arts.comm. Contact: Jill Bernstein, literature director. Fellowships awarded in alternate years to fiction writers and poets. Award: $5,000-7,500. Competition receives 120-150 submissions. Judges: Out-of-state writers/editors. Guidelines available for SASE. Inquiries by fax and e-mail OK. Deadline September 12. Arizona resident poets and writers over 18 years of age only. Winners announced April 1998. Winners notified in writing. List of winners available for SASE.

ARTIST TRUST ARTIST FELLOWSHIPS; GAP GRANTS, (I, II, IV), Artist Trust, 1402 Third Ave., Suite 404, Seattle WA 98101-2118. (206)467-8734. Fax: (206)467-9633. E-mail: arttrust@eskimo.com. Associate Director: Olivia Taguinod. Artist Trust has 2 grant programs for generative artists in Washington State; the GAP and Fellowships. The GAP (Grants for Artist's Projects) is an annual award of up to $1,200 for a project proposal. The program is open to artists in all disciplines. The Fellowship grant is an award of $5,000 in unrestricted funding. Fellowships for Craft, Media, Literature and Music will be awarded in 1997, and Fellowships for Dance, Design, Theater and Visual Art will be awarded in 1998. Competition receives 60-75 (GAP) submissions; 200-250 (Fellowship 1999). Judges: Fellowship—Peer panel of 3 professional artists and arts professionals in each discipline; GAP—Interdisciplinary peer panel of 5 artists and arts professionals. Guidelines available after December for GAP grants; June for Fellowship for SASE. Inquiries by fax and e-mail OK. Deadline February 28 (GAP), mid June (Fellowship). Winners announced December (Fellowship), May (GAP). Winners notified by mail. List of winners available by mail.

‡ARTISTS FELLOWSHIP PROGRAM IN PROSE, Illinois Arts Council, J.R. Thompson Center, 100 W. Randolph, Suite 10-500, Chicago IL 60601. (312)814-4990. Fax: (312)814-1471. E-mail: ilarts@artswire.org. Director of Communication Arts: Richard Gage. Awards to recognize Illinois writers of exceptional talent to enable them to pursue their artistic goals. Biannual competition for short stories and novel excerpts. Award: $500, $5,000, $10,000. Judges: 3 out-of-state jurors. Guidelines available for SASE. Deadline September 1 in odd numbered years. Only Illinois residents are eligible. Students are ineligible. Word length: mss at least 15 pages long and no more than 30 pages long.

ASF TRANSLATION PRIZE, (II, IV), American-Scandinavian Foundation, 725 Park Ave., New York NY 10021. (212)879-9779. Fax: (212)249-3444. E-mail: agyongy@amscan.org. Website: http://www.amscan.org. Contact: Publishing office. Estab. 1980. "To encourage the translation and publication of the best of contemporary Scandinavian poetry and fiction and to make it available to a wider American audience." Annual competition for poetry, drama, literary prose and fiction translations. Award: $2,000, a bronze medallion and publication in *Scandinavian Review*. Competition receives 20-25 submissions. Competition rules and entry forms available with SASE. Inquiries by fax and e-mail OK. Deadline June 1, 1998. Submissions must have been previously published in the original Scandinavian language. No previously translated material. Original authors should have been born within past 200 years. Winners announced in September. Winners notified by letter. List of winners available for SASE. "Select a choice literary work by an important Scandinavian author."

THE ISAAC ASIMOV AWARD, (I, IV), International Association for the Fantastic in the Arts and *Asimov's* magazine, School of Mass Communications, U. of South Florida, 4202 E. Fowler, Tampa FL 33620. (813)974-6792. Awards Administrator: Rick Wilber. "The award honors the legacy of one of science fiction's most distinguished authors through an award aimed at undergraduate writers." Annual award for short stories. Award: $500 and consideration for publication in *Asimov's*. Competition receives 200 submissions. Judges: *Asimov's* editors. Entry fee $5. Guidelines available after January for SASE. Deadline December 15. Unpublished submissions. Full-time college undergraduates only. Winners announced in March. Winners notified by telephone. List of winners available for SASE.

♣ASTED/GRAND PRIX DE LITTERATURE JEUNESSE DU QUEBEC-ALVINE-BELISLE, (III, IV), Association pour l'avancement des sciences et des techniques de la documentation, 3414 Avenue du Parc, Bureau 202, Montreal, Quebec H2X 2H5 Canada. (514)281-5012. Fax: (514)281-8219. E-mail: info@asted.org. Website: http://www.asted.org. President: Josée Valiquette. "Prize granted for the best work in youth literature edited in French in the Quebec Province. Authors and editors can participate in the contest." Annual competition for fiction and nonfiction for children and young adults. Award: $500. Deadline June 1. Contest entry limited to editors of books published during the preceding year. French translations of other languages are not accepted.

THE ATHENAEUM LITERARY AWARD, (II, IV), The Athenaeum of Philadelphia, 219 S. Sixth St., Philadelphia PA 19106. (215)925-2688. Contact: Literary Award Committee. Annual award to recognize and encourage outstanding literary achievement in Philadelphia and its vicinity. Award: A bronze medal bearing the name of the award, the seal of the Athenaeum, the title of the book, the name of the author and the year. Judged by committee appointed by Board of Directors. Deadline December. Submissions must have been published during the preceding year. Nominations shall be made in writing to the Literary Award Committee by the author, the publisher or a member of the Athenaeum, accompanied by a copy of the book. The Athenaeum Literary Award is granted for a work of general literature, not exclusively for fiction. Juvenile fiction is not included.

---

‡ **THE DOUBLE DAGGER** before a listing indicates that the listing is new in this edition. New markets are often the most receptive to submissions by new writers.

AUTHORS IN THE PARK/*FINE PRINT* CONTEST, (I), P.O. Box 85, Winter Park FL 32790-0085. (407)658-4520. Fax: (407)275-8688. Contact: David Foley. Annual competition. Award: $500 (1st prize), $250 (2nd prize), $125 (3rd prize). Competition receives approx. 200 submissions. Guidelines for SASE. Read guidelines before sending ms. Deadline March 31. Word length: 5,000 words maximum. Winners announced in short story collection, *Fine Print*, before December.

‡BAKELESS LITERARY PUBLICATION PRIZES, (I), Bread Loaf Writers' Conference, Middlebury College, Middlebury VT 05753. (802)443-5286. Fax: (802)443-2087. Administrative Assistant: Carol Knauss. Annual award to recognize and publish an author's first novel or short story collection. Award: tuition, room and board at the conference and publication by Middlebury College/University Press of New England. Judges for 1997 were: Garrett Hongo, Joanna Scott and Alec Wilkinson. Entry fee: $10. Guidelines available April 1 for SASE. Unpublished submissions. Length: 150-450 pages. Deadline March 1. Winners announced in August. List of winners available for SASE.

EMILY CLARK BALCH AWARDS, (I), *The Virginia Quarterly Review*, One West Range, Charlottesville VA 22903. Editor: Staige D. Blackford. Annual award "to recognize distinguished short fiction by American writers." For stories published in *The Virginia Quarterly Review* during the calendar year. Award: $500.

‡❦B&A FICTION CONTEST, (I), *Blood & Aphorisms*, P.O. Box 702, Station P, Toronto ONT M5S 2Y4 Canada. (416)535-1233. E-mail: timnancy@ica.net. Publisher: Tim Paleczny. Awards "to discover new writers and generate more excitement for their work in the literary community." Annual competition for short stories from any genre. Awards: The Humber School for Writers Prize (writing course, value up to $1,000); The Random House/Knopf/Vintage Canada Prize (books, value $1,000); The B&A Prize ($500 cash). Contest prizes are valued in Canadian currency. Judge, 1997 contest: David Eddy, author of *Chump Change* (Random House Canada, 1996). Entry fee $18 (US) for entries from outside Canada; $18 (Canadian) from inside. Entrant receives a 1-year subscription to *B&A*. Guidelines for SASE or IRC. Unpublished submissions. Word length: under 2,500. Winning stories will appear in the summer issue of *B&A*. Put name, address, phone and story title(s) on a separate page. Double space, no staples. Make check payable to B&A.

‡BARRINGTON AREA ARTS COUNCIL/WHETSTONE PRIZES, (I), Box 1266, Barrington IL 60010. Fax (847)382-3685. Co-editors: Jean Tolle, Sandra Berris and Marsha Portnoy. Annual competition "to encourage and reward works of literary excellence." Awards: The Whetstone Prize, usually $500 to a single author for best fiction, nonfiction or poetry selected for publication in *Whetstone* (an annual literary journal); The John Patrick McGrath Award, $250 to a single author, for fiction. Competition receives hundreds of entries; all submissions to *Whetstone* are eligible. Judges: editors of *Whetstone*. Guidelines for SASE. Deadline: open until publication; "we read all year." Unpublished submissions. Length: prose up to 25 pages; poetry, 3-5 poems. Sample copies with guidelines $5 postpaid.

MILDRED L. BATCHELDER AWARD, (II), Association for Library Service to Children/American Library Association, 50 E. Huron St., Chicago IL 60611. (312)944-6780, ext. 2163. Fax: (312)280-3257. E-mail: alsc@ala .org. Website: http://www.ala.org/alsc. Program Officer: Stephanie Anton. To encourage international exchange of quality children's books by recognizing US publishers of such books in translation. Annual competition for translations. Award: Citation. Judge: Mildred L. Batchelder award committee. Guidelines available by phone, mail or e-mail. Deadline: December. Books should be US trade publications for which children, up to and including age 14, are potential audience. Winners notified by phone. List of winners available by website, phone.

‡*BCLT/BCLA TRANSLATION COMPETITION, British Centre for Literary Translation/British Comparative Literature Association, % BCLT/EUR, University of East Anglia, Norwich NR4 7TJ England. Phone/fax: +44 1603 592785. E-mail: c.c.wilson@uea.ac.uk. Contact: Christine Wilson, publicity coordinator. Annual competition for translations. Award: £500. Competition receives 300 submissions per category. Judges: a panel. Entry fee £5 cheque or cash. Guidelines available for SASE. Deadline January 31, 1998. Word length: 25 double-spaced A4 single-sided pages. Winners announced July or August. Winners notified by mail.

***BELLETRIST REVIEW* ANNUAL FICTION CONTEST, (I)**, Belletrist Review, P.O. Box 596, Plainville CT 06062-0596. Contact: Marlene Dube, editor. "To provide an incentive for writers to submit quality fiction for consideration and recognition." Annual competition for short stories. Award: $200. Competition receives approximately 100-150 submissions. Judges: Editorial panel of *Belletrist Review*. Entry fee $5. Guidelines available after October for SASE. Deadline July 15. Unpublished submissions. Word length: 2,500-5,000 words. Winners announced in September. Winners notified by phone and mail. List of winners available for SASE. "An interview with the winning author will also be published with the winning story in the September issue."

GEORGE BENNETT FELLOWSHIP, (I), Phillips Exeter Academy, 20 Main St., Exeter NH 03833-2460. Coordinator, Selection Committee: Charles Pratt. "To provide time and freedom from monetary concerns to a person contemplating or pursuing a career as a professional writer." Annual award of writing residency. Award: A stipend ($6,000 at present), plus room and board for academic year. Competition receives approximately 150 submissions. Judges are a committee of the English department. Entry fee $5. SASE for application form and guidelines. Deadline December 1. Winners announced in March. Winners notified by letter or phone. All applicants will receive an announcement of the winner.

‡BERTELSMANN'S WORLD OF EXPRESSIONS SCHOLARSHIP PROGRAM, Bertelsmann USA, 1540 Broadway, New York NY 10036. (212)930-4978. Fax: (212)930-4783. E-mail: bwoesp@bmge.com. Program Manager: Melanie Fallon-Houska. Annual competition for short stories and poems. Award: $1,000-10,000, 46 awards total. Competition receives 2,000 submissions per category. Judges: various city officials, executives, authors, editors. Guidelines for SASE. Deadline March 15, 1998. All the winners must be public New York City high school seniors. Word length: 2,500 words or less.

BEST FIRST NEW MYSTERY AWARD, (I, IV), *New Mystery Magazine*, 175 Fifth Ave., Suite 2001, New York NY 10010. (212)353-1582. Fax: (212)353-3495. E-mail: newmyst@aol.com. Website: http://www.NewMystery.com. Awards coordinator: Miss Linda Wong. Award to "find the best new mystery, crime or suspense writer, and promote high standards in the short story form. For writers who have never been paid for their writing." Annual award for short stories. Award: publication in *New Mystery Magazine*. Competition receives approximately 3,000 submissions. Judges: editorial panel of veteran mystery writers. No entry fee. No guidelines available. Deadline July 4. Unpublished submissions. Word length: 3,000-5,000 words. "Please mark ms 'First Mystery Award.' Study back issues of *New Mystery* for style." Sample copy: $7 plus 9×12 SAE with $1.24 postage. Winners announced in May 1999.

BEST FIRST PRIVATE EYE NOVEL CONTEST, (I, IV), Private Eye Writers of America, Thomas Dunne Books, St. Martin's Press, 175 Fifth Ave., New York NY 10010. Annual award. To publish a writer's first "private eye" novel. Award: Publication of novel by St. Martin's Press. Advance: $10,000 against royalties (standard contract). Judges are selected by sponsors. Guidelines for #10 SASE. Deadline August 1. Unpublished submissions. "Open to any professional or nonprofessional writer who has never published a 'private eye' novel and who is not under contract with a publisher for the publication of a 'private eye' novel. As used in the rules, 'private eye' novel means: a novel in which the main character is an independent investigator who is not a member of any law enforcement or government agency, and who receives a fee for his or her investigative services."

"BEST OF OHIO WRITERS" CONTEST, (I, IV), *Ohio Writer Magazine*, P.O. Box 91801, Cleveland OH 44101. (216)932-8444. Contact: Ron Antonucci, editor. Award "to encourage and promote the work of writers in Ohio." Annual competition for short stories. Awards: $100 (1st prize), $50 (2nd prize), $25 (3rd prize). Competition receives 100 submissions. Judges: "a selected panel of prominent Ohio writers." Entry fee $10; includes subscription to *Ohio Writer*. Guidelines available after September for SASE. Deadline June 30. Unpublished submissions. Ohio writers only. Length: 2,500 words. "No formula plots; we're looking for bright new voices." Winners announced November 1. Winners are notified by phone; confirmed by mail. List of winners available for SASE.

BEST OF SOFT SCIENCE FICTION CONTEST, (II, IV), Soft SF Writers Assoc., 1277 Joan Dr., Merritt Island FL 32952. Contest Director: Lela E. Buis. Award to "encourage the publication of science fiction styles in which emotional content and artistic effect are emphasized rather than plot and deterministic science. Adult issues are encouraged, but gratuitous violence and graphic sex are not the emotional impacts we want." Annual award for short stories. Awards: $100 (1st prize), $50 (2nd prize), $25 (3rd prize). Judges: members of the Soft SF Writers Association. No entry fee. Guidelines for SASE. Entries accepted October 1 through December 15. Entries must have been submitted for publication or published between January 1 and December 15. Word length: 7,000 words. Story must have elements of science fiction, though cross-genre stories are acceptable. Judging criteria: emotional impact, artistic style, clarity, originality, characterization, theme weight, imagery, sensuality; violence or sex added for shock value are discouraged. Format: Send disposable manuscript in standard format. Securely attach name and address.

❀THE GEOFFREY BILSON AWARD FOR HISTORICAL FICTION FOR YOUNG PEOPLE, (II, IV), The Canadian Children's Book Centre, 35 Spadina Rd., Toronto, Ontario M5R 2S9 Canada. (416)975-0010. Fax: (416)975-1839. E-mail: ccbc@lglobal.com. Website: http://www.lglobal.com/~ccbc. Program Coordinator: Jeffrey Canton. "Award given for best piece of historical fiction for young people." Annual competition for novels. Award: $1,000 (Canadian). Competition receives approximately 8-12 submissions. Judged by a jury of five people from the children's literature community. Previously published submissions. Canadian authors only. "Publishers of Canadian children's books regularly submit copies of their books to the Centre for our library collection. From those books, selections are made for inclusion in the Our Choice list of recommended Canadian children's books each year. The shortlist for the Bilson Award is created after the selections have been made for Our Choice, as the book must first be selected for Our Choice to be part of the Bilson shortlist."

IRMA S. AND JAMES H. BLACK CHILDREN'S BOOK AWARD, (II), Bank Street College, 610 W. 112th St., New York NY 10025-1898. (212)875-4455. Fax: (212)875-4558. E-mail: lindag@bnk1.bnkst.edu.

Website: http://www.bnkst.edu/library/clib/isb.html. Award Director: Linda Greengrass. Annual award "to honor the young children's book published in the preceding year judged the most outstanding in text as well as in art. Book must be published the year preceding the May award." Award: Press function at Harvard Club, a scroll and seals by Maurice Sendak for attaching to award book's run. Judges: adult children's literature experts and children 6-10 years old. No entry fee. Inquiries by fax and e-mail OK. Deadline January 1. "Write to address above. Usually publishers submit books they want considered, but individuals can too. No entries are returned." Winners announced in May. Winners notified by phone.

JAMES TAIT BLACK MEMORIAL PRIZES, (III, IV), Department of English Literature, University of Edinburgh, Edinburgh EH8 9JX Scotland. Contact: Professor R.D.S. Jack. "Two prizes are awarded: one for the best work of fiction, one for the best biography or work of that nature, published during the calendar year: October 1st to September 30th." Annual competition. Award: £3,000 each. Competition receives approximately 300 submissions. Judge: Professor R.D.S. Jack, Dept. of English Literature. Guidelines for SASE or SAE and IRC. Deadline: September 30. Previously published submissions. "Eligible works are those written in English, originating with a British publisher, and first published in Britain in the year of the award. Works should be submitted by publishers."

THE BLACK WARRIOR REVIEW LITERARY AWARD, (II, III), P.O. Box 862936, Tuscaloosa AL 35486-0277. (205)348-4518. Website: http://www.sa.ua.edu/osm/bwr. Contact: Christopher Chambers, editor. "Award is to recognize the best fiction published in *BWR* in a volume year. Only fiction accepted for publication is considered for the award." Competition is for short stories and novel chapters. Award: $500. Competition receives approximately 3,000 submissions. Prize awarded by an outside judge. Guidelines available for SASE. Winners announced in the Fall. Winners notified by phone or mail. List of winners available for purchase in Fall 1998 issue.

*BOARDMAN TASKER PRIZE, (III, IV), 14 Pine Lodge, Dairyground Rd., Bramhall, Stockport, Cheshire SK7 2HS United Kingdom. Contact: Mrs. D. Boardman. "To reward a book which has made an outstanding contribution to mountain literature. A memorial to Peter Boardman and Joe Tasker, who disappeared on Everest in 1982." Award: £2,000. Competition receives approx. 15 submissions. Judges: A panel of 3 judges elected by trustees. Guidelines for SASE. Deadline August 1. Limited to works published or distributed in the UK for the first time between November 1 and October 31. Publisher's entry only. "May be fiction, nonfiction, poetry or drama. Not an anthology. Subject must be concerned with a mountain environment. Previous winners have been books on expeditions, climbing experiences; a biography of a mountaineer; novels." Short list, available in September, will be sent to all publishers who have entered books.

BOOK PUBLISHERS OF TEXAS AWARD, (II, IV), The Texas Institute of Letters, TCU Press, TCU Box 298300, Fort Worth TX 76129. (817)921-7822. Secretary: Judy Alter. "Award to honor the best book written for children or young people that was published the year prior to that in which the award is given." Annual competition for children's literature. Award: $250. Competition receives approximately 40 submissions. Judges: Committee selected by TIL. Guidelines available after June 30 for SASE. Deadline January 2. Previously published submissions from January 1 through December 31 of the year prior to the award. "To be eligible, the writer must have been born in Texas or have lived in the state for two years at some time, or the subject matter of the work must be associated with Texas." Winners announced in April. Winners notified by mail or phone. List of winners available for SASE.

‡*BOOKER PRIZE FOR FICTION, Book Trust, Book House, 45 E. Hill, London SW18 2QZ England. 0181 870-9055. Fax: 0181 874-4790. Prizes Manager: Sandra Vince. Award to the best novel of the year. Annual competition for novels. Award: £20,000. Competition receives 100 submissions. Judges: five judges appointed by the Booker Management Committee. Deadline July 1. Published submissions. A full-length novel written in English by a citizen of the Commonwealth or Republic of Ireland.

BOSTON GLOBE-HORN BOOK AWARDS, (II), *Horn Book Magazine, Inc.*, 11 Beacon St., Suite 1000, Boston MA 02108. (617)523-0299. Fax: (617)523-0299. E-mail: info@hbook.com. Marketing Manager: Karen Walsh. Annual award. "To honor excellence in children's fiction or poetry, picture and nonfiction books published within the US." Award: $500 and engraved silver bowl first prize in each category; engraved silver plate for the 2 honor books in each category. Competition receives 2,000 submissions. No entry fee. Guidelines available after January for SASE. Inquiries by fax and e-mail OK. Entry forms or rules for SASE. Deadline May 15. Previously published material from July 1-June 30 of previous year. Winners announced October 6. List of winners available by telephone.

BRAZOS BOOKSTORE (HOUSTON) AWARD (SINGLE SHORT STORY), (II, IV), The Texas Institute of Letters, % TCU Press, TCU Box 298300, Ft. Worth TX 76129. (817)921-7822. Awards Coordinator: Judy Alter. Award to "honor the writer of the best short story published for the first time during the calendar year before the award is given." Annual competition for short stories. Award: $750. Competition receives approximately 40-50 submissions. Judges: Panel selected by TIL Council. Guidelines for SASE. Deadline: January 2.

Previously published submissions. Entries must have appeared in print between January 1 and December 31 of the year prior to the award. "Award available to writers who, at some time, have lived in Texas at least two years consecutively or whose work has a significant Texas theme. Entries must be sent directly to the three judges. Their names and addresses are available from the TIL office. Include SASE."

‡**BRODY ARTS FUND LITERARY FELLOWSHIP, (I, II, IV)**, California Community Foundation, 606 S. Olive St., Suite 2400, Los Angeles CA 90014. (213)413-4042. Contact: Senior Program Secretary. "To recognize and support the work of emerging writers resident in Los Angeles County, California, whose work reflects the ethnic and cultural diversity of the region." Award granted every 3 years for short stories, novels, poetry, plays and screenplays. Award: $5,000 unrestricted fellowship (approximately 5-7 awarded once every 3 years). Competition receives approximately 150 submissions. Judges: A peer panel of local writers and editors. No deadline/applications possible until after January 1. Probable deadline in mid-March 1997. Previously published or unpublished submissions. All applicants must be based in Los Angeles County, California. Guidelines and application forms can be requested by phone or letter, but not until January, 1998.

BRONX RECOGNIZES ITS OWN (B.R.I.O.), (I, IV), Bronx Council on the Arts, 1738 Hone Ave., Bronx NY 10461-1486. (718)931-9500. Fax: (718)409-6445. E-mail: bronsart@artswire.org. Website: http://www.bronx arts.org. Arts Services Associate: Evelyn Collazo. Award to "recognize local artistic talent in Bronx County." Annual competition for novels. Award: $1,500 fellowship (awards 15/year in visual, media, performing and literary arts). Competition receives approximately 55 submissions. Judges: A collective of non-Bronx based artists. Guidelines available mid-December by a phone call or written request. Deadline March. Only Bronx-based individual artists may apply. Proof of Bronx residency required. Word length: 20 typed pages of ms. Winners announced in May. Winners notified by mail. List of winners available for SASE.

✹**GEORGES BUGNET AWARD FOR THE NOVEL, (II, IV)**, Writers Guild of Alberta, 3rd Floor, Percy Page Centre, 11759 Groat Rd., Edmonton, Alberta T5M 3K6 Canada. (403)422-8174. Fax: (403)422-2663. Contact: Darlene Diver, assistant director. "To recognize outstanding books published by Alberta authors each year." Annual competition for novels. Award: $500 (Canadian) and leather-bound book. Competition receives 20-30 submissions. Judges: selected published writers across Canada. Guidelines for SASE. Deadline December 31. Previously published submissions. Must have appeared in print between January 1 and December 31. Open to Alberta authors only.

✹**BURNABY WRITERS' SOCIETY ANNUAL COMPETITION, (I, IV)**, 6584 Deer Lake Ave., British Columbia V5G 2J3 Canada. (604)435-6500. Annual competition to encourage creative writing in British Columbia. "Category varies from year to year." Award: $200, $100 and $50 (Canadian) prizes. Receives 400-600 entries for each award. Judge: "independent recognized professional in the field." Entry fee $5. Contest requirements after March for SASE. Deadline: May 31. Open to British Columbia authors only. Winners announced in September. Winners notified by phone or mail. List of winners available for SASE.

BUSH ARTIST FELLOWSHIPS, (I, IV), The Bush Foundation, E-900 First Nat'l Bank Building, 332 Minnesota St., St. Paul MN 55101. (612)227-5222. Contact: Kathi Polley, program assistant. Award to "provide support for artists to work in their chosen art forms." Annual grant. Award: $40,000 for 12-18 months. Competition receives approximately 500 submissions. Literature (fiction, creative nonfiction, poetry) offered every other year. Next offered 1999 BAF. Applications available August 1998. Deadline October 1998. Must meet certain publication requirements. Judges are writers, critics and editors from outside Minnesota, South Dakota, North Dakota or Wisconsin. Applicants must be at least 25 years old, and Minnesota, South Dakota, North Dakota or Western Wisconsin residents. Students not eligible. Winners announced in April. Winners notified by letter.

BYLINE **MAGAZINE LITERARY AWARDS, (I, IV)**, P.O. Box 130596, Edmond OK 73013-0001. (405)348-5591. Website: http://www.bylinemag.com. Contact: Marcia Preston, executive editor/publisher. "To encourage our subscribers in striving for high quality writing." Annual awards for short stories and poetry including First Chapter of a Novel Award and Genre Short Fiction Contest. Award: $250 in each category. Competition receives 150-200 submissions. Judges are published writers not on the *ByLine* staff. Entry fee $5 for stories; $3 for poems. Guidelines available for SASE. Postmark deadline: November 1. "Entries should be unpublished and not have won money in any previous contest. Winners announced in February issue and published in February or March issue with photo and short bio. Open to subscribers only."

MARKET CATEGORIES: (I) Unpublished entries; **(II)** Published entries nominated by the author; **(III)** Published entries nominated by the editor, publisher or nominating body; **(IV)** Specialized entries.

‡**CALIFORNIA WRITERS' CLUB CONTEST, (I)**, California Writers' Club, 8 Balra Dr., Novato CA 94947-4963. Cash awards "to encourage writing." Competition is held annually. Competition receives varying number of submissions. Judges: Professional writers, members of California Writers' Club. Entry fee to be determined. For the contest rules, write to the Secretary between February 1 and April 30. Unpublished submissions. "Open to all."

JOHN W. CAMPBELL MEMORIAL AWARD FOR THE BEST SCIENCE-FICTION NOVEL OF THE YEAR; THEODORE STURGEON MEMORIAL AWARD FOR THE BEST SCIENCE FICTION SHORT FICTION, (II, III), Center for the Study of Science Fiction, English Dept., University of Kansas, Lawrence KS 66045. (913)864-3380. Fax: (913)864-4298. E-mail: jgunn@falcon.cc.ukans.edu. Website: http://www.falcon.cc.ukans.edu/~sfcenter/. Professor and Director: James Gunn. "To honor the best novel and short science fiction of the year." Annual competition for short stories and novels. Award: Certificate. "Winners' names are engraved on a trophy." Campbell Award receives approximately 150 submissions. Judges: 2 separate juries. Deadline: May 1. For previously published submissions. "Ordinarily publishers should submit work, but authors have done so when publishers would not. Send for list of jurors." Entrants for the Sturgeon Award are selected by nomination only. Winners announced July 10. List of winners available for SASE.

‡**CAPTIVATING BEGINNINGS CONTEST, (I)**, *Lynx Eye*, 1880 Hill Dr., Los Angeles CA 90041. Annual award for stories "with engrossing beginnings, stories that will enthrall and absorb readers." Award: $100 plus publication, first prize; $10 each for 4 honorable mentions plus publication. Entry fee: $5/story. Guidelines available for SASE. Unpublished submissions. Length: 7,500 words or less. "The stories will be judged on the first 500 words." Deadline January 31. Winners announced March 15.

‡**THE CAROLINA NOVEL AWARD, (IV)**, Banks Channel Books, P.O. Box 4446, Wilmington NC 28406. Biennial award to encourage excellence in fiction-writing by Carolina authors. Competition for original novels. Award: $500 advance against royalties and publication by Banks Channel Books. Judges: Banks Channel Books staff. Entry fee: $35. Guidelines for SASE. Deadline July 31. Unpublished submissions. Limited to North and South Carolina residents. Length: 200-400 pages. Winner announced in December. Contest results available for SASE.

RAYMOND CARVER SHORT STORY CONTEST, (I, IV), Dept. of English, Humboldt State University, Arcata CA 95521-4957. Contact: Coordinator. Annual award for previously unpublished short stories. First prize: $500 and publication in *Toyon*. Second Prize: $250 and honorable mention in *Toyon*. Third Prize: honorable mention in *Toyon*. Competition receives 600 submissions. Entry fee $10/story. SASE for rules. Deadline November 1. For U.S. citizens only. Send 2 copies of story; author's name, address, phone number and title of story on separate cover page only. Story must be no more than 6,000 words. Title must appear on first page. For notification of receipt of ms, include self-addressed, stamped postcard. For Winners List include SASE. For a copy of the *Toyon*, send $2. "Follow directions and have faith in your work."

WILLA CATHER FICTION PRIZE, (I, IV), Helicon Nine Editions, 3607 Pennsylvania, Kansas City MO 64111. (816)753-1095. Contact: Gloria Vando Hickok. Annual competition for novels, story collections and novellas. Award: $1,000. Winners chosen by nationally recognized writers. Entry fee $15. Guidelines for SASE. Deadline May 1. Unpublished submissions. Open to all writers residing in the US and its territories. Mss will not be returned. Past judges include Robley Wilson, Daniel Stern, Leonard Michaels, Carolyn Doty.

THE *CHELSEA* AWARDS, (II), P.O. Box 773, Cooper Station, New York NY 10276. *Mail entries to*: Chelsea Awards, %Richard Foerster, Editor, P.O. Box 1040, York Beach ME 03910. Annual competition for short stories. Prize: $750 and publication in *Chelsea* (all entries are considered for publication). Judges: the editors. Entry fee $10 (for which entrants also receive a subscription). Guidelines available for SASE. Deadline June 15. Unpublished submissions. Manuscripts may not exceed 30 typed pages or about 7,500 words. The stories must not be under consideration elsewhere or scheduled for book publication within 8 months of the competition deadline. Include separate cover sheet; no name on ms. Mss will not be returned; include SASE for notification of results. Winners announced August 15. Winners notified by telephone.

CHEVRON AWARD AND WRITERS UNLIMITED AWARD, Writers Unlimited, 910 Grant Ave., Pascagoula MS 39567-7222. (601)762-4230. Contest Chairman: Nina Mason. "Part of an annual contest to encourage first-class writing of poetry and prose." Annual competition for short stories. Prize amounts vary with $50 being the maximum. Competition receives 100 submissions. Deadline September 1. Guidelines available after July 1 for SASE. Winners announced by mail in October.

*****THE CHILDREN'S BOOK AWARD, (II)**, Federation of Children's Book Groups, The Old Malt House, Aldbourne, Marlborough, Wilts SN8 2DW England. Award to "promote good quality books for children." Annual award for short stories, novels, story collections and translations. Award: "Portfolio of children's writing and drawings and a magnificent trophy of silver and oak." Judges: Thousands of children from all over the United Kingdom. Guidelines for SASE or SAE and IRC. Deadline: December 31. Published and previously unpublished submissions (first publication in UK). "The book should be suitable for children."

‡**CHILDREN'S BOOK COMMITTEE AWARD, (III, IV)**, (formerly Child Study Children's Book Award), Children's Book Committee at Bank St. College, 610 W. 112th St., New York NY 10025. (212)875-4540. Fax: (212)875-4759. Website: http://www.bnkst.edu/library/booklist/booklist.html. Contact: Alice B. Belgray, committee chair. Annual award. "To honor a book for children or young people which deals realistically with problems in their world. It may concern social, individual and ethical problems." Only books sent by publishers for review are considered. No personal submissions. Books must have been published within current calendar year. Award: Certificate and cash prize. Winners announced in March. Winners notified by phone.

THE CHRISTOPHER AWARD, (II), The Christophers, 12 E. 48th St., New York NY 10017. (212)759-4050. Contact: Ms. Peggy Flanagan, awards coordinator. Annual award "to encourage creative people to continue to produce works which affirm the highest values of the human spirit in adult and children's books." Published submissions only. Award: Bronze medallion. "Award judged by a grassroots panel and a final panel of experts. Juvenile works are 'children tested.'" Examples of books awarded: *Dear Mr. Henshaw*, by Beverly Cleary (ages 8-10); *Sarah, Plain and Tall*, by Patricia MacLachlan (ages 10-12).

‡**CNW/FFWA FLORIDA STATE WRITING COMPETITION, (I)**, Florida Freelance Writers Association, P.O. Box A, North Stratford NH 03590. (603)922-8338. Fax: (603)922-8339. E-mail: danakcnw@moose.ncia.net. Executive Director: Dana K. Cassell. Award "to recognize publishable writing." Annual competition for short stories and novels. Awards: $75, books, certificate or membership. Competition receives 50-100 submissions. Judges: published authors, teachers, editors. Entry fee varies with membership status. Guidelines available after March 15 for SASE. Previously unpublished submissions.

CONNECTICUT COMMISSION ON THE ARTS ARTIST FELLOWSHIPS, (I, II, IV), One Financial Plaza, Hartford CT 06103-2601. (203)566-4770. Fax: (860)566-6462. E-mail: kdemeo@csunet.ctstateu.edu. Website: http://www.cslnet.ctstateu.edu/cca/. Program Manager: Linda Dente. "To support the creation of new work by creative artists *living in Connecticut*." Biennial competition for the creation or completion of new works in literature, i.e. short stories, novels, story collections, poetry and playwriting. Awards: $5,000 and $2,500. Competition receives 75-100 submissions. Judges: Peer professionals (writers, editors). Guidelines available in January. Inquiries by fax and e-mail OK. Deadline September 1998. Writers may send either previously published or unpublished submissions—up to 20 pages of material. Connecticut residents only. "Write to please yourself . . . if you win . . . that's a bonus." Winners announced in January. Winners notified by mail.

‡**COTTONWOOD FICTION FELLOWSHIP, (IV)**, Cottonwood Cooperative, P.O.Box 4530, Albuquerque NM 87196. (505)255-1544. E-mail: cottonwd@unm.edu. Director: Charli Buono de Valdez. Award "to honor and enable a Southwestern, mid-career writer." Annual competition for short stories, novels and story collections. Award: $1,000. Judges: Panel of Southwestern writers. Entry fee $8. Include SASE for return of ms. Guidelines for SASE. Published or unpublished submissions. Limited to writers from Southwest region (Arizona, Colorado, New Mexico, Oklahoma, Texas and Utah) who have never published a novel or collection of stories. Any genre. "There is particular interest in stories inspired by the Southwest and dealing in some manner with the substance of the Southwest although this preference is by no means definitive." Word length: "Interested authors should submit portfolios—suggested length between 3 and 50 pages. Portfolio may include any number of individual stories and/or a novel excerpt."

‡**COUNCIL FOR WISCONSIN WRITERS ANNUAL WRITING CONTEST, (II, IV)**, Box 55322, Madison WI 53705. Contact: Russell King. "To recognize excellence in Wisconsin writing published during the year in 11 categories." Annual competition for short stories and novels. Award: $500 for 9 categories, $1,000 for 2 categories. Competition receives between 5 and 80 entries, depending on category. Judges: qualified judges from other states. Entry fee $25 for nonmembers and $10 for members. Guidelines for SASE. Previously published submissions. Wisconsin residents only. Official entry form (available in November) required. Deadline mid-January.

‡**CROSSING BOUNDARIES WRITING AWARDS, (I)**, *International Quarterly*, P.O. Box 10521, Tallahassee FL 32302-0521. (850)224-5078. Fax:(850)224-5127. E-mail: vbrock@mailer.fsu.edu. Editor-in-chief/President: Van K. Brock. Award to "reward original creative excellence in four separate categories: fiction, nonfiction, poetry and works that are 'crossing boundaries' of genre and culture." Annual competition for short stories and translations. Awards: publication plus $500 each genre. Competition receives 350 submissions. Judges: *International Quarterly* editors. Entry fee $10 for nonmembers, $5 for members. Guidelines for SASE. Deadline March 1, 1998. Unpublished submissions. Word length: 5,000 for prose, no requirement for poetry. "Original translations into English are also eligible, judged by accuracy and fidelity to original (original and permission should be included), and excellence in English."

THE *CRUCIBLE* POETRY AND FICTION COMPETITION, (I), *Crucible*, Barton College, College Station, Wilson NC 27893. Annual competition for short stories. Award: $150 (1st prize); $100 (2nd prize) and publication in *Crucible*. Judges: The editors. Guidelines for SASE. Deadline April. Unpublished submissions. Fiction should be 8,000 words or less.

DAGGER MYSTERY CONTEST, (I, IV), *Whispering Willow's Mystery Magazine*, 2517 S. Central, P.O. Box 890294, Oklahoma City OK 73189-0294. (405)239-2531. Fax: (405)232-3848. Contact: Peggy D. Farris, editor-in-chief. Annual competition for short stories. Award: $200 plus publication. Competition receives approximately 30 submissions. Judge: Trula Johnson. Entry fee $10. Guidelines for SASE. Deadline March 10. Unpublished submissions. Mystery or mystery/suspense stories only. Length: 500-2,500 words. "No explicit sex, gore, or extreme violence."

DALY CITY POETRY AND SHORT STORY CONTEST, (I), Daly City History, Arts, and Science Commission, % Serramonte Library, 40 Wembley Dr., Daly City CA 94015-4233. (650)992-3179. Contest coordinator: Ruth Hoppin. "To encourage poets and writers and to recognize and reward excellence." Annual competition for short stories. Awards: $40, $25, $10 and $5. Competition receives approximately 50 submissions. Judges are usually teachers of creative writing. Entry fee: $2/story. Guidelines for SASE after January 19. Deadline: January 19. Unpublished submissions. Length: 3,000 words maximum. "No profanity." Winners announced March 1. Winners notified by mail.

‡DANA AWARD IN SPECULATIVE FICTION, (IV), 7207 Townsend Forest Court, Browns Summit NC 27214. (910)656-7009. Chair, Dana Awards: Mary Elizabeth Parker. "To reward work that has been previously unrecognized in the area of speculative fiction (fantasy, futuristic, time travel, psychological suspense/horror). But let authors be aware work must also meet standards of literary complexity and excellence. That is, character development, excellence of style are as important as the plot line." Annual competition for short stories. Awards: guaranteed $500 first prize; "possibility of more—second prize $250, third prize $100 if funds allow." Entry fee $10/short story. Send SASE for complete guidelines. Unpublished submissions and not under contract to any publisher. Word length: no minimum, but no longer than 40 double-spaced pages or 10,000 words.

‡DANA AWARD IN THE NOVEL, 7207 Townsend Forest Court, Browns Summit NC 27214. Chair: Mary Elizabeth Parker. Award to "reward work that has not yet been recognized, since we know from firsthand experience how tough the literary market is." Annual competition for novels. No genre fiction, please. Award: $1,000. Competition receives 140 submissions per category. Judges: nationally-published novelists. Entry fee $20 for each submission. Guidelines for SASE. Deadline October 31. Unpublished submissions. Entries must be first 50 pages of novel only. "Novelists should submit first 50 pages only of a novel either completed or in progress. In progress submissions should be as polished as possible. Multiple submissions accepted, but each must include a separate $20 entry fee. Make checks payable to Dana Awards."

‡THE DOROTHY DANIELS ANNUAL HONORARY WRITING AWARD, National League of American Pen Women, Simi Valley Branch, P.O. Box 1485, Simi Valley CA 93062. Contest Chair: Diane Reichick. Award "to honor excellent writing." Annual competition for short stories. Award: $100 first place. Judges: Pen Women members. Competition receives approximately 150 entries. Entry fee $5/short story. Rules for SASE. Deadline July 30. Unpublished submissions: not currently submitted elsewhere; entries must have received no prior awards. No limit on number of entries. Any person except Simi Valley Pen Women, interns, and their immediate families are eligible. Any genre. Word length: 2,000 words maximum. "Entries must follow rules exactly."

THE JACK DANIEL'S FAUX FAULKNER CONTEST, (I), Jack Daniel Distillery, *Faulkner Newsletter* of Yoknapatawpha Press and University of Mississippi, P.O. Box 248, Oxford MS 38655. (601)234-0909. E-mail: boozernhb@aol.com. Website: http://www.watervalley.net/yoknapatawphapress/index.htm. "To honor William Faulkner by imitating his style, themes and subject matter in a short parody." Annual competition for a 500-word (2-pages) parody. Award: 2 round-trip tickets to Memphis, plus complimentary registration and lodging for the annual Faulkner and Yoknapatawpha Conference at the University of Mississippi. Competition receives approximately 750-1,000 submissions. Judges: George Plimpton, Tom Wicker, John Berendt and Arthur Schlesinger, Jr. (judges rotate every year or so—well-known authors). Guidelines for SASE. Deadline: February 1. Previously unpublished submissions. Winner will be notified April 1—announcement made August 1, at Faulkner's home in Oxford MS. Contestants grant publication rights and the right to release entries to other media—to the sponsors."

MARGUERITE DE ANGELI PRIZE, (I), Bantam Doubleday Dell Books for Young Readers, 1540 Broadway, New York NY 10036. (212)782-8633. Fax: (212)782-9452. "To encourage the writing of fiction for middle grade readers (either contemporary or historical) in the same spirit as the works of Marguerite de Angeli." Open to US and Canadian writers. Annual competition for first novels for middle-grade readers (ages 7-10). Award: One BDD hardcover and paperback book contract, with $1,500 cash prize and $3,500 advance against royalties. Competition receives 300 submissions. Judges: Editors of BDD Books for Young Readers. Guidelines for SASE. Inquiries by fax OK. Deadline: Submissions must be postmarked between April 1 and June 30. Previously unpublished (middle-grade) fiction. Length: 40-144 pages. Winners announced October. Winners notified by phone and letter. List of winners available for SASE.

‡**DEAD METAPHOR PRESS CHAPBOOK CONTEST**, Dead Metaphor Press, P.O. Box 2076, Boulder CO 80306-2076. (303)939-0268. Contact: Richard Wilmarth. Award to "promote quality writing." Annual competition for short stories. Award: 10% of the press run. Competition receives 200 submissions. Judge: Richard Wilmarth. Entry fee $8. Guidelines available for SASE. Deadline October 31. Word length: 24 page limit.

‡**DEEP SOUTH WRITERS CONFERENCE ANNUAL COMPETITION, (I)**, DSWC Inc., English Dept., University of Louisiana at Lafayette, P.O. Box 44691, Lafayette LA 70504. (318)482-6908. Contact: director or contest clerk. Annual awards "to encourage aspiring, unpublished writers." Categories: Novels, short stories, nonfiction, poetry, plays, and French language literature. Awards: Certificates and cash plus possible publication of shorter works. Competition receives 100 submissions. Judges: faculty at University of Southwestern Louisiana. Entry fee $10 for each submission. Contest rules and addition to mailing list for SASE. Deadline July 15. Unpublished submissions. Winners announced September. Winners notified by phone or mail. List of winners available for SASE.

DELACORTE PRESS ANNUAL PRIZE FOR A FIRST YOUNG ADULT NOVEL, (I), Delacorte Press, Department BFYR, 1540 Broadway, New York NY 10036. (212)354-6500. Fax: (212)782-9452. Estab. 1983. Annual award "to encourage the writing of contemporary young adult fiction." Award: Contract for publication of book; $1,500 cash prize and a $6,000 advance against royalties. Competition receives 400 submissions. Judges are the editors of Delacorte Press Books for Young Readers. Contest rules for SASE. Inquiries by fax OK. Unpublished submissions; fiction with a contemporary setting that will be suitable for ages 12-18. Deadline: December 30 (no submissions accepted prior to October 1). Writers may be previously published, but cannot have published a young adult novel before. Winners announced April. Winners notified by phone and letter. List of winners available for SASE

DELAWARE DIVISION OF THE ARTS, (I, IV), 820 N. French St., Wilmington DE 19801. (302)577-8284. Fax: (302)577-6561. E-mail: bking@state.de.us. Website: http://www.dca.net/artsdel. Coordinator: Barbara R. King. "To help further careers of emerging and established professional artists." Annual awards for Delaware residents only. Awards: $5,000 for established professionals; $2,000 for emerging professionals. Competition receives 12 submissions. Judges are out-of-state professionals in each division. Entry forms or rules available after January 1 for SASE. Inquiries by fax or e-mail OK. Deadline March 1. Winners announced in July. Winners notified by mail.

‡**MARTIN DIBNER MEMORIAL FUND FOR MAINE WRITERS**, Maine Community Foundation, 210 Main St., P.O. Box 148, Ellsworth ME 04605. (207)667-9735. Fax: (207)667-9738. Program Officer: Elizabeth Myrick. Award to "provide financial assistance for professional development of writers." Annual competition for poetry and fiction (rotating). Award: $500-1,000 grants. Competition receives 40 submissions per category. Judges: committee of Maine writers. Guidelines available for SASE. Deadline March 15. Maine writers only. Word length: 10-15 poems/pages. "Do not put name on entry—add additional page with name and address."

‡**DOBIE/PAISANO FELLOWSHIPS**, Texas Institute of Letters, P.O. Box 298300, Fort Worth TX 76129. (817)921-7822. E-mail: jalter@gamma.is.tcu.edu. Secretary: Judy Alter. Award to "honor the achievement and promise of two writers." Annual competition for fiction, poetry or nonfiction. Award: $1,200/month for six months and rent-free stay at Paisano ranch southwest of Austin, TX. Judges: committee from Texas Institute of Letters and the University of Texas. Guidelines available for SASE. Deadline January 4. "To be eligible, a writer must have been born in Texas or have lived in the state for at least two consecutive years at some point. The winners usually have notable publishing credits behind them in addition to promising work that is under way."

‡**DOG WRITERS OF AMERICA WRITING COMPETITION**, Dog Writers of America, 31441 Santa Margarita Pky. #A163, Rancho Santa Margarita CA 92688. Competition Co-chair: Betsy Sikora Siino. Award to "reward excellence and professionalism in dog writing." Annual competition for short stories, novels and story collections. Award: Maxwell Medallion and corporate-sponsored cash awards. Judges: A panel of specially selected judges. Entry fee $12 for each story submitted. Guidelines available for SASE. Deadline September. Published submissions.

EATON LITERARY ASSOCIATES' LITERARY AWARDS PROGRAM, (I), Eaton Literary Associates, P.O. Box 49795, Sarasota FL 34230. (941)366-6589. Fax: (941)365-4679. E-mail: eatonlit@aol.com. Contact: Richard Lawrence, vice president. Biannual award for short stories and novels. Award: $2,500 for best book-length ms, $500 for best short story. Competition receives approx. 2,000 submissions annually. Judges are 2 staff members in conjunction with an independent agency. Entry forms or rules for SASE. Inquiries by fax and e-mail OK. Deadline March 31 for short stories; August 31 for book-length mss. Winners announced April and September. Winners notified by mail.

‡**ELF, ANNUAL SHORT FICTION COMPETITION, (I)**, *ELF: Eclectic Literary Forum*, P.O. Box 392, Tonawanda NY 14150. (716)693-7006. Fax: (716)693-7006. E-mail: neubauer@buffnet.net. Website: http://www. pce.net/elf. Award for "fine writing and to encourage emerging authors." Annual competition for short stories. Editor's Awards: $300; 2 honorable mentions at $50 each. Competition receives 200 stories. Judges: editorial staff (all professors of English and published authors). Entry fee $9/story; free to subscribers. Guidelines for SASE. Deadline August 31. Unpublished submissions. Word length: 3,500 words. "Send for complete guidelines or refer to *ELF* on the Web."

❖**ARTHUR ELLIS AWARDS, (II, IV)**, Crime Writers of Canada, Box 113, 3007 Kingston Rd., Scarborough, Ontario M1M 1P1 Canada. E-mail: ap113@torfree.net. Contact: Secretary-Treasurer. "To recognize excellence in all aspects of crime-writing." Annual competition for short stories and novels. Award: statuette (plus *maybe* cash or goods). Competition receives 40 submissions. Judges: panels of members and experts. Guidelines for SASE. Deadline December 31 for published submissions that appeared in print between January 1 and December 31 of that year. Open to Canadian residents (any citizenship) or Canadian citizens living abroad. Four complete copies of each work must be submitted. Every entry must state category entered. Categories include Best Novel, Best First Novel, Best Short Story, Best Nonfiction, Best Play and Best Juvenile. Winners announced May 1998. Winners notified by phone or fax. List of winners available by phone.

‡**EVERGREEN CHRONICLES NOVELLA CONTEST**, Evergreen Chronicles, P.O. Box 8939, Minneapolis MN 55408-0939. (612)823-6638. Fax: (612)722-9005. E-mail: evgrnchron@aol.com. Contact: Louisa Castner, managing editor. Award to "promote work on novellas of gay, lesbian, bisexual or transgender (GLBT) themes/content/experience." Annual competition for novellas. Award: $500/first prize, $100/2nd prize. Competition receives 50 submissions per category. Judges: nationally acclaimed GLBT writers. Guidelines available for SASE. Deadline: September 30. Previously unpublished submissions. Word length: novellas with GLBT themes between 15,000-30,000 words.

EYSTER PRIZES, (II), *The New Delta Review*, LSU/Dept. of English, Baton Rouge LA 70803-5001. (504)388-4079. Contact: Editors. "To honor author and teacher Warren Eyster, who served as advisor to *New Delta Review* predecessors *Manchac* and *Delta*." Semiannual awards for best short story and best poem in each issue. Award: $50 and 2 free copies of publication. Competition receives approximately 400 submissions/issue. Judges are published authors. Guidelines available for SASE. Deadlines: September 15 for fall, February 15 for spring. Winners announced upon acceptance. Winners notified by mail. List of winners available for SASE.

JOAN FASSLER MEMORIAL BOOK AWARD, (II, IV), Association for the Care of Children's Health, 7910 Woodmont Ave., #300, Bethesda MD 20814-3015. (301)654-6549. Fax: (301)986-4553. E-mail: acch@clark.net. Website: http://www.wsd.com/acch.org. "Recognizes outstanding literature that makes a distinguished contribution to a child's or young person's understanding of hospitalization, illness, disabling conditions, dying and death, and preventive care." Annual competition for short stories and novels. Award: $1,000 honorarium and plaque. Competition receives approximately 50-70 submissions. Judges: multidisciplinary committee of 8 ACCH members. Guidelines available after August. Inquiries by fax and e-mail OK. Deadline December 1. Previously published submissions must have appeared in print within previous year. Winners announced March. Winners notified by letter and phone.

VIRGINIA FAULKNER AWARD FOR EXCELLENCE IN WRITING, (II), Prairie Schooner, 201 Andrews Hall, University of Nebraska, Lincoln NE 68588-0334. (402)472-0911. Fax: (402)472-9771. E-mail: lrando lph@unlinfo.uni.edu. Contact: Hilda Raz, editor. "An award for writing published in *Prairie Schooner* in the previous year." Annual competition for short stories, novel excerpts and translations. Award: $1,000. Judges: Editorial Board. Guidelines for SASE. Inquiries by fax and e-mail OK. "We only read mss from September through May." Work must have been published in *Prairie Schooner* in the previous year.

WILLIAM FAULKNER COMPETITION IN FICTION, (I), The Pirate's Alley Faulkner Society Inc., 632 Pirate's Alley, New Orleans LA 70116-3254. (504)586-1609. Fax: (504)522-9725. Contest Director: Joseph J. DeSalvo, Jr. "To encourage publisher interest in writers with potential." Annual competition for short stories, novels, novellas, personal essays and poetry. Award: $7,500 for novel, $2,500 for novella, $1,500 for short story, $1,000 personal essay, $750 poetry and gold medals, plus trip to New Orleans for presentation. Competition receives 200-300 submissions per category. Judges: professional writers, academics. Entry fee $25 for each poem, essay, short story; $30 for novella; $35 for novel. Guidelines for SASE. Inquiries by fax OK. Deadline April 1.

READ THE BUSINESS OF FICTION WRITING section to learn the correct way to prepare and submit a manuscript.

Unpublished submissions. Word length: for novels, over 50,000; for novellas, under 50,000; for short stories, under 20,000. All entries must be accompanied by official entry form which is provided with guidelines. Winners announced August 31. Winners notified by telephone. List of winners available for SASE.

FEMINIST WRITER'S CONTEST, Des Plaines/Park Ridge NOW Chapter, Dept. NSS, P.O. Box 2440, Des Plaines IL 60018. (847)824-7670. E-mail: pat112870@juno.com. Contest Director: Pat Plautz. "To encourage, to reward feminist writers, and to be published in our chapter newsletter." Annual competition for short stories and essays. Award: $100 (1st place), $50 (2nd place). Competition receives approximately 75 submissions. Judges are feminist teachers, writers, political activists, social workers and entrepeneurs. Entry fee $10. Guidelines available after November for SASE. Inquiries by e-mail OK. Deadline August 31 of each year. May be either published or unpublished. "We accept both foreign or domestic entries. Stories/essays may be on any subject, but should reflect feminist awareness." Word length: 3,000 words or less. Winners announced November. Winners notified by phone. List of winners available for SASE.

‡FEMINIST WRITERS GUILD LITERARY ANTHOLOGY/CONTEST, (I), Outrider Press, 1004 E. Steger Rd., Suite C3, Crete IL 60417. (708)672-6630. Competition to collect diverse writings by feminists of all ages, genders and orientations on the theme of "Freedom's Just Another Word." Open to poetry and short stories. Award: publication in anthology; free copy to all published contributors. $100 to the best in each category; $50 for the best submission by an FWG member. Judges: independent panel. Entry fee $16; $11 for members. Guidelines and entry form available for SASE. Deadline December 31, 1997. Unpublished submissions. Word length: 1,750 words or less. Maximum 2 entries per person. Include SASE.

‡FERRO-GRUMLEY AWARDS, The Publishing Triangle, P.O. Box 114, New York NY 10012. E-mail: pubtriangle@nycnet.com. Co-chairs: Jane Perkins and Lawrence Schimel. Award to "honor one work of lesbian fiction and one work of gay male fiction published in the previous year." Annual competition for novels and story collections. Judges: a committee. Published submissions. Work only with lesbian and gay content. Writer must be nominated by publishing Triangle members.

‡FIRST BOOK AWARDS FOR POETRY AND PROSE, Native Writers' Circle of the Americas and the Greenfield Review Literary Center, Greenfield Review Literary Center, P.O. Box 308, Greenfield Center NY 12833. (518)583-1440. Fax: (518)583-9741. Website: http://nativeauthors.com. Contact: Joseph Bruchac, editor/publisher. Annual competition. Award: $500 and publication. Judges: Greenfield Review Literary Center awards committee. Guidelines available for SASE. Deadline between January 1 and March 15 each year. For Native American/American Indian writers who have not yet published a book.

ROBERT L. FISH MEMORIAL AWARD, (II, IV), Mystery Writers of America, Inc., 17 E. 47th St., 6th Floor, New York NY 10017. Estab. 1984. Annual award "to encourage new writers in the mystery/detective/suspense short story—and, subsequently, larger work in the genre." Award: $500 and plaque. Judges: The MWA committee for best short story of the year in the mystery genre. Deadline November 30. Previously published submissions published the year prior to the award. Looking for "a story with a crime that is central to the plot that is well written and distinctive."

‡FJORD DISCOVERIES FIRST NOVEL AWARD, (I), Fjord Press, P.O. Box 16349, Seattle WA 98116-0349. (206)935-7376. Fax: (206)938-1991. E-mail: fjord@halcyon.com. Website: http://www.fjordpress.com/fjord. Editor: Steven T. Murray. "To cultivate first-time novelists." Annual competition for novels. Award: $1,000 and possible publication. Judges: editors of Fjord Press. Entry fee: $20. Inquiries by fax and e-mail OK. Deadline October 15. Previously unpublished. Looking for "high-quality literary mainstream novels only." Word length: 50,000-90,000 words. "Send #10 SASE for official application form and guidelines, which are also available on our website. Study our list to see the kind of novels we publish." Winner announced January 15 and notified by phone or mail. Send SASE for name of winner.

FLORIDA FIRST COAST WRITERS' FESTIVAL NOVEL, SHORT FICTION & POETRY AWARDS, Writers' Festival & Florida Community College at Jacksonville, FCCJ North Campus, 4501 Capper Rd., Jacksonville FL 32218-4499. (904)766-6559. Fax: (904)766-6654. E-mail: hdenson@fccj.ccl.us. Website: http://astro.fccj .cc.fl.us/WritersFestival/. Festival Coordinator/Contest Director: Howard Denson. Conference and contest "to create a healthy writing environment, honor writers of merit, select some stories for *The State Street Review* (a literary magazine) and find a novel manuscript to recommend to St. Martin's Press for 'serious consideration.' " Annual competition for short stories and novels. Competition receives 60 novel, 150-200 short fiction and 300-600 poetry submissions. Judges: university faculty and freelance and professional writers. Entry fees $30 (novels), $10 (short fiction), $5 (poetry). Guidelines available in the fall for SASE. Inquiries by fax and e-mail OK. Deadlines: October 1 all categories. Winners announced at the Florida First Coast Writers' Festival held in April. Unpublished submissions. Word length: none for novel; short fiction, 6,000 words.

‡THE FLORIDA REVIEW EDITORS' AWARDS, (I), *The Florida Review*, Department of English, UCF, Orlando FL 32816. (407)823-2038. Fax: (407)823-6582. Editor: Russell Kesler. Annual competition for short stories, essays, creative nonfiction, poetry. Awards: $500 for each category and publication in summer issue. Competition receives approximately 120 submissions. Judges: *The Florida Review* editorial staff. Entry fee $10 for each entry. Guidelines for SASE after January 1, 1998. Deadline: entries are accepted January through March only. Unpublished submissions. Word length: 7,500 words/prose; grouping of 3-5 poems up to 25 lines maximum. "All submissions must contain a SASE if the contest entrant wants to know the outcome of the Editors' Awards."

FLORIDA STATE WRITING COMPETITION, (I), Florida Freelance Writers Association, P.O. Box A, North Stratford NH 03590-0167. (603)922-8338. Fax: (603)922-8339. E-mail: danakcnw@moose.ncia.net. Executive Director: Dana K. Cassell. "To offer additional opportunities for writers to earn income and recognition from their writing efforts." Annual competition for short stories and novels. Award: varies from $75-125. Competition receives approximately 100 short stories; 50 novels. Judges: authors, editors and teachers. Entry fee from $5-20. Guidelines for SASE. Deadline: March 15. Unpublished submissions. Categories include literary, genre, short short and novel chapter. "Guidelines are revised each year and subject to change. New guidelines are available in fall of each year." Inquiries by fax and e-mail OK. Winners announced May 31. Winners notified by mail. List of winners available for SASE marked Winners.

‡THE FORWARD PRIZE PROGRAM, (IV), The Forward Foundation, Inc., 45 E. 33rd St., New York NY 10016-5336. (212)889-8200. Fax: (212)447-6406. Executive Director: Jonathan Rosen. Award "to promote and develop an understanding of Jewish life and culture. The Foundation will consider submissions from all persons without regard to race, religion or nationality that reflect and support this goal." Annual competition for short stories, novels and story collections. Award: 1997, $10,000, may vary each year. Competition receives 30 submissions. Judges: Independent panel of judges. Entry fee $25 each submission. "Each entry must be accompanied by a summary letter of not more than two pages providing background on the work being submitted and its author." Guidelines for SASE. Submissions published in previous calendar year. Writers may submit their own fiction or work may be nominated by publishers.

✤FOUNDATION FOR THE ADVANCEMENT OF CANADIAN LETTERS CANADIAN LETTERS AWARD, (II, IV), In conjunction with Periodical Marketers of Canada (PMC), South Tower, 175 Bloor St., E., Suite 1007, Toronto, Ontario M4W 3R8 Canada. (416)968-7218. Award Coordinator: Janette Hatcher. "To recognize a Canadian individual who has made an outstanding contribution to writing, publishing, teaching or literary administration." Award: a statuette and a $5,000 donation to the charitable literary organization or educational institution of the winner's choice. Recipient is selected from an independent panel of judges. There is no call for entries.

H.E. FRANCIS SHORT STORY AWARD, (I), Ruth Hindman Foundation, 2007 Gallatin St., Huntsville AL 35801. (205)539-3320. Fax: (205)533-6893. Chairperson: Patricia Sammon. Annual short story competition to honor H.E. Francis, retired professor of English at the University of Alabama in Huntsville. Award: $1,000. Competition receives approximately 500 submissions. Judges: distinguished writers. Entry fee. Guidelines for SASE. Deadline December 1. Unpublished submissions. Winners announced March. Winners notified by telephone. List of winners available for SASE.

＊MILES FRANKLIN LITERARY AWARD, (II, IV), Arts Management Pty. Ltd., Station House, Rawson Place, 790 George St., Sydney NSW 2000 Australia. Fax: 61-2-92117762. E-mail: vbraden@ozemail.com. Associate Director Projects & Artists: Hanne Larsen. "For the advancement, improvement and betterment of Australian literature." Annual award for novels. Award: AUS $27,000, to the author. Competition receives 80 submissions. Judges: Peter Rose, Dagmar Schmidmaier, Jill Kitson and Harry Heseltine. Guidelines for SASE. Inquiries by fax and e-mail OK. Deadline January 31. Previously published submissions. "The novel must have been published in the year prior to competition entry and must present Australian life in any of its phases." Winners announced May/June. Winners notified at award ceremony.

SOUERETTE DIEHL FRASER AWARD, (II, IV), The Texas Institute of Letters, TCU Box 298300, Fort Worth TX 76129. (817)921-7822. Secretary: Judy Alter. "To recognize the best literary translation of a book into English, the translation published between January 1 and December 30 of the year prior to the award's announcement in the spring." Annual competition for translations. Award: $1,000. Judges: committee of three. Guidelines for SASE. Deadline: January 2. "Award available to translators who were born in Texas or who have lived in the state at some time for two consecutive years."

FRENCH BREAD AWARDS, *Pacific Coast Journal*, P.O. Box 23868, San Jose CA 95153. Contact: Stillson Graham, editor. Award with the goal of "finding the best fiction and poetry out there." Annual competition for short stories and poetry. Award: $50 (1st prize), $25 (2nd prize). Competition receives approximately 50 submissions. Judges: Editorial staff of *Pacific Coast Journal*. Entry fee $6. Guidelines for SASE. Deadline December 1. Unpublished submissions. Length: 4,000 words. "Manuscripts will not be returned. Send SASE for winners' list. All entrants will receive issue in which first place winners are published."

‡FRIENDS OF AMERICAN WRITERS AWARDS, (III, IV), #6A, 3000 N. Sheridan Rd., Chicago IL 60657. (773)871-5143. Contact: President. "To encourage high standards and to promote literary ideals among American writers." Annual award for prose writing. Awards: $1,200 (1st prize) and $750 (2nd prize). Judges: a committee of 14 (adults), 9 (juvenile). Deadline: December 31. Manuscripts must have been published during current year. Limited to Midwestern authors who have previously published no more than 3 books; or to authors of books set in the Midwest and have not published more than 3 books previously. Two copies of the book are to be submitted to awards chairman by the publisher of the book. Young Peoples' books awards judged by committee of 9. Awards: $700 (1st prize); $400 (2nd prize). Same limitations. Competition receives approximately 80 submissions per category. Guidelines available for SASE after June. Deadline: December 31. Winners announced February. Winners notified by phone or mail. Lost of winners available April for SASE.

‡GEORGETOWN REVIEW SHORT STORY AND POETRY CONTEST, (I), Georgetown Review, P.O. Box 6309 SS, Hattiesburg MS 39406. (601)583-6940. E-mail: jsfulmer@whale.st.usm.edu. Website: http://www.mindspring.com/~batcat/grwww/. Contact: John Fulmer, editor. "To reward excellent fiction." Annual competition for short stories. Award: $1000 to the winning story. Runner-up stories receive publication and authors receive free subscription. Competition receives approximately 450 submissions. Judges: *GR* editors. Entry fee $10/story. Guidelines for SASE after October 15. Deadline October 1. Unpublished submissions. Word length: 6,500 words. "Must include SASE for return of work." Winners announced January. Winners notified in magazine ad. List of winners available for SASE.

GLIMMER TRAIN'S FALL SHORT-STORY AWARD FOR NEW WRITERS, (I), Glimmer Train Press, Inc., 710 SW Madison St., Suite 504, Portland OR 97205-2900. (503)221-0836. Fax: (503)221-0837. Contest Director: Linda Burmeister Davies. Contest offered for any writer whose fiction hasn't appeared in a nationally-distributed publication with a circulation over 5,000. "Send original, unpublished short (1,200-8,000 words) story with $12 reading fee for each story entered. Guidelines available for SASE. Inquiries by fax OK. Must be postmarked between August 1 and September 30. Title page must include name, address, phone and Short Story Award for New Writers must be written on outside of envelope. No need for SASE as materials will not be returned. Notification on January 2. Winner receives $1,200 and publication in *Glimmer Train Stories*. First/second runners-up receive $500/$300, respectively, and consideration for publication. All applicants receive a copy of the issue in which winning entry is published and runners-up announced."

‡GLIMMER TRAIN'S SPRING SHORT-STORY AWARD FOR NEW WRITERS, (I), Glimmer Train Press, Inc., 710 SW Madison St., Suite 504, Portland OR 97205-2900. (503)221-0836. Fax: (503)221-0837. Contest Director: Linda Burmeister Davies. Contest offered for any writer whose fiction hasn't appeared in a nationally-distributed publication with a circulation over 5,000. "Send original, unpublished short (1,200-8,000 words) story with $12 reading fee for each story entered. Guidelines available for SASE. Inquiries by fax OK. Must be postmarked between February 1 and March 31. Title page must include name, address, phone and Short Story Award for New Writers must be written on outside of envelope. No need for SASE as materials will not be returned. Notification on July 1. Winner receives $1,200 and publication in *Glimmer Train Stories*. First/second runners-up receive $500/$300, respectively, and consideration for publication. All applicants receive a copy of the issue in which winning entry is published and runners-up announced."

‡✦GOD USES INK CHRISTIAN WRITERS' CONTEST, (IV), *Faith Today*, M.I.P. Box 3745, Markham, ONT L3R 0Y4 Canada. (905)479-5885. Fax (905)479-4742. E-mail: ft@efc-canada.com. Website: http://www.efc-canada.com. Award "to encourage Canadian Christian writers in the pursuit of excellence in the craft of print communication." Annual competition for short stories and novels. Awards: from $100-$150. Entry fee $20/book, $1/article. Maximum 3 entries/person. Guidelines for SASE/IRC. Inquiries by fax or e-mail OK. Published submissions. Published entries must have appeared in print between January 1, 1997 and December 31, 1997. Canadian Christian writers only. Writers may submit their own fiction or publisher may nominate the writer's work. "Read entry guidelines and form carefully. Winners announced June 18-20, 1998 (at our writers' conference in Guelph)." Winners notified after June 20 by mail. List of winners available after June 20.

GREAT LAKES COLLEGES ASSOCIATION NEW WRITERS AWARD, Great Lakes Colleges Association, 2929 Plymouth Rd., Suite 207, Ann Arbor MI 48105-3206. (215)735-7300. Fax: (215)735-7373. E-mail: clark@philactr.edu. Director of New Writers Award: Mark Andrew Clark. Annual award. Winners are invited to tour the GLCA colleges. An honorarium of at least $300 will be guaranteed the author by each of the GLCA colleges they visit. Receives 30-40 entries in each category annually. Judges: Professors from member colleges. No entry fee. Guidelines available after August 1. Inquiries by fax and e-mail OK. Deadline February 28. Unpublished submissions. First publication in fiction or poetry. Writer must be nominated by publisher. Four

THE MAPLE LEAF symbol before a listing indicates a Canadian publisher, magazine, conference or contest.

INSIDER REPORT

Lorian Hemingway: "Write first for yourself"

"I didn't choose to write because my name was Hemingway," says Lorian Hemingway. "I wanted to be a doctor. I was interested in chemistry, physics, psychology, the internal working of the body, but particularly hands-on medicine. There's part of me that's really scientific-minded. But I was always drawn back, again and again and again, to expression through the written word." Perhaps that earlier interest in the physicality of life is what attracts Hemingway, as a writer of fiction and poetry, and director of the Lorian Hemingway Short Story Contest, to work that is gutsy, strong, with heart and body, work that seems almost alive.

Lorian Hemingway

Photo by Tom Netting

The granddaughter of Ernest Hemingway, Lorian says she didn't spend time with her grandfather and wasn't aware of his literary influence when, as a child, she began writing poems and stories, that were published in school magazines and small literary journals. "I was published in spite of the name, and maybe at times to spite the name." At times she wrote under different names, to prove to herself she was being taken on her own merits. "It was something I needed to do for myself, just to eliminate the question of whether it helped or hurt. It wasn't of great significance."

In addition to poetry and short stories, she wrote several pieces for the University of Florida Press and published *Walking into the River: A Novel* (Simon & Schuster), in 1992. The fall of 1997 saw the publication of *Walk on Water*, which she says is being called a memoir, although she prefers to describe it as a series of stories. "It's a raw sort of book, not tame, that takes on a lot of my life, which has not been, by any means, your normal life." Hemingway's editor sums up the essential lesson of the book as understanding that the family you end up with in life is the family that you choose or that chooses you, not necessarily the one you are born into.

In addition to her own writing, Hemingway has served for the past 17 years as director of the Hemingway Days Festival Short Story Contest. Due to difficulties affecting the Festival, last year the contest was renamed the Lorian Hemingway Short Story Contest. "We had a scant 70 entries the first year, and I kept doing it. I was very honored and interested. There are so many fine writers out there that don't have the opportunity to be recognized. I do it for the sheer gratification of being able to recognize them. I'm a very strong champion of the talent of others. I'm delighted to be on the ground floor, to find them. The contest is very important to me, a part of my life."

Currently the contest averages 900-1,000 entries. "In April we start receiving stories, and I read through July. I read them all—every story. You hit a point after reading so many that your brain cannot discern. So I often wind up reading a lot of them out loud." Despite the large number of entries, Hemingway says a natural order does arise. "After a

INSIDER REPORT, *Hemingway*

couple of months, you can look back and recall the stories that hit you. They stand out for particular reasons. Our winner this year, "The Blueprint," was the first thing the writer, Lee Deigaard, had sent out. [See the Insider Report with Deigaard also in this section.] That boggles my mind. The strength, the intelligence, the craft and talent, the surety."

In her reading, both for the contest and her own pleasure, Hemingway sees a disturbing trend in fiction. "There is some fine, gutsy writing in America today, but the stuff most publicly available is so sterile at times. And what do writers have to go by [in their writing] but what is being published? I'm also concerned about the teaching of writing and fiction. I've been asked how to get to the heart of what it is that allows you to write effectively. And it's none of the tricks that are so often offered. They can help structure the work but can't compensate for the absence of any viscera in the body of the story."

The challenge for fiction writers today, Hemingway says, is to keep to the integrity of their writing. "At its core, fiction is retelling the human experience. There aren't as many people out there reading. It's daunting, the number of books in bookstores and the type of writing that sells. So many think, 'I'll never make it, no one reads this sort of writing.' It is of the highest importance to keep writing and maintain the integrity of that writing. The appreciation for the writer and for writing itself as a part of the culture seems to be dying. There are a lot of quick fixes out there—'how-to,' 'you can be this,' 'you can be that'—instead of an interior experience that was the reward at the end of the day before television and before computers. A good book of fiction was the entertainment that transported you, that linked you with that commonality of the human experience."

Hemingway does see some cautiously encouraging signs in the world of published fiction. "There is an underground stirring. New fiction imprints are being established. I'd like to predict that it's going to swing back around and there will be a catastrophic awakening in the American conscious. Even if the ground can just be held, with no more erosion, that would be good. But from the sheer magnitude of writing—the volume of books that are out there—getting published is definitely becoming harder. And I won't be the one that goes for the market. I believe that you write first for yourself."

In pursuing publication. Hemingway submitted much of her work to magazines and contests, and feels that is still a good way for a new writer to start. "Study the markets, look at what different magazines accept. Enter stories in contests because there is often a good amount of recognition that goes with winning. Get your material out there."

After writing for so many years, Hemingway has encountered her share of rejection. "I am not one who gives up. I got rejection after rejection, and I didn't quit. I guess that's the thing I try to set across to writers who do have that special something: Don't give up on it." With each rejection, she felt she learned more. "I'm still learning. I hope I never quit. I have this streak of rebellion in me and an 'I'll show you' attitude a continent wide. It can be a real handicap, but it has also been a real asset."

What has worked for her, and what she tries to impart to other writers, is the unflinching commitment she feels to her writing. "What we're talking about is keeping it a personal endeavor that translates to others. It's the returning again and again to what seems to be the undo-able that builds up a degree of strength in a writer. Some of my best days are when I sit down and think, 'Why do you do this?' and I can't possibly write anything of any worth or consequence. Those have ended up being some of my best days. Perhaps when the wall seems the most fortified, what is beyond is probably the greater treasure."

—*Kirsten Holm*

copies of the book should be sent to: Mark Andrew Clark, Director, New Writers Award, GLCA Philadelphia Center, North American Bldg., 121 South Broad St., Seventh Floor, Philadelphia PA 19107. Winners announced in May. Letters go to publishers who have submitted.

GREAT PLAINS STORYTELLING & POETRY READING CONTEST, (I,II), P.O. Box 438, Walnut IA 51577. (712)784-3001. Director: Robert Everhart. Estab. 1976. Annual award "to provide an outlet for writers to present not only their works but also to provide a large audience for their presentation *live* by the writer. Attendance at the event, which takes place annually in Avoca, Iowa, is *required*." Award: 1st prize $75; 2nd prize $50; 3rd prize $25; 4th prize $15; and 5th prize $10. Entry fee: $5. Entry forms available at contest only. Deadline is day of contest, which takes place over Labor Day Weekend. Previously published or unpublished submissions.

GREEN RIVER WRITERS CONTEST, (I, II), Green River Writer, 11906 Locust Rd., Middletown KY 40243-1413. (502)245-4902. Website: http://www.pol.com.greenriver. Contact: Linda Frisa. Annual competition for short stories and novels. Award: for short stories up to 2,000 words, $150; 2,000-3,000 words $150, first chapter of novel, $50. Competition receives 250 submissions. Judges are appointed by sponsors. Entry fee $5 each, $25 total. Guidelines available after March 1 for SASE. Deadline October 31. Unpublished submissions. Word length: up to 3,000 words, depends on category. Winners announced in January. Winners notified by mail. List of winners available January for SASE.

THE GREENSBORO REVIEW LITERARY AWARDS, (I), Dept. of English, UNC-Greensboro, Greensboro NC 27412-5001. (910)334-5459. E-mail: clarkj@fagan.uncg.edu. Contact: Jim Clark, editor. Annual award. Award: $250. Send SASE for contest rules. Deadline September 15. Unpublished submissions. "All manuscripts meeting literary award guidelines will be considered for cash award as well as for publication in *The Greensboro Review.*" Competition receives 1,000 submissions. Winners notified by mail in December.

‡THE GSU REVIEW ANNUAL WRITING CONTEST, GSU Review, Georgia State University, Campus Box 1894, Atlanta GA 30303. (404)651-4804. E-mail: wahoodori@earthlink.net. Contact: Cindy Cunningham, editor. Prize awarded for best poem and for best short story. "This contest widens our scope and allows us to make numerous contacts." Annual competition for short stories. Award: $1,000. Competition receives 200-300 submissions per category. Judge: noted writer. Entry fee $10 for each story submitted. Guidelines available for SASE. Deadline January 15. Previously unpublished submissions. "Fiction should be double spaced. Include SASE for return of manuscript. All contributors receive our spring issue of the journal."

HACKNEY LITERARY AWARDS, (I), Box 549003, Birmingham Southern College, Birmingham AL 35254. (205)226-4921. Fax: (205)226-4931. E-mail: bhopkins@bsc.edu. Director of Special Events: Martha Andrews. Annual award for previously unpublished short stories, poetry and novels. Award: $2,000 (novel); $2,000 (poetry and short stories; 6 prizes). Competition receives approx. 700 submissions. Entry fee: $25 novel; $10 poetry and short story. Rules/entry form for SASE. Inquiries by fax and e-mail OK. Novel submissions must be postmarked on or before September 30. Short stories and poetry submissions must be postmarked on or before December 31. Winners announced at Writing Today Writers' Conference March 21. List of winners available for SASE.

‡LORIAN HEMINGWAY SHORT STORY COMPETITION, (I), P.O. Box 993, Key West FL 33041. (305)294-0320. Fax: (305)292-3653. E-mail: calico2419@aol.com. Co-directors: Carol Shaughnessy and Lorian Hemingway. Award to "encourage literary excellence and the efforts of writers who have not yet had major-market success." Annual competition for short stories. Awards: $1,000 first prize and publication; up to 10 honorable mentions. Judges: A panel of writers, editors and literary scholars selected by novelist Lorian Hemingway. Entry fee $10 for each story postmarked by June 1, 1998; $15 for each story postmarked between June 1 and June 15, 1998. Guidelines for SASE after February 1. Deadline June 1, 1998 and June 15, 1998. Unpublished submissions. "Open to all writers whose fiction has not appeared in a nationally distributed publication with a circulation of 5,000 or more." Word length: 3,000 words maximum. Winners announced before August 1. Winners notified by phone. "All entrants will receive a letter from Lorian Hemmingway and a list of winners by October 1."

HIGHLIGHTS FOR CHILDREN, (I, IV), 803 Church St., Honesdale PA 18431. Editor: Kent L. Brown, Jr. "To honor quality stories (previously unpublished) for young readers." Three $1,000 awards. Stories: up to 500 words for beginning readers (to age 8) and 900 words for more advanced readers (ages 9 to 12). No minimum word length. No entry form necessary. To be submitted between January 1 and February 28 to "Fiction Contest" at address above. "No violence, crime or derogatory humor." Nonwinning entries returned in June if SASE is included with ms. Send SASE for information.

THE ALFRED HODDER FELLOWSHIP, (II), The Council of the Humanities, Princeton University, 122 E. Pyne, Princeton NJ 08544. Program Manager: Marjorie Asbury. "This fellowship is awarded for the pursuit of independent work in the humanities. The recipient is usually a writer or scholar in the early stages of his or her career, a person 'with more than ordinary learning' and with 'much more than ordinary intellectual and literary gifts.' " Traditionally, the Hodder Fellow has been a humanist outside of academia. Candidates for the Ph.D. are not eligible. Award: $44,000. The Hodder Fellow spends an academic year in residence at Princeton working independently. Competition receives 300 submissions. Judges: Princeton Committee on Humanistic Studies. Deadline November 15. Applicants must submit a résumé, a sample of previous work (10 page maximum, not returnable), and a project proposal of 2 to 3 pages. Letters of recommendation are not required.

THEODORE CHRISTIAN HOEPFNER AWARD, (I), *Southern Humanities Review*, 9088 Haley Center, Auburn University AL 36849. Contact: Dan R. Latimer or Virginia M. Kouidis, co-editors. Annual. "To award the authors of the best essay, the best short story and the best poem published in *SHR* each year." Award: $100 for the best short story. Judges: Editorial staff. Only published work in the current volume (4 issues) will be judged.

HONOLULU MAGAZINE/BORDERS BOOKS & MUSIC FICTION CONTEST, (I, IV), *Honolulu* Magazine, 36 Merchant St., Honolulu HI 96813. (808)524-7400. Contact: John Heckathorn, editor. "We do not accept fiction except during our annual contest, at which time we welcome it." Annual award for short stories. Award: $1,000 and publication in the April issue of *Honolulu* Magazine. Competition receives approximately 400 submissions. Judges: Panel of well-known Hawaii-based writers. Rules for SASE. Deadline early December. "Stories must have a Hawaii theme, setting and/or characters. Author should enclose name and address in separate small envelope. Do not put name on story."

L. RON HUBBARD'S WRITERS OF THE FUTURE CONTEST, (I, IV), P.O. Box 1630N, Los Angeles CA 90078. Website: http://www.authorservicesinc.com/wof_home.htm. Contest Administrator: Edith Shields. Estab. 1984. Quarterly. "Foremost contest for new writers of science fiction, fantasy and horror, short stories and novelettes. Awards $2,250 in quarterly prizes, annual $4,000 Grand Prize, five-day Writer's Workshop with major authors, publication in leading international anthology. Outstanding professional judges panel. No entry fee. Entrants retain all rights. For explicit instructions on how to enter send SASE to the above address." Winners announced quarterly. Winners notified by phone and mail.

‡HYPERTEXT PRIZE, (I), *Salt Hill Journal*, English Dept., Syracuse University, Syracuse NY 13244. Website: http://www.hl.syr.edu/cap. Editor: Peter S. Fendrick. Award to "publish the best literary hypertext now being produced." Annual competition for hypertext fiction. Awards: First prize $500 and publication; Second prize $100 and publication. Competition receives 400 submissions. Judge: Final judging by nationally known writer. Entry fee $10 per hypertext entry. Guidelines for SASE. Deadline January 31. Unpublished submissions.

‡IBWA POETRY & SHORT STORY CONTESTS, (IV), International Black Writers & Artists, P.O. Box 43576, Los Angeles CA 90043-0576. (213)964-3721. E-mail: lahughes48@aol.com. Executive Director: L.A. Hughes. Award "to identify and nurture emerging talent, encourage proliferation of cultural literature of the diaspora and create a pool from which to draw projects to be published." Biannual competition for short stories. Competition receives 150 submissions. Judges: a panel. Entry fee $25/story up to 25 pages. Guidelines available in January for SASE. Deadline May 1. Unpublished submissions. "Stories should be well-crafted and concern characters from the diaspora of black peoples." Winners notified June 10. List of winners available for SASE.

‡IDAHO COMMISSION ON THE ARTS LITERATURE FELLOWSHIPS AND WRITER-IN-RESIDENCE AWARD, (IV), Box 83720, Boise ID 83720-0008. (208)334-2119. Fax: (218)334-2488. Contact: Literature Director. Competition to recognize excellence in writing. Held every third year. Award for fiction, creative nonfiction and poetry. Award: $3,500 fellowship; $8,000 writer-in-residence. Competition receives 70-80 entries. Judges: a nationally recognized writer from outside Idaho. Guidelines available for SASE. Deadline January 1998. Entry should have been written in the last 5 years. Award available only to Idaho writers. Word length: 10-20 pages double-spaced. "Please contact the Idaho Commission on the Arts for details."

ILLINOIS ARTS COUNCIL ARTISTS FELLOWSHIPS, (I, IV), Illinois Arts Council, #10-500, James R. Thompson Center, 100 W. Randolph, Chicago IL 60601. (312)814-4990. Fax: (312)814-1471. E-mail: ilarts@arts wire.org. Contact: Richard Gage. Award "to enable Illinois artists of exceptional talent to pursue their artistic goals." Biannual for poetry and prose completed within four years prior to the deadline. Awards: $500, $5,000 and $10,000. Competition receives approximately 250 prose submissions and 140 poetry submissions. Judges: non-Illinois writers/editors of exceptional talent. Guidelines available for SASE. Inquiries by fax and e-mail OK. Deadline September 1 in odd years (next deadline September 1, 1997). Applicants must have been Illinois residents for at least 1 year prior to deadline and cannot be degree-seeking students. Prose applicants limited to 30 pages; poetry limited to 15 pages. Winners announced in December. Winners notified by letter.

‡INDIVIDUAL ARTIST FELLOWSHIP, Nebraska Arts Council, 3838 Davenport, Omaha NE 68131-2329. (402)421-3627. Program Manager: Suzanne Wise. Award to "recognize outstanding achievement by Nebraska writers." Competition every third year for short stories and novels. Award: $5,000 Distinguished Achievement; $1,000-2,000 Merit Awards. Competition receives 70-80 submissions per category. Judges: panel of 3. Deadline

INSIDER REPORT

Time to start getting those stories out there

The winner of the 1997 Lorian Hemingway Short Story Competition almost didn't enter. Lee Deigaard admits she's been bad about submitting her stories. At her farm in Wildwood, Georgia—three miles from the Tennessee border—there is grass to cut and a barn to build. There's a novel, *The Aerialist*, in progress. And for Deigaard, also a sculptor, there's clay to form and wood to carve. But being busy is just part of the problem.

Lee Deigaard

"I have this general commercial bafflement," says the writer of *The Blueprint*, the story that stood out from 625 others to win the respected literary contest. "Sending out stories shouldn't be that complicated, but to me it's daunting. I get caught up in details like 'Do I fold it up? Do I staple it? Do I use a paperclip?' " A writer friend who was already published helped Deigaard write a cover letter and nagged her periodically to submit stories. "I finally said, 'OK. Alright. I'll do it.' "

It's hard to believe the writer of *The Blueprint* could have hesitated. She had been, after all, a Michener Fellow at the University of Texas at Austin, where she earned a Master's in 1996. Writing nearly every day for two years during that fellowship, she learned to do magical things with words. The prose in *The Blueprint* is strong, lyrical and tightly compressed.

"I'm only interested in my own writing if I can make it visually dense—otherwise I get very disappointed in myself," says Deigaard, who admits her perfectionism keeps her from sending out stories. Even after *The Blueprint* won the Hemingway competition, parts of the story still stand out to Deigaard like "big sloppy stitches." What parts are those? Deigaard hesitates, then laughs. "Well, without shooting myself in the foot, I'll just say I can see places where the language has become secondary to having to get somewhere."

But Deigaard is trying hard to live with the "sloppy stitches." A large part of becoming published is realizing your work can never be perfect, she says. "There comes a time when you can do no more. There's a lot to be said for simply getting yourself to a point where you're happy with what you've done. The longer you wait [to send out your work] the harder it gets."

Like many literary writers, Deigaard also struggles with the idea of writing for herself vis-a-vis writing for an audience. "I sometimes worry about the selfish aspects of being a writer. You try to convince yourself that being read by a broader group of people doesn't matter, but it does." And while she doesn't want to be tainted by the market, she doesn't respect the "I express myself perfectly to myself" stance of some literary writers. "I'm starting to realize it's really nice to be read and understood. I know from being a reader that it's worthwhile even if one person who needs your writing finds it." Recalling the connection she feels when reading the works of Eudora Welty and Wallace Stevens, Deigaard says, "It absolutely erases loneliness."

Through the Hemingway competition, Deigaard's work was read, understood and appreciated. *The Blueprint* "was truly unlike anything I have read and it was virtually flawless," says Lorian Hemingway, founder of the competition. "I felt I had to bring everything in me to the reading of it, because it was that strong." (See the Insider Report with Lorian Hemingway also in this section.)

The Blueprint was written in a 12-hour period Deigaard describes as one of the most enjoyable continuous writing experiences she has ever had. "As I was working on it, I started asking myself how memory works and what the impetus to tell a story has to do with the workings of memory. For storage, memories compress—the whole essence of a memory can be contained in one little instant. Then, when they're keyed by something, memories expand. The catalyst is your imagination, which transforms memories into something much larger."

Ironically, *The Blueprint* was born during a bout with writer's block, a period when Deigaard confronted the blank page and came up with nothing. "I had a lot of abstract ideas I wanted to put in the story—which made it very hard to write." Out of frustration, she began writing fragments because "writing in a straight line would have required a full sentence from me," she laughs. "It was almost like I knew the kind of still life I would have drawn of it but had no real idea about how to make it linear—how to put it into language. I'd write words, or parts of sentences and twist them a few degrees." To help her clarify her images, Deigaard spent a lot of time making doodles in the margins until the story resembled "somebody's grocery list gone mad."

To outsmart her writer's block, Deigaard switched off between her computer and writing in longhand. "Anytime I felt the momentum sag at all, I switched mediums. If I couldn't type any more, I'd print it out on hard copy and then edit it and write past it." She likens the experience to "one of those ride-and-tie races with two runners and one horse"— where one person rides the horse to a certain point, dismounts, ties it and starts running and the second person runs to the horse, unties it and rides until he passes the first. "I'd type past where I was in longhand, write past where I was typing. It was a very fun story to write once I got past the writer's block. It was like a dam breaking."

Deigaard doubts she'll ever be "one of those up-at-six, write-'til-two writers. My method seems to be more like a 15-hour spurt and then 3 days of nothing." She's not a discoursive writer. "I don't understand writers who just throw the work out there— regurgitate it. I envy them. But if you've got any other kinds of demands on the language— what could be called poetic concerns—the discoursive method does you no good whatsoever." When writing is more poetic, the rhythm of each sentence determines what follows it, and writers like Deigaard often finds themselves spinning off into entirely separate directions than they had planned.

Deigaard tends to cut her stories as she writes them. "I cut almost more than I produce. I'm not advocating this in the least as any mentally healthy way of working; it's just the only way I can figure it out." But writing a novel, she's learning, is another story. "I'm just figuring out that a big difference between writing stories and writing a novel is that you have to let a novel get to this unwieldly size before you begin cutting too much." Character development is much richer in the novel. "The longer I spend time with the characters, the more I see them as separate from myself." She's often surprised at what comes out of their mouths—how easily one of them puts into words a thought their author

---

INSIDER REPORT, *continued*

feels incapable of expressing.

Deigaard finds herself paying more attention to method and process lately, even to the little rituals writers employ to get them going. "There are processes and tools that free you up and make what you do a pleasure—like sharpening your pencils or writing with your favorite pen. There's a reason people have these rituals. It's important to respect them and enjoy them rather than think of them as some kind of mental crutch—to say, 'This is my method and I will respect this ritual.' "

Sculpture continues to be important to Deigaard. "Writing and the visual artwork are sort of inseparable to me. They're opposite extremes of a continuum—one is so concrete, where you're using your body to push against a resistance or a form, and the other is between your ears, in your brain. I like having the chance to swing between them."

The writing, the sculpture and even the farm work feed on one another, says Deigaard. It's not unusual for her to put down her chisel and scribble bits of a story that come to her mind as she carves. "That's been the real strength of it. Sculpture is such a different form of thought you can actually have part of your mind free for forming sentences." The farm chores are a healthy contrast from sitting in front of a computer screen, which she finds draining.

Winning the Lorian Hemingway prize hasn't changed Deigaard's life very much. (Although after results of the competition were announced in the Chattanooga newspaper, the man who shovels the feed in the feed store stopped his work to congratulate her.) The $1,000 prize was welcome (she used part of it to pay for horseshoes). But the biggest revelation, says Deigaard, is how meaningful it feels to have people read and respond to her writing. It's enough to conquer her anxiety about staples and paper clips—enough to make her take a deep breath and tell herself: "OK—time to start thinking about getting those stories out there."

—Mary Cox

November 15, 2000. Published or previously unpublished submissions. Nebraska residents only. Word length: 50 pages.

‡**INDIVIDUAL ARTIST FELLOWSHIP PROGRAM**, Florida Department of State, Division of Cultural Affairs, The Capitol, Tallahassee FL 32399-0250. (904)487-2980. Arts Consultant: Valerie Ohlsson. Award to "reward work of exceptional merit" Annual competition for short stories and novels. Award: $5,000. Judges: A peer review panel. Guidelines available. Deadline January. Published or previously unpublished submissions. Residents of Florida only; in fiction, short story, poetry and children's literature. Word length: up to 30 pages.

‡**INDIVIDUAL ARTIST FELLOWSHIPS**, Maine Arts Commission, 25 State Horse Station, Augusta ME 04333. (207)287-2724. Fax: (207)287-2335. E-mail: kathy.jones@state.me.us. Associate for Contemporary Arts: Kathy Ann Jones. Unrestricted funds ($3,000) awarded for artistic excellence. Biannual competition for short stories, novels and poetry. Award: $3,000. Competition receives 50 submissions per category. Judges: a jury of experts is selected each time. Guidelines available. Deadline September 1. Published or previously unpublished submissions. Artists must be Maine residents. Word length: fiction or creative nonfiction (maximum 20 pages of prose).

‡**INTERNATIONAL IMITATION HEMINGWAY COMPETITION**, PEN Center USA West, 672 S. Lafayette Park Pl. #44, Los Angeles CA 90057. (213)365-8500. Fax: (213)365-9616. E-mail: rit2writ@ix.netcom.com. Administrative Coordinator: Rachel Hall. Write one page of Imitation Hemingway. It must mention Harry's Bar nicely. Must sound like Hemingway, read like Hemingway, and must be funny. Annual competition. Award: Dinner for 2 at Harry's Bar in Florence. Competition receives 1,000 submissions. Guidelines available for SASE. Deadline March 1. Previously unpublished submissions. Word length: one page.

INTERNATIONAL JANUSZ KORCZAK LITERARY COMPETITION, (II, IV), Braun Center for Holocaust Studies Anti-Defamation League, 823 United Nations Plaza, New York NY 10017. (212)885-7884. Fax: (212)949-6930. Contact: Carol Lister. Biennial award for published novels, novellas, translations, short story collections. "Books for or about children which best reflect the humanitarianism and leadership of Janusz Korczak, a Jewish and Polish physician, educator and author." Inquire for details and deadline. Inquiries by fax OK. List of winners available Spring.

INTERNATIONAL READING ASSOCIATION CHILDREN'S BOOK AWARDS, (II), Sponsored by IRA, P.O. Box 8139, 800 Barksdale Rd., Newark DE 19714-8139. (302)731-1600. Annual awards given for a first or second book in three categories (younger readers: ages 4-10; older readers: ages 10-16 and up; informational book ages 4-16 and up) to authors who show unusual promise in the children's book field. Books from any country and in any language copyrighted during the previous calendar year will be considered. Entries in a language other than English must include a one-page abstract in English and a translation into English of one chapter or similar selection that in the submitter's estimation is representative of the book. The awards each carry a US $500 stipend. Entries must be received by December 1. To submit a book for consideration by the selection committee, send 10 copies to Judith A. Maegher, School of Education, University of Connecticut, 249 Glenbrook Rd., Storrs CT 06268-2064, USA.

‡**INTERNATIONAL WRITERS CONTEST, (I)**, Foster City Arts and Culture Committee, 650 Shell Blvd., Foster City CA 94404. (415)345-5731. Contact: Contest chairman. Annual. "To foster and encourage aspiring writers." Unpublished submissions. Award: 1st prize in each of 4 categories $250, Honorable Mention $125. The 4 categories are: Best Fiction, Best Humor, Best Story for Children, Best Poem. Deadline November 30. Winners announced January. English language entries only. Entry fee $10 to City of Foster City. Contest rules for SASE.

IOWA SCHOOL OF LETTERS AWARD FOR SHORT FICTION, THE JOHN SIMMONS SHORT FICTION AWARD, (I), Iowa Writers' Workshop, 436 English-Philosophy Building, The University of Iowa, Iowa City IA 52242. Annual awards for short story collections. To encourage writers of short fiction. Award: publication of winning collections by University of Iowa Press the following fall. Entries must be at least 150 pages, typewritten, and submitted between August 1 and September 30. Stamped, self-addressed return packaging must accompany manuscript. Rules for SASE. Iowa Writer's Workshop does initial screening of entries; finalists (about 6) sent to outside judge for final selection. "A different well-known writer is chosen each year as judge. Any writer who has not previously published a volume of prose fiction is eligible to enter the competition for these prizes. Revised manuscripts which have been previously entered may be resubmitted."

‡*THE IRISH TIMES LITERATURE PRIZES**, The Irish Times Limited, 10-16 D'Olier St., Dublin 2 Ireland. (01)6792022. Fax: (01)6709383. E-mail: gcavaraph@irish-times.ie. Administrator: Gerald Cavaraph. Co-ordinator: Eleanor Walsh. Biannual competition for novels and story collections. Guidelines available. Deadline between August 1, 1997 and July 31, 1999. Previously published submissions between August 1, 1995-July 31, 1997. Author must have been born in Ireland. Writer must be nominated by screening panel.

JOSEPH HENRY JACKSON AWARD, (I, IV), Intersection for the Arts/The San Francisco Foundation, 446 Valencia St., San Francisco CA 94103. (415)626-2787. Fax: (415)626-1636. E-mail: intrsect@thecity.sfsu.edu. Website: http://ecstatic.com/orgs/intersection. Literary Program Director: Charles Wilmoth. Award "to encourage young, unpublished writers." Annual award for short stories, novels and story collections. Award: $2,000. Competition receives approximately 100 submissions. Entry form and rules available for SASE. Inquiries by fax OK. Deadline January 31. Unpublished submissions only. Applicant must be resident of northern California or Nevada for 3 consecutive years immediately prior to the deadline date. Age of applicant must be 20 through 35. Work cannot exceed 100 double-spaced, typed pages. Winners announced June 15. Winners notified by mail. "Winners will be announced in letter mailed to all applicants."

JAMES FELLOWSHIP FOR THE NOVEL IN PROGRESS, (I), The Heekin Group Foundation, P.O. Box 1534, Sisters OR 97759. Phone/fax: (541)548-4147. E-mail: hgfg1@aol.com. Fiction Director: Sarah Heekin Redfield. Award to "support unpublished writers in their writing projects." Two annual awards for novels in progress. Awards: $3,000. Receives approximately 500 applications. Judges: Invitation of publisher: past judges, Graywolf Press, SOHO Press, Dalkey Archive Press, The Ecco Press, Milkweed Editions. Upcoming judge: Mercury House. Application fee $25. Guidelines for SASE. Deadline December 1. Unpublished submissions. Word length: Submit first 50-75 pages only.

JAPAN FOUNDATION ARTISTS FELLOWSHIP PROGRAM, (IV), 152 W. 57th St., 39th Floor, New York NY 10019. (212)489-0299. Fax: (212)489-0409. E-mail: chris.watanabe@jfny.org. Website: http://www.jfnx.org. Program Assistant: Chris Watanabe. "This program provides artists and specialists in the arts with the opportunity to pursue creative projects in Japan and to meet and consult with their Japanese counterparts." Annual competition. Several artists fellowships from two to six months' duration during the 1997 Japanese fiscal year (April 1-March 31) are available to artists, such as writers, musicians, painters, sculptors, stage artists, movie directors, etc.; and specialists in the arts, such as scenario writers, curators, etc. Benefits include transportation to and from Japan; settling-in, research, activities and other allowances and a monthly stipend. See brochure for more details. Competition receives approximately 30-40 submissions. Judges: Foundation staff in Japan. Guidelines available after August. Inquiries by fax and e-mail OK. Deadline December 1. "Work should be related to Japan. Applicants must be accredited artists or specialists. Affiliation with a Japanese artist or institution is required. Three letters of reference, including one from the Japanese affiliate must accompany all applications. Winners announced March 1998. Winners notified by mail. List of winners available by phone.

JAPANOPHILE SHORT STORY CONTEST, (I, II, IV), *Japanophile*, P.O. Box 223, Okemos MI 48805-0223. (517)669-2109. E-mail: japanlove@aol.com. Website: http://www.voyager.net/Japanophile. Editor: Earl R. Snodgrass. Estab. 1974. Annual award "to encourage quality writing on Japan-America understanding." Award: $100 plus possible publication. Competition receives 200 submissions. Entry fee: $5. Send $4 for sample copy of magazine. Contest rules for SASE. Inquiries by e-mail OK. Deadline December 31. Prefers unpublished submissions. Stories should involve Japanese and non-Japanese characters. Winners notified by mail March.

‡CHARLES JOHNSON AWARD FOR FICTION AND POETRY, (IV), Southern Illinois University at Carbondale, Department of English 4503, Carbondale IL 62901-4503. (618)453-5321. E-mail: cruz@siu.edu. Associate Professor of English: Ricardo Cortez Cruz. Award to "encourage diversity and excellence in creative writing among U.S. college students." Annual competition for short stories. Award: $500 and a signed book. Competition receives 100 submissions. Judges: prominent, nationally known authors/writers. No entry fee. Guidelines for SASE. Deadline January 28, 1998 (a postmark deadline). Unpublished submissions. "Entrants must be enrolled full- or part-time in a U.S. college or university. Only ethnic and racial minority students and students whose work freshly explores the experience/identity of a minority or marginalized culture are considered. 'Ethnic' means of or relating to a racial, national, or cultural group, and includes African American, Native American, Hispanic, Asian, Native Alaskan, Pacific Islander, gay and lesbian, and those that define themselves as 'Other.' " Word length: 20 pages, double-spaced, typed. The Charles Johnson Award has an informational website at http://www.siu.edu/~johnson.

JESSE JONES AWARD FOR FICTION (BOOK), (II, IV), The Texas Institute of Letters, % TCU Press, TCU Box 298300, Fort Worth TX 76129. (817)921-7822. Awards Coordinator: Judy Alter. "To honor the writer of the best novel or collection of short fiction published during the calendar year before the award is given." Annual award for novels or story collections. Award: $6,000. Competition receives 30-40 entries per year. Judges: Panel selected by TIL Council. Guidelines for SASE. Deadline: January 4. Previously published fiction, which must have appeared in print between January 1 and December 31 of the prior year. "Award available to writers who, at some time, have lived in Texas at least two years consecutively or whose work has a significant Texas theme."

JAMES JONES FIRST NOVEL FELLOWSHIP, (I), James Jones Society, Wilkes University, Wilkes-Barre PA 18766. (717)831-4520. E-mail: shaffer@wilkesl.wilkes.edu. Website: http://wilkes.edu/~english/jones.html. Chair, English Department: Patricia B. Heaman. Award to "honor the spirit of unblinking honesty, determination, and insight into modern culture exemplified by the late James Jones by encouraging the work of an American writer who has not published a book-length work of fiction." Annual award for unpublished novel, novella, or collection of related short stories in progress. Award: $2,500. Receives approximately 500 applications. Application fee: $15. Guidelines for SASE. Deadline: March 1. Unpublished submissions. "Award is open to American writers." Word length: 50 opening pages and a two-page thematic outline. "Name, address, telephone number on title page only." Winners announced September 1. Winners notified by phone. List of winners available October 1 for SASE.

EZRA JACK KEATS/KERLAN COLLECTION MEMORIAL FELLOWSHIP, (I, II), University of Minnesota, 109 Walter Library, 117 Pleasant St. SE, Minneapolis MN 55455. (612)624-4576. Fax: (612)625-5525. E-mail: carrie.e.tahtamouni-1@tc.umn.edu. Website: http://160.94.230.174/kerlan/kerlan02.htm. Contact: Carrie Tahtamouni. Award to provide "travel expenses to a talented writer and/or illustrator of children's books who wishes to use the Kerlan Collection for the furtherance of his or her artistic development." Annual competition for books of children's literature. Award: $1,500. Competition receives approximately 10 submissions. Judges: panel of non-Kerlan Collection staff; area professionals, educators, etc. Guidelines available after November for 55¢ SASE. Inquiries by fax and e-mail OK. Deadline early May. Accepts unpublished and previously published

---

MARKET CONDITIONS are constantly changing! If you're still using this book and it is 1999 or later, buy the newest edition of *Novel & Short Story Writer's Market* at your favorite bookstore or order from Writer's Digest Books.

submissions. Winners announced mid June. Winners notified by phone and letter. List of winners available for SASE.

ROBERT F. KENNEDY BOOK AWARDS, (II, IV), 1367 Connecticut Ave. NW, Suite 200, Washington DC 20036. (202)463-7575. Fax: (202)463-6606. E-mail: info@rfkmemorial.org. Website: http://www.rfkmemorial.o rg. Endowed by Arthur Schlesinger, Jr., from proceeds of his biography, *Robert Kennedy and His Times*. Annual. "To award the author of a book which most faithfully and forcefully reflects Robert Kennedy's purposes." For books published during the calendar year. Award: $2,500 cash prize awarded in the spring. Guidelines available after Summer 1998. Inquiries by fax and e-mail OK. Deadline: January 2. Looking for "a work of literary merit in fact or fiction that shows compassion for the poor or powerless or those suffering from injustice." Four copies of each book submitted should be sent, along with a $25 entry fee. Winners announced Spring 1999. Winners notified by phone. List of winners available by phone, fax or e-mail.

KENTUCKY ARTS COUNCIL, KENTUCKY ARTISTS FELLOWSHIPS, (I, IV), 31 Fountain Place, Frankfort KY 40601. (502)564-3757. Fax: (502)564-2839. E-mail: lmeadows@arts.smag.state.ky.us. "To encourage and assist the professional development of Kentucky artists." 10-15 writing fellowships offered every other (or even-numbered) year in fiction, poetry, playwriting. Award: $5,000. Competition receives 75 submissions. Judges are out-of-state panelists (writers, editors, playwrights, etc.) of distinction. Open only to Kentucky residents (minimum one year). Entry forms available for *Kentucky residents in July 1998*." Inquiries by fax and e-mail OK. Deadline September 1998. Winners announced December 1998. Winners notified by mail.

AGA KHAN PRIZE FOR FICTION, *The Paris Review*, 541 E. 72nd St., New York NY 10021. (212)861-0016. Editor: George Plimpton. Best previously unpublished short story. Annual competition for short stories. Award: $1,000. Competition receives approximately 1,000 submissions/month. Guidelines with SASE. Unpublished submissions. Word length: approximately 1,000-10,000 words.

‡**KIRIYAMA PACIFIC RIM BOOK PRIZE, (III)**, Kiriyama Pacific Rim Foundation and University of San Francisco Center for the Pacific Rim, 2130 Fulton St., San Francisco CA 94117-1080. (415)422-5984. Fax: (415)422-5933. E-mail: cuevas@usfca.edu. Website: http://www.usfca.edu/pac_rim/kiriyama.html. Assistant to the Administrators: Jeannine Cuevas. Annual competition for full-length books, fiction or non-fiction. Award: $30,000. Competition receives 200 submissions. Judges: 5 person panel. Guidelines available in February for SASE. Inquiries by fax and e-mail OK. Deadline July 1. Fiction should be published. Published entries must have appeared in print between November 1, 1997 and October 31, 1998. "The prize is open to publishers/ writers world wide. Entries must concern the Pacific Rim. Writer must be nominated by publisher. Writers should prompt their publishers to do so." Winners announced Fall of 1998. Winner notified by phone and announced on website.

‡*****KOREAN LITERATURE TRANSLATION AWARD, (IV)**, The Korean Culture and Arts Foundation, 1-130 Dongsoong-Dong, Chongro-Ku, Seoul South Korea 110-510. Fax: (0)2-760-4700. Biannual competition for translations (of Korean Literature). Award: $50,000 (grand prize), two work-of-merit prizes of $10,000. (If it is decided that there is no work of sufficient merit for the grand prize, the finest entry will be awarded $30,000.) Competition receives approx. 35 submissions. Judges: Translators. Unpublished submissions. Only translations in Korean Literature previously published. (Translators or publishers may submit their works in book.)

LAWRENCE FOUNDATION PRIZE, (I), *Michigan Quarterly Review*, 3032 Rackham Bldg., Ann Arbor MI 48109-1070. (313)764-9265. Contact: Laurence Goldstein, editor. "An annual cash prize awarded to the author of the best short story published in *Michigan Quarterly Review* each year—chosen from both solicited and unsolicited submissions. Approximately eight short stories are published each year." Annual competition for short stories. Award: $1,000. The Review receives approximately 2,000 mss/year. Judges: Editorial Board.

♣**STEPHEN LEACOCK MEDAL FOR HUMOUR, (II, IV)**, Stephen Leacock Associates, P.O. Box 854, Orillia, Ontario L3V 6K8 Canada. (705)325-6546. Chairman, Award Committee: Jean Dickson. Award "to encourage writing of humour by Canadians." Annual competition for short stories, novels and story collections. Award: Stephen Leacock (silver) medal for humour and Laurentian Bank of Canada cash award of $5,000 (Canadian). Receives 40-50 entries. Five judges selected across Canada. Entry fee $25 (Canadian). Guidelines for SASE. Deadline December 30. Submissions should have been published in the previous year. Open to Canadian citizens or landed immigrants only. Winners announced April 15. Winners notified by phone and mail. List of winners available for SASE.

‡*LIBIDO* **SHORT FICTION CONTEST**, Libido: The Journal of Sex & Sensibility, P.O. Box 146721, Chicago IL 60614. (773)275-0842. Fax: (773)275-0752. E-mail: rune@mcs.com. Co-editor: Jack Hafferkamp. Award to "find and reward exceptional short erotic fiction." Annual competition for short stories. Award: $1,000 first prize; $200 second prize. Competition receives 300-400 submissions. Judges: Libido editors. Entry fee $15 for each story submitted. Guidelines available for SASE. Deadline September 1. Previously unpublished submissions. Word length: 1,000-4,000 words. "Winning stories will be well-written, insightful, humorous and arousing.

Contest is open to all orientations and tastes, but the winners will fit Libido's general tone and style. Humor helps."

‡**LIFETIME ACHIEVEMENT AWARD**, Native Writers' Circle of the Americas, English Department, University of Oklahoma, Norman OK 73019-0240. (405)325-6231. Fax: (405)325-0831. E-mail: gearyhobson@ou.edu. Project Historian: Geary Hobson. Award to "honor the most respected of our Native American writers. Our award is the only one given to Native American authors by Native American authors." Annual competition. Author's lifetime work as a writer. Award: $1,000. Writers are voted on for the award by fellow American Indian writers. Writer must be nominated.

LINES IN THE SAND **SHORT FICTION CONTEST**, Le Sand Publications, 1252 Terra Nova Blvd., Pacifica CA 94044-4340. (415)355-9069. Contact: Barbara J. Less, associate editor. "To encourage the writing of good short fiction, any genre." Annual competition for short stories. Award: $50, $25, or $10 and publication in *Lines in the Sand*. January/February awards edition. Honorable mentions will be published as space allows. Competition receives approximately 80 submissions. Judges: the editors. Entry fee $5. Guidelines for SASE. Deadline October 31. Previously published or unpublished submissions. Word length: 2,000 words maximum.

‡*LITERAL LATTÉ* **FICTION AWARD**, Literal Latté, 61 E. 8th St., Suite 240, New York NY 10003. (212)260-5532. E-mail: litlatte@aol.com. Contact: Jenine Gordon Bockman, editor/publisher. Award to "provide talented writers with three essential tools for continued success: money, publication and recognition." Annual competition for short stories. Award: $500 first prize; $200 second prize; $100 third prize; up to 7 honorable mentions. Competition receives 500 submissions. Judges: the editors. Entry fee $10 ($15 includes subscription) for each story submitted. Guidelines available for SASE. Deadline January 18. Previously unpublished submissions. Open to new and established writers worldwide. Word length: 6,000 words maximum. "The First Prize Story in the First Annual Literal Latté Fiction Awards has been honored with a Pushcart Prize."

LONG FICTION CONTEST, (I), White Eagle Coffee Store Press, P.O. Box 383, Fox River Grove IL 60021-0383. (847)639-9200. Contact: Publisher. To promote and support the long fiction form. Annual award for short stories. Winning story receives A.E. Coppard Award—publication as chapbook plus $500, 25 contributor's copies; 40 additional copies sent to book publishers/agents and 10 press kits. Entry fee $12. SASE for results. Deadline December 15. Outside judge. Accepts previously unpublished submissions, but previous publication of small parts with acknowledgements is okay. Simultaneous submissions okay. No limits on style or subject matter. Length: 8,000-14,000 words (30-50 pages double spaced) single story; may have multiparts or be a self-contained novel segment. Send cover with title, name, address, phone; second title page with title only. Submissions are not returned; they are recycled. "Previous winners include Doug Hornig, Christy Sheffield Sanford, Eleanor Swanson, Gregory J. Wolds. SASE for most current information." Winners announced March 15, 1999. Winners notified by phone. List of winners available for SASE.

‡*LOS ANGELES TIMES* **BOOK PRIZES, (III)**, *L.A. Times*, % Public Affairs Dept. Times Mirror Square, Los Angeles CA 90053. (213)237-5050. Fax: (213)237-4609. Contact: Michele Biagioni, director. Annual award. "To recognize finest books published each year." For books published between August 1 and July 31. Award: $1,000 cash prize. "Essays on the winning books and on the Robert Kirsch Award recipient appear in The Times Book Review on the Sunday immediately following the prize ceremony." Entry is by nomination. Juries appointed by the *Times*. No entry fee. "Works must be published during the calendar year." Writers must be nominated by committee members. "The Times provides air fare and lodging for two nights in Los Angeles for the winning authors, their guests and the Kirsch Award winner's principal publisher to attend the *Los Angeles Times* Festival of Books."

‡*LSU/SOUTHERN REVIEW* **SHORT FICTION AWARD (I)**, *The Southern Review*, LSU Dept. of English, 43 Allen Hall, LSU, Baton Rouge LA 70803-5005. (504)388-5108. Fax: (504)388-5098. E-mail: bmacon@unix1. sncc.lsu.edu. Contact: Michael Griffith. Award "to recognize the best first collection of short stories published in the U.S. in the past year." Annual competition for short stories. Award: $500, possible reading. Competition receives approx. 35-40 submissions. Judges: A committee of 4 faculty members at LSU. Guidelines for SASE. Deadline January 31. Submissions must have been published between January 1 and December 31 of previous year. Only books published in the U.S.

MARY McCARTHY PRIZE IN SHORT FICTION, (I, IV), Sarabande Books, Inc., P.O. Box 4999, Louisville KY 40204. Contact: Sarah Gorham, editor-in-chief. "To award publication and $2,000 to an outstanding collection of short stories or novellas or single novella of 150-300 pages." Competition receives approximately 1,000 submissions. Judge: nationally known writer, changes yearly. Entry fee $15. Guidelines for SASE. Unpublished submissions. US citizens. Word length: 150-300 pages. "Writers must submit a required entry form and follow contest guildelines for ms submission. Writers must include a #10 SASE with their inquiries."

THE JOHN H. McGINNIS MEMORIAL AWARD, (I), *Southwest Review*, Box 374, 307 Fondren Library West, Southern Methodist University, Dallas TX 75275. (214)768-1037. Contact: Elizabeth Mills, senior editor.

Annual awards (fiction and nonfiction). Stories or essays must have been published in the *Southwest Review* prior to the announcement of the award. Awards: $1,000. Pieces are not submitted directly for the award but simply for publication in the magazine.

MCKNIGHT ARTIST FELLOWSHIPS FOR WRITERS, Administered by the Loft, (I, IV), The Loft, Pratt Community Center, 66 Malcolm Ave. SE, Minneapolis MN 55414. (612)379-8999. Program Coordinator: Deidre Pope. "To give Minnesota writers of demonstrated ability an opportunity to work for a concentrated period of time on their writing." Annual awards of $10,000; 2 in poetry and 3 in creative prose; 2 awards of distinction of $20,000. Competition receives approximately 275 submissions/year. Judges are from out-of-state. Entry forms or rules for SASE. Deadline November. "Applicants *must* be Minnesota residents and must send for and observe guidelines."

*THE ENID MCLEOD LITERARY PRIZE, (II, IV), Franco-British Society, Room 623, Linen Hall, 162-168 Regent St., London W1R 5TB England. Executive Secretary: Mrs. Marian Clarke. "To recognize the work of the author published in the UK which in the opinion of the judges has contributed most to Franco-British understanding." Annual competition for short stories, novels and story collections. Award: Monetary sum. Competition receives approximately 6-12 submissions. Judges: The Marquis of Lansdowne (FBS President), Martyn Goff and Professor Douglas Johnson. Guidelines for SASE. Deadline December 31. "Writers, or their publishers, may submit 4 copies to the London Office. No nominations are necessary."

MAGGIE AWARD, (I, IV), %Lillian Richey, 4605 Settles Point Rd., Suwanee GA 30174-1988. (770)513-1754. "To encourage and instruct unpublished writers in the romance genre." Annual competition for novels. Award: Silver pendant (1st place), certificates (2nd-4th). 5 categories—short contemporary romance, long contemporary romance, historical romance, mainstream, paranormal. Competition receives 300 submissions. Judges: Published romance authors. Entry fee $25. Guidelines for SASE after April. Deadline is on or about June 15. Unpublished submissions. Writers must be members of Romance Writers of America. Entries consist of 60 pages including synopsis. Winners announced September. Winners notified by phone and mail and announced at Moonlight and Magnolias conference. List of winners sent to all applicants.

MALICE DOMESTIC GRANT, (I, IV), % Bookstore, 27 W. Washington St., Hagerstown MD 21740. (301)797-8896. Fax (301)797-9453. Grants Chair: Pam Reed. Given "to encourage unpublished writers in their pursuit—grant may be used to offset registration, travel or other expenses relating to attending writers' conferences, etc., within one year of award." Annual competition for novels and nonfiction. Award: $500. Competition receives 8-25 submissions. Judges: the Malice Domestic Board. Guidelines for SASE. Unpublished submissions. "Our genre is loosely translated as mystery stories of the Agatha Christie type, that is 'mysteries of manners.' These works usually feature amateur detective characters who know each other. No excessive gore or violence." Submit plot synopsis and 3 chapters of work in progress. Include résumé, a letter of reference from someone familiar with your work, a typed letter of application explaining qualifications for the grant and the workshop/conference to be attended or the research to be funded.

‡*THE MARTEN BEQUEST TRAVELLING SCHOLARSHIP, (I, IV), Arts Management Pty. Ltd., Station House Rawson Place, 790 George St., Sydney NSW 2000 Australia. Awards Coordinator: Hanne Lousen/Louise Roberts. "For the furtherance of culture and the advancement of education in Australia by means of the provision of travelling scholarships as numerous as income will permit, to be awarded entrants who have been born in Australia, and awarded to candidates of either sex between the ages of 21 years and 35 years, who shall be adjudged of outstanding ability and promise." Award granted to writers of prose or poetry every 2 years (next in 1998). Competition for writers of prose or poetry. Award: AUS $18,000 payable in two installments of $9,000 per annum. Guidelines for SASE. Deadline Oct. 31.

MASTERS LITERARY AWARD, (I), Center Press, P.O. Box 16452, Encino CA 91416-6452. Website: http://www.concentric.net/~medianet/index.html. "One yearly Grand Prize of $1,000, and four quarterly awards of 'Honorable Mention' each in either 1) fiction; 2) poetry and song lyrics; 3) nonfiction." Judges: Three anonymous literary professionals. Entry fee $10. Awards are given on March 15, June 15, September 15 and December 15. Any submission received prior to an award date is eligible for the subsequent award. Submissions accepted throughout the year. Fiction and nonfiction must be no more than 20 pages (5,000 words); poetry no more than 150 lines. All entries must be in the English language. #10 SASE required for guidelines.

THE MENTOR AWARD, (IV), *Mentor & Protege Newsletter*, P.O. Box 4382, Overland Park KS 66204. (913)362-7889. Editor: Maureen Waters. "The Mentor Award is given for supporting and promoting the art and practice of mentoring through the written word, and thereby helping to create a new sense of community." Quarterly and annually: Grand Prize ($100) will be awarded each January to the 1 best submission from all quarterly first-prize winners in all categories from the previous year. Competition for short stories (1,000-3,000 words); essay (700-1,500 words); feature article (1,500-3,000 words); interview (1,000-3,000 words); book review (500-1,000 words); and movie review (500-1,000 words). "The Athena Award is for published (after January 1, 1993) material. Entry fee varies by category (book, article, academic dissertation, videos, etc.). All material must be mentoring related. Plaque awarded, no monetary reward." Guidelines for SASE. Deadlines for quarterly competitions: March 31, June 30, September 30, December 31. Previously published (prior to January 1, 1993) and unpublished submissions. Submissions must be about "a mentor or a mentoring relationship."

MIDLAND AUTHORS' AWARD, (II, IV), Society of Midland Authors, P.O. Box 10419, Fort Dearborn Station, Chicago IL 60610-0419. "To honor outstanding books published during the previous year by Midwestern authors." Award: Monetary sum and plaque. Competition receives approximately 400-500 books. Judges are librarians, book reviewers, radio network program reviewers, bookstore executives and university faculty members. Entry forms or rules for SASE. Authors must be residents of Illinois, Indiana, Iowa, Kansas, Michigan, Minnesota, Missouri, Nebraska, Ohio, South Dakota, North Dakota or Wisconsin. Send SASE for entry form. Winners notified April or May by letter. List of winners available for SASE.

MID-LIST PRESS FIRST SERIES AWARD FOR SHORT FICTION, (I, II), Mid-List Press, 4324-12th Ave. South, Minneapolis MN 55407-3218. (612)822-3733. Contact: Lane Stiles, senior editor. To encourage and nurture short fiction writers who have never published a collection of fiction. Annual competition for fiction collections. Award: $1,000 advance and publication. Judges: manuscript readers and the editors of Mid-List Press. Entry fee $15. Deadline July 1. Previously published or unpublished submissions. Word length: 50,000 words minimum. "Application forms and guidelines are available for a #10 SASE."

MID-LIST PRESS FIRST SERIES AWARD FOR THE NOVEL , (I), Mid-List Press, 4324-12th Ave. South, Minneapolis MN 55407-3218. (612)822-3733. Contact: Lane Stiles, senior editor. To encourage and nurture first-time novelists. Annual competition for novels. Award: $1,000 advance and publication. Competition receives approximately 500 submissions. Judges: manuscript readers and the editors of Mid-List Press. Entry fee $15. Deadline February 1. Unpublished submissions. Word length: minimum 50,000 words. "Application forms and guidelines are available for a #10 SASE."

‡**MILTON CENTER FELLOWSHIP, (IV)**, The Milton Center, Kansas Newman College, 3100 McCormick, Wichita KS 67213. (316)942-4291, ext. 326. Fax: (316)942-9658. E-mail: miltonc@ksnewman.edu. Program Director: Essie Sappenfield. Award to "help new writers of Christian commitment complete first book-length manuscript." Annual competition for fiction or poetry. Competition receives 20 submissions. Judges: Milton Center staff. Entry fee $15. Guidelines for SASE. Deadline January 31, 1998. Unpublished submissions. Award available only to writers previously unpublished in poetry or fiction. Submit novel or book of stories: proposal and 3 chapters; poetry: 12-15 poems and proposal.

‡**MIND BOOK OF THE YEAR—THE ALLEN LANE AWARD, (II, IV)**, MIND, Granta House, 15-19 Broadway, London E15 4BQ England. Contact: Ms. A. Brackx. "To award a prize to the work of fiction or nonfiction which outstandingly furthers public understanding of the causes, experience or treatment of mental health problems." Annual competition for novels and works of nonfiction. Award: £1,000. Competition receives approximately 50-100 submissions. Judges: A panel drawn from MIND's Council of Management. Deadline: December. Previously published submissions. Author's nomination is accepted. All books must be published in English in the UK.

MINNESOTA VOICES PROJECT, (IV), New Rivers Press, 420 N. Fifth St., #910, Minneapolis MN 55401. (612)339-7114. Contact: James Cihlar, managing editor. Annual award "to foster and encourage new and emerging regional writers of short fiction, novellas, personal essays and poetry." Requires entry form. Awards: $500 to each author published in the series plus "a generous royalty agreement if book goes into second printing." Competition receives 90 submissions. No entry fee. Send request with SASE for guidelines in October. Deadline: April 1. Restricted to new and emerging writers from Minnesota. Winners announced October.

‡**MISSISSIPPI REVIEW PRIZE**, University of Southern Mississippi/Mississippi Review, P.O. Box 5144 USM, Hattiesburg MS 39406-5144. (601)266-4321. Fax: (601)266-5757. E-mail: fb@netdoor.com. Contact: Rie Fortenberry, managing editor. Award to "reward excellence in new fiction and poetry and to find new writers who are just beginning their careers." Annual competition for short stories. Award: $1,000 plus publication for the winning story; publication for all runners-up. Competition receives 800-1,100 submissions. Judge: guest editor/judge. Entry fee $10/story; limit 2 stories. $5/poem, limit 4 poems. Guidelines available for SASE. Deadline May 31. Previously unpublished submissions. Word length: 6,500 words.

MARKET CATEGORIES: (I) Unpublished entries; **(II)** Published entries nominated by the author; **(III)** Published entries nominated by the editor, publisher or nominating body; **(IV)** Specialized entries.

THE MISSOURI REVIEW **EDITORS' PRIZE CONTEST**, 1507 Hillcrest Hall, Columbia MO 65211. (573)882-4474. Contact: Greg Michalson, managing editor. Annual competition for short stories and essays. Award: Cash ($1,500 for fiction and poetry, $1,000 for essay) and publication in *The Missouri Review*. Competition receives 1,000 submissions. Judges: *The Missouri Review* staff. Page restrictions: 25 typed, double-spaced, for fiction and essays, 10 for poetry. Entry fee $15 for each entry (checks payable to The Missouri Review). Each fee entitles entrant to a one-year subscription to *Missouri Rreview*, an extension of a current subscription, or a gift subscription. Guidelines for SASE. Deadline October 15. Outside of envelope should be marked "Fiction," "Essay," or "Poetry." Enclose an index card with author's name, address, and telephone number in the left corner and, for fiction and essay entries only, the work's title in the center. Entries must be previously unpublished and will not be returned. Winners announced in January. Winners notified by phone. List of winners available for SASE. Enclose SASE for notification of winners. No further guidelines necessary.

♣**MR. CHRISTIE'S BOOK AWARD, (II, IV)**, Christie Brown & Co., 2150 Lakeshore Blvd. W., Toronto, Ontario M8V 1A3 Canada. (416)503-6050. Fax: (416)503-6010. E-mail: myust117@nobisco.ca. Program Coordinator: Marlene Yustin. Award to "honor excellence in the writing and illustration of Canadian children's literature and to encourage the development and publishing of high quality children's books." Annual competition for short stories and novels. Award: Six awards of $7,500 (Canadian) each given in 3 categories to works published in English and French. Competition receives approximately 300 submissions. Judges: Two judging panels, one English and one French. Guidelines for SASE. Inquiries by fax and e-mail OK. Submissions must be published within the year prior to the award ceremony. The author/illustrator must be a Canadian resident. A Canadian is defined as a person having Canadian citizenship or having landed immigrant status at the time of his/her book's publication. Books will be judged based on their ability to: inspire the imagination of the reader; recognize the importance of play; represent the highest standard of integrity; bring delight and edification; help children understand the world both intellectually and emotionally. Winners announced June. Winners notified by telephone.

‡**MODEST CONTEST, (I)**, *New Stone Circle*, 1185 E. 1900 North Rd., White Heath IL 61884. (217)762-5801. Fiction Editor: Mary Hays. Award "to encourage good writing." Annual competition for short stories. Awards: $100 first prize, $50 second, $25 third. Competition receives approximately 65 submissions. Judge: Mary Hays. Entry fee $10. Guidelines for SASE. Deadline October 1. Unpublished submissions.

‡**MONEY FOR WOMEN**, Money for Woman/Barbara Deming Memorial Fund, Inc., Box 40-1043, Brooklyn NY 11240-1043. "Small grants to individual feminists in the arts." Biannual competition. Award: $200-1,000. Competition receives approximately 200 submissions. Judges: Board of Directors. Guidelines for SASE. Deadline December 31, June 30. Limited to U.S. and Canadian citizens. Word length: 6-25 pages. May submit own fiction. "Only for feminists in the arts. Fund includes two additional awards: the Gerty, Gerty, Gerty in the Arts, Arts Arts award for works by lesbians and The Fanny Lou Hamer Award for work which combats racism and celebrates women of color."

‡♣**L.M. MONTGOMERY PEI CHILDREN'S LITERATURE AWARD, (I, IV)**, PEI Council of the Arts, 115 Richmond St., Charlottetown, P.E.I., C1A 1H7 Canada. (902)368-4410. Fax: (902)368-4418. "Awarded by Island Literary Awards to the author of a manuscript written for children within the age range of 5-12." Annual competition for children's stories. Award: $500 (first prize); $200 (second prize); $100 (third prize). Entry fee $6. Deadline February 15. Unpublished submissions. "Open to authors who have been Island residents for six of the last twelve months." Page length: maximum 60 pages. "Must be original and unpublished, submitted with name and address on separate cover sheet for anonymous judging. Entry should be typed, double spaced, one side page only. Work may not have won any other prize competition. SASE will ensure return of manuscript."

MYSTERY MAYHEM CONTEST, (I), *Mystery Time*/Hutton Publications, P.O. Box 2907, Decatur IL 62524. Contact: Linda Hutton, editor. Award "to encourage writers to have fun writing a mystery spoof." Annual competition for short stories. Award: $10 cash and publication in *Mystery Time*. Competition receives approximately 100 submissions. Judge: Linda Hutton, editor of *Mystery Time*. Guidelines for SASE. Deadline September 15 annually. Unpublished submissions. Word length: Must be one sentence of any length. "One entry per person, of one sentence which can be any length, which is the opening of a mystery spoof. Must include SASE. Entry form not required. All material must be typed."

‡♣**THE NATIONAL CHAPTER OF CANADA IODE VIOLET DOWNEY BOOK AWARD, (I, IV)**, The National Chapter of Canada IODE, 254-40 Orchard View Blvd., Toronto, Ontario M4R 1B9 Canada. (416)487-4416. Fax: (416)487-4417. Chairman, Book Award Committee: Marty Dalton. "The award is given to a Canadian author for an English language book suitable for children 13 years of age and under, published in Canada during the previous calendar year. Fairy tales, anthologies and books adapted from another source are not eligible." Annual competition for novels, children's literature. Award: $3,000. Competition receives approx. 80-100 submissions. Judges: A six-member panel of judges including four National IODE officers and two non-members who are recognized specialists in the field of children's literature. Guidelines for SASE. Deadline January 31, 1998. Previously published January 1, 1997 and December 31, 1997. "The book must have been

written by a Canadian citizen and must have been published in Canada during the calendar year." Word length: Must have at least 500 words of text preferably with Canadian content.

NATIONAL ENDOWMENT FOR THE ARTS CREATIVE WRITING FELLOWSHIP, (I), Room 720, 1100 Pennsylvania Ave. NW, Washington DC 20506. (202)682-5428. "The mission of the NEA is to foster the excellence, diversity and vitality of the arts in the United States, and to help broaden public access to the arts." The purpose of the fellowship is to enable creative writers "to set aside time for writing, research or travel and generally to advance their careers." Competition open to fiction writers who have published a novel or novella, a collection of stories or at least 5 stories in 2 or more magazines since January 1, 1993. Award: $20,000. The Endowment now alternates years between fiction and poetry; fiction applications will be accepted in 1999. All mss are judged anonymously. Application and guidelines available upon request.

NATIONAL FEDERATION OF THE BLIND WRITER'S DIVISION FICTION CONTEST, (I), National Federation of the Blind Writer's Division, 2704 Beach Dr., Merrick NY 11566. (516)868-8718. Fax: (516)868-9076. First Vice President, Writer's Division: Lori Stayer. "To promote good writing for blind writers and Division members, blind or sighted." Annual competition for short stories. Award: $40, $25, $15. Competitions receives 20 submissions. Entry fee $5/story. Guidelines for SASE. Inquiries by fax OK. Deadline May 1, 1998 (contest opens 9/1/97). Unpublished submissions. "You don't have to be blind, but it helps. Story must be in English, and typed. SASE necessary." Critique on request, $5. Word length: 2,000 max. Winners announced July 31. Winners notified by mail. List of winners available for SASE.

‡NATIONAL FOUNDATION FOR ADVANCEMENT IN THE ARTS, ARTS RECOGNITION AND TALENT SEARCH (ARTS), (I, IV), 800 Brickell Ave., #500, Miami FL 33131-2914. (305)377-1140. Fax: (305)377-1149. E-mail: nfaa@nfaa.org. Website: http://www.nfaa.org. President: William H. Banchs. "To encourage 17- and 18-year-old writers and put them in touch with institutions which offer scholarships." Annual award for short stories, novels, fiction, essay, poetry, scriptwriting. Awards: $3,000, $1,500, $1,000, $500, and $100. Competition receives 1,200 submissions. Judges: Nationally selected panel. Entry fee $25 before June 1, $35 until October 1. Guidelines for SASE. Inquiries by fax and e-mail OK. 17- and 18-year-old writers only. Applicants must be US citizens or permanent residents of the US. Winners announced in December. Winners notified by mail.

NATIONAL WRITERS ASSOCIATION ANNUAL NOVEL WRITING CONTEST, (I), National Writers Association, 1450 S. Havana, Suite 424, Aurora CO 80012. (303)751-7844. Contact: Sandy Whelchel, director. Annual award to "recognize and reward outstanding ability and to increase the opportunity for publication." Award: $500 first prize; $300 second prize; $100 third prize. Award judged by successful writers. Charges $35 entry fee. Judges' evaluation sheets sent to each entry. Contest rules and entry forms available with SASE. Opens December 1. Deadline: April 1. Unpublished submissions, any genre or category. Length: 20,000-100,000 words.

NATIONAL WRITERS ASSOCIATION ANNUAL SHORT STORY CONTEST, (I), National Writers Association, 1450 S. Havana, Suite 424, Aurora CO 80012. (303)751-7844. Contact: Sandy Whelchel, executive director. Annual award to encourage and recognize writing by freelancers in the short story field. Award: $200 first prize; $100 second prize; $50 third prize. Opens April 1. Charges $15 entry fee. Write for entry form and rule sheet. All entries must be postmarked by July 1. Evaluation sheets sent to each entrant if SASE provided. Unpublished submissions. Length: No more than 5,000 words.

THE NATIONAL WRITTEN & ILLUSTRATED BY . . . AWARDS CONTEST FOR STUDENTS, (I, IV), Landmark Editions, Inc., P.O. Box 270169, Kansas City MO 64127-2135. (816)241-4919. Fax: (816)483-3755. Contact: Nan Thatch. "Contest initiated to encourage students to write and illustrate original books and to inspire them to become published authors and illustrators." Annual competition. "Each student whose book is selected for publication will be offered a complete publishing contract. To ensure that students benefit from the proceeds, royalties from the sale of their books will be placed in an individual trust fund, set up for each student by his or her parents or legal guardians, at a bank of their choice. Funds may be withdrawn when a student becomes of age, or withdrawn earlier (either in whole or in part) for educational purposes or in case of proof of specific needs due to unusual hardship. Reports of book sales and royalties will be sent to the student and the parents or guardians annually." Winners also receive an all-expense-paid trip to Kansas City to oversee final reproduction phases of their books. Books by students may be entered in one of three age categories: A—6 to 9 years old; B—10 to 13 years old; C—14 to 19 years old. Each book submitted must be both written and illustrated by the same student. "Any books that are written by one student and illustrated by another will be automatically disqualified." Book entries must be submitted by a teacher or librarian. Entry fee $1. For rules and guidelines, send a #10 SAE with 64¢ postage. Inquiries by fax OK. Deadline May 1 of each year. Winners announced October. Winners notified by phone.

‡NCWN FICTION COMPETITION, (IV), North Carolina Writers' Network, P.O. Box 954, Carrboro NC 27510. (919)967-9540. Fax: (919)929-0535. E-mail: ncwn@sunsite.unc.edu. Program Coordinator: Frances Dowell. Award to "encourage and recognize the work of emerging and established North Carolina writers." Annual competition for short stories. Awards: $150 first place, $100 second place, $50 third place. Competition receives 100 submissions. Judges change annually. Entry fee $4 for NCWN members; $6 for nonmembers. Guidelines for SASE. Deadline February 27. Unpublished submissions. "The award is available only to legal residents of North Carolina or out-of-state NCWN members." Word length: 6 double-spaced pages (1,500 words maximum).

‡THE NEBRASKA REVIEW AWARD IN FICTION, The Nebraska Review, University of Nebraska at Omaha, Omaha NE 68182-0324. (402)554-3159. Contact: James Reed, fiction editor. Award to "recognize short fiction of the highest possible quality." Annual competition for short stories. Award: publication plus $500. Competition receives 400-500 submissions. Judges: staff. Entry fee $9 for each story submitted. Guidelines available for SASE. Deadline November 30 every year. Previously unpublished submissions. Word length: 5,000 words.

NEGATIVE CAPABILITY SHORT FICTION COMPETITION, (I, IV), *Negative Capability*, 62 Ridgelawn Dr. E., Mobile AL 36608-6116. (334)343-6163. Fax: (334)334-8478. E-mail: negcap@datasync.com. Contact: Sue Walker. "To promote and publish excellent fiction and to promote the ideals of human rights and dignity." Annual award for short stories. Award: $1,000 best story. Competition receives 500 submissions. Judge: Eugene Walter. Reading fee $10, "includes copy of journal publishing the award." Deadline January 15. Length: 1,500-4,500 words. Send one copy without name and a card with name and address. Include SASE for results. Winners announced April. Winner notified by phone. List of winners available by mail, e-mail or fax.

NEUSTADT INTERNATIONAL PRIZE FOR LITERATURE, (III), *World Literature Today*, 110 Monnet Hall, University of Oklahoma, Norman OK 73019-0375. Contact: William Riggan, director. Biennial award to recognize distinguished and continuing achievement in fiction, poetry or drama. Awards: $40,000, an eagle feather cast in silver, an award certificate and a special issue of *WLT* devoted to the laureate. "We are looking for outstanding accomplishment in world literature. The Neustadt Prize is not open to application. Nominations are made only by members of the international jury, which changes for each award. Jury meetings are held in February or March of even-numbered years. Unsolicited manuscripts, whether published or unpublished, cannot be considered."

NEVADA STATE COUNCIL ON THE ARTS ARTISTS' FELLOWSHIPS, (I, IV), 602 N. Curry St., Carson City NV 89703. (702)687-6680. Fax: (702)687-6688. E-mail: sacrosse@lahontan.clan.lib.nv.us. Artists' Services Program Director: Sharon Rosse. Award "to honor individual artists and their artistic achievements to support artists' efforts in advancing their careers." Annual competition for fiction, nonfiction, poetry, playwriting. Award: $5,000 ($4,500 immediately, $500 after public service component completed). Judges: Peer panels of professional artists. Guidelines available, no SASE required. Inquiries by fax and e-mail OK. Deadline April 15, 1998. "Only available to Nevada writers." Word length: 25 pages prose and plays, 10 pages poetry. Winners announced July. Winners notified by mail.

THE NEW ERA WRITING, ART, PHOTOGRAPHY AND MUSIC CONTEST, (I, IV), *New Era Magazine* (LDS Church), 50 E. North Temple, Salt Lake City UT 84150. (801)240-2951. Contact: Richard M. Romney, managing editor. "To encourage young Mormon writers and artists." Annual competition for short stories. Award: partial scholarship to Brigham Young University or Ricks College or cash awards. Competition receives approximately 300 submissions. Judges: *New Era* editors. Guidelines for SASE. Deadline December 31. Unpublished submissions. Contest open only to 12-23-year-old members of the Church of Jesus Christ of Latter-Day Saints.

NEW LETTERS LITERARY AWARD, (I), UMKC, 5101 Rockhill Rd., Kansas City MO 64110-2499. (816)235-1168. Fax: (816)235-2611. E-mail: mccraryg@smptgate.umkc.edu. Awards Coordinator: Glenda McCrary. Award to "discover and reward unpublished work by new and established writers." Annual competition for short stories. Award: $750 and publication. Competition receives 600 entries/year. Entry fee $10. Guidelines for SASE. Inquiries by fax and e-mail OK. Deadline May 15. Submissions must be unpublished. Length requirement: 5,000 words or less. Winners notified by personal letter in September. List of winners available for SASE.

NEW MILLENNIUM WRITING AWARDS, Room 101, P.O. Box 2463, Knoxville TN 37901. (423)428-0389. Fax: (423)428-2302. Website: http://www.mach2.com/books. Contact: Don Williams, editor. Award "to promote literary excellence in contemporary fiction." Semiannual competition for short stories. Award: $1,000 plus publication in *New Millennium Writings*. Competition receives approximately 1,000 submissions. Judges: Novelists and short story writers. Entry fee: $10. Guidelines for SASE. Inquiries by fax OK. Deadlines December

---

MARKET CATEGORIES: (I) Unpublished entries; **(II)** Published entries nominated by the author; **(III)** Published entries nominated by the editor, publisher or nominating body; **(IV)** Specialized entries.

1 and June 1. Unpublished submissions. No required word length. "Provide a bold, yet organic opening line, sustain the voice and mood throughout, tell an entertaining and vital story with a strong ending." Winners announced August 30. Winners notified by mail and phone. All entrants will receive a list of winners, plus a copy of the journal.

NEW WRITING AWARD, (I), *New Writing Magazine*, PO Box 1812, Amherst NY 14226-7812. E-mail: newwriting@aol.com. "We wish to reward *new* writing. Looking for originality in form and content." New and beginning writers encouraged. Annual open competition for prose (novel, novel excerpt, scripts, short story, essay, humor, other) and poetry. Deadline: December 31. Award: up to $3,000 for best entry. Additional awards for finalists. Possible publication. Judges: Panel of editors. Entry fee $10, $5 for each additional plus 15¢/page after 20 pages. Guidelines for SASE. No application form required—simply send submission with reading fee, SASE for manuscript return or notification, and 3×5 card for each entry, including: story name, author and address.

NEW YORK FOUNDATION FOR THE ARTS FELLOWSHIP, (I, II, IV), New York Foundation for the Arts, 14th Floor, 155 Avenue of the Americas, New York NY 10013. E-mail: nyfaafp@artswire.org. Biennial competition for poetry, short stories, plays, screenplays, nonfiction literature and novels. Competition receives approximately 700 submissions per category. Judges: Writers from New York State. Call for guidelines or send SASE. Inquiries by e-mail OK. Manuscript sample (20 pp maximum) may be drawn from published or unpublished work. Applicants must be over 18; must have lived in New York state at least 2 years immediately prior to application deadline; and may not be currently enrolled in any degree program. Deadline: early October. "All submissions must be in manuscript form; copies of published work will not be accepted." Winners announced in July. Winners notified by mail. List of winners available for SASE.

NEW YORK STATE EDITH WHARTON CITATION OF MERIT, (State Author), (III, IV), NYS Writers Institute, Humanities 355, University at Albany, Albany NY 12222. (518)442-5620. Associate Director: Donald Faulkner. Awarded biennially to honor a New York State fiction writer for a lifetime of works of distinction. Fiction writers living in New York State are nominated by an advisory panel. Recipients receive an honorarium of $10,000 and must give two public readings a year.

‡NEW YORK UNIVERSITY PRESS PRIZE, New York University Press, 70 Washington Square S., New York NY 10012. (212)998-2575. Fax: (212)995-3833. Award to "support innovative, experimental and important fiction and poetry by authors who remain unrecognized relative to the quality and ambition of their writing." Annual competition for novels, story collections and poetry. Award: complete publication/marketing of the ms. Competition receives 300-400 submissions per category. Judge: independent committee. Guidelines available for SASE. Deadline May 7. Previously unpublished submissions. "Must include a letter of recommendation from a qualified reader."

JOHN NEWBERY AWARD, (III, IV), American Library Association (ALA) Awards and Citations Program, Association for Library Service to Children, 50 E. Huron St., Chicago IL 60611. Executive Director: S. Roman. Annual award. Only books for children published in the US during the preceding year are eligible. Award: Medal. Entry restricted to US citizens-residents.

CHARLES H. AND N. MILDRED NILON EXCELLENCE IN MINORITY FICTION AWARD, (I, IV), University of Colorado at Boulder and the Fiction Collective Two, English Dept. Publications Center, Campus Box 494, University of Colorado, Boulder CO 80309-0494. (303)492-8938. "We recognize excellence in new minority fiction." Annual competition for novels, story collections and novellas. Award: $1,000 cash prize; joint publications of mss by CU-Boulder and Fiction Collective Two. Competition receives approximately 150 submissions. Judges: Well-known minority writers. Guidelines for SASE. Deadline: November 30. Unpublished submissions. "Only specific recognized US racial and ethnic minorities are eligible. The definitions are in the submission guidelines. The ms must be book length." Winners announced Spring. Winners notified by mail. List of winners available for SASE.

‡THE NOMA AWARD FOR PUBLISHING IN AFRICA, (III, IV), P.O. Box 128, Witney, Oxon OX9 5X4 United Kingdom. (44)1993-775235. Fax: (44)1993-709265. E-mail: maryljay@aol.com. Contact: Mary Jay. Sponsored by Kodansha Ltd. Award "to encourage publication of works by African writers and scholars in Africa, instead of abroad as is still too often the case at present." Annual competition for a new book in any of these categories: Scholarly or academic; books for children; literature and creative writing, including fiction, drama and poetry. Award: $10,000. Competition receives approximately 140 submissions. Judges: A committee of African scholars and book experts and representatives of the international book community. Chairman: Walter Bgoya. Guidelines for SASE. Deadline February 28. Previously published submissions. Submissions are through publishers only. Winners announced September. Winners notified through publishers. List of winners available for SASE.

NORTH AMERICAN NATIVE AUTHORS FIRST BOOK AWARD, (I, II, IV), *The Greenfield Review* Literary Center, P.O. Box 308, Greenfield Center NY 12833. (518)584-1728. Fax: (518)583-9741. Contact: Joe

Bruchac, editor. "To recognize and encourage writing by Native American authors (American Indian)." Annual award for fiction. Award: $500 and publication by the Greenfield Review Press. Competition receives 50-100 submissions. Judges: Anonymous. Guidelines for SASE. Deadline March 15. Published or unpublished (as a book) submissions. Native American authors only. Word length: prose mss no longer than 240 typed double-spaced pages.

NORTH CAROLINA ARTS COUNCIL RESIDENCIES, (IV), 407 N. Person St., Raleigh NC 27601-2807. (919)733-2111, ext. 22. E-mail: dmcgill@ncacmail.dcr.state.nc.us. Literature Director: Deborah McGill. "To recognize and encourage North Carolina's finest creative writers. We offer two- to three-month residencies for two writers at the LaNapoule Foundation in southern France every two years, an annual two- to three-month residency for one writer at Headlands Center for the Arts (California), and an annual one-month master class/residency for one writer at Vermont Studio Center." Judges: Editors and published writers from outside the state. Deadline for France, November 1; for US residencies, early June. Writers must be over 18 years old, not currently enrolled in degree-granting program on undergraduate or graduate level and *must have been a resident of North Carolina for 1 full year prior to applying*. Winners notified by phone.

NTPWA ANNUAL POETRY & FICTION CONTEST, North Texas Professional Writer's Association, P.O. Box 563, Bedford TX 76095-0563. (817)428-2822. Fax: (817)428-2181. E-mail: justel@cris.com. Website: http://www.startext.net/homes/prowritr. Contact: Elaine Lanmon. Award "to recognize and encourage previously unpublished writers." Annual competition for short stories, novels and poetry. Fiction awards: $50 (1st prize), $25 (2nd prize). Poetry awards: $25 (1st prize), $10 (2nd prize). Judges: Published writers. Entry fee: $5 fiction, $3/2 poems. Guidelines for SASE. Inquiries by fax and e-mail OK. Deadline May 31, 1998. Unpublished submissions. Length: 25 pages (fiction); 25 lines (poetry). Winners announced July 15, 1998. List of winners available for SASE.

THE FLANNERY O'CONNOR AWARD FOR SHORT FICTION, (I), The University of Georgia Press, 330 Research Dr., Athens GA 30602. (706)369-6140. Fax: (708)369-6131. Contact: Award coordinator. Annual award "to recognize outstanding collections of short fiction. Published and unpublished authors are welcome." Award: $1,000 and publication by the University of Georgia Press. Competition receives 330 submissions. Deadline June 1-July 31. "Manuscripts cannot be accepted at any other time." Entry fee $10. Contest rules for SASE. Ms will not be returned. Winners announced January 1999. Winners notified by mail.

✦HOWARD O'HAGAN AWARD FOR SHORT FICTION, (II, IV), Writers Guild of Alberta, 3rd Floor, Percy Page Centre, 11759 Groat Rd., Edmonton, Alberta T5M 3K6. (403)422-8174. Fax: (403)422-2663. Contact: Darlene Diver, assistant director. "To recognize outstanding books published by Alberta authors each year." Annual competition for short stories. Award: $500 (Canadian) cash and leather bound book. Competition receives 20-30 submissions. Judges: selected published writers across Canada. Guidelines for SASE. Deadline December 31. Previously published submissions published between January and December 31. Open to Alberta authors only.

‡FRANK O'HARA AWARD CHAPBOOK COMPETITION, Thorngate Road, Campus Box 4240, English Department, Illinois State University, Normal IL 61790-4240. (309)438-7705. E-mail: jmelled@ilstu.edu. Director/Publisher: Jim Elledge. Award to "publish a chapbook-length collection (20 pp. max.) of poetry, prose poems, or cross-genre work (e.g., short short fiction) by lesbian, bisexual, transgendered or gay authors." Annual competition for short short ("flash") fiction. Award: $500 plus 25 copies. Competition receives 150 submissions per category. Judge: an anonymous, nationally-recognized lesbian, bi, transgendered or gay author. Entry fee $15 for each manuscript submitted. Guidelines available for SASE. Deadline February 1, 1998. Published or previously unpublished submissions. "The contest is open to lesbian, bisexual, transgendered or gay authors for short (20 pp. max.) collections of poetry, prose poems or cross-genre texts (e.g., short-short fiction). Individuals may submit as many 20-page manuscripts as they want as long as each is accompanied by the $15 reading fee. Thus far, we've published Kristy Nielsen's *Two Girls: Prose Poems* and Larry Wayne Johns' *An Invisible Veil Between Us: Poems*, both available for $6. During 1997-98, we will be publishing new work by David Trinidad, Karen Lee Osborne, Reginald Shepherd and Maureen Seaton. Write for guidelines."

OHIO STATE UNIVERSITY PRESS, (II), 180 Pressey Hall, 1070 Carmack Rd., Columbus OH 43210-1002. (614)292-6930. Fax: (614)292-2065. E-mail: bucy.4@osu.edu. Website: http://www.ohio-state.edu/osu-press/. **Acquisitions**: Barbara Hanrahan, director. Estab. 1957. "Small-sized university press." Publishes "scholarly books in the humanities and social sciences." Member of Association of American University Presses (AAUP), International Association of Scholarly Publishers (IASP) and Association of American Publishers (AAP). Publishes winners of annual poetry contest and annual short fiction prize. Please write to press for guidelines.

OHIOANA AWARD FOR CHILDREN'S LITERATURE, ALICE WOOD MEMORIAL, (IV), Ohioana Library Association, 65 S. Front St., Room 1105, Columbus OH 43215-4162. (614)466-3831. Fax: (614)728-6974. E-mail: ohioana@urnslo.ohio.gov. Director: Linda Hengst. Competition "to honor an individual whose body of work has made, and continues to make, a significant contribution to literature for children or young adults." Annual award for body of work. Amount of award varies (approximately $500-1,000). Guidelines for SASE. Inquiries by fax and e-mail OK. Deadline December 31 prior to year award is given. "Open to authors born in Ohio or who have lived in Ohio for a minimum of five years." Winners announced Summer 1998. Winners notified by letter. Entrants can call, e-mail or check website for winner.

OHIOANA BOOK AWARDS, (II, IV), Ohioana Library Association, 65 S. Front St., Room 1105, Columbus OH 43215. Contact: Linda R. Hengst, director. Annual awards granted (only if the judges believe a book of sufficiently high quality has been submitted) to bring recognition to outstanding books by Ohioans or about Ohio. Five categories: Fiction, Nonfiction, Juvenile, Poetry and About Ohio or an Ohioan. Criteria: Books written or edited by a native Ohioan or resident of the state for at least 5 years; two copies of the book MUST be received by the Ohioana Library by December 31 prior to the year the award is given; literary quality of the book must be outstanding. Awards: Certificate and glass sculpture (up to 6 awards given annually). Each spring a jury considers all books received since the previous jury. Award judged by a jury selected from librarians, book reviewers, writers and other knowledgeable people. No entry forms are needed, but they are available. "We will be glad to answer letters asking specific questions."

OPUS MAGNUM DISCOVERY AWARDS, (I), C.C.S. Entertainment Group, 433 N. Camden Dr., #600, Beverly Hills CA 90210. (310)288-1881. Fax: (310)288-0257. E-mail: awards@screenwriters.com. President: Carlos Abreu. Award "to discover new unpublished manuscripts." Annual competition for novels. Award: Film rights options up to $10,000. Judges: Industry professionals. Entry fee $75. Deadline August 1 of each year. Unpublished submissions.

ORANGE BLOSSOM FICTION CONTEST, (I), *The Oak*, 1530 Seventh St., Rock Island IL 61201. (309)788-3980. Contact: Betty Mowery, editor. "To build up circulation of publication and give new authors a chance for competition and publication along with seasoned writers." Award: Subscription to *The Oak*. Competition receives approximately 75 submissions. Judges: Various editors from other publications, some published authors and previous contest winners. Entry fee six 32¢ stamps. Guidelines for SASE. Word length: 500 words maximum. "May be on any subject, but avoid gore and killing of humans or animals." Deadline July 1. Winners notified by letter. List of winners available for SASE.

‡OREGON BOOK AWARDS, (IV), Literary Arts, Inc., 720 SW Washington, Suite 700, Portland OR 97205. (503)227-2583. Fax: (503)241-7429. E-mail: la@literary-arts.org. Program Director: Carrie Hoops. Annual award for outstanding authors of fiction, poetry, literary non-fiction, young readers' and drama. Award: $1,000 in each category. Judges: out of state experts. Guidelines available for SASE. Deadline: March 31. Limited to Oregon residents.

OREGON INDIVIDUAL ARTIST FELLOWSHIP, (I, IV), Oregon Arts Commission, 775 Summer St. N.E., Salem OR 97310. (503)986-0082. E-mail: oregon.artscomm@state.or.us. Website: www.das.state.or.us. Contact: Vincent Dunn, assistant director. "Award enables professional artists to undertake projects to assist their professional development." Biennial competition for short stories, novels, poetry and story collections. Award: $3,000. (Please note: ten $3,000 awards are spread over 5 disciplines—literature, music/opera, media arts, dance and theatre awarded in even-numbered years.) Competition receives 150 submissions. Guidelines available for SASE after March. Judges: Professional advisors from outside the state. Guidelines and application for SASE. Deadline: September 1. Competition limited to Oregon residents. Winners announced December. Winners notified by mail. List of winners can be requested from Oregon Arts Commission.

‡OREGON LITERARY FELLOWSHIPS, (IV), Literary Arts, Inc., 720 SW Washington, Suite 700, Portland OR 97205. (503)227-2583. Fax: (503)241-7429. E-mail: la@literary-arts.org. Program Director: Carrie Hoops. "Fellowships will be awarded in two categories: emerging writers and published writers. The intention of the fellowships is to help those in need of funds to initiate, develop or complete a literary project in the areas of poetry, drama, fiction, literary non-fiction and young readers' literature." Award: $500-$2,000. Judges: out of state experts. Guidelines available for SASE. Deadline: June 30. Limited to Oregon residents.

‡PAPYRUS WRITER'S SHOWCASE CONTEST, (I), P.O. Box 270797, West Hartford CT 06127-0797. E-mail: gwhitaker@imagine.com. Website: http://www.ReadersNdex.com/papyrus. Editor: Ginger Whitaker. Competition to award fiction and poetry of interest to African-Americans. Award: $100 in each category and publication. Competition receives 500 submissions. Entry fee $5/category for non-subscribers. Guidelines for SASE. Inquiries by e-mail OK. Deadline January 30. Previously unpublished submissions. Word length: 3,500 words or less. Winner announced April, 1998. Winners notified by mail. List of winners available for SASE.

KENNETH PATCHEN COMPETITION, (I, II), Pig Iron Press, P.O. Box 237, Youngstown OH 44501. (330)747-6932. Contact: Jim Villani. Biannual. Awards works of fiction and poetry in alternating years. Award: publication; $500. Judge with national visibility selected annually. Entry fee $10. Competition receives 300 submissions. Guidelines available for SASE. Reading period: January 1 to December 31. Award for fiction: 1999, 2001, 2003; fiction award for novel or short story collection, either form eligible. Previous publication of individual stories, poems or parts of novel OK. Ms should not exceed 500 typed pages. Winners announced June. Winners notified by mail. List of winners available for SASE.

‡THE PATERSON FICTION PRIZE, The Poetry Center at Passaic County Community College, One College Boulevard, Paterson NJ 07505-1179. (973)684-6555. Fax: (973)684-5843. E-mail: m.gillan@pccc.cc.nj.us. Director: Maria Mazziotti Gillan. Award to "encourage good literature." Annual competition for short stories and novels. Award: $500. Competition receives 400 submissions. Judge: A different one every year. Guidelines available for SASE. Deadline April 1, 1998.

PEARL SHORT STORY CONTEST, (I), *Pearl* Magazine, 3030 E. Second St., Long Beach CA 90803-5163. (562)434-4523. Contact: Marilyn Johnson, editor. Award to "provide a larger forum and help widen publishing opportunities for fiction writers in the small press; and to help support the continuing publication of *Pearl*." Annual competition for short stories. Award: $100, publication in *Pearl* and 10 copies. Competition receives approximately 150 submissions. Judges: Editors of *Pearl* (Marilyn Johnson, Joan Jobe Smith, Barbara Hauk). Entry fee $10 per story. Include copy of magazine featuring winning story. Guidelines for SASE. Deadline December 1-March 15. Unpublished submissions. Length: 4,000 words maximum. Include a brief biographical note and SASE for reply or return of manuscript. Accepts simultaneous submissions, but asks to be notified if story is accepted elsewhere. All submissions are considered for publication in *Pearl*. "Although we are open to all types of fiction, we look most favorably upon coherent, well-crafted narratives, containing interesting, believable characters and meaningful situations." Winners notified by mail June 1998. List of winners available for SASE.

WILLIAM PEDEN PRIZE IN FICTION, (I), *The Missouri Review*, 1507 Hillcrest Hall, University of Missouri, Columbia MO 65211. (573)882-4474. Website: http://www.missouri.edu/~moreview. Contact: Speer Morgan, Greg Michalson, editors. Annual award "to honor the best short story published in *The Missouri Review* each year." Submissions are to be previously published in the volume year for which the prize is awarded. Award: $1,000. No entry deadline or fee. No rules; all fiction published in *MR* is automatically entered.

PEN CENTER USA WEST LITERARY AWARD IN FICTION, (II, IV), PEN Center USA West, 672 S. LaFayette Park Place, #41, Los Angeles CA 90057. (213)365-8500. Fax: (213)365-9616. E-mail: ritzwrit@ix.netcom.com. Program Coordinator: Rachel Hall. To recognize fiction writers who live in the western United States. Annual competition for published novels and story collections. Award: $1,000, plaque, and honored at a ceremony in Los Angeles. Competition receives approximately 100-125 submissions. Judges: panel of writers, booksellers, editors. Entry fee $10 for each story submitted. Guidelines for SASE. Inquiries by fax and e-mail OK. Previously published submissions published between January 1, 1997 and December 31, 1997. Open only to writers living west of the Mississippi. All entries must include 4 non-returnable copies of each submission and a completed entry form. Winners announced May 1998. Winners notified by phone and mail. Call to request press release of winners.

PEN/BOOK-OF-THE-MONTH CLUB TRANSLATION PRIZE, (II, IV), PEN American Center, 568 Broadway, New York NY 10012. (212)334-1660. Awards Coordinator: John Morrone. Award "to recognize the art of the literary translator." Annual competition for translations. Award: $3,000. Deadline December 15. Previously published submissions within the calendar year. "Translators may be of any nationality, but book must have been published in the US and must be a book-length literary translation." Books may be submitted by publishers, agents or translators. No application form. Send three copies. "Early submissions are strongly recommended."

THE PEN/FAULKNER AWARD FOR FICTION, (II, III, IV), c/o The Folger Shakespeare Library, 201 E. Capitol St. SE, Washington DC 20003. (202)675-0345. Fax: (202)608-1719. E-mail: delaney@folger.edu. Website: http://www.folger.edu. Contact: Janice Delaney, PEN/Faulkner Foundation Executive Director. Annual award. "To award the most distinguished book-length work of fiction published by an American writer." Award: $15,000 for winner; $5,000 for nominees. Judges: Three writers chosen by the Trustees of the Award. Deadline October 31. Published submissions only. Writers and publishers submit four copies of eligible titles published the current year. No juvenile. Authors must be American citizens.

PEN/NORMA KLEIN AWARD, (III), PEN American Center, 568 Broadway, New York NY 10012. (212)334-1660. Award Director: John Morrone. "Established in 1990 in memory of the late PEN member and distinguished children's book author, the biennial prize recognizes an emerging voice of literary merit among American writers of children's fiction. Candidates for the award are new authors whose books (for elementary school to young adult readers) demonstrate the adventuresome and innovative spirit that characterizes the best children's literature

• **A BULLET INTRODUCES COMMENTS** by the editor of *Novel & Short Story Writer's Market* indicating special information about the listing.

and Norma Klein's own work (but need not resemble her novels stylistically)." Award: $3,000. Judges: a panel of three distinguished children's authors. Guidelines for SASE. Previously published submissions. Writer must be nominated by other authors or editors of children's books. Next award: 1999.

‡PENNSYLVANIA COUNCIL ON THE ARTS, FELLOWSHIP PROGRAM, (I, IV), 216 Finance Bldg., Harrisburg PA 17101. (717)787-6883. Fax: (717)783-2538. E-mail: csavage@arts.cmicpo1.state.pa.us. Director, Fellowship Program: Caroline Savage. Award "to enable Pennsylvania creative writers of exceptional talent to set aside time to write." Biennial fellowships for fiction, creative nonfiction, and poetry, one year and fiction, creative nonfiction the next year. Award: Up to $10,000. Competition receives approximately 300 submissions for 5-10 awards. Judges: Out-of-state jurors with credentials in the art form. Guidelines for SASE. Inquiries by fax and e-mail OK. Deadline August 1, 1998 for poetry, August 1, 1999 for fiction, creative nonfiction. Applicants must be Pennsylvania residents for 2 years preceding deadline. Word length: 6,250 words maximum (fiction); 10 pages maximum (poetry). Winners announced January 15, 1999. Winners notified by mail.

‡PEW FELLOWSHIP IN THE ARTS, The University of the Arts, (IV), 250 S. Broad St., Suite 400, Philadelphia PA 19102. (215)875-2285. Fax: (215)875-2276. Director: Melissa Franklin. Program Assistant: Christine Miller. "The Pew Fellowships in the Arts provides financial support directly to artists so that they may have the opportunity to dedicate themselves wholly to the development of their artwork for up to two years. A goal of the Pew Fellowships in the Arts is to provide such support at a critical juncture in an artist's career, when a concentration on artistic development and exploration is most likely to contribute to personal and professional growth." Fellowship is awarded in three of nine fields each year. 1998 awards will be for fiction, poetry and 3-D visual arts. Award: up to 12 $50,000 fellowships/year. Judges: a panel of artists and arts professionals. Application and guidelines available for SASE. Limited to 2 year or longer residents of Bucks, Chester, Delaware, Montgomery or Philadelphia counties who are 25 years of age or older. Winners notified by mail.

JAMES D. PHELAN AWARD, (I, IV), Intersection for the Arts/The San Francisco Foundation, 446 Valencia St., San Francisco CA 94103. (415)626-2787. E-mail: intrsect@thecity.sfsu.edu. Literary Program Director: Charles Wilmoth. Annual award "to author of an unpublished work-in-progress of fiction (novel or short story), nonfictional prose, poetry or drama." Award: $2,000 and certificate. Rules and entry forms available after November 1 for SASE. Deadline January 31. Unpublished submissions. Applicant must have been born in the state of California, but need not be a current resident, and be 20-35 years old.

‡PHOEBE FICTION PRIZE, Phoebe, MSN 2D6 George Mason University, 4400 University Dr., Fairfax VA 22030-4444. (703)993-2915. E-mail: phoebe@gmu.edu. Contact: Becky Crane, fiction editor. Award to "find and publish new and exciting fiction." Annual competition for short stories. Award: $500 and publication. Competition receives 200 submissions. Judges: known fiction writers. Entry fee $10 for each story submitted. Guidelines available after July for SASE. Deadline December 15. Previously unpublished submissions. Word length: maximum of 25 pages. "Guidelines only (no submissions) may be requested by e-mail." Winners announced March. Winners notified by phone. List of winners available by e-mail.

PLAYBOY COLLEGE FICTION CONTEST, (I, IV), Playboy Magazine, 680 N. Lake Shore Dr., Chicago IL 60611. (312)751-8000. Contact: Alice K. Turner, fiction editor. Award "to foster young writing talent." Annual competition for short stories. Award: $3,000 plus publication in the magazine. Competition receives 1,000 submissions. Judges: Staff. Guidelines available for SASE. Deadline: January 1. Submissions should be unpublished. No age limit; college affiliation required. Stories should be 25 pages or fewer. "Manuscripts are not returned. Results of the contest will be sent via SASE." Winners notified by letter March.

POCKETS FICTION WRITING CONTEST, (I), Pockets Magazine, Upper Room Publications, P.O. Box 189, Nashville TN 37202-0189. (615)340-7333. Fax: (615)340-7006. (Do not send submissions via fax.) Contact: Lynn Gilliam, associate editor. To "find new freelance writers for the magazine." Annual competition for short stories. Award: $1,000 and publication. Competition receives approximately 600 submissions. Judged by Pockets editors and editors of other Upper Room publications. Guidelines for SASE. Deadline August 15. Former winners may not enter. Unpublished submissions. Word length: 1,000-1,600 words. "No historical fiction or fantasy."

EDGAR ALLAN POE AWARDS, (II, IV), Mystery Writers of America, Inc., 17 E. 47th St., Sixth Floor, New York NY 10017. Executive Director: Priscilla Ridgway. Annual awards to enhance the prestige of the mystery. For mystery works published or produced during the calendar year. Award: Ceramic bust of Poe. Awards for best mystery novel, best first novel by an American author, best softcover original novel, best short story, best critical/biographical work, best fact crime, best young adult, best juvenile novel, best screenplay, best television feature and best episode in a series. Contact above address for specifics. Deadline November 30.

‡POTOMAC REVIEW THIRD ANNUAL SHORT STORY CONTEST, P.O. Box 354, Port Tobacco MD 20677. (301)934-1412. Contact: Eli Flam, editor. Award to "prime the pump for top submissions, spread the word about our 'big little quarterly' and come up with winning entries to publish." Annual competition for short stories. Award: $100 and publication in the fall 1998 issue. Competition receives 50 submissions. Judge: A top writer with no connection to the magazine. Entry fee $15; year's subscription included. Guidelines will be in the winter 1997-1998 issue. Deadline February-March 31. Previously unpublished submissions. There are no limitations of style or promenance. Word length: up to 3,000 words. "We may publish the first runner-up as well."

PRAIRIE SCHOONER THE LAWRENCE FOUNDATION AWARD, (II), 201 Andrews Hall, University of Nebraska, Lincoln NE 68588-0334. (402)472-0911. Fax: (402)472-9771. E-mail: lrandolp@unlinfo2.unl.edu. Website: http://www.unl.edu/schooner/psmain.htm. Contact: Hilda Raz, editor. Annual award "given to the author of the best short story published in *Prairie Schooner* during the preceding year." Award: $1,000. Inquiries by fax and e-mail OK. "Only short fiction published in *Prairie Schooner* is eligible for consideration. Manuscripts are read September-May."

‡PREMIO AZTLAN, (IV), University of New Mexico, Department of English Language and Literature, Albuquerque NM 87131. Contact: Rudolfo Anaya. "National literary prize established for the purpose of encouraging and rewarding new Chicano and Chicana writers." Annual competition. Award: $1,000. Guidelines for SASE. Deadline December 1, 1997. "New writers are those who have published no more than two books of fiction. Any writer or publisher may submit five copies of a work of fiction published in 1997. The 1997 publication may serve as the second book. The writer's current vita must accompany the materials, which will not be returned." Award will be made in the spring of 1998, and the winner will be invited to read his or her work at the University of New Mexico.

THE PRESIDIO LA BAHIA AWARD, (II, IV), The Sons of the Republic of Texas, 1717 8th St., Bay City TX 77414. Phone/fax: (409)245-6644. E-mail: srttexas@tgn.net. Website: www.tgn.net/~srttexas. Contact: Melinda Williams. "To promote suitable preservation of relics, appropriate dissemination of data, and research into our Texas heritage, with particular attention to the Spanish Colonial period." Annual competition for novels. Award: "A total of $2,000 is available annually for winning participants, with a minimum first place prize of $1,200 for the best published book. At its discretion, the SRT may award a second place book prize or a prize for the best published paper, article published in a periodical or project of a nonliterary nature." Judges: recognized authorities on Texas history. Guidelines available after May 1 for SASE. Inquiries by fax and e-mail OK. Entries will be accepted from June 1 to September 30. Previously published submissions and completed projects. Competition is open to any person interested in the Spanish Colonial influence on Texas culture. Winners announced December. Winners notified by phone and mail. List of winners available for SASE.

❧PRISM INTERNATIONAL SHORT FICTION CONTEST, (I), *Prism International*, Dept. of Creative Writing, University of British Columbia, E462-1866 Main Mall, Vancouver, British Columbia V6T 1Z1 Canada. (604)822-2514. E-mail: prism@unixg.ubc.ca. Website: http://www.arts.ubc.ca/prism/. Contact: Publicity Manager. Award: $2,000 first prize and five $200 consolation prizes. Competition receives 650 submissions. Deadline December 15 of each year. Entry fee $15 plus $5 reading fee for each story; years subscription included. SASE for rules/entry forms. Inquiries by e-mail OK. Winners announced July 1999. Winners notified in writing. List of winners available for SASE.

PULITZER PRIZE IN FICTION, (III, IV), Columbia University, 702 Journalism Bldg., Mail Code 3865, New York NY 10027. (212)854-3841. Annual award for distinguished short stories, novels and story collections *first* published in America in book form during the year by an American author, preferably dealing with American life. Award: $5,000 and certificate. Guidelines available for SASE. Deadline: Books published between January 1 and June 30 must be submitted by July 1. Books published between July 1 and December 31 must be submitted by November 1; books published between November 1 and December 31 must be submitted in galleys or page proofs by November 1. Submit 4 copies of the book, entry form, biography and photo of author and $50 handling fee. Open to American authors.

PUSHCART PRIZE, (III), Pushcart Press, P.O. Box 380, Wainscott NY 11975. (516)324-9300. President: Bill Henderson. Annual award "to publish and recognize the best of small press literary work." Previously published submissions, short stories, poetry or essays on any subject. Must have been published during the current calendar year. Award: Publication in *Pushcart Prize: Best of the Small Presses*. Deadline: December 1. Nomination by small press publishers/editors only.

❧QSPELL BOOK AWARDS/HUGH MACLENNAN FICTION AWARD, (II, IV), Quebec Society for the Promotion of English Language Literature, 1200 Atwater, Montreal, Quebec H3Z 1X4 Canada. Phone/fax: (514)933-0878. E-mail: qspell@total.net. Secretary: Julie Keith. "To honor excellence in writing in English in Quebec." Annual competition for short stories, novels, poetry and nonfiction. Award: $2,000 (Canadian) in each category. Competition receives approximately 50 submissions. Judges: panel of 3 jurors, different each year. Entry fee $10 (Canadian) per title. Guidelines for SASE. Inquiries by fax and e-mail OK. Submissions published in previous year from May 16 to May 15. "Writer must have resided in Quebec for 3 of the past 5 years." Books may be published anywhere. Page length: more than 48 pages. Winners announced November 1998.

QUARTERLY WEST NOVELLA COMPETITION, (I), University of Utah, 200 S. Campus Dr., Room 317, Salt Lake City UT 84112-9109. (801)581-3938. Biennial award for novellas. Award: 2 prizes of $500 and publication in *Quarterly West*. Competition receives 300 submissions. Send SASE for contest rules available in June 1998. Deadline: Postmarked by December 31, 1998. Winners announced in May or June. Winners notified by phone. List of winners available for SASE.

SIR WALTER RALEIGH AWARD, (II, IV), North Carolina Literary and Historical Association, 109 E. Jones St., Raleigh NC 27601-2807. (919)733-9375. Awards Coordinator: Jerry C. Cashion. "To promote among the people of North Carolina an interest in their own literature." Annual award for novels. Award: Statue of Sir Walter Raleigh. Competition receive 12-20 submissions. Judges: University English and history professors. Guidelines for SASE. Inquiries by fax OK. Book must be an original work published during the 12 months ending June 30 of the year for which the award is given. Writer must be a legal or physical resident of North Carolina for the three years preceding the close of the contest period. Authors or publishers may submit 3 copies of their book to the above address. Winners announced November. Winners notified by mail. List of winners available for SASE.

‡THE REA AWARD FOR THE SHORT STORY, (IV), Dungannon Foundation, 53 W. Church Hill Rd., Washington CT 06794. (860)868-9455. Contact: Elizabeth Rea, president. Annual award for "a writer who has made a significant contribution to the short story form. Award: $30,000. Judges: 3 jurors. Work must be nominated by the jury. Award announced in April annually.

READ WRITING & ART AWARDS, (I, IV), *Read* Magazine & Weekly Reader Corp., 200 First Stamford Place, P.O. Box 120023, Stamford CT 06912-0023. (203)705-3449. Fax: (203)705-1661. E-mail: eflorain@weekl yreader.com. Website: http://www.weeklyreader.com. Contact: Ellen Flonan, associate editor. "To recognize and publish outstanding writing and art by students in grades 6-12." Annual awards for short story, essay and art. Award: $100 (first prize), $75 (second prize), $50 (third prize); publication of first-prize winner, certificates of excellence. Competition receives approximately 2,000 submissions. Judges: editors of Weekly Reader Corp. Guidelines for SASE after September or phone (860)638-2400. Guideline coupon must accompany each submission. Deadline December 5. Unpublished submissions. Word length: 5-6 pages typed double-space. "Fiction category may include short stories or play formats." Winners announced April. Winners notified by mail. List of winners available May for SASE.

REGINA MEDAL AWARD, (III), Catholic Library Association, 100 North St., Suite 224, Pittsfield MA 01201-5109. Contact: Jean R. Bostley, SSJ executive director. Annual award. To honor continued distinguished lifetime contribution to children's literature. Award: silver medal. Award given during Easter week. Selection by a special committee; nominees are suggested by the Catholic Library Association Membership.

RHODE ISLAND STATE COUNCIL ON THE ARTS, (I, IV), Individual Artist's Fellowship in Literature, 95 Cedar St., Suite 103, Providence RI 02903-1062. (401)277-3880. Contact: Individual Artist Program. Biennial fellowship. Award: $5,000; runner-up $1,000. Competition receives approximately 50 submissions. In-state panel makes recommendations to an out-of-state judge, who recommends finalist to the council. Entry forms for SASE. Deadline: April 1. Artists must be Rhode Island residents and not undergraduate or graduate students. "Program guidelines may change. Prospective applicants should contact RISCA prior to deadline."

HAROLD U. RIBALOW PRIZE, (II, IV), *Hadassah Magazine*, 50 W. 58th St., New York NY 10019. (212)688-0227. Fax: (212)446-9521. E-mail: hadamag@aol.com. Contact: Alan M. Tigay, executive editor. Estab. 1983. Annual award "for a book of fiction on a Jewish theme. Harold U. Ribalow was a noted writer and editor who devoted his time to the discovery and encouragement of young Jewish writers." Book should have been published the year preceding the award. Award: $1,000 and excerpt of book in *Hadassah Magazine*. Deadline is April of the year following publication.

‡THE MARY ROBERTS RINEHART FUND, (III), Mail Stop Number 3E4, English Dept., George Mason University Cretive Writing Program, 4400 University Dr., Fairfax VA 22030-4444. (703)993-1185. E-mail: engl.g rad@gmu.edu. Director: William Miller. Biennial award for short stories, novels, novellas and story collections by unpublished writers (that is, writers ineligible to apply for NEA grants). Award: One grant the amount of which varies depending upon income the fund generates (generally about $1,000). Competition receives approximately 75-100 submissions annually. Rules for SASE. Inquiries by e-mail OK. Next fiction deadline November 30. Writers must be nominated by a sponsoring writer, writing teacher, editor or agent. Winners announced March 1. Winners notified by mail. List of winners available for SASE.

RITE OF SPRING FICTION CONTEST, (I), *Phantasm*, 1530 Seventh St., Rock Island IL 61201. (309)788-3980. Contact: Betty Mowery, editor. "To build up circulation of publication and provide new authors a home for work along with seasoned authors." Competition for short stories. Award: 1 year subscription to Phastasm. Competition receives 25 submissions. Entry fee six 32¢ stamps. Guidelines for SASE. Deadline September 30. "Writers must submit their own fiction of no more than 500 words. We are looking for fiction of quiet horror or fantasy." Winners announced October 2. Winners notified by letter.

SUMMERFIELD G. ROBERTS AWARD, (I, II, IV), The Sons of the Republic of Texas, 1717 8th St., Bay City TX 77414. Phone/fax: (409)245-6644. E-mail: srttexas@tgn.net. Website: http://www.tgn.net/~srttexas. Executive Secretary: Melinda Williams. "Given for the best book or manuscript of biography, essay, fiction, nonfiction, novel, poetry or short story that describes or represents the Republic of Texas, 1836-1846." Annual award of $2,500. Competition receives 10-20 submissions. Guidelines available after June for SASE. Deadline January 15. "The manuscripts must be written or published during the calendar year for which the award is given. Entries are to be submitted in quintuplicate and will not be returned." Winners announced April. Winners notified by mail or phone. List of wiiners available for SASE.

*ROMANTIC NOVELISTS' ASSOCIATION ROMANTIC NOVEL OF THE YEAR AWARD, (II, IV), 3 Arnesby Lane, Peatling Magna, Leicester LE8 SUN England. Tel: 0116/2478330. Contact: Major Award Organiser, Romantic Novelists' Association. "To publish good romantic fiction and therefore raise the prestige of the genre." Annual competition for novels. Award: under consideration. Competition receives approximately 150 submissions. Submissions period: September 1-December 1. For novels "published in the U.K. A modern or historical romantic novel. Three copies of each entry are required. They may be hardback or paperback. Only novels written in English and published in the U.K. during the previous 12 months (December 1-November 30) are eligible. Authors must be domiciled in U.K. or temporarily living abroad whilst in possession of British passport."

BRUCE P. ROSSLEY LITERARY AWARDS, (I, II, III, IV), 96 Inc., P.O. Box 15559, Boston MA 02215. (617)267-0543. Associate Director: Nancy Mehegan. "To increase the attention for writers of merit who have received little recognition." Biennial award for short stories, novels and story collections. Award: $1,000 for the literary award and $100 for Bruce P. Rossley New Voice Award. Competition receives 250 submissions. Judges: Professionals in the fields of writing, journalism and publishing. Entry fee $10. Guidelines for SASE. Deadline September 30. Published or unpublished submissions. "In addition to writing, the writer's accomplishments in the fields of teaching and community service will also be considered." Open to writers from New England. Work must be nominated by "someone familiar with the writer's work."

‡ROTTEN ROMANCE, Hutton Publications, P.O. Box 2907, Decatur IL 62524. Contact: Linda Hutton, editor. Award to "have fun writing a spoof of genre fiction." Annual competition for short stories. Award: $10 and publication. Competition receives 90-100 submissions. Judge: Linda Hutton, editor. Guidelines available for SASE. Deadline Valentine's Day annually. Previously unpublished submissions. Open to anyone. Word length: no more than 1 sentence, any length. "An entry form is available, but not required. Handwritten envelopes and/ or entries will be discarded; all material must be typed. SASE required with entry."

‡PLEASANT T. ROWLAND PRIZE FOR FICTION FOR GIRLS, (IV), Pleasant Company Publications, 8400 Fairway Place, Middleton WI 53562. (608)836-4848. Fax: (608)836-1999. Contact: Submissions Editor. Award to "encourage writers to turn their talents to the creation of high-quality fiction for girls and to reward talented authors of novels that successfully capture the spirit of contemporary American girls and illuminate the ways in which their lives may be personally touched by events and concerns shaping the United States today." Sponsored by Pleasant Company, publisher of The American Girls Collection series of historical fiction, American Girl Library advice and activity books, and *American Girl* magazine. Annual competition for novels appealing to girls ages 8-12. Award: $10,000 cash prize. Winning author will be offered a standard contract with an advance and royalty payments for publication of the book under Pleasant Company's forthcoming contemporary fiction imprint. All entries considered for possible publication by Pleasant Company. Judges: editors of Pleasant Company Publications. No entry fee; 1 entry/person. Guidelines for SASE. Deadline September 1, 1998. Unpublished submissions. No simultaneous submissions. U.S. residents only. Authors whose work is now being published by Pleasant Company not eligible. Employees, their immediate family and suppliers of materials or services to Pleasant Company not eligible. Void where prohibited by law. Word length: 100-200 pages, double spaced. Submissions by authors or agents. "Stories should feature female protagonists between the ages of 8 and 12. We welcome characters of varying cultural backgrounds and family situations." Winner announced shortly after December 31, 1998. Include self-addressed stamped postcard with entry for list of winners.

‡*THE IAN ST. JAMES AWARDS, P.O. Box 60, Cranbrook, Kent TN17 2ZR United Kingdom. 01580 212626. Fax: 01580 212041. Organizer: Merric Davidson. Award to "provide a better way for a writer to take a first step towards a literary career." Annual competition for short stories. Award: £2,000 top prize. Competition receives

---

‡ THE DOUBLE DAGGER before a listing indicates that the listing is new in this edition.

2,500-3,000 submissions. Judges: Writers, publishers. Entry fee £6 per story. Guidelines available for SASE. Deadline April 30. Previously unpublished submissions.

SATIRE WRITING CONTEST, P.O. Box 340, Hancock MO 21750-0340. (301)678-6999. E-mail: satire@intre pid.net. Contact: Larry Logan, editor. Award "to promote the classic literary form/genre that is satire." Short stories, essays, poems, cartoons (under 1,000 words). Entry fee $5 for each story submitted. Three winners will be selected, and each will receive 30% of all entry fees collected, plus their satires will be published in the Summer 1998 issue of *Satire*. Guidelines for SASE. Inquiries by e-mail OK. Deadline January 1. Original, previously unpublished submissions only. Winners announced in March. Winners notified by phone.

THE SCHOLASTIC WRITING AWARDS, (I, IV), Alliance for Young Artists & Writers, Inc., 555 Broadway, New York NY 10012. Program Coordinator: Sarah Fewster. To provide opportunity for recognition of young writers (grades 7-12). Annual award for short stories and other categories. Award: Cash awards and grants. Competition receives 25,000 submissions/year. Judges vary each year. Entry fee: $3. Deadline: varies. "Please request entry form between September and December." Unpublished submissions. Contest limited to junior high and senior high students; grades 7-12. Entry blank must be signed by teacher. "Program is run through school and is only open to students in grades 7 through 12, regularly and currently enrolled in public and non-public schools in the United States and its territories, U.S.-sponsored schools abroad or any schools in Canada." Winners announced May. Winners notified by mail.

SCIENCE FICTION WRITERS OF EARTH (SFWoE) SHORT STORY CONTEST, (I, IV), Science Fiction Writers of Earth, P.O. Box 121293, Fort Worth TX 76121-1293. (817)451-8674. E-mail: sfwoe@flash.net. Website: http://www.flash.net/~sfwoe. SFWoE Administrator: Gilbert Gordon Reis. Purpose "to promote the art of science fiction/fantasy short story writing." Annual award for short stories. Award: $200 (first prize); $100 (second prize); $50 (third prize). Competition receives approximately 150 submissions/year. Judge: Author Edward Bryant. Entry fee $5 for 1st entry; $2 for additional entries. Guidelines for SASE. Inquiries by e-mail OK. Deadline October 30. Submissions must be unpublished. Stories should be science fiction or fantasy, 2,000-7,500 words. "Although many of our past winners are now published authors, there is still room for improvement. The odds are good for a well-written story. Contestants enjoy international competition." Winners announced January 31. Winners notified by phone.

SE LA VIE WRITER'S JOURNAL CONTEST, (I, IV), Rio Grande Press, P.O. Box 71745, Las Vegas NV 89170. Contact: Rosalie Avara, editor. Competition offered quarterly for short stories. Award: Publication in the *Se La Vie Writer's Journal* plus up to $10 and contributor's copy. Judge: Editor. Entry fee $4 for each or $7 for two. Guidelines for SASE. Deadlines: March 31, June 30, September 30, December 31. Unpublished submissions. Themes: slice-of-life, mystery, adventure, social. Length: 500 words maximum.

‡THE SEATON AWARD, Arkansas Review, Department of English, Box 1890, State University AR 72467. (870)972-3043. Contact: Norman Lavers, editor. Award to "encourage good writing from Kansas writers." Annual competition for all genres. Award: $1,000. Judges: Editors. Guidelines available in April issue. "If a writer's work is accepted for publication in Arkansas Review, it is automatically in the running for the prize." Previously unpublished submissions. Writers must have lived in Kansas at least one full year.

SEATTLE ARTISTS PROGRAM, (IV), Seattle Arts Commission, 312 First Ave. N., Suite 200, Seattle WA 98109. (206)684-7310. Fax: (206)684-7172. "Award to support development of new works by individual, generative literary artists." Annual competition for poetry, prose/fiction, scriptwriting, screenwriting, critical writing and creative nonfiction. Award: $2,000 or $7,500. Competition receives approx. 150 submissions. Judges: peer review panels. Guidelines/application for SASE. Deadline: June 1998. Previously published submissions or unpublished submissions. Only Seattle residents or residents with a Seattle studio or office may apply. Word length: Word-length requirements vary; the guidelines must be read.

‡✽CARL SENTNER SHORT STORY AWARD, (I, IV), P.E.I. Council of the Arts, 115 Richmond St., Charlottetown, P.E.I. C1A 1H7 Canada. (902)368-4410. Fax: (902)368-4418. "Awarded by Island Literary Awards to the author of a short story." Annual competition for short stories. Award: $500 (first prize); $200 (second prize), $100 (third prize). Entry fee $6. Deadline February 15. Unpublished submissions. "Competition is open to individuals who have been residents of Prince Edward Island at least six of the last twelve months. Not open to authors with one or more books published in the last five years. Enclose SASE for return of manuscript."

‡7 HILLS SHORT FICTION CONTEST, (IV), Tallahassee Writers Association, P.O. Box 6996, Tallahassee FL 32314. (904)877-0840. E-mail: verna325@aol.com. Fiction Chair: Verna Safran. Competition to "stimulate good writing, to use proceeds for book donations to library and for a college scholarship, to produce a literary magazine." Annual competition for short stories. Awards: $100 first prize, $75 second, $50 third, plus honorable mentions and publication. Judges: different each year. Entry fee $5. Guidelines for SASE. Deadline August 15.

Unpublished submissions and not submitted elsewhere. "We want literary fiction, not genre fiction." Word length: 1,500-2,000.

SEVENTEEN MAGAZINE FICTION CONTEST, (I, IV), *Seventeen Magazine*, 850 Third Ave., New York NY 10022-6258. Contact: Ben Schrank. To honor best short fiction by a young writer. Competition receives 5,000 submissions. Rules published in the November issue. Contest for 13-21 year olds. Deadline April 30. Submissions judged by a panel of outside readers and *Seventeen*'s editors. Cash awarded to winners. First-place story published in the December or January issue. Winners notified by mail in late 1998.

SFWA NEBULA® AWARDS, (III, IV), Science-fiction and Fantasy Writers of America, Inc., 532 La Guardia Place #632, New York NY 10012-1428. President: Michael Capobianco. Annual awards for previously published short stories, novels, novellas, novelettes. Science fiction/fantasy only. "No submissions; nominees upon recommendation of members only." Deadline December 31. "Works are nominated throughout the year by active members of the SFWA."

‡FRANCES SHAW FELLOWSHIP FOR OLDER WOMEN WRITERS, The Ragdale Foundation, 1260 N. Green Bay Rd., Lake Forest IL 60045. (847)234-1063. Fax: (847)234-1075. E-mail: ragdale1@aol.com. Director of Programming, Marketing and Residency: Sylvia Brown. Award to "nurture and support older women writers who are just beginning to write seriously." Annual competition for short stories, novels and poetry. Award: 2 months free residency at Ragdale, plus domestic travel. Competition receives approximately 65 submissions. Judges: a panel of four women writers. Guidelines available for SASE. Deadline February 1. Previously unpublished submissions. Females over 55. Word length: 20 pages/12 short poems.

SHORT AND SWEET CONTEST, (II, IV), Perry Terrell Publishing, M.A. Green Shopping Center, Inc., Metairie Bank Bldg., 7809 Airline Hwy., Suite 215-A, Metairie LA 70003. (504)737-7781. "The purpose is to inspire and encourage creativity in humor. (My personal purpose is to see who has a sense of humor and who doesn't.)" Monthly competition, 1 to 2 months after deadline, for short stories. Award: $5. Receives 15 to 47/ month. Judges: Perry Terrell. Entry fee 50¢/entry. Guidelines for SASE. Send SASE for details."

✿SHORT GRAIN CONTEST, (I), Box 1154, Regina, Saskatchewan S4P 3B4 Canada. E-mail: grain.mag@sk .sympatico.ca. Website: http://www.sasknet.com/corporate/skwriter. ("E-mail entries not accepted.") Contact: J. Jill Robinson. Annual competition for postcard stories, prose poems and dramatic monologues. Awards: $500 (first prize), $300 (second prize) and $200 (third prize) in each category. "All winners and Honourable Mentions will also receive regular payment for publication in *Grain*." Competition receives approximately 1,500 submissions. Judges: Canadian writers with national and international reputations. Entry fee $20 for 2 entries in one category (includes one-year subscription); each additional entry in the same category $5. U.S. and International entries in U.S. dollars. U.S. writers add $4 U.S. postage. International writers add $6 U.S. postage. Guidelines for SASE or SAE and IRC. Deadline January 31. Unpublished submissions. Contest entries must be either an original postcard story (a work of narrative fiction written in 500 words or less) or a prose poem (a lyric poem written as a prose paragraph or paragraphs in 500 words or less), or a dramatic monologue (a self-contained speech given by a single character in 500 words or less). Winners announced April. Winners notified by phone and mail. List of winners available for SASE.

‡SHORT, SHORT FICTION CONTEST, (I), New England Writers, P.O. Box 483, Windsor VT 05089. (802)674-2315. Fax: (802)674-6635. E-mail: newvtpoets@juno.com. Editor: Frank Anthony. Competition for publication in annual *Anthology of New England Writers*. Annual competition for short stories. Award: $250. Competition receives 100 submissions. Judge: Joan Connor, 1998. Entry fee $5. Guidelines available January 1998 for SASE. Inquires by e-mail OK. Deadline June 15, 1998. Unpublished submissions. Word length: 1,000 words maximum. "We want well-crafted stories written for an audience with high standards." Winners announced at annual N.E.W. conference in July. List of winners available for SASE

‡SHORT/SHORT FICTION PRIZE, (I), *Salt Hill Journal*, English Department, Syracuse University, Syracuse NY 13244. Website: http://www.hl.syr.edu/cap. Editor: Peter S. Fendrick. Annual competition to "publish the best short/short fiction being written today." Awards: $500 first prize, $250 second, $100 third, all plus publication; 10 honorable mentions. Judges: final judging by nationally known writer. Entry fee $9/story. Guidelines for SASE. Deadline September 15. Unpublished submissions. Word length: up to 1,500 words/story. Name, address, phone number and word count on first page. Enclose SASE for results; stories not returned. Address submission to Fiction Contest.

SIDE SHOW 8TH SHORT STORY CONTEST, (II), Somersault Press, P.O. Box 1428, El Cerrito CA 94530-1428. (510)215-2207. Contact: Shelley Anderson, M.K. Jacobs and Kathe Stolz, editors. "To attract quality writers for our 300-odd page paperback fiction anthology." Awards: first: $500; second: $200; third: $100; $10/ printed page paid to all accepted writers (on publication). Judges: The editors of *Side Show*. Entry fee $10; year's subscription included. Leaflet available but no guidelines or restrictions on length, subject or style. Sample copy for $10 plus $2 postage. Multiple submissions (in same mailing envelope) encouraged (only one entry fee required for each writer). Manuscripts with SASE critiqued, if requested. No deadline. Book published when we accept 20-25 stories. "A story from *Side Show* was selected for inclusion in *Pushcart Prize XVIII: Best of the Small Presses.*"

BERNICE SLOTE AWARD, (II), *Prairie Schooner*, 201 Andrews Hall, University of Nebraska, Lincoln NE 68588-0334. (402)472-0911. Contact: Hilda Raz, editor. "An award for the best work by a beginning writer published in *Prairie Schooner* during the previous year." Annual award for short stories, novel excerpts and translations. Award: $500. Judges: Editorial board. Guidelines for SASE. Unpublished submissions. Must be beginning writers (not have a book published). "We only read mss September through May."

KAY SNOW CONTEST, (I, IV), Willamette Writers, 9045 SW Barbur Blvd., Suite 5-A, Portland OR 97219. (503)452-1592. Fax: (503)452-0372. E-mail: wilwrite@teleport.com. Contact: Contest Coordinator. Award "to create a showcase for writers of all fields of literature." Annual competition for short stories; also poetry (structured and nonstructured), nonfiction, juvenile and student writers. Award: $200 first prize in each category, second and third prizes, honorable mentions. Competition receives approximately 500 submissions. Judges: nationally recognized writers and teachers. Entry fee $15, nonmembers; $10, members; $5, students. Guidelines for #10 SASE. Inquiries by fax and e-mail OK. Deadline May 15 postmark. Unpublished submissions. Maximum 5 double-spaced pages or up to 3 poems per entry fee with maximum 5 double-spaced pages. Winners announced August. Winners notified by mail and phone. List of winners available for SASE. Prize winners will be honored at the two-day August Willamette Writers Conference. Press releases will be sent to local and national media announcing the winners, and excerpts from winning entries may appear in our newsletter.

SOCIETY OF CHILDREN'S BOOK WRITERS AND ILLUSTRATORS GOLDEN KITE AWARDS, (II, IV), Society of Children's Book Writers and Illustrators, 22736 Vanowen St., Suite 106, West Hills CA 91307. (818)888-8760. Contact: Sue Alexander, chairperson. Annual award. "To recognize outstanding works of fiction, nonfiction and picture illustration for children by members of the Society of Children's Book Writers and Illustrators and published in the award year." Published submissions should be submitted from January to December of publication year. Deadline December 15. Rules for SASE. Award: Statuette and plaque. Looking for quality material for children. Individual "must be member of the SCBWI to submit books."

SOCIETY OF CHILDREN'S BOOK WRITERS AND ILLUSTRATORS WORK-IN-PROGRESS GRANTS, (I, IV), 22736 Vanowen St., Suite 106, West Hills CA 91307. (818)888-8760. Contact: SCBWI. Annual grant for any genre or contemporary novel for young people; also nonfiction research grant and grant for work whose author has never been published. Award: First-$1,000, second-$500 (work-in-progress). Competition receives approximately 180 submissions. Judges: Members of children's book field—editors, authors, etc. Guidelines for SASE. Deadline February 1-May 1. Unpublished submissions. Applicants must be SCBWI members.

SONORA REVIEW **SHORT STORY CONTEST, (I, II)**, Dept. of English, University of Arizona, Tucson AZ 85721-0067. (520)626-2555. Contact: Fiction Editor. Annual contest to encourage and support quality short fiction. $500 first prize plus publication in *Sonora Review*. All entrants receive copy of the magazine. Entry fee $10. Competition receives 150 submissions. Send SASE for contest rules and deadlines.

SOUTH CAROLINA ARTS COMMISSION AND *THE POST AND COURIER* **NEWSPAPER (CHARLESTON, SC) SOUTH CAROLINA FICTION PROJECT, (I, IV)**, 1800 Gervais St., Columbia SC 29201. (803)734-8696. Steve Lewis, director, Literary Arts Program. The purpose of the award is "to get money to fiction writers and to get their work published and read." Annual award for short stories. Award: $500 and publication in *The Post and Courier*. Competition receives between 200 and 400 submissions for 12 awards (up to 12 stories chosen). Judges are a panel of professional writers and Book Editor/Features Assistant Editor for *The Post and Courier*. Deadline: March 15. *South Carolina residents only*. Stories must not be over 2,500 words. Query for guidelines.

SOUTH CAROLINA ARTS COMMISSION LITERATURE FELLOWSHIPS AND LITERATURE GRANTS, (I, IV), 1800 Gervais St., Columbia SC 29201. (803)734-8696. Steve Lewis, director, Literary Arts Program. "The purpose of the fellowships is to give a cash award to a deserving writer (one year in poetry, one year in creative prose) whose works are of the highest caliber." Award: $7,500 fellowship. Matching project grants up to $5,000. Judges are out-of-state panel of professional writers and editors for fellowships, and panels and SCAC staff for grants. Query for entry forms or rules. Fellowship deadline September 15. Grants deadline November 15. *South Carolina residents only*. "The next deadline is for creative prose."

‡**SOUTHEAST TEXAS WRITERS LEAGUE WRITERS CONTEST, (I)**, P.O. Box 5156, Beaumont TX 77726-5156. (409)835-3337. Contact: Druann Wiley, president. Award "to encourage aspiring writers in submissions and to provide valuable critiques from the judges." Biannual competition for short stories, articles and poetry. Award: publication in SETWL Journal. Judges: published writers. Entry fee $5. Guidelines available in early 1998 for SASE. Unpublished submissions. "Only one entry per category per writer." Word length: 3,000 words average. "Do not include writer's name on story, but only on cover page. Include SASE if you wish entry

returned." Winners announced at STWL Conference. Winners notified by mail. List of winners available for SASE.

THE SOUTHERN PRIZE, (I), *The Southern Anthology*, 2851 Johnston St., #123, Lafayette LA 70503. Contact: Dr. R. Sebastian Bennett, managing editor. Award to "promote and reward outstanding writing; to encourage both traditional and avant-garde forms." Annual competition for short stories, novel excerpts and poetry. Award: $600 Grand Prize and publication; six finalists are also published. Judges: Editorial Panel. Entry fee $10. Guidelines for SASE. Postmark deadline: May 30, 1998. Unpublished submissions. "Available to all authors writing in English, regardless of citizenship. There are no form or genre restrictions. Submissions need not address 'Southern' themes. *The Southern Anthology* encourages both traditional and avant-garde writing." Word length: 7,500 words. "*The Southern Anthology* has no restrictions on style. However, we tend to prefer work which is oppositional or formally innovative in nature; which destablilizes established institutions or genres; or which portrays often-overlooked elements of society, avoiding or mimicking stereotypes. We do not subscribe to any political, aesthetic, or moral agenda; and detest conformance to 'political correctness' for its own sake. Often, we publish work which has been deemed 'too risky' for other journals. We also publish a variety of traditional forms."

THE SOUTHERN REVIEW/LOUISIANA STATE UNIVERSITY ANNUAL SHORT FICTION AWARD, (II), *The Southern Review*, 43 Allen Hall, Louisiana State University, Baton Rouge LA 70803. (504)388-5108. Fax: (504)388-5098. E-mail: bmacon@unixl.sncc.lsu.edu. Contact: Editors, *The Southern Review*. Annual award "to encourage publication of good fiction." For a first collection of short stories by an American writer published in the United States appearing during calendar year. Award: $500 to author. Possible campus reading. Guidelines available for SASE early summer 1998. Inquiries by fax and e-mail OK. Deadline a month after close of each calendar year. Two copies to be submitted by publisher or author. Looking for "style, sense of craft, plot, in-depth characters." Winners announced late spring.

‡SPRING FANTASY FICTION CONTEST, Women In The Arts, P.O. Box 2907, Decatur IL 62524. (217)872-0811. Contact: Vice President. Award to "encourage new writers, whether published or not." Annual competition for short stories. Award: At least $30. Competition receives 25-30 submissions. Judges: WITA members who are professional writers. Entry fee $2 for each story submitted. Guidelines available for SASE. Deadline November 15 annually. Published or previously unpublished submissions. Open to anyone not a member of WITA. Word length: 1,500 words maximum. "Entrants must send for our contest rules and follow the specific format requirements."

‡SPRING FANTASY JUVENILE-FICTION CONTEST, Women In The Arts, P.O. Box 2907, Decatur IL 62524. (217)872-0811. Contact: Vice President. Award to "encourage writers of children's literature, whether published or not." Annual competition for short stories. Award: At least $30. Competition receives 10-15 submissions. Judges: WITA members who are professional writers. Entry fee $2 for each story submitted. Guidelines available for SASE. Deadline November 15 annually. Published or previously unpublished submissions. Open to anyone not a member of WITA. Word length: 1,500 words maximum. "Entrants must send for our contest rules and follow the specific format requirements."

‡STAND MAGAZINE SHORT STORY COMPETITION, (I), *Stand Magazine*, 179 Wingrove Road, Newcastle upon Tyne NE4 9DA England. Biennial award for short stories. Award: First prize £1,500; second prize £500; third prize £250; fourth prize £150; fifth prize £100 (or US $ equivalent). Entry fee $8. Guidelines and entry form on receipt of UK SAE or 2 IRCs. Deadline June 30, 1999.

WALLACE E. STEGNER FELLOWSHIP, (I, IV), Creative Writing Program, Stanford University, Stanford CA 94305-2087. (415)723-2637. Fax: (415)725-0755. E-mail: gay-pierce@forsythe.stanford.edu. Program Administrator: Gay Pierce. Annual award for short stories, novels, poetry and story collections. Five fellowships in fiction ($15,000 stipend plus required tuition of $5,000 annually). Competition receive 1,000 submissions. Entry fee $40. Guidelines for SASE. Inquiries by fax and e-mail OK. Deadline: December 1. For unpublished or previously published fiction writers. Residency required. Word length: 9,000 words or 40 pages. Winners announced March. Winners notified by telephone. All applicants receive notification of winners.

‡STONY BROOK SHORT FICTION PRIZE, (IV), State University of New York, Department of English, Humanities Bldg., Stony Brook NY 11794-5350. Contact: Carolyn McGrath. Award "to recognize excellent undergraduate fiction." Annual competition for short stories. Award: $1,000. Judges: Faculty of the Department of English & Creative Writing Program. No entry fee. Guidelines for SASE. Deadline March 2, 1998. Unpublished submissions. "Only undergraduates enrolled full time in American or Canadian colleges and universities for the academic year 1997-98 are eligible. Students with an Asian background are particularly encouraged to participate." Word length: 5,000 words or less. Prize will be awarded by June 1998.

STORY'S SHORT SHORT STORY COMPETITION, STORY Magazine, 1507 Dana Ave., Cincinnati OH 45207. (513)531-2222. Editor: Lois Rosenthal. Award to "encourage the form of the short short and to find stories for possible publication in the magazine." Contest begins June 1 and closes October 31. Award: $1,000 (first prize); $500 (second prize); $250 (third prize); $100 (fourth through tenth prizes); $50 (eleventh through twenty-fifth prizes); plus other prizes that change annually. Entry fee $10. Guidelines are published in the magazine. Word length: 1,500 words or less.

✿SUB-TERRAIN ANNUAL SHORT STORY CONTEST, (I), (formerly Penny Dreadful Annual Short Story Contest), *sub-TERRAIN Magazine*, P.O. Box 1575, Bentall Center, Vancouver, British Columbia V6C 2P7 Canada. (604)876-8710. Fax: (604)879-2667. E-mail: subter@pinc.com. Contact: Brian Kaufman. "To inspire writers to get down to it and struggle with a form that is condensed and difficult. To encourage clean, powerful writing." Annual award for short stories. Prize: $250 and publication. Runners-up also receive publication. Competition receives 150-200 submissions. Judges: An editorial collective. Entry fee $15 for one story, $5 extra for each additional story (includes 4-issue subscription). Guidelines for SASE in November. "Contest kicks off in November." Deadline May 15. Unpublished submissions. Length: 2,000 words maximum. Winners announced in July issue. Winners notified by phone call and press release. "We are looking for fiction that has MOTION, that goes the distance in fewer words."

SUGAR MILL PRESS CONTESTS, (I, II), Perry Terrell Publishing, M.A. Green Shopping Center, Inc., Metairie Bank Bldg., 7809 Airline Hwy., Suite 215-A, Metairie LA 70003. (504)737-7781. "The purpose is to draw manuscripts from all writers, especially new writers, pay the winners first and reserve the right to print all (acceptable) material that is sent to Perry Terrell Publishing in *The Ultimate Writer*, *The Bracelet Charm*, *Amulet* or *The Veneration Quarterly*; also, to choose manuscripts of unique and outstanding quality to recommend to a small movie production company I have been invited to work with in California. (Writers will be notified before recommendation is made.)" Award is granted monthly, 4 to 6 months after contest deadlines. For short stories. Award: $100, $75, $50, $25 and 2 honorable mentions ($5). Competition receives 25 to 75/deadline. Judges: Perry Terrell, editor; Jonathan Everett, associate editor; Julie D. Terrell, features editor. Entry fee $5. Guidelines for SASE. Deadlines are throughout each month. Previously published or unpublished submissions. "Please specify which deadline and/or contest being entered. If not specified, the editor will read, when time permits, and place the entry the next month." Send SASE for theme list. Winners announced 4-6 months after content deadline. Winners notified by mail. List of winners available for SASE.

‡THE RICHARD SULLIVAN PRIZE IN SHORT FICTION, Creative Writing Program, Department of English and University of Notre Dame Press, Department of English, University of Notre Dame, Notre Dame IN 46556. (219)631-7526. Fax: (219)631-8209. E-mail: righter@nd.edu. Director of Creative Writing: William O'Rourke. Award to "publish the second (or later) volume of short stories by an author of demonstrated excellence." Biannual competition for short stories and story collections. Award: $500 and publication by University of Notre Dame Press. Competition receives 150 submissions. Judges: Faculty of the Creative Writing Program. Guidelines available for SASE. Deadline May 1-August 31, 1998. Previously unpublished submissions in book form. Open to any writer who has published at least one previous volume of short stories.

‡✿SURREY WRITERS' CONFERENCE WRITING CONTEST, (I), Surrey School District, 12870 72nd Ave., Surrey British Columbia V3W 2M9 Canada. (604)594-2000. Fax: (604)590-2506. E-mail: Ed_Griffin@compuserve.com. Website: http://www.vcn.bc.ca/swc/. Contact: Ed Griffin, coordinator. Award to "encourage beginning writers." Annual competition for short stories and novels. Award: $75-$250 in each category. Competition receives 150 submissions/category. Judges: appointed by school principal. Entry fee $10; $5 for youth. Guidelines for SASE. Inquiries by e-mail OK. Deadline September 25. Unpublished submissions. Word length: 1,000 words. Winners announced at conference on October 23. Winners not present will be notified by mail. List of winners available for SASE.

TARA FELLOWSHIP FOR SHORT FICTION, (I), The Heekin Group Foundation, P.O. Box 1534, Sisters OR 97759. (503)548-4147. Contact: Sarah Heekin Redfield, fiction director. "To support unpublished, beginning career writers in their writing projects." Two annual awards for completed short stories. Award: $1,500. Receives approximately 600 applications. Judges: Invitation of Publisher judge. Past judges: Graywolf Press, SOHO Press, Dalkey Archive Press, The Ecco Press and the *Threepenny Review*. This year's judge: *Black Warrior Review*. Application fee $25. Guidelines for SASE. Deadline December 1. Unpublished submissions. Word length: 2,500-10,000 words.

‡SYDNEY TAYLOR MANUSCRIPT COMPETITION, Association of Jewish Libraries, 1327 Wyntercreek Lane, Dunwoody GA 30338. Contact: Paula Sandfelder, coordinator. Award to "deepen the understanding of

---

🍁 **THE MAPLE LEAF** symbol before a listing indicates a Canadian publisher, magazine, conference or contest.

Judaism for all children by helping to launch new writers of children's Jewish fiction." Annual competition for novels. Award: $1,000. Competition receives 25 submissions. Judges: 5 children's library. Guidelines available for #10 SASE. Deadline January 15. Previously unpublished submissions. "Children's fiction for readers 8-11 years with universal appeal and Jewish content." Word length: 64 page minimum-200 page maximum, double-spaced.

TENNESSEE ARTS COMMISSION LITERARY FELLOWSHIP, (I, II, IV), 401 Charlotte Ave., Nashville TN 37243-0780. (615)741-1701. Fax: (615)741-8559. E-mail: aswanson@mail.state.tn.us. Contact: Alice Swanson, director of literary arts. Award to "honor promising writers." Annual award for fiction or poetry. Award: At least $2,000. Competition receives approximately 30 submissions. Judges are out-of-state jurors. Previously published and unpublished submissions. Writers must be residents of Tennessee. Word length: 20 ms pages. Write for guidelines. Inquiries by fax and e-mail OK. This year's award is for poetry.

‡TENNESSEE WRITERS ALLIANCE ANNUAL SHORT FICTION/POETRY CONTEST, Tennessee Writer Alliance, P.O. Box 120396, Nashville TN 37212. (615)385-5585. E-mail: tnwral@aol.com. Executive Director: Sallie Bissell. Award to "encourage and reward writing excellence in Tennessee writers, or writers with connections to Tennessee." Annual competition for short stories (odd-numbered years) and poetry (even-numbered years). Award: $500 first prize; $250 second prize; $100 third prize. Competition receives 200 submissions per category. Judge: A Tennessee author or poet. Entry fee $15 ($10 for TWA members) for each story submitted. Guidelines available for SASE. Deadline June 30. Previously unpublished submissions. Tennessee writers or members of the Tennessee Writers Alliance only. Word length: 3,000 words.

TEXAS-WIDE WRITERS CONTEST, (I, IV), Byliners, P.O. Box 6218, Corpus Christi TX 78466. Contact: Contest Chairman. "Contest to fund a scholarship in journalism or creative writing." Annual contest for adult and children's short stories, novels and poems. Award: Novels—1st $75, 2nd $55, 3rd $30; short stories—1st $55, 2nd $40, 3rd $20. Competition receives approximately 30 novel, 60 short story and 45 children's story submissions. Judges: Varies each year. Entry fee $5/story, $10/novel. Guidelines available for SASE. Deadline is February 28 (date remains same each year). Unpublished submissions. Limited to Texas residents and winter Texans. Length: Children's story limit 2,000 words; short story limit 3,000 words; novel 3-page synopsis plus chapter one. "Contest also has nostalgia, article and nonfiction book categories." Winners announced May 16. Winners notified by mail. List of winners available for SASE.

THURBER HOUSE RESIDENCIES, (II), The Thurber House, 77 Jefferson Ave., Columbus OH 43215. (614)464-1032. Contact: Michael J. Rosen, literary director. "Four writers/year are chosen as writers-in-residence, one for each quarter." Award for writers of novels and story collections. $5,000 stipend and housing for a quarter in the furnished third-floor apartment of James Thurber's boyhood home. Judges: Advisory panel. To apply, send letter of interest and curriculum vitae. Deadline: December 15. "The James Thurber Writer-in-Residence will teach a class in the Creative Writing Program at The Ohio State University in either fiction or poetry and will offer one public reading and a short workshop for writers in the community. Significant time outside of teaching is reserved for the writer's own work-in-progress. Candidates should have published at least one book with a major publisher, in any area of fiction, nonfiction, or poetry and should possess some experience in teaching."

‡THE THURBER PRIZE FOR AMERICAN HUMOR, (III), The Thurber House, 77 Jefferson Ave., Columbus OH 43215. (614)464-1032. Fax: (614)228-7445. Literary Director: Michael J. Rosen. Award "to give the nation's highest recognition of the art of humor writing." Biannual competition for novels and story collections. Awards: $5,000, Thurber statuette. Up to 3 Honor Awards may also be conferred. Judges: well-known members of the national arts community. Entry fee $25/title. Guidelines for SASE. Published submissions or accepted for publication in U.S. for first time. No reprints or paperback editions of previously published books. Word length: no requirement. Primarily pictorial works such as cartoon collections are not considered. Work must be nominated by publisher.

♣TICKLED BY THUNDER ANNUAL FICTION CONTEST, Tickled By Thunder, 7385-129 St., Surrey, British Columbia V3W 7B8 Canada. Phone/fax: (604)591-6095. E-mail: thunder@istar.ca. Contact: Larry Lindner, editor. "To encourage new writers." Annual competition for short stories. Award: 50% of all fees, $100 minimum (Canadian), 1 year's (4-issue) subscription plus publication. Competition receives approximately 25 submissions. Judges: The editor and other writers. Entry fee $10 (Canadian) per entry (free for subscribers but more than one story requires $5 per entry). Guidelines available for SASE. Inquiries by e-mail OK. Deadline February 15. Unpublished submissions. Word length: 2,000 words or less. Winners announced in May. Winners notified by mail. List of winners available for SASE.

‡LON TINKLE AWARD, Texas Institute of Letters, P.O. Box 298300, Fort Worth TX 76129. (817)921-7822. E-mail: jalter@gamma.is.tcu.edu. Secretary: Judy Alter. Award to "honor a Texas writer for excellence sustained throughout a career." Annual competition for lifetime achievement. Award: $1,500. Judges: TIL Council. To be eligible, the writer must have a notable association with Texas. Writer must be nominated by a member of TIL

Council. "The TIL Council chooses the winner. Applications for the award are not made, through one might suggest possible candidates to an officer or member of the Council."

TOWSON UNIVERSITY PRIZE FOR LITERATURE, (II, IV), Towson University Foundation, Towson University, Towson MD 21252-0001. (410)830-2128. Fax: (410)830-3999. Contact: Dan L. Jones, Dean, College of Liberal Arts. Annual award for novels or short story collections, previously published. Award: $1,000. Competition receives 5-10 submissions. Requirements: Writer must not be over 40; must be a Maryland resident. SASE for rules/entry forms. Inquiries by fax OK. Deadline May 15. Winners announced December. Winners notified by letter. List of winners available for SASE.

TRAVEL MYSTERY CONTEST, (I, IV), *Whispering Willow's Mystery Magazine*, 2517 S. Central, P.O. Box 890294, Oklahoma City OK 73189-0294. (405)239-2531. Fax: (405)232-3848. Contact: Peggy D. Farris, editor-in-chief. Annual competition for short stories. Award: $200 (1st place), $125 (2nd place), plus publication. Competition receives approximately 30 submissions. Judge: Trula Johnson. Entry fee $10. Guidelines for SASE. Deadline July 1. Unpublished submissions. Mystery or mystery/suspense stories only. Length: 500-2,500 words. "Write about a character in a setting away from his or her home. No explicit sex, gore, or extreme violence."

‡ROBERT TRAVER FLY-FISHING FICTION AWARD, (I), *Fly Rod & Reel Magazine*, P.O. Box 370, Camden ME 04843. (207)594-9544. Fax: (207)594-5144. "The Traver Award is given annually for a work of short fiction that embodies an implicit love of fly-fishing, respect for the sport and the natural world in which it takes place and high literary values." Award: $1,000 and publication. Judges: Independent jury. Last year's jury was headed by Charles Kuralt. Deadline April 17. Include SASE.

STEVEN TURNER AWARD, (II, IV), The Texas Institute of Letters, TCU Box 298300, Fort Worth TX 76129. (817)921-7822. Secretary: Judy Alter. "To honor the best first book of fiction published by a writer who was born in Texas or who has lived in the state for two years at some time, or whose work concerns the state." Annual award for novels and story collections. Award: $1,000. Judges: committee. Guidelines for SASE. Previously published submissions appearing in print between January 1 and December 31.

MARK TWAIN AWARD, (III, IV), Missouri Association of School Librarians, 8049 Highway E, Bonne Terre MO 63628-3771. Estab. 1970. Annual award to introduce children to the best of current literature for children and to stimulate reading. Award: A bronze bust of Mark Twain, created by Barbara Shanklin, a Missouri sculptor. A committee selects pre-list of the books nominated for the award; statewide reader/selectors review and rate the books, and then children throughout the state vote to choose a winner from the final list. Books must be published two years prior to nomination for the award list. Publishers may send books they wish to nominate for the list to the committee members. 1) Books should be of interest to children in grades 4 through 8; 2) written by an author living in the US; 3) of literary value which may enrich children's personal lives.

‡*UPC SCIENCE FICTION AWARD, (I, IV), Universitat Politècnica de Catalunya Board of Trustees, gran capità 2-4, Edifici NEXUS, 08034 Barcelona, Spain. (93)401 43 63. Fax: (34)3 401 7766. E-mail: cscana@rectora t.upc.es. "The award is based on the desire for integral education at UPC. The literary genre of science fiction is undoubtedly the most suitable for a university such as UPC, since it unifies the concepts of science and literature." Annual award for short stories; 1,000,000 pesetas (about 10,000 US $). Competition receives 130 submissions. Judges: Professors of the university and science fiction writers. Deadline: September 12. Previously unpublished entries. Length: 70-115 pages, double-spaced, 30 lines/page, 70 characters/line. Submissions may be made in Spanish, English, Catalan or French. The author must sign his work with a pseudonym and enclose a sealed envelope with full name, a personal ID number, address and phone. The pseudonym and title of work must appear on the envelope. Write for more details. Inquiries by fax and e-mail OK.

‡UTAH ORIGINAL WRITING COMPETITION, (I, IV), Utah Arts Council, 617 E. South Temple, Salt Lake City UT 84102-1177. (801)533-5895. Fax: (801)533-6196. Literary Arts Coordinator: Guy Lebeda. Annual competition for poetry, essays, nonfiction books, short stories, novels and story collections. Awards: Vary; last year between $200-1,000. Competition receives 500 entries. Judges: "Published and award-winning judges from across America." Guidelines available, no SASE necessary. Deadline: Mid-June or later. Submissions should be unpublished. Limited to Utah residents. "Some limitation on word-length. See guidelines for details."
● This writing competition is celebrating its 40th anniversary.

‡VERY SHORT FICTION SUMMER AWARD, Glimmer Train Stories, 710 SW Madison St., Suite 504, Portland OR 97205. (503)221-0836. Fax: (503)221-0837. Contact: Linda Burmeister Davies, editor. Annual award offered to encourage the art of the very short story. Contest opens May 1 and ends July 31; entry must be postmarked between these dates. Awards: $1,200 and possible publication in *Glimmer Train Stories* (first place), $500 (second place), $300 (third place). Entry fee: $10 per story. Guidelines available for SASE. Inquiries by fax OK. Word length: 2,000 words maximum. First page of story should include name, address, phone number and word count. "VSF AWARD" must be written on outside of envelope. No need for SASE as materials will not be returned. Notification on November 1. List of winners available by phone or mail.

‡**VERY SHORT FICTION WINTER AWARD, Glimmer Train Stories**, 710 SW Madison St., Suite 504, Portland OR 97205. (503)221-0836. Fax: (503)221-0837. Contact: Linda Burmeister Davies, editor. Award offered to encourage the art of the very short story. Contest opens November 1 and ends January 31; entry must be postmarked between these dates. Awards: $1,200 and possible publication in *Glimmer Train Stories* (first place), $500 (second place), $300 (third place). Entry fee: $10 per story. Guidelines available for SASE. Word length: 2,000 words maximum. First page of story should include name, address, phone number and word count. "VSF AWARD" must be written on outside of envelope. No need for SASE as materials will not be returned. Notification on May 1. List of winners available by phone, fax or mail.

VIOLET CROWN BOOK AWARD, (I, IV), Austin Writers' League, 1501 W. Fifth St., Suite E-2, Austin TX 78703. (512)499-8914. Fax: (512)499-0441. Executive Director: Angela Smith. Award "to recognize the best books published by Austin Writers' League members over the period September 1 to August 31 in fiction, nonfiction and literary (poetry, short story collections, etc.) categories." Annual competition for novels, story collections, translations. Award: Three $1,000 cash awards and trophies. Competition receives approximately 100 submissions. Judges: A panel of judges who are not affiliated with the Austin Writers' League. Entry fee $10. Guidelines for SASE. Deadline August 31. Previously published submissions between September 1 and August 31. "Entrants must be Austin Writers' League members. League members reside all over the U.S. and some foreign countries. Persons may join the League when they send in entries." Publisher may also submit entry in writer's name. "Awards are co-sponsored by the University Co-op Bookstore. Special citations are presented to finalists."

‡**VOGELSTEIN FOUNDATION GRANTS, (II)**, The Ludwig Vogelstein Foundation, Inc., P.O. Box 277, Hancock ME 04640-0277. Executive Director: Frances Pishny. "A small foundation awarding grants to individuals in the arts and humanities. Criteria are merit and need. No student aid given." Send SASE for complete information after January 1, before June 1.

EDWARD LEWIS WALLANT MEMORIAL BOOK AWARD, (II, IV), 3 Brighton Rd., West Hartford CT 06117. Sponsored by Dr. and Mrs. Irving Waltman. Contact: Mrs. Irving Waltman. Annual award. Memorial to Edward Lewis Wallant offering incentive and encouragement to beginning writers, for books published the year before the award is conferred in the spring. Award: $500 plus award certificate. Books may be submitted for consideration to Dr. Sanford Pinsker, Department of English, Franklin & Marshall College, P.O. Box 3003, Lancaster PA 17604-3003. "Looking for creative work of fiction by an American which has significance for the American Jew. The novel (or collection of short stories) should preferably bear a kinship to the writing of Wallant. The award will seek out the writer who has not yet achieved literary prominence." Winners announced January-February.

‡**WEATHERFORD AWARD**, Appalachian Center, CPO 2336, Berea College, Berea KY 40404-2336. (606)986-9341 ext. 5140. Director: Gordon McKinney. Award to "select the best work about Appalachia, monograph, fiction or poetry." Annual competition for short stories, novels and story collections. Award: $500. Competition receives 15 submissions. Judges: Committee of Appalachian writers. Deadline December 31. Published submissions. Available only to authors who write about the Appalachian Region. "The majority of the winners of the award have been authors of nonfiction works."

WESTERN HERITAGE AWARDS, (II, IV), National Cowboy Hall of Fame, 1700 NE 63rd St., Oklahoma City OK 73111. (405)478-2250. Fax: (405)478-4714. Contact: M.J. Van Deuenter, director of publications. Annual award "to honor outstanding quality in fiction, nonfiction and art literature." Submissions are to have been published during the previous calendar year. Award: The Wrangler, a replica of a C.M. Russell Bronze. Competition receives 350 submissions. Entry fee $35. Entry forms and rules available October 1 for SASE. Inquiries by fax OK. Deadline November 30. Looking for "stories that best capture the spirit of the West. Submit five actual copies of the work." Winners announced April. Winners notified by letter.

‡**WESTERN WRITERS OF AMERICA CONTEST**, 60 Sandpiper, Conway AR 72032. (501)450-0086. Awards Administrator: W.C. Jameson. Award to "honor western and frontier fiction and nonfiction." Annual competition for short stories, novels, children's fiction and scripts. Entry fee $10 for each book, film or story submitted. Guidelines available for SASE. Deadline December 31. Published submissions during the previous

---

MARKET CATEGORIES: (I) Unpublished entries; **(II)** Published entries nominated by the author; **(III)** Published entries nominated by the editor, publisher or nominating body; **(IV)** Specialized entries.

year. Only.work "which is set in the territory west of the Mississippi River or one the early frontier." Send for complete guidelines and entry forms.

‡**BILL WHITEHEAD AWARD**, The Publishing Triangle, P.O. Box 114, New York NY 10012. E-mail: pubtriangle@nycnet.com. Co-Chairs: Lawrence Schimel and Jane Perkins. Award to "honor a significant body of work by a lesbian or gay male author." Annual competition for body of work. Award: $1,000. Judge: A committee. Published submissions. Writer must be nominated by publishing Triangle members. "Awarded in alternate years to a man and to a woman."

LAURA INGALLS WILDER AWARD, (III), American Library Association/Association for Library Service to Children, 50 E. Huron St., Chicago IL 60611. Executive Director: S. Roman. Award offered every 3 years; next year 1998. "To honor a significant body of work for children, for illustration, fiction or nonfiction." Award: Bronze medal. Authors must be nominated by ALSC members.

‡*WIND* **MAGAZINE SHORT STORY COMPETITION, (I)**, P.O. Box 24548, Lexington KY 40524. Editors: Charlie G. Hughes and Leatha F. Kendrick. Annual competition for short stories. Award: $500 and publication (1st prize); finalists receive a one-year subscription. Entry fee $10/story. Deadline April 30. Word length: 5,000 words or less. List of winners available for SASE.

‡**WISCONSIN ARTS BOARD INDIVIDUAL ARTIST PROGRAM, (II, IV)**, 101 E. Wilson St., First Floor, Madison WI 53702. (608)266-0190. Fax: (608)267-0380. E-mail: mfraire@arts.stats.wi.us. Contact: Mark J. Fraire. Biennial awards for short stories, poetry, novels, novellas, drama, essay/criticism. Awards: 5 awards of $8,000. Competition receives approximately 175 submissions. Entry forms or rules upon request. Inquiries by fax and e-mail OK. Deadline September 15 of even-numbered years (1996, 1998 etc.). Wisconsin residents only. Students are ineligible. Winners announced in December-January. Winner notified by mail.

WISCONSIN INSTITUTE FOR CREATIVE WRITING FELLOWSHIP, (I, II, IV), University of Wisconsin—Creative Writing, English Department, 600 N. Park St., Madison WI 53706. Director: Jesse Lee Kercheval. Competition "to provide time, space and an intellectual community for writers working on first books." Two annual awards for short stories, novels and story collections. Awards: $22,000/9-month appointment. Competition receives approximately 400 submissions. Judges: English Department faculty. Required guidelines available for SASE; write to Ron Kuka. Deadline is month of February. Published or unpublished submissions. Applicants must have received an M.F.A. or comparable graduate degree in creative writing and not yet published a book. Limit one story up to 30 pages in length. Two letters of recommendation required.

PAUL A. WITTY SHORT STORY AWARD, (II), International Reading Association, P.O. Box 8139, 800 Barksdale Rd., Newark DE 19714-8139. (302)731-1600. Annual award given to the author of an original short story published for the first time in 1997 in a periodical for children. Award: $1,000. "The short story should serve as a literary standard that encourages young readers to read periodicals." For guidelines write to: Executive Office. Deadline December 1. Published submissions.

THOMAS WOLFE FICTION PRIZE, (I), North Carolina Writers' Network, 3501 Hwy. 54 W., Studio C, Chapel Hill NC 27516. E-mail: ncwn@sunsite.unc.edu. Website: http://sunsite.unc.edu/ncwriters. "Our international literary prizes seek to recognize the best in today's writing." Annual award for fiction. Award: $500 and winning entry will be considered for publication in *Carolina Quarterly*. Competition receives approximately 1,000 submissions. Entry fee $7. Guidelines for SASE. Inquiries by e-mail OK. Deadline August 31. Unpublished submissions. Length: 12 double-spaced pages maximum. Winners announced December 1998. Winners notified by phone in late November or December. List of winners available for SASE.

‡**TOBIAS WOLFF AWARD FOR FICTION, (I)**, Mail Stop 9053, Western Washington University, Bellingham WA 98225. Annual competition for novels and short stories. Award: $1,000 (1st prize); $250 (2nd prize); $100 (3rd prize). Judge: Stuart Dybek. Entry fee $10 for the first entry, $5/story or chapter thereafter. Guidelines for SASE. Deadline March 1. Unpublished submissions. Length: 10,000 words or less per story or chapter. Winner announced July 1998. List of winners available for SASE.

‡**WORLD FANTASY AWARDS**, World Fantasy Awards Association, P.O. Box 1666, Lynnwood WA 98046-0166. Contact: Peter Dennis Pautz, president. Award to "recognize excellence in fantasy literature worldwide." Annual competition for short stories, novels, story collections, anthologies, novellas and life achievement. Award: bust of HP Lovecraft. Judge: Panel. Guidelines available for SASE. Deadline June 30. Published submissions from previous calendar year. Word length: 10,000-40,000 novella, 10,000 short story. "All fantasy is eligible, from supernatural horror to Tolkienesque to sword and sorcery to the occult, and beyond."

‡**WORLD'S BEST SHORT SHORT STORY CONTEST, (I)**, English Department Writing Program, Florida State University, Tallahassee FL 32306-1036. (904)644-4230. Director, Writing Program: Janet Burroway. Annual award for short-short stories, unpublished, under 250 words. Prizewinning story gets $100 and a crate

of Florida oranges; winner and finalists are published in *Sun Dog: The Southeast Review.* Competition receives approx. 3,000 submissions. Entry fee $1. SASE for rules. Deadline February 15. Open to all.Word-length: 250 words.

WRITERS AT WORK FELLOWSHIP COMPETITION, Writers at Work (W@W), P.O. Box 1146, Centerville, UT 84014-5146. (801)292-9285. Fax: (801)294-5417. President: Dawn Marano. Program Administrator: Niquie Love. "Through the recognition of excellence in fiction and poetry, we hope to foster the growth of the supportive literary community which characterizes our annual conference in Utah." Annual competition for short stories, literary fiction, novels (novel excerpts) and poetry. Award: $1,500, a featured reading at and tuition for the afternoon sessions at 1998 conference, and publication in *Quarterly West* literary magazine (first prize); $500, tuition for the afternoon sessions at the 1998 conference and publication in the anthology (second prize). Competition receives 1,500 submissions. Judges: Faculty of Writers at Work Conference. Entry fee $12. Guidelines available for SASE. Inquiries by fax OK. Deadline: March 15. Unpublished submissions. Open to any writer who has not yet published a book-length volume of original work. Word length: 20 double-spaced pages, one story (or excerpt) only; 6 poems, up to 10 total pages. "The 14th Annual Writers At Work Conference is scheduled for July 12-17, 1998." Winners announced May 31. Winners notified by mail.

THE WRITERS COMMUNITY RESIDENCY AWARDS, (II), The YMCA National Writer's Voice of the YMCA of the USA. 5 W. 63rd St., New York NY 10023. (212)875-4261. Program Director: Jennifer O'Grady. Offers semester-long residencies to mid-career writers at YMCAs nationwide. Biannual award for novels and story collections. Award: A semester-long residency. Residents conduct a master-level workshop and give a public reading at their host Writer's Voice center. Honorarium is $6,000. Judges: A committee at each Writer's Voice center. Deadlines vary. "Interested writers should contact their local writer's voice center for deadlines." Previously published submissions in book form. "Writers should apply directly to the Writer's Voice center, as application procedures vary. For a list of Writer's Voice center addresses, send SASE to The Writers Community, YMCA National Writer's Voice, 5 W. 63rd St., New York NY 10023."

WRITER'S DIGEST ANNUAL WRITING COMPETITION, (Short Story Division), (I), *Writer's Digest*, 1507 Dana Ave., Cincinnati OH 45207. (513)531-2222. Contact: Contest Director. Grand Prize is an expenses-paid trip to New York City with arrangements to meet editors/agents in winning writer's field. Other awards include cash, reference books and certificates of recognition. Names of grand prize winner and top 100 winners are announced in the November issue of *Writer's Digest*. Top entry published in booklet ($5.75). Send SASE to WD Writing Competition for rules and entry form, or see January through May issues of *Writer's Digest*. Deadline: May 31. Entry fee $10 per manuscript. All entries must be original, unpublished and not previously submitted to a *Writer's Digest* contest. Length: 2,000 words maximum. No acknowledgment will be made of receipt of mss nor will mss be returned. Contest includes 3 short fiction categories: literary, genre/mainstream and children's fiction.

‡WRITER'S DIGEST NATIONAL SELF-PUBLISHED BOOK AWARDS, *Writer's Digest*, 1507 Dana Ave., Cincinnati OH 45207. (513)531-2222. Contact: Dan Boer or Leanna Wesley. Award to "recognize and promote excellence in self-published books." Annual competition with six categories: Fiction (novel or short story collection), nonfiction, cookbooks, poetry, children's and young adult and life stories. Award: $1,000 plus an ad in *Publishers Weekly*. Category winners receive $300. Judges: WD staff. Entry fee $95 for each book submitted. Guidelines available for SASE. Deadline December 15. Published submissions. Author must pay full cost and book must have been published in year of contest.

‡WRITERS' FILM PROJECT, The Chesterfield Film Co., 8205 Santa Monica Blvd. #200, Los Angeles CA 90046. (213)683-3977. Fax: (310)260-6116. E-mail: www.infoboard.com/chesterfield/. Administrator: Sandra Baker. Award "provides up to 5 (20,000) dollar yearly stipends to promote and foster talented screenwriters, fiction writers and authors of plays." Annual competition for short stories, novels and screenplays. Award: 5 $20,000 awards. Competition receives several thousand submissions. Judges: Mentors, panel of judges. Entry fee $39.50 US dollars for each story submitted. Guidelines available for SASE. Deadline November 7. Published or previously unpublished submissions. "Program open to all age groups, race, religion, educational level etc. Past winners have ranged in age from early 20's to late 50's."

❧WRITERS GUILD OF ALBERTA LITERARY AWARD, (II, IV), Writers Guild of Alberta, 3rd Floor, Percy Page Centre, 11759 Groat Rd., Edmonton, Alberta T5M 3K6 Canada. (403)422-8174. Fax: (403)422-2663. Executive Director: Miki Andrejevic. "To recognize, reward and foster writing excellence." Annual competition for novels and story collections. Award: $500, plus leather-bound copy of winning work. Short story competition receives 5-10 submissions; novel competition receives about 20; children's literature category up to 40. Judges: 3 published writers. Guidelines for SASE. Deadline December 31. Previously published submissions (between January and December). Open to Alberta authors, resident for previous 18 months. Entries must be book-length and published within the current year.

❧WRITERS GUILD OF ALBERTA NEW FICTION COMPETITION, (I, IV), 3rd Floor, 11759 Groat Rd., Edmonton, Alberta T5M 3K6 Canada. (403)422-8174. Fax: (403)422-2663. Project Coordinator: Darlene

Diver. Award "to encourage and publicize Albertan fiction writers." Biannual competition for novels. Award: $4,500 including a 12 month option for motion picture and TV rights. Competition receives approximately 50 submissions. Judges: A jury of respected writers. Entry fee $25. Guidelines for SASE. Deadline December 1. Unpublished submissions. The writer must have been a resident of the province of Alberta for 12 of the last 18 months. Word length: approx. 60,000 words. "On alternate years there is the *Write for Youth* competition. This competition is for children's literature."

WRITERS' INTERNATIONAL FORUM WRITING COMPETITION, (I), *Writers' International Forum*, P.O. Box 516, Tracyton WA 98393. Contact: Sandra E. Haven, editor. Award "to encourage strong storyline in a tight package." Two or more competitions per year for short stories. Awards: Cash prizes and certificates (amounts vary per competition). Competitions receive approximately 200 entries. Judges: *Writers' International Forum* staff. Entry fees vary per competition. Guidelines available for SASE. Previously unpublished submissions. "Length, theme, prizes, deadline, fee and other requirements vary for each competition. Send for guidelines. Entries are judged on creativity, technique, mechanics and appeal." List of winners available one month after closing. Automatically mailed with entrant's return SASE for manuscript.

WRITERS' JOURNAL ANNUAL FICTION CONTEST, (I), Val-Tech Publishing, Inc., P.O. Box 25376, St. Paul MN 55125-0376. Contact: Valerie Hockert, publisher/managing editor. Annual award for short stories. Award: first place, $50; second place, $25; third place, $15. Also gives honorable mentions. Competition receives approximately 500 submissions/year. Judges are Valerie Hockert, Glenda Olsen and others. Entry fee $5 each. Maximum of 3 entries/person. Entry forms or rules for SASE. Maximum length is 2,000 words. Two copies of each entry are required—one *without* name or address of writer.

WRITERS' JOURNAL ROMANCE CONTEST, (I), *Writers' Journal*, Val-Tech Publishing, Inc., P.O. Box 25376, St. Paul MN 55125-0376. Competition for short stories. Award: $50 (first prize), $25 (second prize), $15 (third prize), plus honorable mentions. Entry fee $5/entry. Guidelines for SASE (4 entries/person). Unpublished submissions. Word length: 2,000 words maximum. "Enclose #10 SASE for winner's list."

THE WRITERS' WORKSHOP INTERNATIONAL FICTION CONTEST, (I), The Writers' Workshop, 387 Beaucatcher Rd., Asheville NC 28805. (704)254-8111. Fax: (704)251-2118. Executive Director: Karen Tager. Annual awards for fiction. Awards: $600 (1st prize), $250 (2nd prize), $100 (3rd prize). Competition receives approximately 350 submissions. Past judges have been D.M. Thomas, Mark Mathabane and Robert Creely. Entry fee $18/$15 members. Guidelines for SASE. Deadline: February 25. Unpublished submissions. Length: 20 typed, double-spaced pages per story. Multiple submissions are accepted.

YOUNG READER'S CHOICE AWARD, (III), Pacific Northwest Library Association, Graduate School of Library and Information Sciences, P.O. Box 352930, FM-30, University of Washington, Seattle WA 98195. (206)543-1897. Contact: Carol A. Doll. Annual award "to promote reading as an enjoyable activity and to provide children an opportunity to endorse a book they consider an excellent story." Award: silver medal. Judges: children's librarians and teachers nominate; children in grades 4-8 vote for their favorite book on the list. Guidelines for SASE. Deadline February 1. Previously published submissions. Writers must be nominated by children's librarians and teachers.

‡YOUNG TEXAS WRITERS SCHOLARSHIPS, (IV), Austin Writers' League, 1501 W. Fifth St., Suite E-2, Austin TX 78703. (512)499-8914. Fax: (512)499-0441. E-mail: awl@eden.com. Executive Director: Angela Smith. Award to "recognize outstanding young writing talent enrolled in grades 9-12 in Texas schools." Annual competition for short stories (other categories: essays, poetry, journalism). Awards: 12 cash awards ($50 to $150). Competition receives more than 500 submissions. Judges: experienced writers. Entry fee $5 (one time fee for multiple entries). Fee may be waived. Guidelines for SASE. Deadline January 31, 1998. Entrants must be Texan. Word length: requirements specified on guidelines for each category. Winning entries are published in special anthology.

‡ZOETROPE SHORT STORY CONTEST, (I), Boston Beer Company, 244 Fifth Ave., #2272, New York NY 10001. (617)683-5005. E-mail: 219-3004@mcimail.com. Website: http://www.zoetrope-stories.com. Contact: Adrienne Brodeur, editor-in-chief. Triannual competition for short stories. Award: trip or scholarship worth $4,000. Judges: editors of *Zoetrope: All-Story*. Guidelines available in each issue of the magazine. Previously unpublished. Word length: 3,000 words. Winners announced in November, March and July. Winners notified by mail.

SENDING TO A COUNTRY other than your own? Be sure to send International Reply Coupons instead of stamps for replies or return of your manuscript.

Resources

Resources
Conferences and Workshops

Why are conferences so popular? Writers and conference directors alike tell us it's because writing can be such a lonely business otherwise—that at conferences writers have the opportunity to meet (and commiserate) with fellow writers, as well as meet and network with publishers, editors and agents. Conferences and workshops provide some of the best opportunities for writers to make publishing contacts and pick up valuable information on the business, as well as the craft, of writing.

The bulk of the listings in this section are for conferences. Most conferences last from one day to one week and offer a combination of workshop-type writing sessions, panel discussions, and a variety of guest speakers. Topics may include all aspects of writing from fiction to poetry to scriptwriting, or they may focus on a specific area such as those sponsored by the Romance Writers of America for writers specializing in romance or the SCBWI conferences on writing for children's books.

Workshops, however, tend to run longer—usually one to two weeks. Designed to operate like writing classes, most require writers to be prepared to work on and discuss their work-in-progress while attending. An important benefit of workshops is the opportunity they provide writers for an intensive critique of their work, often by professional writing teachers and established writers.

Each of the listings here includes information on the specific focus of an event as well as planned panels, guest speakers and workshop topics. It is important to note, however, some conference directors were still in the planning stages for 1998 when we contacted them. If it was not possible to include 1998 dates, fees or topics, we have provided information from 1997 so you can get an idea of what to expect. For the most current information, it's best to send a self-addressed, stamped envelope to the director in question about three months before the date(s) listed.

FINDING A CONFERENCE

Many writers try to make it to at least one conference a year, but cost and location count as much as subject matter or other considerations, when determining which conference to attend. There are conferences in almost every state and province and even some in Europe open to North Americans.

To make it easier for you to find a conference close to home—or to find one in an exotic locale to fit into your vacation plans—we've divided this section into geographic regions. The conferences appear in alphabetical order under the appropriate regional heading.

Note that conferences appear under the regional heading according to where they will be held, which is sometimes different than the address given as the place to register or send for information. For example, the Bluegrass Writers Workshop is held in Kentucky and is listed under the Midwest heading, although writers are instructed to write to Princeton, New Jersey, for information.

The regions are as follows:

Northeast (pages 580-584): Connecticut, Maine, Massachusetts, New Hampshire, New York, Rhode Island, Vermont

Midatlantic (pages 585-587): Washington DC, Delaware, Maryland, New Jersey, Pennsylvania

Midsouth (pages 587-588): North Carolina, South Carolina, Tennessee, Virginia, West Virginia

Southeast (pages 588-593): Alabama, Arkansas, Florida, Georgia, Louisiana, Mississippi, Puerto Rico

Midwest (pages 593-598): Illinois, Indiana, Kentucky, Michigan, Ohio

North Central (pages 598-600): Iowa, Minnesota, Nebraska, North Dakota, South Dakota, Wisconsin

South Central (pages 600-603): Colorado, Kansas, Missouri, New Mexico, Oklahoma, Texas

West (pages 603-608): Arizona, California, Hawaii, Nevada, Utah

Northwest (pages 608-611): Alaska, Idaho, Montana, Oregon, Washington, Wyoming

Canada (pages 611-612)

International (pages 612-614)

LEARNING AND NETWORKING

Besides learning from workshop leaders and panelists in formal sessions, writers at conferences also benefit from conversations with other attendees. Writers on all levels enjoy sharing insights. Often, a conversation over lunch can reveal a new market for your work or let you know which editors are most receptive to the work of new writers. You can find out about recent editor changes and about specific agents. A casual chat could lead to a new contact or resource in your area.

Many editors and agents make visiting conferences a part of their regular search for new writers. A cover letter or query that starts with "I met you at the National Writers Association Conference," or "I found your talk on your company's new romance line at the Moonlight and Magnolias most interesting . . ." may give you a small leg up on the competition.

While a few writers have been successful in selling their manuscripts at a conference, the availability of editors and agents does not usually mean these folks will have the time there to read your novel or six best short stories (unless, of course, you've scheduled an individual meeting with them ahead of time). While editors and agents are glad to meet writers and discuss work in general terms, usually they don't have the time (or energy) to give an extensive critique during a conference. In other words, use the conference as a way to make a first, brief contact.

SELECTING A CONFERENCE

Besides the obvious considerations of time, place and cost, choose your conference based on your writing goals. If, for example, your goal is to improve the quality of your writing, it will be more helpful to you to choose a hands-on craft workshop rather than a conference offering a series of panels on marketing and promotion. If, on the other hand, you are a science fiction novelist who would like to meet your fans, try one of the many science fiction conferences or "cons" held throughout the country and the world.

Look for panelists and workshop instructors whose work you admire and who seem to be writing in your general area. Check for specific panels or discussions of topics relevant to what you are writing now. Think about the size—would you feel more comfortable with a small workshop of eight people or a large group of 100 or more attendees?

If your funds are limited, start by looking for conferences close to home, but you may want to explore those that offer contests with cash prizes—and a chance to recoup your expenses. A few conferences and workshops also offer scholarships, but the competition is stiff and writers interested in these should find out the requirements early. Finally, students may want to look for conferences and workshops that offer college credit. You will find these options included in the listings here. Again, send a self-addressed, stamped envelope for the most current details.

The science fiction field in particular offers hundreds of conventions each year for writers, illustrators and fans. To find additional listings for these, see *Locus* (P.O. Box 13305, Oakland CA 94661). For more information on conferences and even more conferences from which to choose, check the May issue of *Writer's Digest. The Guide to Writers Conferences* (ShawGuides, 10 W. 66th St., Suite 30H, New York NY 10023) is another helpful resource now available on their website at http://www.shawguides.com.

Northeast (CT, MA, ME, NH, NY, RI, VT)

‡BECOME A MORE PRODUCTIVE WRITER, P.O. Box 1310, Boston MA 02117-1310. (617)266-1613. E-mail: marcia@yudkin.com. Director: Marcia Yudkin. Estab. 1991. Workshop held approximately 3 times/year. Workshop held on one Saturday in April, September, February. Average attendance 15. "Creativity workshop for fiction writers and others. Based on latest discoveries about the creative process, participants learn to access their unconscious wisdom, find their own voice, utilize kinesthetic, visual and auditory methods of writing, and bypass longstanding blocks and obstacles. Held at a hotel in central Boston."
Costs: $99.
Accommodations: List of area hotels and bed & breakfasts provided.
Additional Information: Conference brochures/guidelines are available for SASE after August. Inquiries by mail, phone or e-mail OK. "Audiotapes of seminar information also available."

BREAD LOAF WRITERS' CONFERENCE, Middlebury College, Middlebury VT 05753. (802)388-3711 ext. 5286. E-mail: blwc@mail.middlebury.edu. Administrative Coordinator: Carol Knauss. Estab. 1926. Annual. Conference held in late August. Conference duration: 11 days. Average attendance: 230. For fiction, nonfiction and poetry. Held at the summer campus in Ripton, Vermont (belongs to Middlebury College).
Costs: $1,600 (includes room/board) (1996).
Accommodations: Accommodations are at Ripton. Onsite accommodations $560 (1996).

EASTERN WRITERS' CONFERENCE, English Dept., Salem State College, Salem MA 01970-5353. (508)741-6330. E-mail: rod.kessler@salem.mass.edu. Conference Director: Rod Kessler. Estab. 1977. Annual. Conference held June 19-20, 1998. Average attendance: 60. Conference to "provide a sense of community and support for area poets and prose writers. We try to present speakers and programs of interest, changing our format from time to time. Conference-goers have an opportunity to read to an audience or have manuscripts professionally critiqued. We tend to draw regionally." Previous speakers have included Nancy Mairs, Susanna Kaysen, Katha Pollitt, James Atlas.
Costs: "Under $100."
Accommodations: Available on campus.
Additional Information: Conference brochure/guidelines are available April 30. Inquiries by e-mail OK. "Optional manuscript critiques are available for an additional fee."

‡FEMINIST WOMEN'S WRITING WORKSHOPS, INC., P.O. Box 6583, Ithaca NY 14851. Directors: Mary Beth O'Connor and Margo Gumosky. Estab. 1975. Workshop held every summer. Workshop duration: 8 days. Average attendance: 30-45 women writers. "Workshops provide a women-centered community for writers of all levels and genres. Workshops are held on the campuses of Hobart/William Smith Colleges in Geneva, NY. Geneva is approximately mid-way between Rochester and Syracuse. Each writer has a private room and 3 meals daily. College facilities such as pool, tennis courts and weight room are available. FWWW invites all interests. Past speakers include Dorothy Allison, National Book Award Finalist for *Bastard Out of Carolina*, and Ruth Stone, author of *Second-Hand Coat, Who Is The Widow's Muse?* and *Simplicity*.
Costs: $535 for tuition, room, board.
Accommodations: Shuttle service from airports available for a small fee.
Additional Information: "Writers may submit manuscripts up to 10 pages with application." Brochures/guidelines available for SASE.

THE FOUNDATIONS OF CREATIVITY® WRITING WORKSHOP, The Elizabeth Ayres Center for Creative Writing, 155 E. 31st St., Suite 4-R, New York NY 10016. (800)843-7353. Founder: Elizabeth Ayres. Estab. 1990. Conference held 10 times/year. Workshops begin every 7 weeks, 1 time/week for 6 weeks. Average attendance: 10. "The purpose of the workshop is to help fledgling writers conquer their fear of the blank page; develop imaginative tools; capitalize on the strengths of their natural voice and style; develop confidence; and interact with other writers in a stimulating, supportive atmosphere." Writers' Retreats also offered 3-5 times/year in weekend and week-long formats. Average attendance: 15. "Retreats provide an opportunity for extended writing time in a tranquil setting with like-minded companions."

Costs: $235 (1997); retreats vary from $300-700 depending on duration.
Additional Information: Workshop brochures and guidelines free after October. Inquiries by mail or phone.

HIGHLIGHTS FOUNDATION WRITERS WORKSHOP AT CHAUTAUQUA, Dept. NM, 814 Court St., Honesdale PA 18431. (717)253-1192. Fax: (717)253-0179. Conference Director: Jan Keen. Estab. 1985. Annual. Workshop held July 18-25, 1998. Average attendance: 100. "Writer workshops geared toward those who write for children—beginner, intermediate, advanced levels. Small group workshops, one-to-one interaction between faculty and participants plus panel sessions, lectures and large group meetings. Workshop site is the picturesque community of Chautauqua, New York." Classes offered include Children's Interests, Writing Dialogue, Outline for the Novel, Conflict and Developing Plot. Past faculty has included Eve Bunting, James Cross Giblin, Walter Dean Myers, Laurence Pringle, Richard Peck, Jerry Spinelli and Ed Young.
Accommodations: "We coordinate ground transportation to and from airports, trains and bus stations in the Erie, PA and Jamestown/Buffalo, NY area. We also coordinate accommodations for conference attendees."
Additional Information: "We offer the opportunity for attendees to submit a manuscript for review at the conference." Workshop brochures/guidelines are available after January for SASE. Inquiries by fax OK.

‡HOFSTRA UNIVERSITY SUMMER WRITERS' CONFERENCE, Hofstra University, UCCE, Hempstead NY 11550-1090. (516)463-5016. Fax: (516)463-4833. E-mail: dcelcs@hofstra.edu. Associate Dean: Lewis Shena. Estab. 1972. Annual (every summer, starting week after July 4). Conference to be held July 13 to July 24, 1998. Average attendance: 50. Conference offers workshops in fiction, nonfiction, poetry, juvenile fiction, stage/screenwriting and, on occasion, one other genre such as detective fiction or science fiction. Site is the university campus, a suburban setting, 25 miles from NYC. Guest speakers are not yet known. "We have had the likes of Oscar Hijuelos, Robert Olen Butler, Hilma and Meg Wolitzer, Budd Schulberg and Cynthia Ozick."
Costs: Non-credit (no meals, no room): approximately $375 per workshop. Credit: Approximately $900/workshop (2 credits).
Accommodations: Free bus operates between Hempstead Train Station and campus for those commuting from NYC. Dormitory rooms are available for approximately $250. Those who request area hotels will receive a list. Hotels are approximately $75 and above/night.
Additional Information: "All workshops include critiquing. Each participant is given one-on-one time of ½ hour with workshop leader. Only credit students must submit manuscripts when registering. We submit work to the Shaw Guides Contest and other Writer's Conferences and Retreats contests when appropriate."

‡IWWG MEET THE AGENTS AND EDITORS: THE BIG APPLE WORKSHOPS, % International Women's Writing Guild, P.O. Box 810, Gracie Station, New York NY 10028-0082. (212)737-7536. Fax: (212)737-9469. E-mail: iwwg@iwwg.com. Website: http://www.iwwg.com. Executive Director: Hannelore Hahn. Estab. 1980. Biannual. 1998 workshops held April 18-19 and October 17-18. Average attendance: 200. Workshops to promote creative writing and professional success. Site: Private meeting space of the New York Genealogical Society, mid-town New York City. Sunday afternoon openhouse with agents and editors.
Costs: $100 for the weekend.
Accommodations: Information on transportation arrangements and overnight accommodations made available.
Additional Information: Workshop brochures/guidelines are available for SASE. Inquires by fax and e-mail OK.

IWWG SUMMER CONFERENCE, % International Women's Writing Guild, P.O. Box 810, Gracie Station, New York NY 10028-0082. (212)737-7536. Fax: (212)737-9469. E-mail: iwwg@iwwg.com. Website: http://www.iwwg.com. Executive Director: Hannelore Hahn. Estab. 1977. Annual. Conference held from August 12-19, 1998. Average attendance: 400, including international attendees. Conference to promote writing in all genres, personal growth and professional success. Conference is held "on the tranquil campus of Skidmore College in Saratoga Springs, NY, where the serene Hudson Valley meets the North Country of the Adirondacks." Sixty-five different workshops are offered everyday. Overall theme: "Writing Towards Personal and Professional Growth."
Costs: $300 for week-long program, plus room and board.
Accommodations: Transportation by air to Albany, New York, or Amtrak train available from New York City. Conference attendees stay on campus.
Additional Information: Features "lots of critiquing sessions and contacts with literary agents." Conference brochures/guidelines available for SASE. Inquires by fax and e-mail OK.

CAN'T FIND A CONFERENCE? Conferences are listed by region. Check the introduction to this section for a list of regional categories.

MANHATTANVILLE COLLEGE WRITERS' WEEK, 2900 Purchase St., Purchase NY 10577. (914)694-3425. Fax: (914)694-3488. Website: http://www.manhattanville.edu. Dean of Adult and Special Programs: Ruth Dowd, R.S.C.J. Estab. 1982. Annual. Conference held June 29-July 3, 1998. Average attendance: 90. "The Conference is designed not only for writers but for teachers of writing. Each workshop is attended by a Master teacher who works with the writers/teachers in the afternoon to help them to translate their writing skills for classroom use. Workshops include children's literature, journal writing, creative nonfiction, personal essay, poetry, fiction, travel writing and short fiction. Manhattanville is a suburban campus 30 miles from New York City. The campus centers around Reid Castle, the administration building, the former home of Whitelaw Reid. Workshops are conducted in Reid Castle. We usually feature a major author as guest lecturer during the Conference. Past speakers have included such authors as Toni Morrison, Mary Gordon, Gail Godwin, Pete Hamill and poet Mark Doty."

Costs: Conference cost was $560 in 1997 plus $40 fee.

Accommodations: Students may rent rooms in the college residence halls. More luxurious accommodations are available at neighboring hotels. In the summer of 1997 the cost of renting a room in the residence halls was $25 per night.

Additional Information: Conference brochures/guidelines are available for SASE in March. Inquiries by fax OK.

‡NEW ENGLAND WRITERS' WORKSHOP AT SIMMONS COLLEGE, 300 The Fenway, Boston MA 02115-5820. (617)521-2090. Fax: (617)521-3199. Conference Administrator: Cynthia Grady. Estab. 1977. Annually in summer. Workshop held 1st week of June. Workshop lasts one week. Average attendance: 45. "Adult fiction: novel, short story or poetry. Boston and its literary heritage provide a stimulating environment for a workshop of writers. Simmons College is located in the Fenway area near the Museum of Fine Arts, Symphony Hall, the Isabella Stewart Gardner Museum, and many other places of educational, cultural, and social interest. Our theme is usually fiction (novel or short story) with the workshops in the morning and then the afternoon speakers either talk about their own work or talk about the 'business' of publishing." Past speakers and workshop leaders have included John Updike, Anne Beattie and Jill McCorkle as well as editors from *The New Yorker*, *The Atlantic* and Houghton Mifflin.

Costs: $550 (1995 included full week of workshops and speakers, individual consultations, refreshments and 2 receptions).

Accommodations: Cost is $150 for Sunday to Saturday on-campus housing. A list of local hotels is also available.

Additional Information: "Up to 30 pages of manuscript may be sent in prior to workshop to be reviewed privately with workshop leader during the week." Conference brochures/guidelines are abailable for SASE in March. Inquiries by fax OK.

ODYSSEY, 20 Levesque Lane, Mount Vernon NH 03057. Phone/fax: (603)673-6234. E-mail: jcavelos@anselm.edu. Website: http://www.edu/odyssey/. Director: Jeanne Cavelos. Estab. 1995. Annual. Workshop to be held June 22 to July 31. Attendance limited to 20. "A workshop for fantasy, science fiction and horror writers. Harlan Ellison will be a special writer-in-residence at the 1998 workshop, his first teaching engagement in over a decade." Conference held at New Hampshire College in Manchester, New Hampshire. Previous guest lecturers included: Hal Clement, Jane Yolen, Elizabeth Hand, Ellen Kushner, Craig Shaw Gardner, Melissa Scott, Esther Friesner and Michael McDowell.

Costs: In 1997: $980 tuition, $337 housing (double room), $20 application fee, $525 food (approximate), $55 processing fee to receive college credit.

Accommodations: "Workshop students stay at a New Hampshire College townhouses and eat at college."

Additional Information: Students must apply and include a writing sample. Students' works are critiqued throughout the 6 weeks. Workshop brochures and guidelines available for SASE.

‡PROVIDENCE WRITERS CONFERENCE, Community Writers Association, P.O. Box 312, Providence RI 02901. (401)846-9884. E-mail: cwa@ici.net. Executive Director: Eleyne Austen Sharp. Estab. 1997. Annual. Conference held from October 11 to October 13. Conference for novel writing, playwriting, screenwriting, book publishing, freelance writing, hypertext fiction, poetry, Rhode Island's film industry, travel and tax incentives, H.P. Lovecraft, humor and writing for children. 1997 speakers included Christopher Keane (screenwriter), Tracy Minkin (freelance writer), Billie Fitzpatrick (book editor), Esmond Harmsworth (literary agent) and others.

Costs: Full tuition, $345 (1997).

Accommodations: Not included. For room availability, contact the Greater Providence/Warwick Convention and Vistors Bureau at (800)233-1636.

Additional Information: Agents, editors, open readings, book sale, author's book signings, raffle. Offers evaluations on mss (short stories, essays and novel chapters). Sponsors the annual CWA Writing Competition. Poetry and short story submissions accepted. Entries judged by a panel of qualified writing professionals. Conference brochures/guidelines available for #10 SASE.

ROBERT QUACKENBUSH'S CHILDREN'S BOOK WRITING & ILLUSTRATING WORKSHOPS, 460 E. 79th St., New York NY 10021-1443. (212)744-3822. Fax: (212)861-2761. Instructor: Robert Quackenbush. Estab. 1982. Annual. Workshop held July 13-17, 1998. Average attendance: limited to 10. Workshops to promote writing and illustrating books for children. Held at the Manhattan studio of Robert Quackenbush, author and illustrator of over 160 books for young readers. "Focus is generally on picture books. All classes led by Robert Quackenbush."
Costs: $650 tuition covers all costs of the workshop, but does not include housing and meals. A $100 nonrefundable deposit is required with the $550 balance due two weeks prior to attendance.
Accommodations: A list of recommended hotels and restaurants is sent upon receipt of deposit.
Additional Information: Class is for beginners and professionals. Critiques during workshop. Private consultations also available at an hourly rate. "Programs suited to your needs; individualized schedules can be designed. Write or phone to discuss your goals and you will receive a prompt reply." Conference brochures are available for SASE. Inquiries by fax OK.

SCBWI CONFERENCE IN CHILDREN'S LITERATURE, NYC, P.O. Box 20233, Park West Finance Station, New York NY 10025. Chairman: Kimberly Colen. Estab. 1975. Annual. Conference held 1st (or 2nd) Saturday in November. Average attendance: 350. Conference is to promote writing for children: picture books; fiction; nonfiction; middle grade and young adult; meet an editor; meet an agent; financial planning for writers; marketing your book; children's multimedia; etc. Held at Union Theological Seminary, 90 Claremont Street, New York City.
Costs: $70, members; $75 nonmembers; $15 additional on day of conference.
Accommodations: Write for information; hotel names will be supplied.
Additional Information: Conference brochures/guidelines are available for SASE. For information, call (214)363-4491 or (718)937-6810.

SCBWI/HOFSTRA CHILDREN'S LITERATURE CONFERENCE, Hofstra University, University College of Continuing Education, Republic Hall, Hempstead NY 11549. (516)463-5016. Co-organizers: Connie C. Epstein, Adrienne Betz and Lewis Shena. Estab. 1985. Annual. Conference to be held May 16, 1998. Average attendance: 150. Conference to encourage good writing for children. "Purpose is to bring together various professional groups—writers, illustrators, librarians, teachers—who are interested in writing for children. Each year we organize the program around a theme. Last year it was The Path to Excellence." The conference takes place at the Student Center Building of Hofstra University, located in Hempstead, Long Island. "We have two general sessions, an editorial panel and five break-out groups held in rooms in the Center or nearby classrooms." Last year's conference featured Diane Roback of *Publishers Weekly* as one of the 2 general speakers, and 2 children's book editors critiqued randomly selected first-manuscript pages submitted by registrants. Special interest groups are offered in picture books, nonfiction and submission procedures with others in fiction.
Cost: $56 (previous year) for SCBWI members; $63 for nonmembers. Lunch included.

‡SEACOAST WRITER'S ASSOCIATION SPRING MEETING AND FALL CONFERENCE, P.O. Box 6553, Portsmouth NH 03802-6553. Membership Director: Majorie Dannis. Annual. Conferences held in May and October. Conference duration: 1 day. Average attendance: 50. "At our spring meeting, we choose the topic of interest to our members. The fall conference offers workshops covering various aspects of fiction, nonfiction and poetry."
Costs: $50.
Additional Information: "We sometimes include critiques. It is up to the speaker." Spring meeting includes a contest. Categories are fiction, nonfiction (essays) and poetry. Judges vary from year to year. Conference brochures/guidelines are available for SASE.

STATE OF MAINE WRITERS' CONFERENCE, P.O. Box 7146, Ocean Park ME 04063-7146. (207)934-9806 June-August; (413)596-6734 September-May. Fax: (413)796-2121. E-mail: rburns0@keaken.rmvnet or wnec.edu (September-May only). Chairman: Richard F. Burns. Estab. 1941. Annual. Conference held August 18-21, 1998. Conference duration: 4 days. Average attendance: 50. "We try to present a balanced as well as eclectic conference. There is quite a bit of time and attention given to poetry but we also have children's literature, mystery writing, travel, novels/fiction and lots of items and issues of interest to writers such as speakers who are: publishers, editors, illustrators and the like. Our concentration is, by intention, a general view of writing to publish. We are located in Ocean Park, a small seashore village 14 miles south of Portland. Ours is a summer assembly center with many buildings from the Victorian Age. The conference meets in Porter Hall, one of the assembly buildings which is listed on the National Register of Historic Places. Within recent years our guest list has included Lewis Turco, Amy MacDonald, William Noble, David McCord, Dorothy Clarke Wilson, John N. Cole, Betsy Sholl, John Tagliabue, Christopher Keane and many others. We usually have about 10 guest presenters a year."
Costs: $85 includes the conference banquet. There is a reduced fee, $40, for students ages 21 and under. The fee does not include housing or meals which must be arranged separately by the conferees.
Accommodations: An accommodations list is available. "We are in a summer resort area and motels, guest houses and restaurants abound."

Additional Information: "We have a list of about 12 contests on various genres that accompanies the program announcement. The prizes, all modest, are awarded at the end of the conference and only to those who are registered." Send SASE for program guide available in May. Inquiries by fax and e-mail OK.

‡VASSAR COLLEGE INSTITUTE OF PUBLISHING AND WRITING: CHILDREN'S BOOKS IN THE MARKETPLACE, Vassar College, Box 300, Poughkeepsie NY 12604. (914)437-5903. E-mail: mabruno@ vassar.edu. Associate Director of College Relations: Maryann Bruno. Estab. 1983. Annual. Conference held in second week of June or July. Conference duration: 1 week. Average attendance: 40. Writing and publishing children's literature. The conference is held at Vassar College, a 1,000-acre campus located in the mid-Hudson valley. The campus is self-contained, with residence halls, dining facilities, and classroom and meeting facilities. Vassar is located 90 miles north of New York City, and is accessible by car, train and air. Participants have use of Vassar's athletic facilities, including swimming, squash, tennis and jogging. Vassar is known for the beauty of its campus. "The Institute is directed by Barbara Lucas of Lucas-Evans Books and features top working professionals from the field of publishing."
Costs: $800, includes full tuition, room and three meals a day.
Accommodations: Special conference attendee accommodations are in campus residence halls.
Additional Information: Writers may submit a 10-page sample of their writing for critique, which occurs during the week of the conference. Artists' portfolios are reviewed individually. Conference brochures/guidelines are available upon request. Inquiries by e-mail OK.

WELLS WRITERS' WORKSHOPS, 69 Broadway, Concord NH 03301. (603)225-9162. Fax: (603)225-3774. E-mail: forbine@forbine.mv.com. Director: Victor A. Levine. Estab. 1988. Held: 2 times/year in Wells, Maine. Conferences held in May and September. Maximum attendance: 6. "Workshop concentrates on short and long fiction, especially the novel. Focus is on the rational structuring of a story, using Aristotelian and scriptwriting insights. Throughout, the workshop balances direct instruction with the actual plotting and writing of the basic scenes of a novel or short story." Workshops located in a "large, airy and light house overlooking the ocean with ample individual space for writers and group conferences. While the purpose of the workshop is to teach the process of plotting as it applies across the board—to all kinds of fiction, including novels, short stories, movies— it strives to meet the specific needs of participants, especially through individual conferences with the instructors."
Costs: $750.
Accommodations: Workshop supplies transportation from/to Portland International Airport—or other places, by arrangement. Workshop supplies accommodations.
Additional Information: Conference brochures/guidelines available for SASE in January. Inquiries by fax or e-mail OK.

WESLEYAN WRITERS CONFERENCE, Wesleyan University, Middletown CT 06459. (860)685-3604. Fax: (860)347-3996. E-mail: agreene@wesleyan.edu. Director: Anne Greene. Estab. 1956. Annual. Conference held the last week in June. Average attendance: 100. For fiction techniques, novel, short story, poetry, screenwriting, nonfiction, literary journalism, memoir. The conference is held on the campus of Wesleyan University, in the hills overlooking the Connecticut River. Meals and lodging are provided on campus. Features readings of new fiction, guest lectures on a range of topics including publishing and daily seminars. "Both new and experienced writers are welcome."
Costs: In 1997, day rate $655 (including meals); boarding students' rate $765 (including meals and room for 5 nights).
Accommodations: "Participants can fly to Hartford or take Amtrak to Meriden, CT. We are happy to help participants make travel arrangements." Overnight participants stay on campus.
Additional Information: Manuscript critiques are available as part of the program but are not required. Participants may attend seminars in several different genres. Scholarships and teaching fellowships are available, including the Jakobson awards for new writers and the Jon Davidoff Scholarships for journalists. Inquiries by e-mail and fax OK.

THE WRITERS' CENTER AT CHAUTAUQUA, P.O. Box 408, Chautauqua NY 14722. (716)483-0381. Fax: (716)489-1281. Director: Janette Martin. Estab. 1987. Annual. Workshops held late June through August "are offered in combination with a vacation at historic Chautauqua Institution, a large cultural resort in western New York for families and singles. Workshops are two hours, Monday-Friday; average attendance is 12." Past workshop leaders: Gloria Frym and Janice Eidus, short story; Judith Bell, novel; Joan C. Connor, fiction; Susan Rowan Masters, writers 6-12 years old and 13-18 years old; Carol H. Behrman and Margery Facklam, Writing for Children.
Costs: In 1997, $70/week. Meals, housing, gate ticket (about $175 per week), parking ($20+) are in addition.
Accommodations: Information is available; but no special rates have been offered.
Additional Information: Each leader specifies the kind of workshop offered. Most accept submissions in advance; information is made available in March on request. Conference brochures/guidelines are available for 55¢ SASE. Inquiries by fax OK.

Midatlantic (DC, DE, MD, NJ, PA)

‡**BALTIMORE SCIENCE FICTION SOCIETY WRITER'S WORKSHOP**, P.O. Box 686, Baltimore MD 21203-0686. (401)563-2737. E-mail: bsfs@bsfs.org. Contact: Steve Lubs. Estab. 1983. Conference/workshop held: roughly, 2 times/year. "Conference dates vary, please write for next date held and other information." Conference duration: 1 day. Average attendance: 8-12. Conference concentration is science fiction and fantasy. "Conference is held in a former movie theater (small) in the process of being renovated."
Costs: Manuscripts are submitted in advance; cost 75¢/page.
Additional Information: "Format will vary from workshop to workshop: some will be manuscript critique, others will be writing exercises. Please read conference description before sending material."

THE COLLEGE OF NEW JERSEY WRITERS' CONFERENCE, (formerly Trenton State College Writers' Conference), English Dept., The College of New Jersey, P.O. Box 7718, Ewing NJ 08628-0718. (609)771-3254. Fax: (609)771-3345. Director: Jean Hollander. Estab. 1980. Annual. Conference held in April. Conference duration: 9 a.m. to 10:30 p.m. Average attendance: 600-1,000. "Conference concentrates on fiction (the largest number of participants), poetry, children's literature, play and screenwriting, magazine and newspaper journalism, overcoming writer's block, nonfiction books. Conference is held at the student center at the college in two auditoriums and workshop rooms; also Kendall Theatre on campus." We focus on various genres: romance, detective, mystery, TV writing, etc. Topics have included "How to Get Happily Published," "How to Get an Agent" and "Earning a Living as a Writer." The conference usually presents twenty or so authors, plus two featured speakers, who have included Arthur Miller, Saul Bellow, Toni Morrison, Joyce Carol Oates, Erica Jong and Alice Walker.
Costs: General registration $45, plus $10 for each workshop. Lower rates for students.
Additional Information: Brochures/guidelines available.

CUMBERLAND VALLEY FICTION WRITERS WORKSHOP, Dickinson College, Carlisle PA 17013-2896. (717)245-1291. Fax: (717)245-1942. E-mail: gill@dickinson.edu Website: http://www.dickinson.edu/depar tments/engl/cvfww.html. Director: Judy Gill. Estab. 1990. Annual. Workshop held June 21-26, 1998. Average attendance: 30-40. "5-day fiction workshop. Workshop is held on the campus of Dickinson College, a small liberal arts college, in Carlisle, PA." Panel: "Writers Roundtable"—faculty responds to wide variety of questions submitted by participants.
Costs: Tuition for 5-day workshop: $350; Room (optional): $150.
Accommodations: Special accommodations made. A residence hall on campus is reserved for workshop participants.
Additional Information: Applicants must submit a 10-page manuscript for evaluation prior to the workshop. Conference brochures/guidelines are available after January for SASE. Inquiries by fax and e-mail OK.

‡**INTERNATIONAL PLATFORM ASSOCIATION CONVENTION**, P.O. Box 250, Winnetka IL 60093. (847)446-4321. Fax: (847)446-7186. Website: http://www.internationalplatform.com. Estab. 1831. Annual. Convention held in summer. Convention duration: 5 days. Average attendance: 300. The convention is held in Washington, D.C. Includes poetry competition, storytelling workshops, creative writing workshop, biographical writing workshop. 1997 speakers included Elizabeth Drew, author; John Seiler, poet; and Jon Spelman, storyteller.
Costs: $265 registration, not including lodging or meals (1997).
Accommodations: No arrangements for transportation. Attendees make own arrangements for hotel; discounts on room rates. On-site accommodations $92/night (1997)
Additional Information Sponsors poetry competition. Request information by e-mail.

MID-ATLANTIC MYSTERY BOOK FAIR & CONVENTION, Detecto Mysterioso Books at Society Hill Playhouse, 507 S. Eighth St., Philadelphia PA 19147. (215)923-0211. Fax: (923)923-1789. Website: http://www.P ACIFIER.com/~alecwest/Bouchercon/Philly.htm. Contact: Deen Kogan, chairperson. Estab. 1991. Annual. Convention held 1997: October 3-5. Average attendance: 450-500. Focus is on mystery, suspense, thriller, true crime novels. "An examination of the genre from many points of view." The convention is held at the Holiday Inn-Independence Mall, located in the historic area of Philadelphia. Previous speakers included Lawrence Block, Jeremiah Healy, Neil Albert, Michael Connelly, Paul Levine, Eileen Dreyer, Earl Emerson, Wendy Hornsby.
Costs: $50 registration fee.
Accommodations: Attendees must make their own transportation arrangements. Special room rate available at convention hotel.
Additional Information: "The Bookroom is a focal point of the convention. Twenty-five specialty dealers are expected to exhibit and collectables range from hot-off-the-press bestsellers to 1930's pulp; from fine editions to reading copies. Conference brochures/guidelines are available by mail or telephone. Inquiries by e-mail and fax OK."

MONTROSE CHRISTIAN WRITER'S CONFERENCE, 5 Locust St., Montrose Bible Conference, Montrose PA 18801-1112. (717)278-1001. (800)598-5030. Fax: (717)278-3061. E-mail: mbc@epix.net. Bible Conference Director: Jim Fahringer. Estab. 1990. Annual. Conference held July. Average attendance: 75. "We try to meet a cross-section of writing needs, for beginners and advanced, covering fiction, poetry and writing for children. We meet in the beautiful village of Montrose, Pennsylvania, situated in the mountains. The Bible Conference provides motel-like accommodations and good food. The main sessions are held in the chapel with rooms available for other classes. Fiction writing has been taught each year."

Costs: In 1997 registration was $100.

Accommodations: Will meet planes in Binghamton NY and Scranton PA; will meet bus in Great Bend, PA. Information on overnight accommodations is available. On-site accommodations: room and board $216-$318/ week; $36-$53/day including food.

Additional Information: "Writers can send work ahead and have it critiqued for $20." Brochures/guidelines are available by e-mail and fax. "The attendees are usually church related. The writing has a Christian emphasis."

JENNY McKEAN MOORE COMMUNITY WORKSHOPS, English Dept., George Washington University, Washington DC 20052. (202)994-8223. Fax: (202)363-8628. Associate Professor: F. Moskowitz. Estab. 1976. Workshop held each semester. Next semester begins September 1997. Length: semester. Average attendance: 15. Workshop concentration varies depending on professor—usually fiction or poetry. Workshop held at university.

Costs: Free.

Additional Information: Admission is competitive and by ms.

NEW JERSEY ROMANCE WRITERS PUT YOUR HEART IN A BOOK CONFERENCE, P.O. Box 513, Plainsboro NJ 08536. (201)263-8477. E-mail: RainyK@juno.com. President: Rainy Kirkland. Estab. 1984. Annual. Conference held in October. Average attendance: 300. Conference concentrating on romance fiction. "Workshops offered on various topics for all writers of romance, from beginner to multi-published." Held at the Holiday Inn in Jamesburg, New Jersey. Offers workshops with a panel of editors and a panel of agents. Speakers have included Diana Gabaldon, Nora Roberts, Alice Orr, Susan Elizabeth Phillips, Tami Hoag, LaVyrle Spencer, Sandra Brown, Kay Hoopes, Pamela Morsie, Mary Jo Putney and Anne Stuart.

Costs: $120 (New Jersey Romance Writers members) and $135 (nonmembers).

Accommodations: Special hotel rate available for conference attendees.

Additional Information: Sponsors Put Your Heart in a Book Contest for unpublished writers and the Golden Leaf Contest for published members of RWA. Conference brochures, guidelines and membership information are available for SASE. "Appointments offered for conference attendees, both published and unpublished, with editors and/or agents in the genre." Mid-Atlantic Booksellers Association promotion available for published conference attendees.

OUTDOOR WRITERS ASSOCIATION OF AMERICA ANNUAL CONFERENCE, 2155 E. College Ave., State College PA 16801. (814)234-1011. E-mail: 76711.1725@compuserve.com. Meeting Planner: Eileen King. Estab. 1927. Annual. Conference held in June. Will be held in California in 1998. Average attendance: 800-950. Conference concentrates on outdoor communications (all forms of media). Featured speakers have included Don Ranley, University of Missouri, Columbia; US Forest Service Chief Michael Dombeck; Nina Leopold Bradley (daughter of Aldo Leopold); Secretary of the Interior, Bruce Babbitt; and Director Bureau of Land Management, Michael Dombeck.

Costs: $130 for nonmembers; "applicants must have prior approval from Executive Director." Registration fee includes cost of most meals.

Accommodations: List of accommodations available after April. Special room rate for attendees.

Additional Information: Sponsors contests, "but all is done prior to the conference and you must be a member to enter them." Conference brochures/guidelines are available for SASE.

SANDY COVE CHRISTIAN WRITERS CONFERENCE, Sandy Cove Bible Conference, North East MD 21901. (800)287-4843. Director: Gayle Roper. Estab. 1991. Annual. Conference begins first Sunday in October. Conference duration: 4 days (Sunday dinner to Thursday breakfast). Average attendance: 200. "There are major, continuing workshops in fiction, article writing, nonfiction books and beginner's and advanced workshops. Twenty-eight one-hour classes touch many topics. While Sandy Cove has a strong emphasis on available markets in Christian publishing, all writers are more than welcome. Sandy Cove is a full-service conference center located on the Chesapeake Bay. All the facilities are first class with suites, single or double rooms available." Past faculty has included William Petersen, editor, Revell; Ken Petersen, editor, Tyndale House; Linda Tomblin, editor, *Guideposts*; Col. Henry Gariepy, editor-in-chief, The Salvation Army; and Andrew Scheer, *Moody Magazine*.

Costs: Tuition is $250.

Accommodations: "If one flies into Philadelphia International Airport, we will transport them the one-hour drive to Sandy Cove. Accommodations are available at Sandy Cove. Information available upon request." Cost is $225 double occupancy room and board, $300 single occupancy room and board for 4 nights and meals.

Additional Information: Special critiques are available—a 1-time critique for $30 and a continuing critique for $75 (one-time is 30-minute appointment and written critique; continuing is 3 30-minute appointments). Conference brochures/guidelines are available for SASE.

TRI-STATE WRITER'S GUILD, 10800 Mt. Fairview Rd. SE, Cumberland MD 21502. (301)724-6842. Director: Petrina Aubol. Estab. 1992. Tri-State Writer's Guild, based in Cumberland, Maryland and an affiliate of the

Allegany Arts Council, has 50 members in Eastern U.S., and holds 2 workshops a year. Retreat is scheduled for second weekend in July at various locations in the Mid-Atlantic region. Conference is held 3rd weekend in October at, and in conjunction with, Allegany College in Cumberland. 1997 speakers included Geraldine Connolly, MA, winner of two NEA creative writing fellowships, co-editor of Poet Lore, author of two books of poems (*The Red Room* and *Food for Winter*), teacher at The Writer's Center of Bethesda; Jeff Minerd, co-editor of Writer's Carousel, monthly publication of The Writer's Center, winner of first F. Scott Fitzgerald Short Story Competition. Stories have appeared in *Blueline, Crescent Review, Wordwrights,* and *The Sulphur River Literary Review*; Children's book author Mary Quattlebaum and editor of *Satire Magazine,* Larry Logan.
Additional Information: Conference brochures/guidelines are available April for SASE.

‡WASHINGTON INDEPENDENT WRITERS (WIW) SPRING WRITERS CONFERENCE, #220, 733 15th St. NW, Suite 220, Washington DC 20005. (202)347-4973. E-mail: washwriter@aol.com. Website: http://www.net-writers.org. Executive Director: Isolde Chapin. Estab. 1975. Annual. Conference held in May. Conference duration: Friday evening and Saturday. Average attendance: 250. "Gives participants a chance to hear from and talk with dozens of experts on book and magazine publishing as well as on the craft, tools and business of writing." Past keynote speakers include Erica Jong, Haynes Johnson and Diane Rehm.
Costs: $100 members; $150 nonmembers; $185 membership and conference.
Additional Information: Brochures/guidelines available for SASE in mid-March.

‡WRITING FOR PUBLICATION, Villanova University, Villanova PA 19085-1099. (215)645-4620. Fax: (610)519-4623. Director: Wm. Ray Heitzmann, Ph.D. Estab. 1975. Semiannual. Conference dates vary, held fall, spring. Next session: TBA Spring, 1998. Average attendance: 15-20 (seminar style). Conference covers marketing one's manuscript (fiction, nonfiction, book, article, etc.); strong emphasis on marketing. Conference held in a seminar room at a university (easy access, parking, etc.). Panels include "Advanced Writing for Publication," "Part-time Writing," "Working With Editors." Panelists include Ray Heitzman, and others.
Costs: $385 (graduate credit); $100 (non-credit) plus $10 registration fee.
Accommodations: List of motels/hotels available, but most people live in area and commute. Special arrangements made on an individual basis.
Additional Information: Critiques available. Voluntary submission of manuscripts. Brochures/guidelines are available. Inquiries by fax OK. "Workshop graduates have been very successful." Emphasis: Nonfiction.

Midsouth (NC, SC, TN, VA, WV)

AMERICAN CHRISTIAN WRITERS CONFERENCES, P.O. Box 110390, Nashville TN 37222. (800)21-WRITE. Website: http://www.ECPA.ORG/ACW (includes schedule). Director: Reg Forder. Estab. 1981. Annual. Conference duration: 3 days. Average attendance: 100. To promote all forms of Christian writing. Conferences held throughout the year in cities such as Houston, Dallas, Minneapolis, St. Louis, Detroit, Atlanta, Washington DC, San Diego, Seattle, Ft. Lauderdale and Phoenix. Usually located at a major hotel chain like Holiday Inn.
Costs: Approximately $199 plus meals and accommodation.
Accommodations: Special rates available at host hotel.
Additional Information: Conference brochures/guidelines are available for SASE.

‡THE CHARLESTON WRITERS' CONFERENCE, Lightsey Conference Center, College of Charleston, Charleston SC 29424. (803)953-5822. Conference Director: Paul Allen; Conference Coordinator: Judy Sawyer. Estab. 1990. Annual. Conference held in March. Conference duration: 3½ days. Average attendance: 165. "Conference concentrates on fiction, poetry and nonfiction. The conference is held at conference center on urban campus in historic setting." Themes are different each year and varied within confines of each conference. 1997 faculty included Tom Paxton, Eleanora Tate, Valerie Sayers, Charleen Swanson, James Kilgo, Chris Huntley, Scott Ely, Carol Houck Smith, Franklin Ashley, David Lee, Brett Lott, Eric Frazier, Susan Ludvigson and Paul Allen.
Costs: Around $125. Includes receptions and breaks.
Accommodations: Special rates available at hotels within walking distance.
Additional Information: "Critiques are available for an extra fee—not a requirement." Those making inquiries are placed on mailing list.

---

‡ THE DOUBLE DAGGER before a listing indicates that the listing is new in this edition. New markets are often the most receptive to submissions by new writers.

HIGHLAND SUMMER CONFERENCE, Box 7014, Radford University, Radford VA 24142-7014. (703)831-5366. Fax: (540)831-5004. E-mail: gedwards@runet.edu. Website: http://www.runet.edu/~arsc. Chair, Appalachian Studies Program: Dr. Grace Toney Edwards. Estab. 1978. Annual. Conference held in mid-June. Conference duration: 12 days. Average attendance: 25. "The HSC features one (two weeks) or two (one week each) guest leaders each year. As a rule, our leaders are well-known writers who have connections, either thematic, or personal, or both, to the Appalachian region. The genre(s) of emphasis depends upon the workshop leader(s). In the past we have had as our leaders Jim Wayne Miller, poet, novelist, teacher; and Wilma Dykemen, novelist, journalist, social critic, author of *Tall Woman*, among others. The Highland Summer Conference is held at Radford University, a school of about 9,000 students. Radford is in the Blue Ridge Mountains of southwest Virginia about 45 miles south of Roanoke, VA."
Costs: "The cost is based on current Radford tuition for 3 credit hours plus an additional conference fee. On-campus meals and housing are available at additional cost. In 1996 conference tuition was $421 for undergraduates, $439 for graduate students."
Accommodations: "We do not have special rate arrangements with local hotels. We do offer accommodations on the Radford University Campus in a recently refurbished residence hall. (In 1996 cost was $18-28 per night.)"
Additional Information: "Conference leaders do typically critique work done during the two-week conference, but do not ask to have any writing submitted prior to the conference beginning." Conference brochures/guidelines are available after February, 1998 for SASE. Inquiries by e-mail and fax OK.

NORTH CAROLINA WRITERS' NETWORK FALL CONFERENCE, P.O. Box 954, Carrboro NC 27510. (919)967-9540. Fax: (919)929-0535. Executive Director: Linda G. Hobson. Estab. 1985. Annual. "1998 Conference will be held in Winston-Salem, NC, November 20-22." Average attendance: 450. "The conference is a weekend full of workshops, panels, readings and discussion groups. We try to have *all* genres represented. In the past we have had novelists, poets, journalists, editors, children's writers, young adult writers, storytellers, puppetry, screenwriters, etc. We take the conference to a different location in North Carolina each year in order to best serve our entire state. We hold the conference at a conference center with hotel rooms available."
Costs: "Conference cost is approximately $130-145 and includes three to four meals."
Accommodations: "Special conference hotel rates are obtained, but the individual makes his/her own reservations. If requested, we will help the individual find a roommate."
Additional Information: Conference brochures/guidelines are available for 2 first-class stamps. Inquiries by fax OK.

‡PRESBYTERIAN COLLEGE WRITERS' WORKSHOP, 503 S. Broad St., Clinton SC 29325. (864)833-8989. Fax: (864)833-8481. E-mail: nmccube@ls1.presby.edu. Estab. 1990. Annual. Workshop held June 4 to June 6. Average attendance: 50."We offer workshops in fiction, poetry, creative nonfiction, screenwriting and children's writing." Workshop is held on the college campus in classroom buildings, dormitories and performance facilities. Past speakers have included Mary Oliver and Tillie Olsen.
Costs: $125; includes meals and lodging. Participants may stay in an area hotel for a reduced fee.
Additional Information: Guidelines available January 1998 for SASE. Inquiries by fax and e-mail OK. "Our past participants and workshop leaders praise the quiet, intimate setting, the relaxed quality of the workshop, and the camaraderie that develops as a result."

‡SEWANEE WRITERS' CONFERENCE, 310 St. Luke's Hall, Sewanee TN 37383-1000. (615)598-1141. Fax: (615)598-1145. E-mail: cpeters@sewanee@edu. Website: http://www.sewanee.edu/writers_conference/home.html. Conference Administrator: Cheri B. Peters. Estab. 1990. Annual. Conference held July 14-26, 1998. Conference duration: 12 days. Average attendance: 110. "We offer genre-based workshops (in fiction, poetry, and playwriting), not theme-based workshops. The Sewanee Writers' Conference uses the facilities of the University of the South. Physically, the University is a collection of ivy-covered Gothic-style buildings, located on the Cumberland Plateau in mid-Tennessee. We allow invited editors, publishers, and agents to structure their own presentations, but there is always opportunity for questions from the audience." The 1997 faculty included Russell Banks, Ernest Gaines, Francine Prose, Diane Johnson, Romulus Linney, Donald Justice and John Hollander.
Costs: Full conference fee (tuition, board, and basic room) is $1,200; a single room costs an additional $50.
Accommodations: Complimentary chartered bus service is available, on a limited basis, on the first and last days of the conference. Participants are housed in University dormitory rooms. Motel or B&B housing is available but not abundantly so. Dormitory housing costs are included in the full conference fee.
Additional Information: "We offer each participant (excluding auditors) the opportunity for a private manuscript conference with a member of the faculty. These manuscripts are due one month before the conference begins." Conference brochures/guidelines are available, "but no SASE is necessary. The conference has available a limited number of fellowships and scholarships; these are awarded on a competitive basis."

Southeast (AL, AR, FL, GA, LA, MS, PR [Puerto Rico])

ALABAMA WRITERS' CONCLAVE, P.O. Box 230787, Montgomery AL 36123-0787. President: Donna Tennis. Estab. 1923. Annual. Conference held for three days, the first week in August. Average attendance: 75-

100. Conference to promote "all phases" of writing. Held at the Ramsay Conference Center (University of Montevallo). "We attempt to contain all workshops under this roof."
Costs: In 1996 fees for 3 days were $35 for members; $45 for nonmembers. Lower rates for 1- or 2-day attendence.
Accommodations: Accommodations available on campus (charged separately).
Additional Information: "We have had a works-in-progress group with members helping members." Sponsors a contest. Conference brochures/guidelines available for SASE. Membership dues are $15. Membership information from Harriette Dawkins, 117 Hanover Rd., Homewood AL 35209.

ARKANSAS WRITERS' CONFERENCE, 6817 Gingerbread, Little Rock AR 72204. (501)565-8889. Director: Peggy Vining. Estab. 1944. Annual. Conference held first weekend in June. Average attendance: 225. "We have a variety of subjects related to writing—we have some general sessions, some more specific, but try to vary each year's subjects."
Costs: Registration: $10; luncheon: $13; banquet: $14, contest entry $5.
Accommodations: "We meet at a Holiday Inn—rooms available at reasonable rate." Holiday Inn has a bus to bring anyone from airport. Rooms average $62.
Additional Information: "We have 36 contest categories. Some are open only to Arkansans, most are open to all writers. Our judges are not announced before conference but are qualified, many from out of state." Conference brochures are available for SASE after February 1. "We have had 226 attending from 12 states— over 3,000 contest entries from 43 states and New Zealand, Mexico and Canada. We have a get acquainted party Thursday evening for early arrivers."

FLORIDA CHRISTIAN WRITERS CONFERENCE, 2600 Park Ave., Titusville FL 32780. (407)269-6702, ext. 202. Conference Director: Billie Wilson. Estab. 1988. Annual. Conference is held in late January. Conference duration: 5 days. Average attendance: 200. To promote "all areas of writing." Conference held at Park Avenue Retreat Center, a conference complex at a large church near Kennedy Space Center. Editors will represent over 30 publications and publishing houses.
Costs: Tuition $360, included tuition, room and board (double occupancy).
Accommodations: "We provide shuttle from the airport and from the hotel to retreat center. We make reservations at major hotel chain."
Additional Information: Critiques available. "Each writer may submit two works for critique. We have specialists in every area of writing to critique." Conference brochures/guidelines are available for SASE.

FLORIDA FIRST COAST WRITERS' FESTIVAL, 3939 Roosevelt Blvd., FCCJ Kent Campus, Box 109, Jacksonville FL 32205. (904)633-8327. Fax: (904)633-8435. E-mail: kclower@fccj.cc.fl.us. Website: http://astro. fccj.cc.fl/WritersFestival/. Budget administrator: Kathy Clower. Estab. 1985. Annual. 1998 Festival: April 3-4. Average attendance: 150-250. All areas: mainstream plus genre. Held on Kent Campus of Florida Community College at Jacksonville.
Costs: Maximum of $75 for 2 days, plus $28 for banquet tickets.
Accommodations: Orange Park Holiday Inn, (904)264-9513, has a special festival rate.
Additional Information: Conference brochures/guidelines are available for SASE. Inquiries by e-mail and fax OK. Sponsors a contest for short fiction, poetry and novels. Novel judges are David Poyer and Elisabeth Graves. Entry fees: $30, novels; $10, short fiction; $5, poetry. Deadline: October 1 in each year.

FLORIDA SUNCOAST WRITERS' CONFERENCE, University of South Florida, Division of Lifelong Learning, 4202 E. Fowler Ave., MGZ144, Tampa FL 33620-6610. (813)974-2403. Fax: (813)974-5732. E-mail: fswc@conted.usf.edu. Directors: Steve Rubin, Ed Hirshberg and Lagretta Linkar. Estab. 1970. Annual. Held in February. Conference duration: 3 days. Average attendance: 450. Conference covers poetry, short story, novel and nonfiction, including science fiction, detective, travel writing, drama, TV scripts, photojournalism and juvenile. "We do not focus on any one particular aspect of the writing profession but instead offer a variety of writing related topics. The conference is held on the picturesque university campus fronting the bay in St. Petersburg, Florida." Features panels with agents and editors. Guest speakers have included Lady P.D. James, Carolyn Forche, Marge Piercy, William Styron and David Guterson.
Costs: Call for verification.
Accommodations: Special rates available at area motels. "All information is contained in our brochure."
Additional Information: Participants may submit work for critiquing. Extra fee charged for this service. Conference brochures/guidelines are available November 1997 for SASE. Inquiries by e-mail and fax OK.

HEMINGWAY DAYS WRITER'S WORKSHOP AND CONFERENCE, P.O. Box 4045, Key West FL 33041-4045. (305)294-4440. Fax: (305)292-3653. E-mail: calico2419@aol.com. Director of Workshop: Dr. James Plath. Festival Director: Carol Shaughnessy. Estab. 1989. Annual. Conference held July 19-22. Conference duration: 3½ days. Average attendance: 60-100. "We deliberately keep it small so that there is a greater opportunity for participants to interact with presenting writers. The Hemingway Days Writer's Workshop and Conference focuses on fiction, poetry and Ernest Hemingway and his work. The workshop and conference is but one event in a week-long festival which honors Ernest Hemingway. The first evening features a reception and presentation

INSIDER REPORT

Carrying on the literary tradition of Key West

When Carol Shaughnessy arrived in Key West in 1977, she embraced its impressive literary culture inspired by Ernest Hemingway. "I was here for two days and I knew I was home." Shaughnessy's 20 years on this island in the Florida Keys have enriched both her own writing craft and the writing ambitions of others. A 1997 co-director of the Lorian-Hemingway Short Story Competition and director of the acclaimed Hemingway Days Festival, Shaughnessy seeks to foster excellence in creative writing and to help short story winners in particular.

Carol Shaughnessy

Photo by Tom Netting

As a publicist, poet, short story writer and travel writer, Shaughnessy exults in this village's love of good writing. Ernest Hemingway's decade-long residence, beginning in 1928, has left its legacy in Key West. The community has been home to Robert Frost, Elizabeth Bishop, Tennessee Williams, and current residents Richard Wilbur and Allison Lurie. Still, the influence of Hemingway can be felt most strongly. Says Shaughnessy, "It is almost impossible to live here and be a writer and not in many ways be immersed in Hemingway."

The Hemingway Days Festival is a blend of frivolity and serious literary endeavor that occurs each summer in Key West. "Key West has a freewheeling atmosphere," says Shaughnessy. "In fact, Ernest Hemingway called it 'the San Tropez of the poor.' "

The ten-day event, begun in 1981, features a Papa Hemingway Look-alike Contest and an arm-wrestling competition, as well as the short story competition and the writer's workshop and conference. The marriage of these events may seem incongruous, but Shaughnessy claims that a remarkable synergy is at work. For instance, some individuals who have entered the Papa Hemingway Look-alike Contest have, years later, entered the short story competition or have presented at the conference as Hemingway scholars.

The conference focuses on fiction writing, poetry writing and Hemingway's work. On the first day an acclaimed writer "whose work epitomizes the creative spirit of Key West" is awarded the Conch Republic Prize for Literature. Previous recipients have included John Updike, James Dickey and Russell Banks. The winner of the prize attends the conference and gives a presentation and reading.

"This year, we're very excited that we're going to be offering more hands-on directed writing sessions than we have ever done before," notes Shaughnessy. The number of conference participants is kept relatively small so that there is a greater opportunity for them to interact with presenting writers. "Writing fiction and poetry can be a lonely business. Getting to know other writers who are going through the same struggles is a way of renewing one's own identity as a writer. Also, the more contact one can make with established writers—unfortunately, today sometimes it's who you know—the greater the likelihood of finding the path to success."

The short story competition was previously named Hemingway Days, but was re-named the Lorian Hemingway Short Story Competition in 1997. Lorian Hemingway, a novelist and journalist, is the granddaughter of Ernest Hemingway and is the competition's founder and guiding force. Shaughnessy, who works closely with Ms. Hemingway, says, "She has an unerring eye for excellence, and that's one of the reasons this competition has been so successful. The integrity of the winning entries has always been impeccable and easily recognizable."

The competition receives between 600 and 1000 entries every year worldwide. Each year, Lorian Hemingway assembles a panel of writers, editors and scholars to serve as judges, and also serves as a judge herself. The first prize is $1,000 and second and third prizes are $500 each. (See an interview with Lorian Hemingway on page 542; an interview with Lee Deigaard, winner of the 1997 competition on page 546; and the listing for the contest on page 544.)

The Lorian Hemingway Short Story Competition has been an invaluable way for fiction writers to attain both recognition and financial support, says Shaughnessy. "Short story writers have never had it easy. Many of the writers who have won tell us the Hemingway competition has given them a boost not only in terms of the validity of their work, but also in a renewed interest from potential markets." The writer Mark Richard, for example, won the Hemingway competition several years ago and went on to publish acclaimed works of fiction.

Shaughnessy offers a few tips for short story writers submitting work to contests. Writers should always research the background and philosophy of each contest and should follow competition guidelines. Although the Lorian Hemingway Competition has "no theme restrictions—we are not expecting the Ernest Hemingway style of writing— generally, we are looking for stories that ring true from people who know their craft. Excellence in craftsmanship and truth in the story are very important aspects of our competition. But if the judges find originality of thought and expression, then that is what particularly shines through." Shaughnessy, although not a judge of the competition, was struck by 1997 winner Lee Deigaard's "The Blueprint" because of its near-flawless execution and the "beautiful tapestry" of its lyricism.

After returning to writing fiction following a hiatus of several years, Shaughnessy says, "I have found such tremendous satisfaction in writing fiction that suddenly an amazing number of doors have opened to me—I'm embracing it like a new convert."

To the novice fiction writer or poet, she believes that "you must read and you must write" on a consistent basis as a necessary tool to hone the craft. In the search for excellent published writing, one should not be afraid to hop genres. Shaughnessy's most inspired reading of late has come from an essay by country songwriter Roseanne Cash in *The Oxford American*, Daphne DuMaurier's mystery novels, and essays on fishing in the recent anthology *Angles*.

"Writing is like working out, for example—the muscles don't become strong except through repetition of effort," notes Shaughnessy. She also recommends writing poetry to improve technique in any genre because poetry "requires that you hone your thought to such a degree that you don't use extra words. It is important for writers to know the elements of good writing and then to let go and listen. If they are very lucky, the stories will come banging on their brains, demanding to be let out."

—*Catherine Fahey*

of the Conch Republic Prize for Literature to a writer whose life's work epitomizes the creative spirit of Key West. Then, one day focuses on the writing of fiction, one day on the writing of poetry, and one day on Ernest Hemingway's life and work. We will be offering more hands-on directed writing sessions in 1998 than ever before, and will combine them with our traditionally-offered presentations and after-sunset readings by critically-acclaimed writers. Most years, we also offer the opportunity for participants to have their own work critiqued. Traditionally, the Workshop & Conference is held at a resort in Key West's historic Old Town section. We expect that to hold true in 1998 as well. Directed writing exercises will take place at a variety of locations in the Old Town area such as gardens and historic sites, while after-sunset readings will take place at an open-air atrium or restaurant."

Costs: $120; includes all panels, directed writing exercises, attendance at all literary receptions and after-sunset readings.

Accommodations: Material available upon request.

Additional Information: Brochures/guidelines are available for SASE. "The conference/workshop is unique in that it combines studies in craft with studies in literature, and serious literary-minded events to celebrate Hemingway the writer with a week-long festival celebrating 'papa' the myth."

‡MOONLIGHT AND MAGNOLIAS WRITER'S CONFERENCE, 4378 Karls Gate Dr., Marietta GA 30068. Phone/fax: (770)513-1754. E-mail: WendyEth@aol.com. Estab. 1982. President, Georgia Romance Writers: Carol Springston. 1998 Conference Chair: Wendy Etherington, 2615 Suwanee Lakes Trail, Suwanee GA 30174-3164. Annual. Conference held 3rd weekend in September. Average attendance: 300. "Conference focuses on writing of women's fiction with emphasis on romance. 1997 conference included ten editors from major publishing houses and five agents. Workshops included: beginning writer track, general interest topics, and professional issues for the published author, plus sessions for writing for children, young adult, inspirational, multicultural and Regency. Speakers included experts in law enforcement, screenwriting and research. Literacy raffle and advertised speaker and GRW member autographing open to the public. Published authors make up 25-30% of attendees. Brochure available for SASE in June. Send requests with SASE to Wendy Etherington. Seventeeth annual conference to be held September 11-13, 1998, at a convenient metro Atlanta hotel with limo service to Hartsfield International Airport.

Costs: Hotel $74/day, single, double, triple, quad (1997). Conference: non GRW members $135 (early registration).

Additional Information: Maggie Awards for excellence are presented to unpublished writers. The Maggie Award for published writers is limited to Region 3 members of Romance Writers of America. Proposals per guidelines must be submitted in early June. Please check with president for new dates. Published authors judge first round, category editors judge finals. Guidelines available for SASE in spring.

‡QUERY LETTER WORKSHOP, P.O. Box 100031, Birmingham AL 35210. (205)907-0140. Estab. 1987. Workshop lasts 1 day. Average attendance: 15-20. Workshop to assist writers with the marketing aspect of their novels. Held in a college classroom. Students receive feedback from a professional editor on actual query letters.

Costs: Vary from $59-99; meals not included.

Additional Information: "Students should bring two copies of their query letters to the workshop for evaluation by a professional editor." Brochure available anytime for SASE. "This is not a creative writing workshop, but is designed to help authors who can already write learn how to sell their work."

‡ROMANCE & MORE, P.O. Box 52505, Shreveport LA 71115-2505. Fax: (318)227-0660. Contact: Linda Lehr, president. Estab. 1985. Annual. Conference held first Saturday of March. Average attendance: 60-70. Conference focuses on fiction. Held at the Holiday Inn-Riverfront. Past themes include "Writing the Bestseller." Guest speakers have included published authors Jennifer Blake, Tami Hoagg and Betina Krohn, and editors Shauna Summers (Bantam) and Cristine Nussner (Silhouette Books).

Costs: $70 (members) and $80 (nonmembers). Includes light breakfast and lunch.

Accommodations: Available at Holiday Inn where conference is held ($60/night for 2).

Additional Information: Sponsors contest for novels. Submit first 3 chapters plus synopsis. First-round judges are published authors; final-round judges are editors. Conference and contest brochures/guidelines are available for SASE. Inquiries by fax OK.

SCBWI/FLORIDA ANNUAL FALL CONFERENCE, 2158 Portland Ave., Wellington FL 33414. (561)798-4824. E-mail: barcafer@aol.com. Florida Regional Advisor: Barbara Casey. Estab. 1985. Annual. Conference held September 12, 1998. Conference duration: one-half day. Average attendance: 70. Conference to promote "all aspects of writing and illustrating for children. The facilities include the meeting rooms of the Library and Town Hall of Palm Springs FL (near West Palm Beach)."

Costs: $50 for SCBWI members, $55 for non-SCBWI members. Ms and art evaluations, $30.

Accommodations: Special conference rates at Airport Hilton, West Palm Beach, Florida.

Additional Information: Conference brochures/guidelines are available July 1998 for SASE. Inquiries by e-mail OK.

SOUTHEASTERN WRITERS CONFERENCE, 5952 Alma Hwy., Waycross GA 31503. (912)285-9159. Secretary: Nelle McFather. Estab. 1975. Annual. Conference held June 21-26, 1998. Conference duration: 1

week. Average attendence: 100 (limited to 100 participants). Concentration is on fiction, poetry and juvenile—plus nonfiction and playwriting. Site is "St. Simons Island, GA. Conference held at Epworth-by-the-Sea Conference Center—tropical setting, beaches. Each year we offer market advice, agent updates. All our instructors are professional writers presently selling in New York."
Costs: $245. Meals and lodging are separate.
Accommodations: Information on overnight accommodations is made available. "On-site-facilities at a remarkably low cost. Facilities are motel style of excellent quality. Other hotels are available on the island."
Additional Information: "Three manuscripts of one chapter each are allowed in three different categories." Sponsors several contests, MANY cash prizes. Brochures are available March for SASE.

SOUTHWEST FLORIDA WRITERS' CONFERENCE, P.O. Box 60210, Ft. Myers FL 33906-6210. (813)489-9226. Fax: (941)489-9051. Conference Director: Joanne Hartke. Estab. 1980. Annual. Conference held Feb. 28-March 1 (always the 4th Friday and Saturday of February). Average attendance: 150. "This year's conference will include fiction, poetry, nonfiction, an agent and others. The purpose is to serve the local writing community, whether they are novice or published writers." The conference is held on the Edison Community College campus.
Costs: "Reasonable." Call or write for conference brochures/guidelines and to be put on mailing list.
Additional Information: Conference brochures/guidelines are available for SASE after November-December. Inquiries by fax OK. "We do sponsor a writing contest annually, with the prizes being gift certificates to local bookstores. A new feature is a coffee critique session, for participant's readings, followed by critique with peers and a published author for immediate feedback."

WRITE FOR SUCCESS WORKSHOP: CHILDREN'S BOOKS, 3748 Harbor Heights Dr., Largo FL 33774-1207. (813)581-2484. Speaker/Coordinator: Theo Carroll. Estab. 1990. Held 3 separate evenings the last 3 weeks in March. Sepearte conference duration: 1 day. Average attendance: 60-110. Concentration is writing for children. Site is the Clearwater, Florida Community Center. "Teaching assignments and classroom/personal critique sessions cover characterization, plotting, the importance of setting, dialogue and more. Assignments given on writing the picture book."
Costs: $85 includes materials. Limo available from Tampa airport. Information on special conference attendee accommodations available.
Additional Information: Brochures for latest seminar are available for SASE.

WRITING STRATEGIES FOR THE CHRISTIAN MARKET, 2712 S. Peninsula Dr., Daytona Beach FL 32118. (904)322-1111. Instructor: Rosemary Upton. Estab. 1991. Seminars given approximately 4 times a year. Conference duration: 3 hours. Average attendance: 10-20. Seminars include Basics I, Marketing II, Business III, Building the novel. Held in a conference room: 3-4 persons seated at each table; instructor teaches from a podium. Question and answer session provided. Critique shop included once a month, except summer (July and August). Instructors include Rosemary Upton, novelist; Kistler London, editor.
Costs: $30 for each 3-hour seminar.
Additional Information: Those who have taken Writing Strategies instruction are able to attend an on-going monthly critiqueshop where their peers critique their work. Manual provided with each seminar. Conference brochures/guidelines are available for SASE. Independent study by mail also available.

WRITING TODAY—BIRMINGHAM-SOUTHERN COLLEGE, Box 549003, Birmingham AL 35254. (205)226-4921. Fax: (205)226-3072. E-mail: bhopkins@bsc.edu. Website: http://www.bsc.edu. Director of Special Events: Martha Andrews. Estab. 1978. Annual. Conference held March 14-15. Average attendance: 400-500. "This is a two-day conference with approximately 18 workshops, lectures and readings. We try to offer workshops in short fiction, novels, poetry, children's literature, magazine writing, and general information of concern to aspiring writers such as publishing, agents, markets and research. The conference is sponsored by Birmingham-Southern College and is held on the campus in classrooms and lecture halls." The 1997 conference featured novelist, Joyce Carol Oates. Joy Harjo, Gay Talese, Nan Talese, Clifton Taulbert, Kevin Arkadie and Patricia Hagan were some of the workshop presenters.
Costs: $90 for both days. This includes lunches, reception and morning coffee and rolls.
Accommodations: Attendees must arrange own transporation. Local hotels and motels offer special rates, but participants must make their own reservations.
Additional Information: "We usually offer a critique for interested writers. We have had poetry and short story critiques. There is an additional charge for these critiques." Sponsors the Hackney Literary Competition Awards for poetry, short story and novels. Brochures available for SASE.

Midwest (IL, IN, KY, MI, OH)

‡**ANTIOCH WRITERS' WORKSHOP**, P.O. Box 494, Yellow Springs OH 45387. Director: Gilah Rittenhouse. Estab. 1984. Annual. Average attendance: 80. Workshop concentration: poetry, nonfiction and fiction.

Workshop located on Antioch College campus in the Village of Yellow Springs. Speakers have included Sue Grafton, Imogene Bolls, George Ella Lyon, Herbert Martin, John Jakes and Virginia Hamilton.

Costs: Tuition is $475—lower for local and repeat—plus meals.

Accommodations: "We pick up attendees free at the airport." Accommodations made at dorms and area hotels. Cost is $16-26/night (for dorms).

Additional Information: Offers mss critique sessions. Conference brochures/guidelines are available after March 1998 for SASE.

‡BLUEGRASS WRITERS WORKSHOP, P.O. Box 3098, Princeton NJ 08543-3098. (609)275-2947. Fax: (609)275-1243. National Director: Karl G. Garson. Estab. 1994. Annual. Workshop held in June. Workshop duration: 2 weeks. Average attendance: 15. "Workshop concentrates on all genres using the horse and/or horse racing as the subject." Held at Churchill Downs racetrack, Louisville, Kentucky. Guest speakers for 1996 will include Gerald Costanzo, founder/director, Carnegie Mellon University Press; Lee K. Abbott, Ohio State University; and Jana Harris, University of Washington.

Costs: Fee for 1995 was $750 (included tuition and daily lunches).

Accommodations: Transportation to workshop site and field trip locations is furnished. Participants are responsible for their travel to and from Louisville. On-campus housing and hotel information is furnished. On-campus housing: $18/single; $13/double, per person, per night. Hotel (Holiday Inn): $35/single or double, per night.

Additional Information: "A representative sample of writing is requested with the workshop application." Conference brochures/guidelines are available for SASE.

THE COLUMBUS WRITERS CONFERENCE, P.O. Box 20548, Columbus OH 43220. (614)451-3075. Fax: (614)451-0174. E-mail: AngelaPL28@aol.com. Director: Angela Palazzolo. Estab. 1993. Annual. Conference held September 27. Pre-conference dinner/program held September 26. Average attendance: 200. The conference is held in the Fawcett Center for Tomorrow, 2400 Olentangy River Road, Columbus OH. "The conference covers a wide variety of fiction and nonfiction topics. Writing topics have included novel, short story, children's, young adult, science fiction, fantasy, humor, mystery, playwriting, screenwriting, travel, humor, cookbook, technical, query letter, corporate, educational and greeting cards. Other topics for writers: finding and working with an agent, targeting markets, research, time management, obtaining grants and writers' colonies." Speakers have included Lee K. Abbott, Lore Segal, Mike Harden, Oscar Collier, Maureen F. McHugh, Ralph Keyes, Stephanie S. Tolan, Dennis L. McKiernan, Karen Harper, Melvin Helitzer, Susan Porter, Les Roberts, Tracey E. Dils, J. Patrick Lewis and many other professionals in the writing field.

Costs: Early registration fee is $89; otherwise, fee is $105. This includes continental breakfast, lunch and afternoon refreshments. Cost for the pre-conference dinner/program is $28.

Additional Information: Call, write, e-mail or send fax to obtain a conference brochure, available mid-summer.

EASTERN KENTUCKY UNIVERSITY CREATIVE WRITING CONFERENCE, Eastern Kentucky University, Richmond KY 40475. (606)622-5861. Conference Director: Dorothy Sutton. Estab. 1962. Annual. Conference held 3rd week in June. Average attendance: 15-20. Conference to promote poetry and fiction. Includes lectures, workshops, private individual and peer group manuscript evaluation. The conference is held on the campus of Eastern Kentucky University "in the rolling hills of Eastern Kentucky, between the horse farms of the Bluegrass and the scenic mountains of the Appalachian chain." Three distinguished visiting writers will teach at the conference. Past speakers have included Donald Justice, Maggie Anderson, Maura Stanton, Richard Marius, Gregory Orr, David Citino and Reginald Gibbons. Also helping with workshops will be EKU faculty Harry Brown, Hal Blythe and Charlie Sweet.

Costs: Approx. $82 for undergraduates ($227 if out-of-state); $120 for graduates ($333 if out-of-state). Cost includes 1 hour of credit in creative writing and is subject to change (please check 1998 brochure for exact charge). Auditors welcome at same price. Dining in the cafeteria is available at reasonable prices.

Accommodations: Air-conditioned dormitory rooms are available for approx. $9 (double) or $12 (single) per night. "Linens furnished. Bring your own blankets, pillow and telephone, if desired. Subject to change. Check brochure."

Additional Information: "Participants are asked to submit manuscript by May 15 to be approved by May 25." For conference brochure, send SASE to English Department (attn: Creative Writing Conference) after February 15, 1998.

CHARLENE FARIS SEMINARS FOR BEGINNERS, 895 W. Oak St., Zionsville IN 46077-1208. Phone/fax: (317)873-0738. Director: Charlene Faris. Estab. 1985. Held 2 or 3 times/year in various locations in spring, summer and fall. Conference duration: 2 days. Average attendence: 10. Concentration on all areas of publishing and writing, particularly marketing and working with editors. Locations have included Phoenix, Los Angeles, Madison WI and Indianapolis.

Costs: $150, tuition only; may attend only 1 day for $80.

Accommodations: Information on overnight accommodations available.

Additional Information: Guidelines available for SASE.

GREEN RIVER WRITERS NOVELS-IN-PROGRESS WORKSHOP, 11906 Locust Rd., Middletown KY 40243. (502)245-4902. Director: Mary E. O'Dell. Estab. 1991. Annual. Conference held March 8-15, 1998.

Conference duration: 1 week. Average attendance: 40. Open to persons, college age and above, who have approximately 3 chapters (60 pages) or more of a novel. Mainstream and genre novels handled by individual instructors. Short fiction collections welcome. "Each novelist instructor works with a small group (5-7 people) for five days; then agents/editors are there for panels and appointments on the weekend." Site is The University of Louisville's Shelby Campus, suburban setting, graduate dorm housing (private rooms available w/shared bath for each 2 rooms). "Meetings and classes held in nearby classroom building. Grounds available for walking, etc. Lovely setting, restaurants and shopping available nearby. Participants carpool to restaurants, etc. This year we are covering mystery, fantasy, mainstream/literary, suspense, historical."
Costs: Tuition—$350, housing $20 per night private, $16 shared. Does not include meals.
Accommodations: "We do meet participants' planes and see that participants without cars have transportation to meals, etc. If participants would rather stay in hotel, we will make that information available."
Additional Information: Participants send 60 pages/3 chapters with synopsis and $25 reading fee which applies to tuition. Deadline will be in late January. Conference brochures/guidelines are available for SASE.

THE HEIGHTS WRITER'S CONFERENCE, P.O. Box 24684, Cleveland OH 44124-0684. Fax: (216)481-2057. E-mail: writersword@juno.com. Director: Lavern Hall. Estab. 1992. Annual. Conference held first Saturday in May. Average attendance: 125. "Fiction, nonfiction, science fiction, poetry, children's, marketing, etc." The conference is sponsored by Writer's World Press and held at the Cleveland Marriott East, Beachwood OH. Offers seminars on the craft, business and legal aspects of writing plus 2 teaching, hands-on workshops. "No theme; published authors and experts in their field sharing their secrets and networking for success."
Additional Information: Conference brochure available March 1 for SASE. Inquiries by e-mail and fax OK.

‡INDIANA UNIVERSITY WRITERS' CONFERENCE, 464 Ballantine Hall, Bloomington IN 47405. (812)855-1877. Fax: (812)855-9535. Director: Patrick Godbey. Estab. 1940. Annual. Conference/workshops held from June 21-26. Average attendance: 100. "Conference to promote poetry, fiction and nonfiction (emphasis on poetry and fiction)." Located on the campus of Indiana University, Bloomington. "We do not have themes, although we do have panels that discuss issues such as how to publish. We also have classes that tackle just about every subject of writing. Ralph Burns, Amy Gerstein, Pinckney Benedict and Sharon Solwit are scheduled to speak and teach workshops at the 1998 conference.
Costs: Approximately $300; does not include food or housing. This price does *not* reflect the cost of taking the conference for credit. "We supply conferees with options for overnight accommodations. We offer special conference rates for both the hotel and dorm facilities on site.
Additional Information: "In order to be accepted in a workshop, the writer must submit the work they would like critiqued. Work is evaluated before accepting applicant. Scholarships are available determined by an outside reader/writer, based on the quality of the manuscript." Conference brochures/guidelines available for SASE in February. "We are the second oldest writer's conference in the country. We are in our 58th year."

‡THE MID AMERICA MYSTERY CONFERENCE, Magna cum Murder, The E.B. Ball Center, Ball State University, Muncie IN 47306. (765)285-8975. Fax: (765)747-9566. E-mail: kkenniso@wp.bsu.edu. Estab. 1994. Annual. Conference held from October 30 to November 1. Average attendance: 400. Conference for crime and detective fiction held in the Horizon Convention Center and Historic Radisson Hotel Roberts. 1997 speakers included Lawrence Block, James Crumley, HRF Keating, Sarah Caudwell, Patricia Moyes, Harlan Coben and James Hess.
Costs: $145, which includes continental breakfasts, boxed lunches, a reception and a banquet (1997).
Additional Information: Sponsors a radio mystery script contest. Brochures or guidelines available for SASE. Inquiries by fax and e-mail OK.

MIDLAND WRITERS CONFERENCE, Grace A. Dow Memorial Library, 1710 W. St. Andrews, Midland MI 48640-2698. (517)835-7151. Fax: (517)835-9791. E-mail: kred@vlc.lib.mi.us. Website: http://www.gracedow library.org. Conference Chair: Katherine Redwine. Estab. 1980. Annual. Conference held June 13. Average attendance: 100. "The Conference is composed of a well-known keynote speaker and six workshops on a variety of subjects including poetry, children's writing, freelancing, agents, etc. The attendees are both published and unpublished authors. The Conference is held at the Grace A. Dow Memorial Library in the auditorium and conference rooms. Keynoters in the past have included Dave Barry, Pat Conroy, Kurt Vonnegut, Roger Ebert."
Costs: Adult - $50 before May 16, $60 after May 17; students, senior citizens and handicapped - $40 before May 17, $50 after May 16. A box lunch is available. Costs are approximate until plans for upcoming conference are finalized.
Accommodations: A list of area hotels is available.
Additional Information: Conference brochures/guidelines are mailed mid-April. Call or write to be put on mailing list. Inquiries by e-mail and fax OK.

‡MIDWEST WRITERS' CONFERENCE, 6000 Frank Ave. NW, Canton OH 44720-7599. (216)499-9600. Fax: (330)494-6121. E-mail: Druhe@Stark.Kent.Edu. Conference Director: Debbie Ruhe. Estab. 1968. Annual. Conference held in early October. Conference duration: 2 days. Average attendance: 350. "The conference provides an atmosphere in which aspiring writers can meet with and learn from experienced and established writers through lectures, workshops, competitive contest, personal interviews and informal group discussions. The areas of concentration include fiction, nonfiction, juvenile literature and poetry. The Midwest Writers' Conference is held on Kent State University Stark Campus in Canton, Ohio. This two-day conference is held in Main Hall, a four-story building and wheel chair accessible."

Costs: $65 includes Friday workshops, keynote address, Saturday workshops, box luncheon and manuscript entry fee (limited to two submissions); $40 for contest only (includes two manuscripts).

Accommodations: Arrangements are made with a local hotel which is near Kent Stark and offers a special reduced rate for conference attendees. Conferees must make their own reservations 3 weeks before the conference to be guaranteed this special conference rate.

Additional Information: Each manuscript entered in the contest will receive a critique. If the manuscript is selected for final judging, it will receive an additional critique from the final judge. Conference attendees are not required to submit manuscripts to the writing contest. Manuscript deadline is early August. For contest: A maximum of 1 entry for each category is permitted. Entries must be typed on 8½×11 paper, double-spaced. A separate page must accompany each entry bearing the author's name, address, phone, category and title of the work. Entries are not to exceed 3,000 words in length. Work must be original, unpublished and not a winner in any contest at the time of entry. Conference brochures and guidelines are available after April 1998 for SASE. Inquiries by e-mail and fax OK.

OAKLAND UNIVERSITY WRITERS' CONFERENCE, 231 Varner Hall, Rochester MI 48309-4401. (248)370-3125. Fax: (248)370-4280. E-mail: gjboddy@oakland.edu. Program Director: Gloria J. Boddy. Estab. 1961. Annual. Conference held in October. Average attendance: 400. Held at Oakland University: Oakland Center: Vandenburg Hall and O'Dowd Hall. Each annual conference covers all aspects and types of writing in 36 concurrent workshops on Saturday. Major writers from various genres are speakers for the Saturday conference and luncheon program. Individual critiques and hands-on writing workshops are conducted Friday. Areas: poetry, articles, fiction, short stories, playwriting, nonfiction, young adult, children's literature. Keynote speaker in 1997: Betty Prashker, executive vice president and editor at Large of the Crown Publishing Group, a division of Random House.

Costs: 1997: Conference registration: $75; lunch, $8; individual ms, $48; writing workshop, $38; writing ms audit, $28.

Accommodations: List is available.

Additional Information: Conference brochure/guidelines available after September 1998 for SASE. Inquiries by e-mail and fax OK.

OF DARK & STORMY NIGHTS, Mystery Writers of America—Midwest Chapter, P.O. Box 1944, Muncie IN 47308-1944. (765)288-7402. Workshop Director: W.W. Spurgeon. Estab. 1982. Annual. Workshop held June. Workshop duration: 1 day. Average attendance: 200. Dedicated to "writing *mystery* fiction and crime-related nonfiction. Workshops and panels presented on techniques of mystery writing from ideas to revision, marketing, investigative techniques and more, by published writers, law enforcement experts and publishing professionals." Site is Holiday Inn, Rolling Meadows IL (suburban Chicago).

Costs: $105 for MWA members; $130 for non-members; $40 extra for ms critique.

Accommodations: Easily accessible by car or train (from Chicago) Holiday Inn, Rolling Meadows $80 per night plus tax; free airport bus (Chicago O'Hare) and previously arranged rides from train.

Additional Information: "We accept manuscripts for critique (first 30 pages maximum); $40 cost. Writers meet with critics during workshop for one-on-one discussions." Brochures available for SASE after February 1.

GARY PROVOST'S WRITERS RETREAT WORKSHOP, % Write It/Sell It, P.O. Box 139, South Lancaster MA 01561-0139. Phone: (508)368-0287. Fax: (918)298-4866. E-mail: wrwwisi@aol.com. Website: http://www.channel1.com/wisi Director: Gail Provost. Assistant Director: Lance Stockwell; Workshop Leader: Carol Dougherty. Estab. 1987. May 1998 workshop held at Marydale Retreat Center in Erlanger, KY (just south of Cincinnati, OH). Workshop duration: 10 days. Average attendance: 25. Focus on fiction and narrative nonfiction books in progress. All genres. "The Writers Retreat Workshop is an intensive learning experience for small groups of serious-minded writers. Founded by the late Gary Provost, one of the country's leading writing instructors and his wife Gail, an award-winning author, the WRW is a challenging and enriching adventure. The goal of the WRW staff is for students to leave with a new understanding of the marketplace and the craft of writing a novel. In the heart of a supportive and spirited community of fellow writers, students are able to make remarkable creative leaps over the course of the 10-day workshop."

Costs: Costs (discount for past participants) $1,595 for 10 days which includes all food and lodging. The Marydale Retreat Center is 5 miles from the Cincinnati airport and offers shuttle services.
Additional Information: Participants are selected based upon the appropriateness of this program for the applicant's specific writing project. Participants are asked to submit a brief overview and synopsis before the workshop and are given assignments and feedback during the 10-day workshop. Brochures/guidelines are available for SASE, or by calling 1-800-642-2494. Inquiries by fax and e-mail OK.

ROPEWALK WRITERS' RETREAT, 8600 University Blvd., Evansville IN 47712. (812)464-1863. E-mail: lcleek.ucs@smtp.usi.edu. Conference Coordinator: Linda Cleek. Estab. 1989. Annual. Conference held June 6-13, 1998: "Celebrating 10 Years in Utopia!" Average attendance: 42. "The week-long RopeWalk Writers' Retreat gives participants an opportunity to attend workshops and to confer privately with one of four or five prominent writers. Historic New Harmony, Indiana, site of two nineteenth century utopian experiments, provides an ideal setting for this event with its retreat-like atmosphere and its history of creative and intellectual achievement. At RopeWalk you will be encouraged to write—not simply listen to others talks about writing. Each workshop will be limited to twelve participants. The New Harmony Inn and Conference Center will be headquarters for the RopeWalk Writers' Retreat. Please note that reservations at the Inn should be confirmed by May 1." 1998 faculty Pam Houston, Bob Shacochis, Ellen Bryant Voigt and Heather MacHugh.
Costs: $395 (1997), includes breakfasts and lunches.
Accommodations: Information on overnight accommodations is made available. "Room-sharing assistance; some low-cost accommodations."
Additional Information: For critiques submit mss approx. 6 weeks ahead. Brochures are available after January 15.

SELF PUBLISHING YOUR OWN BOOK, 34200 Ridge Rd., #110, Willoughby OH 44094-2954. (440)943-3047 or (800)653-4261. E-mail address: fa837@cleveland.freenet.edu. Teacher: Lea Leever Oldham. Estab. 1989. Quarterly. Conferences usually held in February, April, August and October. Conference duration: 2½ hours. Average attendance: up to 25. Conference covers copyrighting, marketing, pricing, ISBN number, Library of Congress catalog number, reaching the right customers and picking a printer. Held at Lakeland Community College, Kirtland, OH (east of Cleveland off I-90). Classrooms are wheelchair accessible.
Additional Information: Conference guidelines are available for SASE. Inquiries by e-mail OK.

WESTERN RESERVE WRITERS & FREELANCE CONFERENCE, 34200 Ridge Rd., #110, Willoughby OH 44094. (440)943-3047 or (800)653-4261. E-mail address: fa837@cleveland.freenet.edu. Coordinator: Lea Leever Oldham. Estab. 1984. Annual. Conference held every September. Conference duration: 1 day. Average attendance: 150. "Fiction, nonfiction, inspirational, children's, poetry, humor, scifi, copyright and tax information, etc." Held "at Lakeland Community College, Kirtland, OH. Classrooms wheelchair accessible. Accessible from I-90, east of Cleveland." Panels include "no themes, simply published authors and other experts sharing their secrets."
Costs: $55 including lunch.
Additional Information: Conference brochures/guidelines are available after July 1998 for SASE. Inquiries by e-mail OK.

WESTERN RESERVE WRITERS MINI CONFERENCE, 34200 Ridge Rd., #110, Willoughby OH 44094. (440)943-3047 or (800)653-4261. E-mail address: fa837@cleveland.freenet.edu. Coordinator: Lea Leever Oldham. Estab. 1991. Annual. Conference held in late March. Conference duration: ½ day. Average attendance: 175. Conference to promote "fiction, nonfiction, children's, poetry, science fiction, etc." Held at Lakeland Community College, Kirtland, OH (east of Cleveland off I-90). Classrooms are wheelchair accessible. "Conference is for beginners, intermediate and advanced writers." Past speakers have included Mary Grimm, Nick Bade, James Martin and Mary Ryan.
Costs: $29.
Additional Information: Conference brochures/guidelines are available after January 1998 for SASE. Inquiries by e-mail OK.

WRITING FOR MONEY WORKSHOP, 34200 Ridge Rd., #110, Willoughby OH 44094. (440)943-3047 or (800)653-4261. E-mail: fa837@cleveland.freenet.edu. Contact: Lea Leever Oldham. Conference held several times during the year. 1997 dates: February 22; March 8; April 19; May 17; July 26; September 27 and October 18. Conference duration: one day. "Covers query letters, characterization for fiction, editing grammar, manuscript preparation and marketing saleable manuscripts." Held at Lakeland Community College, Kirtland, OH. Right off I-90 and in Mayfield, OH, east of Cleveland.
Costs: $39/day.
Additional Information: Workshop brochure/guidelines are available a month prior to class. Inquiries by e-mail OK.

‡**WOMEN WRITERS CONFERENCE**, The University of Kentucky, 931 Patterson Office Tower, Lexington KY 40506-0027. Fax: (606)257-3474. Annual. Conference held from October 22 to October 25. "Gathering of

women writers and scholars—novelists, poets, playwrights, essayists, biographers, journalists—and readers and students of literature. For the past nineteen years, several days of reading, lectures, workshops, musical and theater performances and panel discussions about women writers and women's writing have been held both on campus and out in the community." Panels planned for next conference include "Recovering the Works of 18th Century Women Writers" and "Writing Off the Page." Workshops include hypertext fiction, fiction writing, autobiographical writing, children's literature, on the spot writing, performance art, filmmaking, poetry, song writing, playwriting, performance composition, short story writing, manuscript preparation and reading your own work. Writers and presenters speaking at the conference include Joan Brannon, Norma Cole, Nancy Elliot, Merlene Davis, Kim Edwards, Nancy Grayson Holmes, Sandy Huss, Mary Jefferson, Rhea Lehman, Sharyn McCrumb and Elizabeth Meese.

Costs: $50 for entire conference or $20/day.

Accommodations: A list of area hotel will be provided by the Lexington Chamber of Commerce upon request. Call (606)254-4447.

Additional Information: "Manuscript critiques of pre-submitted fiction, poetry, playwriting and non-fiction by registered conference participants will be provided by regional writers. Feedback will be given in 15-minute private sessions. The fee is $25. Absolute deadline for receipt of manuscripts is October 10. Submit two copies of your double-spaced manuscript, 15 pages maximum in all categories except poetry, where the maximum is six pages." Scholarships are available for those who would otherwise be unable to attend. Attach a brief letter of explanation to the registration form detailing why the conference is important to you.

North Central (IA, MN, NE, ND, SD, WI)

PETER DAVIDSON'S WRITER'S SEMINAR, 982 S. Emerald Hills Dr., P.O. Box 497, Arnolds Park IA 51331. (712)362-7968. Seminar Presenter: Peter Davidson. Estab. 1985. Seminars held about 30 times annually, in various sites. Offered year round. Seminars last 1 day, usually 9 a.m.-4 p.m. Average attendance: 35. "All writing areas including books of fiction and nonfiction, children's works, short stories, magazine articles, poetry, songs, scripts, religious works, personal experiences and romance fiction. All seminars are sponsored by community colleges or colleges across the U.S. Covers many topics including developing your idea, writing the manuscript, copyrighting, and marketing your work. A practical approach is taken."

Costs: Each sponsoring college sets own fees, ranging from $39-59, depending on location, etc.

Accommodations: "Participants make their own arrangements. Usually, no special arrangements are available."

Additional Information: "Participants are encouraged to bring their ideas and/or manuscripts for a short, informal evaluation by seminar presenter, Peter Davidson." Conference brochures/guidelines are available for SASE. "On even-numbered years, usually present seminars in Colorado, Wyoming, Nebraska, Kansas, Iowa, Minnesota and South Dakota. On odd-numbered years, usually present seminars in Illinois, Iowa, Minnesota, Arkansas, Missouri, South Dakota and Nebraska."

GREAT LAKES WRITER'S WORKSHOP, Alverno College, 3401 S. 39 St., P.O. Box 343922, Milwaukee WI 53234-3922. (414)382-6176. Fax: (414)382-6332. Assistant Director: Cindy Jackson, Professional and Community Education. Estab. 1985. Annual. Workshop held during second week in July (Friday through Thursday). Average attendance: 250. "Workshop focuses on a variety of subjects including fiction, writing for magazines, freelance writing, writing for children, poetry, marketing, etc. Participants may select individual workshops or opt to attend the entire week-long session. Classes are held during evenings and weekends. The workshop is held in Milwaukee, WI at Alverno College."

Costs: In 1997, cost was $99 for entire workshop. "Individual classes are priced as posted in the brochure with the majority costing $20 each."

Accommodations: Attendees must make their own travel arrangments. Accommodations are available on campus; rooms are in residence halls and are not air-conditioned. Cost in 1997 was $25 for single, $20 per person for double. There are also hotels in the surrounding area. Call (414)382-6040 for information regarding overnight accommodations.

Additional Information: "Some workshop instructors may provide critiques, but this changes depending upon the workshop and speaker. This would be indicated in the workshop brochure." Brochures are available for SASE after March. Inquiries by fax OK.

GREEN LAKE 1998 WRITERS CONFERENCE, Green Lake Conference Center/American Baptist Assembly, Green Lake WI 54941-9300. (800)558-8898. Estab. 1948. Annual. 1997 conference date is July 4-11. Average attendance: 75. "This conference provides quality instructors who are published authors and experienced at being both friend and coach. Held annually at this 1,000 acre conference center located on a lake offering a wide range of recreational and creative craft opportunities in a hospitable accepting environment." Conference speakers have included Marion Dane Bauer, Ben Logan, Jacqueline Mitchard and many excellent workshop leaders.

Costs: Tuition is $80/person plus room and board.

Accommodations: "We can provide ground transportation from Appleton and Oshkosh airports; the Amtrak

station in Columbus and Greyhound Bus Stop in Fond du Lac for a modest fee. Room costs vary depending on facilities. All rooms are on the American Food Plan. Campground and cabin facilities also available."
Additional Information: Conference brochures are available upon request.

INTERNATIONAL MUSIC CAMP CREATIVE WRITING WORKSHOP, 1725 11th St. SW, Minot ND 58701-6150. (701)838-8472. Fax: (701)838-8472. E-mail: imc@minot.com. Camp Director: Joseph T. Alme. Estab. 1970. Annual.   Conference usually held in July. Conference duration: 6 days. Average attendance: 20. "Conference to promote fiction, poetry, children's writing, plays and mystery stories including feedback from the professionals. The conference is held in the Frances Leach Library at the International Music Camp. The summer Arts camp is located at the International Peace Garden on the border between Manitoba and North Dakota. 3,000 acres of hand-planted flowers, fountains and natural beauty create a perfect setting for a creative writing workshop."
Costs: $190 including room, board and tuition. "The food in the new cafeteria is excellent. Housing in the spacious new dormitories provide privacy and comfort."
Accommodations: Northwest and United Express Airlines fly to Minot, ND. AMTRAK goes to Rugby, ND. A shuttle service is available from both terminals. "Area motels vary in rates. However, the accommodations located on sight are excellent and at no additional cost."
Additional Information: No auditions are required. Critiques are given throughout the week. Conference brochures/guidelines are available for SASE. "A $75 deposit is required. It is refundable until June 1st, 1998. When an application is received, a list of materials needed for the workshop is sent to the student. A promotional video is available upon request." Inquiries by fax and e-mail OK.

IOWA SUMMER WRITING FESTIVAL, 116 International Center, University of Iowa, Iowa City IA 52242-1802. (319)335-2534. E-mail: peggy-houston@uiowa.edu; amy-margolis@uiowa.edu. Website: http://www.edu/~iswfest. Director: Peggy Houston. Assistant Director: Amy Margolis. Estab. 1987. Annual. Festival held in June and July. Workshops are one week or a weekend. Average attendance: limited to 12/class—over 1,300 participants throughout the summer. "We offer courses in most areas of writing: novel, short story, essay, poetry, playwriting, screenwriting, humor, travel, writing for children, memoir, women's writing, romance and mystery." Site is the University of Iowa campus. Guest speakers are undetermined at this time. Readers and instructors have included Lee K. Abbott, Susan Power, Joy Harjo, Gish Jen, Abraham Verghese, Robert Olen Butler, Ethan Canin, Clark Blaise, Gerald Stern, Donald Justice, Michael Dennis Browne, Marvin Bell, Hope Edelman.
Costs: $400/week; $150, weekend workshop (1997 rates). Discounts available for early registration. Housing and meals are separate.
Accommodations: "We offer participants a choice of accommodations: dormitory, $27/night; Iowa House, $56/night; Holiday Inn, $60/night (rates subject to changes)."
Additional Information: Brochure/guidelines are available in February. Inquiries by fax and e-mail OK.

‡REDBIRD WRITING CENTER, 3195 S. Superior St., Milwaukee WI 53207-3074. (418)481-3029. (414)481-3195. E-mail: blankda@execc.com. Website: http://www.execpc.com/redbirdstudios. Estab. 1993. Average attendance: 6-12. "Redbird is an education center and home-port for people who care about writing. From a single Saturday morning workshop, Redbird has grown to include several year 'round and special topic workshops, seminars, conferences and special events. Over 1000 people have attended sessions at the studios." Workshops are held in studio rooms overlooking Lake Michigan. Workshops planned for the next year include suspense, mystery, writing for the children's market, novels and short stories. Past speakers have included Elaine Bergstrom, John Lehman and Sharon Hart Addy.
Costs: $25-$125.
Additional Information: Brochure available for SASE. Inquiries by fax OK. "All sessions are lead by published writers who enjoy helping others."

SCBWI/MINNESOTA CHAPTER CONFERENCES, 7080 Coachwood Rd., Woodbury MN 55125. (612)739-0119. E-mail: kidlit@juno.com. "Although schedule may vary as space is available, conferences are usually held one day in spring and one day in fall. The smaller conference features local authors and editors only. The larger conference features children's book editors from New York publishing houses and well-known authors." Average attendance: 100. Recent speakers have included editors from Houghton Mifflin, authors Phyllis Root and Kathryn O. Galbraith and illustrator Beth Peck.
Costs: Varies: around $20 for local conference or $85 for larger conference with discounts given for SCBWI members and early registration.
Accommodations: Not included in conference cost.
Additional Information: For conference brochure, send SASE no more than 6 weeks in advance. Inquiries by e-mail OK. Ms critiques and portfolio reviews available at larger conference for an additional fee.

SINIPEE WRITERS' WORKSHOP, P.O. Box 902, Dubuque IA 52004-0902. (319)588-7139. E-mail: lcrosset @loras.edu. Director: Linda Crossett. Assistant Director: John Tigges. Estab. 1985. Annual conference held in April. Average attendance: 50-75. To promote "primarily fiction although we do include a poet and a nonfiction writer on each program. The two mentioned areas are treated in such a way that fiction writers can learn new ways to expand their abilities and writing techniques." The workshop is held on the campus of Loras College in Dubuque. "This campus holds a unique atmosphere and everyone seems to love the relaxed and restful mood it inspires. This in turn carries over to the workshop, and friendships are made that last in addition to learning and experiencing what other writers have gone through to attain success in their chosen field." Speakers for 1998: Sandy Whelchel, director of The National Writers Association; Emil Schmit, poet; Cal Lambert, playwright; Sharon Helgens, short story author. New name for the Writing Prizes: The John Tigges Writing Prize for Short Fiction, Nonfiction and Poetry.

Costs: $60 early registration/$65 at the door. Includes all handouts, necessary materials for the workshop, coffee/snack break, lunch, drinks and snacks at autograph party following workshop.

Accommodations: Information is available for out-of-town participants, concerning motels, etc., even though the workshop is 1-day long.

Additional Information: Conference brochures/guidelines are available February/March 1998 for SASE. Limit 1,500 words (fiction and nonfiction), 40 lines (poetry). 1st prize in all 3 categories: $100 plus publication in an area newspaper or magazine; 2nd prize in both categories: $50; 3rd prize in both categories: $25. Written critique service available for contest entries, $15 extra.

‡UNIVERSITY OF WISCONSIN AT MADISON SCHOOL OF THE ARTS AT RHINELANDER, 726 Lowell Hall, 610 Langdon St., Madison WI 53703. Administrative Coordinator: Kathy Berigan. Estab. 1964. Annual. Conference duration: 1 week. Conference held in late July. Average attendance: 300. Courses offered in writing, visual arts, drama, photography, music, folk arts, folk dancing. Conference held in junior high school in the city of Rhinelander in northern Wisconsin (James Williams Junior High School).

Costs: Tuition only—ranges from $149-289. Some courses require materials or lab fee.

Accommodations: Information on overnight accommodations (cabins, motels, camping) made available.

Additional Information: Ms critique workshop available. Request to be put on mailing list.

‡WRITING TO SELL, Minneapolis Writers Conference, Box 24356, Minneapolis MN 55424. Estab. 1985. Annual conference held in August for 1 day. Average attendance: 100. Conference about writing to sell. Held in Minneapolis hotel. 1997 speakers included Pete Hautman and Eleanor Arnason.

Costs: $75 (1997).

Additional Information: Brochure available in May for SASE.

South Central (CO, KS, MO, NM, OK, TX)

‡ASPEN WRITERS' CONFERENCE, Box 7726, Aspen CO 81612. (800)925-2526. Fax (970)920-5700. E-mail: aspenwrite@aol.com. Executive Director: Jeanne McGovern Small. Estab. 1975. Annual. Conference held for 1 week during summer at The Aspen Institute, Aspen Meadows campus. Average attendance: 75. Conference for fiction, poetry, nonfiction and children's literature. Includes general fiction workshops; talks with agents, editor and publisher on fiction. 1997 conference featured George Nicholson, agent, Sterling Lord Litenstic; Carol Honck Smith, editor, W.W. Norton; Tom Auer, publisher, *The Bloomsbury Review*; and special guests Andrea Barrett and Rudolfo Anaya.

Costs: $495/full tuition; $125/audit only (1997)

Accommodations Free shuttle to/from airport and around town. Information on overnight accommodations available. On-campus housing; (800) number for reservations. Rates for 1997: on-campus $60/night double; $85/night single; off-campus rates vary.

Additional Information: Manuscripts to be submitted for review by faculty prior to conference. Conference brochures are available for SASE.

AUSTIN WRITERS' LEAGUE WORKSHOPS/CONFERENCES/CLASSES, E-2, 1501 W. Fifth, Austin TX 78703. (512)499-8914. Fax: (512)499-0441. Executive Director: Angela Smith. Estab. 1982. Programs ongoing through the year. Duration: varies according to program. Average attendance from 15 to 200. To promote "all genres, fiction and nonfiction, poetry, writing for children, screenwriting, playwriting, legal and tax information for writers, also writing workshops for children and youth." Programs held at AWL Resource Center/Library, other sites in Austin and Texas. Topics include: finding and working with agents and publishers; writing and marketing short fiction; dialogue; characterization; voice; research; basic and advanced fiction writing/focus on the novel; business of writing; also workshops for genres. Past speakers have included Dwight Swain, Natalie Goldberg, David Lindsey, Shelby Hearon, Gabriele Rico, Benjamin Saenz, Rosellen Brown, Sandra Scofield, Reginald Gibbons, Anne Lamott, Sterling Lord and Sue Grafton.

Costs: Varies from free to $185, depending on program. Most classes, $20-50; workshops $35-75; conferences: $125-185.

Accommodations: Austin Writers' League will provide assistance with transportation arrangements on request. List of hotels is available for SASE. Special rates given at some hotels for program participants.

Additional Information: Critique sessions offered at some programs. Individual presenters determine critique requirements. Those requirements are then made available through Austin Writers' League office and in workshop promotion. Contests and awards programs are offered separately. Brochures/guidelines are available on request.

HEART OF AMERICA WRITERS' CONFERENCE, Johnson County Community College, 12345 College Blvd., Overland Park KS 66210. (913)469-3838. Fax: (913)469-2565. Program Director: Judith Choice. Estab. 1984. Annual. Conference held in April. Average attendance: 110-160. "The conference features a choice of 16 plus sections focusing on nonfiction, children's market, fiction, journaling, essay, poetry and genre writing." Conference held in state-of-the-art conference center in suburban Kansas City. Individual sessions with agents and editors are available. Ms critiques are offered for $40. Past keynote speakers have included Natalie Goldberg, Ellen Gilchrist, Linda Hogan, David Ray, Stanley Elkin, David Shields, Luisa Valenzuela and Amy Bloom.
Costs: $100 includes lunch, reception, breaks.
Accommodations: Conference brochures/guidelines are available for SASE after December. Inquiries by fax OK. "We provide lists of area hotels."

NATIONAL WRITERS ASSOCIATION CONFERENCE, 1450 S. Havana, Suite 424, Aurora CO 80012. (303)751-7844. Fax: (303)751-8593. E-mail address: sandywriter@aol.com. Executive Director: Sandy Whelchel. Estab. 1926. Annual. Conference held in June. Conference duration: 3 days. Average attendance: 200-300. General writing and marketing. 1997 conference in Denver, CO.
Costs: $300 (approx.).
Additional Information: Awards for previous contests will be presented at the conference. Conference brochures/guidelines are available for SASE.

THE NEW LETTERS WEEKEND WRITERS CONFERENCE, University of Missouri-Kansas City, College of Arts and Sciences Continuing Ed. Division, 215 SSB, 5100 Rockhill Rd., Kansas City MO 64110-2499. (816)235-2736. Fax: (816)235-5279. E-mail: mckinlem@smtpgate.umkc.edu. Estab. in the mid-70s as The Longboat Key Writers Conference. Annual. Runs during June. Conference duration is 3 days. Average attendance: 75. "The New Letters Weekend Writers Conference brings together talented writers in many genres for lectures, seminars, readings, workshops and individual conferences. The emphasis is on craft and the creative process in poetry, fiction, screenwriting, playwriting and journalism; but the program also deals with matters of psychology, publications and marketing. The conference is appropriate for both advanced and beginning writers. The conference meets at the beautiful Diastole conference center of The University of Missouri-Kansas City."
Costs: Several options are available. Participants may choose to attend as a non-credit student or they may attend for 1-3 hours of college credit from the University of Missouri-Kansas City. Conference registration includes continental breakfasts, Saturday dinner and Sunday lunch. For complete information, contact the University of Missouri-Kansas City.
Accommodations: Registrants are responsible for their own transportation, but information on area accommodations is made available.
Additional Information: Those registering for college credit are required to submit a ms in advance. Ms reading and critique is included in the credit fee. Those attending the conference for non-credit also have the option of having their ms critiqued for an additional fee. Conference brochures/guidelines are available for SASE after March. Inquiries by e-mail and fax OK.

NORTHWEST OKLAHOMA WRITER'S WORKSHOP, P.O. Box 5994, Enid OK 73702. Phone/fax: (405)237-2744. E-mail: scrybr8@prodigy.net. Website: http://www.geocities.com/Athens/Acropolis/8817/. Workshop contact: Bev Walton-Porter. Estab. 1991. Annual. Conference held in March or April. Conference duration: 6 hours. Average attendance: 20-30. "Usually fiction is the concentration area. The purpose is to help writers learn more about the craft of writing and encourage writers 'to step out in faith' and submit." Held in Cherokee Strip Conference Center. Past speakers have been Norma Jean Lutz, inspirational and magazine writing; Deborah Bouziden, fiction and magazine writing; Anna Meyers, children's writing; Sondra Soli, poetry; Marcia Preston, magazines, Mary Lynn, manuscript preparation and submission protocol.
Costs: $40; includes catered lunch.
Additional Information: Conference guidelines are available for SASE. Inquiries by e-mail and fax OK.

OKLAHOMA FALL ARTS INSTITUTES, P.O. Box 18154, Oklahoma City OK 73154. (405)842-0890. Fax: (405)848-4538. E-mail: okarts@telepath.com. Website: www.okartinst.org. Contact: Associate Director of Programs. Estab. 1983. Annual. Conference held in late October. Conference duration: 4 days. Average attendance 100. Held at "Quartz Mountain Arts and Conference Center, an Oklahoma state lodge located in southwest Oklahoma at the edge of Lake Altus/Lugert in the Quartz Mountains. Workshop participants are housed either in the lodge itself (in hotel-room accommodations) or in cabins or duplexes with kitchens. Classes are held in special pavilions built expressly for the Arts Institute. Pavilions offer a view of the lake and mountains." No featured panelists. Classes are taught by nationally recognized writers. Evenings include presentations and readings by faculty members and a Friday night chamber music concert.
Costs: $450, which includes double-occupancy lodging, meals, tuition and registration fee.
Accommodations: The Oklahoma Arts Institute leases all facilities at Quartz Mountain Arts and Conference Center for the exclusive use of the Fall Arts Institutes participants. Lodging is included in workshop cost.
Additional Information: Critique is usually done in class. Writers will need to bring completed works with

them. Call or write for Course Catalogues. Inquiries by e-mail and fax OK. The Institutes are open to anyone.

ROCKY MOUNTAIN BOOK FESTIVAL, 2123 Downing St., Denver CO 80211. (303)839-0323. Fax: (303)839-8319. E-mail: ccftb_mm@compuserve.com. Website: http://www.aclin.org/code/ceftb. Program Director: Megan Maguire. Estab. 1991. Annual. Festival held November 1-2. Festival duration: 2 days. Average attendance: 40,000. Festival promotes work from all genres. Held at Currigan Exhibition Hall in downtown Denver. Offers a wide variety of panels. Approximately 300 authors are scheduled to speak at the next festival including Ridley Pearson, Sherman Alexie, Dixie Carter, Dave Barry and Jill Kerr Conway.
Costs: $3 (adult); $1 (child).
Accommodations: Information on overnight accommodations is available.
Additional Information: Brochures/guidelines available for SASE.

‡ROCKY MOUNTAIN CHILDREN'S BOOK FESTIVAL, 2123 Downing St., Denver CO 80205. (303)839-8323. Fax: (303)839-8319. E-mail: ccftb_mm@compuserve.com. Program Director: Megan Maguire. Estab. 1996. Annual festival held in April. Festival duration: 2 days. Average attendance: 30,000. Festival promotes published work for and about children/families. Held at Currigan Exhibition Hall in downtown Denver. Approximately 100 authors speak annually. Past authors include Ann M. Martin, Sharon Creech, Nikki Grimes, T.A. Barron, the Kratt Brothers and Bruce Lansky.
Costs: None.
Accommodations: "Information on accommodations available."
Additional Information: Send SASE for brochure/guidelines.

‡ROMANCE WRITERS OF AMERICA NATIONAL CONFERENCE, Suite 315, 13700 Veteran Memorial Dr., Houston TX 77014-1023. (281)440-6885, ext. 27. Fax: (281)440-7510. Website: http://www.rwanation.com. Executive Manager: Allison Kelley. Estab. 1981. Annual. Conference held in late July or early August. Average attendance: 1,500. Over 100 workshops on writing, researching and the business side of being a working writer. Publishing professionals attend and accept appointments. Keynote speaker is renowned romance writer. Conference will be held in Anaheim, California, in 1998 and Chicago, Illinois, in 1999.
Costs: $300.
Additional Information: Annual RITA awards are presented for romance authors. Annual Golden Heart awards are presented for unpublished writers. Conference brochures/guidelines are available for SASE.

‡SHORT COURSE ON PROFESSIONAL WRITING, University of Oklahoma, Journalism, 860 Van Vleet Oval, Norman OK 73019-0270. (405)325-4171. Fax: (405)325-7565. E-mail: jmdavis@prodigy.net. Estab. 1938. Annual conference held from June 12 to June 14. Average attendance: 200. Conference focuses on writing for publication—all paying markets. Held at the Holiday Inn in Norman. 1997 guest speakers included Clyde Edgerton, Parnell Hall, Mary Lynn and G.E. Stanley.
Costs: $195.
Accomodations: Provides special rates at the Holiday Inn.
Additional Information: "Critiques are optional, but we provide them. Manuscripts must be submitted ahead of time." Brochures available in March for SASE. Inquiries by fax and e-mail OK. "We have sixty years of success with editors, agents and authors. Many successful writers were 'discovered' at the Short Course."

‡SOUTHWEST CHRISTIAN WRITERS ASSOCIATION, P.O. Box 1008, Flora Vista NM 87415-1008. (505)334-0617. Fax: (970)247-8066. President: Kathy Cordell. Estab. 1980. Annual. Conference held the third Saturday in September. Average attendance: 30. For "the beginner as well as the seasoned writer." Conference held at the Hesperus Baptist Camp, 22265 State Hwy. 140, Hesperus, CO. 1997 speaker was Susan Titus Osborne, editor of *The Christian Communicator*. 1998 speaker will be Gayle Roper.
Costs: $47 (meals are offered at camp, $5.50); $5 off early registration and additional $5 off for members.
Additional Information: Conference brochures/guidelines are available for SASE after July. Inquiries by fax OK. "One additional speaker invited (usually from area). Freebies and a booktable available (authors may bring books to sell if attending conference)."

SOUTHWEST WRITERS WORKSHOP CONFERENCE, 1338 Wyoming NE, Suite B, Albuquerque NM 87112-5067. (505)293-0303. Fax: (505)237-2665. E-mail: swriters@aol.com. Website: http://www.us1.net//SWW. Estab. 1983. Annual. Conference held in August. Average attendance: about 400. "Conference concentrates on all areas of writing." Workshops and speakers include writers and editors of all genres for all levels from beginners to advanced. 1997 theme was "The Write Connection: To Dream, To Dare, To Do." Keynote speaker was Jacquelyn Mitchard, bestselling author of *Deep End of the Ocean*. Featured speakers: Tony Hillerman, Christopher Vogler and Erika Holzer. The 1998 keynote speaker will be David Guterson, author of *Snow Falling On Cedars*.
Costs: $265 (members) and $320 (nonmembers); includes conference sessions, 2 luncheons, 2 banquets and 2 breakfasts.

Accommodations: Usually have official airline and discount rates. Special conference rates are available at hotel. A list of other area hotels and motels is available.

Additional Information: Sponsors a contest judged by authors, editors and agents from New York, Los Angeles, etc., and from major publishing houses. Eighteen categories. Deadline: May 1. Entry fee is $24 (members) or $34 (nonmembers). Brochures/guidelines available for SASE. Inquiries by e-mail and fax OK. "An appointment (10 minutes, one-on-one) may be set up at the conference with editor or agent of your choice on a first-registered/first-served basis."

STEAMBOAT SPRINGS WRITERS GROUP, P.O. Box 774284, Steamboat Springs CO 80477. (970)879-9008. E-mail: freiberger@compuserve.com. Chairperson: Harriet Freiberger. Estab. 1982. Annual. Conference held July 11. Conference duration: 1 day. Average attendance: 30. "Our conference emphasizes instruction within the seminar format. Novices and polished professionals benefit from the individual attention and the camaraderie which can be established within small groups. A pleasurable and memorable learning experience is guaranteed by the relaxed and friendly atmosphere of the old train depot. Registration is limited." Steamboat Arts Council sponsors the group at the restored Train Depot.

Costs: $35 before June 15, $45 after. Fee covers all conference activities, including lunch. Lodging available at Steamboat Resorts; 10% discount for participants."

Additional Information: Inquiries by e-mail OK.

TAOS SCHOOL OF WRITING, P.O. Box 20496, Albuquerque NM 87154-0496. (505)294-4601. E-mail: spletzer@swcp.com. Administrator: Suzanne Spletzer. Estab. 1993 by Norman Zollinger. Annual. Conference held in mid-July. Conference duration: 1 week. Average attendance: 60. "All fiction and nonfiction. No poetry or screenwriting. Purpose—to promote good writing skills. We meet at the Thunderbird Lodge in the Taos Ski Valley, NM. (We are the only ones there.) No telephones or televisions in rooms. No elevator. Slightly rustic landscape. Quiet mountain setting at 9,000 feet." Conference focuses on writing fiction and nonfiction and publishing. Previous speakers include David Morrell, Suzy McKee Charnas, Stephen R. Donaldson, Norman Zollinger, Denise Chavez, Richard S. Wheeler, Max Evans and Tony Hillerman.

Costs: $1,200; includes tuition, room and board.

Accommodations: "Travel agent arranges rental cars or shuttle rides to Ski Valley from Albuquerque Sunport."

Additional Information: "Acceptance to school is determined by evaluation of submitted manuscript. Manuscripts are critiqued by faculty and students in the class during the sessions." Conference brochures/guidelines are available for SASE after February. Inquiries by e-mail OK.

WRITERS WORKSHOP IN SCIENCE FICTION, English Department/University of Kansas, Lawrence KS 66045. (913)864-3380. Professor: James Gunn. Estab. 1985. Annual. Conference held June 28-July 12, 1997. Average attendance: 15. Conference for writing and marketing science fiction. "Housing is provided and classes meet in university housing on the University of Kansas campus. Workshop sessions operate informally in a lounge." 1996 guest writers: Frederik Pohl, SF writer and former editor and agent; John Ordover, writer and editor.

Costs: Tuition: $400. Housing and meals are additional.

Accommodations: Several airport shuttle services offer reasonable transportation from the Kansas City International Airport to Lawrence. During past conferences, students were housed in a student dormitory at $12/day double, $20/day single.

Additional Information: "Admission to the workshop is by submission of an acceptable story. Two additional stories should be submitted by the end of June. These three stories are copied and distributed to other participants for critiquing and are the basis for the first week of the workshop; one story is rewritten for the second week." Brochures/guidelines are available for SASE. "The Writers Workshop in Science Fiction is intended for writers who have just started to sell their work or need that extra bit of understanding or skill to become a published writer."

West (AZ, CA, HI, NV, UT)

BE THE WRITER YOU WANT TO BE MANUSCRIPT CLINIC, 23350 Sereno Court, Villa 30, Cupertino CA 95014. (415)691-0300. Contact: Louise Purwin Zobel. Estab. 1969. Workshop held irregularly—usually semiannually at several locations. Workshop duration: 1-2 days. Average attendance: 20-30. "This manuscript

---

CAN'T FIND A CONFERENCE? Conferences are listed by region. Check the introduction to this section for a list of regional categories.

clinic enables writers of any type of material to turn in their work-in-progress—at any stage of development—to receive help with structure and style, as well as marketing advice." It is held on about 40 campuses at different times, including University of California and other university and college campuses throughout the west.
Costs: Usually $45-65/day, "depending on campus."
Additional Information: Brochures/guidelines available for SASE.

‡CALIFORNIA WRITER'S CLUB CONFERENCE AT ASILOMAR, 3975 Kim Court, Sebastopol CA 95472. (707)823-8128. E-mail: GPMansergh@aol.com. Contact: Gil Mansergh, director. Estab. 1941. Annual. Next conference June 26-28, 1998. Conference duration: Friday afternoon through Sunday lunch. Average attendance: 350. Conference offers opportunity to learn from and network with successful writers, agents and editors in Asilomar's beautiful and historic beach side setting on the shores of Monterey Bay. Presentations, panels, hands-on workshops and agent/editor appointments focus on writing and marketing short stories, novels, articles, books, poetry and screenplays for children and adults.
Costs: $435 includes all conference privileges, shared lodging and 6 meals. There is a $90 surcharge for a single room.
Accommodations: Part of the California State Park system, Asilomar is rustic and beautiful. Julia Morgan designed redwood and stone buildings share 105 acres of dunes and pine forests with modern AIA and National Academy of Design winning lodges. Monterey airport is a 15 minute taxi drive away.
Additional Information: First prize winners in all 7 categories of the *California Writers' Club 1998 Writing Contest* receive free registration to the 1998 Conference. $10 entry fee. Contest deadline is May 1, 1998. Brochure and contest submission rules will be available in late February.

‡DESERT WRITERS WORKSHOP/CANYONLANDS FIELD INSTITUTE, P.O. Box 68, Moab UT 84532. (801)259-7750 or (800)860-5262. Executive Director and Conference Coordinator: Karla Vanderzanden. Estab. 1984. Annual. Held first weekend in November. Conference duration: 3 days. Average attendance: 30. Concentrations include fiction, nonfiction, poetry. Site is the Pack Creek Ranch, Moab, Utah. "Theme is oriented towards understanding the vital connection between the natural world and human communities." Faculty panel in 1995 included Mary Sojourner for fiction.
Costs: $440 (members of CFI, $425); $150 deposit required by September 22, which includes meals Friday-Sunday, instruction, field trip, lodging.
Accommodations: At Pack Creek Ranch, included in cost.
Additional Information: Brochures are available for SASE. "Participants may submit work in advance, but it is not required. Student readings, evaluations and consultations with guest instructors/faculty are part of the workshop. Desert Writers Workshop is supported in part by grants from the Utah Arts Council and National Endowment for the Arts. A scholarship is available. College credit is also available for an additional fee."

I'VE ALWAYS WANTED TO WRITE BUT . . . , 23350 Sereno Court, Villa 30, Cupertino CA 95014. (415)691-0300. Contact: Louise Purwin Zobel. Estab. 1969. Workshop held irregularly, several times a year at different locations. Workshop duration: 1-2 days. Average attendance: 30-50. Workshop "encourages real beginners to get started on a lifelong dream. Focuses on the basics of writing." Workshops held at about 40 college and university campuses in the West, including University of California.
Costs: Usually $45-65/day "depending on college or university."
Additional Information: Brochures/guidelines are available for SASE after August.

‡IWWG EARLY SPRING IN CALIFORNIA CONFERENCE, International Women's Writing Guild, P.O. Box 810, Gracie Station, New York NY 10028-0082. (212)737-7536. Fax: (212)737-9469. E-mail: iwwg@iwwg.c om. Website: http://www.IWWG.com. Executive Director: Hannelore Hahn. Estab. 1982. Annual. Conference held March 13 to March 15. Average attendance: 80. Conference to promote "creative writing, personal growth and empowerment." Site is a redwood forest mountain retreat in Santa Cruz, California.
Costs: $100 for weekend program, plus room and board.
Accommodations: Accommodations are all at conference site; $110 for room and board.
Additional Information: Conference brochures/guidelines are available for SASE after August. Inquiries by e-mail and fax OK.

JACK LONDON WRITERS' CONFERENCE, 135 Clark Dr., San Mateo CA 94402-1002. (415)615-8331. Fax: (415)342-9155. Coordinator: Marlo Faulkner. Estab. 1987. Annual. Conference held March 7 from 8:00-4:30. Average attendance: 200. "Our purpose is to provide access to professional writers. Workshops have covered genre fiction, nonfiction, marketing, agents, poetry and children's." Held at the San Francisco Airport Holiday Inn. A partial list of speakers scheduled for 1998 include Robert Mauer, Charles Champlin, Patricia Holt and Meera Lester.
Costs: $95; includes continental breakfast, lunch and all sessions.
Additional Information: "Special rates on accommodations available at Holiday Inn." Sponsors a cash prize writing contest judged by the Peninsula branch of the California Writers Club (requirements in brochure). Brochures/guidelines available for SASE after November. Inquiries by fax OK. The Jack London Conference has

had over 80 professional writers speak and 800 participants. It's sponsored by the Peninsula Branch of the California Writers' Club.

MOUNT HERMON CHRISTIAN WRITERS CONFERENCE, P.O. Box 413, Mount Hermon CA 95041-0413. (408)335-4466. Fax: (408)335-9218. E-mail: mhtalbott@aol.com. Website: http://www.mounthermon.org. Director of Specialized Programs: David R. Talbott. Estab. 1970. Annual. Conference held Friday-Tuesday over Palm Sunday weekend, March 21-25, 1997. Average attendance: 175. "We are a broad-ranging conference for all areas of Christian writing, including fiction, children's, poetry, nonfiction, magazines, books, educational curriculum and radio and TV scriptwriting. This is a working, how-to conference, with many workshops within the conference involving on-site writing assignments. The conference is sponsored by and held at the 440-acre Mount Hermon Christian Conference Center near San Jose, California, in the heart of the coastal redwoods. Registrants stay in hotel-style accommodations, and full board is provided as part of conference fees. Meals are taken family style, with faculty joining registrants. The faculty/student ratio is about 1:6 or 7. The bulk of our faculty are editors and publisher representatives from major Christian publishing houses nationwide." 1998 keynote speaker: John Fischer, songwriting, author, columnist.
Costs: Registration fees include tuition, conference sessions, resource notebook, refreshment breaks, room and board and vary from $485 (economy) to $650 (deluxe), double occupancy (1997 fees).
Accommodations: Airport shuttles are available from the San Jose International Airport. Housing is not required of registrants, but about 95% of our registrants use Mount Hermon's own housing facilities (hotel style double-occupancy rooms). Meals with the conference are required and are included in all fees.
Additional Information: Registrants may submit 2 works for critique in advance of the conference, then have personal interviews with critiquers during the conference. No advance work is required however. Conference brochures/guidelines are available for SASE. Inquiries by e-mail and fax OK. "The residential nature of our conference makes this a unique setting for one-on-one interaction with faculty/staff. There is also a decided inspirational flavor to the conference, and general sessions with well-known speakers are a highlight."

‡NO CRIME UNPUBLISHED® MYSTERY WRITERS' CONFERENCE, Sisters in Crime/Los Angeles, P.O. Box 251646, Los Angeles CA 90025. (213)694-2972. Fax: (310)838-6455. E-mail: jks18@aol.com. Conference Coordinator: Judith Klerman Smith. Estab. 1995. Annual. Conference held in September. Conference duration: 1 day. Average attendance: 200. Conference on mystery and crime writing. Usually held in hotel near Los Angeles airport. Two-track program: Craft and forensic sessions; keynote speaker, luncheon speaker, agent panel, book signings. In 1997: Robert Crais, keynote speaker; Steve Allen, luncheon speaker; authors, agents, forensic experts.
Costs: $85, included continental breakfast, snacks, lunch, souvenir book bag and all sessions (1997).
Accommodations: Airport shuttle to hotel. Optional overnight stay available. Hotel conference rate $89/night. Arrangements made directly with hotel.
Additional Information: Conference brochure available for SASE.

PIMA WRITERS' WORKSHOP, Pima College, 2202 W. Anklam Rd., Tucson AZ 85709. (520)884-6974. Fax: (520)884-6975. E-mail: mfiles@pimacc.pima.edu. Director: Meg Files. Estab. 1988. Annual. Conference held in May. Conference duration 3 days. Average attendance 200. "For anyone interested in writing—beginning or experienced writer. The workshop offers sessions on writing short stories, novels, nonfiction articles and books, children's and juvenile stories, poetry and screenplays." Sessions are held in the Center for the Arts on Pima Community College's West Campus. Past speakers include Michael Blake, Ron Carlson, Gregg Levoy, Nancy Mairs, Linda McCarriston, Sam Smiley, Jerome Stern, Connie Willis and literary agents Judith Riven and Fred Hill.
Costs: $65 (can include ms critique). Participants may attend for college credit, in which case fees are $68 for Arizona residents and $310 for out-of-state residents. Meals and accommodations not included.
Accommodations: Information on local accommodations is made available, and special workshop rates are available at a specified motel close to the workshop site (about $50/night).
Additional Information: Participants may have up to 20 pages critiqued by the author of their choice. Mss must be submitted 2 weeks before the workshop. Conference brochure/guidelines available for SASE. Inquiries by e-mail OK. "The workshop atmosphere is casual, friendly, and supportive, and guest authors are very accessible. Readings, films and panel discussions are offered as well as talks and manuscript sessions."

‡READING AND WRITING THE WEST, Department of English, University of Nevada, Reno NV 89557-0031. (702)784-6689. Fax: (702)784-6266. E-mail: stuchu@powernet.net. Estab. 1991. Annual. Conference held from July 12 to July 24. Average attendance: 30. Conference for "multigenre, reading of western American fiction, nonfiction, poetry and writing of same." The conference is held at the University of Nevada in Reno. The theme for 1998 is "Mapping the West: Landscapes and Literature." 1997 speakers included Bernie Schopen, Mary Webb, Peter Goin and Elizabeth Raymond.
Costs: $300, including 3 university credits.
Accommodations: Attendees must make their own transportation arrangements. Discounts and a list of area hotels are available. Rooms at the University Inn available, $34/night, dormitory suite accommodations possible, $15/night.

Additional Information: Conference brochure/guidelines available for SASE in October. Inquiries by fax and e-mail OK. Conference is "conducted in conjunction with the Great Basin Chautauqua, featuring humanities scholars portraying major intellectual figures."

SAN DIEGO STATE UNIVERSITY WRITERS' CONFERENCE, SDSU College of Extended Studies, San Diego CA 92182-1920. (619)594-2517. E-mail address: ealcaraz@mail.sdsu.edu. Website: http://rohan.sdsu.edu/dept/extstd/writers.html. Assistant to Director of Extension and Conference Facilitator: Erin Grady Alcaraz. Estab. 1984. Annual. Conference held on 3rd weekend in January. Conference duration: 2 days. Average attendance: approximately 350. "This conference is held on the San Diego State University campus at the Aztec Center. The Aztec Center is conveniently located near parking; the meeting rooms are spacious and comfortable and all sessions meet in the same general area. Each year the SDSU Writers Conference offers a variety of workshops for the beginner and the advanced writer. This conference allows the individual writer to choose which workshop best suits his/her needs. In addition to the workshops, read and critique appointments and office hours are provided so attendees may meet with speakers, editors and agents in small, personal groups to discuss specific questions. A reception is offered Saturday immediately following the workshops where attendees may socialize with the faculty in a relaxed atmosphere. Keynote speaker is to be determined."
Costs: Not to exceed $225. This includes all conference workshops and office hours, coffee and pastries in the morning, lunch and reception Saturday evening.
Accommodations: Call or write for a listing of nearby hotels and their rates. Attendees must make their own travel arrangements.
Additional Information: Read and Critique sessions are private, one-on-one opportunities to meet with editors and agents to discuss your submission. Also featured is the research emporium where experts will lecture and answer questions about various topics such as forensics, police procedures, historical clothing and customs, weapons, etc. To receive a brochure, e-mail, call or send a postcard with address to: SDSU Writers Conference, College of Extended Studies, 5250 Campanile Drive, San Diego State University, San Diego CA 92182-1920. No SASE required.

‡SCBWI/NATIONAL CONFERENCE ON WRITING & ILLUSTRATING FOR CHILDREN, 22736 Vanowen St., Suite 106, West Hills CA 91307-2650. (818)888-8760. Executive Director: Lin Oliver. Estab. 1972. Annual. Conference held in August. Conference duration: 4 days. Average attendance: 350. Writing and illustrating for children. Site: Century Plaza Hotel in Los Angeles. Theme: "The Business of Writing."
Costs: $295 (members); $320 (late registration, members); $340 (nonmembers). Cost does not include hotel room.
Accommodations: Information on overnight accommodations made available. Conference rates at the hotel about $115/night.
Additional Information: Ms and illustration critiques are available. Conference brochures/guidelines are available (after June) for SASE.

SCBWI/RETREAT AT ASILOMAR, 1316 Rebecca Dr., Suisun CA 94585-3603. (707)426-6776. Contact: Bobi Martin, Regional Advisor. Estab. 1984. Annual. Conference held during last weekend in February. Attendance limited to 65. "The retreat is designed to refresh and encourage writers and illustrators for children. Speakers are published writers, illustrators and editors. Topics vary year to year and have included writing techniques, understanding marketing, plotting, pacing, etc. The retreat is held at the Asilomar conference grounds in Monterey. There is time for walking on the beach or strolling through the woods. Rooms have private baths and 2 beds. Meals are served semi-cafeteria style and the group eats together. Vegetarian meals also available.
Costs: $225 for SCBWI members; $250 for nonmembers.
Accommodations: "All accommodations are on-site and are included in the cost. All rooms are double occupancy. Disabled access rooms are available." Attendees must make their own transportation arrangements.
Additional Information: Scholarships available to SCBWI members. "Applicants for scholarships should write a letter explaining their financial need and describing how attending the retreat will help further their career. All applications are kept fully confidential." Brochures available for SASE. "Registration begins in October of previous year and fills quickly, but a waiting list is always formed and late applicants frequently do get in."

SOCIETY OF SOUTHWESTERN AUTHORS WRITERS' CONFERENCE, P.O. Box 30355, Tucson AZ 85751-0355. (520)296-5299. Fax: (520)296-0409. Conference Chair: Penny Porter. Estab. 1972. Annual. Three-day conferences held in January. Average attendance: 300. Conference "covers a spectrum of practical topics for writers. Each year varies, but there is a minimum of 16 different classes during the day, plus the keynote speaker." Keynote speakers for 1998: Father Andrew Greeley; Philip B. Osborne, assistant managing editor (Reader's Digest); Stuart James, mystery and suspense writer; N. Scott Momaday, Native American poet and novelist.
Costs: $150 general.
Additional Information: Conference brochures/guidelines are available for SASE.

SQUAW VALLEY COMMUNITY OF WRITERS, 10626 Banner Lava Cap Rd., Nevada City CA 96146. (916)274-8551. (September-June address). P.O. Box 2352, Olympic Valley CA 96146. (916)583-5200. (June-

September address). Programs Director: Ms. Brett Hall Jones. Estab. 1969. Annual. Conference held in July and August. Each program is 1 week. Average attendance approximately 120. "Squaw Valley Workshops include four separate one-week programs—Art of the Wild, Poetry, Fiction and Screenwriting. Each concentrates on its particular discipline except the Art of the Wild which includes poetry, fiction and nonfiction about nature, the environment and the ecological crisis. The workshops are conducted in the Olympic House, a large ski lodge built for the 1960 Winter Olympics. The environment includes pine trees, alpine lakes, rivers and streams; the elevation is 6,200 feet, and we have cool mornings and sunny, warm afternoons."

Costs: Tuition is $555 for the week. Scholarships are available.

Accommodations: "We have vans which will pick up participants at the Reno airport and at the Truckee Bus and train stations. The Community of Writers rents large ski houses in the Valley to house the attendees. This fosters the community atmosphere which makes our experience unique, as well as allowing us to keep the weekly rate reasonable: $160 multi, 220 double and 350 single."

Additional Information: "Acceptance is based on submitted work. Each participant's manuscript is critiqued in depth during the week of the workshop. A written critique is not available for each work submitted. Brochures/guidelines available. Each participant will have an opportunity to have an additional manuscript read by a staff member who will then meet with them for a private conference."

UCI EXTENSION ANNUAL WRITERS' CONFERENCE, P.O. Box 6050, Irvine CA 92616-6050. (714)824-6335. Fax: (714)824-3651. E-mail: newarzer@uci.edu. Website: http://www.unex.uci.edu/~unex. Director, Arts & Humanities: Nancy Warzer-Brady. Estab. 1994. Conference duration: 2-3 days. Average attendance: 100. "Conference to promote nonfiction and fiction writing." Conference held in UCI classroom facility equipped for conference-type meetings. "In addition to the annual summer writers' conference, we offer intensive and 10-week courses and seminars on fiction, nonfiction, and screenwriting on a quarterly basis. A certificate program in screenwriting is also available."

Costs: Fees range from $125 to $275.

Accommodations: Accommodations available for out of town participants if requested.

Additional Information: Conference brochures/guidelines available for SASE after July. Inquiries by e-mail and fax OK.

‡UCLA EXTENSION WRITERS' PROGRAM, 10995 Le Conte Ave., #440, Los Angeles CA 90024. (310)825-9416 or (800)388-UCLA. Fax: (310)206-7382. E-mail: writers@unex.ucla.edu. Website: http://www.unex.ucla.edu/writers. Estab. 1891. Courses held year-round with one-day or intensive weekend workshops to 12-week courses. "The diverse offerings span introductory seminars to professional novel and script completion workshops. The annual Los Angeles Writers Conference and a number of 1, 2 and 4-day intensive workshops are popular with out-of-town students due to their specific focus and the chance to work with industry professionals. The most comprehensive and diverse continuing education writing program in the country, offering over 400 courses a year including: screenwriting, fiction, writing for young people, poetry, nonfiction, playwriting, publishing and writing for interactive multimedia. Courses are offered in Los Angeles on the UCLA campus, Santa Monica and Universal City as well as online over the internet. Adult learners in the UCLA Extension Writers' Program study with professional screenwriters, fiction writers, playwrights, poets, nonfiction writers, and interactive multimedia writers, who bring practical experience, theoretical knowledge, and a wide variety of teaching styles and philosophies to their classes." Online courses are also available. Call for details.

Costs: Vary from $75-425.

Accommodations: Students make own arrangements. The program can provide assistance in locating local accommodations.

Additional Information: Conference brochures/guidelines are available in the Fall. Inquiries by e-mail and fax OK. "Some advanced-level classes have manuscript submittal requirements; instructions are always detailed in the quarterly UCLA Extension course catalog. The Writers' Program publishes an annual literary journal, *West/Word*. Work can be submitted by current and former Writers' Program students. An annual fiction prize, The James Kirkwood Prize in Creative Writing, has been established and is given annually to one fiction writer who was published that year in *WEST/WORD*."

WRANGLING WITH WRITING, (formerly Come Write With Us), Society of Southwestern Authors, P.O. Box 30355, Tucson AZ 85751. (520)296-5996. President: Darrell Beach. Estab. 1971. Annual. Conference held three days January 22-24, 1998. Attendance: limited to 350. Conference "to assist writers in whatever ways we can. We cover many areas." Held at the Inn Suites Hotel with hotel rooms available. Author Father Andrew Greeley, Philip Osborne, assistant managing editor (Reader's Digest), N. Scott Momaday (Native American poet and writer), Stuart James (mystery and suspense writer) are among the featured speakers for the 1998 conference. Plus 25 workshops for all genres of writing.

Costs: $150; includes dinner first day, and continental breakfast and lunch the second day.

Accommodations: Inn Suites Hotel in Tucson. Information included in brochure available for SASE.

Additional Information: Critiques given if ms sent ahead. Sponsors short story contest (2,500 words or less) separate from the conference. Deadline May 31. Awards given September 21. Brochures/guidelines available for SASE.

‡**WRITE TO SELL WRITER'S CONFERENCE**, 8465 Jane St., San Diego CA 92129. (619)484-8575. Director: Diane Dunaway. Estab. 1989. Annual. Conference held in May. Conference duration: 1 day. Average attendance: 300. Concentration includes general fiction and nonfiction; screenwriting to include mystery, romance, children's, television, movies; special novel writing workshop, contacts with top NY agents and editors. Site is the campus of San Diego State University. Panelists include NY editors and agents, bestselling authors and screenwriters.
Costs: $95, includes lunch both days.
Accommodations: Write for details.

WRITE YOUR LIFE STORY FOR PAY, 23350 Sereno Court, Villa 30, Cupertino CA 95014. (415)691-0300. Contact: Louise Purwin Zobel. Estab. 1969. Workshop held irregularly, usually semiannually at several locations. Workshop duration: 1-2 days. Average attendance: 30-50. "Because every adult has a story worth telling, this conference helps participants to write fiction and nonfiction in books and short forms, using their own life stories as a base." This workshop is held on about 40 campuses at different times, inluding University of California and other university and college campuses in the West.
Costs: Usually $45-65/day, "depending on campus."
Additional Information: Brochures/guidelines available for SASE.

WRITERS CONNECTION SELLING TO HOLLYWOOD, P.O. Box 24770, San Jose CA 95154-4770. (408)445-3600. Fax: (408)445-3609. E-mail: info@sellingtohollywood.com. Website: http://www.sellingtohollywood.com. Directors: Steve and Meera Lester. Estab. 1988. Annual. Conference held in August in LA area. Conference duration: 3 days; August 7-9, 1998. Average attendance: 275. "Conference targets scriptwriters and fiction writers, whose short stories, books, or scripts have strong cinematic potential, and who want to make valuable contacts in the film industry. Full conference registrants receive a private consultation with the film industry producer or professional of his/her choice who make up the faculty. Panels, workshops, 'Ask a Pro' discussion groups and networking sessions include over 50 agents, professional film and TV scriptwriters, and independent as well as studio and TV and feature film producers."
Costs: In 1997: full conference by June, $500 members, $525 nonmembers; after June 1, $525 (members); $545 (nonmembers). Includes meals. Partial registration available March 1998; phone, e-mail, fax or send written request.
Accommodations: $100/night (in LA) for private room; $50/shared room. Discount with designated conference airline.
Additional Information: "This is the premier screenwriting conference of its kind in the country, unique in its offering of an industry-wide perspective from pros working in all echelons of the film industry. Great for making contacts." Conference brochure/guidelines available March 1, 1998; phone, e-mail, fax or send written request.

Northwest (AK, ID, MT, OR, WA, WY)

‡**ASHLAND WRITERS CONFERENCE**, 219 E. Main, #14, Ashland OR 97500. (541)488-8627. Fax: (541)482-2783. E-mail: cwright@wpo.sosc.edu.osshe. Estab. 1997. Annual conference held in July or August for 4 days. Average attendance: 102. Conference to focus on better writing. Held at Southern Oregon University. 1997 speakers included Carolyn Forche and Sandra Scofield.
Costs: $275 plus $30 lodging, which includes breakfast.
Accomodations: "Volunteers provide transportation. Dorms and list of hotels provided."
Additional Information: Brochures available in February for SASE. Inquiries by fax and e-mail OK.

CLARION WEST WRITERS' WORKSHOP, 340 15th Ave. E., Suite 350, Seattle WA 98112. (206)322-9083. Contact: Admissions Department. Estab. 1983. Annual. Workshop held June 21-July 31. Workshop duration 6 weeks. Average attendance: 20. "Conference to prepare students for professional careers in science fiction and fantasy writing. Held at Seattle Central Community College on Seattle's Capitol Hill, an urban site close to restaurants and cafes, not too far from downtown." Deadline for applications: April 1.
Costs: Workshop: $1,300 ($100 discount if application received by March 1). Dormitory housing: $750, meals not included.
Accommodations: Students are strongly encouraged to stay on-site, in dormitory housing at Seattle University. Cost: $750, meals not included, for 6-week stay.
Additional Information: "This is a critique-based workshop. Students are encouraged to write a story a week; the critique of student material produced at the workshop forms the principal activity of the workshop. Students and instructors critique manuscripts as a group." Conference guidelines available for SASE. Limited scholarships are available, based on financial need. Students must submit 20-30 pages of ms to qualify for admission. Dormitory and classrooms are handicapped accessible.

FLIGHT OF THE MIND—SUMMER WRITING WORKSHOP FOR WOMEN, 622 SE 29th Ave., Portland OR 97214. (503)236-9862. E-mail: soapston@teleport.com. Director: Judith Barrington. Estab. 1984.

Annual. Workshops held June 19-26 and June 28-July 5. Conference duration: each workshop lasts 1 week. Average attendance: 70. "Conference held at an old retreat center on the Mackenzie River in the foothills of the Oregon Cascades. Right on the river—hiking trails, hot springs nearby. Most students accommodated in single dorm rooms; a few private cabins available. We have our own cooks and provide spectacular food." Five classes—topics vary year to year; 1997 included "Finding Form" by Rosellen Brown and poetry by Toi Deiricotte.
Costs: Approximately $780 for tuition, board and single dorm room. Extra for private cabin; bunk room cheaper alternative.
Accommodations: Special arrangements for transportation: "We charter a bus to pick up participants in Eugene, OR, at airport, train station and bus station." Accommodations and meals are included in cost.
Additional Information: "Critiquing is part of most classes; no individual critiques. We require manuscript submissions for acceptance into workshop. (Receive about twice as many applications as spaces)." Workshop brochures/guidelines are available for 1 first-class stamp (no envelope). "This is a feminist-oriented workshop with a focus on work generated at the workshop."

HAYSTACK WRITING PROGRAM, PSU School of Extended Studies, P.O. Box 1491, Portland OR 97207-1491. (503)725-4186. Fax: (503)725-4840. E-mail: herringtonm@ses.pdx.edu. Website: http://extended.portals. org/haystack.htm. Contact: Maggie Herrington. Estab. 1968. Annual. Program runs from last week of June through first week of August. Workshop duration varies; one-week and weekend workshops are available throughout the six-week program. Average attendance: 10-15/workshop; total program: 325. "The program features a broad range of writing courses for writers at all skill levels. Classes are held in Cannon Beach, Oregon." Past instructors have included William Stafford, Ursula K. LeGuin, Craig Lesley, Molly Gloss, Mark Medoff, Tom Spanbauer, Sallie Tisdale.
Costs: Approximately $320/course weeklong; $150 (weekend). Does not include room and board.
Accommodations: Attendees make their own transportation arrangements. Various accommodations available including: B&B, motel, hotel, private rooms, camping, etc. A list of specific accommodations is provided.
Additional Information: Free brochure available after March. Inquiries by e-mail and fax OK. University credit (graduate or undergraduate) is available.

‡PACIFIC NORTHWEST WRITERS SUMMER CONFERENCE, 2033 6th Ave., #804, Seattle WA 98121. (206)443-3807. E-mail address: pnwritersconf@halcyon.com. Website: http://www.reporters.net/pnwc. Contact: Office. Estab. 1955. Annual. Conference held last weekend in July. Average attendance: 700. Conference focuses on "fiction, nonfiction, poetry, film, drama, self-publishing, the creative process, critiques, core groups, advice from pros and networking." Site is Hyatt Regency, Bellevue WA. "Editors and agents come from both coasts. They bring lore from the world of publishing. The PNWC provides opportunities for writers to get to know editors and agents. The literary contest provides feedback from professionals and possible fame for the winners." The 1997 guest speakers were Jana Harris, Wendy Wossestler and Ridley Pearson.
Costs: $135-165/day. Meals and lodging are available at hotel.
Additional Information: On-site critiques are available in small groups. Literary contest in these categories: adult article/essay, adult genre novel, adult mainstream novel, adult genre short story, adult mainstream short story, juvenile article or short story, juvenile novel, nonfiction book, picture books for children, playwriting and poetry. Deadline: February 15. Up to $7,000 awarded in prizes. Send SASE for guidelines.

‡PACIFIC NORTHWEST WRITERS WINTER CONFERENCE, #804, 2033 6th Ave., Seattle WA 98121. (206)443-3807. E-mail: pnwritersconf@halcyon.com. Website: http://www.reporters.net/pnwc. Estab. 1981. Annual. Weekend conference held in February. Average attendance: 200. "The conference is mostly hands-on workshops: novel, short story, nonfiction, film, poetry, article, children's, getting started, keeping going." Site is the Embassy Suites, Bellevue WA. "The winter conference is a good place to get started. Or a good place to recharge your batteries if your writing is stalled. If you're new in town, it's a good place to meet other writers."
Costs: $85-95/day. Two days for $145-165. Lunch is included in registration.
Accommodations: Lodging is available at the hotel or at surrounding motels.

‡PORT TOWNSEND WRITERS' CONFERENCE, Centrum, Box 1158, Port Townsend WA 98368. (360)385-3102. Director: Carol Jane Bangs. Estab. 1974. Annual. Conference held mid-July. Average attendance: 180. Conference to promote poetry, fiction, creative nonfiction, writing for children. The conference is held at a 700-acre state park on the strait of Juan de Fuca. "The site is a Victorian-era military fort with miles of beaches, wooded trails and recreation facilities. The park is within the limits of Port Townsend, a historic seaport and arts

‡   **THE DOUBLE DAGGER** before a listing indicates that the listing is new in this edition.

community, approximately 80 miles northwest of Seattle, on the Olympic Peninsula." Panels include "Writing About Nature," "Journal Writing," "Literary Translation." There will be 5-10 guest speakers in addition to 10 fulltime faculty.

Costs: Approximately $400 tuition and $200 room and board. Less expensive option available.

Accommodations: "Modest room and board facilities on site." Also list of hotels/motels/inns/bed & breakfasts/private rentals available.

Additional Information: "Admission to workshops is selective, based on manuscript submissions." Brochures/guidelines available for SASE. "The conference focus is on the craft of writing and the writing life, not on marketing."

SITKA SYMPOSIUM ON HUMAN VALUES & THE WRITTEN WORD, P.O. Box 2420, Sitka AK 99835-2420. (907)747-3794. Fax: (907)747-6554. E-mail: island@ptialaska.net. Website: http://www.ptialaska.net/island/index.html. Director: Carolyn Servid. Estab. 1984. Annual. Conference held in June. Conference duration: 1 week. Average attendance: 50. Conference "to consider the relationship between writing and the ideas of a selected theme focusing on social and cultural issues." The Symposium is held in downtown Sitka. Many points of visitor interest are within walking distance. The town looks out over surrounding water and mountains. Guest speakers have included Alison Deming, Scott Russell Sanders, Rina Swentzell, Barry Lopez, William Kittredge, Gary Snyder, Margaret Atwood, Terry Tempest Williams, Robert Hass, Richard Nelson and Linda Hogan.

Costs: $220 before May 1; $250 after May 1.

Accommodations: Accommodation rates are listed on Symposium brochure.

Additional Information: Ms critiques (individually with faculty) are available for people submitting work before May 20. Conference brochures/guidelines are available for SASE. Inquiries by e-mail and fax OK.

SWA WINTER WORKSHOP, Seattle Writers Association, P.O. Box 33265, Seattle WA 98133. (206)860-5207. President: Peter Holman-Smith. Estab. 1986. Annual (February 7, 1998). Workshop 1 day, 9 a.m.-4 p.m. Average attendance: 50. "A 'brown bag' intensive workshop that augments SWA's annual program, e.g.; 1996 workshop presented Elizabeth Lyon on nonfiction book proposals." Site varies. 1997 themes: "What Sells and Why" and "How do editors make their selections?" 1998 theme: "Synopses, Query Letters and Grant Writing." Guest speakers and panelists are regional publishing representatives (editors), radio representatives and booksellers.

Costs: $20; snacks provided, bring lunch.

Additional Information: SWA sponsors "Writers in Performance," a jury selected public presentation of Seattle's best writing. Judges are published and unpublished writers, editors and consultants. Guidelines for SASE. "Workshop 1997 included critique of Tier I of all Writers In Performance 1997 submissions and explained the critique and the selection process."

WILLAMETTE WRITERS CONFERENCE, 9045 SW Barbur, Suite 5-A, Portland OR 97219. (503)495-1592. Fax: (503)495-0372. E-mail: wilwrite@teleport.com. Contact: Conference Director. Estab. 1968. Annual. Conference held in August. Average attendance: 220. "Willamette Writers is open to all writers, and we plan our conference accordingly. We offer workshops on all aspects of fiction, nonfiction, marketing, the creative process, etc. Also we invite top notch inspirational speakers for key note addresses. Most often the conference is held on a local college campus which offers a scholarly atmosphere and allows us to keep conference prices down. Recent theme was 'Making It Work.' We always include at least one agent or editor panel and offer a variety of topics of interest to both fiction and nonfiction writers." Past editors and agents in attendance have included: Marc Aronson, senior editor, Henry Holt & Co.; Tom Colgan, senior editor, Avon Books; Charles Spicer, Senior Editor, St. Martin's Press; Sheree Bykofsky, Sheree Bykofsky Associates; Laurie Harper, Sebastian Agency; F. Joseph Spieler, The Spieler Agency; Robert Tabian and Ruth Nathan.

Costs: Cost for full conference including meals is $195 members; $250 nonmembers.

Accomodations: If necessary, these can be made on an individual basis. Some years special rates are available.

Additional Information: Conference brochures/guidelines are available for catalog-size SASE.

WRITE ON THE SOUND WRITERS' CONFERENCE, 700 Main St., Edmonds WA 98020. (425)771-0228. Sponsored by Edmonds Arts Commission. Estab. 1986. Annual. Conference held first weekend in October. Conference duration: 2 days. Average attendance: 160. "Workshops and lectures are offered for a variety of writing interests and levels of expertise."

Costs: $75 for 2 days, $40 for 1 day; includes registration, morning refreshments and 1 ticket to keynote lecture.

Additional Information: Brochures available in August for SASE.

‡YELLOW BAY WRITERS' WORKSHOP, Center for Continuing Education, University of Montana, Missoula MT 59812-1990. (406)243-2094. Fax: (406)243-2047. E-mail: hhi@selway.umt.edu. Website: www.umt.edu/ccesp/c&i/yellowba. Contact: Program Manager. Estab. 1988. Annual. Conference held mid August. Average attendance: 50-60. Includes four workshops: 2 fiction; 1 poetry; 1 creative nonfiction/personal essay. Conference "held at the University of Montana's Flathead Lake Biological Station, a research station with informal educational facilities and rustic cabin living. Located in northwestern Montana on Flathead Lake, the largest natural freshwater lake west of the Mississippi River. All faculty are requested to present a craft lecture—usually also have an editor leading a panel discussion." 1997 faculty included Kevin Canty, David James Duncan, Jayne Anne Phillips and Jane Hirshfield.

Costs: In 1997, for all workshops, lodging (single occupancy) and meals $825; $800 with double occupancy; $495 for commuters.

Accommodations: Shuttle is available from Missoula to Yellow Bay for those flying to Montana. Cost of shuttle is $40 (1995).

Additional Information: Brochures/guidelines are available for SASE.

Canada

‡✿**THE FESTIVAL OF THE WRITTEN ARTS**, Box 2299, Sechelt, British Columbia V0N 3A0 Canada. (800)565-9631 or (604)885-9631. Fax: (604)885-3967. E-mail: rockwood@sunshine.net. Website: http://www.sunshine.net/rockwood. Estab. 1983. Annual. Festival held: August 6-9. Average attendance: 2,500. To promote "all writing genres." Festival held at the Rockwood Centre. "The Centre overlooks the town of Sechelt on the Sunshine Coast. The lodge around which the Centre was organized was built in 1937 as a destination for holidayers arriving on the old Union Steamship Line; it has been preserved very much as it was in its heyday. A new twelve-bedroom annex was added in 1982, and in 1989 the Festival of the Written Arts constructed a Pavilion for outdoor performances next to the annex. The festival does not have a theme. Instead, it showcases 20 or more Canadian writers in a wide variety of genres each year."

Costs: $10 per event or $120 for a four-day pass (Canadian funds.)

Accommodations: Lists of hotels and bed/breakfast available.

Additional Information: The festival runs contests during the 3½ days of the event. Prizes are books donated by publishers. Brochures/guidelines are available.

✿**MARITIME WRITERS' WORKSHOP**, Extension & Summer Session, UNB Box 4400, Fredericton, New Brunswick E3B 5A3 Canada. (506)453-4646. Fax: (506)453-3572. E-mail: extensin@unb.ca. Website: http://www.unb.ca/web/comed/mww. Coordinator: Glenda Turner. Estab. 1976. Annual. Conference held July 5-11, 1998. Average attendance: 50. "Workshops in four areas: fiction, poetry, nonfiction, writing for children." Site is University of New Brunswick, Fredericton campus.

Costs: $350, tuition; $150 meals; $135/double room; $160/single room (Canadian funds).

Accommodations: On-campus accommodations and meals.

Additional Information: "Participants must submit 10-20 manuscript pages which form a focus for workshop discussions." Brochures are available after March. No SASE necessary. Inquiries by e-mail and fax OK.

‡✿**MEMORIES INTO STORIES**, Hollyhock Box 127, Mansons Landing, British Columbia V0P 1K0 Canada. (800)933-6339. E-mail address: hollyhock1@aol.com. Program Director: Oriane Lee Johnston. Estab. 1993. Conference held irregularly. Conference duration: 5 days. Average attendance: 15-30. "We use memory to tap into creativity and write stories through individual and group exercises. Held at Hollyhock Seminar and Holiday Centre on Cortes Island, British Columbia, 48 acres of forest trails, sandy beaches, hot tub, central dining lodge and individual cabins and meeting rooms." Workshop led by Christine Cohen Park.

Costs: Tuition is $395 (Canadian), meals and accommodations are extra and vary depending on the type of accommodation selected.

Accommodations: "We have a 40-page catalog available listing all Hollyhock Programs, accommodations, travel, etc. Costs from $54-134 (Canadian) person/night, depending on the type of accommodation selected. Hollyhock has everything from tenting, to dorm rooms, to shared and private rooms with shared or private bath. Above prices include 3 meals/day. Brochures/guidelines available at no cost.

✿**SAGE HILL WRITING EXPERIENCE**, Box 1731, Saskatoon, Saskatchewan S7K 3S1 Canada. Phone/fax: (306)652-7395. E-mail: sage.hill@sk.sympatico.ca. Executive Director: Steven Ross Smith. Annual. Workshops held in August and October. Workshop duration 10-21 days. Attendance: limited to 36-40. "Sage Hill Writing Experience offers a special working and learning opportunity to writers at different stages of development. Top quality instruction, low instructor-student ratio and the beautiful Sage Hill setting offer conditions ideal for the pursuit of excellence in the arts of fiction, poetry and playwriting." The Sage Hill location features "individual accommodation, in-room writing area, lounges, meeting rooms, healthy meals, walking woods and vistas in several directions." Seven classes are held: Introduction to Writing Fiction & Poetry; Fiction Workshop; Writing Young Adult Fiction Workshop; Poetry Workshop; Poetry Colloquium; Fiction Colloquium; Playwriting Lab. 1997 faculty included Sharon Pollock, Bonnie Burnard, Don McKay, Di Brandt, Elizabeth Philips, Lee Gowan, Rosemary Sullivan, Tim Lilburn.

Costs: $495 (Canadian) includes instruction, accommodation, meals and all facilities. Fall Poetry Colloquium: $775.

Accommodations: On-site individual accommodations located at Lumsden 45 kilometers outside Regina. Fall Colloquium is at Muenster, Saskatchewan, 150 kilometers east of Saskatchewan.

Additional Information: For Introduction to Creative Writing: A five-page sample of your writing or a statement of your interest in creative writing; list of courses taken required. For intermediate and colloquium program: A resume of your writing career and a 12-page sample of your work plus 5 pages of published work required. Application deadline is May 1. Guidelines are available for SASE. Inquiries by e-mail and fax OK. Scholarships and bursaries are available.

✿**THE VANCOUVER INTERNATIONAL WRITERS FESTIVAL**, 1243 Cartwright St., Vancouver, British Columbia V6H 4B7 Canada. (604)681-6330. Fax: (604)681-8400. E-mail: viwf@axionet.com. Website: http://www.axionet.com/writerfest. Estab. 1988. Annual. Held during the 3rd week of October. Average attendance: 11,000. "This is a festival for readers and writers. The program of events is diverse and includes readings, panel discussions, seminars. Lots of opportunities to interact with the writers who attend." Held on Granville Island—in the heart of Vancouver. Two professional theaters are used as well as Performance Works (an open space). "We try to avoid specific themes. Programming takes place between February and June each year and is by invitation."
Costs: Tickets are $10-15 (Canadian).
Accommodations: Local tourist info can be provided when necessary and requested.
Additional Information: Brochures/guidelines are available for SASE after August. Inquiries by e-mail and fax OK. "A reminder—this is a festival, a celebration, not a conference or workshop."

✿**THE VICTORIA SCHOOL OF WRITING**, Write Away!, 607 Linden Ave., Victoria, British Columbia V8V 4G6 Canada. (250)385-8982. Fax: (250)995-9391. E-mail: writeawy@islandnet.com. Website: http://www.islandnet.com/~writeawy. Contact: Margaret Dyment. Conference held from July 14-17. "Four-day intensive workshop on beautiful Vancouver Island with outstanding author-instructors in fiction, poetry, historical fiction and literary nonfiction."
Cost: $395 (Canadian).
Accommodations: Special hotel rates available.
Additional Information: Workshop brochures available. Inquiries by e-mail and fax OK.

‡✿**A WRITER'S W*O*R*L*D**, Surrey Writers' Conference, 12870 72nd Ave., Surrey, British Columbia V4P 1G1 Canada. (640)594-2000. Fax: (604)590-2506. E-mail: phoenixmcf@aol.com. Principal: Rollie Koop. Estab. 1992. Annual. Conference held in fall. Conference duration: 3 days. Average attendance: 350. Conference for fiction (romance/science fiction/fantasy/mystery—changes focus depending upon speakers and publishers scheduled), nonfiction and poetry. "For everyone from beginner to professional." In 1997: Conference held at Sheraton Guildford. Guest lecturers included authors Diana Gabaldon, Don McQuinn and Daniel Wood; agents and editors.
Accommodations: On request will provide information on hotels and B&Bs. Conference rate, $90 (1997). Attendee must make own arrangements for hotel and transportation.
Additional Information: "A drawing takes place and ten people's manuscripts are critiqued by a bestselling author." Writer's contest entries must be submitted about 1 month early. Length: 1,000 words fiction, nonfiction, poetry, young writers (19 or less). First prize $250, second prize $125, third prize $75. Contest is judged by a qualified panel of writers and educators. Write, call or e-mail for additional information.

International

‡***ART WORKSHOPS IN LA ANTIGUA GUATEMALA**, 4758 Lyndale Ave. S, Minneapolis MN 55409-2304. (612)825-0747. Fax: (612)825-6637. E-mail: artguat@aol.com. Website: http://www.artguat.org. Estab. 1995. Annual. Workshop duration: 10 days. Maximum class size: 10 students per class. The conference is held in either a private home or beautiful hotels. Workshop titles include: Creative Writing—the Short Story with Merna Summers (March 28-April 6, 1998).
Costs: $1,675.
Accommodations: All transportation included.
Additional Information: Conference brochures/guidelines are available.

***EDINBURGH UNIVERSITY CENTRE FOR CONTINUING EDUCATION CREATIVE WRITING WORKSHOPS**, 11 Buccleuch Place, Edinburgh Scotland EH8 9LW. (131)650-4400. Fax: 131 667-6097. E-mail: b.stevens@ed.ac.uk. Website: http://www.ed.ac.uk/~cce/summer. Administrative Director of International

---

🍁 **THE MAPLE LEAF** symbol before a listing indicates a Canadian publisher, magazine, conference or contest.

Summer Schools: Bridget M. Stevens. Estab. 1990. Introductory course July 4-10; short story course July 11-17; playwriting course July 18-31. Average attendance: 15. Courses cover "basic techniques of creative writing, the short story and playwriting. The University of Edinburgh Centre for Continuing Education occupies traditional 18th century premises near the George Square Campus. Located nearby are libraries, banks and recreational facilities. Free use of word-processing facilities."

Costs: In 1997 cost was £195 per one-week course (tuition only).

Accommodations: Information on overnight accommodations is available. Accommodations include student dormitories, self-catering apartment and local homes.

Additional Information: Participants are encouraged to submit work in advance, but this is not obligatory. Conference brochures/guidelines available for SASE. Inquiries by e-mail and fax OK.

*FICTION WRITING RETREAT IN ACAPULCO, 3584 Kirkwood Place, Boulder CO 80304-1938. (303)444-0086. Fax: (303)444-0086. E-mail: basteiner@aol.com. Website: http://www.flyingcolorsart.com. Conference Director: Barbara Steiner. Estab. 1991. Annual. Conference held in November. Conference duration: 1 week. Average attendance: 10. Conference concentrates on creativity and fiction technique/any market. Oceanfront accommodations on private estate of Mexican artist Nora Beteta. Rooms in villa have bath (private) but usually dual occupancy. Swimming in pool or ocean/bay. Classes held on large porches with ocean breeze and views.

Costs: $695 for 1 week includes room, meals, classes.

Accommodations: Airfare separate. Travel agent books flights for groups from Denver. Will book from anyplace in US.

Additional Information: "Writers submit one short fiction piece in advance of workshop. Classes include writing, lecture and assignments." Brochures/guidelines available for SASE after April. Inquiries by e-mail and fax OK.

‡*PARIS WRITERS' WORKSHOP/WICE, 20, Bd du Montparnasse, Paris, France 75015. (33-1)45.66.75.50. Fax: (33-1)40.65.96.53. E-mail: wice@wfi.fr. Website: http://www.wice.org. Co-Directors: Judy Rowley and Ellen Hinsey. Estab. 1987. Annual. Conference held first week in July. Average attendance: 40-50. "Conference concentrates on fiction (2 sections), nonfiction and poetry. Visiting lecturers speak on a variety of issues important to beginning and advanced writers. Located in the heart of Paris on the Bd. du Montparnasse, the stomping grounds of such famous American writers as Ernest Hemingway, Henry Miller and F. Scott Fitzgerald. The site consists of 4 classrooms, a resource center/library, computer room and private terrace."

Costs: $380—tuition only.

Additional Information: "Students submit 2 copies of complete ms or work-in-progress. One copy is sent in advance to writer in residence. Each student has a one-on-one consultation with writer in residence concerning ms that was submitted." Conference brochure/guidelines are available after January. Inquiries by e-mail and fax OK. "Workshop attracts many expatriate Americans and other English language students from all over Europe and North America. We can assist with finding a range of housing, from bare essentials bargains to more luxurious accommodations. We are an intimate workshop with an exciting mix of more experienced, published writers and enthusiastic beginners. Past writers include CK Williams, Carolyn Kizer, Grace Paley, Jayne Anne Phillips and Marilyn Hacker."

‡*SUMMER IN FRANCE WRITING WORKSHOPS, HCOI, Box 102, Plainview TX 79072. Phone/fax: (806)889-3533. E-mail: bettye@plainview.com. Director: Bettye Givens. Annual. Conference: 27 days. Average attendance: 10-15. For fiction, poetry. The classrooms are in the Val de Grace 277 Rue St. Jacques in the heart of the Latin Quarter near Luxeumbourg Park in Paris. Guest speakers include Paris poets, professors and editors (lectures in English).

Costs: Costs vary. Costs includes literature classes, art history and the writing workshop.

Accommodations: Some accommodations with a French family.

Additional Information: Conference brochures/guidelines are available for SASE. Inquiries by e-mail and fax OK. "Enroll early. Side trips out of Paris are planned as are poetry readings at the Paris American Academy and at Shakespeare & Co."

*TŶ NEWYDD WRITER'S CENTRE, Llanystumdwy, Cricieth Gwynedd LL52 OLW, United Kingdom 01766-522811. Fax: 01766 523095. Administrator: Sally Baker. Estab. 1990. Regular courses held throughout the year. Every course held Monday-Saturday. Average attendance: 14. "To give people the opportunity to work

INTERNATIONAL MARKETS, those located outside of the United States and Canada, are marked with an asterisk.

side by side with professional writers, in an informal atmosphere." Site is Ty Newydd. Large manor house. Last home of the prime minister, David Lloyd George. Situated in North Wales, Great Britain-between mountains and sea." Past featured tutors include novelists Beryl Bainbridge and Bernice Rubens.

Costs: £275 for Monday-Saturday (includes full board, tuition).

Accommodations: Transportation from railway stations arranged. Accommodation in TyNewydd (onsite).

Additional Information: Conference brochures/guidelines are available by mail, phone or fax after January. Inquiries by fax OK. "We have had several people from U.S. on courses here in the past three years. More and more people come to us from the U.S. often combining a writing course with a tour of Wales."

*THE WRITERS' SUMMER SCHOOL, SWANWICK, The New Vicarage, Woodford Halse, Daventry, NN11 3RE England. E-mail: bcourtie@aol.com. Secretary: Brenda Courtie. Estab. 1949. Annual. Conference held August 8-14. Average attendance: 300 plus. "Conference concentrates on all fields of writing." In 1997 courses included Plays, Poetry, Beginners, The Novel, Short Stories, New Technology, Nonfiction and Crime. Speakers in 1997 included Robert Barnard, Linda O'Byrne, Martin Shallcross and Kit Wright.

Costs: £190-£300 per person inclusive.

Accommodations: Buses from main line station to conference centre provided.

Additional Information: Conference brochures/guidelines are available after February. Inquiries by e-mail and fax OK. "The Writers' Summer School is a nonprofit-making organization."

‡*ZOETROPE SHORT STORY WRITERS CONFERENCE, Blancaneaux Lodge, Central Farm, P.O. Box B, Cayo District, Belize. 011-501-92-3878. Estab. 1997. Annually. Conference held June 27 to July 4. Average attendance: 20. Conference for short story writers held at Francis Coppola's retreat in Belize. Featured speaker in 1997 was Amy Bloom.

Costs: Depends on accommodations. Varies from $2,000-$3,000 for a full week. Includes three meals a day, deluxe accommodations, trips to Mayan ruins, etc.

Accommodations: "Attendees must arrange for their own travel to Belize City Airport. We take care of everything else."

Additional Information: "We require that the writer bring 10-15 copies of the story he wishes to work on at the workshop." Scholarship available through short story contest. Brochures available for SASE after February.

Organizations and Resources

When you write, you write alone. It's just you and the typewriter or computer screen. Yet the writing life does not need to be a lonely one. Joining a writing group or organization can be an important step in your writing career. By meeting other writers, discussing your common problems and sharing ideas, you can enrich your writing and increase your understanding of this sometimes difficult, but rewarding life.

The variety of writers' organizations seems endless—encompassing every type of writing and writer—from small, informal groups that gather regularly at a local coffee house for critique sessions to regional groups that hold annual conferences to share technique and marketing tips. National organizations and unions fight for writers' rights and higher payment for freelancers, and international groups monitor the treatment of writers around the world.

In this section you will find state-, province-, regional-based groups such as the Arizona Authors Association and the Manitoba Writer's Guild. You'll also find national organizations including the National Writers Association. The Mystery Writers of America, Western Writers of America and the Genre Writer's Association are examples of groups devoted to a particular type of writing. Whatever your needs or goals, you're likely to find a group listed here to interest you.

SELECTING A WRITERS' ORGANIZATION

To help you make an informed decision, we've provided information on the scope, membership and goals of the organizations listed on these pages. We asked groups to outline the types of memberships available and the benefits members can expect. Most groups will provide additional information for a self-addressed, stamped envelope, and you may be able to get a sample copy of their newsletter for a modest fee.

Keep in mind joining a writers' organization is a two-way street. When you join an organization, you become a part of it and, in addition to membership fees, most groups need and want your help. If you want to get involved, opportunities can include everything from chairing a committee to writing for the newsletter to helping set up an annual conference. The level of your involvement is up to you, and almost all organizations welcome contributions of time and effort.

Selecting a group to join depends on a number of factors. As a first step, you must determine what you want from membership in a writers' organization. Then send away for more information on the groups that seem to fit your needs. Start, however, by asking yourself:

- Would I like to meet writers in my city? Am I more interested in making contacts with other writers across the country or around the world?
- Am I interested in a group that will critique and give me feedback on work-in-progress?
- Do I want marketing information and tips on dealing with editors?
- Would I like to meet other writers who write the same type of work I do or am I interested in meeting writers from a variety of fields?
- How much time can I devote to meetings and are regular meetings important to me? How much can I afford to pay in dues?
- Would I like to get involved in running the group, working on the group's newsletters, planning a conference?
- Am I interested in a group devoted to writers' rights and treatment or would I rather concentrate on the business of writing?

FOR MORE INFORMATION

Because they do not usually have the resources or inclination to promote themselves widely, finding a local writers' group is usually a word-of-mouth process. If you think you'd like to join a local writer's group and do not know of any in your area, check notices at your library or contact a local college English department. You might also try contacting a group based in your state, province or region listed here for information on smaller groups in your area.

If you have a computer and would like to meet with writers in other areas of the country, you will find many commercial online services, such as GEnie and America Online, have writers' sections and "clubs" online. Many free online services available through Internet also have writers' "boards."

For more information on writers' organizations, check *The Writer's Essential Desk Reference: A Companion to Writer's Market*, 2nd edition (Writer's Digest Books, 1507 Dana Ave., Cincinnati OH 45207). Other directories listing organizations for writers include the *Literary Market Place* or *International Literary Market Place* (R.R. Bowker, 121 Chanlon Rd., New Providence NJ 07974). The National Writers Association also maintains a list of writers' organizations.

ARIZONA AUTHORS ASSOCIATION, 3509 E. Shea Blvd., Suite 117, Phoenix AZ 85028. (602)867-9001. President: Gerry Benninger. Estab. 1978. Number of Members: 500. Type of Memberships: Professional, writers with published work; associate, writers working toward publication; affiliate, professionals in the publishing industry. "Primarily an Arizona organization but open to writers nationally." Benefits include monthly newsletter, discount rates on seminars, workshops and newsletter ads, discounts on writing books, discounts at bookstores, copy shops, critique groups and networking events. "Sponsors workshops on a variety of topics of interest to writers (e.g., publishing, marketing, structure, genres)." Publishes *Authors Newsletter*, monthly ($25/yr.). Dues: Professional and associate, $40/year; affiliate: $45/year; student: $25/year. Holds monthly critique group, quarterly networking events and annual literary contest. Send SASE for information.

ASSOCIATED WRITING PROGRAMS, Tallwood House, Mail Stop 1E3, George Mason University, Fairfax VA 22030. (703)993-4301. E-mail: awp@gmu.edu. Estab. 1967. Number of Members: 5,000 individuals and 290 institutions. Types of Membership: Institutional (universities); graduate students; individual writers; and *Chronicle* subscribers. Open to any person interested in writing; most members are students or faculty of university writing programs (worldwide). Benefits include information on creative writing programs; grants and awards to writers; a job placement service for writers in academe and beyond. AWP holds an Annual Conference in a different US city every spring; also conducts an annual Award Series in poetry, short story collections, novel and creative nonfiction, in which winner receives $2,000 honorarium and publication by a participating press. AWP acts as agent for finalists in Award Series and tries to place their manuscript with publishers throughout the year. Manuscripts accepted January 1-February 28 only. Novel competition is for writers 32 years of age or younger; winner receives publication by St. Martin's Press and $10,000 in royalties. Send SASE for new guidelines. Publishes *AWP Chronicle* 6 times/year; 3 times/academic semester. Available to members for free. Nonmembers may order a subscription for $20/yr. Also publishes the *AWP Official Guide to Writing Programs* which lists about 330 creative writing programs in universities across the country and in Canada. *Guide* is updated every 2 years; cost is $19.95 plus $5 for first-class mail. Dues: $50 for individual membership and an additional $45 for our placement service. AWP keeps dossiers on file and sends them to school or organization of person's request. Holds two meetings per year for the Board of Directors. Send SASE for information.

AUSTIN WRITERS' LEAGUE RESOURCE CENTER, Austin Writers' League, 1501 W. Fifth, E-2, Austin TX 78703. (512)499-8914. Fax: (512)499-0441. Executive Director: Angela Smith. Estab. 1981. Number of Members: 1,600. Types of Memberships: Regular, student/senior citizen, family. Monthly meetings and use of resource center/library is open to the public. "Membership includes both aspiring and professional writers, all ages and all ethnic groups." Job bank is also open to the public. Public also has access to technical assistance. Partial and full scholarships offered for some programs. Of 1,600 members, 800 reside in Austin. Remaining 800 live all over the US and in other countries. Benefits include monthly newsletter, monthly meetings, study groups, resource center/library-checkout privileges, discounts on workshops, seminars, classes, job bank, discounts on books and tapes, participation in awards programs, technical/marketing assistance, copyright forms and information, Writers Helping Writers (mentoring program). Center has 5 rooms plus 2 offices and storage area. Public space includes reception and job bank area; conference/classroom; library/computer room; and copy/mail room. Library includes 1,000 titles. Sponsors fall and spring workshops, weekend seminars, informal classes, sponsorships for special events such as readings, production of original plays, media conferences, creative writing programs for children and youth; Violet Crown Book Awards, newsletter writing awards, Young Texas Writers awards, contests for various anthologies. Publishes *Austin Writer* (monthly newsletter), sponsors with Texas Commission on the Arts Texas Literary Touring Program. Administers literature subgranting program for Texas Commission on the Arts. Membership/subscription: $40, $35-students, senior citizens, $60 family membership.

Monthly meetings. Study groups set their own regular meeting schedules. Send SASE for information.

THE AUTHORS GUILD, 330 W. 42nd St., 29th Floor, New York NY 10036. (212)563-5904. Fax: (212)564-8363. Executive Director: Paul Aiken. Purpose of organization: membership organization of 7,200 members offers services and information materials intended to help published authors with the business and legal aspects of their work, including contract problems, copyright matters, freedom of expression and taxation. Maintains staff of attorneys and legal interns to assist members. Group health insurance available. Qualifications for membership: book author published by an established American publisher within 7 years or any author who has had 3 works, fiction or nonfiction, published by a magazine or magazines of general circulation in the last 18 months. Associate membership also available. Annual dues: $90. Different levels of membership include: associate membership with all rights except voting available to an author who has a firm contract offer from an American publisher. Workshops/conferences: "The Guild and the Authors Guild Foundation conduct several symposia each year at which experts provide information, offer advice, and answer questions on subjects of concern to authors. Typical subjects have been the rights of privacy and publicity, libel, wills and estates, taxation, copyright, editors and editing, the art of interviewing, standards of criticism and book reviewing. Transcripts of these symposia are published and circulated to members." "The *Authors Guild Bulletin*, a quarterly journal, contains articles on matters of interest to published writers, reports of Guild activities, contract surveys, advice on problem clauses in contracts, transcripts of Guild and League symposia, and information on a variety of professional topics. Subscription included in the cost of the annual dues."

*THE BRITISH FANTASY SOCIETY, 2 Harwood St., Stockport SK4 1JJ United Kingdom. Secretary: Robert Parkinson. Estab. 1971. Open to: "Anyone interested in fantasy. The British Fantasy Society was formed to provide coverage of the fantasy, science fiction and horror fields. To achieve this, the Society publishes its *Newsletter*, packed with information and reviews of new books and films, plus a number of other booklets of fiction and articles: *Winter Chills*, *Mystique*, *Masters of Fantasy* and *Dark Horizons*. The BFS also organises an annual Fantasy Conference at which the British Fantasy Awards are presented for categories such as Best Novel, Best Short Story and Best Film." Dues and subscription fees are £17 (UK); $35 (US); £20 (Europe), £25 (elsewhere). Payment in sterling or US dollars only. Send SASE or IRC for information.

♣BURNABY WRITERS' SOCIETY, 6584 Deer Lake Ave., Burnaby, British Columbia V5G 2J3. (604)435-6500. Corresponding Secretary: Eileen Kernaghan. Estab. 1967. Number of members: 300. "Membership is regional, but open to anyone interested in writing." Benefits include monthly market newsletter; workshops/critiques; guest speakers; information on contests, events, reading venues, etc.; opportunity to participate in public reading series. Sponsors annual competition open to all British Columbia residents; monthly readings at Burnaby Art Gallery; Canada Council sponsored readings; workshops. Publishes *Burnaby Writers Newsletter* monthly (except July/August), available to anyone for $25/year subscription. Dues: $25/year (includes newsletter subscription). Meets second Thursday of each month. Send SASE for information.

‡CALIFORNIA WRITERS' CLUB, 8 Balra Dr., Novato CA 94947-4963. Estab. 1909. Number of Members: 900. Type of Memberships: Associate and active. Open to: "All published writers and those deemed able to publish within five years." Benefits include: speakers—authors, editors, agents, anyone connected with writing—heard at monthly meetings; marketing information; workshops; camaraderie of fellow writers. Sponsors workshops, conferences, awards programs/contests. Publishes a monthly newsletter at state level, monthly newsletter at branch level. Available to members only. Dues: $35/year. Meets monthly. Send SASE for information.

‡♣CANADIAN AUTHORS ASSOCIATION, P.O. Box 419, Campbellford, Ontario K0L 1L0 Canada. (705)653-0323. Fax: (705)653-0593. President: Cora Taylor. Estab. 1921. Number of Members: 800. Type of Memberships: Member (voting); associate (non-voting). "Member must have minimum sales to commercial publications. Associates need not have published yet." National scope (Canada) with 15 regional branches. Branches meet monthly. Benefits include networking, marketing advice, legal advice, several publications, annual conference, awards programs. Sponsors workshops, conferences, awards programs/contests. Publishes *Canadian Author*, quarterly $20 (Canadian)/year; $25 (Canadian) for foreign and *National Newsline* $10 (Canadian)/year, news of members and markets; *Canadian Writer's Guide*, the association's handbook for writers in 12th edition (1997), $30 (Canadian) per copy plus shipping and tax. Dues $115 + guest = $123.05 (Canadian). Send SASE for information.

♣CANADIAN SOCIETY OF CHILDREN'S AUTHORS, ILLUSTRATORS AND PERFORMERS (CANSCAIP), 35 Spadina Rd., Toronto, Ontario M5R 2S9 Canada. (416)515-1559. Fax: (416)515-7022. E-mail: canscaip@interlog.com. Executive Secretary: Nancy Prasad. Estab. 1977. Number of Members: 1,100. Types of membership: Full professional member and friend (associate member). Open to professional active writers, illustrators and performers in the field of children's culture (full members); beginners and all other interested persons and institutions (friends). International scope, but emphasis on Canada. Benefits include quarterly newsletter, marketing opportunities, publicity via our membership directory and our "members available" list, jobs (school visits, readings, workshops, residencies, etc.) through our "members available" list, mutual support through monthly meetings. Sponsors annual workshop, "Packaging Your Imagination," held every October for beginners. Publishes *CANSCAIP News*, quarterly, available to all (free with membership, otherwise $25 Canadian). Dues: professional fees: $60 Canadian/year; friend fees: $25/year; institutional $30/year. "Professionals must have written, illustrated or performed work for children commercially, sufficient to satisfy the membership committee (more details on request)." CANSCAIP National has open meetings from September to June, monthly in Toronto. CANSCAIP West holds bimonthly meetings in Vancouver. Send SASE for information.

‡❦**FEDERATION OF BRITISH COLUMBIA WRITERS**, MPO Box 2206, Vancouver, British Columbia V6B 3W2 Canada. Executive Director: Corey Van't Haaff. Estab. 1982. Number of Members: 800. Types of Membership: regular. "Open to established and emerging writers in any genre, province-wide." Benefits include newsletter, liaison with funding bodies, publications, workshops, readings, literary contests, various retail and educational discounts. Sponsors readings and workshops. Publishes a newsletter 4 times/year, included in membership. Dues: $50 regular. Send SASE for information.

‡**FEMINIST WRITERS GUILD**, Outrider Press, 1004 E. Steger Rd., Suite C3, Crete IL 60417. (708)672-6630. Estab. 1977. Founded by outstanding writers including Adrienne Rich, Marge Piercy, Tillie Olsen and Valerie Miner. Number of members: 150. Open to: all women who write seriously as well as men and women who support feminist writing. Benefits include formal readings, newsletters, open mikes, publications, leadership opportunities and workshops. Dues: $22.

GARDEN STATE HORROR WRITERS, Manalapan Library, P.O. Box 178, Beverly NJ 08010. (908)754-9454. Website: http://www.para-net/~GSHW. President: John Platt. Estab. 1991. Number of Members: 50. Membership levels: active and associate. Open to "anyone interested in pursuing a career in fiction writing." Scope is national. Benefits include "latest market news, use of library meeting rooms, free copies of guidelines for magazine and book publishers, free in-house critique service in person and by mail." Sponsors monthly guest speakers and/or workshops, annual short fiction contest. A future conference/convention is being planned. A free sample of monthly newsletter *The Graveline* is available for SASE. Subscription is included in the cost of any membership. Dues: $30 active; $20 associate/annually. Active members must be 16 years of age. Holds regular monthly meetings. Send SASE for information.

GENRE WRITER'S ASSOCIATION (GWA), P.O. Box 6301, Concord CA 94524. (510)254-7053. Editor: Bobbi Sinha-Morey. The Genre Writer's Association (GWA) is an international service organization dedicated to the promotion of excellence in the fields of Science Fiction, Fantasy, Mystery, Western and Horror. Membership is open to any writer, poet, artist, editor, publisher or calligrapher who participates through his/her creative endeavors in the literary genres espoused by the organization. Members receive: 2 copies of *The Genre Writer's News*; 2 copies of *The Genre Writer's News Market Supplements*; 4 issues of *Horror: The News Magazine of the Horror & Fantasy Field*; a free membership roster (mailed in June/July); The Genre Writer's Association Plaque Awards; and 5-10% off any order to Dark Regions Press or Orinda Press products. "Members enjoy commentary/critique services, reviews, market news, grievance arbitration, promotion of member's work, how-to articles, research services, and much more." Dues for US members are $25, new and renewable. All others $30, new and renewable. Checks payable to GWA. For more information or to join, write with SASE for reply.

HORROR WRITERS ASSOCIATION (HWA), P.O. Box 50577, Palo Alto CA 94303. President: Janet Berlinger. E-mail: hwa@horror.org. Website: http://www.horror.org. Estab. 1983. Number of Members: 700. Type of Memberships: Active—writers who have one published novel or three professional stories. Affiliate—beginning writers and others interested in the horror genre. Sponsors the "Bram Stoker Award" for excellence in horror writing. Publishes newsletter, membership directory and bimonthly market reports. Dues: $55/year (US); $65/year (overseas). Meets once a year. Send SASE for information or visit website.

MYSTERY WRITERS OF AMERICA (MWA), 17 E. 47th St., 6th Floor, New York NY 10017. Executive Director: Priscilla Ridgway. Estab. 1945. Number of Members: 2,600. Type of memberships: Active (professional, published writers of fiction or nonfiction crime/mystery/suspense); associate (professionals in allied fields, i.e., editor, publisher, critic, news reporter, publicist, librarian, bookseller, etc.); corresponding (writers qualified for active membership who live outside the US). Unpublished writers may petition for Affiliate member status. Benefits include promotion and protection of writers' rights and interests, including counsel and advice on contracts, MWA courses and workshops, a national office, an annual conference featuring the Edgar Allan Poe Awards, the *MWA Anthology*, a national newsletter, regional conferences, meetings and newsletters. Newsletter, *The Third Degree*, is published 10 times/year for members. Annual dues: $65 for US members; $32.50 for Corresponding members.

THE NATIONAL LEAGUE OF AMERICAN PEN WOMEN, INC., Headquarters: The Pen Arts Building, 1300 17th St., NW, Washington DC 20036. Phone/fax: (202)785-1997. Contact: National President. Estab. 1897. Number of Members: 5,000. Types of Membership: Three classifications: Art, Letters, Music. Open to: Professional women. "Professional to us means our membership is only open to women who sell their art, writings or music compositions. We have 200 branches in the continental US, Hawaii and the Republic of Panama. Some branches have as many as 100 members, some as few as 10 or 12. It is necessary to have 5 members to form a new branch." Benefits include marketing advice, use of a facility, critiques and competitions. Our facility is The Pen Arts Building. It is a 20-room Victorian mansion. It's most distinguished resident was President Abraham Lincoln's son, Robert Todd Lincoln, the former Secretary of War and Minister of Great Britain. It has a few rooms available for Pen Women visiting the D.C. area, and for Board members in session 3 times a year. Branch and State Association competitions, as well as biennial convention competitions. Offers a research library of books and histories of our organization only. Sponsors awards biennially to Pen Women in each classification: Art, Letters, Music, and $1,000 award biennially in even-numbered year to non-Pen Women in each classification for women age 35 and over who wish to pursue special work in her field. *The Pen Woman* is our membership magazine, published 6 times a year, free to members, $18 a year for nonmember subscribers. Dues: $40/year for national organization, from $5-10/year for branch membership and from $1-5 for state association dues. Branches hold regular meeting each month, September through May except in northern states which meet usually March through September (for travel convenience). Send SASE for information.

NATIONAL WRITERS ASSOCIATION, 1450 S. Havana, Suite 424, Aurora CO 80012. (303)751-7844. Executive Director: Sandy Whelchel. Estab. 1937. Number of Members: 4,000. Types of Memberships: Regular membership for those without published credits; professional membership for those with published credits. Open to: Any interested writer. National/International plus we have 16 chapters in various states. Benefits include critiques, marketing advice, editing, literary agency, complaint service, chapbook publishing service, research reports on various aspects of writing, 4 contests, National Writers Press—self-publishing operation, computer bulletin board service, regular newsletter with updates on marketing, bimonthly magazine on writing related subjects, discounts on supplies, magazines and some services. Sponsors periodic conferences and workshops: short story contest opens April, closes July 1; novel contest opens December, closes April 1. Publishes *Flash Market News* (monthly publication for professional members only); *Authorship Magazine* (bimonthly publication available by subscription $18 to nonmembers). Dues: $65 regular; $85 professional. For professional membership requirement is equivalent of 3 articles or stories in a national or regional magazine; a book published by a royalty publisher, a play, TV script or movie produced. Send SASE for information. Chapters hold meetings on a monthly basis.

NEW HAMPSHIRE WRITERS AND PUBLISHERS PROJECT, P.O. Box 2693, Concord NH 03302-2693. (603)226-6649. Executive Director: Patricia Scholz-Cohen. Estab. 1988. Number of Members: 750. Type of Memberships: Senior/student; individual; business. Open to anyone interested in the literary arts—writers (fiction, nonfiction, journalists, poets, scriptwriters, etc.), teachers, librarians, publishers and *readers*. Statewide scope. Benefits include a bimonthly publication featuring articles about NH writers and publishers; leads for writers, new books listings; and NH literary news. Also discounts on workshops, readings, conferences. Dues: $35 for individuals; $15 for seniors, students; $50 for businesses. Send SASE for information.

NORTH CAROLINA WRITERS' NETWORK, P.O. Box 954, Carrboro NC 27510. (919)967-9540. Fax: (919)929-0535. Executive Director: Linda W. Hobson. Estab. 1985. Number of Members: 1,800. Open to: All writers, all levels of skill and friends of literature. Membership is approximately 1,600 in North Carolina and 200 in 28 other states. Benefits include bimonthly newsletter, reduced rates for competition entry fees, fall and spring conferences, workshops, etc., use of critiquing service, use of library and resource center, press release and publicity service, information database(s). Sponsors annual Fall Conference, Creative Nonfiction Competition, statewide workshops, Writers & Readers Series, Randall Jarrell Poetry Prize, Poetry Chapbook Competition, Thomas Wolfe Fiction Prize, Fiction Competition, Paul Green Playwright Prize. Publishes the 28-page bimonthly *Network News*, and *North Carolina's Literary Resource Guide*. Subscription included in dues. Dues: $35/year, $20/year (students enrolled in a degree-granting program, seniors 65+ and disabled). Events scheduled throughout the year. Send SASE for information.

OZARKS WRITERS LEAGUE, P.O. Box 1433, Branson MO 65616. Estab. 1983. Number of Members: 250. Open to: Anyone interested in writing, photography and art. Regional Scope: Missouri, Arkansas, Oklahoma, Kansas—"Greater Ozarks" area. Benefits include mutual inspiration and support; information exchange. Sponsors quarterly seminars/workshops, two annual writing competitions, one annual photography competition, special conferences. Publishes quarterly newsletter, the *Owls Hoot*. Dues: $15/year. Meets quarterly—February, May, August, November. Send SASE for information.

MARKET CONDITIONS are constantly changing! If you're still using this book and it is 1999 or later, buy the newest edition of *Novel & Short Story Writer's Market* at your favorite bookstore or order from Writer's Digest Books.

PHILADELPHIA WRITERS ORGANIZATION, P.O. Box 42497, Philadelphia PA 19101. (610)630-8670. Administrative Coordinator: Jane Brooks. Estab. 1981. Number of Members: 250. Types of Memberships: Full (voting), associate, student. Open to any writer, published or unpublished. Scope is tri-state area—Pennsylvania, Delaware, New Jersey, but mostly Philadelphia area. Benefits include medical insurance (for full members only), monthly meetings with guest panelists, spring workshop (full day) plus Editors Marketplace. Publishes a monthly newsletter for members only. Dues: $50 (full and associate); $25 (student). Proof of publication required for full members (minimum of 2,000 words). Meets monthly throughout year except July and August. Send SASE for information.

‡ROMANCE WRITERS OF AMERICA (RWA), 13700 Veterans Memorial, Suite 315, Houston TX 77014. (281)440-6885. Fax: (281)440-7510. Executive Manager: Allison Kelley. Estab. 1981. Number of members: over 7,500. Type of Memberships: General and associate. Open to: "Any person actively pursuing a writing career in the romance field." Membership is international. Benefits include annual conference, contests and awards, magazine, forums with publishing representatives, network for published authors, group insurance, regional newsletters and more. Dues: $70/new members; $60/renewal fee. Send SASE for information.

SCIENCE FICTION AND FANTASY WORKSHOP, 1193 S. 1900 East, Salt Lake City UT 84108. (801)582-2090. E-mail: dalton-woodbury@sff.net for more information. Website: http://www.sff.net/people/Dalton-Woodbury/sffw.htp. Director/Editor: Kathleen D. Woodbury. Estab. 1980. Number of members: 400. Type of memberships: "Active" is listed in the membership roster and so is accessible to all other members; "inactive" is not listed in the roster. Open to "anyone, anywhere. Our scope is international although over 96% of our members are in the US." Benefits include "several different critique groups: short stories, novels, articles, screenplays, poetry, etc. We also offer services such as copyediting, working out the numbers in planet building (give us the kind of planet you want and we'll tell you how far it is from the sun, etc.—or tell us what kind of sun you have and we'll tell you what your planet is like), brainstorming story, fragments or cultures or aliens, information on groups who write/critique science fiction and fantasy in your area, etc." Publishes *SF and Fantasy Workshop* (monthly); non-members subscribe for $15/year; samples are $1.50 and trial subscription: $8/6 issues. "We have a publication that contains outlines, synopses, proposals that authors submitted or used for novels that sold. The purpose is to show new and aspiring novelists what successful outlines, etc. look like, and to provide authors (with books coming out) advance publicity. Authors may contact Kathleen about publication. Cost is $2.50/issue or $9/4 issues. We also publish a fiction booklet on an irregular basis. It contains one short story and three critiques by professional writers. Cost to anyone is $5/5 issues or $8/10 issues." Dues: Members pay a one-time fee of $5 (to cover the cost of the roster and the new-member information packet) and the annual $15 subscription fee. To renew membership, members simply renew their subscriptions. "Our organization is strictly by mail though that is now expanding to include e-mail." Or send SASE (or IRC).

SCIENCE FICTION WRITERS OF EARTH, P.O. Box 121293, Fort Worth TX 76121. (817)451-8674. Administrator: Gilbert Gordon Reis. Estab. 1980. Number of Members: 100-150. Open to: Unpublished writers of science fiction and fantasy short stories. "We have a few writers in Europe, Canada and Australia, but the majority are from the US. Writers compete in our annual contest. This allows the writer to find out where he/she stands in writing ability. Winners often receive requests for their story from publishers. Many winners have told us that they believe that placing in the top ten of our contest gives them recognition and has assisted in getting their first story published." Dues: One must submit a science fiction or fantasy short story to our annual contest to be a member. Cost is $5 for membership and first story. $2 for each additional ms. The nominating committee meets several times a year to select the top ten stories of the annual contest. Author Edward Bryant selects the winners from the top ten stories. Contest deadline is October 30 and the awards results are mailed out on January 31 of the following year. Information about the organization is available for SASE or from the Internet: www.flash.net/~sfwoe/.

SCIENCE-FICTION AND FANTASY WRITERS OF AMERICA, INC., 532 La Guardia Place #632, New York NY 10012-1428. President: Michael Capobianco. Estab. 1965. Number of Members: 1,200. Type of Memberships: Active, associate, affiliate, institutional, estate. Open to: "Professional writers, editors, anthologists, artists in the science fiction/fantasy genres and allied professional individuals and institutions. Our membership is international; we currently have members throughout Europe, Australia, Central and South America, Canada and some in Asia." We produce a variety of journals for our members, annual membership directory and provide a grievance committee, publicity committee, circulating book plan and access to medical/life/disability insurance. We award the SFWA Nebula Awards each year for outstanding achievement in the genre at novel, novella, novelet and short story lengths." Quarterly *SFWA Bulletin* to members; nonmembers may subscribe at $15/4 issues within US/Canada; $18.50 overseas. Bimonthly *SFWA Forum* for active and associate members only. Annual *SFWA Membership Directory* for members; available to professional organizations for $60. Active membership requires professional sale in the US of at least 3 short stories or 1 full-length book. Affiliate or associate membership require at least 1 professional sale in the US or other professional sale in the US or other professional involvement in the field respectively. Dues are pro-rated quarterly; info available upon request. Business meetings are held during Annual Nebula Awards weekend and usually during the annual World SF Convention. Send SASE for information.

SEATTLE WRITERS ASSOCIATION, P.O. Box 33265, Seattle WA 98133. (206)860-5207. Fax: (206)483-3519 (contact phone). President: Peter Holman-Smith. Estab. 1986. Number of members: approximately 130. "Open to all writers from the Pacific Northwest, published and unpublished, dedicated to writing professionally and for publication." Benefits include monthly meetings, networking, market advice, critique groups/mss review. Sponsors Winter Workshop and Writers in Performance (contest and performance). Publishes newsletter for members and available upon request. "Writers in Performance" anthology in progress. Dues: $30/year, includes newsletter. Meets first Thursday of month, 7-10 p.m., September through May. Send SASE for information.

SOCIETY OF SOUTHWESTERN AUTHORS, P.O. Box 30355, Tucson AZ 85751-0355. (520)296-5299. Fax:(520)296-0409. President/Chairman: Penny Porter. Estab. 1972. Number of Members: 170. Memberships: Professional, Associate and Honorary. Professional: published authors of books, articles, poetry, etc.; Associate: aspiring writers not yet published; Honorary: one whose contribution to the writing profession or to SSA warrants such regonition. Benefits include conference, short story writing contest, critiques, marketing advice. Sponsors annual conference in January and annual short story writing contest. Publishes *The Write Word* which appears 6 times/year. Dues: $20/year. Meets monthly. Send SASE for information.

WESTERN WRITERS OF AMERICA, Office of the Secretary Treasurer, 1012 Fair St., Franklin TN 37064. (615)791-1444. Secretary Treasurer: James A. Crutchfield. Estab. 1953. Number of Members: 600. Type of Membership: Active, associate, patron. Open to: Professional, published writers who have multiple publications of fiction or nonfiction (usually at least three) about the West. Associate membership open to those with one book, a lesser number of short stories or publications or participation in the field such as editors, agents, reviewers, librarians, television producers, directors (dealing with the West). Patron memberships open to corporations, organizations and individuals with an interest in the West. Scope is international. Benefits: "By way of publications and conventions, members are kept abreast of developments in the field of Western literature and the publishing field, marketing requirements, income tax problems, copyright law, research facilities and techniques, and new publications. At conventions members have the opportunity for one-on-one conferences with editors, publishers and agents." Sponsors an annual four-day conference during fourth week of June featuring panels, lectures and seminars on publishing, writing and research. Includes the Spur Awards to honor authors of the best Western literature of the previous year. Publishes *Roundup Magazine* (6 times/year) for members. Available to nonmembers for $30. Publishes membership directory. Dues: $75 for active membership, $75 for associate membership, $250 for patron. For information on Spur Awards, send SASE.

WILLAMETTE WRITERS, 9045 SW Barbur Blvd., Suite 5A, Portland OR 97219. (503)452-1592. Fax: (503)452-0372. E-mail: wilwrite@teleport.com. Office Manager: Bill Johnson. Estab. 1965. Number of members: 700. "Willamette Writers is a nonprofit, tax exempt corporation staffed by volunteers. Membership is open to both published and aspiring writers. WW provides support, encouragement and interaction for all genres of writers." Open to national membership, but serves primarily the Pacific Northwest. Benefits include a writers' referral service, critique groups, membership discounts, youth programs (4th-12th grades), monthly meetings with guest authors, intern program, annual writing contest, community projects, library and research services, as well as networking with other writing groups, office with writing reference and screenplay library. Sponsors annual conference held the second weekend in August; quarterly workshops; annual Kay Snow Writing Contest; and the Distinguished Northwest Writer Award. Publishes *The Willamette Writer* monthly: a 12-page newsletter for members and complimentary subscriptions. Information consists of features, how-to's, mechanics of writing, profile of featured monthly speaker, markets, workshops, conferences and benefits available to writers. Dues: $36/year; includes subscription to newsletter. Meets first Tuesday of each month; board meeting held last Tuesday of each month. Send SASE for information.

THE WRITER'S CENTER, 4508 Walsh St., Bethesda MD 20815. (301)654-8664. Website: http://www.writer.org. Director: Allan Lefcowitz. Estab. 1977. Number of Members: 2,200. Open to: Anyone interested in writing. Scope is regional DC, Maryland, Virginia, West Virginia, Pennsylvania. Benefits include newsletter, discounts in bookstore, workshops, public events, subscriptions to *Poet Lore*, use of equipment and annual small press book fair. Center offers workshops, reading series, equipment, newsletter and limited workspace. Sponsors workshops, conferences, award for narrative poem. Publishes *Writer's Carousel*, bimonthly. Nonmembers can pick it up at the Center. Dues: $30/year. Fees vary with service, see publications. Brochures are available for SASE.

♣WRITERS' FEDERATION OF NEW BRUNSWICK, P.O. Box 37, Station A, Fredericton, New Brunswick E3B 4Y2 Canada. (902)423-8116. Project Coordinator: Anna Mae Snider. Estab. 1983. Number of Members: 230. Membership is open to anyone interested in writing. "This a provincial organization. Benefits include promotion of members' works through newsletter announcements and readings and launchings held at fall festival and annual general meeting. Services provided by WFNB include a Writers-in-Schools Program and manuscript reading. The WFNB sponsors a fall festival and an annual general meeting which feature workshops, readings and book launchings." There is also an annual literary competition, open to residents of New Brunswick only, which has prizes of $200, $100 and $30 in four categories: Fiction, nonfiction, children's literature and poetry; two $400 prizes for the best manuscript of poems (48 pgs.); the best short novel or collection of short stories and a category for young writers (14-18 years of age) which offers $150 (1st prize), $100 (2nd prize), $50 (3rd prize). Publishes a quarterly newsletter. Dues: $30/year. Board of Directors meets approximately 5 times a year. Annual General Meeting is held in the spring of each year. Send SASE for information.

♣**WRITERS' FEDERATION OF NOVA SCOTIA**, Suite 901, 1809 Barrington St., Halifax, Nova Scotia B3J 3K8 Canada. Executive Director: Jane Buss. Estab. 1976. Number of Members: 500. Type of Memberships: General membership, student membership, Nova Scotia Writers' Council membership (professional), Honorary Life Membership. Open to anyone who writes. Provincial scope, with a few members living elsewhere in the country or the world. Benefits include advocacy of all kinds for writers, plus such regular programs as workshops and regular publications, including directories and a newsletter. Sponsors workshops, two annual conferences (one for general membership, the other for the professional wing), two book awards, one annual competition for unpublished manuscripts in various categories; a writers in the schools program, a manuscript reading service, reduced photocopying rates. Publishes *Eastword*, 6 issues annually, available by subscription for $30 (Canadian) to nonmembers. Dues: $30/year (Canadian). Holds an annual general meeting, an annual meeting of the Nova Scotia Writers' Council, several board meetings annually. Send 5×7 SASE for information.

♣**WRITERS GUILD OF ALBERTA**, Percy Page Centre, 11759 Groat Rd., 3rd Floor, Edmonton, Alberta T5M 3K6 Canada. (403)422-8174. Fax: (403)422-2663. E-mail: writers@compusmart.ab.ca. Website: http://www.writersguildofalberta.ca. Executive Director: Miki Andrejevic. Estab. 1980. Number of Members: 700. Membership open to current and past residents of Alberta. Regional (provincial) scope. Benefits include discounts on programs offered; manuscript evaluation service available; bimonthly newsletter; contacts; info on workshops, retreats, readings, etc. Sponsors workshops 2 times/year, retreats 3 times/year, annual conference, annual book awards program (Alberta writers only). Publishes *WestWord* 6 times/year; available for $55/year (Canadian) to nonmembers. Dues: $60/year for regular membership; $20/year senior/students/limited income; $100/year donating membership—charitable receipt issued (Canadian funds). Organized monthly meetings. Send SASE for information.

WRITERS OF KERN, P.O. Box 6694, Bakersfield CA 93386-6694. (805)871-5834. President: Barbara Gabel. Estab. 1993. Number of members: 100. Affiliated with the California Writer's Club. Types of memberships: Professional, writers with published work; writers working toward publication, students. Open to published writers and any person interested in writing. Benefits of membership: Monthly meetings on the fourth Saturday of every month, except September which is our conference month, with speakers who are authors, agents, etc., on topics pertaining to writing; critique groups for several fiction genres, nonfiction, children's, journalism, poetry and screenwriting which meet weekly or biweekly; several of our members are successfully published and full-time writers; members receive a monthly newsletter with marketing tips, conferences and contests; access to club library; discount to annual conference. Annual conference held the third Saturday in September; annual writing contest with winners announced at the conference. Dues: $35/year, discount for students. Send SASE for information.

THE WRITERS ROOM, INC., 10 Astor Place, 6th Floor, New York NY 10003. (212)254-6995. Executive Director: Donna Brodie. Estab. 1978. Number of Members: 200 fulltime and 40 part-time. Open to: Any writer who shows a serious commitment to writing. "We serve a diverse population of writers, but most of our residents live in or around the NYC area. We encourage writers from around the country (and world!) to apply for residency if they plan to visit NYC for a while." Benefits include 24-hour access to the facility. "We provide desk space, storage areas for computers, typewriters, etc., a kitchen where coffee and tea are always available, bathrooms and a lounge. We also offer in-house workshops on topics of practical importance to writers and monthly readings of work-in-progress." Dues: $175 per quarter year. Send SASE for application and background information.

THE WRITERS' WORKSHOP, P.O. Box 696, 387 Beaucatcher Rd., Asheville NC 28805. (704)254-8111. Executive Director: Karen Ackerson. Estab. 1984. Number of Members: 1,250. Types of Memberships: Student/low income $25; family/organization $60; individual $35. Open to all writers. Scope is national and international. Benefits include discounts on workshops, quarterly newsletter, admission to Annual Celebration every summer, critiquing services through the mail. Center offers reading room, assistance with editing your work, contacts with NY writers and agents. Publishes a newsletter; also available to nonmembers ($18). Offers workshops year-round in NC and the South; 6 retreats a year, 25 readings with nationally awarded authors. Contests and classes for children and teens as well. Advisory board includes Kurt Vonnegut, E.L. Doctorow, Peter Matthiessen, Reynolds Price, John Le Carre and Eudora Welty. Also sponsors international contests in fiction, poetry and creative nonfiction. Brochures are available for SASE.

♣ **THE MAPLE LEAF** symbol before a listing indicates a Canadian publisher, magazine, conference or contest.

Publications of Interest to Fiction Writers

This section features listings for magazines and newsletters that focus on writing or the publishing industry. While many of these are not markets for fiction, they do offer articles, marketing advice or other information valuable to the fiction writer. Several magazines in this section offer actual market listings while others feature reviews of books in the field and news on the industry.

The timeliness factor is a primary reason most writers read periodicals. Changes in publishing happen very quickly and magazines can help you keep up with the latest news. Some magazines listed here, including *Writer's Digest*, cover the entire field of writing, while others such as *The Mystery Review* and *Children's Book Insider* focus on a particular type of writing. We've also added publications which focus on a particular segment of the publishing industry, including *Locus* (science fiction) and *Factsheet Five* (zines).

Information on some publications for writers can be found in the introductions to other sections in this book. In addition, many of the literary and commercial magazines for writers listed in the markets sections are helpful to the fiction writer. Keep an eye on the newsstand and library shelves for others and let us know if you've found a publication particularly useful.

ABOUT CREATIVE TIME SPACES, (formerly Havens for Creatives), ACT I Creativity Center, P.O. Box 30854, Palm Beach Gardens FL 33420. Editor: Charlotte Plotsky, M.S. International sourcebook of information, photos and other materials on retreats, colonies, communities, residencies and other programs for artists of all disciplines, including writers. Send SASE for details.

AWP CHRONICLE, Associated Writing Programs, George Mason University, Tallwood House, Mail Stop 1E3, Fairfax VA 22030. (703)993-4301. E-mail: awp@gmu.edu. Website: http://web.gmu.edu/departmawp. Editor: D.W. Fenza. 6 times/year. Essays on contemporary literature and articles on the teaching of creative writing only. Does *not* publish fiction. Lists fiction markets (back pages for "Submit"). Sample copies available; single copy price $5 (includes postage). Subscription: $20/year; $25/year Canada; $35/year overseas.

‡✽CANADIAN WRITER'S JOURNAL, Box 5180, New Liskeard, Ontario P0J 1P0 Canada. (705)647-6424. Fax: (705)647-8366. E-mail: dranchuk@aol.com. Editor: Deborah Ranchuk. Quarterly. "Mainly short how-to and motivational articles related to all types of writing and of interest to both new and established writers. Fiction is published in limited quantities, and needs are fully supplied through an annual (fall) short fiction contest. SASE for contest rules." Lists markets for fiction. Sample copies available for $5 ($C for Canadian orders, $US for US orders). Subscription price: $15/year; $25/2 years ($C for Canadian orders, $US for US orders).

CHILDREN'S BOOK INSIDER, P.O. Box 1030, Fairplay CO 80440-1030. E-mail: cbi@rmi.net. Website: http://www.write4kids.com. Editor/Publisher: Laura Backes. Monthly. "Publication is devoted solely to children's book writers and illustrators. 'At Presstime' section gives current market information each month for fiction, nonfiction and illustration submissions to publishers. Other articles include writing and illustration tips for fiction and nonfiction, interviews with published authors and illustrators, features on alternative publishing methods (self-publishing, co-op publishing, etc.), how to submit work to publishers, industry trends. Also publishes books and writing tools for both beginning and experienced children's book writers." Sample copy and catalog for SASE with 55¢ postage or e-mail children@mailback.com for free online catalog. Single copy price: $3.25. Subscription price: $29.95/year (US); $35/year (Canadian).

CROW QUARTERLY REVIEW, 147 Vera Marie Lane, Box 340, Rollinsville CO 80474. (303)258-0442. E-mail: kpmc@indra.com. Editor: Kevin McCarthy. Quarterly. "A review of *unpublished* and self-published work—sent to writers, editors, agents and producers. Helps writers market their work. Also serves to bridge the gap between the professions with writer's Crow Bar columns; writer's, editor's, agent's, producer's POV columns, feature articles and classified ads. Send 9×12 SASE for more info." Critiques and reviews unpublished and self-published novels, short story collections and nonfiction. Sample copies available for 9×12 SASE. Also available on the World Wide Web: http://ReadersNdex.com/crow/. "Writers should visit the website or write for info before sending anything.'

FACTSHEET FIVE, P.O. Box 170099, San Francisco CA 94117-0099. Editor: R. Seth Friedman. Biannually. "The definitive guide to the 'zine revolution. *Factsheet Five* reviews over 2,000 small press publications each issue. Send in your independent magazine for review." Sample copy: $6. Subscriptions: $20 for individuals and $40 for institutions.

‡FICTION WRITER'S GUIDELINE, P.O. Box 4065, Deerfield Beach, FL 33442. Editor: Blythe Camenson. Bimonthly. Our publication is "an 8 page newsletter with agent/editor/author interviews, how-to articles on writing fiction and getting it published, fiction markets, conference listings, Q&A column, success stories and more." Sample copies available for $3.50. Subscriptions: $39/year; free to members of Fiction Writer's Connection. "Membership in FWC is $59/year; includes a free newsletter, free critiquing, and a toll-free hotline for questions and free advice. Send SASE for information."

‡GILA QUEEN'S GUIDE TO MARKETS, P.O. Box 97, Newton NJ 07860-0097. Editor: Kathryn Ptacek. "Includes complete guidelines for fiction (different genres), poetry, nonfiction, greeting cards, etc. Also includes 'theme section' each month—science fiction/fantasy/horror, mystery/suspense, romance, western, comics, Canadian, regional, outdoor/sports, etc. and 'mini-markets.' Regular departments include new address listings, dead/ suspended markets, moving editors, anthologies, markets to be wary of, publishing news, etc. Every issue contains updates (of stuff listed in previous issues), new markets, conferences, contests. Publishes articles on writing topics, self-promotion, reviews of software and books of interest to writers, etc." Sample copy: $5. Subscriptions: $34/year (US); $38/year (Canada); $50/year (overseas). Writer's guidelines available for SASE (or IRC).

‡GOTHIC JOURNAL, P.O. Box 6340, Elko NV 89802-6340. (702)738-3520. Fax: (702)738-3524. E-mail: kglass@gothicjournal.com. Website: http://GothicJournal.com/romance/. Publisher: Kristi Lyn Glass. Bimonthly. "*Gothic Journal* is a news and review magazine for readers, writers and publishers of romantic suspense, romantic mysteries, and supernatural, gothic, and woman-in-jeopardy romance novels. It contains articles, reviews, letters, author profiles, market news, book lists and more." Lists fiction markets. Reviews novels and short story collections. Sample copies available for $4 plus $2 postage and handling. Subscriptions: $24/year (6 issues); $30/year (Canada); $36/year (foreign). Note: *As with other listings in this section, this is not a "market," do not send mss.*

GOTTA WRITE NETWORK LITMAG, Maren Publications, 515 E. Thacker, Hoffman Estates IL 60194-1957. Fax: (847)882-8054. E-mail: netera@aol.com. Editor: Denise Fleischer. Semiannually. Zine specializing in writing techniques. "Objective is to support the beginning writer, to teach him/her how to submit work, improve writing skills and look beyond rejection. The magazine is divided into three major sections: general information, Sci-Fi-Galleria and Literary Beat. It includes articles, fiction, interviews, poetry and market news." Sample copy for $5, 9×12 SAE and $1.50 postage. Subscriptions: $12.75/year (US); $15/year overseas.

LOCUS, The Newspaper of the Science Fiction Field, P.O. Box 13305, Oakland CA 94661. Editor: Charles N. Brown. Monthly. "Professional newsletter of science fiction, fantasy and horror; has news, interviews of authors, book reviews, column on electronic publishing, forthcoming books listings, monthly books-received listings, etc." Lists markets for fiction. Reviews novels or short story collections. Sample copies available. Single copy price: $4.50. Subscription price: $43/year, (2nd class mail) for US, $48 (US)/year, (2nd class) for Canada; $48 (US)/year (2nd class) for overseas.

♣THE MYSTERY REVIEW, A Quarterly Publication for Mystery & Suspense Readers, P.O. Box 233, Colborne, Ontario K0K 1S0 Canada. (613)475-4440. Editor: Barbara Davey. Quarterly. "Book reviews, information on new releases, interviews with authors and other people involved in mystery, 'real life' mysteries, out-of-print mysteries, mystery/suspense films, word games and puzzles with a mystery theme." Reviews mystery/suspense novels and short story collections. Send review copies to editor. Single copy price is $5.95 CDN in Canada/$5.95 US in the United States. Subscriptions: $21.50 CDN (includes GST) in Canada; $20 US in the US and $28 US elsewhere.

NEW WRITER'S MAGAZINE, P.O. Box 5976, Sarasota FL 34277. E-mail: newriters@aol.com. (941)953-7903. Editor: George J. Haborak. Bimonthly. "*New Writer's Magazine* is a publication for aspiring writers. It features 'how-to' articles, news and interviews with published and recently published authors. Will use fiction that has a tie-in with the world of the writer." Lists markets for fiction. Reviews novels and short story collections. Send review copies to Editor. Send #10 SASE for guidelines. Sample copies available; single copy price is $3. Subscriptions: $15/year, $25/two years. Canadian $20 (US funds). International $35/year (US funds).

OHIO WRITER, P.O. Box 91801, Cleveland OH 44101. (216)932-8444. Editor: Ron Antonucci. Bimonthly. "Interviews with Ohio writers of fiction and nonfiction; current fiction markets in Ohio." Lists fiction markets. Reviews novels and short story collections. Sample copies available for $2.50. Subscriptions: $12/year; $30/3 years; $18/institutional rate.

PROSETRY, Newsletter For, By, About Writers, P.O. Box 117727, Burlingame CA 94011-7727. Editor: P.D. Steele. Monthly. Estab. 1986. "A newsletter for writers, offering markets, conferences, exercises, information, workshops, and a monthly guest writer column with tips to the fiction and nonfiction writer." Reviews short story and poetry collections. Send review copies to P.D. Steele or E. B. Maynard. Sample copy available for 3 first-class stamps. Subscriptions: $12/year. Guidelines for #10 SASE.

THE REGENCY PLUME, 711 D. St. N.W., Ardmore OK 73401. Editor: Marilyn Clay. Bimonthly. "The newsletter focus is on providing accurate historical facts relating to the Regency period: customs, clothes, entertainment, the wars, historical figures, etc. I stay in touch with New York editors who acquire Regency romance novels. Current market info appears regularly in newsletter—see Bits & Scraps." Current Regency romances are "Previewed." Sample copy available for $3; single copy price is $3, $4 outside States. Subscriptions: $15/year for 6 issues; $18 Canada; $22 foreign. ("Check must be drawn on a US bank. Postal money order okay.") Back issues available. Send SASE for subscription information, article guidelines or list of research and writing aids available, such as audiotapes, historical maps, books on Regency period furniture, Regency romance writing contest, etc.

SCAVENGER'S NEWSLETTER, 519 Ellinwood, Osage City KS 66523. (913)528-3538. Editor: Janet Fox. Monthly. "A market newsletter for SF/fantasy/horror/mystery writers with an interest in the small press. Articles about SF/fantasy/horror/mystery writing/marketing. Now using Flash fiction to 1,200 words, genres as above. No writing-related material for fiction. Payment for articles and fiction is $4 on acceptance." Lists markets for fiction. Sample copies available. Single copy price: $2.50. Subscription price: $17/year, $8.50/6 months. Canada: $20, $10 overseas $26, $13 (US funds only).

SCIENCE FICTION CHRONICLE, P.O. Box 022730, Brooklyn NY 11202-0056. (718)643-9011. Editor: Andrew I. Porter. Monthly. Publishes nonfiction, nothing about UFO's. "Monthly newsmagazine for professional writers, editors, readers of SF, fantasy, horror." Lists markets for fiction "updated every 4 months." Reviews novels, small press publications, audiotapes, software, and short story collections. Send review copies to SFC and also to Don D'Ammassa, 323 Dodge St., E. Providence RI 02914. Sample copies available with 9 × 12 SAE with $1.24 postage; single copy price is $3.50 (US) or £3.50 (UK). Subscriptions: $35 bulk, $42 first class US and Canada; $49 overseas. *Note: As with other listings in this section, this is not a "market"—Do not send mss or artwork.*

‡**THE SMALL PRESS BOOK REVIEW**, P.O. Box 176, Southport CT 06490. (203)332-7629. Editor: Henry Berry. Quarterly. "Brief reviews of all sorts of books from small presses/independent publishers." Addresses of publishers are given in reviews. Reviews novels and short story collections. Send review copies to editor. Published electronically via the Internet.

SMALL PRESS REVIEW/SMALL MAGAZINE REVIEW, P.O. Box 100, Paradise CA 95967. (916)877-6110. Editor: Len Fulton. Monthly. "Publishes news and reviews about small publishers, books and magazines." Lists markets for fiction and poetry. Reviews novels, short story and poetry collections. Sample copies available. Subscription price: $25/year.

‡**SPECULATIONS**, 1111 W. El Camino Real, Suite 109-400, Sunnyvale CA 94087-1057. E-mail: editor@speculations.com. Website: http://www.speculations.com. Editor: Denise Lee. Bimonthly. "Magazine for writers who wish to break into or increase their presence within the science fiction, fantasy, horror or 'other' speculative fiction genres. We publish instruction, advice, editorials, columns, genre-specific articles, questions and answers with the experts, resource guides, interviews with editors, publishers and agents, and—of course—the best market information available anywhere." Sample copies free. Subscriptions: $25/year in US; $30/year in Canada; $40/year overseas.

‡**A VIEW FROM THE LOFT**, 66 Malcolm Ave. SE, Minneapolis MN 55414. (612)379-8999. Editor: Ellen Hawley. Monthly. "Publishes articles on writing and list of markets for fiction, poetry and creative nonfiction." Sample copies available; single copy price is $4 US. Subscriptions: $40 in Twin Cities metro area; $25 elsewhere in US; $35 international, $20 low income student. (Subscription available only as part of Loft membership; rates are membership rates.)

---

‡ **THE DOUBLE DAGGER** before a listing indicates that the listing is new in this edition.

INSIDER REPORT

Everything old is new again

Where are the floating cars? Where are the robot maids? Where are the geodesic domed houses on stilts filled with buttons and gadgets to take all the tedium out of life? Still only in fiction. That fiction, like our houses, cars and maids, is essentially the same as it was 50 and 60 years ago when these concepts of the future were born. Our buildings have foundations, our cars run on internal combustion, and our fiction still comes in magazines or books. And despite the proliferation of fiction on the Internet, the best writing will continue to published on paper, say the editors of *Speculations* magazine.

Kent Brewster

Speculations, which can be found in both print and electronic form, doesn't publish fiction. Instead, its pages hold gems of wisdom and encouragement to help struggling writers of science fiction, fantasy, horror and other genres that fall under the heading of speculative fiction. "I wanted to read a magazine like *Speculations*, only there wasn't one. So I started it myself, if that makes any sense," says publisher Kent Brewster. "What helped me enormously in my multiple attempts to break into the market was the friendly attitude of a few professional writers who spent their free time hanging out on CompuServe and GEnie, two online services. They were willing to patiently answer the same frequently asked questions over and over again, but their answers kept scrolling off into the bit bucket when other messages were posted. So I thought . . . okay, maybe people would pay to read this in a magazine, and maybe those pros would like to get paid for their work. And the rest, as they say, is history."

Kent grouped the concepts of professional advice, peer encouragement and solid market news to make *Speculations* an invaluable assistant to writers, including himself. "I've been writing and selling short stories for about six years; the closest brush with the big time I've had yet was a Nebula nomination this year, for 'In the Pound, Near Breaktime,' published in *Tomorrow Speculative Fiction*." *Speculations* editor Denise Lee is also familiar with the trials of writing. "My editorial experience comes not from speculative fiction," she says, "but mainstream poetry." However, she recently sold her first book, a science fiction novel.

But both of these writers, steeped in the future through their fiction, see publishing in more traditional terms. "There are an awful lot of people out there who are getting the same bright idea at the same time: why not eliminate all the hard work and expense of paper publication and just take the stories straight to the readers, using the Internet?" Brewster says. "Unfortunately, most of these people—with the notable exceptions of Algis Budrys and Ellen Datlow, of *TomorrowSF* and *Omni Online*—don't have any real experience in publishing. So selling them a story is the equivalent of being published in one of

INSIDER REPORT, *Brewster*

those hobby-level zines. The real professionals don't deal with them, their quality of fiction suffers, their readership drops to zero, they go away after a couple of issues, and there's another statistic on the side of the naysayers. Delivering professional fiction on the Internet will require some mechanism to ensure that the writer gets read and gets paid. So far, nobody's come up with anything that makes sense."

Brewster is also skeptical about the "zine revolution." He calls printing "big business" and believes for a magazine to be successful it needs investors who want to see a return on their money. "Maintaining a steady flow of money and putting out a very nice magazine can be done, but it's more of a family-business proposition; look at *Fantasy & Science Fiction* for one excellent example. Corporate backers aren't just interested in steady money; they want bigger money every year, so they can get more for the company when they sell it to somebody else."

So while we still read our fiction the same way we did in the 1920s and '30s, the publishing climate has become much less writer friendly. "You could make a living writing short stories back then," Brewster says. "Unfortunately, the average rate of pay hasn't changed—it's still three to seven cents a word—and the number of truly professional markets has dropped to about five. We've also seen a tremendous dumbing-down of the market since then, mostly due to the evil influence of television, blockbuster movies, and their inevitable spawn, tie-in books. The bookstores sell more Star Trek books, so that's what they stock. That's what they stock, so that's what the kids buy. That's what the kids read, so that's why the kids get tired of reading, since those books contain the same story over and over again, with no real changes or progress in the lives of the characters."

Oddly enough, it's character-driven stories that today's editors hunger for the most. Brewster says, "We've recently interviewed Algis Budrys, Stanley Schmidt, Gardner Dozois, Ellen Datlow, Shawna McCarthy, Bryan Cholfin and Gordon Van Gelder. In general, they all agreed that they're not seeing enough character-driven stories with classical-form plots—you know, all that boring stuff they taught you in Comp 101, like a beginning, middle and end—and satisfying thematic resolution, in which the events transpiring in the story actually turn out to make sense." Lee adds that it's also much harder to break into speculative fiction today. The glut of TV shows and movies makes it even harder for books to win our attention. "Back in the '30s, the fans were hungry for anything with robots, bug-eyed monsters or flying saucers in it." You could submit a story hand-written in crayon (well, almost), and it stood a good chance of being published. Today, the fiction printed in the top speculative markets rivals mainstream fiction in quality. Often, it's better. So you've got to be really good. Ironically, this doesn't at all contradict what Kent said."

In many ways today's speculative fiction market is both better and worse than its heyday in the pulps. The writing has to be top notch to compete in an increasingly competitive market, but the pay is as low as a writer's chance for success. Brewster and Lee agree there is no magic formula to publication. There are no trade secrets to get you through the door. But a little solid marketing advice never hurt anyone.

"The advice I believe in is to always start with the top markets—the ones that pay the most, reach the most readers, and respond in the shortest amount of time—and work down. Once your story has been out to every possible market, you have a choice. You can trunk it for later rewrite—and possible sale to a large market, assuming you break in with something else—or you can start sending it around to the minor leagues. I tend to think that any story that's been rejected by 20 to 80 professional editors probably has something wrong with it, so I trunk 'em. But that's just me. In the end, it's up to you."

"What Kent said," Lee agrees. "Except that in the horror subgenre, few large, professional magazine markets exist. Besides *Cemetery Dance* and *Worlds of Fantasy and Horror*, I can't think of any. Semi-prozine publication in horror may be inevitable if the writer wants exposure." But Lee's best advice for writers no matter what their genre is simple. "Submit, submit, submit. And then submit some more. They can't buy it if it ain't out there."

—Megan Lane

WRITER'S DIGEST, 1507 Dana Ave., Cincinnati OH 45207. (513)531-2690. Editor: Thomas Clark. Monthly. "*Writer's Digest* is a magazine of techniques and markets. We *inspire* the writer to write, *instruct* him or her on how to improve that work, and *direct* him or her toward appropriate markets." Lists markets for fiction, nonfiction, poetry. Single copy price: $3.50. Subscription price: $27.

WRITER'S DIGEST BOOKS–MARKET BOOKS, 1507 Dana Ave., Cincinnati OH 45207. (513)531-2222. Annual. In addition to *Novel & Short Story Writer's Market*, Writer's Digest Books also publishes *Writer's Market*, *Poet's Market*, *Children's Writer's and Illustrator's Market*, *Mystery Writer's Sourcebook*, *Science Fiction and Fantasy Writer's Sourcebook*, *Romance Writer's Sourcebook* and the *Guide to Literary Agents*. All include articles and listings of interest to writers. All are available at bookstores, libraries or through the publisher. (Request catalog.)

WRITERS' JOURNAL, Val-Tech Publishing, Inc., P.O. Box 25376, St. Paul MN 55125-0376. Managing Editor: Valerie Hockert. Bimonthly. "Provides a creative outlet for writers of fiction." Sample copies available. Single copy price: $3.99; $5.75 (Canadian). Subscription price: $19.97; $23.97 Canada.

WRITER'S YEARBOOK, 1507 Dana Ave., Cincinnati OH 45207. (513)531-2690. Editor: Thomas Clark. Annual. "A collection of the best writing *about* writing, with an exclusive survey of the year's 100 top markets for article-length nonfiction." Single copy price: $4.99.

*ZENE, 5 Martins Lane, Witcham Ely, Cambs CB6 2LB England. Editor: Andy Cox. Quarterly (but may be monthly soon). *Zene* is a guide to independent literary markets worldwide. We list complete contributors' guidelines, including subscription details, plus updates, news and feedback from writers. Every issue contains wide-ranging articles by leading writers, editors, publishers, ER, plus interviews, letters, market info, etc. We are international, with correspondents and guidelines from all over the world." Lists fiction markets. Reviews novels, magazines and short story collections. Subscriptions: $16 (AIR), "US checks payable to TTA Press" OK.

Websites of Interest

BY MEGAN LANE

More and more these days, I find myself wondering how I ever lived without the Internet and the World Wide Web. I'm sure I got out more in those ancient times, but I never felt as powerful or as confident about being able to find the answer to any question my inquisitive brain might pose. Even if you refuse to use the Internet, it's virtually impossible to ignore it. Web addresses are popping up in the corners of TV screens, in print ads and even on the packaging of food we eat. But despite all the naying of the naysayers, there is useful information to be found in the vast network of cyberspace. So, enough with the excuses. Even if you don't own a computer, your local library does and now that you can easily access the Internet through your television, you'll have to find some more difficult bit of technology to shun. And even though my eyes are bloodshot from surfing for the past several hours (or is it days?), I've managed to compile a tiny and woefully incomplete listing of websites that fiction writers shouldn't miss.

LITERARY FICTION

The English Server Fiction Collection: http://english-server.hss.cmu.edu/fiction/. "This site offers works of and about fiction collected from our members, contributing authors worldwide, and texts in the public domain." Includes: short fiction, novels, magazines of and about contemporary fiction and criticism, Internet sites publishing fiction, literary criticism, organizations which present awards for excellent fiction, plays, screenplays and dramatic criticism, epic and short verse, and poetic criticism.

Zuzu's Petals Literary Resources: http://www.lehigh.net/zuzu/index.htm. "With 3500+ organized links to helpful resources for writers, artists, performers, and researchers, it is our goal to unearth and present some of the best links and information for the online creative community." Includes links to magazines, readings, conferences, workshops and more.

GENRE FICTION

Children's Literature Web Guide: http://www.ucalgary.ca/~dkbrown/index.html. "The Children's Literature Web Guide is an attempt to gather together and categorize the growing number of Internet resources related to books for children and young adults. Much of the information you can find through these pages is provided by others: fans, schools, libraries, and commercial enterprises involved in the book world." This comprehensive site for children's book writers and illustrators includes links to authors, publishers, booksellers, conferences and events, as well as other sites of interest.

Con-Tour: http://www.con-tour.com. "Con-Tour is a magazine for people who enjoy the fantasy, sci-fi, comic, gaming, and related conventions that are held all over the world. ConTour features listings of upcoming conventions, with highlights and reviews. We also have interviews with guests, fans, artists; and writers; pictures of fans, and nude pictorials of the women (and men) of fandom." The web version includes a list of conventions with hot links to their own websites. A 1-year subscription to the print magazine costs $30. Send a check to ConTour at 196 Alps Rd., Suite 2342, Athens, GA. 30606. The website and magazine are not for the faint of heart, but true fanatics will have fun with what the zany editors throw at them.

LitWeb: A Collection of Literature and Writing Resources: http://www.arcana.com/shannon/litweb.html. A collection of links to sites of interest to fiction writers and readers. Categories include genres like westerns and science fiction. Also includes links to authors' sites.

The Market List: http://www.marketlist.com. Web magazine of genre fiction marketing information. "Each version includes over 100 current markets for genre fiction, with info on response times, genres accepted, payment rates and more."

The Mystery Writers' Forum: http://www.zott.com/mysforum/default.html. "This is a threaded bulletin board system geared specifically for writers and aspiring writers interested in gaining information about the publishing industry, writing advice and business information about the mystery genre." Discussions are separated into categories including agents, bookstores, contests, critique corner, death details and industry news.

Romance Central: http://home1.gte.net/romcen/index1.htm. "Workshops are the heart of Romance Central. When we share knowlege and exchange ideas, we enhance our work and ourselves. Writers should view their peers as brothers and sisters, not competition. And by peers, I mean anyone who feels compelled to put words on paper." Great place for giving and receiving advice about romance writing.

Roundup Online Magazine: http://www.imt.net/~gedison/wwa.html. Official magazine of the Western Writers of America. Includes contest information, reviews of westerns and essays about the genre.

MAGAZINES

Electronic Newsstand: http://enews.com. Massive index of commercial magazines, searchable by title. Provides links to the magazine's website, description of current issue, subscription information and recommendations for similar magazines. A magazine in itself, this site also offers news about the magazine publishing industry and updates on the goings on at individual magazines.

John Hewitt's Writer's Resource Center: http://www.azstarnet.com/~poewar/writer/writer.html. Comprehensive writing site that includes links to consumer, trade and literary magazines. Also catalogs articles by Hewitt covering topics from overcoming writer's isolation to a directory of writers' colonies, associations and organizations of interest to writers.

BOOK PUBLISHERS

A-list Ingram Top Demand: http://www.ingrambook.com/Surf/product_info/category_info/fiction.htm. Lists by category of top 50 books requested from the book distributor Ingram. Includes links to descriptions of the books, complete with publisher names and ISBNs. Great way to see who's publishing the best in each genre. Includes adult, espionage/thriller, fantasy, general fiction, men's adventure, historical, religious, mystery/detective, horror, psychological suspense, romance, science fiction and western.

AcqWeb's Directory of Publisher and Vendors: http://www.library.vanderbilt.edu/law/acqs/pubr.html. Gigantic catalog of links to publishers. Subject headings include: general and multiple subject publishers, associations and institutes, electronic publications including online & CD-ROM, reprints, university presses, literature and fiction, children's literature, poetry, science fiction and fantasy.

Arachnoid Writer's Alliance: http://www.vena.com/arachnoid. This site "presents a collection of books for sale by independent and self-published authors." Gives you an idea of what struggling writers are up to. Includes author bios, contact information and short excerpts from books.

Books A to Z: http://www.booksatoz.com. "This site is intended to be a working tool to enable anyone to produce, distribute or find books. We will also list large numbers of resources for research in books and libraries. All of these areas are neglected and often overlooked in the commercial world. We will not attempt to make a gigantic site listing everything, but we will attempt to provide access to at least some resources in every area of book production, sales and research." Includes links to professional and creative services, production and technical info, bookmaking materials for sale, organizations and groups, events and news, book and music publishers, bookstores and searchers, marketing and distribution, academic and research tools.

Publishers' Catalogs: http://www.lights.com/publisher. This massive site includes a specific geographic index, which lists countries like Albania, Luxembourg, Thailand and Uruguay, as well as the US and UK. The alphabetical lists of publishers link with their websites. But what sets this site apart is its webhosting service for publishers. If a company doesn't have its catalog online, Northern Lights Internet Solutions can do it for them.

ORGANIZATIONS

Canadian Authors Association: http://www.islandnet.com/~caa/national.html. "The Association was founded to promote recognition of Canadian writers and their works, and to foster and develop a climate favorable to the creative arts. Its objectives:
To work for the encouragement and protection of writers.
To speak for writers before government and other inquires.
To sponsor awards and otherwise encourage work of literary and artistic merit.
To publish *Canadian Author, The Canadian Writer's Guide* and other publications designed to improve the professionalism of Canadian writers."

Horror Writers Association: http://www.horror.org. "The Horror Writers Association (HWA) was formed in the 1980s to bring together writers and others professionally interested in horror and dark fantasy, and to foster a greater appreciation of dark fiction among the general public. To this end, among other benefits, the organization issues a regular newsletter, presents the Bram Stoker Awards, and provides members with the latest news on paying markets. We have sponsored a series of successful members-only anthologies. Members also gain access to the private HWA areas on various online services, including Genie's Science Fiction Roundtables (especially SFRT4), Compuserve's SFLitForum 2, SFF-Net, and Dueling Modems, and can, if they choose, receive informational bulletins by e-mail."

Lesbian Writers Guild: http://members.aol.com/lezbnlit/lwg/index.html. "We are a group of women who are dedicated to providing an environment for lesbian writers to showcase their work and gain valuable information on techniques, critiques and industry standards. Whether you are a 'new' writer or a seasoned pro, we hope you will enjoy our pages and provide the stories, poems, interviews and tips we need to contribute to our community."

National Writers Union: http://www.nwu.org/nwu. "The National Writers Union (NWU) is the trade union for freelance writers of all genres. We are committed to improving the economic and working conditions of freelance writers through the collective strength of our members. We are a modern, innovative union offering grievance-resolution, industry campaigns, contract advice, health and dental plans, member education, job banks, networking, social events and much more. The NWU is affiliated with the United Automobile Workers (UAW) and through them with the AFL-CIO. Founded in 1983, the NWU has local and organizing committees throughout the country. Our 4,500 members include journalists, book authors, poets, copywriters, academic authors, cartoonists, and technical and business writers. The NWU has a Supporters Circle open to individuals or organizations who are not writers but wish to support the union.''

PEN American Center: http://www.pen.org. ''PEN American Center, the largest of nearly130 Centers worldwide that compose International PEN, is a membership association of prominent literary writers and editors. As a major voice of the literary community, the organization seeks to defend the freedom of expression wherever it may be threatened, and to promote and encourage the recognition and reading of contemporary literature.''

Romance Writers of America: http://www.rwanational.com. ''RWA is a non-profit professional/educational association of 8,200 romance writers and other industry professionals. We are 'The Voice of Romance.' ''

Society of Children's Book Writers and Illustrators: http://www.scbwi.org. ''The only professional organization dedicated to serving the people who write, illustrate, or share a vital interest in children's literature. Whether you are a professional writer, a famous illustrator, a beginner with a good idea, or somewhere in-between, SCBWI is here to serve you. Our website has a dual purpose: It exists as a service to our members as well as offering information about the children's publishing industry and our organization to non-members.''

The Writers Guild of America: http://www.wga.org. ''Home of the 8,500 professional writers who, since 1933, have created your favorite movies, television shows, and now, many of your favorite interactive games. All of these visions started with a script and a writer. In the beginning was the word. And the word was funny, dramatic, romantic, terrifying and dozens of other things that have entertained, moved and educated you. Here at our website, we hope to make film, television, interactive and other mass media writing—and writers—more familiar and accessible. Whether you are a writer, an aspiring writer, an entertainment professional or purely a member of the viewing public, we are happy to have you visit with us.''

INSPIRATION

Creating a Celebration of Women Writers: http://www.cs.cmu.edu/afs/cs.cmu.edu/user/mmbt/www/women/celebration.html. ''While a number of original sources are already available on the World Wide Web, there are many gaps in the available material. We therefore hope to encourage many people to contribute texts and supporting information about women writers. We propose to make the construction of the exhibit a public process, providing a shared resource for information about the materials in preparation. An initial list of women writers and available online works is provided. We hope that people will commit to scanning or typing in specific works. People are welcome to suggest further additions to the list. We are looking for complete works (not excerpts or single chapters) that are either in the public domain, or authorized by the copyright holder. (Details about copyright restrictions and instructions for submitting works are provided.) As people agree to scan in resources, their names and the works they have agreed to enter will be annotated to the list.'' This site is an amazing resource of links to the works and biographies of women writers throughout history as well as other resources for and about women writers.

Rejection Slips: http://www.linkline.com/personal/bbyun/bryan/rejection/reject.html. ''This page is devoted to my ever-growing pile of rejection slips, amassed over the course of the three years I have been submitting manuscripts to various publishers. It's a fairly tiny stack compared to the collection I'm sure more experienced writers have stored away in their drawers, but I hope to add to it in the future. I created this page in part because I don't know what else to do with these things, aside from tossing them, and also on the off chance that a fellow struggling writer or two might wish to peek into the private hell of another unpublished scribe wallowing in the juices of his own frustrated ambitions." This is a light-hearted look at one man's battle with rejection. Also features articles by Susan Shaughnessy and Anne Lamott about the realities of rejection and the publishing world.

The Unpublished Writer: http://www.unpub.com. "Only writing that has been rejected by other publications, accompanied by that rejection letter, is eligible for publication on this site. With nothing more than the support of friends and simmering anger about having some of my poetry rejected, I started this site for others like myself. Before I knew it, misery found company and the site started becoming populated with other such authors posting some stellar work."

WRITING RULES

Elements of Style by William Strunk, Jr.: http://www.columbia.edu/acis/bartleby/strunk. The full text of the English language's most used guide to grammar.

Grammar Girl's Guide to the English Language: http://www.geocities.com/Athens/Parthe non/1489. If Strunk is too dry for you, try Grammar Girl—a supereditor with an attitude. She's compiled a mass of rules and pet peeves to steer any wayward writer back onto the good grammar track.

The Inkspot: http://www.inkspot.com. "Inkspot is a resource for writers. The Internet is a rich resource of information useful to writers but changes so quickly each day that it is often difficult to keep up with new developments. I started Inkspot for my own personal use but realized that other writers might benefit from it as well." Offers many, many links to writing resources on the Web. Definitely a good place to start looking for answers to any writing-related question.

Mot Juste—Secrets of the Savvy Writer: http://www.ceridwyn.com/motjuste/main.html. This site includes:
"The Best Query Letter Ever!—Find out how you can make an excellent first impression with any publisher or literary agent by writing the best query letter ever. A full listing of good sites for writers is included.
The Savvy Quiz—Are you really ready to send in your manuscript? The Savvy Quiz can help you determine whether you are or aren't.
Ask Ceridwyn—Read this bulletin board moderated by a publishing professional, answering posted questions on various aspects of the publishing industry.
Graphospasm—Contribute to the online watchdog network for writers, designed to help you avoid those agents and publishers whose business practices are a little shady.
PenFriends—The new writer's networking web, PenFriends allows you to post and respond to messages without the aggravation of endless commercial postings!"
Great site especially in its function as a watchdog over the publishing industry. The comments posted by writers about their experiences with agents is extremely enlightening. The Savvy Quiz is also a great way to get a quick refresher course on proper manuscript submission.

William Safire's Rules for Writers: http://www.chem.gla.ac.uk/protein/pert/safire.rules.html. File this under great things to tape next to your computer—a tongue-in-cheek look at some important grammar rules.

RESEARCH RESOURCES

The Crime Writer: http://www.svn.net/mikekell/crimewriter.html. "If you are an author in the areas of true crime or criminology, published or not, this is your site. We hope to provide a meeting place and resources for authors in this genre who use the Internet as a primary source of information gathering, researching and networking." Includes links to resources that provide information on crime, current crime news and the criminal justice system, as well as general writing and news resources.

Directory of Science Sites: http://www.softsolutions.com/links/science.html. To add a little science to your fiction try this collection of scientific sites. Includes NASA Information Services, Space Frontier Foundation and the Voyager Project Home Page, among others. What this page lacks in visual appeal it makes up for in great resources.

ViVa: A Current Bibliography of Women's History in Historical and Women's Studies Journals: http://www.iisg.nl/~womhist/. "ViVa is short for 'Vrouwengeschiedenis in het Vaktijdschrift', which is Dutch for 'Women's history in scholarly periodicals'. Articles in English, French, German and Dutch are selected for ViVa from more than 60 European and American periodicals." Great place to find details about the daily lives of women throughout history. Sample citation: "Anderson, Olive, 'Emigration and marriage break up in mid-Victorian England', Economic History Review 50 (1997) 1, 104-109."

Dr. Jim Weinrich's AIDS and Sexology Page: http://math.ucsd.edu/~weinrich. Don't snicker. This page of information and links is invaluable to any writer of contemporary fiction. The prime rule of fiction—write what you know—should really be write what you can learn a lot about. This site allows you to safely learn the how's and why's of human sexuality as well as its devastating modern consequences.

The best way to find information about specific research topics is through a search engine like Yahoo (http://www.yahoo.com) or Infoseek (http://guide-p.infoseek.com). I did an exact phrase search on Yahoo for "life in" and came up with 478 matches. The websites covered everything from life in concentration camps to life in early Wisconsin to retired life in a motor home to life in ancient Egypt.

It still amazes me how much information waits at our fingertips. Certainly a vast portion of the Internet is taken up by commercial sites and time wasters, but the rest is filled with invaluable resources that are only a deep breath and a few mouse clicks away. If you lack experience with computers or the Internet, the library may be the best place to start. They can offer you friendly advice and a guiding hand. Otherwise, hop on board and start surfing. Your fiction will shine with the details you glean from cyberspace and every little touch can put you that much closer to your ultimate goal—publication.

❦Canadian Writers Take Note

While much of the information contained in this section applies to all writers, here are some specifics of interest to Canadian writers:

Postage: At press time, the cost of one International Reply Coupon in Canada is $3.50 (Canadian). A 7 percent GST tax is required on postage in Canada and for mail with postage under $5 going to destinations outside the country. Since Canadian postage rates are voted on in January of each year (after we go to press), contact a Canada Post Corporation Customer Service Division, located in most cities in Canada, for the most current rates.

Copyright: For information on copyrighting your work and to obtain forms, write Copyright and Industrial Design, Phase One, Place du Portage, 50 Victoria St., Hull, Quebec K1A 0C9 or call (819)997-1936.

The public lending right: The Public Lending Right Commission has established that eligible Canadian authors are entitled to payments when a book is available through a library. Payments are determined by a sampling of the holdings of a representative number of libraries. To find out more about the program and to learn if you are eligible, write to the Public Lending Right Commission at 350 Albert St., P.O. Box 1047, Ottawa, Ontario K1P 5V8 or call (613)566-4378 for information. The Commission, which is part of The Canada Council, produces a helpful pamphlet, *How the PLR System Works,* on the program.

Grants available to Canadian writers: Most province art councils or departments of culture provide grants to resident writers. Some of these, as well as contests for Canadian writers, are listed in our Contests and Awards section. For national programs, contact The Canada Council, Writing and Publishing Section, P.O. Box 1047, Ottawa, Ontario K1P 5V8 or call (613)566-4338 for information or e-mail: silvie.bernier@canadacouncil.ca.

For more information: More details on much of the information listed above and additional information on writing and publishing in Canada are included in the *Writer's Essential Desk Reference: A Companion to Writer's Market,* 2nd edition, published by Writer's Digest Books. In addition to information on a wide range of topics useful to all writers, the book features a detailed chapter for Canadians, Writing and Selling in Canada, by Fred Kerner.

See the Organizations and Resources section of *Novel & Short Story Writer's Market* for listings of writers' organizations in Canada. Also contact The Writer's Union of Canada, 24 Ryerson Ave., Toronto, Ontario M5T 2P3; call them at (416)703-8982 or fax them at (416)703-0826. This organization provides a wealth of information (as well as strong support) for Canadian writers, including specialized publications on publishing contracts; contract negotiations; the author/editor relationship; author awards, competitions and grants; agents; taxes for writers, libel issues and access to archives in Canada.

Printing and Production Terms Defined

In most of the magazine listings in this book you will find a brief physical description of each publication. This material usually includes the number of pages, type of paper, type of binding and whether or not the magazine uses photographs or illustrations.

Although it is important to look at a copy of the magazine to which you are submitting, these descriptions can give you a general idea of what the publication looks like. This material can provide you with a feel for the magazine's financial resources and prestige. Do not, however, rule out small, simply produced publications as these may be the most receptive to new writers. Watch for publications that have increased their page count or improved their production from year to year. This is a sign the publication is doing well and may be accepting more fiction.

You will notice a wide variety of printing terms used within these descriptions. We explain here some of the more common terms used in our listing descriptions. We do not include explanations of terms such as Mohawk and Karma which are brand names and refer to the paper manufacturer. *Getting it Printed*, by Mark Beach (Writer's Digest Books), is an excellent publication for those interested in learning more about printing and production.

PAPER

acid-free: Paper that has a low or no acid content. This type of paper resists deterioration from exposure to the elements. More expensive than many other types of paper, publications done on acid-free paper can last a long time.

bond: Bond paper is often used for stationery and is more transparent than text paper. It can be made of either sulphite (wood) or cotton fiber. Some bonds have a mixture of both wood and cotton (such as "25 percent cotton" paper). This is the type of paper most often used in photocopying or as standard typing paper.

coated/uncoated stock: Coated and uncoated are terms usually used when referring to book or text paper. More opaque than bond, it is the paper most used for offset printing. As the name implies, uncoated paper has no coating. Coated paper is coated with a layer of clay, varnish or other chemicals. It comes in various sheens and surfaces depending on the type of coating, but the most common are dull, matte and gloss.

cover stock: Cover stock is heavier book or text paper used to cover a publication. It comes in a variety of colors and textures and can be coated on one or both sides.

CS1/CS2: Most often used when referring to cover stock, CS1 means paper that is coated only on one side; CS2 is paper coated on both sides.

newsprint: Inexpensive absorbent pulp wood paper often used in newspapers and tabloids.

text: Text paper is similar to book paper (a smooth paper used in offset printing), but it has been given some texture by using rollers or other methods to apply a pattern to the paper.

vellum: Vellum is a text paper that is fairly porous and soft.

Some notes about paper weight and thickness: Often you will see paper thickness described in terms of pounds such as 80 lb. or 60 lb. paper. The weight is determined by figuring how many pounds in a ream of a particular paper (a ream is 500 sheets). This can be confusing, however, because this figure is based on a standard sheet size and standard sheet sizes vary depending on the type of paper used. This information is most helpful when comparing papers of the same type. For example, 80 lb. book paper versus 60 lb. book paper. Since the size of the paper is the same it would follow that 80 lb. paper is the thicker, heavier paper.

Some paper, especially cover stock, is described by the actual thickness of the paper. This is expressed in a system of points. Typical paper thicknesses range from 8 points to 14 points thick.

PRINTING

letterpress: Letterpress printing is printing that uses a raised surface such as type. The type is inked and then pressed against the paper. Unlike offset printing, only a limited number of impressions can be made, as the surface of the type can wear down.

offset: Offset is a printing method in which ink is transferred from an image-bearing plate to a "blanket" and from the blanket to the paper.

sheet-fed offset: Offset printing in which the paper is fed one piece at a time.

web offset: Offset printing in which a roll of paper is printed and then cut apart to make individual sheets.

There are many other printing methods but these are the ones most commonly referred to in our listings.

BINDING

case binding: In case binding, signatures (groups of pages) are stitched together with thread rather than glued together. The stitched pages are then trimmed on three sides and glued into a hardcover or board "case" or cover. Most hardcover books and thicker magazines are done this way.

comb binding: A comb is a plastic spine used to hold pages together with bent tabs that are fed through punched holes in the edge of the paper.

perfect binding: Used for paperback books and heavier magazines, perfect binding involves gathering signatures (groups of pages) into a stack, trimming off the folds so the edge is flat and gluing a cover to that edge.

saddle stitched: Publications in which the pages are stitched together using metal staples. This fairly inexpensive type of binding is usually used with books or magazines that are under 80 pages.

Smythe-sewn: Binding in which the pages are sewn together with thread. Smythe is the name of the most common machine used for this purpose.

spiral binding: A wire spiral that is wound through holes punched in pages is a spiral bind. This is the binding used in spiral notebooks.

Glossary

Advance. Payment by a publisher to an author prior to the publication of a book, to be deducted from the author's future royalties.

All rights. The rights contracted to a publisher permitting a manuscript's use anywhere and in any form, including movie and book club sales, without additional payment to the writer.

Anthology. A collection of selected writings by various authors.

Auction. Publishers sometimes bid against each other for the acquisition of a manuscript that has excellent sales prospects.

Backlist. A publisher's books not published during the current season but still in print.

Book producer/packager. An organization that may develop a book for a publisher based upon the publisher's idea or may plan all elements of a book, from its initial concept to writing and marketing strategies, and then sell the package to a book publisher and/or movie producer.

Cliffhanger. Fictional event in which the reader is left in suspense at the end of a chapter or episode, so that interest in the story's outcome will be sustained.

Clip. Sample, usually from a newspaper or magazine, of a writer's published work.

Cloak-and-dagger. A melodramatic, romantic type of fiction dealing with espionage and intrigue.

Commercial. Publishers whose concern is salability, profit and success with a large readership.

Contemporary. Material dealing with popular current trends, themes or topics.

Contributor's copy. Copy of an issue of a magazine or published book sent to an author whose work is included.

Copublishing. An arrangement in which the author and publisher share costs and profits.

Copyediting. Editing a manuscript for writing style, grammar, punctuation and factual accuracy.

Copyright. The legal right to exclusive publication, sale or distribution of a literary work.

Cover letter. A brief letter sent with a complete manuscript submitted to an editor.

"Cozy" (or "teacup") mystery. Mystery usually set in a small British town, in a bygone era, featuring a somewhat genteel, intellectual protagonist.

Cyberpunk. Type of science fiction, usually concerned with computer networks and human-computer combinations, involving young, sophisticated protagonists.

E-mail. Mail that has been sent electronically using a computer and modem.

Experimental fiction. Fiction that is innovative in subject matter and style; avant-garde, non-formulaic, usually literary material.

Exposition. The portion of the storyline, usually the beginning, where background information about character and setting is related.

Fair use. A provision in the copyright law that says short passages from copyrighted material may be used without infringing on the owner's rights.

Fanzine. A noncommercial, small-circulation magazine usually dealing with fantasy, horror or science-fiction literature and art.

First North American serial rights. The right to publish material in a periodical before it appears in book form, for the first time, in the United States or Canada.

Galleys. The first typeset version of a manuscript that has not yet been divided into pages.

Genre. A formulaic type of fiction such as romance, western or horror.

Gothic. A genre in which the central character is usually a beautiful young woman and the setting an old mansion or castle, involving a handsome hero and real danger, either natural or supernatural.

Graphic novel. An adaptation of a novel into a long comic strip or heavily illustrated story of 40 pages or more, produced in paperback.

Hard-boiled detective novel. Mystery novel featuring a private eye or police detective as the protagonist; usually involves a murder. The emphasis is on the details of the crime.

Horror. A genre stressing fear, death and other aspects of the macabre.

Imprint. Name applied to a publisher's specific line (e.g. Owl, an imprint of Henry Holt).

Interactive fiction. Fiction in book or computer-software format where the reader determines the path the story will take by choosing from several alternatives at the end of each chapter or episode.

International Reply Coupon (IRC). A form purchased at a post office and enclosed with a letter or manuscript to a international publisher, to cover return postage costs.

Juvenile. Fiction intended for children 2-12.

Libel. Written or printed words that defame, malign or damagingly misrepresent a living person.

Literary. The general category of serious, non-formulaic, intelligent fiction, sometimes experimental, that most frequently appears in little magazines.

Literary agent. A person who acts for an author in finding a publisher or arranging contract terms on a literary project.

Mainstream. Traditionally written fiction on subjects or trends that transcend experimental or genre fiction categories.

Malice domestic novel. A traditional mystery novel that is not hard-boiled; emphasis is on the solution. Suspects and victims know one another.

Manuscript. The author's unpublished copy of a work, usually typewritten, used as the basis for typesetting.

Mass market paperback. Softcover book on a popular subject, usually around 4×7, directed to a general audience and sold in drugstores and groceries as well as in bookstores.

Ms(s). Abbreviation for manuscript(s).

Multiple submission. Submission of more than one short story at a time to the same editor. Do not make a multiple submission unless requested.

Narration. The account of events in a story's plot as related by the speaker or the voice of the author.

Narrator. The person who tells the story, either someone involved in the action or the voice of the writer.

New Age. A term including categories such as astrology, psychic phenomena, spiritual healing, UFOs, mysticism and other aspects of the occult.

Nom de plume. French for "pen name"; a pseudonym.

Novella (also novelette). A short novel or long story, approximately 7,000-15,000 words.

#10 envelope. $4 \times 9\frac{1}{2}$ envelope, used for queries and other business letters.

Offprint. Copy of a story taken from a magazine before it is bound.

One-time rights. Permission to publish a story in periodical or book form one time only.

Outline. A summary of a book's contents, often in the form of chapter headings with a few sentences outlining the action of the story under each one; sometimes part of a book proposal.

Payment on acceptance. Payment from the magazine or publishing house as soon as the decision to print a manuscript is made.

Payment on publication. Payment from the publisher after a manuscript is printed.

Pen name. A pseudonym used to conceal a writer's real name.

Periodical. A magazine or journal published at regular intervals.

Plot. The carefully devised series of events through which the characters progress in a work of fiction.

Proofreading. Close reading and correction of a manuscript's typographical errors.

Proofs. A typeset version of a manuscript used for correcting errors and making changes, often a photocopy of the galleys.

Proposal. An offer to write a specific work, usually consisting of an outline of the work and one or two completed chapters.

Protagonist. The principal or leading character in a literary work.

Public domain. Material that either was never copyrighted or whose copyright term has expired.

Pulp magazine. A periodical printed on inexpensive paper, usually containing lurid, sensational stories or articles.

Query. A letter written to an editor to elicit interest in a story the writer wants to submit.

Reader. A person hired by a publisher to read unsolicited manuscripts.

Reading fee. An arbitrary amount of money charged by some agents and publishers to read a submitted manuscript.

Regency romance. A genre romance, usually set in England between 1811-1820.

Remainders. Leftover copies of an out-of-print book, sold by the publisher at a reduced price.

Reporting time. The number of weeks or months it takes an editor to report back on an author's query or manuscript.

Reprint rights. Permission to print an already published work whose rights have been sold to another magazine or book publisher.

Roman à clef. French "novel with a key." A novel that represents actual living or historical characters and events in fictionalized form.

Romance. The genre relating accounts of passionate love and fictional heroic achievements.

Royalties. A percentage of the retail price paid to an author for each copy of the book that is sold.

SAE. Self-addressed envelope.

SASE. Self-addressed stamped envelope.

Science fiction. Genre in which scientific facts and hypotheses form the basis of actions and events.

Second serial (reprint) rights. Permission for the reprinting of a work in another periodical after its first publication in book or magazine form.

Self-publishing. In this arrangement, the author keeps all income derived from the book, but he pays for its manufacturing, production and marketing.

Sequel. A literary work that continues the narrative of a previous, related story or novel.

Serial rights. The rights given by an author to a publisher to print a piece in one or more periodicals.

Serialized novel. A book-length work of fiction published in sequential issues of a periodical.

Setting. The environment and time period during which the action of a story takes place.

Short short story. A condensed piece of fiction, usually under 700 words.

Simultaneous submission. The practice of sending copies of the same manuscript to several editors or publishers at the same time. Some people refuse to consider such submissions.

Slant. A story's particular approach or style, designed to appeal to the readers of a specific magazine.

Slice of life. A presentation of characters in a seemingly mundane situation which offers the reader a flash of illumination about the characters or their situation.

Slush pile. A stack of unsolicited manuscripts in the editorial offices of a publisher.

Social Fiction. Fiction written with the purpose of bringing about positive changes in society.

Speculation (or Spec). An editor's agreement to look at an author's manuscript with no promise to purchase.

Speculative Fiction (SpecFic). The all-inclusive term for science fiction, fantasy and horror.

Splatterpunk. Type of horror fiction known for its very violent and graphic content.

Subsidiary. An incorporated branch of a company or conglomerate (e.g. Alfred Knopf, Inc., a subsidiary of Random House, Inc.).

Subsidiary rights. All rights other than book publishing rights included in a book contract, such as paperback, book club and movie rights.

Subsidy publisher. A book publisher who charges the author for the cost of typesetting, printing and promoting a book. Also Vanity publisher.

Subterficial fiction. Innovative, challenging, nonconventional fiction in which what seems to be happening is the result of things not so easily perceived.

Suspense. A genre of fiction where the plot's primary function is to build a feeling of anticipation and fear in the reader over its possible outcome.

Synopsis. A brief summary of a story, novel or play. As part of a book proposal, it is a comprehensive summary condensed in a page or page and a half.

Tabloid. Publication printed on paper about half the size of a regular newspaper page (e.g. *The National Enquirer*).

Tearsheet. Page from a magazine containing a published story.

Theme. The dominant or central idea in a literary work; its message, moral or main thread.

Trade paperback. A softbound volume, usually around 5×8, published and designed for the general public, available mainly in bookstores.

Unsolicited manuscript. A story or novel manuscript that an editor did not specifically ask to see.

Vanity publisher. See Subsidy publisher.

Viewpoint. The position or attitude of the first- or third-person narrator or multiple narrators, which determines how a story's action is seen and evaluated.

Western. Genre with a setting in the West, usually between 1860-1890, with a formula plot about cowboys or other aspects of frontier life.

Whodunit. Genre dealing with murder, suspense and the detection of criminals.

Work-for-hire. Work that another party commissions you to do, generally for a flat fee. The creator does not own the copyright and therefore cannot sell any rights.

Young adult. The general classification of books written for readers 12-18.

Category Index

Our Category Index makes it easy for you to identify publishers who are looking for a specific type of fiction. [Publishers new to this edition are identified with a double dagger (‡).] The index is divided into types of fiction, including a section of electronic magazines. Under each fiction category are magazines and book publishers looking for that kind of fiction. Publishers who are not listed under a fiction category either accept all types of fiction or have not indicated specific subject preferences. Also not appearing here are listings that need very specific types of fiction, e.g., "fiction about fly fishing only." To use this index to find a book publisher for your mystery novel, for instance, go to the Mystery/Suspense section and look under Book Publishers. Finally, read individual listings *carefully* to determine the mystery publishers best suited to your work.

ADVENTURE

Magazines: Abyss Magazine 311; Acorn, The 96; ‡Advocate 97; Aguilar Expression, The 99; Allegheny Review 102; ‡Ambiguous 103; Amelia 103; Anterior Fiction Quarterly 265; ‡Anthology 266; ‡Armchair Aesthete, The 108; Arnazella 108; artisan 109; Asian Pacific American Journal 109; Aura Literary/Arts Review 110; ‡Bangtale International 266; Barbaric Yawp 112; Belletrist Review, The 113; Black Jack 116; Blue Mesa Review 117; ‡Blue Skunk Companion, The 118; Blueline 118; BookLovers 119; Bouillabaisse 120; Bowhunter Magazine 351; Boys' Life 351; Boy's Quest 268; Brownstone Review, The 122; Buffalo Spree Magazine 351; Bugle 352; Capers Aweigh Magazine 124; ‡Career Focus; College Preview; Direct Aim; Journey; Visions 353; Chinook Quarterly, The 270; Christian Courier 270; Climbing Art, The 129; ‡Clubhouse Magazine 271; ‡Cochran's Corner 271; ‡Compleat Nurse, The 272; ‡Compost Newsletter 130; Cosmopolitan 357; ‡CZ's Magazine 273; Dagger of the Mind 273; Dan River Anthology 135; Dogwood Tales 137; Downstate Story 137; Dream International 274; Drinkin' Buddy Magazine, The 319; Echoes 138; ‡Edge, The 274; 8 139; Elf: Eclectic Literary Forum 140; ‡Etcetera 141; Eureka 141; ‡Evansville Review 142; Expressions 143; Fayrdaw 320; FiberOptic Etchings 276; ‡First Word Bulletin, The 276; Florida Wildlife 360; ‡Forbidden Donut 148; Fugue 149; Georgia Journal 361; ‡Gold and Treasure Hunter 361; ‡Gotta Write Network Litmag 322; Grasslands Review 153; Green Mountains Review 156; Green's Magazine 156; ‡Grit 363; Healing Inn, The 279; Home Times 366; ‡Hybrid Moments 281; i.e. magazine 161; Iconoclast, The 162; ‡Ignite 281; Implosion 367; In the Spirit of the Buffalo 163; ‡Journal of African Travel-Writing, The 167; Junior Trails 369; Lactuca 169; Lines in the Sand 172; Lowell Pearl, The 175; Lynx Eye 176; MacGuffin, The 176; Medicinal Purposes 286; Mediphors 287; Merlyn's Pen 179; Monthly Independent Tribune Times Journal Post Gazette News Chronicle Bulletin, The 326; Musing Place, The 183; My Legacy 288; ‡New England Writers' Network 289; ‡New Spy 375; New Writing 187; Nimrod 188; Nite-Writer's International Literary Arts Journal 189; Northwoods Journal 190; Oak, The 292; Oatmeal & Poetry 192; Out of the Cradle 195; Palo Alto Review 198; Pink Chameleon, The 204; ‡Play the Odds 334; Poetry in Motion 208; ‡Portable Plateau 295; Portland Review 209; Post, The 295; Potpourri 210; Prairie Dog 211; Queen's Quarterly 297; Rag Mag 216; Ralph's Review 335; Reader's Break 217; RE:AL 217; Rosebud™ 298; S.L.U.G.fest 335; Se La Vie Writer's Journal 223; Short Stuff Magazine for Grown-ups 226; Slate and Style 300; Spring Fantasy 235; SPSM&H 235; Storyteller, The 301; Street Beat Quarterly 237; ‡Sunflower Dream, The 239; Surprise Me 239; "Teak" Roundup 241; Texas Young Writers' Newsletter 302; Thema 242; ‡32 Pages 244; ‡Threshold, The 303; Thresholds Quarterly 303; Timber Creek Review 245; Tucumcari Literary Review 246; ‡Ulitarra 246; Unknown Writer, The 340; ‡Villager, The 304; Vincent Brothers Review, The 249; ‡Vintage Northwest 304; Virginia Quarterly Review 304; Volcano Quarterly 304; West Wind Review 251; ‡Womyn's Press 255; Words of Wisdom 256; Writers' International Forum 306; ‡Zone, The 342

Book Publishers: Ariadne Press 393; Arjuna Library Press 419; ‡Avon Flare Books 422; b. dazzle 394; Bethany House Publishers 426; Black Heron Press 426; Books in Motion 428; Bouregy & Company, Thomas 428; Caitlin Press 430; Camelot Books 431; Chinook Press 434; Clarion Books 438; Crossway

Books 441; Crown Publishing 441; Davies Publishing, Robert 443; Dell Publishing 445; ‡Denlingers Publishers 445; Ecopress 397; Fine, Inc., Donald I. 452; Geringer Books, Laura 455; ‡Greycliff Publishing 457; Gryphon Publications 457; Harkey Multimedia 459; Harlequin Enterprises 459; HarperCollins Publishers 463; Harris Literary Agency 398; Holt & Company, Henry 466; Houghton Mifflin Books for Children 466; Intrigue Press 469; Kensington Publishing 471; ‡Landmine Books 400; ‡Lyons Press, The 478; Morrow and Company, William 482; Mountaineers Books, The 483; Nelson Publishers, Thomas 485; Nelson, Tommy 485; ‡Neshui Publishing 485; ‡NWI 488; Our Child Press 402; ‡Patek Press 491; Philomel Books 493; Piñata Books 494; ‡Pocket Books 495; ‡Pride Publications 496; Quixote Press 497; Rain Dancer Books 498; Random House Juvenile Books 499; Random House 499; Review and Herald Publishing 500; Rio Grande Press 500; Riverhead Books 501; St. Martin's Press 503; Severn House Publishers 506; Snowapple Press 407; Story Line Press 512; Vandamere Press 517; Vista Publishing 518; Whispering Coyote Press 521; Willow Creek Press 521; Wordstorm Productions 522; Worldwide Library 522; Writers Press 523

CHILDRENS/JUVENILE

Magazines: ‡Advocate 97; American Girl 347; Associate Reformed Presbyterian, The 348; ‡Bangtale International 266; Boy's Quest 268; Brilliant Star 269; Bugle 352; ‡Calliope 352; Chickadee 353; Child Life 354; Children's Digest 354; Children's Playmate 354; Chinook Quarterly, The 270; Christian Courier 270; Clubhouse 355; ‡Clubhouse Magazine 271; Cobblestone 356; ‡Cochran's Corner 271; ‡Compleat Nurse, The 272; Creative Kids 357; Cricket 357; ‡Crusader 357; ‡CZ's Magazine 273; Discoveries 358; Echoes 138; Faces 359; ‡5th Wall, The 146; Friend Magazine, The 360; ‡Guide Magazine 363; Guideposts for Kids 364; Highlights for Children 365; Hopscotch: The Magazine for Girls 279; Humpty Dumpty's Magazine 366; Jack and Jill 368; Junior Trails 369; Ladybug 370; Lamp-Post, The 170; Majestic Books 286; My Friend 373; My Legacy 288; ‡Newfangled Fairy Tales and Girls to the Rescue 290; Oatmeal & Poetry 192; Odyssey 375; On the Line 379; Pink Chameleon, The 204; Pockets 380; Power and Light 381; R-A-D-A-R 382; Ranger Rick 382; Shofar 384; Skipping Stones 299; Spider 385; Spring Fantasy 235; Stone Soup 235; ‡Story Friends 386; Street Beat Quarterly 237; Surprise Me 239; "Teak" Roundup 241; Turtle Magazine for Preschool Kids 388; Writers' International Forum 306; Young Judaean 307

Book Publishers: Abbeville Kids 416; Absey & Co. 416; Advocacy Press 417; American Diabetes Association 418; Annick Press 418; Arjuna Library Press 419; Arte Publico Press 420; Atheneum Books for Young Readers 420; b. dazzle 394; Bantam/Doubleday/Dell Books for Young Readers 424; Blue Sky Press, The 427; Borealis Press 428; Boyds Mills Press 429; ‡Broadman & Holman Publishers 394; Camelot Books 431; Candlewick Press 431; Carolrhoda Books 431; Cartwheel Books 432; Chariot Children's Books 433; Chariot Victor Publishing 433; Chicago Spectrum Press 434; Chinook Press 434; Christmas 395; Chronicle Books for Children 435; Concordia Publishing House 439; Creative with Words Publications 440; Cross-Cultural Communications 396; Davies Publishing, Robert 443; Dawn Publications 444; Dial Books for Young Readers 446; Down East Books 446; Dutton Children's 447; E.M. Press 448; Eakin Press 448; Éditions du Vermillon, Les 449; Éditions La Liberté 449; Editions Phidal 449; Farrar, Straus & Giroux/ Children's Books 451; Feminist Press, The 452; Focus Publishing 453; Geringer Books, Laura 455; Godine, Publisher, David R. 455; Grade School Press 398; Greene Bark Press 456; Greenwillow Books 456; Grolier Publishing 457; Harcourt Brace & Company 458; Harcourt Brace & Company Children's Books 459; Harkey Multimedia 459; HarperCollins Children's Books 463; HarperCollins Publishers (Canada) 464; Heritage House Publishing 465; Highsmith Press 465; Hohm Press 465; Holiday House 465; Holt & Company Books for Young Readers, Henry 466; Holt & Company, Henry 466; Houghton Mifflin Books for Children 466; Humanics Children's House 467; Hyperion Books for Children 468; Ideals Children's 468; Illumination Publishing 399; Journey Books for Young Readers 471; Just Us Books 471; Key Porter Books 472; Kindred Productions 472; Knopf Books for Young Readers 473; Lee & Low Books 473; Levine Books, Arthur 474; Little, Brown and Company Children's Books 476; Little, Brown and Company 475; Little Tiger Press 476; Living the Good News 476; Lollipop Power Books 400; Lorimer & Co., Publishers, James 477; McElderry Books, Margaret K. 478; Mariner Books 480; Mariposa 480; Meadowbrook Press 481; Milkweed Editions 481; Milkweeds for Young Readers 402; Minstrel Books 482; ‡Misty Hill Press 402; Morehouse Publishing 482; Morrow Junior Books 482; Nelson Publishers, Thomas 485; Nelson, Tommy 485; ‡Neshui Publishing 485; Northland Publishing 487; North-South Books 488; ‡NWI 488; Orca Book Publishers 489; Our Child Press 402; Owen Publishers, Richard C. 490; Pacific Educational Press 490; Pages Publishing Group 403; Pauline Books and Media 491; Peachtree Children's Books 403; Peachtree Publishers 492; Pelican Publishing 492; Pemmican Publications 493; ‡Perfection Learning 493; Perspectives Press 493; Philomel Books 493; Piñata Books 494; Pippin Press 495; ‡Pleasant Company Publications 495; Prep Publishing 496; ‡Pride Publications 496; Puffin Books 497; Quarry Press

CONDENSED NOVEL

ELECTRONIC MAGAZINES

EROTICA

323; Hustler Busty Beauties 366; ‡Hybrid Moments 281; Jack Mackerel Magazine 325; ‡Jackhammer 165; Lactuca 169; Libido 171; Lowell Pearl, The 175; Lynx Eye 176; Manscape 371; ‡Masquerade 286; Matriarch's Way 179; Medicinal Purposes 286; ‡Mini Romances 287; Mississippi Mud 181; ‡New York Stories 187; Nite-Writer's International Literary Arts Journal 189; Northwoods Journal 190; Nugget 375; Old Crow Review 193; Options 379; Paramour Magazine 199; PBW 332; Poetic Space 207; ‡Portable Plateau 295; Portland Review 209; Poskisnolt Press 295; Prairie Dog 211; Prisoners of the Night 296; Rag Mag 216; Rocket Press 220; ‡Salt Hill Journal 221; Salt Lick Press 221; Samsara 221; Sanskrit 221; Screaming Toad Press 223; Shattered Wig Review 225; Slipstream 228; Snake Nation Review 229; SPSM&H 235; ‡Spunk 337; Sub-Terrain 238; Swank 387; ‡Synaethesia Press Chapbook Series 339; ‡32 Pages 244; ‡Threshold, The 303; ‡Ulitarra 246; ‡Unit Circle, The 340; Unknown Writer, The 340; Vox (NM) 341; West Wind Review 251; W!dow of the Orch!d, The 341; ‡Womyn's Press 255; Yellow Silk 258; Zero Hour 259; ‡Zone, The 342

Book Publishers: Arjuna Library Press 419; Artemis Creations Publishing 394; ‡Blue Moon Books 427; Carroll & Graf Publishers 432; Center Press 433; Circlet Press 435; Cleis Press 438; Creative Arts Book Co. 440; Delta Trade Paperbacks 445; Down There Press 397; Ekstasis Editions 449; Forge Books 453; ‡Goddess Dead Publications 455; House of Anansi Press 467; Kensington Publishing 471; ‡Leapfrog Press 400; ‡Masquerade Books 480; Orloff Press 489; ‡Pocket Books 495; Press Gang Publishers 404; ‡Pride Publications 496; ‡Russian Hill Press 502; St. Martin's Press 503; Second Chance Press and the Permanent Press 505; Vandamere Press 517

ETHNIC/MULTICULTURAL

Magazines: ‡About Such Things 95; ACM (Another Chicago Magazine) 96; Acorn Whistle 96; Adrift 97; ‡Advocate 97; African American Review 98; African Voices 346; Aguilar Expression, The 99; Allegheny Review 102; ‡Ambiguous 103; Amelia 103; American Writings 104; Americas Review, The 104; Antietam Review 105; ‡Arba Sicula 107; Arnazella 108; artisan 109; Art:Mag 312; Asian Pacific American Journal 109; Atom Mind 110; Aura Literary/Arts Review 110; Azorean Express, The 110; Bahlasti Papers 313; ‡Baltimore Review, The 111; ‡Bangtale International 266; ‡Barnabe Mountain Review 112; Beneath the Surface 114; Bilingual Review 115; Black Books Bulletin: WordsWork 267; Black Hammock Review, The 115; Black Jack 116; Black Lace 116; ‡Black Lily, The 313; BlackFire 267; Blue Mesa Review 117; ‡Blue Skunk Companion, The 118; BookLovers 119; ‡Boston Review 350; Boy's Quest 268; Briar Cliff Review, The 121; ‡Brilliant Corners 121; Brownstone Review, The 122; Buffalo Spree Magazine 351; Callaloo 123; Canadian Author 124; Capers Aweigh Magazine 124; ‡Career Focus; College Preview; Direct Aim; Journey; Visions 353; Caribbean Writer, The 124; Chinook Quarterly, The 270; Chiricú 127; ‡Chubby Bunny 128; Cicada 128; Climbing Art, The 129; Collages and Bricolages 129; Colorado Review 130; ‡Compleat Nurse, The 272; ‡Compost Newsletter 130; Concho River Review 131; ‡Contraband 272; ‡Crab Orchard Review 132; Cream City Review, The 133; Crucible 134; ‡Curio 134; Curriculum Vitae 318; Dan River Anthology 135; Downstate Story 137; Dream International 274; Drinkin' Buddy Magazine, The 319; Echoes 138; ‡Eclectica 139; ‡Edge, The 274; Elf: Eclectic Literary Forum 140; Eloquent Umbrella, The 275; ‡Entre Nous 140; Epoch Magazine 141; Eureka 141; ‡Evansville Review 142; Expressions 143; Feminist Studies 145; FiberOptic Etchings 276; ‡Filling Station 146; Fish Drum 146; Fish Stories 146; Flying Horse 147; Flying Island, The 148; Footwork 148; Fourteen Hills 149; Fugue 149; Gathering of the Tribes, A 150; Generator 321; Georgetown Review 151; ‡Gerbil 322; Grasslands Review 153; Green Hills Literary Lantern, The 156; Gulf Coast 157; Hadassah Magazine 365; Happy 158; ‡Hawaii Review 158; Hayden's Ferry Review 158; Heartlands Today, The 159; Hill and Holler 160; Home Planet News 160; Horizons 366; Iconoclast, The 162; ‡Ignite 281; ‡In the Family 282; India Currents 368; Inside 368; International Quarterly 164; Intuitive Explorations 282; Iowa Review, The 165; Italian Americana 283; ‡Jackhammer 165; Japanophile 166; Jewish Currents Magazine 283; Jewish Quarterly 283; Jive, Black Confessions, Black Romance, Bronze Thrills, Black Secrets 368; ‡Journal of African Travel-Writing, The 167; Keltic Fringe 284; Kennesaw Review 168; Kenyon Review, The 168; Kerem 169; Left Curve 284; ‡Lies Magazine 285; ‡Lilith Magazine 370; Live 370; Long Story, The 174; Lowell Pearl, The 175; Lullwater Review 175; Lynx Eye 176; MacGuffin, The 176; Mangrove 177; manna 177; Many Mountains Moving 178; Maryland Review 178; Matriarch's Way 179; Medicinal Purposes 286; Midland Review 180; ‡Midstream 373; Mississippi Mud 181; Missouri Review, The 182; Mobius 182; ‡Muse Portfolio 182; Musing Place, The 183; NA'AMAT Woman 374; ‡New England Writers' Network 289; New Laurel Review 185; New Letters Magazine 185; ‡New Thought Journal 290; ‡New York Stories 187; Nimrod 188; North Dakota Quarterly 189; Northeast Arts Magazine 190; Now & Then 191; ‡Now & Then 292; Oatmeal & Poetry 192; Obsidian II: Black Literature in Review 192; Onionhead 193; Oracle Story 194; Orange Coast Review 194; Out of the Cradle 195; ‡Owen Wister Review 195; Oxford Magazine

EXPERIMENTAL

South 131; ‡Contraband 272; Corona 131; Cream City Review, The 133; ‡Crossconnect 134; Crucible 134; ‡Curio 134; Curriculum Vitae 318; ‡Cutting Edge, The 135; ‡CZ's Magazine 273; Dagger of the Mind 273; Dan River Anthology 135; Denver Quarterly 136; ‡Dirigible 136; Dodobobo 137; Downstate Story 137; Dream International 274; Dreams & Nightmares 319; Dreams & Visions 274; ‡Dreams of a Lime Green Catsuit 319; Drop Forge 138; ‡Echo Ink Review 138; Echoes 138; ‡Eclectica 139; ‡Edge, The 274; 8 139; 1812 140; Eloquent Umbrella, The 275; ‡Entre Nous 140; ‡Etcetera 141; Eureka 141; ‡Evansville Review 142; Explorations '98 143; Expressions 143; Fat Tuesday 144; Fault Lines 144; Fayrdaw 320; FiberOptic Etchings 276; Fiction 145; ‡5th Wall, The 146; ‡Filling Station 146; Fish Drum 146; Fish Stories 146; Flipside 147; Florida Review, The 147; Flying Horse 147; Flying Island, The 148; ‡Forbidden Donut 148; ‡Fractal, The 277; Free Focus/Ostentatious Mind 277; ‡Freezer Burn 149; Fugue 149; Gathering of the Tribes, A 150; Generator 321; Georgetown Review 151; Georgia Review, The 151; Gettysburg Review, The 152; ‡Gold and Treasure Hunter 361; Grain 153; Grand Street 153; Grasslands Review 153; Green Hills Literary Lantern, The 156; Green Mountains Review 156; Greensboro Review 157; Gulf Coast 157; ‡Habersham Review 157; Happy 158; Hayden's Ferry Review 158; Heaven Bone 159; ‡Heretic Hollow 323; Home Planet News 160; Hunted News, The 161; Hurricane Alice 279; ‡Hybrid Moments 281; i.e. magazine 161; ‡I Like Monkeys 324; ‡Ignite 281; Implosion 367; ‡In Celebration of Trees 324; Interim 164; International Quarterly 164; Iowa Review, The 165; Iris 165; Jack Mackerel Magazine 325; Kennesaw Review 168; ‡Kenosis 168; Kenyon Review, The 168; ‡Kimera 169; Left Curve 284; Licking River Review, The 171; ‡Lies Magazine 285; Lines in the Sand 172; ‡Liquid Ohio 326; Literal Latté 172; Little Magazine, The 173; Lost and Found Times 174; ‡Lost Worlds 285; Louisville Review, The 174; Lowell Pearl, The 175; Lullwater Review 175; ‡Lummox Journal 175; Lynx Eye 176; MacGuffin, The 176; Madison Review, The 176; Many Mountains Moving 178; Matriarch's Way 179; Maverick Press, The 179; Medicinal Purposes 286; Mediphors 287; Mid-American Review 180; Midland Review 180; Mind in Motion 181; Minnesota Review, The 181; Mississippi Mud 181; Mississippi Review 182; Mobius 182; Monthly Independent Tribune Times Journal Post Gazette News Chronicle Bulletin, The 326; Musing Place, The 183; Neologisms 184; ‡Neologue 327; ‡New Delta Review 184; New Letters Magazine 185; New Methods 289; New Press Literary Quarterly, The 186; New Virginia Review 187; New Writing 187; ‡New York Stories 187; Next Phase 290; ‡Nexus 188; Nimrod 188; Nocturnal Lyric, The 291; North Dakota Quarterly 189; Northwest Review 190; Northwoods Journal 190; ‡Notre Dame Review 191; ‡Now & Then 292; Oak, The 292; Office Number One 329; Ohio Review, The 193; Old Crow Review 193; Onionhead 193; Orange Coast Review 194; Other Voices 194; ‡Owen Wister Review 195; Oxford Magazine 196; ‡Oyster Boy Review 196; Pacific Coast Journal 197; Painted Bride Quarterly 197; Palo Alto Review 198; Pangolin Papers 198; ‡Paper Tigers 331; Paradoxist Literary Movement, The 293; Partisan Review 200; PBW 332; ‡Perceptions 333; Phoebe (NY) 202; Pica 333; Pikeville Review 203; Pink Chameleon, The 204; Pleiades 204; Poetic Space 207; Poetry Forum Short Stories 207; Poetry in Motion 208; ‡Portable Plateau 295; Portland Review 209; Poskisnolt Press 295; Potpourri 210; Prairie Dog 211; ‡Procreation 213; Puckerbrush Review 214; Puerto Del Sol 214; ‡QECE 335; ‡Quarry 215; Quarterly West 215; Queen's Quarterly 297; Rag Mag 216; Rambunctious Review 216; RE:AL 217; Reed Magazine 218; Response 297; ‡Rio Grande Review 218; River Styx 219; RiverSedge 219; Rocket Press 220; Rockford Review, The 220; Rosebud™ 298; Ruby's Pearls 298; S.L.U.G.fest 335; ‡Salamander 220; ‡Salt Hill Journal 221; Salt Lick Press 221; Samsara 221; Sanskrit 221; Screaming Toad Press 223; Seattle Review, The 224; Shattered Wig Review 225; Sidewalks 227; Sierra Nevada College Review 227; Silver Web, The 227; Skylark 228; Slipstream 228; Snake Nation Review 229; Southern California Anthology 231; ‡Spaceways Weekly 300; ‡Sparks 233; spelunker flophouse 233; Spindrift 233; Spout 234; SPSM&H 235; ‡Spunk 337; ‡Stoneflower 236; Story 236; Street Beat Quarterly 237; Struggle 237; Sub-Terrain 238; Sulphur River Literary Review 238; Sycamore Review 239; ‡Sylvia 240; ‡Synaethesia Press Chapbook Series 339; ‡Talking River Review 240; Tampa Review 240; Textshop 242; Thema 242; Thin Air 243; ‡32 Pages 244; This Magazine 244; ‡Threshold, The 303; Transcendent Visions 340; Turnstile 246; ‡Ulitarra 246; ‡Underground, The 247; ‡Unit Circle, The 340; Unknown Writer, The 340; Urbanite, The 247; ‡Verse Unto Us 248; Verve 248; Vincent Brothers Review, The 249; Vox (NM) 341; ‡Washington Square 250; West Coast Line 251; West Wind Review 251; Western Humanities Review 252; Whetstone (Canada) 252; Widener Review 253; W!dow of the Orch!d, The 341; Willow Review 254; Wisconsin Academy Review 305; Wisconsin Review 255; Woman 306; ‡Womyn's Press 255; Writing for Our Lives 257; Xavier Review 257; Yellow Silk 258; ‡Yemassee 259; ‡(000)000-0000 342; Zero Hour 259; ‡Zone, The 342; Zyzzyva 262

Book Publishers: Ageless Press 392; Anvil Press 393; Arjuna Library Press 419; Artemis Creations Publishing 394; BkMk Press 426; Black Heron Press 426; Calyx Books 395; China Books & Periodicals

FAMILY SAGA

FANTASY

Book Publishers: Ageless Press 392; Arjuna Library Press 419; Artemis Creations Publishing 394; Avon Books 421; ‡Avon Eos 421; Avon Science Fiction 422; b. dazzle 394; Baen Books 422; Bantam Books 424; Berkley Publishing 425; Berkley/Ace Science Fiction 425; ‡Blue Star Productions 427; Carroll & Graf Publishers 432; Cartwheel Books 432; Chinook Press 434; Circlet Press 435; Davies Publishing, Robert 443; Daw Books 443; Del Rey Books 444; Delacorte/Dell Books for Young Readers 445; Dutton Signet 447; Geringer Books, Laura 455; HarperCollins Publishers 463; Hollow Earth Publishing 398; Humanitas 468; ‡Masquerade Books 480; ‡Merrimack Books 401; Millennium 482; ‡Neshui Publishing 485; ‡NWI 488; Our Child Press 402; Philomel Books 493; ‡Pocket Books 495; ‡Pride Publications 496; Rain Dancer Books 498; Random House Juvenile Books 499; ‡Red Dragon Press 499; Rio Grande Press 500; ROC 501; St. Martin's Press 503; Savant Garde Workshop, The 406; Severn House Publishers 506; Spectra Books 509; Tor Books 514; Triangle Titles 514; TSR, Inc. 514; W.W. Publications 411; Warner Aspect 520; Whispering Coyote Press 521; Woman in the Moon Publications 411; Write Way Publishing 522

FEMINIST

Magazines: ACM (Another Chicago Magazine) 96; Acorn Whistle 96; Adrift 97; ‡Advocate 97; African American Review 98; Allegheny Review 102; ‡Ambiguous 103; Amelia 103; American Writings 104; Americas Review, The 104; Antietam Review 105; Aphrodite Gone Berserk 106; Arnazella 108; artisan 109; Art:Mag 312; Asian Pacific American Journal 109; Aura Literary/Arts Review 110; Bahlasti Papers 313; ‡Barnabe Mountain Review 112; Beneath the Surface 114; Black Books Bulletin: WordsWork 267; Blue Mesa Review 117; Blue Moon Review, The 117; ‡Bookpress 119; Briar Cliff Review, The 121; Brownstone Review, The 122; Callaloo 123; Calyx 123; Canadian Author 124; Capers Aweigh Magazine 124; Chinook Quarterly, The 270; Chiricú 127; Christian Century, The 354; Collages and Bricolages 129; ‡Compleat Nurse, The 272; ‡Compost Newsletter 130; Contact Advertising 356; Context South 131; ‡Contraband 272; Corona 131; Crucible 134; ‡CZ's Magazine 273; ‡Down Under Manhattan Bridge; ‡Echo Ink Review 138; Echoes 138; ‡Edge, The 274; Elf: Eclectic Literary Forum 140; Eloquent Umbrella, The 275; Emrys Journal 140; ‡Entre Nous 140; ‡Etcetera 141; Eureka 141; ‡Evansville Review 142; Event 142; Expressions 143; Feminist Studies 145; FiberOptic Etchings 276; ‡Filling Station 146; Fish Stories 146; Flying Island, The 148; Free Focus/Ostentatious Mind 277; Frontiers 149; Gathering of the Tribes, A 150; Generator 321; Georgetown Review 151; Green Hills Literary Lantern, The 156; Happy 158; Hayden's Ferry Review 158; ‡Heretic Hollow 323; Home Planet News 160; Horizons 366; Hurricane Alice 279; ‡In the Family 282; Iowa Review, The 165; Iris 165; Kennesaw Review 168; Kenyon Review, The 168; Kerem 169; ‡Lilith 370; Little Magazine, The 173; Long Story, The 174; Lowell Pearl, The 175; Lullwater Review 175; Lynx Eye 176; manna 177; Many Mountains Moving 178; Matriarch's Way 179; Medicinal Purposes 286; Midland Review 180; Minnesota Review, The 181; Mobius 182; Musing Place, The 183; ‡New York Stories 187; North Dakota Quarterly 189; Northwest Review 190; ‡Notre Dame Review 191; ‡Now & Then 292; Obsidian II: Black Literature in Review 192; Onionhead 193; Orange Coast Review 194; Out of the Cradle 195; Oxford Magazine 196; Pacific Coast Journal 197; Painted Bride Quarterly 197; Palo Alto Review 198; Paperplates 199; Phoebe (NY) 202; Pica 333; Pikeville Review 203; Pleiades 204; Poetic Space 207; Poetry Forum Short Stories 207; Portland Review 209; Poskisnolt Press 295; Potato Eyes 209; Primavera 213; Radiance 382; Rag Mag 216; Rambunctious Review 216; RE:AL 217; Response 297; ‡Rio Grande Review 218; River Styx 219; RiverSedge 219; Riverwind 219; ‡Salamander 220; Salt Lick Press 221; Sanskrit 221; Seattle Review, The 224; Shattered Wig Review 225; Side Show 226; Sing Heavenly Muse! 228; Skipping Stones 299; Skylark 228; Snake Nation Review 229; Sojourner 385; Southern California Anthology 231; Southern Exposure 231; Southern Humanities Review 231; ‡Spaceways Weekly 300; spelunker flophouse 233; Spirit 385; ‡Spirit (Of Woman in the Moon), The 234; Spout 234; Spring Fantasy 235; SPSM&H 235; ‡Stoneflower 236; Street Beat Quarterly 237; Struggle 237; Sulphur River Literary Review 238; ‡Sylvia 240; ‡Talking River Review 240; 13th Moon 244; ‡32 Pages 244; This Magazine 244; Timber Creek Review 245; Transcendent Visions 340; ‡Ulitarra 246; ‡Underground, The 247; ‡Unit Circle, The 340; Unknown Writer, The 340; Vincent Brothers Review, The 249; Virginia Quarterly Review 304; Vox (NY) 249; Vox (NM) 341; West Coast Line 251; West Wind Review 251; Willow Review 254; Woman 306; ‡Women's American ORT Reporter 389; ‡Womyn's Press 255; Words of Wisdom 256; Writing for Our Lives 257; Yellow Silk 258; ‡Yemassee 259; Zero Hour 259; ‡Zone, The 342

Book Publishers: Academy Chicago Publishers 416; Ariadne Press 393; Arsenal Pulp Press 419; Arte Publico Press 420; Artemis Creations Publishing 394; ‡Aunt Lute Books 420; ‡Buzz Books 430; Calyx Books 395; Chicago Spectrum Press 434; Chinook Press 434; Circlet Press 435; Cleis Press 438; Creative Arts Book Co. 440; ‡Denlingers Publishers 445; Down There Press 397; ‡Dufour Editions 447; Empyreal

GAY

HISTORICAL

HORROR

HUMOR/SATIRE

Kerem 169; Krax Magazine 284; Lamplight, The 170; ‡Lies Magazine 285; Light Magazine 171; Lines in the Sand 172; ‡Liquid Ohio 326; Literal Latté 172; Little Magazine, The 173; Lowell Pearl, The 175; Lullwater Review 175; Lynx Eye 176; MacGuffin, The 176; Many Mountains Moving 178; Maryland Review 178; Matriarch's Way 179; ‡Mature Living 372; Medicinal Purposes 286; Mediphors 287; Merlyn's Pen 179; Mind in Motion 181; Mississippi Mud 181; Mississippi Review 182; Missouri Review, The 182; Mobius 182; Monthly Independent Tribune Times Journal Post Gazette News Chronicle Bulletin, The 326; Mountain Luminary 288; Musing Place, The 183; My Legacy 288; ‡My Weekly 374; Nebraska Review, The 184; ‡New Delta Review 184; ‡New England Writers' Network 289; New Letters Magazine 185; New Press Literary Quarterly, The 186; new renaissance, the 186; New Writing 187; ‡New York Stories 187; 96 Inc. 188; Nite-Writer's International Literary Arts Journal 189; Nocturnal Lyric, The 291; North Dakota Quarterly 189; ‡Now & Then 292; Nuthouse 329; Oak, The 292; Oatmeal & Poetry 192; Office Number One 329; Onionhead 193; Oracle Story 194; Orange Coast Review 194; Other Voices 194; ‡Outpost, The 331; ‡Owen Wister Review 195; Oxford Magazine 196; Pacific Coast Journal 197; Palo Alto Review 198; Pangolin Papers 198; ‡Panus Index, The 198; Pearl 200; Pegasus Review, The 201; Phoebe (NY) 202; Pica 333; ‡Piedmont Literary Review 203; Pikeville Review 203; Pink Chameleon, The 204; Pipe Smoker's Ephemeris, The 295; Playboy 380; Pleiades 204; ‡Portable Plateau 295; Portland Review 209; Poskisnolt Press 295; Potato Eyes 209; Potpourri 210; Prairie Dog 211; Primavera 213; ‡Procreation 213; Queen's Quarterly 297; Ralph's Review 335; Rambunctious Review 216; ‡Raskolnikov's Cellar and The Lamplight 216; Reed Magazine 218; ‡Reform Judaism 383; Response 297; ‡Rio Grande Review 218; River Styx 219; Riverwind 219; Rocket Press 220; Rockford Review, The 220; Rosebud™ 298; Ruby's Pearls 298; S.L.U.G.fest 335; St. Joseph's Messenger and Advocate of the Blind 384; ‡Salt Hill Journal 221; Sanskrit 221; Satire 222; Screaming Toad Press 223; Se La Vie Writer's Journal 223; Seattle Review, The 224; Sensations 224; Shattered Wig Review 225; Short Stuff Magazine for Grown-ups 226; Side Show 226; Sidewalks 227; Skylark 228; Slate and Style 300; Slipstream 228; Snake Nation Review 229; Southern California Anthology 231; Southern Exposure 231; Southern Humanities Review 231; spelunker flophouse 233; Spout 234; Spring Fantasy 235; SPSM&H 235; ‡Stoneflower 236; Story 236; Storyteller, The 301; Street Beat Quarterly 237; Struggle 237; Sub-Terrain 238; Sulphur River Literary Review 238; ‡Sunflower Dream, The 239; Sycamore Review 239; T.R.'s Zine 339; Talebones 302; ‡Talking River Review 240; Tampa Review 240; "Teak" Roundup 241; Texas Young Writers' Newsletter 302; Thema 242; ‡32 Pages 244; ‡Threshold, The 303; Thresholds Quarterly 303; Timber Creek Review 245; Transcendent Visions 340; Troika 387; Tucumcari Literary Review 246; Turnstile 246; ‡Ulitarra 246; ‡Underground, The 247; ‡Unit Circle, The 340; Unknown Writer, The 340; Urbanite, The 247; Urbanus 247; ‡Verse Unto Us 248; Verve 248; ‡Villager, The 304; Vincent Brothers Review, The 249; ‡Vintage Northwest 304; Virginia Quarterly Review 304; Virtue 388; Volcano Quarterly 304; Vox (NY) 249; Vox (NM) 341; Wascana Review 250; West Wind Review 251; ‡Westcoast Fisherman, The 305; Westview 252; Whetstone 252; Wisconsin Academy Review 305; Woman 306; ‡Women's American ORT Reporter 389; Words of Wisdom 256; Writers' International Forum 306; Writing for Our Lives 257; Xtreme 257; Yarns and Such 307; Yellow Silk 258; ‡Yemassee 259; ‡(000)000-0000 342; Zero Hour 259; ‡Zone, The 342

Book Publishers: Acme Press 392; Ageless Press 392; Ariadne Press 393; ‡Avon Flare Books 422; b. dazzle 394; Black Heron Press 426; Books in Motion 428; Bridge Works Publishing 429; ‡Broadman & Holman Publishers 394; Caitlin Press 430; Camelot Books 431; Cartwheel Books 432; Catbird Press 432; Centennial Publications 432; Center Press 433; Chicago Spectrum Press 434; Chinook Press 434; Clarion Books 438; Cleis Press 438; Coffee House Press 439; Counterpoint 440; Creative with Words Publications 440; Cross-Cultural Communications 396; Crown Publishing 441; ‡Davenport, Publishers, May 443; ‡Exile Press 397; Geringer Books, Laura 455; Harkey Multimedia 459; Harvest House Publishers 464; Holt & Company, Henry 466; Houghton Mifflin Books for Children 466; Ironweed Press 470; Key Porter Books 472; ‡Laugh Lines Press 400; ‡Leapfrog Press 400; Little Tiger Press 476; Morrow and Company, William 482; ‡Neshui Publishing 485; Nightshade Press 487; Orloff Press 489; ‡Patek Press 491; ‡Pocket Books 495; Press Gang Publishers 404; ‡Pride Publications 496; ‡Pudding House Publications 404; Quixote Press 497; Random House Books For Young Readers 498; Random House Juvenile Books 499; Review and Herald Publishing Association 500; Rio Grande Press 500; Riverhead Books 501; ‡Russian Hill Press 502; St. Martin's Press 503; Shields Publishing/NEO Press 406; SJL Publishing 508; Smith, Publisher/Peregrine Smith, Gibbs 508; University of Nevada Press 410; Van Neste Books 411; Vandamere Press 517; Vista Publishing 518; Willow Creek Press 521; Wordstorm Productions 522

LESBIAN

Magazines: ACM (Another Chicago Magazine) 96; Adrift 97; African American Review 98; Allegheny Review 102; ‡Ambiguous 103; Amelia 103; American Writings 104; Aphrodite Gone Berserk 106; Arnazella 108; Art:Mag 312; Asian Pacific American Journal 109; Backspace 313; Bahlasti Papers 313; ‡Barnabe Mountain Review 112; Beneath the Surface 114; Black Lace 116; ‡Black Lily, The 313; Blue Mesa Review 117; Blue Moon Review, The 117; ‡Bookpress 119; Brownstone Review, The 122; ‡Chubby Bunny 128; ‡Compleat Nurse, The 272; ‡Compost Newsletter 130; Contact Advertising 356; ‡Contraband 272; Crucible 134; ‡Cutting Edge, The 135; ‡Down Under Manhattan Bridge; Drinkin' Buddy Magazine, The 319; ‡Echo Ink Review 138; Echoes 138; ‡Edge, The 274; ‡Etcetera 141; ‡Evansville Review 142; Evergreen Chronicles, The 142; Expressions 143; Feminist Studies 145; ‡Filling Station 146; Fish Drum 146; Fish Stories 146; Flying Island, The 148; Fourteen Hills 149; ‡Freezer Burn 149; Frontiers 149; Gathering of the Tribes, A 150; Gay Chicago Magazine 278; Generator 321; Georgetown Review 151; ‡Gerbil 322; Glass Cherry, The 152; Happy 158; ‡Heretic Hollow 323; Home Planet News 160; Horizons 366; Hurricane Alice 279; ‡In the Family 282; Iris 165; Kenyon Review, The 168; Libido 171; ‡Lilith 370; Lowell Pearl, The 175; Lullwater Review 175; Lynx Eye 176; Many Mountains Moving 178; ‡Masquerade 286; Medicinal Purposes 286; Minnesota Review, The 181; Mobius 182; Musing Place, The 183; ‡New York Stories 187; Onionhead 193; Options 379; Orange Coast Review 194; Out of the Cradle 195; Oxford Magazine 196; Painted Bride Quarterly 197; Paperplates 199; PBW 332; ‡Pen & Sword 332; Phoebe (NY) 202; Pica 333; Portland Review 209; Poskisnolt Press 295; Primavera 213; ‡Rio Grande Review 218; River Styx 219; ‡Salt Hill Journal 221; Salt Lick Press 221; Sanskrit 221; Seattle Review, The 224; Sensations 224; Shattered Wig Review 225; Snake Nation Review 229; Southern Exposure 231; ‡Spaceways Weekly 300; ‡Spirit (Of Woman in the Moon), The 234; Spout 234; SPSM&H 235; ‡Sylvia 240; T.R.'s Zine 339; ‡Talking River Review 240; ‡32 Pages 244; This Magazine 244; ‡Threshold, The 303; Transcendent Visions 340; ‡Ulitarra 246; ‡Unit Circle, The 340; Unknown Writer, The 340; Vox (NM) 341; West Wind Review 251; ‡Wit's End Literary Cyberzine 342; Woman 306; ‡Womyn's Press 255; Writing for Our Lives 257; Yellow Silk 258; ‡Yemassee 259

Book Publishers: Alyson Publications 418; Arjuna Library Press 419; Arsenal Pulp Press 419; ‡Aunt Lute Books 420; Braziller, Inc., George 429; Calyx Books 395; Circlet Press 435; Cleis Press 438; Davies Publishing, Robert 443; Down There Press 397; Empyreal Press 450; Faber and Faber 450; Feminist Press, The 452; Firebrand Books 452; ‡Fjord Press 453; Hollow Earth Publishing 398; House of Anansi Press 467; ‡Laugh Lines Press 400; ‡Leapfrog Press 400; Lintel 474; Madwoman Press 401; ‡Masquerade Books 480; ‡Mercury House 481; Morrow and Company, William 482; Naiad Press, The 484; ‡Neshui Publishing 485; New Victoria Publishers 486; Outrider Press 402; Post-Apollo Press, The 403; Press Gang Publishers 404; ‡Pride Publications 496; Ragweed Press/gynergy books 497; ‡Red Dragon Press 499; Rising Tide Press 501; Riverhead Books 501; ‡Russian Hill Press 502; St. Martin's Press 503; Sand River Press 405; ‡Sans Soleil 406; Seal Press 504; Shields Publishing/NEO Press 406; Spinsters Ink 510; Stonewall Inn 512; Third Side Press 408; ‡Thorngate Road 409; Woman in the Moon Publications 411

LITERARY

Magazines: ‡About Such Things 95; ACM (Another Chicago Magazine) 96; Acorn, The 96; Acorn Whistle 96; Adrift 97; ‡Advocate 97; Aethlon 98; African American Review 98; Alabama Literary Review 99; Alaska Quarterly Review 99; Allegheny Review 102; Alpha Beat Press 102; ‡Ambiguous 103; Amelia 103; American Literary Review 104; American Short Fiction 104; ‡American Voice 104; American Writings 104; Americas Review, The 104; Amethyst Review, The 105; Anterior Fiction Quarterly 265; ‡Anthology 266; Antietam Review 105; Antigonish Review, The 106; Antioch Review 106; Aphrodite Gone Berserk 106; Appalachian Heritage 106; ‡Arachne 107; Ararat Quarterly 107; Arnazella 108; ‡Arshile 108; Artful Dodge 108; artisan 109; ‡artisan 311; Art:Mag 312; Ascent 109; Asian Pacific American Journal 109; Atlantic Monthly, The 349; Atom Mind 110; Aura Literary/Arts Review 110; Azorean Express, The 110; ‡Backwater Review 111; Bahlasti Papers 313; ‡Baltimore Review, The 111; B&A: New Fiction 111; ‡Bangtale International 266; Barbaric Yawp 112; ‡Barnabe Mountain Review 112; Bear Essential Magazine, The 349; Belletrist Review, The 113; Bellingham Review, The 113; Bellowing Ark 113; Beloit Fiction Journal 114; Beneath the Surface 114; Berkeley Fiction Review 114; Black Hammock Review, The 115; Black Ice 115; Black Jack 116; ‡Black Lily, The 313; Black River Review 116; Black Warrior Review 117; Blue Mesa Review 117; Blue Moon Review, The 117; ‡Blue Skunk Companion, The 118; Blueline 118; Bone & Flesh 119; BookLovers 119; ‡Bookpress 119; Boston Literary Review (BLuR) 120; ‡Boston Review 350; Bottomfish Magazine 120; Bouillabaisse 120; Boulevard 120; Briar Cliff Review, The 121; ‡Brilliant Corners 121; Brownstone Review, The 122; Buffalo

Libros 462; Harper Perennial 463; HarperCollins Publishers 463; HarperCollins Publishers (Canada) 464; Helicon Nine Editions 465; Hollow Earth Publishing 398; Holt & Company, Henry 466; Houghton Mifflin Books for Children 466; Hounslow Press 467; House of Anansi Press 467; Howells House 467; Hyperion 468; Insomniac Press 469; Ironweed Press 470; Knopf, Alfred A. 473; ‡Landmine Books 400; Laurel Books 473; ‡Leapfrog Press 400; Lincoln Springs Press 474; Livingston Press 476; Loup de Gouttière, Le 477; Macmurray & Beck 479; Macrae Books, John 479; Main Street Books 479; Maritimes Arts Projects Productions 480; Marlowe & Company §Marlowe 480; ‡Mercury House 481; ‡Merrimack Books 401; Milkweed Editions 481; Morrow and Company, William 482; Moyer Bell 483; Multnomah Publishers 483; ‡Neshui Publishing 485; New York University Press 486; Newest Publishers 486; Nightshade Press 487; Noonday Press 487; North Star Line 487; Norton & Company, W.W. 488; Orca Book Publishers 489; Orloff Press 489; Outrider Press 402; Owl Creek Press 490; Peachtree Publishers 492; Philomel Books 493; Picador USA 494; ‡Pocket Books 495; Post-Apollo Press, The 403; Prairie Journal Press 495; Press Gang Publishers 404; ‡Pride Publications 496; Puckerbrush Press 404; ‡Pudding House Publications 404; Quarry Press 497; Rain Dancer Books 498; ‡Rainbow Books 498; Random House 499; Red Deer College Press 499; ‡Red Dragon Press 499; Rio Grande Press 500; Riverhead Books 501; Ronsdale Press 405; ‡Russian Hill Press 502; St. Augustine Society Press 405; St. Martin's Press 503; Sand River Press 405; Sanders & Company, J.S. 503; ‡Sans Soleil 406; Savant Garde Workshop, The 406; Seal Press 504; Second Chance Press and the Permanent Press 505; Seven Stories Press 506; Shaw Publishers, Harold 506; Shields Publishing/NEO Press 406; Simon & Pierre Publishing 507; Smith, Publisher/Peregrine Smith, Gibbs 508; Smith, The 407; Snowapple Press 407; Soho Press 509; Southern Methodist University Press 509; Spectra Books 509; Spirit That Moves Us Press, The 407; Still Waters Poetry Press 511; Stonewall Inn 512; Stormline Press 408; Story Line Press 512; Summit Publishing Group, The 512; Talese, Nan A. 513; Thistledown Press 408; ‡Thorngate Road 409; ‡Turnstone Press 409; Turtle Point Press 410; University of Georgia Press 515; University of Iowa Press 516; University of Arkansas Press, The 410; Van Neste Books 411; Viking 518; Vintage 518; White Pine Press 521; Zephyr Press 412; Zoland Books 524

MAINSTREAM/CONTEMPORARY

Magazines: ACM (Another Chicago Magazine) 96; Acorn, The 96; Acorn Whistle 96; Adrift 97; ‡Advocate 97; African American Review 98; Aguilar Expression, The 99; Alabama Literary Review 99; Alaska Quarterly Review 99; Allegheny Review 102; Amelia 103; American Literary Review 104; American Writings 104; Americas Review, The 104; Anterior Fiction Quarterly 265; Antietam Review 105; Antigonish Review, The 106; Antioch Review 106; Ararat Quarterly 107; Arkansas Review 107; ‡Armchair Aesthete, The 108; Arnazella 108; artisan 109; Art:Mag 312; Asian Pacific American Journal 109; Associate Reformed Presbyterian, The 348; Atlantic Monthly, The 349; Atom Mind 110; Aura Literary/Arts Review 110; Azorean Express, The 110; ‡Baltimore Review, The 111; Barbaric Yawp 112; Belletrist Review, The 113; Bellowing Ark 113; Beloit Fiction Journal 114; Berkeley Fiction Review 114; Black Hammock Review, The 115; Black Jack 116; Black River Review 116; Black Warrior Review 117; Blue Mesa Review 117; Blue Moon Review, The 117; ‡Blue Skunk Companion, The 118; Blueline 118; Bomb Magazine 350; BookLovers 119; Boston Literary Review (BLuR) 120; ‡Boston Review 350; Boulevard 120; Briar Cliff Review, The 121; ‡Brilliant Corners 121; Brownstone Review, The 122; Buffalo Spree Magazine 351; Burnt Aluminum 122; Callaloo 123; Canadian Author 124; Capers Aweigh Magazine 124; Capilano Review, The 124; ‡Career Focus; College Preview; Direct Aim; Journey; Visions 353; Caribbean Writer, The 124; ‡Carousel Literary Arts Magazine 125; Chariton Review, The 125; Chattahoochee Review, The 126; Chicago Review 127; Chinook Quarterly, The 270; Chiricú 127; Chiron Review 127; Christian Century, The 354; Chrysalis Reader 128; ‡Chubby Bunny 128; Cimarron Review 128; Climbing Art, The 129; Clockwatch Review 129; Collages and Bricolages 129; Colorado Review 130; ‡Compleat Nurse, The 272; ‡Compost Newsletter 130; Concho River Review 131; Confrontation 131; ‡Contraband 272; Corona 131; Cosmopolitan 357; Crab Creek Review 132; Cripes! 133; Crucible 134; Curriculum Vitae 318; ‡Cutting Edge, The 135; ‡CZ's Magazine 273; Dan River Anthology 135; Dialogue 358; ‡Dixie Phoenix 318; Dogwood Tales 137; ‡Down Under Manhattan Bridge; Downstate Story 137; Dream International 274; Dreams & Visions 274; Drinkin' Buddy Magazine, The 319; ‡Echo Ink Review 138; Echoes 138; Eckerd Review, The 139; ‡Edge, The 274; 1812 140; Elf: Eclectic Literary Forum 140; Eloquent Umbrella, The 275; Emrys Journal 140; ‡Entre Nous 140; Epoch Magazine 141; Esquire 359; Eureka 141; ‡Evansville Review 142; Event 142; Explorer 143; Expressions 143; Eyes 276; Fayrdaw 320; Feminist Studies 145; FiberOptic Etchings 276; Fiction 145; ‡5th Wall, The 146; ‡Filling Station 146; ‡First Word Bulletin, The 276; Fish Drum 146; Flipside 147; Florida Review, The 147; Flying Horse 147; Flying Island, The 148; Folio 148; Footwork 148; ‡Forbidden Donut 148; Fourteen Hills 149; Free Focus/Ostentatious Mind 277; ‡Freezer Burn 149; Fugue 149; ‡Garnet 150; Gathering of the Tribes,

441; Crown Publishing 441; Daniel and Company, John 442; Davies Publishing, Robert 443; Dell Publishing 445; Denlingers Publishers 445; Dickens Press 397; Dundurn Press 447; Dunne Books, Thomas 447; Dutton Signet 447; Ecopress 397; Éditions La Liberté 449; Ekstasis Editions 449; Eriksson, Publisher, Paul S. 450; Feminist Press, The 452; ‡Fjord Press 453; Forge Books 453; ‡Goddess Dead Publications 455; Goose Lane Editions 455; ‡Greycliff Publishing 457; Griffon House Publications 398; Guernica Editions 457; HarperCollins Publishers (Canada) 464; HarperPaperbacks 464; Harris Literary Agency 398; Harvest House Publishers 464; Helicon Nine Editions 465; Holt & Company, Henry 466; Howells House 467; Hyperion 468; Kensington Publishing 471; Key Porter Books 472; Knopf, Alfred A. 473; ‡Landmine Books 400; ‡Leapfrog Press 400; Lincoln Springs Press 474; Macmurray & Beck 479; Macrae Books, John 479; Morrow and Company, William 482; ‡Neshui Publishing 485; Nightshade Press 487; Orca Book Publishers 489; Orloff Press 489; Our Child Press 402; Owl Books 490; Paper Chase Press 490; Papier-Mache 491; ‡Patek Press 491; Peachtree Publishers 492; ‡Pocket Books 495; Press Gang Publishers 404; ‡Pride Publications 496; Puckerbrush Press 404; Rain Dancer Books 498; ‡Rainbow Books 498; Random House 499; Red Deer College Press 499; Review and Herald Publishing Association 500; Rio Grande Press 500; Riverhead Books 501; ‡Russian Hill Press 502; St. Augustine Society Press 405; St. Martin's Press 503; Savant Garde Workshop, The 406; ‡Scottish Cultural Press 504; Seal Press 504; Second Chance Press and the Permanent Press 505; Seven Buffaloes Press 505; Severn House Publishers 506; Simon & Pierre Publishing 507; Smith, Publisher/Peregrine Smith, Gibbs 508; Snowapple Press 407; Soho Press 509; Southern Methodist University Press 509; Tor Books 514; University of Illinois Press 515; University of Arkansas Press, The 410; Van Neste Books 411; Viking 518; Vintage 518; Weiss Associates, Daniel 520; Woman in the Moon Publications 411; Wordstorm Productions 522; Zephyr Press 412; Zoland Books 524

MILITARY/WAR

Book Publishers: Ariadne Press 393; Avon Books 421; Bantam Books 424; Branden Publishing 429; Crown Publishing 441; Dell Publishing 445; Fine, Donald I. 452; ‡Greycliff Publishing 457; Kensington Publishing 471; Morrow and Company, William 482; Mountain State Press 402; Nautical & Aviation Publishing 484; Naval Institute Press 484; ‡Neshui Publishing 485; ‡Pocket Books 495; Presidio Press 496; ‡Rainbow Books 498; St. Martin's Press 503; Vandamere Press 517; Vanwell Publishing 517

MYSTERY/SUSPENSE

Magazines: ‡Advocate 97; Aguilar Expression, The 99; Allegheny Review 102; ‡Altair 265; Amelia 103; Anterior Fiction Quarterly 265; ‡Anthology 266; ‡Armchair Aesthete, The 108; Arnazella 108; artisan 109; Art:Mag 312; ‡Bangtale International 266; Belletrist Review, The 113; Beneath the Surface 114; bePuzzled 350; ‡Black Lily, The 313; ‡Blue Skunk Companion, The 118; BookLovers 119; Boys' Life 351; Brownstone Review, The 122; Capers Aweigh Magazine 124; ‡Career Focus; College Preview; Direct Aim; Journey; Visions 353; Chinook Quarterly, The 270; Chrysalis Reader 128; Climbing Art, The 129; ‡Cochran's Corner 271; ‡Compleat Nurse, The 272; Cosmopolitan 357; ‡Cozy Detective, The 272; ‡CZ's Magazine 273; Dagger of the Mind 273; Dan River Anthology 135; ‡Dark Starr 318; Dogwood Tales 137; Downstate Story 137; Dream International 274; Drinkin' Buddy Magazine, The 319; Echoes 138; ‡Eclectica 139; ‡Edge, The 274; 8 139; Elf: Eclectic Literary Forum 140; Ellery Queen's Mystery Magazine 358; Eloquent Umbrella, The 275; Eureka 141; ‡Evansville Review 142; Expressions 143; FiberOptic Etchings 276; Flying Island, The 148; ‡Forbidden Donut 148; Free Focus/Ostentatious Mind 277; Fugue 149; ‡Gold and Treasure Hunter 361; Grasslands Review 153; Green's Magazine 156; ‡Grit 363; Hardboiled 278; Hitchcock Mystery Magazine, Alfred 365; ‡Hybrid Moments 281; i.e. magazine 161; Lamplight, The 170; Lines in the Sand 172; Lynx Eye 176; Medicinal Purposes 286; Merlyn's Pen 179; Monthly Independent Tribune Times Journal Post Gazette News Chronicle Bulletin, The 326; Murderous Intent 288; ‡Muse Portfolio 182; Musing Place, The 183; My Legacy 288; Mystery Time 289; ‡New England Writers' Network 289; ‡New Mystery 374; New Press Literary Quarterly, The 186; ‡New Spy 375; Northeast Arts Magazine 190; Northwoods Journal 190; ‡Now & Then 292; Oatmeal & Poetry 192; Oracle Story 194; Outer Darkness 330; Palo Alto Review 198; ‡Perceptions 333; Pink Chameleon, The 204; Pirate Writings 295; ‡Play the Odds 334; Poetry Forum Short Stories 207; Poetry in Motion 208; Portland Review 209; Post, The 295; Potpourri 210; PSI 296; Pulp: A Fiction Magazine 334; Reader's Break 217; Ruby's Pearls 298; Screaming Toad Press 223; Se La Vie Writer's Journal 223; Seattle Review, The 224; Sensations 224; Short Stuff Magazine for Grown-ups 226; Skylark 228; Snake Nation Review 229; Spring Fantasy 235; SPSM&H 235; Storyteller, The 301; Street Beat Quarterly 237; ‡Sunflower Dream, The 239; T.R.'s Zine 339; "Teak" Roundup 241; Texas Young Writers' Newsletter 302; Thema 242; ‡32 Pages 244; Thistle 339; ‡Threshold, The 303; Timber Creek Review 245; Tucumcari Literary Review 246; Urbanus 247; ‡Villager, The 304; Vincent Brothers Review, The 249; ‡Vintage Northwest

NEW AGE/MYSTIC/SPIRITUAL

PSYCHIC/SUPERNATURAL/OCCULT

Writers' International Forum 306; (000)000-0000 342; Zero Hour 259; ‡Zone, The 342

Book Publishers: Avon Books 421; Dell Publishing 445; ‡Hampton Roads Publishing 458; Holmes Publishing Group 466; ‡Llewellyn Publications 477; ‡Masquerade Books 480; NWI 488; ‡Pocket Books 495; ‡Pride Publications 496; ‡Red Dragon Press 499; St. Martin's Press 503; Wilshire Book Co. 521; Woman in the Moon Publications 411; Write Way Publishing 522; Artemis Creations Publishing 394

REGIONAL

Magazines: ‡About Such Things 95; Above the Bridge 265; Acorn, The 96; Acorn Whistle 96; ‡Advocate 97; Allegheny Review 102; Aloha 347; Amelia 103; Anterior Fiction Quarterly 265; Antietam Review 105; Appalachian Heritage 106; ‡Arachne 107; ‡Arachne, Inc. 266; Arnazella 108; Art:Mag 312; Asian Pacific American Journal 109; Aura Literary/Arts Review 110; Azorean Express, The 110; ‡Bangtale International 266; Barbaric Yawp 112; Belletrist Review, The 113; Black Hammock Review, The 115; Blue Mesa Review 117; Blue Moon Review, The 117; ‡Blue Skunk Companion, The 118; Blueline 118; BookLovers 119; ‡Bookpress 119; ‡Boston Review 350; Briar Cliff Review, The 121; Brownstone Review, The 122; Callaloo 123; Canadian Author 124; Capers Aweigh Magazine 124; Cayo 125; Chattahoochee Review, The 126; Chinook Quarterly, The 270; ‡Chubby Bunny 128; Climbing Art, The 129; Clockwatch Review 129; ‡Compleat Nurse, The 272; Concho River Review 131; Confrontation 131; Corona 131; Cream City Review, The 133; Crucible 134; ‡CZ's Magazine 273; Dan River Anthology 135; ‡Dixie Phoenix 318; Downstate Story 137; Drinkin' Buddy Magazine, The 319; ‡Echo Ink Review 138; Echoes 138; Eckerd Review, The 139; ‡Edge, The 274; Elf: Eclectic Literary Forum 140; Eloquent Umbrella, The 275; Emrys Journal 140; Eureka 141; ‡Evansville Review 142; Event 142; Expressions 143; FiberOptic Etchings 276; ‡5th Wall, The 146; ‡Filling Station 146; Fish Drum 146; Fish Stories 146; Fugue 149; Generator 321; Georgia Journal 361; Gettysburg Review, The 152; Grasslands Review 153; Green Hills Literary Lantern, The 156; Gulf Coast 157; ‡Habersham Review 157; ‡Hawaii Review 158; Hayden's Ferry Review 158; Heartlands Today, The 159; Heaven Bone 159; High Plains Literary Review 159; Hill and Holler 160; ‡Huckleberry Press 161; Hunted News, The 161; Image 162; In the Spirit of the Buffalo 163; International Quarterly 164; Japanophile 166; Kennesaw Review 168; Lactuca 169; Left Curve 284; Loonfeather 174; Louisiana Literature 174; Lowell Pearl, The 175; Lullwater Review 175; ‡Lummox Journal 175; Mangrove 177; Manoa 177; Medicinal Purposes 286; Midland Review 180; Musing Place, The 183; My Legacy 288; New Methods 289; ‡New York Stories 187; NeWest Review 187; ‡Nexus 188; Northeast 375; Northwoods Journal 190; Now & Then 191; ‡Now & Then 292; Oatmeal & Poetry 192; Old Crow Review 193; Onionhead 193; Oxford American, The 196; Palo Alto Review 198; Partisan Review 200; Passages North 200; Pikeville Review 203; Pleiades 204; Poetry in Motion 208; Pointed Circle, The 209; ‡Portable Plateau 295; Portland Review 209; Potato Eyes 209; Potomac Review 210; Prairie Dog 211; Prairie Journal of Canadian Literature, The 212; Rag Mag 216; ‡Raven Chronicles, The 216; RE:AL 217; Reed Magazine 218; Response 297; RiverSedge 219; Riverwind 219; Rockford Review, The 220; Rosebud™ 298; S.L.U.G.fest 335; Sanskrit 221; Se La Vie Writer's Journal 223; Seattle Review, The 224; Shattered Wig Review 225; Short Stuff Magazine for Grown-ups 226; Sidewalks 227; Sierra Nevada College Review 227; Skylark 228; Snake Nation Review 229; South Dakota Review 230; Southern California Anthology 231; Southern Exposure 231; Southern Humanities Review 231; Spindrift 233; Spout 234; SPSM&H 235; ‡Stoneflower 236; Storyteller, The 301; Struggle 237; Sycamore Review 239; Sycamore Roots: The Regionalist Papers 338; ‡Talking River Review 240; "Teak" Roundup 241; Thema 242; ‡32 Pages 244; This Magazine 244; Timber Creek Review 245; Tucumcari Literary Review 246; Turnstile 246; TWN 388; Unknown Writer, The 340; Vincent Brothers Review, The 249; Volcano Quarterly 304; West Wind Review 251; ‡Westcoast Fisherman, The 305; Widener Review 253; Willow Review 254; Wisconsin Academy Review 305; ‡Womyn's Press 255; Words of Wisdom 256; Writers' Forum 256; Writers' International Forum 306; Xavier Review 257; Yankee 390; Yarns and Such 307; ‡Yemassee 259; ‡Yorkshire Journal 259; Zyzzyva 262

Book Publishers: Beach Holme Publishers 424; Beil, Publisher, Frederic C. 425; Blair, Publisher, John F. 427; Brown Bear Press 430; ‡Buzz Books 430; Caitlin Press 430; Chinook Press 434; Creative Arts Book Co. 440; Down East Books 446; E.M. Press 448; Feminist Press, The 452; ‡Fjord Press 453; ‡Greycliff Publishing 457; Ice Cube Press 399; Kaya Production 471; ‡Leapfrog Press 400; Lintel 474; ‡Mercury House 481; Mountain State Press 402; New England Press, The 486; Newest Publishers 486; Nightshade Press 487; Northland Publishing 487; Orca Book Publishers 489; Passeggiata Press 491; Peachtree Publishers 492; Philomel Books 493; Pineapple Press 494; Press Gang Publishers 404; Red Deer College Press 499; Rio Grande Press 500; ‡Russian Hill Press 502; Sand River Press 405; Seven Buffaloes Press 505; Southern Methodist University Press 509; Story Line Press 512; Summit Publishing 512; Texas

RELIGIOUS/INSPIRATIONAL

ROMANCE

Book Publishers:

SCIENCE FICTION

Magazines:

Spring Fantasy 235; SPSM&H 235; ‡Starblade 300; ‡Starship Earth 337; Storyteller, The 301; Struggle 237; ‡Sunflower Dream, The 239; Surprise Me 239; ‡Syntax Intergalactic 339; Talebones 302; Terra Incognita 302; Texas Young Writers' Newsletter 302; Thema 242; ‡32 Pages 244; ‡Threshold, The 303; Thresholds Quarterly 303; Tomorrow 245; ‡Ulitarra 246; Urbanite, The 247; Urbanus 247; Vincent Brothers Review, The 249; Volcano Quarterly 304; West Wind Review 251; Woman 306; Writers' International Forum 306; Yellow Silk 258; ‡(000)000-0000 342; ‡Zone, The 342

Book Publishers: Ageless Press 392; Alexander Books 418; Arjuna Library Press 419; Artemis Creations Publishing 394; Avon Books 421; ‡Avon Eos 421; Avon Science Fiction 422; Baen Books 422; Bantam Books 424; Berkley Publishing 425; Berkley/Ace Science Fiction 425; Black Heron Press 426; Books in Motion 428; Carroll & Graf Publishers 432; Cartwheel Books 432; Chicago Spectrum Press 434; Chinook Press 434; Circlet Press 435; Crown Publishing 441; Daw Books 443; Del Rey Books 444; Dutton Signet 447; Ecopress 397; Farthest Star 451; FC2/Black Ice Books 452; Feminist Press, The 452; Gryphon Publications 457; Harkey Multimedia 459; HarperCollins 463; Harris Literary Agency 398; ‡Landmine Books 400; ‡Masquerade Books 480; ‡Merrimack Books 401; Millennium 482; Morrow and Company, William 482; ‡Neshui Publishing 485; ‡NWI 488; ‡Pride Publications 496; Rain Dancer Books 498; ‡Rainbow Books 498; Random House Juvenile Books 499; ‡Red Dragon Press 499; ROC 501; St. Martin's Press 503; Savant Garde Workshop, The 406; Severn House Publishers 506; SJL Publishing 508; Smith, Publisher/Peregrine Smith, Gibbs 508; Spectra Books 509; Tor Books 514; Triangle Titles 514; TSR, Inc. 514; W.W. Publications 411; Warner Aspect 520; Wesleyan University Press 520; Write Way Publishing 522

SENIOR CITIZEN/RETIREMENT

Magazines: Acorn, The 96; ‡Advocate 97; Amelia 103; Aura Literary/Arts Review 110; Brownstone Review, The 122; Canadian Author 124; Christian Courier 270; ‡Compleat Nurse, The 272; ‡Compost Newsletter 130; Dan River Anthology 135; Dialogue 358; Echoes 138; Eloquent Umbrella, The 275; ‡Etcetera 141; ‡Evansville Review 142; Expressions 143; ‡First Word Bulletin, The 276; Gathering of the Tribes, A 150; ‡Gold and Treasure Hunter 361; Grand Times 362; Hayden's Ferry Review 158; Horizons 366; ‡Lilith 370; Lines in the Sand 172; Lowell Pearl, The 175; manna 177; ‡Mature Living 372; Mature Years 372; Medicinal Purposes 286; ‡Montana Senior Citizens News 373; ‡Muse Portfolio 182; My Legacy 288; ‡New York Stories 187; Nite-Writer's International Literary Arts Journal 189; Oatmeal & Poetry 192; Pink Chameleon, The 204; ‡Play the Odds 334; Poetry Forum Short Stories 207; Poskisnolt Press 295; St. Anthony Messenger 383; St. Joseph's Messenger and Advocate of the Blind 384; Snake Nation Review 229; SPSM&H 235; Storyteller, The 301; Struggle 237; Surprise Me 239; T.R.'s Zine 339; Tucumcari Literary Review 246; Vincent Brothers Review, The 249; West Wind Review 251; Writers' International Forum 306

SERIALIZED/EXCERPTED NOVEL

Magazines: Agni 98; Alabama Literary Review 99; American Writings 104; Analog Science Fiction & Fact 347; Art:Mag 312; Asian Pacific American Journal 109; Atom Mind 110; Bahlasti Papers 313; Bellowing Ark 113; Black Jack 116; Bomb Magazine 350; BookLovers 119; Burning Light 269; Callaloo 123; Campus Life 352; Capper's 352; Chiricú 127; ‡Compost Newsletter 130; ‡Contraband 272; Curriculum Vitae 318; Drinkin' Buddy Magazine, The 319; Echoes 138; ‡Emploi Plus 140; ‡Evansville Review 142; Fat Tuesday 144; Generator 321; Gettysburg Review, The 152; Glass Cherry, The 152; Green Mountains Review 156; Hunted News, The 161; Lactuca 169; ‡Lost Worlds 285; Lynx Eye 176; Madison Review, The 176; Manoa 177; Matriarch's Way 179; Mississippi Mud 181; Musing Place, The 183; ‡My Weekly 374; Nassau Review 183; New Laurel Review 185; New Virginia Review 187; Now & Then 191; Oracle Story 194; Orange Coast Review 194; Other Voices 194; Portland Review 209; Potomac Review 210; Prairie Journal of Canadian Literature, The 212; Prism International 213; Puerto Del Sol 214; ‡Quarry 215; River City 219; River Styx 219; Rosebud™ 298; Saturday Night 384; Seattle Review, The 224; Skylark 228; South Dakota Review 230; Southern California Anthology 231; Spindrift 233; ‡Spirit (Of Woman in the Moon), The 234; Summer's Reading, A 238; Trafika 245; ‡Ulitarra 246; Vincent Brothers Review, The 249; Virginia Quarterly Review 304; Volcano Quarterly 304; Vox (NY) 249; ‡Westcoast Fisherman, The 305; Widener Review 253; Willow Springs 254; Xavier Review 257

SHORT STORY COLLECTIONS

Magazines: Ararat Quarterly 107; Aura Literary/Arts Review 110; Painted Bride Quarterly 197

Book Publishers: Absey & Co. 416; Ageless Press 392; Anvil Press 393; Arsenal Pulp Press 419; Arte

Publico Press 420; b. dazzle 394; Beil, Publisher, Frederic C. 425; Books for All Times 394; Branden Publishing 429; Caitlin Press 430; Calyx Books 395; Center Press 433; ‡Champion Books 433; Chicago Spectrum Press 434; Chinook Press 434; Cleis Press 438; Confluence Press 395; Council for Indian Education 440; Counterpoint 440; Creative Arts Book Co. 440; Daniel and Company, Publishers, John 442; Delta Trade Paperbacks 445; ‡Dufour Editions 447; Ecco Press, The 448; Éditions du Vermillon, Les 449; Éditions La Liberté 449; Ekstasis Editions 449; Empyreal Press 450; ‡Exile Press 397; FC2/Black Ice Books 452; Goose Lane Editions 455; Graywolf Press 456; ‡Greycliff Publishing 457; Gryphon Publications 457; HarperCollins Publishers (Canada) 464; Helicon Nine Editions 465; House of Anansi Press 467; Humanitas 468; Insomniac Press 469; Lincoln Springs Press 474; Livingston Press 476; Loup de Gouttière, Le 477; ‡Lyons Press, The 478; Macmurray & Beck 479; ‡Masquerade Books 480; ‡Mercury House 481; ‡Merrimack Books 401; ‡Neshui Publishing 485; North Star Line 487; NWI 488; Orloff Press 489; Outrider Press 402; ‡Patek Press 491; Philomel Books 493; Prairie Journal Press 495; Press Gang Publishers 404; Quarry Press 497; Quixote Press 497; Rain Dancer Books 498; Random House 499; ‡Red Dragon Press 499; Riehle Foundation, The 500; Rio Grande Press 500; Riverhead Books 501; Sarabande Books 503; ‡Scottish Cultural Press 504; Seal Press 504; Seven Buffaloes Press 505; Severn House Publishers 506; Shields Publishing/NEO Press 406; Smith, Publisher/Peregrine Smith, Gibbs 508; Snowapple Press 407; Southern Methodist University Press 509; Story Line Press 512; Third World Press 408; Thistledown Press 408; Triangle Titles 514; University of Missouri Press 410; University of Arkansas Press, The 410; Vintage 518; Vista Publishing 518; White Pine Press 521; Willow Creek Press 521; Woman in the Moon Publications 411; Zephyr Press 412; Zoland Books 524

SPORTS

Magazines: Adventure Cyclist 346; ‡Advocate 97; Aethlon 98; Amelia 103; Anterior Fiction Quarterly 265; Appalachia Journal 348; artisan 109; Aura Literary/Arts Review 110; Balloon Life 349; Beloit Fiction Journal 114; Black Belt 350; BookLovers 119; Bowhunter Magazine 351; Boys' Life 351; Boy's Quest 268; Brownstone Review, The 122; ‡Career Focus; College Preview; Direct Aim; Journey; Visions 353; Chinook Quarterly, The 270; Christian Courier 270; Chrysalis Reader 128; Climbing Art, The 129; ‡Clubhouse Magazine 271; Curriculum Vitae 318; Drinkin' Buddy Magazine, The 319; Echoes 138; Elf: Eclectic Literary Forum 140; Eloquent Umbrella, The 275; ‡Evansville Review 142; Expressions 143; ‡Fan Magazine 144; FiberOptic Etchings 276; Florida Wildlife 360; Fugue 149; Golf Journal 362; Home Times 366; Junior Trails 369; Lowell Pearl, The 175; Medicinal Purposes 286; Nite-Writer's International Literary Arts Journal 189; Northwoods Journal 190; Now & Then 191; Pink Chameleon, The 204; ‡Play the Odds 334; Playboy 380; Riverwind 219; Skylark 228; Spitball 234; Storyteller, The 301; T.R.'s Zine 339; "Teak" Roundup 241; Thema 242; Unknown Writer, The 340; West Wind Review 251; Writers' International Forum 306; ‡You! Magazine 390

Book Publishers: ‡Patek Press 491

THRILLER/ESPIONAGE

Book Publishers: Ageless Press 392; Bookcraft 428; Cleis Press 438; Dutton Signet 447; Ecopress 397; Fine, Donald I. 452; Forge Books 453; Gryphon Publications 457; HarperPaperbacks 464; Hyperion 468; Intrigue Press 469; Kensington Publishing 471; ‡Masquerade Books 480; Morrow and Company, William 482; ‡Neshui Publishing 485; ‡NWI 488; Prep Publishing 496; Presidio Press 496; ‡Russian Hill Press 502; St. Martin's Press 503; Van Neste Books 411; Write Way Publishing 522

TRANSLATIONS

Magazines: ACM (Another Chicago Magazine) 96; Adrift 97; Agni 98; Alabama Literary Review 99; Alaska Quarterly Review 99; ‡Ambiguous 103; Amelia 103; American Writings 104; Antigonish Review, The 106; Antioch Review 106; Aphrodite Gone Berserk 106; Ararat Quarterly 107; Arkansas Review 107; Artful Dodge 108; Art:Mag 312; Asian Pacific American Journal 109; Atom Mind 110; ‡Bangtale International 266; ‡Barnabe Mountain Review 112; Black Ice 115; ‡Black Lily, The 313; Blue Moon Review, The 117; ‡Blue Skunk Companion, The 118; Boston Literary Review (BLuR) 120; ‡Boston Review 350; Callaloo 123; Chariton Review, The 125; Chelsea 126; Chinook Quarterly, The 270; Christian Courier 270; ‡Chubby Bunny 128; Climbing Art, The 129; Colorado Review 130; Columbia 130; ‡Compleat Nurse, The 272; Confrontation 131; ‡Contraband 272; Crab Creek Review 132; ‡Crab Orchard Review 132; Cream City Review, The 133; Curriculum Vitae 318; ‡Dirigible 136; ‡Dixie Phoenix 318; Dream International 274; Eckerd Review, The 139; ‡Eclectica 139; 1812 140; Eloquent Umbrella, The 275; ‡Etcetera 141; Eureka 141; ‡Evansville Review 142; Fault Lines 144; Fiction 145; ‡5th Wall, The 146; ‡Filling Station 146; Flying Horse 147; Folio 148; Fourteen Hills 149; Gathering of the Tribes, A

WESTERN

Press, The 478; Nelson Publishers, Thomas 485; ‡Neshui Publishing 485; ‡NWI 488; Philomel Books 493; ‡Pocket Books 495; Rain Dancer Books 498; Sunstone Press 512; Tor Books 514; University Press of Colorado 411; Walker and Company 519

YOUNG ADULT/TEEN

Magazines: ‡Advocate 97; Associate Reformed Presbyterian, The 348; ‡Bangtale International 266; BookLovers 119; Boys' Life 351; Brilliant Star 269; Campus Life 352; ‡Career Focus; College Preview; Direct Aim; Journey; Visions 353; Chinook Quarterly, The 270; Clubhouse 355; ‡Cochran's Corner 271; ‡Compleat Nurse, The 272; ‡Cozy Detective, The 272; Creative Kids 357; ‡CZ's Magazine 273; Dream International 274; Drinkin' Buddy Magazine, The 319; Echoes 138; ‡Eidolon 274; Eloquent Umbrella, The 275; FiberOptic Etchings 276; ‡First Word Bulletin, The 276; Free Focus/Ostentatious Mind 277; Fudge Cake, The 278; ‡Growing Pains Magazine 322; ‡Guide Magazine 363; ‡Hybrid Moments 281; ‡Jackhammer 165; Lamp-Post, The 170; ‡Lilith 370; Lines in the Sand 172; Majestic Books 286; Medicinal Purposes 286; Merlyn's Pen 179; Message Magazine 372; Mindsparks 287; ‡Mini Romances 287; ‡Muse Portfolio 182; My Legacy 288; New Era Magazine 374; Nite-Writer's International Literary Arts Journal 189; Oatmeal & Poetry 192; On the Line 379; Oracle Story 194; Pink Chameleon, The 204; Poetry Forum Short Stories 207; Poskisnolt Press 295; Seventeen 384; Shadow 225; Skipping Stones 299; Spirit 385; Spring Fantasy 235; Storyteller, The 301; Straight 386; Struggle 237; ‡Sunflower Dream, The 239; Surprise Me 239; "Teak" Roundup 241; Teen Life 387; Teen Magazine 387; Texas Young Writers' Newsletter 302; West Wind Review 251; With 388; Writers' International Forum 306; ‡You! Magazine 390

Book Publishers: Archway Paperbacks/Minstrel Books 419; Arjuna Library Press 419; Arte Publico Press 420; Atheneum Books for Young Readers 420; Avon Books 421; Bantam/Doubleday/Dell Books for Young Readers 424; Beach Holme Publishers 424; Bethany House Publishers 426; Bethel Publishing 394; Borealis Press 428; Boyds Mills Press 429; ‡Broadman & Holman Publishers 394; Caitlin Press 430; Chicago Spectrum Press 434; Chinook Press 434; Chronicle Books for Children 435; Coteau Books 439; Cross-Cultural Communications 396; Crossway Books 441; Delecorte/Dell Books for Young Readers 445; Edge Books 448; Éditions du Vermillon, Les 449; Éditions La Liberté 449; Flare Books 453; Focus Publishing 453; Geringer Books, Laura 455; Godine, Publisher, David R. 455; Grade School Press 398; Harcourt Brace & Company Children's Books 459; Harkey Multimedia 459; HarperCollins Children's Books 463; HarperCollins Publishers (Canada) 464; HarperPaperbacks 464; Holt & Company Books for Young Readers, Henry 466; Holt & Company, Henry 466; Houghton Mifflin Books for Children 466; Hyperion Books for Children 468; Journey Books for Young Readers 471; Just Us Books 471; Lerner Publications 474; Little, Brown and Company Children's Books 476; Living the Good News 476; Lorimer & Co., Publishers, James 477; McElderry Books, Margaret K. 478; Mariner Books 480; Mariposa 480; Morehouse Publishing 482; Morrow Junior Books 482; ‡Neshui Publishing 485; New England Press, The 486; ‡NWI 488; Orca Book Publishers 489; Orchard Books 489; Our Child Press 402; Peachtree Children's Books 403; Peachtree Publishers 492; ‡Perfection Learning 493; Philomel Books 493; Piñata Books 494; Prep Publishing 496; ‡Pride Publications 496; Puffin Books 497; Ragweed Press/gynergy books 497; Rain Dancer Books 498; Random House Books For Young Readers 498; Random House Juvenile Books 499; ‡Raspberry Publications 404; Red Deer College Press 499; Royal Fireworks Press 502; Scholastic 504; Scholastic Canada 503; ‡Scottish Cultural Press 504; Seal Press 504; Snowapple Press 407; ‡Tab Book Club 513; Third World Press 408; Thistledown Press 408; Viking Children's Books 518; W.W. Publications 411; Walker and Company 519; Ward Hill Press 519; Weiss Associates, Daniel 520; Writers Press 523

Markets Index

A double-dagger (‡) precedes listings that are new to this edition. Markets that appeared in the 1997 edition of *Novel & Short Story Writer's Market* but are not included in this edition are identified by a two-letter code explaining why the market was omitted: **(ED)**—Editorial Decision, **(NS)**—Not Accepting Submissions, **(NR)**—No (or late) Response to Listing Request, **(OB)**—Out of Business, **(RR)**—Removed by Market's Request, **(UC)**—Unable to Contact, **(UF)**—Uncertain Future.